DICTIONARY OF LITERARY INFLUENCES

The Twentieth Century, 1914–2000

Edited by John Powell

GREENWOOD PRESS
Westport, Connecticut • London

Library of Congress Cataloging-in-Publication Data

Dictionary of literary influences : the twentieth century, 1914–2000 / edited by John Powell.
   p. cm.
  Includes bibliographical references and index.
  ISBN 0–313–31784–4 (alk. paper)
  1. Celebrities—Books and reading—Europe—History—20th century. 2. Celebrities—
Books and reading—America—History—20th century. 3. Civilization, Modern—20th
century. 4. Intellectuals—Books and reading—Europe—History—20th century.
5. Intellectuals—Books and reading—America—History—20th century. I. Powell, John,
1954– II. Biographical dictionary of literary influences.
Z1039.C45D53 2004
028'.9'0904—dc22   2003049318

British Library Cataloguing in Publication Data is available.

Library of Congress Catalog Card Number: 2003049318
ISBN: 0–313–31784–4

First published in 2004

Greenwood Press, 88 Post Road West, Westport, CT 06881
An imprint of Greenwood Publishing Group, Inc.
www.greenwood.com

Printed in the United States of America

The paper used in this book complies with the
Permanent Paper Standard issued by the National
Information Standards Organization (Z39.48–1984).

10 9 8 7 6 5 4 3 2 1

CONTENTS

Preface   vii

Acknowledgments   xiii

Introduction   xv

The Dictionary   1

Index   573

About the Contributors   609

PREFACE

This work is a continuation of the research begun with *Biographical Dictionary of Literary Influences: The Nineteenth Century, 1800–1914* (Greenwood, 2001). In that volume, an international team of scholars examined the reading habits of 271 men and women who played a prominent role in shaping Western culture. In this work, 156 contributors from 19 countries have done the same for 385 of the Western world's great cultural figures.

DESIGN

The design of the first volume was maintained, with entries arranged alphabetically and composed with an eye toward factual introduction and guidance in research. Contributors were asked to conduct their research with two principal goals in mind: first, to provide a concise summary of literary influences; and second, to provide clear direction for further research. Each entry includes three components:

1. *An introductory section provides basic biographical data,* including educational information and a concise assessment of the contribution of the subject to the development of Western culture. In order to maximize the space available for the project's goals, standard biographical information has been limited. It has been assumed that a researcher wishing to know, for instance, the titles and years of publication of an author's complete oeuvre or a detailed listing of offices held or academic appointments, will consult a regular biographical dictionary.

2. *The body of each article is devoted to an assessment of specific literary works and authors known to have influenced the subject.* The emphasis is factual and specific, though a succinct analysis may be included if the research warrants. As evidence regarding reading habits varies widely, so does the length and nature of the articles themselves. Ironically, advanced technologies of the twentieth century have often led to

less introspection, less information being recorded, and, in recent years, more emphasis on aural or visual influences.

3. *A bibliography includes principal archival collections, standard biographical resources, and published materials relating specifically to the subject's reading.* This section is necessarily uneven from entry to entry, as some figures left excellent sources for reconstructing their reading past, others almost none, and most an odd collection that requires careful reconstruction from a variety of sources.

The Literary Influences project does not indicate that printed mediums are the only, or even the principal, means of transmitting ideas and shaping culture. Many of the cultural giants treated here never wrote a book or published a poem—though a surprisingly large percentage did. All of them read, however. It is the purpose of this project to suggest the broad parameters of literary influence, in its broadest sense, upon the full array of cultural characteristics. While a few preliminary observations will be made in the introduction about the relationship between reading and culture, this work is meant to be suggestive and foundational. On the basis of articles on men and women of influence from widely different fields, scholars may eventually help us all to understand why, for instance, Octavio Paz and Robert Oppenheimer were both drawn to the *Bhagavad-gita*; or why Steven Spielberg, so militantly anticlassic in his reading, went on to produce such traditionally classic films as *Schindler's List* and *Saving Private Ryan*.

PRINCIPLES OF SELECTION

Selecting men and women for inclusion was more difficult for the twentieth century than for the nineteenth. As in the first volume, we began by identifying the people most responsible for the general cultural development of Europe, the Anglo-British world, and the Americas between 1914 and 2000. To be included, a figure

1. must have influenced Western culture in an important way during this time period;
2. must have exerted some influence beyond the local or regional borders of his or her home region; and
3. must have defined his or her career by substantial achievement during the period.

Once again, choosing the top tier of entries was relatively easy. Albert Einstein, Mother Teresa, Martin Luther King Jr., and John Paul II were likely to make anyone's list. The defining madness of World War II and the Cold War threat of global destruction turned many political leaders, good and bad, into figures of enormous cultural importance: Winston Churchill, Adolf Hitler, Josef Stalin, John F. Kennedy, Ronald Reagan, Margaret Thatcher, and Mikhail Gorbachev immediately come to mind.

After the top rank, however, the possibilities were bewildering. Opportunities for learning and avenues of cultural expression were so much greater in the twentieth century than in the nineteenth that influence must be measured in increasingly diverse spheres that often seem to be worlds apart from one another, though they form integral parts of a common culture. Western culture was increasingly shaped by nonwestern influences, though these tended to be diffuse, noncanonical and unevenly spread. Given the reach of European imperialism in the twentieth century, two world wars, massive international migration, and a general Western openness to fresh ideas, Asian and African figures often did much to shape the thought of Western cultural figures. This influence has been acknowledged by the inclusion of, among others, Mohandas Gandhi, Wole Soyinka, and Akira Kurosawa. The case might easily be made for more nonwestern influence, particularly among minority and immigrant communities, and among the general population toward the end of the twentieth century.

As culture evolved in the twentieth century, so did the forms of cultural influence and the degree to which they might be embodied in the lives of individuals. The popularity of professional poets declined precipitously after World War I, and the teaching of philosophy in schools and universities was steadily eroded. Similarly, classical musicians no longer enjoyed the iconic status accorded them in the nineteenth century. On the other hand, more highly advanced and broader applications of technology enhanced the potential cultural influence of scientists, entertainers, and those working in the media generally. In some cases, technology created new categories of influence, including filmmaking and aviation. Professional sport flourished in the twentieth century, taking on a cultural role for which there was no precedent in the previous century. The force of religious thought and conviction declined, but unevenly, and clearly not permanently. Adding further to the difficulty in selecting eminent individuals was the overwhelming influence of the technological mediums themselves. The exploration of space profoundly affected the world in the later twentieth century, but it is not clear who exactly should get the credit—scientists who developed pathbreaking but often isolated technologies, politicians who created space agencies and committed national resources, or the astronauts themselves. News reports from the most remote areas of the earth stream into homes every minute of every day, keeping Western citizens closely informed of local, national, and world affairs in a way that was impossible to imagine even 30 years ago. This access to information is of the utmost significance in democracies that thrive upon education, but it is often difficult to isolate the essential development or achievement. I still wish I could include some *one* who invented television and the Internet.

In choosing among representatives of the diverse ways in which Western culture has been shaped in the twentieth century, we have erred on the side of traditional notions of influence. There are more politicians and military figures here than many might wish to see in a study of "culture." Yet one need only observe the radically different cultural courses of Eastern and Western Europe to see that people like Stalin, Tito, Attlee, de Gaulle, Adenauer, and Brandt altered the cultural lives of tens of millions. High culture remains well represented, most notably among novelists and painters. I have found room for poets Rupert Brooke and Allen Ginsberg, but none for John Ashbery, recently referred to by Harold Bloom as America's "greatest living poet."[1]

Architects, inventors, business figures, and scientists are included but probably underrepresented, mainly because their links to print culture are less explicit. Popular culture is significantly represented, but still in its more elite forms. Film directors have gotten the nod over actors, though cases could certainly be made for including the latter. Some athletes are included—Babe Ruth, Jesse Owens,

Muhammad Ali—but not many, and the number obviously does not represent the collective influence of sport in modern society. Only four acts from the rock era of popular music have been treated: Elvis Presley, Bob Dylan, Bob Marley, and The Beatles. This selection understates the collective cultural power of popular music, but without pandering to simple popularity.[2]

The English-speaking world is undoubtedly privileged in the selections; but then the twentieth century was an age in which English was the principal international medium of intellectual, economic, political, and scientific expression. For good or ill, the United States, and to a lesser degree Britain, had more to do with changing the world—with shaping Western culture—than the other way around. The current wave of anti-Americanism reflects the reality of a widespread belief in Anglocentric cultural encroachment. On the other hand, one must not forget that some three dozen of the cultural figures associated with the United States or Britain were first- or second-generation immigrants from countries around the world, combining their unique cultural perspectives with the freedoms and opportunities afforded in their adoptive homelands. Many others were inspired by and connected to the cultures from which their forbears had come decades earlier. The demographic landscape of *Biographical Dictionary of Literary Influences: The Twenty-first Century* will look considerably different than that of the current volume. The past 20 years have already demonstrated the increasing cultural vitality of Latin America and postcommunist eastern Europe, and a considerable number of entries from these areas are included.

There are at least twice as many worthy figures who might have been included; I hope there are not many who positively should not be here. I cannot claim completeness for this work, but I believe there are enough entries—drawn from a broad range of cultural influences—to suggest both the influence of literature upon our lives and the need for continued exploration of the relationship between reading and culture. By bringing together research on the literary influences on such a variety figures, I believe that scholars will be encouraged to ask fresh questions about the sometimes surprising ways in which literature affects the lives of us all.

NATURE OF THE ENTRIES

The considerable variation in the length and content of the articles in the main reflects the quality of both relevant archives and the degree to which scholars have previously undertaken research in the area. In every case, however, it has been our goal to include enough information on each figure so that the reader may (1) identify key literary influences, (2) assess the possible impact of such reading, and (3) continue research in the most significant published and archival resources. In each case we have encouraged contributors to identify educational and other early literary influences, the most important specific printed works read, and key archival and secondary materials relating to literary influences. What the entries sometimes lack in detail we hope will be made up for in suggestive context and practical bibliographical guidance.

When the text refers to an individual who has his or her own entry, a cross-reference is indicated by **boldface** type.

NOTES

1. Bloom himself has been characterized by Michael Dirda of the *Washington Post* as one of the three most important twentieth-century literary critics writing in English (along with F. R. Leavis and Edmund Wilson). Still, only Wilson is included in this work. "'Greatest Living Poet' Lets Words Slide," CNN.com/Entertainment, posted 8 December 2002, http://www.cnn.com/2002/SHOWBIZ/books/12/wkd.john.ashbery.ap/index.html, accessed 9 December 2002; "Dirda on Books," Washington Post Live Online, 7 June 2001, http://www.washingtonpost.com/wp-srv/liveonline/01/books/dirda060701.htm, accessed 13 December 2002.

2. Elvis Presley was voted greatest rock star of all time in a 2002 ABC poll, more than 30 percentage points ahead of Jimi Hendrix. More importantly, however, 90 percent of the 1,023 adults polled believed he "had a lasting impact upon culture." "Poll: Elvis Greatest Rock Star of All Time," CNN.com/Entertainment, posted 15 August 2002, http://www.cnn.com/2002/SHOWBIZ/Music/08/15/ep.elvis.poll.ap/index.html, accessed 15 August 2002. On the other hand, of artists having one or more of the 20 best-selling albums of all time, only the Beatles made our list: apologies to the Eagles, Michael Jackson, Pink Floyd, Led Zeppelin, Billy Joel, AC/DC, Shania Twain, Fleetwood Mac, Whitney Houston, Boston, Alanis Morissette, Garth Brooks, Hootie and the Blowfish, Bruce Springsteen, Guns 'n Roses, and Elton John.

ACKNOWLEDGMENTS

It has been a pleasure to once again work with the editorial team from *Biographical Dictionary of Literary Influences: The Nineteenth Century, 1800–1914* (Greenwood, 2001). I wish to thank Derek Blakeley for his efforts on this volume, particularly in the area of Britain, Ireland, and the countries of the old British empire. Tessa Powell once again has proven her worth, and I appreciate her work in the preparation of the manuscript. I am grateful to several contributors who devoted considerable time to the project, providing numerous articles, advice, and expertise in their fields of study, among them Eric v. d. Luft, Greg Schnurr, and Yves Laberge. Any editorial shortcomings are, however, my own. The editorial team at Greenwood Press has been superb, as usual. Finally, my best thanks to the contributors, who usually found it necessary to do a great deal more work than is generally thought necessary for such articles.

INTRODUCTION

The study of literary influence is in some ways a very old one. It has often been practiced in relation to novelists, poets, philosophers, and men of letters generally. Because they write, it has been supposed, they are greatly influenced by others who write. Literary influences are less often studied in relation to painters, architects, athletes, musicians, scientists, economists, and businessmen. As they too read, and have in large measure been educated both formally and informally by literature, the impact of the printed word on these cultural figures should be explored. The relationship between their achievements and their reading will not only tell us a great deal about the history of our culture, it will inspire us with a new appreciation for the possibilities of its future.

Because Western civilization in particular has prized the written word, it is not uncommon to find studies of great men and women that pay attention to their reading. One need only note the persistence of Alexander's passion for Homer as an explanatory mechanism, well known in the ancient world and still central to our understanding of his restless energy and unbridled ambition. As Edwyn Bevan wrote at mid-century, when Aristotle came to Pella to tutor the young Macedonian prince, he brought with him a powerful force—literature:

> The great literary achievements of the Greeks . . . lay already far enough behind to have become invested with a classical dignity; the meaning of Hellenic civilization had been made concrete in a way which might sustain enthusiasm for a body of ideal values, authoritative by tradition.[1]

Such stories regarding the power of literature are abundant.

The problem is that while almost everyone agrees that reading plays a fundamental role in the transmission of knowledge and values, in the acquisition of practical and mental skills, and in the fashioning of new ideas, scholars often write as if it were a matter of little consequence. Thus, one authoritative biographer will devote many pages to a subject's reading, while another will ignore it altogether.

One's reading, however, like one's physical appearance or religious attitudes, is essential in coming to appreciate the distinctive personality of a person we will never meet. For the larger purposes of this work, knowledge of the reading habits of those whom we honor as culture-builders is fundamental to understanding the entire process of cultural development. If someone today imagined that J.R.R. Tolkien had drawn his inspiration from the late Victorian revival of medieval romances and "fairy stories," they might well imagine that secondhand knowledge is sufficient in transmitting truth. As Richard Follett has observed in this volume, however, "Middle Earth was not inspired by the works of such predecessors as William Morris or George MacDonald. Rather, Tolkien drew his creative breath directly from the classical epics, from the Norse and Icelandic Sagas, and from Anglo-Saxon poetry." This truth about texts helps to explain the persistence of Tolkien amid the welter of fantasy rip-offs, and why we are still drawn to the cultural mirror he holds to our faces. There is no obvious solution to the determination of some to see the world as they will, regardless of the way it is, but it helps to get useful information before the public.

Another problem one faces in the study of literary influences is one of focus. Should we study the broad realm of ideas contained in published literature, literary texts, the physical books themselves, or the means of distributing them? Each of these areas will suggest important insights; taken together they create the impression of a mechanistic, rather than humanistic, enterprise, an anthropology of literature. In the nineteenth and most of the twentieth centuries, the whole work was generally considered in the context of its creation; more recently the primacy of the text alone has been fashionable. A new group of scholars is now suggesting the need for a broader field of "book studies," that will bring together "specialists in book history, printing history, the book arts, publishing education, textual studies, reading instruction, librarianship, journalism, and the Internet."[2] According to Jonathan Rose:

> It is perfectly legitimate to ask how literature has shaped history and made evolutions, how it has socially constructed race, class, and gender, this, that, and the other. But we cannot begin to answer any of these questions until we know how books (not texts) have been created and reproduced, how books have been disseminated and read, how books have been preserved and destroyed.

All of this is important for understanding the direct relationship between books and culture; it is less important for appreciating the ways in which literature influences men and women to accomplish great things, and thus to transform their cultures.

Another inescapable difficulty in preparing a biographical dictionary of literary influences is the dual nature of the result. Most researchers will probably approach the book wanting to know more about the reading habits of a particular cultural figure—what did Michael Collins read that encouraged him to embrace physical force in the cause of Irish nationalism, what literature enabled Margaret Sanger to imagine a culture that embraced birth control? It is equally valid, however, to examine the "hidden" influences at work on the familiar shapers of our culture—the kind of influence that can only be traced by a careful perusal of the index and resulting reference to a variety of entries. The search for hidden influences—"invisible giants" as they are called in a recent book exploring "formerly famous but now forgotten Americans"—is enjoying a measure of popularity now.[3] This avenue will help one better appreciate the nature of fame and the longevity of influence. Sir Walter Scott, for instance, was clearly one of the most influential literary figures of the nineteenth century, read right across the Western world, from Russia to the United States, and one of the principal progenitors of modern nationalistic movements.[4] Many modern readers will be surprised at his influence in the twentieth century. They will be less surprised that Charles Dickens continued to inspire readers throughout the twentieth century. And there are always surprises, "unknown" people who committed their thoughts to paper without much recognition, or the strange permutations of influence among the powerful. Who would have imagined Josef Stalin as a literary influence on Richard Wright?

Ubiquitous diversity, in terms of ethnicity, opportunity, education, and means of expression, presents its own problems for a study of literary influences in the twentieth century. Whereas there was something approaching a canon of essential literary works in the nineteenth century[5]—the Bible, Greek and Roman classics, Shakespeare, and Sir Walter Scott—it dissipated rapidly in the twentieth. Early reading experience remained important, but became more difficult to delineate. As the twentieth century progressed, early literary influences became embedded in the mental world of children increasingly accustomed to instantaneous aural and visual impressions, often purveying the same kinds of information traditionally found in books. The difficulty of unraveling the literary strand should not deter us from the important cultural exercise it entails. If one recognizes that Andrei Tarkovsky, the Soviet Union's greatest filmmaker of the post–World War II era, was as much influenced by nineteenth-century Russian poets as by any filmmaker, it might encourage a renewed interest in poetry and a heightened appreciation of the role it has played in cultural development.

Two observations regarding literary influences on cultural development have not changed from the first volume. First, it was just as true in the twentieth as the nineteenth century that the motivation for reading varied widely, as did the results. Second, it remained true that individual readers responded uniquely to the written word and thus in unpredictable ways.

In preparing this volume, I wish to acknowledge my debt to many biographers who have carefully ploughed the literary ground in examining the lives of their subjects. These specialized treatments are not always well known outside the discipline of their subjects' work and frequently are not available in local libraries. It is also true that one would need a continuous biographical study of influences from the beginning of written history to the present to establish all the discernible intellectual links involved in the process of cultural change. The *Biographical Dictionary of Literary Influences: The Twentieth Century* nevertheless will identify a number of important links and will serve as a first general guide for researchers, from a variety of disciplines, who seek an introduction to the reading habits and the related intellectual development of the most significant cultural figures in the Western world during the twentieth century.

NOTES

1. Edwyn Robert Bevan, "Alexander III," *Encyclopaedia Britannica*, vol. 1 (Chicago, London, Toronto: Encyclopaedia Britannica, William Benton, 1960), p. 567. On Alexander and Homer, see "Alexander," sec. 8, in Plutarch, *Eight Great Lives*, The Dryden Translation, rev. by Arthur Hugh Clough, ed. C. A. Robinson (New York: Holt, Rinehart, Winston, 1960).

2. Jonathan Rose, speech of January 27, 2001, accepting the American Printing History Association (APHA) Institutional Award for the Society for the History of Authorship, Reading & Publishing (SHARP), http://www.printinghistory.org/htm/mis/awards/2001-SHARP.htm, accessed 29 July 2002.

3. Mark C. Carnes, ed. *Invisible Giants: 50 Americans Who Shaped the Nation but Missed the History Books* (New York: Oxford University Press, 2002).

4. John Powell, ed. *Biographical Dictionary of Literary Influences: The Nineteenth Century, 1800–1914* (Westport, Conn.: Greenwood Press, 2001), p. 4.

5. Ibid., pp. 2–4.

DICTIONARY OF
LITERARY
INFLUENCES

A

ACHEBE, CHINUA (1930–)

Albert Chinualumogu Achebe was born in Nigeria of Christian parents. He attended the Government College in Umuahia from 1944 to 1947 and University College in Ibadan from 1948 to 1953. Afterward, he worked for the Nigerian Broadcasting Corporation in its radio division and began writing during his tenure there (1954–66). His publishing career began with *Things Fall Apart* (1958), which is his most famous and enduring work. He followed his first novel with four more (*No Longer At Ease*, 1960; *Arrow of God*, 1964; *A Man of the People*, 1966; and *Anthills of the Savannah*, 1988) along with several collections of short stories and essays. His support of the separatist government of Biafra during the Nigerian Civil War (1967–69) as a diplomat forced him into exile when the Nigerian government restored its control of the region; consequently, he has primarily lived and taught in the United States since the early 1970s.

The strongest literary influences on Achebe proved to come from two sources: his family and his European-style education. His mother and sister instilled in him a love of storytelling and traditional African culture, which was supplemented by the numerous visitors his father, a clergyman, attracted to their home. As a youth, he was entranced by works such as Sir Walter Scott's *Ivanhoe* and Robert Louis Stevenson's *Treasure Island* because of their setting in exotic times and locales. His university reading, based on the European-based educational system, included works that depicted Africans as simple childlike beings who needed European care-takers in order to have an orderly society. He found this attitude depicted most vividly in Joyce Cary's *Mister Johnson* (1939), and he wrote *Things Fall Apart* par-tially as a response to Cary's novel. Despite his misgivings regarding the European attitudes toward Africans, he particularly admired the works of William Butler Yeats, whose poem *The Second Coming* inspired the title of his first novel. Yeats's use of simple, direct language as well as the passion and intensity of his verse impressed Achebe, and he later sought to imbue his own works with similar simplicity and depth. Combining these elements with his own gifts as a writer quickly made Achebe one of the leading voices in African literature.

Archives

Chinua Achebe Papers: Houghton Library, Harvard University. Contains manuscripts of Achebe's main publications from *Arrow of God* (1964) to *Anthills of the Savannah* (1988), and of a few later occasional writings down to 1993; with some publishers' correspondence.

Printed Sources

Achebe, Chinua. *Home and Exile* (New York: Anchor Books, 2001). Includes three lectures in which he discusses, among other things, literary influences on his works.

Achebe, Chinua, and Bernth Lindfors (eds.). *Conversations with Chinua Achebe*. Literary Conversations Series (Oxford, Miss.: Mississippi University Press, 1997). Interviews.

Ezenwa-Ohaeton. *Chinua Achebe: A Biography* (Bloomington: Indiana University Press, 1997).

Joseph E. Becker

ADAMS, GERALD (1948–)

Gerry Adams was born in West Belfast, Northern Ireland, the eldest of ten children. Educated at St. Mary's Grammar School in Belfast (1961–65), he left at 17 to become a barman but soon devoted himself to the Republican movement, by most accounts serving as an officer in the Provisional Irish Republican Army (IRA). Arrested in 1971, he was released in 1972 to serve on an IRA delegation to England before being interned again in 1973. Upon his release in 1977 Adams became vice president of Sinn Féin, the political counterpart to the IRA. He used his position to encourage the strategy of supplementing IRA violence with politics by contesting elections in Northern Ireland and the Irish Republic. In 1983, Adams became president of Sinn Féin and was elected to Parliament in Westminster for the West Belfast seat (1983–92, 1997–).

Apparently convinced that the goal of a united Ireland could be significantly advanced through political means, Adams attempted to publicly distance himself and his party from the IRA. In 1988 Adams began a dialogue with John Hume of the Social Democratic and Labor Party, the largest Nationalist party in Northern Ireland. These discussions eventually led to meetings with representatives of the Republic of Ireland and the British government, and, in 1994, to permission for Adams to enter the United States. Soon after Adams's much publicized visit to America, the IRA announced a cease-fire. Despite a revival of violence in 1996 and delays in decommissioning the IRA's stockpile of weapons, Sinn Féin participated in the all-party talks that eventually produced the Good Friday Agreement in 1998. Although Adams is not one of his party's representatives to the Northern Irish Assembly, he remains the president of Sinn Féin and the most visible international spokesman for Irish Republicanism.

A frequent contributor to various newspapers in Ireland and the United States, Adams has also written a number of fiction and nonfiction books including *Pathway to Peace* (1988), *Cage Eleven* (1990), *The Street and Other Stories* (1992), *Free Ireland: Towards a Lasting Peace* (1995), and *An Irish Voice: The Quest for Peace* (1997). In his autobiography, *Before the Dawn* (1996), Adams cites Irish Republican literature among his most important early influences; he specifically mentions Charles Kickham's *Knocknagow, or the Homes of Tipperary* (1873) and the writings of labor leader James Connelly.

Archives

Neither Gerry Adams nor Sinn Féin have placed their materials in an archive. Linen Hill Library, Belfast, has an extensive collection of materials on The Troubles.

Printed Sources

Adams, Gerry. *Before the Dawn: An Autobiography* (New York: William Morrow & Co., 1996).
———. *Selected Writings* (Dingle: Brandon Press, 1994).
———. *Signposts to Independence and Socialism* (Dublin: Sinn Féin Publicity Dept., 1988).
Kenna, Colm. *Gerry Adams: A Biography* (Cork: Mercier Press, 1990).
O'Brien, Brendan. *The Long War: The IRA and Sinn Féin, 1985 to Today* (Dublin: O'Brien Press, 1993).
Sharrock, David, and Mark Devenport. *Man of War, Man of Peace?: The Unauthorised Biography of Gerry Adams* (London: Macmillan, 1997).

Padraic Kennedy

ADDAMS, JANE (1860–1935)

Addams's tombstone in the family plot close to her birth house in Cedarville, Illinois, reads: "Hull House and The Women's International League for Peace and Freedom." She was the first American woman to win a Nobel Prize for Peace (1931). Basing Hull House on London's Toynbee Hall, Addams and her colleagues developed need-based social reform work in Chicago. Their model shaped the national Social Settlement Movement, Addams becoming the preeminent woman leader. She had access to Presidents Theodore Roosevelt and Woodrow Wilson. Founder of the Women's Peace Party and presider at the first International Congress of Women at the Hague, Netherlands (1915), she formed the Women's International League for Peace and Freedom, serving as president from 1919 to 1929. She helped establish the National Association for the Advancement of Colored People (1909) and the American Civil Liberties Union (1920). Eleven books, hundreds of articles for ladies' magazines, and countless speeches informed American understanding of immigrants, urban life, social reform, labor unionization, women's suffrage, and peace issues.

John Huy Addams, her father, shaped her in the democratic principles of Abraham Lincoln and a nondogmatic, Quaker approach to religion. At Rockford Female Seminary (1877–81), Addams studied Greek, Latin, and German, absorbing the life wisdom of Socrates and the Greek tragedians, Isaiah's prophetic vision of peace, and the Sermon on the Mount as the ethical bases for life. Reading Thomas Carlyle's *On Heroes, Hero-Worship, and the Heroic in History* (1841), she vowed in college essays that her life would have noble purpose and meaning as did Goethe's, Savonarola's, Frederick the Great's, and Dante's; her reflective postcollege letters to Ellen Gates Starr (cofounder of Hull House) most often quote Carlyle. John Ruskin's studies of art and architecture informed her experience of Europe, and his *Unto This Last* (1859), in its critique of industrial culture and vision of social reform for England, was the basis of much of her literary analysis of the United States. William Morris was the essential influence on the settlement's arts and crafts program.

With Josiah Royce *(The Spirit of Modern Philosophy)* Addams shared central tenets of the Progressive Movement. Intellectual contemporaries were the philosophical pragmatist, William James, and John Dewey, educational reformer, who served on Hull House's board of directors overseeing the Jean Piaget–based kindergarten and the extensive adult continuing education program. Taking the massive study of London by Charles Booth as inspiration, Addams's edition of *Hull House Maps and Papers* became the first American sociological study of a neighborhood.

Count Lev Tolstoy, the father of modern pacifism, was a spiritual example. Addams's international peace activities brought her into close communion with the British Fabian Socialists, especially Sydney and **Beatrice Webb.** She quoted H. G. Wells's pessimism about human nature, and Norman Angell's *The Fruits of Victory* sounded her conviction that war psychology was fatal to social living. Her philosophical book, *Peace and Bread in Time of War* (1922), shared the insights of James G. Frazer's *The Golden Bough* on ancient myths as the origins of culture. *Twenty Years at Hull-House* (1910), combined autobiography with a narrative of programs after the style of Henry Thoreau's *Walden.*

Archives

Jane Addams Hull-House Museum, University of Illinois at Chicago. College themes, essays published in the *Rockford Seminary Magazine,* and copies of correspondence with Ellen Gates Starr.

Swarthmore College Peace Collection, Swarthmore, Pa., *Jane Addams Collection,* Papers from 1838 (bulk 1880–1935). Donated by Addams and her heirs.

Printed Sources

Addams, Jane. *Democracy and Social Ethics.* 1902. Reprint, with an introduction by Anne Firor Scott (Cambridge, Mass.: Harvard University Press, 1964).

Chambers, Clarke A. "Jane Addams." In Leonard Unger (ed.), *American Writers: Supplement I, Part 1* (New York: Charles Scribner's Sons, 1979).

Davis, Allen F. *American Heroine: The Life and Legend of Jane Addams* (London: Oxford University Press, 1973).

Farrell, John C. *Beloved Lady: A History of Jane Addams' Ideas on Reform and Peace* (Baltimore: Johns Hopkins University Press, 1967).

Hurt, James. *"Walden* on Halsted Street: Jane Addams' *Twenty Years at Hull-House," The Centennial Review* 23, 2 (Spring 1979), 185–207.

Levine, Daniel. *Jane Addams and the Liberal Tradition* (Madison: State Historical Society of Wisconsin, 1971).

Schmider, Mary Ellen Heian. "Jane Addams' Aesthetic of Social Reform" (Ph.D. diss., University of Minnesota, 1983). In-depth analysis of nonfiction prose reflecting literary influences, esp. Carlyle and Ruskin.

Mary Ellen Heian Schmider

ADENAUER, KONRAD (1876–1967)

Konrad Adenauer emerged after the Second World War as the central figure in West Germany's economic and political recovery. His career in politics began as a member of the Cologne City Council, and in 1917 he became Lord Mayor of the city. Subsequently, he became president of the Prussian State Council and German

Council of Cities and chairman of the Rhineland Provincial Committee. When the Nazis came to power in 1933, Adenauer, who had not hidden distaste for them, lost his positions, and was forced to go into "exile." The day after the Allied capture of Cologne on May 8, 1945, the Americans asked him to be mayor again, but the British took control of the city and dismissed him. Adenauer then set to work forming a new political party combining Protestants and Catholics into the Christian Democratic Union (CDU). After the Western occupying powers agreed to merge their zones to form a new state in 1948, Adenauer was appointed president of the Parliamentary Council, which hammered out a provisional constitution for West Germany while sustaining the long-term objective of a reunited Germany. After the first West German elections, the CDU and its Bavarian sister party, the Christian Social Union (CSU), emerged as the dominant political force with Adenauer elected chancellor on September 15, 1949. As chancellor, Adenauer's primary focus was a sovereign, democratic West German state firmly anchored in the West. For this West Germany joined the Council of Europe and the International Ruhr Authority. The achievement of national sovereignty, close ties with the free West, reconciliation with France, and the consolidation of social market economy all are landmarks that are inseparably linked with the name of Konrad Adenauer. When it came to rearmament, the memory of World War II created intense fear, among some, of any German national army. On the other hand, the perceived threat of war from the East made pacifist pleas unacceptable. However, Adenauer's position prevailed. In his memorandum of August 29, 1950, Adenauer announced West Germany's willingness to contribute to a European armed force. Normalized relations between Germany and the Western powers were formalized in 1954. As a politician, Adenauer had a long track record as a Francophile and remained sincerely committed to the idea of an integrated Europe. Adenauer also negotiated a compensation agreement with Israel in recognition of the horror perpetrated by **Adolf Hitler** and Germany on the Jews. Adenauer's political career declined after 1961 when the CDU-CSU had to form a coalition with the Free Democratic Party (FDP), and the FDP made it a condition that Adenauer retire in 1963. After retiring, Adenauer traveled and finished his memoirs until his death in 1967.

As a participant in German cultural life, Adenauer's contributions are often submerged in the shadow of his political success. Throughout his life, Adenauer demonstrated his belief in the importance of a German cultural heritage—though with a clear preference for Western Europe. Raised in a Roman Catholic family, Adenauer demonstrated at an early age an interest in poetry and literature. His early exposure to classical literature combined an emphasis on Homer and Virgil with a traditional methodology, emphasizing the memorization of lengthy passages. On the one hand, Adenauer generally rejected works delving into irrationality, socially critical works, such as those of **Heinrich Böll,** and generally those linked with expressionism and neo-romanticism. Rather, Adenauer favored classical writers throughout his life, including Ernst Moritz Arndt, Heinrich Heine, Johann Wolfgang von Goethe, Friedrich Schiller, and Theodor Storm. Adenauer's artistic interests, in comparison, drifted primarily into the sixteenth century and to the figure of Domenicos Theotocopoulos, better known as El Greco. After the Second World War, Adenauer believed Hitler's rise to power to be in many ways a consequence of Germany's departure from its Christian heritage and from its tradition as a tolerant land of diverse thinkers and poets. In foreign policy, Adenauer's sense of religious conviction, combined with a strongly sentimental attachment to elements of classical German literature, no doubt influenced his political commitment to a West German state anchored in the West. In domestic policy, Adenauer stressed the need to return to Germany's Judeo-Christian heritage as the cultural-intellectual foundation capable of inhibiting any revival of German militarism. Consequently, Adenauer did not perceive the rise of Hitler as a consequence of German long-term sociocultural factors, but a short-term deviation from those traditions during the heyday of National Socialism. Adenauer's critics, however, have emphasized the prominence of nationalistic and militaristic elements in works read in his youth as an explanation for his political and social conservatism in his domestic policies.

Archives

Stiftung Bundeskanzler Adenauer Haus (Rhöndorf, Germany) is the primary depository for materials relating to all aspects of Adenauer's life. However, the Bundesarchiv (Koblenz, Germany) and the Auswärtiges Amt (Bonn, Germany) hold vast collections of government documents from Adenauer's tenure as chancellor.

Printed Sources

Adenauer, Konrad. *Erinnerungen 1945–1953* (Stuttgart: Deutsche Verlags-Anstalt, 1965).
——. *Briefe 1945–1955*, 5 vols. (Berlin: Siedler Verlag, 1983–95).
——. *Teegespräche 1950–1963*, 4 vols. (Berlin: Siedler Verlag, 1984–92).
——. *Memoirs 1945–1953*, 4 vols. (Chicago: Henry Regnery, 1965).
Akten zur Auswärtigen Politik der Bundesrepublik Deutschland 1949–52, 2 vols. (München: R. Oldenbourg Verlag, 1989).
Akten zur Vorgeschichte der Bundesrepublik Deutschland 1945–1949, 5 vols. (München: R. Oldenbourg Verlag, 1975–85).
Die Kabinettsprotokolle der Bundesregierung. 1949–1957, 14 vols. (Boppard am Rhein: Harald Boldt Verlag, 1982–2000).
Köhler, Henning. *Adenauer: Eine Politische Biographie* (Berlin: Propyläen, 1994).
Der Parlamentarische Rat 1948–1949. Akten und Protokolle, 4 vols. (Boppard am Rhein: Harald Boldt Verlag, 1975–89).
Schwarz, Hans-Peter. *Adenauer. 1876–1967*, 2 vols. (Stuttgart: Deutsche Verlags-Anstalt, 1986, 1991).
Weymar, Paul. *Adenauer. His Authorized Biography* (New York: Dutton & Co., 1955).

David A. Meier

AITKEN, WILLIAM MAXWELL, FIRST BARON BEAVERBROOK (1879–1964)

William Maxwell Aitken, the son of a Scottish Presbyterian minister, was born in Maple, Ontario. He spent his youth in Newcastle, New Brunswick. Aitken attended the local school, but failed to gain university entrance. He briefly clerked with a law firm before succeeding in insurance and bond sales. By the age of 30 Aitken had brought about the merger of Canada's largest steel manufacturing concerns, riding the Canadian economic boom to millionaire status. In 1910 he relocated to London and became immersed in the Conservative Party.

He made his mark as a politician, a newspaper proprietor, and a historian. Although Aitken sat in the Commons from 1910 to 1916 and then ascended to the Lords, he was most known for his personal associations and intrigues, particularly for his behind-the-scenes involvement in the accession of both David Lloyd George (in 1916) and Bonar Law (in 1923) to the position of prime minister. During World War I he served as Britain's minister of information (1917–18). During World War II long-term friendship with Winston Churchill led to service as minister for aircraft production (1940–41), minister of supply (1941–42), minister of war production (1942), and Lord Privy Seal (1943–45). In 1916 Beaverbrook acquired controlling interest in the *Daily Express*. He founded the *Sunday Express* in 1921 and in 1929 purchased the *Evening Standard*. He attempted to use his newspapers to exert political influence, with mixed results; however their modernized style of presentation set new standards. The *Daily Express* achieved the largest circulation of any newspaper in the world under his personal management. Beaverbrook also collected and greatly restricted access to the papers of major political figures. He utilized them to write controversial histories that have strongly influenced the historical interpretation of World War I and postwar events. His most noted works include *Politicians and the Press* (1925), *Politicians and the War* (2 vols., 1928 and 1932), *Men and Power, 1917–1918* (1956), and *The Decline and Fall of Lloyd George* (1962).

Beaverbrook's identity as a Canadian, a supporter of Empire, and an entrepreneur remained predominant influences throughout his life. He saw himself as an outsider who championed merit. His father's occupation also profoundly (and ambivalently) affected Beaverbrook. He described himself as "a child of the manse" and made frequent biblical references: King David intrigued him and he wrote an unpublished life of Jesus. His father was well read and enjoyed a large library. Robert Louis Stevenson and Walter Scott were Beaverbrook's favorite childhood authors.

As an adult, he was "too impatient to sit down for long with a book or even a newspaper." Secretaries provided summations of important works (Taylor 1972, 9). Beaverbrook kept abreast of breaking news at all times, installing ticker tape in his homes. He calculated his historical interpretation, access to the documents he controlled, and his editorial policies in terms of their immediate contribution to his current political goals. The campaigns of Lord Northcliffe, owner of the *Daily Mail*, initiated Beaverbrook's belief that newspapers offered him his greatest opportunity for political influence.

Beaverbrook sustained intimate friendships with a number of authors, including Rudyard Kipling and Churchill, with whom he exchanged drafts and comments. He also submitted his work to politicians who played a role in events he wrote about, seeking their clarification. Beaverbrook prided himself on his hospitality toward developing talent and cultivated writers as protégés. Some influenced him in return: Arnold Bennett perhaps most strongly.

Archives

Beaverbrook Collection, Harriet Irving Library, University of New Brunswick, Fredericton. Canadian correspondence.

Beaverbrook Papers, House of Lords Records Office, London. Correspondence, draft manuscripts of published works, unpublished works, newspaper clippings, and library.

Printed Sources

Chisholm, Anne, and Michael Davies. *Lord Beaverbrook: A Life* (New York: Alfred Knopf, 1993).

Taylor, A. J. P. *Beaverbrook* (London: Hamilton Hamish, 1972).

Anne Kelsch

AKHMATOVA, ANNA ANDREEVNA (1889–1966)

Anna Akhmatova was born near Odessa, but grew up outside of St. Petersburg in Tsarskoe Selo. In her "Autobiographical Prose," Akhmatova claimed to have learned to read from Lev Tolstoy's *Grammar* and to speak French by the age of five (Akhmatova 1994, 2). She attended school in Tsarskoe Selo and later in Kiev at the Fundukleyevskaya Gymnasium. In 1907 Akhmatova published her first poem and enrolled in the Faculty of Law at the Kiev College for Women. She withdrew from Kiev College a year later to study literature and history in St. Petersburg, where she met her first husband, the Acmeist poet, Nikolay Gumilyov. Between 1910 and 1912 she and Gumilyov traveled to Paris, Switzerland, and Northern Italy. In 1912 Akhmatova published her first volume of poetry, entitled *Evening;* her second book of verse, *Rosary,* appeared in 1914. Three more volumes of poetry came out before she was banned from publishing in 1922. Once silenced, Akhmatova turned her attention to the study of the works of Pushkin and produced three valuable critical studies. She also worked as a translator from French, English, and Italian. Her only son, Lev, was arrested and spent 18 years in prison. Despite years of forced silence, Akhmatova emerged as one of the major voices of Acmeism and published more than a dozen volumes of verse, which included two of her best known works: "Requiem" and "Poem without a Hero."

As a student in Tsarskoe Selo, Akhmatova attended lectures by the Symbolist poet Innokenty Annensky, one of her earliest artistic influences (Reeder 1994, 9). In *My Half Century* she wrote, "I find my own 'origin' in Annensky's poems" (Akhmatova 1992, 111). Ketchian sees the influence as structural; Akhmatova's verse shows "dual-layered correspondences with Annensky, which often hail back to their common source, Alexander Pushkin" (Ketchian 1986, 123). Moreover, Pushkin's influence can be seen in her method of borrowing lines, images, and similes from other writers and transforming them to make them her own (Reeder 1994, 184). Several scholars have noted that Akhmatova conducted "conversations" in this way with a variety of authors (Nayman 1991, 25; Reeder 1994, 183; Ketchian 1986, 121). "Byron, Shelley, Keats, **Joyce** and Eliot are connected with the cycles of 'Cinque' and 'The Wild Rose in Flower' and with 'Poem Without a Hero', no less than Virgil and Horace, Dante, Baudelaire and Nerval" (Nayman 1991, 99). Among the few books she kept with her were the Bible, Dante, a complete Shakespeare, and the collected Pushkin (Nayman 1991, 93).

Archives

Russian Academy of Sciences Institute of Russian Literature (Pushkin House) in St. Petersburg, Russia. The Moscow Central Archive contains 21 notebooks from her last decade. Russian National Library in St. Petersburg, Russia.

Printed Sources

Akhmatova, Anna. "Autobiographical Prose: Sketches, Notes, Diary Entries, and Lectures." In Konstantin Polivanov (ed.) and Patricia Beriozkina (trans.), *Anna Akhmatova and Her Circle* (Fayetteville, Ark.: The University of Arkansas Press, 1994). Includes contemporaries of Akhmatova.
———. *My Half Century*, Ronald Meyer (ed.), (Ann Arbor, Mich.: Ardis, 1992). Includes diary entries, notebook excerpts, prose works on Pushkin, book reviews, public addresses, and correspondence.
Chukovskaya, Lidia. *Zapiski ob Anne Akhmatovoi*, 2 vols. (Paris: YMCA Press, 1976, 1980).

Haight, Amanda. *Anna Akhmatova. A Poetic Pilgrimage* (New York and London: Oxford University Press, 1976).

Ketchian, Sonia. *The Poetry of Anna Akhmatova: A Conquest of Time and Space*, F. D. Reeve (trans.), (München: Verlag Otto Sagner, 1986).

Nayman, Anatoly. *Remembering Anna Akhmatova*, Wendy Rosslyn (trans.), (New York: Henry Holt and Company, 1991). Nayman, a poet and translator, was Akhmatova's literary secretary in her later years.

Reeder, Roberta. *Anna Akhmatova. Poet and Prophet* (New York: St. Martin's Press, 1994).

Erika Haber

ALI, MUHAMMAD (1942–)

Muhammad Ali became heavyweight champion of the world in 1964, at age 22, when he defeated title holder Sonny Liston. Undefeated until February 1978 when he lost the title to Leon Spinks, Ali reclaimed his title during a rematch seven months later. Ali remained undefeated until his retirement in 1981, with 56 wins, including 37 knockouts. Heroically battling Parkinson's disease, during the 1990s he became one of the most popular and widely recognized sports figures in the world.

Cassius Marcellus Clay Jr.—who adopted the name Muhammad Ali in 1964 when he joined the Nation of Islam (Black Muslims)—was born in Louisville, Kentucky, to Cassius Marcellus Clay Sr., a sign painter, and Odessa Gray Clay, a domestic worker. Ali attended segregated elementary and secondary schools in Louisville. He started boxing at age 12. By the time he graduated from high school in 1960, he had fought 108 amateur bouts. He had also won six Kentucky Golden Gloves championships, two National Golden Glove tournaments, and two National Amateur Athletic Union titles. Also in 1960, he won the gold medal at the Olympics in Rome, Italy, as a light-heavyweight.

In 1967, three years after winning the world heavyweight title, Ali was convicted of draft evasion for refusing to be inducted into the armed forces during the Vietnam War due to his religious beliefs. As a result, his boxing license was revoked and he was stripped of his title. Although the Supreme Court reversed his conviction on June 28, 1971, granting him the status of conscientious objector, Ali was forced to fight Joe Frazier to regain his title.

In his autobiography, Ali revealed that he developed his self-promotional "I am the greatest!" tactic after reading about Gorgeous George, a wrestler whose bragging and playful intimidation of opponents drew record crowds. Although his primary focus was physical development, after retirement he wished to learn as much as he could, "because I know nothing compared to what I need to know." As a devout Muslim, he was profoundly influenced by the teachings of **Elijah Muhammad** and the Koran, the foundation of his Islamic faith. Ali's colorful personal life and tumultuous professional career have inspired numerous writers to document his rise from poverty to celebrity, focusing on his love for his people, his generosity, and his refusal to compromise principles, regardless of the consequences.

Archives

Muhammad Ali Center, Louisville, Kentucky.

Printed Sources

Ali, Muhammad, and Richard Durham. *The Greatest: My Own Story* (New York: Random House, 1975). Includes a chronology of key events (1942–72) and Ali's fight record (1960–75).

Early, Gerald (ed.). *The Muhammad Ali Reader* (Hopewell, N.J.: Ecco Press, 1998). Collected articles from various sources.

Hauser, Thomas. *Muhammad Ali: His Life and Times* (New York: Simon & Schuster, 1991). Collected interviews.

Remnick, David. *King of the World: Muhammad Ali and the Rise of an American Hero* (New York: Random House, 1998). Traces Ali's career from 1962 to the late 1990s.

Schulberg, Budd. *Loser and Still Champion: Muhammad Ali* (Garden City, N.Y.: Doubleday, 1972). Focuses on Ali's career following his fight with Joe Frazier.

Torres, Jose. *Sting Like a Bee: The Muhammad Ali Story* (London, New York: Abelard-Schuman, 1971). Biography told from the perspective of a former boxer. Includes preface by Norman Mailer.

Durthy A. Washington

ALLENDE, ISABEL (1942–)

Isabel Allende was born in Lima, Peru to Chilean parents, her father a diplomat. Her formal education ended when she graduated from high school in Santiago, Chile at 16 years old. When she was two, her parents divorced and she and her mother moved in with her maternal grandparents, where her grandmother Memé introduced her to the art of storytelling. Her mother remarried another diplomat, so Allende's adolescent years were spent in Bolivia, the Middle East, and Europe. After high school she worked as a secretary for the Food and Agricultural Organization of the United Nations in Santiago. She left the UN to begin a career in print and broadcast journalism writing a column for a feminist magazine, *Paula*, and hosting a weekly TV show. She also wrote short stories for children and collaborated in writing and producing plays. Chilean politics shaped the rest of her career. When the military dictatorship of Augusto Pinochet Ugarte seized control of Chilean government in 1973, Allende joined church-sponsored groups to provide food and aid to the needy and families of victims of Pinochet's regime. She aided her compatriots in escaping military persecution until 1975, when she fled Chile for Caracas, Venezuela, with her first husband, Michael Frías, and two children, Paula and Nicolás. In political exile, she wrote her first four novels, *Casa de los espiritus/The House of Spirits* (Plaza & Janés, 1982; Knopf 1985), *De amor y de sombra/Of Love and Shadows* (Plaza & Janés, 1984; Knopf 1987), *Eva Luna* (Knopf, 1988). On January 8, 1981, she began *House of Spirits* as a farewell letter to her 100-year-old grandfather, who was still in Chile and dying. Allende has additionally written three other novels, a memoir, an autobiography, and a collection of short stories translated in more than 30 languages, the first woman to share bestseller status with her Latin American male counterparts. Her writing follows the Latin American tradition of blurring the lines between reality and dreams through magical realism.

A member of the first generation of Latin American readers who had access to other Latin American writers, Allende cites as her greatest influences the "great writers of the Latin American boom of literature"; among these she specifically credits Pablo Neruda and **Gabriel García Márquez.** As an adolescent she secretly read *One Thousand and One Nights*, a book that introduced her to the world of imagination and eroticism. Her fiction is influenced by an oral tradition of women telling stories—her mother, her grandmother, and the maids—in addition to radio novellas blasting all day in the kitchen (Crystall and Kuhnheim, 1992). Additionally, she has read English and Russian novelists. In the 1970s, she read European and North American feminists whose ideas affected her life and her work. Because writing is an organic process for Allende, she writes in her native language, Spanish. Now a resident of the United States, Allende says English has influenced her writing style. In *The Stories of Eva Luna* (Atheneum, 1991), she uses more precise language, shorter sentences, and less ornamentation. In *Daughter of Fortune* (Knopf, 1999) and *Portrait in Sepia* (HarperCollins 2000), Allende connects Latin American and North American story and myth.

Archives

Daily letters to and from her mother are known to exist, but are not yet available for research. See, however, "Isabel Allende" n.d., http://www.isabelallende.com, accessed July 30, 2002. Traces literary influences, explains her writing process, lists professional accomplishments, and contains 32 photos from the author's private album.

Printed Sources

Allende, Isabel. *Paula*, Margaret Sayers Peden (trans.), (New York: Harper, 1994). Allende's autobiography chronicles her vigil over her daughter Paula's terminal illness and documents the author's writing and personal life.

Crystall, Elyse, Jill Kuhnheim, and Mary Layoun. "An Interview with Isabel Allende," *Contemporary Literature* 33, 1 (1992), 584–601.

Jill E. Eichhorn

AMADO, JORGE (1912–2001)

Jorge Amado was born on the cacao farm Auricídia, in the rural area of Ferradas, district of Itabuna, in the northeastern state of Bahia, Argentina. He grew up in Ilhéus; at 11 he was sent to the Jesuit college in Salvador. He studied law at the Federal University of Rio de Janeiro, where he graduated in 1935, but he never became a practicing lawyer. Fascinated by Russia, the Russian revolution, and Russian literature, he became a militant of the Brazilian Communist Party, and as such was elected to Congress. He was strongly influenced by the novels of such Russian writers as Aleksandr Fadeyev (*The Rout*, 1927), Aleksandr Serafimovich (*The Iron Flood*, 1927), Isaak Babel (*Red Cavalry*, 1926), Ilya Ilf and Yevgeny Pietrov (*The Twelve Chairs*, 1928), and Ilya Ehrenburg (*The Extraordinary Adventures of Julio Jurenito and His Disciples*, 1922). He also read *Jews without Money* (1930) by Michael Gold, who became his close friend afterward. Mark Twain and Charles Dickens brought to his attention the idea of the deprived childhood as raw material for his early fiction. One of the first books that excited his social conscience was *David Copperfield*, which especially influenced *Captains of the Sands* (1937), a novel that depicts the lives of homeless children living on the streets of Salvador, his most popular novel. Critics prefer *The Two Deaths of Quincas Wateryell* (1961) for its magical realism and *The Violent Land* (1943), a well-structured historical novel and probably his finest narrative.

The novels that exerted more influence upon Brazil and the entire world are *Gabriela, Clove and Cinnamon* (1958), and *Dona Flor and Her Two Husbands* (1966). Both were made into successful movies, television series, and soap operas. The film version of "Dona Flor" (1976) is still the most popular Brazilian movie ever made. These novels helped create a worldwide stereotypical image of Brazil as being an exotic tropical country with spicy ingredients of a folk saga tempered with lusty mulattas, carnival, sex, and Latin machismo. Amado's 25 novels have been translated into 49 languages and have been published in 55 countries.

Archives

Fundação Casa de Jorge Amado built in 1987, and located in Pelourinho, on the historic side of Salvador, maintains a large collection of materials (mainly books, photos, videos, and posters).

Printed Sources

Brower, Keith H. et al. (eds.). *Jorge Amado: New Critical Essays* (New York: Garland, 2001). A comprehensive account of his major works and facets by selected scholars.

Candido, Antonio. "Poesia, documento e história." In *Brigada ligeira e outros escritos* (São Paulo: Editora da Unesp, 1992). Remarkable insights into Brazilian fiction of the 1930s, and on Amado's first novels, especially on *The Violent Land*, by the most reputable Brazilian critic of today.

Duarte, Eduardo de Assis. *Jorge Amado: romance em tempo de utopia* (Natal: UFRN, 1995). A former Ph.D. dissertation is the best source for Amado as a leftist writer. Includes an extensive bibliography and an interview with the novelist.

Galvão, Walnice Nogueira. "Amado: respeitoso, respeitável." In *Saco de Gatos* (São Paulo: Duas Cidades, 1976). A sharp criticism on Amado's works, especially on *Tereza Batista: Home from the Wars*, from a feminist perspective, by one of Brazil's prominent scholars.

Lima, Luís Costa. "Jorge Amado." In Afrânio Coutinho (ed.), *A literatura no Brasil*. 2nd ed., vol. 5 (Rio de Janeiro: Sul Americana, 1970). A restrictive reading of Amado's novels.

Tavares, Paulo. *Criaturas de Jorge Amado*, 2nd ed. (Rio de Janeiro: Record, 1985). The most comprehensive list of characters taken from his fiction published up to 1983. Includes 4,910 entries on characters, animals and birds used as proper names, and places used as settings for his novels.

Gentil de Faria

ANDRIĆ, IVO (1892–1975)

Ivo Andrić was born in the Bosnian town of Travnik. After the death of his father, the two-year-old Andrić was sent to live with relatives in Višegrad, the setting of his most famous novel, *The Bridge on the Drina*. Andrić completed elementary school in Višegrad and studied at the gymnasium in Sarajevo (1903–12), where he became associated with the nationalist movement, Young Bosnia. He enrolled in 1912 at the University of Zagreb, the following year at the University of Vienna, and then, in spring 1914, at Jagiellonian University in Kraków. After the start of World War I he was arrested in Croatia for his connections with Young Bosnia, whose members had carried out the assassination of Archduke Franz Ferdinand, and he was held under guard until 1917. After the war, Andrić edited a journal of South Slavic literature, in which he published his own writings. He entered the Yugoslav Foreign Ministry in 1920 and served at posts throughout Europe over the next two decades. He completed his doctorate in 1924 at Karl Franz University in Graz, submitting the dissertation, "The Development of Spiritual Life in Bosnia under the Influence of Turkish Rule," a critical assessment of Islamic influence in his homeland. Andrić's final diplomatic post was as ambassador to Berlin (1938–41). He resigned in protest against his government's close relations with Nazi Germany and returned to Belgrade. During the war he devoted himself to writing three novels: *The Bridge on the Drina, Bosnian Chronicle,* and *The Woman from Sarajevo.* All three books were published after the liberation in 1945. Andrić supported the communist regime established after the war by Josip Broz Tito. In 1946 he became a member of the Serbian Academy of Sciences and was elected first president of the Yugoslav Writers' Union. In 1950 he was elected to the Federal Assembly, and in 1954 he became a member of the Communist Party. In 1961 he became the first Yugoslav writer to win the Nobel Prize for Literature.

Andrić once remarked on the various literary influences that shaped his style: "Chinese verses, Scandinavians and Poles, French, German, and Russian writers. . . . How could it be possible to extract from that, and far more that has not been mentioned, something that should be called a decisive influence?" (Hawkesworth 1984, 41). His first loves as a reader had been Serbian historical novels and the adventures of Jules Verne, Sir Walter Scott, and Cervantes, which he read in German translation while a student. Andrić mastered the classical languages, German, French, and Italian before he left the gymnasium, and he read widely in those languages. Among his favorite authors as a student were Thomas Mann, whom Andrić appreciated for his contemplation of the power of legend and the irrational; Marcus Aurelius, from whom he gained a stoic outlook and an affinity for reflective literary prose; and Walt Whitman, whom Andrić admired for his celebration of universal brotherhood. Particularly influential was Søren Kierkegaard. When he was arrested at the start of World War I, Andrić was allowed just one volume in his cell: Kierkegaard's *Either-Or* (1843). Andrić found resonance in Kierkegaard's awareness of paradox as a source of passion in life and the melancholy brought by reflection on the divergence of the real and possible. Andrić also counted among his influences nineteenth-century and contemporary writers in Slovene and his native Serbo-Croatian. Most important were the Montenegrin poet Petar Petrović Njegoš and the nineteenth-century collector of Serbian folk songs, Vuk Karadžić. Proof of Andrić's love of reading is the fact that he donated the stipend from his Nobel Prize to purchase books for school libraries in Yugoslavia.

Archives

Personal Fund of Ivo Andrić, Archive of the Serbian Academy of Sciences and Arts, Belgrade, Serbia.

Printed Sources

Hawkesworth, Celia. *Ivo Andrić: Bridge between East and West* (London: Athlone, 1984).

Juričić, Želimir B. *The Man and the Artist: Essays on Ivo Andrić* (Lanham, Md.: University Press of America, 1986).

Mukerji, Vanita Singh. *Ivo Andrić: A Critical Biography* (Jefferson, N.C.: McFarland & Co., 1990).

Bruce R. Berglund

ANGELOU, MAYA (1928–)

Maya Angelou was born Marguerite Johnson in St. Louis, Missouri. Her parents were Bailey Johnson, a doorkeeper and naval dietitian, and Vivian Baxter Johnson, a nurse and real estate agent. Her childhood, which she recounts poetically in the first of her five autobiographies, *I Know Why the Caged Bird Sings*, was spent primarily in Stamps, Arkansas, where she was sent to live when her parents divorced. Angelou attended public schools in Arkansas and California, and she studied music, drama, and dance privately. At the age of sixteen, she had her son, Guy, and began supporting the two of them with a series of jobs, including being a cook, a waitress, a streetcar conductor, and, briefly, a madam. In more recent years, Angelou has been an actress, a singer, a playwright and director, a dance teacher, a civil rights activist, and a lecturer. Her primary literary contribution has been in the field of autobiography; she has also produced five volumes of poetry, as well as several plays and screenplays. Her most prominent themes are the triumph of the human spirit over adversity and the transforming power of art. In 1993, she received national attention when she read her poem "On the Pulse of Morning" at the presidential inauguration of Bill Clinton. She has been visiting writer and lecturer at UCLA, the University of Kansas, and Wichita State University. Since 1981, she has been a professor at Wake Forest University.

In *I Know Why the Caged Bird Sings*, published in 1970, Angelou recounts her early reading of contemporary African American writers. She recalls that she and her brother, Bailey, a prominent figure in this and other works, reject a scene from Shakespeare to memorize, fearing that their strong-willed grandmother would be furious when she discovered the author was white. Instead, the brother and sister choose James Weldon Johnson's "The Creation." Angelou also describes the healing function of reading during her childhood: she is sent back to Stamps after having been raped by a mother's boyfriend in St. Louis, and having responded by remaining mute for five years. During this time, she was tutored by a Mrs. Flowers, a woman she refers to as the "aristocrat of Black Stamps." She read the classics under the tutelage of Mrs. Flowers, and she describes learning from her that the "wonderful, beautiful Negro race" survives "in exact relationship to the dedication of our poets (including preachers, musicians, and blues singers)." She pays homage to her African American literary forbears in some of her titles, including that of her first book, which is taken from Paul Laurence Dunbar's poem "Sympathy"; the title of her fourth book, *The Heart of a Woman*, comes from a poem by Harlem Renaissance writer Georgia Douglas Johnson.

In interviews, Angelou has acknowledged her debt to writers such as Frances Ellen Watkins Harper, Zora Neale Hurston, and James Baldwin. Angelou herself became involved with the Harlem Writers Guild when she was inspired by the social activist writer John Killens to move to Brooklyn in 1958. This group of writers included John Henrik Clarke and Paule Marshall, as well as Baldwin. Angelou was encouraged to write *I Know Why the Caged Bird Sings* by Baldwin and Jules Feiffer, who had heard her stories of her Arkansas childhood. In *Order Out of Chaos: The Autobiographical Works of Maya Angelou*, Dolly McPherson places Angelou in a tradition of African American autobiography, beginning with *The Interesting Narrative of the Life of Olaudau Equiano, or Gastavus Vassa, The African* and continuing through Frederick Douglass, **Paul Robeson**, Zora Neale Hurston, **Malcolm X,** Anne Moody, James Weldon Johnson, and Julius Lester. In an interview with McPherson, Angelou draws comparisons with her autobiographical writing and that of Maxine Hong Kingston. Angelou's life and writing also have been shaped by her involvement in the civil rights movement and social reform. In 1959, she worked as the coordinator for **Martin Luther King**'s Southern Christian Leadership Conference and shortly thereafter lived in Egypt and Ghana, writing about and agitating for social change. Her fifth book, *All God's Children Need Traveling Shoes*, is dedicated to Julian Mayfield and Malcolm X; in it, she recounts her growing appreciation for her African "home."

Archives

Z. Smith Reynolds Library, Wake Forest University, Department of Rare Books: houses many of Angelou's manuscripts and drafts.

Printed Sources

Elliot, Jeffrey M. (ed.). *Conversations with Maya Angelou* (Oxford: University of Mississippi Press, 1989).

McPherson, Dolly A. *Order Out of Chaos: The Autobiographical Works of Maya Angelou* (Camden Town, London: Virago Press, 1991).

Tate, Claudia (ed.). *Black Women Writers at Work* (New York: Continuum, 1983).

Linda A. Barnes

APOLLINAIRE, GUILLAUME (1880–1918)

As part of the avant-garde in French literature at the turn of the twentieth century, Guillaume Apollinaire represents the last of the traditional lyric poets and the first of the modern literary iconoclasts. An enigmatic figure, Apollinaire both courted and scorned intellectualism, perhaps stemming from the secrecy surrounding his illegitimate birth on August 26, 1880. At the age of twenty in 1900, Apollinaire moved to Paris, where he spent the last eighteen years of his life. While there, he cultivated the friendship of artists such as Pablo Picasso, Andre Derain, and his lover, Marie Laurencin. Although best known as an avant-garde poet, he cultivated a reputation as a defender of modern painting and a promoter of new styles in literature and the graphic arts. He continuously used elements of his own life in his literature, so that there was, indeed, no real separation between man and writer. Each poem and story was a commemoration of an event in his life, but he was also acutely aware of the effect his work could have on society.

However, his lifestyle only served to further alienate him from the French people he tried so hard to call his own. He had always considered himself first and foremost a Frenchman, but his fellow français often thought otherwise. Disenchanted, he joined the French army, first in artillery on April 4, 1915, and then in infantry, where he was wounded in March 1916; in total, he spent 11 months on the front, and his celebrated quote, "Ah Dieu! Que la guerre est jolie, risqué fort de ne pas etre si simple" has often been misinterpreted. In other words, although he did not comprehend the reason for the brutality, it, unfortunately, became second nature for him just as it did for every other soldier. The war led to a more questioning Apollinaire, and at 37 at the end of the war, he used the war as a playing field with which to comment on the crisis among young people.

This questioning in turn led to the creation of *Le poete assassine*, a collage of 18 stories detailing a man's life from his birth to his career as a poet to his death at the hands of a mob. The collection of short stories was often broken, and the narrative changes in tone from humorous to serious, yet leaving no doubt regarding his political leanings, since his point of view regarding the Germans remains fluid from beginning to end. In stories such as "Cas du brigadier," the allies fared well, while the German soldier met his fate. Apollinaire intended this work to represent his desire to act as the reconciling party between modernism and traditionalism, and Apollinaire only added one story to this collection of short stories once the war began.

Apollinaire was a French nationalist from the beginning of his career, more because it was tied to his attraction to naturism, and he died a French nationalist. His war poetry demonstrates not only an enthusiasm for war, but an emphasis on the future of society. Although the combination of his prewar nationalism and the nationalist tendencies of the prewar French avant-garde did not guarantee his acceptance in French society, it did cement his celebrity as a literary genius. Ronald St. Onge contends that "the metamorphosis of Apollinaire's political thought led him from a youthful espousal of anarchistic ideals to a manifestation of chauvinistic zeal in his later years" (St. Onge 1971, 516). His family background, his schooling and literary tastes, as well as his political ideologies could have led him to further his anarchistic ideals, yet he remained independent and open to all ideas, including the coinage of some of his own. His position as both an avant-garde artist and a critic caused problems with some of the Nationalist traditionalists, and by defending avant-garde methods and art, he was often attacked and accused of being a Jew or an infidel. With the themes of metamorphism and mimesis, transformation and mimesis, dedoublement and disguise, Apollinaire established himself as poet, art critic, author, and master of many tasks.

Archives

"Guillaume Apollinaire." La Bibliotheque Nationale de France. Le Cabinet des Manuscrits. Musee Guillaume Apollinaire. Stavelot, France.

Printed Sources

Adamson, Walter L. "Apollinaire's Politics: Modernism, Nationalism, and the Public Sphere in Avant-garde Paris," *Modernism/Modernity* 6, 3 (1999), 33–56.

Barry, David. *The Creative Vision of Guillaume Apollinaire: A Study of Imagination* (Saratoga, Calif.: Anma Libri, 1982).

Bates, Scott. *Guillaume Apollinaire* (New York: Twayne Publishers, Inc., 1967).

Bohn, Willard. *Apollinaire and the Faceless Man: The Creation and Evolution of a Modern Motif* (Rutherford, N.J.: Fairleigh Dickinson University Press, 1991).

———. "From Sign to Signature in Apollinaire's 'Le Cheval'." In *Understanding French Poetry: Essays for a New Millennium*, Stamos Metzidakis (ed.), (New York: Garland Publishing, 1994), 51–70.

Pierre, Roland. "Guillaume Apollinaire et L'Avenir," *Europe: Revue litteraire Mensuelle* 421 (1964), 155–65.

St. Onge, Ronald. "Reflections of the Political World in the Works of Guillaume Apollinaire" (Ph.D. diss., Vanderbilt University, 1971).

Jennifer Harrison

ARENDT, HANNAH (1906–1975)

Fleeing from Germany in the 1930s, Hannah Arendt became one of the West's leading political scientists and opponents of totalitarianism. She was born in Hannover, Germany, as Johanna, the daughter of Martha Cohn and Paul Arendt, both educated and prosperous Jews from Königsberg, Prussia. In 1910 they returned to Königsberg, where Arendt began her schooling in Frau Stein's kindergarten and

Frau Sittznik's elementary school. Her father died of tertiary syphilis in 1913 after two years in the Königsberg Psychiatric Hospital. Her mother remarried in 1920. Arendt was always close to her mother but had uneasy and uncertain relationships with her stepfather, Martin Beerwald, and two stepsisters, one of whom committed suicide in 1932 at the age of 30.

Mother and daughter fled to Berlin as soon as World War I erupted. Arendt attended the girls' lyceum in the Berlin suburb of Charlottenburg. She began to appreciate the art of Käthe Kollwitz and the leftist politics of Konrad Schmidt, Eduard Bernstein, Joseph Bloch, Rosa Luxembourg, and Karl Liebknecht. After the war, back in Königsberg, she briefly attended the Luiseschule, the girls' gymnasium, until expelled for insubordination. Nevertheless, two subsequent years as a special student at the University of Berlin earned her the opportunity to take the *Abitur* examination, and thus she received her Luiseschule diploma in 1924. By then she already had read Søren Kierkegaard, Karl Jaspers, and Immanuel Kant and had studied theology under Romano Guardini at Berlin. She learned of the philosopher **Martin Heidegger** in 1923 from her friend Ernst Grumach, who attended Heidegger's earliest lectures at the University of Marburg. Through her lifelong friend, Anne Mendelssohn Weil, a descendant of both Moses and Felix Mendelssohn, Arendt learned about Rahel Varnhagen.

Almost immediately upon matriculating at Marburg in 1924, Arendt began a love affair with her teacher, Heidegger. She also studied under **Rudolf Bultmann** and met fellow student Hans Jonas at Marburg, then after spending a semester in 1925 at Freiburg im Breisgau to learn from Heidegger's mentor, Edmund Husserl, transferred to Heidelberg to become the protégé of Jaspers, under whom she studied Friedrich Nietzsche, August Strindberg, Vincent Van Gogh, **Max Weber,** and Friedrich Wilhelm Joseph von Schelling. There she met Karl Frankenstein, Erich Neumann, Benno Georg Leopold von Wiese, and Erwin Loewenson, and studied German Romanticism under Friedrich Gundolf. Directed by Jaspers, she wrote her doctoral dissertation in 1929 on "The Concept of Love in St. Augustine."

In the 1930s she showed increasing interest in **Bertolt Brecht,** the Zionist Kurt Blumenfeld, Karl Marx, Georg Wilhelm Friedrich Hegel, and Walter Benjamin. The rise of **Adolf Hitler** pushed her toward political philosophy. She was arrested in the spring of 1933, but was released after eight days, and escaped to France via Czechoslovakia and Switzerland. She was naturalized American in 1951.

Archives

The Manuscript Division of the Library of Congress contains 25,000 items in 38 linear feet of Arendt's "correspondence, articles, lectures, speeches, book manuscripts, subject files, transcripts of trial proceedings, notes, and printed matter pertaining to [her] writings and academic career." The co-executors of her literary estate were Lotte Kohler and Mary McCarthy.

Printed Sources

Alte Synagoge Essen. *Hannah Arendt: Lebensgeschichte einer deutschen Jüdin* (Essen: Klartext, 1995).

Clément, Catherine. *Martin and Hannah: A Novel*, Julia Shirek Smith (trans.), (Amherst, N.Y.: Prometheus Books, 2001).

Ettinger, Elzbieta. *Hannah Arendt/Martin Heidegger* (New Haven: Yale University Press, 1995).

Kristeva, Julia. *Hannah Arendt*, Ross Guberman (trans.), (New York: Columbia University Press, 2001).

McGowan, John. *Hannah Arendt: An Introduction* (Minneapolis: University of Minnesota Press, 1998).

May, Derwent. *Hannah Arendt* (Harmondsworth, England: Penguin, 1986).

Prinz, Alois. *Beruf Philosophin, oder die Liebe zur Welt: die Lebensgeschichte der Hannah Arendt* (Weinheim: Beltz & Gelberg, 1998).

Taminiaux, Jacques. *The Thracian Maid and the Professional Thinker: Arendt and Heidegger*, Michael Gendre (trans.), (Albany: SUNY Press, 1997).

Villa, Dana Richard. *Arendt and Heidegger: The Fate of the Political* (Princeton, N.J.: Princeton University Press, 1996).

Young-Bruehl, Elisabeth. *Hannah Arendt: For Love of the World* (New Haven: Yale University Press, 1982).

Eric v.d. Luft

ARMSTRONG, LOUIS (1901–1971)

Louis Armstrong was born in New Orleans, Louisiana, on August 4, 1901. His mother and father separated shortly after his birth, leaving him in the care of his maternal grandmother for several years. At age six, Louis attended the Fisk School for boys. By the middle of the fifth grade, he had dropped out of school. From an early age, Louis worked selling newspapers, hoping to make a few coins for necessities. While working with the Karnofsky brothers on a junk wagon, Louis entertained the children in the streets, playing a tin horn purchased for him by Alex Karnofsky. In later years, Armstrong often recalled the kindness and warmth demonstrated to him by the Karnofskys, especially their assistance with the purchase of his first cornet.

On New Year's Eve 1913, Louis was arrested for firing his stepfather's revolver. He was sent to the Colored Waif's Home. At the home, he received his first formal music instruction from Peter Davis. Davis rewarded Louis's dedication by appointing him leader of the home's band. After his release, Louis earned money by delivering coal and playing cornet in the local honky-tonks. He developed a close relationship with Joe "King" Oliver (1885–1938), a highly recognized cornetist. In *Louis Armstrong, In His Own Words: Selected Writings*, Armstrong describes Oliver's influence, stating: "He was a Creator, with unlimited Ideas, and had a heart as big as a whale when it came to helping the underdog in music, such as me" (Armstrong 1999, 174). After Oliver left for Chicago in 1918, Armstrong took his place in Kid Ory's band. In August of 1922, Armstrong received an invitation from "Papa Joe" to join his Creole Jazz Band in Chicago, making his first recordings the following year.

Armstrong's career spanned more than 50 years, with performances in many countries throughout the world. He was a brilliant trumpet player, bringing many new ideas to jazz improvisation. As a vocalist, he exuded warmth and charisma to audiences worldwide. Armstrong had a deep desire to communicate his innermost thoughts with everyone he came in contact with. He was a prolific writer whose works include two autobiographies, memoirs, notebooks, letters, and numerous magazine articles. In his introduction to *Louis Armstrong, in His Own Words: Selected Writings*, Thomas Brothers discusses some of Armstrong's purposes for writing. According to Brothers, writing helped Armstrong "stay in touch with distant friends and admirers." In addition, writing enabled him to "supply professional writers with material that they could use for publicity purposes." Brothers believes that "Armstrong writes because he sees himself as a writer." Writing was a hobby for Armstrong, and "his portable typewriter became his off-stage passion" (Armstrong 1999, viii–x). When questioned in a radio interview about carrying a dictionary and a book of synonyms and antonyms while traveling, Armstrong explains, "I didn't get much education when I was young, you know, so I'm still learning" (Armstrong 1999, xi).

Despite Armstrong's lack of a formal education, he had a great interest in reading. According to Joshua Berrett, editor of *The Louis Armstrong Companion: Eight Decades of Commentary*, Armstrong's home in Corona, Queens "housed a library of books covering such topics as diet, poetry, biography, history, and race relations." Armstrong's collection also included "special presentation copies from Langston Hughes (*Famous American Negroes*), Richard Avedon, Truman Capote, and others, including a physicist who had been inspired by Louis's trumpet" (Berrett 1999, 102). In his autobiography *Swing That Music*, Armstrong endorses two books on jazz—*Le Jazz Hot* by Hugues Panassie and *On the Frontiers of Jazz* by Robert Goffin. He describes these texts as being "carefully written" and "very interesting to anyone who wants to study modern music" (Armstrong 1936, 104).

Not only was Armstrong a reader, but he also cared deeply about how the written word was communicated. In *Swing That Music*, Armstrong states "I especially want to make this first book on swing truly helpful to students and amateurs and young musicians everywhere" (Armstrong 1936, 117). In another chapter, he explains that the language of swing contains more than 400 words not commonly understood. Armstrong tells his readers: "I hope this book will help to explain it a little—it is the real reason I have tried to write it and kept on after I found out what hard-going writing was for a man who has lived all of his life mostly with a trumpet, not a pencil, in his hand" (Armstrong 1936, 78).

Archives

Hogan Jazz archives, Tulane University, New Orleans, Louisiana.
Institute of Jazz Studies, Rutgers University, Newark, New Jersey.
Louis Armstrong archives, Queens College, Flushing, New York.
Music Division, Library of Congress, Washington, D.C.

Printed Sources

Armstrong, Louis. *Louis Armstrong, in His Own Words: Selected Writings*, Thomas Brothers (ed.), (Oxford: Oxford University Press, 1999).
———. *Satchmo: My Life in New Orleans*, Dan Morgenstern (intro.) [1954] (New York: Da Capo Press, Inc., 1986).
———. *Swing That Music* (London: Longmans, Green and Co., 1936).
Bergreen, Laurence. *Louis Armstrong: An Extravagant Life* (New York: Broadway Books, 1997).
Berrett, Joshua (ed.). *The Louis Armstrong Companion: Eight Decades of Commentary* (New York: Schirmer Books, 1999).
Giddons, Gary. *Satchmo*, produced by Toby Byron/Multiprises (New York: A Dolphin Book-Doubleday, 1988).
Goffin, Robert. *Horn of Plenty: The Story of Louis Armstrong*, James F. Bezou (trans.), (New York: Allen, Towne & Heath, Inc., 1947).

Meryman, Richard. *Louis Armstrong—A Self Portrait* (New York: The Eakins Press, 1966).
Miller, Marc. H. (ed). *Louis Armstrong: A Cultural Legacy* (New York: Queens Museum of Art, in association with University of Washington Press, Seattle and London, 1994).

Marianne Wilson

ARP, JEAN (1887–1966)

Jean Arp was born of mixed French and German descent in Strasbourg, the capital of Alsace-Lorraine. He was privately tutored in his youth and from 1905 to 1907 studied at the Strasbourg School of Arts and Crafts and the Weimar School of Art. Upon graduation he was accepted into the Academie Julian in Paris but rejoined his family in Weggis, Switzerland, in 1910 to study and paint in relative seclusion. In 1911 he exhibited at the Moderne Bund along with Henri Matisse and **Pablo Picasso,** and the following year traveled to Munich where he met **Vassily Kandinsky.** Arp exhibited with the artists of der Blaue Reiter, as well as with the Expressionists at the First Autumn Salon in Berlin. Obtaining exemption from military service during the First World War, Arp completed his first true abstracts in the form of paper cut-outs, wood reliefs, and organic, biomorphic compositions of string on canvas. His experiments in whimsical abstraction led him to become a founding member of the dadaist movement that sprang from Hugo Ball's organization of artists and philosophers in Zurich. Arp participated in the first Surrealist exhibition at the Gallery Pierre in 1925, but in the decade that followed directed his efforts toward more simplified freestanding sculpture. Following a period of seclusion during the Second World War, Arp traveled to the United States where he completed a wood relief for the Graduate Center at Harvard University. Up until the time of his death, Arp traveled and sculpted extensively, and was honored with a retrospective of his work at the Museum of Modern Art in 1958. He was awarded the International Prize for Sculpture at the Venice Biennale (1954) and was the recipient of the Grand Prix National des Arts (1963), the Carnegie Prize (1964), and the German Order of Merit (1965).

Arp loved to read and write poetry, and frequently studied Rene Schickele and Otto Flake of the Sturmer group as well as the German Romantic poet Clemens Brentano. Arp was fascinated by the grace and fantastical imagery of German folk tales such as *Des Knaben Wunderhorn*, which he copied for the sake of preservation. Arp believed that literature, like visual art, need not have deep meaning or cerebral intention to be effective in conveying beauty and harmony. The rationale behind Arp's organic painting and sculpture was based partially on Johann Wolfgang von Goethe's notion that all forms in nature are modifications of a few basic or primal forms. Along with this, Arp's work was influenced by the precepts of Zen Buddhism and those espoused in the Chinese *I Ching*, which stated that chance was always meaningful at the unconscious level of the psyche. Arp would frequently incorporate the accidental into his work, by choosing words at random from newspapers to include in his paintings or letting the play of gravity determine the position of falling pieces of paper that he would assemble into his *papiers dechires*. In this way, his work was allied with that of the surrealist artists and poets such as Paul Eluard and Louis Aragon who valued the part played by the subconscious in artistic production.

Archives

Museum of Modern Art archives, New York, control no. NYMV90-A1.

Archives of American Art, Smithsonian Institution, Washington, D.C., control no. DCAW210187-A.

The Getty Research Institute for the History of Art and the Humanities, Special Collections, control no. CJPA1564998-A.

Printed Sources

Arp, Jean. *On My Way: Poetry and Essays 1912–47* (New York: The Documents of Modern Art, 1948).

Jean, Marcel (ed.). *Arp on Arp: Poems, Essays, Memories* (New York: Viking Press, 1972).

Read, Herbert. *Arp* (London: Thames and Hudson, 1968).

Gregory L. Schnurr

ASTURIAS, MIGUEL ANGEL (1899–1974)

Miguel Angel Asturias was born in La Parroquia, Guatemala, during the presidency of Manuel Estrada Cabrera. His father, a supreme court judge and a Cabrera dissident, subjected his family to three years of self-imposed exile at a remote location in Baja Verapaz. In 1906 the family returned to Guatemala City and Miguel began attending catechism classes at a local Catholic school. He achieved his bachillerato at the state-controlled Instituto Nacional Central de Varones and proceeded to the university, where he studied first medicine, then law. While at the university, Asturias joined the radical Unionista party and wrote politically charged articles for the local student newspaper *El Estudiante*. Upon graduation Asturias traveled extensively throughout Europe, but returned to his native Guatemala in 1931 to teach literature. Under the reign of President Ubico, he was forcibly appointed to a seat in the Guatemalan National Assembly, which he held until the dictator's deposition in 1944. In the decade that followed, Asturias served as ambassador and official diplomat to Mexico, Argentina, and El Salvador under the reformative presidency of Juan Jose Arevalo. Asturias began writing complex and didactic reformative novels in 1946 with *El Señor Presidente*, a work that won the International French Book Award in 1956. This was followed by a string of successful and highly acclaimed novels including *Hombres de maiz* (1949), *El papa verde* (1954), and *Weekend in Guatemala* (1956) within which the almost exclusively indigenous protagonists struggle against social, economic, and political oppression and the detrimental effects of modernization. Asturias won both the William Faulkner Foundation Prize and the Lenin Peace Prize in 1966 and became the first Latin American novelist to be awarded the Nobel Prize for Literature in 1967.

Due to his extensive travels and broad scope of concerns and interests, Asturias's literary influences were extremely eclectic. From his time in France, Asturias became acquainted with the popular literature of Edgar Allan Poe and Walt Whitman, but was fascinated with surrealist texts such as Robert Desnos's *Deuil pour deuil* and *La liberté ou l'amour*. Asturias met with many surrealist authors, including Tristan Tzara, Louis Aragon, and **André Breton,** the latter of which had just published his *Manifeste du Surrealism* a few years prior to Asturias's residency in Paris. Asturias experimented with these authors' automatic writing techniques and employed their rhetorical devices as well as their use of the irrational and the incongruous in his novels. Asturias was also deeply influenced by the literary culture of his homeland. As a student of Georges Raynaud, he was extremely familiar with the indigenous texts of the *Popul Vuh* and the *Annals of Xahil*. Asturias incorporated their nonlinear narrative structure and use of complex symbolism into his paragrammatic novels such as *Hombres de maiz*, wherein the plot develops associatively as opposed to chronologically. Asturias read Jose Vasconcelos's *Prometeo Vencendor* and also the works of the agrarian reform authors Carlos Pellicer and Jaime Torres Bodet, who espoused the fall of modernist dictatorships and a return to a pre-Columbian lifestyle for the indigenous populations of South America. Asturias was also an impassioned reader of the works of the psychologists Sigmund Freud and **Carl Jung,** whose theories of the collective unconsciousness and the shared experience of myth heavily influenced and verified the author's use of parabolic epics and legends in his novels.

Archives

Manuscript collection of the Bibliothèque Nationale, Paris.

Printed Sources

Callan, Richard J. *Miguel Angel Asturias* (New York: Twayne Publishers, 1970).
Henigham, Stephen. *Assuming the Light: The Parisian Literary Apprenticeship of Miguel Angel Asturias* (London: University of Oxford, 1999).
Prieto, Rene. *Miguel Angel Asturias' Archaeology of Return* (Cambridge: Cambridge University Press, 1993).

Gregory L. Schnurr

ATTLEE, CLEMENT (1883–1967)

Clement Attlee, British politician and Labour prime minister, was born in Putney, outside London, in 1883, the youngest son of Henry and Ellen Attlee. His father was a solicitor in the City—a Gladstonian Liberal in politics in a family of Tories—who provided a solidly middle-class home for his family.

Initially educated by his mother at home, Attlee later followed his four older brothers to Haileybury College and the University of Oxford. He remembered his mother as "very well read" and that he "learned to read early and was a voracious reader," being especially fond of poetry (Attlee 1955, 6). His subsequent years in a preparatory school were less fulfilling and he recalled "poor teachers and excessive stress on studying the Bible and biblical history" (Attlee 1955, 9). He continued to read, however, and often finished four books a week (Pearce 1997, 11). Subsequently, he enjoyed the study of history at Haileybury College, did well overall, and remained attached to the school in later years.

He left University College, Oxford, with a second in Modern History, and retained a lifelong interest in the subject. Surprisingly, his favorite author in later years was Sir Arthur Bryant, whose panegyrics to the English past appealed to Attlee's own optimistic view of Britain in the world (Pearce 1997, 9). In this same vein, Rudyard Kipling and John Buchan were among the authors he read to his children. Even as prime minister, he once spent a weekend at Chequers reading Edward Gibbon, as well as finding time for Thomas Hardy, John Milton, "the more sonorous Elizabethans," and Trevelyan's *Social History of England* (Pearce 1997, 11, 104). Alternatively, he might relax to the pages of either *Wisden*—"always good for the settling of the mind"—or the entries of the *Dictionary of National Biography* (Pearce, 123).

Under the influence of his older brother, a Christian Socialist, Attlee became involved in the late Victorian social reform movement and, eventually, the developing socialist party. This stimulus led him not only to read the works of Thomas Carlyle, John Ruskin, and William Morris, but also to become directly involved in the settlement house programs being established in London's East End. From 1907 to 1909, he served as manager of the Haileybury Club—sponsored by his old school—and was also secretary of the better-known Toynbee Hall. Eventually, his reading and practical experience led to an appointment teaching in the Social Sciences Department of the new London School of Economics, which had been established by Sidney Webb.

His personal experience working with the poor gave him a deep understanding of their living conditions but also convinced him that self-help would be insufficient to remedy their plight. Greater social and political changes would be necessary. In 1907, therefore, he joined the local branch of the Independent Labor Party (ILP). One influence in this direction was **Beatrice Webb**'s minority report to the 1909 Poor Law Commission, which called for socialist solutions to poverty. This report also led Attlee onto a more public stage as he became a spokesman for both Webb's report and, in 1911, the National Insurance Act that David Lloyd George and the Liberal government were pushing through Parliament (Attlee, 38). During the First World War, Attlee served in Gallipoli, Mesopotamia, and northern France, rising to the rank of major. He returned to East London and quickly became a fixture in local politics as mayor of Stepney, alderman, and, after 1922, MP for Limehouse.

Despite membership in the ILP, Attlee was not a strict Marxist. Reflecting the views of Ruskin, among others, he recalled later: "The socialist movement in Great Britain began long before Karl Marx. It was derived from native thinkers. It has its economic basis, but still more its ethical basis. . . . a longing for social justice derived from Christian principles" (Brookshire 1995, 9, quoting a speech at the Commonwealth Club of California, May 2, 1945). This moderate political approach was essential to the task Attlee faced when he was called to lead the Labor Party after 1935. It kept the party united through the strains of the late 1930s and subsequently into the wartime coalition of **Winston Churchill** and, ultimately, to sweeping electoral victory in 1945. His moderation sometimes disappointed elements in his own party, but fit the mood of the country, particularly after the publication of the Beveridge Report in 1942. The program of social insurance—most notably a National Health Service—family allowances, and full employment provided the blueprint for postwar reform and reconstruction. It also fit easily within Attlee's pragmatic mind and was quickly adopted by him and the Labour Party and proved to be the basis for the party's 1945 campaign manifesto. In his postwar government, 1945–51, Attlee saw most of the plan put into action and in doing so both radically altered British society and set the framework for the late-twentieth-century political debate in Britain.

Archives

Bodleian Library, Oxford, U.K.
Churchill College, Cambridge, U.K.
Labour Party Archives, National Museum of Labour History, Manchester, U.K.

Printed Sources

Attlee, Clement. *As It Happened* (London: Heinemann, 1955).
Brookshire, Jerry H. *Clement Attlee* (Manchester: Manchester University Press, 1995).
Harris, Kenneth. *Attlee* (London: Weidenfeld and Nicolson, 1982).
Pearce, Robert. *Attlee* (London: Longman, 1997).

Derek W. Blakeley

ATWOOD, MARGARET ELEANOR (1939–)

Margaret Atwood was born in Ottawa, Canada, and spent most of her childhood in Toronto. She studied at Victoria College, University of Toronto (1957–61), and received her M.A. from Radcliffe College, Harvard, where she studied from 1961 to 1962. She began a Ph.D. thesis on the Gothic romance at Harvard in 1965 but returned to Canada in 1967 after winning the Governor General's Award for Poetry. During the 1970s, Atwood held posts at several Canadian universities and served as an editor of House of Anansi Press (1971–73), where she came into contact with the emerging generation of experimental Canadian writers that included Graeme Gibson, who would become her lifelong companion. She was a central figure in Canadian literary criticism for a time after the publication of *Survival: A Thematic Guide to Canadian Literature* (1972), combining the archetypal criticism of Northrop Frye with an unapologetic Canadian nationalism. In the 1970s Atwood became Canada's preeminent poet and novelist and a major public figure, and in the 1980s and 90s she consolidated her international reputation. She has published more than three dozen books and been the recipient of numerous prestigious honors and awards, including the Booker Prize, the Giller Prize, and more than a dozen honorary degrees.

Atwood's literary influences reflect her wide reading of both Canadian and other Western literatures. In *Survival*, Atwood enumerates some of her childhood reading: American comic books, Walter Scott, Edgar Allan Poe, Charles Dickens, Lewis Carroll, Sir Arthur Conan Doyle, and Canadian short fiction, including the works of Sir Charles G. D. Roberts and Ernest Thompson Seton. The autobiographical writings of Susanna Moodie, an early nineteenth-century English immigrant to Canada, provide a creative point of departure for many of Atwood's best-known works and are reflected in her imaginative and thematic interpretations of the Canadian landscape. Other Canadian influences on Atwood's work are numerous, as her critics have revealed, and they include P. K. Page, Margaret Avison, Douglas LePan, Anne Hébert, Phyllis Webb, Gwendolyn MacEwen, bill bissett, John Newlove, Al Purdy, Jay Macpherson, Northrop Frye, D. G. Jones, James Reaney, Eli Mandel, and Dennis Lee (see Carrington 1987 and Mallinson 1985). Atwood's poetic techniques reflect her reading of both contemporary Canadian poetry and the works of prominent modernist poets, including William Butler Yeats, **Ezra Pound, T. S. Eliot,** Wallace Stevens, **William Carlos Williams, W. H. Auden, Dylan Thomas,** and Sylvia Plath (Mallinson 1985). Atwood's fiction draws upon a wide variety of models including the novels of Jane Austen, **Aldous Huxley, Evelyn Waugh,** and William Golding, and a persistent satiric trend in her work reveals her indebtedness to Canadian satirists Thomas Chandler Haliburton, Stephen Leacock, and Robertson Davies (Carrington 1987). Atwood, in turn, became the most influential Canadian writer of her generation.

Archives

Thomas Fisher Rare Book Library, University of Toronto, *The Margaret Atwood Collection:* drafts of Atwood's published works, unpublished poems and fiction, unfinished Ph.D. thesis, correspondence, juvenilia, original artwork.

Printed Sources

Atwood, Margaret. *Survival: A Thematic Guide to Canadian Literature* (Concord, Ont.: House of Anansi Press, 1972).

Carrington, Ildikó de Papp. "Margaret Atwood." In Robert Lecker, Jack David, and Ellen Quigley (eds.), *Canadian Writers and Their Works*, Fiction Series, Vol. 9 (Toronto: ECW Press, 1987). Includes a detailed summary of influences on Atwood's fiction.

Cooke, Nathalie. *Margaret Atwood: A Biography* (Toronto: ECW Press, 1998).

Mallinson, Jean. "Margaret Atwood." In Robert Lecker, Jack David, and Ellen Quigley (eds.), *Canadian Writers and Their Works*, Poetry Series, Vol. 9 (Toronto: ECW Press, 1985). Includes a detailed summary of influences on Atwood's poetry.

Sullivan, Rosemary. *The Red Shoes: Margaret Atwood Starting Out.* (Toronto: Harper-Collins, 1998). A biography of Atwood to 1980 exploring influences on her early career.

Colin Hill

AUDEN, WYSTAN HUGH (1907–1973)

W. H. Auden was born in York, England, and educated at Christ Church, Oxford. He published his first book of poems at the age of 21 and by the 1930s was regarded as one of the leading English language poets. Auden's work often addressed the dislocations of modern industrial life, as in "The Age of Anxiety" and "The Shield of Achilles." Critics have particularly noted the broad scope of topics that caught Auden's eye and also his striking juxtapositions of passion and suffering with the mundane elements of everyday existence.

Auden's father was a physician, and his family had produced a number of Anglican clerics with High Church views. Auden later recalled that his early exposure to church ritual left him with "a conviction . . . that life is ruled by mysterious forces" (Davenport-Hines 1995, 14). He lapsed from religious belief when he was at school, a development some biographers have traced to the contradiction between biblical injunctions and the boy's increasing awareness of his own homosexuality. In the early 1940s, he returned to his faith, influenced in part by the writings of the Christian existentialist Søren Kierkegaard. Many of Auden's subsequent works express a deep piety, including his 1944 Christmas poem, "For the Time Being."

Auden had a strong interest in the study of psychology, dating to his teenage years, when he read his father's medical journals. It is certain that he encountered Sigmund Freud's works during that time, though it remains unclear exactly which ones he read. In 1926, he published an analysis of insanity as portrayed in ancient Greek literature. He was so impressed with Sophocles's clinical accuracy in depicting the madness of the title character in *Ajax* that he classed the dramatist as a medical doctor. As a poet, Auden often used Freudian theory to probe the nature and origins of evil, most famously when alluding to **Adolf Hitler** in the poem, "September 1, 1939."

Auden discovered **Thomas Stearns Eliot** while at Oxford. After reading *The Waste Land*, he destroyed all his poems and proclaimed, "I now see the way I want to write" (Carpenter 1981, 57). Other writers had a greater long-term impact on him, however. Auden later remarked that he drew more from Thomas Hardy's use of colloquial language than he did from Eliot's poetry. Robert Graves was another important figure, partly because of his use of analytic psychology to examine the emotions triggered by poems (Davenport-Hines 1995, 76–78). More fundamentally, Graves's broader search for sources of inspiration, as opposed to Eliot's emphasis on a canon of classic texts, agreed more with Auden's consummately eclectic approach.

Archives

Henry W. and Albert A. Berg Collection of English and American Literature, New York Public Library.

Printed Sources

Auden, W. H. *Collected Poems*, Edward Mendelson (ed.), (New York: Vintage Books, 1991). Princeton University Press has commenced publication of a projected eight-volume series of Auden's writings under the title of *The Complete Works of W. H. Auden*, Edward Mendelson (ed.).
Carpenter, Humphrey. *W. H. Auden: A Biography* (Boston: Houghton Mifflin, 1981).
Davenport-Hines, Richard. *Auden* (London: William Heinemann, 1995).

Christopher Pepus

B

BAECK, LEO (1873–1956)

Leo Baeck was born in Lissa, Prussia, and died in London, England. Leo Baeck's father, Rabbi Dr. Samuel Bäck, had not only pursued a traditional rabbinical education but he also took the unusual step of pursuing a secular education. He received a doctorate in philosophy from the University of Vienna. Leo Baeck emulated this step. He studied at the Jewish Theological Seminary in Breslau, the University of Breslau, the Lehranstalt (a rabbinical school in Berlin), and the University of Berlin. He received his doctorate in philosophy from the University of Berlin in 1895 where he wrote a dissertation on "Benedikt de Spinoza's First Influences on Germany." He studied under such famous professors as Heinrich Graetz, Hermann Cohen, and Wilhelm Dilthey.

He was ordained a rabbi in 1897 at the age of 24 and received an appointment as rabbi in Oppeln, where he met and married Natalie Hamburger, who like himself was the child of a reform-minded rabbi. In 1907, Baeck was invited to become rabbi in Düsseldorf, and in 1912, he became a rabbi in Berlin. In 1914 after the outbreak of World War I, the 41-year-old Baeck, then at the most prominent part of his career, felt ethically compelled to volunteer as a field rabbi (chaplain) in the war. He felt he could not hide away from such a major crisis. At the end of World War I, he returned to Berlin and continued his career as a prominent rabbi, theology professor, and religious philosopher.

In 1943, the Nazis arrested the 70-year-old Baeck and deported him to the concentration camp of Theresienstadt in Czechoslovakia where he was assigned to a labor battalion and forced to pull garbage wagons through the streets. He made it his mission to reduce distress and provide solace to others by preaching theological sermons from the roofs of the concentration camp barracks and giving a lecture series on Spinoza for the benefit of the other inmates. After his liberation from Theresienstadt, Baeck became a theology professor at Hebrew Union College in Cincinnati.

Baeck's major contribution to Jewish theology, *The Essence of Judaism*, first appeared in 1905 and a greatly enlarged version appeared in 1922. The book was originally conceived as a response to the Protestant theologian Adolf von Harnack and his book, *The Essence of Christianity* (1900), which denied that Judaism played a major role in church history. Baeck was greatly influenced by the late nineteenth-century exponents of the "Science of Judaism" school *(Wissenschaft des Judentums)* which rejected the mystical and messianic dimensions of Judaism and limited themselves to rationalistic exegesis. The Science of Judaism school was associated with such names as Leopold Zunz, Eduard Gans, Immanuel Wolf, and Abraham Geiger. This movement had influenced some of Baeck's professors such as Heinrich Graetz and Hermann Cohen, who argued in his 1919 tract, *The Religion of Reason*, that Judaism had adapted itself to the modern world and had become a religion based on rationalistic principles.

Baeck's *The Essence of Judaism* is one of the primary expositions of liberal Judaism. Baeck argues that Judaism is absolutely without dogmas and has no orthodoxy because it consists primarily of moral teachings that work against the development of dogmas. Commandments of virtuous behavior take precedence over articles of belief. Judaism is not a mystical religion. Religion is not to be experienced in a mystical manner, but is to be lived by following principles of just behavior that can lead to a more fulfilled life. Judaism does not believe in miraculous events brought down from heaven to earth and it rejects the notion of sacraments.

This notion of Judaism as a religion of ethics divorced from dogma certainly has it basis in the school of the Science of Judaism, but it also harks back to earlier sources with which Baeck was familiar. Some elements of Baeck's religious philosophy betray the influence of Spinoza's *Tractatus Theologico-Politicus* (1670). Spinoza argued that the best part of our human essence is our powers of reason which lead us to higher orders of perfection. The highest order of perfection depends on the recognition and love of God, which is the source of humankind's most perfect happiness. Whoever makes the effort to love God follows his commandments, because he realizes that love of God is the highest good. Baeck was also influenced by Moses Mendelssohn, who argued in *Jerusalem or On Religious Power and Judaism* (1782) that Judaism is a rationalistic religion whose essence is contained in the ethical principles of the Ten Commandments, principles that are themselves grounded in reason and not in dogma.

Archives

Leo Baeck Institute, New York, N.Y.
Leo Baeck Institute, London, U.K.
Leo Baeck Institute, Jerusalem, Israel.
Jewish Museum, Berlin, Germany.

Printed Sources

Baeck, Leo. *Das Wesen des Judentums* (Berlin: Nathansen & Lamm, 1905).
Baeck, Leo. *Das Wesen des Judentums,* 2nd enlarged ed. (Frankfurt: Kaufmann, 1922).
Baker, Leonard. *Days of Sorrow and Pain: Leo Baeck and the Berlin Jews* (New York: Oxford University Press, 1978).
Friedlander, Albert H. *Leo Baeck: Teacher of Theresienstadt* (New York: Holt, Rinehart, and Winston, 1968).

Peter R. Erspamer

BAKER, JOSEPHINE (1906–1975)

Josephine Baker was born in St. Louis, Missouri. Notorious for dancing only with a girdle of bananas, her erotic dancing style influenced Parisian choreography in the 1920s while proving to audiences that black was beautiful. However, she was most influential for her distinctive style of dance, which fused elements of ballet, the Charleston, and Cuban and South American influences. Baker's singing abilities were noted in the 1930s, and she appeared in two films that showcased all her talents: *ZouZou* (1934) and *Princess Tam-Tam* (1935). Briefly returning to the United States during 1935–36 to star in the Ziegfield *Follies*, she returned to Europe before the outbreak of World War II and became a French citizen. Joining the Resistance as a courier and liaison officer, Baker was a lieutenant in the Women's Auxiliary Air Force and was awarded the Rosette de La Resistance. France awarded her the Croix de Guerre in 1946. While touring the United States in 1951 Baker confronted restaurant and hotel owners over racial discrimination and segregation, which led to an official Josephine Baker Day (May 21) in Harlem. The same year she was named the NAACP's woman of the year. Baker and her husband Jo Bouillon adopted twelve children, deemed the "Rainbow Tribe," from different ethnic backgrounds to prove that racial harmony was possible. Baker continued entertaining and working for racial equality. She died in Paris in 1975 only two days after a revue celebrating the fiftieth anniversary of her Parisian debut. Baker was the first American-born woman to receive a state funeral in France.

Two major literary influences upon Baker were Grimm's *Fairy Tales* and histories of European royalty. Her Grandmother McDonald gathered Baker on her lap and told her the stories of "Little Red Riding Hood," "The Three Little Pigs," "Snow White," and "Sleeping Beauty" (Haney 1981, 11). In fact, Baker's imagination overflowed with stories whose characters eventually overcame great obstacles to triumph in the end. Still learning to read through her adolescence, she often discovered friends backstage who encouraged her to improve her reading and writing skills. After filming *ZouZou* (1934) Baker wrote, "I had little time for reading and limited myself to detective stories, which were like a game. Books were not for me. They taught me nothing about life. Life was meant to be breathed and touched and smelled, books tried to package experience. I like my living fresh" (Baker 1977, 99). However, Ginette Renaudin wrote that by 1960 Baker read constantly (Baker 1977, 224).

Archives

Beinecke Rare Book and Manuscript Library, Yale University, New Haven, Conn.: Henry Hurford Janes–Josephine Baker Collection. James Weldon Johnson Collection in the Yale Collection of American Literature contains letters, manuscripts, research notes, clippings, printed works, photographs, and miscellaneous materials gathered by Henry Hurford Janes, which document his acquaintance with Josephine Baker between 1943 and 1975. The collection spans the years 1926–86, with the majority of the material falling within the dates 1943–75. Additionally, there is an unprocessed collection of Josephine Baker's papers from 1930–71.

Printed Sources

Baker, Josephine, and Jo Bouillon. *Josephine* (New York: Harper & Row Publishers, 1977).
Haney, Lynn. *Naked at the Feast: A Biography of Josephine Baker* (New York: Dodd, Mead & Company, 1981).

Rose, Phyllis. *Jazz Cleopatra: Josephine Baker in Her Time* (New York: Doubleday, 1989).

Rebecca Tolley-Stokes

BAKHTIN, MIKHAIL MIKHAILOVICH (1895–1975)

Mikhail Bakhtin was born in Orel, Russia. A controversial Russian philosopher and scholar, Bakhtin emerged by the mid-1980s as an important twentieth-century thinker in the West. The influence of Bakhtin and the Bakhtin Circle was profound, crossing national and ideological boundaries and disciplinary lines. Paradoxically, by the late 1990s, as controversy grew, "Bakhtin's theories" continued to shape intellectual discourse in areas as different as philosophy, religion, language, communication, semantics, art, sociology, anthropology, literature, and cultural studies, spawning a "Bakhtin Industry" in Russia and the West.

Bakhtin left very few letters and no diaries. In interviews with Viktor Dmitrievich Duvakin (1970s), a fragile Bakhtin provided a fragmentary autobiographical account. According to Duvakin's transcript, Mikhail Bakhtin, along with his older brother Nikolai Mikhailovich (1894–1950), received a classical education and a grounding in European culture at home. Mikhail read the *Iliad* and the *Odyssey* in German by age 9, works by Fyodor Dostoyevsky by age 11, and Immanuel Kant's *Critique of Pure Reason* (1781) by age 13. The family moved often, and Mikhail attended secondary schools in Vilnius, Orel, and Odessa. He began his university studies in Odessa (1913), where he read the works of Søren Kierkegaard and Friedrich Wilhelm Nietzsche, studied with the linguist Aleksandr Ivanovich Tomson (1860–1935), and developed a lifelong passion for the neo-Kantian Marburg School. In Petrograd University, Bakhtin claimed as his teachers the neo-Kantian classicist Fadei Frantsevich Zelinskii and the linguist Baudoin de Courtenay, who taught the theories of Ferdinand de Saussure and counted among his students members of the St. Petersburg Formalists—OPOYAZ—a group that Bakhtin came to know only later. To date, however, no official school records have been found, leading to new controversial theories that challenge Bakhtin's account and contend that Bakhtin probably had very little formal schooling and for political reasons appropriated biographical facts from his brother's life.

Members of the Bakhtin Circle (1919–28) represented various fields and included Matvei Isaevich Kagan, a student of Hermann Cohen, the founder of the Marburg School; Lev Vasilievich Pumpianskii; the musicians Ivan Ivanovich Sollertinskii and Maria Veniaminovna Judina. Members of the Circle discussed philosophy, music, art, culture, religion, and literature, shaping new theories as they explored world literature, works by Kant, Cohen, Ernst Cassirer, Karl Marx, and Sigmund Freud, among others.

Bakhtin identified the "dialogues" of the Bakhtin Circle as formative. Key texts—*Freudianism* (1927), *Marxism and the Philosophy of Language* (1929), and *The Formal Method in Literary Scholarship* (1928)—that were attributed to Bakhtin, authorship Bakhtin neither claimed nor disclaimed, were published by Voloshinov and Medvedev, respectively. In interviews, Bakhtin expressed interest in **György Lukács**'s *The Theory of the Novel* (1920), Kant, and Cassirer's *The Philosophy of Symbolic Forms* (1923–29), a work underpinned, in part, by the philosophy of Georg Wilhelm Friedrich Hegel. Brian Poole in "Bakhtin and Cassirer" identified German idealist philosophy, Johann Wolfgang von Goethe, Friedrich von Schlegel, and traces of Cassirer's texts in Bakhtin's works on François Rabelais *(Rabelais and His World)* and the novel.

Archives

Bakhtin's fragmentary papers are held in restricted personal archives. The Duvakin tapes are located in Moscow State University Library.

Printed Sources

Adlam, Carol, and David Shepherd (eds.). *The Annotated Bakhtin Bibliography* (London: MHRA Publications, 2000). MHRA Bibliographies, no. 1.

Bakhtin Centre: http://www.utm.edu/research/iep/b/bakhtin.htm, accessed October 18, 2003.

Brandist, Craig. *The Bakhtin Circle: A Philosophical and Historical Introduction* (London: Pluto, 2002).

Clark, Katerina, and Michael Holquist. *Mikhail Bakhtin* (Cambridge: Harvard University Press, 1984).

Duvakin, V. D. *Besedy V.D. Duvakina s M. M. Baktinym* (Moscow: Progress, 1996).

Emerson, Caryl. *Critical Essays on Mikhail Bakhtin* (New York: G.K. Hall, 1999).

———. *The First Hundred Years of Mikhail Bakhtin* (Princeton: Princeton University Press, 1997).

Poole, Brian. "Bakhtin and Cassirer: The Philosophical Origins of Bakhtin's Carnival Messianism." In *Bakhtin/"Bakhtin": Studies in the Archive and Beyond.* Special Issue. *The South Atlantic Quarterly* 97:3/4 (1998), 537–78.

Shepherd, David. *The Contexts of Bakhtin: Philosophy, Authorship, Aesthetics* (Amsterdam, Netherlands: Harwood Academic Publishers, 1998).

Yurchenko, T. G. (ed.). *M.M. Bakhtin v zerkale kritiki* (Moscow: Labirint, 1995).

Ludmilla L. Litus

BALDWIN, STANLEY (1867–1947)

Stanley Baldwin, industrialist, MP, and Conservative prime minister on three different occasions, was born August 3, 1847, at Bewdley, Worcestershire, the son of Alfred and Louisa (Macdonald) Baldwin. The family's commercial bent was tempered by a strong religious heritage, and Baldwin counted both missionaries and clerics among his forebears. He attended Harrow (1881–85) and Trinity College, Cambridge (1885–88), where he took a third class in the historical tripos. After graduation from Cambridge he entered the family business and became active in local politics. In 1908 he was elected to Parliament for Bewdley, a seat he would hold until his retirement in 1937. Baldwin forged strong ties with Andrew Bonar Law and served as his personal parliamentary secretary. He was joint financial secretary to the Board of Trade from 1917 to 1921, president of the Board of Trade from 1921 to 1922, and chancellor of the Exchequer from 1922 to 1923. He became prime minister for the first time upon Bonar Law's sudden resignation in 1923. Baldwin's elevation came as a surprise to most observers, including Bonar Law and Baldwin himself, who expected Lord Curzon, the foreign secretary, to receive the call. The first Baldwin government fell in November 1923 as a result of its bid to reintroduce protection, but the Conservatives regained power with Baldwin at the helm in November 1924. This government lasted until its defeat at the polls in 1929. Baldwin was lord president of the Council in MacDonald's government from 1931 to 1935 and served once again as prime minister from 1935 to

1937. Growing deaf and in declining health, he retired from Parliament in May 1937 and was created First Earl Baldwin of Bewdley in June 1937. He died at Astley, the family home, on December 14, 1947. Though he was the quintessential Conservative, Baldwin portrayed himself as a man not so much above as outside party who personified a spirit of national unity. His public reputation suffered gravely from his association with the specter of British decline, the aftermath of the First World War, the policy of appeasement, and the Depression.

The suite of cultural influences that formed Baldwin's thinking is both complex and ambiguous. For years scholars used the four volumes of his collected speeches published between 1926 and 1937 as the standard source for determining the origins of his ideas. They reveal a homespun man of wide reading who bore the deep impress of Victorian values and who was steeped in English literature. Indeed, Rudyard Kipling was his first cousin, and a maternal aunt was married to Edward Burne-Jones. His public utterances also revealed Baldwin as first an Englishman rather than a member of the Conservative Party. His oft-quoted desire to retire to the countryside to keep pigs (*The Times*, May 25, 1923) embodied the essential Baldwin for many if not most Britons. He had a strong distrust of intellectuals verging on dislike. The vocabulary of the public Baldwin included Shakespeare, John Bunyan, Jane Austen, and the Bible. At the same time, Baldwin was on the cutting edge of twentieth-century political practice in his use of speechwriters, and virtually all his public addresses were at least in part the work of others, most notably of Thomas Jones, a civil servant and advisor to a number of Conservative politicians. Jones later wrote the entry on Baldwin for the *Dictionary of National Biography*. Baldwin usually edited the drafts his writers presented to him until the words sounded as if they were his own (Williamson 1999, 159–63), though his more impromptu presentations and responses to questioners bore a remarkable resemblance to his formal utterances. It is not possible to verify all the authors noted above in his reading, and the evidence available in his correspondence and other sources indicates influences that are at once more specific and less broad. From an early age Baldwin took advantage of the family library, and by the time he was nine he had read aloud to his mother and indulgent aunts Sir Walter Scott's *Ivanhoe*, *Guy Mannering*, and *Rob Roy*, among others. By the time he was sent to Harrow he also had read Lamb's *Tales from Shakespeare*, and it may be from this source rather than the plays themselves that he derived his knowledge of the Bard's works. Baldwin acknowledged spending a good deal of time with Bunyan's *Pilgrim's Progress*, and he made some headway in Sir Thomas Mallory's *La Morte D'Arthur*. He also read Kingsley's *Heroes*, Dickens's *Pickwick Papers* and *A Tale of Two Cities*, and later in life indicated some familiarity with Mark Twain's *Tom Sawyer* and *Huckleberry Finn*. He displayed little taste for poetry, and among the authors his mother tried to introduce to him only Blake took. Probably most important as a formative literary influence was the Bible lesson he heard each Sunday at Bewdley, and as he remembered in old age, "the English Bible leaves its mark on you for life" (Hyde 1973, 15).

The sum of elements from this varied collection produced a habit of mind that is best characterized as flexible conservatism, that is, as retaining nineteenth-century values while taking into account the exigencies of modern life. Baldwin's ideas on economics and industrial relations were a combination of the cultural influences of his youth, his work in the family firm, and his early political experience, but they bent to accommodate the realities of the postwar world. He believed in free trade, the harmony of class interests, and the noninterventionist state, but through the 1920s and especially in the 1930s, as prosperity dimmed and class antagonisms sharpened, he admitted that protectionism, greater spending on social services, and state intervention in the economy were desirable. Fearful of mass democracy before the war, he realized after 1918 that the Conservative Party must develop a broader appeal to the working classes if it were to enjoy continued electoral success. Baldwin had an almost naïve belief that religion could act as a healing national balm, and, as a result, he often intertwined contradictory notions such as individual freedom alongside mutual interdependence, and the virtues of Little England with a reinvigorated imperialism. These odd fusions had their roots in the peculiarly Victorian notion that Christianity, properly understood and applied, could create order and cohesion in an increasingly fractious society. Above all, Baldwin absorbed and exemplified moral seriousness, self-reliance, community, and respect of the classes for one another, and in a world in upheaval, he stood as a beacon of traditional virtues.

Archives

Fourth Earl of Bewdley: Baldwin personal and family papers, including correspondence and miscellaneous family papers.

Worcester County Public Records Office, Worcester: Baldwin Family Papers, consisting of materials dealing with Baldwin's parents and the family business.

Cambridge University Library, Cambridge: Baldwin's political papers, materials used by Thomas Jones to construct the biographical sketch of Baldwin in the *Dictionary of National Biography*, and miscellaneous correspondence.

Printed Sources

Adams, R. J. Q. *Bonar Law* (Stanford, CA: Stanford University Press, 1999).

Hyde, H. Montgomery. *Baldwin: The Unexpected Prime Minister* (London: Hart-Davis, MacGibbon, 1973).

Jenkins, Roy. *Baldwin* (London: Collins, 1987).

Middlemas, Keith, and John Barnes. *Baldwin: A Biography* (London: Macmillan, 1969).

Williamson, Philip. *Stanley Baldwin* (Cambridge: Cambridge University Press, 1999).

Young, G. M. *Stanley Baldwin* (London: R. Hart-Davis, 1952).

Young, Kenneth. *Stanley Baldwin* (London: Weidenfeld and Nicolson, 1976).

George Mariz

BARTH, KARL (1886–1968)

Karl Barth was born in Basel, Switzerland, in 1886. He was raised in Bern where his father, Johann Friedrich (Fritz) Barth was professor of New Testament and early church history. Karl studied reformed theology at the University of Bern, developing a keen interest in the theology of Friederich Schleiermacher. Barth understood himself in sharp opposition to Schleiermacher's "liberal" theology and conducted a running battle with his thought throughout his lifetime. Barth then studied church history under Adolf von Harnack in Berlin, New Testament under Adolf Schlatter at Tübingen in 1907, and systematic theology under the premier Kantian theologian in Germany, Wilhelm Herrmann at Marburg. After ordination as a minister in the Swiss Reformed Church, Barth worked as a pastor in Safenwil,

Switzerland, from 1911 to 1921, where he became greatly interested in questions of social justice. Karl Barth is regarded as the leading Protestant systematic theologian in the twentieth century.

Karl Barth's theological output may be divided into the early period and the later period. His commentary on *Romans*, the German edition of which appeared in 1919, has been called a bombshell in the playground of the theologians. In this work we see the strong influence of Franz Overbeck, Johann Christian Blumhardt, Christoph Blumhardt, Fyodor Dostoyevsky, and Søren Kierkegaard, who made clear to Barth the antimony between Christianity and culture (James B. Torrance 1987, 69). In this early period Barth was associated with "dialectical theology," a movement of thought in German theology after World War I that argued that theology needed to be God-centered rather than man-centered. Dialectical theology emphasized the transcendence or otherness of God, finding its classic formulation in Barth's second edition of his *Epistle to the Romans*. In the 1930s as **Adolf Hitler** rose to power, Barth sided with the Confessing Church in Germany and was the principal author of the famous *Barmen Declaration* of 1934.

The later Barth authored the 10 volumes of the massive *Church Dogmatics* in which the analogy of faith takes the place of the dialectics found in the *Epistle to the Romans*. If the early Barth stresses the distance between God and humanity, the latter Barth emphasizes the nearness of God to humanity in Christ. One may compare Barth's thought to an hourglass. The constriction in the middle of the hourglass through which all the sand passes is the revelation of Christ. This is Barth's christological concentration and apart from it there exists no link between God and humanity. And just as the sand in the hourglass moves from top to bottom, so too does the revelation of God move only in one direction from top (God) to bottom (humanity). In the *Church Dogmatics* we see the influence of St. Anselm of Canterbury, St. Augustine, St. Athanasius, Martin Luther, and especially John Calvin. Barth's theology made its greatest impact in English-speaking countries in the 1930s.

Archives

Karl Barth archives, Basel, Switzerland.

Printed Sources

Busch, Eberhard. *Karl Barth: His Life from Letters and Autobiographical Texts* (Philadelphia: Fortress Press, 1976). The most authoritative biography.

Hunsinger, George. *How to Read Karl Barth: The Shape of His Theology* (New York: Oxford University Press, 1991).

Jungel, Eberhard. *Karl Barth: A Theological Legacy* (Edinburgh: Scottish Academic Press, 1986).

Kung, Hans. *Justification: The Doctrine of Karl Barth and a Catholic Reflection* (Philadelphia: Westminster Press, 1981).

McCormack, Bruce L. *Karl Barth's Critically Realistic Dialectical Theology: Its Genesis and Development 1900–1936* (New York: Oxford University Press, 1995).

Sykes, S. W. (ed.). *Karl Barth: Studies of His Theological Method* (New York: Oxford University Press, 1979).

Torrance, James B. "Barth, Karl," In *The Encyclopedia of Religion*, vol. 2, Mircea Eliade (ed.), (New York: Macmillan Publ. Co., 1987), 68–71.

Torrance, T. F. *Karl Barth: An Introduction to his Early Theology, 1910–1931* (Edinburgh: T & T Clark, Ltd., 2000, 1962).

Von Balthasar, Hans Urs. *The Theology of Karl Barth: Exposition and Interpretation*, Edward T. Oakes (trans.) (San Francisco: Communio Books, Ignatius Press, 1992).

Wildi, H. M. *Bibliographie Karl Barth* (Zurich: Theologischer Verlag, 1984).

Richard Penaskovic

BARTHES, ROLAND (1915–1980)

Roland Barthes was born in Cherbourg, France. He studied at the Lycée Louis-le-Grand in Paris (1930–34) and at the Sorbonne (1935–39). His education was interrupted by tuberculosis, but his periods of convalescence were marked by a thorough reading of French writers, especially **André Gide** (1869–1951), **Jean-Paul Sartre** (1905–80), and **Albert Camus** (1913–60). Brought up by a Protestant mother, Barthes does not reveal a particular interest in religion in his work. He held several academic and nonacademic posts over the course of his career, including teaching positions in Romania and Egypt. His lack of an advanced degree, however, made it difficult to find regular academic work, but toward the end of his career (1976) he was named professor at the Collège de France, where he remained until his death. Although his work is difficult to categorize, Barthes's influential writings have made major contributions to structuralism, semiology, and literary theory and have provided the groundwork for later developments in cultural studies.

In a 1964 interview, Barthes states "I don't believe in influences" (Barthes 1985, 27) but "to my mind, what is transmitted is not 'ideas' but 'languages,' i.e. forms which can be filled in different fashions" (26). In his view, "books are 'currency' rather than 'forces'" (27). In his autobiographical text *Roland Barthes by Roland Barthes* (1975), Barthes lists four major "phases" of his career, for each providing an "intertext," a "genre," and his own works corresponding to the phase. His early period of productivity he terms "social mythology," a phase during which he composed *Writing Degree Zero* (1953), *Mythologies* (1957), and various writings on theater. Barthes responds directly to Sartre's *What Is Literature?* (1947) in "What is Writing?"—the key essay in *Writing Degree Zero*—by adding a notion of "écriture" (writing) to Sartre's famous style/language distinction (see Sontag 1968). A Marxist-inflected "language" can also be located in *Mythologies* and in his writings on the theater (see Roger 1997). His second "phase" is characterized by a rewriting of Saussurian linguistics, as in *Elements of Semiology* (1964) and *The Fashion System* (1967). His period of "textuality" contains traces of Philippe Sollers, **Jacques Derrida,** Jacques Lacan, and his student Julia Kristeva (1941–), and is represented in his works by *Sade, Fourier, Loyola* (1971), *Empire of Signs* (1970), and especially *S/Z* (1970), in which Barthes looks at "narrative codes" at play in the Balzacian realist text "Sarrasine." His final "morality" phase is marked by the "currency" of Friedrich Nietzsche (1844–1900), in *The Pleasure of the Text* (1973) and *Roland Barthes by Roland Barthes* (1975).

Archives

Institut Mémoires de l'édition contemporaine, Paris, France. Includes manuscripts, notes, journals, and letters.

Printed Sources

Barthes, Roland. "I Don't Believe in Influences." In *The Grain of the Voice*, Linda Coverdale (trans.), (New York: Hill and Wang, 1985).

————. *Oeuvres completes*, 4 vols. (1993–95, Paris: Editions du Seuil, 1993–2002).

————. *Roland Barthes by Roland Barthes*, Richard Howard (trans.), (New York: Hill and Wang, 1977).

Calvet, Louis Jean. *Roland Barthes: A Biography*, Sarah Wykes (trans.), (Bloomington: Indiana University Press, 1994).

Roger, Philippe. "Barthes with Marx." In *Writing the Image after Roland Barthes*, Jean-Michel Rabaté (ed.), (Philadelphia: University of Pennsylvania Press, 1997).

Sontag, Susan. "Preface." In Roland Barthes, *Writing Degree Zero*, Annette Lavers and Colin Smith (trans.), (New York: Hill and Wang, 1968).

Ungar, Steven, and Betty R. McGraw. "Introduction." In *Signs in Culture: Roland Barthes Today*, Steven Ungar and Betty R. McGraw (eds.), (Iowa City: University of Iowa Press, 1989). On Saussure and Barthes.

Todd W. Reeser

BARUCH, BERNARD MANNES (1870–1965)

Bernard Baruch was born in Camden, South Carolina, the son of Simon Baruch, a Jewish surgeon who fled East Prussia for the United States in 1855 to escape German military conscription, later serving in the Confederate Army, and Belle Wolfe, the plantation-born daughter of an old-established Southern Jewish family. In 1881 Baruch's family moved to New York City, though Baruch always identified strongly with the American South and eventually bought a South Carolina estate. Baruch's mother insisted her family not only follow strict Jewish religious observances but also respect the Christian Sunday. Baruch considered himself first an American and opposed Zionism; he assimilated substantially, marrying an Episcopalian who raised their children as Christians, but still attended synagogue on high holidays, and believed that his Jewish origins precluded any political career for him. Baruch's father not only pioneered public hygiene, but was also profoundly committed to philanthropic and community service, values transmitted to his admiring son, who generously supported numerous charities from the fortune he accumulated through skillful stock speculation. His other lifelong political idol was President **Woodrow Wilson**, a fellow Southerner who appointed prominent Jews to office, including Baruch, who headed the War Industries Board in 1917–18, after American intervention in World War I, coordinating wartime raw materials procurement. Baruch thenceforth became a munificent Democratic contributor, particularly close to the party's conservative Southern power-brokers. In peacetime he preached voluntary business cooperation, in wartime governmental economic direction and rationing; above all he opposed inflation, even at the price of high unemployment. Increasingly unsympathetic to 1930s New Deal Democratic economic policies, in World War II the anti-German Baruch rallied support for industrial mobilization. As a postwar adviser on nuclear energy, he effectively recommended that his country retain its atomic monopoly. Throughout, a well-oiled publicity machine ably promoted Baruch's image as unofficial "adviser to presidents," though from the late 1940s his influence waned.

Baruch recalled hearing traditional Southern folktales such as Br'er Rabbit from his black childhood nurse. He imbibed the romance of the Southern "Lost Cause," once staying up all night devouring a biography of Robert E. Lee, the Southern commander (Coit 1957, 8–15). Helped by an inspiring teacher, whose gift of novels by Charles Dickens, a favorite author, he treasured all his life, at fourteen Baruch graduated second in his class from New York Public School No. 59 before entering the City College of New York. Despite a retentive memory for facts, Baruch, who later described himself as "intellectually lazy" (Schwarz 1981, 13), performed poorly in classics and science, though he subsequently recalled that his courses in political economy, especially on the law of supply and demand, enthralled him and permanently influenced his thinking. Somewhat to his regret, his literary and intellectual range was always limited; Baruch once described "account books" and corporate reports as his "favorite reading" (Baruch 1957, 55, 78), found performances of plays by William Shakespeare overly demanding, and spoke poorly in public. He often quoted Woodrow Wilson and Thomas Macaulay, but preferred popular novels and employed ghost writers to polish all his published works.

Archives

Bernard M. Baruch Papers. Seeley G. Mudd Manuscripts Library, Princeton University, Princeton, N.J., United States. Baruch's personal and semi-official correspondence, writings, and other materials.

Printed Sources

Baruch, Bernard M. *My Own Story* (New York: Holt, Rinehart, 1957).
———. *The Public Years* (New York: Holt, Rinehart, 1960).
Coit, Margaret L. *Mr. Baruch* (Boston: Houghton Mifflin, 1957).
Schwarz, Jordan A. *The Speculator: Bernard M. Baruch in Washington, 1917–1965* (Chapel Hill: University of North Carolina Press, 1981). Fullest biography.

Priscilla Roberts

THE BEATLES

The Beatles' legendary career began in 1957, when Liverpool teenager John Lennon (1940–80) organized his first musical group, The Quarry Men. By the summer of 1958, Paul McCartney (1942–) and George Harrison (1943–2001) had become permanent members of Lennon's band. In 1962, the group, now known as The Beatles and managed by Brian Epstein (1934–67) successfully auditioned for producer George Martin (1926–) of EMI Parlophone Records in London. Shortly after their audition, drummer Ringo Starr (1940–) joined the band and The Beatles made their first record for EMI in September 1962. The Beatles conquered Britain in 1963, and in February 1964 they arrived in the United States. Bolstered by an appearance on *The Ed Sullivan Show*, Beatlemania overwhelmed America. During the 1960s, The Beatles released groundbreaking recordings such as *Rubber Soul* (1965), *Revolver* (1966), *Sgt. Pepper's Lonely Hearts Club Band* (1967), and *Abbey Road* (1969). The Beatles revolutionized not only the sound and lyrics of rock music, but also the visual arts, film, fashion, and hairstyles of the 1960s. The Beatles officially disbanded in 1970, and founder John Lennon was assassinated in New York City in 1980.

Early in The Beatles' career, John Lennon was tagged the "literary" Beatle, due in part to the publication of his book, *In His Own Write* (1964), which was "compared favorably with the works of Edward Lear" (Schaffner 1977, 27). Lennon claimed that the first time he "consciously put (the) literary part" of himself into a lyric was in the autobiographical ballad "In My Life" (1965), "inspired by Kenneth Alsopf, the British journalist, and **Bob Dylan**" (Sheff and Golson 1981, 151).

Lennon specifically cited the influence of Lewis Carroll and Oscar Wilde in his creative work (Sheff and Golson 1981, 93). Carroll's influence is evident in "Strawberry Fields Forever" (1967), whose images were "from *Alice In Wonderland*. It was Alice in the boat" (Sheff and Golson 1981, 153). Similarly, Lennon's "I Am the Walrus" (1967) borrowed images from Carroll's poem "The Walrus and the Carpenter," and featured Humpty Dumpty's final words, "Goo goo goo joob," from **James Joyce**'s *Finnegans Wake*. The opening lines from Lennon's "Tomorrow Never Knows" (1966) were taken from the *Tibetan Book of the Dead*.

Paul McCartney fell in love with literature after his English teacher introduced him to Chaucer's "Miller's Tale." McCartney was equally enthralled by the great playwrights: "We did *Hamlet*, which I immediately started to eat up. I became a director in my own mind. I started reading a lot of plays, Oscar Wilde's *Salome*, **Tennessee Williams**'s *Camino Real*, then a lot of Shaw's stuff, Sheridan, Hardy" (Miles 1997, 41–42). Beatles historian Nicholas Schaffner suggests that McCartney's nostalgic "Penny Lane" (1967) "may have been inspired by 'Fern Hill' a poem by **Dylan Thomas** who Paul revealed he had been reading" (68). The lyrics for McCartney's "Golden Slumbers" (1969) were taken, nearly verbatim, from the 1603 poem "Golden Slumbers" by Thomas Dekker (1570–1632).

George Harrison's search for spiritual enlightenment frequently resulted in songs with lyrics rooted in *Bhagavad Gita* and other religious texts. The lyric to "The Inner Light" (1967) came from a translation from the *Tao Te Ching* (Harrison 1980, 118). Even Harrison's best-known rock-and-roll composition, "While My Guitar Gently Weeps" (1968), was inspired by a spiritual source. Harrison was reading *I Ching—the (Chinese) Book of Changes* "which seemed to be based on the Eastern concept that everything is relative to *everything* else. As opposed to the Western view that things are merely coincidental. . . . I decided to write a song based on the first thing I saw upon opening any book. . . . I picked up a book at random—opened it—saw 'Gently weeps'—then laid the book down again and started the song" (Harrison 1980, 120).

Ringo Starr's literary influences are more difficult to discern, as Ringo composed few songs for The Beatles. But, as an actor, Starr seemed particularly drawn to the works of American author Terry Southern, whose novels *Candy* (1968) and *The Magic Christian* (1969) were both adapted as films starring Ringo. "Appropriately, perhaps, Ringo had the words 'Buy a Terry Southern book' included in the sleeve notes of his *Goodnight Vienna* (1974) album" (Harry 1992, 615).

Collectively, The Beatles seemed to have been interested in **J.R.R. Tolkien**'s *Lord of the Rings*, as it was briefly considered for their third film project following *Help!* (1965). Literary figures were also prominent in the collection of personal heroes chosen for display on the cover of *Sgt. Pepper's Lonely Hearts Club Band* (1967). Among those pictured are Edgar Allan Poe, Terry Southern, **William Burroughs**, H. G. Wells, Stephen Crane, Lewis Carroll, and George Bernard Shaw. Clearly, The Beatles were inspired, not only by the pioneers of rock and roll, but also by a variety of pioneering authors, and the band's innovative mixture of musical and literary styles forever changed the sound and grammar of popular music.

Archives

There is no central archival source. Some Beatles manuscripts have been loaned to the British Library by Paul McCartney and Hunter Davies. Other materials are known to be in the hands of Yoko Ono and the estate of George Harrison.

Printed Sources

Harrison, George. *I Me Mine* (New York: Simon and Schuster, 1980).

Harry, Bill. *The Ultimate Beatles Encyclopedia* (New York: Hyperion Books, 1992).

Miles, Barry. *Paul McCartney: Many Years from Now* (New York: Henry Holt and Company, Inc., 1997).

Schaffner, Nicholas. *The Beatles Forever* (Harrisburg: Cameron House, 1977).

Sheff, David, and G. Barry Golson. *The Playboy Interviews with John Lennon and Yoko Ono* (New York: Playboy Press, 1981).

Keith D. Semmel

DE BEAUVOIR, SIMONE LUCIE-ERNESTINE-MARIE-BERTRAND (1908–1986)

Simone de Beauvoir symbolized the socially committed woman of the post–World War II era, living her life in conformity with the tenets of existentialism. An eminent French existentialist writer and feminist, she was raised in a bourgeois Catholic family, the eldest of two daughters. Her childhood was relatively happy, and she developed a lifelong love of reading at her grandfather's estate in Limousin. De Beauvoir attended private schools and eventually became an atheist, determining that the intellectual and the spiritual approaches to life were incompatible. She graduated from the Sorbonne (1929) with a thesis on Gottfried Wilhelm Leibniz, and in the same year met **Jean-Paul Sartre,** who became her lifelong companion. De Beauvoir is remembered as much for her relationship with Sartre as for her writings. They attempted to live according to their intellectual principles, rejecting traditional marriage and other bourgeois conventions in favor of a bond of "essential" love, permanent but not excluding other sexual relationships. After teaching high school (1931–43), she founded the monthly review *Le Temps modernes* (1945). De Beauvoir won the Prix Goncourt for *Les Mandarins* (1954). She achieved world-wide recognition for *Le Deuxième Sexe* (*The Second Sex,* 1949), a pioneering feminist study of the social and historical position of women. Other autobiographical works included *Memoires d'une jeune fille rangee* (*Memoirs of a Dutiful Daughter,* 1958), *La Force de l'age* (*The Prime of Life,* 1960), *La Force des choses* (*The Force of Circumstance,* 1963), *Toute compte fait* (*All Said and Done,* 1972), and *La Cérémonie des adieux* (*Adieux: A Farewell to Sartre,* 1981). Strongly committed to and engaged in political activism, she wrote widely, including books of philosophy, travel, and essays.

Leibniz provided the fundamental philosophical influence on her work. She was also strongly influenced by Jean-Paul Sartre's existentialism: his *L'Être et le néant* has been regarded as the original source of some of de Beauvoir's works, including *Pyrrhus et Cenéas* (1944) and *Pour une morale de l'ambiguité* (*The Ethics of Ambiguity,* 1947). Thinkers including Edmund Husserl (a visible influence on *Pour une morale de l'ambiguité* and *La Force de l'age*), G.W.F. Hegel, Immanuel Kant, and **Martin Heidegger** were important parts of her philosophical framework (Tidd 1999, 18–19). In her writings on lesbianism, de Beauvoir was influenced by Renée Vivien's work and the theories of sexuality suggested by Pierre Janet and Alfred Kinsey (in his *Sexual Behaviour in the Human Male*). She also drew extensively on the work of realist writers Nelson Algren and **Richard Wright** (especially *Native Son, Black Boy,* and *A Record of Childhood and Youth*); of autobiographers **Colette,** Marie Bashkirtsev, Sophie Tolstoy, Violette Leduc, and Michel Leiris. **Virginia Woolf**'s *Mrs. Dalloway* provided answers to de Beauvoir's questions on language and novel writing (Tidd 1999, 138). Émmanuel Lévinas, Alexandre Kojève, Alfred Adler, and Merleau-Ponty's *Phenomenologie de la perception* were also important points of reference for de Beauvoir, especially for *Le Deuxième Sexe*. Gunnar Myrdal's writings on racism influenced her *L'Amerique au jour le jour* (1954). F. R. Chateaubriand and Louisa May Alcott *(Little Women)* were especially important in the construction of her narrative methodologies and testimonial discourses, especially in *Mémoires d'une jeune fille rangée* (1958). Finally, de Beauvoir also read Fyodor Dostoyevsky, Charles Baudelaire, Emile Zola, Nathalie Barney, Henri Bergson, Søren Kierkegaard, George Eliot, Jean Jacques Rousseau, and Montaigne.

Archives

Libraire Gallimard, Montreal. For an account of the de Beauvoir archives, see Ursula Tidd, *Simone de Beauvoir: Gender and Testimony* (Cambridge: Cambridge University Press, 1999).

Printed Sources

Ascher, Carol. *Simone de Beauvoir, A Life of Freedom* (Brighton: Harvester, 1981).

Bair, Deirdre. *Simone de Beauvoir, A Biography* (London: Jonathan Cape, 1990).

Beauvoir, Simone de. *All Said and Done*, 4 vols., Patrick O'Brian (trans.), (New York: Putnam, 1974). Most important autobiographical source, evoking the mood of the age, as well as carefully chronicling her life.

Crosland, Margaret. *Simone de Beauvoir: The Woman and Her Work* (London: Heinemann, 1992).

Evans, Mary. *Simone de Beauvoir, a Feminist Mandarin* (London: Tavistock, 1985).

Mahon, Joseph. *Existentialism, Feminism and Simone de Beauvoir* (Basingstoke: Macmillan, 1998).

Marks, Elaine. *Simone de Beauvoir: Encounters with Death* (New Brunswick, N.J.: Rutgers University Press, 1973). Perceptive study of de Beauvoir's literary and autobiographical works, including underlying philosophies.

Moi, Toril. *Simone de Beauvoir: The Making of an Intellectual Woman* (Oxford: Blackwell, 1994).

Monteil, Claudine. *Simone de Beauvoir, Le Mouvement des femmes, Mémoires d'une jeune fille rebelled* (Monaco: Du Rocher, 1996).

Tidd, Ursula. *Simone de Beauvoir: Gender and Testimony* (Cambridge: Cambridge University Press, 1999).

Vintges, Karen. *Philosophy as Passion, The Thinking of Simone de Beauvoir* (Bloomington and Indianapolis: Indiana University Press, 1996).

Winegarten, Renée. *Simone de Beauvoir* (Oxford: Berg, 1988).

Cyana Leahy

BEAVERBROOK, LORD

See Aitken, William Maxwell.

BECKETT, SAMUEL BARCLAY (1906–1989)

Samuel Beckett was born in Foxrock, Ireland, to a low-church Protestant family. He attended Portora Royal School at Enniskillen, excelling in sports and French, and read for a degree in modern languages at Trinity College Dublin with poet and scholar Thomas Rudmose-Brown. In 1928 he was awarded a lectureship at the

École Normale Supérieure. In Paris he came in touch with the literary circles around Thomas MacGreevy, Eugene Jolas, and **James Joyce** and published his first writings, an essay on *Finnegans Wake* (1929) and a long poem called *Whoroscope* (1930). The desire for a literary career soon overshadowed any academic aspirations, although it could not offer him any financial or emotional security. Troubled by psychosomatic ailments, for which he underwent psychoanalytic treatment with Wilfred Bion, and disillusioned about his writing career and life in general, he permanently left Ireland in 1936. Recognition of his talents arrived with *More Kicks than Pricks* (1934) and *Murphy* (1938), yet finding publishers remained difficult. During the war he worked for the Resistance and lived in hiding for three years in Rousillon, while *Watt* (1953) remained an unpublished manuscript. As a relaxation from prose and fiction, he turned to writing in French (a language without style, he said) and to drama, leading to his first real successes with the performance of *En attendant Godot* in 1953, directed by Roger Blin, followed by *Fin de partie* in 1957. Beckett continued experimenting with theater and fiction, writing stories, short plays, radio and television scripts, and even a movie, *Film* (1964), starring Buster Keaton; nonetheless, his longer works, such as the Trilogy (*Molloy* [1951], *Malone Dies* [1956], *The Unnamable* [1958]) and *Krapp's Last Tape* (1958) were still received unfavorably. In 1969 he received the Nobel Prize, but did not accept the prize in person. Living practically in seclusion, he further purified his writing to the barest essentials; his literary production decreased as he devoted his time to supervising productions of his plays across Europe. In 1986 he was diagnosed with emphysema and he moved to a nursing home. He died three years later.

With Beckett influence is a contested matter, and one rather speaks of affinity than of literary precursors. He produced very little criticism (an essay, *Proust* [1931], and his contribution on "Dante . . . Bruno. Vico . . . Joyce" to *Our Exgamination round his Factification for Incamination of Work in Progress*) and few writings bear the weight of his influences; nonetheless most of his work is strewn with allusions to Dante, the Bible, Descartes, Schopenhauer, Malebranche, and Mauthner. For many authors, such as Dante and Racine, Beckett showed a lifelong predilection; but mostly influence is a matter of borrowing abstractions: the axiom of Arnold Geulincx, a Belgian disciple of Descartes, "Ubi nihil vales, ibi nil velis" (Where you can do nothing, there wish nothing), pervades Beckett's existentialism and absurdism; silent movies and the filmic types of Buster Keaton and **Charlie Chaplin** inspired his dramatic techniques; **Carl Jung**'s theory on the presence of fragmentary personalities in the unconscious stimulated his sense of characterization; Bion's "grid system" in the field of group therapy returns in the schematic structures of his writings. Furthermore, Beckett took his sense for structure, synthesis, and abstraction largely from chess and from his reading of **Marcel Duchamp** and Vitali Halberstadt's manual *Opposition et cases conjugées sont reconciliées* (1932). Other affinities reveal themselves through transposition: the romantic nostalgia in Jack B. Yeats's paintings Beckett interpreted as a feeling of alienation; the truth or untruth of Schopenhauer's metaphysics was secondary to his attempt to justify unhappiness; even Dante works on an existential level as infernal doom represents the futility of desiring a paradisiacal state. That Beckett was troubled by influence shows in his relationship to Joyce; styling himself as adopting the "Joyce method" as a young man, he spent great efforts during his career trying to distance himself from Joyce's shadow.

Archives

University of Reading, U.K.: Manuscripts and typescript drafts, theatrical notebooks, published works, translations, ephemera, including programs, recordings and press, personal art collection, secondary criticism.

Harry Ransom Humanities Research Center, University of Texas, Austin, Texas: Manuscripts and typescripts, correspondence, publication announcements, interviews, press cuttings.

Printed Sources

Bair, Deirdre. *Samuel Beckett: A Biography* (New York: Harcourt Brace Jovanovich, 1978).

Carey, Phyllis, and Ed Jewinski (eds.). *Re: Joyce'n Beckett* (New York: Fordham University Press, 1992). A collection of essays on various interconnections between Joyce and Beckett that range from the biographical to the intertextual, including the use of allusion and the common influence of Dante.

Coe, Richard. *Samuel Beckett* (New York: Grove Press, 1964). Examines philosophical ideas in Beckett and their parallel with the ideas of, among others, Proust, Descartes, Geulincx, and Wittgenstein.

Corcoran, Neil. *After Yeats and Joyce: Reading Modern Irish Literature* (Oxford: Oxford University Press, 1997). Traces the literary legacy of Yeats and Joyce through twentieth-century Irish literature, including their influence on Beckett, Kinsella, Friel, and Heaney.

Cronin, Anthony. *Samuel Beckett: The Last Modernist* (New York: HarperCollins, 1997).

Esslin, Martin. "Samuel Beckett: The Search for the Self." *The Theatre of the Absurd*, 3rd ed. (Harmondsworth: Penguin, 1980), 29–91. General survey of influences for Beckett's drama.

Farrow, Anthony. *Early Beckett: Art and Allusion in* More Pricks than Kicks *and* Murphy (Troy, N.Y.: Whitston, 1991).

Fletcher, John. *Samuel Beckett's Art* (London: Chatto & Windus, 1967). Contains a chapter on "Sources and Influences."

Kennedy, Sighle. *Murphy's Bed: A Study of Real Sources and Sur-Real Associations in Samuel Beckett's First Novel* (Lewisburg, Pa.: Bucknell University Press, 1971). Traces Vico, Bruno, Dante, Homer, and Joyce as well as the influence of surrealism and other modernist movements in *Murphy*.

Knowlson, James. *Damned to Fame: The Life of Samuel Beckett* (New York: Simon and Schuster, 1996).

Murray, Patrick. *The Tragic Comedian: A Study of Samuel Beckett* (Cork: Mercier Press, 1970). Chapter on "Beckett and Tradition" places Beckett in context of Anglo-Irish influences.

Pilling, John. *Samuel Beckett* (London: Routledge, Kegan Paul, 1976). Thorough analysis of Beckett's personal, intellectual, cultural, and literary development.

Robinson, Michael. "From Purgatory to Inferno: Beckett and Dante Revisited," *Journal of Beckett Studies* 5 (1979), 69–82.

Scruton, Roger. "Beckett and the Cartesian Soul." *The Aesthetic Understanding: Essays in the Philosophy of Art and Culture* (London: Methuen, 1983). On Beckett's philosophical influences.

Wim van Mierlo

BELL, DANIEL (1919–)

Daniel Bell was born in the Lower East Side of New York City. He attended the City College of New York (1935–38), and spent the following 20 years as a journalist working as writer and editor for *New Leader* and *Fortune* magazines. He also entered into academia at various times, teaching social science at the University of

Chicago for three years in the mid-1940s and occasionally acting as an adjunct lecturer in sociology at Columbia University in the 1950s. In 1958 Bell was accepted as a full-time professor at Columbia and received his Ph.D. in 1960 with the acceptance of a collection of his previously published work. He moved to Harvard in 1969 and was appointed Henry Ford II Professor of Social Sciences in 1980 until he retired in 1990. Bell's main influence stemmed from his analysis of the nature of postindustrial society and his later conservative readings of contemporary culture.

Like most sociologists in America after World War II, Bell was influenced by the major intellectual figures of Western thought including Karl Marx, Emile Durkheim, and Thorstein Veblen. But Bell always acknowledged that his major intellectual inspiration for the study of modernity came from the sociological writings of **Max Weber.** Bell even described Weber's *The Protestant Ethic and the Spirit of Capitalism* as the most important sociological work of the twentieth century. But Bell was also heavily influenced by his association with the New York intellectuals, the community of independent scholars and thinkers including Nathan Glazer, Sidney Hook, and Irving Kristol who profoundly influenced American intellectual life in the latter half of the twentieth century. Bell's famous 1960 declaration concerning the "end of ideology in the West" and the exhaustion of Marxism as a political tool was a phrase borrowed from the writings of the French philosopher **Albert Camus,** and an idea developed in connection with the Congress for Cultural Freedom in 1955, attended by Raymond Aron, Michael Polanyi, Edward Shils, and Seymour Martin Lipset. Bell readily acknowledged the importance of Raymond Aron's *The Opium of the Intellectuals* (1955) as a source of inspiration. Bell's analysis of the "coming of post-industrial society" was influenced by the growing body of sociological literature after the Second World War concerned with the transformation in the nature of capitalism. Bell mentioned the importance of Ralf Dahrendorf's *Class and Class Conflict in an Industrial Society* (1959), David Riesman's essay, "Leisure and Work in Post-Industrial Society" (1958), and W. W. Rostow's *Stages of Economic Growth* (1960). His understanding of the importance of technological changes to economic development was influenced by the work of the economist Joseph Schumpeter, in particular his *Capitalism, Socialism and Democracy* (1942). Bell mentioned the influence of Colin Clark's *Condition of Economic Progress* (1940) in his understanding of the changing composition of the workforce. Bell's analysis of the relationship between economics, culture, and social change in works such as *The Cultural Contradictions of Capitalism* (1976) was shaped by the literary criticism of Lionel Trilling and Irving Howe, the economic writings of Robert Heilbroner, and in particular the work of Max Weber.

Archives

Daniel Bell Files, Tamiment Institute Library, New York University, New York.

Printed Sources

Brick, Howard. *Daniel Bell and the Decline of Intellectual Radicalism* (Madison: Wisconsin University Press, 1986).

Dittberner, Job L. *The End of Ideology and American Social Thought, 1930–1960* (Ann Arbor, Mich.: UMI Research Press, 1979).

Leibowitz, Nathan. *Daniel Bell and the Agony of Modern Liberalism* (Westport, Conn.: Greenwood Press, 1985).

Rose, Margaret. *The Post-Modern and the Post-Industrial* (Cambridge: Cambridge University Press, 1991).

Walker, Malcolm. *Daniel Bell* (London: Routledge, 1996).

Robert Genter

BENDA, JULIEN (1867–1956)

Julien Benda was born in Paris and educated at the lycées Charlemagne and Condorcet 1876–84; he studied engineering at the Ècole Centrale and later received a *License ès lettres* from the Sorbonne.

Although little read today, Benda was one of the leading lights of the Third Republic's literary culture. Benda's distinction was that he was a complete contrarian. Throughout his long career he was reluctant to ally with any school of, and remained a trenchant critic of, contemporary thought. Much of his best-known writing is to be found in Charles Péguy's *Cahiers de la Quinzaine* and **André Gide**'s *La Nouvelle Revue Francaise*, yet he consistently quarreled and eventually broke with both men. His most famous work by far, *La Trahison des Clercs* (translated *The Treason of the Intellectuals*), was a ringing condemnation of what he saw as current intellectuals' surrender to material and lay forces. The upshot, Benda argued, was the politicization of all aspects of life, and the unleashing of irrational passions throughout society. Benda preferred the notion of clerk over that of intellectual in that the former was devoid of contemporary connotations. The virtue of the clerk consisted in its devotion to reason and the universal as opposed to the contingent and particular. In the light of 1927, Benda's assault on intellectuals stirring the fires of nationalist and class hatred appeared timely and prescient.

Benda was born into a privileged and secularized Jewish household. Although he was never active in the Parisian synagogue, he closely identified with Jews as a people and as a historically persecuted group. Indeed, his first public writings addressed the Dreyfus Affair. Benda was an ardent Dreyfussard, and his first work, *Dialogues à Byzance* (1900), focused on the leading intellectuals of the anti-Dreyfussard movement—Ferdinand Brunetière, Maurice Barrès, and Jules Lemaître. Benda's focus was less on the innocence or guilt of Dreyfus, but rather on the employment of authoritarian and irrationalist arguments on the part of the anti-Dreyfussards (Sarocchi 1968, 17). From the outset Benda was thus concerned with the activity of letters and ideas in the realm of public affairs.

In the immediate post-Dreyfus period Benda was torn in a number of different directions. On the one hand, he associated with Péguy and Georges Sorel and the circle associated with the *Cahiers de la Quinzaine*. There were frequent discussions of socialism, and group expeditions to **Henri Bergson**'s philosophy lectures at the Collège de France. At the same time Benda pursued a more independent tack and read deeply in the works of the philosopher Charles Renouvier and the psychologist Théodule Ribot (Nichols 1978, 57, 61). Renouvier and Ribot were pillars of establishment Third Republic philosophy. Benda employed the staid elder statesmen's neo-Classical and neo-Kantian rationalism in shaping a multipronged attack on Bergson. The work *Le Bergsonisme* (1912) dealt less with the technical philosophical aspects of Bergson's writing than it did with teasing out what Benda saw as the dangerous implications of Bergson's thought. Essentially, Benda argued that Bergson's stress on intuition and élan vital were an upshot of late-romanticism and irrationalism (Grogin 1978, 27). He was especially scornful of the salon crowd that touted Bergson.

Le Bergsonisme generated a great deal of discussion and paved the way for Benda's prolific career. *La Trahison* extended Benda's deeply negative critique to all modernist turns-of-thought ranging from Nietzsche to Marx. Although he valorized Spinoza, Kant, and Renan as exemplars of dispassionate reason, his own style was most frequently bitter and polemical. In other words, his own writings stood in sharp contrast to those he held out as models. Despite his loathing of most forms of modernism he was not a simple reactionary (Revah 1991, 209–10). As the political situation degenerated in the 1930s his writings took an increasingly political cast, and he most frequently sided with the left.

Benda was outspoken in his denunciation of the rise of Nazism. He was forced to flee Paris following the occupation, and his library and papers were destroyed by the authorities. Following the war Benda once again achieved notoriety through his strident defense of the execution of collaborators (Schalk 1979, 45). He would write up to his last days in 1956, but clearly his star had peaked with the publication of *La Trahison*.

Archives

Bibliothèque nationale, Départment des manuscrits, Fonds Benda.

Printed Sources

Cornish, Martin. "Catalyst for Intellectual Engagement: The Serialization of Julien Benda's *La Trahison des clercs* in the *Nouvelle Revue Francaise*, 1927–1932," *French Cultural Studies* 4 (1993), 31–49.

Grogin, Robert C. "Rationalists and Anti-Rationalists in pre–World War I France: The Bergson-Benda Affair," *Historical Reflections/Reflexions Historiques* 5, 2 (1978), 223–31.

Nichols, Ray. *Treason, Tradition and the Intellectual: Julien Benda and Political Discourse* (Lawrence: The Regents Press of Kansas, 1978). The most comprehensive book on Benda in English. The extensive bibliography of Benda's works is especially helpful.

Niess, Robert J. *Julien Benda* (Ann Arbor: University of Michigan Press, 1956). An early, searching commentary on Benda's works.

Revah, Louis-Albert. *Julien Benda: Un Misanthrope juif dans la France de Maurras* (Paris: Plon, 1991).

Sarocchi, Jean. *Julien Benda: Portrait d'un intellectuel* (Paris: A.G. Nizet, 1968). The standard French biography.

Schalk, David L. *The Spectrum of Political Engagement: Mounier, Benda, Nizan, Brasillach, Sartre* (Princeton: Princeton University Press, 1979). This fine work situates Benda within the intellectual landscape of interwar France.

Jim Millhorn

BENEŠ, EDVARD (1884–1948)

Edvard Beneš was born in Kožlany, in the present-day Czech Republic. The son of a prosperous peasant, Beneš studied between 1904 and 1909 at the Czech University in Prague, the Sorbonne, and the University of Dijon, earning a degree in law from Dijon in 1908 and a doctorate in philosophy from Prague in 1909. While a student, he began publishing theoretical works on socialism, sociological studies, and commentaries on Czech national politics. After his return to Prague, he taught at the Czech Commercial Academy and collaborated with his former professor,

Tomáš Garrigue Masaryk (1850–1937), on issues of Czech national politics. In 1915, Beneš followed Masaryk into exile and worked closely with him to secure Allied support for an independent Czech state. After the creation of Czechoslovakia in 1918, he became foreign minister, representing the new republic at the Paris Peace Conference and later the League of Nations. In 1935 Beneš succeeded Masaryk as president of Czechoslovakia. On September 30, 1938, Beneš accepted the Munich Agreement between Britain, France, and Germany in order to prevent war between Czechoslovakia and Germany. He resigned the presidency and went into exile in London in October 1938. After the start of World War II in 1939, Beneš formed a Czechoslovak government-in-exile in London. Once again he succeeded as a diplomat, gaining the Allies' denunciation of the Munich Agreement and a treaty of alliance with the Soviet Union. He returned home to a hero's welcome in 1945, following the Soviet Army's liberation of Czechoslovakia. In poor health after the war, Beneš was unable to stave off the Czechoslovak Communist Party's encroachments against its partners in a coalition government. In February 1948 he accepted a realignment of the cabinet that allowed the Communists to take control of the government. In June of that year, he resigned the presidency for the second time. Three months later a stroke took his life.

Beneš regarded himself not only as a master politician and diplomat, but also as a prescient analyst of democracy and international relations. He believed himself to be a scientific student and practitioner of politics, someone who could dispassionately dissect a given set of circumstances and determine a rational solution. In an interview with his biographer, the British author Compton Mackenzie (1883–1972), Beneš cited Charles Darwin (1809–82) as a principal influence on his intellectual development and his reliance on the scientific method. He was also inclined toward Social Darwinism, a philosophy that fit well with his personality: prudish, socially isolated, and arrogant, Beneš as a politician held many of his colleagues in disdain and exhibited little solidarity with the citizenry. His political opinions were shaped in part by his brother Václav, 19 years his senior, with whom Beneš lived while a student at the gymnasium in Prague. A teacher and editor, Václav Beneš leaned toward socialism, and he introduced his brother to socialist texts. As a student, Beneš also read the novels of Emile Zola (1840–1902), and he translated *L'Assomoir* into Czech when he was 19. Beneš considered himself a socialist throughout his entire political career, although more from the conviction that socialism was the next logical step in Europe's political development than from a concern about social justice. He viewed Karl Marx (1818–83) and his proponents through a critical lens, arguing that Marx's thought presupposed a spiritual conception of the equality of humanity, something that Marxist thinkers and politicians, especially Communists, did not recognize. Beneš himself, although irreligious, did not hold to a fully materialistic view of the world. He believed that a spiritual understanding of humanity and an acceptance of transcendent moral norms undergirded a successful democratic and socialist society: ideas gained from his association with Tomáš Masaryk. Beneš's professor and political mentor was the most important influence upon both his philosophical and political thinking. In memoirs and interviews, Beneš cited the influence of René Descartes (1596–1650), Emile Dürkheim (1858–1917), and **Henri Bergson** (1859–1941) upon his thinking as a student. Yet he pointed out that he viewed these thinkers anew after studying with Masaryk. During his political career, he regarded himself as the inheritor of

Masaryk's mantle and the protector of his mentor's conception of a republic built upon humanitarian ideals.

Archives

Archive of the National Museum, Prague, Czech Republic: Edvard Beneš and Hana Benešová Papers. Personal correspondence of Beneš and his wife, photographs.

Archive of the T. G. Masaryk Institute, Czech Academy of Sciences, Prague, Czech Republic: Beneš Archive and London Archive. Diplomatic and presidential papers from interwar period and exile in London (1938–45), manuscripts of speeches, press clippings, miscellaneous correspondence.

Hoover Institution Archive, Hoover Institution for War, Revolution, and Peace, Stanford University, Stanford, Calif.: Eduard Táborský Collection. Personal and official papers of Beneš's personal secretary in London exile, Táborský's wartime diary.

Printed Sources

Lukes, Igor. *Czechoslovakia between Stalin and Hitler: The Diplomacy of Edvard Beneš in the 1930s* (New York: Oxford University Press, 1996).

Mackenzie, Compton. *Dr. Beneš* (London: Harrap, 1946).

Taborsky, Eduard. *President Beneš between East and West, 1938–1945* (Stanford: Hoover Institution Press, 1981).

Zeman, Zbyněk, and Antonín Klimek. *The Life of Edvard Beneš, 1884–1948: Czechoslovakia in War and Peace* (Oxford: Oxford University Press, 1997).

Bruce R. Berglund

BEN-GURION, DAVID (1886–1973)

David Ben-Gurion was born in the town of Plonsk, in Russian-dominated Poland. His primary education was in the traditional Jewish manner, learning the Bible, the Talmud, and books of prayer in small rabbinical schools. Tzarist rules restricting the number of Jewish students in Eastern Europe and the lack of financial means to study in Western Europe prevented him from getting a high school or vocational education, and he was self-taught. He was a polyglot and well-read person. In 1906, Ben-Gurion went to Palestine as a pioneer and in 1911, he went to Constantinople to study law, but after the outbreak of World War I, he was expelled from the Ottoman Empire and never pursued formal studies.

Ben-Gurion's biographers tend to divide his public life after his return to Palestine in 1918 into three phases: some 15 years as general secretary of Histadrut, the federation of labor (1920–35), 13 years as chairman of the executive committee of the Jewish Agency (1935–48), leading the Jews' struggle for independence from British rule, and 15 years as Israel's first prime minister (1948–63). His role in the proclamation of the State of Israel and its construction as a modern democratic state had made him, in the eyes of many, the greatest Jewish leader in modern history. Moreover, Ben-Gurion stood out as one of the great world leaders of the twentieth century in combining a far-reaching vision with a strong sense of pragmatism. His political leadership, characterized by the effective utilization of knowledge and manipulation of power in the service of an encompassing vision of state-guided social transformation, served as a model for a modern Western culture in search of a balance between social ideology and political realism.

Ben-Gurion's disciple, Shimon Peres, has shown how Ben-Gurion's reading was related to the skills he deemed necessary in each stage of his career. As leader of the Histadrut he read a great deal of socialist and revolutionary literature as well as books about mass psychology. As head of the Jewish Agency he was greatly concerned with the history of the Jewish people and the prerequisites of a Jewish state. As prime minister of Israel, he was deeply involved with science. The literary and intellectual treasures that influenced Ben-Gurion's thought can be divided into four categories:

1. *The Old Testament:* Ben-Gurion was strongly versed in the Old Testament, from which he derived the right of the Jewish people to establish a state in Palestine. He wrote several essays on biblical issues reflecting his identification with biblical leaders related to the conquest of the Land of Canaan, especially Moses and Joshua.[1]

2. *Rationalist philosophy:* Ben-Gurion often mentioned the influence of Plato and Spinoza on his thought. A great admirer of both, he believed that human beings, as an organic part of the material and spiritual world, have the gift of deducing the secrets of nature and of the human conscience. The influence of the two philosophers can also be detected in the cosmic proportions of his model of the Jewish state.

3. *National literature:* Ben-Gurion made a great effort to mobilize writers to inspire the state-building process, an effort influenced by his admiration of intellectual national leaders, especially Gandhi, and by early modern literature supporting the development of the nation-state, such as Cervantes's *Don Quixote*.

4. *Modern Israeli literature:* Ben-Gurion was strongly affected by Yizhar Smilansky's novel *The Days of Ziklag* (1958) and by Nathan Alterman's poems relating to public affairs. He saw both writers as manifesting "a supreme human quality,"[2] which, he believed, could only come to bear in a literature produced by Jews living in the land of Israel.

Archives

Ben-Gurion Archives, Ben-Gurion Heritage Institute and Research Center, Sde-Boker, Israel.

The Ben-Gurion archives online: http://bgarchives.bgu.ac.il/archives/frame.asp?arc.

Printed Sources

Aronson, Shlomo. *David Ben-Gurion: The Renaissance Leader and the Waning of an Age* (Beer-Sheva: Ben-Gurion University Press, 1999). In Hebrew.

Hazony, Yoram. *The Jewish State: The Struggle for Israel's Soul* (New York: Basic Books, 2001).

Keren, Michael. *Ben-Gurion and the Intellectuals: Power, Knowledge and Charisma* (DeKalb, Illinois: Northern Illinois University Press, 1983).

Teveth, Shabtai. *Ben-Gurion: The Burning Ground, 1886–1948* (Boston: Houghton Mifflin, 1987).

Notes

1. David Ben-Gurion, *Ben-Gurion Looks at the Bible*. Jonathan Kolatch, trans. (London: W. H. Allen, 1972).

2. David Ben-Gurion to Nathan Alterman, letter, August 12, 1960. Ben-Gurion Archives, Ben-Gurion Heritage Institute and Research Center, Sde-Boker, Israel.

Michael Keren

BERGMAN, INGMAR (1918–)

Born in Uppsala, Sweden, on July 14, 1918, the second son of a severe Lutheran minister often explained that he had a bad conscience during childhood, and at 18 years of age he lost his faith and left his parents. His few happy moments came in living with his grandmother, away from his violent father who beat him, as depicted in Bergman's final masterpiece, *Fanny and Alexander* (1982). He disliked his university years in Stockholm, but admitted the influence of his professor of Swedish Literature, Martin Lamm (Bergman 1973, 24). Although he became famous in the late fifties for his cold movies about inner life and conflicted souls, Ingmar Bergman began his career as a stage director for many Swedish theater companies; he did some 70 projects, from 1944 until the late eighties, in all kinds of genres: staging plays (and some operas) by Molière, Shakespeare, **Bertolt Brecht, Albert Camus,** Jean Anouilh, August Strindberg, and many Swedish playwrights, including himself. Many of Bergman's first movies as a director were adapted from plays, and some of them were comedies; his debut was *Crisis* (1945), adapted from *Morderdyret*, a Danish play by Leck Fisher; *It Rains on Our Love* (1947) was adapted from a Norwegian play by Oscar Braathen, *Decent People*. Bergman was an unique film director, who succeeded perfectly in representing fundamental feelings into pure images and dialogues: the humiliation in *The Naked Night* (1953); the fear of death in *The Seventh Seal* (1956) and *Wild Strawberries* (1957); the doubt about the existence of God in *Winter Light* (1962); the impossibility of communication in *The Silence* (1963) and *Persona* (1966); impressions of guilt in *The Shame* (1967) and *Cries and Whispers* (1972). Among the many projects he never made, Bergman wrote a script from Camus's book, *The Downfall*, but the latter's death stopped that collaboration, even though both men exchanged a correspondence (Bergman 1973, 26).

In *Laterna Magica*, Bergman recalls the strong influence of August Strindberg, Hjalmar Bergman, and Molière. He was not impressed by Strindberg's *The People of Hemsö*, but more by *Black Banners* (*Svarta Fanor*), and *The Red Room*, whose opening chapter he knew "virtually by heart" (Bergman 1973, 23). Franz Kafka was another major influence (Bergman 1973, 27). At 16, Bergman staged plays for a kind of family theater, including Strindberg's *Lucky Per's Travels* and *Master Olof* and Maeterlinck's *Blue Bird* (Bergman 1973, 9). He was fascinated by the city of Berlin, both from personal visits and "an early collection of short stories about Berlin by Siegfried Siwertz" (Bergman 1973, 181). He also remembers Hans Fallada's novels *Kleiner Mann was nun?*, *A Wolf among Wolves*, and Brecht and Weill's *Threepenny Opera* (Bergman 1973, 181).

In a long interview given in 1968 to three Swedish film critics, Bergman remembered the first film he saw, a silent adaptation of *Black Beauty* around 1924 at the Sture Cinema in Stockholm, "how it excited me, and how afterwards we bought the book of *Black Beauty* and how I learned the chapter on the fire by heart—at that time I still hadn't learned to read" (Bergman 1973, 6). Bergman also admitted that his masterpiece *Wild Strawberries* (with Victor Sjöström as an actor) was influenced specifically by Strindberg's *The Dream Play* and *To Damascus*, but also by an obscure Swedish novelist and dramatist, Jonas Love Almqvist (Bergman 1973, 138).

Archives

Svenska Filminstitutet Archiv, Stockholm.

Printed Sources

Bergman, Ingmar. *Laterna Magica* (Paris: Gallimard, 1987).

Bergman, Ingmar. With Stig Björkman, Torsten Manns, Jonas Sima (eds.). *Bergman on Bergman* [1970] (London: Secker & Warburg, 1973). By far the best book about Bergman's literary influences.

Bergom-Larsson, Maria. *Ingmar Bergman and Society*, Barrie Selman (trans.), (London: Tantivy Press; South Brunswick, N.J.: A. S. Barnes, with the Swedish Film Institute and the Swedish Institute, 1978).

Gervais, Marc. *Ingmar Bergman: Magician and Prophet* (Montreal: McGill-Queen's University Press, 1999).

Jones, G. William. *Talking with Ingmar Bergman* (Dallas: SMU Press, 1983).

Steene, Birgitta. *Ingmar Bergman: A Guide to References and Resources* (Boston: G.K. Hall, 1987).

Yves Laberge

BERGSON, HENRI LOUIS (1859–1941)

Henri Bergson was born in Paris, France, the second oldest of seven children of immigrant Jews, Kate Levison from London, England, and Michael Bergson, a musician from Warsaw, Poland. After graduating from the Lycée Condorcet in 1878, he enrolled in the École Normale Supérieure, receiving his baccalaureate in philosophy in 1881 and his D.Litt. in 1889 with a Latin dissertation on Aristotle. He taught philosophy at the Angers Lycée from 1881 to 1883; the Blaise Pascal Lycée, Clermont-Ferrand, from 1883 to 1888; the Collège Rollin, Paris, from 1888 to 1889; Lycée Henri Quatre, Paris, from 1889 to 1897; the École Normale Supérieure from 1897 to 1900; and the Collège de France from 1900 until his retirement in 1921. He was elected to the Académie Française in 1914, the same year that the Vatican placed his works in the *Index of Prohibited Books*. In 1927 he won the Nobel Prize for literature. He nearly converted to Roman Catholicism in the late 1930s, but refused to break solidarity with the oppressed Jews of Europe. He died of pneumonia caught while standing in line in the winter to register as a Jew in occupied France.

At Condorcet he studied classics, showed an aptitude for mathematics, and read Nikolai Ivanovich Lobachevski, Jules Lachelier, Farkas Bolyai, Blaise Pascal, George Friedrich Bernhard Riemann, and Jules Tannéry. His puzzlement over the paradoxes of Zeno of Elea first pushed him toward philosophy. At first he was a disciple of Herbert Spencer and admired Charles Darwin and John Stuart Mill, but gradually came under the sway of German Romantics such as Friedrich Wilhelm Joseph von Schelling and Novalis. This led him to study Plotinus, Baruch Spinoza, Gottfried Wilhelm Freiherr von Leibniz, Immanuel Kant, Johann Gottlieb Fichte, Georg Wilhelm Friedrich Hegel, Charles Renouvier, Jean Gaspard Félix Lacher Ravaisson-Mollien, Jaime Luciano Balmès, Antoine Augustin Cournot, Alfred Jules Émile Fouillée, Marie Jean Guyau, Hippolyte Adolphe Taine, and Joseph Ernest Renan at the École Normale Supérieure, where among his teachers were Léon Ollé-Laprune and Émile Boutroux and among his classmates was Jean Léon Jaurès. His earliest publications concerned Pascal (1878), James Sully (1883), and Lucretius (1883).

In psychology Bergson was inspired by Paracelsus, Franz Anton Mesmer, Charles Richet, Jean Martin Charcot, Claude Bernard, Eduard von Hartmann, Rudolf Hermann Lotze, James Ward, William James, Maine de Biran, Théodule Armand Ribot, Auguste Penjon, Joseph René Léopold Delboeuf, Arthur Schopenhauer, and Friedrich Nietzsche. Bergson and **Marcel Proust** knew each other from a young age and strongly impressed each other. Bergson married Proust's cousin, Louise Neuberger, in 1892. It is also said that Bergson and Claude Debussy enjoyed mutual influence. In any case, Bergson's philosophical concept of *durée* (the continuity of consciousness) suggests the gentle flow of impressionistic music. Pierre Paul Royer-Collard and Claude Henri de Rouvroy, Comte de Saint-Simon, influenced Bergson's political thought. Émile Durkheim and Bergson steadfastly opposed each other's sociological views all their lives.

Archives

Bergson's letters, papers, and memorabilia are dispersed in repositories throughout France. Significant collections are at the Fonds Bergson de la Bibliothèque Doucet, the Bibliothèque Nationale, the Académie Française, and the various institutions where he studied or taught.

Printed Sources

Antliff, Mark. *Inventing Bergson: Cultural Politics and the Parisian Avant-Garde* (Princeton, N.J.: Princeton University Press, 1993).

Chevalier, Jacques. *Henri Bergson*, Lilian A. Clare (trans.), (New York: AMS Press, 1969).

Gunter, Pete Addison Y. *Henri Bergson: A Bibliography* (Bowling Green, Ohio: Philosophy Documentation Center, 1986).

Hude, Henri. *Bergson* (Paris: Éditions Univérsitaires, 1989).

Kolakowski, Leszek. *Bergson* (South Bend, Ind.: St. Augustine's Press, 2000).

Lacey, Alan Robert. *Bergson* (London: Routledge, 1993).

Moore, Francis Charles Timothy. *Bergson: Thinking Backwards* (New York: Cambridge University Press, 1996).

Mullarkey, John. *Bergson and Philosophy* (Notre Dame, Ind.: University of Notre Dame Press, 2000).

Scharfstein, Ben-Ami. *Roots of Bergson's Philosophy* (New York: Columbia University Press, 1943).

Soulez, Philippe. *Bergson: Biographie* (Paris: Flammarion, 1997).

Eric v.d. Luft

BERLIN, IRVING (1888–1989)

Israel Baline (Berlin's name at birth) was born in Mohilev, Russia, on May 11, 1888. His father, Moses, was a cantor in a local synagogue. At age five, the family immigrated to the United States, taking up residence on the Lower East Side in New York City. "Izzy" attended public school as well as religious instruction. Occasionally, Izzy sang in the synagogue with his father. In his biography *As Thousands Cheer: The Life of Irving Berlin*, Laurence Bergreen illustrates Moses Berlin's influence on his son, quoting Berlin: "'I suppose it was singing in *shul* that gave me my musical background,' he recalled. 'It was in my blood'" (Bergreen 1996, 12).

At the age of 14, Izzy quit school and left home. Residing in Lower East Side lodging houses, Izzy earned money singing in Bowery saloons. He entertained his customers by composing and performing parodies of popular songs. Collaborating with pianist Mike Nicholson, Berlin wrote his first song, "Marie from Sunny Italy" in 1907. In 1911, Berlin served as both composer and lyricist for his first major hit, "Alexander's Ragtime Band." Within three years, Berlin formed his own music publishing company, Irving Berlin, Inc.

Berlin describes the joy of reading in his song "Lazy," published in 1924. In *Irving Berlin: American Troubadour*, Edward Jablonski mentions Berlin's extraordinary library at his 130 East End Avenue residence. Jablonski states: "Berlin was especially proud of his collection of rare first editions and often compared his acquisitions with those of another avid collector, Jerome Kern" (Jablonski 1999, 154).

According to Berlin biographer Philip Furia, Berlin had developed an interest in the poetry of the eighteenth-century British satirist Alexander Pope. Furia compares "Pope's ability to compress his observations on politics, manners, and art within the confines of ten syllables" to "Berlin's devotion to the restrictions of the thirty-two bar chorus" (Furia 1998, 96).

Berlin was a member of the Algonquin Round Table, a group of playwrights, artists, journalists, critics, and actors. The Round Table provided an intellectually stimulating social environment for Berlin. Among the group's original members were Berlin's biographer and theater critic Alexander Woollcott, Deems Taylor, George S. Kaufman, Robert Benchley, Harold Ross, Heywood Broun, and Robert E. Sherwood.

Berlin's rise to fame was unlike the average songwriter or playwright, who often produced one hit followed by years of misses. He contributed countless hits as a songwriter, a composer of music for the Broadway stage, and as a film score composer for several major Hollywood musicals. Despite Berlin's lack of a formal education, he dedicated himself to self-improvement. Laurence Bergreen presents Berlin's intentions toward self-study: "'I never had a chance for much schooling,' he now explained with endearing candor, 'so I couldn't read the good books I wished to because I had to look up too many of the big words. I'm taking time now to look those words up. I'm trying to get at least a bowing acquaintance with the world's best literature, and some knowledge of history, and all of the famous dead people'" (Bergreen 1996, 115).

Archives

Irving Berlin Archive, Library of Congress, Washington, D.C.

Printed Sources

Bergreen, Laurence. *As Thousands Cheer: The Life of Irving Berlin* [1990] (New York: Da Capo Press, 1996).

Freedland, Michael. *Irving Berlin* [1974] (New York: A Scarborough Book–Stein and Day Publishers, 1978).

Furia, Philip. *Irving Berlin: A Life in Song* (New York: Schirmer Books, 1998).

Hamm, Charles. *Irving Berlin: Songs from the Melting Pot: The Formative Years, 1907–1914* (New York: Oxford University Press, 1997).

Jablonski, Edward. *Irving Berlin: American Troubador* (New York: Henry Holt and Company, 1999).

Kimball, Robert, and Linda Emmet (eds.). *The Complete Lyrics of Irving Berlin* (New York: Alfred A. Knopf, 2001).

Marianne Wilson

BERNSTEIN, LEONARD (1918–1990)

Leonard Bernstein was born on August 25, 1918, in Lawrence, Massachusetts. His mother, Jennie (née Resnick), and his father, Sam, were Russian immigrants. As a young child, "Lenny" enjoyed listening to all types of music. While attending services at Temple Mishkan Tefila with his family, Lenny gained an appreciation for the music of his Jewish heritage. When he was 10, Aunt Clara gave her piano to his family. Shortly thereafter, Lenny began studying piano with Frieda Karp, making outstanding progress.

In 1929, Bernstein graduated from William Lloyd Garrison Grammar School. He continued his education at the Boston Latin School for the next six years. In 1935, Bernstein attended Harvard University, majoring in music. In addition to his piano studies with Heinrich Gebhard, Bernstein "studied English literature, and claimed to have read all the plays of Shakespeare . . . " (Burton 1994, 35). He wrote music criticism for *Modern Music* and the *Harvard Advocate*. Upon his graduation from Harvard in 1939, Bernstein enrolled at the Curtis Institute in Philadelphia, studying conducting with Fritz Reiner. During the summer of 1940, Bernstein was a conducting student of Serge Koussevitzky at the Berkshire Music Center in Tanglewood. While Bernstein was working as the assistant conductor of the New York Philharmonic Orchestra in 1943, guest conductor Bruno Walter unexpectedly became ill. Bernstein made his dramatic debut, filling in for Walter on November 14, 1943.

From a young age, Bernstein observed his father's dedicated reading of the Talmud. Bernstein's collection of writings, entitled *Findings*, contains an essay (dated February 11, 1935) that he wrote while attending Boston Latin School. Referring to his father, Sam, Bernstein states, "his life's textbook is the Talmud." He further states that his father uses the Talmud as his guide to both "business ethics and economic construction" and "moral and social ethics" (Bernstein 1982, 13). Bernstein was exposed to literature and poetry while attending both Boston Latin and Harvard University. In *Leonard Bernstein*, author Humphrey Burton illustrates Bernstein's reading assignments at Boston Latin: "A scribbled list of titles on the opposite page of his 1934–1935 exercise book gives a hint of the breadth of Leonard's required reading in his final year: *The Story of Philosophy*, *The Mind in the Making*, *Why Men Fight*, *Roads to Freedom*, *The Arts* and *The Meaning of Liberal Education*" (Burton 1994, 28). In his preface to *Bernstein Remembered*, violinist Isaac Stern recalls Lenny's "incredible mind, insatiable in its lust for knowledge, devouring volumes of poetry, history, biography, and philosophy, reveling in the power and beauty of ideas, driven to share his wonder at these human treasures with all who were around him—most particularly young people" (Stern 1991, 7). He later adds, "Russian novels, French poems, Shakespeare, the Bible, the written history of man's mind, were his roaming fields . . . " (7). In his book *Conversations about Bernstein*, William Westbrook Burton asks the composer Lukas Foss: "How important do you think a literary stimulus was to his composition?" Within his reply, Foss states, "I would say Lenny was the most well-read composer I have ever met; for example, he knew a large amount of poetry from memory" (Burton 1995, 12).

Many of Bernstein's compositions reveal his love of poetry and literature. *The Age of Anxiety, Symphony No. 2* for Piano and Orchestra (1949) was inspired by **W. H. Auden**'s poetry. Bernstein's *Candide* (1956; book by Lillian Hellman) is a comic operetta based on Voltaire's satire. The musical *West Side Story* (1957; book by Arthur Laurents) is a twentieth-century interpretation of Shakespeare's *Romeo and Juliet*. Bernstein's songs and choral works feature numerous twentieth-century poets as well as lyrics written by Bernstein. Other works by Bernstein were inspired by biblical or liturgical texts. His *Jeremiah, Symphony No. 1* (1942), was based upon material from the Old Testament. The *Kaddish, Symphony No. 3* for Orchestra, Boys' Choir, Speaker, and Soprano Solo (1963), has a religious text written by Bernstein. *Mass*, A Theatre Piece for Singers, Players and Dancers, uses text from the Roman Mass as well as additional lyrics by Stephen Schwartz and Leonard Bernstein.

Archives

The Leonard Bernstein Archive, Library of Congress, Washington, D.C.

Printed Sources

Bernstein, Leonard. *Findings* (New York: Simon and Schuster, 1982).
———. *The Infinite Variety of Music* (New York: Simon and Schuster, 1962).
———. *The Joy of Music* (New York: Simon and Schuster, 1954).
———. *The Unanswered Question: Six Talks at Harvard* (Cambridge, Mass.: Harvard University Press, 1976).
Burton, Humphrey. *Leonard Bernstein* (New York: Doubleday, 1994).
Burton, William Westbrook (ed.). *Conversations about Bernstein* (New York: Oxford University Press, 1995).
Gottlieb, Jack (ed.). *Leonard Bernstein's Young People's Concerts*, newly rev. and expanded ed. (New York: Anchor Books–Doubleday, 1992).
Gradenwitz, Peter. *Leonard Bernstein: The Infinite Variety of a Musician* (Leamington Spa, U.K.: Oswald Wolff Books–Berg Publishers, 1987).
Peyser, Joan. *Bernstein: A Biography* (New York: Beech Tree Books–William Morrow, 1987).
Secrest, Meryle. *Leonard Bernstein: A Life* (New York: Alfred A. Knopf, 1994).
Stern, Isaac. Preface. *Bernstein Remembered*, Jane Fluegel (ed.), (New York: Carroll & Graf Publishers, Inc., 1991).

Marianne Wilson

BETHMANN HOLLWEG, THEOBALD VON (1856–1921)

Born in Hohenfinow, Brandenburg, Bethmann was educated at the elite school *Schulpforta* and at the universities of Strassburg, Leipzig, and Berlin, where he studied law. A Protestant from a family risen to patent nobility two generations earlier, he became Prussian minister of the interior in 1905 and Imperial state secretary of the interior in 1907. In 1909 he succeeded chancellor Bernhard von Bülow. Bethmann favored modest reform bringing about comprehensive insurance and association laws, and greater autonomy for Alsace-Lorraine. His attempt to modernize Prussia's electoral system failed because of conservative resistance. Without solid support in the Reichstag, he was forced to look for changing majorities. His negotiations with the British over reduction of naval armaments remained unsuccessful because of the opposition by Admiral von Tirpitz backed by emperor William II. After the assassination of the Austro-Hungarian successor to the throne, Bethmann gave a "blank check" to the Austrian government for measures against Serbia. He took the calculated risk of Russia going into action in favor of Serbia, thus setting in motion the alliances and general staff planning culminating in a war among the great powers. Although he would have preferred a negotiated peace, Bethmann made critical concessions to nationalist–expansionist feeling and to military demands. In 1916 his room for maneuver was further diminished by the political influence of the new military leadership under Hindenburg and Ludendorff. Bethmann resisted unrestricted submarine warfare to keep the United States neutral. But he angered the conservatives by taking up again the idea of electoral reform. He had to resign during the debates on the peace resolution passed by the Reichstag in July 1917.

Bethmann's education exposed him to the study of the classical authors of antiquity, in which he excelled. He was enamored of the correspondence with his younger schoolmate Wolfgang von Oettingen revolving around their poetry. Still in retirement the former chancellor expressed to his Germanist friend how much he valued his letters and poetry. Bethmann extensively read and idealized Johann Wolfgang von Goethe and wrote in 1877: "*Wilhelm Meister*, just reread, spooks around in my head, so much so that I want to cry" (Jarausch 1973, 434).

Young Bethmann's idealism was challenged by the stress on struggle he discovered in the works of Charles Darwin and David Friedrich Strauss. The chancellor's emphasis on the Hegelian primacy of the state and on evolutionary political development—that he explicated with reference to an article by his friend, the historian Karl Lamprecht, in 1910—might be attributed to those influences. More obvious is the indebtedness of the chancellor's rhetoric to the leading apologist of the liberalized monarchical bureaucratic state, Rudolf von Gneist, who had been his teacher in Leipzig.

During World War I Bethmann's person and political program were subject to heavy criticism in the press. He made broad use of censorship, confiscating among others Pan-German leader Heinrich Class's annexationist brochure and the volumes of the volkish publicist Hans von Liebig.

In retirement Bethmann participated in the debate over German war guilt by writing his *Betrachtungen zum Weltkriege* but also by encouraging publications by Admirals von Müller and von Pohl as well as the recollections of Gottlieb von Jagow (former foreign secretary), Otto Hammann (former foreign office press chief), and Karl Helfferich (former vice chancellor); the latter Bethmann found disappointing.

Archives

Bundesarchiv, Berlin: Bethmann's personal papers were destroyed during World War II, but the federal archives hold the documents of the imperial chancellery and various other pertinent public records and personal papers.

Printed Sources

Bethmann Hollweg, Theobald von. *Betrachtungen zum Weltkriege*, 2 vols. (Berlin: Hobbing, 1921–22).

———. *Kriegsreden*, Friedrich Thimme (ed.), (Stuttgart: Deutsche Verlags-Anstalt, 1919).

Fischer, Fritz. *Griff nach der Weltmacht. Die Kriegszielpolitik des kaiserlichen Deutschland 1914/18* (Düsseldorf: Droste, 1964).

Jarausch, Konrad. *The Enigmatic Chancellor: Bethmann Hollweg and the Hubris of Imperial Germany* (New Haven: Yale University Press, 1973).

Vietsch, Eberhard von. *Bethmann Hollweg. Staatsmann zwischen Macht und Ethos* (Boppard: Harald Boldt Verlag, 1969).

Alexander Sedlmaier

BLOCH, MARC (1886–1944)

Marc Bloch was born in Lyon, France, where his father, Gustave, a renowned historian of Roman antiquities, was lecturing at the University. In 1888 Gustave Bloch was appointed to the École Normale Supérieure in Paris. Here, Marc attended the elite lycée Louis-le-Grand. In 1904 he was admitted at the École Normale Supérieure. After passing the *agrégation* in 1908, he spent one year in Berlin and Leipzig, studying principally economic history. In 1909 he was granted a fellowship permitting him to concentrate on his doctoral thesis. This work was interrupted by World War I, most of which Bloch spent in the trenches. In 1919 he was integrated into the newly established French University of Strasbourg, where he was appointed as lecturer in medieval history. Having published his thesis *Rois et serfs* (1920), Bloch was promoted to the position of associate professor in 1921, becoming a full professor in 1927. In the meantime he had published his magistral work *Les rois thaumaturges* (1924). In 1931 followed *Les caractères originaux de l'histoire rurale française*, in 1939 and 1940 the great two-volume synthesis *La société féodale*. After two failed attempts to secure an academic position in Paris, he finally succeeded in 1936, being nominated at the Sorbonne. At the outbreak of war he volunteered, notwithstanding his age. Because of his Jewish origin he was removed from his academic positions and joined the Résistance. In March 1944 he was arrested by the Gestapo and executed at Saint-Didier-de-Formans on June 16. Posthumously were published *L'étrange défaite*, an astute analysis of the French defeat in 1940, and *Apologie pour l'histoire*, Bloch's methodological reflections on history, which have been received as the author's professional testament.

Marc Bloch is one of the most influential historians of the twentieth century, even though his fame suffered a partial eclipse until the 1970s and 1980s, when he was rediscovered by the *"nouvelle histoire"* as one of its ancestors. *Les rois thaumaturges* were a pioneering example of historical anthropology; in *Les caractères originaux* Bloch investigated in the perspective of *"longue durée"* the rural landscape of France, and in *La société féodale* he explored an entire civilization in an attempt of *"histoire totale."* Furthermore, Bloch advocated interdisciplinarity and campaigned for comparative history. Essential to Bloch's fame is the fact that he was, along with Lucien Febvre (1878–1956), the cofounder of the *Annales* journal.

Marc Bloch was a prolific reader, which makes it difficult to single out particular literary influences. Still, among the authors having marked Bloch is Numa-Denis Fustel de Coulanges whose republicanism may have filtered to Bloch through his father, who had been Fustel's student (David 1997, 102–7). Another source of influence may have been the so-called "French geographical school of Paul Vidal de la

Blache." Its impact, however, was recently minimized in favor of the thriving German *"Landesgeschichte"* and German economic history (Toubert 1988, 9, 16–24). Indeed, Bloch's familiarity with German historical writing is illustrated by about 500 reviews of German books and articles, including eight substantial review articles for the *Revue historique* between 1928 and 1938 (Schöttler 1999, 55). As to Émile Durkheim's influence on Bloch, it is not easy to evaluate. It has been claimed that Durkheimian sociology was seminal for Bloch's thinking (Rhodes 1978, 46–51). Indeed, *Les rois thaumaturges* are built upon concepts such as "collective opinion" or "collective representations," and Jacques Le Goff perceives Durkheim's shadow looming behind Bloch (Le Goff 1983, xxxv). Yet Durkheim is not particularly referred to in this book. On the other hand, Bloch does occasionally speak of Durkheim, for instance in his *Apologie*. There he acknowledges the methodological rigor of the Durkheimian school, but criticizes its schematism. Bloch reproved positivist historiography for its lack of imagination, though in his own oeuvre he always valued its craftsmanship.

Archives

The Bloch papers are in the archives Nationales, Paris (fonds Marc Bloch, AB XIX). Consultation requires special authorization. The edition of the Bloch–Febvre correspondence is planned in three volumes, the first of which was published in 1994: Müller, Bertrand (ed.). *Marc Bloch, Lucien Febvre et les Annales d'Histoire Économique et Sociale: Correspondance I 1928–1933* (Paris: Fayard, 1994). Private and other public archival collections are listed in Fink, 355–58.

Printed Sources

David, Jean-Michel. "Marc Bloch et Gustave Bloch, l'Histoire et l'étude de la cité, l'héritage de Fustel de Coulanges." In *Marc Bloch, l'historien et la cité*, Pierre Deyon, Jean-Claude Richez et Léon Strauss (eds.), (Strasbourg: Presses Universitaires, 1997).

Dumoulin, Olivier. *Marc Bloch* (Paris: Presses de Sciences Po, 2000).

Fink, Carole. *Marc Bloch: A Life in History* (Cambridge: Cambridge University Press, 1989).

Gasnault-Beis, Marie-Claude. "Bibliographie [des oeuvres de Marc Bloch]." In Marc Bloch, *Mélanges historiques II* (Paris: École Pratique des Hautes Études, 1963).

Le Goff, Jacques. "Préface." In Marc Bloch, *Les rois thaumaturges* (Paris: Gallimard, 1983).

Rhodes, R. Colbert. "Emile Durkheim and the Historical Thought of Marc Bloch," *Theory and Society* 5, 1 (January 1978), 45–73.

Schöttler, Peter. "Marc Bloch und Deutschland." In Peter Schöttler (ed.), *Marc Bloch: Historiker und Widerstandskämpfer* (Frankfurt/Main: Campus, 1999).

Toubert, Pierre. "Préface." In *Marc Bloch, Les caractères originaux de l'histoire rurale française* (Paris: Armand Colin, 1988).

Georg Modestin

BOHR, NIELS HENRIK DAVID (1885–1962)

Niels Bohr was born in Copenhagen, Denmark, the son of Christian Bohr, professor of physiology at Copenhagen University. His mother was Ellen (Adler) Bohr. According to Bohr, his father greatly influenced his revolutionary and original studies in physics. Bohr matriculated in 1891 at the Gammelholm Grammar School. In 1903, he entered Copenhagen University, where he studied under Professor C. Christiansen, an original and erudite physicist in his own right. Bohr received his master's degree in physics in 1909 and his doctorate in 1911. He briefly studied at Cambridge under J. J. Thompson before moving to Victoria University in Manchester to work under Ernest Rutherford.

In 1911, Rutherford had proposed an atomic model which described the hydrogen atom as a small heavy nucleus surrounded by an electron with a fixed circular orbit, an arrangement completely at odds with the laws of classical physics. Bohr's genius was to propose that an electron might orbit the nucleus without emitting energy. The two of them formed a close working relationship which resulted in Bohr producing his theory of the hydrogen atom in 1913 at the age of 27.

After lectureships at Copenhagen University (1913–14) and Victoria University (1914–16), and appointment as professor of theoretical physics at Copenhagen University (1916–20), Bohr was appointed as head of the Institute for Theoretical Physics at Copenhagen University, a post held until his death in 1962. In 1922, he was awarded the Nobel Prize for physics. In 1965 the organization which he had headed for more than four decades was renamed the Niels Bohr Institute.

Bohr was strongly influenced by the ideas, lectures, and writings of **Max Planck.** By introducing conceptions borrowed from Planck's Quantum Theory, Bohr succeeded in working out and presenting a picture of atomic structure that, with later improvements (mainly as a result of Werner K. Heisenberg's ideas in 1925), still serves as an explanation of the physical and chemical properties of the elements. In September 1927 Bohr espoused his principle of complementarity, which gave a physical interpretation of Heisenberg's uncertainty relations.

During Sunday dinners and at parties, Bohr would often read poetry, including his favorite, Goethe's "Zueignung." He greatly admired Goethe's works, especially his poems and dramas. Bohr also had extensive knowledge of the Danish classics, and could quote from the Icelandic "Eddas" at length.

In 1938 Otto Frisch, who had worked closely with Bohr in Copenhagen, introduced Bohr to Lise Meitner. Meitner explained her theory of uranium fission to Bohr, hypothesizing that by splitting the nucleus of the atom, it was possible to create the explosive and destructive power of many thousands of pounds of dynamite. At a conference held in Washington in January 1939, Bohr explained the possibility of creating nuclear weapons based partially on Meitner's ideas. After some work with Enrico Fermi, Bohr showed that only the radioisotope uranium-235 would undergo fission with slow neutron decay.

Bohr continued with his research after Denmark was invaded by the German Army. With help from the British Secret Service, Bohr and his family escaped to Sweden in 1943. After moving to the United States he joined Robert Oppenheimer, Edward Teller, Enrico Fermi, and many others as part of the Manhattan Project to develop the atomic bomb. After the Second World War Bohr returned to Denmark where he argued for strict controls on the manufacture of nuclear weapons.

Archives

Niels Bohr Institute Blegdamsvej 17 DK—2100 Copenhagen, Denmark.
American Institute of Physics, Center for History of Physics, Niels Bohr Library, One Physics Ellipse, College Park, Maryland 20740-3843, U.S.A.

Printed Sources

Aaserud, Finn. *Redirecting Science: Niels Bohr, Philanthropy, and the Rise of Nuclear Physics* (New York: Cambridge University Press, 1990).

Blædel, Niels. *Harmoni og enhed (Harmony and Unity: the Life of Niels Bohr)* (New York: Springer Verlag, 1988).

Favrholdt, David. *Niels Bohr's Philosophical Background* (Copenhagen: Munksgaard, 1992).

Pais, Abraham. *A Tale of Two Continents, A Physicist's Life in a Turbulent World* (Princeton: Princeton University Press, 1997).

Peter E. Carr

BOJAXHIU, AGNES GONXJA (1910–1997)

Mother Teresa of Calcutta was born Agnes Bojaxhiu to a prosperous Albanian merchant family in Skopje, Serbia. She was the youngest of three children. The death of her father in 1919 reduced the family to economic hardship but engendered in young Agnes an appreciation of nonmaterial virtues. By age 12, Agnes had determined that she wanted to become a Catholic nun, and for the following six years, she, her family, and her church leaders tested the strength of her vocational commitment. In 1928, Agnes left Skopje to join the Sisters of Loreto, a missionary order based in Dublin, Ireland, but conducting missionary efforts in Calcutta, India, where the young nun was soon sent. Agnes assumed the name Sister Mary Teresa, reflecting her affinity for St. Thérèse of Lisieux, the French Carmelite nun whose best-selling autobiographical *Story of a Soul* recounted her devotional path of humble simplicity. After nearly twenty years of teaching in Calcutta, Sister Teresa was overcome with a desire to serve God by administering to the poorest of the poor in India, an inspiration she had described as "a call within a call." Soon afterward, Sister Teresa embarked on a unique mission to minister to society's most needy, hungry, diseased, and outcast members. She was granted Indian citizenship in 1949 and, one year later, her missionary work among India's poorest people was given the papal stamp of approval when Pope Pius XII approved the foundation of her Order of the Missionaries of Charity. Leading the order she founded over the course of 50 years, what began as a personal vocation to minister to the poor aided by a few of her former students from Calcutta evolved into a worldwide network of shelters, dispensaries, and homes for the sick and dying. In appreciation for the sizable effects of her order's small works of mercy, Mother Teresa was honored with the Nobel Prize for peace in 1979. By the time of her death in 1997, the Missionaries of Charity boasted more than 4,000 sisters in some 130 countries.

In keeping with her adherence to devotional simplicity, Mother Teresa's literary influences are themselves simple, though some embody foundational precepts of the Catholic faith. Her missionary vocation was shaped early on from reading letters and reports of Indian missionary work published in the periodical *Catholic Missions* during the 1920s, and some of her own letters from abroad were afterward published in the journal's pages. Mother Teresa's own work and writings were heavily influenced by the New Testament, especially chapter 25, verse 35 of St. Matthew's Gospel, which admonishes Christians to recognize Christ in all those in need. "For I was hungry and you gave me food; I was thirsty and you gave me to drink; I was a stranger and you welcomed me, sick and you visited me, in prison and you came to see me" (Spink 1997, 24). Mother Teresa often spoke of her ministering to the lepers, the dying, and the unloved as a mission of caring for Jesus himself "in the distressing disguise of the poorest of the poor" (Mother Teresa et al. 1996, 19). In addition to recognizing Christ in the poor, Mother Teresa credits her faith in the seminal Catholic doctrine of transubstantiation, the actual presence of Christ in the Eucharist, with strengthening herself and her sisters for their daily work among the people. Mother Teresa also found special inspiration in St. Thérèse of Lisieux's autobiography and its overarching message of childlike surrender to God. Just as St. Thérèse understood herself to be an instrument of God's work on earth, "a ball in the hands of the Child Jesus," Mother Teresa described herself as "a pencil in God's hands" (Varday 1995, xxi). "I chose her as my namesake," Mother Teresa said of the saint, "because she did ordinary things with extraordinary love" (Mother Teresa 1995, 64).

Archives

There is no public Mother Teresa archive available. In August of 2001, some 35,000 pages of documents were delivered to the Congregation for Sainthood Causes in Vatican City. Here, these documents will be analyzed with a view toward canonizing Mother Teresa. Meanwhile, they remain confidential.

Printed Sources

Mother Teresa. *A Simple Path* (New York: Ballantine Books, 1995).
Mother Teresa et al. *My Life for the Poor* (New York: Ballantine Books, 1996).
Sebba, Anne. *Mother Teresa: Beyond the Image* (New York: Doubleday, 1997).
Spink, Kathryn. *Mother Teresa: A Complete Authorized Biography* (New York: HarperCollins, 1997).
Varday, Lucinda. "Introduction." In Mother Teresa, *A Simple Path* (New York: Ballantine Books, 1995).

Todd Douglas Doyle

BÖLL, HEINRICH (1917–1985)

Heinrich Böll, born in 1917 in Cologne, entered secondary school in 1928 and obtained his school-leaving certificate in 1937. He began an apprenticeship as a bookseller in Bonn, Germany, but left soon afterward due to a call up for "labour service." In 1939 he enrolled at the University of Cologne to study German and classic philology, but was not able to graduate due to an induction to military service. Böll's education was largely coined by his parents' Catholicism, although their relation to the Catholic church has always been distanced and critical. Therefore, his reading during childhood and adolescence was "ziemlich kanonisch und im Ganzen besonders anti-aufklärerisch" (Schröter 1982, 44).

Böll was awarded the most important literary prize in the German-speaking countries, the Georg-Büchner-Prize in 1967. In 1972 he received the Nobel Prize for literature "for his writing which through its combination of a broad perspective on his time and a sensitive skill in characterization has contributed to a renewal of German literature." In 1973 he was given the honorary doctoral degrees of the universities of Dublin, Birmingham, and Uxbridge. Furthermore, he was an honorary member of the American Academy of Arts and Letters. The author's novels, narrations, short stories, and essays reflect the problems of postwar Germany to a large extent. His early novels such as *The Silent Angel* (published posthumously in 1992), *The Train Was on Time* (1949), and *Stranger, Bear Word to the Spartans We . . .* (1950) draw upon his experience of the Nazi era and the war and, beyond that, depict the societal development of postwar Germany. During his lifetime, Böll took an active part in the peace movement and in supporting persecuted writers such as the expatriated Russian **Alexander Solzhenitsyn** and civil rights activist Angela Davis. His works not only comprise literary writings but also numerous essays and articles. Next to Günter Grass and Siegfried Lenz, Böll became Germany's most important writer after World War II.

Early in his childhood, Böll became acquainted with a variety of authors, including Daniel Defoe, Karl May, Jack London, Johann Peter Hebel, Charles Dickens, Honoré de Balzac, and Fyodor Dostoyevsky. Dickens, Balzac, and Dostoyevsky served him as a model for covering a whole epoch in a literary work. Léon Bloy and Georges Bernanos are known to have influenced Böll to a large extent: both had a critical but willful attitude toward Catholicism. Bloy, passionately opposed to all free-thinkers, republicans, protestants, and Jews, left an impression on Böll because of his anticapitalistic praise of poverty. In 1936, Böll read Bloy's novel *Das Blut der Armen (The Blood of the Poor)*, which had appeared in German translation in the same year. Georges Bernanos, who belonged to a group of writers intending to renew Catholicism *(Renouveau catholique)* finally gave rise to Böll's own writing.

During regular visits to Ireland, Böll and his wife became concerned with Irish literature. In the 1950s Annemarie Böll began to translate Irish authors into German with the sometime assistance of her husband, among them George Bernard Shaw, Sean O'Casey, Flann O'Brien, and Brendan Behan.

Archives

Heinrich-Böll-Archiv der StadtBibliothek Köln, Cologne. Secondary literature, newspaper clippings, correspondence. www.stbib-koeln.de/boell.

Printed Sources

Butler, Michael (ed.). *The Narrative Fiction of Heinrich Böll. Social Conscience and Achievement* (Cambridge: Cambridge University Press, 1994).
Conrad, Robert C. *Heinrich Böll* (Boston: Twayne Publishers, 1981).
———. *Understanding Heinrich Böll* (Columbia, S.C.: Columbia University Press, 1992).
Reid, James H. *Heinrich Böll: Withdrawal and Re-emergence* (London: Wolff, 1973).
Schröter, Klaus. *Heinrich Böll* (Reinbek: Rowohlt, 1982).

Ernst Grabovszki

BONHOEFFER, DIETRICH (1906–1945)

Dietrich Bonhoeffer, born in Breslau (Wroclaw, Poland) in 1906, was the son of Karl Bonhoeffer, a well-known professor of psychology and neurology at the University of Berlin. He enrolled at Tübingen in 1923–24, and then transferred to the University of Berlin where he studied under such luminaries as Adolf Deissman, Karl Holl, Reinhold Seeberg, and Adolf von Harnack, receiving his doctorate in 1927. In 1928–29 Bonhoeffer served as an assistant minister to a Lutheran congregation in Barcelona. In 1930 Bonhoeffer did postdoctoral research at Union Theological Seminary in New York City, then returned in 1931 to lecture at the University of Berlin where he was identified with the ecumenical movement, which sought to unite Christians throughout the world. Bonhoeffer left Germany to protest the Nazi enforcement of anti-Jewish legislation in 1933 and worked in a German parish in London until 1935, when he returned to Germany to become head of a clandestine seminary of the German Confessing Church at Finkenwalde, Pomerania, until the Nazis shut it down in 1937. Bonhoeffer was involved in the German Resistance movement and in 1943 was arrested and imprisoned until 1945 when he was hanged at Flossenburg. Initial attention focused on Bonhoeffer's discussion of Christianity and modernity in his *Letters and Papers from Prison* under the heading "religionless Christianity in a world come of age." Later studies addressed his writings on ethics and social philosophy, Christian discipleship and community life, biblical interpretation, ecumenism, and Jewish-Christian relations.

Bonhoeffer's *Habilitationsschrift, Act and Being,* is heavily influenced by such philosophers as Paul Natorp, Edmund Husserl, Max Scheler, **Martin Heidegger,** Hermann Cohen, and Erich Przywara. While in prison Bonhoeffer read the Bible in addition to such diverse writers as Euripides, Plutarch, Quintus Septimius Florens Tertullian, St. Cyprian of Carthage, Johann Wolfgang von Goethe, Rainer M. Rilke, and the philosophers Immanuel Kant, Wilhelm Dilthey, Nicholai Hartmann, and **José Ortega y Gasset.** Educated in the liberal theology of Berlin, Bonhoeffer became an ally of **Karl Barth** and was also deeply influenced by Martin Luther, **Rudolf Bultmann,** and Adolf von Harnack. He was strongly affected by the novels of Georges Bernanos. Bonhoeffer's theology has the uncanny ability to extend into new intellectual arenas without deserting its historical context.

Archives

Die Staaatsbibliothek, Berlin, Germany is the best archive for the original Bonhoeffer material.

Bonhoeffer Collection at the Burke Library, Union Theological Seminary, New York City. This archive has primary sources in German, English, and some other languages, microfiche of the Bonhoeffer papers, and secondary literature, both published and unpublished.

Printed Sources

Bethge, Eberhard. *Dietrich Bonhoeffer: A Biography.* Victoria J. Barnett (rev. and ed.), (Minneapolis: Fortress Press, 2000). This volume and others by Bethge, a friend and relative of Bonhoeffer, are authoritative.

De Gruchy, John W. (ed.). *The Cambridge Companion to Dietrich Bonhoeffer.* Cambridge Companions to Religion (Cambridge: Cambridge University Press, 1999).

Feil, Ernst. *Bonhoeffer Studies in Germany. A Survey of Recent Literature,* James Burtness (ed.), Jonathan Sorum (trans.), (Philadelphia: International Bonhoeffer Society, 1997).

Floyd, Wayne Whitson Jr., and Clifford J. Green. *Bonhoeffer Bibliography: Primary Sources and Secondary Literature in English* (Evanston, Ill.: American Theological Library Association, Inc., 1992).

———. *The Wisdom and Witness of Dietrich Bonhoeffer* (Minneapolis: Fortress Press, 2000).

Green, Clifford J. *Bonhoeffer: A Theology of Sociality,* rev. ed. (Grand Rapids: William B. Eerdmans, 1999).

Kelly, Geoffrey B., and F. Burton Nelson. *A Testament to Freedom: The Essential Writings of Dietrich Bonhoeffer,* rev. ed. (San Francisco: Harper San Francisco, 1998).

Marsh, Charles. *Reclaiming Dietrich Bonhoeffer: The Promise of His Theology* (New York: Oxford University Press, 1994).

Rasmussen, Larry. *Dietrich Bonhoeffer, His Significance for North Americans* (Philadelphia: Fortress Press, 1990).

Wustenberg, Ralf K. *A Theology of Life: Dietrich Bonhoeffer's Religionless Christianity*, Doug Stott (trans.), (Grand Rapids: Eerdmans, 1998).

Young, Josiah Ulysses III. *No Difference in the Fare: Dietrich Bonhoeffer and the Problem of Racism* (Grand Rapids: Eerdmans, 1998).

Richard Penaskovic

BORGES, JORGE LUIS (1899–1986)

Jorge Borges was born in Buenos Aires to Jorge Guillermo Borges, lawyer and psychology teacher, and Leonor Acevedo de Borges, descended from a long line of soldiers. Both of his parents spoke and read English, and Jorge and his younger sister Norah were bilingual. In 1908 Borges began to attend school but he found it a sad experience: the moral and intellectual level of the other students was much lower than his, and his admiration for the English culture and literature and his adoption of an English style of dress were considered provocative. In 1914 the whole family moved to Geneva, and the Borges children attended the high school at College Calvin, learning Latin, German, and French. During these years Borges developed a taste for symbolist literature, discovering through the works of Verlaine, Rimbaud, and Mallarmé a new, abstract way of depicting the world. He was also deeply interested in Arthur Schopenhauer and fascinated by Walt Whitman's poems. The works of **Franz Kafka, Virginia Woolf,** and G. K. Chesterton influenced his own writing, too. In March 1921 the Borges family returned to Buenos Aires, where Borges fell under the influence of the poet Macedonio Fernandéz, who explained to him the thought of Berkeley and Hume. By this time Borges had already published some poems and short stories, but it was in the 1930s that he became famous with the publication of *Historia universal de la infamia* (*A Universal History of Infamy*, 1933–34) and of *Historia de la eternidad* (*A History of Eternity*, 1936). The complete blindness of his father forced him to accept a job as first assistant in the Miguel Cané branch of the Municipal Library. He remained in the library for nine years, and though it was an unhappy period, Borges was able to spend most of his working hours in the basement, reading the classics or translating modern fiction into Spanish. Soon after leaving the library he accepted positions as lecturer on American and English literature. Even though the Perón regime made life difficult for him and his family, he published his major books of short stories, *Ficciones* (1944) and *Aleph* (1949), and *Otras inquisiciones* (*Other Inquisitions*, 1952) shortly before being appointed director of the National Library in Buenos Aires. The 1960s saw him travel across America and Europe together with his mother—he was by now, like his father, completely blind—giving lectures and writing short stories, essays, and poems: *El informe de Brodie* (*Dr. Brodie's Report*, 1970), *El libro de arena* (*The Book of Sand*, 1975), *El libro de los seres imaginarios* (*The Book of Imaginary Beings*, 1967), *Nueve ensayos dantescos* (*Nine Essays on Dante*, 1982). He died on June 14, 1986, in Geneva of liver cancer.

Borges's main heritage consists in a very particular elaboration of the concepts of time and space and in a close number of symbols that can reproduce the whole world. His influence is most clearly seen in Italo Calvino, **Umberto Eco,** Carlos Fuentes, **Gabriel García Márquez,** Ernesto Sabato, Bruce Chatwin, **Salman Rushdie,** and José Saramago.

Archives

Special Collections Department at the University of Virginia Library: manuscripts and letters.

The Helft Collection–Buenos Aires: autographed books, letters, manuscripts, and books corrected and annotated by Borges.

University of Notre Dame: one script of a conference, one handwritten short poem, a letter dictated and signed by Borges.

Printed Sources

Bloom, Harold (ed.). *Jorge Luis Borges* (New York: Chelsea House, 1969).
Lennon, Adrian. *Jorge Luis Borges* (New York: Chelsea House, 1992).
McMurry, George R. *Jorge Luis Borges* (New York: Ungar, 1980).

Maria Tabaglio

BOURKE-WHITE, MARGARET (1904–1971)

Margaret Bourke-White was born in New York City. After graduating from Cornell University in 1927, she moved to her mother's home in Cleveland, Ohio, and worked as a freelance commercial photographer. Her experimental photographs taken inside steel mills gained the notice of Henry Luce and earned her a job as the first staff photographer for *Fortune*. She took the first cover photo for *Life* and remained a staff photographer from 1935 to 1969. Bourke-White traveled overseas on assignment regardless of war or peace and was in fact the first woman war photographer, covering multiple fronts during World War II. She wrote eleven books detailing her adventures and including her remarkable photographs. Bourke-White became the first woman photographer of the U.S. Air Force. She photographed **Josef Stalin, Winston Churchill, Franklin D. Roosevelt,** and later **Mahatma Gandhi** during India's fight for independence. After covering the Korean conflict in 1952, Bourke-White discovered that she had early symptoms of Parkinson's Disease. This decreased both her photographic and writing ability, yet she put her last efforts toward completing her autobiography, *A Portrait of Myself* (1963). She died at her home in Darien, Connecticut, in 1971.

Passionate about insects and nature, she read the Jean-Henri Fabre classics *The Hunting Wasps* (1916) and *The Life of the Grasshopper* (1917) and lived with Anna Botsford Comstock's *Handbook of Nature-study* (1911). She and her first husband, Everett Chapman, enjoyed reading many of the same authors, mentioned in Goldberg's biography: John Milton, **Carl Sandburg,** and Henry James. Additionally, Goldberg notes several other literary influences: **Jane Addams**'s *A New Conscience and an Ancient Evil* (1912), Frances Donovan's *The Woman Who Waits* (1920), and Ellen Key's *The Woman Movement* (1912). Goldberg also includes a list of books that most influenced Bourke-White: *The Education of Henry Adams* (1907), John Strachey's *The Coming Struggle for Power* (1933), and Raymond L. Ditmars's *Reptiles of North America* (1907). While working on *Eyes on Russia* (1931), she completed Tolstoy's *War and Peace* (1930). When she met author John Buchan, he loaned her several books to read, two of which he wrote, the *Green Mantle* (1916) and *Thirty-Nine Steps* (1915), which she was delighted with. Though natural history and herpetology books captured her interests, she also enjoyed detective stories. For her trip to Russia in 1941 she took 28 paper-bound detective stories. While exploring the shelves of a bookstore in Lanchow, China, which she had to travel through to get to Russia, she bought a textbook for English students that contained short stories by Sir Arthur Conan Doyle. When she read James R. Newman's *Tools of War* (1942) in bed, she wrote "always I have been an incurable reader in bed; even war could not break me of the habit" (Bourke-White 1944, 66–67). Never without a book to read, she often carried books on her person and read while waiting atop her suitcases or in bomb shelters.

Archives

George Argents Research Library, Syracuse University, Syracuse, N.Y.: chief repository of her papers including biographical materials, correspondence, writings, memorabilia, and photographic equipment.

Printed Sources

Bourke-White, Margaret. *A Portrait of Myself* (New York: Simon and Schuster, 1963).
———. *They Called it "Purple Heart Valley"* (New York: Simon and Schuster, 1944).
Goldberg, Vicki. *Margaret Bourke-White: A Biography* (New York: Harper & Row Publishers, 1986).

Rebecca Tolley-Stokes

BRADBURY, RAY (1920–)

Ray Bradbury was born in Waukegan, Illinois. The family moved to Los Angeles in 1934 where Ray began writing short stories and for school publications. While selling newspapers for income, 1940–43, Bradbury broke into the professional market in 1941 with a story cowritten with Henry Hasse. As Bradbury's reputation grew, Arkham House published a book-length collection of his short stories, *Dark Carnival* (1947). The fantasy and horror stories written in his distinctive poetic style were readily accepted by genre magazines, but Bradbury published increasingly in the mainstream *Mademoiselle, Harper's*, and *The New Yorker*, and in short story collections. *The Martian Chronicles* (1950) legitimized science fiction's growing respectability among mainstream critics. Film director John Huston took Bradbury to Ireland in 1956 to write the screenplay for *Moby Dick*, and this experience provided material for several stories and plays and sparked Bradbury's interest in Herman Melville. His first novel, *Fahrenheit 451* (1953), is revered as both an attack on censorship and the growing power of television in the mass culture. Between the 1960s and 1970s Bradbury focused on dramatic writing and poetry. He returned to fiction and short stories in the 1980s and published a fourth novel, *From the Dust Returned* (2001), based on his fantasy short stories about the Elliot family in *The October Country*.

Bradbury's influences range from serious writers to comic books. He has written that his first literary influences were "Edgar Allan Poe when I was eight, Buck Rogers at nine, [Edgar Rice Burroughs's] Tarzan at ten, and all the science fiction magazines from these same years," the traditional ghost stories of Charles Dickens and H. P. Lovecraft, and later Henry Kuttner, Robert Bloch, Clark Ashton Smith, and his friend Leigh Brackett (Nolan 1975, 6; Bradbury 1990, 14, 26). He left his brief infatuation with Thomas Wolfe's writing style for the spare, controlled works of Jessamyn West, **Sinclair Lewis,** Sherwood Anderson, and Katherine Anne Porter, all recommended by Henry Kuttner in 1944 (Nolan 1975, 55; Bradbury 1990, 26). He credits as influences on his writing style William Shakespeare and **Robert Frost,** the plays of George Bernard Shaw, **John Steinbeck**'s novels, the short stories of Eudora Welty and John Collier, and **Edith Wharton** *(Santa Barbara)*. Robert Heinlein's humanistic science fiction "influenced me to dare to be human instead of mechanical" (Kelley 1996). As a boy he read Jules Verne and H. G. Wells, but Bradbury believes "you should read in your own field only when you're young. . . . I went on to Alexander Pope and John Donne and Moliére to mix it up" (Kelley 1996). Bradbury thinks he "was born a collector of metaphors. I'm deeply influenced by Greek mythology, Roman mythology. The colorful stuff, anything magical." The Bible story of Daniel in the lion's den "influenced my story 'The Veldt' where the lions come out of the walls and eat the parents" (Mesic 1998–99, *Cosmic Ray*). Bradbury said he goes "back to Mark Twain all the time, and to Melville . . . because he was deeply influenced by Shakespeare and the Old Testament," both of which have shaped Bradbury's own work (Mesic 1998–99, "Ray's Faves").

Archives

Bowling Green State University, Libraries, Center for Archival Collections, Bowling Green, Ohio. Correspondence, interviews.

Department of Special Collections, University Library, University of California, Los Angeles, Calif. 21-hour audiotaped interview in 1961.

Printed Sources

Bradbury, Ray. *Zen in the Art of Writing* (New York: Bantam, 1990).

Kelley, Ken. "Playboy Interview: Ray Bradbury," *Playboy* 43, no. 5 (May 1996), 47–56, 149–50. Reprinted http://www.raybradbury.com/articles_playboy.html.

Mesic, Penelope. "Cosmic Ray." *Book Magazine*, Dec. 1998/Jan. 1999. Reprinted http://www.raybradbury.com/articles_book_mag.html, accessed October 21, 2003.

———. "Ray's Faves." *Book Magazine*, Dec. 1998/Jan. 1999. Reprinted http://www.raybradbury.com/articles_rays_faves.html, accessed October 21, 2003.

Mogen, David. *Ray Bradbury* (Boston: Twayne, 1986).

Nolan, William F. *The Ray Bradbury Companion* (Detroit: Gale Research; Bruccoli Clark, 1975).

Spalding, John D. "The Bradbury Chronicles." *Santa Barbara Magazine*, Jan./Feb. 1992. Reprinted http://www.raybradbury.com/articles_santa_barbara.html, accessed October 21, 2003.

Susan Hamburger

BRANCUSI (BRÂNCUŞI), CONSTANTIN (1876–1957)

Brancusi was born in the village of Hobişa in Oltenia, a rural region of western Romania. His primary-school instruction was basic and his attendance infrequent: it has been suggested that he taught himself to read and write so as to enroll in the School of Arts and Crafts in the regional capital Craiova (1894–98); this is uncertain, although his mother was illiterate, and his own handwriting and orthography in both French and Romanian remained shaky. After Craiova, he graduated from the Academy of Fine Arts in Bucharest (1898–1902). A government grant enabled him to attend the Académie des Beaux-Arts, Paris (1905–7); although made to leave because he was over 30, he expressed no regrets, saying that "in any case, I learnt more from life" (Miller 1995, 97). Thenceforth Brancusi lived and worked in Paris and came to be recognized as one of the most innovative and influential sculptors of the twentieth century. His masterpieces include *The Kiss* (1912), *The Beginning of the World* (1924), and the memorial to the war dead at Târgu Jiu, Romania, including the *Endless Column* (1938) and the *Table of Silence* (1938).

Brancusi was generally evasive about literary influences on his work. Early presentations of him as a simple peasant genius have been somewhat modified now that it is known that he underwent a thorough French academic training, albeit one in which technical instruction prevailed over the theoretical or aesthetic. But folk influences should not be discounted. An early sculpture, *Maiastra* (1908–12, lost; the prototype for *Bird in Space*, 1919) takes its theme from a Romanian fairy tale: Brancusi's relation of it does not resemble existing published versions (Brezianu 1998, 227). When erotic elements in his sculpture *La princesse X* were attributed to his unconscious desires, he replied that "I have a very low opinion of psychoanalysis."

Many visitors to Brancusi's studios from the 1920s onward reported his enthusiasm for philosophical and mystic writers such as Plato, Lao-Tse, and especially the eleventh-century Tibetan monk Milarepa; but the latter was only translated into French in 1925 when Brancusi was nearly 50 and his artistic conceptions and practices had long been crystallized. His few published writings—aphorisms, postcards to friends, a 100-word fantastic story—show possible folk influences, but also the immediate contact he enjoyed with friends such as **Guillaume Apollinaire, Ezra Pound,** Tristan Tzara, **Marcel Duchamp,** Eric Satie, and other luminaries of the Parisian avant-garde. About 160 books in his possession at the time of his death have been preserved (Lemny 1997, II, 1–57). Of these nearly 50 were gifts from friends and admirers which reveal much about the artists gravitating around him but cannot automatically be considered as representative of his own preferences. There are some classics (Ovid, La Fontaine, Aesop), some philosophical works (Jean-Jacques Rousseau, Henri Poincaré, **Henri Bergson**), some lives of artists (Botticelli, da Vinci), and three technical manuals of geometry and mechanics. The only book he illustrated was the Romanian surrealist poet Ilarie Voronca's *Plante şi animale—terase* (1929).

Archives

Musée National d'Art Moderne, Centre Georges Pompidou, Paris, Fonds Brancusi (currently closed to researchers but a detailed analytical account can be found in Lemny, *Le milieu*).
Arhivele Statului, Craiova/Arhivele liceului industrial; Craiova (school certificates).

Printed Sources

Brezianu, Barbu. *Brancusi en Roumanie* (Bucarest: Bic All, 1998).
Istrati, Alexandru, and Natalia Dumitrescu. *Constantin Brancusi* (Paris: Flammarion, 1986).
Lemny, Doïna. "Le milieu artistique et culturel de Brancusi. Essai d'investigation à partir du legs au Musée Nationale d'art moderne," 2 vols. (Doctoral thesis, Université de Paris I, 1997).
Miller, Sanda. *Constantin Brancusi: A Survey of his Work* (Oxford: Oxford University Press, 1997).

Alexander Drace-Francis

BRANDEIS, LOUIS DEMBITZ (1856–1941)

Louis Brandeis was born in Louisville, Kentucky, to Bohemian Jewish parents. He attended public schools in Louisville and spent three years in the Annen Realschule in Dresden, Germany. Brandeis returned to the United States to study at Harvard Law School, where he received his LLB in 1877 and his graduate degree in 1878. After practicing law for less than a year in St. Louis, he returned to Boston, where he earned the title of "the people's attorney" for his vigorous defense of the public interest, often for no retainer. In the 1908 case, *Muller v. Oregon*, Brandeis submitted his most famous argument, the so-called Brandeis Brief. Marshalling a wide variety of economic and sociological data, he argued for the constitutionality of a state law limiting working hours for women. Beginning in 1912 Brandeis was also a public supporter of Zionism. On August 31, 1914, he became chairman of the Provisional Executive Committee for General Zionist Affairs, serving until June 1921. In 1916, **Woodrow Wilson** appointed Brandeis to the Supreme Court, where he developed a reputation for the mistrust of unchecked governmental power and monopolistic business practices, both usually conducted in the name of the public interest. Brandeis retired from the bench on February 13, 1939.

Before traveling to Europe in 1872, Brandeis acquired a copy of Dr. John Todd's *Index Rerum*, a blank book into which he collected useful literary quotations for later reference. At Harvard Brandeis started a second notebook filled with references, quotations, and his own thoughts on books he had read, including Shakespeare, Milton, Emerson, Swift, Tennyson, Longfellow, Robert Louis Stevenson, Algernon C. Swinburne, Horace Walpole, James Russell Lowell, and Matthew Arnold. Brandeis was especially impressed by Emerson and his thoughts on self-reliance, optimism, and care for one's neighbor, as well as his preference for flexibility over so-called consistency. Furthermore, he adopted a lifestyle of simplicity, living in a relatively Spartan manner and, as a consequence, accumulating a respectable fortune at a young age. When Brandeis began practicing law in Boston he spent a significant amount of time trying to meet Henry Adams, Emerson, and other literary celebrities living in the area. Brandeis's views on labor, capital, and the public interest all seemed influenced by his Puritanical education. Although in his youth neither Louis nor either of his parents exhibited any strong sense of Jewish identity, Brandeis was brought into contact with thousands of Jewish workers during a New York cloak-making strike he arbitrated in 1910. He eventually adopted a Zionistic philosophy (first publicly articulated in March 1913) but remained restrained and pragmatic on the subject. Brandeis was inspired by the post-Biblical wisdom book of Ben Sira. Jews, he believed, were in need of a movement loyal to the fundamental principles of Judaism.

Archives

Albany archives, University Libraries, State University of New York at Albany, Albany, New York: copies of letters to family, friends, and colleagues, 1870–1941, judicial activity.

Louis D. Brandeis School of Law Library, University of Louisville, Louisville, Kentucky: correspondence, drafts of speeches and publications, scrapbooks, reference files, pamphlets, reports, and legal documents.

Robert D. Farber University archives and Special Collections Department, Brandeis University, Boston, Massachusetts: notebooks (including those mentioned above, in Box III.I.a.2), books, articles, photographs, memorabilia.

Printed Sources

Gal, Allon. *Brandeis of Boston* (Cambridge: Harvard University Press, 1980).

Mason, Alpheus Thomas. *Brandeis: A Free Man's Life* (New York: The Viking Press, 1956).

Paper, Lewis J. *Brandeis: An Intimate Biography of One of America's Truly Great Supreme Court Justices* (Englewood Cliffs, N.J.: Prentice-Hall, 1983).

Strum, Philippa. *Louis D. Brandeis: Justice for the People* (Cambridge: Harvard University Press, 1984).

Paul Allan Hillmer

BRANDT, WILLY (1913–1992)

Willy Brandt was born Herbert Ernst Karl Frahm, the illegitimate child of Martha Frahm, a shop assistant in Lübeck, and one John Möller, whom he never met. He grew up in a working-class milieu of Social Democratic convictions. Brandt's mother, stepfather, a foreman bricklayer, and his grandfather, Ludwig Frahm, a former farm laborer in Mecklenburg and then truck driver in Lübeck, were members of the Social Democratic Party (SPD). Ludwig Frahm exerted the strongest influence on the young Herbert, making him, among other things, see Socialism as a way of life and an ideal community without injustice and poverty. It was he who spurred on Herbert to enter the world of Social Democratic working-class associations from the early age of nine, a world which became a home to the boy soon. Herbert attended the St. Lorenz-Knaben-Mittelschule not far away from his home for seven years, went on to a Realschule (1927–28) and then, on a scholarship, on to four years at the Johanneum, where he graduated in 1932. In 1930 he was accepted as a member of the SPD, although still two years away from the age of eighteen usually obligatory for admission into the party. In 1933, the nineteen-year-old fled to Scandinavia, first to Denmark, then to Norway, and after the German invasion in 1940 to Sweden, to escape persecution by the National Socialists, assuming what was to become his official name in 1949, Willy Brandt. His achievements as a politician are multifarious. Brandt was governing mayor of Berlin from 1957 to 1966—that is, during the years of the second Berlin crisis, at the time of the erection of the Wall in 1961 and the visit of President **John F. Kennedy.** As foreign minister (1966–69) of a coalition government with the conservative party, he initiated the so-called policy of small steps toward East Germany, part of the concept to change the relations between the two German states by means of a rapprochement. As the first Social Democratic Chancellor (1969–74) in Germany since 1930, Brandt enacted, most important of all, a new "Ostpolitik," a new policy toward East Germany, Poland, and the Soviet Union, which culminated in the treaties with Warsaw and Moscow in 1970 and East Berlin in 1972. This fundamental change in German foreign policy ushered in a German conciliation with her World War enemies and a better understanding between the superpowers, so that, in the long run, it turned out to be the first step toward German reunification. It was to earn Brandt the Nobel Peace Prize in 1971.

Brandt's grandfather had introduced him to the ideas of Ferdinand Lassalle and, a lifelong interest, August Bebel—the subject of his final paper in history at the Johanneum. In his youth, as he puts it in one of his autobiographies, reports on social conditions, biographies, and novels that had something to say interested him most (Brandt 1960, 35), among them books by the Dane Martin Andersen-Nexö, **Erich Maria Remarque, Thomas Mann,** whose novel about the Lübeck patrician family, *Die Buddenbrooks*, Brandt knew well, Maxim Gorki, **Upton Sinclair,** B. Traven, Jack London, and Ernst Toller's *Masse Mensch*. He started to get acquainted with the writings of Karl Marx while still at school, quoting from the *Communist Manifesto* in the small pieces he started to write and publish from the age of 14. While in Oslo, he collaborated in the first translation of Marx's *Das Kapital* into Norwegian, though the work failed to make him a convert to dogmatic Marxism. An avid reader throughout his life, he held on to his favorite subjects of history, politics, biographies—preferably of statesmen whose lives could offer him inspiration, for instance of **Walter Rathenau, Gustav Stresemann,** even **Konrad Adenauer** and Otto von Bismarck—and semi-documentary novels, generally speaking books dealing with political and social matters that were uppermost in his mind.

Brandt was married three times and had four children, a daughter with his first, three sons with his second wife. He died of cancer in his house in Unkel near Bonn in October 1992.

Archives

Willy-Brandt-Archiv im Archiv der sozialen Demokratie der Friedrich-Ebert-Stiftung, Bonn.

Printed Sources

Binder, David. *The Other German: Willy Brandt's Life and Times* (Washington, D.C.: New Republic Book Co., 1975).

Brandt, Willy. *Erinnerungen* (Berlin, Frankfurt am Main: Ullstein, 1989), transl. as *My Life in Politics* (London, New York: Hamish Hamilton, 1992).

———. *Mein Weg nach Berlin. Aufgezeichnet von Leo Lania* (München: Kindler, 1960), transl. as *My Road to Berlin* (London: Peter Davies, 1960).

Marshall, Barbara. *Willy Brandt: eine politische Biographie* (Bonn: Bouvier, 1993), transl. as *Willy Brandt: A Political Biography* (London: Macmillan Press; New York: St. Martin's Press, 1997).

Prittie, Terence. *Willy Brandt: Portrait of a Statesman* (London: Weidenfeld & Nicolson, 1974).

Angela Schwarz

BRAQUE, GEORGES (1882–1963)

Georges Braque was born in Argenteuil-sur-Seine near Paris and moved to Le Havre at the age of eight, where he studied at the Ecole Nationale des Beaux-Arts. Upon graduation, Braque worked as a house painter and faux finisher until he was called to perform one year of obligatory military service in 1901. The following year, Braque traveled to Paris to study painting at the Academie Humbert and attended the Fauvist exhibition of 1905 where he viewed the colorful and emotive work of Henri Matisse and André Derain. Braque exhibited at the 1906 Salon des Independants and the Salon d'Automne of 1907 and met **Pablo Picasso** during his first one-man exhibition at Kahnweiler's Gallery in Paris. The following year the two artists began a collaboration that would lead to the development of analytical and, later, synthetic cubism. In works such as *Violin and Pitcher* (1910), Braque neutralized the color of his subject matter and divided it into complex patterns of faceted forms to reflect a variety of possible viewpoints. He also incorporated collage into his paintings, pasting pieces of newspaper and wood grained and patterned paper onto the surfaces of canvasses such as *Fruit Dish and Glass* (1912). In 1914 Braque enlisted in the French army, and obtained a severe head wound at

Carency, for which he was awarded the Croix de Guerre and made a chevalier of the Legion d'Honneur. Three years later he resumed his artistic career, remaining steadfast to the principles of cubism, which he found to be an infinitely flexible and variable means of expression. Braque won First Prize at both the Carnegie International Exhibition of 1937 and the 1948 Venice Biennale, and in 1961 he was the first artist to be honored with a one-man exhibition at the Louvre.

Unlike a variety of artists of his era, Braque did not bind surrealist concepts to his artistic production and abandoned the model for freely invented signs and symbols that poets such as Pierre Reverdy utilized in their literature. While a great deal of Braque's paintings and papiers collés demonstrate relationships between images that reflect psychological meaning, this meaning was never arrived at with the aid of the artist's subconscious. Influenced by Friedrich Nietzsche, Braque believed that to have an aim was to be in a position of servitude, and he approached his work with a spirit of freedom and experimentation. In this way he shared the belief that all art surrendered to predestination, as espoused by his friend, the poet Francis Ponge. In developing cubism, Braque was influenced by many of the same authors who had made their marks on Paul Cézanne and the Fauvist painters, such as **Henri Bergson.** In works such as *Creative Evolution* (1907), Bergson expressed his essential belief that painting need not represent the natural. Following this thought, Braque not only broke with traditional representation of subject matter, but with how mass, distance, and color had formerly been depicted as well. Braque's simplicity and conservatism was fostered by the artist's frequent referencing of D. T. Suzuki's *Essais sur le Bouddhisme Zen*, which he acquired during his period of recuperation throughout the First World War. Braque was also a regular reader of Greek mythology, including Hesiod's *Theogony*, which he illustrated with a series of etchings.

Archives

Archives of American Art, Smithsonian Institution, Washington, D.C., control no. DCAW210148-A.

The Getty Research Institute for the History of Art and the Humanities, Special Collections, control no. CJPA86-A133.

Printed Sources

Clement, Russell T. *Georges Braque* (Westport: Greenwood Press, 1994).

Wilkin, Karen. *Georges Braque* (New York: Abbeville Press, 1991).

Zurcher, Bernard. *Georges Braque, Life and Work* (New York: Rizzoli, 1988).

Gregory L. Schnurr

BRAUDEL, FERNAND (1902–1985)

Fernand Braudel, eminent historian of the Mediterranean and of the material life of early modern Europe, was born in Lumeville, a small village in eastern France, although he grew up largely in the countryside outside Paris. He graduated from the Sorbonne and became a schoolteacher in French Algeria. At this time the official French school curriculum permitted no deviation from great events and figures, and, as Braudel himself states, the young historian did not think beyond these terms. However, the influential *Annales* school, a group of French historians dedicated to stressing the importance of social, geographic, and economic forces in history, began to change his thinking. Braudel gradually conceived of a history of the Mediterranean which would owe less to political events and statesmen than to the land and people. Braudel left Algeria and held teaching positions in Brazil and Paris while developing this thesis and remaining in contact with *Annales* school historians (the name *Annales* comes from the title of a journal devoted to social and economic history).

During World War II, Braudel served as an officer in the French army. He was captured by the Germans and spent the years 1940–45 as a prisoner of war. It was during this time that Braudel wrote, from memory, what was to become his masterpiece, *The Mediterranean and the Mediterranean World in the Age of Philip II*. After the war, Braudel submitted his manuscript to the Sorbonne, which granted him the *docteur des lettres* degree. *La Mediterranée et le monde mediterraneen à l'epoque de Philippe II* appeared in France in 1949.

During the 1950s and 1960s, Braudel assumed leadership of the *Annales* school from his mentor Lucien Febvre (1878–1956). In 1966 a second edition of *La Mediterranée* appeared in France, solidifying its stature as a classic. In 1972, *The Mediterranean* was translated into English, formalizing Braudel's international historical reputation. Braudel's other great work, the multivolume *The Structure of Everyday Life: The Limits of the Possible* appeared in French in 1979 and was translated into English in 1982. *Structure* echoed *Mediterranean* in painting the geographical and material life of the world's history between the fifteenth and eighteenth centuries. Braudel died in 1985.

Fernand Braudel's influences have been discussed both by Braudel himself and observers. Braudel invokes Henri Berr, a French professor of history responsible for an earlier journal similar to the later *Annales*. Of course, the most direct influences were the founders of the *Annales* school, Febvre and **Marc Bloch** (Bloch was killed by German forces during the war). Febvre's chief works are *A Geographical Introduction to History* (1922), *Martin Luther* (1928), and *The Coming of the Book: The Impact of Printing, 1450–1800* (1958). Marc Bloch wrote *The Royal Touch* (1924), *French Rural History: An Essay on Its Basic Characteristics* (1931), and *Feudal Society* (1939–40). Both Febvre and Bloch wrote numerous scholarly articles that appeared in the *Annales* and elsewhere.

The *Annales* school itself was an evolved synthesis that drew on the work of previous intellectuals. Chief among these were Fustel de Coulanges (*The Ancient City*, 1864), François Simiand, and the great sociologist Emile Durkheim, author of *The Division of Labor in Society* (1893), *Rules of Sociological Method* (1895), *Suicide: A Study in Sociology* (1897), and *Elementary Forms of the Religious Life* (1912).

Archives

Not available.

Printed Sources

Braudel, Fernand. "Personal Testimony," *Journal of Modern History* 4 (Dec. 1972), 448–67.
Braudel, Paule. "Les origins intellectuelles de Fernand Braudel: Un Temoignage," *Annales: Economies, Societes, Civilisations* 47, 1 (1992), 237–44.
Burke, Peter. *The French Historical Revolution: The Annales School, 1929–89* (Stanford, CA: Stanford University Press, 1991).

Daix, Pierre. *Braudel* (Paris: Flammarion, 1995).

Hexter, J. H. "Fernand Braudel and the *Monde Braudellien . . .*," *Journal of Modern History* 4 (Dec. 1972), 480–539.

Siegel, Martin. "Henri Berr's *Revue de Synthèse Historique*," *History and Theory* 9, 3 (1970), 322–34.

Trevor-Roper, H. R. "Fernand Braudel, the *Annales*, and the Mediterranean," *Journal of Modern History* 4 (Dec. 1972), 468–79.

Charles Allan

BRAUN, WERNHER VON (1912–1977)

Wernher von Braun was born in Wirsitz, Germany, the second of three sons to Magnus von Braun, an Imperial administrator, and Emmy von Quistorp. The latter awakened Wernher's interest in the sciences, even giving him a telescope for his Lutheran confirmation. Transferred on account of poor grades from the French gymnasium (high school) in Berlin to the Hermann-Lietz boarding school near Weimar and later to its Spiekeroog site on the North Sea, von Braun came under the spell of the rocket fad that gripped Germany in the 1920s. He later studied at the University of Berlin. While completing his dissertation in physics he was hired by the army weapons laboratory in 1932. There, von Braun worked on a series of rocket projects which culminated in the development of the A-4 ballistic missile (also known as V2) during World War II. In the meantime, he joined the SS in 1940. Surrendering to American troops in 1945, von Braun came to the United States with other German scientists under Project Paperclip. He became a U.S. citizen in 1955. He served as technical director for the Army Ballistic Missile Agency in Huntsville, Alabama, later the George C. Marshall Flight Center. In this position, he directed the development of several launchers, including the Saturn moon rocket project. In 1970, he was named NASA Deputy Associate Administrator in charge of planning, but he resigned in 1972 when the space budgets were cut back. He then joined Fairchild Industries. He died of cancer five years later.

Although he experienced a classical education, von Braun's interest in the sciences affected his readings. In 1963, he recalled reading avidly the major science-fiction classics, including Jules Verne's *From the Earth to the Moon*, H. G. Wells's *War of the Worlds*, and German science-fiction writer Kurd Lasswitz's *Auf zwei Planeten* (in honor of which von Braun and his fellow enthusiasts of the German Society for Space Travel named their 1931 test rocket "The Repulsor"). He also read the popular works by Max Vallier, who tested Fritz von Opel's rocket car, and of Willy Ley, a journalist fascinated with rocketry and space travel.

In 1925, while practicing astronomy in his spare school time, von Braun saw an ad for a book about space travel and ordered it. Written by Transylvanian mathematician Hermann Oberth, *Die Rackete zu den Planetenraumen* ("The Rocket into Interplanetary Space") theorized about the science necessary for rocket flight. Oberth's book was the first that showed von Braun how rocketry might become a means of space travel. Frustrated with the mathematics that filled much of the book, he began to focus his studies on calculus and trigonometry and read astronomy classics by Johannes Kepler and French astronomer Camille Flammarion, whom von Braun cited in a high school paper.

Archives

Bundesarchiv Koblenz, papers of Magnus von Braun, correspondence with his sons.
Deutsches Museum, Munich, Peenemünde Archive.
Space and Rocket Center, Huntsville Alabama, von Braun papers (unordered).
University of Alabama at Huntsville Library, Willy Ley collection.
National Archives and Records Administration, Berlin Document Center records, Project Paperclip records.

Printed Sources

Braun, Magnus von. *Von Ostpreussen bis Texas* (Stollhamm: Rauschenbusch, 1955).
Braun, Wernher von, and Frederick I. Ordway. *History of Rocketry and Space Travel* (New York: Crowell, 1966).
———. *The Rocket's Red Glare* (New York: Doubleday, 1976).
Neufeld, Michael J. *The Rocket and the Reich* (Cambridge, Mass.: Harvard University Press, 1997).
———. "Weimar Culture and Futuristic Technology: The Rocketry and Spaceflight Fad in Germany, 1923–1933," *Technology and Culture* 31, 4 (1990), 725–52.
———. "Wernher von Braun, the SS and Concentration Camp Labor: Questions of Moral, Political, and Criminal Responsibility," *German Studies Review* 25, 1 (Feb. 2002), 57–78.
Stuhlinger, Ernst, and Frederick I. Ordway. *Wernher von Braun, Crusader for Space* (Malabar, Fla.: Krieger, 1994).

Guillaume de Syon

BRECHT, BERTOLT EUGEN FRIEDRICH (1898–1956)

Berthold (originally) Brecht was born in Augsburg in 1898. In 1904 he entered the grammar school, then in 1908, the Städtisches Realgymnasium in Augsburg. At the age of 16, Brecht started to publish poems and short stories. In 1917 he enrolled at the University of Munich to study medicine but exmatriculated in 1921. During the 1920s Brecht studied Marxism in evening courses. From that point on, Marxist viewpoints became more prominent in his plays.

Brecht's notion of theater was coined mainly by the attempt to eliminate the identification with figures and plot, to avoid mere entertainment and to promote a political consciousness and commitment. For him, theater was a pedagogic discipline that should be conducive for political enlightenment and activation of the proletarian masses. His theory of theater is based on Friedrich Schiller's idealistic notion of the theater as a medium of education and humanistic refinement. Beyond that, Brecht's poetry has become as highly esteemed as his dramatic works.

Brecht's first play, *Baal* (1918), was conceived as a counterpart to Hanns Johst's conventional play *Der Einsame* (1918), whereas the image of Baal, a young poet, was influenced by François Villon and Arthur Rimbaud. Both poets served as a model in Brecht's early dramatic and poetic writings. His new conception of political theater was coined early in his life. Already his second play, *Trommeln in der Nacht* (1919), influenced by Georg Büchner and Frank Wedekind, is characterized by the audience's reduced identification with the the action on stage, effects of dramatic alienation, popular language, and increased application of mimic art and pantomime. Further early one-act plays such as *Lux in Tenebris, Er treibt den Teufel aus*, and *Die Kleinbürgerhochzeit* are influenced by the comedian Karl Valentin's laconic irony and sense of the absurd. Brecht gained to a large extent from east Asian authors and dramatic tradition. His plays *Der Jasager und der Neinsager* (1930) and

Die Maßnahme (1930), for instance, are based on the play *Taniko* by the Japanese author Zenchiku (1405–68). Further prose works (e.g., *Die höflichen Chinesen*) and poems (e.g., *Legende von der Entstehung des Buches Taoteking auf dem Weg des Laotse in die Emigration*) demonstrate Brecht's interest in Asian literature.

Brecht adapted a number of foreign-language plays, such as Christopher Marlowe's *The Troublesome Raigne and Lamentable Death of Edward II, King of England* and works by William Shakespeare, Sophocles, and Molière. Brecht's most popular adaptation is John Gay's *Beggar's Opera*, which he made into his *Dreigroschenoper* (1929), with music by Kurt Weill. Brecht himself once stated that he copied Japanese, hellenistic, and Elizabethan drama.

Archives

Bertolt-Brecht-Archiv der Akademie der Künste der DDR, Berlin. Letters, books, newspaper clippings, films, photographs.

Institut für Literaturwissenschaft, University of Karlsruhe. Primary and secondary literature.

Printed Sources

Ewen, Frederic. *Bertolt Brecht. His Life, His Art and His Time* (New York: Citadel Press, 1992).

Fuegi, John. *Bertolt Brecht* (Cambridge: Cambridge University Press, 1987).

Jameson, Frederic. *Brecht and Method* (London: Verso, 1998).

Lee, Sang-Kyong. *Nô und europäisches Theater* (Frankfurt/M.: Peter Lang, 1983).

Mittenzwei, Werner. *Das Leben des Bertolt Brecht oder Der Umgang mit den Welträtseln*, 2 vols. (Frankfurt: Suhrkamp, 1987).

Willet, John. *The Theatre of Bertolt Brecht* (London: Methuen, 1977).

Ernst Grabovszki

BRETON, ANDRÉ (1896–1966)

A very handsome man who couldn't accept concessions or compromises, French author André Breton was born in Tinchebray (Orne) on February 18, 1896, the son of a clerk at the local police station who later became a shopkeeper in a crystal manufactory in Pantin, near Paris. André Breton spent his early childhood with his grandfather in Saint-Brieuc, on the Brittany coast (until 1900) and went to the Collège Chaptal in Paris from 1907 to 1914. He got a religious education from his mother but lost faith before his teens. While he studied medicine and neurology (from 1915), he worked as a hospital attendant in Nantes and Verdun and later in Paris during World War I. Breton published his first articles in 1919; he also worked for a short period in 1920 as an assistant for **Marcel Proust.** The next year, he was librarian in Paris for collector Jacques Doucet and remained in that post until 1924. Breton was a member of the Dada movement between 1920 and 1923; he was interested in communism between 1925 and 1935, but he soon was disgusted by Stalinism and politics in general. André Breton is known as the founder in 1923 and leader of the *mouvement surréaliste*, which had many followers including important French writers (Louis Aragon, Philippe Soupault, Paul Éluard, Benjamin Péret), artists (director **Luis Bunuel** and photographer Man Ray), and painters (**Salvador Dali, Joan Miro,** Max Ernst). In 1924, Breton published the *Manifeste du surréalisme*, followed by *Second Manifeste du surréalisme* in 1929. All members of the group wrote in select avant-garde journals, such as *La révolution* *surréaliste*. Even though the movement faded in the late 1930s, the surrealist influence was very strong in Europe, even in *Mai 68*. During World War II, Breton spent five years in the Americas: Martinique, Haiti, Canada (Gaspésie) and mainly New York City, where he worked for a French radio station. Back in France in 1946, he remained active and productive, writing books and giving papers until his death in 1966.

It is difficult to indicate specific literary influences for a man who was a constant reader from his early childhood. André Breton admitted he was shocked upon first reading Arthur Rimbaud's poetry in 1914; during that early period, he also read poets he admired, such as Paul Valéry, Charles Baudelaire, Stéphane Mallarmé, Saint-Pol Roux, and Paul Fort. His strongest literary impression was in 1916, when he became aware of Sigmund Freud's interpretations of the meaning of dreams and his discovery of the unconscious mind; that inspired him to experiment with a totally new method of creation, the *écriture automatique* (automatic writing), a process he used first with Philippe Soupault for their common book, *Les Champs magnétiques* (1919). Other surrealist authors such as Paul Éluard, Robert Desnos, and Antonin Artaud used that same approach in order to find a free way to write without any kind of censorship. Among Breton's main influences were unknown authors that he considered precursors of surrealism, such as the Comte de Lautréamont (born Isidore Ducasse), who wrote *Les Chants de Maldoror* (a book Breton discovered in 1918), and poet Raymond Roussel, who wrote a strange novel, *Impressions d'Afrique*. André Breton hated consecrated writers such as Anatole France and François Mauriac but admitted he owed a debt to audacious French authors like the Marquis de Sade and **Guillaume Apollinaire** (whom Breton met in 1916). He also was inspired by **Leon Trotsky**'s enthusiastic book about Lenin; that idealized energy gave Breton the strength to write his most beautiful book, *Nadja*, a fascinating autobiographical story about astonishing coincidences and his love for a mysterious woman, written in 1927. Among many books, Breton also published in 1938 an *Anthologie de l'humour noir*, banned in France in 1940. Breton's influence is clear on authors like **Eugène Ionesco, Samuel Beckett,** Alain Robbe-Grillet, and other French writers of the nouveau roman and the theater of the absurd.

Archives

Fonds Breton, Bibliothèque littéraire Jacques Doucet, 8 et 10 Place du Panthéon, Paris, France. Manuscripts, correspondence, personal archives, annotated books.

Printed Sources

Balakian, Anna, and Rudolph E. Kuenzli. *André Breton Today* (New York: Wethis Locker and Owens, 1989).

Breton, André. *Anthology of Black Humor*, Mark Polizzotti (trans.), (San Francisco: City Lights Books, 1997).

———. *Mad Love*, Mary A. Caws (trans.), (Lincoln: University of Nebraska Press, 1988).

———. *Manifestoes of Surrealism*, Helen R. Lane (trans.), Richard Seaver (trans.), (Ann Arbor: University of Michigan Press, 1989).

———. *Nadja*, Richard Howard (trans.), (New York: Grove/Atlantic, Inc., 1976).

———. *What Is Surrealism?: Selected Writings*, Franklin Rosemont (ed.), (New York: Pathfinder Press, 1985).

Breton, André, and Philippe Soupault. *The Magnetic Fields: Facsimile of the Manuscript* [1919] (Paris: Éditions Lachenal et Ritter, 1988).

Breton, André, Philippe Soupault, and Paul Éluard. *Automatic Message:* The Magnetic Fields *and* The Immaculate Conception, David Gascoyne (trans.), Antony Melville (trans.), (London, Serpent's Tail, 1998).

Gracq, Julien. *André Breton. Quelques aspects de l'écrivain* (Paris: Éditions José Corti, 1948).

Raymond, Marcel. *De Baudelaire au surréalisme* [1933] (Paris: José Corti, 1972).

Sheringham, Michael. *André Breton: a Bibliography* (London: Grant & Cutler, 1972; new ed., 1992, with Elza Adamowicz). Extensive list of books, articles, tracts by André Breton.

Yves Laberge

BRITTEN, BENJAMIN (1913–1976)

Benjamin Britten was born in Lowestoft, Suffolk, England. Educated locally, he studied piano early, followed by private instruction in the viola. Beginning to write music as a child, he impressed British composer Frank Bridge with several of his compositions and subsequently became his private pupil. After two years at Gresham's School in Holt, Norfolk, he entered the Royal College of Music (London) in 1930 where he studied composition with John Ireland and piano with Arthur Benjamin. At a rehearsal for a broadcast performance of his early choral work, *A Boy Was Born* (1933), he met tenor Peter Pears. So began a lifelong personal and professional relationship in which Pears became the appointed soloist in many of Britten's song, choral, and operatic premieres. In 1935, while working for the GPO Film Unit, he met the poet **W. H. Auden.** Matching Auden's social criticism with Britten's satirical and virtuoso musical style, their collaboration, beginning with the orchestral song cycle, *Our Hunting Fathers* (1936), proved to be a highly creative one. While living in the United States during the early war years, he came across an article by **E. M. Forster** (*The Listener,* May 29, 1941) on the Suffolk poet George Crabbe. His poem *The Borough,* especially its section on Peter Grimes, moved the composer to write his first and most enduring opera. The premiere of *Peter Grimes* in 1945 was an immediate success and established Britten as a formidable musical dramatist. Generally considered as his nation's greatest composer since Henry Purcell (1659–1695), Britten's world reputation centered on his operatic output and, to some extent, his choral and vocal music for solo voice. His best-known instrumental composition is *Young Person's Guide to the Orchestra* (1946).

Britten's most distinctive work was influenced by language and the texts he found among poets and librettists. Superb poetry meant a great deal to him. His library at Aldeburgh contained a rich compendium of anthologies and individual poets' works. As a frequent traveler, he was never without his favorite anthology, Horace Gregory's 1943 volume, *The Triumph of Life, Poems of Consolations* (Ford 1994, xii). Britten said that the person most responsible for his love of poetry was Auden, and it was he, as well as Pears, who suggested most of the texts for Britten's vocal works (Ford 1994, xiv).

He drew upon some of the world's giant literary figures for inspiring the libretti for many of his finest operas. Among them are Herman Melville for *Billy Budd* (1951), Henry James for *The Turn of the Screw* (1954), William Shakespeare for *A Midsummer Night's Dream* (1960), and **Thomas Mann** for *A Death in Venice* (1973). The composer expressed a lifelong admiration for the novels of Charles Dickens and even thought of turning *David Copperfield* into an opera but found the overall structure nearly impossible to master (Mitchell and Reed 1998, II, 233–4).

If Auden spoke of Britten's "extraordinary musical sensibility in relation to the English language," the composer's setting of French poet Arthur Rimbaud's *Les*

Illuminations (1939) captured the beauty of the rise and flow of another language as well (Ford 1994, xiii). While visiting Japan in 1956 he saw a Noh play and was immediately impressed by Japanese classical drama and its close general affinities with English medieval morality plays (Mellers 1992, 42–45). Out of this fascination Britten would later write his quasi-operatic parables *Curlew River* (1964), *The Burning Fiery Furnace* (1966), and *The Prodigal Son* (1968).

Britten's willingness to combine literary texts—the searing poems of Wilfred Owen, a young English soldier who fell during World War I, with the traditional Latin Mass for the Dead—produced his most powerful work, the *War Requiem*, which premiered on May 30, 1962 at the consecration of the restored Coventry Cathedral. The church had been destroyed during World War II and Britten wrote the piece as a prayer for peace. It was an immediate success and furthered the composer's public recognition.

Only toward the end of Britten's life was his long and strong attraction to **T. S. Eliot**'s poetry finally realized with his *Canticle IV: Journey of the Magi* (1971). After Britten's heart surgery in 1973, Eliot was one of the few poets he was able to read.

Archives

The Britten–Pears Library, Aldeburgh, Suffolk, United Kingdom: Correspondence to and from Britten, literary works, including those of W. H. Auden, E. M. Forster, Wilfred Owen, and others.

Printed Works

Carpenter, H. *Benjamin Britten: A Biography* (London: Faber & Faber, 1992).

Ford, Boris (ed.). *Benjamin Britten's Poets: The Poetry He Set to Music* (Manchester: Carcanet Press, 1994).

Mellers, Wilfrid. "Letters from a Life," *New Republic*, Jan. 20, 1992, 42–45.

Mitchell, Donald. *Britten and Auden in the Thirties: The Year 1936* (Woodbridge: The Boydell Press, 1981).

Mitchell, Donald, and P. Reed (eds.). *Letters from a Life: Selected Letters and Diaries of Benjamin Britten*, 2 vols. (London: Faber & Faber, 1991, 1998).

Geoffrey S. Cahn

BRODSKY, JOSEPH ALEKSANDROVICH (1940–1996)

Joseph Brodsky was born in Leningrad, died in Brooklyn, and is buried in Venice, Italy. Brodsky received his unremarkable early education from public schools in Leningrad but read voraciously throughout his life. He left school at the age of 15 and took a series of odd jobs that allowed him time to write. In 1964 Brodsky was arrested and charged with "parasitism" for writing poetry without being a member of the Soviet Writers' Union. He served 18 months of his five-year sentence. During this time, his first collection of verse came out in the West. According to his friend Lev Loseff, Brodsky was arrested because he continued the work of the Russian modernists—**Vladimir Mayakovsky**, Marina Tsvetaeva, **Boris Pasternak**—and successfully managed to transplant "Western-European metaphysical poetics to Russian soil" (Loseff 1990, 35). Exiled from the Soviet Union in 1972, Brodsky settled in the United States, where he taught, toured, and published more than a dozen volumes of poetry and essays. Brodsky received the Nobel Prize in literature in 1987 and served as Poet Laureate of the United States in 1991 and 1992.

Living between two cultures, Brodsky's literary influences reflect his life's circumstances. Russian writers and poets shaped his style, and Anglophone modernists helped him develop his mature voice. Brodsky considered his contemporaries Boris Slutsky and Yevgeny Rein his early mentors. Rein advised him to use nouns more than any other part of speech (Bethea 1994, 32). From Slutsky he learned how to use language from all strata of society, which gave his poetry a "potential absurdist streak." (Bethea 1994, 30). Brodsky also drew from the talents of previous generations. He developed his restrained tone and stylistic complexity from the nineteenth-century poet Evgeny Baratynsky (Polukhina 1989, 7). His early baroque tendencies can be traced from seventeenth-century poetry and Russian classicists like Antioch Kantemir and Gavrila Derzhavin (Volkov 1998, 14). In the 1960s, he studied the Russian religious philosophers Nikolai Berdyaev and Lev Shestov, read the Bible and Mikhail Dostoyevsky, which gave his poetry its philosophical bent (Volkov 1998, 13). After his forced emigration, Brodsky translated George Herbert, John Donne, **Bertolt Brecht,** and **Tom Stoppard** (Volkov 1998, 14). This work increased his love for the English metaphysical poets and anglophone modernists. In conversations with Solomon Volkov, Brodsky admitted that he belonged to Anna Akhmatova's circle but that Tsvetaeva had a greater influence on his poetry; he greatly admired her complex syntax (Volkov 1998, 39). In his Nobel Lecture, Brodsky expressed his debt to his favorite poets: Osip Mandelstam, Marina Tsvetaeva, **Robert Frost, Anna Akhmatova,** and **W. H. Auden** (Brodsky 1990, 1). He admitted that in his better moments he considered himself their sum total, though invariably inferior to any one of them individually (Brodsky 1990, 2).

Archives

The Russian National Library in Saint Petersburg, Russia.

Printed Sources

Bethea, David M. *Joseph Brodsky and the Creation of Exile* (Princeton: Princeton University Press, 1994).

Brodsky, Joseph. "Nobel Lecture, 1987." In Lev Loseff and Valentina Polukhina (eds.), *Brodsky's Poetics and Aesthetics* (London: Macmillan, 1990).

Loseff, Lev. "Politics/Poetics." In Lev Loseff and Valentina Polukhina (eds.), *Brodsky's Poetics and Aesthetics* (London: Macmillan, 1990).

MacFadyen, David. *Joseph Brodsky and the Soviet Muse* (Montreal and Kingston: McGill-Queen's University Press, 2000). Excellent discussion of literary influences.

Polukhina, Valentina. *Joseph Brodsky. A Poet for Our Time* (Cambridge: Cambridge University Press, 1989).

Volkov, Solomon. *Conversations with Joseph Brodsky. A Poet's Journey through the Twentieth Century.* Marian Schwartz (trans.), (New York: The Free Press, 1998). Includes Brodsky's own admissions of influence.

Erika Haber

BROOKE, RUPERT (1887–1915)

Rupert Brooke was born in Rugby, England, and educated in classics at Rugby School, where his father was a housemaster, and at King's College, Cambridge (1906–10). His interest in Greek and Latin literature faded during his undergraduate years, and he turned instead to earlier English drama, especially Christopher

Marlowe, John Marston, and John Webster. Rejecting Christianity and embracing socialism, he represented an upper-class version of the rebellion against conventional beliefs associated with **D. H. Lawrence.** His personal beauty and talent for networking made him the leader of a group of Cambridge students and friends who went on camping trips, bathed in the nude, and were nicknamed "Neo-Pagans" by their half-envious seniors of the Bloomsbury Group. His first book of poems (1911) showed great promise but shocked many reviewers by its realism. His King's College fellowship thesis in the new discipline of English (1912) took a sharply revisionary approach to Shakespeare and his contemporaries; his views on literary tradition partially anticipate those later propounded by **T. S. Eliot.** He helped his friend (Sir) Edward Marsh to compile the anthology of contemporary writers published in 1912 as *Georgian Poetry;* this volume and its four successors defined a movement away from Victorian modes to a more direct style. In 1914 Brooke wrote sonnets on the outbreak of war, one of which, "The Soldier," was enthusiastically adopted as the expression of English heroism. Brooke's death from blood-poisoning on the way to Gallipoli on April 23, 1915, welded the image of the youthful poet to the poem so firmly that for most of the twentieth century he was regarded as the poster-boy for a naive patriotism that perished in the useless slaughter of the Somme.

Since 1980 masses of letters long withheld have been published or made accessible to scholars, and Brooke's literary innovations can now be understood as closely linked to emotional struggles of his personal life. When he was in his teens, the work of Algernon Charles Swinburne influenced not only the style of his own poems but also introduced him to the issues he would concern himself with in later years, the Elizabethan dramatists and sexual identity. For the son of a Rugby schoolmaster, the elegant aestheticism of Walter Pater and fin de siècle writers of the 1890s provided an ideal means to express rebellion. Oscar Wilde was influential at this stage, and while his recent conviction for homosexual activities was clearly relevant to Brooke's adolescent homoerotic leanings, his writings also paved the way for Brooke's conversion to socialism and reading of George Bernard Shaw, H. G. Wells, and Sydney and **Beatrice Webb.** Brooke read widely in the plays of Henrik Ibsen, though in later years he admired August Strindberg more; he was one of the first English admirers of the German playwright Frank Wedekind.

Archives

King's College Archive Centre, Cambridge, England: letters and literary papers.

Department of Manuscripts and Literary Archives, Cambridge University Library: letters and literary papers.

Printed Sources

Brooke, Rupert. *John Webster and the Elizabethan Dramatists* (London: Sidgwick and Jackson, 1916). Brooke's fellowship thesis, written 1911–12, published as a memorial.

Delany, Paul. *The Neo-Pagans: Rupert Brooke and the Ordeal of Youth* (New York: Free Press, 1987). Contextualizes Brooke's conflicted intellectual and emotional positions.

Jones, Nigel. *Rupert Brooke: Life, Death & Myth* (London: Richard Cohen, 1999). Comprehensive biography, based on archival material, crucial elements of which were not available before.

Lehmann, John. *The Strange Destiny of Rupert Brook* (New York: Holt, 1980). First showed the significance of Brooke's breakdown in 1912 to understanding his career.

John D. Baird

BRYAN, WILLIAM JENNINGS (1860–1925)

William Jennings Bryan was born in Salem, Illinois. He attended Whipple Academy and graduated from Illinois College in Jacksonville in 1881. Studying law at Union Law School in Chicago, he passed the bar in 1883. Bryan moved to Lincoln, Nebraska, in 1887, establishing a law partnership with a Union classmate. In 1890 he was elected to Congress where he forcefully argued for both tariff and monetary reforms. After serving two terms, Bryan's strong advocacy of the free coinage of silver cost him the favor of President Cleveland and his seat. He continued his crusade by becoming editor of the Omaha *World Herald.* Prosilver delegates controlling the 1896 Democratic convention made Bryan the party's candidate after he delivered his famous "Cross of Gold" speech. Losing the 1896 election, Bryan became a longstanding critic of the policies of the Republican majority. Though he ran unsuccessfully for the presidency on two more occasions, Bryan was named secretary of state by President **Woodrow Wilson.** Known for instigating numerous "treaties of reconciliation" with other countries, Bryan resigned in 1915, believing Wilson's responses to the sinking of the *Lusitania* would lead to America's involvement in the Great War. In the last years of his life, Bryan focused on moral issues, including prohibition. In 1925 he went to Dayton, Tennessee, to defend a state law forbidding the teaching of evolution in public schools. Though Bryan initially won the case remembered as the "Scopes Monkey Trial," he was humiliated by his opponent, Clarence Darrow, who put Bryan on the stand as an expert on the Bible and attacked his apparent hypocrisy and pomposity. Dying shortly after the trial, Bryan's last campaign served to obscure his many years of dedicated service to issues of reform.

Bryan was influenced from his earliest days by the Bible, especially its moral teachings as found in the Ten Commandments and Christ's Sermon on the Mount. Though Bryan is usually associated with fundamentalism, he read the works of social gospel thinkers such as Washington Gladden. He corresponded with Charles Sheldon, the author of *In His Steps,* and also sent a letter to Richard T. Ely thanking him for sending a copy of his *Political Economy.* He sympathetically read, though did not always agree with, more socialist-leaning social gospel figures such as Walter Rauschenbusch, George Herron, and William D. P. Bliss, as well as single-tax advocate Henry George. Lists of books in his personal library, found in his Library of Congress papers, include a wide variety of reform-themed titles: Henry D. Lloyd's *Wealth Against Commonwealth,* Thomas More's *Utopia,* Edward Bellamy's *Looking Backward* and *Equality,* Benjamin Kidd's *Social Evolution,* J. P. Putnam's *The Kingdom of Heaven Is at Hand,* Josiah Strong's *The Twentieth Century City* and *Our Country,* Jacob Riis's *The Children of the Poor* and *How the Other Half Lives,* **Jane Addams**'s *Democracy and Social Ethics,* and the collected works of Lev Tolstoy. To his dying day, Bryan's favorite poem was one he learned from his parents: William Cullen Bryant's "To a Waterfowl."

Archives

Manuscripts Division, Library of Congress, Washington, D.C.: correspondence, notes, miscellaneous writings (Boxes 23 and 51 contain lists of books from his library).

Printed Sources

Ashby, LeRoy. *William Jennings Bryan: Champion of Democracy* (Boston: Twayne Publishers, 1987).

Cherny, Robert W. *A Righteous Cause: The Life of William Jennings Bryan* (Boston: Little, Brown, and Co., 1985).

Smith, Willard H. "Bryan and the Social Gospel." In *William Jennings Bryan: A Profile*, Paul Glad (ed.), (New York: Hill and Wang, 1968).

Williams, Charles Morrow. *The Commoner: William Jennings Bryan* (Garden City, N.Y.: Doubleday and Co., 1970).

Paul Allan Hillmer

BUBER, MARTIN (1878–1965)

Martin Buber was born in Vienna, Austria, in 1878 and grew up in Lvov, Galicia (present-day Ukraine), at the home of Solomon Buber, his grandfather and a scholar of Talmudic literature, responsible for critical editions of the Midrash. Buber studied art history, literature, and philosophy at the University of Vienna from 1897 to 1898 and at the University of Zurich in the summer of 1899, where he met the woman he would marry, Paula Winkler. He found his path through a form of Jewish mysticism known as Hasidism through his wife's encouragement, writing three books on Hasidism and changing scholarly opinion on the subject. He received his doctorate from the University of Vienna in 1904 with a dissertation on German mysticism. Buber began a monthly magazine, *Der Jude*, in 1916. In 1922 Buber published his most important book, *Ich und du* (*I and Thou*), which contained his philosophy of dialogue, and he was made professor of comparative religion at the University of Frankfurt from 1925 to 1933. After Jews were barred from German educational institutions, Buber moved to Palestine in 1938, becoming a professor at the Hebrew University. Buber was a strong advocate of an Arab-Israeli state and lectured widely throughout the world. He died in Jerusalem in 1965.

Such mystics as Jakob Boehme and Meister Eckhart influenced Martin Buber. The book *I and Thou* established his reputation as a religious existentialist. Buber argues that human existence is dynamically relational, a dialogue occurring either in an objectifying mode (I–It) or a value-conferring mode of personal mutuality and openness (I–Thou). In this work we see the influence of Immanuel Kant, Friedrich Nietzsche, and Søren Kierkegaard. Buber spoke of the Jewish–Christian relationship as a dialogue, arguing that both religions were authentic paths to God. Buber, along with Franz Rosenzweig, inaugurated a major shift in the focus of the Jewish–Christian dialogue in the 1950s. Buber was also greatly influenced by Gustav Landauer, a socialist, who saw a communal settlement in a new age of art, beauty, and religious dedication. Buber wrote widely on social and ethical problems and was influenced by German social theorists such as Georg Simmel, Max Weber, and Ferdinand Toennies.

Archives

Martin Buber Archive, The Jewish National & University Library, Jerusalem, Israel.

Printed Sources

Anderson, R., and K. N. Cissna. *Martin Buber–Carl Rogers Dialogue: A New Transcript with Commentary* (Albany, N.Y.: State University of New York Press, 1997).

Avnon, Dan. *Martin Buber: The Hidden Dialogue* (Lanham, Md.: Rowman & Littlefield Publishers, 1998).

Buber, Martin, and Judith Buber-Agassi (eds.). *Martin Buber on Psychology and Psychotherapy: Essays, Letters and Dialogue* (Syracuse: Syracuse University Press, 1999).

Buber, Martin, and Gilya Gerda Schmidt (eds.). *The First Buber: Youthful Zionist Writings of Martin Buber* (Syracuse: Syracuse University Press, 1999).

Cohn, Margot, and Rafael Buber. *Martin Buber: A Bibliography of His Writings, 1897–1978* (Jerusalem and New York: Magnes Press, Hebrew University, 1980). A first-rate bibliography of Buber's writings.

Friedman, M. S. *Martin Buber: The Life of Dialogue*, 3rd ed. (Chicago: University of Chicago Press, 1976). Best introduction in English to Buber's thought.

Glatzer, N. N., and H. Bloom. *On the Bible: Eighteen Studies by Martin Buber* (Syracuse: Syracuse University Press, 2000).

Haim, G., and J. Bloch. *Martin Buber: A Centenary Volume* (New York: Ktav, for the Faculty of Humanities and Social Sciences, Ben Gurion University of the Neger, 1984).

Kirsch, Hans-Christian. *Martin Buber: Biographie eines deutschen Juden* (Freiburg im Breisgau: Herder, 2001).

Mendes-Flohr, P. "Buber, Martin." In R. J. Zwi Werblowsky and G. Wigoder (eds.), *The Oxford Dictionary of the Jewish Religion* (New York: Oxford University Press, 1997), 141–42.

Silberstein, L. J. "Martin Buber." In Mircea Eliade (ed.), *The Encyclopedia of Religion 2*, (New York: Macmillan, 1987), 316–18.

Shapira, Avraham, and J. Green. *Hope for Our Time: Key Trends in the Thought of Martin Buber* (SUNY Series in Judaica, Hermeneutics, Mysticism and Religion), (Albany: State University of New York Press, 1999).

Richard Penaskovic

BUKHARIN, NIKOLAI IVANOVICH (1888–1938)

Nikolai Bukharin was born in Moscow, Russia. His father, Ivan Gavrilovich, played an important role in the young Bukharin's education, especially with respect to natural history, world literature, and painting. Like many revolutionaries, Bukharin's parents were devout Russian Orthodox and politically conservative. After the completion of primary school in 1900, Bukharin entered one of the best classical humanities gymnasiums and earned excellent grades. By the 1905 Revolution, Bukharin was a member of an illegal radical student group. A year later he joined the Bolshevik political party. In the fall of 1907, Bukharin passed his entrance examinations to Moscow University while working as a Bolshevik organizer and propagandist. He studied economics and jurisprudence there until his administrative exile in 1910. Between 1912 and 1914, Bukharin published a number of articles and books such as *The Economic Theory of the Leisure Class* (1914) that defended orthodox Marxism against the revisionist theorists of the Austro-Marxists. After the October Revolution, Bukharin's theoretical writings were centered around the problem of building a new socialist society in Russia. He became the editor of the party's official newspaper, *Pravda*, in 1918. By 1921 Bukharin published two more major theoretical works that earned him a reputation as the foremost Bolshevik social theorist: *Historical Materialism* (1921) and *Imperialism and World Economy* (1917). Receptive to Marxist criticism and highly influenced by Karl Marx's (1818–83) critics, Bukharin did not regard Marxism as a closed system of thought. After 1925, when his economic program had become official party doctrine, Bukharin became vulnerable to opposition attacks. The Stalinist majority formally denounced Bukharin in 1928. **Josef Stalin** attacked his ideas, political

83

supporters, and friends. Bukharin spent the last eight years of his life relegated to a minor political post. He was sentenced, tried, and executed as an "enemy of the people" in 1938.

Bukharin's early, unsystematic reading of world literature under the direction of his father constituted an important part of his education. By the time he joined the Bolshevik party at the age of 17, Bukharin had familiarized himself with French, German, and English. An early influence on the young Bukharin was the nihilism of the Russian social thinker Dmitri Pisarev. When he began to attend Moscow University, his interests shifted to economics, philosophy, sociology, and contemporary, non-Marxist theories. Like many young intellectuals of his day, Bukharin read and admired the work of Marx and Friedrich Engels. The Marxist philosopher Alexander Bogdanov had a deep influence on his most important book, *Historical Materialism* (1921). After 1917 Bukharin turned to an analysis of Marx's critics such as Vilfredo Pareto, Robert Michels, and Max Weber. Particularly the writings of the Austro-Marxism school, represented by Otto Bauer, and Rudolf Hilferding's *Finance Capital: The Newest Phase in the Development of Capitalism*, left a lasting impression on Bukharin. Unlike most Bolshevik leaders, such as Vladmir Lenin, Bukharin was deeply influenced by twentieth-century social thought. The "new sociology" of Emile Durkheim, Benedetto Croce, Weber, and Michels had a profound impact on the intellectual development of Bukharin.

Archives

Rossiiskii gosudarstvennyi arkhiv sotsial'no-politicheskoi istorii (RGASPI) [Russian State Archive of Socio-Political History], Moscow, Russia: Bukharin's personal papers, correspondence.

Printed Sources

Bergmann, T., G. Schaefer, and M. Selden (eds.). *Bukharin in Retrospect* (Armonk: M.E. Sharpe, 1994).

Cohen, Steven F. *Bukharin and the Bolshevik Revolution* (Oxford: Oxford University Press, 1980).

Gluckstein, Donny. *The Tragedy of Bukharin* (Boulder: Pluto Press, 1994).

Kozlov, N. N. and E. D. Weitz (eds.). *Nikolai Ivanovich Bukharin: A Centenary Appraisal* (New York: Greenwood Press, 1990).

Larina, A. *This I Cannot Forget: The Memoirs of Nikolai Bukharin's Widow* (New York: Norton and Co., 1993).

Eugene M. Avrutin

BULTMANN, RUDOLF KARL (1884–1976)

Rudolf Bultmann was born in Wiefelstede, Germany, the son of Helene Stern and Arthur Bultmann, a Lutheran minister. Both his grandfathers were also clergymen. After attending the elementary school in Rastede from 1892 to 1895 and the humanistic gymnasium in Oldenburg from 1895 to 1903, he matriculated in theology at the University of Tübingen. He spent three semesters there, then two at the University of Berlin, taught at the Oldenburg Gymnasium in 1906 and 1907, and received his Lic.Theol. from the University of Marburg in 1910 with a thesis on St. Paul, directed by Johannes Weiss and Wilhelm Heitmüller. After completing his habilitation thesis on Theodore of Mopsuestia, directed by Adolf Jülicher, in 1912, he taught at Marburg until 1916, the University of Breslau until 1920, the University of Geissen for one year, then, as Heitmüller's successor, again at Marburg from 1921 until he retired in 1951.

Besides the Bible, Martin Luther, and Søren Kierkegaard, most of Bultmann's strongest influences came from his teachers and his early colleagues. Professors such as Karl Müller, Adolf Schlatter, Theodor Haering, and Heinrich Maier at Tübingen; Hermann Gunkel, Adolf von Harnack, Julius Kaftan, and Gustav Hoennicke at Berlin; and Wilhelm Herrmann, Karl Budde, Carl Mirbt, Martin Rade, Johannes Bauer, and Paul Natorp at Marburg all contributed positively to his development as a theologian and New Testament scholar. Although Bultmann never took a course from Hermann Cohen, the neo-Kantian spirit pervaded his Marburg student experience. As a Marburg student he also became friends with Rade, editor of *Die Christliche Welt (The Christian World)*. Teaching at Marburg in the 1920s, Bultmann found himself not always agreeing with but always stimulated by his fellow faculty, including Rudolf Otto, who succeeded Herrmann; Hans von Soden, who succeeded Jülicher; Gustav Hölscher, who succeeded Budde; Walter Baumgartner, **Martin Heidegger,** Paul Friedländer, Hans-Georg Gadamer, Gerhard Krüger, Karl Löwith, Heinrich Schlier, and Günther Bornkamm. Equally fruitful were his exchanges with thinkers from outside Marburg, such as **Karl Barth,** Friedrich Gogarten, Karl Jaspers, Erich Frank, and Julius Ebbinghaus.

Archives

The most significant collection of Bultmann material is at the University of Tübingen, but much else is in other repositories in Europe and America, including four linear feet at Syracuse University. Some is in private hands. Bultmann's literary executor, his daughter Antje Bultmann Lemke, explained some of her decisions regarding the fate of his extensive legacy of papers and correspondence in "Der unveröffentlichte Nachlass von Rudolf Bultmann," in *Rudolf Bultmanns Werk und Wirkung*, edited by Bernd Jaspert (Darmstadt: Wissenschaftliche Buchgesellschaft, 1984), 194–207. She and Eberhard Jüngel, Rudolf Smend, and Eduard Lohse formed a committee in the 1980s to choose materials for occasional publication. Jaspert has brought out two volumes: Bultmann's correspondence with Karl Barth and Bultmann's notes from his seminars on the New Testament from 1921 to 1951. Additional details are available in *Rudolf Bultmann (1884–1976): Nachlassverzeichnis*, edited by Harry Wassmann, Jakob Matthias Osthof, and Anna-Elisabeth Bruckhaus (Wiesbaden: Harrassowitz, 2001).

Printed Sources

Ashcraft, Morris. *Rudolf Bultmann* (Peabody, Mass.: Hendrickson, 1991).

Baasland, Ernst. *Theologie und Methode: Eine historiographische Analyse der Frühschriften Rudolf Bultmanns* (Wuppertal: Brockhaus, 1992).

Bultmann, Rudolf. "Autobiographical Reflections." in *Existence and Faith*, Schubert M. Ogden (trans.), (New York: Meridian, 1960), 283–86.

Evang, Martin. *Rudolf Bultmann in seiner Frühzeit* (Tübingen: Mohr, 1988).

Fergusson, David. *Bultmann* (London: Chapman, 1992).

Johnson, Roger A. *The Origins of Demythologizing: Philosophy and Historiography in the Theology of Rudolf Bultmann* (Leiden: Brill, 1974).

Malet, André. *The Thought of Rudolf Bultmann*, Richard Strachan (trans.), (Garden City, N.Y.: Doubleday, 1971).

Smart, James D. *The Divided Mind of Modern Theology: Karl Barth and Rudolf Bultmann, 1908–1933* (Philadelphia: Westminster, 1967).

Young, Norman James. *History and Existential Theology: The Role of History in the Thought of Rudolf Bultmann* (London: Epworth, 1969).

Eric v.d. Luft

BUNUEL, LUIS (1900–1983)

One of the most original film directors of the twentieth century, Luis Bunuel was born in Calanda, Spain, on February 22, 1900. Though he was Spanish, he worked mainly in Mexico (where he emigrated in 1934) but made his most famous movies in France. Oddly, *Land without Bread, Viridiana,* and *Tristana* are the only three films he directed in his native country. After his first film, *Un chien andalou* (*An Andalousian Dog,* 1928), a 20-minute surrealist essay co-scripted with his friend **Salvador Dali,** Bunuel became in 1929 an official member of the *Mouvement surréaliste* with many important writers (**André Breton,** Paul Éluard, Benjamin Péret) and painters (Salvador Dali, **Joan Miro,** Max Ernst). The surrealist influence can be seen in such movies as *L'Âge d'or* (1930), *El Angel Exterminator* (*Exterminating Angel,* 1962), *Le Fantôme de la liberté* (*The Phantom of Liberty,* 1974), and in his unforgettable last movie, *Cet obscur objet du désir* (*That Obscure Object of Desire,* 1977).

In his childhood, Bunuel had a very religious Catholic education, first at the Corazonistas, then at the Jesuit College del Salvador in Saragossa, Spain. Bunuel had an excellent knowledge of the Bible, but he lost his faith when he read Darwin's *The Origin of Species* at 17. Between 1917 and 1925, Bunuel went to Madrid to pursue his studies in engineering. There he met **Federico Garcia Lorca** and Dali.

Bunuel became anticlericalist during the 1920s. The result was films about religion and priests in a very satiristic approach, such as *L'Âge d'or* (1930), *Nazarin* (1958), *Simon du désert* (1965), *La Voie lactée* (1968). Tiny anticlerical attacks are relevant in almost every Bunuel movie: in *Robinson Crusoe* (1952), the isolated Robinson uses a copy of the Bible as a hammer to build a fence around his camp. In *Le charme discret de la bourgeoisie* (1972), a bishop is looking for a job as a gardener.

In his autobiography, titled *My Last Sight,* Bunuel devotes an entire chapter to explaining his main literary influences. Oddly, the book he preferred was an old and precise dissertation about insects, in ten volumes, titled *Souvenirs Entomologiques,* written by a French "amateur" with no scientific degree, Jean-Henri Fabre (1823–1915). The director admits his debt toward French authors such as the Marquis de Sade, and this is clearly relevant in many of his films, such as *L'Âge d'or* (1930), *El* (1951; not to be confused with another film he made the next year, titled *El Bruto*), and *Cet obscur objet du désir* (1977). The best example of Sade's strong influence can be seen in *El,* when a jealous husband wants to "sew" his wife while she is sleeping. Other artists he admired were composer Richard Wagner and director **Fritz Lang.** After Bunuel's death, his friend and co-screenwriter Jean-Claude Carrière explained that the three books Luis Bunuel admired most were novels (written in French) that he discovered during the 1920s before he left Spain: *Le Journal d'une femme de chambre* (*Diary of a Chambermaid,* by Octave Mirbeau), *La femme et le pantin* (by Pierre Louÿs) and *Là-bas* (by Joris-Karl Huysmans). The director was lucky enough to adapt the two first books (the second became *Cet obscur objet du désir*); nonetheless, a complete script of his never-made movie adapted from *Là-bas* was written in French and published in 1993.

Archives

Luis Bunuel Archives, Filmoteca Española, Institut de la Cinematografia y de las artes audio-visuales, Madrid.

Printed Sources

Bouhours, Jean-Michel, and Nathalie Schoeller (eds.). *Les Cahiers du Musée national d'art moderne:* "L'Âge d'or. Correspondance Luis Bunuel et Charles de Noailles. Lettres et documents 1929–1976," special issue (Paris, Éditions du Centre Georges-Pompidou, 1993).

Bunuel, Luis. *Là-bas,* Jean-Claude Carrière (preface) [1976] (Paris, Éditions Écriture, 1993).

———. *My Last Sigh* (New York: Alfred A. Knopf, 1983).

———. *An Unspeakable Betrayal: Selected Writings of Luis Bunuel,* Garrett White (trans.), (Berkeley: University of California Press, 2000).

Bunuel, Luis, and Salvador Dali. *L'Âge d'or,* Paul Hammond (ed.), (Berkeley: University of California Press, 1998).

Buñuel, 100 Years: It's Dangerous to Look Inside (Buñuel, 100 años: es peligroso asomarse al interior), (New York: Instituto Cervantes: Museum of Modern Art, 2001).

Yves Laberge

BURROUGHS, WILLIAM SEWARD II (1914–1997)

William S. Burroughs was born in St. Louis, Missouri. He attended John Burroughs School, St. Louis (1925–29), the Ranch School, Los Alamos, New Mexico (1929–31), and Harvard University (1932–36). He enrolled in medical school at the University of Vienna (1936), but left the same year, and in 1937 started graduate studies in psychology (Columbia University, New York) and archeology (Harvard), but dropped both. From 1939 to 1946 Burroughs lived in New York, where he met **Jack Kerouac** and **Allen Ginsberg,** got involved in petty crime, started using heroin, and met Joan Vollmer, later his common-law wife. Burroughs moved to New Waverly, Texas, in 1947, where his son was born, then to Algiers, Louisiana (1948) and Mexico City, Mexico (1949). He studied Mayan and Mexican architecture at Mexico City College. In 1951 Burroughs killed his wife while attempting to shoot a glass off her head. Afterward he began writing in earnest, going from reportorial novels about his drug use and homosexuality (*Junky* and *Queer*) to such experimental works as *Naked Lunch* and the *Nova* trilogy (*The Soft Machine, The Ticket That Exploded, Nova Express*). In Colombia in 1953, he experimented with hallucinogens (see *The Yage Letters*). Subsequently he lived in Tangier (1954–58), Paris (1958–60), and London (1966–73). A major figure in the Beat Generation, Burroughs's novels and lifestyle were pivotal to the development of the post-1950s counterculture. He settled in New York in 1974, then moved to Lawrence, Kansas, in 1981.

Burroughs's early writings included collaborations with Kells Elvin ("Twilight's Last Gleaming") and Jack Kerouac ("And the Hippos Were Boiled in Their Tanks"). He constructed *Naked Lunch* from manuscript with help from Allen Ginsberg, Peter Orlovsky, and Alan Ansen. Brion Gysin inspired Burroughs's use of cut-ups and fold-ins in the *Nova* trilogy. A book Burroughs read at thirteen, Jack Black's *You Can't Win,* spurred his interest in crime and provided a pattern for his first published novel, *Junky.*

At Harvard, John Livingston Lowes's course on Samuel Taylor Coleridge stimulated Burroughs's interest in connections between drugs and creativity. Burroughs heard Count Alfred Korzybski, author of *Science and Sanity*, lecture in 1939, drawing from his works ideas about language, either/or dichotomies, and thinking in pictures. In 1947 Burroughs became interested in Wilhelm Reich's theories about connections between sexual repression, drug use, and cancer, as explored in Reich's book *The Cancer Biopathy*. Many direct references to Reich appear in *Naked Lunch*, and links between social repression and neurosis recur in Burroughs's novels. After his wife's death, Burroughs found inspiration to write in Denton Welch's writings. Burroughs's frequent cutting of other authors' works into his own, as well as his constant allusions, confound the concept of literary "influence" as such, but clear instances of direct influence appear in *The Wild Boys*, for which Poul Anderson's science-fiction work *The Twilight World* provided a source, and "The Examination" scene of *Naked Lunch*, which reflects Joseph Conrad's novel *Under Western Eyes*.

Archives

Arizona State University Library, Tempe. Draft manuscripts, dream notes, clippings, Burroughs's magazine collection.

Butler Library, Columbia University, New York. Letters, manuscripts, galley proofs.

Printed Sources

Goodman, Michael. *William S. Burroughs: An Annotated Bibliography of His Works and Criticism* (New York: Garland, 1975).

Grunberg, Serge. "A la recherche d'un corps": *Langage et silence dans l'œuvre de William S. Burroughs* (Paris: Editions du Seuil, 1979).

Johnston, Allan. "The Burroughs Biopathy: William S. Burroughs' *Junky* and *Naked Lunch* and Reichian Theory," *Review of Contemporary Fiction* (Spring 1984), 107–20.

Lydenberg, Robin. *Word Cultures: Radical Theory and Practice in William S. Burroughs' Fiction* (Urbana: University of Illinois Press, 1987).

Morgan, Ted. *Literary Outlaw: The Life and Times of William S. Burroughs* (New York: Henry Holt, 1988).

Mottram, Eric. *William Burroughs: The Algebra of Need* (London: Marion Boyars, 1977).

Allan Johnston

C

CAMUS, ALBERT (1913–1960)

Albert Camus, the son of Lucien Camus and Hélèn Sintès, was born and spent his boyhood in the French-controlled Algeria. After his father's death in World War I, Albert's mother, who was semideaf and illiterate, was forced to raise her son in extreme poverty—living in a squalid apartment near the Arab quarter of Algiers. Camus escaped his dismal conditions by immersing himself in academics and athletics at the local schools. He came to the attention of one of his teachers, Louis Germain, who tutored the intellectually gifted young man and enabled him to pass the entrance exams to the lycée in 1923. He attended the University of Algiers, majoring in philosophy, before illness forced him to cease being a full-time student.

During the early- to mid-1930s, he worked in a series of menial jobs and had a short-lived marriage. In 1934, he became involved in socialist political activism and remained an ardent leftist for the remainder of his life. From the mid-1930s, Camus wrote for and edited several socialist newspapers.

He participated in the French Resistance during World War II and managed to write his classic novel, *L'étranger,* which was published in 1941. During the same year, he met **Jean-Paul Sartre,** whose existentialist ideas and literary endeavors became a major influence on Camus. From the 1940s through the 1950s, Camus wrote novels and plays which focused primarily on existentialist themes. He was awarded the Nobel Prize in Literature in 1957 and continued to write until his life was cut short by an automobile accident in Paris in 1960. He left unfinished a novel, *The First Man,* which was published posthumously in the mid-1990s.

Camus had several major literary influences. He was fascinated by the works of René Descartes who wrote about ideas of revolt and rebellion and the philosopher's concept of existence preceding essence. Though he admired much in Nietzsche, Camus was not fond of the German philosopher, nor did he find the ideas of Karl Marx particularly inspiring—a point which would eventually damage his relationship with Jean-Paul Sartre. Camus noted that the works of **André Gide** were particularly influential with regard to his own aesthetic development and that he admired the ideas of **Henri Bergson,** the early twentieth-century French philosopher. Gide, Bergson, and Sartre were all important in shaping Camus's existentialist and moralist philosophical tendencies.

Archives

Carlton Lake Manuscript Collection at the Harry Ransom Humanities Research Center at the University of Texas, Austin. Contains manuscripts and letters, including the manuscript of *Le Malentendu*, corrected page proofs of *Les Justes*, and the manuscript of *Discours de Suède*, Camus's Nobel Prize acceptance speech.

George A. Smathers Libraries, Special Collections, University of Florida. Contains unpublished correspondence with Lucette Françoise Maeurer—including 45 autograph letters, 1 telegram, 1 convocation, and 3 envelopes.

Printed Sources

Bronner, Stephen. *Camus: Portrait of a Moralist* (Minneapolis: Minnesota University Press, 1999).

Lottmann, Herbert R. *Albert Camus: A Biography* (New York: Doubleday, 1979); reprint, Gingko Press, 2002.

Todd, Olivier. *Albert Camus: A Life*, Benjamin Ivry (trans.), (New York: Knopf, 1997).

Joseph E. Becker

ČAPEK, KAREL (1890–1938)

Karel Čapek was born in Malé Svatoňovice (now in the Czech Republic) and lived most of his adult life in Prague. He studied at the universities of Prague, Berlin, and Paris, completing a doctorate in philosophy in 1915. He began working in 1917 as a journalist, first for the newspaper *Národní listy* and then, from 1921 until his death, for the respected Czech daily *Lidové noviny.* He published his first humorous short stories in 1916 with his brother Josef Čapek, who also was an important writer and modernist artist in interwar Czechoslovakia. During his career, Čapek authored collections of short stories, travel essays, feuilletons, translations of French poetry, detective stories, novels, and a biography of Czechoslovak President **Tomáš Masaryk.** Czech readers, including novelist **Milan Kundera,** and scholars of his work regard Čapek's short stories and novels, especially the trilogy *Hordubal* (1933), *Meteor* (1934), and *An Ordinary Life* (1934), as his best literary work. He gained greatest acclaim, however, for his plays, especially the utopian drama *R.U.R.*, which premiered in Prague in 1921 and was performed in New York in 1922 and London in 1923. The play introduced the Czech word "robot" to the universal lexicon and brought Čapek international recognition. Other plays were also produced throughout Europe and in North America, most notably *From the Life of Insects* (1921) and *The Macropolous Case* (1922), which composer Leoš Janáček made into an opera in 1928. As president of his country's PEN Club (1925–33), Čapek was the principal representative of Czech arts and letters. His death on Christmas Day 1938, weeks after the Munich Agreement had dismembered Czechoslovakia, was regarded by Czechs as a symbolic end to the vibrant culture of the interwar republic.

Čapek wrote once of his literary influences: "I could name three or four authors who did not influence me; otherwise, I try to learn from anything that comes to my hands; I do not think much of originality" (Bradbrook 1998, 119). Indeed, Čapek's early literary work, written collaboratively with his brother Josef, reflects the influence of a succession of disparate authors and movements: Czech decadent modernism, Paul Ernst and German neoclassicism, French unanism and **Henri Bergson**'s ideal of élan vital. The brothers' upbringing (sons of a country physician, they devoted much time to exploring the woods and gardening) inclined them toward naturalism and fostered a skepticism of modernism's extreme subjectivity. The start of World War I, which coincided with his final years of university studies, fully jarred Čapek from his earlier influences. He adopted a rational, objectivist philosophy that he maintained throughout his life. His doctoral dissertation followed the ideas of German art historians Ernst Grosse and August Schmarsow in arguing for an objective history and criticism of art. He also wrote at this time the essay "Pragmatism," which advocated the ideas of William James (1842–1910) and **John Dewey** (1859–1952). Čapek found in pragmatism a philosophy for a humanistic democracy, one which allowed for a spirit of tolerance and a belief that discernible truth could be grasped in a manner both objective and embracing a range of viewpoints. Čapek saw cubism as an artistic corollary to this philosophy. He regarded himself as a "literary cubist," taking different approaches to a character or situation in order to present it in the fullest light. As for contemporary writers, Čapek took inspiration from the utopian tales of H. G. Wells, the detective stories of G. K. Chesterton, and the dramas of George Bernard Shaw, all of whom he befriended. Critics and scholars have pointed in particular to Wells's *Island of Dr. Moreau* (1896) as an inspiration for Čapek's most famous work, *R.U.R.*, as well as to *Gas I* (1918) by Georg Kaiser, *Frankenstein* (1818) by Mary Shelley, and the legend of the Prague Golem.

Archives

Archive of the National Literature Museum, Prague, Czech Republic: Karel Čapek Collection (73 boxes), personal papers, manuscripts of published works, miscellaneous correspondence, photographs, drawings.

Printed Sources

Bradbrook, Bohuslava R. *Karel Čapek: In Pursuit of Truth, Tolerance, and Trust* (Brighton: Sussex Academic Press, 1998).
Harkins, William E. *Karel Čapek* (New York: Columbia University Press, 1962).
Makin, Michael, and Jindřich Toman (eds.). *On Karel Čapek* (Ann Arbor: Michigan Slavic Publications, 1992).

Bruce R. Berglund

CAPRA, FRANK (1897–1991)

Born in Bisaquino, Italy, Frank Capra was just six years old when his family emigrated from Sicily to California in May 1903. They came from a rural and Catholic background. First he went to the local primary school on Castelar Street, in a poor Los Angeles neighborhood called "Little Sicily," where he completed primary school in less than four years. Capra had to work his way through the Manual Arts High School. He received a university diploma in chemical engineering from the California Institute of Technology in Pasadena (1915–18). Always ambitious, Capra went on to become one of the most popular film directors in the United States, the incarnation of the "New Deal." In Capra's movies, anybody could succeed because everyone had equal chances; you just had to be honest and sincere.

In his autobiography, Capra defined himself as an idealist and considered his personal vision similar to that of artists such as Hemingway, Gauguin, Homer, and Plutarch. Although Capra admitted he was fascinated by classical works such as Tolstoy's *Anna Karenina* and Dostoyevsky's *Crime and Punishment*, he openly preferred American popular novels such as Maxwell Anderson's *Valley Forge* and Clarence Buddington Kelland's *Opera Hat*. Capra could easily make a film from an unknown novel he read in *Cosmopolitan*, as he did with Samuel Hopkins Adams's "Night Bus," a story that became *It Happened One Night*, in 1934.

After working for years as a second assistant and gagman with Mack Sennett, Capra emerged as a film director in 1922. By 1936 he had become the first filmmaker to define himself as an author and therefore ask for his name to be placed before the movie's title in the list of credits (*Mr. Deeds Goes to Town*, 1936). Capra's most influential movies were produced during the 1930s: *Platinum Blonde* (1931), *It Happened One Night* (1934), *Mr. Deeds Goes to Town* (1936), and *Mr. Smith Goes to Washington* (1939). Twelve of his films were made with the help of playwright Robert Riskin (1897–1955). During the 1940s, Capra made two important movies: *Meet John Doe* (1941) and *It's a Wonderful Life* (1947). But the director had much less success in the two next decades; Capra's optimism and populism were not popular during and after the McCarthy years. Innocence was then seen as an excess of sentimentality. In *American Vision: The Films of Frank Capra*, Raymond Carney ranks Frank Capra's movies in the tradition of American transcendentalism, along with artists such as Thomas Eakins, John Singer Sargent, and Edward Hopper and writers such as Ralph Waldo Emerson, Edgar Allan Poe, Nathaniel Hawthorne, William James, and Henry James.

Archives

Frank Capra Archives, Wesleyan University, Middletown, Connecticut.

Film Archives

The following are in the Library of Congress:
Meet John Doe Test Footage, LC Control Number: 97513985.
The Donovan Affair—Excerpt Footage, LC Control Number: 95513440.
Turning point. Interview with Frank Capra, 1959. LC Control Number: 94838473.

Printed Sources

Basinger, Jeanine (ed.). *The It's a Wonderful Life Book* (New York: Knopf, 1990).
Capra, Frank. *The Name Above the Title. An Autobiography* (New York: MacMillan, 1971).
Carney, Raymond. *American Vision: The Films of Frank Capra* (University Press of New England, 1996).
Gehring, Wes D. *Populism and the Capra Legacy* (Westport, Conn.: Greenwood Press, 1995).
Sklar, Robert, and Vito Zagarrio (eds.). *Frank Capra: Authorship and the Studio System* (Philadelphia: Temple University Press, 1998).

Yves Laberge

CARNAP, RUDOLF (1891–1970)

Rudolf Carnap was born in Ronsdorf, Germany, into the pious family of Johannes Carnap, a business manager, and Anna Dörpfeld. After his father died in 1898, Carnap, his mother, and his sister moved to nearby Barmen, where, as a student at the Barmen Gymnasium, his favorite subjects were mathematics and Latin. In 1909 they moved to Jena. Carnap studied philosophy, mathematics, and physics at the Universities of Jena and Freiburg im Breisgau from 1910 to 1914. Among his Jena professors were neo-Kantian Bruno Bauch, under whom he participated in a year-long slow reading of Immanuel Kant's *Critique of Pure Reason*; mathematical logician Gottlob Frege, who became his mentor and through whom he learned of **Bertrand Russell** and Georg Cantor; and Hegelian scholar Hermann Nohl. He read Sigmund Freud, Johann Wolfgang von Goethe, Ernst Heinrich Philipp Haeckel, Wilhelm Ostwald, and Baruch Spinoza.

Carnap had just begun to plan a doctoral dissertation in physics when World War I broke out. He served as a frontline soldier until 1917, when he was ordered to Berlin as a physics research officer. Since **Albert Einstein** was then in Berlin as director of the Kaiser Wilhelm Institute for Physics, Carnap used that opportunity to learn the theory of relativity. Back at Jena after the war and influenced by the neo-Kantianism of Paul Gerhard Natorp and Ernst Cassirer and the empiricism of Hermann von Helmholtz and Moritz Schlick, he wrote his dissertation, "Space" *(Der Raum)*, under Bauch's direction with suggestions from physicist Max Wien. For five intense years after receiving his doctorate in 1921, he privately studied Russell, Richard Avenarius, Hugo Dingler, Ernst Mach, Jules Henri Poincaré, Richard von Schubert-Soldern, Wilhelm Schuppe, and the Gestalt psychology of Max Wertheimer and Wolfgang Köhler, and wrote copiously on logic and the philosophical foundations of science.

Carnap met Hans Reichenbach, with whom he had corresponded for some time, Heinrich Behmann, Paul Hertz, and Kurt Lewin at a philosophy conference in Erlangen in 1923. In 1926 he moved to Vienna and became part of the "Vienna Circle," the famous group of logical positivist philosophers that met from 1922 to 1938. Besides Schlick, the Circle included Gustav Bergmann, Herbert Feigl, Philipp Frank, Kurt Gödel, Hans Hahn, Bela von Juhos, Felix Kaufmann, Viktor Kraft, Karl Menger, Otto Neurath, Friedrich Waismann, and Edgar Zilsel. It discussed David Hilbert, Mach, Russell, **Max Planck, Ludwig Wittgenstein,** Ludwig Boltzmann, **Karl Popper,** Reichenbach, and many others germane to its philosophical program. Beginning in 1930 it had contact with the Warsaw group of logicians, including Alfred Tarski. Carnap moved to Prague, Czechoslovakia, in 1931, and to the United States in 1935.

Archives

The major repository of Carnap's manuscripts, correspondence, and personal papers is the Archives of Scientific Philosophy, Special Collections Department, University of Pittsburgh. Microfilm copies are available in several libraries worldwide.

Printed Sources

Cirera, Ramon. *Carnap and the Vienna Circle: Empiricism and Logical Syntax*, Dick Edelstein (trans.), (Amsterdam; Atlanta: Rodopi, 1994).

Creath, Richard (ed.). *Dear Carnap, Dear Van: The Quine-Carnap Correspondence and Related Work* (Berkeley: University of California Press, 1990).

Friedman, Michael. *A Parting of the Ways: Carnap, Cassirer, and Heidegger* (Chicago: Open Court, 2000).

Hausman, Alan, and Fred Wilson. *Carnap and Goodman: Two Formalists* (Iowa City: University of Iowa Press, 1967).

Hintikka, Jaakko (ed.). *Rudolf Carnap, Logical Empiricist: Materials and Perspectives* (Dordrecht; Boston: Reidel, 1975).

Mayhall, C. Wayne. *On Carnap* (Belmont, Calif.: Wadsworth/Thomson Learning, 2002).

Michalos, Alex C. *The Popper-Carnap Controversy* (Hague: Nijhoff, 1971).

Sarkar, Sahotra (ed.). *Decline and Obsolescence of Logical Empiricism: Carnap vs. Quine and the Critics* (New York: Garland, 1996).

———. *Logical Empiricism at Its Peak: Schlick, Carnap, and Neurath* (New York: Garland, 1996).

Schilpp, Paul Arthur (ed.). *The Philosophy of Rudolf Carnap* (La Salle, Ill.: Open Court, 1963).

Eric v.d. Luft

CARSON, RACHEL LOUISE (1907–1964)

Rachel Carson was born on May 27, 1907. Carson grew up in a Pennsylvania homestead near the Allegheny River, in a community whose rural charm was being replaced by industries. She inherited from her mother a passion for bird-watching and nature. She was interested in reading and writing at an early age and submitted a number of juvenile stories, poems, and essays as well as drawings to leading youth magazines such as *St. Nicholas* magazine, regarded by many as the best magazine ever published for children.

Carson's stories and drawings reflected not only her keen observation of bird and animal life but also the kind of children's literature read at her time. Her favorites were the animal stories by Beatrix Potter with their detailed drawings (*The Tale of Peter Rabbit*, for instance). She also discovered the novels of Gene Stratton Porter, who wrote about wildlife and nature as a source of moral virtue. Later, she became keenly interested in authors who wrote stories and poems about the ocean and the sea, such as Herman Melville, Joseph Conrad, and Robert Louis Stevenson.

Carson obtained her B.A. in English from Pennsylvania College for Women (now Chatham College) in 1928, and her M.A. in marine zoology from Johns Hopkins University in 1932. Writer, scientist, and ecologist, she is one of the most important voices that rose in the twentieth century. She expressed her love of nature both as a writer and as a marine biologist. In the early 1930s, she wrote radio scripts on marine life for broadcast programs such as "Romance under the Seas" and articles on natural history for the *Baltimore Sun*. In 1936 she began her career in the U.S. Bureau of Fisheries as a scientist and editor and finally became the editor-in-chief of all publications for the U.S. Fish and Wildlife Service, writing pamphlets on conservation and natural resources and editing scientific articles.

In her spare time she turned to more lyrical prose, as can be read in her article published in 1937 in the *Atlantic Monthly*, "Undersea," showing her fascination for the natural world and confirming her dual talent as both a literary writer and scientist. She was thus encouraged to publish her first book, *Under the Sea-Wind* in 1941. Although she worked full-time, she pursued her research on marine life. In 1951, she published her first study of the ocean, *The Sea around Us*, which won the National Book Award and remained on the best-seller lists for 86 weeks. In the same year, she received the Guggenheim Foundation Fellowship. She then undertook the writing of a book on the ocean's shoreline, which was published as *The Edge of the Sea* in 1955 and remained a best seller for 23 weeks, in which she expressed her philosophy of ecology. Among her other writings were articles such as "Our Ever-Changing Shore" published in 1957 and "Help Your Child to Wonder" published in *Woman's Home Companion* in 1956 and posthumously in 1965 as a book, *The Sense of Wonder*, glorifying the mysteries of the universe for children. Her writings were aimed at drawing public attention to the wonders of the natural world, and they brought her fame as a naturalist and popular science writer.

In 1958, Carson decided to write an article on the impact of DDT, and this venture turned into her most influential publication by far, *Silent Spring*, in 1962, in which she not only challenged the use of post–World War II synthetic pesticides but also called for a change in humans' attitude toward the natural world. The following year she testified before the U.S. Congress, calling for new federal environmental policies, and was attacked by chemical industries at a moment when she was struggling for her life against breast cancer. Considered as a seminal work in environmentalism, *Silent Spring* has been translated into most of the languages in the world and is still in print in the United States 39 years after its first publication. It soon became the source of inspiration for deep ecology, grassroots environmentalism, and ecofeminism, and her legacy led to the creation of the Environmental Protection Agency and mobilized public opinion on Earth Day 1970.

Archives

Beinecke Rare Book and Manuscript Library at Yale University holds the Rachel Carson Papers.

Charles E. Shain Library at Connecticut College holds Linda Lear's archive of materials used for her biography, as well as personal papers given to Lear by Carson's colleagues and friends.

Ferdinand Hamburger Archives, Milton Eisenhower Library at Johns Hopkins University, holds papers related to Carson's days as a graduate student in marine biology during the early 1930s.

Ladd Library at Bates College holds the Dorothy Freeman Collection, letters of Rachel Carson and Dorothy Freeman.

Printed Sources

Brooks, Paul. *The House of Life: Rachel Carson at Work* (Boston, Mass.: Houghton-Mifflin Company, 1972).

Freeman, Martha (ed.). *Always Rachel: The Letters of Rachel Carson and Dorothy Freeman, 1952–1965* (Boston, Mass.: Beacon Press, 1995).

Graham, Frank Jr. *Since Silent Spring* (Boston, Mass.: Houghton-Mifflin Company, 1970).

Lear, Linda. *Rachel Carson: Witness for Nature* (New York: Henry Holt &Company, 1997).

Gelareh Yvard-Djahansouz

CARTER, JAMES EARL JR. (1924–)

Jimmy Carter was born in Plains, Georgia, the first son and child of James Earl and Lillian Gordy Carter. Young Carter, who would become the thirty-ninth president of the United States, grew up on his father's farm at Archery, Georgia, attended high school and junior college near his home, then attended Georgia Technological Institute in Atlanta, and graduated from the United States Naval Academy in 1946. He married Rosalynn Smith promptly thereafter, and in time they became the parents of four children. After a distinguished career as an officer in the navy specializing in nuclear submarines, he returned to Plains in 1953 to operate his late father's lucrative agribusiness. He served in the Georgia state senate from 1962 to 1966 and as governor of Georgia from 1971 to 1975. By championing racial equality, he forced his state into the modern age and attracted national attention. A Democrat who showed extraordinary interest in human rights at both the domestic and international levels, he served as president of the United States from 1977 to 1981. In 1986 he and his wife dedicated the Carter Presidential Center in Atlanta, Georgia. Through that center, they advance health and agriculture in the developing world, resolve conflicts, protect human rights, and promote world peace, taking up difficult cases not attended by governments or other international agencies. Renowned as one of the great peacemakers of the twentieth century, Carter had published fifteen books by 2001. His career has been driven by his love for his family, his Southern Baptist religion, and a passionate interest in reading that dated from his childhood. He was awarded the Nobel Peace Prize in December 2002.

The books that had the greatest impact upon Carter's intellectual development include the Bible, James Agee's *Let Us Now Praise Famous Men* (1941), the poetry of Welshman **Dylan Thomas,** the writings of the neo-orthodox theologian **Reinhold Niebuhr,** and Lev Tolstoy's *War and Peace.* Agee's book deals with impoverished Georgians during the Great Depression, Dylan Thomas offers faith and hope to innocent and underprivileged people, Niebuhr affirms that Christians can work within an immoral political structure, and Tolstoy dramatizes the lives of all types of people, great and small, in Russian society at the time of the Napoleonic invasion in 1812. Carter's insatiable thirst for knowledge led him to read works on agriculture and science, politics and theology, literature and biography, and treatises on the American presidency. The books he read notably influenced his public career of service to humanity, and they are often reflected in his own autobiographical writings. From his campaign autobiography, *Why Not the Best?* in 1975, to his powerful memoir of his boyhood, *An Hour Before Daylight* in 2001, the themes of his favorite writers come to life in the details of his autobiography. He describes the southern political milieu that cast him into public life brilliantly in *Turning Point: A Candidate, a State, and a Nation Come of Age* (1992). His books that describe his own political career, approach to public service, and commitment to world peace include *A Government as Good as Its People* (1977), *Keeping Faith: Memoirs of a President* (1982), *Negotiation: The Alternative to Hostility* (1984), *The Blood of Abraham: Insights into the Middle East* (1985), and *Talking Peace: A Vision for the Next Generation* (1993). His interest in spiritual guidance, outdoor life and conservation, and self-help is expressed in *Living Faith* (1996), *Sources of Strength: Meditations on Scripture for a Living Faith* (1997), *An Outdoor Journal: Adventures and Reflections* (1988), *Everything to Gain: Making the Most of the Rest of Your Life* (with Rosalynn Carter, 1987), and *The Virtues of Aging* (1988). He published a children's story, *The Little Baby Snoogle-Fleeger* (1995), which was illustrated by his daughter Amy. His most penetrating probe into his own life and psyche is found in his single volume of poetry, *Always a Reckoning and Other Poems* (1995).

Archives

The principal archives are the Jimmy Carter Presidential Library in Atlanta, Georgia. The Georgia Department of Archives and History in Atlanta contains his governor's correspondence.

Printed Sources

Anderson, Patrick. *Electing Jimmy Carter: The Campaign of 1976* (Baton Rouge: Louisiana State University Press, 1994).

Bourne, Peter G. *Jimmy Carter* (New York: Scribner, 1997).

Brinkley, Douglas. *The Unfinished Presidency: Jimmy Carter's Journey Beyond the White House* (New York: Viking, 1998).

Carter, Hugh A. *Cousin Beedie and Cousin Hot* (Englewood Cliffs, N.J.: Prentice-Hall, 1978).

Carter, Rosalynn. *First Lady from Plains* (Boston: Houghton Mifflin Co., 1984).

Fink, Gary M. *Prelude to the Presidency* (Westport, Conn.: Greenwood Press, 1980).

Glad, Betty. *Jimmy Carter: In Search of the Great White House* (New York: Norton, 1980).

Godbold, E. Stanly Jr. "Dusty Corners of the Mind: Jimmy Carter's Poetry," *Studies in the Literary Imagination* 30 (Spring 1997), 107–77.

Hargrove, Erwin C. *Jimmy Carter as President: Leadership and the Politics of the Public Good* (Baton Rouge: Louisiana State University Press, 1988).

Schramm, Martin. *Running for President* (New York: Pocket Books, 1976).

Stroud, Kandy. *How Jimmy Won* (New York: Morrow, 1977).

Witcover, Jules. *Marathon* (New York: Simon and Schuster, 1977).

E. Stanly Godbold Jr.

CASTRO, FIDEL (1926–)

Fidel Alejandro Castro Ruz was born to a wealthy landowning family in Oriente Province, Cuba, on August 13, 1926 (1927 according to some sources). He first attended public school, then the private Colegio La Salle, Colegio Dolores, and Colegio Belen, from which he graduated in 1945. At Belen, he studied Cuban history and Jose Martí, the father of the Cuban independence movement. Castro continued his education at the University of Havana Law School, receiving his law degree in 1950. At Havana he became increasingly interested in politics, joining the Ortodoxo Party led by Eduardo Chíbas. Chíbas lost the presidential election in 1948 and ran again in 1952, but committed suicide before the election was held. After Chíbas's suicide and before the election, Fulgencio Batista led a bloodless coup and took control of the Cuban government. Castro appeared before Cuba's highest court to argue that Batista had violated the 1940 Constitution, but the action was in vain. Castro then organized and launched an attack against the Moncada military barracks at Santiago de Cuba on July 26, 1953. The attack failed and Castro was captured. At his closed trial, Castro delivered the "La Historia Me Absolvera" ("History Will Absolve Me") speech. He was sentenced to 15 years in prison, but released as part of a general amnesty for political prisoners in 1955. Castro immediately fled to Mexico and organized the 26th of July Movement with the goal of ousting Batista. An invasion of the north coast of Oriente Province on December 2, 1956, was unsuccessful, and only 12 men evaded capture, including Castro, his brother Raúl, and the Argentine revolutionary **Ernesto "Che" Guevara.** Castro's group hid in the Sierra Maestra Mountains and engaged in guerrilla warfare against the Batista regime. Within two years, Batista's support in Cuba had dissipated, and he fled the island on January 1, 1959. Although initially refraining from formally consolidating power, Castro soon became head of state. Later in 1959, he passed an agrarian reform bill and reestablished normal relations with the Soviet Union. Castro personally led forces repulsing an American-sponsored invasion force of Cuban exiles authorized by President **John F. Kennedy** at the Bay of Pigs in April 1961 and, in response, suspended the 1940 Constitution and established stronger ties with the Soviet Union. In late 1961, Castro publicly declared himself a Marxist-Leninist and soon announced his intention to make Cuba a socialist nation. Tension between Cuba, the United States, and the Soviet Union came to a head the following year with the Cuban Missile Crisis. Soviet premier **Nikita Khrushchev** removed nuclear weapons from Cuba, and Kennedy promised not to invade the island, but an angry Castro was excluded from the negotiations. As he continued his program of socialist reform at home, Castro aligned himself increasingly with global revolutionary groups. Castro remains in power in Cuba.

Castro's influences are perhaps best evaluated by separating the periods before and after he assumed power. As a young revolutionary, many of Castro's most formative influences were Cuban precursors, including Carlos Manuel de Céspedes, Father Félix Varela y Morales, Enrique José Varona, Carlos B. Baliño, and Juan Antonio Mella. The most prominent revolutionary precursors were Antonio "Tony" Guiteras, whose employment of guerrilla warfare and leftist vision of Cuba in the 1920s and 1930s were highly significant for Castro, and Jose Martí, Castro's personal hero dating to his youth, who carried the mantle of Cuba's war for independence until his death in 1895. Among Castro's revolutionary comrades, the most significant is clearly Che Guevara, both from the standpoint of developing a coherent pragmatic approach to fomenting revolution and also from the standpoint of developing an increasingly coherent, and increasingly Marxist-Leninist, theoretical foundation. Ideologically, Castro's most prominent influences became Karl Marx, Friedrich Engels, and **Vladimir Lenin,** although scholars generally agree that Castro became a revolutionary prior to, and not as a result of, becoming a Marxist-Leninist (which Castro has frequently claimed). Che Guevara also encouraged Castro to read the works of **Antonio Gramsci.** Fundamentally, however, Castro's thinking represents a melding of Marxist-Leninist theory, which emphasized the nature of socialism and communism but was insufficient for applying its theories to the Cuban experience, and the less theoretical but in many cases more immediately relevant writings of his Cuban revolutionary precursors.

Archives

Castro's papers are tightly controlled in Cuba. See, however, the Latin American Network Information Center, *Castro Speech Database*, http://www.lanic.utexas.edu/la/cb/cuba/castro.html, accessed October 19, 2003.

Printed Works

Bunck, Julie Marie. *Fidel Castro and the Quest for a Revolutionary Culture in Cuba* (University Park: The Pennsylvania State University Press, 1994).

Castro, Fidel. *History Will Absolve Me* (Secaucus, N.J.: Lyle Stuart Inc., 1961).

Draper, Theodore. *Castroism: Theory and Practice* (New York: Frederick A. Praeger, 1965).

Fagen, Richard. *The Transformation of Political Culture in Cuba* (Stanford: Stanford University Press, 1969).

Liss, Sheldon B. *Fidel!: Castro's Political and Social Thought* (Boulder: Westview Press, Inc., 1994).

Lockwood, Lee. *Castro's Cuba, Cuba's Fidel* (Boulder: Westview Press, Inc., 1990).

Paterson, Thomas. *Contesting Castro: The United States and the Triumph of the Cuban Revolution* (New York: Oxford University Press, 1994).

Perez-Stable, Marifeli. *The Cuban Revolution: Origins, Course, and Legacy* (New York: Oxford University Press, 1993).

Phil Huckelberry

CATHER, WILLA (1873–1947)

Born on December 7, 1873, in Back Creek Valley, Virginia, Willela Cather invented the name Willa for herself. She was known through the publication of her first four novels as Willa Sibert Cather, after which she dropped the adopted middle name. When she was nine years old, her family moved to Nebraska, where Cather gathered those indelible impressions that would become the seeds of her fiction.

In 1884, the family settled in the prairie town of Red Cloud where Cather had access to the personal library of Charles Wiener, a local merchant whose library included French classics, the German edition of Walter Scott's novels, and English translations of Friedrich Schiller. Cather's own family library contained many nineteenth-century authors such as Charles Dickens, Scott, William Makepeace Thackeray, Edgar Allan Poe, Nathaniel Hawthorne, John Ruskin, Ralph Waldo Emerson, and Thomas Carlyle; in addition there were volumes of William Shakespeare, history books, romances, and translations of Latin and Greek classics. During her time in Red Cloud, Cather took lessons in Latin and Greek and read portions of the *Iliad* and the *Aeneid*. A love for reading and keen observation skills shaped Cather's youth in Nebraska so that at 14, she identified her hobbies as "snakes and Sheakspear." Cather wrote and performed plays in high school, and after entering the University of Nebraska, she began writing drama criticism for the *Nebraska State Journal* in 1893 and later for the *Pittsburgh Leader*. Reflecting on her childhood in Nebraska, Cather wrote in her Pittsburgh book column that among the books "essential to a child's library" are *Pilgrim's Progress* and *The Swiss Family Robinson*.

After a six-year tenure as managing editor at *McClure's Magazine*, Cather ventured full-time into fiction writing. As a young writer, Cather was influenced by two poets in particular: Poe and A. E. Housman, whom she visited in England and whose work influenced her poetry collection *April Twilights* (1903). In those years, Cather much admired Dickens, Thackeray, Emerson, Lowell, Longfellow, and Hawthorne. She attempted to imitate Henry James in some of her short stories in *The Troll Garden* (1905) and in her first novel, *Alexander's Bridge* (1912). Cather described James as "a mighty master of language and keen student of human action and motives" (Woodress 1987, 108). But a powerful and more lasting influence on Cather was her brief friendship with Sarah Orne Jewett who, taking on a mentoring role, advised Cather to explore the region she knew best.

In midcareer, after her own literary success with *O Pioneers!* (1913), *My Ántonia* (1918), and *One of Ours* (1923), Cather paid tribute to Jewett by editing a collection of her stories. Cather wrote, "If I were asked to name three American books which have the possibility of a long, long life, I would say at once, *The Scarlet Letter*, *Huckleberry Finn*, and *The Country of the Pointed Firs*" (Woodress 1987, 357). Cather personally knew many of her literary contemporaries such as William Dean Howells, Theodore Dreiser, and **D. H. Lawrence,** but she preferred the streamlined style of Stephen Crane, whom she called "one of the first post-impressionists" (Woodress 1987, 100).

Archives

Nebraska State Historical Society, Lincoln; Houghton Library, Harvard; Love Library, University of Nebraska, Lincoln; Willa Cather Historical Center, Red Cloud; Beinecke Rare Book and Manuscript Library, Yale.

Printed Sources

Gerber, Philip. *Willa Cather* (New York: Twayne Publishers, 1995).

Lewis, Edith. *Willa Cather Living* (Athens: Ohio University Press, 1989).

McDonald, Joyce. *The Stuff of Our Forebears: Willa Cather's Southern Heritage* (Tuscaloosa: University of Alabama Press, 1998).

Rosowski, Susan J. *The Voyage Perilous: Willa Cather's Romanticism* (Lincoln: University of Nebraska Press, 1986).

Ryder, Mary Ruth. *Willa Cather and Classical Myth: The Search for a New Parnassus* (Lewiston: Edwin Mellen Press, 1990).

Urgo, Joseph R. *Willa Cather and the Myth of American Migration* (Urbana: University of Illinois Press, 1995).

Woodress, James. *Willa Cather: A Literary Life* (Lincoln: University of Nebraska Press, 1987).

Annette Trefzer

CEAUŞESCU, NICOLAE (1918–1989)

Nicolae Ceauşescu was born into a family of peasants in Scorniceşti in southern Romania and received a summary primary education in the village school before moving to Bucharest in December 1928 to assist in his brother-in-law's cobbler's shop. The exact circumstances of his first contacts with communist and labor activists are not known, but he was only 15 when, on October 23, 1933, he was arrested for distributing pamphlets. The rest of his early years were spent between underground militant activities and jail until his release in August 1944 when Soviet troops arrived in Romania. The years before his rise to power did not, then, offer any opportunity for a developed education, a situation which was changed only slightly by his attendance at a few courses at the Moscow Military Academy from 1950 to 1951. Ceauşescu's accumulation of power may be summarized as follows: elected member of the Central Committee of the Romanian Communist Party, 1945–48 and 1952–89; member of the politburo 1955; first secretary of the Communist Party from 1965; president of the republic in 1974. He was overthrown by a popular revolt on December 22, 1989, and shot on Christmas Day following a summary trial.

There is little reliable documentation on Ceauşescu's education or on the instruction he received in Communist circles inside or outside of prison. His school certificates have been shown to be unreliable (Kunze 2000, 21), and the claims made in Communist propaganda (e.g., Ardeleanu; Matichescu) that Ceauşescu had access in jail not only to works by Marx and Engels but also to progressive Romanian writers (Nicolae Bălcescu, Constantin Dobrogeanu-Gherea, A. D. Xenopol) are unverifiable. There is no record of Ceauşescu's personal library: his interior designer recently revealed that Ceauşescu had no interest in arranging books in his many homes by any other criterion than the shiny appearance of their spines (Petcu & Roguski 2001, 97). Contemporaries and colleagues who have given interviews or published memoirs since 1989 agree both that Ceauşescu was poorly educated and that he showed little interest in acquiring further instruction through books (Betea 1995, 66–71; Betea & Bârlădeanu 1998, 45–46; Câmpeanu 2002, 21–25, 69–71). It appears, however, that he had some taste for nineteenth-century Romantic nationalist poets such as Dimitrie Bolintineanu and George Coşbuc, whose sentimental patriotism and use of easy-to-remember folk rhythms may have appealed to Ceauşescu's temperament.

Archives

Documents (of questionable authenticity, as noted above) relating to Ceauşescu's youth and early career were formerly held at the memorial house in his home village of Scorniceşti, Romania; and at the Doftana prison museum, Romania: both these were ransacked after his fall from power in 1989 and remain closed. Abundant documentation relative to Ceauşescu's political career can be found in the Archives of the Central Committee of the Romanian Communist Party, kept at the National Archives in Bucharest.

Printed Sources

Ardeleanu, Ion. "Doftana: temniţă şi universitate," *Magazin istoric,* II, nr.7–8 (1968), 101–3.

Betea, Lavinia (interviewer). *Maurer şi lumea de ieri. Mărturii despre stalinizarea României* (Arad, Romania: Fundaţia culturală "Ioan Slavici," 1995).

Betea, Lavinia (interviewer), and Alexandru Bârlădeanu. *Alexandru Bârlădeanu despre Dej, Ceauşescu şi Iliescu* (Bucureşti: Evenimentul românesc, 1998).

Câmpeanu, Pavel. *Ceauşescu, anii numărătorii inverse* (Iaşi: Polirom, 2002).

Fisher, Mary Ellen. *Nicolae Ceauşescu: A Study in Political Leadership* (Boulder, Colo.: Lynne Rienner, 1989).

Gabbanyi, Anneli Ute. *The Ceauşescu Cult* (Bucureşt: FCR, 2000).

Kunze, Thomas. *Nicolae Ceauşescu. Eine Biographi* (Berlin: Ch. Links, 2000).

Matichescu, Olimpiu. *Doftana, simbol al eroismului revoluţionar* (Bucureşti: Editura politică, 1979).

Petcu, Mirela, and Camil Roguski. *Ceauşescu: adevăruri din umbră* (Bucureşti: Evenimentul Românesc, 2001).

Alexander Drace-Francis

CÉSAIRE, AIMÉ (1913–)

Aimé Césaire was born in Basse-Pointe, Martinique. He attended Lycée Victor Schoelcher (1924–31) before traveling to Paris, France, where he enrolled in the Lycée Louis-le-Grand (1932–35) as well as the École Normale Supérieure (1935–39). While in Paris, he met the Senegalese writer, Léopold Sédar Senghor, with whom he collaborated in editing the short-lived review, *L'Etudiant noir* (1934–36) and helped found the "négritude" movement—defined by Senghor as "the totality of the cultural values of the black world." Returning to Martinique in 1939, Césaire embarked on a literary career. He and a group of associates founded a review, *Tropiques,* which criticized the social order and the pro-Nazi Vichy government. The review's political content led to his political involvement. For 14 years, he was a member of the Communist party (breaking with them in 1956 after the Soviet invasion of Hungary), and helped win Martinique the status of overseas *départment* of France. His literary output consisted of a number of volumes of poetry (e.g., *Cahier d'un retour au pays natal* [*Notebook of a Return to My Native Land,* 1939], *Les Armes miraculeuses* [*Miraculous Weapons,* 1944], and *Soleil cou coupé* [*Beheaded Sun, 1948*]). In addition, he wrote several dramas along with political writings and other documents produced by his long tenure as mayor of Fort-de-France. As one of the founders of the *négritude* movement, his influence has been extensive in both Caribbean and Francophone literature.

Césaire's principle literary influences stem from his association with Senghor in Paris in the 1930s. There he read Paul Claudel's *Tête d'Or*, as well as works by Stéphan Mallarmé, Fyodor Dostoyevsky, and Arthur Rimbaud. The latter proved to be extremely influential and led Césaire toward the surrealism that permeates his works. Other influences during the 1930s were the writings produced by members of the Harlem Renaissance in the United States—particularly work by Langston Hughes. The ideas of Karl Marx and Sigmund Freud influenced his work as well. The existentialist philosopher René Le Senne and Louis Lavelle with his "doctrine of participation" motivated Césaire to incorporate some of their theoretical components into his literary endeavors throughout the course of his career.

Archives

Special Collections, La Bibliothèque Schoelcher: Rue de la Liberté, Fort-de-France, Martinique. Manuscripts and papers.

La Bibliothèque Marxiste de Paris: 21 rue Barrault, Paris, France. Contains records (correspondence, etc.) of Césaire's involvement with the Communist Party.

Printed Sources

Davis, Gregson. *Aimé Césaire* (Cambridge: Cambridge University Press, 1997).

Hale, Thomas A. *Les Écrits d'Aimé Césaire: Bibliographie commentée* (Montréal: Presses de l'Université de Montréal, 1978). Exhaustive listing of Aimé Césaire's works (books, articles, correspondence, governmental documents, etc.), ca. 1935 to ca. 1975.

Joseph E. Becker

CHAGALL, MARC (1887–1985)

Marc Chagall was born on July 7, 1887, in Vitebsk, Russia. In 1907 he went to St. Petersburg to study at the Academy of Arts and, dissatisfied, went to the private school of Leon Bakst. He traveled to Paris and remained in the capital from 1910 to 1914 where he painted extensively. After the war, he moved back to Russia and created the Academy des Beaux Arts. Returning to Paris in 1923, he organized retrospective exhibits and created many works. He resided in New York in 1941, and after 1944 settled in a small village of France, St. Paul de Vance, where he enjoyed painting, which he interspersed with extensive travel around the world.

Chagall had a long and prolific career. Raised in the traditional values and readings of the Torah, his family valued the Hassidistic tradition of Jews, who worship the omnipresence of God and a constant living communion between God and man. The artist remained faithful to this Jewish ritual and popular tradition in his work. His excellent knowledge of the Bible and the episode of the Garden of Eden would be a recurrent theme in his paintings. His illustrations for the Bible (1931–39 and 1962–63), in their intensity and visionary force, their pathos and human understanding, bring to mind Rembrandt, whom he greatly admired.

The artistic climate of Paris (1910–14) offered a stimulating contrast to the artist's cultural background. The aesthetics of the Ecole de Paris and his intense artistic activity with Chaim Soutine, **Constantin Brancusi,** and Amedeo Modigliani brought him to reconsider his work with deeper shades and elongated forms.

His renditions of animals, circus people, flowers, and trees were constructed with a deep interplay of colors that was inspired by the Russian avant-garde of Larionov, Sonia Delaunay, and Natalia Gontcharova, which, as expounded in their *Realistic Manifesto* of 1920, aimed at concentrating on the absolute value of art and its independence from the society, be it capitalist or communist. His meeting with the French publisher of *La revue Blanche* (1902), Apollinaire, the French avant-garde poet and theoretician of *The Cubist Painters-Aesthetic Meditations* (1913), was crucial: he was able to develop new themes based on movements, curvilinear distortions, and fragmentation with cubist friends **Pablo Picasso** and **Paul Klee.** He also experimented with colors in the Orphist movement (Robert Delaunay), and worked with futurist artists Umberto Boccioni and Carlo Carra. The main characteristic of futurism was its intention to become involved in all aspects of modern life, and its first manifesto (signed by Filippo Tommaso Marinetti), published in 1909, led him to develop more diversified themes in his paintings. The theory of surrealism by **André Breton,** *Manifeste du surréalisme* (1924–30), inspired him to explore the association of dreams, but his paintings, imbued with psychological depth and the mysticism of Eastern European Jewish culture, remained original. The racial persecution carried out under **Adolf Hitler'**s rule and his reading of *Mein Kampf* (1923) prompted Chagall to deal with more dramatic characters. His *Crucifixion* series (1955–70) reflect his anguish over the plight of his own people in Europe during the Second World War and to some extent would inspire works of **Salvador Dali.** His constant preoccupation with poetry, opera, and novels led him to illustrate La Fontaine's *Fables* (1929–31), the Russian novelist Nikolai Gogol's *Dead Souls* (1914), and passionate and exuberant lithographs of the *Arabian Nights* (1946).

Traditionally recognized as one of the most important painters of the twentieth century, he brought poetry back into painting through subject matter. Harmony and joy radiate through a very distinctive set of colors and a world of recurrent characters such as fiddlers, circus acrobats, flowers, and robins.

Archives

Bibliothèque Nationale de Paris; Centre Pompidou; Le Louvre; Metropolitan Museum of Art, New York; Walker Art Center, Minneapolis.

Printed Sources

Chagall, Marc, and Charles Sorlier. *Les céramiques et sculptures de Marc Chagall* (Monte Carlo: A. Sauret, 1973).

Chatelain, Jean. *Le message biblique. Marc Chagall* (Cologne: Fernand Mourlot, 1972).

Christ, Dorothea. *Marc Chagall* (Berne: Hallwag, 1973).

Fineberg, Jonathan David. *Art since 1940; Strategies of Being* (London: Calmann & King, Ltd., 2000).

Marceau, Jo (ed.). *Art. A World History* (New York: DK Publishing, 1998).

Shwob, René. *Chagall et l'âme juive* (Paris: Correa, 1939).

Martine Sauret

CHAMBERLAIN, ARTHUR NEVILLE (1869–1940)

Neville Chamberlain was born in Birmingham, England, in 1869 at the height of England's reputation as the shopkeeper to the world. Born into a politically conscious family, Chamberlain grew up following in the footsteps of his father, Joseph—the radical Liberal leader of the late nineteenth century who broke with Gladstone over the Irish Question before bringing his rump Liberal Unionist Party into coalition with the Conservatives at the turn of the century—and his older half-brother, Austen, a rising political star.

Like Austen, Neville Chamberlain attended Rugby, but did not enjoy the experience, having little interest in sports. Following Rugby, he attended Mason College, the forerunner of the University of Birmingham, an institution that provided a more "practical" education than the traditional universities. There he studied metallurgy and science. Unlike most of his contemporaries in politics, therefore, Chamberlain did not receive the traditional Oxbridge education still stressing classical knowledge; he would later complain that he "neither knew nor cared anything" about art and music—although he did enjoy traveling across Europe with his sisters to view both (Feiling 1946, 214). After two years of study, Chamberlain joined a firm of chartered accountants and then spent several years on the island of Andros in the Bahamas overseeing a failed family business venture growing sisal.

From an early age, Chamberlain had been encouraged to pursue a variety of intellectual pursuits. A love of gardening began as a young child and broadened into a general interest in natural history while at Rugby and Mason College, which included reading Darwin and other works on the subject. While in the Bahamas, he returned to these interests to fill the hours and combat the isolation, reading particularly works on the native flowers and birds. He later recalled that Edward Grey's *The Charm of Birds*, with its descriptions of bird songs, was a favorite (Dilks 1984, 27). While in the Caribbean, he read broadly, from political biography—Carlyle's biography of Cromwell, among others—to history, J. R. Green's *History of England*, to fiction, including *Middlemarch* and contemporary German novelists (Feiling 1946, 23–27). His letters home to his sisters, especially Beatrice, provided a running commentary on his readings.

Although the Bahamian venture failed, he gained valuable experience, which he then used to launch a successful business career at home in Birmingham. During World War I, the successful businessman was appointed the Lord Mayor of Birmingham, an office held by his father many years before. His first foray into national politics was as director general of the National Service during the First World War, and he was first elected to Parliament at the age of 49, serving as the Conservative MP for the Ladywood division of Birmingham. In 1922, Chamberlain joined the Conservative front bench, beginning his national career as postmaster general. In 1937, he would attain the height, becoming prime minister following the retirement of Stanley Baldwin.

Chamberlain's political ideas were primarily inherited from his father, Joseph, from whom he inherited a reforming ideology and a belief in protectionist legislation and imperial ties, but his mental outlook was also shaped by his business experience and scientific interests. As one biographer has written, he became prime minister as a result "of a proved record of administrative ability, forensic skill and knowledge of the party" (Dilks 1984, 326). These contributed to a tendency to see everything through a practical lens, guided by principles such as economic solvency and a technocrat's reliance on figures and expert opinion.

Often this served Chamberlain well. In the 1920s, Chamberlain came to be associated with a number of initiatives aimed at reforming the Poor Law, which also laid the foundation for the British welfare state that would emerge following the Second World War. As a technocrat, Chamberlain was the perfect minister. Although wary of **Adolf Hitler** before their first meeting, Chamberlain changed his mind and believed he could deal with the Nazi leader. After the 1938 resignation of **Anthony Eden,** Chamberlain assumed the role of de facto foreign minister and conducted the most important diplomatic negotiations himself. He was, however, a man ill-suited to the role by both temperament and inclination. He was strong-willed to the point of stubborn. As a result, it could be argued that he had a disastrous impact on the European situation prior to the outbreak of war in 1939. It can similarly be argued that, like all men of his age, he was profoundly impacted by the carnage and waste of the First World War. He saw as his mission the prevention of a new general war in Europe. It was a vision soon to founder in the seas of World War II.

Chamberlain's biographer noted that he had "few indoor relaxations beyond music and reading" and habitually read each evening before retiring to bed. As in the Bahamas, his reading list was broad, and he possessed "wide but well-defined tastes." In these, he cared little for poetry, except Shakespeare. Fiction from Eliot to Twain, detective stories, the classics of history (Gibbon, Macaulay, Trevelyan, Acton), contemporary biography, and books on a variety of more specific topics all occupied his time, and he maintained a running inventory of his library throughout his life (Dilks 1984, 388). Despite lacking the traditional Oxbridge education—perhaps because he had not had one—he developed a great faith in his own knowledge and ability.

Archives

Neville Chamberlain Papers, University of Birmingham, Birmingham, England. Much material on Neville Chamberlain's career is also to be found in the papers of his half-brother, Austen, his half-sister, Beatrice, and his sisters, Ida, Hilda, and Ethel—especially his regular letters home to the sisters reporting on his activities. These collections are also held at the University of Birmingham.

The Public Record Office, Kew Gardens, London, contains the official records of his political career.

Printed Sources

Dilks, David. *Neville Chamberlain* (Cambridge: Cambridge University Press, 1984).

Dutton, David. *Neville Chamberlain* (London: Arnold, 2001).

Feiling, Keith. *The Life of Neville Chamberlain* (London: Macmillan, 1946).

Parker, R. A. C. *Chamberlain and Appeasement: British Policy and the Coming of the Second World War* (New York: St. Martin's Press, 1993).

Ruggiero, John. *Neville Chamberlain and British Rearmament: Pride, Prejudice and Politics,* (Westport, Conn.: Greenwood Press, 1999).

Rock, William. *Neville Chamberlain* (New York: Twayne Publishers, 1969).

Phyllis Soybel

CHAPLIN, CHARLES SPENCER (1889–1977)

Charlie Chaplin was born in Walworth, England, on April 16, 1889, to parents who performed in music halls. His father died of alcoholism; his mother went insane a few years later. Chaplin began his career by accident, at five years old, at the Aldershot's Cantine, replacing his mother who had a malaise. In 1908, young

Chaplin played in many theaters for Fred Karno's Speechless Comedians. He toured in Britain and France and went to the United States as an actor in 1910, when his troupe was on tour. He went back to England, but in 1912 returned to New York City with a one-way ticket. Two years later in Hollywood, he made his first short film for Keystone Film Company, inventing the unforgettable character of the tramp. Chaplin was one of the four cofounders of United Artists in 1919. The 1920s was his most important period, mixing comedy with social criticism in *The Kid* (1920) and *The Gold Rush* (1926). The next five feature films became his most famous: *City Lights* (1931), *Modern Times* (1936), *The Great Dictator* (1940), *Monsieur Verdoux* (1947), and *Limelight* (1952). Chaplin left the United States for the London premiere of *Limelight* in 1952 when his U.S. visa could not be renewed. He settled in Corsier-sur-Vevey, Switzerland, in 1953, where he lived until his death at 88. Chaplin was the first complete author in film history: scriptwriter, director, actor, producer, and music composer for his soundtracks.

In his autobiography, Chaplin recalled the first book he read, *Oliver Twist*, admitting he was fascinated with Dickens's characters, especially the old man in *The Old Curiosity Shop*. He also remembered that he read a lot in 1912, on tour in the United States, when he discovered Robert Ingersoll's *Essays and Lectures*. That book made Chaplin realize how cruel the Old Testament was. Chaplin says he bought at that time Schopenhauer's famous *World as Will and Representation*, and often read parts of it over the next 40 years, though he never finished the book. Chaplin also appreciated Emerson's essay on independence. He liked Mark Twain, Edgar Allan Poe, Nathaniel Hawthorne, Washington Irving, and William Hazlitt; he always disliked Walt Whitman's *Leaves of Grass*. Chaplin wrote that he partly agreed with Max Eastman's book titled *A Sense of Humour*. Director **Luis Bunuel** once said that he saw for the first time **Leni Riefenstahl**'s documentary *Triumph des Willens* (1935) with Chaplin, in a private screening at the Museum of Modern Art in New York. Bunuel recalled that he was horrified by what he saw on screen, but was surprised to observe Chaplin frequently laughing. Maybe he was already imagining scenes that would appear in *The Great Dictator*. It is interesting to notice that Chaplin never adapted a novel or a play for his feature films, preferring to write original subjects.

Archives

Chaplin Archives, Geneva, Switzerland. Manuscripts, hand-written orchestrated scores.

The Cineteca di Bologna, Italy. Scripts, notes, drawings, photographs, production and promotional materials.

Chaplin Archives, Museum of the Moving Image in London.

Federal Bureau of Investigation, Washington, D.C. *FBI Files on Charlie Chaplin*. For an unofficial guide to the files, see http://www.fadetoblack.com/foi/charliechaplin/, last accessed October 19, 2003.

Printed Sources

Chaplin, Charles. *My Autobiography* (London: Bodley Head, 1964).

Lyons, Timothy James (ed.). *Charles Chaplin: A Guide to References and Resources* (Boston: G.K. Hall, 1979).

Maland, Charles J. *Chaplin and American Culture: The Evolution of Star Image* (Princeton, N.J.: Princeton University Press, 1991).

Yves Laberge

CHÁVEZ, CÈSAR (1927–1993)

Cèsar Chávez was a Mexican American reformer who dedicated his life to improving the working conditions for farm laborers on both sides of the U.S.–Mexico border. He was born in Yuma, Arizona, to Mexican immigrants, Librado and Juana, who spoke Spanish to young Cèsar at home, inculcated in him traditions of the Roman Catholic Church, and raised him as if he were Mexican. When the Chávez family grocery store went bankrupt during the Great Depression, they became migrant farm workers. Because the family crisscrossed the Southwest in pursuit of jobs harvesting crops, Chávez skipped from school to school. In eighth grade, when Cèsar's father was injured in a car accident, he dropped out of school permanently to help support his family. Ultimately, his migrant lifestyle inspired Chávez's lifelong dedication to reform agribusiness practices whose exploitation he and his family experienced.

Those reforms primarily came about through his creation of a labor union called the United Farm Workers (U.F.W.) in 1966. Among other goals, U.F.W. worked to raise wages for laborers, outlaw unsafe harvesting practices, and improve health policies. Chávez used grassroots activism to launch community-wide strikes, motivate consumers to boycott specific produce companies, and march on the government in protest of unfair labor practices. Perhaps the most famous of Chávez's protests was the Delano grape strike and boycott of the late 1960s. By joining with striking Filipino workers, Chávez ultimately attracted the attention and earned the support of thousands of white, middle-class Americans who sided with David rather than Goliath. Ultimately, Chávez's forces defeated the parent grape companies who conceded to the workers' demands for increased pay.

Chávez's lifelong commitment to community activism brought about reform. In 1986, the U.S. government passed the Immigration Reform and Control Act, which granted amnesty to undocumented Mexican migrants working in the United States. In addition, the Mexican government passed an act to afford social security benefits to Mexicans working in the United States and affiliated with U.F.W. Today Chávez's legacy is larger than such legislative changes might suggest. Rather than a union leader, he is viewed as a spiritual leader of the Chicano movement and celebrated along with fellow heroes of the 1960s, such as **John F. Kennedy, Martin Luther King Jr.,** and **Malcolm X.**

Chávez's impressive career can be attributed, in part, to several literary influences that stem from **Mohandas Gandhi** and the Roman Catholic Church. Chávez first encountered Gandhi's ideas while helping a local priest, Father Donald McDonnell, who provided Chávez with readings on papal encyclicals on labor, the teachings of St. Francis of Assisi, and readings by Gandhi (Griswold del Castillo and Garcia 1995, 23). Chávez was so struck by Gandhi's values that he read Louis Fisher's biography, *The Life of Gandhi*, on his own initiative. In *Cèsar Chávez: A Triumph of Spirit*, the author explains how Ghandi's philosophies resonated with Chávez's personal experience: "Ghandi spoke about the complete sacrifice of oneself for others, about the need for self-discipline and self-abnegation in order to achieve a higher good. These were values that Mexican farm workers could understand" (Griswold del Castillo and Garcia 1995, 23). The principle of nonviolence later would become a hallmark of Chávez's leadership in protest movements against the agribusiness industry.

The Catholic Church was also a major influence in Chávez's life. Traditionally, the Chávez family was strongly devoted to a rich spiritual life that transcended secular activities. Regardless of where the family resided, they regularly attended mass, honored the holy sacraments, learned church history, and loyally celebrated church feast days. There is ample evidence of the important role of the Church in Chávez's life as a reformer. Under his guidance, for example, strikers would often transform Chávez's station wagon into a shrine to Our Lady of Guadaloupe. He would also invite local priests to pray on behalf of a community strike or he'd encourage them to participate in boycotts. Finally, Chávez reshaped protest marches into spiritual pilgrimages. In 1966, he called for a march from Delano to Sacramento, California, to inform then-governor Pat Brown of farm labor abuses. The religious fervor that Chávez ignited on the march resembled that inspired by Martin Luther King Jr. on his journey from Selma to Montgomery, Alabama.

Archives

A Guide to the Archives of Labor History and Urban Affairs, Wayne State University, Detroit, Michigan. Holdings include published and unpublished sources from the late 1960s and early 1970s, photographic essays, issues of *El Malcriado* (the union's newspaper), and biographies written since the mid-1970s.

Printed Sources

Brown, Mary Elizabeth. "Cèsar Chávez." In *Shapers of the Great Debate on Immigration: A Biographical Dictionary* (Westport: Greenwood Press, 1999).

Day, Mark. *Forty Acres: Cèsar Chávez and the Farm Workers* (New York: Praeger Publishers, 1971). One of the most comprehensive sources by a union insider; the book is written from the perspective of Catholic social teaching and principles of nonviolence.

Dunne, John. *Delano, Story of the California Grape Strike* (New York: Farrar, Straus and Giroux, 1967). First book to thoroughly address the grape strike of 1965–67 along with the conflicts between the Filipino and Mexican members of the U.F.W.

Fodell, Beverly. *Cèsar Chávez and the United Farm Workers: A Selective Bibliography* (Detroit: Wayne State University, 1974). A bibliographic source citing journal and newspaper articles about Chávez; text may need to be supplemented by a follow-up bibliography titled *Selected Bibliography: United Farm Workers, 1973–1976*.

Griswold del Castillo, Richard, and Richard Garcia. *Cèsar Chávez: A Triumph of Spirit* (Oklahoma Press: University of Oklahoma Press, 1995).

Levy, Jacques E. *Cèsar Chávez: Autobiography of La Causa* (New York: W.W. Norton, 1975).

Mathhiessen, Peter. *Sal Si Puedes: Cèsar Chávez and the New American Revolution* (New York: Random House, 1969). Narrative of Chávez's early life and of the Delano, California, Grape Strike.

Taylor, Ronald. *Chávez and the Farm Workers* (Boston: Beacon, 1975).

Rosemary King

CHOMSKY, (AVRAM) NOAM (1928–)

Noam Chomsky, the son of Russian-Jewish immigrants to the United States, was born in Philadelphia, Pennsylvania. His father, William (Zev) Chomsky, principal of Philadelphia's Jewish Mikveh Israel school and president of Gratz College, fled Russia in 1913 to avoid conscription into the Czarist army, gained a doctorate from Johns Hopkins University, and became one of the world's leading scholars of Hebrew language. His highly intellectual mother, Elsie Simonofsky, a Hebrew teacher, was a political and social activist. From the ages of 2 to 12 Chomsky attended the Deweyite experimental Oak Lane Country Day School, run on non-competitive lines designed to encourage individual development; he then moved to Mikveh Israel School, excelling academically though he thought it overly competitive. In 1945 Chomsky, aged 16, entered the University of Pennsylvania, studying Arabic, philosophy, languages, and logic. At this time Chomsky, like his parents a disciple of the unorthodox Zionist Asher Ginsburg, who opposed the creation of a distinctly Jewish state, was already deeply interested "in efforts at Arab–Jewish cooperation within a socialist framework" (Chomsky 1987, 7) and briefly considered emigration to Palestine. His most influential teacher at Pennsylvania was the pioneering structural and descriptive linguist and politically radical Zellig Sabbetai Harris, under whose direction—though he often differed from his mentor—Chomsky subsequently gained master's and doctoral degrees. In 1955 Chomsky joined the Massachusetts Institute of Technology's Department of Linguistics and Philosophy, where his numerous writings, including *Syntactic Structures* (1957) and *The Logical Structure of Linguistic Theory* (written in 1955–56, though only published in 1975), revolutionized linguistic studies. By the late 1990s he had published over 70 books and 1,000 articles and was the most cited living academic author. Chomsky also became a prominent political activist, best known for his condemnation from radical perspectives of United States policies in Vietnam and other Third World countries as undemocratic and detrimental to those nations. He also criticized many aspects of Israel's treatment of Palestinians and other Arabs.

As a child Chomsky was a precocious and competitive student, at the age of seven reading through much of *Compton's Encyclopedia*. An avid reader, at elementary school he devoured works by nineteenth-century realist novelists, including Jane Austen, Charles Dickens, Fyodor Dostoyevsky, George Eliot, Thomas Hardy, Victor Hugo, Lev Tolstoy, Ivan Turgenev, Mark Twain, and Emile Zola. Heavily influenced by his father's interests, Chomsky studied Hebrew language and literature, including the Bible and books by nineteenth-century Hebrew renaissance and turn-of-the-century Yiddish-Hebrew writers. At the age of 12 Chomsky read one of his father's draft manuscripts, later stating: "My idea of the ideal text is still the Talmud. I love the idea of parallel texts, with long, discursive footnotes and marginal commentary, texts commenting on texts" (Barsky 1997, 10). Once he started high school Chomsky made numerous trips to New York, haunting bookstores and, assisted by his uncle, a hunchbacked socialist newsvendor, meeting numerous radical intellectuals. Reading voraciously in both Marxist and non-Marxist left-wing works, including those of Karl Marx, Rosa Luxembourg, **Leon Trotsky, Vladimir Ilich Lenin,** and many others, Chomsky quickly gravitated toward anarcho-syndicalists, finding Rudolf Rocker's works particularly persuasive. The writings of **George Orwell** on the Spanish Civil War, especially *Homage to Catalonia*, permanently influenced Chomsky, who found Spanish anarcho-syndicalists far preferable to orthodox Marxists. At his uncle's urging the teenaged Chomsky also read Sigmund Freud's psychoanalytic works and was "much impressed," though "on re-reading years later I was appalled, frankly" (Barsky 1997, 50). In the later 1940s he read devotedly the New York anarchist and pacifist magazine *Politics*, published by Dwight and Nancy Macdonald. Academically, in his early career Chomsky rather ignored the predominant structural linguistic school. His linguistic studies were heavily influenced by the philosophical works of **Rudolf Carnap,** Gottlob Frege,

Ludwig Wittgenstein, and **Bertrand Russell,** the British mathematician, philosopher, and peace activist, whose career became an inspiration and model for his own.

Archives

In private possession.

Printed Sources

Barsky, Robert F. *Noam Chomsky: A Life of Dissent* (Cambridge, Mass.: MIT Press, 1997). Comprehensive biographical study.

Chomsky, Noam. *The Chomsky Reader.* James Peck (ed.), (New York: Pantheon, 1987). Includes Chomsky's own account of his early intellectual development.

Haley, Michael C., and Ronald F. Lunsford. *Noam Chomsky* (New York: Twayne, 1994).

Jacoby, Russell. *The Last Intellectuals: American Culture in the Age of Academe* (New York: Basic Books, 1987).

Leiber, Justin. *Noam Chomsky: A Philosophic Overview* (Boston: Twayne, 1975).

Otero, Carlos P. (ed.). *Noam Chomsky: Critical Assessments*, 4 vols. (London: Routledge, 1994).

Salkie, Raphael. *The Chomsky Update: Linguistics and Politics* (London: Unwin-Hyman, 1990).

Priscilla Roberts

CHURCHILL, WINSTON LEONARD SPENCER (1874–1965)

Born in 1874 to Lord Randolph Churchill and his American wife, Jennie Jerome, Winston Churchill was born into wealth and the upper echelons of British society. His grandfather, the Duke of Marlborough, represented the tradition of land and aristocracy that still permeated British society in the nineteenth century. Although Churchill never accepted a peerage, this worldview influenced him throughout his entire life.

Sent to Harrow for schooling, he had little interest in the classics—and did poorly in them—but developed both a love of history and "an aptitude for the use of the English language" that would serve him well in the future (Jenkins 2001, 18). Overall he did well academically at Harrow, although he later fostered the notion that he had struggled (Rose 1994, 28). Instead of university, Churchill went on to the British military academy at Sandhurst and entered the army, being first stationed in India. It was during this time that Churchill's interest in writing and history came to the fore. He seems to have discovered a value in learning and in reading that had not manifested during his years at school.

While serving in India, he became a voracious reader of history, philosophy, economics, and other subjects, reading Gibbon, Macaulay, Hallam, and Adam Smith. These historians remained a primary influence on his writing and historical outlook throughout his life (Plumb 1969, 140). He also began his career as a journalist, reporting on the campaigns to which he was assigned for London papers, then turning these articles into his first books on the North–West Frontier and Omdurman campaigns. At various points during his long political career, Churchill continued to serve as a freelance writer, primarily to supplement his income.

In later years, he published numerous well-received histories detailing the history of the English-speaking nations, as well as his personal histories of both World Wars. His six-volume *The Second World War* received the Nobel Prize for Literature in 1953. He also wrote major biographies both of his father, Lord Randolph Churchill, the maverick Tory Democrat of the 1880s, and his forebear, the first duke of Marlborough, John Churchill. In his writings, his style "drew heavily on Macaulay—'crisp and forcible'—and Gibbon—'stately and impressive'" (Rose 1994, 55). In his historical works, he had a tendency to overlook the faults of his heroes, particularly his father, and to adopt a Whiggish interpretation of British history. In this he was influenced by his reading of the traditional histories of England by J. R. Green, G. M. Trevelyan, and others (Plumb 1969, 134–37).

Like his father, Churchill went into politics upon leaving the army, beginning as a conservative MP in 1900, moving to the Liberal Party in 1904, and returning to the Conservatives following the end of World War I. In his political career, Churchill would serve as the president of the Board of Trade, first lord of the Admiralty (twice), chancellor of the Exchequer, and would conclude his career with two turns as prime minister, first during World War II and again from 1953 to 1955. While his political career often suffered as many reverses as advances, his triumphant lead as prime minister from 1940 to 1945 firmly established his reputation—as well as providing him the opportunity to apply both his knowledge of history and his writing ability in his public rhetoric.

Churchill died in 1965 and became only one of select few outside the monarchy to be given a state funeral at Westminster Abbey. It is hard to measure Churchill's influence on the twentieth century, if only because he inspires the strongest of emotions and because he was frequently seen as never wholly belonging to the twentieth century, despite living in it for 63 years. This influence of the past was marked by his contemporaries. **Clement Attlee** compared Churchill to a layer cake: "One layer was certainly seventeenth century. The eighteenth century in him is obvious. There was the nineteenth century, and a large slice, of course, of the twentieth century; and another, curious layer which may have been the twenty-first" (Manchester 1983–88, 12).

Never quite accepted by either party, Churchill's major interest lay in ensuring the future of Great Britain and the British Empire. In his writing, this worldview is most apparent. Violet Bonham Carter wrote that, although quick to adapt new technology, fundamentally Churchill was "imbued with a historic sense of tradition, he was untrammeled by convention" (Bonham Carter 1965, 11).

Equally apparent was his interest in the military and its role in statecraft. More than half of the 56 books Churchill wrote dealt with war and warriors. One biographer held that Churchill believed, like Nietzsche, Carlyle, and Gobineau, and contrary to his contemporaries, that the "great issues of his day would be decided on the battlefield . . . that war was a legitimate political instrument . . . " (Manchester 1983–88, 14). Indeed the great ideologies of his day were tested on the battlefields of Europe and Asia, in several great and bloody conflicts, again a historical fact of which Churchill was profoundly aware. He took a special interest in defense matters, actually serving as first lord of the Admiralty twice. During World War II, he took an active role, not always welcome, in strategy and policy. But to insist that Churchill was so rooted in tradition, military glory, and history is to ignore the political survivor.

Winston Churchill lasted almost sixty years in the House of Commons as a member of two political parties. He was prime minister twice and chancellor of the Exchequer once. He also nearly cashiered his career in the 1930s, running afoul of the Conservative leadership, including **Stanley Baldwin** and **Neville Chamberlain,** but emerged as one of the few consistent critics of the rising dictators such as **Adolf Hitler.** He remained a member of parliament for his entire career, a place where his oratory made a difference, whether in defense or opposition of policy or proposed legislation.

In a century with few larger-than-life figures, Winston Leonard Spencer Churchill seems to loom larger than most as a result of both his actions and, importantly, his own literary legacy—itself influenced in large part by the historical giants of the nineteenth century and the Whig tradition they fostered. As times change, the Whig influence has become more suspect, but its optimistic depiction of the evolution of the British past was certainly one Churchill returned to throughout his life.

Archives

Churchill's papers have been deposited in the Churchill Archives at Churchill College, Cambridge.

There are also copies of his correspondence with Franklin D. Roosevelt at the Roosevelt Presidential Library, Hyde Park, New York.

Documents on Churchill's official career are in the Public Records Office, Kew Gardens, London.

Printed Sources

Alldritt, Keith. *Churchill the Writer: His Life as a Man of Letters* (London: Hutchinson, 1992).

Barrett, Buckley Barry. *Churchill: A Concise Bibliography* (Westport, Conn: Greenwood Press, 2000). A comprehensive list of both the writings of Churchill and those that have been produced about all aspects of his life and career.

Bonham Carter, Lady Violet. *Winston Churchill: An Intimate Portrait,* (New York: Harcourt, Brace and World, Inc., 1965).

Churchill, Randolph S., *Winston S. Churchill,* 2 vols. (London: Heinemann, 1966–67).

Gilbert, Martin. *Churchill: A Life* (London: Heinemann, 1991). The one-volume condensation of the official biography.

———. *Winston S. Churchill,* 6 vols. (London: Heinemann, 1971–88). The official biography, the first two volumes by Randolph Churchill, the subsequent six by Martin Gilbert. There are 16 volumes of companion papers to the official biography, edited by Gilbert, and published between 1967 and 2000.

Holley, Darrell. *Churchill's Literary Allusions: An Index to the Education of a Soldier, Statesman and Litterateur* (Jefferson, N.C.; London: McFarland & Co., 1987).

Jenkins, Roy. *Churchill* (London: Farrar, Straus and Giroux, 2001).

Manchester, William. *The Last Lion, Winston Spencer Churchill* (Boston: Little, Brown, 1983–88).

Plumb, J. H. "The Historian." In A. J. P. Taylor et al., *Churchill Revised: A Critical Assessment* (New York: Dial Press, 1969), 133–69.

Rose, Norman. *The Unruly Giant* (New York: Free Press, 1994).

Phyllis Soybel

COLETTE, SIDONIE-GABRIELLE (1873–1954)

Colette was a French writer born at Saint-Saveur-en-Puisaye, France, where she attended grammar school. In 1893, she married the writer and critic Henri Gauthier-Villars ("Willy"), age 35. Indifferent to religion or convention, her true loyalty was to writing. Her husband forced her to write but had her work published under his own name. Colette left her husband in 1906. During this time, she met the Marquise de Balbeuf, an affluent lesbian. Colette's divorce from Willy was finalized in 1910, and in 1912 she married Henry de Jouvenel, the editor-in-chief of *Le Matin*. In 1934, Colette divorced Henry de Jouvenel. One year later, she married Maurice Goudeket, who was also a writer. Colette was elected to the Belgian Royal Academy in 1935. She was also made a grand officer of the Legion d'honneur. In 1945, she became the first woman elected to the Académie Goncourt. Colette died in Paris on August 3, 1954.

Colette's earliest works made up the collection that would henceforth be called the "Claudine" novels. These novels were inspired by Colette's own experiences. Colette's familiarity with the music hall and the time that she spent in the company of the Marquise inspired two additional novels. From 1913, she published novels that treated the romantic relationships that existed between men and women, semi-autobiographical works that looked back upon life in the countryside and the innocent childhood that she had spent there, and works that focused on characteristics of female sexuality.

It was both her father's literary connections and those of her first husband, Willy, that permitted Colette to become involved in writing. Willy had access to the most important artistic, literary, and musical circles of the era, and Colette soon became intimate with members of the most important literary groups. Colette frequented the Paris of the 1890s. This was the Paris of **André Gide, Marcel Proust,** Émile Zola, and Paul Valéry. As a young woman of 20, she plunged herself into the novels and poems of these famous writers, all of whose works Colette had esteemed. She admired Gide's novel *L'Immoraliste* (1902), which was a study of how ethical concepts conflict with traditional conventions of morality, and Zola's famous "J'accuse" letter (1898), in which Zola attacked French officials for their persecution of the French artillery officer Alfred Dreyfus, who had been found guilty of treason. Colette's favorite writers, and those that influenced her the most, were Honoré de Balzac and her contemporary Marcel Proust, born two years before she was.

Colette's literary works have affinities with both Balzac and Proust. Like her contemporary Proust, she was a diligent and determined writer who struggled persistently through revision after revision in order to find the perfect expression to convey to her reader her thoughts. Like Balzac's characters, hers are often larger than life, and like Balzac she tended to recycle characters throughout various novels in order to show their character development over time. Like his *La Comédie humaine* (1842–48), which Colette read, loved, and admired, her works examine individuals of a certain social milieu at a certain time in order to show a slice of life on the literary page. Nevertheless, Colette's literary creations are much more autobiographical in nature than those of Balzac.

Archives

La Bibliothèque Nationale de France, Paris, France, Colette, Cabinet des Manuscrits.
University of Texas at Austin, Collection "Manuscrits," Colette, Carlton Lake Collection.

Printed Sources

Lottman, Herbert R. *Colette: A Life* (London: Minerva, 1991).
Thurman, Judith. *Secrets of the Flesh: A Life of Colette* (New York: Ballantine Books, 2000).

Richard J. Gray II

COLLINS, MICHAEL (1890–1922)

Michael Collins was born in 1890 near Clonakilty, County Cork, an area of constant conflict between Irish tenant farmers and landlords. Michael was the youngest of the eight children of Michael Sr. and Marianne Collins. His father, who died when Michael was six, was an educated Catholic farmer and a member of the Irish Republican Brotherhood (IRB). Michael was educated at the Lisavaird National School under the tutelage of Denis Lyons, also an active member of the IRB. Lyons eagerly taught the physical force republicanism of Theobald Wolfe Tone, and according to Collins, infused in him "a pride of the Irish as a race." Collins trained for the postal examination at the Clonakilty National School and worked as a postal clerk and stockbroker in London (1906–15) prior to joining the IRB and participating in the Easter Rising of 1916. Following imprisonment, he became an influential member of the Irish Republican Army and the Irish Volunteers. Elected to the Dail from South Cork, Collins served as minister of home affairs and minister of finance. During the Anglo-Irish War he coordinated military strategies and organized highly effective urban guerrilla warfare against the British. As minister of finance, Collins reluctantly helped negotiate the Anglo-Irish treaty. With the outbreak of the Irish Civil War in 1922, he was named commander in chief of the Free State army, but was assassinated in August by anti-treaty Irregulars.

Even at a young age Collins read eclectically. Along with the works of Shakespeare and other English classics, he read the traditional Irish novels, poems, ballads, and Fenian folklore that helped to form a historical and cultural basis for his nationalism. The works of John Banim and Thomas Kickham, describing the plight of oppressed Irish tenants, were among his favorite Irish novels. According to **Frank O'Connor,** he wept over the peasant sufferings depicted in Kickham's *Knocknagow.* Collins enjoyed the theater, especially the plays of Shaw and Barrie. He also read works by **W. B. Yeats,** Padraig Colum, James Stephens, Oscar Wilde, Thomas Hardy, George Meredith, H. G. Wells, Arnold Bennet, Joseph Conrad, and Algernon Swinburne. Wilde's "Ballad of Reading Gaol" became especially poignant during his imprisonment.

Collins drew political inspiration from the writings of Thomas Davis, propagandist of the Young Ireland revolt of 1848, and from the songs and stories of A. M. Sullivan, T. D. Sullivan, and Thomas Moore. Analytical editorials by Arthur Griffith in the *United Irishmen* and D. P. Moran in *The Leader* provided systematic criticism of the social and economic struggles of the Irish people and established a political tone that Collins eventually adopted, somewhere between the wildness of perpetual violence and the propriety of the Irish Parliamentary Party, which he dismissed as "slaves of England" (Coogan 1996, 14). Collins seems to have been influenced in his approach to the Anglo-Irish War by G. K. Chesterton's *The Man Who Was Thursday*—given to him by Joseph Plunkett—in which the main anarchist suggests that "If you don't seem to be hiding, nobody hunts you out." According to O'Connor, Collins's "reading regularly outdistanced his powers of reflection," and the sources of his action are almost always to be found in the tales and experiences of his youth (O'Connor 1965, 19).

Archives

State Paper Office of Ireland, Dublin. Official papers. His private papers are widely scattered, many in private hands. See Coogan 1996, 461–63.

Printed Sources

Coogan, Tim Pat. *Michael Collins: The Man Who Made Ireland* (Boulder, Colo.: Roberts Rinehart, 1996).

O'Connor, Frank. *The Big Fellow*, rev. ed. (Dublin: Clonmore and Reynolds, 1965).

John Grady Powell

COPLAND, AARON (1900–1990)

Aaron Copland was born on November 14, 1900, in Brooklyn, New York. His father, Harris, and his mother, Sarah (née Mittenthal), immigrated to America from Russia. A year before their marriage in 1885, Harris Copland opened a department store in Brooklyn. Aaron, along with his four brothers and sisters, helped in the family store. The Coplands belonged to a synagogue in Brooklyn and observed the Jewish high holy days.

At age six, Aaron attended School No. 111, graduating from School No. 9 in 1914. His oldest brother Ralph studied violin, while his sister Laurine played the piano. Laurine also took singing lessons at the Metropolitan Opera School. Inspired by his older brother and sister, Aaron soon became very interested in music. At age 14, he began his piano studies with Leopold Wolfsohn. As early as 1915, Copland had decided to pursue a career in music. In 1917, Copland commenced studies in composition with Rubin Goldmark. After his graduation from Boys' High in 1918, Copland decided not to attend college. Instead, he continued his private studies in piano and composition while working as a pianist. In 1921, Copland left for three years of study in Paris. While attending the summer program in the Palace of Fontainebleau, Copland met Nadia Boulanger, who was to become his composition teacher during his stay in Paris. Before his return to America, Boulanger introduced Copland to the conductor, Serge Koussevitzky. At Koussevitzky's suggestion, Copland composed his first major work, which was to feature Boulanger as soloist. The Symphony for Organ and Orchestra premiered on January 11, 1925, with the New York Symphony Orchestra conducted by Walter Damrosch.

In his book *Copland: 1900–1942* (written in collaboration with Vivian Perlis), Copland makes many references to his love of reading. He recalls looking forward to lunch breaks while working on Wall Street during the summer of 1918, "because I had come upon a basement bookstore that sold second-hand books in French. It was there that I invested in my first French book, a battered copy of Alphonse Daudet's play *Sappho*" (Copland 1984, 25). Copland's close friend, Aaron Schaffer, was a student of French and French literature at Johns Hopkins University. Describing Schaffer's influence, Copland states, "My new friend advised me about literature, his own field, and at about this time I began to read voraciously, adding French literature to the Horatio Alger and Mark Twain I was already familiar with" (Copland 1984, 26). For Copland, "reading became a passion second only to music" (Copland 1984, 28–29). He frequented the Brooklyn Public Library, familiarizing himself with the writings of Sigmund Freud and Havelock Ellis, as well as Romain Rolland's *Jean Christophe* and Walt Whitman's *I Hear America Singing* (Copland 1984, 28). Finally, in an undated letter written to his parents from Paris, Copland acknowledges the importance of reading in his life, stating, "I read not to learn anything, but from the pure love of it" (Copland 1984, 82).

Copland's lifelong appreciation of reading provided inspiration for many of his compositions. Richard Barnefield, Edward Arlington Robinson, **Ezra Pound, E. E. Cummings,** Alfred Hayes, George Meredith, John Barbour, Genevieve Taggard, and Emily Dickinson are among the many poets represented in Copland's works. He wrote scores for several films based on the literary works of Alex Karmel, Henry James, **John Steinbeck, Thornton Wilder,** and Lillian Hellman. Copland's other compositions include two operas, incidental music for several plays, ballet music, symphonies and concerti, music for the piano, chamber music, and songs.

In addition to his accomplishments as a composer, pianist, conductor, and educator, Copland was a prolific writer. He wrote numerous magazine and newspaper articles, illustrating both the trends and controversies surrounding twentieth-century American music. He strongly expressed his faith in the future of the American composer and his music. His four books—*What to Listen for In Music, Our New Music* (later renamed *The New Music 1900–1960*), *Music and Imagination*, and *Copland on Music*—are written for a broad audience and can be appreciated by the non-musician as well as the specialist.

Archives

Copland Collection at the Library of Congress, Washington, D.C.
New York Public Library.

Printed Sources

Berger, Arthur. *Aaron Copland.* [1953] (Westport, Conn.: Greenwood Press, 1971).
Butterworth, Neil. *The Music of Aaron Copland* (New York: Toccata Press–Universe Books, 1985).
Copland, Aaron. *Copland on Music* (Garden City, N.Y.: Doubleday and Company, Inc., 1944).
———. *Copland Since 1943* (New York: St. Martin's Press, 1989).
———. *Music and Imagination* [1952] (Cambridge: Harvard University Press, 1980).
———. *The New Music 1900–1960*, rev. and enlarged ed. (New York: W. W. Norton & Company, Inc., 1968). Reprint of *Our New Music*, 1941.
———. *What To Listen For In Music*, rev. ed. (New York: McGraw Hill, 1957).
Copland, Aaron, and Vivian Perlis. *Copland: 1900–1942* (New York: St. Martin's/Marek, 1984).
Pollack, Howard. *Aaron Copland: The Life and Work of an Uncommon Man* (New York: Henry Holt and Company, 1999).
Skowronski, Joann. *Aaron Copland: A Bio-Bibliography.* Bio-Bibliographies In Music, Number 2 (Westport, Conn.: Greenwood Press, 1985).

Marianne Wilson

COWARD, SIR NOËL PEIRCE (1899–1973)

Noël Coward was born on December 16, 1899, at Teddington, Middlesex, to Arthur and Violet Coward, both of whom had a passion for music. Coward's formal education was "sporadic" and often interrupted, so much of his learning was self-directed. Coward's mother frequently took him to the theater, and by age 12 he was acting professionally; by 14 he was famous. He did several shows with Sir Charles Hawtrey, from whom he learned the mechanics of writing and theatrical production. In June 1915, Mrs. Astley Cooper invited Coward to stay at her manor house at Hambleton, a visit which brought him into contact with the world of England's upper classes, from which he would derive much of his support as well as material for much of his comedy. By 1916 Coward was writing his own songs and plays. After brief service in the army in 1918, Coward returned to the theater. In 1920 he first performed in his own play, *I'll Leave It to You*. Though praised by reviewers, the play closed quickly. His first critical and financial success came in 1924 with *The Vortex*, a serious play about drug addiction. After this came a rush of successes, and by the mid-1930s, Coward was well established as a darling of the London and New York stages, though less as an actor, and more and more as a writer, producer, and composer. During the Second World War he produced several shows, including his longest-running comedy, *Blythe Spirit* (1941) and the war film *In Which We Serve* (1942). After the war, his comedy was less well received, though Coward continued to have commercial success. A few more plays and his only novel appeared in the 1960s. During this time he was "rediscovered," and in 1970 he received a knighthood in England and a special Tony Award in America. He died at home in Jamaica on March 26, 1973. As Somerset Maugham had predicted, Coward greatly influenced English theater from the 1930s through the 1950s, but he has also been honored for giving the British some of their most beloved songs of the midcentury. Coward's lifestyle, having come from modest origins to summering in Switzerland and wintering in the Caribbean, as much as anything reflected the growing impact of theater and film on the culture of the twentieth century.

Because his education was picked up between performances, it is not surprising that many of his influences were theatrical. In youth Coward read Oscar Wilde, Laurence Hope, Omar Khayyam, **Marcel Proust,** and Hector Hugh Munro, better known as Saki. Saki proved to be the single greatest influence on Coward, especially in the emphasis on youth and in the style of his "homosexual but very English sensibility" (Hoare 1996, 41). In 1922, Coward produced his play *The Young Idea*, which borrowed "shamelessly" from George Bernard Shaw's *You Never Can Tell*. Shaw, not offended, warned Coward that he ought not to imitate him, lest he be out of date too soon, a criticism Coward took to heart. Prior to the start of World War II, Coward had gathered a close-knit group of friends—his "family" he sometimes called them—which included Cole Lesley, Graham Payn, Joyce Cary, Lorn Loraine, and Gladys Calthrop, from whom he gained both insight and encouragement. Although not immune to the barbs of critics, he often acknowledged their justice and was aware that his personality and flair for performance often overshadowed his writing.

Archives

Diaries, correspondence, some letters, and other papers. Birmingham University Special Collections Department.

Other correspondence is spread among many archives and one is encouraged to search the Historical Manuscript Commission databases and the *Location Register of Twentieth-Century English Literary Manuscripts and Letters* (Boston: G. K. Hall, 1988).

Printed Sources

Hoare, Philip. *Noël Coward: a Biography* (New York: Simon and Schuster, 1996). Most widely respected and accessible biography.

Lesley, Cole. *The Life of Noël Coward* (New York: Penguin Books, 1978). An early "official" biography from one who knew him well.

Levin, Milton. *Noël Coward, Updated Version* (Twayne's English Author Series, Boston: Twayne Publishers, 1989). Provides a helpful introduction to Coward's plays and writings.

Richard R. Follett

CROCE, BENEDETTO (1866–1952)

Benedetto Croce was born in Pescasseroli, Italy, the son of rich landed gentry on both sides. He wrote in his autobiography that at the age of six or seven his greatest love was already books. His mother encouraged his reading, which in his childhood included the romances of Father Antonio Bresciani, Tommaso Grossi, and, in Italian translation, Canon Christoph von Schmid, Marie Risteau ("Sophie") Cottin, and Sir Walter Scott. He attended exclusive Catholic schools in Naples, where he read, sometimes on the sly, Bertrando Spaventa, Silvio Pellico, Ferdinando Martini, Francesco De Sanctis, and Giosuè Carducci. When both his parents and a sister were killed by an earthquake in 1883, Croce, severely injured, became the ward of his father's cousin, the politician Silvio Spaventa, in Rome. At first miserable there and contemplating suicide, he recovered his spirits by sequestering himself in the Dominican library of Casanatense.

Croce's turn toward philosophy came during his second year in Rome when he attended Antonio Labriola's lectures at the university. The doubts he had secretly entertained in Naples about his mother's traditional Catholic piety now grew more forceful. Returning to Naples in 1886, he immersed himself for the next six years in Neapolitan history and began writing for publication. In 1893, influenced by Giambattista Vico's *New Science*, Croce wrote his first of many works on the philosophy of art. Encouraged by Labriola, he began intensive study of Karl Marx, Friedrich Engels, Giovanni Gentile, and Johann Friedrich Herbart. On his own he became familiar with Georg Wilhelm Friedrich Hegel, St. Augustine, Alexander Baumgarten, René Descartes, Antonio Rosmini, Wilhelm Dilthey, Herbert Spencer, Gabriele d'Annunzio, medieval scholasticism, and Immanuel Kant. By 1905 he was an articulate, self-taught philosopher.

In the 1890s Croce contributed articles to leftist journals such as *Le Devenir* and corresponded with Georges Sorel and Vilfredo Pareto. In 1902 he founded his own bimonthly journal, *La Critica*, which lasted until 1943 and was noted for being quite derogatory toward academic philosophers, especially Antonio Fogazzaro, Giovanni Pascoli, and d'Annunzio. He engaged the psychological theories of Cesare Lombroso, Paolo Mantegazza, Émile Zola, and Claude Bernard. As a philosopher, he sided with idealism against the then dominant positivism, neo-Kantianism, utilitarianism, and scientism of Spencer, John Stuart Mill, Auguste Comte, Roberto Ardigò, Hippolyte Taine, and others, drawing inspiration from Hegel, Friedrich Wilhelm Joseph von Schelling, Bernard Bosanquet, and even early British empiricists such as John Locke and George Berkeley. Yet the main sources of his thought remained mostly Italian, primarily Vico.

Archives

The Croce Library (Biblioteca Benedetto Croce) was created in Naples in 1955 along with the organization that oversees it, the Croce Foundation (Fondazione Benedetto Croce). Collaborating with the Italian Institute for Historical Studies (Istituto Italiano per gli Studi Storici), part of its mission is to preserve Croce's personal library and papers and to collect primary research materials about him.

Printed Sources

Brescia, Giuseppe. *Croce Inedito: 1881–1952* (Napoli: Società Editrice Napoletana, 1984).

Corsi, Mario. *Le Origini del Pensiero di Benedetto Croce* (Napoli: Giannini, 1974).

Croce, Benedetto. *An Autobiography*, Robin George Collingwood (trans.), (Freeport, N.Y.: Books for Libraries, 1970).

De Feo, Italo. *Croce: L'Uomo e l'Opera* (Milano: Mondadori, 1975).

Franchini, Raffaello. *Note Biografiche di Benedetto Croce* (Torino: Edizioni Radio Italiana, 1953).

Marra, Dora. *Conversazioni con Benedetto Croce su Alcuni Libri della sua Biblioteca* (Milano: Hoepli, 1952).

Orsini, Gian N. G. *Benedetto Croce: Philosopher of Art and Literary Critic* (Carbondale: Southern Illinois University Press, 1961).

Roberts, David D. *Benedetto Croce and the Uses of Historicism* (Berkeley: University of California Press, 1987).

Scirocco, Giovanni. *Croce: La Vita, l'Itinerario, il Pensiero* (Milano: Academia, 1973).

Sprigge, Cecil Jackson Squire. *Benedetto Croce: Man and Thinker* (New Haven, Yale University Press, 1952).

Eric v.d. Luft

CUMMINGS, EDWARD ESTLING (1894–1962)

Popularly known as "e.e.cummings," he was born in Cambridge, Massachusetts, on October 14, 1894, and died in North Conway, New Hampshire, September 3, 1962. He was educated at Cambridge Latin School and at Harvard College, where in 1915 he received his A.B., graduating *magna cum laude* in Greek and English; he received his A.M. from Harvard in 1916. Cummings's father was a Unitarian minister whose influence in the development of his son's open, playful, and free-from-dogma approach to the world cannot be doubted. There was an early period of personal rebellion against Unitarian piety and the settled ethos of Cambridge. Cummings's great love for his father and for his mother, a strong-willed and fearless person, is clearly shown in an autobiographical presentation he gave at Harvard in 1953: *i–six nonlectures*. By 1918, Cummings had created his highly eccentric poetic style. That style, which broke with standard grammatical rules and usage, placed him in the vanguard of experimental, radical, and "frontier-breaking" literary achievement. His corpus of over 500 poems, produced from his start as early as 1916 until his death 46 years later, has received ample critical acclaim and establishes unquestionably that Cummings's oeuvre contributed significantly in the larger domain of poetry in English.

Cummings's career as an innovator did not emerge suddenly, without experience or acquaintance with the conventional Western literary tradition. He learned from earlier poetic and prose forms: the Pindaric ode, Elizabethan song, eighteenth-century satire, the works of Henry Thoreau, Ralph Waldo Emerson, and Emily Dickinson. His nonlecture about himself at Harvard reveals his reading in Aeschylus, Homer, and the French troubadours. He had gained skill in poetic forms with definite rules: villanelle, roundel, ballade royale, and sonnet. Thus solidly based, he forged ahead in his work as a poet, playwright, novelist, and essayist in a highly individualistic, confident, and enlivening way.

Cummings was also well-read in other authors pertinent to his studies: Geoffrey Chaucer, Dante Gabriel Rossetti, Gaius Valerius Catullus, and Sappho. Henry Wadsworth Longfellow was his early idol. He was drawn away from him and guided in replacing him with John Keats by one of his early mentors, Theodore A. Miller.

There remain three other fields which must be mentioned in his growth as an artist. First, Cummings was a lover of the circus and believed acrobats to be miraculous. He wanted his poems to create movement, and the movement is akin to the tension and release acrobats create in their viewers. Next, Cummings loved burlesque. He saw artful life in it, enough so that when asked for his theory of poetic technique, he answered that he was like a burlesque comedian. Finally, Cummings's post–World War I years in Paris and his settling in Greenwich Village furthered his aesthetic development, leading to his concern for creating an instantaneous surround of understanding. He admired Paul Cézanne, **Marcel DuChamp, Pablo Picasso,** and **Constantin Brancusi** and read such books as Willard Huntington Wright's *Modern Art*.

Archives

Houghton Library, Harvard University, Cambridge, Mass. Cummings's letters, diaries, sketchbooks, manuscripts, personal library, and miscellaneous papers.

Additional manuscripts can be found at the Humanities Research Center, University of Texas; Clifton Waller Barrett Library, University of Virginia; Sibley Watson Collection, Rochester, New York; Beinecke Library, Yale University; Princeton University Library, New Jersey.

Printed Sources

Cummings, E. E. *Selected Letters of E. E. Cummings*, F. W. Dupee and George Stade (eds.), (New York: Harcourt Brace Jovanovich, 1969).

Friedman, Norman. *E. E. Cummings: The Growth of a Writer* (Carbondale, Ill.: Southern Illinois University Press, 1964).

Kennedy, Richard. *Dreams in the Mirror: A Biography of E. E. Cummings* (New York: Liveright, 1980).

Kidder, Rushworth. *E. E. Cummings: An Introduction to the Poetry* (New York: Columbia University Press, 1979).

Schmider, Carl L. "Precision Which Creates Movement: The Stylistics of E. E. Cummings" (Ph.D. diss., University of Denver, 1972).

Carl L. Schmider

D

DALI, SALVADOR (1904–1989)

Salvador Domenech Felipe Jacinto Dali was born in Figueras, Catalonia, Spain, where he acquired a fascination for drawing and painting at the age of ten. He attended the Colegio Hermanos de las Escuelas Cristianas, a private school administered by the Brothers of the Marist order, and during the evenings took classes at the municipal drawing school under Juan Nuñez. Later, Dali studied at the Academia de San Fernando in Madrid, where he lived at the infamous Residencia de Estudiantes. By 1925 Dali had assimilated a number of different artistic styles, including cubism and illustrative seventeenth-century Dutch realism. In 1928 he traveled to Paris and formally joined the surrealist painters, under whose influence Dali produced his best-known work, including *The Persistence of Memory* (1931). Dali's autobiographical and sometimes shocking paintings were paralleled by his surrealist films *Un chien andalou* and *L'Age d'or*, directed by **Luis Bunuel.** In 1940, Dali fled European Nazism and settled in the United States with his wife, Helena Diakonova, also known as Gala. Dali's later works such as *Crucifixion* (1954) and *The Sacrament of the Last Supper* (1955) frequently reflected religious themes that were absent in his earlier work.

From a very early age, Dali had access to an extraordinary amount of literature, as he was regularly loaned books from his uncle Anselmo, a bookseller and bibliophile who lived in Barcelona. Dali became interested in philosophy as a youth, and read Friedrich Nietzsche's *Thus Spake Zarathustra*, Voltaire's *Philosophical Dictionary*, as well as the works of Immanuel Kant, Rene Descartes, and Benedict Spinoza. From the French magazine *Litterature*, Dali became acquainted with the writings of **André Breton** and the poet Philippe Soupault, who, along with the authors Paul Valery and **André Gide,** promoted an experimental playfulness and irreverence that would eventually spawn the surrealist movement in both art and literature. Surrealist poets such as Louis Aragon and Paul Eluard often used imagery inspired by their unconscious minds and brought to the conscious realm through the use of automatism, or automatic writing. While Dali's work was not a product of automatism, it was certainly based on images from the subconscious. Dali was an avid reader of Sigmund Freud, especially his *Interpretation of Dreams*, and believed that in dreams, unconscious and repressed primal desires become manifest. Dali believed that by approximating the nonsensical quality of dreams through art, access to the real workings of the mind could be gained. Accordingly, Dali's art often contained images and objects juxtaposed in irrational ways that served to shock viewers, without the spectators possessing conscious knowledge of why the images were disturbing. Dali read the psychiatrist Jacques Lacan's *Of Paranoiac Psychosis in Its Relationship to Personality*, and afterward developed his paranoiac-critical method of determining the content of his art. Dali would descend into a temporary state of self-hypnosis, wherein he would develop imagery based on delirious associations of personal ideas and past experiences. Dali's work therefore contained limitless combinations of extremely personal images, reflecting the artist's own desires and fears that most often manifested themselves in symbols of eroticism and decay.

Archives

Pierpont Morgan Library, Department of Literary and Historical Manuscripts, control no. NYPR106454-A.
Columbia University Rare Book and Manuscript Library, New York, control no. NYCR88-A76.
The Getty Research Institute for the History of Art and the Humanities, Special Collections, control no. CJPA1546454-A.

Printed Sources

Dali, Salvador. *Dali by Dali* (New York: Harry N. Abrams, 1970).
Parinaud, Andre. *The Unspeakable Confessions of Salvador Dali* (New York: William Morrow and Company Inc., 1976).
Smith, Meredith Etherington. *The Persistence of Memory: A Biography of Dali* (London: Smith, Sinclair and Stevenson, 1992).

Gregory L. Schnurr

DAY, DOROTHY MAY (1897–1980)

Dorothy Day was born in Brooklyn, New York. Though not from a religious family, she was baptized in the Episcopal Church at age 12. At 16 she won a scholarship to study at the University of Illinois, Urbana, where she began to call herself a socialist. She left university after two years to return to New York where she wrote for several socialist journals. As part of the radical and intellectual scene in Greenwich Village of the 1920s, she knew such writers as **Eugene O'Neill, John Dos Passos,** Malcolm Cowley, and Kenneth Burke. In 1927, she baptized her infant daughter in the Catholic Church; Day's own baptism followed later that year, the beginning of her life as a Catholic activist. With Peter Maurin, she established the *Catholic Worker* newspaper, first distributed on May 1, 1933, and the Catholic Worker movement. Day wrote for the *Worker*, and for other Catholic journals, all her life. They grounded the movement in their ideas about manual labor, voluntary poverty, a decentralized society, nonviolence, and, especially, the Works of Mercy (Matt. 25:31–46). Known particularly as a pacifist, Day is considered by many to be the most important lay figure in American Catholicism. After her death, she was proposed for sainthood by the Claretians.

An ardent reader, Day often reflected on her readings in her various writings, particularly in *The Long Loneliness* and *From Union Square to Rome*. In both she recalls reading the Bible and the Psalms while a young girl and adolescent. Day grew up in Chicago, and **Upton Sinclair**'s *The Jungle* and the works of Jack London had particular effect on her social consciousness (Day 1938, 34). Her adolescent reading included St. Augustine's *Confessions*, William James's *Varieties of Religious Experience*, and Thomas à Kempis's *Imitation of Christ*. She had a lifelong admiration of the great Russian writers, particularly Dostoyevsky and Tolstoy (Day 1938, 39). She credited Prince Peter Kropotkin for bringing to her attention the plight of the poor (Day 1952, 38). After her conversion, Joris-Karl Huysmans's novels helped her feel at home in the church (Day 1952, 107, 142). From Maurin, a Frenchman, she learned of the French Catholic personalists such as Emmanuel Mournier and Jacques Maritain. She wrote often about the influences of the lives of the saints, particularly St. Francis of Assisi, St. Teresa of Avila, St. Catherine of Siena, and St. Thérèse of Liseux, about whom she wrote a biography. In talks with Robert Coles late in her life, she spoke of many writers who influenced her, including **Simone Weil, George Orwell,** Charles Dickens, Georges Bernanos *(Diary of a Country Priest)*, **Graham Greene,** François Mauriac, and, in particular, **Ignazio Silone** (especially in *Bread and Wine*) (Coles 1987, 174).

Archives

Marquette University, Milwaukee, Wisconsin.

Day's correspondence and other materials; archives of the *Catholic Worker* at http://www.mu.edu/library/collections/archives/day.html.

The Catholic Worker Web site (www.catholicworker.org) includes an annotated bibliography of her writing searchable by keywords or names.

Printed Sources

Coles, Robert. *Dorothy Day: A Radical Devotion* (Reading, Mass.: Addison-Wesley Publishing Co. Inc., 1987).

Day, Dorothy. *From Union Square to Rome* (Silver Spring, Md.: Preservation of the Faith Press, 1938).

———. *Loaves and Fishes* [1963] (Maryknoll, N.Y.: Orbis Books, 1997). History of the Catholic Worker movement.

———. *The Long Loneliness: An Autobiography* [1952] (San Francisco: Harper & Row, 1981).

Klejment, Anne, and Alice Klejment. *Dorothy Day and the Catholic Worker: A Bibliography and Index* (New York: Garland Publishing, Inc. 1986).

Merriman, Brigid O'Shea. *Searching for Christ: The Spirituality of Dorothy Day* (Notre Dame: University of Notre Dame Press, 1994). Traces the literary and other influences on Day's spirituality and activism.

Miller, William D. *Dorothy Day* (New York: Harper, 1982).

Linda C. Macrì

DEBS, EUGENE VICTOR (1855–1926)

Eugene V. Debs was born in Terre Haute, Indiana. He attended a secondary institution for boys, the Old Seminary School in Terre Haute (1860–67), where he was heavily influenced by one of the school's teachers, Abbie Flagg, who helped him develop a command of proper English. Flagg presented Debs with a Bible containing the inscription "Read and Obey," neither of which appealed to him (Constantine 1990, Volume One, xlix). While Debs's close-knit family had Christian ties (his father had attended Protestant churches and his mother had been a Catholic), Debs distrusted established religion. He attended public high school (1867–70), where he was involved in literary and debate societies, although he left school at the age of 14. He then worked a number of jobs, including as a railroad fireman and finally as a billing clerk for a grocer. Debs established the Occidental Literary Club in Terre Haute and he invited a number of individuals to speak, including Robert Green Ingersoll (1833–99) and Susan B. Anthony (1820–1906), both of whom profoundly impressed him. He joined the Brotherhood of Locomotive Firemen in 1875, and eventually became editor of the *Fireman's Magazine*. He was elected to the Indiana State Legislature as a Democrat in 1884. The following year, he was imprisoned for six months for his role in a railroad strike, and he became a socialist while in prison. In 1897, Debs helped establish the Social Democracy of America, and later the Social Democratic Party of America, on whose ticket he ran for President in 1900. In 1901, he was instrumental in the formation of the Socialist Party and ran as its Presidential candidate in 1904, 1908, 1912, and finally in 1920 while serving time in prison for making an antiwar speech.

Debs was not an intellectual, but rather a committed political activist, and his literary influences generally reflect his political interests. His early reading, however, included Voltaire's *Philosophical Dictionary* (1764), Victor Hugo's *Les Miserables* (1862), which heavily impressed him, and the partially fictitious *Appleton's Cyclopedia* (1887–89), which Debs hoped would help teach him "what I needed to know" (Constantine 1990, Volume One, xlix–li). In "How I Became a Socialist," Debs records that "socialism gradually laid hold of me in its own irresistible fashion" and he specifically cites the writings of Edward Bellamy, especially *Looking Backward* (1888), and Robert Blatchford, as well as Lawrence Gronlund's *The Cooperative Commonwealth* (1884) (Tussey 1972, 48–49; Debs 1948, vii). He treasured a copy of Karl Marx's *Capital* (1887) given to him by fellow socialist Victor L. Berger. Moreover, Debs found the writings of Marxist philosopher Karl Kautsky "so clear and conclusive that I readily grasped not merely his argument, but also caught the spirit of his utterance . . . " (Tussey 1972, 48). Debs's reading habits were therefore critical in informing his political views and he thanked "all who helped me out of darkness into light" (Tussey 1972, 48).

Archives

Special Collections Division, Cunningham Memorial Library, Indiana State University, Terre Haute, Indiana.

The Eugene V. Debs Foundation, Terre Haute, Indiana.

Printed Sources

Constantine, Robert J. (ed.). *Letters of Eugene V. Debs*, 3 vols. (Urbana, Ill.: University of Illinois Press, 1990).

Debs, Eugene V. *Writings and Speeches of Eugene V. Debs*. Arthur M. Schlesinger Jr. (intro.), (New York: Hermitage Press, 1948).

Radosh, Ronald (ed.). *Debs: Great Lives Observed* (Englewood Cliffs, N.J.: Prentice-Hall, 1971).

Salvatore, Nick. *Eugene V. Debs: Citizen and Socialist* (Urbana, Ill.: University of Illinois Press, 1982).

Tussey, Jean Y. (ed.). *Eugene V. Debs Speaks.* James P. Cannon (intro.), (New York: Pathfinder Press, 1972).

Scott Lupo

DE GAULLE, CHARLES (1890–1970)

Charles de Gaulle, president of France and leader of the Free French, provided firm domestic leadership and restored French influence in European affairs after the Second World War. A staunch nationalist and anti-Communist, de Gaulle's individualistic and authoritarian style inclined him to employ a heavy hand in addressing domestic issues and adopt a highly competitive stance in European and international affairs.

De Gaulle's father, Henri de Gaulle, instilled in him an appreciation for classical literature and philosophy. His father and his early exposure to the Jesuit scholars endowed de Gaulle with an extensive humanist education. Evidence of this came with de Gaulle's regular ability to publicly quote the Greek authors, including Aeschylus and Sophocles as well as the philosophers Heraclitus, Parmenides, and especially Plato. De Gaulle also studied the works of Roman and Greek historians including Thucydides, Xenophon, Polybius, Sallust, Tacitus, Livy, Julius Caesar, and their literary counterparts, including Horace. De Gaulle's knowledge of prominent Latin authors also included Saint Augustine and early modern figures, including Jean de Joinville, François Rabelais, and Michel de Montaigne. He also took an interest in later figures including the Marquis de Vauvenargues, Nicolas Chamfort, Antoine, comte de Rivarol, and André Chénier. He was philosophically inclined toward the moralistic writings of La Rochefoucauld, Jean de La Bruyère, René Descartes, Blaise Pascal, Cardinal de Retz, Comte de Saint-Simon, and Vicomte de Chateaubriand. As for more modern authors, de Gaulle read the works of Victor Hugo, Honoré de Balzac, Alfred de Musset, Benjamin Constant, Paul-Louis Courier, Barney d'Aurevilly, Villiers de Lisle Adam, Stendhal, Gustave Flaubert, Walter Scott, Jules Verne, Maurice Barrès, Charles Péguy, Joan Psichari, Étienne Boutroux, **Henri Bergson,** Paul Bourget, Anatole France, Pierre Loti, and Claude Farrère. De Gaulle also appreciated the poetry of Charles Baudelaire, Paul Verlaine, and Albert Sarrain. Finally, he had a strong interest in the historians of his day.

His chosen career path, however, was the military. Trained as a future officer at St. Cyr, de Gaulle was wounded during the First World War and fell into German hands. As a prisoner of war, de Gaulle learned to speak German. After the war, de Gaulle remained in the French military serving in Poland and then Germany. A promising junior officer, de Gaulle rose to the rank of colonel in 1937 and promoted in numerous works his vision of a modernized French army. France's youngest general in May 1940, de Gaulle fled France for London in the wake of the German invasion in 1940. Rising quickly as the central figure among the Free French, de Gaulle headed the provisional government in France (September 1944) and quickly rose farther in post-war French political life.

De Gaulle's political decline came just as quickly. Forced from office for his critique of the Fourth Republic's constitution, de Gaulle pursued the creation of an alternative political movement opposed to the creation of the European Defense Community as well as West Germany's entrance into NATO. French national elections in 1953 destroyed the nascent movement and de Gaulle withdrew from politics to write his memoirs. Domestic instability and an open revolt against France in Algeria propelled de Gaulle back onto the political stage in 1958 as France's new president. De Gaulle's strong-handed approach to domestic unrest and swift resolution of the Algerian question earned him the strong support of the electorate again in 1961.

As president, de Gaulle's domestic agenda focused on constitutional reforms to strengthen the hand of the president. Internationally, de Gaulle sought a reconciliation with the West German state and its chancellor, **Konrad Adenauer.** On the continent, de Gaulle sought to prevent further British involvement economically while continuing to build French–German relations. Concerned about France's decline as a world power, de Gaulle pushed the creation of a French nuclear arsenal and a foreign policy with the Soviet Union unencumbered by Britain or the United States. In 1966, de Gaulle withdrew from the military component of NATO. The following year, de Gaulle traveled through eastern Europe and the Soviet Union expressing his support for the continued existence of two German states and the recognition of the Oder-Neisse border between Poland and the German Democratic Republic. De Gaulle's political career declined with the student revolts in 1968 and declining popular support in 1969. De Gaulle died one year later in 1970.

While his military and political careers are well known, de Gaulle's career as a writer and his cultural interests have been largely forgotten. De Gaulle wrote numerous works based on his military and political careers, including *La discorde chez l'ennemi* (1924), *Vers l'armee de metier* (1934), *La France et son armee* (1938), and his war memoirs, *Le fil de l'epee* (1944), *L'appel* (1954), *L'unite* (1956), and *Le salut* (1959).

Archives

Centre historique des Archives nationales (1945–68), Paris.
Fondation et Institut Charles de Gaulle, Paris.
Archives du Quay d'Orsay, 1944–46, Paris.
Archives du Rassemblement du peuple français, Paris.
Archives de l'armée de terre, Vincennes.
Private Archives Georgette Elgey and Jean Mauriac.

Printed Sources

Boissieu, Alain de. *Pour combattre avec de Gaulle (1940–1946)* (Paris: Plon, 1982).
———. *Pour servir le Général (1946–1970)* (Paris: Plon, 1982).
Crawley, Adrian. *De Gaulle* (New York: Bobbs-Merrill Co., 1969).
Crozier, Brian. *De Gaulle, The First Complete Biography* (New York: Charles Scribner's Sons, 1973).
Hatch, Alden. *The de Gaulle Nobody Knows: An Intimate Biography of Charles de Gaulle* (New York: Hawthorn Books, 1960).
Kersaudy, François. *Churchill and de Gaulle* (London: Collins, 1981).
Lacouture, Jean. *André Malraux* (New York: Pantheon, 1975).
———. *De Gaulle—the Rebel, 1890–1944* (New York: W. W. Norton, 1990).
———. *De Gaulle—the Ruler, 1945–1970* (New York: W. W. Norton, 1993).
Linsel, Knut. *Charles de Gaulle und Deutschland 1914–1969* (Sigmaringen: Jan-Thorbecke-Verlag, 1998).

Malraux, André. *Felled Oaks: Conversation with de Gaulle* (London: Hamish Hamilton, 1971).

Malraux, André, and James Burham. *The Case for de Gaulle* (New York: Random House, 1948).

Ménil, Lois P. de. *Who Speaks for Europe?* (London: Weidenfeld & Nicholson, 1977).

Schunck, Peter. *Charles de Gaulle. Ein Leben für Frankreichs Grösse* (Berlin: Propyläen, 1998).

Thomson, David. *Two Frenchmen: Pierre Laval and Charles de Gaulle* (London: The Cresset Press, 1951).

Werth, Alexander. *De Gaulle: A Political Biography* (New York: Simon and Schuster, 1966).

Williams, Charles. *The Last Great Frenchman: a Life of General de Gaulle* (London: Little, Brown, 1993).

David A. Meier

DE KOONING, WILLEM (1904–1997)

Willem de Kooning was born in Rotterdam, Holland, and received eight years of instruction at the State Academy. After brief apprenticeships with commercial decorators and sign painters, de Kooning moved to Belgium to further his studies in painting at the Academie Royal des Beaux-Arts in Brussels. In 1926, de Kooning traveled as a stowaway to the United States, eventually settling in Manhattan where he painted with Fernand Leger and shared a studio with experimental painter Ashile Gorky. De Kooning began to paint on a full-time basis under funding from the Federal Arts Project of 1936, and the following year his mural designs for the Hall of Pharmacy at the New York World's Fair were accepted. During the early 1940s, de Kooning's work gained popularity as the shift toward abstraction in painting became increasingly acceptable to the American public with the influx of immigrant European artists. Paintings from this period such as *Seated Woman* (1940) demonstrate de Kooning's wild abstraction of the female form, the result of which earned him fame as a pioneer of the American abstract expressionist movement. He held his first one-man show at New York's Egan Gallery in 1948 and frequently exhibited at the Whitney Museum and the Museum of Modern Art throughout the next decade. While he was teaching at Black Mountain College and the Yale Art School in New Haven, de Kooning's productions such as *Attic* (1949), *Excavation* (1951), and *Woman I* (1952) continued to push the boundaries of American abstract art. His mid-century masterpieces such as *Easter Monday* (1956) exhibited the dynamism and chaos of New York's urban landscape in a way unknown to his predecessors. In later work, de Kooning would frequently integrate both the figure and its surroundings into frenzied yet unified abstract compositions.

The central themes of de Kooning's work were mirrored in the literature of his era. Man's alienation from society and the nightmares of industrialization were frequent themes in the writings of Fyodor Dostoyevsky and **Martin Heidegger.** De Kooning reflected these concepts on his canvasses through the placement of abstracted figures in a "non-environment," merging both inside and outside space to reflect the metaphysical concept of man's loss of place. De Kooning's experimental and spontaneous application of paint as well as his acceptance of the chance and accidental in his work owed much to the theories of automatism developed by surrealism's literary innovator **André Breton.** The dislocation and juxtaposition of disparate elements in his paintings were often conscious acts, however, as his technique demonstrated calculated reworking of the canvas. This dualistic approach to painting can be paralleled with Friedrich Nietzsche's concept of the "frenzy of will" as outlined in his *Gotzen-Dammerung*. This idea that art is created through alternating periods of conscious calm and spontaneous action was also espoused by the French poet Paul Valery in *The Esthetic Invention*, a work that de Kooning referenced frequently. Finally, John D. Graham's *System and Dialectics in Art* (1937) encouraged de Kooning's spontaneity and improvisation as well as his reliance on the unconscious as a source for his abstract paintings. Graham championed the work of **Carl Jung** and Sigmund Freud, and believed that through expressive action painting, the artist became involved in an act of existential self-creation.

Archives

Archives of American Art, Smithsonian Institution, Washington, D.C., control no. DCAW209606-A.
Museum of Modern Art Library, New York, control no. NYMX91-A4.

Printed Sources

Hess, Thomas B. *Willem de Kooning* (New York: George Braziller Inc., 1959).
Scrivani, George (ed.). *The Collected Writings of Willem de Kooning* (New York: Hanuman Books, 1988).
Waldman, Diane. *Willem de Kooning* (London: Thames and Hudson, 1988).

Gregory L. Schnurr

DEMILLE OR DE MILLE, CECIL BLOUNT (1881–1959)

The man who sometimes was identified as "the founder of Hollywood" was born in Ashville, Massachusetts, on August 12, 1881, but spent most of his childhood in New Jersey. His father, Henry DeMille, very active at the local Prompton Christ Church, had different jobs, including as a playwright. Shortly after his father's premature death in 1893, his mother opened a school at home, the DeMille School. She already was president of the Women's Guild and began to write plays as well. Between 1896 and 1898, Cecil B. DeMille went to the Pennsylvania Military College in Chester but never got a diploma. Later in 1900, Cecil graduated from a two-year acting course at the American Academy of Dramatic Arts in New York City. As an actor, he played Osric in *Hamlet* and Colin de Cayeulx in *If I Were King* (DeMille 1959, 52). Between 1914 (*The Squaw Man*) and 1956 (*The Ten Commandments*), DeMille directed some sixty films; more than half were silent. Many of his early stories were written or adapted by Jeannie MacPherson. He touched many genres, including westerns, comedies, dramas, and epic movies. He often made remakes of his own films: *The Squaw Man* in 1914, 1918, and 1931; *The Ten Commandments* in 1923 and 1956. DeMille was a fervent anticommunist during the 1950's, favoring loyalty oaths and writing conservative columns in the press. He died on January 21, 1959.

DeMille's name means flamboyant and epic movies, often inspired by religious stories. In his posthumous *Autobiography*, he recalled memories from 1892 when his father used to read the Bible: "I remember best the evenings, I think, when he read to us a chapter from the *Old Testament*, a chapter from the *New*, and often a chapter from American or English or European history or from Thackeray or Victor Hugo or some other classic" (DeMille 1959, 31). The director explained the links with his most famous movies: "*The King of Kings* and *The Ten Commandments* were born in those evenings in Prompton, when father sat under the big lamp and read and a small boy sat near his chair and listened" (DeMille 1959, 31). Another reading by his father, in fact an old play about Sepoy Rebellion, *Jesse Brown*, also inspired DeMille's movie, *Unconquered* (1946; DeMille 1959, 398). DeMille wrote that his childhood hero, the "Champion Driver," inspired his recreation of some of his characters, such as Richard "Lionheart" in *The Crusades* (1935), the pirate Jean Lafitte in *The Buccaneer* (1937), Jeff "Bucko" in *Union Pacific* (1939), and Captain Chris Holden in *Unconquered* (1946; DeMille 1959, 40). DeMille was proud of his complete collection of *The Illustrated London News* (DeMille 1959, 123). But the strongest impressions came from foreign movies he saw as early as 1914. "It was Italian films, like *Cabiria* and *The Last Days of Pompeii*, which gave me my first full conception of the possibilities of great spectacles on the screen, of photographing massive movements, whole battles, whole cities, whole nations almost" (DeMille 1959, 124). Above all, DeMille admired American director David Wark Griffith (DeMille 1959, 125). In his historical movies, DeMille worked with a team of scriptwriters and historians; in his *Cleopatra* (1934; adapted from Tite-Live, Plutarque), he worked with scriptwriter Bartlett Cormack; for *The Plainsman* (about Buffalo Bill), DeMille worked with four scriptwriters. The famous director even got assistance in finding new subjects and ideas. From 1945, DeMille asked his research consultant, Henry S. Noerdlinger, "to read for me now on the subjects of what, at my age, will probably be my last pictures" (DeMille 1959, 393). Cecil's older brother, William C. de Mille (with a small "d") was also a film director during the silent era and professor of theater at the University of Southern California. The legendary director played his own character in Billy Wilder's *Sunset Boulevard* (1950).

Archives

DeMille Archives, Arts and Communication Archives, Harold B. Lee Library, Brigham Young University, Provo, Utah. Collected papers, correspondence, production files, and photographs of Cecil B. DeMille.

Eastman House collection, Rochester, N.Y. The largest collection of DeMille silent movies.

The American Film Institute Collection in the Library of Congress, Washington, D.C. Silent films.

The UCLA Film and Television Archive's Research and Study Center (ARSC), Los Angeles. Films.

Printed Sources

D'Arc, James V. (comp. and ed.). *The register of the Cecil B. DeMille archives: MSS 1400* with a biographical essay by Sumiko Higashi (Provo, Utah: Brigham Young University, Harold B. Lee Library, 1991).

DeMille, Cecil B. *The Autobiography of Cecil B. DeMille*, Donald Hayne (ed.), (Englewood Cliffs, N.J.: Prentice-Hall, 1959).

Higashi, Sumiko. *Cecil B. De Mille and American Culture: The Silent Era* (Los Angeles: University of California Press, 1994).

——— (ed.). *Cecil B. DeMille: a Guide to References and Resources* (Boston: G.K. Hall, 1985).

Noerdlinger, Henry S. *Moses and Egypt; The Documentation to the Motion Picture* The Ten Commandments, Cecil B. de Mille (intro.), (Los Angeles: University of Southern California Press, 1956).

Yves Laberge

DERRIDA, JACQUES (1930–)

Jacques Derrida was born in El-Biar near Algiers to Aimé Derrida and Georgette Safar. Derrida enrolled at the Lycée Ben Aknoun in 1941, but was expelled on the first day of the school year as the school had exceeded its quota of Jews. He returned to the Lycée Ben Aknoun, which he attended from 1943 to 1947. He spent the next year at the Lycée Gauthier in Algiers before going to the Lycée Louis-le-Grand in Paris from 1949 to 1952 to study philosophy. He attended the Ecole Normale Supérieure from 1952 to 1953, where he met fellow Algerian Pierre Althusser, with whom he formed an enduring friendship. In the following year he wrote his higher studies dissertation, "The Problem of Genesis in the Philosophy of Edmund Husserl." In 1957 he passed the *agrégation* and received a grant as a special auditor at Harvard University to study the unpublished work of phenomenologist philosopher Edmund Husserl. In this same year, Derrida also began to read the works of **James Joyce.** Under the literary influence of Joyce, Derrida produced what may be regarded as his first major work, a "philosophical" introductory essay to his translation of Husserl's *The Origin of Geometry*, perhaps the first work of what has come to be known in the popular imagination as "deconstruction."

Thus can Derrida's deconstructive writing be considered as the complex result of both literary *and* philosophical influences, although it is irreducible to neither. Derrida's main concern is the deconstruction of the "metaphysics of presence." **Martin Heidegger**'s *Being and Time* originally diagnosed the metaphysics of presence as Western philosophy's bias toward the eternal presence of the "essence" of an object, denoted by the present tense of the verb "to be." This means that ever since Plato, Western philosophy has privileged the essence or idea (Greek, *eidos*) as being that which truly "is" over those mundane objects which are mere representations or copies of those ideas. In *Of Grammatology*, *Writing and Difference* and *Speech and Phenomena: An Essay on Husserl's Theory of Signs*, Derrida examines how this "present" bias of Western metaphysics represses the nonpresence of what he calls "writing." Derrida extends the traditional notion of writing by using it to designate the iterable, or repeatable, products of what Derrida calls *différance*. *Différance* is a neologism which combines the senses of the French verb *différer*, which means both to differ and to defer. It thus resists being simply present. Through iteration, a written mark is shot through with a future and a past that disrupts presence by deferring and differentially spacing it. Derrida analyzes these written or *différantial* structures at work in both Husserl's analysis of the spoken sign in phenomenology and Ferdinand de Saussure's analysis of the sign in semiology. As such, the sign— both written and spoken—is, to a degree, incommensurable with the metaphysics of presence inherent in a philosophical or literary Platonism that seeks to return to the more real presence of the form or idea.

In addition to what may be regarded as philosophical texts, Derrida also reads a wealth of literary and artistic texts which trace the nonpresent inscription of "writing." He has written two pieces on James Joyce, "Ulysses Gramophone: Hearsay Yes in Joyce" and "Two Words for Joyce," which explore Joyce's texts as a site of nonrepresentative writing. Derrida also finds nonpresent inscription at work in the "disseminative" word-play of Stéphane Mallarmé's poetry to the extent that it refuses the imposition of a preexistent sense *(Dissemination)*, the quasi-literary trope of catachresis which writes in a rigorously non-Platonic fashion *(The Margins of Philosophy)*, the disruption of masculine/feminine binarism through the mechanism of "antherection" found throughout Genet's writing *(Glas)*, the inside/outside of a work of art through Immanuel Kant's discussion of the *"parergon"* or margin *(Truth in Painting)*, and the disruption of the true "addressee" of a piece of writing on a "post-card" *(The Post-Card: From Socrates to Freud and Beyond)*.

Derrida's works have been a major influence on the field of literary theory. Literary theorists and critics such as Derek Attridge, Jean-Michel Rabaté, Margot Norris, Lorraine Weir, and Claudette Sartiliot have all explored the literary debts Derrida has said he owes literature. Derrida's deconstructive strategies have also been adapted by cultural and political theorists such as Drucilla Cornell, Eve Kosofsky-Sedgwick, and Judith Butler to other texts in a non-essentialist manner.

Archives

University of California, Irvine, Critical Theory Archive; Department of Special Collections and Archives.

Printed Sources

Attridge, Derek (ed.). *Post-structuralist Joyce: Essays from the French* (Cambridge: Cambridge University Press, 1984).

Butler, Judith. *Bodies That Matter: On the Discursive Limits of "Sex"* (New York: Routledge, 1993).

Cornell, Drucilla. *Deconstruction and the Possibility of Justice* (New York: Routledge, 1992).

———. (ed.). *The Cambridge Companion to James Joyce* (Cambridge: Cambridge University Press, 1990).

Derrida, Jacques. *The Archaeology of the Frivolous: Reading Condillac*, John P. Leavey Jr. (trans.), (Lincoln: University of Nebraska Press, 1987).

———. *Dissemination*, Barbara Johnson (trans.), (London: Athlone, 1981).

———. *Margins of Philosophy*, Alan Bass (trans.), (Chicago: University of Chicago Press, 1982).

———. *Of Spirit: Heidegger and the Question*, Rachel Bowlby and Geoffrey Bennington (trans.), (Chicago: University of Chicago Press, 1989).

———. *Writing and Difference*, Alan Bass (trans., intro.), (London: Routledge, 1978).

Husserl, Edmund. *L'Origine de la géométrie*, Jacques Derrida (trans., intro.), (Paris: Presses Universitaires de France, 1962). English trans. John P. Leavey Jr. (Brighton: Harvester, 1978).

Kosofsky-Sedgwick, Eve. *The Epistemology of the Closet* (Berkeley: University of California Press, 1990).

Norris, Margot. *The Decentered Universe of* Finnegans Wake: *A Structuralist Analysis* (Baltimore: Johns Hopkins University Press, 1976).

Rabaté, Jean-Michel. *James Joyce, Authorized Reader* (Baltimore: Johns Hopkins University Press, 1991).

———. *Joyce upon the Void: The Genesis of Doubt* (London: MacMillan, 1991).

Sartiliot, Claudette. *Citation and Modernity: Derrida, Joyce, and Brecht* (Norman: University of Oklahoma Press, 1993).

Weir, Lorraine. *Writing Joyce: A Semiotics of the Joyce System* (Bloomington: Indiana University Press, 1989).

Peter Mahon

DE VALERA, EAMON (1882–1975)

Eamon Edward George Coll de Valera was born in New York City of an Irish immigrant mother and Spanish father. When his father died in 1885, de Valera was sent to Ireland to be raised by his uncle Edward Coll in Bruree, County Limerick. Educated at Blackrock College (1898–1901) and the Royal University in Dublin (1901–4), he taught mathematics at various colleges and universities around Dublin from 1904 to 1916. His involvement in the Gaelic League led him to join the Irish Volunteers in 1913, rising to command a detachment of Volunteers during the Easter Rising in Dublin in 1916. Although he was court-martialed and sentenced to death, his sentence was commuted to life imprisonment, and he was released under a general amnesty the next year. In 1917, he was elected president of Sinn Féin, which called for the establishment of an Irish Republic, and was elected to Parliament at Westminster as the representative of East Clare. De Valera also became commander in chief of the Irish Volunteers. Rearrested in 1918, he escaped from Lincoln prison in January 1919 and shortly later was elected president of Dail Eireann, the legislature of the newly proclaimed Irish Republic. As the Anglo-Irish War intensified, de Valera traveled throughout the United States raising funds. He returned to Ireland in December 1920 and took part in negotiations with the British government in early 1921. However, he did not join the delegation that traveled to London later that year and rejected the Anglo-Irish Treaty the delegates signed, objecting to the oath of allegiance to the British crown and the continued partition of Ireland. When the Dail narrowly approved the Treaty in 1922, de Valera withdrew from the government and sided with the republicans in the ensuing Irish Civil War. In 1926, he split with the republicans and left Sinn Féin to form his own party, Fianna Fail. Advocating separation from Britain and an end to partition, in 1932 Fianna Fail won a majority of seats in the Dail, and de Valera became prime minister or Taoiseach (1932–48, 1951–54, 1957–59) as well as minister for external affairs. De Valera also became president of the council of the League of Nations in 1932 and president of the assembly of the League six years later. As Taoiseach, de Valera won passage of a new constitution for Ireland (1937) which deleted references to Britain and recognized the special position of the Roman Catholic Church. He negotiated another Anglo-Irish agreement (1938) to regain control of certain Irish ports, and refused to relinquish these ports during World War II, when Ireland declared its neutrality. In 1959, his eyesight failing, de Valera stepped down as Taoiseach and was elected to two terms as president of Eire (1959–73). He died in 1975.

Although de Valera considered Shakespeare his favorite author and praised the Anglo-Irish writers such as Jonathan Swift, Edmund Burke, and Oliver Goldsmith (Bromage 1956, 45; Cronin 1982, 7), his own speeches, writings, and policies were most obviously influenced by romantic nationalists such as Thomas Davis, John Mitchel, Charles Gavan Duffy, and A. M. Sullivan, who were associated with the movement known as Young Ireland. In a speech on St. Patrick's Day, 1943, that outlined his view of the Irish past and its present mission, de Valera particularly celebrated the work of the Young Irelanders, whose writings "inspired our nation and moved it spiritually as it had hardly been moved since the golden age of Irish civilization" (de Valera 1980, 466).

Archives

Franciscan Library Dun Mhuire, Killiney, County Dublin: de Valera's correspondence and private papers. This material is currently being catalogued by the University College Dublin Archives as part of an agreement between the two institutions.

House of Lords Record Office: The Parliamentary Archives: correspondence with David Lloyd George, 1921–22.

Public Record Office, Kew: Dublin Castle Papers. Official files and captured de Valera correspondence.

Printed Sources

Bowman, John. *De Valera and the Ulster Question, 1917–1973* (Oxford: Clarendon Press, 1982).

Bromage, Mary. *De Valera and the March of a Nation* (New York: Noonday Press, 1956).

Coogan, Tim Pat. *De Valera: Long Fellow, Long Shadow* (London: Hutchinson, 1993).

Cronin, Anthony. *Heritage Now: Irish Literature in English* (New York: St. Martins Press, 1982).

de Valera, Eamon. *Speeches and Statements of Eamon de Valera 1917–73*, Maurice Moynihan (ed.), (Dublin: Gill & Macmillan, 1980).

Dwyer, T. Ryle. *De Valera: The Man and the Myths* (Swords: Poolbeg, 1991).

Longford, Frank Pakenham, Earl of, and Thomas O'Neill. *Eamon de Valera* (London: Hutchinson, 1970).

O'Carroll, J. P., and J. A. Murphy (eds.). *De Valera and His Times* (Cork: Cork University Press, 1986).

Travers, Pauric. *Eamon de Valera* (Dundalk: Dundalgan, 1994).

Padraic Kennedy

DEWEY, JOHN (1859–1952)

Born in Burlington, Vermont, to Archibald S. Dewey, a Civil War veteran, and Lucina A. Rich, John was the oldest of three surviving sons. He enjoyed the outdoors. His mother, a strong Calvinist, encouraged him to join the First Congregational Church at the age of 11. His father gave him a deep interest in British literature and urged him to read widely. Faculty members of the University of Vermont were often guests in Dewey's home. Dewey graduated in 1879. At the university Dewey read Thomas H. Huxley's *Lessons in Elementary Physiology* and studied with G. H. Perkins, an evolutionist. He also read Scottish moral realism and Hegelianism with H.A.P. Torrey, whose influence was significant. Elements of Hegel and Darwin remained with Dewey throughout his life. Naturalism and historicism gradually replaced Christianity theology in his thought, but he maintained a life-time commitment of reformism from Protestantism.

In 1884 Dewey graduated from Johns Hopkins University with a Ph.D. in philosophy. George Sylvester Morris, an Hegelianist, and G. Stanley Hall, a Darwinian psychologist, significantly influenced Dewey at Hopkins. After teaching philosophy for 10 years, by 1894 Dewey established a laboratory school at the University of Chicago. He also stopped attending church. After a dispute with university authorities, Dewey went to Columbia in 1904. He retired in 1930. He remained active in political reforms (often a form of Protestant uplift) and writing until his death.

He once observed that "the forces that have influenced me have come from persons and from situations more than from books—not that I have not, I hope, learned a great deal from philosophical writings, but that what I have learned from them has been technical in comparison with what I have been forced to think upon and about because of some experience in which I found myself entangled." Because of that thought, Dewey celebrated the Vermont of his youth. "I shall never cease to be grateful that I was born at a time and a place where the earlier ideal of liberty and the self-governing community of citizens still sufficiently prevailed so that I unconsciously imbibed a sense of its meaning."

His significant influences are notable in three areas. Dewey was a founder of progressive education wherein the child's interests form the core of the educational program. *The School and Society* (1899) was his major educational contribution.

Dewey was a reformer. Instrumentalism, his version of pragmatism, was reform in behalf of democracy. People should be able to make individual choices, and, because they live in an industrial and urban context, government, as a balancing presence, must protect the individual as expressed in *The Public and Its Problems* (1927).

Dewey's third area of influence was as an academic philosopher. Dewey modified his Hegelianism but he was never completely divorced from German idealism. Darwinian naturalism with its appeal of scientific certainty meant that Dewey grounded his inquiry in the biological nature of the human organism. Dewey accepted the methodologies and results of experimental science. As inherited from pre-Darwinian philosophy and science, teleology was highly misleading. *Reconstruction in Philosophy* (1920), *Human Nature and Conduct* (1922), and *The Quest For Certainty* (1929) were Dewey's major publications.

Archives

Center for Dewey Studies, Southern Illinois University, Carbondale.

Printed Sources

Coughlan, Neil. *Young John Dewey* (Chicago: University of Chicago Press, 1975). Explains Hegel's impact on Dewey's thought.

Dewey, John. *The Collected Works of John Dewey*, 37 vols., Jo Ann Boydston (chief ed.), (Carbondale: Southern Illinois University Press, 1967–91).

Dykhuizen, George. *The Life and Mind of John Dewey* (Carbondale: Southern Illinois University Press, 1975).

Westbrook, Robert B. *John Dewey and American Democracy* (Ithaca: Cornell University Press, 1991). The best detailed account of Dewey's activities as a philosopher and citizen.

Donald K. Pickens

DICKEY, JAMES (1923–1997)

James Dickey was born in Atlanta, Georgia. He attended Clemson University but during his first semester left to join the Army Air Corps from 1942 to 1946. He began writing and publishing poems during officer training. After the war, Dickey completed his B.A. (1949) and M.A. (1950) in English at Vanderbilt University. During his first teaching job, Dickey was recalled to active duty in the Korean War. After his discharge, Dickey received a *Sewanee Review* fellowship that enabled him to move to Europe for a year to write poetry. Upon his return, Dickey accepted a teaching position at the University of Florida, but resigned in 1956 after a controversial poetry reading. Dickey became an advertising copywriter for a succession of agencies where he spent equal time writing narrative poetry characterized by myth, violence, fearful cruelty, and compassion. He published his first book-length collection of poems, *Into the Stone*, in 1960. A Guggenheim fellowship allowed him to quit advertising to work on his third book, *Helmets* (1964). The publication of *Buckdancer's Choice* (1965) brought Dickey his first major recognition, the National Book Award in poetry in 1966, and a two-year appointment as consultant in poetry at the Library of Congress. His self-described "barnstorming for poetry" across the country brought him greater notoriety as he promoted both poetry and himself. From 1969 until his death, Dickey taught poetry at the University of South Carolina. In the 1970s and 1980s, Dickey published books of poetry, his popular novel *Deliverance*, the autobiographical *Self-Interviews*, and his second novel, *Alnilam*. His collected poems, essays, and a third novel, *To the White Sea*, appeared in the early 1990s.

Dickey acknowledged literary influences on him during various stages of his writing career. He culled bits of philosophy from different poets and writers, absorbing and incorporating them into his own work. Dickey counted the poets Theodore Roethke, **Dylan Thomas,** and Gerard Manley Hopkins as early influences. George Barker's sense of style, Kenneth Patchen's attitude, W. S. Graham's method and diction, Rainer Rilke's insight and attitude, Stephen Spender's idealism, Randall Jarrell's humanistic feeling of compassion, and Robert Penn Warren's violence were qualities he emulated (Dickey 1970, 27–28, 34). He got creative stimulation from philosopher Heraclitus's evocative images and parables, and admired James Agee's verbal sensibility (Dickey 1970, 69, 75). Dickey cited Thomas Hardy's inventiveness with forms and **T. S. Eliot**'s use of the Osiris myth as influences on his first book (Dickey 1970, 84–85). In a letter to his wife in 1953, Dickey said he was striving for "fast, athletic, imaginative, and muscular vigor that I want to identify as my particular kind of writing." Dickey taught himself to read French and wrote, "the French writers have done me much good . . . I want to [develop] the sense of immediacy in poetry, the controlled spontaneity that I am convinced my writing should have . . ." (Sept. 25, 1954, in Dickey 2003, 226-28). A voracious reader of writers he disliked as well as admired, Dickey purchased a breadth of books on existential philosophy (**Albert Camus,** Søren Kierkegaard, Friedrich Nietzsche), mythology and primitive religion, literary biographies (Agee, Warren, Roethke), apocalyptic poetry, and French poetry (Jules Superveille, Pierre Reverdy, André Frenaud, René Guy Cadon).

Archives

Special Collections Department, Thomas Cooper Library, University of South Carolina, Columbia, S.C. Dickey's 18,000-volume personal library.

Special Collections Department, Robert W. Woodruff Library, Emory University, Atlanta, Ga. Notebooks and correspondence (published 1996 and 1999).

University Archives, John West Campus Library and Conference Center, Washington University, Clayton, Mo. Unpublished essays and addresses.

Printed Sources

Calhoun, Richard J., and Robert W. Hill. *James Dickey* (Boston: Twayne, 1983).

Dickey, Christopher. *Summer of Deliverance; a Memoir of Father and Son* (New York: Simon & Schuster, 1998).

Dickey, James. *The One Voice of James Dickey: His Letters and Life, 1942-1969.* Gordon van Ness (ed.), (Columbia: University of Missouri Press, 2003).

Dickey, James. *Self-Interviews.* Recorded and edited by Barbara and James Reiss (Garden City, N.Y.: Doubleday, 1970).

Susan Hamburger

DIETRICH, MARLENE (1901–1992)

Marlene Dietrich was born as Marie Magdalene Dietrich in Schöneberg, near Berlin, the daughter of police lieutenant Louis Dietrich, who died in 1907. When her mother, Josephine Felsing, remarried, Marie acquired the surname of her stepfather, army officer Eduard von Losch. About this time she contracted "*Marie Magdalene*" to "Marlene." She and her older sister Elisabeth, tutored at home by their mother and governesses, were each fluent in both French and English by the age of 12. Her mother also fostered her talent for voice, piano, and violin, hiring private teachers for the two instruments in 1915. After Colonel von Losch was killed in World War I, Frau von Losch urged Marlene toward a career as a concert violinist. Marlene moved from Berlin to Weimar in 1919 to continue her violin studies. There she met Alma Mahler-Gropius and immersed herself in the Bauhaus culture and Gustav Mahler's legacy. Her diligent concentration on her instrument gained her admission to the prestigious Hochschule für Musik in Berlin in 1921. She practiced so hard that she did severe neurological damage to her left wrist and had to give the violin up in 1922.

Swallowing her bitter disappointment, and idolizing Henny Porten, she determined to become an actress instead. To spare her disapproving mother's feelings, she changed her surname back to "Dietrich." The prominent producer/director Max Reinhardt accepted her into his Deutsche Theaterschule on her second attempt, and by the end of 1922 she was playing small roles in his repertory productions of several plays, including Shakespeare's *The Taming of the Shrew*. Her success on stage came to the attention of Georg Jacoby, who directed her in her first film, *Der kleine Napoleon*, in 1923. With the release of *Der blaue Engel* in 1930, she was famous throughout Germany. Josef von Sternberg, the director of that film, brought her to America in 1930, directed her in *Morocco*, released *The Blue Angel*, and directed her in five more films. Many critics accused von Sternberg of being her Svengali, but her outspoken independence soon proved them wrong. When he unilaterally ended their professional relationship in 1935, her stardom as both actress and singer was secure. His career never again reached such heights, but she later triumphed in *Destry Rides Again, Stage Fright, Witness for the Prosecution, Judgment at Nuremberg*, and on nightclub stages around the world.

Dietrich was familiar with German drama from Johann Wolfgang von Goethe to Hugo von Hofmannsthal to **Bertolt Brecht** and beyond. She was friends with and knew the works of **Ernest Hemingway, Erich Maria Remarque, Noël Coward,** Jean Cocteau, Alfred Kerr, Kenneth Tynan, **André Malraux**, and Carl Zuckmayer. She knew many poems of Goethe and Rainer Maria Rilke by heart.

Archives

In 1993 Dietrich's entire estate, including about 300,000 leaves of papers and correspondence and about 15,000 photographs, was moved to Berlin to create the permanent Marlene Dietrich Collection at the Stiftung Deutsche Kinemathek.

Printed Sources

Bach, Steven. *Marlene Dietrich: Life and Legend* (New York: Morrow, 1992; Da Capo, 2000).
Dickens, Homer. *The Complete Films of Marlene Dietrich* (New York: Carol, 1992).
Dietrich, Marlene. *Ich bin, Gott sei Dank, Berlinerin* (Frankfurt am Main: Ullstein, 1987), trans. as *Marlene* by Salvator Attanasio (New York: Grove, 1989).

Frewin, Leslie. *Dietrich: The Story of a Star* (New York: Stein and Day, 1967).

Higham, Charles. *Marlene: The Life of Marlene Dietrich* (New York: Norton, 1977).

Morley, Sheridan. *Marlene Dietrich* (London: Elm Tree, 1976; New York: McGraw-Hill, 1977).

O'Connor, Patrick. *Dietrich: Style and Substance* (New York: Dutton, 1991).

Riva, Maria. *Marlene Dietrich: By Her Daughter* (New York: Knopf, 1993).

Silver, Charles. *Marlene Dietrich* (New York: Pyramid, 1974).

Spoto, Donald. *Blue Angel: The Life of Marlene Dietrich* (New York: Doubleday, 1992).

Eric v.d. Luft

DIMAGGIO, JOSEPH PAUL (1914–1999)

Joe DiMaggio was born in Martinez, California. The eighth of nine children born to Sicilian immigrants Giuseppe and Rosalie DiMaggio, the young DiMaggio grew up in the North Beach section of San Francisco, California. Days for DiMaggio and his immediate circle of friends were spent playing hooky, hanging out at the docks, fishing off the pier, and playing poker for pennies. The classroom was not DiMaggio's favorite place to be, with childhood friend Frank Venezia recalling DiMaggio's shyness and the reclusiveness of Giuseppe and Rosalie, who spoke only Italian. Relatively quickly, DiMaggio distinguished himself in the neighborhood as a ballplayer, finding in baseball something he could do well and earn a living playing, eventually capping his West Coast career with a season for the San Francisco Seals. In the early years of DiMaggio's thirteen seasons in center field for the New York Yankees, Lefty Gomez recalls a shy DiMaggio who took a small radio on a two-week road trip and listened to big-band music and quiz shows like Dr. IQ, and read the sports pages. Throughout the course of his career in Yankee pinstripes, DiMaggio remained a private figure while contributing to nine World Series titles, winning three American League Most Valuable Player awards and two batting titles, and serving for two years in the U.S. Army. DiMaggio's record for hitting safely in 56 consecutive games in the 1941 season stands today. DiMaggio's post-Yankee years were marked by his brief marriage to Marilyn Monroe, broadcasting and coaching efforts for the Oakland As, spokesman roles for Mr. Coffee products and Bowery Savings Bank, and recognition until his death as baseball's greatest living player.

Throughout most of his playing career, DiMaggio was a figure brought to life for fans through the play-by-play of radio broadcasters and the words of sports writers. For his steady, fabled presence on the field and regular appearances at Toots Shor's in New York, DiMaggio remained an intensely private person. During his years as a Yankee, DiMaggio studied the game itself. Not an avid reader, DiMaggio is reputed to have read Norman Mailer's *The Naked and the Dead*, and had his favorite sports columnists, including Looie Effrat from the *New York Times*, Jimmy Cannon, Bill Corum, Grantland Rice, Red Smith, and Arthur Daley. In addition to being a fan of their writing style, DiMaggio enjoyed their relaxed company and off-the-record confidences at Toots Shor's. Columnist and friend Walter Winchell took DiMaggio out for late drives listening to the police scanner. Jackie Gleason made DiMaggio laugh, and fights at Madison Square Garden stoked his competitive spirit. DiMaggio also kept his eye on Wednesdays when the latest issue of Superman comics appeared on the stands, often asking others, like Lefty Gomez, to buy the comic book for him. DiMaggio's brief marriage to Marilyn Monroe exposed him to Antoine de Saint-Exupery's *The Little Prince*, Mickey Spillane, and Jules Verne. Monroe also kept the Bible, Walt Whitman's *Leaves of Grass*, **Ernest Hemingway**'s *The Old Man and the Sea*, **James Joyce**'s *Ulysses*, Lev Tolstoy's *War and Peace*, **Carl Sandburg**'s *Abraham Lincoln, vols. 1–6*, Ralph Waldo Emerson's *Essays*, and Sigmund Freud's *Psychology of Everyday Life* on her shelves, though it is not known whether DiMaggio read the books. Throughout his entire life, including his time with Marilyn Monroe, DiMaggio remained a fan of movie and television westerns. Several sources cite the post-Yankee DiMaggio's favorite book as being Thomas J. Stanley and William Danko's *The Millionaire Next Door: The Surprising Secrets of America's Wealthy*. In his later years, DiMaggio educated himself by devouring newspapers, including the editorial pages, and nurturing an addiction to 24-hour news, including CNN, CNBC, and C-Span. The mystique of DiMaggio carried over to the realm of stories with Ernest Hemingway's Santiago telling the boy he would like to take the great DiMaggio fishing, while Simon and Garfunkle's 1968 "Mrs. Robinson" asked "Where have you gone, Joe DiMaggio," searching for lost heroes.

Archives

Major League Baseball archives, New York, New York.
Player Clipping Files, National Baseball Library, Cooperstown, New York.

Printed Sources

Allen, Maury. *Where Have You Gone, Joe DiMaggio?* (New York: E.P. Dutton & Company, Inc., 1975).
Cramer, Richard Ben. *Joe DiMaggio: The Hero's Life* (New York: Simon & Schuster, 2000).
Johnson, Dick, and Glenn Stout. *DiMaggio, An Illustrated Life* (New York: Walker and Company, 1995).
Moore, Jack B. *A Bio-bibliograph*. (Westport, Conn.: Greenwood Publishing Group, 1986).
———. *Joe DiMaggio: Baseball's Yankee Clipper* (Westport, Conn.: Greenwood Publishing Group, 1986).
Whittingham, Richard (ed.). *The DiMaggio Albums: Selections From Public and Private Collections Celebrating the Baseball Career of Joe DiMaggio* (New York: G.P. Putnam's Sons, 1989).

Devon Niebling

DISNEY, WALTER ELIAS (1901–1966)

Walt Disney was a hard-working midwesterner born in Chicago without money or advantages who created an unmatched American entertainment empire. Walt Disney found success due to his ability to innovate, to sense what the public would like, and to pursue his dreams with workaholic intensity. Unlike many entrepreneurs for whom amassing wealth is the end goal, Disney's goal was the creation of entertainment for families and, ultimately, the bettering of life through entertainment. From cartoons to live-action films to educational nature documentaries, Disney continually moved into new entertainment areas, including amusement parks and planned communities of the future. For a political conservative, Disney's interest in innovation was remarkable. He was the first to work with storyboards (now a standard feature film tool) and the first to match sound with animation. He embraced Technicolor and nearly every other technological innovation he felt could make his entertainment products better. He was the first film mogul to embrace television. In fact, Disney was so linked to innovation that it was long rumored that Disney had asked that his body be frozen upon death so that if future science progressed, he might be unfrozen and revived. While false, the rumor shows the intense originality and spirit of innovation associated in the public mind with Disney by the time of his death. His President's Medal of Freedom (1964) citation read "Artist and impresario, in the course of entertaining an age, he has created an American folklore." Disney changed the face of American popular culture. This midwestern "go-getter" who moved to Los Angeles with just $40 in his pocket has had a lasting impact on the U.S. entertainment industry. Disney's dual import as entrepreneur and entertainer is reflected in the fact that when *Time Magazine* recognized the turn of the century by naming in 2001 the top 100 leaders of the past century, Walt Disney's name appeared among the top ten entertainment leaders as well as among the top ten "Builders and Titans," something no other entry achieved. In 2002, the company he founded was the world's second-largest media company.

Taught to read by his mother, Disney was an average student, perhaps because he held a variety of jobs outside of school. He graduated from Benton School, Kansas City, in 1917 and enrolled that year in McKinley High School in Chicago upon his family's return to Chicago. He studied anatomy, pen technique, and cartooning three nights a week at the Chicago Art Institute. However, after only one year of high school, Disney joined the Red Cross Ambulance Corps in November 1918 as World War I concluded and never returned to high school.

According to biographer Bob Thomas, Disney read everything by Mark Twain, whose Missouri childhood was similar to his own. Disney was fascinated by the success stories of Horatio Alger. Disney enjoyed the storytelling of Robert Louis Stevenson, Sir Walter Scott, and Charles Dickens. Disney was keenly influenced by his early twentieth-century childhood in his literary tastes. His entertainment empire's products reflect that taste, with films based on late nineteenth-century literature, including Lewis Carroll's *Alice in Wonderland*, Rudyard Kipling's *The Jungle Book*, Robert Louis Stevenson's *Treasure Island*, and Jules Verne's *20,000 Leagues Under the Sea* as well as folk and fairy tales such as "Snow White" and "Cinderella." He used American folklore as well, producing films like "Davy Crockett." Disney sought all literary materials that could be transformed into film and television shows that would serve the public's need for family entertainment. Disney's 1946 film *Song of the South* was based on the Uncle Remus stories of Joel Chandler Harris, which he had enjoyed since childhood. Disney and his staff plumbed literature that might be successfully adapted to film and television, always with family entertainment and good storytelling the high priorities. For example, *Mary Poppins* (1964) had its beginnings twenty years earlier when Disney saw the book on his daughter's bedside table, and after reading it himself adapted the collection of stories about a nanny to film. All who knew him agree Disney was most keenly skilled not in art and animation but in story-editing and storytelling. The phrase "Disney version" has come to mean in popular culture the "cleaned up" version of a once-violent fairy tale or other story, made fit by the Disney sensibility for families to hear, rather than the unvarnished violence, crude humor, or risqué materials created by other entertainment firms.

Archives

The Walt Disney Archive, Walt Disney Corporate Headquarters, 500 South Buena Vista, Burbank, California.

Printed Sources

Schickel, Richard. *The Disney Version: The Life, Times, Art and Commerce of Walt Disney* (New York: Simon & Schuster, 1968).

Thomas, Bob. *Walt Disney: An American Original* (New York: Hyperion, 1976).

Ann Shillinglaw

DJILAS, MILOVAN (1911–1995)

Milovan Djilas was born in Podbišće, Montenegro. Desiring a just social order, in contrast to the rule of clans and blood feuds in his native land, Djilas became a supporter of communism while a student in secondary school and was an active member of the Party at the University of Belgrade in the early 1930s. He was imprisoned by Yugoslavia's royal dictatorship for his political activities (1933–36). A convinced Stalinist, he acted as a propagandist and recruiter for the Party in the late 1930s. During World War II, Djilas served as a principal lieutenant to **Josip Broz Tito** (1892–1980) in the Partisan army. Near the end of the war and immediately afterward, he visited Moscow as a representative of Tito and the Yugoslav communists. These visits became the basis of his book *Conversations with Stalin* (1962), a seminal portrait of the Soviet dictator. Djilas held the posts of vice president of communist Yugoslavia and president of the Federal Assembly following the war. His warnings against the expanding bureaucratic state and calls for intellectual freedom led to his ouster from leadership in January 1954. In March 1954 he resigned from the Party. Between 1956 and 1966 he was tried six times for crimes against the state and imprisoned for a total of nine years. Djilas continued to write during this time, publishing his works outside Yugoslavia. Among his books are the classic critiques of the communist state: *The New Class* (1957), *The Unperfect Society* (1969), and *Fall of the New Class* (1998). In the late 1980s and 1990s Djilas turned his criticism to the nationalist regime of Slobodan Milošević.

In the diary he kept during his imprisonment under the Communist regime, Djilas noted in one entry three authors as major influences on his literary and intellectual development: Njegoš, Dostoyevsky, and Marx. Primary among these was Petar Petrović Njegoš (1813–51), the national bard of Djilas's native Montenegro. Djilas drew from Njegoš's epic poetry a romantic vision and an awareness of the individual's proclivities to both good and evil, and he paid homage to Njegoš by writing a biographical study (*Njegoš: Poet, Prince, Bishop*, 1966) that he hoped would introduce the poet to a non-Yugoslav audience. Djilas discovered Fyodor Dostoyevsky when Djilas was a student in secondary school. Initially moved by the Russian writer's depiction of the realities of human existence and the belief of his characters in a more just society, Djilas cited Dostoyevsky as one of the principal influences in his move toward communism. Later, after his imprisonment, he reread many of Dostoyevsky's works and understood that Dostoyevsky proposed an entirely different philosophical path: "He is not only an author of genius and a thinker, but he also creates a new spiritual world. It may be that he is even a new civilization" (Djila 1975, 110). Because Djilas had adopted communism out of a sincere desire for social justice and equality, inspired by his reading of Dostoyevsky and authors such as Immanuel Kant and Jean Jacques Rousseau, he was already an adherent to the ideology when he first read Karl Marx. Even after his resignation from the League of Yugoslav Communists and his realization that Marxism's claims to universal truth were false, Djilas maintained an appreciation for Marx's humanistic critique of capitalism and his vision of an ideal society. Djilas believed that his warning against the bureaucratic state, *The New Class*, was a Marxist book, and he held that twentieth-century Marxist regimes had nothing in common with Marx's original ideas.

Archives

Yugoslav Biographical Files I, 1948-1991, in the Records of Radio Free Europe/Radio Liberty Research Institute, Open Society Archives at Central European University, Budapest. Clippings from Yugoslav and foreign press, news agency releases, Radio Free Europe/Radio Liberty research papers, and excepts from Yugoslav radio broadcasting on Djilas.

Printed Sources

Djilas, Milovan. *Parts of a Lifetime*, Michael and Deborah Milenkovitch (eds.), (New York: Harcourt Brace Jovanovich, 1975).
Reinhartz, Dennis. *Milovan Djilas: A Revolutionary as Writer* (Boulder: East European Monographs, 1981).

Bruce R. Berglund

DOS PASSOS, JOHN (1896–1970)

John Dos Passos was born in a Chicago hotel room, the son of an illegitimate union between a successful married corporate lawyer, John R. Dos Passos, who could recite entire scenes from Shakespeare's plays, and the widowed Lucy Addison Sprigg, whom he eventually married in 1910. John Madison—he would not take his father's name until he was sixteen (Pizer 1988, 12)— would become one of the primary post–World War I chroniclers of American culture. Dos Passos's childhood was varied, having no stable home, friends, routine, or consistent company of his father. After beginning his education miserable in an English boarding school, Dos Passos entered the Choate School in Connecticut under the name of John Madison in 1907. He remained there until 1911. In 1912, at the age of 15, Dos Passos entered Harvard University. After graduating from Harvard in 1916, Dos Passos served three tours in World War I, in the Norton-Harjes ambulance service in France, the American Red Cross ambulance service in Italy, and in 1918 he enlisted in the U.S. Army Medical Corps. After leaving the army, Dos Passos, then an ardent socialist though reluctant to associate himself officially with the Communist party, began his prolific literary career. Dos Passos's socialist leanings were apparent in his writing for *The New Masses* and *The Daily Worker*, and his direction of the New Playwright's Theatre in New York (1926–29). In the following decades, Dos Passos produced a series of novels that would make him one of the most innovative of a generation of important novelists of the post–World War I period, including **Ernest Hemingway** (who sustained a decade-long friendship with Dos Passos) and **F. Scott Fitzgerald.** In his greatest novels, Dos Passos described "the Great Betrayal" following the First World War. In *Three Soldiers* (1921), *Manhattan*

Transfer (1925), and his trilogy *U.S.A.* (published as a single volume in 1938), Dos Passos attempts to capture and recreate the manifold complexities (political, economic, cultural) of the United States in the years following World War I.

It was at Harvard that Dos Passos's unique novelistic technique began to develop. While there, Dos Passos discovered both impressionistic painting and the forming literary modernist movement, reading early Eliot poems in *Blast* (Becker 1974, 22). Dos Passos was also influenced by the budding imagist movement, reviewing the work of Edgar Lee Masters, **T. S. Eliot,** and **Ezra Pound** for the Harvard *Advocate*. The movement differed drastically from Dos Passos's other influences, which included the realist novels of Flaubert, to whom Dos Passos credits his having learned an "obsession with the *mot juste*" (Becker 1974, 17), and those of Theodore Dreiser, whom Dos Passos befriended. Noting that while at Harvard "many of us chose to live in the 1890's," Dos Passos cites *The Yellow Book* (ed. Henry Harland), *The Hound of Heaven* (Francis Thompson), and Arthur Machen's *The Hill of Dreams* as particularly important in his formative college years (Knowles 1981, 219). These fantastical texts, coupled with his readings of **James Joyce**'s *Ulysses*, Thorstein Veblen's *Theory of the Leisure Class*, and the Belgian poet Emile Varharen, all contributed to Dos Passos's later themes of socialism, travel, and recording the inner voices of his characters. Additionally, in a 1960 interview, Dos Passos cites Frank Norris, the Italian futurists, Arthur Rimbaud, Stendahl's *Chartruse De Parme*, William Makepeace Thackeray's *Vanity Fair*, Daniel Defoe, Henry Fielding, and Tobias Smollett as all being influential on his writing (Pizer 1988, 239). As early as 1915, Dos Passos declared, "by all the gods of Flaubert, of Homer, of modern realism and the new poetry, . . . that Prize fights are every bit as good a subject for poetry as fine ladies and illicit love affairs" (Becker 1974, 17). Thus, Dos Passos's influences include lyrical imagism coupled with realist subject matter, contemporary political and cultural motifs, and varied political stances, which all converged to make Dos Passos one of the most important observers, chroniclers, and novelists of the twentieth century.

Archives

John Dos Passos Archive at the University of Virginia, Special Collections, University of Virginia Library, Charlottesville, Virginia.

John Dos Passos Collection, Mcfarlin Library, University of Tulsa, Tulsa, Oklahoma.

John Dos Passos Collection, Founders Memorial Library, Northern Illinois University, De Kalb, Illlinois.

John Dos Passos Collection, The Lilly Library, Indiana University, Bloomington, Indiana.

Printed Sources

Becker, George. *John Dos Passos* (New York: Frederick Ungar Publishing Co., 1974).

Davis, Robert. *John Dos Passos* (Minneapolis: University of Minnesota Press, 1962).

Knowles, A.S. Jr. "John Dos Passos." In *Dictionary of Literary Biography*, vol. 9 (Detroit: Gale Research Group, 1981), 217–36.

Ludington, Townsend. *John Dos Passos: A Twentieth Century Odyssey* (New York: Dutton, 1980).

——— (ed.). *The Fourteenth Chronicle; Letters and Diaries of John Dos Passos* (Boston: Gambit, 1973).

Pizer, Donald. *Dos Passos' U.S.A.: A Critical Study* (Charlottesville: The University of Virginia Press, 1988).

———— (ed.). *John Dos Passos: The Major Nonfiction Prose* (Detroit: Wayne State University Press, 1988).

Spencer Carr, Virginia. *Dos Passos: A Life* (Garden City, N.Y.: Doubleday, 1984).

Wagner, Linda. *Dos Passos: Artist as American* (Austin: University of Texas Press, 1979).

James Mellis

DUBČEK, ALEXANDER (1921–1992)

Alexander Dubček was born in Uhrovec, in western Slovakia. His father, a carpenter and Communist Party member, brought the family to the Kirghiz Soviet Republic in 1925 to help build the new socialist state. The family lived in Kirghizstan until 1930, when they moved to Gorky (now Nizhni Novgorod) where Dubček completed his schooling. The family returned to Slovakia in 1938, and Dubček held a variety of menial jobs. During the war he took part in the communist-led resistance against the Nazi-client regime in Slovakia, and he was wounded in the armed uprising of 1944 that was put down by German troops. Following the Czechoslovak Communist Party's takeover in February 1948, Dubček rose quickly in the ranks. He was sent to the Party's High Political School in Moscow (1955–58), was named committee secretary in the Slovak capital of Bratislava upon his return, became First Party secretary in Slovakia in 1963, and was a member of the Party Presidium from 1962 to 1969. An advocate of political and economic reform and a defender of Slovak interests in the multinational state, Dubček succeeded the hardliner Antonín Novotný as first secretary of the Czechoslovak Communist Party in January 1968. As head of the Party leadership in Prague, Dubček elevated reform-minded members, who drafted a blueprint for the creation of a "new model of socialist democracy." The Action Program, adopted in April 1968, was official policy during the period of dramatic reforms known as the Prague Spring. On August 21, 1968, these reforms came to an end as Soviet forces invaded Czechoslovakia. Dubček was kidnapped by KGB troops and forced in Moscow to agree to concessions. He resigned his leadership post in April 1969 and was expelled from the Party in 1970. He worked as a mechanic in Slovakia until November 1989, when he returned to Prague, appearing alongside **Václav Havel** at the antiregime demonstrations. After the fall of the communist government, he served as chairman of the Federal Assembly until his death in a car accident on September 1, 1992.

Dubček's early education was sporadic and marred by Soviet ideology: the school in the Kirghiz town where his family settled lacked sufficient textbooks and trained teachers, while his schooling in Gorky took place under the most rigid years of Stalinism. As Dubček recalled, "Even when the instruction was good in strictly pedagogical terms, it was too heavily burdened with Marxist-Leninist ideology and hardly conducive to independent thinking" (Dubček, 25–26). Although he was uncertain about the Party's explanation of the purges, Dubček could not bring himself to question the rule of Stalin and the Communist Party. Dubček first studied Marxism-Leninism when he was sent to High Political School in 1955. While in Moscow, he took particular interest in the lesser-known writings of Karl Marx (1818–1883), including *The 18th Brumaire of Louis Napoleon* (1852). He questioned the limited perspective of the Party school's curriculum, and he also became aware of the incongruities between the ideas of Marx and those of **Vladimir Lenin.** In particular, he questioned why the focus of socialist activities should not be in an advanced industrial state, such as Czechoslovakia or East Germany, rather than backward Russia. Another important influence on his political thinking was events in Moscow during his time there; his studies at the High Political School coincided with the beginnings of de-Stalinization in the Soviet Union, including the 1956 "Secret Speech" by **Nikita Khrushchev** (1894–1971) denouncing **Josef Stalin**'s cult of personality. Upon becoming head of the Czechoslovak Communist Party in 1968, Dubček was convinced of the need for economic reform and greater participation in governance. Consistent throughout Dubček's life was his love of the Slovak nation, and he took pride in the fact that he had been born in the same house as the poet L'udovit Štur (1815–56), the founder of the Slovak literary language.

Archives

Archive of the Central Committee of the Czechoslovak Communist Party, State Central Archive, Prague, Czech Republic.

Printed Sources

Dubček, Alexander, with Andra Sugar, *Dubcek Speaks* (London: I.B. Tauris, 1990).
———. *Hope Dies Last: The Autobiography of Alexander Dubček*, Jiří Hochmann (trans. and ed.), (New York: Kodansha, 1993).
Shawcross, William. Dubcek: *Dubček and Czechoslovakia 1918–1990* (London: Hogarth, 1990).

Bruce R. Berglund

DUCHAMP, MARCEL (1887–1968)

Marcel Duchamp, one of the most influential artists of the twentieth century, first achieved notoriety with his painting, *Nude Descending a Staircase, No. 2* (1912), which was singled out at the Armory Show (1913). He invented "readymades," everyday objects elevated to the status of art, left his *Large Glass* (1915–23) "definitively unfinished," constructed a female alter ego for himself in Rrose Sélavy (1920), and played chess obsessively. In the 1920s and 1930s he came into contact with the European Dada groups, then was courted by **André Breton** and the surrealists.

Duchamp was born in Blainville, a suburb of Rouen, and received an upper-middle-class education at the Lycée Corneille. He later sporadically attended the Académie Julian, a private art school. He worked briefly as a librarian at the Bibliothèque Sainte-Geneviève in Paris (1913–14). Later in life he admitted, perhaps too modestly, to being unable to read complex works. This has not prevented scholars from searching for hermeneutic keys to his art that have included alchemical and cabalistic literature. Altogether, he is regarded as a most literary artist because of the importance of language in his art. When he did admit to influences, he cited authors rather than artists. Duchamp was influenced by the Symbolists of the 1880s and 1890s, particularly the poetry of Stéphane Mallarmé and Jules Laforgue. Duchamp liked Laforgue's prose narratives, *Moralités légendaires (Moral Tales)*, especially his ironic retelling of *Hamlet*, and a group of drawings from 1911and 1912 have direct references to Laforgue's poetry ("Encore á cet astre," for instance). Early in his career, while Duchamp was still allied to the cubists, he was encouraged by **Guillaume Apollinaire.** On a trip to Switzerland in 1912, Duchamp heard the poet read *Zone* for the first time. His *Large Glass* (1915–23), a monumental glass piece filled with parodic mechanical imagery, may reflect its influence. Duchamp was decisively influenced by his experience of avant-garde theater, especially the absurdist plays of Alfred Jarry and Raymond Roussel. A 1912 performance of Roussel's *Impressions d'Afrique*, a proto-surrealist burlesque about a group of shipwreck survivors, galvanized Duchamp's interests in linguistic invention and, as he said, "the madness of the unexpected." His pieces that utilize the effects of chance may demonstrate the artist's appreciation for Alfred Jarry's satirical "pataphysics" as articulated in Jarry's novel, *Gestes et opinions du docteur Faustroll, pataphysicien* (written 1898; published in 1911). Additionally, Jarry's short, blasphemous "The Passion Considered as an Uphill Bicycle Race" (1903) may have inspired Duchamp's 1914 drawing *To Have the Apprentice in the Sun* (1914). Finally, Duchamp's *Large Glass* (1915–23) may demonstrate an awareness of the bizarre mechanomorphism of Jarry's *Le Surmâle* (*The Supermale*, 1902) in which an oversexed hero makes love mechanically to an American girl. Along similar lines, the splintery nude woman in Duchamp's *Nude Descending a Staircase, No. 2* (1912) has been linked to the future woman in Villier de L'Isle Adam's *L'Eve future* (1886).

Archives

The preponderance of Duchamp's artworks are housed in the Philadelphia Museum of Art as part of the Walter and Louise Arensberg Collection. Yale University and the Museum of Modern Art, New York, have other works. Examples of Duchamp's box projects, reproductions, and multiples exist in collections worldwide.

Philadelphia Museum of Art, Arensberg Archives, Philadelphia, Penn. Unpublished material and correspondence.

Printed Sources

Cabanne, Pierre. *Entretiens avec Marcel Duchamp* (Paris: Belfond, 1967); *Dialogues with Marcel Duchamp*, Ron Padgett (trans.), (New York: Viking Press, 1977).

Duchamp, Marcel. *Salt Seller: The Writings of Marcel Duchamp*. Michel Sanouillet and Elmer Peterson (eds.), (New York: Oxford University Press, 1973).

Schwarz, Arturo. *The Complete Works of Marcel Duchamp* (Milan: Schwarz, 1997).

Tomkins, Calvin. *Duchamp: A Biography* (New York: Henry Holt and Company, 1996).

Mark B. Pohlad

DUMONT, FERNAND (1927–1997)

Born in Montmorency (now a quarter of Québec City, Canada) on June 24, 1927, French-Canadian social scientist Fernand Dumont is an example of a son of proletarians who became one of the most influential intellectuals in his country. After going to a local Catholic school in Beauport (1933–41) and high school at the Collège des Frères du Sacré-Cœur de Limoilou in Québec City (1942–45), Fernand Dumont went to the Petit Séminaire de Québec (1946–49) and then to the Université Laval (1949–53) in Québec City, where he got a master's degree in social sciences. He did two Ph.D. theses: the first in Paris (June 1967) in sociology and the second at Université Laval (1987) in theology. His writings range among field studies, sociology, anthropology, philosophy, theology, history, and social theory, but also include poetry and essays. From 1955 to 1995, he was professor of sociology at Université Laval, where he cofounded an academic journal, *Recherches sociographiques*, in 1960. He also cowrote the *Livre blanc* (*White Book*, 1977), which created Bill 101 regarding the importance of French language in Québec, in 1977. Dumont won many prizes for his books, including in 1969 the governor of Canada's prestigious prize for his most influential book, *Le Lieu de l'homme. La culture comme distance et mémoire* (1968), introducing his theory of primary and secondary culture. He was the first president of the Institut québecois de recherche sur la culture (now INRS—Culture et société), in Québec City. He died of cancer on May 1, 1997.

When he was about ten years old, Dumont received as a school prize a copy of Robert Rumilly's *Mercier.* He read this biography of the premier of the province of Québec, Honoré Mercier (1840–94) many times. Dumont began to read serious books around the age of thirteen under the guidance of his first school mentor, Brother George, who suggested Corneille's plays and other French classics (Dumont and Cantin 2000, 43). While in tenth grade, Dumont worked at the Parlement Library in Québec City. There he discovered reading, as most of his previous schools had not had libraries. In his autobiography, *Récit d'une émigration. Mémoires,* Dumont remembered reading during this period Plato, G.W.F. Hegel, Alexis de Tocqueville, Émile Durkheim, Karl Jaspers, and Emmanuel Levinas (Dumont 2000, 54). While he was still young, he was impressed by a biography of Louis Pasteur *(La vie de Pasteur)* written by Pasteur's grandson, René Vallery-Radot. He also read articles by influential polemicists from Montreal, including historian Lionel Groulx and journalist André Laurendeau in journals such as *L'Action française* and *L'Action nationale.* While a student at Université Laval, Dumont appreciated Montesquieu and Auguste Comte. He didn't like Karl Marx's *Capital,* preferring Hegel's *Phenomenology of Spirit.* Among sociologists, Dumont was fond of the French tradition in sociology, with authors such as Durkheim, François Simiand, Maurice Halbwachs, Célestin Charles Alfred Bouglé, and Marcel Mauss. With notable exceptions such as Everett C. Hughes's famous study (*French Canada in Transition,* 1943), Dumont seldom mentioned authors from the United States, although many of his professors at Université Laval had studied in American universities. Later, while he lived in Paris (1953–55), Dumont said he was strongly influenced by his favorite professor at La Sorbonne, French philosopher Gaston Bachelard, especially by his book on epistemology *(La philosophie du non: essai d'une philosophie du nouvel esprit scientifique).* Along with Bachelard, Dumont considered Emmanuel Mounier and another French philosopher, Maurice Blondel, as his intellectual masters. Apart from philosophy and sociology, the young Dumont also read playwrights such as Georges Bernanos, Charles Péguy, Paul Claudel, and Shakespeare. A research chair on culture with the name of Fernand Dumont was created in Québec City in 1998; he is still considered the most important sociologist in Canadian history.

Archives

Chaire Fernand-Dumont, INRS Culture, société et urbanisation, Québec City, Canada. http://chaire_fernand_dumont.inrs-ucs.uquebec.ca/pdf/corpus_fernand-dumont.pdf.

Printed Sources

Dumont, Fernand. *Récit d'une émigration. Mémoires* (Montréal: Boréal, 1997). This intellectual autobiography details literary influences.

———. *Un témoin de l'homme.* Serge Cantin (ed.), (Montréal: Hexagone, 2000). Transcriptions of interviews given by Fernand Dumont between 1965 and 1996.

———. *The Vigil of Quebec* [1971]; Sheila Fischman and Richard Howard (trans.), (Toronto: University of Toronto Press, 1974). Dumont's only book translated in English, about the Canadian political crisis of October 1970.

Weinstein, Michael A. *Culture Critique. Fernand Dumont and New Québec Sociology* (New York: St. Martin Press, 1985).

Yves Laberge

DÜRRENMATT, FRIEDRICH (1921–1990)

Friedrich Dürrenmatt was born in Konolfingen, Switzerland, the son of Hulda Zimmermann and Reinhold Dürrenmatt, the village pastor, and the grandson of the poet, satirist, and politician Ulrich Dürrenmatt. He attended elementary school in nearby Grosshochstetten from 1933 to 1935, when his family moved to Bern because his father was appointed Protestant chaplain of the Salem Hospital. Dürrenmatt attended the Freies Gymnasium, Bern, from 1935 to 1937, then, despite failing to be promoted in 1939, graduated from the Humboldtianum School, Bern, in 1941. His father wanted him to become a minister, but, inspired more by his grandfather's works than by his father's conservative respectability, Dürrenmatt diverged toward art and literature.

Except for the 1942–43 winter semester at the University of Zürich, Dürrenmatt was enrolled from 1941 to 1946 at the University of Bern. He was not a good student and sometimes felt ashamed that after 10 semesters he still had no degree. Originally he intended to study literature and become a painter, but his interests soon shifted toward the study of philosophy and the goal of becoming an author and playwright. Among the philosophers he read were Plato, Aristotle, Immanuel Kant, Georg Wilhelm Friedrich Hegel, Arthur Schopenhauer, Friedrich Nietzsche, and **Martin Heidegger.** He also read some theology and was particularly impressed by **Karl Barth**'s commentary on the Epistle to the Romans.

Among his Zürich professors was Emil Staiger, but Dürrenmatt thought him "highly pathetic" and gained more from informal evening sessions at the home of expressionist painter Walter Jonas, where the group would discuss the unconventional literature of Georg Büchner, Georg Heym, Ernst Jünger, **Franz Kafka,** Robert Musil, Georg Trakl, and others. Dürrenmatt may also have discovered **Albert Camus**, one of his most significant influences, around this time.

At Bern he studied under Fritz Strich, Emil Ermatinger, and Richard Herbertz. He spoke of writing a dissertation on Søren Kierkegaard's philosophy of tragedy, but never did. Instead he began writing plays that expressed the Kierkegaardian existentialist/absurdist point of view more poignantly than a prose essay could. The grotesqueness of Hieronymus Bosch's and George Grosz's paintings affected Dürrenmatt's subsequent stories and plays as much as did the absurdity of Kafka's fiction.

Among the dramatists, poets, and literary authors he read in the early 1940s were Euripides, Sophocles, William Shakespeare, Johann Wolfgang von Goethe, Johann Christoph Friedrich von Schiller, Christoph Martin Wieland, Gotthold Ephraim Lessing, Friedrich Hölderlin, August Strindberg, Johann Nepomuk Nestroy, Gerhart Hauptmann, **Thornton Wilder, Bertolt Brecht,** Max Frisch, and his favorite, Aristophanes. Soon after he met his first wife, actress Lotti Geissler, in 1946, she starred in one of Henrik Ibsen's plays at the Stadttheater in Basel.

Archives

Dürrenmatt's papers and memorabilia are at the Centre Dürrenmatt in Neuchâtel, Switzerland, the gift of his widow, Charlotte Kerr, in collaboration with the Schweizerisches Literaturarchiv (Swiss Archives of Literature) and the Friedrich-Dürrenmatt-Stiftung (Friedrich Dürrenmatt Foundation).

Printed Sources

Arnold, Armin. *Friedrich Dürrenmatt* (New York: Ungar, 1972).

Crockett, Roger Alan. *Understanding Friedrich Dürrenmatt* (Columbia: University of South Carolina Press, 1998).

Fritzen, Bodo, and Heimy F. Taylor (eds.). *Friedrich Dürrenmatt: A Collection of Critical Essays* (Normal, Ill.: Applied Literature Press, 1979).

Jenny, Urs. *Dürrenmatt: A Study of His Plays*, Keith Hamnett and Hugh Rorrison (trans.), (London: Eyre Methuen, 1978).

Lazar, Moshe (ed.). *Play Dürrenmatt* (Malibu: Undena, 1983).

Peppard, Murray B. *Friedrich Dürrenmatt* (New York: Twayne, 1969).

Tiusanen, Timo. *Dürrenmatt: A Study in Plays, Prose, Theory* (Princeton, N.J.: Princeton University Press, 1977).

Whitton, Kenneth S. *Dürrenmatt: Reinterpretation in Retrospect* (New York: St. Martin's, 1990).

———. *The Theatre of Friedrich Dürrenmatt: A Study in the Possibility of Freedom* (London: Wolff; Atlantic Highlands, N.J.: Humanities, 1980).

Eric v.d. Luft

DYLAN, BOB (1941–)

Dylan was born Robert Zimmerman in Duluth, Minnesota, and grew up in Hibbing. He briefly attended the University of Minnesota, 1959–60, before dropping out to pursue his musical career beginning in the off-campus area known as Dinkytown. Bobby Zimmerman became the folksinger Bob Dillon and finally Bob Dylan. After reading Woody Guthrie's autobiography, *Bound for Glory* (1943), Dylan moved to New York City's Greenwich Village. He frequently visited the ailing Guthrie in his New Jersey hospital room where Dylan internalized Guthrie's speech patterns and movements. When Dylan met Joan Baez in 1961, she became one of his biggest supporters, recording his songs and bringing him on stage to sing with her. A recording contract with Columbia Records led to the John Hammond–produced first album, *Bob Dylan* (1962). Dylan initially made his mark as a writer of protest songs but quickly moved on to successfully experiment with poetic lyrics unparalleled among contemporary songwriters of the 1960s. Defying stylistic trends, three-minute song length limits, and simplistic rhymes, Dylan set a standard for musical and artistic freedom that influenced generations of musicians. With each successive album, Dylan moved into fresh territory, exploring psychedelia (*Blonde on Blonde*, 1966), country (*John Wesley Harding*, 1968, and *Nashville Skyline*, 1969), rock and roll (*Blood on the Tracks*, 1975), and religion (*Slow Train Coming*, 1979). Of Jewish parentage, Dylan became a born-again Christian one year after the dissolution of his eleven-year marriage to Sara Lownds in 1977, but returned to his Jewish roots by 1983.

Rarely has Dylan given straight answers to interviewers' questions. Literary influences on his songwriting can be garnered from examining his lyrics and from interviews with close friends. The books of **John Steinbeck** and Woody Guthrie played pivotal roles in the development of his "Bob Dylan" persona. Early 1960s girlfriend Suze Rotolo and Dylan read a lot of poetry together, particularly Lord Byron and Arthur Rimbaud, and the playwright **Bertolt Brecht** (Hadju 2001, 108). He absorbed the ideas, style, and content of Beat poets Kenneth Patchen and **Allen Ginsberg,** who in turn acknowledged Dylan as an influence on his own later work. Michael Gray devotes a chapter in *Song & Dance Man III* to Dylan and the literary tradition, and throughout the book meticulously examines Dylan's lyrics for British and American literary influences, particularly Robert Browning, **T. S. Eliot,** John Donne, **D. H. Lawrence,** Edgar Allan Poe, Walt Whitman, **Jack Kerouac, W. H. Auden, William Burroughs, Franz Kafka,** and Charles Baudelaire. Gray defines the central theme of Dylan's entire output as the quest for salvation. A primary source for lyrics and inspiration, consistently recurring since his first album, is the Bible and biblical themes.

Archives

Department of Special Collections, Library, Stanford University, Stanford, Calif. Correspondence with, 1970–89, and interview by Allen Ginsberg, 1977.

Experience Music Project, Seattle, Wash. Robert Shelton Collection.

Minnesota Historical Society, St. Paul, Minn. Dennis Anderson's scholarly Bob Dylan research collection.

Printed Sources

Dylan, Bob. *Lyrics 1962–1985* (New York: Alfred A. Knopf, 1996).

Gray, Michael. *Song & Dance Man III: The Art of Bob Dylan* (London and New York: Cassell, 2000).

Hadju, David. *Positively 4th Street: The Lives and Times of Joan Baez, Bob Dylan, Mimi Baez Fariña, and Richard Fariña* (New York: Farrar, Straus and Giroux, 2001).

Mellers, Wilfrid. *A Darker Shade of Pale: A Backdrop to Bob Dylan* (New York: Oxford University Press, 1985).

Scaduto, Anthony. *Bob Dylan: An Intimate Biography* (New York: Grosset & Dunlap, 1971).

Shelton, Robert. *No Direction Home: The Life and Music of Bob Dylan* (New York: William Morrow/Beech Tree Books, 1986).

Susan Hamburger

E

EARHART, AMELIA (1897–1937)

Amelia Earhart was born in Atchison, Kansas. Because of her father's alcoholism, the family was forced to move repeatedly and she consequently attended six different high schools. In 1916, she enrolled in Ogontz School, a small college outside Philadelphia, but dropped out to tend to military veterans suffering in the Great Flu Epidemic of 1918. Shortly thereafter, she enrolled in Columbia University as a medical student, but later quit because she could not afford tuition. She fell in love with aviation in 1920 after her first plane ride. A female pioneer in the field, she set numerous flying records and promoted airplanes as a safe form of transportation. Perhaps the best-known female pilot of the twentieth century, she served as a role model for women who seek professions beyond those traditionally prescribed for them by society. Her legacy continues today because of the mysterious manner in which she died: she disappeared over the Pacific Ocean during an attempt to fly around the world in 1937.

Books were an important influence on Earhart's childhood. Before her father's alcoholism emerged, the family celebrated literature in the household. In *The Fun of It*, her autobiography, Earhart writes, "I was exceedingly fond of reading" and "Books have meant much to me. Not only did I myself read considerably, but Mother read aloud to my sister and me, early and late (Earhart 1932, 6). Each Sunday evening, both of her parents would read from the Bible or John Bunyan's *Pilgrim's Progress*. She fondly recalls her father Edwin's humorous interpretation of Charles Dickens's *Pickwick Papers* and how "he could define the hardest words as well as the dictionary" (Earhart 1932, 6–7). She and her sister, Muriel, would also read aloud while doing household chores such as washing or dusting. Amelia often recited excerpts from "Horatius at the Bridge," Matthew Arnold's *Sohrab and Rustum*, and Robert Browning's "That Toccato of Gallupis" (Putnam 1939, 26; Earhart 1932, 6–7). She loved poetry. Her husband, George Palmer Putnam, offers an example of Amelia's tastes in *Soaring Wings* as Amelia lauds Vachel Lindsay's whimsical poem, "The Broncho That Would Not Be Broken of Dancing" (Putnam 1939, 16). At her grandparents' home, the sisters also took advantage of the family library, which was stocked with works by Victor Hugo, Alexandre Dumas, Sir Walter Scott, George Eliot, and Thackeray as well as magazines such as *Youth's Companion, Harper's Weekly,* and *Puck* (Earhart 1932, 6). Her father even bought a complete set of Rudyard Kipling on the installment plan (Morrissey 1963). Given that the family was never far from bankruptcy, Edwin's purchase of the collection shows the value the Earharts placed on literature.

Books offered Amelia courage and solace as her father's drinking problem grew. "Where before he loved to hear the girls quote poetry," explains biographer Carol Pearce, "now he wasn't interested" (Pearce 1988, 35). Because Amelia's father was not able to make any payments on the Kipling texts, her mother paid for the books by scrounging money from a meager household budget (Pearce 1988, 13). On one occasion, Amelia recited "Horatius at the Bridge" to her father when he nearly struck her for pouring a bottle of whisky down the drain (Pearce 1988, 18). Shortly thereafter, Edwin disappointed the family again one night when he was supposed to return home to take the sisters to see a performance of *Twelfth Night* at church. When he didn't show up because of his drinking, Muriel sobbed all evening while Amelia "read herself to sleep" (Rich 1989, 10–11).

Biographies illustrate Amelia's burgeoning assertiveness that would, later in life, allow her to engage in activities precluded to women. During Amelia's senior year at a Chicago high school, an incompetent, deaf English teacher outraged Amelia, who circulated a petition among the students demanding a more responsible instructor; as a compromise, the school allowed her to spend her English period in the library, where she read "about four times the required number of books" (Goldstein and Dillon 1997, 20; for another account, also see Rich 1989, 12). Amelia demonstrated a similar crusade while attending Ogontz, where the headmistress, Abby Sutherland, assigned Ibsen's *A Doll's House.* Amelia asked to read *Ghosts* and *Hedda Gabler,* but Sutherland denied the request because such controversial subject matter was unsuitable for young women (Morrissey 1963, 99). On another occasion, Amelia flustered Sutherland by asking her, during a formal meal with multiple guests, to explain the meaning of Wilde's *The Picture of Dorian Gray* (Rich 1989, 17). In fact, the teachers at Ogontz were later surprised when Amelia failed to pursue a career in literature, given the fact that her room was "filled with books, which she avidly perused during the day and half the night" (Pearce 1988, 23). Eventually, Earhart did pursue such a career in part by writing her memoirs, *20 Hours and 40 Minutes* (1928), *The Fun of It* (1932), and *Last Flight* (published posthumously by her husband in 1937).

Archives

"Records Relating to Amelia Earhart," U.S. Navy Operational Archives, Naval Historical Center, Washington D.C., www.history.navy.mil/faqs/faq3-2.htm.

"Amelia Earhart," FBI Declassified Documents, FBI Documents Released Under the Freedom of Information Act, Washington D.C., www.foia.fbi.gov/earhart.htm. Records contain correspondence by individuals speculating about her death.

"Earhart, Amelia and Amy Otis," Vol. 9, The Manuscript Inventories, Catalogs of Manuscripts, Books and Photographs, Radcliffe College Schlesinger Library on the History of Women in America, Cambridge.

Purdue University Library, West Lafayette, Indiana. Collection organized around historic flights.

National Air and Space Museum at the Smithsonian Institution, Washington, D.C.

"AE Memorabilia," International Women's Air and Space Museum, Centerville, Ohio.

The Ninety-Nines, International Women's Pilots Organization, Will Rogers World Airport in Oklahoma City, Okla.

Printed Sources

Butler, Susan. *East to the Dawn: The Life of Amelia Earhart* (Reading, Mass.: Addison Wesley, 1998).

Earhart, Amelia. *The Fun of It* (New York: Brewer, Warren and Putnam, 1932).

Goldstein, Donald M., and Katherine V. Dillon. *Amelia: The Life of the Aviation Legend* (Washington: Brassey Inc., 1997).

Lovell, Mary S. *The Sound of Wings* (New York: St. Martin's Press, 1989). This text addresses the relationship between Amelia and her husband, George Palmer Putnam.

Morrissey, Muriel. *Courage Is the Price* (Kansas: McCormick–Armstrong, 1963). Written by Amelia's sister, this book focuses on family relationships.

Morrissey, Muriel, and Carol L. Osborne. *Amelia, My Courageous Sister* (Santa Clara: Osborne Publisher, 1987).

Pearce, Carol A. *Amelia Earhart* (New York: Facts on File, 1988).

Putnam, George Palmer. *Soaring Wings* (New York: Harcourt, Brace & Co., 1939). The account of Earhart's husband.

———. *Wide Margins.* (New York: Harcourt, Brace & Co., 1942).

Rich, Doris. *Amelia Earhart: A Biography* (Washington D.C.: Smithsonian Institution Press, 1989).

Ware, Susan. *Still Missing: Amelia Earhart and the Search for Feminism* (New York: W.W. Norton, 1994).

Rosemary King

ECO, UMBERTO (1932–)

Umberto Eco, Italian philosopher, cultural theorist, and novelist, was born and educated in Alessandria. Eco graduated with a degree in philosophy from the University of Turin in 1954, where he began to lecture in aesthetics (1961–64). After holding academic positions in Florence (1966–69) and Milan (1969–71), he taught semiotics at the University of Bologna, where he remains as a professor, in conjunction with appointments and honorary degrees at universities worldwide. Eco's theoretical contribution—dozens of books, among which are *A Theory of Semiotics* (1976), *The Role of the Reader* (1979), and *The Limits of Interpretation* (1990)—goes hand in hand with a creative production culminating with the novels *The Name of the Rose* (1980; tr. 1983), *Foucault's Pendulum* (1988; tr. 1989), *The Island of the Day Before* (1994; tr. 1995), and *Baudolino* (2000).

As an adolescent, Eco manifested a passion for reading and a gift for parodic writing. His ironic and desecrating attitude coexists with a serious cultural commitment. Attracted to the poetry of Rimbaud, Mallarmé, Verlaine, Ungaretti, Quasimodo, and especially Montale during high school, he later turned to medieval philosophy and wrote a dissertation on Thomas Aquinas. Eco reads Aquinas's aesthetics as the prefiguration of methodological and rhetorical principles that reemerge in the modern world, from the modernist poetics of James Joyce—one of his favorite authors—to New Criticism and the multimedia theories of Marshall

McLuhan. This eclectic connection between diverse cultural forms as medieval allegorism and the contemporary avant-garde is the pivot of *The Open Work* (1962; tr. 1989), the book that earned Eco a European reputation for its reconceptualization of the structure of the work of art as "*chaosmos*" (Eco 1989, 41), a polyvalent, open, but not undefined aesthetic order.

Eco's interest in the form of avant-garde art as a field of possibilities is also sparked by experimental artists like musician Luciano Berio, with whom Eco collaborated at the Italian National Broadcasting Company (RAI) as the person responsible for television cultural programs (1954–58), and writer Edoardo Sanguineti, a leading member of the neo-avant-garde movement "Gruppo 63," which Eco joined in 1963. This intellectual and creative experience consolidated Eco's notion of the open work as an antiauthoritarian and innovative construction rather than as a stable, content-oriented cognitive model. Hence, it paved the ground for Eco's subsequent studies in reception theory and mass communication and also anticipated the erosion of differences between elitist and popular forms of culture, crucial to Eco's shift toward semiotics in the 1970s.

Rejecting Ferdinand De Saussure's ontological idea of structure and endorsing Charles Peirce's notion of unlimited semiosis, according to which signs refer to other signs and not to objective referents or universal ideas, Eco now treats the totality of culture as "a system of systems of signification" (Eco 1976, 28). Yet signs and their codes are for Eco sociohistorical creations to be interpreted through an inferential process requiring contextual validation.

The coexistence of a theoretical and a pragmatic approach to communication, the dialogue between past and present, and the blend of high and low culture persist in Eco's novelistic activity. Inspired by **Jorge Luis Borges**'s *Ficciones* as well as by John Barth's postmodern notions of literary exhaustion and replenishment, *The Name of the Rose* revives Eco's medieval erudition together with his enduring passion for the popular genre of detective fiction, with the aim of a narrative renewal based upon an ironic quotation of literary tradition. The openness of Eco's exploration of a textual world leading back to other books rather than to a referential reality is reasserted in *The Island of the Day Before*, whereas *Foucault's Pendulum*, recalling Edgar Allan Poe's fictional universe as much as **Michel Foucault**'s notion of decenteredness, adopts the detective story to denounce overinterpretation, the danger of the reader's excessive heuristic freedom in his endless quest for meaning.

Archives

No archival sources yet available.
Eco's curriculum vitae: http://www.dsc.unibo.it/dipartimento/people/eco/CURRICUL.htm.

Printed Sources

Bondanella, Peter. *Umberto Eco and the Open Text* (Cambridge: Cambridge University Press, 1997).
Capozzi, Rocco (ed.). *Reading Eco. An Anthology* (Bloomington: Indiana University Press, 1997).
Eco, Umberto. *The Open Work* (Cambridge: Harvard University Press, 1989).
———. *A Theory of Semiotics* (Bloomington: Indiana University Press, 1976).
Ganeri, Margherita. *Il caso Eco* (Palermo: Palumbo, 1991).

Nicoletta Pireddu

EDEN, ROBERT ANTHONY (1897–1977)

Anthony Eden was born in County Durham, England. The scion of an aristocratic family, he was educated at Eton and Christ Church, Oxford, and entered Parliament as a Conservative just five years after surviving the First World War. A foreign policy expert, Eden rose to the rank of foreign secretary in 1935, but in 1938 he resigned in protest against Prime Minister **Arthur Neville Chamberlain**'s policy of appeasement toward Germany and Italy. Thereafter, Eden aligned himself with **Winston Churchill** and spent many years as Churchill's chief lieutenant. Eden became prime minister in 1955, but resigned in disgrace a few months after the 1956 Suez Crisis, in which Britain and France attempted to take control of the Suez Canal from Egypt by force, ultimately withdrawing under United States economic pressure. Eden's reputation as prime minister gets reexamined with every new wave of Arab militancy. However, attempts to rehabilitate him are limited by the fact that his government secretly endorsed an Israeli invasion of Egypt in order to create a pretext for seizing the canal, a matter about which Eden lied to Parliament.

At Eton, Eden had a particular interest in foreign languages. "I preferred Greek to Latin and French to either," he later wrote (Eden 1977, 45). At Oxford, he took a first class degree in oriental languages, specializing in Persian and Arabic, and serving as president of the university's Asiatic Society. Some writers have seen a connection between Eden's interest in other languages and cultures and his later specialization in foreign policy issues, and his Oxford tutor in Persian predicted (correctly) that Eden would be foreign secretary before he turned 40 (Rhodes James 1986, 60). Though he professed not to have been too interested in politics until his twenties, that subject accounted for a large quantity of his early reading. While in his teens he studied parliamentary debates and elections so closely that on train trips he could name the MP of each town passed, along with statistics from the constituency's last election (Rhodes James 1986, 26). Lord Curzon's writings on foreign policy likewise prodded him to choose a political career (Rhodes James 1986, 62). However, Eden's experience as an infantry officer during the war had a larger impact on him than any of his studies, and he did not attend Oxford until after the armistice. He saw frontline action during the war and lost many friends and also a brother in the navy. His strong support for the League of Nations and the United Nations was an obvious consequence of his wartime experience. In that light, Eden's maverick military action at Suez is all the more puzzling, despite the parallels he tried to draw between Egypt's Gamal Abdel Nasser and the fascist dictators of the 1930s.

Archives

Avon Papers, Special Collections, University of Birmingham Library.
Public Record Office, Kew, London (site of Eden's Foreign Office Papers).

Printed Sources

Eden, Robert Anthony. *Another World* (Garden City, N.Y.: Doubleday and Co., 1977).
———. *Facing the Dictators* (Boston: Houghton Mifflin, 1962).
———. *Full Circle* (Boston: Houghton Mifflin, 1960).
———. *The Reckoning* (Boston: Houghton Mifflin, 1965).
Rhodes James, Robert. *Anthony Eden* (New York: McGraw-Hill, 1986).

Christopher Pepus

EINAUDI, LUIGI (1874–1961)

Luigi Einaudi, born in Carrù, Piedmont, was an economist, statesman, and journalist. From 1902 he was professor of public finance at the University of Turin, and in 1908 he became managing editor of *Riforma sociale*. In 1919 he became a lifelong Senator of the Kingdom of Italy. An opponent of Fascism, in 1935 he was forced to stop editing *Riforma sociale*. An exile in Switzerland in 1943, he mediated the case for a European federation. In 1945 he was appointed governor of the Bank of Italy. In 1946 he was elected as Liberal deputy at the Assemblea Costituente, and he played a part in writing many articles of the new Italian constitution. In 1947 he became budget minister in the fourth **Alcide de Gasperi** cabinet and successfully "rescued" the Italian lira from inflation. In 1948, he was elected president of the republic.

Einaudi's literary work as a professional economist and journalist is enormous. His bibliography amounts to more than 3,800 items, and his articles appeared in more than 150 different Italian and foreign periodicals. He contributed almost 300 articles dealing with the economic and financial situation of Italy during the interwar years to the *Economist* (London). As a specialist in public finance, his favorite topic was the trade-off between equity and efficiency of taxation. In 1912 he started from the phenomenon of the so-called double taxation of saving, already stated by John Stuart Mill, in order to advocate a tax system levied on non-necessary consumption; in 1929 he discussed the properties of the "optimal" tax—that is, one that does not disturb the economic equilibrium. The evolution of his thought in financial matters shows a shift from a partial equilibrium approach à la Marshall to a general equilibrium approach à la Walras.

As a political thinker, he was much influenced by the Smith-Burke tradition, and considered the individual liberty from the state as the main feature of freedom. He was one of the founders of the libertarian Mont Pelerin Society, and praised **F. A. von Hayek**'s *The Road to Serfdom*. In fact, both Hayek and Einaudi considered collectivism as the most serious menace to Western civilization. Moreover, he was in correspondence with the Dutch historian Johan Huizinga and the German economist Wilhelm Roepke, who were concerned with the negative features of modern industrialism and mass civilization. On the other hand, he learned the lesson of John Stuart Mill (whose book *On Liberty* he prefaced in 1925) in the sense of a more democratic and "popular" liberalism. Therefore, he accepted the idea of some relevant public tasks (mainly in education) in order to allow for everybody "the equality of the starting-points."

Einaudi's laissez-faire libertarianism was very different from J. M. Keynes's attitude toward an active role of the state in economic policy. He did not approve of the "Keynes plan" (1933) as a remedy to depression and unemployment. The Keynesian investment-saving sequence via the multiplier was rejected by Einaudi in favor of the reverse traditional sequence going from private saving and accumulation to investment. In the monetary field, he rejected Keynes's "liquidity preference" concept and reaffirmed the everlasting validity of the quantity theory of money, considering the transaction motive for keeping money as the rule. Finally, he discussed with the liberal philosopher **Benedetto Croce** (1866–1952) the relationship between political liberalism and economic libertarianism. While Croce identified liberalism with the "religion of liberty" in some metaphysical sense quite independently from historical circumstances, Einaudi pointed out that if one gives to liberalism no empirical content (i.e., a certain amount of laissez-faire and free enterprise), the result would be an empty abstraction.

Archives

Fondazione Luigi Einaudi, Torino, *Carte di Luigi Einaudi.*

Printed Sources

Caffè, F. "Luigi Einaudi." In *The New Palgrave*, 4 vols. (London and Basingstoke: Macmillan, 1987).

Einaudi, Luigi. *Cronache economiche e politiche di un trentennio (1893–1925)*, 8 vols. (Turin: G. Einaudi, 1959–65).

———. *"From Our Italian Correspondent": Luigi Einaudi's Articles in the Economist, 1908–1946*, R. Marchionatti (ed.), (Florence: Olschki, 2000).

———. *Prediche inutili* (Turin: G. Einaudi, 1964).

———. *Saggi sul risparmio e l'imposta* (Turin: G. Einaudi, 1941).

———, and B. Croce, *Liberismo e liberalismo*, 2nd ed. (Milan-Naples: R. Ricciardi, 1957).

Faucci, Riccardo. *Luigi Einaudi* (Turin: Unione tipografico-editrice torinese, 1986).

Robbins, Lionel, Steven G. Medema, and Warren J. Samuels. *A History of Economic Thought. The LSE Lectures* (Princeton: Princeton University Press, 1998).

Schumpeter, J. A., and Elizabeth Boody Schumpeter. *History of Economic Analysis* [1954] (London: Routledge, 1997).

Ricardo Faucci

EINSTEIN, ALBERT (1879–1955)

Albert Einstein was born on March 14, 1879, in Ulm, Germany, the eldest child of Jewish middle-class merchants. He attended a Catholic elementary school in Munich from 1884 to 1889 and then the Luitpold Gymnasium, where he studied until 1894, at which time he left school to join his parents, who had moved to Milan, Italy. He finished his final year of secondary education at a cantonal school in Aarau, Switzerland, from which he graduated in 1896. He then traveled to Zurich to begin his studies at the Eidgenössische Technische Hochschule (ETH), receiving his diploma in 1900. Einstein held numerous teaching positions through the course of his life, including tenures at the German University in Prague, the ETH, the Prussian Academy of Sciences in Berlin, and visiting professorships at Princeton University and the California Institute of Technology in Pasadena, California.

From an early age, Einstein exhibited a resistance to formal methods of education that relied on fear, force, and artificial authority. Such an approach, in his view, weakened "that divine curiosity which every healthy child possesses" (Einstein 1950, 33). Einstein's childhood curiosity led him to pursue his own course of studies outside of the classroom. Under the tutelage of Max Talmud, a young medical student who dined weekly with his family, he read Aaron Bernstein's *Naturwissenschaftliche Volksbücher (Popular Books on Physical Science)*, Ludwig Büchner's *Kraft und Stoff (Force and Matter)*, and Immanuel Kant's *Kritik der Reinen Vernunft (Critique of Pure Reason)*, as well as texts on geometry and advanced mathematics. In addition to his scientific and philosophical studies, Einstein also developed a passionate and abiding interest in literature, including the works of Honoré de Balzac, Charles Dickens, and Fyodor Dostoyevsky (particularly *The Brothers Karamazov*).

In 1905, which later became known as Einstein's *annus mirabilis*, or "miraculous year," he worked in a patent office in Bern, Switzerland. There, as he later described it, he thought: "If a person falls freely he will not feel his own weight. I was startled. This simple thought made a deep impression on me. It impelled me toward a theory of gravitation." This vision gave birth to his special theory of relativity and later would form the basis of general relativity. Others had addressed the issue of relativity prior to Einstein, including Hendrik Antoon Lorenz and Jules Henri Poincaré. However, Einstein's special theory, published in 1905 in the journal *Annalen der Physik,* was revolutionary in its approach. He also published two other papers in 1905: one on Brownian motion that confirmed the atomic theory of matter, and one on the photo-electric effect that resolved difficulties in **Max Planck**'s quantum theory. These works stunned the scientific community, but their enormous significance was yet to be fully demonstrated.

Like Isaac Newton before him, who invented calculus to provide a mathematical description of gravity, Einstein needed a similar mathematical tool to describe his general theory of relativity. He found it with the help of Georg Pick, a mathematician at the German University in Prague, who introduced him to the works of Italian mathematicians Gregorio Ricci and Tullio Levi-Cività. Einstein then teamed up with his oldest friend, Marcel Grossman, a mathematics professor at the ETH, who recommended the works of Bernhard Riemann, a pioneering nineteenth-century mathematician specializing in the geometry of curved space. Einstein completed his general theory of relativity in 1916, and its subsequent verification during an eclipse in 1919 created an entirely new understanding of gravitation and made him an international celebrity. He was awarded the Nobel Prize for physics in 1921 for his work on the photo-electric effect.

In 1950, Einstein published a collection of essays titled *Out of My Later Years* in which he recorded his thoughts on science, education, politics, and religion. He was deeply influenced by H. G. Wells's *The Outline of History,* which emphasized an educational system that promotes the progress of global civilization as opposed to national dominance. Having witnessed the horrors of two world wars, both of which he saw as having been driven by a perverse and oppressive nationalism, he advocated an international governing body, similar to the League of Nations, but which could enforce its decisions with military force if needed. He cited Lord Davies's *Force* as "an excellent expression of this conviction" (Einstein 1950, 209). Einstein's support for the development of atomic weapons in 1939 undercut his own political views against the use of science for military purposes. That he never envisioned the use of these weapons, however, is evident in his later writings. Peace among nations and the preservation of freedom for all people was, in his view, the goal of science. "Without such freedom there would have been no Shakespeare, no Goethe, no Newton, no Faraday, no Pasteur and no Lister" (Einstein 1950, 149).

Archives

Albert Einstein Archives, Jewish National and University Library, Hebrew University of Jerusalem; houses the literary estate of Albert Einstein.

Einstein Papers Project, California Institute of Technology; joint project with Princeton University Press to publish *The Collected Papers of Albert Einstein* in 25 volumes, comprising scientific, professional, and personal papers, manuscripts, and correspondence.

Printed Sources

Einstein, Albert. *Out of My Later Years* (New York: Philosophical Library, 1950).
———. *The World as I See It* (New York: Carol Publishing Group, 1991).

Highfield, Roger, and Paul Carter. *The Private Lives of Albert Einstein* (London: Faber and Faber, 1993).

Jammer, Max. *Einstein and Religion* (Princeton: Princeton University Press, 1999).

White, Michael, and John Gribbin. *Einstein: A Life in Science* (New York: Dutton, 1993).

Philip Bader

EISENHOWER, DWIGHT DAVID (1890–1969)

Dwight Eisenhower was born in Denison, Texas, to a devout Christian family with Mennonite roots. In 1891 they moved to Abilene, Kansas, where Eisenhower graduated from high school in 1909. His early years involved family Bible reading and memorization; in addition, he read John Bunyan's Christian allegory *Pilgrim's Progress* several times (Tobin 1966, 32). He also loved reading ancient history. In his 1967 memoir, *At Ease: Stories I Tell to Friends*, Eisenhower recalls that his childhood hero was the Roman leader Hannibal.

After two years as a creamery refrigeration engineer, Eisenhower received an appointment to West Point and earned a commission as an infantry officer in 1915, graduating 61 of 164. Eisenhower wanted to lead soldiers into battle during World War I but instead ran training camps and coached football—work he excelled at. While in the Tank Corps at Fort Meade, Maryland (1919–22), George S. Patton introduced Eisenhower to General Fox Conner, who made him his aide in Panama (1922–24). Although West Point had made history an "out-and-out memory course" (Eisenhower 1967, 185), Conner rekindled Eisenhower's interest by sharing his library. They discussed books during horseback rides together in Panama, starting with novels like *The Crisis*, an epic about the Civil War by the American novelist Winston Churchill. They read Plato, Cicero, Tacitus, the *Federalist Papers*, and even Nietzsche—which Eisenhower admittedly quit halfway through (Tobin 1966, 32). He also read Civil War memoirs by Ulysses S. Grant, another general who later became President. Grant's plain style would serve as a model for Eisenhower's own writing (Perret 1999, 379).

Conner's sponsorship combined with Eisenhower's grasp of military strategy and writing ability propelled him to staff assignments in Washington, D.C. (1927–35) and with **General Douglas MacArthur** in the Philippines (1935–39). Eisenhower's favorable impression on high-level commanders culminated in his rapid ascension from lieutenant colonel (1941) to five-star general by the end of World War II (1944–45). Under the direction of Army Chief of Staff **George C. Marshall**, Eisenhower led Allied campaigns in North Africa and Italy (1942–43) and the Normandy Invasion in June 1944—operations requiring collaboration with British Prime Minister **Winston Churchill** and Free French leader **Charles de Gaulle**. As Supreme Commander of the Allied Forces, Eisenhower brought an end to World War II in May 1945. He succeeded Marshall as chief of staff (1945–48) before retiring to become president of Columbia University (1948–50). As the cold war intensified, President **Harry S. Truman** recalled Eisenhower to duty as NATO commander (1950–52). Eisenhower, who since World War II had resisted pressure to run for president, in 1952 ran successfully and served two terms (1953–61). In 1961 Eisenhower and his wife, Mamie, retired to a farm in Gettysburg, Pennsylvania, where he painted, wrote, and continued to be consulted on national security matters until his death in 1969.

Among the most influential works Eisenhower read while under General Conner's mentorship was *On War* by nineteenth-century Prussian soldier-philosopher Karl von Clausewitz, who described war as a "continuation of political intercourse with an admixture of other means" (quoted in Pickett 1985, 23). The horrors of war Eisenhower had witnessed in World War II led him to avoid those "other means" once he gained political power: he ended fighting in Korea quickly and countered Soviet advances and other Cold War threats peacefully—despite his advisors' recommending otherwise several times (Ambrose 1983–84, 2:626); Eisenhower said he drew inspiration from poet **Robert Frost,** who dedicated this line of poetry to him: "The strong are saying nothing until they see" (quoted in Eisenhower 1967, 168).

Eisenhower Library archivist Barbara Constable summarizes White House responses to inquiries about Eisenhower's favorite reading: "The Bible—because of his early training by deeply religious parents; [Mark Twain's] *Connecticut Yankee in King Arthur's Court*—because it is a wonderful satire; Shakespeare—because of the author's penetrating thought on an infinite variety of subjects." In a 1940 letter, Eisenhower responded to his son John's suggestion that man is just chemicals by appealing to literature: "The plays of Shakespeare, the Bible, the Gettysburg Address and [Thomas] Gray's Elegy are *not* merely mixtures of natural elements" (Eisenhower 1998, 465).

Archives

Dwight D. Eisenhower Library, Abilene, Kansas: Personal and official papers, books from the Eisenhower family home.
Eisenhower National Historic Site in Gettysburg, Pennsylvania: Personal belongings including books.

Printed Sources

Ambrose, Stephen E. *Eisenhower: Soldier, General of the Army, President-Elect* (vol. 1); *The President* (vol. 2), (New York: Simon and Schuster, 1983–84). The definitive biography.
Eisenhower, Dwight D. *At Ease: Stories I Tell to Friends* (Garden City, N.Y.: Doubleday, 1967). Chapters III and XIII discuss Eisenhower's reading.
———. *The Prewar Diaries and Selected Papers,* Daniel D. Holt and James W. Leyerzapf (eds.), (Baltimore: Johns Hopkins University Press, 1998).
Lee, R. Alton (comp.). *Eisenhower: A Bibliography of His Times and Presidency* (Wilmington: Scholarly Resources Inc., 1991). Comprehensive bibliography dealing with Eisenhower and his cultural surroundings.
Perret, Geoffrey. *Eisenhower* (New York: Random House, 1999). Tracks the importance of reading throughout Eisenhower's life.
Pickett, William. "Eisenhower as a Student of Clausewitz," *Military Review* 65, 7 (July 1985), 21–27.
Tobin, Richard. "Dwight D. Eisenhower: 'What I Have Learned'," *Saturday Review* Sept. 10, 1966, 29–34.

Stephen J. Rippon

EISENSTEIN, SERGEI MIKHAYLOVICH (1898–1948)

Sergei Eisenstein was born in Riga, Latvia, and became the most noted filmmaker of the Soviet Communist regime as well as one of the most instrumental filmmakers in the history of movies. Eisenstein moved to St. Petersburg in the

1910s and trained as an architect and engineer at the Institute of Civil Engineering. He witnessed the 1917 October Revolution and volunteered for the Red Army in 1918, serving as a construction and defense engineer and producing troop entertainment. Later, he joined the First Worker's Theatre of Proletcult in Moscow, working as the assistant stage designer and codirector. Convinced that he could translate his political agenda to the movie screen after being drawn toward film with an appreciation of **D.W. Griffith**'s work, Eisenstein's first cinema work was a 1923 newsreel parody titled *Glumov's Diary*. In 1924 he directed his first film, *Strike*, and published his first article on the theories of montage editing in the review *Lef*, in which he proposed that the effect and statements of a movie are made through visuals rather than dialogue. He also employed the technique of "typeage"—to cast nonprofessionals in leading roles. Despite his pioneering ideas, Eisenstein only completed seven films, most done under the intrusion of the communist system so they could not escape criticisms of serving as propaganda vehicles. Eisenstein's other movies include *The Battleship Potemkin, October (Ten Days That Shook the World), Alexander Nevsky*, and *Ivan the Terrible*. Voted by *Sight and Sound* in 1958 as the greatest movie ever made, *The Battleship Potemkin* (1925) was filmed in the Black Sea port of Odessa to commemorate the Revolution of 1905 and brought Eisenstein world fame. Banned in several countries, *Potemkin* contains his most famous montage editing sequence, the massacre on the Odessa steps, which was so realistic viewers believed they were watching newsreel footage and clashed with police outside the USSR. Eisenstein started the 1930s with a trip to Europe and the United States to research the techniques of employing sound with film. He was hailed as a hero and became friends with people as diverse as **Albert Einstein, Charlie Chaplin, Walt Disney**, D.W. Griffith, and **Upton Sinclair**, among others. Sinclair helped Eisenstein with financial assistance to shoot his only American film, *Que Viva Mexico!*, but under **Josef Stalin**'s orders, who feared Eisenstein's defection, Russian government officials intercepted it to be edited later by others. During his trip, Eisenstein witnessed several cultural and political differences that would help lead to a nervous breakdown because he could not settle into Soviet hopes for a Stalinist Hollywood in the USSR. In 1935, an All-Union Conference of Cinema Workers even vilified him. He became a devoted teacher and scholar after taking the head of the Direction Department at the Moscow film school in 1932. After *Potemkin*, Eisenstein's most popular work was probably *Alexander Nevsky* (1938), a monumental costume epic and attack on Nazi Germany, as well as an international success that won him the Order of Lenin. Yet, it was pulled from distribution after the 1939 Non-Aggression Pact. During World War II, Eisenstein started *Ivan the Terrible*, his last major work of the cinema. While Stalin admired the sixteenth-century Ivan IV, after the release of the first part in 1943, the Soviet Film Trust withheld the second part until 1958 because Stalin believed the movie was a mask of Eisenstein's attitudes toward him as a bloodthirsty tyrant. While Stalin allowed him to start work on the third part for some reason, Eisenstein died of a heart attack in 1948 before its conclusion.

During his career, several literary sources influenced Eisenstein. As the leading figure of Soviet film, one of Eisenstein's goals for montage editing was to represent Karl Marx's dialectic and to utilize cinematic techniques for the common man. Yet, Eisenstein also expanded filmmaking by including influences beyond the Soviet machinery. While in the military, Eisenstein studied theater, philosophy, psychology, and linguistics, and staged and performed in several productions for which he designed sets and costumes. He was also interested in Richard Wagner's work and drew on his interest in Japanese Kabuki theater and Noh drama and their use of masks, making *Ivan the Terrible*'s gestures, sound, costumes, sets, and colors into one powerful, synthetic experience. The use of these art forms was completely consistent with Eisenstein as a modernist who did not want to separate cinema from other art forms, but place it within the context of those forms. His modernist focus can be traced to influences from his early study as an architect and engineer when he came into contact with the work of Leonardo da Vinci, Sigmund Freud, and Karl Marx. Da Vinci's work influenced Eisenstein with Renaissance conceptions of space, later interpreted for their psychological impact by Freud. Based on Freud's interpretations, Eisenstein believed he could use the technology of film to distort space and get machine-age sensations into the style of the Renaissance, translating those sensations into Marxist humanism to serve Communist propaganda. During his later trip West, he became good friends with many modernist writers and architects, including **James Joyce,** Abel Gance, **Le Corbusier,** and **Gertrude Stein,** who all encouraged his ideas of how to use the cinema.

Archives
The Museum of Modern Art Film Stills Library, New York: stills and archival material.

Printed Sources
Bergan, Ronald. *Eisenstein: A Life in Conflict* (London: Little, Brown, and Co., 1997).
Bordwell, David. *The Cinema of Eisenstein* (Cambridge, Mass.: Harvard University Press, 1993).
Christie, Ian, and Richard Taylor (eds.). *Eisenstein Rediscovered* (New York: Routledge, 1993).
Goodwin, James. *Eisenstein, Cinema, and History* (Urbana, Ill.: University of Illinois Press, 1993).

Christopher C. Strangeman

ELIOT, THOMAS STEARNS (1888–1965)

T. S. Eliot was born into a prosperous Unitarian home in St. Louis, Missouri, the youngest of seven children. He spent his summers at the family home in Worcester, Massachusetts. He would later use images of the sea in his poems, while also retaining the influence of his "Southern" upbringing.

Eliot was educated at Smith Academy, which had been founded by his grandfather, and Harvard University (B.A., 1906–10). As a master's and Ph.D. philosophy student at Harvard, he attended Oxford University in 1914 and remained in England for the rest of his life. He completed his dissertation but never received the Ph.D., and after marriage to Vivien Haigh-Wood in 1915, he went to work for Lloyd's Bank in London, where he remained for eight years. He rose through the ranks while writing poetry and criticism at night. The pressure of this schedule and his wife's mental illness wore on him; he spent two months in a Swiss sanatorium in 1921. Eliot separated from Haigh-Wood in 1933; she died in 1947. He married Valerie Fletcher in 1957.

While still at Lloyd's Bank, Eliot was assistant editor of the *Egoist* (1917–19). He founded the *Criterion* in 1922 and remained its editor until 1939. Eliot used the *Criterion* to publish his own poems, including his most famous poem, *The Waste*

Land, in the fall of 1922. In 1925, he began working for Faber and Faber publishers, where he remained until his death. Eliot's writing career comprised poetry, criticism, and drama. His greatest poems are considered "The Love Song of J. Alfred Prufrock" (1920), *The Waste Land,* and *The Four Quartets* (1935–42). It has been said that he invented modern poetry in English (Bergonzi 1972, 11). Eliot's criticism appeared in such works as *The Sacred Wood* (1920), *Selected Essays, 1917–1932* (1932), *The Use of Poetry and the Use of Criticism* (1933), and *Notes towards a Definition of Culture* (1948). His plays include *Murder in the Cathedral* (1935), *The Family Reunion* (1939), and *The Cocktail Party* (1950). As one of the most influential literary figures of the twentieth century, Eliot received the Nobel Prize for literature in 1948. He died in London in 1965, having been made a British subject in 1927.

As a child, Eliot enjoyed the poems of Thomas Babington Macaulay, Charles Wolfe, and Alfred Lord Tennyson. At 14, he read *The Rubáiyát of Omar Khayyam;* two years later his first published poem appeared in the *Smith Academy Record.* As an undergraduate at Harvard, Eliot composed four of his most important poems: "Portrait of a Lady," "The Love Song of J. Alfred Prufrock," "Preludes," and "Rhapsody on a Windy Night." They were influenced by Dante's *Divine Comedy,* first read in 1910, as well as the metaphysical poets, the Jacobean dramatists, and the French symbolists. Of this last group, Eliot was particularly attracted to Jules Laforgue. Laforgue, Eliot said, was "one of those which have affected the course of my life." Laforgue's influence on Eliot continued until 1912 but in the end was less profound than that of Dante and Charles Baudelaire (Bergonzi 1972, 9). Dante's poetry was "the most persistent and deepest influence upon my own verse," Eliot wrote in his essay "What Dante Means to Me" (*To Criticize the Critic,* 1965). Throughout his works, Eliot echoes Dante's forms, techniques, and subject matter—from "Prufrock" to 1942's "Little Gidding."

The Waste Land, first published in 1922, exhibits Eliot's most important influences. It is most of all a symbolist poem, full of suggestion and implication but little explanation. At the same time, its sharp visual images owe much to Dante. The subject of Eliot's doctoral dissertation, philosopher F. H. Bradley, also contributes to the poem, in the feeling that time has no objective reality. How much of *The Waste Land* was also influenced by its editor, Ezra Pound, was not known until 1968, when Eliot's original manuscript was discovered. Eliot did not accept all of Pound's suggestions, but Pound's editing did make *The Waste Land* into a single poem, rather than a group of separate poems.

Eliot's graduate studies also brought much to bear on his poetry. For his doctoral studies in philosophy and Oriental studies, he read Sanskrit poetry and the *Bhagavad-Gita.* He refers to the *Bhagavad-Gita* in "The Dry Salvages" (1941), and Sanskrit tags appear at the end of *The Waste Land.* Western religion was the subject of his later poems. While Eliot's early poems dealt with the isolation and chaos of modern life, his later poems, like *Ash Wednesday* and the *Four Quartets,* showed his turn toward spiritual hope. In 1927, he had become a member of the Anglican Church.

Archives

T. S. Eliot Collection, King's College Archive Centre, Cambridge University, Cambridge, England. Correspondence, literary manuscripts, and papers.

T. S. Eliot Collection, Houghton Library of the Harvard College Library, Cambridge, Mass. Correspondence, literary manuscripts, and papers.

T. S. Eliot Collection, New York Public Library, New York, N.Y. Correspondence, literary manuscripts, and papers.

Printed Sources

Bergonzi, Bernard. *T. S. Eliot* (New York: The Macmillan Company, 1972).

D'Ambrosio, Vinnie-Marie. *Eliot Possessed: T. S. Eliot and FitzGerald's Rubáiyát* (New York: New York University Press, 1989).

Eble, Kenneth (ed.). *T. S. Eliot* (Boston: Twayne Publishers, 1982).

Eliot, T. S. *The Letters of T. S. Eliot, 1888–1965* (San Diego, Calif.: Harcourt Brace Jovanovich, 1988).

Eliot, T. S. *T. S. Eliot: The Complete Poems and Plays, 1909–1950* (New York: Harcourt, Brace & World, Inc., 1971).

Mackinnon, Lachlan. *Eliot, Auden, Lowell: Aspects of the Baudelairean Inheritance* (London: Macmillan, 1983).

Manganiello, Dominic. *T. S. Eliot and Dante* (New York: St. Martin's Press, 1989).

Melissa Stallings

F

FANON, FRANTZ (1925–1961)

Frantz Fanon was born in Martinique, French West Indies. He attended lycée in Fort-de-France, Martinique (1939–43), studying with **Aimé Césaire,** but quit to join the Free French in World War II (1943–45), earning the Croix de Guerre. In 1946 he reentered the lycée and helped Césaire campaign for mayor of Fort-de-France. Fanon studied dentistry (University of Paris, 1947), then switched to psychiatry (University of Lyon), defending his thesis in 1951. His 1952 marriage to Josie Dublé, a white woman, was controversial. Fanon practiced psychiatry at the Hospital of Saint-Ylie (1952), then did residency at the Hospital of Saint-Alban under Dr. François Tosquelles, who strongly influenced Fanon's psychiatric practice. In 1953 Fanon worked at Pontseron, Normandy/Brittany, then moved to Algeria as *chef de service* of the Blida-Joinville psychiatric hospital, introducing treatment methods inspired by his residency. He became involved with the *Front de liberation nationale* (FLN) in its fight for Algerian liberation. In 1957, Fanon was expelled from Algeria for political reasons. Moving to Tunisia, he served the FLN as a propagandist, spokesperson, and diplomat, and wrote for *El Moudjahid*, taught at the University of Tunis, and practiced psychiatry. Surviving several assassination attempts in 1959, he became a representative of the provisional Algerian government in 1960. That year he was diagnosed with leukemia. In 1961 Fanon sought a position in Cuba, his model of a successful revolution. He died undergoing leukemia treatments in Bethesda, Maryland.

Many forces influenced Fanon. Aimé Césaire, his teacher and intellectual mentor, introduced him to the ideology of the négritude movement, inspiring his quest to discover his authentic self and recognize the beauty of being black. Fanon quotes Césaire's *Cahier d'un retour au pays natal* in *Peau noire masques blancs*. **Jean-Paul Sartre** influenced Fanon's consciousness of race prejudice and of how the other shapes identity. Fanon read Sartre's *Anti-Semite and Jew, Being and Nothingness,* and *Orphée noir,* originally an introduction to a négritude poetry anthology. When defining his identity under the concept of négritude in *Peau noire masques blancs*, Fanon discusses Sartre's views regarding the situation of Jews and blacks, criticizing Sartre's evaluation of négritude as a passing phase but finally agreeing with it. The two met in 1961 to arrange Sartre's writing of the preface to *Les damnés de la terre*. Fanon's analysis of violence in *Les damnés de la terre* derives from Hegel via Sartre. Fanon also read **Leon Trotsky, V. I. Lenin,** and Karl Marx. *Peau noire masques blancs* hints at universalist solutions for social and racial oppression reminiscent of Marxist philosophy. Direct structural parallels exist between Marx's *The Eighteenth Brumaire of Louis Bonaparte* and Fanon's *L'An V de la révolution algerienne*. "Concerning Violence" in *Les damnés de la terre* parodies Marx's and Friedrich Engels's "Preface to a Contribution to the Critique of Political Ideology." Psychiatric influences on *Peau noire masques blancs* include Alfred Adler's *Understanding Human Nature* and *The Nervous Character* and Sigmund Freud. The "Lordship and Bondage" section of Georg Wilhelm Friedrich Hegel's *Phenomenology of Spirit* (Jean Hyppolite, translator) underlies Fanon's critique of Hegel's master–slave relation (*Peau noire masques blancs*, chapter seven). Friedrich Nietzsche's Superman (*Thus Spake Zarathustra*) impressed Fanon greatly, while Karl Jaspers shaped Fanon's existentialist education. Other influences include the négritude periodical *Présence africaine*, **Martin Heidegger,** Søren Kierkegaard, and Maurice Merleau-Ponty, Fanon's teacher at Lyon.

Archives

Bibliothèque populaire Frantz Fanon, Riviere-Pilote, Martinique, French West Indies.

Printed Sources

Bulhan, Hussein Abdilahi. *Frantz Fanon and the Psychology of Oppression* (New York: Plenum Press, 1985).

Geismar, Peter. *Fanon* (New York: The Dial Press, 1971).

Gendzier, Irene L. *Frantz Fanon: A Critical Study* (New York: Pantheon, 1973).

Hansen, Emmanuel. *Frantz Fanon: Social and Political Thought* (Columbus: Ohio State University Press, 1977).

Macey, David. *Frantz Fanon: A Biography* (London: Granta Books, 1998).

Guillemette Johnston

FASSBINDER, RAINER WERNER (1945–1982)

Born in Bad Wörishofen, not far from Munich, (West) Germany, on May 31, 1945, Rainer Werner Fassbinder often pretended he was born in 1946. From the age of 18, he wanted to be a filmmaker, and he determined to release 30 feature films before the age of 30. He succeeded, but had to cheat one year on his date of birth. After his parents divorced, young Fassbinder lived in Munich, mainly with his mother, who was a translator. He went to the Rudolf-Steiner elementary school between 1951 and 1955. From 1956 to 1961, Fassbinder went to several high schools in Munich and Augsburg. From 1963, he went to drama schools including the Jungen Akademie, in Munich, where he won in 1966 the third prize for his play titled *Nur eine Scheibe Brot (Only a Slice of Bread)*. The same year, he was refused twice by the new Deutschen Film und Fernsehakademie in West Berlin, because of his "lack of talent." Fassbinder directed his first short films and began working as an actor and director in a collective pseudo-avant-garde theater troupe in Munich in 1967, freely adapting classic plays by Henrik Ibsen *(A Doll's House)* and August Strindberg *(Miss Julie)*. His first 10 films (1969–71) were weak; but after discovering Douglas Sirk's melodramas, his style changed into flamboyant melodramas, with a sense of Brechtian distance. He released his most famous films between 1972 and 1981: *Fontane Effi Briest* (1974), *Fox and his Friends* (1974), *The Marriage of Maria Braun* (1979), *Lola* (1981). Fassbinder also wrote plays and song lyrics (with composer Peer Raben) for actress Ingrid Caven. Rainer Werner Fassbinder died in Berlin on June 10, 1982, from a mixture of alcohol and pills. He was only 37. He had created some 40 films in just 13 years.

Fassbinder often said that Alfred Döblin's book, *Berlin Alexanderplatz*, changed his life when he discovered it in his teenage years. In many of his first movies, there is a character named after Döblin's hero, Franz Biberkopf, played by Fassbinder himself. When Fassbinder uses a pseudonym (as a film editor), he chooses "Franz Walsh," mixing his double identification with Biberkopf and filmmaker Raoul Walsh. Fassbinder often wrote his own scripts and sometimes adapted famous novels into his best films: **Vladimir Nabokov**'s *Despair*, a novel written in the thirties, became one of Fassbinder's masterpieces, *Despair* (1978), from a script written by **Tom Stoppard**; Jean Genet's *Querelle de Brest* inspired his posthumous *Querelle* (1982), a very sinister and baroque movie. Fassbinder also adapted his own plays *The Bitter Tears of Petra von Kant* (1972) and *Bremer Freiheit* (1973). But his masterpiece is probably the 15-hour adaptation of Döblin's famous book, *Berlin Alexanderplatz* (1980), which is in the *Guinness Book of Records* as the longest feature film in the history of cinema. The film's epilogue explains how Döblin's universe has shaped the filmmaker's baroque imagery. Fassbinder also was a film buff; as a teenager, he went to see movies almost every day and admired French directors such as Claude Chabrol, Éric Rohmer, **Jean-Luc Godard,** and Robert Bresson. He also admired Luchino Visconti's *The Damned* (1969), **Luis Bunuel**'s *Viridiana* (1961), Alexander Kluge, and Douglas Sirk. Fassbinder was fascinated by a book written in the sixties by a German female author (who committed suicide), *Man of Jasmine*, by Unica Zürn. Fassbinder was a constant reader who was receptive to all influences; when he read a German translation of Henri de Montherlant's novel, *Pitié pour les femmes*, he created a female character who writes every day to the author she admires; that character is in Fassbinder's provocative movie, *Satan's Brew* (1976). The director read all kinds of magazines, from the leftist *Spiegel* to popular German sensation tabloids such as *Konkret*, that inspired melodramatic films such as *I Only Want You to Love Me* (1975) and *Mother Kusters Goes to Heaven* (1975). He later adapted popular biographies: Lale Anderson's autobiography, *Der Himmel hat viele Farben*, about a popular singer in Nazi Germany became the controversial *Lili Marleen* (1980); German actress Sybille Schmitz's sad life inspired his most beautiful film, *Veronika Voss* (1982). Although he didn't read many history books, Fassbinder's movies could each tell a bit of Germany's history in the twentieth century through many wonderful "portraits de femmes."

Archives

The Rainer Werner Fassbinder Foundation, Berlin. Personal archives, manuscripts, correspondence, films, scripts.

Filmverlag der Autoren, Munich. Manuscripts, correspondence.

Deutsche Stiftung Kinemathek, Berlin. Manuscripts, costumes, correspondence, film scripts.

Printed Sources

Elsaesser, Thomas. *Fassbinder's Germany: History, Identity, Subject* (Amsterdam: Amsterdam University Press, Serie: Film culture in transition, 1996).

Fassbinder, Rainer Werner, *The Anarchy of the Imagination: Interviews, Essays, Notes*, Michael Toteberg (ed.), Krishna R. Winston (trans.), (Baltimore: Johns Hopkins University Press, 1992).

Lardeau, Yann. *Rainer Werner Fassbinder* (Paris: Seuil, 1990).

Schmid, Marion, and Herbert Gehr (eds.). *Rainer Werner Fassbinder: Dichter, Schauspieler, Filmemacher* (Catalog) (Berlin: Argon, 1992).

Shattuc, Jane. *Television, Tabloids, and Tears: Fassbinder and Popular Culture* (Minneapolis: University of Minnesota Press, 1995).

Watson, Wallace Steadman. *Understanding Rainer Werner Fassbinder: Film as Private and Public Art* (Columbia: University of South Carolina Press, 1996).

Yves Laberge

FAULKNER, WILLIAM CUTHBERT (1897–1962)

William Faulkner was born in New Albany, Mississippi, but moved with his family to Oxford, Mississippi, in 1902. Initially home-schooled, he entered public school when he was eight years old. Faulkner was reared in the Methodist Church, but became a nominal Episcopalian in adulthood. Leaving high school in 1915, he befriended Yale law student Phil Stone. Both he and Stone shared a fascination with modern literature, and under Stone's guidance Faulkner began to read the works of authors whose styles would later influence his own writing. Rejected for American military service in World War I, he went to Canada, trained with the Royal Air Force, but saw no action abroad. Back in Oxford, Faulkner was enrolled briefly at the University of Mississippi, where he contributed book reviews and artwork to campus publications. In the early 1920s he made literary pilgrimages to New Orleans and Paris. The first of his 19 novels, *Soldiers' Pay* (1926) and *Mosquitoes* (1927), failed to attract an appreciative readership. Not until the publication of *Sartoris* and *The Sound and the Fury* in 1929 did Faulkner become widely known. His bold use of the stream-of-consciousness technique prompted critics to hail the Mississippian as a remarkable talent and as a leading figure in the Southern literary renascence. But his greatest accomplishment lay in his skill to make universal the characters and events in his mythical Yoknapatawpha County. Forced by economic necessity to work as a Hollywood screenwriter in the 1930s and 1940s, he saw his literary fortunes plummet until critic Malcolm Cowley edited and issued *The Portable Faulkner* (1949). Other significant novels include *As I Lay Dying* (1930), *Sanctuary* (1931), *Light in August* (1932), *Absalom, Absalom!* (1936), *The Hamlet* (1940), *Go Down, Moses* (1942), *Intruder in the Dust* (1948), *A Fable* (Pulitzer Prize, 1954), and *The Reivers* (Pulitzer Prize, 1962). Awarded the Nobel Prize for literature in 1949 (conferred in 1950), Faulkner was appointed writer-in-residence and lecturer at the University of Virginia in 1957. He died in Byhalia, Mississippi.

As a child, Faulkner read the works of Henry Fielding, Joseph Conrad, Rudyard Kipling, Edgar Allan Poe, William Shakespeare, Voltaire, Victor Hugo, and Honoré de Balzac. Later, with Stone's encouragement, he delved into the writings of the modernists: **James Joyce, Thomas Mann,** Sigmund Freud, **Henri Bergson,** the French symbolist poets (especially Stéphane Mallarmé), **Marcel**

Proust, Sir James G. Frazer, **Gertrude Stein,** and Sherwood Anderson. Joyce's *Ulysses* moved Faulkner to use the interior monologue in such works as *The Sound and the Fury* and *Absalom, Absalom!* Mann's *Buddenbrooks* may have inspired *The Sound and the Fury.* The influence of Freud's *Interpretation of Dreams* is evident in the free-association monologues in *As I Lay Dying* and *The Sound and the Fury.* Bergson's *Creative Evolution* had a pronounced effect on Faulkner's theology. The symbolists' doctrine that words—as symbols—should "suggest" rather than "state," encouraged what many have seen as Faulkner's "faults" as a novelist, among them obscurity and delayed revelation. Proust's toyings with time in *À la récherche du temps perdu* perhaps led to the creation of various time levels in *The Sound and the Fury.* Faulkner's interest in myths and legends owes much to Frazer's *The Golden Bough;* Faulkner even chose the name of his Oxford home, Rowan Oak, after consulting this volume. His often-anguished stream-of-consciousness passages echo Stein's use of leitmotifs. Impressed with Anderson's attack-on-the-village theme in *Winesburg, Ohio,* Faulkner was moved to create his own fictitious realm, Yoknapatawpha County. Twice in 1924 he journeyed to New Orleans just to meet Anderson, who was for a time the young writer's mentor. In a 1956 interview Faulkner cited numerous other literary influences: the Old Testament, Charles Dickens, Miguel de Cervantes, Gustave Flaubert, Fyodor Dostoyevsky, Lev Tolstoy, Christopher Marlowe, Robert Herrick, Thomas Campion, Ben Jonson, John Donne, John Keats, Percy Bysshe Shelley, A. E. Housman, Mark Twain, and George Washington Harris (Forkner and Samway 1986, 668-71). Joseph Blotner notes Faulkner's respect for Jeremy Taylor's *Holy Living* and *Holy Dying* (Blotner 1976, 2:1760, 1806). Faulkner's debt to the 1611 Authorised Version of the Bible is obvious, as we see in such titles as *Sanctuary, Absalom, Absalom!, Father Abraham,* and *Go Down, Moses,* and in the plots of *The Sound and the Fury, Pylon,* and *A Fable.*

Archives

Alderman Library, University of Virginia, Charlottesville, Va.: Faulkner's personal library (partial), draft manuscripts, correspondence.

John Davis Williams Library, University of Mississippi, University, Miss.: Draft manuscripts, Nobel Prize citation and medallion, and artwork and book reviews from Faulkner's student days.

Rowan Oak, Old Taylor Road, Oxford, Miss.: Faulkner's personal library (partial), other items.

Printed Sources

Blotner, Joseph Leo. *William Faulkner: A Biography,* 2 vols. (New York: Random House, 1976).

Brooks, Cleanth. *Toward Yoknapatawpha and Beyond* (New Haven: Yale University Press, 1978).

Forkner, Ben, and Patrick Samway (eds.). *A Modern Southern Reader,* rev. 4th edition (Atlanta: Peachtree Publishers, 1986).

Stein, Jean. *Writers at Work: The Paris Review Interviews, First Series* [Interview with William Faulkner], Malcolm Cowley (ed.), *The Paris Review,* 1957, 1958.

Webb, James W. *William Faulkner of Oxford* (Baton Rouge: Louisiana State University Press, 1965).

Harry McBrayer Bayne

FELLINI, FEDERICO (1920–1993)

Federico Fellini was born in Rimini, Italy, in 1920, son of Ida Barbiani, housewife, and Urbano Fellini, a sales representative. He received a Roman Catholic education at both the primary and the high schools in Rimini that strongly influenced his artistic life and spent free time reading comics, playing the puppet theater, and watching American movies. His favorite authors were Gustave Flaubert, **Jean-Paul Sartre,** Carlos Castaneda and **Samuel Beckett.** After the school-leaving-examination he matriculated to the Faculty of Jurisprudence but never graduated. In 1938 he left Rimini for Florence and Rome, where he worked as a writer and cartoonist and toured with a theater company. His meeting with Aldo Fabrizi, an Italian actor, introduced him to the world of films, though he earned his living with *The Funny Face Shop*, which specialized in caricatures and photographs of American soldiers. In 1943 he married a young actress named Giulietta Masina, who appeared in many of his most successful films.

Fellini's career as film writer, assistant, collaborator, and finally film director began in 1940 and was, at the beginning, subject to the restraints of Fascism. But censorship hit many of his films even in later years because of the audacity of some scenes (*Fellini-Satyricon*, 1969) or because of the representation of a generation without moral ideals (*La Dolce Vita*, 1959, which was condemned also by the Roman Catholic Church). His collaboration with film directors including **Roberto Rossellini,** Alberto Lattuada and Pietro Germi, begun in the 1940s, is considered to have produced some of the most poetic films in the history of cinematography. Fellini won many international prizes: Academy Awards for *La Strada* (1954), for *Le Notti di Cabiria* (1957), for *8 1/2* (1963), for *Amarcord* (1973), and in 1992 for career achievement. He also received a Leone d'Argento (Silver Lion) for *I Vitelloni* (*The Young and Passionate*, 1953) and for *La Strada*, and a Leone d'Oro (Gold Lion) at the Venice Film Festival in 1985 for his career. *La Dolce Vita* won the Golden Palm in Cannes in 1960. After *Amarcord*, a moving representation of Fellini's inner and outer worlds mixing autobiography and quotation, memory and fantasy, dream and reality, the film director shot *La Città delle Donne* (*City of Women*, 1979), *E la Nave va* (*And the Ship Sails On*, 1983), and *Ginger e Fred* (*Ginger and Fred*, 1984), starring once again his wife Giulietta Masina together with Marcello Mastroianni, the favorite protagonist of his films. Fellini's last film was *La Voce della Luna* (*The Voice of the Moon*, 1989). He died in 1993.

Archives

Fondazione Federico Fellini, Rimini.

Printed Sources

Alpert, Hollis. *Fellini, A Life* (New York: Atheneum, 1986).
Baxter, John. *Fellini* (London: Fourth Estate, 1993).
Burke, Frank. *Fellini's Films: From Postwar to Postmodern* (New York: Twayne, 1996).
Fellini, Federico. *Fellini on Fellini* (London: Methuen, 1976).
Salachas, Gilbert. *Federico Fellini* (New York: Crown Publishers, 1998).

Maria Tabaglio

FITZGERALD, FRANCIS SCOTT KEY (1896–1940)

F. Scott Fitzgerald was born in St. Paul, Minnesota. He attended Princeton University between 1913 and 1917 but failed to graduate, and from 1918 to 1919 he was a member of the army. He married in 1920 and achieved overnight success with the publication of his first novel, *This Side of Paradise*. Stories in *The Saturday Evening Post*, *Scribner's Magazine*, and H. L. Mencken's *Smart Set* followed. In 1922 Fitzgerald published *Tales of the Jazz Age* and his second novel, *The Beautiful and Damned*. His most accomplished and critically acclaimed book, *The Great Gatsby*, followed in 1925 and portrayed the American Dream corrupted. The Fitzgeralds lived and traveled primarily in Europe between 1924 and 1931, a period marked by personal turmoil and excess. *Tender Is the Night* (1934), a novel nine years in the making, reproduces the incipience of the mental illness of Fitzgerald's wife and depicts the collapse of Western ideals. Between 1927 and 1940 Fitzgerald worked as a Hollywood screenwriter. He moved to Los Angeles in 1937 and began writing *The Last Tycoon* (1941), an unfinished novel posthumously edited by Edmund Wilson. Fitzgerald died of a heart attack in Los Angeles on December 21, 1940, after which Wilson edited *The Crack-Up* (1945), a collection of Fitzgerald's essays and letters.

As a child, Fitzgerald subscribed "to the *St. Nicholas*, a popular children's magazine published by Charles Scribner's Sons" (Bruccoli 1981, 19), and he later remembered being "filled . . . with the saddest and most yearning emotion" upon reading an unidentified "nursery book" about lost innocence (quoted in Bruccoli 1981, 19). The young Fitzgerald also read the poetry of Edgar Allan Poe and Lord Byron, and an early interest in history attracted him to Sir Walter Scott's *Ivanhoe* (1819), the G. A. Henty books, and Edward Stratemeyer's Tom Swift series. In early adulthood Fitzgerald admired the intelligence and technique of Joseph Conrad, imitating Conrad's style from the preface to *The Nigger of the "Narcissus"* (1897), *Lord Jim* (1899–1900), and "The Secret Sharer" (1910) in the themes, conclusion, and unreliable narrator of *The Great Gatsby*. Famous at a young age, Fitzgerald eagerly promoted the careers of fellow writers, introducing acquaintance Ernest Hemingway to Scribner's editor and friend Maxwell Perkins and recommending, through favorable reviews and personal references, Nathanael West, **Franz Kafka,** Erskine Caldwell, **John Dos Passos,** and Ring Lardner, the latter of whom he thought possessed a "noble dignity." In Europe, Fitzgerald met several authors whom he read and admired: **Gertrude Stein, Edith Wharton,** John Galsworthy, Theodore Dreiser, and **James Joyce.** He sought to emulate the style of Gustave Flaubert and Hemingway and advised Thomas Wolfe to write more sparingly, prompting Wolfe to depict Fitzgerald unflatteringly in *You Can't Go Home Again* (1941). Yet Wolfe later wrote a letter, included in *The Crack-Up*, in praise of Fitzgerald's talent. Toward the end of his life, Fitzgerald knew **T. S. Eliot** and novelist John O'Hara, and worked with legendary film producer Irving Thalberg, model for the protagonist of *The Last Tycoon*.

Archives

Firestone Library, Department of Rare Books and Special Collections, Princeton University, N.J.: extensive collection of photographs, book illustrations, correspondence, manuscripts.

Thomas Cooper Library, University of South Carolina, Columbia, S.C.: over 12,000 holdings; revised manuscripts, galley proofs of *The Great Gatsby*, only extant copies of play from Princeton years, revised pages from early short stories, *For Whom the Bell Tolls* inscribed to Fitzgerald by Hemingway, correspondence, personal items.

Printed Sources

Bruccoli, Matthew J. *Some Sort of Epic Grandeur* (N.Y.: Harcourt Brace Jovanovich, 1981).
LeVot, André. *F. Scott Fitzgerald: A Biography*, William Byron (trans.), (N.Y.: Doubleday, 1983).
Meyers, Jeffrey. *Scott Fitzgerald: A Biography* (N.Y.: Harper Collins, 1994).

Tiffany Aldrich

FORD, HENRY (1863–1947)

Henry Ford was born on a farm in Springwells Township, Wayne County, Michigan, the second of eight children born to William Ford, a farmer of Protestant Irish descent, and his wife Mary, née Litogot. His formal education was limited to classes at a one-room school he attended when not working on the farm between 1871 and 1879. Leaving for Detroit in 1879 to seek employment as a mechanic, Ford was barely proficient in writing and reading but had already shown an intuitive understanding of machinery. After his apprenticeship in a machine shop, Ford worked as an engineer for several firms, among them Westinghouse and the Edison Illuminating Company, while spending some of his spare time experimenting on an internal combustion engine to power an automobile. In 1899 he founded the first company to manufacture motorcars in Detroit, four years later the Ford Motor Company. It was this company that in 1908 advertised Ford's Model T or "Tin Lizzy," which was to change America economically, socially, and culturally. It catapulted the nation, especially the rural population, into the modern age. Intended to be an object of utility for the masses, particularly for farmers, not one of luxury for the rich, 15.5 million Model T cars were sold in the United States alone until production ceased in 1927: the first mass-produced car only to be surpassed half a century later by the VW Beetle. A success like this needed more than a knack for constructing an engine and a car. Ford revolutionized industrialism when he introduced assembly-line production and with his view of capitalism summed up as "Fordism." He realized that reduction of costs meant market expansion, that higher wages meant more buying power. From 1914 onward he paid his workers the highest wages in the industry if the employees had proved eligible by conforming to their employer's notion of social outlook and moral behavior. This made Ford the target of much criticism. People reacted critically, too, to a series of antisemitic articles published under his name in the early 1920s and combined in the book *The International Jew* (1922)—said to have made Adolf Hitler an admirer of Ford.

To many of his contemporaries the epitome of capitalism and an age dominated by the machine, Henry Ford was deeply rooted in the concepts and values of his rural Midwest upbringing. The staple diet of his—and many other nineteenth-century children's—reading at school, the *McGuffey's Eclectic Readers*, impressed him so much that he not only felt some of his moral precepts and his respect for wildlife and nature reinforced by certain passages, but collected editions of the Readers when he became a successful car manufacturer, ending up with a collection second only to that of the university where William Holmes McGuffey had taught. Obsessed with the common man and a rural life that the advent of the Model T had done much to destroy, Ford accumulated American objects from everyday life, utensils, tools, furnishings, machines, and even completely furnished rooms and buildings, including a reconstruction of his own country school room, Thomas Alva Edison's laboratory at Menlo Park, and the birthplace of McGuffey. These Americana were later housed and displayed at the Henry Ford Museum and Greenfield Village in order to educate the public in pioneer virtues such as hard work, self-reliance, and thrift.

In sending a Model T as a gift to the naturalist and poet John Burroughs, whose works the manufacturer had read "with great pleasure" (quoted in Gelderman 1981, 189), Ford again demonstrated his life-long endeavor to reconcile nature and technology, to see the machine firmly placed and accepted in the garden. Burroughs discussed with Ford other influential writers on nature and human existence in communion with it, notably Ralph Waldo Emerson and Henry David Thoreau. It was on their writings that much of Ford's reading centered. The ideas he found in them converged with some of his own values, his love for nature, his idealization of the simple life, and his anti-city bias. In Henry Ford, these existed side by side with a fascination for the machine and a concept of the car as a necessity to ordinary people.

In 1888, Ford had married Clara Jane, née Bryant, the daughter of a neighboring farmer. Their only child, Edsel, had been born to them in 1896. Henry Ford died at his Fair Lane estate, 10 miles west of Detroit, in 1947.

Archives

Ford Archives of the Edison Institute in Dearborn, Michigan.

Printed Sources

Ford, Henry. *My Life and Work* (New York: Doubleday, 1922).

Gelderman, Carol. *Henry Ford. The Wayward Capitalist* (New York: The Dial Press, 1981).

Lacey, Robert, *Ford: The Man and the Machine* (Boston: Little, Brown and Company, 1986).

Lewis, David L. *The Public Image of Henry Ford: An American Folk Hero and his Company* (Detroit: Wayne State University Press, 1976).

Nevins, Allan, and Frank Ernest Hill. *Ford: Decline and Rebirth: 1933–1962* (New York: Charles Scribner's Sons, 1962).

———. *Ford: Expansion and Challenge: 1915–1933* (New York: Charles Scribner's Sons, 1957).

———. *Ford: The Times, the Man, the Company* (New York: Charles Scribner's Sons, 1954).

Angela Schwarz

FORD, JOHN (1894–1973)

Born John Martin Feeney, in Cape Elizabeth, Maine, on February 1, 1894 (although he often said he was Sean Aloysius O'Feeney, born in 1895), future film director John Ford first chose the pseudonym "Jack Ford" when he began to work for Universal Studios in 1914 and adopted "John Ford" only in 1923. He was the thirteenth and last child of Irish Catholic parents who often spoke Gaelic at home. His parents had emigrated from Galway in 1872 and married three years later. The young boy went to the Emerson Grammar School in Portland. In 1914, John Feeney got his degree from the Portland High School; according to Ford himself, his history teacher, William B. Jack, "was the most influential figure in his life after his father" (Gallagher 1986, 6). In 1914, he went to Hollywood, where his older brother Francis "Ford" worked as a film director, scriptwriter, and actor. The future John Ford became a stuntman and assistant between 1914 and 1917. Between 1917 and 1966, he directed some one hundred thirty films, almost half of them silent movies (many of those are lost). Apart from numerous westerns (such as *Stagecoach* in 1939, *My Darling Clementine* in 1946, and *The Man Who Shot Liberty Valance* in 1962), he also made melodramas, biographies (*The Adventures of Marco Polo*, 1938; *Young Mister Lincoln*, 1939; *The Long Grey Line*, 1955) and even some propaganda films produced by the United States Navy (*The Battle of Midway*, 1942; *This is Korea!*, 1951; *Korea: Battleground for Liberty*, 1959). In the Monument Valley studios in Arizona, he created a whole vision of the American West. Ford contributed to the recognition of western movies as a respected cinematographic genre.

Ford discovered books at the age of eight, during a long convalescence after a diphtheria attack. "Ford was quoted as having always dreamed of filming Conan Doyle's *White Company*, which he claimed to have read each year since he was eight" (Gallagher 1986, 452). Among filmmakers, Ford admired **D. W. Griffith,** with whom he worked once as an extra in *Birth of a Nation* (1915), his favorite movie (Gallagher 1986, 14 and 452). He met German director F. W. Murnau in Berlin in 1927 and said that Murnau's *Sunrise* was "the greatest picture that has been produced" (Gallagher 1986, 50). Expressionist influence can be noticed in Ford's *Four Sons* (1928), *Hangman's House* (1928), and *The Informer* (1935). Ford said he respected some early **Cecil B. DeMille** movies, but not the person. Ford also appreciated films directed by his friends: Leo McCarey, **Frank Capra,** Raoul Walsh, Tay Garnett, Henry King, and Samuel Fuller (Gallagher 1986, 453). Apart from some of his first silent short films (written with the help of his brother Francis Ford, writer Dudley Nichols, and actor Harry Carey), Ford scarcely wrote scripts, preferring various screenwriters (more than a hundred in half a century) who freely adapted short stories, biographies, and popular novels (by authors such as James Warner Bellah and many Irish writers). Notable exceptions are **John Steinbeck**'s *Grapes of Wrath* (1940) and **Graham Greene**'s *The Power and the Glory* for *The Fugitive* (1947). On the visual side, Tag Gallagher (1986, 258) notes strong influences by such artists as Frederic Remington, Eugène Delacroix, and Matthew Brady. It is interesting to observe Ford's tribute to his Irish ancestors in less typical movies such as *Mary Stuart* (1936), *The Plough and the Stars* (1936), *The Quiet Man* (1952), *The Rising of the Moon* (1957; these two were shot in Ireland), and *Donovan's Reef* (1963).

Archives

The John Ford Papers, Lilly Library, Indiana University. Reminiscences, correspondence.

John Ford archives at the Metropolitan Museum of Art. Personal papers, manuscripts, correspondence.

John Ford files at the Academy of Motion Picture Arts and Sciences, Hollywood, California. Films.

John Ford archives at the Universal Studios, Hollywood, California. Personal papers, photographs.

Printed Sources

Darby, William. *John Ford's Westerns: A Thematic Analysis, with a Filmography* (Jefferson, N.C.: McFarland & Company, Inc. Publishers, 1996). Includes a chapter on Ford's western literary sources and their adaptations.

Eyman, Scott. *Print the Legend: The Life and Times of John Ford* (Baltimore: Johns Hopkins University Press, 2001).

Gallagher, Tag. *John Ford. The Man and His Films* (Berkeley: University of California Press, 1986).

Levy, Bill. *John Ford: A Bio-Bibliography* (Westport, Conn.: Greenwood Press, 1998).

Peary, Gerald, and Jenny Lefcourt (eds.). *John Ford Interviews* (University Press of Mississippi, 2001).

Studlar, Gaylyn, and Matthew Bernstein (eds.). *John Ford Made Westerns: Filming the Legend in the Sound Era* (Indianapolis: Indiana University Press, 2001).

Yves Laberge

FORSTER, EDWARD MORGAN (1879–1970)

E. M. Forster, novelist and critic, was born in London. From 1893 to 1897 he attended Tonbridge School, studying Greek and Latin, and proceeded to King's College, Cambridge, with disappointing results in classics (1900) and history (1901). During his years at Cambridge he abandoned his religious faith and recognized that he was homosexual, two steps that shaped the rest of his life. His early novels critique the conventions of Edwardian society and protest the spread of suburbia. *Howards End* (1910), a sensitive articulation of the clash between commercial imperialism and personal morality, established him as an important writer on both sides of the Atlantic. In the last novel published during his lifetime, *A Passage to India* (1924), Forster depicts Hindus and Muslims as unable to shake off prejudices inherited from the past and their British rulers as more culpably prejudiced, since they reject the liberal tradition of their own culture in order to avoid the duty of understanding the peoples they govern. Forster's fiction, like the essays, radio talks, and other writings with which he occupied the remainder of his long life, is a humanist's plea for responsibility and mutual understanding in an increasingly complex and mechanized world.

Forster's reading practices are illustrated in the Commonplace Book he kept fitfully from 1924 to 1964. In preparing the lectures published as *Aspects of the Novel* (1927), he read (following the advice of **Virginia Woolf**) key works of eighteenth-century English fiction; five years later he read widely in tragic drama, though no significant writing of his own resulted. His entries include passages which stimulated his thinking on larger issues and passages which struck him as remarkable in themselves or strikingly relevant to contemporary events. A sense of the wide range of Forster's reading is supplied by his essay collections, *Abinger Harvest* (1936) and *Two Cheers for Democracy* (1951). He pays tribute to Samuel Butler's *Erewhon* (1872), an appealingly unpretentious work of genius which showed him that satire can be amusing without losing its incisiveness. Another work of skeptical irony, Gibbon's *Decline and Fall of the Roman Empire*, belongs with Dante's *Divine Comedy* in Forster's lists of great books which had influenced him, along with Shakespeare and his favorite novelist, Jane Austen. He greatly admired **Marcel Proust**, ranking *A la Récherche du Temps Perdu* as the next greatest novel after Tolstoy's *War and Peace*. In these authors, as in Emily Brontë, he found clarity of vision and honesty in presentation, qualities he strove to achieve in his own writing. His 1930 obituary of **D. H. Lawrence** affirming his genius was controversial, but Forster refused to recant. In 1935 he almost became the first biographer of **T. E. Lawrence,** whose *Seven Pillars of Wisdom* had moved him deeply. Despite his rejection of Christianity, Forster had no doubt of the reality of evil, something he found adequately rendered in literature only by Dostoyevsky and Herman Melville, whose *Billy Budd* he helped to adapt for Benjamin Britten's opera (1950). An influence of a different kind was the books of Edward Carpenter (1844–1929), follower of Walt Whitman and an exponent of simple living and "homogenic love." A visit to Carpenter's community at Milthorpe in Yorkshire in 1913 inspired the novel *Maurice*, not published until after the author's death (1971).

Archives

King's College Archive Centre, Cambridge, England: letters, literary manuscripts, personal papers.
Harry Ransom Humanities Center, University of Texas, Austin: letters, literary manuscripts.

Printed Sources

Forster, E. M. *Commonplace Book*, Philip Gardner (ed.), (London: Scolar, 1985).
Furbank, P. N. *E. M. Forster: A Life*, 2 vols. (London: Secker, 1977–78).
Lago, Mary. *E. M. Forster: A Literary Life* (New York: St. Martin's, 1995).

John D. Baird

FOUCAULT, MICHEL (1926–1984)

Michel Foucault was born in Poitiers, France. His family was Catholic but rather anticlerical, and the young Foucault was not fond of religion. He studied at the Collège St. Stanislas in Poitiers (1940–45), the Lycée Henri-IV in Paris (1945–46), and the Ecole Normale Supérieure (1946–50). Foucault studied philosophy, psychology, and psychopathology, earning a degree in the latter from the Institut de Psychologie in 1952. He held teaching positions in France, Sweden, Tunisia, and the United States, and he was elected to the Collège de France in 1969. Foucault's corpus is highly diverse, but it often focuses on ways in which so-called human nature is changeable and on how power functions in and through discourse. His work has been particularly influential in cultural studies, literary theory, historiography, sociology, political science, the history of sexuality, and queer theory.

As was often the case in the postwar period, Georg Wilhelm Friedrich Hegel and phenomenology were dominant intellectual influences in the Parisian educational establishment, and Foucault's intellectual training, marked in particular by the teaching of Jean Hyppolite at Henri-IV, was no exception. In a 1978 interview, however, he explains that Friedrich Nietzsche, Pierre Klossowski, Maurice Blanchot, and Georges Bataille were the writers that allowed him to free himself from Hegel and phenomenology since "they didn't have the problem of constructing systems" but had "direct, personal experiences" (Foucault 1991, 30). Reading Nietzsche in the 1950s produced a "philosophical shock," strongly influencing the subsequent composition of *Madness and Civilization* (1961) in the preface of which Foucault defines the long-term goal of his work as "under the sun of the great Nietzschean quest" (see Miller 1993, 67). The genealogical aspect of this quest is discussed in "Nietzsche, Genealogy, History" (1971). Foucault returned to reading

Nietzsche in the 1970s as well, as evidenced by *Discipline and Punish* (1975). His work also engages with Karl Marx, often to reject his influence. The first volume of his *History of Sexuality* (1976) famously argues against Freudian psychoanalysis and the repressive hypothesis. His well-known lecture "Nietzsche, Marx, Freud" (1964) displays the influence of the three thinkers, but with a clear preference for the first. Other influential German philosophers included **Martin Heidegger** and Immanuel Kant. Foucault acknowledges the influence of Kantian "critique" in *The Order of Things* (1966) and at the beginning of "Foucault," an encyclopedia entry Foucault wrote on himself near the end of his life (see Miller 1993, 137–42).

Archives

Institut Mémoires de l'édition contemporaine (IMEC), Paris: Recordings of lectures and a few unpublished manuscripts available to researchers. Because of Foucault's popularity, most of his writings and interviews have been published.

Printed Sources

Eribon, Didier. *Michel Foucault*, Betsy Wing (trans.), (Cambridge, Mass.: Harvard University Press, 1991).

Faubion, James D. (ed.). *Aesthetics, Method, and Epistemology: Essential Works of Foucault* (1954–84), vols. II, III (New York: The New Press, 1994).

Foucault, Michel. *Politics, Philosophy, Culture: Interviews and Other Writings 1977–1984*, Lawrence D. Kritzman (ed.), Alan Sheridan (trans.), and others (New York: Routledge, 1988).

———. *Remarks on Marx: Conversations with Duccio Trombadori*, R. James Goldstein and James Cascaito (trans.), (New York: Semiotext[e], 1991).

Macey, David. *The Lives of Michel Foucault: A Biography* (New York: Pantheon Books, 1993).

Miller, James. *The Passion of Michel Foucault* (New York: Simon and Schuster, 1993).

Todd W. Reeser

FRANCO BAHAMONDE, FRANCISCO (1892–1975)

Francisco Franco was born in El Ferrol, Galicia, Spain, to a middle-class naval family. He attended two primary schools in El Ferrol, *Sagrado Corazón* and *Colegio de la Marina*. During Franco's formative years, his father separated from his family. His mother, María del Bahamonde, a conservative, moralistic Catholic, influenced her son's pious religious and moral views. He trained as an army cadet in Toledo's Academy of the Alcázar and was accepted into the officer corps. Franco was posted to Morocco, Africa (1912), where he developed his military reputation and subsequently became Europe's youngest brigadier general (1926). He directed the Military Academy of Zaragoza (1927), commanded the Brigade of Infantry, La Coruña (1932), and was promoted to major general and returned to Morocco (1934). Franco considered military intervention against the Second Republic (1934–36) because of "undesirable ideology." With the left-wing election victory and the outbreak of civil war (1936), Franco conspired to overthrow the government.

Supported by the Falange in 1938, he seized Spanish state and military powers when the Spanish Civil War ended (1939). His worldview was of limited cultural and economic training with fascist political ideas rooted in his military experience during Spain's decline. Franco's major accomplishment was to become the head of the Spanish state through military achievements and remain Spain's self-appointed *Caudillo* from 1938 to 1975. He linked Spain to **Adolf Hitler, Benito Mussolini,** and the Axis powers, and guided Spain out of civil war and into international isolation. With the advent of the Cold War, he signed a treaty with the United States (1953), which led to a more open Spain of economic and social reform.

Franco read, wrote, and influenced Spanish literature. During his seminal period, Franco read the Bible, memorized texts of the Roman Catholic dogma, and studied military history. Franco was fascinated with the medieval ballad *El Cantar del Mío Cid* and wanted to emulate El Cid—Spain's great warrior, legend, and savior. He studied the Spanish military textbook, *Reglamento provisional para la instrucción de las tropas de Infantería*, in which he read about military philosophy, discipline, moral virtues, bravery, rules, obedience, loyalty, patriotism, and the army as the nation's guardian. The young Franco was disturbed by press reports of domestic anarchy and loss of civil control. In the early 1920s, he penned the autobiographical novel, *Raza*, and his diary *Diario de una bandera* (1922). Franco espoused "Regenerationism," a literary and philosophical movement that aimed to reinvigorate and reform Spain, born out of the loss of the Spanish–American War and other colonial holdings in 1898. Franco's own production ranged from early books (e.g., *Masonería*) to his numerous speeches and treatises when he served as head of state. He maintained correspondence with protagonists of the day such as **Winston Churchill** and **Franklin Roosevelt.** Later Franco would be characterized in works of historical fiction such as *Autobiografía del general Franco* by Manuel Vázquez Montalbán (1992) offering interpretative insights into Franco's literary formation and writings.

Franco both read and used Spain's rightist monarchist newspaper, the *ABC*, to promote his regime. Literature and journalism of the Franco period were permeated by Franco's presence. After the civil war, Spanish literary figures were exiled abroad to avoid Franco's censorship (e.g., Jorge Guillén, Rafael Alberti). However, within Francoist Spain a viable moderate literary and intellectual culture worthy of critical attention evolved. Literary language of the Franco period was characterized by vagueness, metaphor, double-speak, and a language of silence. Most fiction of the Franco era avoided fantasy and underscored social conditions.

Archives

Ministerio de Asuntos Exteriores, Archivo General, Madrid.
Serrano Suñer Papers, Madrid.
Templewood Papers, University Library, Cambridge.

Printed Sources

Bardavío, Joaquín, and Justino Sinova. *Todo Franco: Franquismo y antifranquismo de la A a la Z* (Barcelona: Plaza y Janés, 2000).

Cierva, Ricardo de la. *Historia del franquismio. Aislamiento, transformación, agonía* (1945–75) (Barcelona: Planeta, 1978).

Franco Bahamonde, Francisco. *Pensamiento político de Franco (Antología)*, 2 vols. (Madrid: Ediciones del Movimiento, 1975).

Herzberger, David. "History as Power, Fiction as Dissent: Writing the Past in Franco's Spain," *West Virginia University Philological Papers*, 44 (1998–99), 1–9.

Ilie, Paul. "Dictatorship and Literature: The Model of Francoist Spain," *Ideologies and Literature* 4, 17 (1983), 238–55.

Preston, Paul. *Franco: A Biography* (New York: Basic Books, 1994).

Sheri Spaine Long

FRIEDAN, BETTY (1921–)

Betty Friedan was born Bettye Naomi Goldstein in Peoria, Illinois, just six months after the ratification of the Nineteenth Amendment to the U.S. Constitution extended the franchise to women. She studied at Smith College from 1938 to 1942, began graduate work at the University of California, Berkeley, that same year, and ultimately chose to decline a Ph.D. fellowship in psychology. She has since received a number of honorary degrees from universities across the United States. Known for both her publication of *The Feminine Mystique* in 1963 and her role in founding the National Organization for Women (NOW) in 1966, Friedan has earned an international reputation as a leader, writer, speaker, lobbyist, and activist for equality. Early experiences with gender bias and antisemitism stimulated Friedan to care deeply about social justice and to engage the cause fearlessly.

By excelling in school and reading socially conscious fiction by Theodore Dreiser and **Sinclair Lewis,** young Friedan came to love reading so much that she dreamed of a career as a librarian. Her affinity for the written word instead helped make her the author who would challenge and sharpen the thinking of her many readers, admirers and detractors alike. Although an avid reader as a child, Friedan was introduced to great literature in college. She delighted in courses exposing her to such formative feminist texts as Virginia Woolf's *Mrs. Dalloway* and *A Room of One's Own*. While at Smith, Friedan also took many writing courses, and her short stories bore the influence of the social fiction of **John Steinbeck** (1902–68) and **John Dos Passos** (1896–1970). By the time she graduated, Friedan combined her interests in humanistic psychology and protest literature with cultural commentaries on social class by Karl Marx (1818–83) and Thorstein Veblen (1857–1929). Years later, as she prepared to write her first book, *The Feminine Mystique*, many readings shaped her thinking, but none more than the writings of **Simone de Beauvoir** (1908–86). Advocating women's autonomy as de Beauvoir had before her, Friedan rebutted all those in the 1950s—from psychological theorists to editors of popular magazines—contending that careers, higher education, political rights, and independence posed threats to women's vitality and femininity. Most conspicuously, she critiqued gender bias in the psychoanalytic writings of Sigmund Freud (1856–1939) as "sexual solipsism." Friedan drew from Thomas S. Kuhn's *The Structure of Scientific Revolutions* the concept of paradigm shifts, to suggest a redefinition of gender perception. In doing so, Friedan framed a cultural critique that would play a definitive part in the women's movement.

As an agent for change, Friedan has aligned her activism not only with NOW, but also with such organizations as the National Women's Political Caucus and the National Abortion and Reproduction Rights Action League. Since penning *The Feminist Mystique*, Friedan has maintained her role in promoting civil rights for women and has worked to fight age discrimination in much the same way she took on sexism earlier in her career. She serves as Distinguished Visiting Professor at Cornell University and director of the New Paradigm Program. Her other books include *It Changed My Life: Writings on the Women's Movement* (1976), *The Second Stage* (1981), *The Fountain of Age* (1993), *Beyond Gender: The New Politics of Work and Family* (1997), and a memoir, *Life So Far* (2000). Friedan's work to advance equality has, in turn, influenced the lives and writings not only of subsequent feminists, but also of countless others who seek to combat bias in language, law, and everyday life.

Archives

Friedan's personal and professional papers spanning 1933–93, including clippings, writings as a student, manuscripts and typescripts, lectures and materials from her teaching career, and items associated with her organizational affiliations, including NOW, can be found in the Schlesinger Library, Radcliffe Institute for Advanced Study, at Radcliffe College, Cambridge, Mass. Supplementary material is available through the Smith College Archives and the Peoria Public Library.

Printed Sources

Friedan, Betty. *Life So Far* (New York: Touchstone Books, 2001).

Hennessee, Judith. *Betty Friedan: Her Life* (New York: Random House, 1999).

Horowitz, Daniel. *Betty Friedan and the Making of* The Feminine Mystique: *The American Left, the Cold War, and Modern Feminism* (Amherst, Mass.: University of Massachusetts Press, 1998).

Sherman, Janann (ed.). *Interviews with Betty Friedan* (Oxford, Miss.: University Press of Mississippi, 2002).

Linda S. Watts

FRIEDMAN, MILTON (1912–)

Milton Friedman was born in Brooklyn, New York. Friedman's parents, his wife, and many of his intellectual mentors were immigrants, therefore strongly influencing his views on open immigration. He was Jewish but considered himself a complete agnostic. Friedman earned the equivalent of two bachelor of arts degrees from Rutgers University (1932) in mathematics and economics. He earned a master of arts degree from the University of Chicago (1933) and a doctorate from Colombia University (1946); both were in the area of economics. On June 25, 1938, Friedman married Rose Director, whom he met in Jacob Viner's economic theory course while they were graduate students at the University of Chicago. Rose, an accomplished economist in her own right, played a substantial role in reading and critiquing everything Milton published (Friedman and Friedman 1998, xii). Friedman held a variety of positions with government research departments. He served as associate economist for the National Resources Committee (1935–37) and as a research member of the National Bureau of Economic Research (1937–46, 1948–81). Additionally, he served as the principal economist for the Division of Tax Research, U.S. Treasury Department (1941–43) and associate director of the Statistical Research Group, Division of War Research, Columbia University (1943–45). Friedman also held a number of academic positions including posts at Columbia University (1937–40), the University of Wisconsin (1940–41), the University of Minnesota (1945–46), and the University of Chicago (1946–82), filling the position that had been Jacob Viner's.

In 1976, Friedman was awarded the Nobel Prize in economic science. From 1977, Friedman held a senior research position at the Hoover Institute on War, Revolution and Peace in Stanford, California. Friedman is widely regarded as the leader of the "Chicago school" of monetary economics. He has written extensively on public policy and was a contributing editor to *Newsweek* magazine (1966–84). Friedman's public-policy writing always had a primary emphasis on the preservation and extension of individual freedom. The success of his advocacy has been enormous, and opinion in Western countries has moved decisively in its preference for those economic freedoms that he so eloquently advocated.

Friedman considers two of the most influential individuals in his life to be Arthur Burns and Homer Jones, both Rutgers faculty members. In one of the former's seminars, Friedman and another student spent the semester going over a draft of Burns's doctoral dissertation, *Production Trends in the United States.* In addition to introducing Friedman to highly sophisticated scientific research, Burns influenced Friedman by having him read Alfred Marshall's works, especially *Principles of Economics* (1898). Homer Jones, a disciple of Frank Knight, introduced Friedman to what would be known as the Chicago school view of individual freedom. Especially influential was Knight's book *Risk, Uncertainty and Profit* (1921). These two professors instilled a love of economics that led Friedman to change his aspiration away from an actuarial career. Jones's connections at the University of Chicago influenced Friedman's choice of graduate school.

At Chicago, Friedman recalls being heavily influenced by Jacob Viner, Frank Knight, Henry Schultz, and an outstanding group of graduate students. Especially important, according to Friedman's memoirs, was Viner's class in economic theory. Friedman has described his time working under Viner as the greatest intellectual experience of his life. The year at Chicago was followed by graduate work at Columbia University where Harold Hotelling's course in mathematical statistics and Wesley C. Mitchell's mentoring and empirical emphasis had a great influence on Friedman's later intellectual work. An important book that reinforced Friedman's understanding of economic theory applied to empirical problems was John Maurice Clark's *Studies in the Economics of Overhead Costs* (1923). After leaving Columbia, Friedman spent a year as a research assistant on Henry Schultz's *The Theory and Measurement of Demand* (1938). Friedman remarked that working on Schultz's book shaped his future approach to the theory of business cycles.

Friedman's work during the New Deal and World War II honed his practical application of empirical data to economic theory. The data collected at the National Resources Committee for a large consumer budget study facilitated some of Friedman's early ideas on consumption function that were more fully developed later. In 1937, Friedman went to work for Simon Kuznets, another future Noble laureate, at the National Bureau of Economic Research. This research served as the basis for Friedman's Ph.D. dissertation and was published jointly, with Kuznets, as *Incomes from Independent Professional Practice* (1946). Here for the first time, Friedman introduced the important distinction between "permanent" and "transitory" income. This was one of the two principal components of his consumption theory, later developed fully in *Theory of the Consumption Function* (1957). In 1941, Friedman took up an appointment with the Division of Tax Research of the U.S. Treasury. His experience there dealing with macroeconomic policy, Keynesian economics, and the relative importance of monetary and taxation policy started Friedman on the road to the key economic concepts that would become his principal professional interest.

Archives

Register of the Milton Friedman Archives, 1931–91, Hoover Institution on War, Revolution and Peace, Stanford University, Stanford, California.

Printed Sources

Breit, William, and Roger W. Spencer (eds.). *Lives of the Laureates: Thirteen Nobel Economists* (Cambridge, Mass.: MIT Press, 1995).

Friedman, Milton, and Rose D. Friedman. *Two Lucky People: Memoirs* (Chicago: The University of Chicago Press, 1998).

Leube, Kurt R. (ed.). *The Essence of Friedman* (Stanford, Calif.: Hoover Institution Press, 1987).

Craig T. Cobane

FROST, ROBERT LEE (1874–1963)

Robert Frost was born in San Francisco, California. After his father died in 1885, the family relocated to New Hampshire, near his father's parents in Lawrence, Massachusetts. His Scottish Presbyterian-turned-Swedenborgian mother read aloud from William Shakespeare, William Wordsworth, and Ralph Waldo Emerson—poets Frost cited as precedents for his musical, colloquial diction (Frost 1966, 4). Emerson's "Monadnoc" was a powerful early influence (Frost 1995, 693). Frost also acknowledged debt to the ancients; in 1958, Frost named Homer's *The Odyssey* and Catullus's poems as "Books That Have Meant the Most," just behind the Old Testament (Frost 1995, 852).

Frost graduated from Lawrence High School in 1892 as covaledictorian, gifted in Greek and Latin. After spending one semester at Dartmouth College, Frost withdrew and worked as a teacher, miller, and newspaperman. Meanwhile, he studied Shakespeare and English lyric poems from Francis Palgrave's *Golden Treasury*, along with scientific works like Richard Proctor's *Our Place Among the Infinities*, Mrs. William Starr Dana's *How to Know the Golden Flowers*, and Charles Darwin's *The Voyage of the Beagle*.

In 1897 Frost enrolled at Harvard, where he read William James's *Psychology: The Briefer Course* and studied under George Santayana (Parini 1999, 61–62). After quitting Harvard in 1899, Frost raised poultry and taught in New Hampshire to support his wife, Elinor (his covaledictorian) and their children. Their first son, Elliott, died in 1900. In 1901 Frost read Henry David Thoreau's *Walden*; he later said *Walden* and Ivan Turgenev's *Sportsman's Sketches* "had a good deal to do with the making of me" (Frost 1964, 182). Frost's reading reinforced Emerson's idea that natural objects correspond to larger truths. He observed his neighbors' speech, too, and wrote those "sentence sounds" at his kitchen table at night. In 1911 Frost read **Henri Bergson**'s *Creative Evolution*, which praised poets' ability to transcend a scientific worldview (Parini 1999, 110).

In 1912 Frost took his family to England, published his first book, *A Boy's Will*, and met **William Butler Yeats** and **Ezra Pound**. Yeats's colloquialism and Pound's imagism influenced Frost (Parini 1999, 243, 254). Pound and others favorably reviewed Frost's book; when Frost returned to America in 1915, he had an audience.

Over the next four decades, Frost held positions at Amherst College, the University of Michigan, Dartmouth, and Harvard while lecturing nationwide. He received 44 honorary degrees and won four Pulitzer Prizes while facing the loss of two more children, his son Carol by suicide in 1940.

Frost's later poetry touched on politics; he opposed **Franklin D. Roosevelt**'s New Deal—in 1934 Frost said he admired the self-sufficiency in Daniel Defoe's

Robinson Crusoe (Frost 1995, 738). He became friendly with both **Dwight D. Eisenhower**'s and **John F. Kennedy**'s administrations, becoming the first poet to read at a presidential inauguration, for Kennedy in 1961. In 1962, a few months before his death, Frost flew to the Soviet Union and met with Premier **Nikita Khruschev** and poet **Anna Akhmatova.**

Archives

Major collections housed at Dartmouth College (Frost's notebooks); New York University's Fales Library (Frost's books); Amherst College's Robert Frost Memorial Library; and the Jones Library, Amherst, Massachusetts.

Printed Sources

Frost, Robert. *Collected Poems, Prose, and Plays.* Richard Poirier and Mark Richardson (eds.), (New York: Library of America, 1995).

———. *Interviews with Robert Frost.* Edward Connery Lathem (ed.), (New York: Holt, Rinehart, Winston, 1966).

———. *Selected Letters, Robert Frost.* Lawrance Thompson (ed.), (New York: Holt, Rinehart, Winston, 1964).

Parini, Jay. *Robert Frost: A Life* (New York: Henry Holt, 1999).

Poirier, Richard. *Robert Frost: The Work of Knowing* (New York: Oxford University Press, 1977). Discusses philosophical influences.

Thompson, Lawrance. *Robert Frost*, 3 vols. (New York: Holt, Rinehart, Winston, 1966, 1970, 1976). The definitive biography.

Tuten, Nancy Lewis, and John Zubizarreta (eds.). *Robert Frost Encyclopedia* (Westport, Conn.: Greenwood Press, 2001).

Stephen J. Rippon

G

GALBRAITH, JOHN KENNETH (1908–)

John Kenneth Galbraith was born in southwestern Ontario, Canada. He received a B.S. degree in animal husbandry from Ontario Agricultural College, now the University of Guelph, in 1931. That same year he won a fellowship to the University of California at Berkeley, where in 1933 he received an M.S. degree and in 1934 a Ph.D. in agricultural economics. In 1937 he married Katherine Atwater and became a United States citizen. He has spent most of his academic career at Harvard University, where in 1949 he became the Paul W. Warburg Professor of Economics. He served as ambassador to India for the Kennedy Administration in the early 1960s, and in 1970 was elected president of the American Economic Association. A gifted writer, Galbraith's books and articles have been read and appreciated by a large public audience. Because of the popularity of his writings, Galbraith can be considered one of the most influential economists of the twentieth century. His major contribution to economic thought has been his study of power relationships in economic systems and the social and ideological factors that support those relationships.

At Harvard, Galbraith wrote his most influential books, which include *The Affluent Society* (1958), *The New Industrial State* (1967), and *Economics and the Public Purpose* (1973). These books provide us with insights into some of the major influences on his literary development, but it is his essays written for different magazines and journals that give us the greatest insight of which thinkers and writers influenced him the most. Galbraith wrote in an essay "Writing and Typing" (Galbraith 1979, 286) that those who influenced him early in his writing career were not literary figures, but teachers and editors. By far, the most important person at this time that influenced his career and style of writing was Henry Robinson Luce, who Galbraith worked for at *Fortune Magazine* in the 1940s.

Known for his voracious reading habits, Galbraith mentioned many authors he enjoyed reading, but only a handful of literary figures that significantly influenced him. A common characteristic of these authors is their ability to write clear and witty sentences. Of this group of writers two stand out: The first is **Evelyn Waugh,** who Galbraith considers to be one of the best novelists of the twentieth century. Waugh influenced Galbraith's use of the English language, his ability to come up with the right word or phrase in his writing, and developing sentences that end with irony and wit. Having been introduced to Waugh's novels in 1945, Galbraith continued to read Waugh's *Scoop* every summer. Next to Waugh, Galbraith put H. L. Mencken for his ability to express ideas clearly and distinctly. Other literary influences include Anthony Trollope, particularly his novels *Barchester Towers, The Warden,* and *The Last Chronicle of Barset.* Of economists who have influenced Galbraith's literary style, Thorstein Veblen stands out for the clarity of his thought and subtle wit and irony. Finally, a late literary influence on Galbraith comes from a fellow Canadian, Robertson Davies, known for his Deptford trilogy that includes *Fifth Business, The Manticore,* and *World of Wonders.* Galbraith characterizes Davies as " . . . one of the most learned, amusing and otherwise accomplished novelists of our century" (Galbraith 1986, 98).

Archives

John Fitzgerald Kennedy Library, Boston, Massachusetts, 02125-3398.

Printed Sources

Galbraith, J. K. *Annals of an Abiding Liberal* (New York: New American Library, 1979).
————. *A View from the Stands* (Boston: Houghton Mifflin, 1986).
Hession, Charles. *John Kenneth Galbraith and His Critics* (New York: New American Library, 1972).
Reisman, David. *Galbraith and Market Capitalism* (New York: New York University Press, 1980).
Sharpe, M. E. *John Kenneth Galbraith and the Lower Economics* (White Plains, N.Y.: International Arts and Sciences Press, 1973).
Stanfield, James R. *John Kenneth Galbraith* (New York: St. Martin's Press, 1996).

Richard P. F. Holt

GANDHI, MOHANDAS KARMCHAND (1869–1948)

Mohandas Gandhi, the Indian nationalist leader and champion of nonviolent activism, remains a cultural and spiritual icon around the world to this day. One of the inner circle of the Indian National Congress, Gandhi mobilized a great cross-section of the Indian populace in his determined, yet peaceful, campaign to end British rule in India. He became known around the world for his activities, from marching to the sea to break the British ban on making salt in 1930 to his negotiations with British viceroys in their imperial palaces, his desperate attempts to end the Hindu–Muslim violence which erupted at India's partition in 1947, and finally his 1948 assassination by a Hindu extremist who resented Gandhi's embrace of Muslims as fellow Indians. Gandhi's legacy of nonviolent activism has remained profound since his death, influencing among others the American civil-rights leader, Dr. **Martin Luther King Jr.** Since Gandhi's death, however, there has also been a tendency to portray Gandhi simply as a saint, an icon, or as a one-dimensional figure, whether it be in feature films or advertising campaigns for personal computers. The Mahatma ("Great Soul") was in fact a complex and complicated man, one of great insight, imagination, and belief, but also one who remained intellectually curious, sometimes frustrated, and occasionally maddeningly stubborn.

One can see the extent of Gandhi's wide-ranging and active intellect simply by reviewing the great number of literary works and figures that influenced both his spiritual and political development. He titled his autobiography "My Experiments with Truth," reflecting in part his lifelong engagement with works of philosophy, theology, and history. It was a process begun in his youth in Gujarat in western India and continued through his sojourns in Britain, South Africa, and his later life in India. Jailed for his activities, first in South Africa, then in British India, Gandhi often spent his confinement in study and intensive reading. Much of his wide reading—everything from the Koran to the Bible to Ralph Waldo Emerson—informed his evolving philosophy of duty, nonviolence, and social justice, but there were particular works that were of fundamental importance to him personally and philosophically.

As a law student in London in the early 1900s, Gandhi fell in with members of the Theosophist movement, who introduced him to Hindu scriptures, works which had not been part of Gandhi's English-style education in India. One in particular, the *Bhagavad Gita*, part of the larger epic *Mahabharata*, remained a central part of the rest of Gandhi's life. As one of his biographers has put it, the *Gita* "became the supreme authority in his daily life" (Brown 1989, 77). The *Gita*, which recounts the god Krishna's advice to the warrior Arjuna, focuses on the importance of duty and of nonattachment—that is, of distance from the world and its material and emotional ties, all in the aid of truth and spiritual discipline. The theme of renunciation remained key in Gandhi's life, reflected in his embrace of fasting, simple clothing, and even *brahmacharya* (voluntary celibacy).

To Gandhi, the *Gita* instructed man to search for truth (God), something which could only be done through a life of service to one's fellow beings and thus an embrace of all God's creation. There were, however, two other works which greatly influenced the sort of service Gandhi would undertake and the way in which he would pursue his quest. These works profoundly shaped his first public activism, during his time in South Africa from 1893 to 1914 on behalf of the rights of Indian "coolies" or indentured laborers. In 1910, Gandhi founded his first experiment in simple, communal living, and named it Tolstoy Farm. A few years before, he had encountered the Russian author's work, *The Kingdom of God Is Within You*, a plea for a communitarian Christian life, based on the ideas of love through service and, even more important for Gandhi, of the rejection of aggression or violence, though not of activism in the service of justice. The other significant work Gandhi encountered in South Africa was John Ruskin's *Unto This Last*, a critique of the inequalities of modern economies and of the science of political economy which promoted such inequality as necessity, and which ended with the declaration "There is no wealth but life." Gandhi embraced Ruskin's call for an egalitarian, moral economy, as became apparent in Gandhi's 1910 publication, *Hind Swaraj*, which saw India's regeneration possible only through a rejection of Western economic thought and a return to a simpler model based on agriculture and the moral economy of the rural village. Gandhi's rejection of social distinctions and hierarchy was also apparent in his criticism of the treatment of Hindu "untouchables" in India in the 1930s.

These works were all significant in shaping Gandhi's thought and actions, but they were hardly the only influences. To use a term from the anthropologist

Claude Lévi-Strauss, Gandhi was a "bricoleur," a jack-of-all-trades, embracing ideas and philosophies from a wide range of sources, constantly searching for social justice and equity, and, until the day he died, always "experimenting" in a quest for the truth that was his God.

Archives

Nehru Memorial Library, University of Delhi: Includes some private papers.

Printed Sources

Brown, Judith. *Gandhi: Prisoner of Hope* (London and New Haven: Yale University Press, 1989).

Chatterjee, Margaret. *Gandhi's Religious Thought* (Notre Dame, Ind.: University of Notre Dame Press, 1983).

Fox, Richard. *Gandhian Utopia: Experiments with Culture* (Boston: Beacon Press, 1989).

Gandhi, M. K. *An Autobiography: The Story of My Experiments with Truth* (Boston: Beacon Press, 1957).

———. *Collected Works of Mahatma Gandhi* 6th rev. ed., 100 vol. (New Delhi: Publications Division, Ministry of Information and Broadcasting, Government of India, 2000–2001).

Andrew Muldoon

GARCIA LORCA, FEDERICO (1898–1936)

The best-known poet of the Generation of 1927 was born in Fuentevaqueros, a small town in Granada of a well-to-do family. As a child, he grew up listening to the legends and traditions of Andalusia. A gifted artist, he combined his passion for poetry with music and painting. He studied music under composer Manuel de Falla. His father had opened an account at a local bookstore in Granada and young Federico and brother Paco amassed an impressive library. In Lorca's youthful autobiography *My Village*, he recounts his readings of Voltaire's *Candide*, Darwin's *Origin of Species*, both scandalous at the time, and the classics, such as the Platonic *Dialogues*, Hesiod's *Theogony*, and Ovid's *Metamorphoses*, about which he later exulted: "It has everything." During his adolescent years, his readings were more soul-searching: as diverse as the Bible, Saint Teresa's *Life*, the poems of Saint John of the Cross, Unamuno's essays, Hindu philosophy, the *Rubáiyát* of Omar Khayyám, and Oscar Wilde's *De Profundis*.

Lorca's first poems were already being recited in the social scene of Granada even before the publication of his early book of prose, *Impresiones y paisajes* (1918), which expresses his feelings through places visited in Spain. Lorca studied law and in 1919 departed for Madrid to enroll at the elitist *Residencia de Estudiantes* where he befriended many important artists such as **Salvador Dali** and film director **Luis Bunuel.** At the time, the surrealistic movement launched by **André Breton** projected a revolutionary trend promoting the liberation of the unconscious and the transformation of existing social values. Lorca was also influenced by Charles Baudelaire and the French symbolists Paul Verlaine, Arthur Rimbaud, and Stephane Mallarmé. Above all at this time, the modernist Nicaraguan poet Rubén Darío inspired Lorca's poetry with exotic imagery, unusual meter, technical virtuosity, and transcendent belief in art and beauty.

The magnetism of his personality and exceptional artistry quickly made Lorca a center of attention in Madrid's artistic circles. His book *El Romancero Gitano* (1928), inspired by the folklore and landscape of his native Granada, brought him immediate local and international success. Disagreeing with the artistic vanguard mission, Lorca's reaction is the use of traditional *romance* or ballads with contemporary poetry. Speaking of a popular Andalusian farce, *La zapatera prodigiosa* (1926), Lorca declares: "The restless letters I was receiving from my friends in Paris (probably from both Dali and Bunuel), who were engaged in the handsome and bitter struggle to create abstract art, led me to produce this almost banal fable with its direct reality" (Stainton 1999, 148).

Other of Lorca's traditional sources include the old epics "cantares de gesta" or narrative poems celebrating the exploits of battle; the contributions of poetic schools like the Galician-Portuguese "cancioneros" in the thirteenth and fourteenth centuries; the "nanas infantiles" or nursery rhymes of his native region; and the eroticism of Arabic–Andalusian. In a literary world dominated by Juan Ramón Jiménez, Lorca was already acclaimed with international recognition.

In 1929 his visit to the United States inspired his *Poeta en Nueva York* (1930). He was profoundly affected by this experience and spoke of alienation, minority race issues, and disillusion with modern civilization, expressing his horror in a poetic bizarre juxtaposition of images and metaphors. It is one of the best examples of surrealist poetry in Spanish letters. His avant-garde perception of reality and artistry had also influenced certain American Beat poets, such as **Allen Ginsberg** and Lawrence Ferlinghetti.

After returning to Spain in 1932, he founded the highly praised La Barraca (The Cabin), an experimental drama company that brought the Spanish Golden Age drama and plays by Miguel de Cervantes, Lope de Vega, and Calderón to the most remote villages in Spain. This initiative was very celebrated during the Spanish Republic.

Inheriting from the Spanish tradition of Arciprestre de Hita, Lope de Vega, Luis de Góngora, José Zorrilla, the Duque de Rivas, the popular and the cult, the irrational and the traditional are characteristic of his work. Lorca admired the plastic sensitivity and technical mastery of de Góngora who invents, according to Lorca, "a new method for hunting and shaping metaphors, and thinks, without saying it, that the eternity of a poem depends on the quality and structure of its images." About another great poet of the Spanish Golden Century, Lorca declares: "Quevedo is Spain." Distancing from the realism of Jacinto Benavente's theater, the lyrical and dramatic of Lorca's trilogy of rural tragedies use fantasy, poetry, music, and ballet to express unrestrained passion in *Bodas de Sangre* (1933) and frustrated maternity in *Yerma* (1934). *La casa de Bernarda Alba* (1936), written a month before his death, mixes honor and the repressed feminine passion. The absurd and the irrational are intertwined with popular values in Andalusia, thus creating a world that explores universal human feelings: freedom versus suppression, hatred and desire, sex and maternity, blood and revenge, foreboding, passion, pride, and superstition. The characters of his plays are gypsies and bullfighters, the Civil Guard, the Spanish peasantry, and the stoic Spanish saints and *beatas*. The theater is the culmination of his poetry, it is dramatic poetry. Lorca conceived works of daring themes which dramatists such as Tennessee Williams later exploited successfully.

Another inestimable poetic resource for Lorca was *el cante jondo*. This is a variant of deep song flamenco characterized by a tragic vision of life. Bearing close analogy to the hieratic melodies of India and the primitive Christian chant, *cante jondo* is a gypsy lament and an expression of pagan and sacred religion and art. *Llanto por Ignacio Sánchez Mejías* (1935), his supreme poetic achievement, shows his talent for the musicality, rhythm, and the plasticity of its verses, equaling Lope de Vega's mastery of the ballad form.

After visiting several Latin American countries, Lorca returned to Spain in 1935. His poetry was radicalized as he began to write about the situation of women and homosexuals. His play *El Público* was not completely published until 1978. Lorca, a strong advocate for individual freedom and education, was arrested and executed by Spanish fascists during the Civil War (1936–39).

Archives

Fundación García Lorca-Archivo Residencia de estudiantes-Consejo Superior de Investigaciones Científicas, Madrid.
Museo Casa Natal Federico García Lorca, Fuentevaqueros, Granada.
Museo García Lorca, Granada.

Printed Sources

Cobb, Carl W. *Federico García Lorca* (New York: Twayne, 1967).
Delgado, Morales, and Alice J. Poust. *Lorca, Buñuel, Dalí: Art and Theory* (Lewisburg: Bucknell University Press, 2001).
Durán, Manuel, and Francesca Collecchia. *Essays on Lorca's Life, Poetry and Theater* (New York: P. Lang, 1991).
Gibson, Ian. *Federico García Lorca: A Life* (New York: Pantheon, 1989).
Johnston, David. *Federico García Lorca* (Somerset, England: Absolute Press, 1998).
MackCurdy, G. Grant. *Federico García Lorca: Life, Work, and Criticism* (Fredericton, N.B.: York, 1986).
Predmore, Richard L. *Lorca's New York Poetry: Social Injustice, Dark Love, Lost Faith* (Durham: Duke University Press, 1980).
Stainton, Leslie. *Lorca: A Dream of Life* (New York: Farrar, Straus and Giroux, 1999).

Andrés Villagrá

GARCÍA MÁRQUEZ, GABRIEL JOSÉ (1928–)

Born on March 6, 1928, in Aracataca, a small village in northern Colombia, Gabriel José García Márquez was raised primarily by his grandparents in a large house filled with stories, folklore, and the presence of a large extended family of aunts and uncles. He remained there until the age of eight, when he returned to the house of his mother and father in Sucré. García Márquez was deeply influenced by the years he spent in Aracataca. Regarding his life there, he wrote, "I feel that all my writing has been about the experiences of the time I spent with my grandparents." While his grandfather served as an "umbilical cord with history and reality," his grandmother was "the source of the magical, superstitious and supernatural view of reality" that appears throughout his novels and short fiction.

García Márquez attended boarding school in Baranquilla before winning a scholarship to the Liceo Nacional in Zipaquíra. Upon graduation and at the request of his parents, he enrolled in the Universidad Nacional in Bogotá to study law in 1946. Finding that his studies did not satisfy him, he turned his attention to poetry and writing. He was given a copy of **Jorge Luis Borges**'s translation of *The Metamorphosis* by **Franz Kafka,** and the book transformed him. "I thought to myself that I didn't know anyone was allowed to write things like that. If I had known, I would have started writing a long time ago." That same year, García Márquez published his first short story, "The Third Resignation," in the politically left-wing Bogotá newspaper *El Espectador*, and he immersed himself in reading and writing.

By 1950, García Márquez decided to give up his studies and devote himself full-time to writing. He returned to Baranquilla and joined a literary circle of writers and artists called *el grupo de Baranquilla*. Under their influence, García Márquez began to devour the literature of **Ernest Hemingway, James Joyce, Virginia Woolf, Albert Camus, John Dos Passos,** Erskine Caldwell, and **William Faulkner** as well as classical writers like Sophocles, whose *Oedipus Rex* remains one of his favorite works. Influenced heavily by Faulkner's fictional county of Yoknapatawpha, Mississippi, García Márquez began to envision such a device for his own writing. In 1952, he completed a novella, *La hojarasca* (*Leaf Storm*, 1979), which was set in Macondo, a fictional village named after a banana plantation in his home town of Aracataca. The manuscript was initially rejected for publication, and he put it aside. He had found the setting he needed but had not yet found the story.

In 1965, while vacationing in Mexico with his family, García Márquez had a revelation. He spent the next eighteen months writing, and in 1967 he published *Cien años de solidad* (*One Hundred Years of Solitude*, 1970), a novel deeply imbued with the characters and life of his grandparents' home in Aracataca, and set in his fictional Maconda. The novel was an instant success and secured his international reputation as a writer of the highest rank. He was awarded the Nobel Prize in literature in 1982.

In his Nobel lecture before the Swedish Academy, García Márquez delivered a politically charged speech that encompassed the breadth of his research into Latin American history and that reflected the influence of his career as a journalist in Colombia and abroad on his writing. He had lived through years of tyranny and corruption, of massacres and assassinations, and of aging tyrants who refused to let go of the reins of power. Images of death, decay, and political obstinacy, expressed in early works like *El otoño del patriarca* (*The Autumn of the Patriarch*, 1976) and *La mala hora* (*In Evil Hour*, 1968) continued to inform such later writings as *Love in the Time of Cholera, El general en su labertino* (*The General in His Labyrinth*, 1990), *Doce cuentos peregrinos* (*Strange Pilgrims*, 1994), and *Del amor y otros demonios* (*Love and Other Demons*, 1995).

Archives

No archives yet established.

Printed Sources

Bell, Michael. *Gabriel García Márquez: Solitude and Solidarity* (New York: St. Martin's Press, 1993).

Bell-Villada, Gene H. *García Márquez: The Man and His Work* (Chapel Hill: University of North Carolina Press, 1990).

Hahn, Hannalore. *The Influence of Franz Kafka on Three Novels by Gabriel García Márquez*, Comparative Cultures and Literatures, vol. 4 (New York: Peter Lang Publishing Group, 1994).

Philip Bader

GARVEY, MARCUS (MOZIAH, JR.) (1887–1940)

Marcus Garvey, champion of American Black identity, was born on August 17, 1887, in St. Ann's Bay, Jamaica, to racially pure decedents of the Maroons, African slaves who escaped to Jamaica. Young Marcus's early education ended when he was forced to move to Kingston to be apprenticed to a professional printer. His first effort at social protest came when he led a futile strike of printers in 1907, the failure of which left Garvey with a lifelong distrust of labor unions as voices of the downtrodden. He tried his luck in Costa Rica and Panama, but soon returned to Jamaica where he organized the Universal Negro Improvement and Conservation Association and African Communities League, which he hoped would bring worldwide Negro racial pride and unity.

Marcus Garvey moved to New York in 1916 in an attempt to spread his message of racial pride. By 1919 Garvey had established UNIA chapters in many major American cities. To tie African Americans together, Garvey established the Negro Factories Association, which was owned by Negro stockholders. One of Garvey's major failures was his inability to establish a Black homeland in Liberia. Garvey was convicted of mail fraud in 1925 for his fund-raising efforts for his Black Star Line shipping company and was sentenced to five years in the Atlanta Federal Penitentiary. His sentence was commuted the same year by President Calvin Coolidge. Garvey moved to London in 1934, where he died on June 10, 1940, at the age of 52.

Although his education was sporadic, Marcus Garvey was a voracious reader. During his first visit to England in the early years of the century, Garvey discovered the edicts of Pan African champion Duse Mohammed Ali in his journal *African Times and Orient Review* and then soon began working for the publication. However, the works which proved most influential in the development of Marcus Garvey were the sociological works of J. E. Casely Hayford, which introduced him to the concept of African pride and unity, and Booker T. Washington's autobiography *Up from Slavery* (1900), which argued that anyone could better one's own life through work. Later, the works of the Black American intellectual and founder of the National Association for the Advancement of Colored People (NAACP), W.E.B. DuBois, provided Garvey with ammunition to question the real worth of DuBois and his organization because Garvey felt that neither represented the entirety of America's Black population.

As strange as it might seem, Garvey utilized the words of such colonial leaders as Patrick Henry to demonstrate how seemingly futile ideas can become central to the founding of a nation or separatist movement. Garvey's strongest voicing of his philosophy of Black pride is to be found in his two-volume *The Philosophy and Opinions of Marcus Garvey* (1923, 1925).

Archives

Schomburg Center for Research in Black Culture, Harlem, New York City.
Fish University Library, Nashville, Tennessee.
The Marcus Garvey and UNIA Papers Project, James S. Coleman African Studies Center, UCLA. An attempt to gather Garvey papers from numerous other collections.

Printed Sources

Cronon, Edmund David. *Black Moses: The Story of Marcus Garvey and the Universal Negro Improvement Association* (Madison: University of Wisconsin Press, 1955). The first scholarly biography of Garvey.

Garvey, Marcus. *The Philosophy and Opinions of Marcus Garvey; or, Africa for Africans*, 2 vols., Amy Jacques Garvey (ed.) [1923, 1925] (Dover, Mass.: The Majority Press, 1986). Provides the clearest picture of Garvey's thoughts.

Hill, Robert A. (ed.). *Marcus Garvey, Life and Lessons: A Centennial Companion to the Marcus Garvey and Universal Negro Improvement Association Papers* (Berkeley: University of California Press, 1987). A guide for the Garvey Papers.

Tom Frazier

GASPERI, ALCIDE DE (1881–1954)

Alcide de Gasperi was born in Pieve Tesino (Trentino), Austria-Hungary, of middle-class parentage. In 1905 he graduated with a degree in philology at the University of Vienna; six years later, he was elected to the Austrian parliament by the Trentine Catholic regionalist party. After the Trentino was annexed by Italy at the end of the First World War, de Gasperi joined the newly formed Italian Popular Party, won election to the Chamber of Deputies in 1921, and served as the party's last leader prior to its disbanding in 1926. Accused of clandestine activities and then imprisoned for nine months by the Fascist Regime, de Gasperi was released with Vatican assistance. He spent the next decade working as a librarian at the Vatican and studiously laying the organizational and intellectual foundations for the Christian Democratic party. Much of the party's postwar program may be traced back to de Gasperi's *Reconstructive Ideas of Christian Democracy*, circulated in Rome in July 1943, just after Mussolini's fall from power. Between December 1945 and July 1953, de Gasperi headed eight successive governments, serving as the Italian Republic's first, and to this day most durable, prime minister. Relying initially upon Socialist and Communist support, de Gasperi expelled those parties from governing coalitions in 1947. The watershed 1948 elections garnered the Christian Democrats an absolute majority of seats in the Italian Chamber of Deputies. Nevertheless, de Gasperi bucked Vatican pressures and retained a multiparty governing coalition with the Social Democrats and several other small, centrist lay parties. A staunch supporter of the Western alliance and NATO, de Gasperi also espoused European federalism. In the eyes of his countrymen, however, de Gasperi was most appreciated for his leadership in reconciling Italy's Catholic and its liberal, secular national traditions.

His worldview was shaped, appropriately enough, by a combination of traditional Christian and more recent reformist writings—both spiritual and secular. Deeply versed in the scriptures, he habitually scribbled favorite biblical passages in the margins of committee minutes or other official documents. A pessimist by temperament, he was drawn to Job in the Old Testament and to the apostle Paul (especially the Letters to the Romans) in the New. Among the church fathers, St. Augustine exercised the strongest influence on de Gasperi. Like many fellow northern Italians of his day, he revered Alessandro Manzoni's Risorgimento classic *The Betrothed* (1825–27). De Gasperi insisted that Catholicism address everyday realities, that it mean more than simple piety and the observation of the sacraments. His understanding of modern industrial and class relations bore the indelible stamp of Catholic Social Teaching, particularly as articulated in Leo XIII's watershed encyclical *Rerum Novarum* (1893) and in the writings of progressive Catholic political economist Giuseppe Toniolo.

De Gasperi understood parliamentary politics as a vocation possessing its own professional standards and ethos. During the quiet decade he spent working at the Vatican library, de Gasperi researched the experience of pioneer Belgian, French, and Austrian Christian Democrats, as well as the German Center Party. He drew on the legacies of these European forerunners, and on the writings of such contemporaries as French neoscholastic Jacques Maritain in refining his own, distinctive political philosophy. De Gasperi's celebrated 1948 Brussels address, "The Moral Bases of Democracy," echoed both Maritain's *Christianity and Democracy* (1943) and the wartime Christmas radio messages of Pius XII. For all of his personal piety, however, de Gasperi was no integralist: in one biographer's words, he disliked those who "say their prayers on street corners" (Carrillo 1965, 149). This sensibility contributed in no small measure to the trust he inspired among a broad spectrum of postwar lay political leaders. Even Italian Communist Party chieftain Palmiro Togliatti, writing four years after de Gasperi's death, acknowledged the unusual "disinterestedness" and personal probity of his erstwhile political nemesis.

Archives

De Gasperi's personal papers remain closed and in the private custody of family members.

Printed Sources

Andreotti, Giulio. *De Gasperi e il suo tempo* (Milan: Mondadori, 1954).

Carrillo, Elisa. *Alcide de Gasperi: The Long Apprenticeship* (South Bend, Ind.: Notre Dame University Press, 1965). Details de Gasperi's intellectual debts to Catholic social teaching, especially pp. 106–9 and 170n.

Catti de Gasperi, Maria Romana. *De Gasperi, uomo solo* (Milan: Mondadori, 1964).

De Capua, Giovanni, (ed.). *Processo a de Gasperi: 211 testimonianze* (Rome: EBE, 1976).

De Gasperi, Alcide. *De Gasperi scrive. Corrispondenza con capi di Stato, cardinali, uomini politici, giornalisti, diplomatici, M. R. Catti de Gasperi* (ed.), (Brescia: Morcelliana, 1974).

Durand, Jean-Dominique. "Alcide de Gasperi ovvero la politica ispirata." *Storia Contemporanea* 16, 4 (Aug. 1984), 545–91. Documents the sources and significance of de Gasperi's spirituality.

Scoppola, Pietro. *La proposta politica di de Gasperi* (Bologna: Il Mulino, 1977).

Steven F. White

GATES, WILLIAM HENRY, III (1955–)

Bill Gates was born in Seattle, Washington, the second of three children of William Gates Jr., a Seattle lawyer, and Mary Maxwell Gates, a schoolteacher and heiress to two successive generations of banking fortunes. Gates was educated at Seattle's leading prep school, Lakeside, from seventh to twelfth grades. Here, the young software magnate kindled an important and long-lasting friendship with Paul Allen (1953–), future Microsoft cofounder. Together the two engrossed themselves in computer programming using a computer owned by General Electric and linked to Lakeside via a teletype machine. Eventually, the two subsidized the computer's expensive rental time fees by developing computer applications for Lakeside and for third parties. After Lakeside, Gates spent two years at Harvard University before taking a leave of absence (that would later become permanent) to form Microsoft with Allen in 1975. Gates was the primary software architect for a number of instrumental computer programming codes including Microsoft's

BASIC (Beginner's All Purpose Symbolic Instruction Code), and MS DOS, a disk operating software code used by IBM. Gates and Allen expanded on their initial success to build Microsoft into a multi-billion-dollar software empire whose "Windows" software appears on millions of computer desktops worldwide. Other top-selling Microsoft programs include "Outlook," an e-mail application, "Excel," a spreadsheet tool, and "Internet Explorer," an Internet browser. As chairman and chief executive officer of Microsoft, Gates earned the distinction of becoming the world's richest man before he reached the age of 40.

Gates has frequently described himself as an avid reader, and his preference for works on the social sciences reflects his secular enlightenment outlook. He has evinced a particular interest in biography, especially the lives of inventors and military leaders. For example, Gates's own writings have alluded to biographical and autobiographical works of and by the likes of the **Wright brothers,** Napoleon, the Chinese military strategist Sun-tzu, and Leonardo da Vinci, whose *Codex Leicester* (ca. 1508), one of 21 da Vinci notebooks known to exist, he purchased for $30.8 million in 1994. In addition, Gates has confessed a penchant for biological texts, especially those having to do with genetics and the workings of the human brain (Gates, *New York Times* column, 1995). The present-day Microsoft campus is graced with a sizable reading library that Gates frequents assiduously. He regularly reads, and has contributed essays to, the *Wall Street Journal*, the Sunday *New York Times*, *Forbes*, *USA Today*, and his personal favorite, the *Economist*, as well as other weekly news magazines. One seminal literary influence, often mentioned in writings by and about Gates, was the January 1975 issue of *Popular Electronics*. The issue's feature article on the MITS Altair 8080 computer entitled "World's First Microcomputer Kit to Rival Commercial Models" spurred Gates and Allen to develop a simple and user-friendly BASIC program for the computer in keeping with its layman's appeal. Upon the initial success of the Altair programming venture, inspired by this article, Microsoft was launched (Wallace and Erickson 1992, 67–81). Other noteworthy influences have included Alfred P. Sloane's *My Years with General Motors*, which Gates admires for its recounting of Sloane's objective, fact-based management style, and Michael Hammer and James Champy's *Reengineering the Corporation: A Manifesto for Business Revolution* (rev. ed. New York: HarperBusiness, 1997) which Gates has commended for its advocating of simple, streamlined business processes (Gates 1999, 6–11; 294–97).

Archives

There is no single public repository of Bill Gates's personal papers. An electronic archive of his essays and speeches may, however, be accessed at: http://www.microsoft.com/ billgates/default.asp.

Printed Sources

"The Bill Gates Interview: a Candid Conversation with the Sultan of Software about Outsmarting his Rivals," *Playboy*, July 1994. Gates speaks about his regular weekly and daily reading lists.

Gates, William H., III. *Business @ the Speed of Thought* (New York: Warner Books, 1999). Reflections by the Microsoft founder on the future of technology and strategies that make businesses succeed.

Gates, William H., III. *New York Times* column, http://www.microsoft.com/billgates/ columns/pastQ&A.asp. An archive of past Q & A columns written by Gates for the *New*

York Times. Several columns from 1995 discuss Gates's literary influences (1/17/95, 2/15/95, 5/9/95).

Gatlin, Jonathan. *Bill Gates: The Path to the Future* (New York: Avon Books, 1999). A compilation of biographical information and excerpts from speeches and writings by and about Gates.

Wallace, James, and James Erickson. *Hard Drive: Bill Gates and the Making of the Microsoft Empire* (New York: John Wiley, 1992).

Todd Douglas Doyle

GERSHWIN, GEORGE (1898–1937)

George Gershwin was born in Brooklyn to Russian immigrant parents on September 26, 1898. His father, Morris, worked at a number of different professions. Rose Gershwin (née Bruskin), George's mother, was actively involved with Morris in his business pursuits. George spent a good deal of time playing sports and scuffling with his buddies in the streets, often neglecting his schoolwork. One of his first contacts with music was through a talented younger schoolmate, Max Rosenzweig (later known as the violin soloist Max Rosen). George listened attentively to Max's recital from outside the school building. The Gershwins purchased a piano in 1910 with the intention of providing an instrument for George's brother Ira to practice on. George impressed his family with his ability to play compositions that he had learned on his own. He began taking piano lessons from a variety of teachers, the most influential being Charles Hambitzer.

Despite Rose's attempts to steer George into a traditional career path, George left the High School of Commerce in May of 1914. He went to work as a pianist for Jerome H. Remick & Company, an important Tin Pan Alley song publisher. During this time, George developed into an impressive performer. He also began composing songs. In 1919, Gershwin's first major success was "Swanee," with lyrics by Irving Caesar. His first Broadway show, *La La Lucille*, opened on May 26, 1919. At the invitation of Paul Whiteman, Gershwin composed *Rhapsody in Blue* for piano and orchestra (1924), his first large-scale work incorporating popular styles with music for the concert hall.

Regardless of George's lack of interest in school, he became a well-read and cultured musician. While working at Remick's, Gershwin became acquainted with the songwriter Herman Paley. He attended gatherings in his home, meeting many literary and artistic people. According to Edward Jablonski, Gershwin "was aware of the currents in contemporary music, he attended concerts and recitals of 'modern' music, he subscribed to Henry Cowell's avant-garde quarterly, *New Music*, collected scores and recordings, with Stravinsky and Sibelius sharing shelf space with Bach, Schubert and Hindemith" (Jablonski 1987, xi). In his book *A Smattering of Ignorance*, Oscar Levant reveals that Gershwin's reading matter included "such standard fact books as the Grove Dictionary and Cobbett's *Cyclopaedic Survey of Chamber Music*," as well as "virtually every worthwhile musical book of his own time, and many older ones" (Levant 1940, 194–95). Gershwin was impressed with DuBose Heyward's novel *Porgy*. Working closely with Heyward, Gershwin brought *Porgy's* characters to life in his American opera, *Porgy and Bess*. The opera opened in New York at the Alvin Theater on October 10, 1935.

Perhaps the greatest influence on George's career was the close relationship that he had with his brother, Ira (1896–1983). In contrast to George, Ira was a student and a reader. He had a gift for writing both witty and sentimental song lyrics. Their first collaboration was a tune called "The Rag" in 1918. In *Fascinating Rhythm: The Collaboration of George and Ira Gershwin*, Deena Rosenberg quotes Ira's description of his working relationship with George: "We are both pretty critical and outspoken, George about my lyrics and I about his music . . ." (Rosenberg 1991, 154). According to their mutual friend, Oscar Levant, "The brightness of Ira's thought acted as a spur to George's musical resources and produced many songs that departed from the conventions they had found. They also strongly influenced others" (Levant 1940, 203–4).

Archives

George and Ira Gershwin Collection, Museum of the City of New York.
George Gershwin Memorial Collection, Fisk University.
Gershwin Collection, Library of Congress, Washington, D.C.
New York Public Library, Music and Theater Divisions.

Printed Sources

Gilbert, Steven E. *The Music of Gershwin* (New Haven: Yale University Press, 1995).
Jablonski, Edward. *Gershwin* (New York: Doubleday, 1987).
Kendall, Alan. *George Gershwin* (New York: Universe Books, 1987).
Kresh, Paul. *An American Rhapsody: The Story of George Gershwin*. Jewish Biography Series (New York: Lodestar Books–E. P. Dutton, 1988).
Levant, Oscar. *A Smattering of Ignorance* (New York: Doubleday, Doran & Co., Inc., 1940).
Peyser, Joan. *The Memory of All That: The Life of George Gershwin* (New York: Simon & Schuster, 1993).
Rosenberg, Deena. *Fascinating Rhythm: The Collaboration of George and Ira Gershwin* (New York: Dutton-Penguin Books, 1991).
Schneider, Wayne (ed.). *The Gershwin Style: New Looks at the Music of George Gershwin* (New York: Oxford University Press, 1999).
Schwartz, Charles. *Gershwin: His Life and Music* (Indianapolis: The Bobbs-Merrill Company, 1973).

Marianne Wilson

GHEORGHIU-DEJ, GHEORGHE (1901–1965)

Gheorghe Gheorghiu-Dej was born in Bîrlad, a small town on Romania's eastern frontier, the son of a laborer. After four years' elementary schooling, he was apprenticed in various trades before becoming an electrician, working in railway yards in Galaţi, a large port on the Danube, and Griviţa, Bucharest (1916–33; military service 1921–23). His entry into the then-outlawed Romanian Communist Party is not clearly documented but definitely occurred before February 1933, when he was arrested for his involvement in the Griviţa railway workers' strike, the most significant Communist-backed labor protest in interwar Romania. The next 10 years were spent in and out of prisons. In 1936, as one of the few native working-class Romanian activists, he was elected to the Central Committee of the Party. After the Soviet military occupation of Romania in 1944, he was released from Târgu Jiu internment camp. He was elected secretary-general of the Party from October 1945, held various ministerial posts, and in 1951 became prime minister, following which various purges of the "Muscovite" wing of the Party in Romania were organized. Elected president of the State Council in 1961, he held this post until his death in 1965.

An election propaganda article published in the Communist paper *Scânteia* (*The Spark*, 8 November 1946), relates that Dej became a communist in 1930 on finding a leaflet lying in the street commemorating the anniversary of a strike. On attending a workers' meeting, he spoke using the language of the leaflet and was sought out afterward by a party agent. This conversion parable was clearly composed more to inculcate an exemplary model of the effectiveness of propaganda than to convey a historical event. Those who worked closely with Dej have stressed his limited educational horizons in favorable or unfavorable contrast to intellectual or Moscow-trained rivals. His main induction into Marxism-Leninism almost certainly took place in Doftana prison (1938–1944), where **Nicolae Ceauşescu** was also interned; it is also here that he is said to have learned Russian and possibly Yiddish under the instruction of veteran communist Gheorghe Stoica.

His close collaborator and successor as prime minister, Ion Gheorge Maurer, affirmed that Dej had little understanding of Leninism except through Stalin's ideas, but stressed his shrewdness (Betea 1995, 18). Alexandru Bârlădeanu, once his economics minister, claimed that Maurer helped Dej write one of his few theoretical publications, *O politică românească* (*A Romanian politics*, 1944). Romanian communists joked in the 1950s, at the height of efforts to Sovietize the Romanian economic system, that "maybe we should put off the construction of socialism till Gheorghe gets his high-school certificates" (Betea and Bârlădeanu 1998, 74). However, the same sources also emphasize Dej's eagerness to "cultivate" himself: he apparently enjoyed the novels of the distinguished critic and writer George Călinescu, namely *Bietul Ioanide* (*Poor Ioanide*, 1953) and *Scrinul negru* (*The Black Chest*, 1960), which portray the experiences of intellectuals adapting to the new regime (Betea and Bârlădeanu 1998, 45–46). Paul Sfetcu, his long-serving deputy *chef de cabinet*, writes that "he read a lot, particularly political literature" without going into more details, but also that he took no particular interest in organizing the display bookshelves in his office.

Archives

Archives of the Central Committee of the Romanian Communist Party, National Archives, Bucharest.

Printed Sources

Betea, Lavinia (interviewer). *Maurer şi lumea de ieri. Mărturii despre stalinizarea României* (Arad, Romania: Fundaţia culturală "Ioan Slavici," 1995).

Betea, Lavinia (interviewer), and Alexandru Bârlădeanu. *Alexandru Bârlădeanu despre Dej, Ceauşescu şi Iliescu* (Bucureşti: Evenimentul românesc, 1998).

Deletant, Dennis. *Communist Terror in Romania: Gheorghiu-Dej and the Police State, 1948–1965* (London: Hurst, 1999).

Sfetcu, Paul. *13 ani în anticamera lui Dej* (Bucureşti: Fundaţia culturală română, 2000).

Tismăneanu, Vladimir. *Fantoma lui Gheorghiu-Dej* (Bucureşti: Univers, 1995).

Alexander Drace-Francis

GIBRAN, KAHLIL (1883–1931)

A Lebanon-born writer who lived in Boston and New York City for most of his life, Kahlil Gibran is best known as the author of *The Prophet* (1923), the loosely organized tale of a mystic philosopher who speaks in parables. Other notable works include *The Broken Wings* (1912), *A Tear and a Smile* (1914), *The Madman* (1918), *Sand and Foam* (1926), *Jesus, Son of Man* (1928), and the posthumous *The Garden of the Prophet* (1933).

Gibran was born in Bsharri, a Maronite Christian community in what is now modern-day Lebanon. The family emigrated to Boston in 1895. By chance Gibran caught the attention of a number of prominent Bostonians who encouraged and supported the young immigrant. Gibran returned to Lebanon for college. He returned to America after his studies, but personal tragedy struck the young Gibran when he lost his sister, half-brother, and mother all within a few months of his return. Gibran continued to live in Boston, largely supported by his benefactors. After studying abroad in Paris (where he met Auguste Rodin) and London for short durations, Gibran settled permanently in New York City from 1911 until his death in 1931. Gibran never acquired American citizenship, having become involved in Lebanese patriotism and the movement for Lebanese independence from Syria. Upon his death, Gibran willed his personal effects, including his papers, to his hometown of Bsharri, Lebanon.

Gibran naturally gravitated to the introspective and mystic, owing equally to his outsider immigrant status, early family tragedy, and personal inclination. He absorbed a good number of influences, the majority of which seemed to have been American, French, and British writers. Boston's rich transcendental tradition of Henry David Thoreau (*Walden*, 1854), Ralph Waldo Emerson (*Essays*, 1841 and *Essays*, 1844) and Walt Whitman (*Leaves of Grass*, 1855) were both an inspiration for and affirmation of his beliefs. The Belgian writer and dramatist Maurice Maeterlinck (*The Treasure of the Humble*, 1897), a name more prominent then than now, was an important early influence. Artist-poet-mystic William Blake was a kindred spirit and an influence on the young philosopher-writer. Friedrich Nietzsche's *Thus Spake Zarathustra* (1885) provided the format for Gibran's *Prophet*. Other important formative influences included **William Butler Yeats,** Edward Carpenter, Ernest Renan, and Algernon Charles Swinburne.

Gibran was more concerned with formulating philosophical ideas in his prose and poetry than crafting fiction. Together with his interest in drawing and painting, his writing makes him a sort of Renaissance man or man-of-letters. Gibran's influence, based chiefly on *The Prophet*, grew steadily after his death. Annual sales reached the millions during the 1960s and 1970s and remain strong today.

Archives

Kahlil Gibran Museum in Bsharri, Lebanon.

Printed Sources

Ditelberg, Joshua L. "Kahlil Gibran's Early Intellectual Life, 1883–1908" (M.A. thesis, University of Pennsylvania, 1987).

Gibran, Jean, and Kahlil Gibran. *Kahlil Gibran: His Life and World* (New York: Interlink Books, 1974).

Ostle, Robin. "The Romantic Poets." In Muhammad M. Badawi (ed.), *Modern Arabic Literature* (Cambridge: Cambridge University Press, 1992), 82–131.

Waterfield, Robin. *Prophet: The Life and Times of Kahlil Gibran* (New York: St. Martin's Press, 1998).

Charles Allan

GIDE, ANDRÉ (1869–1951)

André Gide was born and educated in Paris, at Pension Keller (now Reid Hall), Ecole Alsacienne, and Lycée Henri IV. Gide experimented with the full spectrum of literary genres but is remembered less as fiction writer than as autobiographical chronicler equally revealing of himself and his times. Perhaps no other author until our day has so relentlessly (perhaps narcissistically) observed, dramatized, and analyzed his life and world. This greatest French moralist and immoralist of the last century, alternately Protestant puritan and pagan hedonist, was awarded the Nobel Prize for literature in 1947 and placed on the Papal Index in 1952.

His early life wavered between opposite poles: the Bible, carried in his coat pocket, and the Arabian Nights, which his father had also read to him. His first conscious act was onanism, ages five to nine, followed from age 13 by obsession with older cousin Madeleine: their unconsummated marriage came in 1895, soon after his mother's death. By 15 was established another precocious passion, reading. Young Gide devoured daily at least one book. His childhood readings were in religion (François Fénélon's *Traité de l'existence de Dieu*, Bishop Bossuet's *De la connaissance de Dieu*, Augustine's *Confessions*) rather than in poetry, which would have suited him better. His late father's "bookcase of poets" was locked until Gide was almost 16, when his mother opened its glass doors to him. Following the "most moving discovery" of Heinrich Heine's lyrics he conceived a "passionate predilection" for verse. Gide memorized Victor Hugo from a "charming little edition" given to his mother and discovered in the Leconte de Lisle translations given to him those Greeks "who have had such a decisive influence on my mind," such as the *Iliad* and the *Oresteia*. "Through them, I beheld Olympus, and the suffering of man, and the smiling severity of the gods." Christian and Apollonian ideals were not then contradictory for Gide. Instead, "everything contributed to making me as I am today." His virtually lifelong diary, kept "out of a need to give shape to a chaotic inner agitation," began just months after conceiving a "most sincere" admiration for *Amiel's Journal* (1883), lent him by his tutor. At 16, when reading Heine's *Book of Songs* in translation, he underwent the headier influence of younger Alsacienne classmate Pierre Louÿs. At 18 through Louÿs he discovered Faust, a closer elective affinity: Gide preferred comparison to Johann von Goethe over Voltaire. His "initiation into philosophy" was Arthur Schopenhauer's *World as Will and Idea* in 1889. In 1903 he said his youth was much affected by German literature, but in the long term "what Goethe, Heine, Schopenhauer, Nietzsche perhaps taught me best was their admiration for France." Gide entered Stephen Mallarmé's influential symbolist circle in 1891. His encounter with Oscar Wilde that year and with North Africa in 1893 liberated him from Victorianism and facilitated the acceptance of his homosexuality. He had left his beloved Bible at home in France.

"Concerning Influence in Literature" (1900) is Gide's apologia for all influences, unavoidable and necessary. Genuine affinity, not hack work, is reflected in his translations or presentations of Goethe (universal curiosity, said **Thomas Mann**), Wilde (vice authorized), Montaigne and Walt Whitman (self-celebratory confessional), Fyodor Dostoyevsky ("l'acte gratuit"), Rabindranath Tagore and Blake (mystic lyricism), Joseph Conrad's *Typhoon*, and Shakespeare's *Hamlet*. By his definition he authored only one novel, *The Counterfeiters*. His youthful desert-island lists included no extended prose fiction and comparatively few French authors. When he accepted to prepare a roster of the 10 leading French novels,

Stendhal's *Charterhouse of Parma* and Laclos's *Dangerous Liaisons* came first. From his long career and massive output Gide in 1946 said if only one work of his were to survive, he would choose the *Journal*.

Archives

Bibliothèque Doucet, Paris, has correspondence, manuscripts, and papers, some unpublished.

Printed Sources

Davenport, William Wyatt. *An Old House in Paris: The Story of Reid Hall* (Paris: Reid Hall, 1969).
Delay, Jean. *The Youth of André Gide* (Chicago: University of Chicago, 1963).
Gide, André. *Dostoevsky* (New York: New Directions, 1961).
———. *If It Die* (Harmondsworth: Penguin, 1977).
———. *Imaginary Interviews* (New York: Knopf, 1944).
———. *The Journal*, 4 vols. (New York: Knopf, 1947–51).
———. *Montaigne* (New York: McGraw-Hill, 1964).
———. *Oscar Wilde* (New York: Philosophical Library, 1949).
———. *Pretexts* (New York: Delta, 1964).
Fayer, Mischa. *Gide, Freedom and Dostoevsky* (Burlington: Lane, 1946).
Fryer, Jonathan. *André and Oscar* (New York: St. Martin's, 1997).
Guggenheim, Michel. "Gide and Montaigne," *Yale French Studies* 7 (1951), 107–14.
Lang, B. Renée. *André Gide et la pensée allemande* (Paris: Egloff, 1949).
Sheridan, Alan. *André Gide: A Life in the Present* (Cambridge: Harvard, 1999).

Roy Rosenstein

GINSBERG, ALLEN (1926–1997)

Irwin Allen Ginsberg, American poet and social activist, was born June 3, 1926, in Newark, New Jersey, and raised in nearby Paterson. He died April 5, 1997, in New York City of a heart attack, shortly after being diagnosed with liver cancer. His parents were Louis Ginsberg, a high school English teacher, poet, and socialist; and Naomi (Levy) Ginsberg, a Marxist, who suffered from chronic mental illness. Allen's interest in poetry came early, probably influenced by his father reading poetry aloud at home. By age 11 he was writing his own poems. Naomi's struggles with mental illness had a profound impact on her son. *Kaddish*, one of his two most critically acclaimed works, is drawn from her life and from the family's Jewish heritage. According to biographer Barry Miles, "He became the poet advocate of the underdog" and "the most famous living poet on earth" (Miles 1989, 533).

Ginsberg entered Columbia University in September 1943 and received an A.B. degree in 1948, though he later said his formal education had been a waste of time. He began his studies in prelaw, but changed to literature and studied with traditionalists Mark Van Doren and Lionel Trilling. Their influence on him waned when he met and became friends with the personalities and writers who would form the core of the Beat Generation: Lucien Carr, **William Burroughs, Jack Kerouac,** John Clellon Holmes, Neal Cassady, and Gregory Corso. Burroughs introduced him to the works of **Franz Kafka,** W. B. Yeats, Céline, Arthur Rimbaud, and most importantly, to the poetry of William Blake, whose voice appeared to Ginsberg in an "auditory vision" in 1948. He heard Blake reciting *Ah! Sunflower* and *The Sick Rose* from *Songs of Innocence and Experience* and opened to levels of perception and consciousness beyond the ordinary. The experience was so profound he spent the next 15 years seeking to expand his consciousness through the use of psychedelics. Kerouac impressed upon him the idea of "spontaneous prose," which emphasized writing what one felt at the moment and not revising. Kerouac thought revision destroyed the creation of the moment and lessened the work. Neither Burroughs nor Kerouac had been published at the time, but Ginsberg did read Burroughs's notes for his first novel, *Junky*, published in 1950. Kerouac shared his journals and experimental writings, which were the basis for his 1957 breakthrough novel *On the Road*.

Ginsberg developed a long breath line poetry that was personal and based on speech rhythms and imagery drawn from everyday language. He first heard his high school English teacher read Walt Whitman's *Leaves of Grass*. This was a poetry that was personal and that spoke with an American voice. His own long breath style was derived from Whitman's long lines. He was also reading **William Carlos Williams** in high school, and it was Williams who most influenced his early poems. In 1947 he wrote a favorable review of the first book of Williams's five-book epic *Paterson* in his hometown newspaper. He met the poet in 1950 and Williams impressed upon him the importance of verse capturing the actual sounds and rhythms of American speech. He began to rework his own writings and submitted them to Williams for critique. Williams liked what he read and became a mentor, writing the introductions to *Howl* and *Empty Mirror*. Ginsberg was also influenced by the precise speech emphasis and "direct treatment of the thing" in the poetry of **Ezra Pound,** as in *The Cantos* and earlier works.

Ginsberg moved to California in 1954 and became part of the San Francisco Poetry Renaissance, a group of writers including Kenneth Rexroth, Lawrence Ferlinghetti, Gary Snyder, Michael McClure, Philip Lamantia, Robert Duncan, and Philip Whalen. There he also met Peter Orlovsky, who would be his companion and lover for most of the rest of his life. His reading of *Howl* at the Six Gallery in October 1955 catapulted him and the Beat movement into public awareness. He lived in San Francisco for about three years, then in Tangier and Paris before traveling in India and the Far East during 1962–63. When he returned to the United States, he made New York his home.

Buddhism became a significant influence on Ginsberg's work from the time he was introduced to it by Kerouac, Snyder, and Whalen in the mid-1950s. When he and Orlovsky traveled in India and on his own solo trip through parts of the Far East, he sought out holy men to deepen his spiritual awareness. His growing identification of himself as a "Buddhist–Jew" and the poverty he saw in India influenced him to abandon his obsession with drug-induced attempts to expand his consciousness and led him toward a life of social activisim and serious Buddhist practice. In 1970 he met Chogyam Trungpa, Rinpoche who told him he should make up poems on the spot, and who became a spiritual and literary mentor until his death in 1987. In 1989 Tibetan Lama Ngawang Gelek, Rinpoche became Ginsberg's friend and spiritual mentor.

Archives

Allen Ginsberg Papers, M0733, Dept. of Special Collections, Stanford University Libraries, Stanford, Calif. http://www.oac.cdlib.org/dynaweb/ead/stanford/mss/m0733. The collection contains Ginsberg's personal papers through 1997, including literary manuscripts, journals, correspondence, photographs, and tape recordings as well as his library.

Printed Sources

"Allen Ginsberg," in *Dictionary of Literary Biography, Volume 169: American Poets Since World War II, Fifth Series*. A Bruccoli Clark Layman Book. Joseph Conte (ed.), (State University of New York at Buffalo: The Gale Group, 1996), 116–36.

Miles, Barry. *Ginsberg: A Biography* (New York: Simon and Schuster, 1989).

Morgan, Bill. *The Response to Allen Ginsberg, 1926–1994: A Bibliography of Secondary Sources* (Westport, Conn.: Greenwood Press, 1996).

———. *The Works of Allen Ginsberg, 1941–1994* (Westport, Conn.: Greenwood Press, 1995).

Schumacher, Michael. *Dharma Lion: A Biography of Allen Ginsberg* (New York: St. Martin's Press, 1992).

Jerry Shuttle

GODARD, JEAN-LUC (1930–)

Jean-Luc Godard was born in Paris. In 1940, he became a Swiss citizen but returned to Paris in 1949 to study ethnology at the Sorbonne. In the 1950s, he regularly attended the Cinéclub and the Cinémathèque, where he met other future *nouvelle vague* filmmakers such as **François Truffaut,** Éric Rohmer, Claude Chabrol, and Jacques Rivette. During this time, Godard began writing for the *Cahiers du cinéma*, founded by André Bazin, whose ideas on film greatly influenced these young men. In 1960, his first feature-length film, *À bout de souffle*, was released in Paris, marking the turning point not only for Godard's own career, but for the *nouvelle vague* as a whole. In the 1960s, Godard produced some of his most cinematically innovative films. As he aligned himself with far-leftist and militant movements, his films became more overtly political. At the same time, he founded the Dziga Vertov Group with Jean-Pierre Gorin, which embodied the ideal of collective filmmaking. It was during this period that he met and married Anne Wiazemsky. In the 1970s, Godard divorced Wiazemsky and founded his own film and video production studio with Anne-Marie Miéville, with whom he continues to make and produce provocative and innovative films.

Godard's influences are literary and political as well as cinematic. The numerous quotations in his films are testimony to his vast knowledge of literature and philosophy (see the interview *Les livres et moi* in Bergala 1985, 1988, II, 432–39). His films, critical writings, and interviews also reveal his numerous cinematic influences. He particularly admired the films of Howard Hawks, as is evident in his *Défense et Illustration du découpage classique* (1952). In the same article, he praises the techniques and aims of **Sergei Eisenstein,** the influence of whom can also be seen in Godard's other theoretical writings, *Pour un cinéma politique* (1950) and *Montage, Mon Beau Souci* (1956). The films of such diverse directors as **D. W. Griffith, Alfred Hitchcock,** Jean Renoir, Jean Rouch, and **Roberto Rossellini,** among many others, are referred to constantly by Godard and informed his ideas on filmmaking.

Godard's education exposed him to ideas which formed the basis of his theories on cinema. His thoughts on the semiology of film are rooted in Brice Parain's *Recherches sur la nature et les fonctions du langage* (1942) (Parain later appeared in *Vivre sa vie*), and the work of Ferdinand de Saussure. It is likely that Maurice Merleau-Ponty's thoughts on cinema informed some of Godard's own reflections on film as perception. The ideas of **Bertolt Brecht** on the role of the spectator also play a large part in his theory. In his *Défense*, Godard proposes a dialectic cinema, showing his debt to Friedrich Hegel. His politics are greatly influenced by Karl Marx and Louis Althusser, while his more militant views are rooted in the ideas of Mao Zedong. The writings of all three thinkers are quoted extensively in Godard's films.

Archives

No single collection, although major film archives housing prints of films, stills, clippings, and screenplays are listed in Lesage 1979, 419–21.

Printed Sources

Bergala, Alain (ed.). *Godard par Godard*, 2 vols. (Paris: Cahiers du cinéma/Étoile, 1985, 1998). Collected writings, interviews, and photographs.
Dixon, Wheeler Winston. *The Films of Jean-Luc Godard* (Albany: SUNY Press, 1997).
Lesage, Julia. *Jean-Luc Godard. A Guide to References and Resources* (Boston: G. K. Hall, 1979).
Monaco, James. *The New Wave* (New York: Oxford University Press, 1977).
Roud, Richard. *Jean-Luc Godard*, 2nd rev. ed. (London: Thames and Hudson in association with the British Film Institute, 1970).

Linda Ness

GOEBBELS, JOSEPH PAUL (1897–1945)

Joseph Goebbels was born in Rheydt, Germany. He was raised a Roman Catholic and was known as a reserved yet scholarly boy in school. He was teased relentlessly by his peers due to his crippled foot, the result of a bout with polio. This disability, along with his small stature and his dark features (children taunted him for looking "Jewish," which he loathed) haunted him for the rest of his life. After completing his education in the gymnasium in Rheydt, Goebbels was accepted at the University of Heidelberg, where he studied for his doctorate in German literature and history. As a member of the Catholic student fraternity "Unitas," Goebbels received an Albertus Magnus Society loan for poor Catholics, a loan whose repayment he would shirk his entire life. His professor, Dr. Friedrich Gundolf, a Jewish literary historian, Goethe scholar, and disciple of the poet Stefan Georg, ironically became one of Goebbels's favorite instructors. His doctoral thesis was entitled *Wilhelm von Schaetz as Dramatist: A Contribution to the History of the Drama of the Romantic School*. Goebbels even wrote a novel, *Michael: Ein deutsches Schicksal in Tagebuchblaettern* (1926), which was not well received. However, Goebbels's childhood had affected him strongly, even as an adult. In a effort to compensate for his stature, the "Little Doctor," as he later came to be called, turned to strong anti-Semitic rhetoric and right-wing extremism as the Nazis surged into power in the late 1920s and early 1930s. He had switched to **Adolf Hitler**'s party in 1926 and became a master propagandist as well as a cultural dictator. He created all sorts of myths and dredged up old historical legends against Jews to advance Hitler's cause and the Nazi propaganda against the Jews. He built up Hitler into the powerful force he became, a fact for which Hitler was truly grateful.

In 1933, Goebbels became the Reichsminister for Public Enlightenment. He also staged the famous book-burning in Berlin on May 10, 1933. Marxist, Jewish, and other "undesirable" authors had their works destroyed in massive bonfires.

Under Goebbels's instructions, Jews were banned from law, medicine, public offices, and entertainment. This hatred was fed to the public in large doses and became a way to mobilize the masses into supporting the Nazis' values. He was especially interested in the use of film as a propaganda tool and enticed many German actors into performing in his films. One director, **Fritz Lang** (1890–1976), managed to elude Goebbels's requests for films by quickly emigrating.

After Hitler committed suicide in 1945, Goebbels had an SS doctor inject his children with poison, while he and his wife, Magda, had themselves shot by an SS orderly on May 1, 1945.

As a student of literature, Goebbels was introduced to a world of great German literature. He was especially influenced by Johann Wolfgang von Goethe's works, such as *Wilhelm Meisters Lehrjahre* (1795–96) and *Faust* (1808), both of which reflect the richness of the literature of the romantic era in Germany. Hoffmann von Fallersleben's poem *Lied der Deutschen* (1841), in which the greatness of Germany is expressed, had a particularly strong influence upon Goebbels. Falsely interpreted by the Nazis, this poem of the romantic era supplied the words to the German national hymn. Karl Marx's writings, among them *The Communist Manifesto* (1848), aided in deepening his hatred of the Jews and their "invention" of Communism. However, Goebbels also appears to have been greatly influenced by his own doctoral thesis in drama, having studied Friedrich Schiller's *Kabale und Liebe* (1792) and Gotthold Ephraim Lessing's *Nathan der Weise* (1779). Drama had been used in the Enlightenment and the romantic period as an educational tool for the audience. Indeed it is from his own study of drama that Goebbels turned to film in order to advance his propaganda cause. He had also read Hitler's *Mein Kampf* (1925), which became especially influential in his lending his wholehearted support to Hitler's manifest against the Jews.

Archives

National Archives, Modern Military Branch, Washington, D.C. Films, correspondence, historical records on World War II.

Bundesarchiv, Koblenz, Germany. Propaganda films, correspondence, war records, historical records on World War II.

Munich Film Archives (Reichsfilmarchiv), Munich, Germany. Propaganda films.

Holocaust Museum, Washington, D.C. War records, Holocaust records, photography archive and other audio-visual recordings.

Printed Sources

Boelke, Willi A. *The Secret Conferences of Dr. Goebbels: The Nazi Propaganda War, 1939–1943,* Willi A. Boelke (ed.), Ewald Osers (trans.), (New York: E.P. Dutton, 1970).

Goebbels, Joseph. *Die Tagebuecher von Josef Goebbels: Saemtliche Fragmente.* Hsg. Elke Froehlich im Auftrag des Instituts fuer Zeitgeschichte und in Verbindung mit dem Bundesarchiv (Muenchen: K.B. Sauer, 1987).

———. *The Goebbels Diaries, 1939–1941,* Fred Taylor (ed. and trans.), (New York: Putnam, 1983).

Moeller, Felix. *The Film Minister: Goebbels and the Cinema in the Third Reich* (Stuttgart: Edition Axel Menges, 2000).

Riess, Curt. *Josef Goebbels: A Biography* (Garden City, N.Y.: Doubleday, 1948).

Cynthia A. Klima

GOMPERS, SAMUEL (1850–1924)

Samuel Gompers was born in London, attending the Jewish Free School in London from 1856 to 1860. However, owing to his family's poverty, he left school at the age of 10. Emigrating with his family to the United States in 1863, Gompers followed his father into the cigar-making trade and became a naturalized citizen in 1872. In 1873 he went to work for David Hirsch, who ran the only union cigar shop in New York City. Attending a conference of unions in 1881 where a loose affiliation called the Federation of Organized Trades and Labor Councils was formed, Gompers was named its first leader. Owing to its poor organization, Gompers reorganized the Federation into American Federation of Labor (AFL) in 1886. By 1892 the AFL had over one million members. Gompers served as president of the AFL from 1886 to 1924. During an era when the public was largely hostile to unions, Gompers developed the philosophy of "voluntarism," which stressed the union's use of strikes, boycotts, and other efforts deleterious to business. Gompers emphasized the development of a powerful union of skilled workers rather than widening the AFL's membership to include unskilled labor. After remaining politically neutral for many years, the AFL endorsed William Jennings Bryan for president in 1908 after courts declared many union tactics illegal. Gompers attended the Versailles Treaty negotiations, where he helped create the International Labor Organization, an arm of the League of Nations. Gompers died while attending the Congress of the Pan-American Federation of Labor, which sought to establish trade unions in Mexico.

Most of Gompers's biographers describe him as a man who rarely read and whose labor philosophies came as much from hard-won experience as from any literary influence. Louis Reed described him as practical and anti-intellectual. However, it is important to note that, as a worker in David Hirsch's cigar shop, Gompers was exposed to a wide variety of literature through the shop readers, whose job it was to keep workers' minds occupied. Readers also provided information from many of the labor papers of the day, including *The Workingmen's Advocate*, published by A. C. Cameron in Chicago, and the *National Labor Tribune*, published by John M. Davis in Pittsburgh. Henry George's *Progress and Poverty*, first published, as Gompers recalled, in pamphlet form in the *Irish World*, was also read to the workers and provided grist for many discussions. Hirsch, as well as many of his employees, were German exiles whose revolutionary activities had led to their expulsion from Hamburg. Swede Karl Malcolm Ferdinand Laurrell, the shop's intellectual leader, gave Gompers a copy of Karl Marx's *Communist Manifesto*. Determined to appreciate its full meaning, Gompers learned German, reading not only the *Manifesto*, but also works by Friedrich Engels, Ferdinand Lassalle, and others. Gompers was especially fond of German socialist Carl Hillman's pamphlet, entitled *Emancipationswinke (Emancipation Hints)*, which awakened Gompers to the potential power of trade unions.

Archives

M. P. Catherwood Library, Cornell University, Ithaca, N.Y.: notebooks, scrapbooks, correspondence.

Rare Books and Manuscripts Division, New York Public Library, New York City, N.Y.: scrapbooks, testimonials, and memorials, photographs, certificates, printed matter, and ephemera.

State Historical Society of Wisconsin, Madison, Wisc.: correspondence, speeches, writings, reports, clippings, miscellaneous material.

Printed Sources

Gompers, Samuel. *Seventy Years of Life and Labour* (New York: Augustus M. Kelley Publishers, 1925).

Kaufman, Stuart Bruce. *Samuel Gompers and the Origins of the American Federation of Labor, 1848–1896* (Westport, Conn.: Greenwood Press, 1973).

Mandel, Bernard. *Samuel Gompers: A Biography* (Yellow Springs, Ohio: Antioch Press, 1963).

Reed, Louis. *The Labor Philosophy of Samuel Gompers* (Port Washington, N.Y.: Kennikat Press, Inc., 1930).

Paul Allan Hillmer

GORBACHEV, MIKHAIL SERGEYEVICH (1931–)

Mikhail Gorbachev was born in Privolnoye in the Stavropol territory of Southern Russia. Gorbachev started his career as a farm machinery operator, but at the age of 19 was accepted into the prestigious Moscow State University, where he studied history, literature, and physics before turning his attention to law. He graduated with a law degree in 1952 and became a full member of the Communist Party. Publicly loyal to the policies of **Josef Stalin** but privately critical of the leader's severe actions throughout the Second World War, Gorbachev agreed with **Nikita Khrushchev** that the Soviet government was in need of reform and modernization. In 1960, Gorbachev became the leader of Stavropol's communist newsgroup and by 1963 was in charge of the territory's collective farms. He studied and completed a degree in agronomy and began to restructure the local agricultural system to increase productivity. Scaling the political ladder, Gorbachev became secretary of the Stavropol Communist Organization in 1970, where he met Yuri Andropov and Konstantin Chernenko. He was appointed by Andropov to the Secretariat of the Communist Central Committee in 1971, and later became the Party secretary in charge of agriculture (1978) and the youngest full member of the Politburo (1980). After the death of Chernenko in 1985, Gorbachev was elected as Soviet general secretary and party head. Under Gorbachev's policies of perestroika (reform) and glasnost (openness), the entire structure of the Soviet Union was changed. The consumption of alcohol was limited, a free market economy was implemented and public elections were instituted for party officials. As well, relationships with the West were strengthened and the production of nuclear arms significantly limited. His Communist Party failed to hold the fragmenting Soviet Union together, and after a major coup in 1991, Gorbachev resigned as party head as waves of former Soviet republics declared their independence. For his contributions to world peace, Gorbachev was awarded the Nobel Peace Prize in 1990. Upon his retirement he became head of a political research group in Moscow and is still active in politics.

Gorbachev frequently modernized the writings of **Vladimir Ilyich Lenin,** the founder of the Soviet State, and applied them to the political and social situation within the Soviet Union at the time of his leadership. Gorbachev's glasnost was directly derived from the Leninist concept of free and frequent criticism of the state. Under Gorbachev's rule, this would include the expansion of media freedoms (and consequently an increase in government scrutiny), as well as a critical reexamination of Soviet history. Lenin's *Imperialism, the Highest Stage of Capitalism* (1916) was also influential to Gorbachev's decentralizing reform efforts through its criticism of the dictatorial and complex nature of Western bureaucracy. His concept of democratic centralism allowed for a freedom of discussion, criticism, and debate that was firmly rooted in Lenin's original treatises. Along with studying Karl Marx's *Das Kapital*, Gorbachev also read Thomas Aquinas's *Summa Theologica*, Thomas Hobbes's *The Elements of Law, Natural and Politic* and John Locke's *Two Treatises of Civil Government*, whose common emphasis on natural law and the innate rights of the individual helped to structure his humanitarian reform efforts. Finally, Gorbachev's decentralization of the Soviet State was supported in the writings of economist Abel Aganbegyan and the social critic Tatyana Zaslavskaya, both of whom published their work in the era immediately previous to his leadership.

Archives

Russian State Historical Archives (RGIA), St. Petersburg, Russia.
The Library of Congress, Washington, D.C. Control # 2001052443. Includes 71-page notebook (1994) and interviews conducted by Zdnek Mlynar.

Printed Sources

Brown, Archie. *The Gorbachev Factor* (London: Oxford University Press, 1996).
Gorbachev, Mikhail. *Memoirs* (New York: Doubleday, 1995).
Sakwa, Richard. *Gorbachev and His Reforms, 1985–1990* (Upper Saddle River, N. J.: Prentice Hall, 1991).

Gregory L. Schnurr

GORDIMER, NADINE (1923–)

Nadine Gordimer, South African novelist, essayist, and short-story writer, was born in Springs, a mining town near Johannesburg. Born to Jewish parents, Gordimer spent her early years in a convent school, but when she was 11, her mother removed her from formal schooling, claiming that the child had a heart condition. From age 11 through 16, Gordimer was tutored at home. This period was one of extensive self-direction, in which Gordimer read widely from British and European novels. In 1943, Gordimer began studying at the University of Witwatersrand but left after one year. Thereafter, she began publishing regularly. Her first book of short stories, *Face to Face*, was published in 1949. *The Lying Days*, her first novel, appeared in 1953. To date, she has published 13 novels, over 150 short stories, and over 200 nonfictional essays. She has been the recipient of many literary prizes, including the Booker Prize (1974) and the Nobel Prize for literature (1991).

Gordimer was first influenced by the British tradition, in particular **E. M. Forster, D. H. Lawrence,** and **Virginia Woolf.** Many critics note the influence that British fictional forms have had on Gordimer's fiction, citing in particular her association with the liberal humanist tradition and its emphasis on the individual, social realism, and familial themes. We see this influence primarily in her early stories and novels, which show an intense focus on character development and psychological enlightenment. Also in her early years, Gordimer was influenced by the social upheaval expressed by nineteenth-century Russian writers, most significantly Anton Chekhov and Ivan Turgenev, as well as by the style of Guy de Maupassant, **Thomas Mann, James Joyce,** and **Marcel Proust,** whom she calls her "great mentor." One of Gordimer's noted achievements is her ability to combine British/European literary techniques with an African consciousness. The literary theorist most often connected to Gordimer's work is **György Lukács,** especially his concept of critical realism, which has been useful in identifying her increasing concern with bringing together style and theme. Especially in her later novels, she incorporates radical continental ideas, experimenting with new forms of the novel (fragmented points-of-view, gaps), irony, and ambiguity. Gordimer admires contemporary developments in the novel from Latin American writers, especially **Gabriel García Márquez** and **Jorge Luis Borges,** among others. Moreover, she is an important contributor to the discussion of African writing and has noted her personal connection with **Chinua Achebe, Wole Soyinka,** and Kofi Awoonor. In addition, she has published comments on Naguib Mahfouz and identified **Edward Said** as a major influence on her thoughts about non-European perspectives and traditions. Gordimer's writing career spans the duration of official apartheid in South Africa. Her writing chronicles the effects of the system on individual lives. She insists, however, that hers are not political novels. Instead, understanding the situation in South Africa was part of becoming a writer in her particular place and at her particular time in history.

Archives

Harry Ransom Humanities Research Center, University of Texas, Austin. Manuscripts of early work, including 13 short stories from *Friday's Footprint* and the novel *A World of Strangers.*

National English Literary Museum, Grahamstown, South Africa. Manuscripts, interviews, letters from 1960 to 1975.

Printed Works

Bazin, Nancy Topping, and Marilyn Dallman Seymour (eds.). *Conversations with Nadine Gordimer.* Literary Conversations Series (Jackson: University Press of Mississippi, 1990).

Clingman, Stephen R. *The Novels of Nadine Gordimer: History from the Inside* (London: Allen & Unwin, 1986).

JanMohamed, Ahdul, R. *Manichiean Aesthetics: The Politics of Literature in Colonial Africa* (Amherst: University of Massachusetts Press, 1983). Places Gordimer in the context of an African writing tradition.

Newman, Judie. *Nadine Gordimer.* Contemporary Writers Series (London: Routledge, 1988). Consideration of postmodern techniques and influences.

Shwartz, Ronald B. *For the Love of Books: 115 Celebrated Writers on the Books They Love Most* (New York: Grosset/Putnam, 1999).

Holly Messitt

GÓRECKI, HENRYK MIKOŁAJ (1933–)

Composer Henryk Górecki was born on December 6, 1933, in a village of Czernica in Upper Silesia, Poland, and is best known for the poignant Symphony No. 3, *The Symphony of Sorrowful Songs* (1976), based on Polish religious and folk material. After graduating from high school in 1951, Górecki taught in a primary school while pursuing his musical training. He studied composition with Bolesław Szabelski at the State Higher School of Music (PWSM) in Katowice (1955–60), graduating with highest honors. His engagement with literature began with a teacher-training course in Rybnik and continued through his life. Performances of his compositions at the Warsaw Autumn Festivals from 1958 onward led to a national recognition of his musical talent. He won many Polish and international competitions, including UNESCO Composers' Rostrum (Paris, 1967 and 1973). Unlike his compatriots, Krzysztof Penderecki and Witold Lutosławski, Górecki did not travel to conduct and publicize his music abroad; he stayed in Silesia focusing on composition and teaching. Since 1965 he has taught at the PWSM in Katowice; from 1975 to 1979 he became its rector. The rise and fall of the Solidarity movement heightened Górecki's resolve to withdraw from public life; he settled in the Podhale area of the Tatra Mountains, where he is surrounded by his favorite tradition of Polish folklore (his music features numerous references to the music of this area). The astounding global fascination with the Symphony No. 3 gradually broke this self-imposed exile: in the late 1990s the composer began traveling to receive honorary doctorates (Concordia University, Montreal, 1998; University of Victoria, B.C., 2000) and attend premieres and festivals of his works.

As a composer, he has favored the genres of vocal and vocal–instrumental music for which he carefully selects texts of a religious or deeply personal nature (he is a devoted Catholic who lost his mother at the age of two and suffered several serious illnesses). His music evolved from large-scale avant-garde compositions (Symphony No. 1 "1959") to rigorously constructed works of a great emotional intensity and sparse musical material, often based on quotations from early music or folksong (*Old Polish Music*, 1969; Symphony No. 3). The religious inspiration is expressed in a series of monumental pieces to texts including brief fragments of Latin psalms, hymns, or treatises (Symphony no. 2, *Copernican*, 1972; *Beatus vir*, 1979; *Miserere*, 1981). Musical allusions to "Bogurodzica" (Mother of God)—the earliest Polish anthem—permeate Górecki's oeuvre. Many choral compositions use religious texts (*Amen* 1975; *Totus tuus*, 1987) or Polish folk poetry (*Szeroka woda*, 1979; *Wisło moja, Wisło szara*, 1981). Górecki's fascination with romantic poetry is clearly expressed in the choice of poems for his songs: by Juliusz Słowacki (*Three Songs*, 1956), Cyprian Kamil Norwid (*Blessed Raspberry Songs*, 1980), and Stanisław Wyspianski (*Trzy Fragmenty*, 1996). Other favorite poets are Maria Konopnicka, Adam Mickiewicz, Kazimierz Przerwa Tetmajer, and Julian Tuwim, whose last words provided the text for Górecki's *Epitafium* (1958). The only foreign poet that has inspired the composer is **Federico Garcia Lorca,** though his poetry appears in Polish translation (*Nocturne*, 1956; *Two Songs*, 1980). Górecki's texts are consistently either in Polish or Latin; he often has used brief fragments, or he coins the needed phrase himself, preferring countless repetitions of one word to extensive texts (*Ad Matrem*, 1971, and other choral pieces). Finding a suitable phrase sometimes takes years of archival research (for example, the prisoner's phrase for the second movement of Symphony No. 3). In addition to reading poetry and studying history, Górecki has acknowledged an interest in scholarly writings in the areas of literature, music, and theology. In the latter domain, he has proclaimed a complete faithfulness to the teachings of the pope.

Archives

Boosey & Hawkes Music Publishers, London office. Press clippings, concert programs, miscellaneous publications, scores, videos, etc.

Górecki's Personal Archives, village Ząb, Podhale, Poland (unavailable for study). Manuscripts, sketches, correspondence, library.

Printed Sources

Droba, Krzysztof. "From *Refrain* to *Beatus Vir*, or Concerning Constructivist Reductionism and Expressionism in the Music of Henryk Mikołaj Górecki." In Leszek Polony, ed., *Przemiany techniki dzwiekowej, stylu I estetyki w polskiej muzyce lat 70tych* (Krakow: PWM, 1986), 85–97. Based on the author's 1971, M.A. thesis.

Homma, Martina. "Das Minimale und das Absolute: Die Musik Henryk Mikołaj Góreckis vor the Mitte der sechziger Jahre bis 1985," *MusikTexte* 44 (1992), 40–59. Detailed analysis of Górecki's major compositions and the main aspects of his style and aesthetics.

Howard, Luke. "'A Reluctant Requiem:' The History and Reception of Henryk M. Górecki's Symphony no. 3 in Britain and the United States" (Ph.D. diss., University of Michigan, 1997). Extensive study of the phenomenon of the Symphony No. 3, its genesis, content, and detailed reception history, including marketing and music criticism.

Jacobson, Bernard. *A Polish Renaissance* (London: Phaidon Press, 1996). Popular study, with one chapter on Górecki, with material from interviews and films not available in print.

Thomas, Adrian. *Górecki.* Oxford Studies of Composers (Oxford: Clarendon Press, 1997). The first monograph about the composer, written by an expert in Polish music and a long-time Górecki friend. With detailed analysis of works, annotated list of compositions, discography, and bibliography.

Trochimczyk, Maja (ed.). *The Music of Henryk Górecki* (Los Angeles: Polish Music Center at USC, forthcoming). Includes interviews with the composer from 1958, 1997, 1998, and 2002.

Maja Trochimczyk

GÖRING, HERMANN WILHELM (1893–1946)

Hermann Göring was born in Rosenheim, Bavaria. Between the ages of 6 and 11, he attended schools near Nuremberg, in Fürth, and in Ansbach. He then enrolled in military school in Karlsruhe, and graduated at 16. He entered an officer's training school, and upon finishing, served with German land forces. Göring joined the air force in 1915, where he became the successor to Baron Manfred von Richthofen. Göring was later awarded the Iron Cross and the *Pour le Mérite*. He returned to civilian life, and took courses in political science and history at the University of Munich. Göring met **Adolf Hitler** around 1921, and by 1922, became a member of the Nazi party. He was proud of his connections with Hitler, and described *Mein Kampf* as a major influence. Hitler appointed Göring head of the *Sturmabteilungen* (storm troopers), and on November 9, 1923, Göring led the Munich *Putsch*. Göring also married his first wife, Baroness Karin von Kantzow, the same year. She died eight years later of tuberculosis. In 1928, Göring was elected to Parliament. In 1933, Hitler appointed Göring as Minister Without Portfolio. Göring held many offices, including Prussian minister of the interior and *Reichsminister* of the *Luftwaffe*. In April 1933, Göring founded the *Gestapo*, designed to suppress all opposition to Nazism. He remained in charge of the *Gestapo* until 1934. In April 1935, Göring married Emmy Sonnemann, an actress, and in 1938, his only child, Edda, was born. Göring also later ordered the "Aryanization" of all Jewish businesses. In 1939, he was appointed Hitler's heir and *Reichsmarshall*. Göring was partially responsible for developing the concentration camps. During the summer of 1941, he authorized Reinhard Heydrich to come up with a *Lösung*, or solution to the "Jewish question." After his *Luftwaffe* failed at plans to invade England, Göring lost favor with Hitler. In May 1945, he was captured by American forces and was placed on trial at Nuremberg, where he was found guilty of war crimes, including conspiracy and crimes against humanity. On October 15, 1946, hours before he was scheduled to die by hanging, Göring committed suicide by swallowing a smuggled vial of poison.

After World War I, Göring lacked direction, but Hitler's *Mein Kampf* gave him a purpose, both personally and politically. Hitler called Göring, who was influenced by military history, a "Renaissance man" (Fest 1970, 119). Göring read several accounts of Napoleon I, one of which he brought to Hitler's attention (Göring 1972, 63). He referenced Napoleon in a 1942 speech, where he compared Napoleon's and Hitler's Russian campaigns. Göring was also fond of detective novels (Davidson 1966, 93). In addition, books about animals and nature influenced him. He was an animal activist and attempted to ban all vivisection in Germany. In his official biography, which he edited, he was described as having a nightly book hour, during which he read newspapers as well as art and history books (Gritzbach 1973, 197). His private library contained important historical works that dealt with Nordic countries, as well as classic literature and texts that were historically representative of the entire world. Other personal influences include books on German history and military (Gritzbach 1973, 249). While courting Emmy, he bought every book he could find on the theater (Göring 1972, 27). While not all titles of books he read are known, Emmy asserted that Göring had a love of reading, second to his true passion, collecting art. Göring published many of his speeches and wrote a book entitled *Aufbau einer Nation*. In 1944, he published an atlas, as he was also fond of geography.

Archives

Civilian Agency Records, Records of the American Commission for the Protection and Salvage of Artistic and Historic Monuments in War Areas (RG 239) Department of State and Foreign Affairs Records, Washington, D.C.

National Archives and Records Service, Records of the International Military Tribunal (IMT) at Nuremberg (RG 238), College Park, Maryland.

Printed Sources

Davidson, Eugene. *The Trial of the Germans: An Account of the Twenty-Two Defendants before the International Military Tribunal at Nuremberg* (New York: The Macmillan Company, 1966).

Fest, Joachim. *The Face of the Third Reich: Portraits of Nazi Leadership* (New York: Ace Books, 1970).

Göring, Emmy. *My Life with Göring* (London: David Bruce and Watson, 1972).

Gritzbach, Erich. *Hermann Göring: The Man and His Work* [1939] (New York: AMS Press, 1973).

Sax, Boria. *Animals in the Third Reich: Pets, Scapegoats, and the Holocaust* (New York and London: Continuum, 2000).

Wendy A. Maier

GRAHAM, WILLIAM FRANKLIN (1918–)

Billy Graham, the most renowned Christian evangelist in postwar American history, was born near Charlotte, North Carolina, to a devoutly Presbyterian family of Scottish descent. Graham's formative years were spent on the family's dairy farm outside of Charlotte, a rural upbringing that he later idealized. He attended Sharon High School, where he was a mediocre student, but a conversion experience at the revival meeting of an itinerant preacher named Mordecai Ham changed Graham's perspective, and he soon decided to pursue a career in the ministry. He entered Bob Jones College in Tennessee in the fall of 1936, before transferring to the Florida Bible Institute in Tampa (1937–40), from which he graduated in 1940. He then furthered his education at Wheaton College in Illinois (1940–43), graduating with an undergraduate degree in anthropology. Graham rose to fame as a result of revival meetings in Los Angeles in 1949 that captured the attention of newspaper publisher **William Randolph Hearst.** Hearst's coverage of the campaign made Graham a celebrity. Graham adroitly maintained this notoriety during the next five decades as he expanded his evangelistic efforts. He effectively used the mass media through programs such as his "Hour of Decision" radio broadcast and televised revivals in cities around the nation and the world to bring his message to millions of people. Graham also became noted for his frequent meetings with political leaders, including each United States president since **Harry S. Truman.**

Although Billy Graham demonstrated an active mind throughout his career, his literary influences are narrow, a fact that has often led to the label of a "country preacher." Graham records that he had been familiar with the Bible "almost since infancy"(Graham 1997, 36), and biblical passages were the most important literary sources for informing his intellectual and cultural outlook. As a boy, Graham also devoured tales about such figures as Tarzan, Tom Swift, Robin Hood, and Zane Grey, although his mother encouraged him to do more serious reading and pressed him to memorize the Westminster Shorter Catechism, published by the Presbyterians, as well as an encyclopedia entitled *The Book of Knowledge* (Graham 1997, 15; see also Martin 1991, 60). As Graham's intellectual interests matured and as he perceived that he would enter the ministry, he read biographies of Christian preachers and missionaries as well as an abridged edition of the eighteenth-century historian Edward Gibbon's multivolume *Decline and Fall of the Roman Empire* (1776–88). Yet Graham's lack of literary breadth appeared to haunt him: he later confessed that he wished he had been more attentive to his studies. Ironically, his own limited literary awareness contributed to the adoption of a simple yet popular evangelistic style that deemphasized the intellectual aspects of Christianity.

Archives

Graham's papers, which contain numerous documents related to his evangelistic campaigns, are housed at the Billy Graham Center Archives at Wheaton College in Wheaton, Ill.

Printed Works

Aikman, David. *Great Souls: Six Who Changed the Country* (Nashville: Word, 1998).

Barnhart, Joe E. *The Billy Graham Religion* (Philadelphia: United Church Press, 1972). Although dated, this work is a critical account of Graham's career, highlighting how he reflected American cultural and intellectual trends in both his personal outlook and ministry.

Frady, Marshall. *Billy Graham: A Parable of American Righteousness* (Boston: Little, Brown, 1979).

Frost, David. *Billy Graham: Personal Thoughts* (Colorado Springs: Victor Books, 1997).

Graham, Billy. *Just as I Am: The Autobiography of Billy Graham* (New York: HarperCollins, 1997). Graham's autobiography contains his recollections of his early literary interests.

Martin, William. *A Prophet with Honor: The Billy Graham Story* (New York: William Morrow, 1991).

Pollock, John. *Billy Graham: The Authorized Biography* (New York: McGraw-Hill, 1966).

Scott Lupo

GRAHAM, MARTHA (1894–1991)

Martha Graham—dancer, teacher, choreographer, and founder of American modern dance—was born in Allegheny, Pennsylvania, to George Greenfield Graham, a physician, and Jane Beers Graham. She attended the Cumnock School in Los Angeles from 1913 to 1916 and then became a lead dancer at the Denishawn School of Dancing in Los Angeles under the training of Ruth St. Denis and Ted Shawn from 1916 to 1923. The Martha Graham Dance Group debuted in New York City in 1926 and Graham shortly began her influential career as a teacher and choreographer when she developed the seminal Graham Technique, which centered on the principles of muscular contraction and release. Her long-term collaborations with composer Louis Horst and set designer Isamu Noguchi helped complete the Graham style: angular, sharp, and emotional dances set to modern music amid stark, symbolic sets. In 1932 she was the first dancer to win a Guggenheim Fellowship and began to participate in the Bennington College Summer Dance Program in 1934. In 1937 Graham became the first American dancer to perform at the White House, and her most well known work, *Appalachian Spring*, for which composer Aaron Copland won the Pulitzer Prize, debuted at the Library of Congress in 1944. In the 1950s, the Graham Company toured under the auspices of the State Department's Department of Cultural Presentations. Graham was awarded the U.S. Medal of Freedom in 1976, was honored for lifetime achievement by the Kennedy Center in 1979, received the French *Légion d'Honneur* in 1984 and the U.S. National Medal of Arts in 1985. Graham retired from dancing in 1970 but continued to choreograph until her death.

Graham's influences were diverse, ranging from literature to modern art, and she famously confessed to her *Notebooks*, "I am a thief—and I am not ashamed. I steal from the best wherever it happens to me—Plato, **Pablo Picasso**, Bertram Ross . . . I steal from the present and from the glorious past" (Ross 1973, xi). She incorporated into her work a wide selection of subjects, including the Bible and Native American religious rites (*Primitive Mysteries*, 1931) and American history (*Appalachian Spring*, 1944). She was often inspired by the work of individuals, including the sermons of Jonathan Edwards (*American Document*, 1938), the poetry of Emily Dickinson (*Letter to the World*, 1940) and the lives and novels of the Brontë sisters (*Deaths and Entrances*, 1943). Works such as *Clytemnestra* (1958) and *Phaedra* (1962) reveal the strong influence of psychology and classical mythology; Graham read **Carl Jung**, scholarly literature on mysticism, fairy and folk tales, and was greatly influenced by *The Masks of God: Occidental Mythology* (1964), written by her friend Joseph Campbell.

Archives

Martha Graham Archives. Music Division, Library of Congress, Washington, D.C.

Printed Sources

De Mille, Agnes. *Martha: The Life and Work of Martha Graham* (New York: Random House, 1991).

Freedman, Russell. *Martha Graham: A Dancer's Life* (New York: Clarion Books, 1998).

Graham, Martha. *Blood Memory* (New York: Doubleday, 1991).

McDonagh, Don. *Martha Graham: A Biography* (New York: Praeger Publishers, 1973).

Ross, Nancy Wilson (ed.). *The Notebooks of Martha Graham* (New York: Harcourt Brace Jovanovich, 1973).

Stodelle, Ernestine. *Deep Song: The Dance Story of Martha Graham* (New York: Schirmer Books, 1984).

Jill Silos

GRAMSCI, ANTONIO (1891–1937)

Antonio Gramsci, Italian socialist political theorist, was born in Ales, in the Sardinian province of Cagliari. Despite family financial difficulties, he successfully graduated from secondary school in Santu Lussurgiu (1908), and from the lyceum in Cagliari. In 1911 he enrolled in the Faculty of Letters in Turin, but quit in 1915 to join the Italian Socialist Party and the editorial staff of *L'Avanti*. In 1919 he founded the periodical *L'Ordine Nuovo* with Palmiro Togliatti and other left-wing intellectuals and began to play an important role in the newly created Italian Communist Party. Elected deputy to the Italian parliament after living in Moscow as a delegate to the Communist International (1922–23), he was arrested in 1926 for his anti-Fascist stance despite his parliamentary immunity and died after a 10-year detention in prison and hospital.

A withdrawn youngster with a lively intellectual curiosity, Gramsci spent considerable time reading during his high school years. **Benedetto Croce,** Gaetano Salvemini, Emilio Cecchi, Giuseppe Prezzolini, and Carolina Invernizio were among his favorite authors. However, he objected to Sardinian writers like Sebastiano Satta and Grazia Deledda for their allegedly sentimental and idealized depiction of their regional reality. Sensitive to the problems of Sardinia, from illiteracy to malaria, starvation, and the terrible conditions of miners, Gramsci felt more attuned to the thought of Karl Marx, which he discovered in this period. Although he did not frequently refer to Marx in his writings until 1917, he already participated in local socialist groups and wrote for newspapers like *L'Unione Sarda*, urging Sardinia's independence and emphasizing the need to transcend social and economic differences and to free the masses from ignorance. These issues will become central to *L'Ordine Nuovo*.

The 1917 Russian Revolution drove Gramsci fully to abandon his contemplative intellectual stance. **Vladimir Lenin's** ideas, translated into Italian from French sources, soon overtook the work of Francesco De Sanctis, Friedrich Hegel, Romain Rolland, and Henri Barbusse in Gramsci's readings, providing the model of a political and economic organization in which the masses act as conscious protagonists. With this more practical and antideterministic attitude to historical change, Gramsci deepened his knowledge of Marx's texts, complemented by Antonio Labriola's *The Materialist Conception of History*, hence setting the premises of the most mature phase of his political thought, that of the prison years.

In his posthumous letters and *Prison Notebooks*, Gramsci resolutely opposed one of his earlier literary models, Benedetto Croce, denouncing him as a reactionary and bourgeois intellectual and investigated the aesthetic, philosophical, and moral standards necessary to the creation of a proletarian civilization. The need for a connection between intellectuals and the working masses sparked Gramsci's notion of a "national-popular" culture that would lead to an independent working-class worldview. In the rich array of books that Gramsci received in prison thanks to the economist Piero Sraffa, Niccolò Machiavelli's *The Prince* was pivotal. It provides Gramsci with insights into "hegemony," which, unlike the coercive strategy of "domination," is for him a political power legitimized by the intellectual and moral consensus of a system of class alliances expressing a collective will. The relationship that Gramsci established between Machiavelli and Marx revealed to him that the success of the socialist revolution depended less upon a direct attack on the state than upon its ability to undermine the ideology of the ruling class.

Archives

Archivio Fondazione Istituto Gramsci, Rome, Italy. Letters, *Prison Notebooks*, photographs, documents about Gramsci's university years and trials.

Printed Sources

Davidson, Alastair. *Antonio Gramsci: Towards an Intellectual Biography* (London: Merlin Press, 1977).
Dombroski, Robert S. *Antonio Gramsci* (Boston: Twayne Publishers, 1989).
Gramsci, Antonio. *Letters from Prison*, Frank Rosengarten (ed.), Raymond Rosenthal (transl.), (New York: Columbia University Press, 1994).
———. *Vita attraverso le lettere (1908–1937)*, Giuseppe Fiori (ed.), (Torino: Einaudi, 1994).
Sassoon, Ann Showstack (ed.). *Approaches to Gramsci* (London: Writers and Readers, 1982).

Nicoletta Pireddu

GREENE, HENRY GRAHAM (1904–1991)

Born on October 2, 1904, in Berkhamsted, Hertfordshire, Greene attended the school where his father served as headmaster and then went to Balliol College, Oxford, after which he worked for the *Nottingham Journal*. There he met Vivien Dayrell-Browning, whom he later married (1927; although never divorced, they separated in 1948) and through whom he was introduced to the Catholic Church, into which he was received in 1926. From 1926 to 1930 he worked as a subeditor for the London *Times*, leaving that position to devote full time to his writing, although he continued as a film critic (1935–39) and literary editor (1940–41) for *The Spectator*. His popular *The Man Within* appeared in 1929. A long series of over 60 "entertainments" and serious novels followed thereafter along with intermittent journalistic pieces, screen-writing and other cinematography, autobiographical works, and extensive travel writing, including *Stamboul Train* (1932), *It's a Battlefield* (1934), *England Made Me* (1935), *Journey Without Maps* (1936), and *A Gun For Sale* (1936).

Greene's first major novel, *Brighton Rock*, was published in 1938. During the Second World War he worked for the Secret Service in Sierra Leone, and the nature of his work can be noted in different ways in *The Lawless Roads* (1939), *The Confidential Agent* (1939), *The Ministry of Fear* (1943), *The Third Man* (1950), *The Quiet American* (1955), and *Our Man in Havana* (1958). Clearly among his best works are *The Power and the Glory* (1940), *The Heart of the Matter* (1948), and *A Burnt-Out Case* (1961).

Following the war he served as director of Eyre & Spottiswoode publishers in London (1944–48) and director of Bodley Head publishers, London (1958–68). In 1954 he was the Indo-China correspondent for *The New Republic* (1954). Other major novels, travel books, and autobiographical reflections followed from the 1960s on, including *In Search of a Character: Two African Journals* (1961), *A Sense of Reality* (1963), *The Comedians* (1966), *Travels with My Aunt* (1969), *A Sort of Life* (1971), *The Honorary Consul* (1973), *Ways of Escape* (1980), and *Monsignor Quixote* (1982).

Like **Evelyn Waugh,** his contemporary and the British Catholic convert novelist with whom he is regularly linked, Greene was most influenced by his own immediate experience: his travel, his wartime service (in Greene's case, unlike Waugh's, his work in espionage), his Catholicism, and his literary and other personal associations. His wide-ranging reading, reviews, and comments on authors he admired makes it difficult to narrow the range of those authors who had the greatest impact on his work. Certainly H. Rider Haggard's (1856–1925) novels had an early attraction for him, as he noted in his autobiography, and the psychoanalytic help and friendship of Kenneth Richmond (and his wife Zoe), who introduced him to dream analysis and encouraged him in his literary pursuits, cannot be ignored. At Balliol College, Oxford, he gained an interest in drama (which would blossom throughout his life in close study and knowledge of the cinema and his use of cinematic techniques in his writing; the figure of Mae West, for example, in *Brighton Rock*'s Ida) and an early attraction to espionage is marked in undergraduate trips to Ireland and Germany. By 1923 he spoke of himself as being "converted to Sitwellianism," and in 1925 joined the Communist Party, although his attraction to Vivien at the time and his resulting growing interest in Catholicism redirected his formal Marxist ideology.

On a trip to visit fellow party members in Paris he purchased a copy of **James Joyce**'s *Ulysses,* but he was much more firmly drawn to **T. S. Eliot** and Herbert Read ("the two great figures of my young manhood" [*Ways of Escape,* 33]), and his work and his autobiographical reflections indicate the far greater influence of Joseph Conrad (1857–1924) on his early thought and style. Among the critical work which he cites as important for him is Percy Lubbock (*The Craft of Fiction,* 1921), and noteworthy as well was the wide range of writers and artists he knew through the Lady Ottoline Morrell circle, members of which he used as models for characters in his writing. (Note in particular Morrell herself as Lady Caroline and John Middleton Murray as Mr. Surrogate in *It's a Battlefield.*) The list of writers established by Duran in his *Graham Greene* ("Literature and the Nobel Prize," 43–53) is too general to be of great use in establishing influences, though it does support some of Greene's own reflections, particularly in its placement of Ford Madox Ford's *The Good Soldier* as first in Greene's list of the best novels he knew, a positioning supported in Greene's "Some Famous Writers I Have Known" dream diary, *A World of my Own* (1992).

Much of the influence to be traced in his work is marked primarily in the individual compositions themselves and not greatly beyond them. Thus one may suggest that his reflections on the nature of evil generally may be shaped by the work of Frederick Rolfe (1860–1913), but it is more useful to narrow the perspective in individual cases and note, for example, the importance of a work like that of Father Wilfrid Parsons, *Mexican Martyrdom* (1936) and the place of the historical martyr, Padre Miguel Pro (1891–1927), in the case of *The Power and the Glory* than to seek some more complex philosophical or theological source in contemporary British Catholic figures such as Bede Jarret (1881–1934).

Archives

Georgetown University, Special Collections, Lauinger Library: correspondence and papers.

Boston College Libraries: residual library and archives.

University of Texas at Austin, Harry Ransom Humanities Research Center Library: Manuscript of *The Power and the Glory*.

Reading University Library: 1963–78; letters (52) to the Bodley Head Ltd.

Pierpont Morgan Library: 1945–55; letters (62) to Herbert Greene.

National Library of Wales, Department of Manuscripts and Records: 1940–88; correspondence with Emyr Humphreys.

Oxford University, Bodleian Library, Special Collections and Western Manuscripts: 1977–78; letters to Jack Lambert, with Lambert's interview, notes.

British Film Institute: 1968–74; correspondence with Joseph Losey.

Sussex University Library Special Collections: 1958–65; correspondence with *New Statesman* magazine.

London University, University College London (UCL) Manuscripts Room; 1943–59: letters from Mervyn Peake.

Printed Sources

Bloom, Harold (ed.). *Graham Greene* (New York: Chelsea House Publishers, 1987).

Couto, Maria. *Graham Greene: On the Frontier: Politics and Religion in the Novels* (New York: St. Martin's Press, 1988).

Duran, Leopoldo. *Graham Greene* (London: HarperCollins, 1994).

Gorra, Michael Edward. *The English Novel at Mid-century: From the Leaning Tower* (New York: St. Martin's Press, 1990).

Meyers, Jeffrey (ed.). *Graham Greene: A Revaluation: New Essays* (New York: St. Martin's Press, 1990).

Pendleton, Robert. *Graham Greene's Conradian Masterplot: The Arabesques of Influence* (New York: St. Martin's Press, 1996).

Sharrock, Roger. *Saints, Sinners and Comedians: The Novels of Graham Greene* (Tunbridge Wells: Burns & Oates, 1984).

Sherry, Norman. *The Life of Graham Greene*, 3 vols. (London: Jonathan Cape, 1989–)

West, W. L. *The Quest for Graham Greene* (London: Weidenfeld and Nicholson, 1997).

Peter C. Erb

GRIFFITH, DAVID WARK (1875–1948)

Born on a farm in Floydsfork, near Crestwood in Oldham County (Kentucky) on January 22, 1875, D. W. Griffith is known as the director of epic, flamboyant silent movies such as *Birth of a Nation* (1915), *Intolerance* (1916), and the melodrama *Broken Blossoms* (1919). Griffith was raised as a Methodist and later became freemason (Schickel 1984, 33). Actor Ralph Graves described Griffith as slightly illiterate and "a bit of a humbug" (quoted in Schickel 1984, 412). Griffith's father died when David was 10, forcing him to leave primary school early. Among many jobs, Griffith sold newspapers in Louisville when he was 14 and four years later was clerk at Flexner's Book Store. He began touring in New York and New England as an actor in 1902, playing roles in *The Gypsy Cross* and later in *Miss Petticoats* (the latter from a novel by Dwight Tilton; Schickel 1984, 62). In Oakland, California, in 1906, Griffith had a huge success in Anthony Hope's *The Prisoner of Zenda*. One of the cofounders of United Artists (1919), Griffith is sometimes known as "the man who invented Hollywood." After his first film, a short titled *The Adventures of Dollie* (1908), he directed more than 450 movies (many now lost), mostly shorts (one or two reels), and all silent with the exception of *Abraham Lincoln* (1930) and his last, *The Struggle* (1931). Although he was much criticized for his reactionary ideas, even in his most famous films Griffith is nevertheless recognized as the filmmaker who from 1908 invented narration modes and visual techniques such as "cross-cutting" (*The Fatal Hour*, 1908; *The Lonely Villa*, 1909), and "fade-outs," still used in today's movies.

Edmund Rucker recalls that young Griffith occasionally went to the Polytechnic Library where he read Dickens (whom he admired above all), and also "Browning, possibly Tolstoy and even Hardy, as well as Civil War history" (Schickel 1984, 41). Griffith often acknowledged that Dickens was the master of efficient storytelling, and later adapted *The Cricket on the Hearth* to film (1909; Schickel 1984, 113). Among newspapers, Griffith's parents would read *Leslie's Weekly* (Schickel 1984, 27). Griffith was much influenced by a popular book, Jack London's *The Call of the Wild* (1903), showing a mythical portrait of the nation as it would appear in *Birth of a Nation* (1915; Schickel 1984, 66). On stage, in 1905, Griffith played a role in an adaptation of Helen Hunt Jackson's novel, *Ramona*, which he later filmed. Many Griffith films were adapted from American history and from numerous novels by Edgar Allan Poe, Jack London, Guy de Maupassant, Shakespeare, Robert Louis Stevenson, Dickens, and many playwrights. He directed *Resurrection* (1909) from Tolstoy, *The Death Disc* (1909) from Mark Twain, and *A Corner in Wheat* (1909) from Frank Norris's *A Deal in Wheat*. Griffith adapted Alfred Lord Tennyson's *Enoch Arden* on three different occasions. Griffith also had a strong identification with Edgar Allan Poe (Schickel 1984, 56), adapting *The Avenging Conscience* (1914). While Griffith admired Walt Whitman, he found Voltaire "rather too cynical" (Schickel 1984, 194). Griffith also appreciated the tale "The Chink and the Child," in Thomas Burke's bestseller *Limehouse Nights* (1917), adapted as *Broken Blossoms* (1919). From 1920, Griffith declared he wanted to make only films adapted from "the theatrical and literary classics of his time," but these were all failures (Schickel 1984, 425). As a pioneer, D. W. Griffith was admired by the most important film directors, including **Sergei Eisenstein, John Ford, Orson Welles,** and **François Truffaut.**

Archives

D. W. Griffith Papers. Museum of Modern Art, New York City. Includes manuscripts, unpublished writings, Griffith Corporation scrapbooks, correspondence. Most of this has been reproduced on 36 reels of microfilm. See *D.W. Griffith Papers, 1897–1954: A Guide to the Microfilm Edition*. Produced by the Museum of Modern Art, New York, University of Louisville, Louisville, Kentucky, Microfilming Corporation of America, Sanford, North Carolina. Sanford, N.C: The Corporation, 1982.

United Artists Archives (and Paramount Archives), at the Wisconsin Center for Theatre Research, Madison, Wisconsin. Official papers and contracts.

Printed Sources

Barry, Iris (ed.). *D. W. Griffith: American Film Master* [1940] (New York: Museum of Modern Art, distributed by Doubleday, Garden City, N.Y., 1965).

Griffith, D. W. *The Man Who Invented Hollywood; The Autobiography of D. W. Griffith*, James Hart (ed.), (Louisville: Touchstone Pub. Co., 1972).

Schickel, Richard. *D. W. Griffith: An American Life* (New York: Simon and Schuster, 1984). By far the best biography of Griffith.

Yves Laberge

GROPIUS, WALTER ADOLPH (1883–1969)

Walter Gropius, the son of a Prussian architect, was born in Berlin and studied at that city's Technical University from 1903 to 1907. Upon graduation, Gropius gained a three-year apprenticeship as chief assistant to the German architect and functionalist industrial designer Peter Behrens. Rejecting historical precedent and ornament for standardization and the use of materials such as glass and steel, Gropius quickly developed what would become known as the modern or international style of architecture, best exemplified in his Fagus Shoe Works Factory in Alfeld, Germany (1910) and the factory buildings for the Werkbund Exposition in Cologne (1914). Gropius served in the army during World War I and upon the completion of his duty was appointed director of the Weimar School of Art, which he subsequently reorganized as the famous Staatliches Bauhaus in 1919. Following the Bauhaus philosophy to eliminate the distinction between the fine and applied arts, Gropius hired prominent visual artists including **Wassily Kandinsky, Paul Klee,** and **Ludwig Mies van der Rohe** to teach a complete and diverse regimen of disciplines. In 1925, Gropius moved the Bauhaus to Dessau, with classes being housed in 26 new buildings that he had personally designed. Three years later he resigned as director and began a private practice in Berlin. During the Nazi uprising of the early 1930s, Gropius fled to England to establish a practice with the architect Maxwell Fry. In 1937, Gropius became chairman of the Department of Architecture at Harvard University, a position he held until 1952. By 1946, he had formed The Architects Collaborative, within which he continued to produce outstanding works of modernist architecture, including the Pan Am Building in New York City (1958), the U.S. Embassy in Athens (1959), the University of Baghdad (1961), and the Grand Central Building in New York (1963). Gropius died in Boston at the age of 86.

Gropius believed that the form of a building should be derived from both the intrinsic qualities of its materials and the function that the structure would ultimately serve. This was directly influenced by the neoclassical and positivist writings of theorists such as Lyonel Feininger who were proponents of a widespread artistic movement known as De Stijl. Inside of this framework, Gropius based his style on a severe geometry of form and an overall economy of modern materials. This decision was supported in literature by the writings of William Morris and Johannes Itten, who espoused the beauty of the mass-produced, the standardized, and the plain, and encouraged architects to place individual creativity over the prototypes of their heritage. In the socialist writings of Karl Marx and **Vladimir Lenin,** Gropius had read of the concept of dialectical materialism, which stated that historical change is accomplished through a struggle of opposites that can only be resolved through synthesis. Gropius's theory of objective formalism extended this idea into the realm of design by fusing all preexisting forms of art and craft into a single universally recognizable style. It was this new vision of design that Gropius believed would act as a catalyst for the idealistic social reform movements the architect had read of in works such as Oswald Spengler's *The Decline of the West.*

Archives

The Bauhaus Archive/Museum of Design, Berlin.
Houghton Library, Harvard College Library, Harvard University. Call No. Ms Ger 208.
Special Collections Department, University Libraries, Virginia Tech, Blacksburg, Va. Call No. Ms 92-052.

Printed Sources

Fitch, James Martson. *Walter Gropius* (New York: George Braziller, 1960).
Sharp, Dennis. *Bauhaus Dessau Walter Gropius* (London: Phaidon Press, 1993).
Zanichelli, Nicola. *Walter Gropius* (Bologna: Editore S.P.A., 1983).

Gregory L. Schnurr

GROTOWSKI, JERZY MARIAN (1933–1999)

Grotowski was born in Rzeszów, Poland. He studied acting at the State Theatre School in Kraków (1951–55) and then directing at the State Institute of Theatre Arts (GITIS) in Moscow (1955–56) and the State Theatre School in Kraków (1956–58). Grotowski was brought up as a Catholic, but his mother, Emilia Kozłowska Grotowska, practiced "the most ecumenical Catholicism" (Schechner and Wolford 1997, 251) and encouraged Grotowski to read books about Buddhism, Hinduism, and Judaism (including Hasidism), as well as Christian books that the Church had forbidden. In 1959, Grotowski was named artistic director of the Theatre of Thirteen Rows in the provincial town of Opole, where, together with Ludwik Flaszen, the company's literary manager, he established an experimental theater—which changed its name first to the Laboratory Theatre of Thirteen Rows, and later, after its move to Wrocław (a larger, more cosmopolitan city), the Laboratory Theatre-Institute for Research in Acting Method (known outside of Poland as the Polish Laboratory Theatre)—that became renowned worldwide for its extremely detailed psychophysical acting style and its equally well-developed vocal technique. During this period of his work (later called the "Theatre of Productions"), Grotowski and his company produced some extraordinary performances, the most famous of which were *Akropolis* (1962), *The Constant Prince* (1965), and *Apocalypsis cum Figuris* (1969); he also evolved a method of actor training, a distinctive style of mise-en-scène, and a method of textual montage. Largely because of Grotowski's work during this period of his activity, he is now considered, in Richard Schechner's words, "[one] of the five great forces in European theatre in the twentieth century" (Schechner and Wolford 1997, 464). Nevertheless, in about 1969–70, Grotowski announced his "exit from the theatre," and never created any new productions again. His post-theatrical work went through several phases: "Paratheatre" (1969–78), "Theatre of Sources" (1976–82), "Objective Drama" (1983–86), and "Art as Vehicle," (1986–99). Theatre had always been for Grotowski a means, rather than an end, and all these phases were concerned with using the elements of performance as a means by which human beings can access a deeper level of perception. Grotowski remained tremendously influential in the theater world (especially among alternative theater groups) during this post-theatrical phase, and Lisa Wolford suggests that the significance of his work in this period lies "in his radical reconceptualization . . . of what performance is and what it can be used for" (Schechner and Wolford 1997, 18).

Grotowski's earliest productions showed the influence of Russian constructivism, especially the thinking of Vsevelod Meyerhold, whose work he had studied as a student in Moscow. The most famous productions of the Laboratory Theatre, despite being quite outside the mainstream of Polish theater practice in the 1960s, drew upon two common streams of Polish thought: the sacred images of Catholicism (often treated by Grotowski in a blasphemous way) and Polish romanticism (especially the writings of Adam Mickiewicz, Juliusz Słowacki, and the neo-romantic

Stanisław Wyspiański). From the beginning of his activity, he also emphasized research into the fundamental principles of the actor's art and took actor training ideas from Meyerhold, Konstantin Stanislavsky, and Juliusz Osterwa (one of the founders of the Reduta Theatre, a Polish interwar commune/theater company) and added his own approach to their work. In *Towards a Poor Theatre*, Grotowski wrote that he wanted to create a method to fulfill Antonin Artaud's vision that "Actors should be like martyrs burnt alive, still signaling us from their stakes" (Grotowski 1968, 93); in the same book, he also indicated that he found **Bertolt Brecht**'s theories intriguing, but as an aesthetic rather than a method (Grotowski 1968, 173). From his student days onward, Grotowski had studied Indian and Chinese philosophy and traveled widely in Central Asia, India, and China; he continued to draw upon these interests and experiences during both his theatrical and post-theatrical phases. Grotowski's interest in ritual, evident even in his "Theatre of Productions" phase, became even more pronounced during the "Theatre of Sources" and "Objective Drama" phases, during which he worked with a core, multinational group that explored "source techniques" from various native cultures, such as Haitian voodoo, the Yoruba culture of Nigeria, the Huichol Indians of Mexico, and yogis in India. Schechner also points out Grotowski's connections with G. I. Gurdjieff, Carlos Castaneda (whom Grotowski met), Sufism, Hasidism, and American youth culture of the late 1960s and early 1970s (Schechner and Wolford 1997, 474–87).

Archives

Archiwum, Ośrodek Badań Twórczości Jerzego Grotowskiego i Poszukiwan Teatralno-Kulturowych (Center for Research on Jerzy Grotowski's Work and Theatrical-Cultural Pursuits), Wrocław, Poland: films and videos, photographs, some costumes and fragments of scenery, audiotapes, personal and official documents, posters, leaflets, brochures, magazine articles, and books, all connected with the activity of the Laboratory Theatre; in addition, there are materials connected with some Grotowski-derived groups and with the Grotowski Center itself.

Printed Sources

Grotowski, Jerzy. *Towards a Poor Theatre* (New York: Simon and Schuster, 1968).
Kumiega, Jennifer. *The Theatre of Grotowski* (London: Methuen, 1985).
Osiński, Zbigniew. *Grotowski I jego Laboratorium* (Warsaw: Państwowy Instytut Wydawniczy, 1980); trans. and abridged as *Grotowski and His Laboratory* by Lillian Vallee and Robert Findlay (New York: PAJ Publications, 1986).
Schechner, Richard, and Lisa Wolford (eds.). *The Grotowski Sourcebook* (London: Routledge, 1997).

Kathleen M. Cioffi

GUEVARA, ERNESTO "CHE" (1928–1967)

Che Guevara, the Marxist revolutionary and guerrilla leader, was born in Rosario, Argentina. Prompted to study medicine by childhood asthma, Guevara received his medical degree from the University of Buenos Aires in 1953. During and after medical school, Guevara embarked on numerous trips from Argentina to explore Central and South America.

In December of 1953, he arrived in Guatemala, where he became involved with a leftist revolution and met exiled Cuban revolutionaries. Guevara escaped to Mexico when U.S.-supported forces overthrew the Guatemalan government in 1954. While in Mexico City during the summer of 1955, Guevara met Raul and **Fidel Castro**. Inspired, Guevara joined Castro as one of 82 rebels who landed in Cuba in December of 1956. Though originally a medical assistant for the rebel army, Guevara was promoted to commander of his column in 1957. After the triumph of the Cuban revolution in 1959, Castro appointed Guevara as director of the Industrial Department of the National Institute of Agrarian Reform (INRA), president of the National Bank of Cuba, and minister of industry.

To further his adamant opposition to dictatorships and U.S. imperialism throughout Latin America, Guevara wrote *Guerrilla Warfare* (1960) as a guide for revolutionary insurrections. Guevara held that such insurrections would liberate Latin America. In 1965, he resigned as minister of industry and left Cuba to start guerrilla campaigns in Congo and Bolivia. Bolivian troops executed Guevara on October 9, 1967.

Hindered by childhood asthma, Guevara spent much of his early years in bed reading classic American and European adventure novels. As an adolescent he turned his attention to the works of Jack London, Charles Baudelaire, Sigmund Freud, **Albert Camus,** and **Franz Kafka.**

In 1945, Guevara took his first philosophy course, studying *The Communist Manifesto* and *Das Kapital* of Karl Marx and Friedrich Engels. During this course, he began to record thoughts on his philosophical readings in a series of notebooks. Over the next seven years he would complete 10 such notebooks covering the works of Pablo Neruda, Frederich Nietzsche, **Adolf Hitler**'s *Mein Kampf,* H. G. Wells's *Brief History of the World,* and advanced readings of **V. I. Lenin.** As a university student, Guevara indexed the literature he read and continued his readings in social philosophy, including **Benito Mussolini** (Fascism), **Josef Stalin** (Marxism), and the speeches of Lenin.

In Guatemala in 1954, Guevara met his first wife, Hilda Gadea, who introduced him to the works of Mao Zedong (*New China*), Walt Whitman, **Jean-Paul Sartre,** Alfred Adler, and **Carl Jung.** While living in Mexico City in 1955, together they read Pancho Villa's memoirs and general accounts of the Mexican revolution. Guevara also borrowed numerous Russian works, including those of Aleksandr Pushkin and Mikhail Lermontov, from the Instituto Cultural Ruso-Mexicano. Still in Mexico City in 1956, he and other rebels under Castro's command began training for their Cuban invasion. Guevara studied the economic theory of Adam Smith and John Maynard Keynes and condensed his philosophical notebooks into one volume.

While in the Sierra Maestra Mountains of Cuba (1957–59), Guevara kept a copy of Mao's *On Guerrilla Warfare,* despite fellow rebels' ongoing suspicion of his "Red" book collection. Throughout the remainder of the Cuban revolution and into his term of office under Castro, Guevara continued to read and write on guerrilla warfare, economic and agrarian reform policy, anti-imperialism, and accounts of peasant revolts.

Archives

Guevara's journals are in the private collection of his widow, Aleida March. They include his "Diccionario Filisofico" and "Indice Literario," which provide detailed accounts of what he read between the ages of 17 and 28.

Printed Sources

Anderson, Jon Lee. *Che Guevara: A Revolutionary Life* (New York: Grove Press, 1997). Deals extensively with Guevara's reading.

Castañeda, Jorge G. *Companero: The Life and Death of Che Guevara* (New York: Knopf, 1997).

J. Brandon Hinman

GUTIERREZ MERINO, GUSTAVO (1928–)

Gustavo Gutierrez was born in Lima, Peru. Born with osteomyelitis, he was left with a permanent limp, a condition that inspired him to study medicine at San Marcos University from 1947 to 1950. At San Marcos, he read the works of Karl Marx and joined the Christian student movements that challenged the political order in Peru. His teachers, Cesar Arrospide and Geraldo Alacro, stimulated Gutierrez's interest in spirituality, an interest that led to his decision to study theology at the Catholic University in Santiago de Chile. Continuing his theological studies, Gutierrez entered the Catholic University at Louvain, Belgium, where he earned a master's degree in 1955. His thesis focused on the work of Sigmund Freud. After Louvain, Gutierrez moved to the University of Lyon in France, gaining exposure to the progressive Roman Catholic movement known as *la nouvelle theologic*. It was during this time that he read Henri de Lubac's *The Mystery of the Supernatural* (1950) and Karl Rahner's *Theological Investigations* (1954). After earning a master's degree at Louvain in 1959, he enrolled at the Gregorian University in Rome and was ordained a priest in 1959.

Gutierrez returned to Peru in 1960 and became interested in **Albert Camus,** Karl Marx, and the poet Cesar Vallejo. As a Roman Catholic priest, Gutierrez was certainly influenced by the documents of the Second Vatican Council, *Gadium et Spes* (1962), which encourage a commitment to the poor. Gutierrez's commitment to the oppressed was further enhanced by reading the socialist José Mariategui's *Peranicemosal Peru* (Lima, 1970). Gutierrez contributed to, and was influenced by, the final documents of the Latin American Bishops Conference at Medellin, Colombia, in 1968. These writings emphasize the church's responsibility to the downtrodden. Gutierrez embarked upon a close friendship with the novelist José Maria Arguedas in the late 1960s, whose novels *Todas Las Sangres* and *El Zorro de ariba e el zorro de a baja* heightened his interest in popular religion.

Gutierrez, among other liberation theologians, redefined the study of Western theology. His work helped to move theology away from purely metaphysical questions and placed it squarely in the lives and struggles of the poor. Gutierrez broadened this enterprise when serving as a visiting professor at New York's Union Theological Seminary in 1976, where he engaged in close dialogue with James Hal Cone, author of *A Black Theology of Liberation* (1970). Gutierrez maintains that the sixteenth-century friar, Bartolome de las Casas, inspires much of his work. The most significant influences on Gutierrez's writings are the voices of the Peruvian poor, written in their struggle for liberation.

Archives

Instituto Bartolome de Las Casas, Rimac, Lima, Peru. Gutierrez's personal library and writings.

Printed Sources

Cadorette, Curt. *From the Heart of the People: The Theology of Gustavo Gutierrez* (Oak Park, Ill.: Meyer Stone Books, 1988).

Ellis, Mark, and Otto Maduro (eds.). *Expanding the View: Gustavo Gutierrez and the Future of Liberation Theology* (Maryknoll, N.Y.: Orbis Books, 1988).

McAffee Brown, Robert. *Gustavo Gutierrez: An Introduction to Liberation Theology* (Maryknoll, N.Y.: Orbis Books, 1990).

Carl Mirra

HAILE SELASSIE (1892–1975)

Lij Tafari Makonnen was born in Harar, capital of one of Ethiopia's important provinces. His father was (Ras) Prince Makonnen of Showan and the first cousin and close advisor of the celebrated Ethiopian emperor, Menilek II. Tafari's mother, Yeshi-immabet Ali was not of Ethiopia's elite class. It was this fact, as well as his father's Christian example of feeding the poor, that influenced the emperor's benevolent policies toward the non-elite. Tafari, who through his father's ancestral line was believed to be a direct descendant of King Solomon and the Queen of Sheba, began moving up the royal ranks during his early teens. At age 14 he was confirmed as a *dejazmach* or earl. A year later he became governor of a part of Sidamo Province in southern Ethiopia. Tafari later became governor of his birthplace, Harar; however, Lij Iyasu, impetuous heir to the throne and Tafari's longtime political rival, demoted the future emperor to the governorship of a remote and impoverished province in southwestern Ethiopia. He later resumed his governorship of Harar under the empress Zauditu. Tafari and Zauditu engaged in a 10-year power struggle in which Tafari was the victor. In 1930 Zauditu was forced to declare Tafari *negus* or king. Tafari became the last emperor of Ethiopia and adopted his baptismal name Haile Selassie. During his 60-year reign he accomplished major land reform, abolished slavery, and revised a constitution that provided universal suffrage. Nevertheless, his failure to secure socioeconomic reform forced him to abdicate in 1974. He was held under house arrest until his death in 1975.

Haile Selassie's literary influences are sketchy. In *The Autobiography of Emperor Haile Selassie 1892–1937*, he merely noted that his father prized Western civilization and thus hired private tutors to provide the future emperor with a European education. Selassie studied French extensively, but the bulk of his education was provided by the Catholic mission school. Like his father, the emperor believed that his country and people could "learn much from Western lore and life. . . . He was an avid reader, and his study was filled with books in French in all subjects" (Marcus 1987, 56). The economist and progressive writer Gebre Heywet Baykedagn greatly influenced the young emperor to initiate domestic reforms. Being well versed in the Western intellectual tradition enabled Selassie to form alliances with Western powers. Of all of the literary texts Selassie read, the Bible appears to have been the most influential. Many of his speeches were laced with scriptural references. Like his father, Selassie was a devout Christian and believed he was appointed by God to lead his people to modernization and prosperity.

Archives

Institute of Ethiopian Studies, Addis Ababa University.

Printed Sources

Marcus, Harold G. *Haile Selassie I: The Formative Years 1892–1936* (Berkeley: University of California Press, 1987).

Selassie, Haile. *The Autobiography of Emperor Haile Selassie: My Life and Ethiopia's Progress 1892–1937* (New York: Oxford University Press, 1976).

Arika L. Coleman

HAMMARSKJÖLD, DAG HJALMAR AGNE CARL (1905–1961)

Dag Hammarskjöld was born in Jönköping, Sweden, the fourth son of Agnes Maria Karolina Almqvist and Knut Hjalmar Leonard Hammarskjöld, a prominent Swede who served as prime minister from 1914 to 1917, governor of Uppland from 1907 to 1930, and chairman of the Nobel Prize Foundation from 1929 to 1947. Before turning to law and politics, Hjalmar Hammarskjöld was a scholar of Germanic languages and literature, especially fond of **Hermann Hesse,** Hugo von Hofmannsthal, and August Platen. He instilled this love of learning and reading in his son Dag. Another strong influence in his home was traditional Lutheran piety, involving a sense of duty in general and noblesse oblige in particular. Hjalmar wanted to build an Augustinian "City of God" in Sweden. In contrast to Hjalmar's severity and aloofness, Dag's mother was romantic, friendly, and effusive, yet equally pious and literary.

For most of Dag's childhood the Hammarskjölds lived in Uppsala, where they were friends with the family of Archbishop Nathan Söderblom. On the advice of Yvonne Söderblom, the archbishop's wife, he read Blaise Pascal's *Pensées*, which was thereafter his favorite book. After achieving a brilliant record in primary and secondary schools in Uppsala, Hammarskjöld matriculated at the University of Uppsala at 17 and earned his bachelor's degree just two years later, majoring jointly in literature, French, philosophy, and political economy. Among the authors he studied were Joseph Conrad, **Thomas Mann,** Thomas Wolfe, Emily Dickinson, and Katherine Mansfield. He knew Sundar Singh and Rabindranath Tagore personally through the archbishop.

Continuing his studies, he received a licentiate in economics from Uppsala in 1928, a bachelor of laws from Uppsala in 1930, and a doctorate in economics from the University of Stockholm in 1933. He taught political economy at Stockholm from 1933 to 1936, then embarked on the political career that eventually led to his becoming the second secretary general of the United Nations. During this period he read Albert Schweitzer, Jacques Rivière, Paul Claudel, Charles Pierre Péguy,

Bertil Ekman, Gabriel Marcel, Erik Gustaf Geijer, and Léon Bloy. He began but never finished a Swedish translation of **Martin Buber**'s *I and Thou.*

Hammarskjöld's fragmented, poetic, spiritual autobiography, *Markings,* was discovered as a manuscript in his New York apartment after his death, bequeathed to his friend Leif Belfrage, who published it in Swedish in 1963 and, with translation by Leif Sjöberg and **Wystan Hugh Auden,** in English in 1964. Hammarskjöld saw it only as a diary, but sensitive literary minds and religious souls consider it a masterpiece. The mysticism that pervades this book came to Hammarskjöld in the 1930s, primarily through the works of St. John of the Cross, Thomas à Kempis, Meister Eckhart, and St. Teresa of Avila.

Archives

Hammarskjöld's letters and papers are held in many libraries worldwide, including the Dag Hammarskjöld Library at the United Nations in New York City, but the largest and most significant collection is in the Manuscripts Section of the Royal Library of Sweden, Stockholm.

Printed Sources

Beskow, Bo. *Dag Hammarskjöld: Strictly Personal: A Portrait* (Garden City, N.Y.: Doubleday, 1969).

Gillett, Nicholas. *Dag Hammarskjöld* (London: Heron Books, 1970).

Henderson, James Lewis. *Hammarskjöld: Servant of a World Unborn* (London: Methuen, 1969).

Kelen, Emery. *Dag Hammarskjöld: A Biography* (New York: Meredith, 1969).

Simon, Charlie May Hogue. *Dag Hammarskjöld* (New York: Dutton, 1967).

Stolpe, Sven. *Dag Hammarskjöld: A Spiritual Portrait*, Naomi Walford (trans.), (New York: Scribner, 1966).

Thelin, Bengt. *Dag Hammarskjöld: Barnet, Skolpojken, Studenten* (Stockholm: Carlsson, 2001).

Urquhart, Brian. *Hammarskjold* (New York: Harper & Row, 1984).

Van Dusen, Henry Pitney. *Dag Hammarskjöld: A Biographical Interpretation of "Markings"* (London: Faber & Faber, 1967).

———. *Dag Hammarskjöld: The Statesman and His Faith* (New York: Harper & Row, 1967).

Eric v.d. Luft

HAŠEK, JAROSLAV (1883–1923)

Jaroslav Hašek was born and lived most of his life in Prague, the city whose streets and pubs were the setting for the adventures of his famous character, the good soldier Švejk. From an early age, Hašek displayed a contempt for authority and a love of high jinks, which earned him expulsion from gymnasium. He completed studies at the Commercial Academy in Prague in 1902 and held a succession of jobs—bank clerk, editor of a nature journal, reporter for a political newspaper, proprietor of a dog-breeding business—that he usually lost due to his irreverence and fondness for a day at the pub. Hašek paid for his mugs of beer by writing. During his lifetime, he published some 1,200 pieces, including commentaries for Anarchist newspapers, short stories and feuilletons inspired by his travels in Austria-Hungary and Germany, mock-serious articles describing fictional species for the nature journal he edited, and polemics in support of whichever political party agreed to pay him (he sometimes carried on debates with himself in rival partisan dailies). In 1911 Hašek

229

published his first short story featuring Švejk (pronounced "Shvake"), basing his tale on the experiences of friends in the Austro-Hungarian army. Hašek himself joined the army in January 1915 and was captured on the Russian front in September of that year. He later joined the Czechoslovak Legion, formed in Russia of prisoners-of-war, and served as a propagandist for the unit. After the October Revolution in 1917, he turned to the Bolsheviks and held various official positions in Siberia and central Asia. In 1920 he returned to Prague, planning to take part in a Communist revolution that was aborted before his arrival. Branded a Bolshevik and a traitor to the Czech national cause, Hašek turned to Švejk to make ends meet, publishing in 1921 the first volume of *The Fortunes of the Good Soldier Švejk in the Great War* (*Osudy dobrého vojáka Švejka za světové války*). He completed three volumes of the novel before his death due to alcoholism.

Hašek was a naturally gifted writer who would write and submit hundreds of pages without making an edit. His literary efforts owed more to his remarkable abilities of observation and mimicry than to any influential author or style. He was neither a devoted reader of literature nor a habitué of any literary circle, although he was friends with other Prague artists, such as cartoonist Josef Lada (1887–1957), who completed a famous series of illustrations of scenes from *Švejk*, and playwright František Langer (1888–1965), with whom he collaborated on various satiric projects. Hašek was a wide-ranging reader whose writings do make direct and indirect references to other literary works. Hašek drew from, commented upon, and often satirized a variety of sources, from newspapers, political journals, humor magazines, and pulp novels to sacred texts and classic works of literature. *The Good Soldier Švejk* cites some twenty Czech, German, and Hungarian periodicals; historical, philosophical, and psychiatric studies; the New Testament and Indian sacred texts; the works of François Rabelais, Miguel de Cervantes, and William Shakespeare; and those of Aleksandr Pushkin, Heinrich Heine, and Victor Hugo. One example of these literary references is at the close of part I, chapter 12, when the military chaplain, Otto Katz, falls asleep with the *Decameron* by Boccaccio (1313–75) in his hands. These references indicate that Hašek was familiar with a variety of classic literary works, and both scholars and contemporary critics, including the Prague critic Max Brod (1884–1968), have commented upon the parallels between Hašek's *Švejk* and other texts, such as Cervantes's *Don Quixote*, Rabelais's *Gargantua and Pantagruel*, and *The Pickwick Papers* of Charles Dickens (1812–70).

Archives

Archive of the National Literature Museum, Prague, Czech Republic: Jaroslav Hašek Collection (8 boxes); correspondence, manuscripts of *The Good Soldier Švejk* and other prose and poetry, photographs.

Printed Sources

Gaifman, Hana Ari. "Problems and Issues in Hašek's *The Adventures of the Good Soldier Švejk*." In Walter Schamschula (ed.), *Proceedings of the International Hašek Symposium* (Frankfurt: Peter Lang, 1989).

Parrott, Cecil. *The Bad Bohemian: The Life of Jaroslav Hašek, Creator of the Good Soldier Švejk* (London: The Bodley Head, 1978).

———. *Jaroslav Hašek: A Study of Švejk and the Short Stories* (Cambridge: Cambridge University Press, 1982).

Bruce R. Berglund

HAUPTMANN, GERHART (1862–1946)

Gerhart Hauptmann was born at Obersalzbrunn (today's Bad Salzbrunn), Germany. After elementary school, Hauptmann entered into junior high school at Zwinger/Breslau but left school in 1878 to learn farming with his uncle Gustav Schubert. In 1880 he was accepted at the Breslau School for Arts to become a sculptor. A year later, Hauptmann became engaged to Marie Thienemann, a wealthy merchant's daughter and, financially secure, he began to study history at the University of Jena (1880–83). After traveling around southern Europe, Hauptmann settled in Rome in 1883, where he intended to live and work as a sculptor. However, he was forced to go back to Germany in 1883 when he suffered a life-threatening typhus infection. Hauptmann married Marie in 1885 and they decided to move to Erkner, a town near Berlin, as he wanted to live close to his artistic friends. In 1885, Hauptmann began writing the epos *Promethidenlos*, poetry, and his novellas *Fasching* (1887) and *Bahnwärter Thiel* (1887). His naturalistic play *Vor Sonnenaufgang (Before Daybreak)* made Hauptmann instantly famous in 1889. The highly critical social drama *Die Weber* was based on the brutal suppression of the revolting Silesian weavers in 1844 and caused an enormous scandal in Berlin in 1892. His biggest success as a dramatist was his rather uncontroversial fairy-tale-like *Die versunkene Glocke* (1896). In 1912, Hauptmann was awarded the Nobel Prize for literature.

During his one-year apprenticeship on a farm in Silesia, Hauptmann came under the influence of Count Nikolaus von Zinzendorf (1700–60), one of the leaders of German pietism in the eighteenth century. His verse epos *Promethidenlos* (1885) alludes to Lord Byron's style and tone. The dogmatic leader of the German naturalist movement, Arno Holz, was personally involved in Hauptmann's writing of *Vor Sonnenaufgang* (1889). Hauptmann, however, distanced himself from Holz and was much more indebted to Henrik Ibsen's social dramas. *Vor Sonnenaufgang* was clearly inspired by Ibsen's *The Wild Duck* (1884) and *Das Friedensfest (The Coming of Peace*, 1890) was influenced by Ibsen's *Ghosts* (1881) and *Rosmersholm* (1886). In his novella, *Der Apostel* (1890), Hauptmann incorporated motives from Georg Büchner's novella *Lenz* (posthumously published in 1839) and Fyodor Dostoyevsky's *The Idiot* (1868–69). Hauptmann based his play *Elga* (1896) on Friedrich Grillparzer's *Das Kloster bei Sendomir* (1827). In 1922, Hauptmann published the story "Phantom. Aufzeichnungen eines ehemaligen Sträflings," which resembles Dostoyevsky's *Crime and Punishment* (1866). In his later years, Hauptmann considered himself a true successor of Johann Wolfgang von Goethe and frequently alluded to Goethe's oeuvre. In the 1920s and 1930s, Hauptmann also evoked various works by Shakespeare in *Die Insel: Paraphrase zu Shakespears "Sturm"* (1920), *Hamlet in Wittenberg* (1928), *Die goldene Harfe* (1933), and *Im Wirbel der Berufung* (1936). Hauptmann's epos *Der große Traum* (1942) was influenced by Dante's *Divine Comedy* (1310–14).

Archives

Staatsbibliothek zu Berlin, Preußischer Kulturbesitz, Berlin, Germany: Largest collection of Hauptmann's manuscripts and his entire unpublished works.

Gerhart-Hauptmann-Museum, Erkner, Germany: Some of Hauptmann's manuscripts and correspondence.

University of Wroclaw, Poland: Smaller collection of Hauptmann's correspondence.

Printed Sources

Hilscher, Eberhard. *Gerhart Hauptmann: Leben und Werk* (Frankfurt: Athäneum, 1988).

Hoefert, Sigfrid. *Das Drama des Naturalismus* (Stuttgart: Metzler, 1993).

Marx, Friedhelm. *Gerhart Hauptmann* (Stuttgart: Reclam, 1998).

Maurer, Warren R. *Understanding Gerhart Hauptmann* (Columbia: University of South Carolina Press, 1992).

Osborne, John. *Gerhart Hauptmann and the Naturalist Drama* (Amsterdam: Harwood, 1998).

Poppe, Reiner. *Gerhart Hauptmann: Leben und Werk* (Husum: Husum, 1998).

Tschörtner, H. D., and Sigfrid Hoefert. *Gespräche und Interviews mit Gerhart Hauptmann (1894–1946)* (Berlin: Erich Schmidt, 1994).

Gregor Thuswaldner

HAVEL, VÁCLAV (1936–)

Václav Havel was born in Prague into a wealthy family. After the Czechoslovak Communist Party gained power in 1948, his family's status was a strike against him. Barred from the Academy of Performing Arts, Havel studied at a technical university and served in the army before gaining work in 1960 at Prague's Theater on the Balustrade. He soon became the theater's principal playwright, authoring absurdist dramas, such as *The Garden Party* (1962), *The Memorandum* (1965), and *The Increased Difficulty of Concentration* (1968), that subtly criticized the communist regime. In 1968 Havel turned to politics, writing speeches and articles in support of the reform program of **Alexander Dubček.** Following the Soviet invasion in August 1968, Havel was denounced for his political activities. He found work in a brewery and continued to write, although his plays could only be staged secretly in Czechoslovakia. In 1975 Havel wrote the first of his political essays: a letter to President Gustav Husák (1913–91) decrying the stagnation of Czechoslovak culture. Two years later he and philosopher Jan Patočka drafted Charter 77, which criticized the regime for failing to protect human rights. In the following years, Havel was arrested on several occasions for his dissident activities, and between 1977 and 1989 he spent a total of five years in prison. During one term in prison (1979–82), Havel engaged in a correspondence with his wife and his younger brother, Ivan, which was published later as *Letters to Olga* (1984). Havel also wrote criticisms of the regime that were published in *samizdat*, most notably his essay "Power of the Powerless" (1978), as well as the plays *Largo Desolato* (1984) and *Temptation* (1986). In November 1989 he was the leading figure in Civic Forum, which negotiated with the regime while hundreds of thousands of people demonstrated in the streets of Prague. Following the government's collapse, Havel was elected president of Czechoslovakia on December 29, 1989. He led the country through the initial years of transition, resigned in 1992 in protest against the proposed split of Czechoslovakia, and took office as president of the Czech Republic in January 1993. As head of state in a parliamentary system, Havel exercised little political power in the 1990s.

As a playwright, Havel is often grouped with the absurdist writers **Eugene Ionescu** and **Samuel Beckett.** Havel did read both authors, and his early dramatic work for the Theater on the Balustrade demonstrates their influence, particularly in presenting dehumanized characters. Havel also admired the leading Czech writers of the 1920s, **Karel Čapek** and **Jaroslav Hašek,** and he had a great affinity for the other leading Prague literary figure of that period, **Franz Kafka.** The clearest statement of Havel's personal philosophy is in the volume *Letters to Olga.* In the letters, Havel explains his belief in Being, a transcendent absolute that Havel describes in various instances as "the order of existence" and "the final horizon." Although Havel's Being has similarities to a personal God, he refuses to describe it as such. Havel admits admiration for religious believers; however, he denies any orthodox belief or religious affiliation. Rather, the primary influence on Havel's notion of Being was the philosopher **Martin Heidegger.** Havel read Heidegger in prison, he quotes the philosopher in *Letters to Olga,* and he employs Heideggerian terms in his writings: "Being" (*Sein*), "existence in the world" (*Dasein*), and "thrownness" (*Geworfenheit*). Havel's philosophy is also based upon the work of Czech phenomenologist Jan Patočka, who viewed ideology as another ill-used product of the rationalism of the modern era. Rather than following the "totalizing untruths" of party doctrines or ideologies, Havel urges people to "live in truth," a concept taken from Patočka. In his actions as president, Havel has cited as a model the first president of Czechoslovakia, **Tomáš G. Masaryk**. Masaryk based his politics on morality, Havel stated in his first New Year's address as president; "Let us try in a new time and a new way to restore this concept of politics" (Havel 1991, 395).

Archives

Josef Škvorecký Collection, Hoover Institution of War, Peace, and Revolution, Stanford University, Stanford, Calif. Correspondence between Havel and his North American publisher, Czech novelist Josef Škvorecký.

Archive of the Coordinating Committee of Civic Forum, Institute of Contemporary History, Czech Academy of Sciences, Prague, Czech Republic.

Printed Sources

Findlay, Edward F. "Classical Ethics and Postmodern Critique: Political Philosophy in Václav Havel and Jan Patočka," *The Review of Politics*, 61, 3 (1999), 403–39.

Goetz-Stankiewicz, Marketa, and Phyllis Carey (eds.). *Critical Essays on Václav Havel* (Boston: Twayne, 1999).

Havel, Václav. *Letters to Olga: June 1979–September 1982*, Paul Wilson (trans.), (New York: Henry Holt, 1989).

———. *Open Letters: Selected Writings, 1965–1990*, Paul Wilson (trans.), (New York: Alfred A. Knopf, 1991).

Keane, John. *Václav Havel: A Political Tragedy in Six Acts* (New York: Basic Books, 2000).

Sire, James. *Václav Havel, The Intellectual Conscience of International Politics: An Introduction, Appreciation, and Critique* (Downers Grove, Ill.: InterVarsity, 2001).

Bruce R. Berglund

HAYEK, FRIEDRICK AUGUST VON (1899–1992)

Friedrick von Hayek was born in Vienna, Austria. He came from a family of intellectuals; his father and both his grandfathers were published scholars. Hayek studied at the University of Vienna (1918–23), earning degrees in law and political science, and spent a year at New York University while attending lectures at Columbia University (1923–24). Hayek, along with such future intellectuals as Fritz Machlup, Eric Vögelin, and Gottfried Haberler, attended the biweekly "private seminars" organized and led by **Ludwig von Mises** from 1924 to 1931. During this time, with the assistance of Mises, Hayek founded and directed the Austrian Institute for Business Cycle Research (1927). He later became a lecturer in economics at the University of Vienna (1929–31). Hayek then took a faculty position as the Tooke Professor of Economic Science and Statistics, London School of Economics (1931–50). In 1947, Hayek founded the Mont Pelerin Society and served as president for twelve years, bringing together intellectuals to exchange ideas regarding the nature of a free society. Later, Hayek was professor of Social and Moral Science in the Committee on Social Thought, University of Chicago (1950–62) and then professor at the Albert-Ludwigs University in Freiburg, Germany (1962–68). In 1974, Hayek shared the Nobel Prize in economic science with Gunnar Mydral. Hayek is considered to have played a key role in the twentieth-century revival of classical liberalism. Hayek's ideas are at the forefront of the movement toward a society based on freedom and the rule of law and away from society based upon the arbitrary control of central government.

Hayek describes the major influences in his precollegiate life, aside from his family, as drama and theater. He read seventeenth- and eighteenth-century Spanish and French dramas, although Hayek considered Goethe the greatest literary influence on his early thinking (Ebenstein 2001, 13). During Hayek's service in World War I he read socialist pamphlets and was led to his early Fabian Socialist views by the writings of **Walter Rathenau**. During his first year at the University of Vienna, Hayek's major interest was philosophical psychology (the nature of human mental understanding of the physical world). The physicist and philosopher Ernst Mach (*Analysis of Sensations*, 1914) influenced Hayek's thinking, stimulating the ideas that were published in *The Sensory Order: An Inquiry into the Foundations of Theoretical Psychology* (1952). Another strong influence on Hayek's research was **Ludwig Wittgenstein**'s *Tractatus Logico-Philosophicus* (1921). *Tractatus* influenced not only the style and substance of *The Sensory Order*, but also Hayek's picture of science and knowledge (see, for example, his essays in *Collectivist Economic Planning* [1935]).

After his first year at the University of Vienna, Hayek's interests turned to economics, and he credits Carl Menger, Eugen von Böhm-Barwerk and Friedrich von Wieser (the founders of the Austrian school of economics) as exerting the greatest intellectual influence on him. Wieser represented the more corporatist and intervention-oriented branch of the Austrian perspective and thus attracted the early Fabian Hayek. Hayek was later introduced to the writings of Menger and considered *Principles of Economics* (1871) and *Investigations into the Method of the Social Sciences* (1883) as crystallizing much of his thinking. Although Wieser would advise his thesis, Hayek came to work with Ludwig von Mises (who represented the Böhm-Barwerk anti-intervention branch). The time spent and the intellectual stimulation accorded by Mises's private seminar was vital to Hayek's scholarly development. Hayek also considered Mises's book *Socialism* (1951) as one of the two most influential books he had ever read (the other was Menger's *Principles*). Through Mises's assistance Hayek spent a year at the New York University and was influenced by Wesley Clair Mitchell.

In his professional career Hayek noted the influence of his tenure at the London School of Economics and the importance of his shared seminar with Lionel Robbins in advancing his economic views (Ebenstein 2001, 47). **Karl Popper** was another person who deeply influenced Hayek. One of the ongoing debates among

Hayek scholars is the role of Popper in influencing Hayek's methodological leanings. This debate aside, there is no doubt Hayek acknowledges an intellectual debt to Popper, especially *Logic of Scientific Discovery* (1959). Throughout his career Hayek balanced his empirical training with his normative theoretical leanings. An examination of Hayek's four major works of societal philosophy—*The Road to Serfdom; The Constitution of Liberty; Law, Legislation and Liberty;* and *The Fatal Conceit*—reveals that the most cited individuals are David Hume, Adam Smith, J. S. Mill, Popper, and Mises.

Archives

Register of the Friedrich A. von Hayek Papers, 1906–92. Hoover Institution on War, Revolution and Peace, Stanford University, Stanford, California.

UCLA Oral History Program, Department of Special Collections, Charles E. Young Research Library: a valuable collection of interviews with Hayek.

The University of Salzburg, in Austria, purchased Hayek's personal library in 1969. It still owns the collection.

Printed Sources

Ebenstein, Alan. *Friedrick Hayek: A Biography* (New York: Palgrave, 2001).

Hennecke, Hans Jörg. *Friedrick August von Hayek. Die Tradition der Freiheit* (Düsseldorf: Wirtschaft und Finanzen, 2000).

Kresge, Stephen, and Leif Wenar (eds.). *Hayek on Hayek: An Autobiological Dialogue* (Chicago: The University of Chicago Press, 1994).

Craig T. Cobane

HEANEY, SEAMUS (1939–)

Seamus Heaney was born in County Derry, Northern Ireland, at "Mossbawn," the family farm. He is the eldest of nine children in a Catholic family. His cultural surroundings and awareness of the political divide between Anglo-Protestant domination and the native Irish land left an indelible imprint on his poetry. He was a boarder at St. Columb's College, Derry (1957–61) and studied English at Queen's University, Belfast (1957–61). After obtaining his Teacher Training Diploma (1962), he got his first teaching post in Belfast. During this period he came in contact with Irish poets and began writing himself. His first collection, *Death of a Naturalist*, appeared in 1966, followed by *Door into the Dark* (1969) and *Wintering Out* (1972). His poetry sold well and received widespread praise; gradually assuming the role of public poet, he spent in 1970–71 his first year abroad at Berkeley. In 1972, he relocated to Glanmore in the Irish Republic. This event marked an important turning point in his writing, because it was accompanied with feelings of guilt for fleeing the political "troubles" of Northern Ireland; he considered himself a writer in exile and identified with William Wordsworth, whose sojourn in Dove Cottage at Grasmere and writing of the *Prelude* followed political disillusions. Around the same period *North* (1975) was published, a book of poetry that, like its successor *Field Work* (1979), confronted the social and political situation in Northern Ireland. In 1984 Heaney was appointed Boylston Professor of Rhetoric at Harvard. From 1988 to 1994 he was professor of poetry at Oxford. In the intervening years he published *Station Island* and *Sweeney Astray* (1984), *The Haw Lantern* (1987), *Seeing Things* (1991), and *Sweeney's Flight* (1992). His most recent publications include *The*

Spirit Level (1996), a translation of *Beowulf* (1999), and *Electric Light* (2001). In 1995 Heaney received the Nobel Prize.

Heaney's influences can mostly be gleaned from explicit allusions in his poetry, from interviews, and from his essays, particularly the volumes *Preoccupations* (1980) and *The Government of the Tongue* (1988); he has made translations from Dante, Sophocles, and *Beowulf*. In *Station Island* (1984) he defines influence as the dilemma between guiding and being guided: while the modern poet seeks guidance from his predecessors, he ultimately needs to reshape his models to forge an original poetic voice. The development of Heaney's poetry reflects the legacy of two literary traditions: one is specifically Anglo-Irish (**W. B. Yeats, James Joyce,** Patrick Kavanagh), coupled to an acute awareness of the language and speech patterns as he experienced them in Northern Ireland; the other is English and cosmopolitan (including Thomas Wyatt, William Wordsworth, **T. S. Eliot,** Ted Hughes, Dante, Anton Chekhov, Osip Mandelstam, Zbigniew Herbert, **Czeslaw Milosz**), and served Heaney to see the familiar and the local as part of a wider poetic horizon. The influence of Dante and other exilic poets like Herbert and Milosz hinges on the delicate balance between poetic autonomy and political engagement and concerns the problem of reconciling the poet's independence with public responsibility. Heaney invokes Wordsworth's political disillusionment to elucidate the problem of the poet's spiritual alienation either from himself or from the world in *Place and Displacement* (1984), and in the pastoral "Glanmore Sonnets" (1975); the "spots of time" feature as a technique of memory in *Stations* (1975). The most obvious use of Dante appears in *Field Work* (1979), *Station Island* (1984)—noted for its presence of the *Inferno* and *Purgatorio* interwoven with a pilgrimage to Saint Patrick's Purgatory—and *The Spirit Level* (1996). The archeological element in Heaney that sees historical memory preserved in the native soil found its inspiration from P. V. Glob's *The Bog People* (1969), a study of ritual sacrifice in prehistorical Jutland.

Archives

None currently available.

Printed Sources

Buttell, Robert. "Seamus Heaney." In *Dictionary of Literary Biography*. Vol. 40: *Poets of Great Britain and Ireland, since 1960*, Part I (Detroit, Mich.: Gale, 1985), 179–201. Still the most complete biographical sketch to date; others can be found in interviews and various introductory volumes to Heaney's poetry.

Corcoran, Neil. *After Yeats and Joyce: Reading Modern Irish Literature* (Oxford: Oxford University Press, 1997). Traces the literary legacy of Yeats and Joyce through twentieth-century Irish literature, including their influence on Beckett, Kinsella, Friel, and Heaney.

Garret, Robert F. (ed.). *Critical Essays on Seamus Heaney* (New York: G.K. Hall, 1995). Contains a section on "Poetic Contexts" with essays on "Heaney and Dante" by Carla De Petris; "The Poet as Archeologist: W. B. Yeats and Seamus Heaney," by Jon Stallworthy; "Irish Poetry after Joyce (Heaney and Kavanagh)," by Dillon Johnston; and "Orthodoxy, Independence, and Influence in Seamus Heaney's *Station Island*," by Carolyn Meyer.

———. *Modern Irish Poetry: Tradition and Continuity from Yeats to Heaney* (Berkeley: University of California Press, 1986). Places Heaney within the context of the Irish literary tradition, particularly its attempt to forge a cultural identity, and discusses Heaney's own uncertainties about his place in that tradition.

Hart, Henry. *Seamus Heaney: Poet of Contrary Progressions* (Syracuse: Syracuse University Press, 1992). The chapter on "Ghostly Colloquies" reviews the literary personae who feature in Heaney's poetry as guides or as travelers on their exilic night journeys.

Molino, Michael R. *Questioning Tradition, Language, and Myth: The Poetry of Seamus Heaney* (Washington, D.C.: Catholic University of America Press, 1994). A detailed analysis of tradition and identity in Heaney's work with particular reference to Anglo-Irish literature and the Field Day company.

Morrison, Blake. *Seamus Heaney* (London: Methuen, 1982). An introduction to Heaney's work that places him within the broad tradition of romantic poetry.

Murphy, Andrew. *Seamus Heaney.* 2nd ed. (Plymouth: Northcote House, British Council, 2000). This critical introduction to Heaney contains the most recent and up-to-date timeline of Heaney's life, besides discussing in passing the most obvious cases of influence.

O'Donoghue, Bernard. *Seamus Heaney and the Language of Poetry* (New York: Harvester Wheatsheaf, 1994). Contains a chapter on "Heaney's *ars poetica*: Mandelstam, Dante, and the Government of the Tongue" and Heaney's definition in his critical writings of the poet's poetical and political roles through reference to poets with whom he shares certain affinities.

Wim van Mierlo

HEARST, WILLIAM RANDOLPH (1863–1951)

William Randolph Hearst was born in San Francisco. His father was the multi-millionaire miner and rancher George Hearst. He attended public grammar schools, then received private tutoring while touring Europe before entering preparatory school at St. Paul's School in Concord, New Hampshire. He studied at Harvard but did not complete his senior year. He was baptized an Episcopalian but attended the Presbyterian church and Bible school throughout his childhood. Creator of a vast publishing empire and the Hearst Corporation, he was a dominating and innovative figure in twentieth-century communications. During his career in newspapers, magazines, radio, and film, he changed the way mass media functioned. Sometimes sensationalizing and manipulating the news, he used his vast media empire to espouse causes he believed in. Many historians point to the anti-Spanish outcry in Hearst's newspapers as one factor influencing the United States' entry into war with Spain in 1898. His newspapers initially supported liberal policies such as public ownership, antitrust laws, and labor unions, but they turned to vigorous opposition to **Franklin Roosevelt**'s New Deal policies on taxes, trusts, and labor. Hearst became a staunch conservative and anticommunist and opposed the United States' entry into World War II. At the peak of his influence in the mid-1930s, his newspapers were so powerful as vehicles of public opinion in the United States that **Adolf Hitler**, **Benito Mussolini**, and **Winston Churchill** all wrote for him. He served two terms in Congress, ran for presidential nomination in 1904, and was for a half century a major force in U.S. political thought and discourse.

Young Hearst was well read in both history and literature, enjoying the wit of William Makepeace Thackeray and the pageantry of Sir Walter Scott, but Charles Dickens was Hearst's "literary hero for all time" and *Dombey and Son* was his favorite novel, according to his first biographer, who knew Hearst personally (Older 1936, 40). Hearst wrote to his political columnist Paul Mallon in 1935, "You ask me how I developed my own particular style . . . I wish I could write books that live, like Dickens or Thackeray; or like our own Americans, Mark Sullivan, Frank Simonds, or **Carl Sandburg**" (Hearst 1952, 4). Much of Dickens's style is reflected in the humor and compassion of Hearst's *In the News* opinion columns, which debuted in the *Los Angeles Examiner* in 1940. The Bible also influenced Hearst throughout his life, and he often quoted scripture and referred to the Bible in his columns. "The Bible means to me the accumulation of the wisdom of the ages," he wrote. "It means also the expression and establishment of moral and religious standards . . . I want the familiar passages to speak to me . . . in the words that I learned in my youth." Young Hearst also "delighted in" theater, and "never forgot" the productions of *Shakespeare* performed by the best actors of the day (Older 1936, 40). While on a 20-month tour of Europe before entering preparatory school, Hearst immersed himself in German, French, and Italian history. He read *Legends of the Rhine* on the German riverbank (P. A. Hearst to Husband, June 30, 1873, PAH Papers, Bancroft Library; Procter 1998, 20), delivered *Cicero's* orations on the site where they were spoken (P. A. Hearst to Husband, July 13, 1873, PAH Papers, Bancroft Library; Procter 1998, 20), and went to Verona reading *Romeo and Juliet* (P. A. Hearst to Husband, July 19, 1873, PAH Papers, Bancroft Library; Procter 1998, 20). Hearst revered the American founders and collected their writings. While at Harvard he telegraphed his father requesting allowance to pay for a rare edition of Alexander Hamilton's *Federalist Papers* (Older 1936, 61). Hearst was always a voracious reader of newspapers, beginning with a subscription to the *London Times* while a teen at St. Paul's (Older 1936, 44). A letter from Hearst to his father in 1885 compares the family-owned *San Francisco Examiner* unfavorably to Joseph Pulitzer's *New York World* and demonstrates his growing depth of understanding about newspapers. Hearst urged his father to adjust every aspect of the *Examiner* to make it more like the *World* and suggested "all these changes be made not by degrees but at once" (Procter 1998, 42). Hearst's practice of analyzing newspapers continued after his father turned the *Examiner* over to him. Writes one biographer, "He spread the pages of *The World* about his room—a habit that he continued throughout his life—in an attempt to dissect the different features of the day's edition. And such an examination further confirmed his ideas for overhauling *The Examiner*" (Procter 1998, 42). Hearst also demonstrated a talent for discovering gifted writers. Among the budding writers Hearst engaged to contribute to his editorial pages was Ambrose Bierce. The contract allowed Bierce the time and means to write some of his best-known works. While Hearst's political views and allegiances shifted throughout his life, he always identified with Thomas Jefferson and referred to himself as a Jeffersonian Democrat. He looked to Jefferson for political inspiration and made numerous pilgrimages to Monticello. Indeed, Hearst, once a presidential hopeful and always an active political force in American democracy, may well have drawn analogy between Jefferson's intellectual retreat and his own mansion with its magnificent, 4,000-volume library at San Simeon.

Archives

Bancroft Library, University of California, Berkeley: Hearst family letters, papers, documents, records, certificates. Unpublished transcripts of taped interviews.

Printed Sources

Hearst, William Randolph. *William Randolph Hearst: A Portrait in His Own Words*, Edmond Coblentz (ed.), (New York: Simon and Schuster, 1952). Thoughtful analyses of Hearst's belief system based on his writings. Coblentz reprints published works and private letters and supplies historical context—commentary includes numerous references to Hearst's readings.

Nasaw, David. *The Chief: The Life of William Randolph Hearst* (New York: Houghton Mifflin Company, 2000). Utilizes some previously unavailable archival material, but mostly relies on same archival material as previous biographers.

Older, Cora. *William Randolph Hearst: American* (New York: D. Appleton Century Company, 1936). Numerous direct references to Hearst's reading, but lacks citations.

Procter, Ben. *William Randolph Hearst: The Early Years, 1863–1910* (New York: Oxford University Press, 1998). Includes text of numerous letters between Hearst and his parents, many previously unpublished.

Robinson, Judith. *The Hearsts: An American Dynasty* (Newark: University of Delaware Press, 1991). Includes text of numerous letters between Hearst and his parents, many previously unpublished.

Swanberg, W. A. *Citizen Hearst* (New York: Charles Scribner's Sons, 1961). Oft-cited first posthumous biography of Hearst. Includes information gleaned from author's personal interviews with Hearst's wife.

Richard N. Swanson

HEIDEGGER, MARTIN (1889–1976)

Martin Heidegger, the son of Johanna Kempf and master cooper Friedrich Heidegger, was born in the town of Messkirch, Baden, a solidly Roman Catholic area of southern Germany. His intellectual talent was noticed early by the local Catholic priest, Camillo Brandhuber, who taught him Latin and encouraged him in every way. He prepared for the Catholic priesthood at the archepiscopal gymnasium, the Konradihaus, Constance, from 1903 to 1906, and at Berthold's Gymnasium, Freiburg im Breisgau, from 1906 to 1909, then was briefly a Jesuit novitiate in Austria in 1909. In Constance he came under the tutelage of Matthäus Lang, reading Catholic authors such as St. Augustine, St. Bonaventura, and Hermann Schell.

Heidegger enrolled at the University of Freiburg im Breisgau in 1909 to study theology. He learned hermeneutics, biblical exegesis, and church dogmatics, but his favorite course was Carl Braig's systematic theology. Under Braig he studied Aristotle, Thomas Aquinas, Francisco Suárez, Friedrich Wilhelm Joseph von Schelling, and Georg Wilhelm Friedrich Hegel. In 1910 Heidegger's first publications concerned the theologian Friedrich Wilhelm Foerster and the poet Johannes Jørgenson. Shortly thereafter he reviewed books by Friedrich Klimke, Josef Geyser, and Otto Zimmermann. In 1911 he switched to mathematics and philosophy, studied Christian philosophy under Arthur Schneider and history under Heinrich Finke, received his doctorate in 1913, and wrote his habilitation thesis on John Duns Scotus in 1915.

The revolutionary character of Heidegger's thought seems to have been prompted by Franz Brentano's *The Multivalent Meaning of Being in Aristotle*, which he received as a gift from Conrad Gröber, a prominent Catholic clergyman, in 1907. Heidegger as a Freiburg student engaged the phenomenology of Edmund Husserl and was steeped in the neo-Kantianism of Wilhelm Windelband, Heinrich Rickert, and Emil Lask. Since neo-Kantianism is mostly a reaction against Hegelianism, Heidegger there intensified his lifelong study of Hegel. Other writers who absorbed his interest at this time include Sextus Empiricus, Blaise Pascal, Friedrich Hölderlin, Immanuel Kant, Johann Gottlieb Fichte, Søren Kierkegaard,

Friedrich Nietzsche, Georg Simmel, Max Scheler, **Henri Bergson,** and representatives of early Protestant theology, such as Martin Luther, John Calvin, and Huldreich Zwingli.

After noncombatant army service in World War I, Heidegger began teaching philosophy at Freiburg in 1918 and became Husserl's assistant there in 1919. For the next decade he considered Husserl his mentor. By the early 1920s he was friends with Karl Jaspers and **Rudolf Bultmann** and knew the work of Ernst Cassirer and **Karl Barth.** From 1923 until 1928 he taught at the University of Marburg, where, even though married to Elfride Petri since 1917 and already the father of two boys, he started a love affair in 1924 with his student **Hannah Arendt.**

Heidegger's 1927 publication of *Being and Time*, dedicated to Husserl, quickly made him world famous. He succeeded to Husserl's chair of philosophy at Freiburg in 1928, began supporting Nazism in 1931, became rector of that university in 1933, soon disavowed or ignored Husserl, Arendt, Karl Löwith, and other Jews, and collaborated with the Nazis even after he resigned the rectorship in 1934. Captured by the French in 1945, he was tried by a denazification committee and forbidden to teach until 1949. Thereafter he lived nearly as a recluse, always under the shadow of his mysterious and perhaps cowardly actions during the Nazi era, a controversy that continues into the twenty-first century.

Heidegger's central concept of *Dasein* acquired much from Wilhelm Dilthey's concept of *Leben* (life), and the Heideggerian hermeneutic circle has much in common with Dilthey's version of *Verstehen* (understanding). Meister Eckhart also had a profound effect on Heidegger, readily seen in Heidegger's 1959 essay, *Gelassenheit* ("Release"). A detractor once said that most of Heidegger's good ideas, especially his philosophy of time, were derived from Augustine, but that most of his bad ideas were his own. Despite the strong presence of Augustine, the pre-Socratics, Plato, Hegel, and many other speculative thinkers in Heidegger's thought, Aristotle and Husserl always remained his two greatest influences.

Archives

Significant collections of Heidegger's manuscripts, personal papers, and correspondence are in Germany at the Schiller-Nationalmuseum/Deutsches Literaturarchiv, Marbach, and the University of Freiburg im Breisgau. The Martin-Heidegger-Archiv was under construction in 2002 in Messkirch, supported by the Martin-Heidegger-Gesellschaft, founded there in 1975, and the Messkircher-Martin-Heidegger-Stiftung (Martin Heidegger Foundation of Messkirch). Klostermann Verlag began in 1975 to publish Heidegger's complete works *(Gesamtausgabe)*. By 2000, 59 of the projected 102 volumes had appeared.

Printed Sources

Clark, Timothy. *Martin Heidegger* (New York: Routledge, 2002).

Gadamer, Hans Georg. *Heidegger's Ways*, John W. Stanley (trans.), (Albany: SUNY Press, 1994).

Kisiel, Theodore J. *The Genesis of Heidegger's "Being and Time"* (Berkeley: University of California Press, 1993).

Kisiel, Theodore J., and John van Buren. *Reading Heidegger from the Start: Essays in His Earliest Thought* (Albany: SUNY Press, 1994).

May, Reinhard. *Heidegger's Hidden Sources: East Asian Influences on His Work*, Graham Parkes (trans.), (London: Routledge, 1996).

Ott, Hugo. *Martin Heidegger: A Political Life*, Allan Blunden (trans.), (Hammersmith, England: HarperCollins; New York: Basic Books, 1993).

Pöggeler, Otto. *The Paths of Heidegger's Life and Thought*, John Bailiff (trans.), (Amherst, N.Y.: Humanity Books, 1998).

Rockmore, Tom. *On Heidegger's Nazism and Philosophy* (Berkeley: University of California Press, 1992).

Safranski, Rüdiger. *Martin Heidegger: Between Good and Evil*, Ewald Osers (trans.), (Cambridge, Mass.: Harvard University Press, 1998).

Van Buren, John. *The Young Heidegger: Rumor of the Hidden King* (Bloomington: Indiana University Press, 1994).

Eric v.d. Luft

HEMINGWAY, ERNEST (1899–1961)

Ernest Hemingway was born in Oak Park, Illinois. Upon completing high school in 1917, he became a cub reporter for the Kansas City *Star* in Missouri. In 1818 he volunteered as a Red Cross ambulance driver in World War I Italy where, as recreated in *A Farewell to Arms* (1929), he was injured in an explosion. In 1920 Hemingway wrote for the *Toronto Star* and the Chicago magazine *The Cooperative Commonwealth*, and in 1921 in Chicago, he met Sherwood Anderson, author of *Winesburg, Ohio* (1919), and poet **Carl Sandburg,** and he married. Hemingway moved to Paris in the same year and wrote fiction while working as a newspaper correspondent, experiences recounted in the posthumously published novel *A Moveable Feast* (1964). Hemingway's first book, *Three Stories and Ten Poems*, was published in 1923. Among his other published fiction are *In Our Time* (1925), *The Sun Also Rises* (1926), *To Have and Have Not* (1937), *For Whom the Bell Tolls* (1940), and the Nobel and Pulitzer Prize-winning novella, *The Old Man and the Sea* (1952). In 1930 Hemingway left Europe to live in Key West, Florida, and in 1940 moved to Cuba. He became a United States war correspondent in 1944 and was awarded the Bronze Star for his war efforts. No longer able to write, and worn from many years of depression, Hemingway shot and killed himself on July 2, 1961, in Ketchum, Idaho.

As a young man, Hemingway admired the realism and naturalism of Theodore Dreiser and Frank Norris, and the "mannerism of Jack London and O. Henry . . . crept into the short stories he wrote during his high school years" (Lynn 1987, 24). He was deeply impressed by Mark Twain's *The Adventures of Huckleberry Finn* (1885), which he dubbed the progenitor of modern American literature. In his youth Hemingway also read Theodore Roosevelt's *African Game Trails* (1910), Owen Wister's *The Virginian* (1902), **Sinclair Lewis's** *Main Street* (1920), Somerset Maugham's *The Moon and Sixpence* (1919), and Joseph Conrad's *The Nigger of Narcissus* (1897); he is likely, too, to have encountered the novels of fellow Oak Park resident Edgar Rice Burroughs. Hemingway's critics note Sherwood Anderson's and Ring Lardner's influence on his craft, and although Hemingway later resented the comparison, he initially praised and emulated the simplicity of Anderson's writing and modeled elements of his own abbreviated yet expressive style after Lardner's journalistic mode. Hemingway's stories are further reminiscent of Lardner's in that they are told colloquially and reveal the first-person narrator's character. Anderson encouraged Hemingway to move to Paris and provided letters of introduction to revolutionary modernist writers **Gertrude Stein, James Joyce,** and **Ezra Pound.** It was Stein whom Hemingway quoted in the epigraph to *The Sun Also Rises* (1926) as saying, "You are all a lost generation"; both quotation and book succeeded in defining the postwar age. In Paris, Hemingway also became acquainted with **John Dos Passos, F. Scott Fitzgerald,** Archibald MacLeish, and Ford Madox Ford and read Ivan Sergeyevich Turgenev's *A Sportsman's Sketches* (1895), **D. H. Lawrence**'s *Sons and Lovers* (1913), and Joyce's *Ulysses* (1922), the latter of which Hemingway had a small hand in getting published.

Archives

Firestone Library, Princeton University, Princeton, N.J.: autographed manuscripts of articles and short stories; signed carbon of *The Torrents of Spring*, inscribed to the Fitzgeralds; correspondence; photographs.

Harry Ransom Humanities Research Center, University of Texas, Austin: manuscripts of *Death in the Afternoon* and "The Snows of Kilimanjaro"; family papers, correspondence.

Hemingway Room, John F. Kennedy Library, Boston, Mass.: immense collection, approximately 600 manuscripts, including short stories, articles, poetry, stages of books; over 1,100 letters and 10,000 photographs; Grace Hemingway's scrapbooks of son Ernest.

Printed Sources

Lynn, Kenneth S. *Hemingway* (New York: Simon and Schuster, 1987).

Mellow, James R. *Hemingway: A Life Without Consequences* (New York: Houghton Mifflin Co., 1992).

Meyers, Jeffrey. *Hemingway: A Biography* (New York: Harper & Row, 1985).

Reynolds, Michael S. *Hemingway's Reading, 1910–1940: An Inventory* (Princeton, N.J.: Princeton University Press, 1981).

Spilka, Mark. *Hemingway's Quarrel with Androgyny* (Lincoln: University of Nebraska Press, 1990).

Tiffany Aldrich

HESSE, HERMANN (1877–1962)

Hermann Hesse was born in Calw, Germany, into a pietistic Christian family. From his early years, school held little interest and led to a succession of brief stints at the Latin School in Göppingen (1890–91), the Protestant church school in Maulbronn (1891–92), schools for the emotionally disturbed and handicapped in Bad Boll and Stetten (1892), and finally the gymnasium in Cannstatt (1892–93). Largely self-educated, his early aestheticism and romanticism eventually fused with a more realistic assessment of the world, which itself was tempered by Indian and Eastern influences and Jungian psychology. Hesse's quest for identity, influenced by his dualistic view of man as spirit and matter, found voice in his autobiographical novellas and poems. Opposing the virulent nationalism and militarism of World Wars I and II from his home in Switzerland, having become a citizen in 1919, Hesse gained acclaim after both wars as a moral guide amid cultural crisis and chaos. He received the Nobel Prize for literature in 1946.

Hesse's literary awakening can be traced to his years in Calw (1893–95) and his time as an apprentice in a Tübingen bookshop (1895–99). His readings in eighteenth- and nineteenth-century German literature formed his aesthetic and romantic inclinations. Although Hesse expressed his greatest indebtedness to

Johann Wolfgang von Goethe, he also drew inspiration from the romantic Novalis as well as Joseph Eichendorff, Heinrich Heine, Ernst Theodor Amadeus (E.T.A.) Hoffmann, Maurice Maeterlinck, Ludwig Tieck and the Swabian poets Friedrich Hölderlin and Eduard Friedrich Mörike, among others. For Russian literature, he maintained great respect and interest, especially for the works of Lev Tolstoy, Fyodor Dostoyevsky, and Ivan Sergeyevich Turgenev. Stylistically and thematically influenced by medieval literature and the Italian Renaissance, notably the hagiography of St. Francis of Assisi, the Latin literature embodied in Cäsarius von Heisterbach and the novellas of Giovanni Boccaccio—and later still the novellas of Gottfried Keller—Hesse also drew from the historical learning of Jacob Burckhardt and the philosophies of Friedrich Nietzsche and Arthur Schopenhauer. Nietzsche's pervasive sense of life's loneliness and suffering and the need for a morality beyond good and evil found expression in Hesse's *Demian: Die Geschichte einer Jugend von Emil Sinclair* (1919; translated 1923 as *Demian*) while Schopenhauer's philosophy embodied in *Die Welt als Wille und Vorstellung* (1818; translated 1966 as *The World as Will and Representation*) melded with Hesse's Eastern religious influences. Underlying Hesse's canon is a cosmopolitan religion of love and the soul, which is governed by a pietistically dominated mystic Christianity and subsequently influenced by his readings of Hinduism and Indian Brahmanism, especially the *Upanishads* and the *Bhagavad Gita*, and the discourses of the Buddha (ca. sixth to fourth century B.C.). Later still, the teachings of Confucius (551–479 B.C.) and Lao Tzu (ca. sixth century B.C.) find expression as well as the psychology of **Carl Gustav Jung.** Ever attempting to understand himself, his works are largely autobiographical reflections unfolding the inherent inner struggles in the myriad of influences in his life.

Archives

Hermann-Hesse-Archiv, Schiller-Nationalmuseum, Marbach am Neckar, Germany: most extensive collection of Hesse's literary remains.

Hesse Sammlung, Schweizerische Landesbibliothek (Swiss National Library), Bern, Switzerland: large collection of Hesse's correspondence, personal documents and items, manuscripts and typescripts.

Printed Sources

Freedman, Ralph. *Hermann Hesse: Pilgrim of Crisis: A Biography* (New York, Pantheon Books, 1978).

Hesse, Hermann. *My Belief: Essays on Life and Art*, Theodore Ziolkowski (ed.) and Denver Lindley (trans.), (New York: Farrar, Straus and Giroux, 1974).

Mileck, Joseph. *Hermann Hesse: Life and Art* (Berkeley: University of California Press, 1978).

Ziolkowski, Theodore. *Hesse: A Collection of Critical Essays* (Englewood Cliffs, N.J.: Prentice Hall, 1973).

Rouven J. Steeves

HINDENBURG, PAUL VON (1847–1934)

Paul von Hindenburg was born to an officer's family in the garrison town of Posen in Eastern Prussia, present day Poznan, Poland. With a family military tradition extending as far back as the thirteenth century, Hindenburg was destined to continue his family's profession and lived a typical Prussian Junker's childhood.

Between Hindenburg's parents he received the necessary education for a career officer; his father instructed him in geography and history and his mother was responsible for his religious training. Hindenburg began gymnasium in 1859 before transferring a year later to the Cadet School in Wahlstatt, Silesia. In 1865, Hindenburg completed Cadet School in Lichterfelde outside Berlin. These military schools were harsh and enforced brutal discipline, and by all accounts Hindenburg loved this time of his life. Only reluctantly, however, did Hindenburg enter the more intellectually challenging War Academy in 1873 as a means to enter the vaunted General Staff. Hindenburg had an unremarkable military career before retiring in 1911. Three years later he was called out of retirement and together with Erich Ludendorff emerged as virtual military dictator of Germany between 1916 and 1918. Hindenburg's most important position was as two-term president of the fragile Weimar Republic. Hindenburg was a simple man whose loyalty and character were considered by most Germans as beyond reproach. These personal qualities made Hindenburg an ideal caretaker of the otherwise chaotic Weimar government.

Hindenburg once stated proudly, "Since my days as a cadet, I have never read a book that did not deal with military affairs." There is every reason to believe that he was telling the truth. Hindenburg is one of those rare historical figures with no discernible intellectual influence whatsoever. Hindenburg's mentor was Alfred von Schlieffen and his personal hero was Frederick the Great (1712–86), but Hindenburg found no value in reading anything but the Bible in his spare time. Hindenburg excelled in math because of its military utility, but otherwise he despised all intellectual endeavors, preferring physical education, map reading, and military history. His most difficult period was enduring the War Academy's classical curriculum requiring foreign languages and philosophy. Hindenburg was known as a slow learner who never bothered to ask the question "why?" Hindenburg's biographers note that the civilian world barely penetrated his Spartan lifestyle, although Hindenburg did marry in 1879. Hindenburg's devotion to God, King, and country endeared him to confused voters seeking stability in the 1920s, but his simplicity also made him vulnerable to the political machinations of less scrupulous politicians.

Archives

Nachlass Paul von Hindenburg, Bundesarchiv-Militärarchiv Freiburg, Germany. Contains official and some nonofficial correspondence from his 45-year military career.

Significant papers concerning Hindenburg's First World War career can be found in the *Kriegsministerium* record group (PH 2) also in Freiburg.

Printed Sources

Dorpelan, Andreas. *Hindenburg and the Weimar Republic* (Princeton: Princeton University Press, 1964).

Goldsmith, Margaret, and Frederick Voigt. *Hindenburg: The Man and the Legend* (Freeport, N.Y.: Books for Libraries Press, 1930).

Marchs, Erich. *Hindenburg: Feldmarschall und Reichspräsident* (Böttinsen: Masterschmidt Verlag, 1963).

Ruge, Wolfgang. *Hindenburg: Porträt eines Militaristen* (Berlin: Veb Deutscher Verlag, 1974).

Weterstetten, Rudolph, and A. M. K. Watson. *The Biography of President von Hindenburg* (New York: The Macmillan Company, 1930).

Brian Crim

HITCHCOCK, ALFRED (1899–1980)

Born in London on August 13, 1899, Alfred Joseph Hitchcock received a Catholic Jesuit education at the Saint Ignatius's College in London. He first wanted to study engineering, but his family couldn't afford the tuition. Hitchcock left school in 1914 and found a job as a technical agent at the W. T. Henley's Telegraph Works in London, where he worked until 1921. During this period, Hitchcock published his first short stories in the company's small journal, *The Henley Telegraph*. He was hired as a set-designer by the Londonian Famous Players Lasky Film Studio in 1921, and four years later directed his first film, *The Pleasure Garden*. In 1926 he married a colleague scriptwriter, Brompton Alma Reville, who assisted him throughout his career. *The Lodger* (1926) was his first thriller, and *Blackmail* (1929) his first talking picture. In 1940, Hitchcock released his first Hollywood movie and the only one to ever win an Oscar, *Rebecca*, an adaptation of the Daphne Du Maurier novel, produced by David O. Selznick. He released his best films during the 1950s: *I Confess* (1952), *Rear Window* (1954), *Vertigo* (1958), *North by Northwest* (1959). The greater commercial successes in *Psycho* (1960) and *The Birds* (1963) actually mark the beginning of his decline. His last film, *Family Plot*, was released in 1976.

As a teenager, Alfred Hitchcock often bought the *Lloyd's Bulletin* to help him locate the English boats sailing on the seas. His fascination with the ocean appears in his *Lifeboat* (1943), specially written for Hitchcock by **John Steinbeck.** In a 1976 interview with John Russell Taylor (reprinted in Gottlieb 1999–2000, 1995), Hitchcock says that in his prime, he read novels by John Buchan (who wrote *The Thirty-Nine Steps*), but also "all the real-life crime stories I could get a hold of . . ." (Gottlieb 1999–2000, 60). Hitchcock liked to quote Thomas de Quincy's essay, *Murder as One of the Fine Arts.* Hitchcock worked with scriptwriter John Michael Hayes for some movies in the fifties: *Rear Window, To Catch a Thief* (1955), *The Trouble with Harry* (1956), and his remake of his own British movie from 1935, *The Man Who Knew Too Much* (1956). It was after seeing the French film *Les Diaboliques* (1955) by Henri-Georges Clouzot, from a novel by Pierre Boileau and Thomas Narcejac, that Hitchcock asked the two authors to write a story for his next movie; that project would become *Vertigo* (1958), his most beautiful masterpiece. In a half century, Alfred Hitchcock made 53 movies, most of them adapted from almost as many authors, including Charles Bennett, Somerset Maugham, and Campbell Dixon.

Archives

Hitchcock Collection at the Margaret Herrick Library, Academy of Motion Picture Arts and Sciences. Manuscripts, diaries, scripts, storyboards, notebooks.

The Alfred Hitchcock Files, The Cinema-Television Library and Archives of the Performing Arts, University of Southern California, Los Angeles, California.

The David O. Selznick Collection, University of Texas, Austin, Texas. Correspondence with Hitchcock. http://www.lib.utexas.edu/Libs/HRC/HRHRC/DOS/DOSUTCAT2.html.

Printed Sources

DeRosa, Steven. *Writing with Hitchcock: The Collaboration of Alfred Hitchcock and John Michael Hayes* (London: Faber and Faber, 2001).

Garncarz, Joseph. "German Hitchcock," *Hitchcock Annual*, 2000–2001, 73–99.

Garrett, Greg. "The Men Who Knew Too Much: The Unmade Films of Hitchcock and Lehman," *North Dakota Quarterly* 61, 2 (Spring 1993), 47–57.

Gottlieb, Sidney. "Early Hitchcock: The German Influence." *Hitchcock Annual*, 1999–2000, 100–130.

Gross, Larry. "Parallel Lines: Hitchcock the Screenwriter," *Sight & Sound* 9:8 (August 1999 supplement), 38–44.

Hitchcock, Alfred. *Hitchcock's Notebooks: An Authorized and Illustrated Look Inside the Creative Mind of Alfred Hitchcock*, Dan Auiler (ed.), (New York: Spike, 1999).

———. *Hitchcock on Hitchcock: Selected Writings and Interviews*, Sidney Gottlieb (ed.), (Los Angeles: University of California Press, 1995).

Krohn, Bill. *Hitchcock at Work* (London: Phaidon, 2000).

Leff, Leonard J. *Hitchcock and Selznick: The Rich and Strange Collaboration of Alfred Hitchcock and David O. Selznick in Hollywood* (Berkeley: University of California Press, 1999).

Marantz Cohen, Paula. *Alfred Hitchcock: The Legacy of Victorianism* (Lexington: University Press of Kentucky, 1995).

Perry, Dennis R. "Bibliography of Scholarship Linking. Alfred Hitchcock and Edgar Allan Poe," *Hitchcock Annual*, 2000–2001, 163–73.

Sloan, Jane E. *Alfred Hitchcock: A Filmography and Bibliography* (Los Angeles: University of California Press, 1995).

———. *Alfred Hitchcock: A Guide to References and Resources* (New York: Maxwell Macmillan International, 1993).

Truffaut, François, and Helen G. Scott. *Hitchcock*, rev. ed. (New York: Touchstone Books, 1985).

Yves Laberge

HITLER, ADOLF (1889–1945)

Adolf Hitler was born in Braunau am Inn, Austria, to a despotic 51-year-old customs official, Alois Hitler, who had changed his name from Schicklgruber in 1876, and his long-suffering 28-year-old wife, Klara, née Pölzl, whom Hitler professed to love dearly. Hitler was baptized and enrolled in school as "Adolfus." He attended various schools near Linz, Austria, including a Benedictine monastery school for two years. After his father, whom he actively hated, died in January 1903, Hitler lived with his mother and sister in Urfahr, near Linz. He nearly failed at the Linz high school, blaming his teachers for his bad grades, but admired science teacher Theodor Gissinger and history teacher Leopold Poetsch. Having transferred to the Staatsrealschule in Steyr, Austria, he remained a poor student, except in drawing and athletics, and dropped out in September 1905 shortly before he was to take his final examinations. He then went to Munich, his first time in Germany, and studied briefly at the private art school of a Professor Gröber.

Back in Linz early in 1906, at the beginning of the happiest three years of his life, he discovered Richard Wagner, who soon became his greatest influence. Hitler not only listened to Wagner's music, but also read Wagner's tracts against Jews, cultural degeneration, national disunity, and racial pollution. Because of Wagner, Hitler became a vegetarian. He moved to Vienna in 1907, frequented the concert halls, museums, galleries, and theaters, and twice failed to gain admittance to the prestigious Vienna Academy of Fine Arts. He hoped to become a painter, architect, or writer, but could not convince anyone of his talent. His mother's death from breast cancer in December 1908 plunged him into poverty, despair, and the saddest four years of his life. He came to hate the masses of Slavs, Jews, and other non-Germans in Vienna who all seemed to be faring better than he was. As his racist, nationalist, anti-democratic views took shape, he became attracted to Georg Ritter von Schoenerer's Pan-German Nationalist Party and Karl Lueger's Christian Social Party. Frustrated by Lueger's tolerance of the Jews, he moved to Germany in May 1913.

The outbreak of World War I was a godsend to Hitler's fortunes. He volunteered in August 1914 for the Sixteenth Bavarian Reserve Infantry Regiment, served with distinction until 1920, was wounded in 1916 and gassed in 1918, achieved the rank of corporal, and was decorated four times, including the Iron Cross, First Class, for bravery. When the war ended in November 1918, Hitler was convinced that the German army was not beaten in the field, but sabotaged by Jewish financiers and industrialists. He joined the German Workers' Party in 1919, had its name changed to the National Socialist German Workers' Party in 1920, and became its leader in 1921. Sentenced to five years in Landsberg am Lech prison for his role in the "Beer Hall Putsch," the unsuccessful Bavarian coup d'état of 1923, he took that opportunity to dictate his ideological autobiography, *Mein Kampf (My Struggle)*, to his secretary, Rudolf Hess. Released after only nine months and now a national celebrity, he gained strength and followers throughout the 1920s and 1930s, was named chancellor by President **Paul von Hindenburg** in 1933, realized dictatorial power by 1934, and plunged the world into the most horrible war in history in 1939. He committed suicide in 1945 just before the Soviet army entered Berlin.

There is no evidence that Hitler ever read much. He knew no languages besides German. Nevertheless, he seems to have had a fair grasp of German and Austrian history. He was certainly familiar as a young man with *The Protocols of the Wise Men of Zion*, a vicious, subversive, often translated, and widely circulated piece of Russian propaganda designed to reveal a worldwide Jewish plot to undermine legitimate governments and corrupt wholesome societies. Aside from that, he seems to have gathered most of his knowledge, formulated most of his opinions, and honed most of his demagogic skills in the streets of Vienna and Munich.

Contrary to a frequently attested belief, Hitler was not influenced by the philosophy of Georg Wilhelm Friedrich Hegel, or, if he was, it was only through the distorted and simplistic Hegelianism derived from the German popular imagination. The case is similar with Friedrich Nietzsche. There is a famous photograph, reminiscent of Rembrandt's *Aristotle Contemplating the Bust of Homer*, depicting Hitler at the Nietzsche-Archiv in Weimar in about 1932 staring at the bust of Nietzsche. But Hitler had no real knowledge of Nietzsche. Facile misinterpretations of Nietzschean thought can be made consonant with Nazi ideology, but Nietzsche himself preferred the Jews and the Poles to the Germans, disliked militarism, hated nationalism, and held above all other values the high cultural creativity of individual artists in the world-historical future. He relinquished his German birthright and became a naturalized Swiss. His image of the "blond beast," which the Nazis used as a metaphor for the Aryan superman, was in fact only a lion.

Archives

Most of Hitler's personal papers and effects were destroyed by the Soviets in the last days of the Nazi regime. Some material may be in repositories in Russia or other former Soviet states.

Printed Sources

Birken, Lawrence. *Hitler as Philosophe: Remnants of the Enlightenment in National Socialism* (Westport, Conn.: Praeger, 1995).

Gassert, Philipp, and Daniel S. Mattern. *The Hitler Library: A Bibliography* (Westport, Conn.: Greenwood, 2001).

Hamann, Brigitte. *Hitler's Vienna: A Dictator's Apprenticeship* (New York: Oxford University Press, 1999).

Heiden, Konrad. *Der Fuehrer: Hitler's Rise to Power* (Boston: Houghton Mifflin, 1944).

Hitler, Adolf. *Hitler's Table Talk, 1941–1944: His Private Conversations* (New York: Enigma, 2000).

————. *Mein Kampf* (New York: Reynal & Hitchcock, 1939).

Müller, Michael Berthold. *Der junge Hitler: eine Biographie der ersten dreissig Lebensjahre* (Frankfurt am Main: Haag & Herchen, 2000).

Schwaab, Edleff H. *Hitler's Mind: A Plunge Into Madness* (New York: Praeger, 1992).

Scobie, Alexander. *Hitler's State Architecture: The Impact of Classical Antiquity* (University Park: Pennsylvania State University Press, 1990).

Shirer, William L. *The Rise and Fall of the Third Reich: A History of Nazi Germany* (New York: Simon and Schuster, 1960).

Weinreich, Max. *Hitler's Professors: The Part of Scholarship in Germany's Crimes against the Jewish People* (New Haven: Yale University Press, 1999).

Eric v.d. Luft

HOFMANNSTHAL, HUGO VON (1874–1929)

Hugo von Hofmannsthal was born at Vienna, the capital of the Austro-Hungarian Empire. He began publishing poetry at the age of 16 and wrote book reviews for Viennese periodicals under the pseudonym "Loris." Hofmannsthal read from his poems in Viennese coffeehouses, the gathering places of Viennese poets and authors at the turn of the century. The authors Arthur Schnitzler (1862–1931) and Hermann Bahr (1863–1934) were deeply impressed by Hofmannsthal's talent. The German symbolist poet Stefan George (1868–1933) was intellectually but most likely also physically attracted to Hofmannsthal. After a personal, unspecified disagreement, Hofmannsthal's relationship toward George changed, but he agreed to write short verse plays and poems for George's journal *Blätter für die Kunst*. However, Hofmannsthal distanced himself from George and his quasi-esoteric symbolist school and broke off all contact in 1906. After 1902, Hofmannsthal turned away from symbolism and poetry and concentrated on librettos for Richard Strauss's operas, such as *Der Rosenkavalier* of 1910 and *Die Frau ohne Schatten* of 1919. His later period was dominated by religious allegories and political pessimism. Hofmannsthal also wrote numerous essays, plays, and an unfinished novel, *Andreas*, which was posthumously published in 1932. In 1920, his neo-baroque play *Jedermann* was performed in front of the Salzburg Cathedral, which marked the beginning of the Salzburg Festival. Hofmannsthal's collaboration with the director Max Reinhardt proved to be very fruitful as their yearly festival became internationally renowned within a few years.

In his youth, Hofmannsthal was primarily influenced by baroque plays he had seen at the Viennese Burgtheater and also by French symbolists such as Stéphane Mallarmé, Paul Verlaine, and Charles Baudelaire. However, Hofmannsthal did not become an epigone, as some critics claimed, but found his own distinctive voice.

He had already been fascinated by French symbolism when he met the German symbolist poet Stefan George.

At the turn of the century, Hofmannsthal's skeptical notions concerning language in general reached their climax. Contemporary writers such as Robert Musil and Hermann Bahr also voiced their doubts that reality could be represented by language in a meaningful way. Hofmannsthal's predicament was surely triggered by the physicist Ernst Mach, whose lectures Hofmannsthal attended at the University of Vienna. Hofmannsthal wrote about his "language crisis" in "Ein Brief" (1902). In his "Märchen der 672. Nacht" (1895) and in *Die Frau ohne Schatten* (1914), he alluded to oriental stories of *The Thousand and One Nights*. Hofmannsthal's story "Das Erlebnis des Marschalls von Bassompierre" retells an anecdote in Goethe's *Unterhaltungen deutscher Ausgewanderter* (1795). Furthermore, Hofmannsthal was influenced by Elizabethan drama when he based his *Das gerettete Venedig* (1905) on Thomas Otway's *Venice Preserv'd* (1682). He also turned to Greek drama and motives in his librettos *Elektra* (1904), *Ariadne auf Naxos* (1910), and *Die ägyptische Helena* (1929). In his later years, Hofmannsthal was drawn to morality plays from the baroque era. His allegorical *Jedermann* (1911) is loosely based on the fifteenth-century English play *Everyman*. Hofmannsthal's unfinished novel *Andreas* (1932) clearly refers to the bildungsroman tradition of Goethe, Novalis, and Gottfried Keller.

Archives

Hofmannsthal-Archiv des Freien Deutschen Hochstifts, Frankfurter Goethe-Museum, Frankfurt am Main, Germany: majority of Hofmannsthal's draft manuscripts, librettos, stories, poems, plays, essays, correspondence, and photographs.

Deutsches Literaturarchiv, Schiller Nationalmuseum, Marburg am Neckar, Germany: various poems, plays, correspondence.

Houghton Library, Harvard University, Cambridge, Mass.: majority of Hofmannsthal's posthumous works, first editions, correspondence.

Printed Sources

Janik, Allen, and Stephen Toulmin. *Wittgenstein's Vienna* (New York: Simon & Schuster, 1973).

Mayer, Mathias. *Hugo von Hofmannsthal* (Stuttgart: Metzler, 1993).

Schorske, Carl. *Fin-de-Siècle Vienna: Politics and Culture* (New York: Knopf, 1980).

Steinberg, Michael P. *The Meaning of the Salzburg Festival: Austria as Theater and Ideology, 1890–1938* (Ithaca: Cornell University Press, 1990).

Vilain, Robert. *The Poetry of Hugo von Hofmannsthal and French Symbolism* (Oxford: Oxford University Press, 2000).

Gregor Thuswaldner

HOLLAND, AGNIESZKA (1948–)

Agnieszka Holland was born in Warsaw to a Catholic mother and a Jewish father, both of whom were prominent journalists. Following very much in her parents' footsteps, the young Agnieszka began writing plays at an early age. Tragically, when she was 13 years old her father was arrested by the KGB and died in the most mysterious of circumstances during interrogation.

Later as a student, Holland studied film directing at the Prague Film Academy, during which time she would meet her future husband. Holland was politically active during the Czech Spring Uprising and was subsequently imprisoned for several weeks. On her return to Poland in 1971 she gained prominence as a directorial assistant to Krzysztof Zanussi for the film *Illuminations* (1973). Concurrent with her directing and screenwriting apprenticeship in the 1970s, Holland also forged something of an acting career for herself, playing minor roles in film and television productions. In 1976 she codirected with Paweł Kędzierski *Out Takes*, playing at the same time the acting part of a director. It was Holland's collaboration with Andrzej Wajda on the screenplay to his celebrated film *Man of Marble* (1976) that first brought her to the attention of critics outside of Poland. It was not until 1978, however, that Holland made her own impact on Polish cinema by making her independent directing debut with the film *Provincial Actors*, achieving instant international acclaim and marking the beginning of a cinematic odyssey through numerous themes and film genres. The following films *Fever* (1980) and *A Lonely Woman* (1981) enjoyed equal critical success, thus cementing Holland's position at the heart of European cinema. It was while promoting this film in Sweden that martial law was declared in Poland, and due to her political activities with the Solidarity movement, Holland was forced to flee to France. For the next few years Holland maintained herself in France by translating and producing screenplays for film and television. Her rebirth as a director came in 1985 with the German film *Angry Harvest*, which told the story of a Polish Catholic farmer hiding a Jewish girl during the Nazi occupation. Here Holland's efforts were awarded with an Oscar nomination in the best foreign film category. Agnieszka Holland chose France as the place for her 1988 production, *To Kill a Priest*, featuring an American and English ensemble of actors, which told the story of the Polish priest, Jerzy Popiełuszko, who had become a spiritual leader for the Solidarity movement in the early 1980s but was murdered by a unit of Poland's secret police. This film was followed in 1991 by *Europa, Europa*, which recounted the survival of a Jewish teen in Nazi Germany as he is forced to hide within the ranks of the Hitler Youth. *Europa, Europa* enjoyed considerable commercial success in America and was nominated for an Oscar in the best original screenplay category. Her following film *Olivier, Olivier* (1992) is a comparable film to Krzysztof Kieślowski's *The Double Life of Veronique*—notably, Holland penned the screenplay to Kieślowski's *Three Colours—Blue* (1993). The film was sumptuously shot and set in the French countryside, telling the troubling story of a boy's disappearance and the disintegration of his family following the incident. The mystery deepens as the child resurfaces many years later, and the question of his lost years divides both his parents and his suspicious sister.

Following *Olivier, Olivier*, Holland was offered to direct the Hollywood production of *The Secret Garden* (1993), based on the Frances Hodgson Burnett tale. Holland's take on the classic story pleased both critics and audiences alike. Her next film, the independently made *Total Eclipse* (1995), relating the tempestuous relationship of Arthur Rimbaud and Paul Verlaine, failed to find a wide audience. However, Holland's 1997 film *Washington Square*, based on the novel by Henry James, received wide critical praise. In 1999 Holland made *The Third Miracle*, featuring Ed Harris (who also starred in the film *To Kill a Priest*) as a priest who must determine the candidacy of a dead woman for sainthood and the authenticity of the miracles which seemed to be taking place in the inner-city neighborhood where she had lived. Agnieszka Holland's latest movies have treated difficult and gritty subjects. *Shot in the Heart* (2001), filmed for HBO, recounts the family tragedy of Gary

Gilmore, whose execution by firing squad in the late 1970s—instigated at his own request—acted as a catalyst for the death penalty to be reintroduced in many American states. *Julia Walking Home* (2001), on the other hand, is the story of a woman who, having been betrayed by her husband, takes her terminally ill son to Poland to be treated by a Russian faith healer.

Throughout her career Agnieszka Holland has maintained an independent path, and each film stands as unique unto itself. Holland's Polish-Jewish heritage is explored often, and it is impossible to separate her own life-history from many of her films. In addition, the extreme circumstances of Holland's life resulted in a keen insight into the lot of individual man swept up by the tide of history. An avid reader, Holland's films are often filled with literary motifs, and she is not averse to infusing her films with traces of the supernatural.

Printed Sources

Doportowa, Mariola Jankun. *Gorzkie Kino Agnieszki Holland (The Bitter Cinema of Agnieszka Holland)* (Warsaw: Słowo/Obraz Terytoria, 2001).
Kornatowska, Maria. *Magia I pieniadze (Magic and Money)* (Cracow: Znak, 2002).

Barry Keane

HONECKER, ERICH (1912–1994)

Erich Honecker was born the fourth of six children on August 25, 1912 in Neunkirchen, Saar, near the German–French border and attended the local primary school. Honecker's father, Wilhelm, was a coal miner and a member of the Social Democratic Party (SPD). Nominally Protestant, Honecker neither attended nor received religious instruction and officially left the church at age 14. Young Erich had an early exposure to politics through his father, a militant member of the coal-miner's union and after 1919 the Communist Party (KPD). Honecker was active in communist youth groups after age 10 and in 1929 devoted himself to full-time political work, initially as head of propaganda and agitation for the local communist youth league. He joined the KPD in 1929, and during 1930–31 attended the Lenin School in Moscow. After 1933 Honecker performed underground work for the KPD; he was arrested in 1935, imprisoned, and only released in April 1945. While in prison Honecker cemented numerous political relationships. In 1945 Honecker settled in the Soviet sector of Berlin; from 1945 to 1955 he performed Party work with the Free German Youth, rising to lead this organization. In 1949 he became a member of the Central Committee of the Socialist Unity Party, a Stalinist-style melding of SPD and KPD. Honecker's rapid rise in the party structure was primarily due to a strong ideological and political allegiance to the German Democratic Republic (GDR) state and party leader **Walter Ulbricht.** In 1957 Honecker became head of GDR security forces; in this role he carried through plans in August 1961 to construct the Berlin Wall. Opposed to liberalization during the 1960s, in 1971 Honecker replaced Ulbricht when the latter lost the support of the Soviet Union over the question of relations with West Germany. From 1971 to 1989 Honecker held the most important political offices in East Germany, controlling party, state, and armed forces. The emergence of Gorbachev in the Soviet Union in the mid-1980s brought new pressures for economic and political reform, which Honecker rejected. Demonstrations throughout the GDR led to his ouster in October 1989. Charged by authorities with corruption and misuse of power, Honecker fled in March 1991 to Moscow, but in July 1992 was turned over to a German court. After a brief time in prison he was released and went into exile in Chile, where he died on May 29, 1994.

The union and political activities of his father exposed Honecker early to radical influences. As a youth he sat at meetings where the messages of Karl Liebknecht and Karl Marx were preached. During his late teenage years he read Marx, but also Zinoviev and Bukharin. He was also supportive of **Josef Stalin**'s policies; the Soviet leader's *Foundations of Leninism* was a key influence. The impact on young Honecker of the year in Moscow (1930–31) cannot be overestimated; his schooling there cemented his belief that class conflict was the key to understanding history and his belief in the need to work tirelessly for revolution. While at the Lenin School, he read a wide range of standard Marxist texts, notably Marx, **Friedrich Engels, V. I. Lenin,** and Stalin, and specifically Bukharin's *ABC of Communism.* Outside of political tracts he read little during his life; when he did, he chose socialist-realist novels by lesser-known Soviet and East German authors. These presented working-class heroes and revolutionary situations, conforming to Honecker's view of the world and how it should be.

Archives

Bundesarchiv Potsdam. Records of GDR Council of State.

Central Archive of the Former GDR Ministry of State Security, Berlin. Records of GDR Council of Ministers, other state bodies.

Printed Sources

Herzberg, Andert. *Der Sturz: Honecker im Kreuzverhör* (Berlin: Aufbau Verlag, 1991). Insightful interview conducted after fall from power.

Honecker, Erich. *From My Life (Aus meinem Leben)* (New York: Pergamon, 1981). Autobiography.

Honecker, Erich. *Zu dramatischen Ereignissen* (Hamburg: Runge, 1992). Honecker's version of 1989.

Lippmann, Heinz. *Honecker and the New Politics of Europe* (New York: Macmillan, 1972). Solid on formative years.

Thomas Saylor

HOOVER, HERBERT C. (1874–1964)

Herbert Hoover was born in West Branch, Iowa. Raised in a Quaker family, he later recalled that his early reading consisted of the Bible, the encyclopedia, and temperance tracts. Orphaned at age nine, he moved to Oregon where for three years he attended Friends Pacific Academy, founded by his uncle. As an adolescent Hoover worked in a land development company. A local school teacher, Miss Jennie Gray, introduced him to literature beginning with *Ivanhoe* and *David Copperfield* and progressing to William Thackeray, Washington Irving, and biographies of George Washington, Abraham Lincoln, and Ulysses Grant. At night school, he obtained a rudimentary education in business subjects.

As the youngest member of Stanford University's pioneer class, Hoover focused on geology and engineering, placing priority on fieldwork. Over the next two decades, he made a fortune as a mining engineer and financier. He assisted his wife,

Lou Henry Hoover, in translating a sixteenth-century Latin mining and metallurgical text, *De Re Metallica* (1556) by "Georgius Agricola" (Georg Bauer), which they privately published in 1912. Claremont College houses their extensive library of mining and engineering books. Hoover frequently subsidized book acquisitions for members of the Stanford faculty. He gave the university a collection of more than 500 volumes about China. And Mrs. Hoover collected manuscripts related to the Boxer Rebellion, which occurred during their residency in Tientsin.

By 1914, Hoover was a millionaire and considered entering public life. Human suffering in occupied nations of Europe in World War I drew him into extensive relief activities that involved much travelling. Long sea voyages offered unprecedented opportunities to remedy gaps in his reading, particularly historical works. Inspired by Andrew D. White's example of acquiring documents about the French Revolution, Hoover recognized a unique opportunity to collect "fugitive publications" of the day. Thus began the vast archival collections of the Hoover Institution on War, Revolution and Peace on the campus of Stanford University.

America's declaration of war in 1917 brought Hoover home to head the U.S. Food Administration. After postwar relief work, he served as secretary of commerce from 1921 to 1928 under Presidents Warren G. Harding and Calvin Coolidge. Articulating a major defining principle of that era, Hoover described his concept of United States citizenship in *American Individualism* (1922). The small book is more the product of his own experiences, especially as an American living abroad, than of any particular literary influence.

Elected president of the United States in 1928, Hoover served one term, blighted by the onset of the Great Depression. Returning to private life in 1933, he engaged in Republican Party politics, opposed American entry into World War II, and tried unsuccessfully to provide relief to European democracies after the outbreak of war in 1939. With the death of **Franklin Roosevelt,** President **Harry S. Truman** recalled Hoover to service, sending him on a world tour to combat famine in 1946 and on a follow-up visit to Germany and Austria in 1947. Truman and his successor, **Dwight D. Eisenhower,** recruited Hoover to head two commissions on reorganization of the executive branch of government.

Hoover published prolifically after his presidency. *The Challenge to Liberty* (1934) launched his critique of the New Deal. It was followed by eight volumes of *Addresses upon the American Road*, speeches and press statements covering 1933 to 1960. Three volumes of *Memoirs* (1951–52) told his story in his own way. Another four of *An American Epic* (1959–64) provided an edited documentary record of food relief. At the time of his death, Hoover was preparing *Freedom Betrayed*, his still unpublished examination of U.S. foreign policy after his presidency.

Archives

Herbert Hoover Presidential Library, West Branch, Iowa. Hoover's personal and official manuscripts. Many manuscript collections of associates. Museum, including personal and contextual artifacts.

Hoover Institution on War, Revolution and Peace, Stanford University, Stanford, California. Archives of relief organizations. Manuscript collections of associates.

Printed Sources

Best, Gary Dean. *Herbert Hoover: The Postpresidential Years* (Stanford, Calif.: Hoover Institution Press, 1983).

Burner, David. *Herbert Hoover: A Public Life* (New York: Knopf, 1979).

Nash, George H. *The Life of Herbert Hoover*. Vol. I: *The Engineer, 1874–1914*. Vol. 2: *The Humanitarian, 1914–1917*. Vol. 3: *Master of Emergencies, 1917–1918* (New York: W. W. Norton & Company, 1981, 1988, 1996).

Nash, Lee (ed.). *Understanding Herbert Hoover: Ten Perspectives* (Stanford, Calif.: Hoover Institution Press, 1987).

Smith, Richard Norton. *An Uncommon Man: The Triumph of Herbert Hoover* (New York: Simon and Schuster, 1984).

Wilson, Joan Hoff. *Herbert Hoover: Forgotten Progressive* (Boston: Little, Brown and Company, 1975).

Susan Eastbrook Kennedy

HUSÁK, GUSTÁV (1913–1991)

Gustáv Husák was born in Dubrávka, Slovakia. He was a political leader for the Slovaks in the beginning of his career as a statesman and later became Communist Party secretary of Czechoslovakia in 1969, after the Soviet invasion of Prague. Like most Slovaks, he had been raised with the Catholic religion, but he rejected all religion when he turned to the Communist Party.

Husák studied law at Komenius University in Bratislava, Slovakia. In 1933, as a member of the Communist Party, he assisted in leading the Slovak uprising against the Nazis. In 1951, during the Communist Party purges and puppet trials, Husák was arrested and jailed for nine years, gaining release in 1960. In 1963 he received permission to rejoin the Party and became a very outspoken critic of Antonín Novotný, whose policies and politics were viewed as anti-Slovak by Husák and Slovak Nationalists. Novotný resigned in 1968, and Husák became the deputy premier of Czechoslovakia and developed the reforms in 1968 before the Soviet invasion of Czechoslovakia. After the invasion, Husák became very pro-Soviet and assisted the government in creating one of the most tightly controlled Communist regimes in Europe. Husák created a large network of vicious goverment informers who spied upon the people, while the economy and government turned itself more deeply into the Soviet-style form of Communism. In 1975, Husák became president of Czechoslovakia but resigned in 1989 with the collapse of the Berlin Wall and Communist rule. He was replaced by Václav Havel as president.

Husák was a prolific Communist writer and wrote many speeches that were published as pamphlets in both Czech and Slovak languages. He was greatly influenced as a Communist writer by Karl Marx and Friedrich Engels, who cowrote *The Communist Manifesto* (1848). Marx's *Das Kapital* (1867–95), as well as Friedrich Engels's work *The Condition of the Working Class in England* (1844), which critiques the squalor and misery created in Manchester, England, by greedy capitalist factory owners, served as models for Husák's writing and thinking. Husák also read the works of **Vladimir Illych Lenin** (1870–1924) such as *What Is to Be Done* (1901–02), *Imperialism: The Highest Stage of Capitalism* (1916), and *Lessons of the Moscow Uprising* (1906), as well as the works by Czech writer Julius Fučík, who wrote *Božena Němcová bojující* (1939; *Božena Němcová is Fighting*) and *V zemi, kde zítra již znamená včera* (1932; *In the Country Where Tomorrow No Longer Means Yesterday*). These works reflected not only a defiance against the Nazis' rise to power but also brought forth a creative method of socialist realism. Palmiro Togliatti's *Jalta Memorandum* (1964), which was written for the Italian Communist Party, was also a basis for Husák's writing.

Archives

Národní knihovna v Praze (National Library in Prague at the Klemintinum in Prague, Czech Republic): Husák's speeches and writings, material on Communist Party in Czechoslovakia. Newspapers, magazines, and photos.

Archív hlavního města Prahy (Prague City Archives, Prague 4-Chodov, Prague, Czech Republic): Manuscripts, documents on the Communist Party in Czechoslovakia. Newspapers, magazines, and photos.

Státní ústřední archív (State Central Archive in Prague, Czech Republic): Photos, documents, manuscripts.

Printed Sources

Kennedy, Michael D. *The End to Soviet-Type Society and the Future of Post-Communism* (Ann Arbor: University of Michigan Press, 1991).

Motková, Eva Victoria. "Václav Havel and Lech Walesa: Networks for Peaceful Transformation, Truth and Freedom" (Thesis). Eckerd College, St. Petersburg, Fla., 2001.

An Outline of the History of the CPCz (Communist Party of Czechoslovakia) (Prague: Orbis, 1985).

Sviták, Jan. *The Unbearable Burden of History: The Sovietization of Czechoslovakia. Vol. 2. Prague Spring Revisited* (Praha: Akademia, 1990).

Cynthia A. Klima

HUXLEY, ALDOUS (1894–1963)

Aldous Huxley was born at Laleham, Godalming in Surrey. He entered Eton in 1908, had to withdraw in 1911 due to illness, but was still able to matriculate to Balliol College, Oxford in 1913. He left Oxford with a first class degree in 1916 and took up a teaching position at Eton. However, literature emerged as a more important vocation as he began to publish a number of significant novels during the 1920s. *Crome Yellow* (1921), *Mortal Coils* (1922), and *Antic Hay* (1923) are all indicative of Huxley's growth as a novelist. However, it was *Point Counter Point* (1928), which caught the turbulence of postwar Europe, and *Brave New World* (1932), which presaged a future in which science, technology, and mass-production would form a bland, lifeless society, that established his reputation as a critical twentieth-century voice. In 1938 Huxley moved to California, where he would live for the last 25 years of life; while he continued to produce a range of literary works (plays, novels, and film scripts), this period of his life has also been remembered for his exploration of both Eastern religions and experimental drug use.

While Huxley was remembered at Oxford as someone who had "read everything," his intellectual formation was largely the product of pedigree. To begin with, he was at once the great grandson of Dr. Thomas Arnold of Rugby, the grandson of Thomas Henry Huxley, the grand nephew of Matthew Arnold, the nephew of the novelist Mrs. Humphry Ward, and the brother of Julian Huxley, who would ultimately become a successful scientist and writer. In addition, as a teacher and scholar, his father made a significant contribution in his own right, while his mother founded a school. Given this background, Aldous Huxley's development was shaped as much by family habit as it might have been by exposure to a given set of ideas.

Huxley did, nevertheless, bear the stamp of a generation that understood itself to be significantly different than its predecessors, a sentiment which would later find expression as the "revolt against Victorianism." For the young Huxley it meant an open stance toward the future shape of society and, on a more immediate level, a rethinking of personal and sexual boundaries; both of these orientations would later mean that critics would identify Huxley with literary modernism.

Huxley's career, then, depended upon what he learned from key personal relationships. Literary scholars have discerned that Huxley's development was affected by the friendship which he developed with **D. H. Lawrence** (whose letters he would publish), who he claimed was a "great man." Huxley also benefited from the patronage of Lady Ottoline Morrell, who introduced him to the household society of Garsington (about six miles from Oxford). At Garsington Huxley would begin to form friendships with Leonard and **Virginia Woolf, Bertrand Russell** ("lucid and intellectual"), **John Maynard Keynes** ("always fascinating"), Clive Bell ("extremely stimulating"), and Roger Fry ("from whom I learned a great deal"). These relationships were personal before they were literary, but they amounted to a significant intellectual resource for the young Huxley to draw from.

Given these wide influences, it is not surprising that Huxley never developed a series of central ideas or core of thought. Instead, he maintained an unusual curiosity and breadth of interest in intellectual questions. These concerns ultimately involved what he perceived to be the struggle for human freedom. As such, he tended to remain hostile to conservatism and traditional Christianity while embracing social experimentation and divergent forms of spiritual life.

After his relocation to California, Huxley's outlook and interests would again be decisively shaped by personal encounters. Both Jiddu Krishnamurti and Swami Prabhavananda helped him become even more sensitive to Hinduism. These relationships bore fruit in a number of ways: in the emphasis on Eastern mysticism which helps to define Huxley's later writings and in his attempts to help Gerald Heard in the establishment of a religious community called Trabuco College.

Archives

Aldous Huxley Collection, William Andrews Clark Memorial Library, UCLA, Los Angeles, California.

Printed Sources

Bedford, Sybille. *Aldous Huxley. A Biography*, 2 vols. (New York: Knopf, 1973–74).

Dunaway, David King. *Aldous Huxley Recollected: An Oral History* (New York: Caroll and Graf, 1995).

Huxley, Aldous. *The Letters of Aldous Huxley*, Grover Smith (ed.), (New York: Harper and Row, 1969).

Huxley, Sir Julian. *Memories*, 2 vols. (New York: Harper and Row, 1970).

Huxley, Laura Archera. *This Timeless Moment: A Personal View of Aldous Huxley* (New York: Farrar, Straus and Giroux, 1968).

Stephen L. Keck

I

IONESCO, EUGÈNE (ROMANIAN SPELLING: IONESCU, EUGEN) (1909–1994)

Eugène Ionesco was born in Slatina, a small town in western Romania, to a Romanian father and a French mother of Jewish origin. He spent the years 1913–22 in France before returning to Romania, where he attended high schools in Bucharest and Craiova and obtained a degree in French language and literature from Bucharest University. In the 1930s, he gained a reputation as the enfant terrible of Romanian literary journalism and criticism—winning a prize for his iconoclastic collection of essays *Nu* (No) in 1934—while earning a living as a French teacher. In 1938 he left for Paris, taking up a French government scholarship to do a thesis on Baudelaire's poetry; henceforth, apart from a brief spell between 1940 and 1942, he lived in France for the rest of his life. His groundbreaking play *La cantatrice chauve* was first performed in Paris in 1950, and over the next two decades he established himself in France, Britain, and America as one of the leading lights of the post–World War II theatrical avant-garde with works such as *La leçon* (1954), *Rhinocéros* (1960), and *Le roi se meurt* (1962). In his later life Ionesco also took up painting. He died in 1994.

Besides his early literary criticism, Ionesco gave a large number of interviews and published several volumes of journals, in which a complex but relatively consistent pattern of literary influence can be established. He was an obsessive reader with an exceptionally acute critical faculty; he repeatedly attacked both consecrated writers and the concept of the literary canon, while at the same time engaging in an intense search for meaning in life and literature: the title of his 1987 volume, *La quête intermittente*, describes this process well. In *Nu* and other Romanian criticism, Ionesco was ruthless about the provincial, imitative aspect of Romanian literature. He made exceptions for the rationalist critic Titu Maiorescu, the romantic poet Mihai Eminescu, and the satirical dramatist Ion Luca Caragiale, for whom he retained a lifelong affection (Ionesco 1962, 117–21; Ionesco 1987, 76) and whose dramatic technique clearly influenced his own (Hamdan 1993, 138–74). He also admired Romanian surrealists including Tristan Tzara, and claimed to have arrived at the techniques of the theater of the absurd independently of **Samuel Beckett.** In the early 1930s a deprecatory aside about Romanians in **Aldous Huxley**'s novel *Point Counter Point* both offended him and made him aware of the impossibility of achieving European distinction while writing in a minor cultural language (Ionesco 1934, 57). In 1935 he wrote a hilarious travestied biography of Victor Hugo, but later expressed admiration for Hugo's attempts at theatrical innovation.

Early critics of his theater related his work to the traditions of French modernism and the surrealist avant-garde: he admitted that of Gustave Flaubert, Alfred Jarry, and the poets Paul Claudel and Jammes and Maurice Maeterlinck (interview in Hayman 1972, 1–17), although his immediate inspiration for *La cantatrice chauve* was not a literary text but a series of dialogues in an English-teaching manual (*Englezeşte fără profesor*, 1948 repr. with French translation in Hamdan 1993, 175–201). Philosophically, he found Arthur Schopenhauer, Fyodor Dostoyevsky, Emile Durkheim and **Carl Jung** more interesting than Friedrich Nietzsche ("indigestible"), Søren Kierkegaard (whom "I never managed to understand very well"; Ionesco 1987, 101ff.), or Sigmund Freud. The influence of religious thought on Ionesco's work is not to be ignored. He took great interest in the "personalist" Christian writer Emmanuel Mounier, especially during the war when French and Romanian intellectual life seemed to him to have lost all moral direction (Hayman 1972, 3; Ionesco 1968, 166), while the writings of St. John of the Cross remained important to him in what he saw as a desacralized world in which "reason, in its mediocrity, prevents us from having faith" (Ionesco 1987, 95). He explicitly rejected, however, the false promises of materialist prophecy (Marx), the possibility of art to convey messages (**Bertolt Brecht, Jean-Paul Sartre**), or the mystical eschatology of the extreme right.

Archives

Ionesco's correspondence remains mostly in private hands; however, he gave many interviews during his lifetime and published numerous volumes of journals which shed light on the question of literary influence (see Printed Sources). The manuscripts of some of his plays have been deposited at the Bibliotheque Nationale de France, Paris.

Printed Sources

Hamdan, Alexandra. *Ionescu avant Ionesco. Portrait de l'artiste en jeune homme* (Berne: Peter Lang, 1993).

Hayman, Ronald. *Eugene Ionesco* (London: Heinemann, 1972).

Heitmann, Klaus. "Ein religiöser Denker unserer Tage: Eugene Ionesco." In Alfonso de Toro (ed.), *Texte, Kontexte, Strukturen. Beiträge zur französischen, spanischen und hispanoamerikanischen Literatur, Festschrift zum 60. Geburtstag von Karl Alfred Blüher* (Tübingen: Gunter Narr, 1987), 113–36.

Ionesco, Eugène. *Antidotes.* (Paris: Gallimard, 1977).

———. *Conversations with Eugene Ionesco*, Claude Bonnefoy (ed.), Jan Dawson (trans.), (London: Faber and Faber, 1970).

———. *Découvertes* (Genève: A. Skira, 1969).

———. *Journal en miettes* (Paris: Mercure de France, 1967).

———. *Notes et contre notes* (Paris: Gallimard, 1962).

———. *Nu* (Bucureşti: Vremea, 1934).

———. *Présent passé, passé présent* (Paris: Mercure de France, 1968).

———. *Ruptures de silence: rencontres avec André Coutin* (Paris: Mercure de France, 1995).

———. *La quête intermittente* (Paris: Gallimard, 1987).

Ionescu, Gelu. *Les débuts littéraires roumains d'Eugène Ionesco (1926–1940)*, Mirella Nedelco-Patureau (trans.), (Heidelberg: Carl Winter, 1989).

Petreu, Marta. *Ionescu în țara tatălui* (Cluj-Napoca: Apostrof, 2001).

Alexander Drace-Francis

J

JAMES, CYRIL LIONEL ROBERT (1901–1989)

C.L.R. James was born in Trinidad into a middle-class family. Several years after he completed his education, James taught at his alma mater, Queen's Royal College. In 1932, at the age of 31, James left Trinidad and moved to England with hopes of becoming a novelist. There, James worked as a cricket reporter for the *Manchester Guardian*. In 1933, he became involved in the Trotsky revolutionary movement. James felt that Trotskyism could be used to aid Africans and people of African descent in their struggle for equality and, in some cases, independence. This interest was at the core of his involvement with the 1930s African Independent Movement. However, at the signing of the Hitler-Stalin Pact, he became disillusioned with the Trotsky movement and eventually broke from it (Grimshaw 1996, 6–7). In 1936, James wrote, produced, and acted in a play, *Toussaint L'Ouverture*, choosing **Paul Robeson** to play the lead role. Two years later, the activist moved to the United States. While there, he traveled in literary circles, forming relationships with figures such as **Richard Wright,** Ralph Ellison, and Carl Van Vechten. He married Constance Webb and the couple had a son, but the marriage was not successful. During the McCarthy era, James was imprisoned on Ellis Island for his left-wing political affiliations. Consequently he was deported from the United States in 1953. James traveled throughout Europe and Africa until he returned to Trinidad in 1958 and he joined the People's National Movement drive for Trinidadian independence. In 1968, he returned to the United States, where he lectured at universities and continued to write. James eventually settled in Brixton, London, where he died.

James's work reflects his interest in the ordinary person, the working class or proletariat. Before he became involved in Trotskyism, he wrote a biography on Andre Cipriani, *The Life of Captain Cipriani: An Account of British Government in the West Indies* (1932). In an interview, James said he was interested in Cipriani because of the Trinidadian labor leader's ideas about self-government and his concern with the "barefooted man" (Farred 1996, 118). By the time James published this biography, he had written a novel, *Minty Allen* in 1929 (although it was not published until 1936) and short stories, including "Triumph," which were, according to James, about "ordinary people" (Farred 1996, 119). When he began to study Trotskyism, he was particularly interested in **Leon Trotsky**'s three-volume *History of the Russian Revolution.* He also studied Karl Marx, G.W.F Hegel, **V. I. Lenin,** and **Josef Stalin** (Farred 1996, 105). James read a variety of authors including the works of Pan-Africanist W.E.B. DuBois and Universal Negro Improvement Association leader **Marcus Garvey.** Further, he so admired Herman Melville's *Moby Dick* that he wrote about it in a book entitled *Mariners, Renegades and Castaways: The Story of Herman Melville and the World We Live In* (1953). According to James, he was intrigued by Melville's "instinctive revolutionary development" and his ability to make the crew of ordinary people distinctive (Farred 1996, 41). These ideas are at the heart of *Black Jacobins: Toussaint L'Ouverture and the San Domingo Revolution* (1938). James was also fond of Aeschylus and Shakespeare, whom he credits as being artists who used new methods of expression.

Archives

C. L. R. James Institute, New York City.

Printed Sources

Buhle, Paul. *C.L.R. James: The Artist as Revolutionary* (London: Verso, 1988).
Farred, Grant (ed.). *Rethinking C.L.R. James* (Cambridge: Blackwell, 1996).
Grimshaw, Anna (ed.). *Special Delivery: The Letters of C.L.R. James to Constance Webb, 1939–1948* (Cambridge: Blackwell, 1996).
Nielsen, Aldon Lynn. *C.L.R. James: A Critical Introduction* (Jackson University Press of Mississippi, 1997).
Worcester, Kent. *C.L.R. James: A Political Biography* (Albany: State University of New York Press, 1996).

Tara D. Green

JANION, MARIA (1926–)

Maria Janion, a scholar in the history of Polish literature, a historian of ideas, and a feminist, spent her childhood and World War II in Vilnius (at that time in Poland). She studied Polish literature at the Lódz and Warsaw Universities (1945–49). From 1948 she worked in the Institute of Literary Research at the Polish Academy of Sciences (IBL PAN), writing extensively on the history of ideas, Polish romanticism, Polish literature and feminist thought. From 1979 she also worked at the Gdansk University where her pioneering views on women's identity in general and in Poland in particular resulted in seven volumes entitled "Transgressions" (1981–88), a collective piece written under Janion's direction by young writers from the "New Privacy" generation. The central concept of crossing various cultural borders and prohibitions becomes synonymous with individual freedom. The works focus on usually marginalized aspects of humanity such as loneliness, cruelty, madness, or eroticism and on the condition of a genius, an artist, a child, a rebel, and a woman. These volumes became one of the earliest publications on feminism in post–Communist Poland. Janion's work influenced a younger generation of writers, including Krystyna Lars and Izabella Fillipiak, who shared Janion's assumption that transgressing various types of social and cultural norms leads to freedom.

Janion's unique erudition makes it difficult to pinpoint the major influences on her, although she was influenced by the works of Adam Mickiewicz, the greatest Polish romantic poet, by German romantic fantastic literature, and perhaps by French surrealism. Janion has rarely talked or written about herself, though in her most personal book, *Zyjac tracimy zycie* (*We Lose Life While Living It*; 2001), she discusses her fascination with Honore de Balzac's novel, *The Magic Skin* (1831) and his concept of continuous ending of human life.

Janion's greatest accomplishments lie in two areas of research: her work on Polish romanticism and her innovative work on feminist thought. Her extensive research on Polish romanticism examines the strengths of romanticism in Polish literature, including the postwar literature (1945–90) and its importance in understanding cultural constructs of Polish national identity. Janion often worked with Maria Zmigrodzka, also a scholar of Polish romanticism, who was likely the major influence on Janion's philosophy. Janion's monographs—*Lucjan Siemienski, poeta romantyczny* (*Lucjan Siemienski, the Romantic Poet*; 1955); *Zygmunt Krasinski, Debiut i dojrzalosc* (*Zygmunt Krasinski: The Debut and the Maturity*; 1962)—as well as her works analyzing the major themes of romantic thought are devoted to the mythology of patriotism, the cultural construct of tragedy, the concept of romantic individualism, irrationalism, and demonism. These include *Romantyzm: Studia i ideach i stylu* (*Romanticism: Studies about Ideals and Style*; 1969); *Goraczka romantyczna* (*The Romantic Fever*; 1975); *Czas formy otwartej: Tematy i media romantyczne* (*The Time of the Open Form: Romantic Themes and Mediums*; 1984); and *Romantyzm i historia* (*Romanticism and History*), co-authored with Maria Zmigrodzka (1978).

Janion's latest writings prove the exhaustion of the romantic myths in Polish post-communist society and its inability to create a different model for the experiences of the twentieth century. These works include *Wobec zla* (*Facing Evil*; 1989); *Zycie posmiertne Konrada Wallenroda* (*The Afterlife of Konrad Wallenrod*; 1990); and *Projekt krytyki fantazmatycznej: Szkice o egzystancjach ludzi i duchow* (*The Project of Phatasmatic Criticism: Sketches on the Existence of People and Spirits*; 1991). Janion's views on history bear some influence of the historians of the so-called Warsaw school of the history of ideas, especially those of Bronislaw Baczko and Leszek Kolakowski.

Archives
None available.

Printed Sources

Hawkesworth, C. (ed.). *A History of Central European Women's Writing* (New York: Palgrave, in association with School of Slavonic and Eastern European Studies, University College, London, 2001).

Janion, Maria. *Zyjac tracimy zycie* (Warsaw: Wydawn, W.A.B., 2001).

Walczewska, S. *Damy, rycerze i feministki: kobiecy dyskurs emancypacyjny w Polsce* (Krakow: Wydawn EFKA, 1999).

Katarzyna Zechenter

JIMÉNEZ, JUAN RAMÓN (1881–1958)

Juan Ramón Jiménez was called an "essential poet." He expressed his conviction that beauty and poetry are real entities rather than simply a belief in beautiful objects or poetic verses. For Jiménez, there existed the harmony of both the aesthetic qualities of reality and the aesthetic sensibilities of the poet, in a sense responding to Charles Baudelaire's pure poetry distinction between ethics and aesthetics. From the sentimental subjectivism of his early years, his poetry evolved to objectivity and finally toward a philosophical, metaphysical poetry. His poetry was elitist and introspective and is largely free of literary trends and fashion.

Jiménez was born in Moguer, in the south of Spain. He studied law in Seville, where he initiated his poetic writings and read the Spanish romantic poets of the nineteenth century: Gustavo Adolfo Bécquer, José de Espronceda, Rosalía de Castro; the mystics, such as Saint John of the Cross; and medieval Arabic-Andalusian poetry.

At 20, Jiménez left for Madrid. After having met the Nicaraguan poet Rubén Darío, he spoke of "destino," a crucial episode in his career that introduced him to modernism. During these years, Jiménez enjoyed reading and also declaiming poetry of Alphonse Lamartine, Lord Byron, Heinrich Heine, Gabriele D'Annunzio, and Parnassianism. In an autobiographical note published in *Renacimiento*, Jiménez spoke of his heritage: "My blood circulated in *romance* (ballads), I could hear it. That was a folk song, cultured because of the unconsciously reflected model of Heine, of Bécquer and of Musset, whose *Intermezzo* and whose *Nights* I was then reading. Musset gave it seriousness and Heine the second accent" (Jiménez 270). Jiménez admired symbolist poet Paul Verlaine, "the most estrange and sweet soul that has been on Earth." He published his first modernist books of poems *Ninfeas* (1900) and *Almas de Violeta* (1900) that were filled with the musicality and beauty of language. Years later, irritated by the preciosity of this writing, Jiménez tried to destroy all the volumes he could lay his hands on.

His father's sudden death resulted in Jiménez suffering several nervous breakdowns. During his convalescence, he read the aphoristic prose of Friedrich Nietzsche and the poetry of William Shakespeare, Johann Wolfgang von Goethe, and Percy Bysshe Shelley. After returning to Madrid in 1911, Jiménez was already an acclaimed poet. He moved to the *Residencia de Estudiantes*, the famous college frequented by prominent artistic and intellectual figures such as **Miguel de Unamuno, José Ortega y Gasset,** and later **Federico García Lorca, Luis Bunuel,** and **Salvador Dali,** as well as **John Maynard Keynes, Albert Einstein,** and Paul Valéry.

In 1913, while at the *Residencia de Estudiantes*, Jiménez met a young student, Zenobia Camprubí, the American educated daughter of a wealthy Spaniard. Their stormy courtship is reflected in two books of poetry: *Estío* (1914, published 1915) and *Sonetos espirituales* (1914–15, published 1917) based on the sonnet tradition of Shakespeare and Garcilaso de la Vega.

Returning to Spain from a honeymoon in the United States, he led a secluded and solitary life writing poetry. He worked persistently on poetry, prose, reviews, prefaces, and introductions and kept informed of literary movements in Spain and Spanish America and the world. He was director of several poetic journals that attracted the most important poets at the time, including Pedro Salinas, Jorge Guillén, and Rafael Alberti, among others. *Platero y yo*, a pseudo-autobiographical masterpiece of literary prose, was published in 1914.

At the beginning of the Spanish Civil War in 1936, the couple left for the United States, where Jiménez was cultural attaché until 1939. They traveled in Latin America, and he later taught at several U.S. universities. In 1950, he established himself in Puerto Rico where Zenobia died in 1956, a few days after her husband received the Nobel Prize for literature. Jiménez died two years later in 1958.

The literary work of Jiménez can be divided into three stages. Before 1916, his poetry followed the modernist trend. His *Arias tristes* (1903) and *Jardines Lejanos* (1904) were influenced by musicians such as Franz Schubert and Felix Mendelssohn-Bartholdy. From 1907, his longtime friend Luisa Grimm de Muriedas introduced him to the poetry of **William Butler Yeats**, Francis Thompson, and Lord Byron.

After this stage, his poetry became independent of any school. Filled with symbolism in search of absolute beauty, it is the period of *Poesía pura* (naked poetry). It is a dehumanized and intellectual poetry that simplifies the vocabulary and any unnecessary complexity in a ceaseless meditation on love, poetry, and death. In 1917 he published *Diario de un poeta recién casado* and *Estación total* (written between 1923 and 1936).

Zenobia had a great influence in his life, collaborating in translating many authors into Spanish, including Rabindranath Tagore's *The Crescent Moon*. In the United States, Jiménez read the works of **Robert Frost** and **Ezra Pound** and, later, Emily Dickinson. He also established contact with prestigious American intellectual institutions. The Hispanic Society of America published an anthology, *Poesías escogidas: 1899–1917*.

After 1949, he concentrated on more spiritual writing; some critics have talked of "neomisticismo" (neomysticism) parallel to Saint John of the Cross. In *Tiempo y muerte* Jiménez stated that God is in each one of us and is what joins us to another. His latest works were complex and filled with emotions, especially *Romances de Coral Gables* (139–42, published 1948) and *Animal de fondo* (1949).

Jiménez was the teacher of the so-called "Generation of 1927" poets (including García Lorca and Rafael Alberti, among others). He had a great influence on Spanish poetry by opening new poetic expressions and horizons for Hispanic writers. For his originality and independence, Jiménez has always been at the forefront of twentieth-century Spanish poetry.

Archives

Fundación Juan Ramón Jiménez, centro de estudios Juan Roamonianos, Moguer, Huelva, Spain.

Casa-Museo, Moguer, Huelva, Spain.

"Sala Zenobia y Juan Ramón Jiménez" in the Biblioteca General, Universidad de Puerto Rico, Río Piedras.

Archivo Histórico Nacional, Biblioteca Nacional, Madrid.

Printed Sources

Albornoz, Aurora de. *Juan Ramón Jiménez* (Madrid: Taurus, 1983).

Fogelquist, Donald F. *Juan Ramón Jiménez* (Boston: Twayne Publishers, 1976).

Garfias, Francisco. *Juan Ramón Jiménez* (Madrid: Taurus 1958).

Jiménez, Juan Ramón. *Por el cristal amarillo*. Francisco Garfias (ed.), (Madrid: Aguilar, 1961).

Juliá, Mercedes. *El universo de Juan Ramón* (Madrid: Gredos 1989).

Palau de Nemes, Graciela. *Vida y obra de Juan Ramón Jiménez: La poesía desnuda*, 2 vols. (Madrid: Gredos, 1975).

Wilcox, John C. *Self and Image in Juan Ramón Jiménez* (Urbana: University of Illinois Press, 1987).

Young, Howard. *The Line in the Margin: Juan Ramón Jiménez and His Readings on Blake, Shelley, and Yeats* (Madison: University of Wisconsin Press, 1980).

Andrés Villagrá

JOHN XXIII (1881–1963)

Pope John XXIII was born Angelo Giuseppe Roncalli in the village of Sotte il Monte, Italy, the third of thirteen children and the first son of Giovanni and Marianna Roncalli. He was educated in Bergamo and at the Apollinare seminary in Rome, receiving his doctorate in theology and ordination as a priest in 1904. From 1904 to 1914 he was secretary to the bishop of Bergamo. Following national service in World War I, Roncalli's career in the church progressed steadily but uneventfully. His appointments as archbishop in 1925 and then as the Vatican's diplomatic representative (nuncio) to Bulgaria, Turkey, Greece, and France broadened his perceptions as well as his horizons. During the dangerous years before and during the Second World War, Roncalli was able to use his official (and geographical) positions in combination with his natural charm to secure safe passage for thousands of Jews away from the onslaught of the Third Reich. In 1953 he was named cardinal and patriarch of Venice. In the autumn of 1958, as he approached the age of 77, this son of tenant farmers was elected pope of the Roman Catholic Church. Roncalli took John as his papal name, in honor of his father and of John the Baptist, who was patron saint of his home village; the name choice also countered and cancelled the anti-pope John XXIII of the fifteenth century. As Pope John XXIII, Roncalli continued to mix politics with religion via morality and ethics, noting significantly that "justice comes before charity" (Cahill 2002, 169). He cultivated relationships with Eastern Orthodox, Jewish, Islamic, Protestant, and Shinto leaders. He was consultant and confidant to both U.S. President **John F. Kennedy** and Soviet Premier **Nikita Khrushchev;** indeed, they were dubbed "The Triumvirate." And he was the instigator and driving force behind the Second Vatican Council ("Vatican II," 1962–65) and its reforming advocacy of integration and ecumenicalism, for which *Time* magazine named him the Man of the Year for 1962. Both before and after his assumption of the pontificate, Roncalli's personality transcended religion, race, and culture.

As might be expected, the future pope's early literary experiences circled around the Bible. Roncalli's father showed his young son the carved and glassed depictions of biblical tales in the local church. The poetry of the mass and the rosary was a daily event. In the evenings of his childhood, Roncalli's Uncle Zaviero would regale the Roncalli children with vivid readings of Bible stories. Zaviero Roncalli, a prolific reader, was also a member of the socialist group Catholic Action and mixed readings from the socialist newspapers with the biblical recitations. For Angelo Roncalli, ever afterward, religion and socialism would not be conflicting ideologies; the church and the well-being of ordinary people were inexorably tied. His formal study of the Bible, and subsequently of the Christian fathers and of the Greek and Roman classics, began when he was seven and sent to learn Latin from a local priest. Roncalli's subsequent acceptance to seminary took him to the nearby city of Bergamo—"the most Catholic of cities," according to *L'Osservatorre Romano* (Elliott 1973, 21)—known for its arts and its agitations for social reform. Bergamo was also the setting of Alessandro Manzoni's hugely popular historical epic *The Betrothed* (1826). Considered Italy's first modern novel, *The Betrothed (I promessi sposi)* was approvingly described by one reviewer as "Scott, Dickens, and Thackeray rolled into one" (Hebblethwaite 1985, 19). A compassionate and deeply Catholic novelist and poet, Manzoni wrote about the conflict between formal, devotional Catholicism and popular expressions of faith, bringing them into harmony. Roncalli first read *The Betrothed* as a young seminarian and, throughout his life, would frequently recommend it as valuable reading, especially the last chapter, for priests in conflict. Manzoni's poetry held equal appeal, particularly *La Pentacoste*, when Pope John began envisioning a new Vatican Council.

Roncalli had been well familiar with Dante, Petrarch, and Tasso as well as St. Augustine and Manzoni since his teenage years and continued reading and referencing them. His later literary interests also included Charles Péguy, the twentieth-century poet and proponent of Catholic socialism, and Nicolas Gogol, especially the *Spiritual Letters*. He was also a regular reader of newspapers but, for the most part, Roncalli preferred reading varied and various histories and biblical commentaries. He was, after all and for most of his life, a publishing historian as well as churchman; and he combined the two when he opened Vatican II by saying "History is the teacher of life" (Trevor 1967, 100). In seminary Roncalli's readings in church history gave him a base from which to evaluate modern concerns. He was a classical linguist, mastering Greek and Hebrew along with Latin (and then there were the Romance and Slavonic languages which he also acquired). Cicero and Juvenal were perpetually favored authors, with Cicero's humane good sense having a natural appeal to Roncalli. In what became his *Journal of a Soul*, the young seminarian Roncalli writes of having "a restless longing to know everything, to study all the great authors . . . ," which disingenuously implied also those authors on the [Catholic] Index of Forbidden Books (Cahill 2002, 87). Years on an interviewer described the bookshelves of Roncalli's quarters in Sofia, Bulgaria, as being stocked with works by the Greek fathers, Petrarch, Dante, and Manzoni. And, as a denizen of Paris's book shops, the portly papal nuncio to France was seen scrambling around on the floor of a bookstore, hunting for a work by John Henry Newman but retrieving just as happily a translation of Dom Guéranger. For the pope as well as for the young seminarian, the value of great writers and the importance of good writing was perpetual. In a mild chastisement to newspaper reporters regarding the content of their reporting on Vatican II, Pope John offered for contemplation the words of Alessandro Manzoni: "Truth is holy and I have never betrayed it" (Elliott 1973, 273; Hatch 1963, 190).

Archives

Acta Apostolicae Sedis. The official collection of papal and curial documents, Vatican Library, Rome.

Printed Sources

Aimé-Azam, Denise. *L'Extraordinaire Ambassadeur* (Paris: La Table Ronde, 1967). First-hand anecdotal account of Roncalli's Parisian mission.

Cahill, Thomas. *Pope John XXIII* (New York: Viking, 2002).

Capovilla, Loris. *Giovanni XXIII, Quindici Letture* (Rome: Storia e Lettertura, 1970). Primary sources and unpublished material.

———. *Ite Missa Est* (Padua: Messegero, and Bergamo: Grafica e Arte, 1983). Documentation of Roncalli's childhood and youth and of significant episodes during the pontificate.

Cugini, Davide. *Papa Giovanni nei suoi primi passi a Sotto il Monte* (Bergamo: Istituto Italiano d'Arti Grafiche, 1965). Reminiscences by a friend about Roncalli's childhood and youth.

Elliott, Lawrence. *I Will Be Called John: A Biography of Pope John XXIII* (New York: E.P. Dutton, 1973).

Hatch, Alden. *A Man Named John* (New York: Hawthorn Books, 1963).

Hebblethwaite, Peter. *Pope John XXIII: Shepherd of the Modern World* (New York: Doubleday, 1985).

Lercaro, Giacomo. "Suggestions for Historical Research." In Giacomo Lercaro and Gabriele De Rosa (authors), Dorothy White (trans.), *John XXIII, Simpleton or Saint?* (London: Geoffrey Chapman, 1967).

Pepper, Curtis Bill. *An Artist and the Pope* (New York: Grosset & Dunlap, 1968). Based on personal recollections of the sculptor Giacomo Manzu.

Roncalli, Angelo Giuseppe (Pope John XXIII). *Giovanni XXIII, il Pastore*, Giambattista Busetti (ed.), (Padua: Messegero, 1980). Roncalli's letters from 1911 to 1963 to his diocesan congregation, the Priests of the Sacred Heart.

———. *Journal of a Soul*, Loris Francesco Capovilla (ed.), Dorothy White (trans.), (London: Geoffrey Chapman, 1980; Italian original: Rome: Storia e Letteratura, 1967). Roncalli's spiritual diary, begun when he was 14 years old.

———. *Letters to his Family, 1901–1962*, Loris Francesco Capovilla (ed.), Dorothy White (trans.), (London: Geoffrey Chapman, 1970; Italian original: Rome: Storia e Letteratura, 1968.)

———. *The Teachings of Pope John XXIII*, Michael Chinigo (ed.), Arthur A. Coppotelli (trans.), (London: George G. Harrap, 1967).

Trevor, Meriol. *Pope John* (London: Macmillan, 1967).

E. D. Lloyd-Kimbrel

JOHN PAUL II (1920–)

Karol Wojtyła was born in Wadowice, southern Poland. In his youth, he wrote his first poetic works and, as an amateur actor, he performed in local theaters. After 1938, he studied Polish philology and later theology at the Jagiellonian University in Krakow. During the war, in 1941, he helped create and acted in the clandestine Rhapsodic Theater of Mieczysław Kotlarczyk. In 1942, Wojtyła decided to enter the priesthood by enrolling in an underground theological seminary in Krakow. After being ordained a priest in 1946, he studied at Angelicum University in Rome, where, in 1948, he received a doctorate in theology (his dissertation was titled: *The Doctrine of Faith in St. John of the Cross*). Afterward he taught at various theological seminaries, and in 1954 he became a professor of philosophy and ethics at the Catholic University of Lublin, Poland. In 1958, he was consecrated a bishop of Krakow. In 1963, he became an archbishop and in 1967 he was made a cardinal. Wojtyła participated in the Second Vatican Council (1962–65). On October 16, 1978, he was elected as pope and thus became the first non-Italian bishop of Rome since 1522. His new position as head of the Roman Catholic Church revolutionized the church and renovated the papacy. While closely guarding all the traditional values and moral imperatives of the Roman Catholic Church (something that warranted his critics to accuse him of conservatism), he managed to implement a new church policy representing its openness to the problems of the modern world. He is credited for the full implementation of the directives of Vatican II, the redefinition of inter-religious dialogue (especially concerning Judaism), the introduction of ecumenism into Catholicism, and the elucidation of the moral challenges facing contemporary society. He is also commended for his contribution to dismantling communism and promoting world peace. Being a religious leader who goes with his teachings to people by traveling to numerous countries throughout the world, John Paul II is an unconventional and charismatic pope. He has provided personal inspiration that has affected the lives of both Christians and non-Christians. His pontificate is regarded as the most consequential since the Reformation.

As expressed in his early poetry and plays and later in his philosophical works, papal documents, and teachings, John Paul's thought was inspired by various authors and sources. Before the war, he wrote traditional poetry containing folklore elements of his hometown region. During his early university studies in Krakow, his literature teachers were two eminent professors, Stefan Kołaczkowski and Stanisław Pigoń, whose ideas influenced his view of literature, especially Polish romantic poetry. During the war, he authored his first dramatic works, *David* (1939), *Job* (1940), and *Jeremiah* (1940), which were clearly inspired by the Old Testament, ancient Greek drama, Polish history, and the ideas of his friend, the creator of the "living word" theater, Kotlarczyk. In his war-time letters to Kotlarczyk (Letters–Pakosiewicz collection) Wojtyła indicated several Polish romantic and neo-romantic poet–prophets and playwrights whose works he read, admired, and often performed as an actor in the Kotlarczyk's Rhapsodic Theater. The list includes Adam Mickiewicz, his national epic poem *Pan Tadeusz* (1834); Juliusz Słowacki, his mystical work *King-Spirit* (1845–49), digressive poem *Beniowski* (1841), and play *Samuel Zborowski* (1845); Zygmunt Krasiński, his prophetic drama *Un-divine Comedy* (1835); Stanisław Wyspiański, his national drama *The Wedding* (1901); Jan Kasprowicz, his visionary poetic cycle *Hymns* (1902), and poems from his *The Book of the Poor* (1916). The form and content of Wojtyła's own plays as well as poetry suggest that he was influenced by these poets and works but also point to an especially strong impact of Cyprian Norwid, a poetic innovator and profound Catholic thinker. *Our God's Brother* (1945–50), Wojtyła's most complex play, contains in turn clear references to Krasiński's *Un-divine Comedy*. Having very meditative, religious, and intellectual character, Wojtyła's other postwar plays and poems reveal such additional sources of inspiration and influence as the Bible, the medieval liturgical drama, the Renaissance poetry of Jan Kochanowski (1530–84), the intellectual poetry and drama of **T. S. Eliot,** and the phenomenological ideas of Max Scheler. The most significant influence came from the writings of the great mystics, especially St. John of the Cross, and the church fathers, especially St. Thomas Aquinas. The great literary tradition of Polish poetry and the indicated mystical and philosophical writings are strongly present not only in John Paul's literary compositions, but also in his philosophical and theological works. His postdoctoral thesis (1959) addresses the problem of Christian ethics and the thought of Scheler. One of the thesis readers was the phenomenologist and theoretician of literature Roman Ingarden, who influenced strongly Wojtyła's future intellectual development. His other main philosophical works, especially *Love and Responsibility* (1960) and *Person and Deed* (1969), deal integrally with the ideas of Thomism, the phenomenology of Edmund Husserl, and personalism. John Paul's numerous papal encyclicals, apostolic constitutions, letters, exhortations, addresses, and other discourses likewise draw upon these philosophies and contain some traces of the indicated literary influences.

Archives

Archiwum Kurii Metropolitalnej, Krakow, Poland: manuscripts of published literary works, miscellaneous documents.

Biblioteca Apostolica Vaticana: Archivio Segreto Vaticano, Città del Vaticano, Vatican City State: records of John Paul II's pontificate.

Katolicki Uniwersytet Lubelski: Biblioteka Uniwersytecka KUL and Instytut Jana Pawła II, Lublin, Poland: miscellaneous manuscripts, documents, and works.

Letters of Karol Wojtyła to Mieczysław Kotlarczyk (1939/40): private collection of Aniela Pakosiewicz (cf. Ciechowicz, Jan. *Dom opowieści. Ze studiów nad Teatrem Rapsodycznym Mieczysława Kotlarczyka* [Gdańsk: Wydawn. Uniwersytetu Gdańskiego, 1992], 119).

Printed Sources

Buttiglione, Rocco. *Karol Wojtyla: The Thought of the Man Who Became Pope John Paul II*, Paolo Guietti and Francesca Murphy (trans.), (Grand Rapids, Mich.: Eerdmans, 1997).

Ciechowicz, Jan. "Światopogląd teatralny Karola Wojtyły," In Jan Ciechowicz, *Dom opowieści. Ze studiów nad Teatrem Rapsodycznym Mieczysława Kotlarczyka* (Gdańsk: Wydawn. Uniwersytetu Gdańskiego, 1992), 114–28.

Crosby, John F., and Geoffrey Gneuhs. *The Legacy of Pope John Paul II: His Contribution to Catholic Thought* (New York: Crossroad Pub., 2000).

Dybciak, Krzysztof. "Jan Paweł II." In Wincenty Granat and Feliks Grylewicz (eds.), *Encyklopedia katolicka*, 7 vols. (Lublin: Tow. Nauk. Katolickiego Uniwersytetu Lubelskiego, 1973–97).

———. *Karol Wojtyła a literatura* (Tarnów: Biblos, 1991).

Maciejewski, Jarosław. "Karol Wojtyła i Jan Paweł II wobec literatury," *W drodze* 7, 8 (1983).

Malinski, Mieczyslaw. *Pope John Paul II: The Life of Karol Wojtyla* (New York: Crossroad, 1981).

Weigel, George. *Witness to Hope: The Biography of Pope John Paul II* (New York: Cliff Street Books, 1999).

Williams, George Huntston. *The Mind of John Paul II: Origins of His Thought and Action* (New York: Seabury Press, 1981).

Zieba, Maciej. *The Surprising Pope: Understanding the Thought of John Paul II*, Karolina Weening (trans.), (Lanham, Md.: Lexington Books, 2000).

Andrzej Karcz

JOHNSON, LYNDON BAINES (1908–1973)

"LBJ" was one of the most powerful political figures in twentieth-century America. Born in the barren central hill country of Texas, the hint of poverty forever influenced Johnson's political beliefs. Johnson entered Southwest Texas State Teacher's College in 1927 before briefly teaching at a poor, Hispanic school in rural Texas. In college, Johnson was active on the debate team and in campus politics and also edited the school newspaper. But it was not reading and studying that exemplified LBJ's college days; it was extracurricular activities and his burgeoning political ambition.

In 1934, at the tender age of 28, Johnson was elected to Congress. The ever-ambitious Texan immediately set his sights on higher offices. Running for the U.S. Senate, Johnson was narrowly defeated in his initial try but was elected to that distinguished body in 1948. During the interim years, he married, started a family, and crafted a series of investments that made him prosperous for the remainder of his life. In 1954, he was named senate majority leader—becoming the most powerful member of the Senate. LBJ tried for the White House in 1960, but he was no match for the charismatic **John Fitzgerald Kennedy.** Johnson was, however, selected as Kennedy's vice-presidential running mate and helped the ticket gain a razor-slim victory in the November election. On November 22, 1963, Johnson became president when Kennedy was killed by an assassin in a Dallas, Texas, motorcade.

Johnson's presidency (1963–69) was marked by both tremendous legislative gains and devastating political disappointments. During his term, he created the Great Society—an effort to end poverty in the United States. He established Medicare, poured money into education and cities, and advanced civil rights legislation. His Great Society and War on Poverty helped him win a landslide victory in the 1964 election. But foreign policy proved to be Johnson's downfall. A commitment of American troops in Vietnam was beginning to intensify by 1965, and Johnson fell into the quagmire. By 1968, his administration had committed over 500,000 troops to the Vietnam War. With mounting American casualties and no clear goals, Johnson began losing political support. As he committed money, troops, and his credibility to the unwinnable war, his political fortunes sagged. Once considered a sure bet to win reelection in 1968, he was challenged within his own party and finally decided not to run. Johnson retired to his Texas ranch where he wrote his memoirs. Suffering from long-term heart ailments, LBJ suffered a massive heart attack and died on January 22, 1973.

Lyndon Johnson was never an avid reader. One biographer estimated that Johnson read almost no books after college. The literary influences that did affect Johnson concerned his life's passion: politics. It was political ambition that drove his intellectual development. Johnson himself said that he wanted to know people—he was never interested in theories or philosophical principles. One of Johnson's close friends explained that LBJ did study and learn, not from books, but from people.

As a youth, his mother couldn't get him to read fiction—if a story was made up, young Lyndon would not read it. Johnson became, however, an avid reader of newspapers and other political publications. Throughout his legislative career and into his presidency, Johnson devoured three to four newspapers per day, including the *New York Times* and the *Washington Post.* He was also an avid reader of *The Congressional Record,* a publication that examines legislative bills and governmental activities. And during his presidency, Johnson was known to have viewed the three major television news programs simultaneously in order to see how each network interpreted his administration and its policies.

No one ever questioned Johnson's intelligence. Yet, he himself worried about his cultural and literary knowledge—especially around the Kennedys. Though he was not overly impressed with the university intellectuals that permeated Washington in the 1960s, Johnson dreaded having to attend state dinners for writers, artists, and classical musicians. Rarely could he talk to them and later said that those formal occasions reminded him of musty museums or lecture halls.

Lyndon Baines Johnson was an intellectual anomaly—politically well read and intelligent, but culturally and philosophically uninterested. It was an irony of his life that he reached the presidency at a time when intellectual knowledge was on the ascendancy. Had he become president a decade or two earlier, his "literary" interests—people and politics—would have been more appreciated. But helped by the Kennedy administration, the youth movement, and the counterculture, Johnson found himself in an era in which he didn't seem to belong—where his particular skills were misunderstood. Historically he is remembered for his Great Society, War on Poverty, and Vietnam policies. Johnson is also remembered by many for being crude and uncultured. In an era and decade of intellectual, literary, and cultural growth, Johnson the president and master politician was the antithesis. In comparison, Johnson was simply a back-slapping politician from another era who read little and had no higher philosophy than to win votes. His literary and intellectual shortfalls, coupled with the Vietnam debacle, made Johnson a semi-tragic figure during the turbulent 1960s.

Archives

Lyndon B. Johnson Library, University of Texas, Austin, Texas. This comprehensive collection holds Johnson's papers, family correspondence, his House of Representatives and Senate papers and correspondence, speeches, letters, numerous oral histories, and papers of several of his cabinet members and aides.

Printed Sources

Caro, Robert. *The Years of Lyndon Johnson: The Path to Power* (New York: Knopf, 1982); *The Years of Lyndon Johnson: Means of Ascent* (New York: Knopf, 1990); *The Years of Lyndon Johnson: Master of the Senate* (New York: Knopf, 2002). Well-researched works on the life of Johnson. Best in looking at Johnson's rise in politics and methods he used to gain power.

Dallek, Robert. *Lone Star Rising: Lyndon Johnson and His Times, 1908–1960* (New York: Oxford University Press, 1991); *Flawed Giant: Lyndon Johnson and His Times, 1961–1973* (New York: Oxford University Press, 1998). Well-written biographies which stress politics and Johnson's fall from grace during the Vietnam debacle.

Johnson, Lyndon B. *The Vantage Point: Perspectives of the Presidency, 1963–1969* (New York: Johnson, Holt, Reinhart & Winston, 1971). A biased justification of his own policies.

Kearns, Doris. *Lyndon B. Johnson and the American Dream* (New York, Signet, 1976). Impressive work by author who had access to Johnson. The history is very good—the psycho-history is even more interesting.

Unger, Irwin, and Deb Unger. *LBJ: A Life* (New York: John Wiley & Sons, 1999). Best current one-volume biography of LBJ.

David E. Woodard

JOYCE, JAMES AUGUSTINE (1882–1941)

James Joyce was born in Dublin to a lower-middle-class family. His father, a garrulous bon vivant whose early retirement and heavy drinking led his family to poverty, and his Jesuit education determined the growth of Joyce's mind. After obtaining a degree from University College Dublin, Joyce intended to study medicine in Paris but abandoned his plans and set out on a literary career instead. Feeling cramped by Dublin provincialism, he eloped in 1904 with Nora Barnacle to the Continent, where his son Giorgio (1905) and his daughter Lucia (1907) were born. He sustained himself with various teaching posts in Pola and Trieste while he finished *Dubliners* (1914) and wrote the autobiographical *Stephen Hero* (1944), the early version of *A Portrait of the Artist as a Young Man* (1917). He spent the war in Zurich, while *A Portrait* brought him some international recognition. Encouraged by **Ezra Pound** and sponsored by Harriet Shaw Weaver, he later settled in Paris, where *Ulysses* was published in 1922. This novel about a day in the life of Mr.

Leopold Bloom was a *succès de scandale* and banned in the United Kingdom and the United States. As Joyce's financial security increased, his eyesight deteriorated, and during the 1920s and 1930s he underwent numerous operations for glaucoma. In the early 1930s, moreover, the signs of Lucia's schizophrenia became increasingly apparent. After 17 years of writing, *Finnegans Wake* (1939) was published, but the feat was eclipsed by the outbreak of war. He moved back to Zurich, where he died on 13 January 1941 of a perforated ulcer and was buried at Flüntern cemetery.

Joyce's notes, published in the *James Joyce Archive*, contain the traces of his reading. With the exception of *Dubliners*, written in a scrupulously realist mode, and *Exiles*, a play in imitation of Ibsen, Joyce's influences are summed up by two quotations—one early from *Stephen Hero*, "applied Aquinas," one late from *Finnegans Wake*, "the last word of stolentelling"—signifying the intent behind his literary appropriations. Aristotle and Aquinas are the major sources for Joyce's aesthetic theories as they are found in fictional form in *A Portrait of the Artist* and its precursor *Stephen Hero*. *Ulysses* follows schematically Homer's *Odyssey* (Joyce's major source for the Homeric parallel is Victor Bérard's *Les Phoeniciens et l'Odysee* [1902–3] on the Semitic origins of the *Odyssey*), while the hyperrealistic underpinnings of the novel come from contemporary newspapers and Thom's Dublin directory for 1904. His stream-of-consciousness style Joyce said derived from a relatively unknown novel, *Les lauriers sont coupées* (1887) by Édouard Dujardin (to Freud he revealed a remarkable resistance). For *Finnegans Wake* hundreds of sources have been identified, as Joyce attempted to put as much "world" into the book as possible, from newspaper excerpts to popular hagiographic writings and histories, from Dublin lore to Buddhism; the major principles behind the *Wake*'s encyclopedic nature are based on Vico's cyclical view of history in *The New Science* (1744), Quinet's idea of immutability (through Metchnikoff's *La civilisation et les grands fleuves historiques* [1889]), Giordano Bruno's and Nicholas of Cusa's notion of the "coincidence of contraries," the Celtic art in the *Book of Kells*, and the Egyptian *Book of the Dead*. Other influences in his writing can be traced to the Bible, Dante, Shakespeare, and Flaubert, as well as to appropriations from popular literature and to his love for music, especially Irish ballads, music hall songs, Renaissance music, and Richard Wagner.

Archives

British Museum: Manuscripts, typescripts, page proofs for *Finnegans Wake*; Harriet Shaw Weaver correspondence.

Poetry/Rare Books Collection, University of Buffalo, N.Y.: Manuscripts, typescripts, page proofs for *Ulysses*; notebooks for *Ulysses* and *Finnegans Wake*; Beach and miscellaneous correspondence; personal library; published works; press cuttings; photographs.

Harry Ransom Humanities Research Center, University of Texas, Austin, Texas: Correspondence; page proofs for *Ulysses*; personal library; published works.

Princeton University Library, Princeton, N.J.: Correspondence; miscellaneous manuscripts and typescripts; published works; Beach papers relating to Shakespeare & Co.

National Library Dublin, Ireland: Léon correspondence; manuscripts.

Printed Sources

Atherton, James. *The Books at the Wake: A Study of Literary Allusions in James Joyce's Finnegans Wake* (New York: Viking, 1960). Critical discussion of structural and thematic influences; includes an alphabetic list with page references of allusions.

Aubert, Jacques. *The Aesthetics of James Joyce* (Baltimore: Johns Hopkins University Press, 1992). Analysis of Joyce's aesthetic influences in the early works, including a discussion of Joyce's notes on Aquinas and Aristotle.

Boldereff, Frances M. *Hermes to His Son Thoth: Being Joyce's Use of Giordano Bruno in Finnegans Wake* (Woodward, Penn.: Classic Non-Fiction Library, 1968). Line-by-line identifications of Bruno's philosophy in the *Wake;* not always reliable.

Bowen, Zack. *Musical Allusions in the Works of James Joyce: Early Poetry through Ulysses* (Albany: State University of New York Press, 1974). A reference tool but also a critical study of music in terms of style, structure, and theme.

Connolly, Thomas E. *The Personal Library of James Joyce; A Descriptive Bibliography* (Buffalo: University of Buffalo, 1955). Describes the items that survived from Joyce's personal library in Paris.

Ellmann, Richard. *The Consciousness of Joyce* (London: Faber and Faber, 1977). A concise study of Joyce's major sources for *Ulysses;* includes a description of Joyce's Trieste library.

———. *James Joyce*, rev. ed. (New York: Oxford University Press, 1982).

Groden, Michael et al. (eds.). *The James Joyce Archive* (New York: Garland, 1977–79). A facsimile edition of available notebooks, drafts, typescripts, and page proofs for all of Joyce's writings.

Kershner, R. B. *Joyce, Bakhtin, and Popular Literature: Chronicles of Disorder* (Chapel Hill: University of North Carolina Press, 1989). An intertextual reading of Joyce's borrowings from and attitudes toward popular literature; discusses a wide array of possible and actual sources.

Reynolds, Mary T. *Joyce and Dante: The Shaping Imagination* (Princeton: Princeton University Press, 1981). Traces Joyce's Dantean affinities and allusions through the major works.

Seidel, Michael. *Epic Geography: James Joyce's Ulysses* (Princeton: Princeton University Press, 1976). Critical study of Joyce's use of Homeric myth, focusing on structural parallels, and with particular reference to Odysseus's travels; includes maps and a discussion of Joyce's specific borrowings from Bérard.

Tysdahl, Bjorn J. *Joyce and Ibsen: A Study in Literary Influence* (Oslo: Norwegian Universities Press, 1968). Traces Ibsen's influence in Joyce from the early works to *Finnegans Wake.*

Verene, Donald Philip (ed.). *Vico and Joyce* (Albany: State University of New York Press, 1987). Collection of essays by historians and literary critics that trace affinities between Joyce and Vico in terms of structure, language, and myth.

Wim van Mierlo

JUAN CARLOS I DE BOURBON (1938–)

Juan Carlos was born in Rome's Anglo-American hospital, the third child to Don Juan de Borbón y Battenberg, Count of Barcelona, and Doña María de las Mercerdes de Borbón-Siciles, who had married in the Italian capital in 1935 and settled there two years later, after being forced to leave Cannes by the French Popular Front government. Juan Carlos was grandson to Spain's last ruling monarch, Alfonso XIII. Following the collapse of the monarchy, the Spanish royal family went into exile in France and later Italy. By the mid-1930s many of those who wished to overthrow the Republic and set up an authoritarian system of government in its place no longer regarded the former constitutional monarch, Alfonso XIII, as a suitable figurehead and began to look to his son, Juan Carlos's father, for leadership. Juan Carlos entered Spain for the first time on November 9, 1948, after having been schooled in Switzerland, where his grandmother resided from 1948, and in Spain (by agreement between his father and General **Francisco Franco**). Juan Carlos earned commissions in the army, navy, and air force (1955–59) and studied at the University of Madrid (1959–61). In 1962 he married Princess Sophia of Greece, and they have three children. Ostensibly, his presence on Spanish soil would contribute to Franco's acceptance by Western democracies and would fuel hope for the restoration of the monarchy at the end of Franco's reign. On settling in Spain, Juan Carlos found himself competing with others, including his own exiled father, for the post of successor to General Franco, until his nomination in 1969 eventually paved the way for his proclamation as king of Spain in 1975 after Franco's death. Instead of upholding the Franco dictatorship (as had been intended), he decisively presided over Spain's democratization, helping to defeat a military coup (1981) and assuming the role of a constitutional monarch.

An unknown figure (except for his athletic prowess, his dedication to work, and his determination to keep the army behind him), Juan Carlos took the throne after Francisco Franco's death under the shadow of his creator. Yet the future monarch exposed himself to a wide variety of books and serials that, in retrospect, suggest the transition from dictatorship to democracy that his reign initiated. He read with interest Calvo Serer's *Las nuevas democracias* (*The New Democracies*, 1964) and Emilio Romero's *Cartas a un Príncipe* (*Letters to a Prince*, 1964), and he justified a post-Franco era that would recognize the diverse political forces in Spain. So, too, the young and impressionable Juan Carlos was a frequent reader of the two periodicals that provided weekly commentaries on current events: *Cambio 16* (*Change 16*) and *Actualidad Económica* (*Current Economics)* and the newspaper *La Vanguardia (The Vanguard)*. Such readings led him to preside decisively over Spain's democratization, helping to defeat a military coup (1981) and assuming the role of a constitutional monarch.

The behavior of Juan Carlos in the critical years following Franco's death contributed immensely to the compromise, consensus, mutual trust, and legitimacy that were essential for the consolidation of the parliamentary monarchy—the only form of state which could be viewed as legitimate by both opponents and supporters of the authoritarian regime. Due to the absence of suitable precedents, Juan Carlos was constantly forced to break new ground by shaping the institution in his own image—a gradual evolution toward a Western-type democracy without a constitutional break; that is, using the Francoist institutions to reform Francoism. There were the extension of freedoms and civil rights and the reform of "the representative institutions" (i.e., the *Cortes*); political parties were allowed to hold open meetings and congresses; demonstrations were authorized; freedom of the press was guaranteed. The king of Spain's current prestige and reputation largely reflect popular recognition of his decisive role during Spain's transition to democracy and his contribution to "order and stability" during a difficult period in Spain's history. He has shown that the monarchy is capable of adapting to the changing needs of Spanish society.

Archives

Ministerio de Asuntos Exteriores (Madrid). Archivo General: Serie de Archivo Renovado (MAE/R files).
Public Record Office (London). Foreign Office General Correspondence.

Printed Sources

Carr, Raymond, and Juan Pablo Fusi. *Spain: Dictatorship to Democracy* (London: George Allen & Unwin, 1979).

Podolny, Joel. "The Role of Juan Carlos I in the Consolidation of the Parliamentary Monarchy." In Richard Gunther (ed.), *Politics, Society, and Democracy. The Case of Spain* (Boulder, Colo.: Westview Press, 1993), 88–112.

Powell, Charles T. *Juan Carlos of Spain: Self-Made Monarch* (New York: St. Martin's Press, 1996).

Elena M. De Costa

JUNG, CARL GUSTAV (1875–1961)

C. G. Jung was born in Kesswil, Switzerland, to a melancholy, disinclined Protestant pastor, Johann Paul Achilles Jung, and his alternately joyful and diabolical wife, Emilie Preiswerk. His formal education began at the village school in Kleinhüningen, near Basel. After age six, his father taught him Latin. From 1886 to 1895 he attended the Basel Gymnasium, then until 1900 studied science and medicine at the University of Basel, receiving his M.D. in 1900, although his doctoral dissertation on the psychopathology of the occult was not complete until 1902. In the 1890s he also studied archeology, paleontology, and philology on his own. He became Eugen Bleuler's assistant at the Burghölzli psychiatric clinic, Zürich, in 1900, but spent the winter semester of 1902–3 studying in Paris at the Salpetrière under Pierre Janet. From 1905 to 1913 he taught psychiatry at the University of Zürich. He resigned from Burghölzli in 1909 because of conflict with Bleuler. Thereafter he was in private psychiatric practice, writing copiously, traveling widely, and lecturing frequently.

At a very early age, Jung learned to escape from the oppressive loneliness of his miserable family into his own myth-world. He believed that his grandfather, the physician Carl Gustav Jung, was the illegitimate son of Johann Wolfgang von Goethe. This fantasy inspired his lifelong enthusiasm for Goethe's works, especially *Faust*. Always fascinated by religion, though distrustful of organized religion, Jung as a child knew the Bible, Greek and Germanic mythology, and local superstition and folklore thoroughly, and had a rudimentary knowledge of Hinduism. As a teenager he admired German literature, English literature in German translation, the medieval mysticism of Meister Eckhart, the philosophies of Immanuel Kant, Arthur Schopenhauer, the pre-Socratics and Plato, and the historical novels of Johann Heinrich Daniel Zschokke and Friedrich Gerstäcker, but was disappointed in the scholastic theology of Thomas Aquinas, the dogmatic theology of Alois Emanuel Biedermann, the historicist theology of Albrecht Ritschl, and the philosophies of Aristotle, Wilhelm Traugott Krug, and Georg Wilhelm Friedrich Hegel. Many of these books, except the philosophical, he found in his father's library.

As a university student, Jung read Jakob Burckhardt, Carl Gustav Carus, Eduard von Hartmann, Richard von Krafft-Ebing, and Buddhist texts. His favorite medical professor was Friedrich von Müller. Enthralled by spiritualism and the occult around 1896, he devoured the works of William Crookes, Carl du Prel, Karl August von Eschenmayer, Joseph von Görres, Justinus Kerner, Johann Carl Passavant, Emanuel Swedenborg, and Johann Karl Friedrich Zoellner. His intense love/hate relationship with the works of Friedrich Nietzsche, especially *Thus Spake Zarathustra*, started in 1898. Jung probed the innermost nuances of Zarathustra's character and personality but saw mostly the dark, lonely side of Nietzsche through Schopenhauerian eyes.

The first two decades of the twentieth century were the most fruitful period for Jung's development of his psychological, religious, and philosophical thought. At Burghölzli, Jung used the ideas of Gustav Aschaffenburg, Francis Galton, G. Stanley Hall, William James, Emil Kraepelin, and Krafft-Ebing. He read cover-to-cover all the volumes of *Allgemeine Zeitschrift für Psychiatrie* from its inception in 1844. He immersed himself in the psychological works of Janet, Josef Breuer, Alfred Binet, and Théodore Flournoy, the theology of Rudolf Otto, the philosophy of Jakob Friedrich Fries, the arcane works of Gnostics and mystics, and the mythologies of numerous religious and cultural traditions from around the world. He discerned in the alchemical, astrological, and spiritualist writings of Paracelsus foreshadowings of both Goethe's *Faust* and Nietzsche's *Zarathustra*. But his most profound learning came from Sigmund Freud, with whom he began a long and famous correspondence in 1906 and whom he met in 1907. Freud committed the drug-addicted psychiatrist Otto Gross to Burghölzli in 1908 so that Gross and Jung could psychoanalyze each other. Freud, Jung, and Sandor Ferenczi lectured together in 1909 at Clark University, Worcester, Massachusetts, where they met James and Hall. Initially Freud and Jung were smitten with each other, but by 1913 philosophical and personal differences had torn them apart. The break from Freud plunged Jung into depression.

Archives

Most of Jung's correspondence, papers, and manuscripts are in the History of Science Collections of the Eidgenössische Technische Hochschule, Zürich. Some autobiographical materials, compiled by Aniela Jaffé, are in the Library of Congress in Washington, D.C.

Printed Sources

Brockway, Robert W. *Young Carl Jung* (Wilmette, Ill.: Chiron, 1996).

Donn, Linda. *Freud and Jung: Years of Friendship, Years of Loss* (New York: Collier Macmillan, 1990).

Homans, Peter. *Jung in Context: Modernity and the Making of a Psychology* (Chicago: University of Chicago Press, 1995).

Jung, C. G. *Memories, Dreams, Reflections*, Aniela Jaffé (ed.), Richard and Clara Winston (trans.), (New York: Pantheon Books, 1963). Jung's autobiography.

McLynn, Frank. *Carl Gustav Jung* (New York: St. Martin's, 1997).

Noll, Richard. *The Aryan Christ: The Secret Life of Carl Jung* (New York: Random House, 1997).

Smith, Robert C. *The Wounded Jung: Effects of Jung's Relationships on His Life and Work* (Evanston, Ill.: Northwestern University Press, 1996).

Stern, Paul J. *C.G. Jung: The Haunted Prophet* (New York: Braziller, 1976).

Stevens, Anthony. *On Jung* (Princeton: Princeton University Press, 1999).

Wehr, Gerhard. *Jung: A Biography*, David M. Weeks (trans.), (Boston: Shambhala, 1987).

Eric v.d. Luft

K

KAFKA, FRANZ (1883–1924)

Franz Kafka was the greatest German-Jewish writer of Prague. He studied literature, earned a law doctorate in 1906, then toiled mornings as a civil servant in workers' accident insurance until 1922. His heightened sensitivity and incipient tuberculosis broke his health but not his spirit. Kafka's life saw no formative events, no major encounters, no long *Wanderjahre*. Although he never knew exile, he seems an isolated figure, triply alienated as German-speaking Jew surrounded by ethnic Czechs, as Jew within the non-Jewish German community, and as atheist in his own immediate Jewish circle. Was Kafka more influential than influenced? Who were his precursors, **Luis Borges** tantalizingly wondered. Substantially none, he concluded, while acknowledging Kafka's devotion to Blaise Pascal (whom he read ardently) and Søren Kierkegaard (whose biography he studied and whose work he grew to know in 1917).

Brod says Kafka preferred biographies and autobiographies, fictional or otherwise, in the confessional mode (Dostoyevsky, Goethe, Kierkegaard, Kleist, Strindberg) and especially the lives of inveterate bachelors (Flaubert, Grillparzer). He cited these often with sympathy, as with Kierkegaard's broken engagement ("his case is very similar to mine"). Gogol also belongs in this category: Kafka read him and saw his *Inspector General* performed. If Kafka felt akin to all who sacrificed themselves on the altar of literature, he was most directly influenced by Freud, Goethe, Flaubert, and Jewish fables. *The Interpretation of Dreams* (1900) may have oriented his written nightmares. Kafka acknowledged having "thoughts about" Freud when writing "The Judgment." His dearest masters after Goethe were Flaubert and Dickens. In Prague in 1912 Goethe and Flaubert were popular. Under the influence of a professor, Kafka had long admired Goethe and chose him as the subject of his final high school presentation. Kafka suggested to Brod that they together read Flaubert in French. He liked to quote Flaubert on those raising a family: "Ils sont dans le vrai." *Sentimental Education* was a bedside book: he speaks of it and other Flaubert titles between 1912 and 1921. When Kafka bought Flaubert's letters for Oskar Baum, he also gave Janouch *David Copperfield*, to which his novel *Amerika* owed much.

Kafka's library and diaries confirm he read Dostoyevsky. Raskolnikov in *Crime and Punishment* is an inescapable model for Kafka's indecisive protagonists. References to Dostoyevsky are frequent during the writing of *The Trial*, July–December 1914. In 1921 Kafka ordered a Dostoyevsky biography for Robert Klopstock. But he himself wanted to read the Bible then. Kafka is a fable-writer in the Jewish tradition. Never profoundly moved by Judaism as creed, beginning around 1910 he came to discover Yiddish theater and appreciate the force of Talmudic parables, lecturing on Yiddish in 1912 and studying Hebrew in 1917. He said to Rudolf Steiner that his work had put him in a trancelike state and jokingly claimed that his work was a new cabala.

Finally, there are 29 heavily annotated volumes of Strindberg among the surviving 200 books from Felice Bauer's library, suggesting that she too turned to them for clues to her fiancé's behavior.

Archives

Memorial of National Literature, Prague: correspondence.
Franz Kafka Society, Prague: personal library.
Bodleian Library, Oxford: Most of the manuscript materials. Others are scattered: Vienna, Marbach, New York.

Printed Sources

Bernheimer, Charles. *Flaubert and Kafka* (New Haven: Yale, 1982).
Binder, Hartmut. *Kafka-Handbuch* (Stuttgart: Kröner, 1979).
Borges, Jorge Luis. "Kafka and His Precursors." In *Selected Non-Fictions*, Eliot Weinberger (ed.), (N.Y.: Viking, 1999), 363–65.
Born, Jurgen. *Kafkas Bibliothek* (Frankfurt: S. Fischer, 1990). Catalogs Kafka's library.
Brod, Max. *Franz Kafka* (New York: Schocken, 1963).
Dodd, W. J. *Kafka and Dostoyevsky* (New York: St. Martin's, 1992).
Gravier, Maurice. "Strindberg et Kafka." *Etudes germaniques* 8 (1953), 118–40.
Hayman, Ronald. *Kafka: A Biography* (New York: Oxford, 1982).
Janouch, Gustav. *Conversations with Kafka* (New York: Praeger, 1953).
Kafka, Franz. *Diaries* (New York: Vintage, 1999).
Kaus, Rainer J. *Kafka und Freud* (Heidelberg: Winter, 2000).
Nagel, Bert. *Kafka und die Weltliteratur* (Munich: Winkler, 1983).
———. *Kafka und Goethe* (Berlin: Schmidt, 1977).
Rolleston, James. "Kafka's Principal Works and His Recorded Private Reading." In *Twentieth Century Interpretations of The Trial* (Englewood Cliffs, N.J.: Prentice-Hall, 1976), 105–7.
Spilka, Mark. *Dickens and Kafka* (Bloomington: Indiana University Press, 1963).
Struc, Roman. "Categories of the Grotesque: Gogol and Kafka." In *Franz Kafka: His Place in World Literature* (Lubbock: Texas Tech, 1971), 135–53.
Thieberger, Richard. "Franz Kafka's Grillparzer-Reception." In *Kafka's Contextuality*, Alan Udoff (ed.), (Baltimore: Gordian, 1986), 57–82.

Roy Rosenstein

KAHLO, FRIDA (1907–1954)

Frida Kahlo was born Magdalena Carmen Frieda Kahlo y Calderon in Coyoacan, Mexico. A *mestiza* of European and Mexican ancestry, Kahlo was isolated from her peers at an early age as a result of childhood polio and entered the National Preparatory School in Mexico City at the delayed age of 15. In 1925 her intentions to pursue a career in medicine were banished as she sustained near-fatal injuries in a bus accident. Effectively immobilized, Kahlo began to paint from her bed, producing works that reflected her internal anguish. In 1929 she married muralist **Diego Rivera,** a union which both encouraged and publicized her unique style. Her most famous work, such as *What the Water Gave Me* (1938) and *The Two Fridas* (1939), expresses the highly personal and rather sanguinary themes that would become the staples of her production. Kahlo rarely exhibited publicly and produced much of her work in isolation. She taught at La Esmeralda School of Art starting in 1942 and acquired a loyal following of students dubbed *Los Fridos.* Kahlo's dependence on alcohol and prescription pain medications became contributing factors in her untimely death one year after gangrene claimed her right leg.

Kahlo's literary influences were diverse. She was a proponent of the ethic of *Mexicanidad,* the fervent wave of nationalism that accompanied the Mexican Revolution of 1910. Paintings such as *My Nurse and I* reflect Arielist views that Kahlo developed as a youth under the literary reforms of education minister Jose Vasconcelos. Vasconcelos opened state publishing houses to popularize literature by South American authors such as Jose Enrique Rodo, who criticized Porfirian ideology and the positivism of the dictator Diaz in favor of embracing pre-Hispanic Mexican history and culture. Kahlo's use of a deliberately naïve style, vivid colors, and primitive subject matter clearly link her work to traditional Mexican folk art. The French surrealist movement also had a direct influence on Kahlo's paintings. Surrealist authors incorporated irrational and fantastic elements into their writing and through the use of automatism sought to gain access to the unconscious mind to produce work patterned on Sigmund Freud's concept of the ego. Kahlo was certainly familiar with Freud and based her painting *Moses* (1945) on his book *Moses and Monotheism.* She met and read the work of surrealism's founder **André Breton,** and frequently incorporated surrealist literary techniques into her productions, artistically celebrating the chance and the accidental by connecting randomly placed spots of fallen ink to begin her preparatory sketches and drawings. Kahlo often practiced automatic drawing techniques in an effort to bypass conscious process and utilized fantastic and irrational subject matter to produce compositions that juxtaposed her conscious and unconscious self. Communist doctrine and the ideology of Marxism pervaded Kahlo's life and work as well. The artist had a casual relationship with the activist and photographer Tina Modotti and in 1937, a brief affair with exiled leader **Leon Trotsky.** Kahlo's early relationship with Rivera was strengthened by the couple's mutual acceptance of Marxist ideology and their membership in the Young Communist League. Both Kahlo and Rivera supported leftist political causes in Mexico and abroad and frequently incorporated Communist slogans and symbols into their art.

Archives

Archives of American Art, Smithsonian Institution, Washington, D.C., control no. DCAW212397-A.

Printed Sources

Herrera, Hayden. *Frida: A Biography of Frida Kahlo* (New York: Harper and Row, 1983).

Kahlo, Frida. *The Diary of Frida Kahlo: An Intimate Self Portrait* (New York: Harry N. Abrams Inc., 1995).

Kahlo, Frida, and Martha Zamora (eds.). *The Letters of Frida Kahlo: Cartas Apasionadas* (San Francisco: Chronicle Books, 1995).

Gregory L. Schnurr

KANDINSKY, VASSILY VASIL'YEVICH (1866–1944)

Vassily Kandinsky was born in Moscow, Russia. He studied economics, ethnography, and law at the University of Moscow (1886–93) and wrote a dissertation on the legality of laborers' wages. Although Kandinsky did not attend church regularly, Christianity in general was deeply ingrained in the artist's conscience. He regarded the city of Moscow as the origin of his artistic ambitions. In 1896 Kandinsky left for Munich to study art. Six years later he met Gabriele Münter, who became his companion and an important figure in his artistic and intellectual development. He and Münter traveled throughout Europe, observed the paintings of Paul Gauguin and Henri Matisse, and participated in art exhibitions in St. Petersburg, Moscow, Berlin, and Paris. In 1911 he and Franz Marc prepared for publication *The Blaue Reiter Almanac*, which reveals his interest in a grand synthesis of the arts. After the October Revolution of 1917, Kandinsky worked for Narkompros (the People's Commissariat for Enlightenment). Between 1917 and 1921, he painted watercolors and canvases, sketched many drawings, and taught and wrote in the Department of Visual Arts in Narkompros. Kandinsky moved to Berlin in 1922. At the Bauhaus in Weimar, Kandinsky distanced himself from Russian avant-garde art and centered his work around geometric shapes and objects. After the Nazis closed the Bauhaus in 1933, Kandinsky moved to Paris.

Kandinsky's Russian heritage, especially the Russian Orthodox Church and Moscow, was an important and lasting influence on the mature artist. Although Kandinsky's early work was heavily indebted to the decorative art of Jugendstil, his small oil sketches, influenced by the work of Russian symbolists, began to abandon representational art and move into the direction of the abstract. After 1908, Kandinsky's work depicted abstract geometric forms and objects in a compressed space. Drawing on theosophy and anthroposophy and especially the theoretical writings of Rudolf Steiner and Madame Blavatsky, Kandinsky developed the concept of the external representation of inner conscience in his most important book, *On the Spiritual in Art* (1911). Kandinsky was well-read in Russian classical literature. In his personal library (now in Paris), French, English, and German literature and philosophy are also well represented. Most important to Kandinsky's intellectual development and to his transition to abstract art were the Russian symbolists such as the poets Alexander Blok, Dmitri Merezhkovsky, Andrei Bely, and the religious philosopher Vladimir Soloviev. He was especially interested in spiritual and mystical philosophy. Sufism, the mystic, heretic branch of Islam, also played an important role in his conception of the spiritual in art. Russian avant-garde art, represented by such artists as Alexander Rodchenko, Vladimir Tatlin, and Kazimir Malevich, affected his artistic development. When Kandinsky moved from Berlin to Dessau in 1925, **Paul Klee**'s art was reflected in Kandinsky's later paintings.

Archives

Museé National d'Art Moderne, Paris, France: Kandinsky's personal library contains Russian, German, French, and English literature and philosophy.

Archives of the Gabrielle Münter and Johannes Eichner Foundation (which will be turned over to the Städtische Galerie), Munich, Germany: Münter's library, where Kandinsky's books can be found.

Printed Sources

Hanl-Koch, J. *Kandinsky* (New York: Rizzoli International Publications, 1993).

Lindsay, K. C., and Vergo, P. (eds.). *Kandinsky: Complete Writings on Art*, 2 vols. (Boston: G. K. Hall and Co., 1982). Excellent English translation of Kandinsky's published writings.

Long, Rose-Carol Washton. *Kandinsky: The Development of an Abstract Style* (Oxford: Clarendon Press, 1980).

Weiss, P. *Kandinsky and Old Russia: The Artist as Ethnographer and Shaman* (New Haven: Yale University Press, 1995).

———. *Kandinsky in Munich: The Formative Jugendstil Years* (Princeton: Princeton University Press, 1979).

Eugene M. Avrutin

KARAMANLIS, KONSTANTINOS (1907–1998)

Konstantinos Karamanlis was born at Proti (former Kiupkioi), an east Macedonian village which was at that time part of the Ottoman Empire. His childhood years were marked by the struggle between Greeks, Bulgarians, and Serbians over the annexation of the European provinces of the Ottoman Empire. The experience of struggle, of the realization and defense of "national interests," came to form Karamanlis's scheme of perception and thinking. Throughout his political life he referred continually to "national interests" as an independent and guiding principle of his action. Karamanlis studied law at Athens (1925–29), where he became closely acquainted with the conflict between the Liberals and the Royalist Conservatives over the new form that Greek society should take following the collapse of irredentist nationalism (1922). He joined the Conservatives, who opposed the modernization and liberalization of the country, and was voted a representative of his home province in the parliamentary elections of 1935 and 1936. Immediately after the Second World War, Karamanlis again entered the political life of the country as a functionary of the Conservative Party. Conservatives established a regime that allowed the coexistence of democratic institutions (parties, elections, parliament), authoritarian measures (state syndicates, deportations, persecution of heterodox views), and informal powers (the army). From 1946 to 1955 Karamanlis was a member of parliament and held different posts as a minister of the Conservative governments. In 1955 he succeeded in assembling the whole conservative camp under his new party, winning the elections and becoming prime minister (1956–63). To legitimize his authoritarian measures, he insistently alleged communist plans for the violent seizure of power and the alienation of parts of Greece on the northern neighbor states. In his view, his party's interest in keeping power was equivalent to the "national interest." In 1963 he came into conflict with the informal powers and was forced to resign. He immigrated to Paris, where he lived until 1974. After the occupation of Northern Cyprus by the Turkish army (1974), Karamanlis was recalled by the Greek military to help avoid war with Turkey and to manage the country's transition to a democratic regime. With his new party, "New Democracy," Karamanlis won the elections. His appointment as prime minister (1974–80) gave him the chance to establish the institutions of the Third Greek Republic in accordance with the ideas of a semi-liberal, elitist democracy ("radical liberalism" was the name of his program). He rejected the ideas of both the nationalists and the populists, who called for a Greece culturally and politically independent of the West. He proclaimed Greece to be an integral part of western Europe and achieved its membership in the European Community. His ideas about democracy were based primarily on an equal competition of two strong parties and his continued distrust of the ability of the citizenry to act with political wisdom.

Karamanlis was not part of the educated elite of the country. Unlike many other important politicians of his generation (as, for example, P. Anayiotis Kanellopoulos), he was not educated in the large universities of western Europe. During debates between intellectuals, politicians, and men of letters about themes of policy, national culture, literature, and morality, he never articulated his own views. Karamanlis did not write articles or essays and never documented his concepts of conservatism. He was a man of political practice par excellence, and so there are only available his speeches and interviews. During the period before World War II, the conservative Karamanlis, like other Conservative politicians, was influenced by historians such as Konstantinos Paparighopoulos and by nationalist authors such as Ion Dragoumis. Another great influence at that time came from intellectuals who wrote for the political-literary journal *Idea*, such as Spyros Melas. After the Second World War Karamanlis was acquainted with the philosopher, literary critic, and politician K. Tsatsos (in the 1930s Tsatsos founded a school which referred to the ideas of Plato and demanded the establishment of an aristocratic democracy). Karamanlis at once adopted the ideas of Tsatsos, who had an overwhelming influence upon him for the next decades. During his stay in Paris, Karamanlis read the works of famous historians, of political philosophy, and political sciences. Part of his reading matter was ancient Greek philosophy—mainly the works of Plato and Aristotle—and historiography—principally Thucydides and Plutarch. But at the same time he was interested in other political authors, such as Cicero, and philosophers such as **Henri Bergson,** which shows his great interest in the western European history of ideas. After his return to Greece he often referred to Plato and especially to Aristotle when discussing political maneuvers. He recruited Socrates for his idea of the European reunion. The speeches of Karamanlis show that he stood also under the influence of reports about "psychology of the masses" and "national characters." His favorite newspapers were the Greek *Kathimerini* and *Le Monde*.

Archives

Karamanlis—Archive, Karamanlis Foundation, Athens.
Transcripts of the Greek Parliament, 1946–63, 1974–80.

Printed Sources

Genevoix, Maurice. *The Greece of Karamanlis* (London: Doric Publications, 1972).

Karamanlis, Konstantinos. *Konstantinos Karamanlis: Archeio – Gegonota kai Keimena*, 12 vols. K. Svolopoulos (ed.), (Athens: Ekdotiki Athinon, 1992–97).

———. *Oi Logoi tou K. Karamanlis* (Athens: n.p., 1974–81).

———. *O Karamanlis tis metapolitefsis: oi megales paremvaseis 1974–1992*, E. Kartakis (ed.), (Athens: Roes, 1993).

Tsatsos, Konstantinos. *O agnostos Karamanlis: mia prosopographia* (Athens: Ekdotiki Athinon, 1984).

Tzermias, Pavlos. *Konstantinos Karamanlis: Versuch einer Würdigung* (Tübingen: Francke Verlag, 1992).

Woodhouse, C. M. *Karamanlis: The Restorer of Greek Democracy* (Oxford: Clarendon Press, 1982).

Theodoros Lagaris

KAZANTZAKIS, NIKOS (1883–1957)

Nikos Kazantzakis was born in Iraklion, Crete, during a period of intense civil strife. He was educated at the University of Athens, where he received a law degree in 1906; concurrently, he began publishing plays and essays. In 1907 he moved to Paris to study philosophy under **Henri Bergson,** completing a dissertation on the work of Friedrich Nietzsche in 1909. For the next 30 years he alternated residence in Greece and several European countries as he worked to earn a living as a writer. He also traveled extensively in Spain, the Soviet Union, and Japan, later writing several books about his experiences and observations in these countries. In 1911, he married Galatea Alexiou, but divorced her in 1926; before his divorce he had begun a relationship with Eleni Samiou, whom he eventually married. For nearly three decades he supported himself by writing travelogues, textbooks, and encyclopedia articles as he worked on *The Odyssey: A Modern Sequel* (1938) and various novels and plays. During World War II he was confined to Aegina during the German occupation of Greece. Though some of his fiction and poetry was published before the war, the bulk of his literary work became available to an international audience during the following decade. His postwar reputation rested largely on the publication of novels that celebrate the struggle of the individual to achieve personal salvation. In 1946, Kazantzakis served as an official for UNESCO, but spent the last decade of his life engaged with publishers and translators and traveling. On a trip to China in 1957, he contracted influenza; he died in a sanatorium in Freiburg, Germany, in October 1957.

The literary influences on Kazantzakis are manifold, but certainly among the most important is Homer, whose epics inspired Kazantzakis's *Odyssey: A Modern Sequel.* The plotting of his more popular novels displays a confluence of ideas from mainstream European fiction, existentialist philosophy, and Eastern ideology such as Buddhism and Taoism. While he cannot be identified as a slavish follower of any literary master, two important figures shaped Kazantzakis's understanding of humankind's quest for salvation and spiritual fulfillment and provided the impetus for virtually all of his writing.

The first of these is Bergson, the French philosopher who espoused the concept of the élan vital, a life force that exists from generation to generation and inspires individuals to love life and seek fulfillment from their experiences. As Kazantzakis's tutor in Paris, Bergson had direct and frequent contact with the writer for nearly two years. Not surprisingly, a number of Kazantzakis's characters exhibit this élan vital, most notably Alexis Zorba in *Zorba the Greek* (1946), Captain Mihalis in *Freedom or Death* (1953), and Odysseus.

The second and perhaps greater influence on Kazantzakis's work is the philosopher Friedrich Nietzsche, the subject of Kazantsakis's doctoral dissertation. Nietzsche's concept that humans must create meaning in their own lives inspired in Kazantzakis the drive to create existentialist heroes who struggle to make their lives meaningful. Zorba, Captain Mihalis, and Odysseus carry out this quest, as do two other important figures that Kazantzakis appropriates from the Christian tradition: St. Francis of Assisi (in *Saint Francis* [1956]) and Jesus Christ himself (in *The Last Temptation of Christ* [1955]), both of whom strive to live moral lives in this world, not knowing if there is a life after death in which their struggles will be rewarded.

Archives

Historical Museum of Crete, Heraklion, Crete: miscellaneous manuscripts and personal items.

Nikos Kazantzakis Museum, Myrtia, Crete: personal items, manuscripts, letters, first editions, documentation of dramatic productions, secondary source materials.

Printed Sources

Bien, Peter. *Kazantzakis: Politics of the Spirit* (Princeton: Princeton University Press, 1989). An intellectual biography focusing on the first three decades of Kazantzakis's professional career; discusses many of the shaping influences that affected his worldview.

Dombrowski, Daniel A. *Kazantzakis and God* (Albany: State University of New York Press, 1997). Analysis of Kazantzakis's spirituality; gives special attention to the influence of Bergson and Nietzsche.

Kazantzakis, Helen. *Nikos Kazantzakis: A Biography Based on His Letters* (New York: Simon & Schuster, 1968). Reveals many of the influences that shaped his thought and helped focus his critical and creative genius.

Lea, James F. *Kazantzakis: The Politics of Salvation* (University, Ala.: University of Alabama Press, 1979). Examines the political dimensions of Kazantzakis's writings, emphasizing the debt he owes to both Western and Eastern philosophers for the ideas that shape his prose and poetry.

Levitt, Morton. *The Cretan Glance: The World and Art of Nikos Kazantzakis* (Columbus, Ohio: Ohio State University Press, 1980). Critical reading of Kazantzakis's fiction, emphasizing the existential basis of his work.

Middleton, Darren. *Novel Theology* (Macon, Ga.: Mercer University Press, 2000). Traces the parallels between Alfred North Whitehead's process theology and Kazantzakis's fiction.

Middleton, Darren, and Peter Bien (eds.). *God's Struggler: Religion in the Writings of Nikos Kazantzakis* (Macon, Ga.: Mercer University Press, 1996). Collection of essays exploring the religious dimensions of Kazantzakis's writings.

Laurence W. Mazzeno

KENNAN, GEORGE FROST (1904–)

George Frost Kennan was born in Milwaukee, Wisconsin, the son of Kossuth "Kent" Kennan, a prosperous lawyer of Scotch-Irish descent, then aged 52, and his German-American wife, Florence James, who died two months later. In his career, Kennan consciously emulated an older cousin and namesake, whom he met once in his childhood, who had explored Russia and exposed czarist political prison conditions. Kennan attended St. John's Military Academy in Delafield, Wisconsin, which instilled learning, patriotism, and discipline, before entering Princeton University in 1921, where he was academically undistinguished. In 1926 Kennan joined the United States Foreign Service, receiving intensive specialized Russian training at Berlin University and Riga and spending five years in the American embassy in Moscow when the United States resumed relations with Russia in 1933. After spells in Prague, Berlin, Lisbon, and London, Kennan returned to Moscow as minister-counselor in 1944. In his influential February 1946 "Long Telegram," he argued the internal dynamics of Russian communism made genuine Soviet-Western understanding unattainable. Recalled to Washington, from 1947 to 1950 Kennan was the first director of the State Department's policy planning staff, exercising his greatest immediate impact upon American foreign policy. In a famous 1947 article, "The Sources of Soviet Conduct," published anonymously in *Foreign Affairs*, Kennan enunciated the "containment" doctrine, which became the basis of United States cold war strategy toward the Soviet Union. By 1949, however, his opposition to the creation of NATO and pressures to enhance United States military spending divided him from Secretary of State Dean Acheson, and Kennan took a one-year sabbatical at Princeton. In 1952 Kennan was briefly ambassador to the Soviet Union, but his outspoken criticism of Stalin's regime quickly brought his expulsion.

In 1953 the new Republican administration dispensed with Kennan's diplomatic services, and he began a lengthy career as a historian and influential political commentator whose prolific, well-publicized, and iconoclastic writings, often questioning prevailing orthodoxies among the foreign policy elite, habitually obtained at least a respectful hearing. In 1958 Kennan controversially urged the unification and neutralization of both Germanies. In the early 1960s he spent three years as ambassador to Yugoslavia. Primarily Eurocentric, in 1969 Kennan turned decisively against the American war in Vietnam, which he had earlier considered a questionable overcommitment of resources to a strategically insignificant area, diverting American attention from European concerns. Kennan nonetheless disliked radical critics of the war, particularly student protesters, whose violence, intolerance, and incivility he thought symptomatic of broader American malaises. Kennan subsequently advocated that the United States reduce its overseas commitments and eschew first use of nuclear weapons. More broadly, he suggested that wider concerns, particularly the environment, resources, population growth, and arms control, were the most critical international issues confronting the United States.

From childhood, Kennan, a solitary boy with a distant, elderly father, always read voraciously, especially in European and American literature and history. Linguistically adept, in 1912 he became fluent in German after six months' family residence in Kassel, while learning Latin and French at school. Romantic admiration for **F. Scott Fitzgerald**'s *This Side of Paradise* impelled him to apply to Princeton. Often anti-democratic, Kennan greatly admired earlier, more elitist periods of European and American history and was particularly influenced by two massive classics, Edward Gibbon's *Decline and Fall of the Roman Empire* and Alexis de Tocqueville's *Democracy in America*. After leaving Princeton, Kennan immersed himself in German culture for several months, reading Oswald Spengler's *Decline of the West* and Goethe's *Faust* in the original. As a trainee diplomat Kennan did likewise with Russian at Riga and Berlin University, acquiring his encyclopedic knowledge of Russian literature and history. His rather intimidating breadth of learning characterized all Kennan's writings, diplomatic and scholarly, as did the elegant prose style he consciously cultivated. Both greatly enhanced his ability to present a bureaucratic case and to attract and convince a broader general audience.

Archives

Mudd Manuscripts Library, Princeton University, Princeton, N.J.: repository for Kennan's personal papers.

National Archives II, College Park, Md.: holds Department of State records relating to Kennan's diplomatic service.

Printed Sources

Hixson, Walter L. *George F. Kennan: Cold War Iconoclast* (New York: Columbia University Press, 1989).

Kennan, George F. *Memoirs*, 2 vols. (Boston: Little, Brown, 1967–72).

Mayers, David. *George Kennan and the Dilemmas of US Foreign Policy* (New York: Oxford University Press, 1988).

Miscamble, Walter D. *George F. Kennan and the Making of American Foreign Policy, 1947–1950* (Princeton: Princeton University Press, 1992).

Stephanson, Anders. *Kennan and the Art of Foreign Policy* (Cambridge, Mass.: Harvard University Press, 1989).

Priscilla Roberts

KENNEDY, JOHN FITZGERALD (1917–1963)

John F. Kennedy was born in Brookline, Massachusetts, the second son of Joseph P. Kennedy, a prominent Irish Catholic businessman, speculator, and politically active Democrat, and his wife Rose Fitzgerald, the daughter of a popular former mayor of Boston who, like his grandson and namesake, was a passionate reader. Despite briefly experiencing some religious doubts in his twenties, Kennedy, his skeptical turn of mind notwithstanding, almost automatically embraced his family's traditional political and Catholic faiths. After spells at the Edward Devotion School and the exclusive Dexter School in Boston and the Riverdale, New York, Country Day School, in 1930 Kennedy's parents enrolled him in preparatory school, first the Catholic Canterbury School in New Milford, Connecticut, and one year later the elite Episcopalian Choate School in Wallingford, Connecticut, from which he graduated in 1935. Besides spending brief periods at the London School of Economics, Princeton University, and Stanford Business School, Kennedy majored in politics at Harvard University. After highly decorated wartime combat service, in 1946 Kennedy won election to Congress, representing the Massachusetts eleventh congressional district, and then, in 1954, as junior Senator for Massachusetts. Elected president in 1960, Kennedy was known for his wit, charm, and stirring rhetoric. Embracing cold war orthodoxy, as president Kennedy mounted a botched invasion of Cuba and widened American involvement in the developing Vietnam War, but skillfully defused the October 1962 Cuban missile crisis and after some hesitation embraced the growing civil rights movement. Nationally and internationally his assassination in November 1963 brought an outpouring of grief.

Unlike most of his largely nonintellectual family, from early childhood Kennedy, who until the mid-1950s repeatedly endured lengthy bouts of ill health, read voraciously; as president his speedreading skills and near-photographic recall became famous. His mother believed her habit of reading childhood classics to him helped during early illnesses, including the works of Walter Scott and Rudyard Kipling (Kennedy 1974, 94, 111–112; Hellmann 1997, 12–14; Parmet 1980, 17–18). Academically Kennedy was a mediocre student until his senior year at Harvard, when he painstakingly researched a thesis attempting to explain Britain's tardiness in opposing Hitler, subsequently published as *Why England Slept* (1940), which implicitly challenged his father's notoriously isolationist views.

History remained a lifelong passion; Kennedy's knowledge of United States presidential and political history and biography and of Britain's past were alike encyclopedic. He particularly admired and read all the voluminous works of one political idol, Britain's wartime prime minister **Winston Churchill.** The mature Kennedy rarely read novels, but admitted to enjoying Ian Fleming's James Bond thrillers (Schlesinger, 104–6). To brief himself on specific issues, from his late twenties onward Kennedy regularly devoured formidable stacks of reading matter. William Lederer and Eugene Burdick's bestseller, *The Ugly American* (1958), which questioned the effectiveness of United States diplomatic practices in the third world, apparently influenced Kennedy in establishing the Peace Corps and espousing counterinsurgency doctrines (Hellmann 1997, 141). Although Kennedy already knew Shakespeare well and quoted Dante during his first political campaign, following his 1953 marriage to Jacqueline Bouvier, his wife's love of poetry and literature probably brought more literary allusions into his speeches. Kennedy's favorite books included John Buchan's memoir, *Pilgrim's Way*, and David Cecil's biography of Lord Melbourne. Buchan's description of his friends, the group of idealistic and talented young men Lord Milner assembled in South Africa who subsequently enjoyed distinguished careers, possibly inspired Kennedy's attempts to instill similar camaraderie within his own administration's inner circles. Kennedy's personal role models apparently included Buchan's brilliant friend Raymond Asquith, killed in World War I; the aristocratic Lord Melbourne, a retiring and bookish second son who became a Whig prime minister; and Lord Byron, the clubfooted poet-rake who seduced Melbourne's wife and died fighting for Greek independence (Hamilton 1992, 544–45, 549–50; Hellmann 1997, 27–35; Kennedy 1995, xxxv–xxxvii, 119; Schlesinger 1965, 87, 100). Kennedy's embrace of a romantic, even doomed, personal image informed his rhetoric, his 1955 book *Profiles in Courage*, and his love of Alan Seeger's poem "I Have a Rendezvous with Death," perhaps reflecting his belief that persistent health problems limited his life expectancy. Kennedy's commitment to in-depth research, his detached, analytical Harvard thesis, and the pragmatic policies he adopted demonstrated his paradoxically skeptical, rational, and realistic political outlook (Schlesinger 1965, 98, 109–10).

Archives

John F. Kennedy Presidential Library, Boston, Mass.: depositary for all the John Fitzgerald Kennedy Papers and those of many family members and political and personal associates.

Printed Sources

Hamilton, Ian. *JFK: Reckless Youth* (London: Random, 1992).

Hellmann, John. *The Kennedy Obsession: The American Myth of JFK* (New York: Columbia University Press, 1997).

Kennedy, John F. *Prelude to Leadership: The European Diary of John F. Kennedy: Summer 1945*, Deirdre Henderson (ed.), (Washington, D.C.: Regnery Publishing Inc., 1995).

Kennedy, Rose Fitzgerald. *Times to Remember* (Garden City, N.Y.: Doubleday, 1974).

Parmet, Herbert S. *Jack: The Struggles of John F. Kennedy* (New York: Dial Press, 1980).

Schlesinger, Arthur M., Jr. *A Thousand Days: John F. Kennedy in the White House* (Boston: Houghton Mifflin, 1965).

Priscilla Roberts

KENNEDY, ROBERT FRANCIS (1925–1968)

Robert F. Kennedy was an American political figure who, even in a relatively short career, had a lasting impact on U.S. history and culture. Born in Massachusetts to a wealthy Irish-Catholic family, his multimillionaire father, Joseph P. Kennedy, was a Wall Street trader and U.S. ambassador to England. His oldest brother, Joseph P. Kennedy Jr., was killed in an air combat mission during World War II. Another older brother, **John Fitzgerald Kennedy,** became president of the United States in 1961. Robert Kennedy briefly served in the navy during World War II before earning a law degree at the University of Virginia. During the 1950s, his brother John Kennedy began his rapid ascend into national politics—and younger brother Robert became an integral part of that rise. As his brother's campaign manager and principal advisor, Robert Kennedy proved to be a brilliant strategist and political organizer, helping his brother win two terms in the United States Senate as well as a razor-thin victory over **Richard M. Nixon** in the 1960 presidential contest.

President-elect John F. Kennedy surprised the nation by appointing his brother Robert as attorney general. It was during Kennedy's tenure that the federal government was summoned to enforce civil rights laws in the South. He was equal to the challenge and helped Washington begin to fulfill its responsibility of providing equal justice throughout the land. In November 1963, President Kennedy was assassinated, and Robert Kennedy's political rival, **Lyndon B. Johnson,** became president. With his political future unclear, Kennedy resigned his cabinet post in 1964 to run for a United States Senate seat in New York. Kennedy was elected by a comfortable margin and immediately became a leader in national politics.

By 1968, Kennedy was having doubts about the nation's Vietnam War policies—and party leaders were urging the New York senator to challenge President Johnson for the Democratic nomination. Kennedy entered the race and appeared to have a formidable chance to win his party's nomination and carry on his brother's political heritage. But on June 5, 1968, after a victory in the important California primary, Kennedy was shot and killed by an assassin. He died the following day and was buried near the grave of his brother at Arlington National Cemetery in Washington, D.C.

Robert Kennedy's early reading choices do reveal future political tendencies. One of his favorite childhood books was John Buchan's spy thriller, *The Thirty-Nine Steps.* And Buchan's autobiography, *Pilgrims's Way,* was a favorite of both Kennedy brothers. One can see a connection between Buchan's plots and the Kennedy administration's covert foreign policy actions in Cuba and Vietnam. Later, Robert Kennedy moved on to other spy stories, specifically Ian Fleming's James Bond novels. Kennedy saw the adventuresome heroes in these novels as nothing like the bland and bureaucratic CIA agents he witnessed in Washington.

Kennedy was always self-conscious about his intellect and spent years in a quest for self-improvement. He read many American Civil War books—Bruce Catton being his favorite author. During the Vietnam War, he even sent President Johnson a copy of Catton's *Never Call Retreat,* a book explaining how President Abraham

Lincoln had stood up to both his generals and meddlesome politicians. RFK was also intrigued with Barbara Tuchman's *The Guns of August* and E. S. Creasy's *Fifteen Decisive Battles of the World*. Kennedy even held monthly seminars at his Virginia estate of Hickory Hill where he and wife Ethel invited national and world leaders to speak on various subjects.

Kennedy's intellectual and philosophical development blossomed after his brother was assassinated. His faith was tested and he began questioning life's meaning. During his intense mourning in 1963, his brother's widow, Jacqueline Kennedy, gave him a copy of Edith Hamilton's *The Greek Way*—a book about history and tragedy in fifth-century Greece. Kennedy read the book for hours, underlining numerous passages. Seeking to make sense of his brother's death, he found some answers in Greek history. And it was in Hamilton's book that Kennedy was introduced to Greek writers and poets like Sophocles, Euripides, and Aeschylus. Kennedy began to find some solace in Greek poetry. His two particular favorites were by Aeschylus: *Oresteia* and *Prometheus*. Both examined topics such as injustice, fate, and the arrogance of great and powerful men.

In 1965, RFK began reading Ralph Waldo Emerson, nineteenth-century American poet, writer, and essayist. Kennedy owned an old copy of Emerson's *Essays*—which he kept with him and often quoted in speeches and in conversation. He was particularly influenced by Emerson's ideas about self-trust and self-reliance. Kennedy discovered French writer **Albert Camus** in 1966. Kennedy was impressed with Camus's idea that because of life's constant tragedy and unpredictability, man should begin anew each day. Kennedy, by 1966, agreed that fate and suffering were perpetual—but one had to move on. His favorite Camus works included *The Stranger*, *Notebooks*, and *Resistance, Rebellion, and Death*. Kennedy often had his secretary type Camus quotes on index cards. By the end of his life, Robert Kennedy had become an iconoclastic politician—often quoting Greek poets and citing passages from radical existential writers.

Archives

John F. Kennedy Library, Boston, Massachusetts. There are numerous RFK sources at the John F. Kennedy Library: RFK's Senate Papers, 1965–68; the Papers of Adam Walinsky (a Kennedy advisor), which also contains *The Bedford-Stuyvesant Development Project Overview: A Working Paper*; the Papers of Peter Edelman (a Kennedy advisor); and the Joseph P. Kennedy Papers.

Printed Sources

Halberstam, David. *The Best and the Brightest* (New York: Random House, 1969). One of the most critically acclaimed books about the Kennedy administration and the Vietnam War. Author David Halberstam chronicles the inner workings of the Kennedy White House, including Robert Kennedy's role as policymaker and principal advisor to his brother.

Kennedy, Robert. *Thirteen Days: A Memoir of the Cuban Missile Crisis* (New York: Norton, 1969). Robert Kennedy was part of the now famous executive committee that helped President Kennedy settle the turbulent Cuban Missile Crisis of 1962. This postcrisis memoir shows the close personal and professional relationship that existed between President Kennedy and his brother.

———. *To Seek a Newer World* (Garden City, N.Y.: Doubleday, 1967). Robert Kennedy's speeches and policy statements during his senate years. This book offers insights into his views on the major public issues of the times: race, urban affairs, Vietnam, nuclear war.

Schlesinger, Arthur. *Robert Kennedy and His Times* (Boston: Houghton Mifflin, 1978). The first comprehensive biography of RFK. Schlesinger's massive book—over 1,000 pages—is impressive in both scope and detail. But when the book was written, many national security documents, especially concerning Vietnam and Cuba, were still classified.

Thomas, Evan. *Robert Kennedy: His Life* (New York: Simon & Schuster, 2000). Best contemporary biography of Robert Kennedy. This book examines national security issues using a variety of declassified information that Schlesinger did not have in the 1970s.

David E. Woodard

KEROUAC, JACK (1922–1969)

Jack Kerouac was born on March 12, 1922, in Lowell, Massachusetts. Kerouac attended Horace Mann Prep School in New York City and later Columbia University in 1941. He eventually quit Columbia and spent time as a merchant seaman. Kerouac completed his first novel, *The Town and the City*, in 1948, after which he began to write *On the Road*, the novel that was to make him famous. Kerouac completed several trips across the country during the 1950s, a subject that he visited in *On the Road*. In 1954 Kerouac began studying Buddhism during a stay in California. Throughout the 1950s and 1960s Kerouac published many novels and works of poetry including *The Subterraneans*, *The Dharma Bums*, *Mexico City Blues*, and *Big Sur*. Kerouac maintained his nomadic lifestyle for most of the 1950s, living in places such as Tangier, Mexico City, Florida, California, and New York. Kerouac's constant battle with alcohol plagued him for most of his life. He died on October 20, 1969, in St. Petersburg, Florida. Kerouac's main contribution was the inspiration he gave to the emerging Beat generation of writers, poets, and musicians that prefigured the cultural radicalism of the 1960s and helped challenge the tone of conformity that plagued American culture in the 1950s. Likewise, his use of spontaneous writing techniques and his improvisational style help set the tone for much of postwar American literature.

Kerouac's first novel, *The Town and the City* (1950), was heavily influenced by the dynamic literary style of Thomas Wolfe (1900–1938). At Columbia University Kerouac befriended many writers and poets who were to compose the Beat Generation and who were to influence Kerouac's own writings and philosophy. His friendship with **William Burroughs** and **Allen Ginsberg** introduced Kerouac to the liberating possibilities within the aesthetic form. Kerouac's intense interest in the process of "automatic writing" was influenced by surrealist themes in the writings of **André Breton** and Phillippe Soupault as well as the French symbolist Arthur Rimbaud. Kerouac's prose style was also influenced by his reading of Oswald Spengler's *The Decline of the West* (1926) and L. F. Celine's *Journey to the End of the Night* (1934). His interest in novels narrating the liberating aspects of voyage and travel was influenced by John Galsworthy's *Forsyte Saga* (1928). Like many countercultural writers of the postwar period, Kerouac was influenced by the psychoanalyst Wilhelm Reich and his theories concerning the psychological harm of sexual repression. Kerouac also maintained an interest in Eastern philosophies, particularly through his reading of Ashvaaghosa's *The Life of Buddha* and the anthology of Buddhist scriptures entitled *The Buddhist Bible* (1932). Kerouac's interest in Buddhism developed after studying the work of Henry David Thoreau and other American transcendentalists. During the time Kerouac spent in northern California, he was introduced to and influenced by the emerging San Francisco renaissance of poets including Kenneth Rexroth, Philip Whalen, Lawrence Ferlinghetti, and others. Kerouac's writing style was also enormously influenced by his lifelong interest in jazz, particularly the music of Lester Young, Charlie Parker, and Dizzy Gillespie.

Archives

Kerouac's unpublished work remains in the possession of the Kerouac estate in Lowell, Massachusetts.

Printed Sources

Charters, Ann. *Kerouac: A Biography* (San Francisco: Straight Arrow Books, 1973).
Hunt, Tim. *Kerouac's Crooked Road* (Hamden, Conn.: Archon Books, 1981).
Jarvis, Charles. *Visions of Kerouac* (Lowell, Mass.: Ithaca Press, 1973).
McNally, Dennis. *Desolate Angel: A Biography of Jack Kerouac* (New York: Random House, 1979).
Miles, Barry. *Jack Kerouac, King of the Beats* (London: Virgin Publishing Ltd., 1998).
Weinreich, Regina. *The Spontaneous Poetics of Jack Kerouac* (Carbondale: Southern Illinois University Press, 1987).

Robert Genter

KEYNES, JOHN MAYNARD (1883–1946)

John Maynard Keynes was born in Cambridge, England, on June 5, 1883. He died at his country home, Tilton, in Sussex, England, in 1946 of a heart attack at the age of 62. With the help of a scholarship he went to Eton and then to King's College at the University of Cambridge where he took a degree in mathematics in 1905. In 1908 he began his academic career at Cambridge with a lectureship in economics. It was around this time that he got involved with the famous Bloomsbury group, an eclectic group of writers and artists who had a strong literary and artistic influence on Keynes.

With the beginning of World War I, Keynes took a leave of absence from Cambridge and joined the Treasury Department. He advanced quickly up the ranks in the department and in 1919 became the principal treasury representative at the Peace Conference at Versailles. He strongly disagreed with the position of the English government and resigned his post. His first major publication was on the political consequences of the conference, *Economic Consequences of the Peace* (1920). He went back to Cambridge and in 1925 married the Russian ballerina Lydia Lopokova. It was in the 1920s and 1930s that he wrote or published his most influential books: *A Tract on Monetary Reform* (1923), *A Treatise on Money* (1930), *The General Theory of Employment, Interest and Money* (1936), *Essays in Persuasion* (1931), and *Essays in Biography* (1933).

The publication of Keynes's collected writings from 1971 to 1982, with the bibliography and index in 1989, has provided scholars with an opportunity to see and evaluate the chief intellectual influences on Keynes's writings and thinking. By far the two most influential thinkers on Keynes were G. E. Moore and Edmund Burke. As a young man Keynes admired the work of both of these thinkers, and their influence can be found in his economic and literary writings throughout his career. In his essay "My Early Beliefs," Keynes describes the importance of Moore's classic work *Principia Ethica* on his intellectual development. Keynes also felt Moore's influence in a more indirect way through the writings of his Bloomsbury friends, many of whom were associated with the secret society at Cambridge University called the Apostles. The views of Moore on ethics, aesthetics, and friendship can be seen in the art, literature, and politics of fellow Apostles like Leonard Woolf, **Lytton Strachey,** and **E. M. Forster,** Roger Fry, Sir Ralph Hawtrey, H. O. Meredith, Saxon Sydney-Turner, and Desmond Turner, who were all friends or close associates of Keynes and influenced his literary taste and artistic development deeply.

The influence of Burke dates back to Keynes's days at Eton. In 1904 he wrote a 99-page essay on "The Political Doctrines of Edmund Burke," which won the university's English Essay Prize. From Burke he took away the importance of looking at reform instead of revolution in societal change and recognizing the limits of individual behavior compared to the state in providing political and economic stability for all. Keynes used Burke's writings as the bedrock for his political views on what is good government, which should focus on means and not ends.

Archives

The primary archives of J. M. Keynes's unpublished writings can be found in the Marshall Library, Cambridge; University, King's College, Cambridge; and the Royal Economic Society, London.

Printed Sources

Harrod, R. F. *The Life on John Maynard Keynes* (New York: Harcourt Brace Jovanovich, 1962).

Keynes, John M. *The Collected Works of John Maynard Keynes*, 30 vol., D. E. Moggridge (ed.), (London: Macmillan, for the Royal Economic Society, 1971–89).

Moggridge, D. E. *Keynes* (Toronto: University of Toronto Press, 1976).

Skidelsky, R. *John Maynard Keynes: The Economist as Saviour 1920–1937* (London: Macmillan, 1994).

———. *John Maynard Keynes: Fighting for Britain 1937–1946* (London: Macmillan, 2000).

———. *John Maynard Keynes: Hopes Betrayed 1883–1920* (London: Macmillan, 1986).

Richard P. F. Holt

KHRUSHCHEV, NIKITA SERGEYEVICH (1894–1971)

Nikita Khrushchev was born of peasant stock in Kalinovka, Kursk Province, in the Ukraine, part of the Russian Empire, to Sergei Nikanorovich Khrushchev, a coal miner, and his wife, Aksinia Ivanova. During the winters an elementary parochial school, where Russian Orthodox worship was compulsory, taught Khrushchev, in childhood a shepherd and farmhand, to read and write. Fascinated by everything mechanical, at 15 Khrushchev was apprenticed as a fitter in Donbass, an industrial city. Employed in the Rutchenkov mines as a metal worker, he quickly became a labor activist, from around 1913 helping to organize numerous strikes. An enthusiastic Bolshevik supporter, although he only formally joined the Communist Party in 1918, from November 1917 Khrushchev headed the local mineworks committees soviet. During the Russian Civil War he became a Red Army military commissar, and in 1921 the Rutchenkov mines deputy manager. Shortly thereafter the Yuzovka Mining Institute worker's training school gave him secondary and further party instruction. In 1914 Khrushchev married Yefrosinya Ivanovna, who died of typhus during the Civil War. In 1924 he remarried, to Nina

Petrovna Kukharchuk, a well-educated Communist activist and instructor. Appointed party secretary of Petrovsko-Mariinsk, Yuzovka, in 1925, the energetic Khrushchev moved steadily up the Ukrainian party hierarchy in Kharkov and Kiev, aligning himself with **Josef Stalin,** the emerging Soviet dictator. In 1929 he studied metallurgy at the Stalin Industrial Institute in Moscow, winning influential party contacts, and in 1931 moved to Moscow, becoming first secretary of the Moscow city region in 1935. One of only three provincial secretaries to weather Stalin's purges, Khrushchev conformed and survived. From 1939 he was a full Politburo member and, until 1949, first secretary of the Ukraine. As a Second World War lieutenant general in the Soviet military, he handled political liaison and stimulated civilian resistance. In 1949 Khrushchev resumed his old Moscow responsibilities, simultaneously becoming secretary of the Communist Party's Central Committee.

On Stalin's death in 1953 Khrushchev contended ruthlessly for supreme power, becoming first secretary of the Soviet Communist Party in 1955 and Soviet premier in 1958. Khrushchev soon demonstrated an unanticipated reformist streak, in 1956 secretly condemning the excesses of Stalin's one-man rule, personality cult, and purges, and releasing millions of political prisoners even as he repressed dissident intellectuals and forcibly suppressed the 1956 Hungarian rebellion. He attempted to humanize Soviet Communism, emphasizing the production of consumer rather than military goods, and instituting wide-ranging though ultimately unsuccessful agricultural reforms. Khrushchev also sought to defuse cold war nuclear tensions through arms control agreements with the West. In 1964 perceived international Soviet humiliations over Berlin and Cuba and Khrushchev's agricultural failures and erratic personal behavior brought his overthrow in a Politburo coup. In retirement Khrushchev lived quietly, writing lengthy memoirs which were gradually published abroad and in Russia.

A bookloving fellow miner and poet, Pantelei Makhinia, whose verses Khrushchev often recited later, introduced him to both Russian literary classics and revolutionary writings, including the *Communist Manifesto* and the French novelist Emile Zola's *Germinal.* Khrushchev subsequently recalled his intense emotional empathy with such works and those of Karl Marx. In 1914 Khrushchev began distributing a labor broadsheet, *The Miners' Leaflet,* and in 1915 the new Communist journal *Pravda* and other underground materials, devouring them voraciously. Unlike the cosmopolitan first generation of "Old Bolshevik" intellectual Communist leaders, Khrushchev received limited formal education, much of it being technological or ideological. Yet his memoirs demonstrate his familiarity with works by numerous Soviet novelists and poets, and he subsequently regretted his refusal to authorize the Russian publication of **Boris Pasternak**'s novel *Dr. Zhivago.*

Archives

The following Russian archives contain official former Soviet materials (some still closed) relating to Khrushchev: Archive of the President of the Russian Federation, Moscow; Archive of Foreign Policy of the Russian Federation, Moscow; State Archive of the Russian Federation, Moscow; Russian Center for Preservation and Study of Documents of Contemporary History, Moscow; Central Archive of Social Movements of the City of Moscow; Central State Archive for Social Organization of Ukraine, Kiev, Ukraine.

Printed Sources

Khrushchev, Nikita S. *Khrushchev Remembers*, Strobe Talbott (ed.), (Boston: Little, Brown, 1970).

———. *Khrushchev Remembers: The Glasnost Tapes*, Jerrold L. Schechter (ed.), (Boston: Little, Brown, 1990).

———. *Khrushchev Remembers: The Last Testament*, Strobe Talbott (ed.), (Boston: Little, Brown, 1974).

Taubman, William, Sergei Khrushchev, and Abbott Gleason (eds.). *Nikita Khrushchev* (New Haven: Yale University Press, 2000).

Priscilla Roberts

KING, MARTIN LUTHER JR. (1929–1968)

Heralded as "a spokesman for the conscience of America," Martin Luther King Jr. was one of the key leaders of the civil rights movement. A staunch advocate of nonviolent resistance against injustice, Dr. King's struggle for human rights began with the 1955 Montgomery bus boycott sparked by Rosa Parks and ended with his assassination on April 4, 1968, in Memphis, Tennessee, where he was to lead a protest march for the city's sanitation workers. King's activism was instrumental in the passage of key civil rights legislation, such as the Voting Rights Act of 1965 and the Civil Rights Acts of 1964 and 1968.

Michael Luther King Jr. (whose name was changed to Martin at age six) was born January 15, 1929, in Atlanta, Georgia, to Martin Luther King Sr., a Baptist minister, and Alberta (Williams) King, a teacher and minister's daughter. After graduating from Booker T. Washington High School in Atlanta, King—following in the footsteps of his father and grandfather—enrolled at Morehouse College. At Morehouse, college president Benjamin Mays and philosophy professor George Kelsey—both ordained ministers—inspired him to enter the ministry. In 1947, while still a student at Morehouse, King joined his father as co-pastor of Ebenezer Baptist Church. After earning his B.A. degree, King went on to earn a B.D. degree from Crozer Theological Seminary in Chester, Pennsylvania, and a Ph.D. degree in systematic theology from Boston University.

In September 1954, King moved to Montgomery, Alabama, to accept a post as pastor of Dexter Avenue Baptist Church. To encourage his parishioners to become involved in community affairs, he organized a committee that focused on social and political issues such as black voter registration. Two years later, King emerged as a leader of the civil rights movement when, as president of the Montgomery Improvement Association, he led the Montgomery bus boycott, which after 382 days resulted in Blacks being able to ride integrated city buses.

In February 1957, King, an executive member of the National Association for the Advancement of Colored People (NAACP), was elected president of the newly formed Southern Christian Leadership Conference. Over the next decade, his continued dedication to civil and human rights and his commitment to nonviolent resistance earned him worldwide recognition as an empathetic, compassionate leader as well as numerous honorary degrees and awards from religious and civic organizations. In 1963—the same year he was arrested in Birmingham for defying a court order barring demonstrations for fair hiring practices and the desegregation of local facilities and wrote his "Letter from a Birmingham Jail"—he was chosen as

Man of the Year by *Time* magazine. In 1964, at age 35, King became the youngest recipient of the Nobel Peace Prize, which he accepted on behalf of the civil rights movement. On January 14, 1994, President Bill Clinton proclaimed King's birthday a federal holiday.

A devout follower of the teachings of Jesus and **Mohandas K. Gandhi,** King once commented that he gained his ideals from his Christian background and his technique of passive resistance from Gandhi. An avid reader, King was especially influenced by the philosophical works of G.W.F. Hegel, Henry David Thoreau, **Paul Tillich,** and E. S. Brightman. He was also inspired by the poetry of Langston Hughes and Paul Laurence Dunbar. King's literary legacy includes five books that chronicle his journey from local minister to international spokesman for civil and human rights: *Stride toward Freedom: The Montgomery Story* (1958); *Strength to Love* (1963); *Why We Can't Wait* (1964); *Trumpet of Conscience* (1968); and *Where Do We Go from Here: Chaos or Community* (1967).

Archives

Martin Luther King Jr. Archives, Atlanta, Georgia.
Dr. Martin Luther King Jr. Memorial Center, Atlanta, Georgia.
The Martin Luther King Jr. Center for Nonviolent Social Change, Inc., Atlanta, Georgia.

Printed Sources

Bennett, Lerone Jr. *What Manner of Man: A Biography of Martin Luther King, Jr.* (Chicago: Johnson Publishing, 1964).
King, Martin Luther. *The Papers of Martin Luther King, Jr.*, Carson Clayborne (senior ed.), (Berkeley: University of California Press, 1992–2000). Vol. 1: *Called to Serve* (Jan. 1929–Sept. 1951); Vol. 2: *Rediscovering Precious Values* (July 1951–Nov. 1955); Vol. 3: *Birth of a New Age* (Dec. 1955–Dec. 1956); Vol. 4: *Symbol of the Movement* (Jan. 1957–Dec. 1958). First volumes of a projected 14-volume series.
Moses, Greg. *Revolution of Conscience: Martin Luther King, Jr., and the Philosophy of Nonviolence* (New York: Guilford Press, 1997). Focuses on King's political philosophy.

Durthy A. Washington

KISSINGER, HENRY (1923–)

Henry Kissinger, former secretary of state for two presidents, was destined for a public life. It is not apparent, however, from his early years. Kissinger was born in Furth, Germany, in 1923. Despite a happy young childhood, his life would be forever changed by the assumption of power by the Nazis in 1933. In 1938, his family fled to the United States and settled in New York City. As an adult, he would return to Germany as part of the occupying American army. Once discharged, he resumed his college career, finishing his undergraduate and graduate degrees at Harvard University, where he would later become a tenured, full professor in the Department of Government. In 1969, he was tapped to join the State Department and in 1973, he became secretary of state under President **Richard Nixon.** He would remain in that post under Gerald Ford. Since then, Kissinger has continued to teach, to write, and to comment on a number of issues concerning American foreign policy.

Although not particularly religious later in life, as a young boy in Furth, Kissinger had been exposed to and discussed the Torah on a regular basis (Isaacson

1992, 25). This interest did not survive the Nazi era in Germany. One constant through more than 70 years of his existence was his mother, Paula Stern Kissinger. Two individuals would have profound impact on Kissinger's intellectual growth: Fritz Kraemer, who pulled the young private out of the ranks to handle postwar denazification and occupation duties in a small town in Germany, and his dissertation advisor, William Elliot, a professor of government at Harvard.

Kissinger is one of the twentieth century's pre-eminent practitioners of the Bismarckian concept of *realpolitik*. As such, he has advanced the concept of balance of power within the twentieth-century superpower structure. He has shown the influence of nineteenth-century foreign policy practitioners like Klemens Von Metternich, Austrian foreign minister (1813–1848), and Otto von Bismarck, German chancellor (1862–1890), in both his historical works.

Kissinger is a conservative. His foreign policy closely mirrored that of Metternich and Bismarck. Indeed his doctoral dissertation was an examination of the balance-of-power system created in the aftermath of the Napoleonic wars in the early nineteenth century. In his writings, one can pick up the influence of European politicians and intellectuals of the nineteenth century, including Fyodor Dostoyevsky, G.W.F. Hegel, and Immanuel Kant (Isaacson 1992, 31). One childhood friend recalled that "[Kissinger] was always reading about politics and history . . . " (Isaacson 1992, 36).

Henry Kissinger broke away from the idealistic tone of the young individuals who had surrounded **John F. Kennedy** and who were kept on by **Lyndon Johnson**. Instead, like Richard Nixon, Kissinger looked at the reality of the situation and, instead of believing in the goodness of humans, seemed to hold that foreign policy should instead focus on how to insure that two superpowers, and the nations they used, held a balance of power. While he was certainly anti-fascist and anti-communist, Kissinger attempted to work with the Soviet Union to ensure that neither side so threatened the other as to cause a nuclear war. He was one of the few to survive Nixon's fall from power, but not without some cost. He continued to write books, articles, and commentary pieces that in themselves continued to influence new generations of historians, politicians, and political scientists.

Archives

Public papers of Kissinger can be found in various government archives, such as the National Archives, particularly the State Department and the records of the National Security Council. The Richard M. Nixon and Gerald R. Ford Libraries also hold some public documents.

Printed Sources

Bell, Coral. *The Diplomacy of Detente: the Kissinger Era* (New York: St. Martin's Press, 1977).

Isaacson, Walter. *Kissinger: A Biography* (New York: Simon and Schuster, 1992).

Kalb, Bernard, and Marvin Kalb. *Kissinger* (Boston: Little, Brown, 1974).

Kissinger, Henry. *American Foreign Policy* (New York: Norton, 1977).

———. *Diplomacy* (New York: Simon and Schuster, 1994).

———. *Does America Need a Foreign Policy?: Towards a Diplomacy for the 21st Century* (New York: Simon and Schuster, 2001).

———. *For the Record: Selected Statements, 1977–1980* (Boston: Little, Brown, 1981).

———. *Nuclear Weapons and Foreign Policy* (New York: W.W. Norton, 1969).

———. *Observations: Selected Speeches and Essays, 1982–1984* (Boston: Little, Brown, 1985).

———. *White House Years* (Boston: Little, Brown, 1979).

———. *A World Restored: Metternich and Castlereagh and the Problems of Peace, 1812–1822* (Boston: Houghton Mifflin, 1957).

———. *Years of Renewal* (Boston: Little, Brown, 1999).

———. *Years of Upheaval* (Boston: Little, Brown, 1982).

Mazlish, Bruce. *Kissinger: The European Mind in American Policy* (New York: Basic Books, 1976).

Schulzinger, Robert D. *Henry Kissinger: Doctor of Diplomacy* (New York: Columbia University Press, 1989).

Phyllis Soybel

KLEE, PAUL (1879–1940)

Paul Klee was born in Munchenbuchsee, Switzerland, and at the age of ten entered the gymnasium, where he became fascinated with the study of literature, music, and fine art. Graduating in 1898, Klee moved to Germany to pursue private studies in art and eventually enrolled in the Munich Academy to become a fellow student of **Wassily Kandinsky.** His early etchings and pencil drawings reflected the fantasy and satire of Francisco Goya and William Blake, but his numerous travels in middle age to locales such as Tunisia, Paris, and Italy exposed Klee to a wide variety of styles and ideas. In 1911 he joined Der Blaue Reiter and perfected his expressionist and abstract technique. After a brief stint in the military during the First World War, Klee was appointed to the Bauhaus in Weimar, where he taught until he accepted the position of professor of fine art at the Dusseldorf Academy in 1931. In the following years, the Nazis dismissed Klee's work as degenerate and he was forced to seek refuge in Bern. Klee was a lifelong proponent of simplicity and conservatism in art. A master of exact, fluid line, his work transformed traditional romantic motifs into a visual language appropriate to the scale of children. In 1935 Klee contracted scleroderma and his once playful and colorful compositions such as *Twittering Machine* (1922) and *Pastoral* (1927) became brooding and sombre works, epitomized by creations such as *Death and Fire* (1940). Klee was admitted to the Victoria Sanatorium in Muralto and died before the full effects of his influence on the American abstract expressionist movement could be felt.

Klee was a voracious reader of fiction. His diaries are filled with entries regarding his daily literary conquests, including the fantastical short stories of Edgar Allan Poe and Adolf von Wilbrandt, Honoré de Balzac's *Les Contes Drolatiques,* Voltaire's *Candide,* and Miguel de Cervantes's *Don Quixote.* His interest in the alternate realities that fiction could create was heightened by the work of playwrights Henrik Ibsen and Friedrich Hebbel (whose journals Klee frequently referenced) as well as by the early writings of Aristophanes, Plautus, and Sophocles. Authors of a more serious nature that Klee read included Fyodor Dostoyevsky and Lev Tolstoy, although the artist often found their works to be overtly ethical and lacking in humor. Klee was an ardent proponent of early twentieth-century German idealistic metaphysics and believed that the visible world was one of many latent realities behind which existed a deeper state of being. To explain his theories regarding the science of design, Klee wrote *The Thinking Eye.* This monumental work contained the idea that painters could produce visual equivalents for spiritual states on their canvasses, that music in the form of eighteenth-century counterpoint could be translated directly from aural to visual motifs demonstrating gradations of value and color, and that fantasy was legitimate subject matter for painting, as the world had no final reality. Klee frequently incorporated symbols and emblems into his work as well to introduce the viewer to deeper meanings beyond the apparent subject matter. This idea that visual art is simultaneously surface and symbol was espoused by Oscar Wilde in his *Aesthetic Manifesto*, a work that Klee read along with the author's *Man's Soul under Socialism* and *The Picture of Dorian Gray*.

Archives

The Getty Research Institute for the History of Art and the Humanities, Special Collections, control no. CJPA89-A318.

Printed Sources

Grohmann, Will. *Paul Klee* (New York: George Braziller, 1962).
Klee, Felix. *Paul Klee* (New York: George Braziller, 1962).
———— (ed.). *The Diaries of Paul Klee 1898–1918* (Berkeley: University of California Press, 1964).

Gregory L. Schnurr

KOESTLER, ARTHUR (1905–1983)

Arthur Koestler was born in Budapest, the only child of assimilated Jews: a Hungarian father and Austrian mother. After scientific studies in Vienna and a kibbutz stay in Palestine, he became a roving journalist, foreign editor, and Communist propagandist. He survived Franco's jails (1937), internment in France (1939–40), the French Foreign Legion (1940), and the British Pioneer Corps (1941–42), becoming a British national after the war but remaining a citizen of the world. With his third wife he committed suicide, reaffirming private dignity and individual liberties, the values he had championed for much of his life.

The turning point in Koestler's development was his joining the Communist Party on December 31, 1931. By the time he left the Party in 1938, the unfinished debate over "noble ends and ignoble means," between morality and expediency, was yielding to his quest for an understanding of individual psychology beyond collective rhetoric and abstract ideologies. Koestler turned increasingly inward, to **Henri Bergson, Carl Jung,** and especially Sigmund Freud, whom he finally met with awe in London in autumn 1938 but from whom he would distance himself in subsequent works. "Freud or Marx?" asked **George Orwell** in reviewing Koestler, who acknowledged these two strands to his development. The binary opposition between chronic indignation (Marxism, Zionism, anti-Fascism) and oceanic relativism (Freudianism, mysticism, creativity) is reflected in the antithetical titles of his many writings, in which he rejects both Communism and psychoanalysis. Versed in each but dismissive of both, Koestler long flogged these same "dead horses." He thrived on reconciling opposites, pursuing the impossible synthesis, representing differences as contraries.

Koestler's personal reading tastes began with Knut Hamsun, from whom he and **Ernest Hemingway** learned conciseness. He considered Hemingway the greatest writer of the twentieth century. The "heroes of [his] youth" were "Darwin and Spencer, Kepler, Newton, and Mach; Edison, Hertz and Marconi." His "Bible" was a nineteenth-century classic, Ernst Haeckel's *Mysteries of the Universe*, of which one riddle remained unresolved: free will. To two "knowing ones" he remained devoted until their deaths: Vladimir Jabotinsky, Zionist, and Willy Muenzenberg, Communist (Koestler 1952, 50–55). Among more literary figures, he "adored Dostoyevsky," particularly *Crime and Punishment* and *The Possessed:* Raskolnikov is the starting point and foil to Koestler's characters in grappling with free will. As a youth he also "loved Oscar Wilde" and "admired Stendhal." After the modern Hungarian poet Endre Ady he favored "Rilke, Goethe, Heine, Hölderlin, and Byron, approximately in that order." (Hölderlin was added to this list in 1975.) In his mature years Koestler's "Pantheon became overpopulated" (Koestler 1975, 47–50). How to encompass the immense territory of this polyglot and polymath's readings? The diversity of critics addressing his work highlights its underpinnings in literature, politics, philosophy, science, and beyond. For *Insight and Outlook* the publisher reported Koestler had invested five years in studying biology, neurology, and psychology; he himself confirmed that his research for *The Gladiators* had been equally comprehensive. For the unfinished third volume of his autobiography, Cynthia Koestler lists a sampling of books he ordered almost weekly in 1950, spanning volumes of Freud's complete works alongside Hemingway, **Ignazio Silone,** and Stephen Spender, all representing the literature of antifascism. In that generation which was his own, he particularly respected George Orwell's model of moral integrity and artistic professionalism: "the only writer of genius among the littérateurs of social revolt between the wars" (Koestler 1980, 269). When pressed in an interview to identify influences (not imitation but "feeding and digesting"), he cited Alfred Döblin, **Thomas Mann,** Hemingway, and the early **Thornton Wilder** (Rosner and Abt 1970, 144). In his final interview he was asked about imaginative writers important to him but replied, "No comment. That's list-making" ("Arthur Koestler" 1984, 195).

Archives

Edinburgh University: manuscripts and papers.

Printed Sources

"Arthur Koestler." *The Paris Review* 92 (1984), 183–201.
Cesarani, David. *Arthur Koestler: The Homeless Mind* (New York: Free Press, 1998).
Crossman, Richard (ed.). *The God That Failed* (New York: Harper, 1949).
Day, Frank. *Arthur Koestler: A Guide to Research* (New York: Garland, 1987).
Hamilton, Iain. *Koestler: A Biography* (London: Secker and Warburg, 1982).
The Koestler Archive in Edinburgh University Library: A Checklist (Edinburgh: Edinburgh University Library, 1987).
Koestler, Arthur. *Arrow in the Blue* (New York: Macmillan, 1952).
———. *Bricks to Babel* (New York: Random, 1980).
———. *The Invisible Writing* (New York: Macmillan, 1954).
———. "Lectures de jeunesse." In *Arthur Koestler,* Pierre Debray-Ritzen (ed.), (Paris: L'Herne, 1975), 47–50.
Koestler, Arthur, and Cynthia Koestler. *Stranger on the Square* (New York: Random, 1984).
Orwell, George. "Freud or Marx?" *Manchester Evening News,* Dec. 9, 1943, 2.
Rosner, Stanley, and Lawrence E. Abt (eds.). *The Creative Experience* (New York: Grossman, 1970), 131–53.

Roy Rosenstein

KOHL, HELMUT (1930–)

Helmut Kohl, known as the "Chancellor of Unity" for his role in Germany's 1989–90 reunification and as the Federal Republic of Germany's sixth chancellor (1982–98), grew up in a staunchly Catholic family in Ludwigshafen. After completing high school in 1950, Kohl's university studies focused first on law at Frankfurt am Main and then history at Heidelberg. Completed in 1958, Kohl's doctorate focused on the revival of political life in post-1945 western Germany.

Kohl identified early with Konrad Adenauer's Christian Democratic Union (CDU) in Rhineland-Pfalz. Inspired by the CDU's conservative vision and its leadership, Kohl rose quickly within the CDU, serving on its various regional and national committees, throughout the 1950s and 1960s. In 1969 Kohl succeeded Peter Altmeier as minister-president of Rhineland-Pfalz. As minister-president (1969–76), Kohl held to policies emphasizing the modernization of Rhineland-Pfalz, its educational system, and centralized planning within the state. Paralleling his rise in state politics, Kohl's image as a national leader rose. Under Kohl's increasing leadership, CDU embraced principles balancing the needs of a competitive market with a moral responsibility to sustain a social welfare system. Kohl succeeded Helmut Schmid as chancellor in October 1982 while the CDU surged ahead in subsequent elections. While confronted with an economy in decline, Kohl's foreign policy revitalized his political career. After East Germany's collapse in late 1989, Kohl sought to realize the CDU's long-term objective of German reunification. In March 1990, East Germans voted into office a collection of pro-unification political parties, and Kohl's popularity rose accordingly, keeping him in office for another eight years. Nevertheless, Kohl's domestic policies failed to remedy the ailing economy, growing unemployment, and outbursts of xenophobia. Kohl's support for a long-term policy leading to Europe's political unification, as outlined in the Maastricht Treaty, did not satisfy the electorate at a time of economic decline. Kohl's critics emphasized an apparent lack of intellectual depth and emphasis upon internal political machinations as an explanation for his political longevity. In 1998, Gerhard Schröder succeeded Kohl as German chancellor.

Helmut Kohl's clearest contribution to German culture is in architecture. Visible evidence of Kohl's inclination for modernism and sense of history can be gleaned from many of the federal structures in both Bonn and Berlin dating back to his days as chancellor. Bonn's Art Museum (Kunstmuseum) and Haus der Geschichte der Bundesrepublik Deutschland and Berlin's Kulturforum, the new chancellery, and the restructured Reichstag are particularly stunning examples of the merger of these themes.

Helmut Kohl's earthy charisma, large stature, and simple style often made him a target his critics could not resist. Overall, his contributions to German cultural life moved along several paths. Kohl admired **Konrad Adenauer** and shared with him a belief in the importance of a German cultural heritage. While less enthusiastic than Adenauer about classical literature, Kohl seemed to agree with Adenauer's distaste for socially critical authors, such as Günther Grass. Of those works he favored, Kohl's memoirs suggest that he preferred contemporary political figures to classical authors. Like Adenauer, Kohl believed **Adolf Hitler**'s rise represented a departure from Germany's Christian heritage and constituted a break with its traditional cultural ties with its neighbors. Nevertheless, Kohl did not believe that past events should determine the future cultural growth of his fellow Germans.

Archives

Zwischenarchiv des Bundesarchivs, Hangelar. Temporary location for documents being transferred to the national archives, but still in the formal posession of the issuing ministries.

Bundesarchiv, Koblenz. National Archival holdings.

Bundeskanzleramt, Bonn. Papers held by the Office of the Federal Chancellor.

Archive fur Christlich-Demokratische Politik, Sankt Augustin. Official archive of the Christian Democratic Union.

Buro des Bundesvorsitzenden der CDU, Konrad-Adenauer-Haus, Bonn.

Privatarchive und Dokumentensammlung Werner Weidenfelds, Munich. Documents used by Karl-Rudolf Korte to write on the German unification process. Holdings of personal advisors to Kohl and not generally accessible to researchers.

Printed Sources

Clemens, Clay, and William E. Paterson (eds.). *The Kohl Chancellorship*, special issue of *German Politics* 7, 1 (April 1998).

Geschichte der deutschen Einheit in 4 Bänden (Stuttgart: Deutsche Verlags Anstalt, 1998–99).

Kohl, Helmut. *Ich wollte Deutschlands Einheit* (Berlin: Ullstein, 1996).

Maser, Werner. *Helmut Kohl: Der Deutsche Kanzler* (Frankfurt am Main: Ullstein, 1990).

Muenchler, Guenter, and Klaus Hofmann. *Helmut Kohl: Kanzler der Einheit* (Bonn: Presse- und Informationsamt der Bundesregierung, 1992).

David A. Meier

KUNDERA, MILAN (1929–)

Kundera Milan was born in Brno, Czechoslovakia. His father was a concert pianist and musicologist. Kundera himself studied music theory at Charles University in Prague as well as film at the Academy of Performing Arts. In 1947 he joined the Czechoslovak Communist Party like many Czech students of the time. However, due to his opposition to socialist realism, Kundera was expelled from the Party in 1950. Reinstated in 1956, Kundera gained a teaching position in the Film Faculty of the Academy of Performing Arts, where his students included Miloš Forman and Jiří Menzel, both of whom later won Academy Awards. Kundera established himself as one of the most important literary figures in Czechoslovakia during the 1960s, publishing a play and two collections of short stories before his first novel, *The Joke* (1967). Kundera was an avid supporter of the political reforms of **Alexander Dubček,** and he was cast into official disfavor following the Soviet invasion of Czechoslovakia in August 1968. He emigrated to France in 1975, taking a teaching position at the University of Rennes. In 1980 he became a professor at the École des hautes études en sciences sociales in Paris. After his emigration, Kundera published the novels that gained him acclaim as one of the most important European writers of the late twentieth century: *The Farewell Party* (1976), *The Book of Laughter and Forgetting* (1979), *The Unbearable Lightness of Being* (1984), and *Immortality* (1990). He also has written a play, *Jacques and His Master* (written in Czech in 1971, first performed in French in 1981), and two collections of essays, *The Art of the Novel* (1986) and *Testaments Betrayed* (1995). His essay collections and his two novellas, *Slowness* (1995) and *Identity* (1996), were written originally in French rather than his native Czech.

Kundera's primary concern with existence in a world without God and the digressions he takes in his novels (often halting the narrative to comment to the reader on his characters or historical events) have earned him the label of "philosophical" author. But, just as he eschewed the label of "dissident," so does Kundera reject the idea that he is a philosophical writer. Instead, he sees himself as a novelist, someone who explores questions of existence through the actions of imaginary characters. According to Kundera, the novel is the defining art form of the modern era in that it allows writers and readers to investigate various facets of existence with humor, moral ambiguity, and the search for knowledge as the sole guiding principle. In his essay collections, Kundera describes a history of the novel, offering a survey of some of his literary influences: principal among them are Cervantes, Gustave Flaubert, and especially **Marcel Proust** and **James Joyce,** who used the novel to meditate upon time and consciousness. Kundera also highlights four Central Europeans whom he regards as the defining "post-Proustian" novelists: **Franz Kafka,** Austrian novelists Robert Musil and Hermann Broch, and Polish writer Witold Gombrowicz. These writers plumbed the central questions of an existence constricted by forces that are "impersonal, uncontrollable, incalculable, and inescapable," in particular the dilemma of trying to control one's own life when confronted by the irrationality of history. Another important influence on Kundera's fiction, in terms of style and structure, is classical music. Critics have pointed to the musical structure of Kundera's most famous novel, *The Unbearable Lightness of Being*, with its recurrence of motifs, the development of variations upon themes, and the counterpunctual layering of narratives. Kundera seemingly acknowledges this structuring with his references to Beethoven's final quartet and its musical motif of "Es muss sein."

Archives

Josef Škvorecký Collection, Hoover Institution of War, Peace, and Revolution, Stanford University, Stanford, Calif. Correspondence between Kundera and his North American publisher, Czech novelist Josef Škvorecký.

Printed Sources

Banerjee, Maria Němcová. *Terminal Paradox: The Novels of Milan Kundera* (New York: Grove Weidenfeld, 1990).

Kundera, Milan. *The Art of the Novel*, Linda Asher (trans.), (New York: Grove, 1988).

———. *Testaments Betrayed*, Linda Asher (trans.), (New York: HarperCollins, 1995).

Misurella, Fred. *Understanding Milan Kundera: Public Events, Private Affairs* (Columbia: University of South Carolina Press, 1993).

Petro, Peter (ed.). *Critical Essays on Milan Kundera* (New York: G.K. Hall, 1999).

Bruce R. Berglund

KUROSAWA, AKIRA (1910–1998)

Akira Kurosawa was born in the Omori district of Tokyo at the end of Japan's Meiji period. He attended Morimura Gakuen School, Kuroda Primary School, and Keika Middle School, where he excelled in the arts, kendo, and calligraphy. At the Tokyo Academy of Fine Arts, Kurosawa trained formally as a painter and joined the Proletarian Artists League. He voiced his political concerns by contributing articles to many socialist publications throughout the early 1930s. Kurosawa was hired at Tokyo's Photo Chemical Laboratory in 1935 and apprenticed with renowned filmmaker Kajiro Yamamoto, studying all aspects of movie-making from set construction to editing. Kurosawa filmed his first work, *Sanshiro Sugata*, in 1943, and within a decade was recognized as Japan's foremost director. His films reflected the social conflicts inherent in postwar Japanese society and the struggle to maintain an Eastern identity in the wake of rising Western social values. Kurosawa's 1951 film *Roshomon* won first prize at the Venice Film Festival and served as a gateway to introducing his work to Western audiences. The classics *The Seven Samurai* (1954), *Yojimbo* (1961), and *Akahije* (1965) demonstrate Kurosawa's advanced knowledge of on-screen choreography and his ingenious use of the anamorphic frame and multi-camera filming. Kurosawa's films often combined long tracking shots with spectacular action scenes, slow-motion sequences, and fast-paced editing. Despite a period of desperation that included a suicide attempt, Kurosawa produced epic films into his eighth decade. His final full-length motion pictures *Kagemusha* (1980) and *Ran* (1985) continued to emphasize the dignity and worth of the individual.

In his youth, Kurosawa's father would frequently take him to view the storytellers who pantomimed their tales in the public halls around Kagurazaka. As such, the young director learned to express narrative visually as well as through written language. Kurosawa spent his formative years studying the works of master painters such as Vincent van Gogh and Edgar Degas in the heavily discounted art books of the Japanese depression era. Utilizing the theories of Western impressionist painters and Japanese printmakers such as Hokusai, Kurosawa developed a new way of establishing interesting arrangements of elements on film by emphasizing planar composition. Often, in the manner of a cubist painter, Kurosawa would treat the object caught on film as something to be dissected or broken down visually into a number of separate segments for analysis. His love of epic and dramatic tales drew him to Russian literature, where he perused such works as Ivan Turgenev's *The Rendezvous*, and Fyodor Dostoyevsky's *The Idiot* and *The Brothers Karamazov*. Like Dostoyevsky, Kurosawa frequently used children as emblems of vulnerability in his work, and many of his darker cinematographic moments reflect the Russian novelist's complex written portrayals of spiritual and physical poverty. Kurosawa also read the works of the popular Japanese novelists Natsume Soseki, Mori Ogai, and Kunikida Doppo, as well as Sei Shonagon's *Pillow Book* from the middle of the Heian period. He was a student of the precepts of traditional Japanese Noh drama as espoused by the medieval theorist Ze-ami in his treatise, *Kadensho*. Kurosawa fused these established notions of performance with the theories of modern artists and the techniques of cinematographers such as **Sergei Eisenstein** and **John Ford** to produce his truly unique and original, moving works of art.

Archives

The Getty Research Institute for the History of Art and the Humanities, Special Collections.

Printed Sources

Boch, Audie E. (ed.). *Akira Kurosawa: Something Like an Autobiography* (New York: Alfred A. Knopf, 1982).

Prince, Stephen. *The Warrior's Camera: The Cinema of Akira Kurosawa* (Princeton: Princeton University Press, 1991).

Yoshimoto, Mitsuhiro. *Kurosawa: Film Studies and Japanese Cinema* (Durham: Duke University Press, 2000).

Gregory L. Schnurr

LAMPEDUSA, DUKE OF PALMA AND PRINCE OF

See Tomasi, Giuseppe.

LANG, FRITZ (1890–1976)

Born in Vienna on December 5, 1890, to Anton Lang, architect, and a converted Jewish mother named Paula Schlesinger, Fritz Lang received a Catholic education that he qualified "puritanist." He had an older brother only, Adolf Lang, born in 1884, of whom he never spoke. The young Fritz Lang went to a Viennese Catholic high school, the K. und K. Staatsrealschule, from 1901. In 1913, at 22, he traveled through Europe and spent some time in Paris, where he studied painting at the École de peinture Maurice Denis and at the Académie Julien. He had to go back to Vienna in 1914 as World War I began. Lang wrote his first scripts in 1917 and became a film director in 1919 in Berlin. He made his most famous masterpieces during the 1920's: *Der Mude Tod* (*Destiny*, 1920), *Dr Mabuse* (1922), *Siegfried* (*Die Nibelungen*, 1924), *Metropolis* (1927), and *M* (1931). Lang left his wife and Nazi Germany for France in 1933. The German director made most of his films in Hollywood, from 1935 to 1957. In 1963, the director played (in French) his own character in **Jean-Luc Godard**'s feature film, *Le Mépris (Contempt)*. Lang's influence is unique in film history. **Alfred Hitchcock, Orson Welles, Ingmar Bergman, Luis Bunuel, François Truffaut,** and Jean-Luc Godard all owe something to the German master. American directors Ford Beebe and Robert Hill copied many scenes from *Metropolis* in their 1938 *Flash Gordon's Trip to Mars*, as did Ridley Scott in *Blade Runner* (1983). His 1929 *Woman on the Moon* was the first film to include a countdown, a suspense strategy invented by Lang himself. Even Madonna's videoclip "Express Yourself" is a pastiche of a scene from Lang's *Metropolis*.

Fritz Lang grew up in a bourgeois family, where he read books by Jules Verne, Willi Gail, Kurd Lasswitz, and Hans Dominik. When he was at the Realschule, Lang also learned French and English and discovered authors such as Friedrich Nietzsche, Arthur Schopenhauer, Søren Kierkegaard, Friedrich Schiller, Johann von Goethe, William Shakespeare, Heinrich Heine, and playwright Hans Sachs. His film classic *Metropolis* combines numerous uncredited influences from French novelist Villiers de l'Isle-Adam's *L'Ève future* to Georg Kaiser's play *Coral*. From 1920 until 1933, Lang co-wrote 10 German films with his wife Thea von Harbou, who also wrote novels and scripts (without her husband) for influential directors such as F. W. Murnau (four films between 1922 and 1924, including *Phantom*) and Arthur von Gerlash (*Zur Chronik von Grieshuus*, 1925). After adapting *Liliom*, a play by Ferenc Molnar, in 1934, Lang left Paris for the United States. The next step was Hollywood, and after many projects that didn't work, Lang released his first American masterpiece, *Fury*, in 1936. In the next three decades spent in Hollywood, Lang directed films in many genres: dramas (*You Only Live Once*, 1937), anti-Nazi films (*Hangmen Also Die*, co-written with **Bertolt Brecht** in 1943; *Ministry of Fear*, 1944) and even westerns, among the best in film history, such as *The Return of Frank James* (1940), *Western Union* (1941), and *Rancho Notorious* (1952). To explain his fascination with the American West, Lang admits he read Karl May's numerous stories about Indians and cowboys while he was a teenager. Lang also did two remakes (*Scarlet Street*, 1945, and *Human Desire*, 1954) of Jean Renoir's movies, of which he wasn't very proud. Lang's last film, a fantastic thriller titled *The Thousand Eyes of Dr. Mabuse*, was shot in Western Germany in 1960. For Lang, it was the third adaptation of Luxembourgois novelist Norbert Jacques's 1922 story about the mysterious Dr. Mabuse.

Archives

Stiftung Deutsche Kinematek, Berlin, Germany. Films, photos, personal papers, and the Lang–Von Harbou divorce records.

Fritz Lang Archives, Cinémathèque française, Paris, France. Photos, miscellaneous correspondence.

Paramount Collection at the Margaret Herrick Library of the Academy of Motion Picture Arts and Science, Beverly Hills, California. Photos, posters.

The Fritz Lang Files, The Cinema-Television Library and Archives of the Performing Arts, University of Southern California, Los Angeles, California. The most important files about Lang, with personal and professional papers, correspondence, diaries, film scripts.

Printed Works

Elsaesser, Thomas. *Metropolis* (University of California Press, 2000).

Jacobsen, Wolfgang, Cornelius Schnauber, and Rolf Aurich (eds.). *Fritz Lang: His Life and Work. Photographs and Documents* (Jovis Verlags und Projektburo, 2001).

Kaplan, E. Ann (ed.). *Fritz Lang: A Guide to References Resources* (New York: Macmillan, 1981).

McGilligan, Patrick. *Fritz Lang: The Nature of the Beast* (New York: St. Martin's Press, 1997).

Yves Laberge

LAWRENCE, DAVID HERBERT (1885–1930)

D. H. Lawrence was born at Eastwood, Nottinghamshire. Lawrence was raised a Congregationalist, and although he eventually broke from the Congregational chapel around 1907, its emphasis on the Bible and revelation, freedom, and independent self-governance was a formative influence. Lawrence studied on scholarship at Nottingham High School (1898–1901) but left after three years. In 1906, after he placed in the first division of the King's Scholarship exam, he began to study at Nottingham University College for a teacher's certificate and qualified for such in 1908. In 1911 illness forced Lawrence to stop teaching. In May 1912 Lawrence traveled with Frieda Weekley (née von Richthofen), wife of a University of Nottingham professor, to Germany and Italy and thus began a nomadic life. Any assessment of Lawrence's work on the development of Western culture in the twentieth century would consider his exploration of the volatility of essential human emotions and his examination of the paramount importance of humankind's primal relation to cosmic nature.

Some key influences on Lawrence are mentioned in one of his early stories, "A Modern Lover" (1909–10). Of the sources cited, those of note include Charlotte Brontë, George Eliot, Thomas Carlyle, John Ruskin, Arthur Schopenhauer, Friedrich Nietzsche, William James, Honoré de Balzac, Guy de Maupassant, and Henrik Ibsen. In some cases Lawrence was impressed by particular works, such as *Jane Eyre* (1847) by Charlotte Brontë; *The Mill on the Floss* (1860) by George Eliot; *Modern Love* (1862), a long poem by George Meredith; *Anna Karenina* (1873–77) by Lev Tolstoy; *Pragmatism* (1907) by William James. Lawrence also admired the work of Ivan Turgenev.

Lawrence benefited from Meredith's and Eliot's close observation of nature and critical examination of the relationship between men and women. Foremost, however, is Thomas Hardy, without question a significant influence on Lawrence, who wrote *Study of Thomas Hardy* (composed 1914; published entirely 1935). Nature, natural forces, the extent of any one person's freedom and free will are key themes in Hardy and in Lawrence. The German metaphysical philosopher of pessimism and will, Arthur Schopenhauer, had influenced Hardy. Lawrence read (and annotated) a translated, redacted version of some of Schopenhauer's essays and was deeply affected (see Roberts and Poplawski 2001).

In 1915, Lawrence read about the early Greek pre-Socratic philosophers and began to visualize more fully his belief of fundamental principles operating in the cosmic order, especially the notions of duality and polar opposites, ideas already rooted in him from the German philosophers. From his study of Hardy, and his reading of Schopenhauer, Nietzsche, Carlyle, and William James, Lawrence developed his thinking on the exceptional individual struggling to make meaning in a confused and threatening world. In 1918 Lawrence read *On the Psychology of the Unconscious* (1917) by **Carl Gustav Jung,** a reader of Schopenhauer and Nietzsche who emphasized that all human minds share vast primordial contexts.

As a major poet, Lawrence's early, fundamental influences are Meredith and Hardy. More extensive influences include the prophetic style of William Blake and the autobiographical nature meditations of William Wordsworth. Walt Whitman is the most complex and enduring influence on Lawrence's poetry. Around 1914, Lawrence was captivated by Filippo Tommaso Marinetti and his ideas of futurism.

Archives

The University of Nottingham, Manuscripts and Special Collections, University Park, Nottingham, England: manuscripts, literary papers, correspondence, photographs, artistic works, early biographical holdings, miscellanea, George Lazarus manuscript bequest.

Harry Ransom Humanities Research Center, The University of Texas, Austin: numerous drafts, manuscripts, and typescripts of the majority of works.

See Roberts and Poplawski for numerous other holdings.

Printed Sources

Brunsdale, Mitzi M. *The German Effect on D.H. Lawrence and His Works 1885–1912* (Berne: Peter Lang, 1978).

Dircks, Mrs. Rudolf. *Essays of Schopenhauer* (London: Walter Scott, 1903). The collection annotated by Lawrence.

Ellis, David. *D.H. Lawrence: Dying Game 1922–1930* (Cambridge: Cambridge University Press, 1998).

Kinkead-Weekes, Mark. *D.H. Lawrence: Triumph to Exile 1912–1922* (Cambridge: Cambridge University Press, 1996).

Meyers, Jeffrey (ed.). *D.H. Lawrence and Tradition* (Amherst: University of Massachusetts Press, 1985).

Milton, Colin. *Lawrence and Nietzsche: A Study in Influence* (Aberdeen: Aberdeen University Press, 1987).

Roberts, Warren, and Paul Poplawski. *A Bibliography of D.H. Lawrence*, 3rd ed. (Cambridge: Cambridge University Press, 2001).

Worthen, John. *D.H. Lawrence: The Early Years 1885–1912* (Cambridge: Cambridge University Press, 1991).

Gregory F. Tague

LAWRENCE, T. E. (1888–1935)

Thomas Edward Lawrence was born the illegitimate son of Thomas Chapman and Sarah Lawrence in North Wales. He attended Jesus College, Oxford University (1907–10), studied military history, wrote a thesis on crusader castle architecture in Syria, and received first class honors. He worked as an archaeologist at Carchemish in Syria (1911–14), where he learned to speak Arabic. In World War I, he served on Cairo's general staff as a "temporary second-lieutenant interpreter" and cartographer. In 1916, he went to western Arabia to aid the Arab Revolt against the Ottoman Empire, where he began working closely with the Hashemite Sharif, Faysal ibn Husayn, as British liaison officer. From March 1917 to October 1918, he coordinated attacks by small groups of Arab irregular soldiers on the Hejaz railway, gathered information on the geography and peoples of northern Arabia and Syria, led a surprise capture of the port of Aqaba, and helped to consolidate Arab control of Damascus after its capture. He was awarded the Distinguished Service Order, Companion of Bath, and Croix de Guerre, but declined knighthood. After the war, Lawrence was mythologized as "Lawrence of Arabia," emerging in the media as an enigmatic, romanticized hero. G. B. Shaw, Siegfried Sassoon, H. G. Wells, Thomas Hardy, and **Winston Churchill** considered his self-analytical war memoirs, *Seven Pillars of Wisdom*, among the greatest contemporary works in English. Lawrence died in 1935 following a motorcycle accident.

Lawrence read voraciously and recommended his favorites to his correspondents. Lawrence's initial travels to Syria were informed by studies of the Bible, A. H. Layard's works on the excavation of ancient Nineveh, and John Ruskin's *Stones of Venice* (1851–53). He enjoyed romantic renderings of medieval history, such as Tennyson's *Idylls of the King* (1859–85), Maurice Hewlett's *Life and Death of Richard Yea-and-Nay* (1900), and above all William Morris's *Hollow Land and Other*

Tales, Roots of the Mountains, Sigurd the Volsung, Well at the World's End, and *Wood Beyond the World*. Lawrence once commented: "I suppose everybody loves one writer unreasonably . . . I'd rather Morris than the world." He carried copies of his favorite books with him in Arabia; for example, a British officer saw him reading Sir Thomas Malory's *Morte d'Arthur* (1469) in a mess tent. He also studied orientalist travel narratives: Charles Doughty's *Travels in Arabia Deserta* (1888) and David Hogarth's *A Wandering Scholar in the Levant* (1896), but disliked Richard Burton, whom he considered "vulgar." Lawrence's descriptions of the Arabs reflected both orientalist imagery and imperialist concepts; he often compared educated, nationalist Syrians unfavorably to the idealized "unspoiled" Bedouin. Lawrence later became a book collector, favoring war literature and poetry.

Archives

Bodleian Library, Oxford: Reserve Manuscript Collection.
British Library Additional Manuscripts Collection, London: diaries, letters to Charlotte Shaw.
Public Record Office, Kew: Arab Bureau files, Foreign Office and War Office files, Intelligence files.
Houghton Library, Harvard University, Cambridge: letters to Robert Graves.

Printed Works

English, J. A. "Kindergarten Soldier: The Military Thought of Lawrence of Arabia," *Military Affairs* (Jan. 1987), 7–11.
Lawrence, A. W. (ed.). *T. E. Lawrence by His Friends* (London: Jonathan Cape, 1937). This edition includes titles in Lawrence's book collection.
Lawrence, T. E. *Letters of T. E. Lawrence*, David Garnett (ed.), (London: Jonathan Cape, 1939). Some contentious material edited out.
———. *T. E. Lawrence: The Selected Letters*, Malcolm Brown (ed.), (New York: Norton, 1989). Updated collection; indexed references to books, plays, and poetry.
———. *Seven Pillars of Wisdom, A Triumph* (London: Jonathon Cape, 1935). Account of the Arab Revolt of 1916–18; includes literary references and quotations.
Wilson, Jeremy. *Lawrence of Arabia, the Authorized Biography* (London: Heinemann, 1989). A cautious and reliable study; excellent bibliography.

Indira Falk Gesink

LEARY, TIMOTHY FRANCIS (1920–1996)

Timothy Leary, the only child of affluent Roman Catholic parents, was born in Springfield, Massachusetts. When he was 13, his alcoholic father abandoned him and his mother. He attended Classical High School in Springfield from 1935 until 1938, when he was nearly expelled for truancy and insubordination. Because his principal refused to recommend him to the prestigious colleges he wanted, he spent two years at the College of the Holy Cross in Worcester, Massachusetts, while waiting for admission to the U.S. Military Academy at West Point. Shortly after becoming a plebe in 1940, he was officially ostracized, or "silenced," for drunkenness and lying. Eventually his enemies among the upperclassmen hounded him into resigning in 1941. That fall he matriculated at the University of Alabama, but was expelled a year later for sleeping in the girls' dormitory. Drafted, he earned his bachelor's degree in the army in 1944. After receiving his M.S. in psychology from Washington State University in 1946 and his Ph.D. in clinical psychology from the University of California at Berkeley in 1950, he taught at Berkeley and the University of California at San Francisco until 1956 and directed psychological research at the Kaiser Foundation Hospital, Oakland, from 1952 to 1957. He taught at the University of Copenhagen in 1958 and lived briefly in Italy before joining the Harvard University psychology faculty in 1959. Fired by Harvard in 1963 for giving psychedelic drugs to students, he established an experimental drug commune in Millbrook, New York, and founded the League for Spiritual Discovery.

As a preteen, Leary read 8 or 10 books a week, mostly novels, history, and biography, not children's books. He was reading Mark Twain's *Life on the Mississippi* when his grandfather praised him as the only reader among his nine children and six grandchildren. Leary's father's bookshelves were full of British and Celtic poetry. At Holy Cross he enjoyed classical Latin authors. He found being shunned by his fellow cadets an advantage at West Point, because it created a monastic atmosphere in which he read Plato, Aristotle, Immanuel Kant, Arthur Schopenhauer, Will Durant, Buddhism, and mysticism. Immediately after his dismissal from West Point, he checked out **James Joyce**'s *Ulysses* from the restricted collection at Springfield Public Library, simply because it had been forbidden. In the 1950s and early 1960s, his interest in psychoactive drugs was sparked by Frank Barron, **William S. Burroughs,** Neal Cassady, Nick Chewelos, Walter H. Clark, Sidney Cohen, Keith Ditman, **Allen Ginsberg,** Gerald Heard, Abram Hofer, Michael Hollingshead, **Aldous Huxley,** Oscar Janiger, **Jack Kerouac,** John Lilly, Jack London, Fitz Hugh Ludlow, Humphrey Osmond, Edgar Allan Poe, Robert Gordon Wasson, and Alan Watts. While a fugitive in Switzerland in 1971, Leary met Albert Hofmann, the inventor of LSD. Among the other major influences Leary cited in his autobiography, *Flashbacks*, are Giordano Bruno, Carlos Castañeda, Aleister Crowley, Dante, Ralph Waldo Emerson, Margaret Fuller, Georges Ivanovitch Gurdjieff, **Hermann Hesse,** *I Ching*, William James, Ken Kesey, **Arthur Koestler,** Julien Offroy de La Mettrie, Paolo Mantegazza, **Marshall McLuhan,** Gerard K. O'Neill, Paracelsus, Sri Krishna Prem, Thomas Pynchon, Wilhelm Reich, and Robert Anton Wilson.

Archives

A small collection of Leary's papers is at the University of Texas at Austin, but most of his effects remain in private hands.

Printed Sources

Forte, Robert (ed.). *Timothy Leary: Outside Looking In* (Rochester, Vt.: Park Street, 1999).
Gilmore, Mikal. "Timothy Leary, 1920–1996," *Rolling Stone,* July 11–25, 1996.
Kleps, Art. *Millbrook: A Narrative of the Early Years of American Psychedelianism: Recension of 1994* (Austin: Neo-American Church of Texas, 1994).
———. *Millbrook: The True Story of the Early Years of the Psychedelic Revolution* (Oakland, Calif.: Bench, 1977).
Leary, Timothy Francis. *Flashbacks: A Personal and Cultural History of an Era: An Autobiography* (Los Angeles: Tarcher, 1990).
Mansnerus, Laura. "Timothy Leary, Pied Piper of Psychedelic 60's, Dies at 75," *New York Times,* June 1, 1996.
Slack, Charles W. *Timothy Leary, the Madness of the Sixties, and Me* (New York: P.H. Wyden, 1974).

Eric v.d. Luft

LE CORBUSIER (1887–1965)

Charles Edouard Jeanneret was born in La Chaux-de-Fonds, Switzerland. At the age of thirteen he left conventional school to follow in his father's footsteps as a watch dial engraver. In 1902, Jeanneret enrolled in a local art school under the tutelage of Charles L'Eplattenier, who steered the young student toward studies in architecture. He graduated from college in 1907, and traveled throughout Europe to study reinforced concrete techniques under August Perret in Paris and the theories of the Bauhaus school of design under Peter Behrens. As a young architect, Jeanneret developed a highly effective iron-concrete skeletal system for producing structurally superior skyscrapers. During the 1920s he adopted the name Le Corbusier after a maternal forbear and established a design studio in his native Switzerland. Le Corbusier's minimalist dwellings became known as "machines for living" due to the basic geometric design of their floor plans and their overall regularity and simplicity. Le Corbusier wrote prolifically on both residential and urban planning in such works as *Towards a New Architecture*, *The City of Tomorrow* and *The Decorative Art of Today*. Le Corbusier codified his style of architecture in designs for the League of Nations during the 1930s and in his urban planning efforts to aid in the restructuring of European cities in the aftermath of the Second World War. He founded the International Congress of Modern Architecture and produced many successful (albeit aesthetically controversial) projects throughout the 1950s, such as the National Museum of Western Art in Tokyo, the Church of Notre Dame du Haut at Ronchamp, France, and the Unite d'Habitation in Marseille. He was also commissioned to modernize and transform the urban plan of Chandigarh, the capital city of the Indian state of Punjab, through the design and construction of such structures as the Palace of Justice and the Secretariat Building. He drowned in the Mediterranean Sea off the coast of Cap Martin, France, at the age of 78.

Le Corbusier's so-called "international style" of architecture was directly influenced by a movement known as purism, formulated by Amedee Ozenfant. Purism rejected complicated abstractions of form and advocated a return to simple geometric planning as the basis for residential design. Ozenfant's *Apres Le Cubisme* explained the principals of his functionalist architectural design and espoused a rejection of ornament and unnecessary detail in the exterior and interior designs of buildings. The idea that universal beauty and truth is revealed through the abandonment of the complicated and the realistic in favor of the geometric and stylized is one that Le Corbusier inherited from many sources, however. For centuries, the need for this type of minimalist design had been espoused by prominent theorists such as Maurice Deufrene and Karl Grosz as well as in Edward Shure's *Les Grand Inites* and Owen Jones's *Grammar and Ornament*. The respected architect and writer Adolf Loos also published his work *Ornament and Crime* in 1908, which defined functionalism and simplicity as the primary prerequisites of all good modern design. Le Corbusier closely studied Loos's precepts, as well as those of Adolf Zeising and Gustav Fechner, whose principles of the "Golden Section" directly influenced the way in which Le Corbusier divided his modular residential units according to the intricate measurements of the human body.

Archives

The Getty Institute for the History of Art and the Humanities, 1200 Getty Center Drive, Los Angeles, California.

Printed Sources

Brooks, H. Allen. *Le Corbusier's Formative Years* (Chicago: University of Chicago Press, 1997).

Curtis, William J. R. *Le Corbusier: Ideas and Forms* (New York: Rizzoli International Publications, 1986).

Serenyi, Peter (ed.). *Le Corbusier in Perspective* (Upper Saddle River, N. J. : Prentice Hall, 1975).

Gregory L. Schnurr

LENIN, VLADIMIR ILICH (1870–1924)

Vladimir Ilich Lenin was born in Simbirsk, Russia. His parents, Ilya and Maria Ulyanov, had a lasting influence on the young and mature Lenin, especially with respect to his educational and work values. He studied at the Simbirsk Classical Gymnasium, where he learned Latin, Greek, French, and German. In 1886 Lenin's father died, and his brother Alexander, who had joined a revolutionary organization that attempted to assassinate Alexander III, was tried and executed. These were two important turning points in the young Lenin's life. After his brother's execution, Lenin joined terrorist organizations dedicated to agrarian-socialist ideals. Lenin chose to study jurisprudence at the same university where his father studied, the Imperial Kazan University (1887–1891). In 1893 Lenin moved to St. Petersburg, where a group of young Marxists such as Petr Struve and Sergei Bulgakov published on the Russian economy and society. Lenin published his first article, "New Economic Trends in Peasant Life," in 1893. Two years later, Lenin left for Switzerland to meet the father of Russian Marxism, Georgi Plekhanov, whose interpretations of Karl Marx and Friedrich Engels greatly influenced his own. During the same year, he met his future wife, Nadezhda Krupskaya (1869–1939). In January 1897 Lenin was exiled to Siberia for revolutionary activity. After his exile, Lenin left for Zurich to join Plekhanov in 1900. During this trip, Lenin helped organize the Marxist newspaper *Iskra* (*The Spark*), which was a mouthpiece for revolutionary propaganda. In 1901 Lenin published a small booklet, *What Is to Be Done?*, in which he outlined the organizational tactics of an illegal political party. During the Second Party Congress of the Russian Social-Democratic Labor Party in 1903, a major tactical and organizational disagreement between Lenin and Yuli Martov broke the party into two camps: Lenin's followers became the Bolsheviks and Martov's, the Mensheviks. After the 1905 Revolution, Lenin showed a willingness to break with conventional orthodox Marxism, which stipulated that there would first occur a "bourgeois" revolution and subsequently a socialist revolution led by the working class. In April 1917, after the fall of the Russian monarchy, Lenin considered bypassing the first conventional stage of the revolutionary process. In his "April Thesis" he argued that Russia was ready for the consolidation of the revolutionary process. Lenin's most important role in the October Revolution was as a political strategist and inspirer. After the consolidation of Bolshevik power, Lenin's health increasingly deteriorated. He suffered fatigue and bad nerves. He endured a number of massive strokes and an assassination attempt. Although Lenin continued to write and work in the remaining three years of his life, his role as a political and organizational leader was limited.

Lenin was in every respect a nineteenth-century intellectual. His favorite authors and thinkers were from the nineteenth century. During his gymnasium days, he read and translated to Russian the Latin and Greek classics. As a young boy, he read nineteenth-century classical Russian literature and especially admired the novels of Nikolai Gogol, Ivan Turgenev, Lev Tolstoy, and Fyodor Dostoyevsky. However, his favorite novel in his adolescent years was Harriet Beecher Stowe's *Uncle Tom's Cabin*. After the assassination of his older brother, Alexander, the young Lenin turned to the Russian radical author Nikolai Chernyshevski, whose novel *What Is to Be Done?* was not only a favorite of his brother's, but had an immense effect on Lenin's consciousness and direction in life. Lenin's earliest expression of a distinctive "Leninism" was in the 1902 pamphlet titled *What Is to Be Done?* During university days, he familiarized himself with David Ricardo, Charles Darwin, Henry Buckle, Marx, and Engels. He read and admired Marx's *Capital* and *The Poverty of Philosophy; Anti-Dühring* and *The Condition of the Working Class* by Engels; and *Our Disagreements* by Plekhanov. Agrarian socialists such as Pëtr Tkachëv and Sergei Nechaev and the Jacobins of the French Revolution commanded respect as well. The populist author of short stories Gleb Uspensky should also be mentioned as an important influence on Lenin. However, unlike some of the other leading Marxist thinkers, such as Alexander Bogdanov, **Nikolai Bukharin,** and Anatoly Lunacharsky, who greatly admired twentieth-century social thought, Lenin was not interested in fashionable, contemporary ideas. He constantly returned to his four principal figures for intellectual stimulus: Marx, Engels, Plekhanov, and Karl Kautsky.

Archives

Rossiiskii gosudarstvennyi arkhiv sotsialno-politicheskoi istorii (RGASPI; Russian State Archive of Socio-Political History), Moscow, Russia: Lenin's archive (Fond 2) Manuscripts. Documents of Lenin's family. Activities of Lenin.

Printed Sources

Haimson, Leopold. *The Russian Marxists and the Origins of Bolshevism* (Cambridge: Harvard University Press, 1955).
Harding, N. *Lenin's Political Thought*, 2 vols. (London:Macmillan, 1977–1981).
Pipes, Richard. (ed.). *The Unknown Lenin: From the Secret Archive* (New Haven: Yale University Press, 1996).
Service, Robert. *Lenin: A Biography* (Cambridge: Harvard University Press, 2000).
———. *Lenin: A Political Life*, 3 vols. (London: Macmillan, 1985–95).
Volkogonov, D. A. *Lenin: A New Biography* (New York: Free Press, 1994).

Eugene M. Avrutin

LEVI, PRIMO (1919–1987)

Primo Levi lived most of his life in the same apartment in which he was born on July 31, 1919, in Turin, Italy. Raised as an assimilated Jew with no real ties to religion, Levi grew up in a family devoted to books. He studied chemistry at the University of Turin, from which he received his doctorate in 1941. Meanwhile, in 1938, the Fascist regime in Italy had enacted a series of anti-Semitic regulations that, among other things, required the expulsion of Jews from universities. With great difficulty, Levi managed to complete his studies.

Following the Nazi invasion of northern Italy in 1943, Levi was deported to Auschwitz. He attributed his survival in part to his training as a chemist, to the kindness of a fellow inmate—an Italian bricklayer who supplied him with extra food—and to luck. His work in the synthetic rubber factory attached to the camp spared him from much of the harsh weather, physical labor, and ultimately the gas chambers that awaited most inmates of Auschwitz.

Following his liberation in 1945 and eight months spent as a refugee in Russia, Levi returned home to Turin and resumed his work as a chemist, married Lucia Morpurgo, and raised two children. He began to write in his spare time, and his experiences in Auschwitz became the source of a vivid and remarkable body of literature that continues to astonish readers today with its precise scientific perspective and its insights into the broader human condition.

In 1947, a small publisher issued Levi's memoir *Se questo è un uomo* (*Survival in Auschwitz*, 1959), which initially generated little interest. Not until its reissue in an expanded edition and the many translations that followed did the world recognize the profundity of Levi's work. He followed this with *La tregua* (*The Reawakening*, 1965), an account of the eight months among European refugees in Russia following his liberation. He retired from his career in chemistry in 1977 to pursue writing full time and produced the crowning achievement of his literary career, *Il sistema periodico*, (*The Periodic Table*, 1986). Using Mendeleyev's table of physical elements as his framework, Levi created a masterful series of autobiographical stories that linked the physical properties of matter with the psychological properties of the events he recounted.

Levi's unlikely career as a writer is rooted in his survival of the holocaust. "My uncommon experience as a concentration camp inmate and as a survivor has deeply influenced my later life and has turned me into a writer." In 1981, Levi published *La ricerca della ridici* (*The Search for Roots: A Personal Anthology*, 2001), a work that would "bring to light the possible traces of what has been read on what has been written." Among his recorded favorite writers were Joseph Conrad, **Thomas Mann,** Isaac Babel, Paul Célan, and **T. S. Eliot.** Levi's anthology also includes such varied sources of personal and literary inspiration as scientist and science fiction novelist Arthur C. Clarke, the Greek poet Homer, Dante Alighieri's *The Divine Comedy*, the Old Testament book of Job, and the French satirist and novelist François Rabelais, "to whom," Levi wrote, "I have been faithful for forty years without in the least resembling him or knowing exactly why." What links these seemingly disparate influences is, for Levi, a common tension. "More or less all show the effects of the fundamental dichotomies customary in the destiny of every conscious person" (Levi 2001, 8).

Archives

Lawrence Sheldon Rudner Papers, Special Collections Department, North Carolina State University Library, 218.6.22, notes, articles.

Printed Sources

Anissimov, Myriam. *Primo Levi: Tragedy of an Optimist*, Steve Cox (trans.), (New York: Overlook Press, 1999).

Homer, Frederic D. *Primo Levy and the Politics of Survival* (Columbia: University of Missouri Press, 2001).

Kremer, Roberta S. (ed.). *Memory and Mastery: Primo Levi as Writer and Witness* (Albany: State University of New York, 2001).

Levi, Primo. *The Search for Roots: A Personal Anthology*, Peter Forbes (trans.), (London: Allen Lane, 2001).

Patruno, Nicholas. *Understanding Primo Levi* (Columbia: University of South Carolina Press, 1995).

Philip Bader

LÉVI-STRAUSS, CLAUDE GUSTAVE (1908–)

Claude Lévi-Strauss, Belgian philosopher and anthropologist, was born on November 28, 1908, to a Jewish family in Brussels, Belgium. Lévi-Strauss spent his formative years in France where he attended a Parisian lycée and later the Sorbonne, where he studied philosophy. Following his formal education, Lévi-Strauss taught for several years in numerous provincial French schools before developing a deep interest in anthropology, which would remain with him for the rest of his life. With this new interest, Lévi-Strauss accepted the post of professor of sociology at Sao Paulo University in Brazil from 1935 to 1939, at which time he began his own research into the lives of primitives. When World War II erupted, Lévi-Strauss returned to France to serve in the French army's futile stand against the Nazis from 1939 to 1941. With the fall of France and his being Jewish, Lévi-Strauss was forced to flee to the United States where he had secured a teaching position at the New School for Social Research in New York (1942–45).

At the war's end, Lévi-Strauss returned to France, where he began to build his reputation as a researcher and thinker and became a leader in the structural anthropological school of thought while gaining a reputation as a teacher at the École Pratique des Hautes Etudes in Paris from 1950 to 1974 and at the College de France until 1982. Lévi-Strauss spent his life of writing and teaching espousing the utilization of structuralism when considering all aspects of human society, especially mankind's myths, about which he wrote extensively in his four-volume *Mythologiques* (1964, 1966, 1968, 1972).

Although considered an eclectic genius in his own right, Lévi-Strauss freely acknowledged the influences other thinkers had upon him. He credits the Austrian-born American anthropologist Robert Harry Lowie with turning the young Lévi-Strauss to ethnography, especially through his work with the culture of American Plains Indians in *Primitive Society* (1920) and in *The History of Ethnological Thought* (1937). It was through the influence of Lowie that Lévi-Strauss was introduced to theory of the unconscious in cultural phenomenon espoused by Franz Boas and to the investigations into the unconscious by Sigmund Freud.

Like many young aspiring anthropologists, Lévi-Strauss experienced the substantial intellectual sway of Émile Durkheim and his nephew Marcel Mauss during his student days in Paris. Most influential was Durkheim's journal *L'Année Sociologique*, which Mauss took over at his uncle's death. Both Durkheim and Mauss were concerned with primitives' developing an identity through their music and rites of mourning, a concept which they stressed as the thesis of their major collaboration *Primitive Classification* (1903). But it was when he arrived in New York for his teaching stint at the New School that Lévi-Strauss became aware of the two scholars who would formalize his perception of the structural construction and investigation of all anthropological concerns. The application of structuralism to abstract concepts was most clearly demonstrated in the works of Lévi-Strauss's teaching colleague and Russian linguist Roman Jakobson and Ferdinand de Saussure, both of which touted language as a system of abstract rules that could be investigated through structuralism just as any other human intellectual activity could.

Archives

Laboratoire D'Anthropologie Sociale, College de France, Paris. Contains most of his papers and manuscripts.
Musee de l'Homme, Paris. Fieldwork materials.

Printed Sources

Champagne, Roland A. *Claude Lévi-Strauss* (Boston: Twayne, 1987).
Henaff, Marcel. *Claude Lévi-Strauss and the Making of Structural Anthropology* (Minneapolis: University of Minnesota Press, 1998).
Lévi-Strauss, Claude. *Structural Anthropology* [1958], Monique Layton (trans.), (Chicago: University of Chicago Press, 1983). The seminal work in the Lévi-Strauss canon.

Tom Frazier

LEWIS, C. S. (1898–1963)

Clive Staples Lewis was born on November 29, 1898, near Belfast in Ireland. Clive decided to go by "Jack" when still young, and "C. S." became a pen name. When only nine, his mother died, and Jack was sent to a series of preparatory schools, ending with Malvern College. From 1914 to 1917, he studied with a private tutor, William Thompson Kirkpatrick, who recognized both his gifts and his limitations, writing to Lewis's father that "You'll make a writer or a scholar of him, but you'll not make anything else" (Lewis 1955, 183). He entered University College, Oxford, in April 1917 but was called up for military service soon after. Wounded at the Battle of Arras in April 1918, Lewis recovered in time to return to Oxford at the start of 1919. In 1924 he took a temporary post as lecturer at University College and was elected to a fellowship in Magdalen College in 1925, a position he held until 1954, when he accepted the Chair of Medieval and Renaissance English at Cambridge University. His first work on medieval literature, *The Allegory of Love* (1936), though now superceded in its particulars, opened up the academic study of emotion in literature. Lewis's scholarship contributed to establishing the continuity between medieval and Renaissance literature. While at Oxford, Lewis underwent a conversion to Christianity and returned to the Anglican confession of his youth. His books and essays on Christian living and apologetics have formed an ongoing and ecumenical following, which sees him as perhaps the twentieth century's best presenter of a "reasonable Christianity." Finally, his fiction continues to amuse and educate. Lewis married Joy Davidman Gresham in 1956; she died from cancer in 1960. Lewis taught until he suffered a heart attack in July 1963 and died later that year on November 22.

By the time he was eighteen, Lewis had read most of the classics of English literature from Spenser's *Faerie Queen* to Keats and Dickens and even the American Mark Twain, had mastered Norse, Greek, and Roman mythologies, and was beginning to read ancient and medieval philosophy in Greek and Latin. This classical background appears in all his works, perhaps most complexly in his retelling of the

Cupid and Psyche myth, *Till We Have Faces* (1956). At the age of 10 he read Milton's *Paradise Lost;* its continued impact on him is evidenced in his *Preface to "Paradise Lost,"* published in 1942. Stylistic and thematic aspects of the fantasy-romances of William Morris and George MacDonald are reflected in Lewis's allegorical *Narnia Chronicles;* indeed, MacDonald is portrayed as Lewis's mentor in his theological fantasy *The Great Divorce.* Lewis loved the science fiction of H. G. Wells (though not his naturalism), but it was David Lindsay's *Voyage to Arcturus* that revealed to him the imaginative possibility of the genre as a "spiritual adventure" (Sayer 1988, 153). The influence of both writers appears in Lewis's space trilogy *Out of the Silent Planet, Perelandra,* and *That Hideous Strength,* which is one of the first fictional works in which humankind is shown as more menacing than the extraterrestrials. The apologetic writings of G. K. Chesterton were particularly important for Lewis and are often quoted in his own essays. Besides these predecessors, Lewis was influenced by the participants in the "Inklings," the semi-formal philosophical and literary discussion group Lewis gathered together in Oxford, especially his older brother Warren H. Lewis, Charles Williams, and **J.R.R. Tolkien,** whose *Hobbit* and *Lord of the Rings* were first read in this group, as indeed were Warren's histories and Jack's novels.

Archives

The Lewis Papers, including 11 volumes compiled by W. H. Lewis. Buswell Memorial Library, Wheaton College, Wheaton, Illinois, with a copy at the Bodleian Library, Oxford, England.
Correspondence and Literary Manuscripts, Bodleian Library, Oxford, England.

Printed Sources

Cantor, Norman. *Inventing the Middle Ages: The Lives, Works, and Ideas of the Great Medievalists of the Twentieth Century* (New York: William Morrow, 1991). Assesses Lewis's scholarly impact.
Green, Roger Lancelyn, and Walter Hooper. *C. S. Lewis: a Biography,* rev. ed. (New York: Harcourt Brace & Company, 1994).
Lewis, C. S. *Surprised by Joy: The Shape of My Early Life* (New York: Harcourt Brace Jovanovich, 1955). Retells his progression from atheist to Christian believer; provides an account of literary influences to about 1931.
Sayer, George. *Jack: C. S. Lewis and His Times* (San Francisco: Harper & Row, 1988). Perhaps the most insightful biography to date.
Wilson, A. N. *C. S. Lewis: a Biography* (New York: W. W. Norton, 1990). Good biography from an unsentimental observer.

Richard R. Follett

LEWIS, JOHN LLEWELLYN (1880–1969)

John Lewis was born in Lucas County, Iowa, to Welsh immigrants. Lewis's father, Thomas, a coal miner in Lucas, was blacklisted for union-organizing activities, forcing the Lewis family to move repeatedly while John was young. He quit school before completing eighth grade and entered the workforce. The Lewis family returned to Lucas after the blacklists were removed and John briefly joined his father in the mines. After five years' traveling, Lewis returned to Lucas to become a labor organizer. He married Myrta Bell in 1907, and then Lewis moved his entire family to the coal town of Panama, Illinois, where he quickly moved up the ranks of the United Mine Workers (UMW) local. Lewis's activities in Panama caught the attention of American Federation of Labor (AFL) President **Samuel Gompers,** for whom Lewis worked as an AFL organizer from 1911 until 1916. Lewis left the AFL to work at UMW headquarters in Indianapolis, where he rose from statistician to vice president and then to acting president in 1919. He was elected UMW president in 1921 and consolidated union power throughout the 1920s. The election of **Franklin Delano Roosevelt** and the institution of his New Deal programs sparked a reversal of early Depression-era union fortunes. Lewis successfully portrayed himself as a tough but moderate leader of an increasingly militant union and became the nation's most visible labor leader and a potential candidate for the presidency. Lewis broke from the AFL and cofounded the Conference of Industrial Organizations (CIO) in 1935. As CIO leader, Lewis was instrumental in the success of the United Auto Workers' (UAW) sit-down strike against General Motors in 1937. After 1937 Lewis's overall prominence in the labor movement waned, but he remained the most visible national labor leader, breaking with Roosevelt, leading a highly criticized UMW strike in 1943, and blasting mine safety standards in the aftermath of mine disasters in Centralia, Illinois, and West Frankfort, Illinois, in 1947 and 1950. Lewis retained the UMW presidency until retiring in 1960.

Lewis's limited formal education belies his gift for oration and writing. There is disagreement on the part of Lewis's biographers as to how he developed his command of language, evidenced by his book *The Miners' Fight for American Standards.* One biographer argues that Lewis's wife, Myrta, "organized Lewis's reading habits" and was "the most important single force in the life of John L. Lewis" (Alinsky 1949, 17). Other biographers reject this notion, pointing to Lewis's involvement with productions at the Lucas Opera House and citing *Bartlett's Familiar Quotations* and the Bible as Lewis's most consistent references. According to these biographers, when he was older Lewis's primary reading fare included military history, westerns, mysteries, and the magazine *American Heritage* (Dubofsky and Van Tine 1986, 16). Certainly Lewis's attention to labor issues stemmed largely from his own father's activities. One definite influence in this area was Samuel Gompers, whom Lewis seems to have viewed as both a model of what a powerful labor leader could be and also as a contrast from which to develop his own leadership qualities. In terms of his approach to organizing, however, Lewis developed his own style. By the time of Lewis's ascendancy to the UMW presidency, he had already developed the intellectual basis that would undergird his actions over the next three decades.

Archives

State Historical Society of Wisconsin, Madison: The John L. Lewis papers, 1879–1969.
United Mine Workers of America Archives, Washington, D.C.: official UMW and CIO papers of John L. Lewis.

Printed Sources

Alinsky, Saul. *John L. Lewis: An Unauthorized Biography* (New York: G. P. Putnam's Sons, 1949).
Dubofsky, Melvyn, and Warren Van Tine. *John L. Lewis: A Biography,* abridged ed. (Urbana: University of Illinois Press, 1986).
Lewis, John L. *The Miners' Fight for American Standards* (Indianapolis: The Bell Publishing Company, 1925).

Phil Huckelberry

LEWIS, SINCLAIR (1885–1951)

Sinclair Lewis was born and reared in Sauk Centre, Minnesota. He attended preparatory school at the Oberlin Academy in Oberlin, Ohio, for six months (1902–3) before entering Yale University (1903–6; 1907–8). Lewis left Yale at the beginning of his senior year, although he eventually returned and graduated. During this hiatus from school he engaged in a variety of tasks, including living and working for a month at Helicon Hall, the communal home established near Englewood, New Jersey, by Upton Sinclair. There were already indications of the direction that Lewis's life would take. On a visit to Sauk Centre in the summer of 1905, he envisioned writing a novel that would be a biting exposé of life in small-town America. The novel was published as *Main Street* in 1920. It was a popular success, and it established the trajectory of his literary contributions. In his heyday, Lewis became known as a capable satirist, one who could wield his pen to expose the fictions of life in twentieth-century America. He followed with other novels, including *Babbitt* (1922), which was a critique of self-promoting middle-class values, *Arrowsmith* (1925), which undermined the supposed objectivity of science and medicine, and *Elmer Gantry* (1927), which gave an unflattering portrait of American fundamentalism. Lewis was nominated for the Pulitzer Prize in 1926, although he declined to accept it, suggesting that his works were designed to undermine dominant images of American life rather than to uphold them, which the award was intended to recognize. In 1930, he became the first American to receive the Nobel Prize for literature.

As a boy, Lewis enjoyed the romances of Thomas Malory and Sir Walter Scott (Grebstein 1962, 20), and he remained an avid fan of Charles Dickens, from whom he gained an early appreciation of social criticism and whom he admired for his expert creation of lively characters (Light 1975, 21–22). Lewis likewise venerated the novelist H. G. Wells, whom he considered "the greatest living novelist" (Light 1975, 22). Lewis especially enjoyed Wells's *The History of Mr. Polly* (1910) and *Tono-Bungay* (1909), which Lewis identified as having a more profound influence on him than any other work of fiction (Light 1975, 23). Wells's reform impulses are evident in these novels and Lewis's early works reflect a similar style and themes, indicating the enormity of Wells's influence. Another significant literary influence on Lewis was his contemporary, H. L. Mencken (1880–1956), to whom Lewis dedicated *Elmer Gantry* "with profound admiration." Mencken, who distrusted "Middle America" and took issue with many of the same subjects as Lewis, including the Midwest, preachers, and politicians, became a role model for him. In the final years of Lewis's life, Mencken urged him to revive his flagging career by re-focusing on his satirical gifts, suggesting that the United States "swarms" with subjects, such as bogus experts and idiotic labor leaders, for him to explore (Light 1975, 26).

Archives

Beinecke Rare Book and Manuscript Library, Yale University, New Haven, Conn.
Harry Ransom Humanities Research Center, University of Texas, Austin, Texas.
St. Cloud State University Archives, St. Cloud, Minn.

Printed Sources

Bloom, Harold (ed.). *Modern Critical Views: Sinclair Lewis* (New York: Chelsea House Publishers, 1987).

Grebstein, Sheldon Norman. *Sinclair Lewis* (New York: Twayne, 1962).

Light, Martin. *The Quixotic Vision of Sinclair Lewis* (West Lafayette, Ind.: Purdue University Press, 1975). An excellent source for Lewis's literary influences. Light includes an informative chapter entitled "Reading."

Lingeman, Richard. *Sinclair Lewis: Rebel from Main Street* (New York: Random House, 2002).

Schorer, Mark. *Sinclair Lewis* (Minneapolis: University of Minnesota Press, 1963).

Scott Lupo

LINDBERGH, CHARLES AUGUSTUS (1902–1974)

Charles Lindbergh was born in Detroit, Michigan, the only son of Charles August Lindbergh, a lawyer and liberal Republican congressman for Minnesota, and his wife, Evangeline Lodge Land, a science teacher and daughter of a prominent Detroit dentist. An undistinguished student, from the age of eight Lindbergh almost annually switched schools in Washington, D.C., California, and Little Falls, Minnesota. Entering the University of Wisconsin at Madison in 1920 as an engineering student, Lindbergh excelled only in the Reserve Officer Training Corps and was expelled in 1922. After some time barnstorming, Lindbergh joined the Army Air Service, acquiring systematic study habits and graduating first in his class at the Kelly Field Advanced Flying School, and then became an airmail pilot. On May 21, 1927, Lindbergh instantaneously became a national hero and international celebrity when he completed the first nonstop transatlantic flight, from New York to Paris, in thirty-three hours in his monoplane the *Spirit of St. Louis.*

In 1929 Lindbergh married Anne Spencer Morrow, the literary daughter of a prominent New York investment banker and Republican politician. Lindbergh subsequently undertook pioneering flights in the Americas, Asia, Europe, and Africa to develop commercial aviation routes and was an early supporter of research in rocket technology. His growing interest in medical science led him to develop a perfusion pump, whose invention facilitated future organ transplants. Tragedy struck in 1932 when the Lindberghs' two-year-old son Charles was kidnapped and murdered, impelling them to live in Britain and France until 1939. In the later 1930s Lindbergh believed German airpower greatly surpassed that of any other European state and feared Britain and France could not prevail in a European conflict, which would only destroy Western civilization. Lindbergh strongly supported his country's aviation defense buildup, but—perhaps influenced by his father's vigorous World War I opposition to intervention—when World War II began he joined the anti-interventionist America First Committee, which opposed United States aid to the Allied nations or entry into the war. Ill-considered speeches permanently damaged his reputation, generating lingering charges he was anti-Semitic and pro-Nazi. Denied a commission after Pearl Harbor, as a civilian Lindbergh developed and tested military aircraft and in 1944 flew 50 combat missions in the South Pacific. In his final decades Lindbergh remained deeply involved in medical and aviation research, the development of commercial flying, and conservation.

A brilliantly innovative flyer and scientist, Lindbergh was a convinced rationalist without political acumen or a sense of self-preservation, traits his wife later attributed to the fact that he "was not a great reader" (Herrmann 1992, 322). Lindbergh spoke and understood no language but English but in his teens devoured tales of Arctic exploration, flying sagas, and the Yukon frontier poems of

Robert W. Service, unsophisticated tastes that embarrassed his Smith College–educated fiancée, herself a respected writer, as Lindbergh himself would also eventually become. Lindbergh's marriage greatly extended his literary range; visiting his younger sister-in-law's freshman English class, he apparently commented knowledgeably on *Paradise Lost* (Milton 1993, 208). In the 1930s the Social Darwinist outlook and writings of Lindbergh's Nobel Prize–winning scientific collaborator, Dr. Alexis Carrel, apparently reinforced his almost obsessive beliefs on race, eugenics, and the need to preserve Western civilization against communism and barbarism. Carrel's surprising mysticism perhaps inspired Lindbergh's similarly paradoxical interest in the supernatural and nonrational. While he believed "no one culture or religion had a monopoly on truth" (Berg 1998, 558), the teachings of both Jesus Christ and Lao Tzu profoundly influenced Lindbergh, and from the 1930s onward he explored the tenets of most major faiths and thinkers, featuring a medley of readings from several at his funeral. Lindbergh's later interest in conservation was also fueled both by his increasingly profound regard for the writings of David Henry Thoreau and by his growing feeling that the technological advances he had helped pioneer were in numerous respects environmentally and socially detrimental.

Archives

Yale University Library, New Haven, Conn.: Lindbergh's personal papers, together with those of his wife.
Missouri Historical Society, St. Louis, Mo.: Lindbergh's papers relating to aviation and rocket research, 1927–33.

Printed Sources

Berg, A. Scott. *Lindbergh* (New York: Putnam, 1998). Best biographical source.
Herrmann, Dorothy. *Anne Morrow Lindbergh: A Gift for Life* (New York: Ticknor & Fields, 1992).
Lindbergh, Charles A. *Autobiography of Values* (New York: Harcourt Brace Jovanovich, 1977).
———. *The Wartime Journals of Charles A. Lindbergh* (New York: Harcourt Brace Jovanovich, 1970).
Milton, Joyce. *Loss of Eden: A Life of Charles and Anne Morrow Lindbergh* (New York: Harper Collins, 1993).

Priscilla Roberts

LIPPMANN, WALTER (1889–1974)

Born in New York City to Jacob and Daisy Lippmann, second-generation highly assimilated German Jews, Walter had a privileged childhood of wealth, European travel, and education by private tutors. The first chapter, entitled "The Only Child," in Ronald Steel's biography, *Walter Lippmann and the American Century* (1980), clearly reveals the influences on Lippmann's life. In 1915 he remarked that a "man's philosophy is his autobiography; you may read in it the story of the conflict with life." In time his conflict consisted of politics and political philosophy, the search for the good society and human control over the forces of modernism. Because of his cosmopolitan lifestyle, Lippmann was comfortable with gentile norms. While scholars have debated Judaism's impact, Lippmann was never concerned about having a Jewish heritage.

He entered Harvard as a member of the famous class of 1910. From his early years, Lippmann was an idealist tempered by twentieth-century war, politics, and economic depression. William James and George Santayana shaped Lippmann's undergraduate experiences: James's pragmatism liberated him from previous dogma and inclined him toward instrumental reason; Santayana provided an aristocratic attitude based on philosophical materialism and skepticism. Lippmann served as Santayana's teaching assistant. Later Lippmann wrote, "I love James more than any other man I ever saw but increasingly I find Santayana inescapable." Santayana's influence was lifelong.

After leaving Harvard, Lippmann was involved in socialist politics. He wrote about two dozen books of social and cultural criticism. Over the years they were critical of mass democracy and a civic morality that bordered on ethical relativism. Lippmann was a speechwriter for the American delegation to the Peace Conference at end of the Great War. He helped write President **Woodrow Wilson**'s Fourteen Point Speech. He was a columnist for several New York newspapers; he did not write news stories. His greatest influence came from his more reflective pieces on the varied significance of passing events. He was a close student of American life. Married twice, he never had children.

Lippmann began his syndicated column, "Today and Tomorrow," in 1931 for the *New York Herald-Tribune*. The relationship lasted for nearly forty years. Passing judgment on politics, he correctly noted the development of something before it was generally recognized, such as the cold war and the policy disaster that was the Vietnam War. His initial low opinion of **Franklin D. Roosevelt** was an example of one his few errors in judgment. While celebrating American ideals, the nation's tendency toward moral self-indulgence and smug acceptance of conventional wisdom disappointed him. In his way, his writings prepared the American public to understand the world and the cost of global leadership.

Generally, Lippmann's books dealt with the conjunction of political theory, politics, and philosophy. From *The Stakes of Diplomacy* (1915) to *Essays in Public Philosophy* (1955), he moved from pragmatism to higher law tradition. He intellectually migrated from pragmatism's liberal reform to the transcendent conservatism of natural law. His core concern was the legitimacy and duty that constituted authority, an order that transcended mere historicism. Lippmann's desire for a meaningful scheme of values endeared him to his readers. In that desire he combined the wisdom of his two major influences on his life, William James and George Santayana.

Archives

The Lippmann Papers are in the Sterling Library, Yale University, New Haven, Connecticut, a massive collection of original manuscripts and letters.

Printed Sources

Blum, D. Steven. *Walter Lippmann, Cosmopolitanism in the Century of Total War* (Ithaca: Cornell University Press, 1984). A brief, thoughtful analysis of Lippmann's views on foreign policy.

Diggins, John Patrick. "From Pragmatism to Natural Law: Walter Lippmann's Quest for the Foundations of Legitimacy," *Political Theory* 19 (November 1991), 519–37. In a close critical analysis, Lippmann's intellectual odyssey is traced from reformist liberalism to a conservative defense of an eternal verity. At the end as a conservative, Lippmann defended liberty and the course of reform.

Forcey, Charles. *The Crossroads of Liberalism: Croly, Weyl, Lippmann and the Progressive Era, 1900–1925* (New York: Oxford, 1961). Deals with Lippmann's contribution to the *New Republic* magazine and its influence on future liberal reform.

Steel, Ronald. *Walter Lippmann and the American Century* (Boston: Atlantic Monthly Press, 1980). Nearly a definitive biography.

Donald K. Pickens

LLOSA, MARIO VARGAS (1936–)

Mario Vargas Llosa was born in Arequipa, Peru. He spent his early childhood in Bolivia, returning to Peru at the age of 10. His strict father enrolled him in a Lima military academy, hoping to cure young Mario of his love for literature and poetry. However, Vargas Llosa continued to read and write at a frenzied pace. Some of his short stories appeared in the late fifties, garnering the young college graduate an invitation to Paris from a French literary magazine. For the next decade, Vargas Llosa would live in Paris while he established his career as an author. His first novel, *The Time of the Hero*, appeared in 1963. *The Green House* (1966) and *Conversation in the Cathedral* (1969) followed, winning Vargas Llosa recognition as an important Latin American writer and intellectual.

With other intellectuals from developing countries, Vargas Llosa shared a generational passion for indigenous culture and socialist concerns about third world exploitation and social injustice at home. However, even during this time, Vargas Llosa identified with the plight of the human condition inside political rhetoric—a concern that ideological excesses could impinge upon human rights. This position brought Vargas Llosa into disfavor with the more extreme elements of the Left.

Vargas Llosa returned to Peru in 1974, where he continues to make his main residence. Works that followed included *Captain Pantoja and the Special Service* (1973) and *Aunt Julia and the Scriptwriter* (1977). Perhaps his best-known book, *The War at the End of the World*, appeared in 1981. By the late 1970s to early 1980s, Vargas Llosa had secured a place as one of the preeminent figures of the Latin American literary boom and as one of the world's few truly international literary figures. Always concerned with the state of his native Peru, Vargas Llosa became more and more involved with political activity. This engagement culminated in his running for the presidency of Peru in 1990. After losing the election to Alberto Fujimori, Vargas Llosa recounted the experience in his book *A Fish in the Water* (1993). Vargas Llosa left politics and returned to his life as a writer.

Like many writers from the underdeveloped world, Vargas Llosa was attracted to intellectuals who stressed the importance of one's indigenous culture. Vargas Llosa's native heroes were essayist José Carlos Mariátegui, ethnologist José María Arguedas, poet César Moro, and playwright Sebastián Salazar Bondy. The Marxist and nativist convictions of their works reflected the deep convictions of many intellectual Peruvians. In Vargas Llosa's case, the existentialist writings of **Jean-Paul Sartre** and **Albert Camus** provided the necessary human element to overly strident political discourse. In addition to politically committed literature, Vargas Llosa also loved the world literary masterpieces he read so avidly in his youth. The young bibliophile Vargas Llosa absorbed virtually the entire canon of classic nineteenth- and twentieth-century literature, especially the entertaining adventure stories of French writer Alexandre Dumas (more, perhaps, for their value as expert entertainment than depth). Among more contemporary writers, **William Faulkner** (*The Wild Palms* and the entire Yoknapatawpha saga) deeply impressed the young Peruvian. Vargas Llosa's lifelong fascination with nineteenth-century French novelist Gustave Flaubert and his classic work *Madame Bovary* is a favorite topic of discussion with the author himself (see Vargas Llosa's own *Perpetual Orgy*). Vargas Llosa's work may be described as a combination of Peruvian subject material within highly sophisticated literary forms of international origin.

Archives

Mario Vargas Llosa Papers, Firestone Library, Princeton University.

Printed Sources

Castro-Klaren, Sara. *Understanding Mario Vargas Llosa* (Columbia, S.C.: University of South Carolina Press, 1990).

Kristal, Efrain. *Temptation of the Word: The Novels of Mario Vargas Llosa* (Nashville, Tenn.: Vanderbilt University Press, 1998).

Vargas Llosa, Mario. *A Fish in the Water*, Helen Lane (trans.), (New York: Faber and Faber, 1993).

———. *The Perpetual Orgy: Gustave Flaubert and Madame Bovary*, Helen Lane (trans.), (New York: Farrar, Straus and Giroux, 1986).

Charles Allan

LLOYD GEORGE, DAVID (1863–1945)

David Lloyd George was born in Manchester, England, of Welsh parents. His father, a schoolmaster, died in 1864. He grew up in North Wales in the bilingual home of his uncle, a shoemaker and lay preacher, and attended a National (Anglican) School from 1866 to 1877. Raised as a Baptist, he became an agnostic at 18 but throughout life was inspired by Nonconformism. He qualified as a solicitor in 1884, practicing law in North Wales until elected to Parliament in 1890 as a Liberal. Previously a radical backbencher and opponent of the Boer War (1899–1902), in 1905 he became trade minister in the Liberal cabinet and in 1908 chancellor of the exchequer. He sponsored many reforms and is recognized as one of the founders of the welfare state. In the First World War Lloyd George was munitions minister (1915–16) and war minister (1916), but in 1916 broke with his Liberal colleagues over policy and became prime minister of a coalition cabinet (1916–22). Famed as "the man who won the war," he represented Great Britain at the 1919 Paris Peace Conference. Out of office he remained politically active, leading the Liberal party between 1926 and 1931. He became Earl Lloyd-George of Dwyfor in 1945.

Belittled by university-trained politicians for his modest formal education, Lloyd George was in fact well-read. Tutored by his autodidact uncle and a cultured schoolmaster, he avidly absorbed geography, history, biography, and literature. Notes of his youthful reading are preserved in his papers.

From his deceased father Lloyd George inherited a substantial library, supplemented by his uncle's well-stocked bookshelves. In childhood and adolescence he read William Shakespeare, John Bunyan, Daniel Defoe, Edward Gibbon, Sir Walter Scott, Thomas Babington Macaulay, and Ralph Waldo Emerson, among many others. The American Civil War and the life of Abraham Lincoln were special interests. Iconoclast Thomas Carlyle, skeptic Ernest Renan, and positivist Frederic Harrison influenced his religious and philosophical thinking. He was thoroughly familiar with the Bible, however skeptical of its veracity, and could accurately quote scores of passages.

Young Lloyd George was familiar with the writings of social thinkers from Karl Marx to John Ruskin to Henry George, as well as eighteenth- and nineteenth-century economists including Adam Smith and John Stuart Mill. Later, sociologist Seebowm Rowntree and radical journalist/politician Charles Masterman influenced his thinking on social issues. Lloyd George's best-loved work of fiction was the socially conscious novel *Les Miserables* by Victor Hugo, a dog-eared cheap edition of which he carried with him. He was also fond of novelists Charles Dickens, Alexandre Dumas, Charles Reade, Charles Kingsley, and Robert Louis Stevenson. He admitted to being bored by Jane Austen, Anthony Trollope, and George Eliot and thought Joseph Conrad gloomy. He enjoyed traditional Welsh poetry. His preferred English-language poets were John Milton, Robert Burns, and Lord Byron, but he expressly disliked the twentieth-century poets Edith Sitwell and **T. S. Eliot.**

In Lloyd George's later life, the serious reading of his formative years was increasingly replaced by recreational reading of popular fiction, especially mystery and adventure novels and Wild West tales. The American western novelist Zane Grey was a favorite.

Archives

Lloyd George Papers, House of Lords Record Office, London. Papers from the 1880s to 1945, including reading notes and jottings.

Lloyd George Papers, National Library of Wales, Aberystwyth. Correspondence and notebooks, 1870s to 1940s.

Printed Sources

Cregier, Don M. *Bounder from Wales: Lloyd George's Career Before the First World War* (Columbia, Mo.: University of Missouri Press, 1976).

George, W. R. P. *The Making of Lloyd George* (London: Faber, 1976).

Rowland, Peter. *Lloyd George* (London: Barrie & Jenkins, 1975).

Don M. Cregier

LONERGAN, BERNARD (1904–1984)

Bernard Lonergan was born in Buckingham, Quebec, Canada, in 1904 of anglophone Catholic-convert parents. After studying at Loyola College in Montreal, he entered the Society of Jesus in 1922 at Guelph, Ontario, studying at Heythorp College, the University of London, England, and the Gregorian University, Rome. He was ordained to the priesthood in 1936, earned a doctorate at the Gregorian in 1940, and taught theology at the Collège de L'Immaculée Conception, Montréal (1940–47); Regis College, Toronto (1947–53, 1965–75); the Gregorian University, Rome (1953–65); and was Stillman Professor at Harvard University (1971–72). In 1957 he published his most important book, *Insight: A Study of Human Understanding*, and in 1972 his *Method in Theology*. He died in 1984. Working from within a form of the neo-Thomistic tradition often described as transcendental Thomism, Lonergan attempted to develop an epistemology that would take seriously the Kantian turn and at the same time afford a place for metaphysical speculation.

Although first trained according to the philosophic methods of the Spanish Thomist Francisco Suarez, then much in use among the Jesuits, Lonergan was early attentive to the work of the English thinker John Henry Newman, in particular the latter's epistomological study, *A Grammar of Assent* (1870), a work focused on the factual and empirical nature of human thinking and the manner by which human persons come to certitude in the use of their "illative sense" and that insisted on the moral and religious dimension of all human knowing. Shortly after his first engagement with Newman at Heythorp College, Lonergan undertook a careful examination of Plato's theory of ideas through a careful study of John Alexander Stewart's work on the Greek philosopher; in 1933 he was much influenced by his reading of Augustine's Cassiacum dialogues and two years later a review of Christopher Dawson. At this time Lonergan took up Aquinas's *Summa Theologica* once again, but now in the context of studies he had read by the Dutch Jesuit, Peter Hoenen, and his American confrere, Leo W. Keeler, the former leading him to reflect more closely on Thommasio de Vio Cajetan's interpretation of Thomas, the latter directing attention to Thomas's view of judgment in human knowledge. Among all the Thomists he studied, however, the most influential was the Belgian Jesuit, Joseph Maréchal, a figure of primary importance for the development of Transcendental Thomism in general, whose work *Le point de départ de la métaphysique: leçons sur le développement historique et theorique du problème de la connaissance* (5 vols., 1923–47), a work which attempted to overcome the seeming divisions between Thomas and Kant.

Archives

Heythorp College, London.
Pontifical Gregorian University, Rome.
Lonergan Research Institute, Regis College, Toronto, Ontario.
Lonergan Institute, Boston College, Boston, Mass.

Printed Sources

The fullest bibliography of primary works is available in the ongoing work of Terry J. Tekippe (http://ARC.TZO.COM/PADRE/pri.htm). For a detailed secondary bibliography see the regular updates in the *Lonergan Studies Newsletter* and the electronic version (http://www.lonergan.on.ca/bib/LSN_Bib_1980_to_2000.pdf).
Crowe, Frederick E. *Lonergan* (London: Geoffrey Chapman, 1992).
Liddy, Richard. *The Transforming Light: Intellectual Conversion in the Early Lonergan* (Collegeville, Minn.: Liturgical Press, 1993).
Lonergan, Bernard J. F. *The Collected Works of Bernard Lonergan*, Frederick Crowe and Robert M. Doran (eds.), 25 vols. (Toronto: Published by University of Toronto Press for Lonergan Research Institute of Regis College, 1988–).
Meynell, Hugo Anthony. *An Introduction to the Philosophy of Bernard Lonergan* (Toronto: University of Toronto Press, 1991).
———. *The Theology of Bernard Lonergan* (Atlanta, Ga.: Scholars Press, 1986).
Stebbins, J. Michael. *The Divine Initiative: Grace, World-Order, and Human Freedom in the Early Writings of Bernard Lonergan* (Toronto: University of Toronto Press, 1995).
Tracy, David. *The Achievement of Bernard Lonergan* (New York: Herder and Herder, 1970).
Tyrrell, Bernard. *Bernard Lonergan's Philosophy of God* (Notre Dame, Ind.: University of Notre Dame Press, 1974).

Peter C. Erb

LUCE, HENRY ROBINSON (1898–1967)

Henry Luce was born in Tengchow, China, the son of Presbyterian missionaries. At 10, he was sent to a British boarding school at Chefoo on the China coast. Luce entered the Hotchkiss School in Lakeville, Connecticut, at 15. He graduated from Yale and then studied history at Oxford University. Creator of *Time, Life,* and *Fortune* magazines, Luce at his peak had a weekly audience of more than 40 million people and arguably influenced his era more than any other publisher. Luce's news magazines were innovative in that they aimed to sift through the facts for their readers by summarizing and explaining events and trends in politics, business, arts, and sciences. Luce's journalistic formula spread to competing news services in radio and television and spawned a transformation in American news media from information to synthesis. Luce is controversial because he believed objective reporting is impossible and encouraged his writers and editors to express his own views in their articles. *Time* often reflected his personal leanings, which were Republican, Christian, staunchly anticommunist, and in favor of U.S. intervention in global politics.

At an early age Luce consumed books in the family's substantial library and read the many American periodicals to which the Luces subscribed (Baughman 1987, 11). Having been exposed to Sunday sermons of the mission elders, he excelled at a family parlor game based on the Biblical scriptures (Kobler 1968, 25) and one Christmas young Luce received at his request "an American Revised Standard Bible, sets of Shakespeare and the Victorian novelists" (Kobler 1968, 26). He was a devoted reader of the boy's magazine *St. Nicholas,* to which he submitted a letter-to-the-editor at age 10. Luce at 14 was criticizing James Bryce's *American Commonwealth* for being out-of-date and recommending periodicals to his father (Luce to parents, January 26, 1913, McCormick Papers; Baughman 1987, 14). While at Hotchkiss, Luce wrote a paper in which he praised Benjamin Franklin's *Autobiography.* "The ardent way in which he strove was the secret to his own personal and moral uplift," wrote Luce (school theme attached to letter to parents, November 4, 1913, Luce Family Correspondence; Baughman 1987, 14). Luce would refer to and quote Franklin throughout his publishing career. In a speech at the Franklin Award dinner in New York on January 18, 1954, he said, "When I was first introduced to [Franklin] at school by a very dull teacher, I was appalled by the narrow and thrifty maxims of *Poor Richard.* Later I came to know the brilliant, versatile 18th-century mind, questing, restless and yet serene, the master of all trades—printer, editor, publisher . . . and—after his own relaxed fashion, Christian." Longtime Luce writer and editor John Jessup described his boss as "all his life a steady reader in many fields, especially popular fiction, theology, history and political philosophy" (Luce 1969, 6). A well-worn Bible was always upon Luce's bedside table, yet his favorite hero of legend was Prometheus, a man who defied the gods. Luce's attempts to reconcile Christian humility with personal ambition and Christian mysticism with scientific reason are recurrent themes in his speeches and writings. He was interested in theological efforts to modernize the idea of God and was attracted to the quasi- and liberal Christian philosophies of William Ernest Hocking, **Paul Tillich,** Arnold Toynbee, Gerald Heard, and John Courtney Murray. He introduced Toynbee's *A Study of History* to a mass audience in *Life Magazine* in 1948. Teilhard de Chardin came closest to a scientific model of Christian hope for Luce. Luce often quoted Cardinal Manning's assertion that politics is a branch of morality. Luce often quoted **Ortega y Gasset**'s *The Revolt of the Masses* in the 1930s, and, in emphasizing the difficult choices facing civilization during World War II, his favorite quotations were from **Alfred North Whitehead.** Later he repeatedly quoted Walt Whitman. Luce read Karl Marx, **V. I. Lenin, Max Weber,** and the Christian Socialists, but he revered the American founding fathers above all political thinkers and heralded Alexander Hamilton's *Federalist Papers* as containing universal political truths. In the mid-1960s Luce yearned for a new U.S. policy toward China and often countered Rudyard Kipling's dictum that "East is East and West is West, and never the twain shall meet" with hopes of cooperation and communication between the United States and China. **Walter Lippman**'s writing on the state of journalism greatly influenced Luce and the cofounder of *Time Magazine*, Briton Hadden. Lippman asserted that journalism needed to be more analytical. Luce and Hadden showed Lippman their prototype of *Time* and often quoted him extensively when describing the magazine's mission.

Archives

Time Inc. Archives, Time-Life Building, New York, New York. Interoffice memoranda, Luce letters and speeches, business documents and historical data. Restricted access.

McCormick Papers, State Historical Society of Wisconsin, Madison. Luce letters between Henry and family and between Henry and family benefactor Nettie Fowler McCormick.

Printed Sources

Baughman, James. *Henry R. Luce and the Rise of the American News Media* (Boston: Twayne Publishers, 1987). Luce biography containing the most references to Luce's reading practices.

Herzstein, Robert. *Henry R. Luce: A Political Portrait of the Man Who Created the American Century* (New York: Charles Scribner's Sons, 1994).

Kobler, John. *Luce: His Time, Life and Fortune* (New York: Doubleday and Company Inc., 1968). Contains several references to childhood reading practices, without citations.

Luce, Henry. *The Ideas of Henry Luce*, John Jessup (ed.), (New York: Atheneum, 1969). A collection of Luce's speeches, put into historical and biographical context by Jessup.

Swanberg, W. A. *Luce and His Empire* (New York: Charles Scribner's Sons, 1972). Contains numerous reprints of Luce family correspondence.

Richard N. Swanson

LUDENDORFF, ERICH (1865–1937)

Erich Ludendorff was born in a small town outside of Posen in eastern Prussia to a poor but socially prominent family. Ludendorff began his education in the local school before deciding on a military career. He attended Cadet School in Plön in 1877 and concluded the training at Berlin-Lichterfelde in 1880. Ludendorff continued his education at the War Academy in Berlin between 1893 and 1897 before beginning his meteoric rise in the General Staff. Ludendorff was known as an excellent student but a poor athlete. He became quartermaster general during the First World War and shared responsibility for the overall war effort with Field Marshal **Paul von Hindenburg** between 1916 and 1918. Whereas Hindenburg survived the war as a sympathetic figure, Ludendorff was shattered by the collapse in 1918 and became radicalized by the experience. Ludendorff believed he was made the scapegoat for the military defeat and the ensuing revolution. After returning from exile in Scandinavia, Ludendorff began what can be called his second career as a right-wing revolutionary and *völkisch* ideologue. Ludendorff distinguished himself as an early supporter of the Nazi Party and a prolific author of racist literature throughout the Weimar period.

Like Hindenburg, Ludendorff revealed no real discernible intellectual interest outside of military affairs during his career. Ludendorff lived a Spartan life with his wife, Margarethe. After the war, however, the intellectual influences on Ludendorff can only be described as poisonous. Ludendorff was perennially involved in putschist conspiracies against the Weimar Republic. These plots endangered his wife, whom Ludendorff began to view as a hindrance to his political battles. Ludendorff lived in Munich, the hot bed of *völkisch* radicalism in the 1920's, where he was revered by younger personalities such as **Adolf Hitler** and *Freikorps* commander Hermann Ehrhardt. The person who influenced Ludendorff the most during the postwar years was a widow living in the town next to him. Mathilde Kemnitz studied medicine at the University of Freiburg where she became interested in genetics. A devout racist, Kemnitz believed strongly in the tenets of eugenics and gravitated naturally to the National Socialist Party. Kemnitz introduced Ludendorff to the racial ideas of Houston Stewart Chamberlain, whose *Foundations of the Twentieth Century* (1899) delineated the differences between the races. Chamberlain's pseudoscience lauded the Aryan race and confirmed that Jews were the most dangerous race. For an embittered man who looked for scapegoats while believing himself to be one, Kemnitz's anti-Semitism made sense to Ludendorff. In 1926 Ludendorff divorced his wife at the age of sixty-one and married Kemnitz. They lived in her house and together published dozens of anti-Semitic pamphlets. Ludendorff and his guru Kemnitz feared international forces, specifically the unholy trinity of Jews, Freemasons, and the Catholic Church. Ludendorff, who more than likely was mentally ill by the late 1920's, began to attack former allies for their supposed links to one or more of the trinity. Ludendorff accused the veterans' group *Stahlhelm* of harboring Freemasons and Hitler of joining forces with "Rome."

Archives

Nachlass Erich Ludendorff (N 77) Bundesarchiv-Militärarchiv Freiburg, Germany. Contains an index of Ludendorff's racist and political writings, along with some original copies. Unfortunately, Ludendorff's personal papers remain in control of the family and can only be accessed with written permission. Ludendorff's official correspondence is found in several record groups in Freiburg.

Printed Sources

Goodspeed, D. J. *Ludendorff: Soldier, Dictator, Revolutionary* (London: Rupert Hart-Davis, 1966).

Parkinson, Roger. *Tormented Warrior: Ludendorff and the Supreme Command* (New York: Stein and Day, 1978).

Tschuppik, Karl. *The Tragedy of a Military Mind*, W. H. Johnson (trans.), (New York: Houghton Mifflin Co., 1932).

Brian Crim

LUKÁCS, GYÖRGY (1885–1971)

György, or Georg, Lukács, the son of a self-made Jewish financier in Budapest, Hungary, was a melancholy boy, barely communicating with his mother or brother and only superficially with his father and sister. He always felt alienated from his family's bourgeois society and resisted their conventional philistinism. They preached success in business, did not support his intellectual aspirations, and generally did not take him seriously. He made no friends but escaped by reading the literature of Europe and America. At the age of nine he adored Hungarian prose translations of Homer's *Iliad* and James Fenimore Cooper's *The Last of the Mohicans* and soon thereafter Mark Twain's *Tom Sawyer* and *Huckleberry Finn*. As a teenager he read Berthold Auerbach, Charles Baudelaire, Gustave Flaubert, **Gerhart Hauptmann,** Friedrich Hebbel, Henrik Ibsen, John Keats, Gottfried Keller, Max Nordau, William Shakespeare, Percy Bysshe Shelley, Johann Friedrich von Schiller, Algernon Swinburne, Paul Verlaine, and Émile Zola. He met his first true friend, Marcell Benedek, son of Elek Benedek, at 15.

Lukács attended the Protestant Gymnasium in Budapest, then the University of Budapest, receiving degrees in political science in 1906 and philosophy in 1909. In the first decade of the twentieth century, Lukács became familiar with the works of Jakob Burckhardt, Wilhelm Dilthey, Fyodor Dostoyevsky, József Eötvös, Johann Gottlieb Fichte, Immanuel Kant, Alfred Kerr, Søren Kierkegaard, Imre Madách, Friedrich Nietzsche, Georges Sorel, Baruch Spinoza, Max Stirner, Alexis de Tocqueville, Lev Tolstoy, and Ferdinand Tönnies. In Berlin and Heidelberg before World War I, he met Ernst Bloch, **Martin Buber,** Paul Ernst, Emil Lask, Emil Lederer, Georg Simmel, and **Max Weber,** and became attracted to the neo-Kantianism of Heinrich Rickert and Wilhelm Windelband. Impressed by the plays of Sándor Bródy and the politics of Rosa Luxemburg, he later transposed his appreciation of the realism of Shakespeare, Honoré de Balzac, and Stendhal into defenses of the realism of **Thomas Mann, Bertolt Brecht,** and Anna Seghers.

In 1917 Lukács rejected all his work to date and deposited a large cache of manuscripts, correspondence, notes, and his 1910–11 diary in a vault at the Deutsche Bank in Heidelberg. These papers, recovered in 1973, are the richest source of information about his early intellectual life. From just after World War I until his death, the two greatest influences on Lukács were Georg Wilhelm Friedrich Hegel and Karl Marx. His major work consisted in re-Hegelianizing Marx to develop a specifically Hegelian version of Western Marxism that he called "Critical Realism," but scholars such as George L. Kline have noticed the strong influence of Friedrich Engels in Lukács's Marxism and significant deviations from Hegel in Lukács's Hegelianism. In 1971 Lukács told *The New Left Review*, "there are only three truly great thinkers in the West, incomparable with all others: Aristotle, Hegel and Marx."

Archives

Lukács Archives, Institute of Philosophy, Hungarian Academy of Sciences.

Printed Sources

Arato, Andrew, and Paul Breines. *The Young Lukács and the Origins of Western Marxism* (London: Seabury, 1978).

Congdon, Lee. *The Young Lukács* (Chapel Hill: University of North Carolina Press, 1983).

Feenberg, Andrew. *Lukács, Marx, and the Sources of Critical Theory* (New York: Oxford University Press, 1986).

Gluck, Mary. *Georg Lukács and His Generation, 1900–1918* (Cambridge, Mass.: Harvard University Press, 1985).

Joós, Ernest (ed.). *George Lukács and His World: A Reassessment* (New York: Peter Lang, 1988).

Kadarkay, Arpad. *Georg Lukács: Life, Thought, and Politics* (Cambridge, Mass.: Blackwell, 1991).

Löwy, Michael. *L'évolution politique de Lukacs, 1909–1929: Contribution à une sociologie de l'intelligentsia révolutionnaire* (Lille: Atelier Reproduction des Thèses, Université Lille III; Paris: Champion, 1975).

Lukács, György. *Georg Lukács: Selected Correspondence, 1902–1920: Dialogues with Weber, Simmel, Buber, Mannheim, and Others* (New York: Columbia University Press, 1986).

———. *Record of a Life: An Autobiographical Sketch* (London: Verso, 1983).

Marcus, Judith, and Zoltan Tar (eds.). *Georg Lukács: Theory, Culture, and Politics* (New Brunswick, N.J.: Transaction, 1989).

Eric v.d. Luft

M

MACARTHUR, DOUGLAS (1880–1964)

Douglas MacArthur was born in Little Rock, Arkansas, the third son of Arthur MacArthur, a well-connected high-ranking United States career soldier of Scottish descent, and his wife, Mary Pinkney Hardy of Norfolk, Virginia. Educated initially at grade schools in frontier army posts and Washington, in 1897 MacArthur graduated first in his class from a newly founded Episcopalian private school, West Texas Military Academy near Fort Sam Houston, which combined military discipline, compulsory chapel, and high academic standards. Following family tradition, in 1899 MacArthur entered West Point Military Academy, graduating as first captain and excelling academically, though due to lack of interest his subsequent performance in Army Engineering School was mediocre. During World War I he fought flamboyantly with the 42nd Division in France, winning promotion to brigadier general. From 1919 to 1922 as superintendent of West Point, MacArthur introduced reforms to broaden the curriculum and modernize army training. He later claimed that Philippine assignments during the 1920s gave him special insight into "Oriental psychology."

Appointed army chief of staff in 1930, for six years from 1935 MacArthur, who retired from the United States army two years later, was military adviser to the newly independent Philippine Commonwealth Government. In 1941 the War Department recalled MacArthur to active duty to command United States Far Eastern army forces while exercising similar authority over the Filipino troops. When Japanese forces overran the islands in 1942, MacArthur escaped to Australia and was appointed commander of the Southwest Pacific Area Theater. Although the American navy was primarily responsible for victory in the Pacific campaign, MacArthur's forces provided important support. As supreme commander of the Allied occupation forces in Japan from 1945 to 1950, MacArthur authorized extensive political, economic, and military reforms. As the cold war intensified he demanded a major American anti-Communist initiative in Asia. When North

Korea invaded the South in June 1950, quickly overrunning most of the country, MacArthur was appointed commander of the United Nations forces that intervened in Korea. In September 1950 he devised the risky Inchon landing operation that turned the tide in Korea. MacArthur's subsequent insistence on crossing the former Thirty-Eighth Parallel dividing North and South Korea and attempting to reunite the country led Chinese Communist "volunteer" forces to enter the war, initially precipitating a near-rout of the United Nations forces, though the situation eventually stabilized somewhere near the parallel. After MacArthur demanded the use of nuclear weapons against China, in April 1951 President **Harry S. Truman** dismissed him for insubordination. Returning to the United States, MacArthur was welcomed as a national hero but nonetheless failed to win the coveted 1952 Republican presidential nomination. MacArthur subsequently lived in relative seclusion in New York City, writing his memoirs. His self-serving ambition, egotism, and self-promotion and his indifference to constitutional restraints undoubtedly vitiated his indisputably outstanding military abilities. MacArthur's career embodied many of the overall strengths and weaknesses of broader twentieth-century American policies toward Asia.

MacArthur's high-school education included Latin and Greek classics and most of the then-accepted canon of English literature, history, and poetry. Determined to be a scholar-soldier, MacArthur's ambitious father, his son's greatest role model, always read avidly, and in the 1880s he submitted a report urging United States expansion into the Asia-Pacific area. A nine-month Asian tour with his parents in 1905–6 likewise permanently convinced the son of the significance of Asia, which he perceived as Western civilization's last frontier, imbibing Social Darwinist views on Anglo-Saxons' superiority to Asians. The adult MacArthur read voraciously, often consuming three volumes a day, and acquired a library of seven to eight thousand volumes, many inherited from his father. Military history, especially the Civil War and biographies of Confederate generals, was a particular interest, but he also followed international affairs closely, habitually perusing numerous newspapers and periodicals. While largely reflecting MacArthur's existing preoccupations, his choice of reading matter perhaps encouraged his grandiloquent tendency to glorify himself and inflate events in which he participated.

Archives

Douglas MacArthur Memorial, Norfolk, Va.: repository for MacArthur's personal papers.

National Archives II, College Park, Md.: repository of Department of State and Modern Military Records relating to MacArthur's official career.

Printed Sources

James, D. Clayton. *The Years of MacArthur*, 3 vols. (Boston: Little, Brown, 1970–85). Most significant biographical work.

MacArthur, Douglas. *Reminiscences* (New York: McGraw Hill, 1964).

Manchester, William. *American Caesar* (Boston: Little, Brown, 1978).

Perret, Geoffrey. *Old Soldiers Never Die: The Life of Douglas MacArthur* (New York: Random House, 1996).

Schaller, Michael. *Douglas MacArthur: The Far Eastern General* (New York: Oxford University Press, 1989).

Priscilla Roberts

MACMILLAN, MAURICE HAROLD (1894–1986)

Harold Macmillan was born in Cadogan Place, London, and educated at Eton and Balliol College, Oxford (1912–14). Strongly influenced in his youth by Ronald Knox, later a leading convert to Catholicism, Macmillan nevertheless remained faithful to the Church of England. After serving as an officer on the Western Front in the Great War, he entered the family publishing house in 1920, a life that continued alongside the political career begun by his election as Conservative MP for Stockton in 1924. Macmillan was an outsider in the Conservative Party of interwar Britain. Opposed to what he saw as socialism's bureaucracy and politics of envy, he nevertheless repeatedly called for planning to level up society during the 1930s, culminating in his *The Middle Way* (1938). He was also an ardent anti-appeaser. It was not until the Second World War that he obtained office, serving alongside **Dwight D. Eisenhower** in North Africa in 1943–45. The **Clement Attlee** government (1945–51) tempered his enthusiasm for planning. Returning to office as minister of housing and local government in 1951–54, he liberalized regulation and used the private sector to deliver the Conservative pledge to build 300,000 houses per annum. Briefly minister of defense (1954–55), he tried hard to encourage détente when foreign secretary (April–December 1955). Overseas problems, notably the cold war, Middle East conflict, European integration, Anglo-American relations and decolonization, continued to dominate his concerns as chancellor of the exchequer (1955–57) and prime minister (1957–63). Macmillan's vision for European integration did not win out, and he failed to secure British membership of the EEC (European Economic Community) in 1961–63. However, he was more successful in managing Anglo-American relations, as well as presiding over the smooth demission of the vast bulk of Britain's colonial empire. Domestically, his policies remain exemplars of pragmatic, compassionate conservatism.

As befitted a publisher, Macmillan was a voracious reader, meticulously recording each work read in the diaries he kept from 1943 to 1945 and 1950 to 1966. Even in his first full year as prime minister in 1958, he read 73 books. Famously the prime minister who regularly went to bed with a Trollope, he also favored other nineteenth-century novelists, notably Charles Dickens, Jane Austen, and Sir Walter Scott (and more occasionally Tolstoy). These staples he consistently returned to, as they helped him to unwind in periods of tension. His reading of contemporary novelists was more selective, though **Aldous Huxley** seems to have been a favorite. Biography, however, could be equally relaxing. Macmillan commented on July 23, 1959, "I find these 19th century memoirs soothing. They had just as many difficulties and crises as we do. But they did not live in the terrible world produced by 2 wars, with its frightful losses and the prospect of a third" (Macmillan 2003–). Generally speaking, less than half of Macmillan's reading was of fiction. Apart from occasional forays into theology or literary criticism, the rest was made up of biographies, memoirs, diaries, and history. Eighteenth- and nineteenth-century political history was particularly favored, but Macmillan's historical interests went much wider. Occasionally this reading was prompted by current concerns; for instance, he prepared for his 1959 trip to Moscow by reading Vasili Klyuchevsky's *Peter the Great*. Generally, he preferred a history of events and individuals, as can be seen from the fact that about a quarter of his reading was of biographies.

Archives

Macmillan's diaries and papers are held at the Bodleian Library, Oxford. Much relevant material from his ministerial career can also be found in the Public Record Office, London, notably the PREM11 class list covering the Prime Minister's office 1951–64.

Printed Sources

Horne, Alistair. *Macmillan*, 2 vols. (London: Macmillan, 1988–89).
Macmillan, Harold. *The Macmillan Diaries*, 2 vols. (London: Macmillan, 2003, 2005).
———. *Memoirs*, 6 vols. (London: Macmillan, 1966–73).
———. *War Diaries: The Mediterranean 1943–1945* (London: Macmillan, 1984).

Peter P. Catterall

MALCOLM X (EL-HAJJ MALIK EL-SHABAZZ) (1925–1965)

Malcolm Little, who adopted the name Malcolm X when he became a member of the Nation of Islam (Black Muslims), was born May 19, 1925, in Omaha, Nebraska, to Louise Norton Little, a homemaker, and Earl Little, a Baptist minister and supporter of Black Nationalist leader **Marcus Garvey**. Threatened by the Ku Klux Klan for "stirring up trouble" in the Black community with his "back to Africa" sermons, Earl Little moved his family to Milwaukee, Wisconsin, and then to Lansing, Michigan, where he continued to preach. On November 7, 1929, the Littles' home was burned to the ground. Less than two years later, Earl Little was run over by a streetcar. Ten years later, Louise Little suffered a nervous breakdown. Declared legally insane, she was committed to the State Mental Hospital at Kalamazoo, where she remained for 26 years, leaving her children in the hands of distant relatives and foster parents.

Deemed unmanageable, Malcolm was placed in a juvenile detention center in Lansing. In 1946, after being arrested for a series of drug-related crimes, Malcolm (also known as "Detroit Red") spent several years in prison, where he was introduced to the teachings of Black Muslim leader **Elijah Muhammad.** Upon his release, Malcolm dedicated his life to the Nation of Islam and eventually assumed the role of minister of New York Temple No. 7, where he met his future wife, Betty Sanders (Shabazz). On February 21, 1965, Malcolm was assassinated while addressing an audience at Harlem's Audubon Ballroom on the goals of his fledgling Organization of Afro-American Unity, the secular branch of Muslim Mosque, Inc., designed "to bring the Negro struggle from the level of civil rights to the level of human rights." As noted in *The Autobiography of Malcolm X*, Malcolm's conversion to the Nation of Islam ignited his lifelong passion for learning. And although he eventually severed his ties with the Black Muslims and changed his name from Malcolm X to El-Hajj Malik El-Shabazz following a pilgrimage to Mecca—a decision that caused a rift with his friend **Muhammad Ali**—Malcolm credited the organization with saving his life.

Although his formal education ended with the eighth grade, Malcolm read voraciously. His readings included a broad spectrum of linguistic and historical works, including *Webster's English Dictionary*, the Koran, the complete works of Shakespeare, and Frederick Bodmer's *The Loom of Language*. Convinced that "[o]f all our studies, history is best qualified to reward our research," Malcolm focused his attention on historical works ranging from ancient Egypt to the present. He also admired the works of renowned photojournalist Gordon Parks and the writings of James Baldwin, whom he considered to be one of the few Black writers who told the truth.

Archives

Archives at Emory University Library, Atlanta, Georgia: Personal and official letters and other documents.

Printed Sources

Carson, Clayborne. *Malcolm X: The FBI File*, David Gallen (ed.), (New York: Carroll & Graf, 1991). A transcript of the files maintained by the Federal Bureau of Investigation on Malcolm X from 1953 until his death.

Gallen, David. *Malcolm X: As They Knew Him* (New York: Carroll & Graf, 1992). Twenty-five men and women who knew Malcolm X share their stories.

Malcolm X. *Autobiography of Malcolm X* (as told to Alex Haley) [1964] (New York: Ballantine Books, 1973).

———. *Malcolm X: By Any Means Necessary*, George Breitman (ed.), (New York: Betty Shabazz and Pathfinder Press, 1992). A collection of speeches from the last year of his life.

———. *Malcolm X on Afro-American History* (New York: Betty Shabazz and Pathfinder Press, 1985). Excerpts from various speeches and *The Autobiography*.

———. *Malcolm X: The Final Speeches*, Steve Clark (ed.), (New York: Pathfinder Press, 1992). Malcolm X's final speeches reflect his changing attitude from Black Nationalism to internationalism.

———. *Malcolm X Speaks*, George Breitman (ed.), (New York: Pathfinder Press, 1976). Includes "Message to the Grass Roots," "The Ballot or the Bullet," and "To Mississippi Youth."

———. *Malcolm X: Speeches at Harvard*, Archie Epps (ed.), (New York: Paragon House, 1991). Includes three speeches presented at Harvard Law School Forum.

Durthy A. Washington

MALRAUX, ANDRÉ GEORGE (1901–1976)

Born in 1901 in Paris, France, André Malraux was the only son of Fernand and Berthe Malraux. His parents separated when he was four, and Malraux was raised by his mother and grandmother in the Paris suburb of Bondy. He attended the École de Bondy from age 5 to age 13, and the École Primaire Supérieure until the age of 17, after which he periodically attended lectures at the École des Langues Orientales and the École de Louvre. His vast knowledge of literature and art, cultivated by years of voracious reading in the public library at Bondy and among the bookstalls of Paris, allowed him to move easily within the fervid literary culture of Paris in the 1920s. He wrote articles and book reviews for numerous literary journals and quickly made a name for himself as a critic and scholar of unusual scope and brilliance.

Despite his intellectual accomplishments, however, Malraux craved a life of action. He came of age amid the devastation of France by the First World War. "We were surrounded by corpses. We were people whose fields had been ploughed up by history" (Lacouture 1975, 17). With other nations, similarly ravaged by history, Malraux felt a certain solidarity. He fought on the Loyalist side during the Spanish Civil War. He opposed the French colonial governments in Morocco and

Indochina. He joined the French Resistance during the Second World War. As France's minister of cultural affairs from 1958 to 1969, he established exhibitions of little-known works of art from India, Persia, and Egypt, and a celebrated exhibit of works from sixteenth-century France.

Malraux had a staggering knowledge of literature, art, and philosophy, due in large part to a lifetime of reading as well as his personal relationships with the writers and artists of his own generation, including **Pablo Picasso, André Gide,** and **Albert Camus.** As a child, he read the novels of Alexander Dumas, James Fenimore Cooper, and Sir Walter Scott. Other important books included Gustave Flaubert's *Bouvard et Pécuchet* and *Salammbô,* and the novels of Victor Hugo and Honoré de Balzac (particularly *Les Chouans*). Malraux also claimed aesthetic influences that included the French writers Charles Baudelaire, **Guillaume Apollinaire**, Tristan Corbière, and Paul Claudel, the German philosopher Friedrich Nietzsche, and the Russian novelist Fyodor Dostoyevsky. Perhaps the greatest influence on the youthful Malraux, however, was the cubist poet Max Jacob (Lacouture 1975, 31), to whom Malraux dedicated his first book, *Lunes en papier* (1921).

As an art director for his own publisher, Gaston Gallimard, Malraux was responsible for introducing the works of **D. H. Lawrence, William Faulkner,** and Dashell Hammett to the Gallimard catalogue, and he contributed two of his most famous prefaces to editions of Lawrence and Faulkner (Lacouture 1975, 136). In **T. E. Lawrence,** Malraux found a dim reflection of his own aspirations as a writer and revolutionary as well as a fellow admirer of Nietzsche and Dostoyevsky. Malraux also admired **Leon Trotsky** for his opposition to **Joseph Stalin.** However, the man who seemed best to combine Malraux's political and aesthetic ideals was **Charles de Gaulle,** with whom Malraux served in the French Resistance and to whom he remained a loyal friend and supporter through de Gaulle's tumultuous postwar political career.

Archives

Robert Payne Collection, State University of New York at Stony Brook, Subgroup II, Box 9, letters.

Nicola Chiaromonto Papers, Beinecke Rare Book and Manuscript Library, Yale University, Box 1, Folder 55, letters; Box 5, Folder 146, manuscript.

Roger Caillois Collection, Valery Larbaud Médiathèque, letters.

Printed Sources

Cate, Curtis. *André Malraux: A Biography* (London: Hutchinson, 1995); *André Malraux,* Marie-Alyx Revellat (trans.), (Paris: Flammarion, 1994).

Lacouture, Jean. *Malraux, une vie dans le siècle* (Paris: Seuil, 1973); *André Malraux,* Alan Sheridan (trans.), (New York: Pantheon, 1975).

Lyotard, Jean-François. *Signed, Malraux,* Robert Harvey (trans.), (Minneapolis, Minn.: University of Minnesota Press, 1999).

———. *Soundproof Room: Malraux's Anti-Aesthetics,* Robert Harvey (trans.), (Stanford: Stanford University Press, 2001).

Malraux, André. *Antimémoires,* Terence Kilmartin (trans.), (New York: Holt, Rinehart, Winston, 1968).

Todd, Olivier. *André Malraux: une vie* (Paris: Gallimard, 2001).

Philip Bader

MANDELA, NELSON ROLIHLAHLA (1918–)

Nelson Mandela was born at Mveza, in the Umtata district of the Transkei, eight hundred miles east of Cape Town. He received his early education from the Wesleyan Methodist institutions at Mqhekezweni, Clarkebury, and Healdtown. "We were taught and believed," Mandela recalled of his missionary schooling, "that the best ideas were British ideas, the best government was British government, and the best men were Englishmen" (Mandela 1994, 27). He studied English, anthropology, and politics at Fort Hare University, completing his degree in 1942. Mandela's introduction to the African protest movement came following his move to Johannesburg in the early 1940s and intensified following the installation of the Nationalist Party government in 1948. He was put on trial for treason in 1957 and again in 1964, when he was sentenced to life in prison. Mandela served 18 of his 27 years in captivity at the infamous prison on Robben Island, and he was released, at last, on February 11, 1990. The overwhelming victor in the first fully democratic election in the Republic of South Africa, Mandela became president in 1994 and served a full term before his retirement from office in 1999.

Mandela's political initiation came through his contact with activists in Johannesburg—for example, the African nationalist Anton Lembede, who espoused a philosophy of African self-sufficiency and independence. He nevertheless befriended militants in the Indian protest movement, such as Ismail Meer and Jaydew Sing. He also associated with members of the South African Communist Party, including Bram Fischer and Ruth First. Mandela's mistrust of whites led him to resist close collaboration with the Communist Party. However, as his political activity intensified, Mandela's opposition to Marxism began to erode. During the early 1960s Mandela read the complete works of Karl Marx and became increasingly interested in books on liberation movements, including Mao Tse-Tung and Edgar Snow on the Chinese revolution, Menachem Begin on Israel, and Louis Taruc's account of the Philippine uprising, *Born of the People*. "Marxism's call to revolutionary action," Mandela noted, "was music to the ears of a freedom fighter." He subscribed to the fundamental tenet of Marxist doctrine, "from each according to his ability, to each according to his needs" (Mandela 1994, 104–5). Mandela's prison experiences, especially regular contact with white guards, eventually softened much of his militancy. As a politician he came to recognize the necessity of cooperation with white society and industry in order to successfully build a new South Africa.

During his prison years on Robben Island, Mandela engaged in intense political debates with fellow prisoners over the future of the protest movement and was instrumental in the creation of lessons to educate young prisoners in the program of the African Nationalist Congress. Known as "Robben Island University," the curriculum trained an entire generation of African political leaders. Mandela himself also took a correspondence course in law from London University. When prison authorities banned him from continuing his studies, Mandela enthusiastically turned to works of fiction. He read the works of liberal South African authors such as **Nadine Gordimer,** many of whom he befriended following his release. He greatly admired Lev Tolstoy's *War and Peace* and saw parallels between the plight of the migrant workers in **John Steinbeck**'s *The Grapes of Wrath* and the difficulties faced by African laborers under apartheid (Mandela 1994, 428). Political biographies also helped to prepare Mandela for his later political career. "While the comrades were reading *Das Kapital*," recalled a fellow prisoner, "Mandela was reading **Churchill**'s war memoirs, or biographies of **Kennedy** or Vorster" (Sampson 1999, 282).

Many of the prisoners on Robben Island also expressed high regard for the works of Shakespeare and frequently recited long passages from the historical plays. Mandela identified the following passage from *Julius Caesar* as his particular favorite (Sampson 1999, 231–2):

> Cowards die many times before their deaths;
> The valiant never taste of death but once.
> Of all the wonders that I yet have heard,
> It seemed to me most strange that men should fear;
> Seeing that death, a necessary end,
> Will come when it will come.

Archives

Shell House, Johannesburg: African National Congress Archives.
William Cullen Library, Witwatersrand University, and the Brenthurst Library, Johannesburg: Extensive materials on South African political protest movements.

Printed Works

Benson, Mary. *Nelson Mandela: The Man and the Movement* (London: Penguin, 1994).
Mandela, Nelson Rolihlahla. *Long Walk to Freedom* (New York: Little, Brown and Company, 1994).
———. *No Easy Walk to Freedom*, Ruth First (ed.), (London: Heinemann, 1965).
———. *The Struggle Is My Life* (London: International Defense and Aid Fund for South Africa, 1978).
Meredith, Martin. *Nelson Mandela* (New York: St. Martin's Press, 1997).
Sampson, Anthony. *Mandela: The Authorized Biography* (New York: Knopf, 1999).

Michael A. Rutz

MANN, HEINRICH (1871–1950)

Heinrich Mann was born in Lubeck in 1871. He and his brother Thomas attended the private school of Professor Bussenius and then enrolled in the Gymnasium Katharineum but left the school before the final examinations. He began his career as a writer in the 1880s, after failing as a publisher's apprentice, and audited the philosophy lessons at the University of Berlin. German culture was in this decade strongly dominated by the trans-European movements of naturalism, symbolism, and decadence, introduced in Germany through the work of Hermann Bahr and Georg Brandes. Heinrich grew up in this cultural climate: his education can be considered more European than German, and his novels, though accurately reflecting German culture and society, go beyond the limits of nationalism. As critic and essayist he wrote *Eine Freundschaft: Gustave Flaubert und George Sand* (1905), *Voltaire—Goethe* (1910), and *Zola* (1915), works which demonstrate a sympathy for the social and democratic ideals of the French left. As a novelist he published *Im Schlaraffenland* (*In the Land of Cockaigne*, 1900), *Die Göttinnen* (1903), and *Professor Unrat* (*Small Town Tyrant*, 1905). Adaptations for cinema by Joseph von Sternberg—*The Blue Angel*, 1930, *Die kleine Stadt* (*The Small Town*, 1909), *Der*

Untertan (*The Patrioteer*, 1914)—brought him considerable fame. By reason of his stance on the democratic ideals and against the accession to power of **Adolf Hitler,** Mann was forced to flee to France (1933) and then to the United States (1940). To the French period belong the two novels *Die Jugend des Königs Henri Quatre* (*Young Henry of Navarre*, 1935) and *Die Vollendung des Königs Henri Quatre* (*Henry, King of France*, 1938), while his last narrative period saw the publication of *Lidice* (1943) and *Der Atem* (*The Breath*, 1949) and his autobiography *Ein Zeitalter wird besichtigt* (*An Age is Examined*, 1945). Heinrich Mann died in Santa Monica, California, in 1950.

Mann's participation in the theatrical club Freie Bühne of Berlin induced him to write dramas: *Varieté* (1910), *Schauspielerin* (1911), *Die grosse Liebe* (1912), *Madame Legros* (1913), and *Der Weg zur Macht* (1919). He met many intellectuals and artists, which encouraged creativity: in Italy he met the writer Gabriele D'Annunzio and the composer Giacomo Puccini, while, during his French stay, he associated with a group of political exiles who met in Sanary sur Mer: **Bertolt Brecht,** Franz Werfel, Alfred Döblin, Erwin Piscator, Ludwig Marcuse, Joseph Roth, and Stefan Zweig. He also collaborated with **Aldous Huxley** and **André Gide** for the review *Die Sammlung*. Mann formulated in his works the role of the intellectual as deeply engaged in society, working and operating in the interest and to the advantage of the masses, and fighting the cruelty of capitalism and industrialism. Mann's cultural influence is more evident in the model of the modern intellectual committed to the defense of social rights than in stylistic–literary aspects. Mann's exploration of different expressive possibilities (novel, essay, cinema, theater, articles) also made him a complex and a multiform writer.

Archives

Heinrich Mann Collection Inventory in the Feuchtwanger Memorial Library Archives—University of Southern California.
Heinrich Mann Archiv—Berlin.

Printed Sources

Gross, David. *The Writer and Society: Heinrich Mann and Literary Politics in Germany, 1890–1940* (Atlantic Highlands: New Jersey Humanities Press, 1980).
Hamilton, Nigel. *The Brothers Mann: The Lives of Heinrich and Thomas Mann, 1871–1950 and 1875–1955* (London: Secker Warburg, 1978).
Roberts, David. *Artistic Consciousness and Political Conscience: The Novels of Heinrich Mann 1900–1938* (Berne: Lang, 1971).

Maria Tabaglio

MANN, PAUL THOMAS (1875–1955)

Thomas Mann was born in Lübeck, Germany, and there attended the Katharineum (1889–94). Earning his diploma in 1894, he joined his mother in the intellectual and artistic milieu of Munich. Mann enrolled for several courses at the Teschnische Universität in Munich before achieving critical acclaim for his novel *Buddenbrooks: Verfall einer Familie* (1901; translated 1924 as *Buddenbrooks*). As embodied in this tale of the generational decline of a family, Mann established himself as a novelist of ideas. His works served as forums to examine philosophical issues, including the upheavals of his own time, the more transcendent issues underlying Western civilization, and the ever-recurring leitmotif of the artist as different—often above—society. The craftsmanship and complexity of his fictional and political works embodying humor, poignant irony, and parody established him as one of the foremost thinkers and novelists of the twentieth century and earned him the Nobel Prize for literature in 1929. **Adolf Hitler**'s rise to power in 1933 only quickened Mann's progression from his support of authoritarianism as expressed in *Betrachtungen eines Unpolitischen* (1918; translated 1983 as *Reflections of a Nonpolitical Man*) to a more humane and democratic understanding. Having sought exile first in Switzerland, he moved to the United States in 1938 and became a citizen in 1940. Mann spoke fervently against European fascism, although his political views still embodied an ambiguous tension between a romanticized, apolitical German burgher and a universalized humanity increasingly associated with social democracy. He returned to Europe in 1953 in light of the hysteria of McCarthyism.

Mann credited the roots of his leitmotif to his parental influences: "From my father the 'serious approach to life,'" and from his mother "artistic-sensual direction and—in the widest sense of the word—the 'urge to story-telling'" (quoted in Prater 1995, 4). During his time at the Teschnische Universität, the lectures on Nordic mythology and the literature of the Middle Ages provided important material for Mann's works. However, the majority of his learning took place outside of academia. A vivid imagination coupled with his avid reading of Friedrich von Schiller, Heinrich Heine, and Theodor Storm led to his first expressions of verse in Lübeck. In the 1890s, following in the footsteps of his literate brother, Heinrich Mann, the influence of Hermann Bahr becomes evident. Also noticeable during this period is Mann's transition from naturalism to neo-romanticism. Mann read extensively French, Scandinavian, and Russian literature marking the influences of Guy de Maupassant, Jonas Lie, Alexander Kielland, Anton Chekhov, Fyodor Dostoyevsky, and Ivan Turgenev. Ideas and details from his readings, travels to the Baltic coast as a child, and his time in Italy in the 1890s filled notebooks with ideas and details that would be incorporated in later works. However, greater influences on his work were already observable during his Lübeck years, where Mann was deeply drawn to Richard Wagner's operatic music renowned for its intensity, complexity, and epic grandeur. Parallels between Mann's literary leitmotifs and Wagner's musical ones are found throughout Mann's works. Interest in Wagner soon led Mann to explore the works of Arthur Schopenhauer and Friedrich Nietzsche, specifically Schopenhauer's *Die Welt als Wille und Vorstellung* (1818; translated 1966 as *The World as Will and Representation*) and Nietzsche's *Jenseits von Gut und Bose* (1886; translated 1967 as *Beyond Good and Evil*) and *Der Fall Wagner* (1888; translated 1967 as *The Case of Wagner*). In the artistic suburb of Schwabing, Munich, his mother's elite circle of friends exposed Mann to poet Stefan George's decadent movement of *l'art pour l'art* and a culture of nihilism and pessimism. These themes conflicted with the influence Johann Wolfgang von Goethe exerted on Mann, specifically his view of the burgher as a human being and romantic individualist. The juxtaposition of these various facets is reflected in most of Mann's works.

Archives

Thoman-Mann-Archiv, Eidgenössische Technische Hochschule Zürich, Switzerland: majority of Thomas Mann's original works, including manuscripts, diaries, notebooks, and letters and a wide array of recorded and secondary material.

Thomas Mann Collection, Yale University, New Haven, Conn.: manuscript items, correspondence and special files, and a large collection of printed materials by and about Mann.

Printed Works

Prater, Donald. *Thomas Mann: A Life* (New York: Oxford University Press, 1995).

Winston, Richard. *Thomas Mann: The Making of an Artist, 1875–1911* (New York: Knopf, 1979; London: Constable, 1982).

Rouven J. Steeves

MARCUSE, HERBERT (1898–1979)

Herbert Marcuse was born in Berlin on July 19, 1898, to Carl and Gertrud Marcuse. He briefly attended the Humboldt University in Berlin but eventually transferred to the Albert-Ludwig University of Freiburg-im-Breisgau, studying German literature and philosophy with figures such as Edmund Husserl. In 1922 Marcuse completed his dissertation on the figure of the artist-hero in the German novel. He then studied at Freiburg University as a postdoctoral student, working in particular with the German philosopher **Martin Heidegger.** Just prior to **Adolf Hitler**'s rise to power in Germany, Marcuse accepted a position at the Institute for Social Research, commonly known as the Frankfurt School, working with figures such as Max Horkheimer, Leo Lowenthal, and Freidrich Pollock. Marcuse eventually fled to America in 1934 when the threat of fascism became too great. In the United States Marcuse taught at many schools, including Columbia University, Brandeis University, and the University of California at San Diego. His scholarship included an influential reading of G.W.F. Hegel entitled *Reason and Revolution* (1941), a critique of neo-Freudianism entitled *Eros and Civilization* (1955), and a scathing critique of modern industrial society called *One-Dimensional Man* (1964). Marcuse's writings covered a wide range of topics from traditional philosophical concerns and aesthetic theory to overtly political tracts. Outside of his scholarship, Marcuse's major impact stemmed from the inspiration and encouragement he gave to the New Left and the student movement during the 1960s. Marcuse died on July 29, 1979, in Starnberg, Germany.

Early in his academic career Marcuse was influenced by his studies of German phenomenology with Edmund Husserl and Martin Heidegger. But his interest in German literature, in particular German romanticism, introduced him to the aesthetic theories of Friedrich Schiller, which influenced his understanding of the emancipatory potential of the aesthetic form. He was also drawn to surrealism as an art form, in particular the program of **André Breton.** Marcuse also made continual reference to the work of literary figures such as Johann Wolfgang von Goethe, **Samuel Beckett,** Arthur Rimbaud, and Charles Baudelaire, which spoke to his interest in modern literature. Marcuse's relationship with the Frankfurt school introduced him to the work of Theodor Adorno and Erich Fromm, which influenced his understanding of psychoanalysis, social science, and critical theory. Like many other German intellectuals, Marcuse was deeply indebted to the work of Hegel, Karl Marx, and Sigmund Freud and spent much of his academic career attempting to reconcile the work of these three towering figures. The publication in 1932 of the recently discovered early manuscripts of Karl Marx entitled *Economic and Philosophical Manuscripts of 1844* influenced Marcuse's understanding of Marxism and helped him to ground his phenomenological claims. Marcuse's two studies of Hegel reflected his continued interest in dialectical materialism. His work on Sigmund Freud also spoke to his continual preoccupation with psychoanalysis as a form of critical analysis. Marcuse's understanding of industrial development and economic change was also influenced by his reading of the work of Rudolf Bahro and Franz Neumann.

Archives

Herbert Marcuse Archive, City and University Library, Frankfurt am Main, Germany.

Printed Sources

Bokina, John, and Timothy J. Lukes (eds.). *Marcuse: From the New Left to the Next Left* (Lawrence: University of Kansas Press, 1994).

Katz, Barry. *Herbert Marcuse and the Art of Liberation* (London: Verso, 1982).

Kellner, Douglas. *Herbert Marcuse and the Crisis of Marxism* (Berkeley: University of California Press, 1984).

Lipshires, Sidney. *Herbert Marcuse: From Marx to Freud and Beyond* (Cambridge, Mass.: Schenkman, 1974).

Schoolman, Morton. *Imaginary Witness: The Critical Theory of Herbert Marcuse* (New York: Free Press, 1980).

Robert Genter

MARLEY, NESTA ROBERT (1945–1981)

Bob Marley was born in Nine Mile, Jamaica. He completed his formal education at the age of 16 from Model Private School in Kingston, Jamaica. Before the age of six, one of Bob Marley's first musical influences occurred through his attendance at a Christian church with his mother in Nine Mile. Here he was exposed to gospel songs, such as *Let the Lord Be Seen in You* and *Take My Hand Precious Lord* (Talamon et al. 1994, 16). In 1966, Bob Marley became Rastafarian, which is a messianic cult religion. His religious beliefs, combined with the current social issues of his time, would be the focal point for the messages in his songs. Due to his music's prevailing themes against political oppression, he eventually became an international symbol of freedom. After Marley signed a contract with Island Records in 1972, he brought Reggae music to the foreground of the Western culture's musical scene. He is also accredited with educating white Europeans and Americans to pay "rapt attention to his songs of black retribution," while, at the same time, exposing them to Jamaican Creole culture (White 1983, 4).

When Marley was an adolescent attending Model Private School, he held a special regard for history and quickly became interested in the torment and oppression inflicted upon the Maroons (White 1983, 129). His history lessons gave him insight into the contemporary (1950s) oppressive forces that plagued his people. These insights would later develop into themes for his music. In 1959, Joe Higgs, a Reggae performer, started tutoring Marley in singing. Marley's first band was formed with Higgs's encouragement and help. Higgs taught Marley that songs should hold messages about faith and resistance. Another influential figure in Marley's life was Mortimo Planno, his Rastafarian guru. The Rastafarian bible is the *Holy Piby*, which was compiled by Robert Athlyi Rogers from 1913 to 1917. This religion's ideological premises come from some of the teachings of back-to-Africa advocate

Marcus Mosiah Garvey. In addition to the religious teachings, the songs and chants from the *Holy Piby* also influenced Marley. He turned one of the chants into the song *Rasta Man Chant.* The song *War,* from the album *Rastaman Vibration,* took its lyrics from a speech made by the former Ethiopian emperor, **Haile Selassie I,** to the United Nations. The Rastas believed that Selassie was the true messiah. Bob Marley's songs *Jah Live* and *Crazy BaldHeads* were written in protest against the purported murder of Selassie. Marley brought his spiritual messages to the Western world through his unique interplay of Jamaican idioms, folklore, and metaphors. Marley had a unique way of connecting with his audience, especially his listeners in his homeland of Jamaica. He used his music as a means to educate the world about the political injustices that occurred in Jamaica.

Archives

Bob Marley Museum, Kingston, Jamaica: Two international rooms with newspaper clippings from 1973 to 1980, artifacts, memorabilia, numerous writings, and photographs.

The National Library of Jamaica in Kingston: Bibliographical information including books, articles, a selection of articles published in *Daily Gleaner* 1976–March 1977, and audiovisual materials.

Rock & Roll Hall of Fame, Cleveland: Marley musical memorabilia.

Roger Steffens Reggae ARCHIVES, Los Angeles, California: Last videotape ever made of Marley (in hospital bed), an audiotape from his bedroom "musical diary," and Marley artifacts and memorabilia.

Printed Sources

Salewicz, Chris, Adrian Boot, and Chris Blackwell. *Reggae Explosion: The Story of Jamaican Music* (New York: Harry N. Abrams, 2001).

Talamon, W. Bruce, Roger Steffens, and Timothy White. *Bob Marley: Spirit Dancer* (New York and London: Norton & Company, 1994).

White, Timothy. *Catch a Fire: The Life of Bob Marley* [1983] (New York: Henry Holt and Company, 1998).

White, Timothy. "The Importance of Being Bob Marley." May 17, 2002. Web site of Bob Marley Inc., http://www.bobmarley.com/life/legacy/interview/, accessed October 23, 2003.

Rose Giltzow

MARSHALL, GEORGE CATLETT (1880–1959)

George Marshall was born in Uniontown, Pennsylvania, the second son and last child of George Catlett Marshall Sr., a prominent businessman, and Laura Bradford. Both his parents came from established Virginia and Kentucky families. Marshall accepted nearly unquestioningly his family's Episcopalian Christian faith and regarded the local minister as a boyhood mentor. Educated at local private and public schools, at 16 Marshall entered the Virginia Military Institute, graduating in 1901 as first captain and near the top of his class in engineering and military studies. The following year he married Elizabeth "Lily" Carter Coles of Lexington, Virginia, and was commissioned a second lieutenant of infantry. When the United States entered the First World War, in June 1917 Marshall went to France; he became the First Army's chief of operations and then aide to the chief of staff, General John J. Pershing. During three years in China, Marshall acquired proficiency in Mandarin Chinese; in five as assistant commandant of the Infantry School, Fort Benning, Georgia, he introduced curriculum reforms and trained numerous future

American generals. In 1930 Marshall, a widower since 1927, married Katherine Tupper Brown, a widow with three children who had also been a successful actress.

In 1938 Marshall, already a general, transferred to the general staff in Washington and in September 1939 became chief of staff of the United States Army. As World War II began, Marshall energetically rebuilt the United States military, supervising an increase in United States armed forces from two hundred thousand in December 1941 to a wartime peak of eight million. Marshall retired in November 1945 and for fourteen months unsuccessfully sought to mediate the continuing Chinese civil war between the Nationalist Government and Communist rebels. In January 1947 Marshall became secretary of state as the developing cold war presented new challenges to his country. His most visible accomplishments were the Marshall Plan, a coordinated $10 billion five-year scheme to rehabilitate the Western European economies, and American membership in the North Atlantic Treaty Organization, the first permanent security pact the United States had ever entered. Marshall left office in January 1949, but when the Korean War began in June 1950, President **Harry S. Truman** persuaded him to become secretary of defense, and for 15 months Marshall again built up manpower and war production. In December 1953 a Nobel Peace Prize recognized his efforts for European recovery.

Evening family readings from classic histories, novels, and adventure stories, often with an earlier American historical background, enthralled Marshall. He particularly enjoyed historical novels by G. A. Henty and Arthur Conan Doyle, especially the latter's *The Refugees* and *Sir Nigel*, Eugene Sue's *The Wandering Jew*, the novels of Charles Dickens, and stirring western stories. An erratically mediocre high school student, Marshall nonetheless excelled in history, later regretting that the Virginia Military Institute college curriculum omitted history and international affairs and provided inadequate language teaching, deficiencies he considered detrimental to his country's international interests. Although Marshall readily passed various undemanding army examinations, he only acquired rigorous study habits in his four years from 1906—two as student, two as instructor—at the reformed Infantry and Cavalry School, Fort Leavenworth, Kansas. He passed the demanding initial year first in his class, reading intensively in military history, strategy, and tactics. Throughout his life he voraciously consumed volumes of history; in 1943, for instance, to sidetrack his fellow history enthusiast, Britain's Prime Minister **Winston Churchill,** from more sensitive subjects, Marshall discussed with him Lord Macaulay's account of Warren Hastings's impeachment, which he had recently read. Marshall's imaginative historical empathy and his professional training both facilitated his ultimate emergence as a leading architect of the "American century" of United States international dominance.

Archives

George C. Marshall Library, Virginia Military Institute, Lexington, Va.: repository for the personal papers of Marshall and many of his associates, and copies of materials on Marshall collected from other sources.

National Archives II, College Park, Md.: holds numerous Department of State and Modern Military records from Marshall's official career.

Printed Sources

Cray, Ed. *General of the Army: George C. Marshall, Soldier and Statesman* (New York: Norton, 1990).

Marshall, George C. *The Papers of George Catlett Marshall*, Larry I. Bland (ed.), 4 vols. to date (Baltimore: Johns Hopkins Press, 1981–).

———. *Interviews and Reminiscences for Forrest C. Pogue*, Larry I. Bland (ed.), (Lexington, Va.: Marshall Foundation, 1991).

Pogue, Forrest C. *George C. Marshall*, 4 vols. (New York: Viking Press, 1963–1987).

Stoler, Mark A. *George C. Marshall: Soldier–Statesman of the American Century* (Boston: Twayne, 1989).

Priscilla Roberts

MASARYK, TOMÁŠ GARRIGUE (1850–1937)

Masaryk was born in Hodonín, Moravia (now part of the Czech Republic), the son of a Slovak father and a German-speaking Czech mother. He studied at gymnasia in Brno (1865–69) and Vienna (1869–72) before enrolling in 1872 at the University of Vienna, where he completed degrees in philosophy (1875 PhDr., 1878 doc.). During a one-year sabbatical at the University of Leipzig, Masaryk met Charlotte Garrigue, daughter of a wealthy Brooklynite. They married in 1877, and Masaryk adopted his wife's maiden name as his own middle name. Raised a Roman Catholic, Masaryk left the church in 1870 following the declaration of papal infallibility. He remained, however, an advocate of religious belief and expressed a Protestant faith that borrowed from Unitarian theology (his wife belonged to the Unitarian Church) and the intellectual traditions of the fifteenth-century Hussite movement and the seventeenth-century Church of the Czech Brethren. After teaching as a docent at the University of Vienna (1878–82), Masaryk was appointed in 1883 as professor of sociology at the newly created Czech University in Prague, a position he held until 1914. He was a prolific and iconoclastic writer, and he sparked controversy with his books and articles on philosophy, Czech history and culture, and the political and social situation in the Habsburg Empire. In 1890 he was elected to the Austrian Parliament. After the start of World War I he went abroad and worked with his former student **Edvard Beneš** (1884–1948) to lobby the governments of France, England, the United States, and Russia for the dismantling of Austria-Hungary. He returned to independent Czechoslovakia in December 1918 as the republic's first president. During the 1920s and 1930s, Masaryk was revered by Czechs as "Papa Masaryk" and hailed in western Europe and the United States as the model of the "philosopher-president." He was a vocal spokesman of democracy, national self-determination, and a republican state built upon a humanitarian, responsible citizenry. In 1935 he was succeeded as president by Beneš, his foreign minister.

Masaryk was an insatiable reader. In addition to Czech, Slovak, and German, Masaryk also read in the classical languages, French, English, Italian, Russian, and Polish. An entire chapter of *Talks with T. G. Masaryk*, the biography by Czech writer **Karel Čapek,** recounts Masaryk's lifetime of reading and the authors who had influenced him. The most important works in the development of his social and political philosophy were Plato's dialogues and the Bible. Of the former, Masaryk maintained that he was a lifelong Platonist, and he appreciated in particular the philosopher's striving for a unity of knowledge and a harmony of theory and practice. His idealism was further shaped by his reading of Johann Gottfried Herder. Masaryk was attracted to Herder's notions of humanity as an ideal, the providential causation of history, the role of the nation in history's progress, and the important role of the Slavs. His view of Herder was shaped by leading Czech and Slovak cultural figures of the nineteenth century who had been adherents of the German philosopher: Czech linguists Josef Dobrovský and Josef Jungmann, historian František Palacký, journalist Karel Havlíček, and Slovak poet Ján Kollár. Masaryk also sought to balance his idealism with a strong measure of Enlightenment skepticism and rationality. He cited David Hume, Auguste Comte, and John Stuart Mill as particularly important for the development of his "realist" politics, a program that addressed the immediate needs of the people while also aiming for a lofty, humanitarian goal. Masaryk's skepticism and emphasis on rationality also shaped his views of religion. He revered the heritage of the Czech Reformation and its leaders Jan Hus and Jan Amos Komenský, and he followed Palacký's interpretation that Protestant faith was at the core of Czech national identity. He maintained that religious faith was necessary for the responsible, ethical life in the modern era, and he often cited the teachings of Jesus Christ. He summarized his guiding philosophy as president as "Christ, not Caesar."

Archives

Archive of the T. G. Masaryk Institute, Czech Academy of Sciences, Prague, Czech Republic: Masaryk Archive. Presidential and personal papers, papers relating to Masaryk's efforts in exile during World War I, manuscripts of articles and books, collections of Masaryk's wife, Charlotte, and their children: Herbert, Alice, Olga, and Jan.

Printed Sources

Čapek, Karel. *Talks with T. G. Masaryk* (North Haven, Conn.: Catbird Press, 1995).
Hanak, Harry (ed.). *T. G. Masaryk (1850–1937)*, vol. I, *Statesman and Cultural Force* (New York: St. Martins, 1990).
Pynsent, Robert (ed.). *T. G. Masaryk (1850–1937)*, vol. II, *Thinker and Critic* (New York: St. Martin's, 1989).
Skilling, H. Gordon. *T. G. Masaryk: Against the Current, 1882–1914* (University Park: Pennsylvania State University Press, 1994).
Szporluk, Roman. *The Political Thought of Thomas G. Masaryk* (Boulder: East European Monographs, 1981).
Winters, Stanley (ed.). *T. G. Masaryk (1850–1937)*, vol. III, *Thinker and Politician* (London: Macmillan, 1990).

Bruce R. Berglund

MASLOW, ABRAHAM HAROLD (1908–1970)

Abraham Maslow, regarded as the founder of humanistic psychology, was born in Brooklyn, New York, the eldest of seven children of uneducated Jewish immigrants from Russia. He earned degrees in psychology at the University of Wisconsin: his B.A. in 1930, his M.A. in 1931, and his Ph.D. in 1934. Professor Harry Harlow, who supervised Maslow's dissertation, was at the time researching behavior in baby rhesus monkeys. Maslow subsequently worked as a professor at Brooklyn College (1937–51) and at Brandeis University (1951–61).

Several important mentors influenced Maslow including Erich Fromm, Kurt Koffka, Karen Horney, and Alfred Adler. Maslow advanced his theory of human motivation based on the study of two of his mentors, anthropologist Ruth Benedict and Gestalt psychologist Max Wertheimer.

Maslow's relationship with Wertheimer was especially influential. Wertheimer's lecture entitled "Being and Doing" prompted Maslow to study Eastern philosophy.

Wertheimer also emphasized the role of "values" in human life, something that would also dominate Maslow's own theories. One Wertheimer article, "Some Problems in the Theory of Ethics," condemned the relativist views of the period. In "A Story of Three Days," Wertheimer criticized the emphasis by many psychologists on the study of mental illness, advocating instead that they direct more attention toward the study of the mental health of individuals. In this article, Wertheimer also alluded to what Maslow would ultimately label as "peak-experiences."

The theories that Maslow advanced differed dramatically from others since they did focus upon the mental health, the human strengths, and upon the potential of the individual. Maslow's seminal work, *Motivation and Personality* (1954), expanded his arguments by depicting a "hierarchy of needs," thus shifting the focus of motivation theory away from the deprivation of a person and toward the gratification of the individual. This work presented a new humanistic model consisting of five broad categories of human needs, in ascending order: physiological needs, safety and security needs, social or love needs, esteem needs, and finally self-actualization needs. Maslow argued that the gratification of each successive need led to the activation of the next level in the hierarchy.

On June 8, 1970, Abraham Harold Maslow died of a massive heart attack.

Archives

Maslow, Abraham, Papers. Archives of the History of American Psychology, University of Akron, Akron, Ohio. 65 linear feet. Materials in the collection date between 1929 and 1972 and include class notes, manuscripts, diaries, annotated books, and audiotapes. Topics of correspondence include self-actualization; peak experiences; T-Groups; Eupsuchian Philosophy; humanists; the Esalen Institute; and work with Blackfoot Indians.

Dreikurs, Rudolf, Papers, Library of Congress, Manuscript Division, Washington, D.C. Correspondence with Abraham Maslow.

Wertheimer, Max, Papers. New York Public Library, New York, N.Y. 9 cartons. Letters (1902–43) to Wertheimer from European colleagues relating to his work in Gestalt psychology; manuscripts. of his lectures and writings including *Productive Thinking* (1945); notes, notebooks, and miscellaneous papers.

Printed Sources

Hoffman, Edward. *The Right to Be Human: A Biography of Abraham Maslow* (Los Angeles: Jeremy P. Tarcher, Inc., 1988). A well-written book that uses many sources including diaries, notes, writings, and correspondence. This work also includes an excellent bibliography.

———— (ed.). *Future Visions: The Unpublished Papers of Abraham Maslow* (Thousand Oaks, Calif.: Sage Publications, 1996).

Maslow, Abraham H. *Motivation and Personality* (New York: Harper and Row, 1954). Maslow's epochal work that advanced his psychological theory of a "hierarchy of needs" and shifted the study of psychology toward a humanistic direction.

Wertheimer, Max. *Productive Thinking*, English ed. (New York: Harper, 1959).

————. "Some Problems in the Theory of Ethics," *Social Research* 2 (1935), 353–67. Reprinted in Mary Henle (ed.), *Documents of Gestalt Psychology* (Berkeley: University of California Press, 1961).

————. "A Story of Three Days." In R. N. Anshen (ed.), *Freedom: Its Meaning* (New York: Harcourt, Brace, 1940). Reprinted in Mary Henle (ed.), *Documents of Gestalt Psychology* (Berkeley: University of California Press, 1961).

Robert O. Marlin IV

MAYAKOVSKY, VLADIMIR VLADIMIROVICH (1893–1930)

Vladimir Mayakovsky was born and lived in Bagdadi (now Mayakovsky), Georgia, until 1906 when his family moved to Moscow. A self-admitted poor student, Mayakovsky was thrown out of several schools as a boy. In his autobiography "I, Myself," Mayakovsky explained that he received his haphazard education from his mother and older sisters (Mayakovsky 1978, 29). Before the age of 16, Mayakovsky had been arrested three times for bolshevik agitation and spent more than six months in prison, most of it in solitary confinement. After his release, Mayakovsky attended the Moscow Institute for the Study of Painting, Sculpture and Architecture, where he met the modernist poet and painter David Burlyuk. Having persuaded Mayakovsky to pursue poetry over painting, Burlyuk was a decisive influence in his life and Mayakovsky called him "my true teacher" (Mayakovsky 1978, 38). In his short lifetime, Mayakovsky produced several volumes of lyrical poetry and political verse, four narrative poems, graphic art for advertising, propaganda slogans, thirteen film scenarios, and two plays. Thus, although Mayakovsky began his career as a member of the cubist movement in Russian painting in 1911, he is remembered today as an innovative poet, playwright, and one of the founding members of Russian futurism.

In his autobiography, Mayakovsky boasted that the second book he ever read was *Don Quixote*; he also claimed to have read Jules Verne at an early age (Mayakovsky 1978, 30). Despite these early literary adventures, Mayakovsky admitted that he read little fiction growing up; he preferred the writings of G. W. F. Hegel and especially Marx (Mayakovsky 1978, 33). During his solitary confinement in prison, he finally read Lord Byron, William Shakespeare, and Lev Tolstoy's *Anna Karenina* (Mayakovsky 1978, 35). Then he discovered his contemporaries the Russian symbolists and read Andrey Bely and Konstantin Balmont (Mayakovsky 1978, 34). He was inspired by the formal innovation of the symbolists, and tried his hand at applying their methods to his own subject matter. These verses written in prison in 1909 were his first attempts at poetry. Edward Brown suggests that Mayakovsky's debt to Bely can be seen in his mature verse as well, especially in his frequent use of sun imagery and unconventional stanzaic structure, based on a system of emotional emphasis that first appeared in Bely's *Gold on Azure* (Brown 1973, 38). Soviet scholarship prefers to trace Mayakovsky's roots to the poetry of Nikolai Nekrasov and Gavrila Derzhavin. Kozhinov claims that Nekrasov and Derzhavin provide the model for Mayakovsky's mixing of speech styles, shocking imagery, and preoccupation with the common cause (Kozhinov 1976, 74). The hallmarks of Mayakovsky's style and the reasons for his lasting influence—his radical rhymes, his offbeat metaphors, and his unconventional diction—are his own brilliant innovations.

Archives

Russian State Archive of Literature and Art (RGALI) in Moscow.
The Mayakovsky Museum in Moscow.

Printed Sources

Brown, Edward J. *Mayakovsky: A Poet in the Revolution* (Princeton: Princeton University Press, 1973). Contains an excellent bibliography.

Jakobson, Roman. "On a Generation That Squandered Its Poets." In *Major Soviet Authors: Essays in Criticism*, E. J. Brown (ed. and trans.), (New York: Oxford University Press, 1973).

Katsis, L. F. *Vladimir Mayakovsky. Poet v intellektual'nom kontekste epoxi* (Moscow: Yazyki russkoi kultury, 2000).

Kozhinov, Vadim. "Mayakovsky and Russian Classical Literature." In *Vladimir Mayakovsky: Innovator*, Alex Miller (trans.), (Moscow: Progress Publishers, 1976).

Mayakovsky, V. V. "Ia sam" ("I, Myself"). In *Sochineniia v trekh tomakh* (Moscow: Khudozh-estvennaya literatura, 1978). A short autobiography.

Shklovsky, Viktor. *Mayakovsky and His Circle*, Lily Feiler (ed. and trans.), (New York: Dodd, Mead & Co., 1972).

Terras, Victor. *Vladimir Mayakovsky* (Boston: Twayne Publishers, 1983).

Erika Haber

McLUHAN, HERBERT MARSHALL (1911–1980)

Marshall McLuhan, born at Edmonton Alberta, Canada, spent his youth in Winnipeg, Manitoba. After graduating from the University of Manitoba (B.A., 1933; M.A. 1934) he received a doctorate in English literature from Cambridge University (1943). His thesis involved a review of the trivium from its classical beginnings through to the early Renaissance as a way of interpreting the works of Thomas Nashe. Raised as a "loose" Protestant—he attended Baptist, Methodist, and Anglican Churches in Winnipeg—later, heavily influenced by the writings of G. K. Chesterton, he formally converted to Roman Catholicism in 1937. Throughout his doctoral studies and later career he read extensively in the anti-Nicene fathers and the writings of St. Thomas Aquinas. McLuhan, who became the image of media studies in the 1960s and early 1970s, emerged again in the 1990s when *Wired* magazine adopted him as their saint, one of the prime figures anticipating the growth of digiculture. From the perspective of literary history and history of the arts, McLuhan is the main conduit by which the traditions from Egypt and the Near East through Greece and Rome and the Middle Ages to the *symbolistes* and the radical avant-garde were implicated in the prehistory of cyber-culture.

The major influences on McLuhan's program involved the literature on classical education in grammar, logic, and rhetoric (particularly Aristotle, Cicero, and Seneca), Ovid and the Ovidian tradition, the Menippean satirists (Lucian, Apuleius, Varro), and their Renaissance and neo-Augustan successors (Desiderius Erasmus, Thomas More, François Rabelais, Jonathan Swift, Alexander Pope, Laurence Sterne). His thesis, soon to be published by Gingko Press *(Thomas Nashe and the Learning of His Time)*, is the most extensive account of the classical influences and secondary sources. His first and earliest literary interests were in the Renaissance period, in which he had extensive knowledge of the canon of Elizabethan and Tudor drama. His particular interests were Shakespeare and Ben Jonson, the latter particularly as a precursor of **James Joyce.** His Renaissance interests were by no means limited to English drama. Francis Bacon, Michel Montaigne, and Blaise Pascal were crucial figures in the shaping of his complex, ambivalent, satiric essay style. The centrality of these issues in his writings can be seen in his first recognized publication, *The Gutenberg Galaxy* (1962), which opens with his argument being supported by a scene from Shakespeare's *King Lear* and concludes with the unfolding argument about the rise and fall of print being related to Pope's *The Dunciad*.

Contemporary literature, art, and architecture were primary influences on all of his works. The most central figures were Joyce and Wyndham Lewis, whom he viewed as Menippean satirists, along with **Ezra Pound, T. S. Eliot,** and the major French *symbolistes*, particularly Stephane Mallarmé, Arthur Rimbaud, Jules LaForgue, Charles Baudelaire, and Paul Valéry. Joyce is one of the most cited writers in all of his works and provides virtually the whole grounding for his *essai concrete*, *War and Peace in the Global Village*. Far more than any commentary, McLuhan's own writings provide insight into his literary and artistic interests, especially *From Cliche to Archetype* and *The Vanishing Point*. On the artistic side, it is important to note that his first work, *The Mechanical Bride*, adopted its title from Marcel Duchamp's *Large Glass* and that Sigfreid Giedion, Laszlo Moholy-Nagy, and Lewis Mumford were important influences both in the writing and the presentation of his first *essai concrete*.

The still not fully recognized contribution of McLuhan to discourse about culture, communication, and technology is that he transmitted both a long-range and a short-range history to the evolution and understanding of electronic and digital media and their impact on traditional oral, written, and print culture. The major discussions of these aspects of McLuhan are to be found in the books listed below.

Archives

The Marshall McLuhan collection in the National Archives of Canada, Ottawa. Contains extensive notes and correspondence relating to literary and personal sources as well as some of McLuhan's course materials for his graduate and undergraduate English courses.

Printed Sources

Cavell, Richard. *McLuhan in Space: A Cultural Geography* (Toronto: University of Toronto Press, 2002).

Gordon, Terence. *Marshall McLuhan: Escape into Understanding* (Toronto: Stoddart, 1997).

Kroker, Arthur. *Technology and the Canadian Mind: Innis/McLuhan/Grant* (Montreal: New World Perspectives, 1984).

Languirand, Jacques. *De McLuhan à Pythagore* (Ottawa: Ferron éditeur, 1972).

McLuhan, Marshall. *The Medium and the Light*, Eric McLuhan and Jacek Szklarek (eds.), (Toronto: Stoddart, 1999).

Marchand, Philip. *Marshall McLuhan: The Medium and the Messenger* (Toronto: Random House, 1989).

Moos, Michael A. (ed.). *Marshall McLuhan Essays: Media Research: Technology, Art, Communication* (Amsterdam: G & B Arts, 1997).

Stearn, Gerald (ed.). *McLuhan Hot & Cool: A Critical Symposium* (New York: Dial, 1977).

Theall, Donald. *The Medium Is the Rear View Mirror: Understanding McLuhan* (Montreal: McGill-Queen's University Press, 1971).

Theall, Donald (with E. S. Carpenter). *The Virtual Marshall McLuhan* (Montreal: McGill-Queen's University Press, 2001).

Toye, William. "Commentaries and Annotations." In *The Letters of Marshall McLuhan*, Matie Molinaro, Corinne McLuhan, and William Toye (eds.), (Toronto: Oxford University Press, 1987).

Zingrone, Frank, and Eric McLuhan (eds.). *Essential Marshall McLuhan* (Toronto: Anansi, 1995).

Donald F. Theall

McPHERSON, AIMEE SEMPLE (1890–1944)

McPherson, the first major female revivalist in the United States, was born near Ingersoll, Ontario, Canada, to James and Minnie Kennedy. Her father was a Methodist, and her mother was active in the Salvation Army. As a result, Aimee was early exposed to her father's traditional piety and her mother's activist theology. As a student at the Ingersoll Collegiate High School (1905–8), Aimee was introduced to Charles Darwin's theory of evolution, which shook her Christian belief. Her faith was later restored, largely as a result of the sermons of Robert Semple, a young Pentecostal evangelist. Aimee married Semple and traveled with him as a missionary to China, but he died soon afterward. Aimee relocated to the United States, married Harold McPherson, and settled in Providence, Rhode Island. She began work as an itinerant evangelist, eventually divorced her husband, and moved to Los Angeles with her mother in 1918. McPherson continued her revivals, built the spacious Angelus Temple to accommodate them, and acquired a radio station. She emphasized the "foursquare gospel"—regeneration, divine healing, the Second Coming of Christ, and the baptism of the Holy Ghost (Thomas 1970, 20)—and she named her organization the International Church of the Foursquare Gospel. In 1926, she disappeared from a California beach, reemerging two months later in Arizona and claiming that she had been kidnapped. Her disappearance was alleged by many to have been a lover's tryst, however, and the scandal cast a shadow over the remainder of her career. She died of an apparent accidental overdose of a prescribed sedative in 1944.

Evidence of McPherson's early literary influences is scant, but she apparently owed much of her resourcefulness and resolve to lessons that she learned from Alice Caldwell Hagen's childhood story, *Mrs. Wiggs of the Cabbage Patch* (Blumhofer 1993, 19). McPherson's most significant literary influence, however, was the Bible, and its narratives informed her outlook on the world. At the age of five, she could recite whole chapters of biblical books (Thomas 1970, 3). This sheltered outlook received a severe shock when she encountered the theory of evolution in her high school textbook, *High School Physical Geography*. In an attempt to discover the truth about God's existence, McPherson delved into the works of such thinkers as Voltaire, Robert Ingersoll, Thomas Paine, and Charles Darwin, and she gained a command of contemporary science (Epstein 1993, 31). Eventually, McPherson rejected Darwinism, and the Bible again became her primary intellectual and literary reference. In fact, she derived her "foursquare gospel" in part from the visions in the biblical book of Ezekiel (Blumhofer 1993, 190–92). In a course entitled "Foursquare Fundamentals" that McPherson taught at her L. I. F. E. Bible college, she also cited John Wesley, Dwight L. Moody, and Albert Benjamin Simpson, a Canadian evangelist who emphasized a "Fourfold Gospel," as individuals whose work informed her beliefs (Epstein 1993, 432–33).

Archives

Heritage Department, International Church of the Foursquare Gospel, Los Angeles, Calif. McPherson left no private papers or correspondence and these materials are related to her career.

Printed Sources

Bahr, Robert. *Least of All Saints: The Story of Aimee Semple McPherson* (Englewood Cliffs, N.J.: Prentice-Hall, 1979).

Blumhofer, Edith L. *Aimee Semple McPherson: Everybody's Sister* (Grand Rapids, Mich.: William B. Eerdmans, 1993).

Epstein, Daniel Mark. *Sister Aimee: The Life of Aimee Semple McPherson* (New York: Harcourt Brace Jovanovich, 1993).

Thomas, Lately. *Storming Heaven: The Lives and Turmoils of Minnie Kennedy and Aimee Semple McPherson* (New York: William Morrow, 1970).

———. *The Vanishing Evangelist: The Aimee Semple McPherson Kidnaping Affair* (New York: Viking, 1959).

Scott Lupo

MEAD, MARGARET (1901–1978)

Margaret Mead was born in Philadelphia, Pennsylvania. Her parents, Edward Sherwood Mead and Emily Fogg Mead, were both academics and encouraged their oldest daughter's intellectual questions. Her paternal grandmother, Martha Ramsey Mead, was her first teacher and schooled her at home until she was eight. Mead's formal education was interspersed with years of home schooling and permission from her parents to come and go from classes as she pleased. Margaret was attracted to a religious life, even though her family was not. She explored several denominations before settling on the Episcopal faith at age 11. In 1919 she attended her father's alma mater, DePauw College in Indiana, intent on becoming a writer. She transferred to Barnard where she found her niche in the psychology department. After graduating with a B.A. from Barnard in 1923, Mead completed an M.A. in psychology 1924 and a doctorate in anthropology in 1929 at Columbia, studying with Franz Boas and Ruth Benedict. Mead's first field trip was to Samoa where her work on adolescent girls resulted in her book, *Coming of Age in Samoa* (1928). A tireless researcher, Mead continued to study the peoples of the Pacific Islands. Her base throughout her life was as a curator at the American Museum of Natural History in New York. Later in life Mead turned to studies on contemporary life that focused on diet, mental health, and technology. Mead married three times. With Gregory Bateson, her third husband, she developed ethnographic film techniques still considered important. Mead's legacy is her cross cultural work which focuses on keen observations of places and people, especially adolescents and children.

In an essay included in *A History of Psychology in Autobiography*, vol. VI (1974), Mead describes her reading practices. As a young girl, Mead read poetry and novels, children's books of her grandmother's generation and plays of her mother's liking. She also read classical mythology and all of Charles Dickens. In college psychology Mead studied the work of Sigmund Freud and **Carl Jung,** whose theories affected her anthropological work. Edward Sapir's book *Language: An Introduction to the Study of Speech* (1921) was significant to Mead and she passed it on to her daughter Catherine when she left for college. Prior to her fieldwork in Samoa, she read everything she could find on the Pacific Islands including Bronislaw Malinowski's book, *Argonauts of the Western Pacific*. Margaret Mead enjoyed long relationships with many colleagues whose work influenced her throughout her life. The manuscript of Ruth Benedict's *Patterns of Culture* (1934) arrived while Mead was in the field in New Guinea. She read Franz Boas's *The Mind of Primitive Man* (1911) as an undergraduate. Scholars who developed tests, such as **Jean Piaget** and Erik Erickson, influenced the way Mead constructed her field experiments.

Theodora Mead Abel's cross-cultural work on Rorschachs "enlivened" her own studies of Pacific cultures. Interdisciplinary reading was vital to Mead's work and she mourned the lack of it in younger colleagues.

Archives

Margaret Mead Administrative Correspondence, Interviews (1925–80), American Museum of Natural History, New York, N.Y.

Margaret Mead Archives, Pacific Ethnographic Archives, 1838–1987 (bulk 1911–78), Library of Congress, Washington, D.C. 1,800 boxes of diaries, correspondence, manuscripts, and photographs, over 500 films, over 1,000 recordings.

Printed Sources

Bateson, Mary Catherine. *With a Daughter's Eye: A Memoir of Margaret Mead and Gregory Bateson* (New York: William Morrow & Company, Inc., 1984).

Howard, Jane. *Margaret Mead: A Life* (New York: Simon & Schuster, 1984).

Mead, Margaret. *Blackberry Winter: My Earlier Years* (New York: William Morrow & Co., Inc., 1972).

———. "Margaret Mead." In Gardner Lindzey (ed.), *A History of Psychology in Anthropology*, vol. 6 (Englewood Cliffs, N.J.: Prentice-Hall, Inc. 1974).

Millie Jackson

MEIR, GOLDA (1898–1978)

Golda Mabovitch, the prime minister of Israel from 1969 to 1973, was born in Kiev, Russia. Due to hardship and extreme poverty, her family immigrated to the United States in 1906 and settled in Milwaukee, Wisconsin. Following in the footsteps of her sister Sheyna, nine years her senior, she joined the Socialist-Zionist Poale Zion in 1915. She enrolled in the Milwaukee Normal School and then the Teachers' Training College in 1916. A year later she married Morris Myerson, a sign painter, who introduced her to classical music, Lord Byron, Percy Bysshe Shelley, John Keats, and the *Rubáiyát* of Omar Khayyám. The young couple left for Palestine in 1921, settling first in Kibbutz Merhavia and then moving to Tel Aviv and Jerusalem, where they started a family—a son, Menachem, was born in 1924 and a daughter, Sarah, was born in 1926. In 1928 Meir embarked on a lifelong political career as she joined the Women's Labor Union. In 1934, she became a member of the executive committee of the Israel Labor Union and later headed its political department. During the 1940s, as the head of the political department of the Jewish Agency, she actively negotiated concessions with the British mandatory government. Upon the establishment of the state of Israel in 1948, Meir was appointed the first ambassador to Moscow, a position she held until April 1949. Later that year, as a new member of the Israeli Parliament, she became the minister of labor. From 1956 to 1965, Meir served as the first female foreign minister of Israel, developing new relationships between Israel and various African, Asian, and Latin American countries and gaining acclaim worldwide. On retirement from the foreign ministry, she accepted the post of the secretary general of the Labor Party. In 1969 after the sudden death of Prime Minister Levi Eshkol, Meir became the world's second female prime minister after Madame Sirimavo Bandaranaike of Sri Lanka. She resigned in 1974, deeply distraught by the conclusions of the Agranant Inquiry Commission, ruling that the Israeli Defense Forces (IDF) and Meir's government had erred in assessing the imminent danger posed to the nation before the Yom Kippur War in 1973.

Regina Medzini, Meir's lifelong friend, recalls that young Golda preferred reading to play and socialization. She frequented the local library, consuming works of Russian authors such as Nikolai Gogol, Lev Tolstoy, and Fyodor Dostoyevsky; French authors such as Victor Hugo, Guy de Maupassant, and Anatole France; and English and American authors such as Arnold Bennett, Charles Dickens, Mark Twain, and **Sinclair Lewis.** The greatest influence in Meir's life, apart from her husband, was her elder sister Sheyna, a radical socialist, who introduced her to Socialism and Zionism. While living with her sister in Denver, Meir studied the writings of Pëter Kropotkin and Emma Goldman and the theories of anarchism, pacifism, and feminism. She also became enamored with the Yiddish literature of Mendele Mokher Safarim, Sholem Aleichem, and Y. L. Peretz. In "The Zionist Purpose," a speech delivered at Dropsie College in November 26, 1967, Meir talked about the enormous admiration she felt for the works of four writer-activists who had a paramount effect on the Jewish population of pre-state Israel and on her own convictions: Aaron David Gordon's *Selected Essays*, Berl Katzenelson's *What Is Socialist Zionism? Aims and Principles of the United Zionist Party*, Samuel Yavnieli's *A Journey to Yemen and Its Jews* (Hebrew) and Rachel Bluwstein's *Flowers of Perhaps*. These revolutionary socialist-Zionists, founders of the kibbutz movement, strongly believed that only self-labor can emancipate Jews from their ghetto mentality and warrant them a moral and historical right to the land of Israel, where they can erect a model society.

Archives

Israel State Archives, Quiryath Ben Gurion, Jerusalem, includes the official and private documents of Golda Meir.

Archives for the Labour Movements, Lavon Institute, Tel-Aviv, includes official and private documents.

The Ben Gurion Archives, The Ben Gurion Research Center, Sde Boker Campus, Israel, maintains a correspondence file between David Ben Gurion and Golda Meir.

In the United States, extensive collections can be found at the Golda Meir Library at the University of Wisconsin, Milwaukee, and the Golda Meir Center for Political Leadership in Denver, Colorado.

Printed Sources

Mann, Peggy. *Golda: The Life of Israel's Prime Minister* (New York: Coward, McCann & Geoghegan, 1971).

Martin, Ralph G. *Golda: The Romantic Years* (New York: Scribner's, 1988).

Meir, Golda. *Golda Meir Speaks Out*, Marie Syrkin (ed.), (London: Weidenfeld and Nicolson, 1973).

———. *A Land of Our Own: An Oral Autobiography*, Marie Syrkin (ed.), (New York: Putnam's, 1973).

———. *My Life* (New York: Putnam's, 1975).

———. *This Is Our Strength: Selected Papers* (New York: Macmillan, 1962).

Meir, Menahem. *My Mother Golda Meir: A Son's Evocation of Life with Golda* (New York: Arbor House, 1983).

Noble, Iris. *Israel's Golda Meir: Pioneer to Prime Minister* (New York: J. Messner, 1972).

Dina Ripsman Eylon

MENCKEN, HENRY LOUIS (1880–1956)

H. L. Menken was born in Baltimore, Maryland, to comfortably bourgeois German-American parents, August Mencken, co-owner of a cigar store, and Anna Margaret Abhau. Mencken's German-born paternal grandfather, Burkhardt Mencken, instilled in both his son and grandson a fierce pride in their seventeenth- and eighteenth-century German ancestry of prominent jurists and scholars. Although he attended Sunday school and was confirmed as a Lutheran Protestant, Mencken shared the rationalist, freethinking skepticism of his father and grandfather. Mencken attended a private school, Knapp's Institute, Baltimore, patronized largely by middle-class German-Americans, and Baltimore Polytechnic, graduating in 1896 as class valedictorian. Under parental pressure, Mencken worked briefly in the family cigar factory, but his father's death in 1899 freed him to follow the journalistic career he preferred. Mencken initially worked for the *Baltimore Morning Herald*, winning rapid successive promotions, and when that journal ceased publication in 1906 he joined the *Baltimore Sun*, remaining there until 1948, when a stroke forced him into retirement. Mencken quickly won a reputation far surpassing that of a journalist, as an iconoclastic political, literary, and cultural critic whose prolific writings, including newspaper columns, drama criticism, reviews, and essays in a wide variety of periodicals, together with numerous books, were perceived as defining a new, twentieth-century American outlook. From 1908 onward Mencken traveled extensively, acquiring greater familiarity with European cultural trends, but he urged Americans to develop their own robust national literary and aesthetic tradition, reflecting all their country's variegated racial roots, and reject prevailing establishment assumptions that American literature should be Anglo-Saxon, idealistic, polite, and morally uplifting. Several successive editions of *The American Language*, his seminal work on linguistics, demonstrated that enormous differences in usage separated British and American English. Before American intervention in both world wars, Mencken expressed politically contentious and somewhat maverick pro-German views. A leading liberal, modernist intellectual voice dissenting from the complacency of 1920s America, Mencken spoke out vigorously on such socially controversial issues as political intolerance, race, prohibition, evolution, education, and sexual morality. He also introduced numerous new writers, such as **James Joyce** and **Aldous Huxley,** to the American public. In the 1930s Mencken's economically conservative and anti-Soviet, pro-German views placed increasing distance between him and the American left. In the 1980s and 1990s, long after his death, the posthumous publication of Mencken's diaries and autobiography and the illiberal, racist, and anti-Semitic sentiments they contained again made him a controversial figure.

From childhood Mencken foraged voraciously among British and American literature from his father's bookshelves and Baltimore's Enoch Pratt Free Library. His leading literary inspirations and models included Thomas Henry Huxley, William Makepeace Thackeray, Rudyard Kipling, George Bernard Shaw, O. Henry, Stephen Crane, Mark Twain, Theodore Dreiser, Frank Norris, and Ambrose Bierce, and the critics George Ade, Percival Pollard, and James Huneker, who fueled his conviction that the critic's function was to challenge accepted beliefs and oppose all censorship, especially the tyranny of majority views to which democracy was liable. Mencken's strong German-American self-identification bolstered this outlook and contributed to his pro-German sympathies in both world wars, as did his admiration for Friedrich Nietzsche's brutally competitive philosophy, on which Mencken published a book-length study in 1908. Mencken's boyhood reading of and admiration for scientific works by Huxley, Charles Darwin, and Herbert Spencer, from whom he derived his staunch faith in evolution and also in social and international competition as an engine of progress, probably triggered his lifelong interest in medicine and natural sciences. Writings by William Graham Sumner, Spencer's leading American admirer, strengthened Mencken's economic conservatism and commitment to capitalism. His extensive reading also instilled a romantic admiration for an idealized version of eighteenth-century Southern plantation society, which perhaps helped to account for some of his racially controversial statements.

Archives

H. L. Mencken Papers, New York Public Library, New York. A massive collection of Mencken's literary correspondence and writings.

H. L. Mencken Manuscripts, Enoch Pratt Free Library, Baltimore, Maryland. Extensive biographical and literary materials, including voluminous diaries and autobiographical manuscripts.

Printed Sources

Hobson, Fred. *Mencken: A Life* (New York: Random House, 1994). The leading biography.

Mencken, H. L. *The Diary of H. L. Mencken*, Charles A. Fecher (ed.), (New York: Alfred A. Knopf, 1989).

———. *Happy Days, 1880–1892* (New York: Alfred A. Knopf, 1940).

———. *Heathen Days, 1890–1936* (New York: Alfred A. Knopf, 1943).

———. *My Life as Author and Editor*, Jonathan Yardley (ed.), (New York: Alfred A. Knopf, 1993).

———. *Newspaper Days, 1899–1906* (New York: Alfred A. Knopf, 1941).

Priscilla Roberts

MIES VAN DER ROHE, LUDWIG (1886–1969)

Ludwig Mies van der Rohe was born in Aachen, Germany, and, with **Frank Lloyd Wright** and **Le Corbusier,** would become one of the twentieth century's most important architects. At age 19, he left Aachen for Berlin, where he would lead a modernist revolt against the imperial and nationalist architecture of Wilhelmine Germany. He served in the army for a short time in 1905 and came of age as an architect between 1906 and 1923, completing his Riehl House (1906) as a real start at designing and completing his plan for the Freidrichstrasse Office Building (1921) as passing German architecture into modernity. During the years in between he developed a nearly adversarial rivalry with **Walter Gropius** (who opened the Bauhaus in 1919), saw Frank Lloyd Wright's work for the first time, and worked as a postwar editor for the functionalist journal *G*. He also tackled the problems of the tall building with his first truly modernist work, the rejected Honeycomb (1921) competition entry for an office building in Berlin. Rohe's strict modernism would keep him limited to the tall office building and the house of single, open space during the rest of his career. In Rohe's remaining years in Germany, he completed the Weissenhofsidelung housing colony in 1927 as the representation of a real international style, in 1928 presented his masterpiece (the German Pavilion of the Barcelona International Exposition), accepted the directorship of the Bauhaus in 1930 (later closed in 1932 by the Nazis), and joined a group under propaganda minister **Joseph Goebbels** given the task of designing projects for the 1935 World's Fair that were never completed. He left Germany in 1938 after accepting a position as head of the Armour Institute of Technology in Chicago and after an unexpected visit by Gestapo agents. Rohe's first design opportunity in America occurred in 1939 with the entire Armour campus, renamed the Illinois Institute of Technology (IIT) after a merger. His first completed project for the school's campus was the Minerals and Metals Research Building in 1943. After a Museum of Modern Art retrospective of his work in 1947, Rohe became the most potent public architect of postwar America, and his office enjoyed over 100 design commissions on three continents. Among his credits are the 860–880 Lake Shore Drive twin apartment buildings (1949–51), the towers of 900 Esplanade and Commonwealth Promenade of Diversey Parkway (1959) in Chicago, and the Seagram Building in New York City (1958), generally considered the most important tall building of the post–World War II period. At 72 years old, Mies formally retired from IIT in 1958. His last major building before his death in 1969 was the Berlin National Gallery (1962–67).

Despite postmodernist attacks against modern architecture as sterile and inhumane, Mies's position as a pre-eminent architect remains. During his career, Rohe's influences were largely literary and philosophic, ranging as far as Oswald Spengler, St. Thomas Aquinas, and St. Augustine. As early as his days in Aachen, Rohe found a copy of the *Die Zukrunft (The Future)* journal while cleaning out a desk and credited interest in the journal as a point leading him to thinking about spiritual matters, philosophy, and culture. With his first client, Professor Alois Riehl, Rohe was introduced into philosophy circles, and as his work as a modernist emerged, he moved toward a Spenglerian-Aquinaian argument that there was an overreaching truth that culture depended on and the role of an architect was in recognizing and presenting this truth. While he denied in several interviews that he was influenced by Spengler, he owned both the 1918 and 1922 copies of *Decline of the West* in his library. Though he abandoned organized religion upon becoming an architect, Rohe admired the philosophies of Aquinas and Augustine, because they echoed his own beliefs that creativity was distillation rather than inspiration, and their arguments that the work of God could be studied and understood through scientific method. His interest in Aquinas and Augustine may have led him in his later years to read the work of major scientists, including Julian Huxley, Arthur Eddington, Sigmund Freud, Werner Heisenberg, and Erwin Schrodinger, to help him view science as a rational religion containing a higher unifying system than just theoretical postulates. Rohe also seems to have been influenced by the philosophy of Plato, whom he was reading during work on the Honeycomb design.

Archives

Mies van der Rohe Archive at the Museum of Modern Art, New York: most of his professional files and many personal papers, over 1,000 of his drawings.
Library of Congress, Washington, D.C.: archival material.

Printed Sources

Blake, Peter. *The Master Builders: Le Corbusier, Mies van der Rohe, Frank Lloyd Wright* (New York: W.W. Norton & Co., 1996).

Campbell, Joan. *The German Werkbund: The Politics of Reform in the Applied Arts* (Princeton: Princeton University Press, 1977).

Mies Reconsidered: His Career, Legacy, and Disciple (Chicago: Art Institute of Chicago, 1996).

Schulze, Franz. *Mies van der Rohe: A Critical Biography* (Chicago: University of Chicago Press, 1985).

Christopher C. Strangeman

MILLER, ARTHUR (1915–)

Arthur Miller was born on October 17, 1915, in New York City. His family later moved to Brooklyn. Miller's mother, Augusta, enrolled him in Abraham Lincoln High School one year before he graduated grade school. As a teenager, he worked at several odd jobs, including carpentry and delivering bakery goods, in order to raise money for college. Miller, who began writing plays at the age of 20, later went to the University of Michigan where in 1938 he graduated with a bachelor of arts degree. While at the university, Miller was first recognized as an up-and-coming author and playwright, winning two awards. In 1939, he wrote *The Man Who Had All the Luck*. In 1940, he married his first wife, Mary Grace Slattery. They had two children, a son Bob and a daughter Jane. *The Man Who Had All the Luck* went to Broadway in 1944, but was a failure. Miller still worked at various jobs but continued to write plays as well as scripts for radio. In 1947, he wrote *All My Sons*, for which he won the New York Drama Critics Circle Award. *Death of a Salesman* went on Broadway in 1949, won the Pulitzer Prize, and remains one of Miller's most popular plays. By 1950, Miller was one of America's favorite playwrights. In 1951, through mutual friend Elia Kazan, Miller first met Marilyn Monroe. *The Crucible*, which went on Broadway in 1953 and subsequently won a Tony Award, was another success. In 1955, he wrote *A View from the Bridge*, which failed. Miller divorced Mary Grace and married Monroe in 1956. While married to Monroe he wrote the screenplay *The Misfits*, which became a movie in which she starred. In 1961, Monroe and Miller divorced. The marriage to Monroe may have affected some of Miller's works, including his play *After the Fall*, seen perhaps not only as a thinly disguised portrait of Monroe's troubled life, but as representative of human vulnerability and an illustration of private anguish. In 1962, he married photographer Inge Morath with whom he subsequently had a daughter, Rebecca. Later works included *Incident at Vichy*, *The Price*, *The Creation of the World and Other Business*, *The American Clock*, and *Broken Glass*. Miller also wrote the script for *Playing for Time*, a 1980 television film about a women's orchestra in a Nazi concentration camp, for which he won an Emmy Award. In 1987, Miller published his autobiography *Timebends: A Life*, and in the summer of 2001, *The Man Who Had All the Luck* was staged at the Williamstown Theatre Festival in Massachusetts.

In *Timebends* Miller cited that two of the most important literary influences on him as an author were not writers or even particular titles of books, but his mother Augusta and his aunt Stella (Miller 1987, 36). Miller further cited Russian authors Dostoyevsky and Tolstoy as having influenced his work; he said both writers were representative of the world's best authors (Miller 1987, 94). Miller described Marion Starkey's *The Devil in Massachusetts*, Charles W. Upham's *Salem*

Witchcraft, and investigations led by Senator Joseph McCarthy in the 1950s as having all influenced *The Crucible* (Miller 1987, 330). He also named **Franz Kafka**'s *The Castle* as a definitive work that influenced his literary style. Written in a simple yet exploratory style, *The Castle* continually provided Miller with a frame of reference on how to write. Other major literary influences included a book Miller read while in high school, *The Brothers Karamazov*, which he felt stimulated his love of Russian literature. Richard Hughes's *A High Wind in Jamaica* was another work that Miller described as so influential that he never forgot it (Shwartz 1999, 184).

Archives

Harry Ransom Humanities Research Center at University of Texas at Austin. The Center holds an enormous amount of Miller-related papers, including correspondence, notes, scripts, and sketches.

Special Collections Department, 7th Floor, Harlan Hatcher Graduate Library, The University of Michigan, Ann Arbor, Mich., 48109-1205.

Printed Sources

Bigsby, Christopher W. (ed.). *The Cambridge Companion to Arthur Miller* (Cambridge: Cambridge University Press, 1997).

Miller, Arthur. *Timebends: A Life* (New York: Grove Press, 1987).

Shwartz, Ronald B. *For the Love of Books: 115 Celebrated Writers on the Books They Love Most* (New York: Grosset/Putnam, 1999).

Wendy A. Maier

MILOSZ, CZESLAW (1911–)

Milosz Czeslaw is today the best known Polish poet in part owing to his receiving the Nobel Prize. Milosz grew up in a Polonised noble family in Lithuania that was then a part of the Russian Empire. He studied at the University of Vilnius (1930–34) and remains influenced by the city's cultural and religious diversity of Catholic, Judaic, Orthodox, and Protestant thought. He was also influenced by gnosticism, which is responsible for his rather stark views on nature, and by the pagan elements in Lithuanian folklore. Milosz's religious ideas at that time were influenced by Marian Zdziechowski, a Christian thinker and professor at the University of Vilnius, in addition to Russian writers including Lev Tolstoy and Vladimir Sergeyevich Solovyov. The list of Milosz's intellectual inspirations is vast and includes writers as diverse as Emanuel Swedenborg, William Blake, and especially his own relative, Oscar Milosz, "a Parisian recluse and a visionary" who interested him in mysticism and metaphysics and who gave him a deeper insight into the religion of the Old and New Testaments. During World War II, Milosz became interested in English and American poetry and began translating various poets who "intellectualize poetry" and influenced his poetic language. Among them are **T. S. Eliot,** whose use of irony Milosz admired, Edgar Allan Poe, Walt Whitman, and Robert Browning.

Milosz's early poems in *Trzy zimy* (*Three Winters*, 1936) present the world through a catastrophic lens and reflect the aura of the deepening prewar crisis in Europe. Milosz's catastrophist views owed much to Stanislaw Ignacy Witkiewicz, the playwright, philosopher, painter, and novelist whose work was the precursor of the theater of the absurd in the early 1920s.

After the war Milosz worked as a cultural attaché of the People's Poland, but in 1951 he requested political asylum in Paris. Two years later he published his famous and innovative study about the interdependence between a totalitarian state and the intellectuals who supported it (*Zniewolony umysl [The Captive Mind]*, 1953). As a consequence, his writings were banned in communist Poland for the next 30 years. He published extensively in France and then in the United States (*Traktat poetycki [Treatise on Poetry]*, 1957; *Miasto bez imienia [City without Name]*, 1969; *Kroniki [Chronicles]*, 1987), and in 1980 he received the Nobel Prize for literature. The language of Milosz's mature poetry is unique but he acknowledges the influence of Adam Mickiewicz, Poland's greatest romantic poet. He is also indebted to Stanislaw Brzozowski, a philosopher, critic, and novelist, in particular to his intellectual, nonemotional approach to ethical questions.

At the core of Milosz's writing is an ethical dilemma for the poet: choosing between detachment from life, which might be morally unacceptable but is necessary for writing, on the one hand, and full participation in life, which precludes writing about it, on the other. His notion of a poet's "double vision" of seeing life from very close and simultaneously maintaining a distance was influenced by Selma Lagerlöf's *Wonderful Adventures of Nils*, a book he read as a boy, and later by works of **Simone Weil** and her concept of distance as "the soul of beauty." He credited these writers in his Nobel lecture on December 8, 1980, and acknowledged "the generations who wrote in his native tongue as every poet inherits styles and forms elaborated by those who lived before him." Milosz rejected preoccupation with aestheticism in the name of poetry's moral obligation (*Traktat moralny [Treatise on Morals]*, 1948) and favored poetry that is understood as "an instrument of intelligence" such as the poetry of **W. H. Auden** and Karl Shapiro. Milosz's poetry is emotionally restrained, intellectual yet sensual, metaphorically dense, contemplative, and sometimes prophetic. It is rooted in his native Lithuania yet he felt more privileged than the Western poets for being able to write from the point of view of an outsider speaking with many voices. His extraordinary erudition and familiarity with poetry of Asia, especially the Indian poet Kabir, and with Japanese haiku, demonstrate his openness to diverse influences. His latest poetry has moved toward acceptance of the world as the poetic persona reaches *apokatastasis*, the state of equilibrium, absent from his earlier poems.

Although primarily a poet, Milosz has written several novels, including some with strong autobiographical elements. The autobiographical novel *The Valley of the Issa* (*Dolina Issy*, 1955) presents the world in a Manichean context, while *Native Realm* (*Rodzinna Europa*, 1959) is written from the viewpoint of an East European attempting to explain his "otherness" to the Western reader.

Archives

None available.

Printed Sources

Carpenter, Bogdana. "The Gift Returned," *World Literature Today* 4, 73 (Autumn 1999), 631–36.

Fiut, Aleksander. *The Eternal Moment: The Poetry of Czeslaw Milosz*, Theodosia S. Robertson (trans.), (Berkeley: University of California Press, 1990).

Haven, Cynthia L. "A Sacred Vision: An Interview with Czeslaw Milosz," *The Georgia Review* 57, no. 2 (2003), 303–14.

Milosz, Czeslaw. *Between Anxiety and Hope: The Poetry and Writing of Czeslaw Milosz*, Edward Możejko (ed.), (Edmonton: University of Alberta Press, 1988).

———. *Conversations with Czeslaw Milosz*, Ewa Czarnecka and Aleksander Fiut (eds.), Richard Lourie (trans.), (San Diego: Harcourt Brace Jovanovich, 1987).

Nathan, Leonard, and Arthur Quinn. *The Poet's Work: An Introduction to Czeslaw Milosz* (Cambridge: Harvard University Press, 1991).

Pinsky, Robert. "Czeslaw Milosz," *Partisan Review* 46 (1999), 145–53.

Katarzyna Zechenter

MIRO, JOAN (1893–1983)

Fundacio Joan Miro was born in Barcelona, Spain, and from an early age attended informal drawing lessons at La Llotja School of Fine Art. Despite pursuing further artistic studies at the Academia Gali, Miro worked for a number of years as a bookkeeping clerk in a specialty imports firm. Suffering from the effects of typhoid fever as well as a nervous breakdown, Miro resigned from his previous employment, endeavoring to use art as a means of rehabilitation. Possessing a life-long resistance to depicting the human form, Miro fused the styles of the fauvists, cubists, and impressionists into his own nonfigural, colorful biomorphic abstractions. After his first one-man exhibition in 1918, Miro moved to France to produce such masterpieces as *The Farm* (1922) and *Harlequin's Carnival* (1925). His atmospheric oneiric and Dutch interior paintings of 1925–28 were followed by two years of collage experimentation, after which Miro's work began to reflect the serious atmosphere surrounding the Second World War. In 1942 Miro returned to Barcelona, where he embarked on his self-proclaimed "assassination of painting," using a wide range of innovative materials and techniques that would influence American abstract expressionists such as Jackson Pollock. Miro won the Grand Prize for engraving at the 1955 Venice Biennale and in 1959 completed two large ceramic murals for the UNESCO building in Paris. In 1966 he was honored with a retrospective at the Tokyo and Kyoto Museums of Modern Art in Japan, but he continued to pioneer new artistic avenues well into the 1970s.

Joan Miro's art was truly a product of the literature of his era. In the Barcelona of his youth, Miro was exposed to two opposing literary movements. Noucentism was essentially new Mediterranean classicism based on Catalonian culture and best typified by the writings of Eugenio d'Ors, whose novels, including *La ben plantada*, Miro read as a youth. In opposition to this movement were the modernistes, authors whose external influences such as the symbolism of Belgian writer Maurice Maeterlinck led them down more expressionist and fantastical paths. The young Miro incorporated both the established and the creatively progressive in his work, an act that was reinforced and paralleled by his reliance on both traditional poetry and the work of his Paris contemporaries in later life. After 1920, Miro became acquainted with the French poets **Guillaume Apollinaire** and Pierre Reverdy, as well as the surrealist proponents Tristan Tzara, **André Breton,** Louis Aragon, and Phillipe Soupault. Although he failed to attend surrealist meetings, Miro incorporated the surrealists' sense of experimentation and innovation into his artistic productions and often formulated the subject matter of his pieces from unconscious impulses and dream experiences. Moreover, Miro would occasionally include the titles and contents of contemporary French poetry in his paintings, etchings, and sculptures. Coupled with this interest in the literature of his day was Miro's fascination with traditional spiritual authors. Miro was an avid reader of the Christian author St. Francis of Assisi, whose *Canticle of the Sun* he often referenced while completing his detaillist paintings of 1918–20. The work of early Eastern authors such as Lao-Tsu and the Tibetan ascetics influenced Miro as well. From these sources, Miro learned to keep his visual compositions uncluttered and simplistic and to concentrate through acts of meditation while awaiting inspiration for his work.

Archives

The Getty Research Institute for the History of Art and the Humanities, Special Collections, control no. CJPA86-A995.

Printed Sources

Dupin, Jacques. *Miro* (New York: Harry N. Abrams, 1993).
Erben, Walter. *Joan Miro: The Man and His Work* (New York: Taschen, 1998).
Lassaigne, Jacques. *Miro: Biographical and Critical Study* (Geneva: Skira Publishers, 1963).

Gregory L. Schnurr

MISES, LUDWIG VON (1881–1973)

Ludwig von Mises was born at Lemberg (today's Lviv, Ukraine), then a city in the Austro-Hungarian Empire. After attending the prestigious Akademisches Gymnasium in Vienna (1892–1900), he studied law at the University of Vienna (1900–1906). In 1906 Mises received his doctoral degree in both Canon and Roman Laws and from 1906 until 1912 he held a teaching position at the Wiener Handelsakademie für Mädchen (Viennese Commercial Academy for Girls). Mises was also employed as an economist by the Vienna Chamber of Commerce (1909–34) and after World War I he became the main economic advisor to the Austrian government. He was attending Eugen von Böhm-Bawerk's economics seminar at the University of Vienna (1904–14) when he published his first important theoretical book, *Theorie des Geldes und der Umlaufsmittel*. Mises began lecturing at the University of Vienna in 1913 but was called up soon after the outbreak of World War I to serve as a captain of the cavalry mainly on the eastern front. After the war, Mises took up lecturing at the University of Vienna (1918–34) but was unable to secure a tenure-track position. Between 1920 and 1934, he conducted a private seminar in his office for post-doctoral students and other invited guests and founded the Österreichische Institut für Konjunkturforschung (Austrian Institute for Business Cycle Research) in 1927. After **Adolf Hitler** had gained control in Germany, Mises accepted a professorship of International Economic Relations at the Graduate Institute of International Studies in Geneva, Switzerland, in 1934 before he emigrated to the United States in 1940. At New York University he was offered a visiting professorship from 1945 until 1969.

As a student of the Akademisches Gymnasium, Mises was especially interested in economic issues, but he was disappointed with the predominant German historical school. His main advisor at the university, Carl Grünberg, was influenced mainly by the German economic historian Georg Friedrich Knapp, one of the leading thinkers of the younger German historical school. Mises, however, found that the Grünberg-Knapp methodology did not provide scientific explanations of economic history. In his posthumously published autobiographical sketches, *Notes and Recollections* (1978), Mises claimed that his reading of Carl Menger's work *Principles of Economics* (German edition 1871) in December 1903 had the profoundest influence on his thinking about economics. As a result, he turned away from a left-liberal and interventionist position and embraced Menger's free-market liberalism. Mise's breakthrough as an economist was his *Theorie des Geldes und der Umlaufsmittel (The Theory of Money and Credit)*, which was published in 1912. The book questioned the Anglo-American quantity theory and Irving Fisher's "equation of exchange." Moreover, it proved the British Currency School and David Ricardo right. Drawing on Menger and Böhm-Bawerk, Mises predicted in his second major work, *Socialism: An Economic and Sociological Analysis* (German edition 1922), the downfall of socialism because, as he said, socialism was unable to undertake "economic calculation." Eugen von Böhm-Bawerk's influence on Mises cannot be overestimated as Böhm-Bawerk clearly criticized Karl Marx and his followers. The so-called "Austrian School of Economics," which was founded by Carl Menger, Böhm-Bawerk, and Friedrich von Wieser, was revived by Mises's radical laissez-faire doctrine.

Archives

Ludwig von Mises Institute, Auburn, Ala.: All of Mises's manuscripts and correspondence.

Printed Sources

Hazlitt, Henry. "Understanding 'Austrian' Economics," *The Freeman* (February 1981), 67–78.
Kirzner, Israel M. *Ludwig von Mises: The Man and His Economics* (ISI: Wilmington, 2001).
Mises, Ludwig von. *Notes and Recollections* (South Holland, Ill.: Libertarian Press, 1978).
———. *On the Manipulation of Money and Credit* (Dobbs Ferry: Free Market Books, 1978).
———. *Socialism: An Economic and Sociological Analysis* (Indianapolis: Liberty Classics, 1981).
———. *The Theory of Money and Credit* (Indianapolis: Liberty Classics, 1980).
Rothbard, Murray N. "Ludwig von Mises." In Holcombe, Randall G. (ed.), *15 Great Austrian Economists* (Auburn: Ludwig von Mises Institute, 1999).

Gregor Thuswaldner

MITTERAND, FRANÇOIS (1916–1996)

Born in Jarnac, a small village of west central France, François Mitterand studied law at the Ecole Libre des Sciences Politiques in 1934. He worked with a Vichy government agency but quickly broke his association with the Vichy regime in 1943 on account of its anti-Semitic actions. He joined the Resistance, but did not get along with de Gaulle. During the Fourth Republic, Mitterand served eleven governments with different ministerial titles. He joined the UDSR party (Union Démocratique des Socialistes de la Résistance). His constant opposition to de Gaulle propelled him to the political forefront. He received the control of the socialist party in 1971 and was elected president in 1981. His first seven-year term started with socialist ministers and ended with a period of coalition (1986–88). Reelected in 1988, he first appointed socialist ministers. But in 1993 a new coalition government occurred and lasted until 1995.

Mitterand was influenced by the socialist doctrine. He quickly showed a great talent for analyzing and synthesizing some French socialist movements such as Saint-Simon (1760–1825) in *Le catéchisme des industriels* (1823–24), Jean-Joseph

Proudhon in *La philosophie de la misère* (1848), and Louis Blanqui and Flora Tristan when they attacked the notion of propriety, underlined the power of democratic election, and requested the right of peaceable assembly. Following in the footsteps of Jules Ferry, who aimed to achieve free education, free press, and development of unions, he was also inspired by Jean Jaures, founder of *L'Humanité* and writer of *Histoire socialiste*, when he wanted to apply to France a more socioeconomic and dynamic power while encouraging the separation of church and state and a strong educational system. Mitterand's vision of nationalization of resources, social security, and added paid vacation was also inspired by Leon Blum, who governed France during *Le Front populaire* in 1936. Mendès France's articles about his decision to finish the Indochina war and his objections to CED (Communauté Européenne de Défense) would affect his decisions when president. But Mitterand developed his own political style in a mixture of complex and ideological dogma.

He was also influenced by important literary figures such as the romantic figures of Victor Hugo's *Les Misérables* (1866) and Lamartine's *Histoire des Girondins* (1847) in their fight to obtain democratic election and redistribution of wealth. **Albert Camus**'s point of view in *La Peste* (1947) on the absurdity of the human condition following the Second World War played a strong role in Mitterand's pursuit of peace and freedom for the world. A special mention is deserved for Charles Peguy with *Les cahiers de la quinzaine* (1900–1914) and Émile Zola with *Les Rougon-Macquart, histoire naturelle et sociale d'une famille sous le second empire* (1871–93): their socialist ideas in newspaper articles and their strong commitment for justice found echo in Mitterand. Strongly affected by the war, his constant quest for freedom and social change was in total conflict with General **Charles de Gaulle**'s *Mémoires de guerre* (1954–59). The stylistic approach of Marguerite Yourcenar in *Mémoires d'Hadrien* (1951) and **Marcel Proust**'s *A la recherche du temps perdu* (1913–27), stressing the delicate intricacy of past and present, the concept of death and literature, influenced both his books *Le grain et la paille* (1975) and *L'abeille et l'architecte* (1978). His friends who were journalists (Jean Daniel, *Le Nouvel Observateur*), writers (Marguerite Duras, *L'amour*, 1971), poets (Louis Aragon, *Le crève-coeur*, 1941) and architects (Louis Pei, *cour Napoléon*, 1986–88) brought him new perspectives on the value of man, beauty, and politics and were expressed in interviews and political speeches.

His principal changes following the presidential election reflected some ideals of the 1968 "May revolution," as well as socialist concepts, philosophy expressed in Voltaire's *Lettres philosophiques* (1734) and Jean-Jacques Rousseau's *Discours sur l'origine et les fondements de l'inégalité parmi les hommes* (1758) in their pursuit of equality and justice for all. **Michel Foucault**'s *Les mots et les choses* (1966), in his criticism of human sciences and fragmentation of history, and Gilles Deleuze's *Qu'est-ce que la philosophie* (1986), in which he stressed the notion of "difference," were reflected in Mitterand's speeches.

Mitterand's complex international, artistic, and theoretical formation led him to mix genres in politics. But his words were not always followed by corresponding actions, and it is true that his frequently changing course disappointed many of those who had carried him to power in 1981.

Archives

Archives Nationales de Paris; Bibliothèque Nationale de Paris; Socialist Party Headquarters, Paris.

Printed Sources

Bell, D. S., and Byron Criddle. *The French Socialist Party. The Emergence of a Party of Government* (Oxford: Clarendon Press, 1988).

Cole, Alistair. *François Mitterand. A Study in Political Leadership* (London and New York: Routledge, 1989).

Duhamel, Alain. *Une Ambition Française* (Paris: Plon, 1999).

Dupin, Eric. *L'Après Mitterand. Le parti Socialiste à la dériv* (Paris: Calmann-Lévy, 1991).

Mamère, Noel. *Ma République* (Paris: Seuil, 1999).

Mitterand, François. *L'abeille et l'architecte* (Paris: Seuil, 1978).

———. *Le grain et la paille* (Paris: Seuil, 1975).

Price, R. *A Concise History of France* (Cambridge, Mass.: Cambridge University Press, 1993).

Martine Sauret

MONDRIAN, PIETER CORNELIS (1872–1944)

Piet Mondrian was born in Amersfoort, the Netherlands. Upon completion of elementary studies he pursued a teaching diploma and taught for a brief time at a school that his father administered. In 1892 Mondrian moved to Amsterdam and studied fine art at the Rijksacademie, copying paintings from the Rijksmuseum and receiving additional private lessons from instructors. His early works exhibited a calm semi-naturalism that was quickly abandoned upon his introduction to cubism in 1911. Mondrian exhibited at the Salon des Independants in Paris before moving to Holland for four years during the First World War. In 1917 Mondrian founded De Stijl, an avant-garde style of art based on his concept of neoplasticism. Through his productions such as the nonrepresentational *Composition with Red, Yellow and Blue* (1937), Mondrian strove to express underlying universal absolutes through the use of flat primary colors, planar elements, and straight lines. Unable to sell his abstract work, Mondrian was forced to paint canvasses of flowers throughout the 1920s to earn enough to survive. He moved to New York in 1940 and two years later held his first one-man exhibition, showcasing work such as *Broadway Boogie-Woogie* (1942) that demonstrated his use of chain-link patterns of color. Mondrian died of pneumonia in the Murray Hill Hospital in New York City on February 1, 1944.

Mondrian's substitution of symbolic color for natural color and of nonrepresentational signs for perceived reality was directly linked to the literature of his era, especially that of the theosophist writers Henry Olcott and Madame Helena Blavatsky. Theosophy synthesized oriental religions, Western magic, Asian scripture, and Rosicrucian mythology into a type of organized occultism that espoused that knowledge of the laws of the universe could be obtained by discarding the immediate and the tangible. Mondrian, who was a member of the Theosophical Society, believed that by banishing nature from art one could also expel the irrational and emotional to expose universal truths. This nineteenth-century idea was closely linked to that of ancient philosophers such as Plato, who espoused that universal order and higher consciousness could be demonstrated through the use of perfect solids. Artists contemporary to Mondrian, such as **Constantin Brancusi,** also believed that the essence of things was not expressed in their external form and that it was impossible for artists to express anything essentially by imitating the exterior. It was this belief that art could provide a transition to regions of deeper, spiritual reality that led Mondrian to champion the use of the nonrepresentational over the traditional and figural in his art. Mondrian was not interested in the formal design aspects of his work or in achieving correct mathematic proportions in painting. His principles of neoplasticism clearly reflected the ideas of contemporary religious writers such as Jan Greshoff, Martinus Nijhoff, and Adrian Roland Holst as well as the popular poets **T. S. Eliot** and **William Butler Yeats**. These authors' more mystical and supernatural outlook on the universe and man's relationship to his environment filled a vacuum in the Western psyche that the numerous attacks on conventional religious belief, issued by the writings of Friedrich Nietzsche, Charles Darwin, and Sigmund Freud, had left barren.

Archives

The Getty Research Institute for the History of Art and the Humanities, Special Collections, control no. CJPA1366111-A.
Archives of American Art, Smithsonian Institution, Washington, D.C., control no. DCAW211732-A.

Printed Sources

Holtzman, Harry, and Martin S. James (eds.). *The New Art–the New Life: The Collected Writings of Piet Mondrian* (New York: Da Capo, 1993).
Janssen, Hans et al. *Piet Mondrian* (Toronto: Bulfinch Press, 1994).
Milner, John. *Mondrian* (London: Phaidon, 1994).

Gregory L. Schnurr

MONNET, OMER MARIE GABRIEL JEAN (1888–1979)

Jean Monnet was born at Cognac, France, the son of a small brandy grower and freethinking radical socialist who advised his son to think for himself rather than read books (Brinkley and Hackett 1991, 123). Despite a devoutly religious mother and later a wife who was a nominal Roman Catholic, Monnet rarely if ever demonstrated substantial interest in religion. Educated locally near Pons and in Cognac, he left school at sixteen after passing his first *baccalauréat*, joining his father's business. Monnet spent World War I in the inter-Allied economic bureaucracy, and from 1919 to 1923 was deputy secretary general of the new League of Nations, subsequently resuming his business career with a New York–based investment bank. A Free French economic expert during World War II, he devised the postwar Monnet Plan to facilitate France's recovery. Convinced that only full-scale European cooperation would prevent future devastating wars, from 1945 onward Monnet quietly but relentlessly crusaded for this, playing central roles in establishing the 1951 European Coal and Steel Community, of which he became first president, and its 1957 successor, the European Economic Community, which ultimately evolved into the European Union. For 20 years beginning in 1955, Monnet—virtually universally considered unified Europe's preeminent founder—headed the Action Committee for the United States of Europe, working constantly to strengthen existing institutions.

Notoriously unintellectual, possessing no university degrees and indifferent to theory, Monnet was "no great reader, except of newspapers," rarely made literary allusions (Brinkley and Hackett 1991, 122–23), and disliked metaphors and studied stylistic effects (*Témoignages* 1989, 182, 355). While Monnet's activities effectively exemplified many of their precepts, friends believed him unfamiliar with the philosophical works of René Descartes or Immanuel Kant or such contemporaries as Raymond Aron (Brinkley and Hackett 1991, 40; Bossuat and Wilkens 1999, 484). Yet Monnet frequently quoted his favorite writer, the nineteenth-century Swiss diarist Henri-Frédéric Amiel, on the necessity to preserve individuals' accomplishments by establishing appropriate permanent institutions (Monnet 1976, 393). Similarly influential was the prominent French poet-essayist Paul Valéry, whose warning against being constrained by historical precedents Monnet cited approvingly, marking up and frequently rereading his *Regards sur le monde actuel* (Roussel 1996, 21; *Témoignages* 1989, 573). An inspirational anthology, *The Spirit of Man* (1916), its compiler British poet laureate Robert Bridges, was his favorite bedside book, and though he supposedly "never read novels," Monnet relaxed with Peter Cheyney's hard-boiled detective stories (Duchêne 1994, 401; Brinkley and Hackett 1991, 13, 121–22, 124). Although he was incapable of memorizing Corneille's verse, he apparently did recognize the plot of Shakespeare's *Merchant of Venice* (Brinkley and Hackett 1991, 21, 119). More broadly, an associate believed the Judeo-Christian tenets of European history, Greek philosophy, and the Bible implicitly pervaded Monnet's efforts for European unity (Bossuat and Wilkens 1999, 484).

Archives

Fondation Jean Monnet pour l'Europe, Ferme de Dorigny, Lausanne, Switzerland: the great bulk of Monnet's surviving personal papers, though many pre-1940 materials disappeared during World War II.

French National Archives, Paris, France: Ministry of Foreign Affairs records include portions of Monnet's private papers for 1939–40.

Printed Sources

Bossuat, Gérard, and Andreas Wilkens (eds.). *Jean Monnet, l'Europe et les Chemins de la Paix* (Paris: Publications de la Sorbonne, 1999).

Brinkley, Douglas G., and Clifford P. Hackett (eds.). *Jean Monnet: The Path to European Unity* (New York: St. Martin's Press, 1991).

Duchêne, François. *Jean Monnet: The First Statesman of Interdependence* (New York: Norton, 1994).

Monnet, Jean. *Mémoire* (Paris: Fayard, 1976).

Monnet, Jean, and Robert Schuman. *Correspondance, 1947–1953* (Lausanne: Fondation Jean Monnet, 1986).

Roussel, Eric. *Jean Monnet 1888–1979* (Paris: Fayard, 1996).

Témoignages à la mémoire de Jean Monnet (Lausanne: Fondation Jean Monnet, 1989).

Priscilla Roberts

MONTINI, GIOVANNI BATTISTA

See Paul VI.

MOORE, HENRY (1898–1986)

Henry Moore was born in the coal-mining town of Castelford, Yorkshire, England, where he attended elementary and secondary school. Moore began a teaching career in 1915, but was called to war at the age of 18 where he served with the Civil Service Rifles and suffered a gas attack at the battle of Cambrai, France. Moore returned to study art as the only sculpture student at the newly inaugurated Leeds University and at the same time attended informal evening pottery classes. On scholarship, Moore traveled to London to study at the Royal College of Art and became a frequent visitor to the Victoria and Albert Museum. He also toured Italy on a six-month traveling scholarship, studying the work of the old masters. In 1928 Moore was granted his first public sculpture commission and held his first one-man exhibition at the Warren Gallery in London. He later accepted a seven-year appointment as instructor at the Royal College of Art and for an additional seven years held the position of department head at the Chelsea School of Art, during which time he produced monumental works such as his *Reclining Figure* (1936). Moore became a master of such materials as wood, stone, bronze, and marble, producing works centered around specific and recurring themes such as the mother and child. In 1941 Moore served as an official war artist and was recognized for his drawings of the London citizenry huddled in air raid shelters. He received an honorary doctorate from the University of Leeds (1945), won international sculpture prizes at the Venice, Tokyo, and San Paulo Biennales, and was a trustee of both the Tate and National Galleries in London. He became a Companion of Honor in 1955, received the British Order of Merit (1963) and the Erasmus Prize (1968), and produced commissioned works for the UNESCO Headquarters in Paris, the Lincoln Center of Performing Arts in New York, Toronto City Hall, and the National Gallery of Art in Washington, D.C.

Moore's monumental figures have been stylistically compared to the reclining figures of Chac-mool, Toltec-Mayan sculptures that would have been familiar to the artist through his readings of Frans Blom and Oliver LaFarge's *Tribes and Temples* (1926). Moore also read **D. H. Lawrence**'s *The Plumed Serpent* and was fascinated by the harshness of execution and truth to materials inherent in South American sculpture. As a youth, Moore read an abundance of classic literature, including the works of William Shakespeare, the French poet Charles Baudelaire, and contemporary authors such as **T. S. Eliot** and Lawrence. As an art student, Moore read Roger Fry and Clive Bell's *Vision and Design*, which contained numerous essays on ancient American and African sculpture that influenced the artist in his handling of material and expressive exaggeration of form. The writings of Henri Gaudier-Brzeska and **Vassily Kandinsky**'s *The Art of Spiritual Harmony* stated that sculpture should serve to express the emotions of the artist and need not be adjunct to existence. Moore adhered to these ideas as well as to those of the constructivists, who advocated that art, through transmission of meaning, is positive and enriching to its viewers.

Archives

Archives of American Art, Smithsonian Institution, Washington, D.C., control no. DCAW212069-A.
Museum of Modern Art, New York, control no. NYMX92-A2.

Printed Sources

James, Philip (ed.). *Henry Moore on Sculpture: A Collection of the Sculptor's Writings and Spoken Words* (New York: Da Capo Press, 1992).

Moore, Henry, and John Hedgecoe. *Henry Moore—My Ideas, Inspiration and Life as an Artist* (New York: Collins and Brown, 1999).

Parker, William. *Henry Moore: An Illustrated Biography* (London: Weidenfield and Nicolson, 1985).

Gregory L. Schnurr

MORRISON, TONI (1931–)

Toni Morrison was born in Lorain, Ohio, on February 18, 1931, the second of four children. She was named Chloe Anthony Wofford, a name she changed to Toni in college when people could not pronounce her first name. Her father, George Wofford, migrated from Georgia to Lorain. He worked as a welder, often holding three jobs to support the family. Her mother, Rahmah, was the daughter of Alabama sharecroppers who had migrated north in search of a better life. She ran the home and worked at what Morrison called "humiliating jobs" to help support the family. Her parents' views of white people influenced Morrison during her youth. Her father did not trust or believe any white person while her mother hoped that the white race would improve. The Woffords taught their children to rely on their own race and not to trust the society at large.

Morrison attended integrated schools in Lorain. She was the only Black child in her first grade class and the only one who could read. Morrison graduated with honors from Lorain High School in 1949. She then went to Howard University in Washington, D.C., where she earned a B.A. in English and classics in 1953. Following her graduation, she attended Cornell University, where she earned an M.A. in English. Her thesis explored suicide in Virginia Woolf's and William Faulkner's literature.

Morrison pursued a teaching career following college. She taught at Texas Southern University and Howard University. At Howard she met her husband, Harold Morrison, a Jamaican architect. They had two sons but the marriage ended in divorce. Morrison went on to work in publishing for Random House. She rose to the position of senior editor and shepherded writers such as Toni Cade Bambara, Angela Davis, and Gayle Jones through the editing process. Morrison has been Robert F. Goheen Professor in the Council of Humanities at Princeton University since 1989.

Numerous awards have been granted for Morrison's work. *The Bluest Eye* was her first novel, followed by *Sula, Song of Solomon, Beloved, Tar Baby, Jazz,* and *Paradise. Sula* won the National Book Award in 1974. *Beloved* was awarded the Pulitzer Prize in 1988 and was made into a film. Morrison was awarded the Nobel Prize for literature in 1993, the first African American woman to win it.

The roles of storyteller and listener are important to Toni Morrison. Stories, myths, folk tales, and family stories shaped Morrison's feeling for language at a young age. From these stories she gained an understanding of the importance of narrative structure. By the time she entered first grade she could read. As an adolescent she read Jane Austen, Fyodor Dostoyevsky, and Gustave Flaubert. Morrison recalls the specific details of culture and experience that the authors used in their books. She imitated that trait in her work when she became a writer. Her research on William Faulkner was also valuable, and Faulkner's style often can be seen in Morrison's work. In interviews Morrison frequently comments on the importance of reading and research. The seeds of history often appear in her work. For the *Black Book*, she collected materials that ranged from the period of slavery through the 1940s. These included accounts from newspapers, bills of sale, sheet music, letters, photographs, and other artifacts. The first-hand documents that she read for this project influenced other books as well. Researching a town, a history, or an era is often an important part of writing a novel for Morrison.

Archives

None available.

Printed Sources

Heinze, Denise. "Toni Morrison." In James R. Giles and Wanda H. Giles (eds.), *American Novelists Since World War II (Third Series). Dictionary of Literary Biography*, vol. 143. (Detroit: Bruccoli Clark Layman Book, Gale Research Inc., 1994).

Morrison, Toni. *Toni Morrison—Nobel Lecture. December 7, 1993.* http://www.nobel.se/literature/laureates/1993/morrison-lecture.html (accessed June 30, 2002).

Samuels, Wilfred D., and Clenora Hudson-Weems (eds.). *Toni Morrison* (Boston: Twayne Publishers, 1990).

Taylor-Guthrie, Danielle (ed.). *Conversations with Toni Morrison* (Jackson: University Press of Mississippi, 1994). A collection of the major interviews with Toni Morrison.

Millie Jackson

MOSLEY, OSWALD ERNALD (1896–1980)

Oswald Mosley was born at Rollaston Hall, Staffordshire. He studied at Winchester (1909–13) and was there confirmed as a member of the Church of England. Entering Sandhurst in 1914, he was commissioned into the cavalry before transferring to the Royal Flying Corps. Invalided out of active service, Mosley spent the rest of the war at the Ministry of Munitions and the Foreign Office. Beginning his political career as a Conservative MP in 1918, he broke with that party to sit first as an Independent before joining the Labour Party and becoming an MP and then a junior minister in the government of 1929–31. Following the rejection of his proposals to mitigate the effects of the Slump, Mosley founded the New Party, which failed at the polls in 1931. After this he took the step which would make him notorious, founding the British Union of Fascists (BUF) in 1932, which he led until interned as a security risk in 1940. Although framing innovative solutions for Britain's problems, Mosley became most associated in the British public mind with violence and anti-Semitism. This view of him ensured that his attempts to re-enter politics after 1945 were doomed to failure.

The pattern of Mosley's reading reflected the vicissitudes of his career. During times of intense commitment he relied on the research of assistants but periods of enforced idleness were seized upon for personal study. He described his reading whilst recuperating from wartime injuries—including Thomas Macaulay, Edward Gibbon, and theosophist works—as "omnivorous and voracious." Having decided to enter politics, he read the speeches of great parliamentarians. The hiatus in his parliamentary career in the 1920s and the year before the founding of the BUF were similar periods of concentrated study. In this respect at least, Mosley lived up to his ideal of the man of thought *and* action. His thought is distinctive in his attempt to synthesize a reasoned critique of liberal capitalism and proposals for its transformation with the stress on authoritarianism and vitalism more commonly associated with fascism. During the 1920s his economic ideas were influenced by **John Maynard Keynes**'s *Tract on Monetary Reform* (1923) and the "underconsumptionist" thesis of J. A. Hobson espoused by the Independent Labour Party. The other side of Mosley's thinking was influenced in the 1920s and after by George Bernard Shaw, in particular *The Perfect Wagnerite* (1898), *Caesar and Cleopatra* (1901), and *Back to Methuselah* (1921). Shaw remained an intellectual hero for Mosley throughout his life, but Mosley also read more widely during the 1930s, including Friedrich Nietzsche's *Thus Spake Zarathustra* (1883–91), and he was strongly influenced by Oswald Spengler's critique of European society, *The Decline of the West* (1918–22). During his wartime internment (1940–43), Mosley learned German and immersed himself deeply in modern and classical philosophy, drama, and literature—although, apart from Stendhal's *The Red and the Black* (1831), he never cared much for the novel. Of his wartime reading, **Carl Jung** and Johann Wolfgang von Goethe probably had the most influence on him. He committed many passages from Goethe's *Faust* (1808, 1832) and *Die Wahlverwandtschaften* (1809) to memory and later wrote an introduction for a translation of the former.

Archives

Mosley Papers, Special Collections, University of Birmingham Library.

Printed Sources

Mosley, Diana. *Loved Ones: Pen Portraits* (London: Sidgwick & Jackson, 1985).

Mosley, Nicholas. *Beyond the Pale: Sir Oswald Mosley and Family, 1933–1980* (London: Secker and Warburg, 1983).

———. *Rules of the Game: Sir Oswald and Lady Cynthia Mosley, 1896–1933* (London: Secker and Warburg, 1982).

Mosley, Oswald. *My Life* (London: Nelson, 1968).

Ritchel, Daniel. *The Politics of Planning: The Debate on Economic Planning in Britain in the 1930s* (Oxford: Clarendon, 1997).

Skidelsky, Robert. *Oswald Mosley* [1975] (London: Papermac, 1990).

Philip M. Coupland

MUHAMMAD, ELIJAH (1897–1975)

Muhammad was born Elijah Poole in Sandersville, Georgia, to a family of former slave sharecroppers. His father was a Baptist preacher. He received only two years of formal education, and left home at age 16. He married Clara Evans in 1919. Muhammad moved to Detroit, Michigan, in 1923, where he worked as a manual laborer until he was laid off in 1929. During the Great Depression he was forced to live on government relief for two years. In 1931 he met Wali Fard Muhammad (Wallace D. Fard), founder and leader of the "Lost-Found Nation of Islam in the Wilderness of America" (NOI). He joined the organization and soon became Fard's most trusted lieutenant. In 1932 he was sent to Chicago and successfully established Temple No. 2 of the NOI. After Fard's mysterious disappearance in 1934, Elijah assumed leadership of the NOI. Because of internal schisms, he relocated the headquarters to Chicago. In these years Fard was deified as Allah. Elijah Muhammad was instituted as the messenger of Allah and was always addressed with the title "the Honorable." In 1942, at the age of 45, he was arrested for discouraging young Black men from serving in the armed forces, but was acquitted. In the same year he was imprisoned for four years for refusing to comply with the Selective Service Act. As a leader he had his best and most difficult moments with **Malcolm X** (El-Hajj Malik El-Shabazz), who played a crucial role in the NOI from 1952 until his resignation in 1964. Under Elijah Muhammad's leadership, the NOI established more than a hundred temples. In accordance with its slogan "Build Black, Buy Black," the NOI created and operated a wide range of businesses, including farms, supermarkets, and a newspaper and even ran its own educational system. His radical message, which equated Christianity with racist oppression, shook the foundations of the Black Christian community and created a distinct voice outside of the mainstream civil rights movement. His message of Black liberation and self-awareness and his principled abstention from politics influenced the lives of numerous African Americans. At the popular level he became an inspiration for many Blacks who were suffering economic and social inequalities. His leadership is known for nurturing pride, self-sufficiency, and solidarity among African American Muslims. The NOI promoted a strong work ethic, banned criminal activity, and required members to be clean-cut and wear suits. Alcohol, tobacco, narcotics, and adultery were prohibited, and unhealthy food was derided as "slave food." In the final years of his life he toned down his criticism of Christianity, which encouraged dialogue among the major faiths, especially in the urban centers. Elijah Muhammad died in Chicago on February 25, 1975.

Muhammad's traumatic childhood during one of the harshest periods of Southern segregation played an important role in shaping his worldview as did his deep discussions on religion with his eldest brother, Billie, while he was unemployed during the Great Depression. His thinking was also shaped by various faiths, doctrines, and social movements that challenged the segregated, discriminatory social environment of the country. These included Bishop Henry McNeal Turner's International Migration Society and its later incarnation, the Universal Negro Improvement Association of Marcus Garvey; a mythical notion of history called *Ethiopianism*; and Noble Drew Ali's Moorish Science Temple Movement, with its "home made" *Holy Koran of the Moorish Science Temple*. Muhammad was also influenced by the self-help and solidarity-based Peace Mission Movement of Father Divine (George Baker), sundry eschatological and millenarian doctrines, and the Harlem Renaissance, which fostered an earnest sense of Black pride and resistance. The greatest influence upon his teaching and philosophy was Fard Muhammad's "The Supreme Lessons."

Archives

None known to exist.

Printed Sources

Clegg, Claude Andrew, III. *An Original Man: The Life of and Times of Elijah Muhammad* (New York: St. Martin's Press, 1997).

Evanzz, Karl. *The Messenger: The Rise and Fall of Elijah Muhammad* (New York: Pantheon Books, 1999).

Gardell, Mattias. *In the Name of Elijah Muhammad: Louis Farrakhan and the Nation of Islam* (Durham, N.C.: Duke University Press, 1996).

Lee, Martha F. *The Nation of Islam: An American Millenarian Movement* (Syracuse, N.Y.: Syracuse University Press, 1996).

McCloud, Aminah Beverly. *African American Islam* (New York: Routledge, 1995).

Muhammad, Elijah. *History of the Nation of Islam*, Nasir Makr Hakim (ed.), (Cleveland: Secretarius, 1994).

Turner, Richard Brent. *Islam in the African American Experience* (Bloomington, Ind.: Indiana University Press, 1997).

White, Vibert L. *Inside the Nation of Islam: A Historical and Personal Testimony by a Black Muslim* (Gainesville: University Press of Florida, 2001).

Yücel Demirer

MUNCH, EDVARD (1863–1944)

Edvard Munch was born in Loten, Norway, and moved to present day Oslo with his family in 1867. Both his mother and sister Sophie died prematurely, and in 1879 Munch escaped his traumatic childhood and entered college to study engineering. After a year of study, Munch's interests turned to art history, and he entered the Oslo School of Design, supervised by the academician Christian Krohg. This was followed by informal study at Frits Thaulow's open-air academy, wherein Munch became one of the "Christiania Boheme," a group of slightly radical students with a shared interest in modern art. In 1895 Munch painted *The Sick Child* and was awarded a grant from the Finne Bequest to travel to Paris and Antwerp. He held his first one-man show in 1889 and received a second and third scholarship to study European art in 1890 and 1891 respectively. During this time Munch initiated his *Frieze of Life*, a series of intimately symbolic and expressive paintings that portrayed the fragile cycle of life, death, and love. His best-known work, *The Scream* (1893), was part of this extensive grouping, and prints of Munch's work were popularized throughout Europe following its production. Munch exhibited at the Paris Salon des Independents (1898), participated in the 1899 Venice Biennale, and became associated with the Berlin succession painters in 1904. Suffering a nervous breakdown, Munch entered a Copenhagen clinic in 1908 but the following year began work on a series of three large murals for the assembly hall at Oslo University. By the time of his death at his home in Ekely, Munch's prodigious output had paved the way for German expressionism.

Munch's use of art as therapeutic self-presentation was linked to the beliefs of authors such as Emile Zola who espoused that art must not simply convey nature but existentially reveal the essence of its creator, offering a form of salvation in the process. Munch turned to Zola's work *L'Oeuvre* (1886) as justification for abandoning his naturalistic approach to painting in favor of a more expressionist style. Charles Henry's theories on the emotive power of color were also read by the artist, whose use of poignant hues and symbolist subject matter expressed his experiences transformed by time, emotions, and memory. This externalization of mood and experience was paralleled by the literature of Munch's era, including the Norwegian Knut Hamsun's novel *Sult*, which externalized the internal suffering of the urban poor and destitute. Authors such as Fyodor Dostoyevsky, Jens Peter Jacobsen, and Herman Bang also portrayed the often weary and hopeless mood of their era in dark and numinous novels and poems. The mystical content of much of Munch's art was influenced by monism, a spiritual viewpoint shared by many of his contemporaries including Ernst Haeckel and the Swedish author August Strindberg. Contributing to Munch's diversion from traditional Christian theology was his study of various neospiritual works of literature such as the novels of Stanislaw

Pryzbyszewski, Hans Jaeger's *Homo Sapiens*, and Theodor Daubler's *Northern Lights*. Munch was also known to have studied Arthur Schopenhauer's *Philosophie der Kunst* and Søren Kierkegaard's *Concept of Dread*, as well as Charles Darwin's *Origin of the Species* (1860) and *Descent of Man* (1871).

Archives

The Getty Research Institute for the History of Art and the Humanities, Special Collections, control no. CJPA86-A173.

Van Pelt Library, University of Pennsylvania, Philadelphia, Special collections, control no. PAUR93-A1088.

Printed Sources

Heller, Reinhold. *Munch: His Life and Work* (Chicago: University of Chicago Press, 1984).

Hodin, J. P. *Edvard Munch* (New York: Praeger Publishers, 1972).

Stang, Ragna Thiis. *Edvard Munch: The Man and His Art* (New York: Abbeville, 1979).

Gregory L. Schnurr

MUSSOLINI, BENITO AMILCARE ANDREA (1883–1945)

Benito Mussolini was born at Verano di Costa near Forlì, Italy. His father was a blacksmith and ardent socialist internationalist in a rural community near Bologna, then the focus of violent revolutionary spirit. From socialist roots and internationalism, Mussolini turned to nationalism, the extreme manifestation of which was the Fascist dictatorship for which he was assassinated.

Mussolini was born within two years of the deaths of Giuseppe Garibaldi and Karl Marx. At different stages of his life both influenced him. His father was a staunch atheist, his mother a devout Catholic schoolteacher. There are contradictory myths about Mussolini's childhood: the boy tearing apart live chickens; the reclusive bookworm. Fascist supporters later embroidered stories of his violent youth, the brutality and aggression, when probably he had a normal, happy childhood, though under the influence of his father's lessons on social injustice. He had a good education in church and secular schools and excelled academically despite his growing violence. He read Robert Ardigo's *Positivist Morality*, Francesco Fiorentino's *History of Philosophy*, and Victor Hugo's *Les Miserables*.

At 18 he became a schoolteacher, later traveling to Switzerland in pursuit of socialists and anarchists and avoiding military service. He became fluent in French and German. He read the works of Angelica Balabanoff, a socialist lecturer at the University of Lausanne. He did manual jobs like bricklaying but eventually concentrated on study, reading socialist and anarchist literature including Marx, Friedrich Engels, Karl Kautsky, Peter Kropotkin, Mikhail Bakunin, Rugnd Bebel, and Gustave Hervé, some of whom he translated into Italian. His favorite author was Georges Sorel because of his contempt for parliamentary compromise and reformism. He returned to military service in Verona in 1904, later saying a man must learn to obey before he can command. From 1909 he edited the socialist newspaper *L'Avvenire del Lavoratore* in Trentino, still under Austrian rule and torn between Italian nationalism, supported by the bourgeoisie, and socialism, represented by the Austrian Social

Democrats. Suspected as an anarchist, he was returned to the Italian authorities. In Forlì he wrote *Claudia Particella*, a novel about an ambitious courtesan who seduces a cardinal, and *Il Trentino veduto da un socialista*. He edited an extremist local newspaper, *La Lotta di Classe*, writing and acting in opposition to Italy's invasion of Libya and war with Turkey in 1911. He was imprisoned. Working out his philosophy from his reading, he embodied a strange mixture of pacifism and interventionism, socialism and totalitarianism, idealism and realism, romanticism and opportunism.

From 1912 he edited *Avanti!*, the Italian Socialist Party's daily newspaper published in Milan. During riots and strikes he called for mob violence to fight state violence, in the cause of proletarian power. He was disillusioned at socialists willing to engage in skirmishes but ultimately afraid to overthrow authority. In 1914 when many socialist parties in Europe turned from international ideals toward their individual states and war, the Italian party firmly opposed war. Mussolini wrote that the situation demanded flexibility and favored Italian intervention with the Allies against Germany, not least because the majority of Italians wanted it. Forced to resign from *Avanti!*, he established his own newspaper, *Il Popolo d'Italia*, calling for Italy to join what he described as a just, democratic war. He was conscripted in 1915, fighting on the Austrian front until he was wounded. He supported continuing war to absolute victory, calling the socialists traitors. As the Italian army collapsed, resigned, and deserted, Mussolini condemned pacificism and blamed weak government. He believed the crisis called for dictatorship as the only route to democracy. More than any other writer, Mussolini admired Machiavelli. But his interpretation of *The Prince* was narrow and personal and selectively peppered with Marx, Max Stirner, Friedrich Nietzsche, Sorel, Vilfredo Parreto, Gustave Le Bon, Giuseppe Prezzolini, Pyotr Alekseyevich Kropotkin, and Arthur Schopenhauer, reinterpreted into the cocktail that became fascism. In 1919 he founded the national Fasci di Combattimento, uniting groups in existence since their call for intervention in the war in 1914. They demanded universal suffrage, proportional representation, abolition of the Senate, and creation of national economic councils. In the 1919 election Fascist candidates, including Mussolini, were defeated by the Socialists, winning no seats. Fascism as a political force appeared dead. But the threat of Bolshevism alarmed Europe. As workers' action spread through northern Italy, the economy declined. The middle classes turned to fascism to fight the threat of anarchy.

From this time Mussolini was less influenced by literature than himself influential. He followed no one, acting on an ad hoc basis without a single guiding philosophy. His unselective interpretation of socialist and anarchist writers created an unpredictable mixture of violence, jargon, and personal aggrandisement. He successfully fought the 1921 election in the name of nationalism, citing the lives and work of Dante, Galileo, Giuseppe Verdi, Garibaldi, Giuseppe Mazzini, and Gabriele D'Annunzio. Clashes with socialists continued in and out of parliament, Mussolini alternating between skillful parliamentarian and mob supporter. He founded an intellectual paper, *Gerarchia*, promoting overthrow of democracy in favor of state control. He encouraged violent fascist squads organized on military lines to put down socialism and strikes. In 1922, under threat of a fascist siege of Rome, the king invited Mussolini to form a government. The Fascists had no majority, but Mussolini as prime minister held all necessary power. By 1924 he had a majority, an international reputation, and was admired not least by **Adolf Hitler.** By 1926 parliamentary democracy was dead and Mussolini was the Fascist dictator.

The positive side effects included suppression of the Sicilian Mafia while fascism lasted. Despite the dictatorship, freedom of discussion was tolerated, there was a revolution in architecture, emphasis on education, better working conditions, health care, and, so the myth goes, the trains ran on time. But even Mussolini failed to save Italy from the Depression or growing fears of war with Germany. In 1935 Italy invaded Ethiopia despite British opposition. Mussolini's support against Hitler was more important to Britain than the freedom of Ethiopia or Libya, his imperial plans, or his growing racism. But international pressures, including economic sanctions, forced Mussolini into alliance with Hitler. Convinced that Germany would win, he declared war on the Allies in 1940. When it was clear that Italy would fall to the Allies, Mussolini was overthrown and the Fascist regime fell. In prison, Hitler sent him a copy of Nietzsche's works. The Germans rescued Mussolini, taking him to Munich. He returned to German-occupied northern Italy, establishing the Italian Social Republic in Salò and denouncing the Savoia monarchy, but he was overpowered by Italian Communist partisans and executed.

Archives

The primary surviving source of archival material by Mussolini is his *Opera omnia*, 35 volumes edited by Edoardo e Duilio Susmel at the Biblioteca Nazionale in Firenze, 1951–62.

The Archivio Centrale di Stato in Rome, Segreteria Particolare del Duce, contains Mussolini's office papers and some correspondence, although much was destroyed, probably by Mussolini himself, in 1945.

St Antony's College, Oxford, has photocopies of other Mussolini papers.

Printed Sources

De Felice, Renzo. *Mussolini*, 5 vols. (Firenze: Le Monnier, and Torino: Giulio Einaudi, 1975–97).

Gregor, Anthony James. *Young Mussolini and the Intellectual Origins of Fascism* (Berkeley: University of California Press, 1979).

Mack Smith, Denis. *Mussolini* (London: Weidenfeld and Nicolson, 1981).

Pini, Giorgio, and Duilio Susmel. *Mussolini: l'uomo e l'opera*, 4 vols. (Firenze: Biblioteca Nazionale, 1953–55).

Ridley, Jasper. *Mussolini* (London: Constable, 1997).

Gillian Fenwick

NABOKOV, VLADIMIR VLADIMIROVICH (1899–1977)

Vladimir Nabokov, the Russian-born American writer, playwright, poet, critic, translator, scholar, and lepidopterist, was born in St. Petersburg to liberal aristocrats Elena Rukavishnikov and Vladimir Dmitrievich Nabokov. Celebrated for his brilliant, self-conscious prose, Nabokov is known best for *Lolita* (1955), his controversial novel that propelled him to world fame and perhaps cost him the Nobel Prize.

English Arthurian legends awakened Nabokov's imagination. He composed verse in three languages before enrolling in Tenishev's progressive school (1910–19). By age 15, he read hundreds of books in the original, including works by Robert Browning, Ivan Bunin (Nobel Prize, 1933), Anton Chekhov, Charles Darwin, Charles Dickens, Gustave Flaubert, John Keats, Mayne Reid, Arthur Rimbaud, Miguel de Cervantes Saavedra, William Shakespeare, Lev Tolstoy, Paul Verlaine, H. G. Wells, and by writers who later lost their appeal—Nikolay Chernyshevsky, Fyodor Dostoyevsky, Sir Arthur Conan Doyle, Edgar Allan Poe, and Jules Verne. Inspired by first love and Russia's silver-age poets, Nabokov published his first collection of poetry at age 17.

Fleeing Russia after the revolution (1919), he enrolled in Trinity College, graduating with a degree in romance and Slavic languages (1922). In Cambridge, he read Russian, English, and French classical works, developing an affinity for Russian and French medieval literature. He translated Romain Rolland's *Colas Breugnon*, Lewis Carroll's *Alice's Adventures in Wonderland*, and published the first of 18 Lepidoptera papers. Devoted to Vladimir Dahl's *Dictionary of the Living Russian Language*, *The Song of Igor's Campaign*, and Alexander Pushkin's *Eugene Onegin*, he later produced translations of the epic (1960) and the verse novel (1964).

In 1925, Nabokov married Véra Slonim (1902–91), his muse. In 1926, already the author of many short works, Nabokov (pseud. V. Sirin) completed his first Russian novel, *Mashen'ka* (*Mary*, 1970). Before leaving for the United States to teach

Russian literature (1941–59), he wrote his first English novel, *The Real Life of Sebastian Knight* (1938), and produced some two thousand pages of lecture notes.

Essays in *The Garland Companion* explore Nabokov's relationship to others, including Chernyshevsky, Dostoyevsky, **Franz Kafka**, and **James Joyce**. Nabokov consistently denied outside influences. He attributed his fundamental belief in the existence of a higher order of being to his mother and his moral code, and appreciation of "the thrill of a great poem" to his father, a former member of Alexandr Kerensky's government and a social critic. He credited his early memories of his idyllic childhood and his passions—butterfly collecting and chess—for shaping his oeuvre, acknowledging only a general debt to Pushkin, Nikolay Gogol, Shakespeare, and Russia's silver age.

Nabokov considered Alexander Blok the best Russian poet of his time, and *Petersburg* (Andrey Bely), *Metamorphosis* (Kafka), *Ulysses* (Joyce), and *In Search of Lost Time* (**Marcel Proust**) the greatest twentieth-century novels. He esteemed Vladislav Khodasevich, Alfred Housman, François-René Chateaubriand, **Henri Bergson**, Alain Robbe-Grillet, **Jorge Luis Borges**, J. D. Salinger, and **John Updike**; valued **Boris Pasternak**'s poetry but intensely disliked *Dr. Zhivago*; admired **Alexander Solzhenitsyn**'s courage but harshly judged his artistry. He had no use for Sigmund Freud, **Thomas Mann, Albert Camus, Ernest Hemingway,** and **William Faulkner.**

Archives

The Berg Collection in New York's Public Library, the Library of Congress, Washington, D.C., and the Nabokov Museum in St. Petersburg hold the largest collections of Nabokov's papers.

Printed Sources

Alexandrov, Vladimir E. (ed.). *The Garland Companion to Vladimir Nabokov* (New York: Garland, 1995).

Boyd, Brian. *Vladimir Nabokov: The American Years* (Princeton: Princeton University Press, 1991).

———. *Vladimir Nabokov: The Russian Years* (Princeton: Princeton University Press, 1990).

Juliar, Michael. *Strong Opinions* (New York: McGraw-Hill, 1973).

———. *Vladimir Nabokov: A Descriptive Bibliography* (New York: Garland, 1986).

Karlinsky, Simon (ed.). *The Nabokov–Wilson Letters, 1940–1971* (New York: Harper & Row, 1979).

Nabokov, Dmitri, and Matthew J. Bruccoli (eds.). *Vladimir Nabokov: Selected Letters, 1940–1977* (San Diego: Harcourt Brace Jovanovich, 1989).

Nabokov, Vladimir Vladimirovich. *Perepiska s sestroi* (Ann Arbor: Ardis, 1985).

———. *Speak, Memory: An Autobiography Revisited* (New York: Alfred A. Knopf, Inc., 1999).

Ludmilla L. Litus

NADER, RALPH (1934–)

Ralph Nader was born in Winfred, Connecticut, to Lebanese immigrants Nathra and Rose (Bouziane) Nader. The Nader family remained in Winfred throughout Ralph's childhood. Nader studied at Princeton (1951–55) and then at Harvard Law School (1955–58) where he also served in multiple positions, including editor-in-chief, for the Harvard Law School *Record*. After graduating from Harvard Law School, Nader served a six-month term with the U.S. Army as a cook at

Fort Dix, New Jersey. When his term was complete in 1959, he established a law practice in Hartford, Connecticut, and published the article "The Safe Car You Can't Buy" in *Nation*. Nader maintained his Hartford practice and traveled throughout the world until accepting a consultant position in 1964 under Assistant Secretary of Labor Daniel Patrick Moynihan. In November 1965, *Unsafe at Any Speed*, a sweeping critique of American automobile manufacturer safety standards, was published, catapulting Nader to national recognition. Buoyed by his accomplishments in bringing automobile safety standards to national attention, Nader branched out and became the nation's best-known consumer advocate. Since the late 1960s, Nader has formed multiple organizations (including the Public Research Interest Group, Public Citizen, and the Project for Corporate Responsibility), influenced hundreds of pieces of legislation, and recruited hundreds of young lawyers ("Nader's Raiders") to follow through on his many efforts. Nader's activities fall into three basic categories: empowering consumers, fostering mechanisms of government accountability, and promoting the "public interest." In recent years, Nader has reemerged in the national spotlight, running as the Green Party candidate for president in 1996 and again in 2000, when he visited all 50 states and received over 2,500,000 votes.

Nader's essential political philosophy seems to be threefold: the public interest comes first; the public is best qualified to determine what its interest is; and the public is the best guarantor that its interest is served. There is much of Thomas Jefferson's championing of the people here, but the emphasis on protecting the "public interest" has been formulated largely by Nader himself. His most prominent influences, by most accounts, are Nathra and Rose Nader. His parents emphasized hard work and debate and fostered a mentality of putting people first. Nader's ideas of the power and roles of citizen-consumers and journalists were strongly influenced by the muckrakers Ida Tarbell, Lincoln Steffens, **Upton Sinclair,** and George Seldes. Nader's early emphasis on automobile safety was invigorated by a 1955 *Harvard Law Review* article by Harold A. Katz and aided by working for Daniel Patrick Moynihan.

Archives

Currently there is no archive of Nader's personal papers.

Baker Library, Harvard Business School, Cambridge: Vincent W. Gillen Papers, 1963–91 (Gillen investigated Nader for General Motors; personal correspondence with Nader is included in his papers).

Printed Sources

Bollier, David. *Citizen Action and Other Big Ideas: A History of Ralph Nader and the Modern Consumer Movement* (published on the World Wide Web at http://www.nader.org/history_bollier.html. Last accessed 11 August 2002).

Buckhorn, Robert F. *Nader: The People's Lawyer* (Englewood Cliffs, N.J.: Prentice-Hall, Inc., 1972).

McCarry, Charles. *Citizen Nader* (New York: Saturday Review Press, 1972).

Nader, Ralph. *Crashing the Party: Taking on the Corporate Government in an Age of Surrender* (New York: Thomas Dunne Books, 2002).

———. *The Ralph Nader Reader* (New York: Seven Stories Press, 2000). Collection of articles by Nader.

———. *Unsafe at Any Speed.* (New York: Grossman Publishers, 1965).

Phil Huckelberry

NAGY, IMRE (1896–1958)

Imre Nagy was born in Kaposvar, Hungary, to a family of devoted Calvinists. He graduated from high school and worked as a mechanic until World War I (1914–18), when he was drafted into the Austro-Hungarian Army and sent to the Russian front. In December 1944, he reappeared in Hungary to become one of the pillars of the Hungarian Communist Party. Early in 1948, the Communist Party gained full control of Hungary, and the state was proclaimed a People's Republic in 1949. Nagy, who served as a minister of agriculture, was responsible for gathering peasants onto large, state-supervised collective farms. In 1949, Nagy twice appealed to the Hungarian Central Committee, criticizing the party's position on the "peasant question" and advocating the delay of collectivization. For this Nagy was dismissed, but one year later was returned to office. By 1953 constant economic difficulties and peasant resentment of collectivization had led to a profound crisis in Hungary. The new set of liberalizing policies of a satellite government that Nagy introduced during his first premiership became known as the "New Course." Nagy's New Course de-emphasized forcible collectivization and loosened police controls. Nagy idealized Karl Marx, who was a disciple of G.W.F. Hegel. Marx built on Hegel's ideas of the class struggle, and Nagy, deeply shaken by past and current events, internalized Marx's manifesto, "Workers of the World Unite!" which was at the heart of both *The Communist Manifesto* and of *Wage-Labor and Capital.* Nagy, deeply devoted to his cause and his faith unshaken, was well aware of all the major works of Marx and Engels, **V. I. Lenin,** and even **Josef Stalin.** For example, he referred to Stalin's article "Workingwomen and Peasantwomen Remember and Carry Out Lenin's Behests," published in the magazine *Rabotnitsa,* No. 1, January 1925, to support his programs. In his manuscript, *On Communism: In Defence of the New Course,* Nagy lays out his principles, policies, and plans which establish the need for liberalization within a framework of communism. But Marxist dogma, as interpreted by Stalinist bureaucrats, was bound to reject Nagy's promising, albeit naive perspective. During the revolution of 1956, Nagy emerged as a symbol of liberalism within the Communist Party. During the few days of liberty, political development in Hungary was rapid. Nagy was revered as a national hero, promising free elections and a Soviet withdrawal from Hungary. The fate of Imre Nagy and the revolution of the Hungarian people was sealed by the counter-revolution that took place only a week later. Nagy was arrested by Soviet police and in 1957 was returned to the custody of the new Hungarian regime headed by Janos Kadar. His secret trial and execution were announced in 1958. After many years as a one-party Marxist state, Hungary became a multiparty parliamentary democracy in 1989. In the same year, Imre Nagy was officially rehabilitated and reburied with full honors. Attempts at a historical reconstruction of the events prompted a lawsuit by Imre Nagy's daughter; however the court refused to express an opinion on matters of history.

Some Nagy files were found in the KGB archives after 1989. As in many cases in which KGB materials were released, it was for a concrete, political purpose. Rumors about Imre Nagy's affiliation with the Soviet secret police, code-named "Agent Volodya," have circulated widely. The initial search for Soviet archival materials on Nagy may have been triggered by an inquiry from Hungarian reformist political figures, who requested that all documents pertaining to Nagy's sentence and his activities while in the Soviet Union be declassified. A number of damaging materials were declassified in Moscow in an attempt to compromise Nagy's importance as a historical symbol. Although it seems that the documents are authentic, they were carefully selected to discredit Nagy and undermine democratic trends in Hungary. Scholars should be cautious when evaluating them.

Archives

Zamchevskii, I. About Imre Nagy and his politics with the Yugoslav leaders, Archive of Foreign Policy of Russian Federation, Arkhiv Vneshnei Politiki Rossiiskoi Federatsii (AVP RF).

Russian Centre for the Preservation of Contemporary Documents, Tsentr Khranenia Sovremennoi Dokumentatsii (TsKhSD).

Printed Sources

Calhoun, F. Daniel. *Hungary and Suez, 1956: An Exploration of Who Makes History* (Lanham, Md.: University Press of America, 1991).

Gati, Charles. *Hungary and the Soviet Bloc* (Durham, N.C.: Duke University Press, 1986).

Nagy, I. *On Communism: In Defense of the New Course* (New York: Frederick A. Praeger, 1957).

Rainer, M. Janos. *Nagy Imre. Politikai eletrajz (Imre Nagy: A Political Biography)*, Vol. I, 1896–1953 (Budapest: 1956-os Intezet, 1996).

Eva Dobozy

NAIPAUL, VIDIADHAR SURAJPRASAD (1932–)

V. S. Naipaul, the recipient of the Nobel Prize for literature in 2001, has achieved acclaim and attracted some controversy throughout his prolific career as a novelist, essayist, and critic. Born in Trinidad in the Caribbean as the descendant of an Indian indentured laborer, Naipaul first commanded critical attention in 1961 with the publication of *A House for Mr. Biswas*, a family saga set in Trinidad which some scholars maintain is Naipaul's finest work. In 1971 he received the Booker Prize for *In a Free State*. Over the past 30 years, Naipaul has garnered both praise and criticism for his depictions of African and Asian societies, and most recently of Islam in particular, in novels such as *A Bend in the River* and travel narratives such as *An Area of Darkness* and *Among the Believers*. Accused at times of caricaturing non-Western societies, Naipaul has defended himself with the characteristic acerbity that continues to mark his writing and to attract, in equal measure, both laudatory words and vigorous dissent.

Naipaul has throughout his career identified some important influences on his work. These include Charles Dickens and H. G. Wells, both of whom Naipaul encountered in his boyhood; critics have pointed to these two authors as particularly significant in the creation of *A House for Mr. Biswas* with its elaborate plotting and familial setting. In his fiction, and especially in his travel writing and criticism, Naipaul has, by his own admission, drawn on other nineteenth-century writers whom he admires for their realism, lack of pretense, and "breakneck prose" (Naipaul 1987, 7). Among them are the Victorian polemicists and essayists William Hazlitt and William Cobbett.

Naipaul's own life, however, has played the largest role in shaping his work, a fact he has readily acknowledged. An Indian born into the multiethnic Trinidad created by slavery, indentured labor, and imperial rule, Naipaul has consistently marked himself as a product of both a colonial and a postcolonial world in which identities, borders, and sensibilities are fluid and unstable. Though resident in Great Britain since the mid-twentieth century, Naipaul still considers himself an exile, someone who remains an outsider, no matter whether he is in Trinidad, Britain, or India. This sense of himself permeates even his most recent work, including the novel *The Enigma of Arrival*, a meditation on immigration and belonging in modern Britain. Some scholars and reviewers have also pointed to Naipaul's sense of himself as an observer as the driving force behind the relentless travel which has marked much of his career as well, from the American South to central Africa and southeast Asia.

More controversially, Naipaul has employed his own memories in formulating a sense of a bifurcated world. He has described the Trinidad of his youth, and even today, as a "half-made society," unlike the fully-evolved Europe where he now lives. This view of postcolonial states as less mature or even childish entities seems to have affected greatly Naipaul's descriptions of the non-European or non-Western world, leading some prominent critics to see him as a purveyor of old colonial nostrums and stereotypes. Naipaul has in fact modified his own once-derogatory views of India, and some of his depictions of misrule and corruption in postcolonial Africa have unfortunately proved prescient. His recent and highly critical excursions into the Islamic world, however, have not met with much scholarly or literary approval.

In his sense of exile and of being a product of a lesser society, Naipaul has identified himself explicitly with one particular novelist: Joseph Conrad. Naipaul sees the Polish-born Conrad as a forebear and an influence in that Conrad was himself not only born into a "half-made" society, but lived as an exile in Britain and spent years as an itinerant traveler and observer in European colonies in Africa. In this way, Conrad was an exile and a realist; Naipaul defines himself similarly to this day.

Archives

McFarlin Library at the University of Tulsa in Oklahoma is the major repository of Naipaul's letters and papers.

Printed Sources

Hamilton, Iane. "Without a Place: An Interview with V. S. Naipaul" *Times Literary Supplement*, 30 July 1971, 897–98.

Hammer, Robert (ed.). *Critical Perspectives on V. S. Naipaul* (Washington, D.C.: Three Continents Press, 1977).

King, Bruce. *V. S. Naipaul* (London: Macmillan, 1993).

Mustafa, Fawzi. *V. S. Naipaul* (Cambridge: Cambridge University Press, 1995).

Naipaul, V. S. "Conrad's Darkness," *New York Review of Books*, 17 October 1974, 16–21.

———. "On Being a Writer," *New York Review of Books*, 23 April 1987, 7.

———. *A Way in the World: A Sequence* (London: Heinemann, 1994).

Nixon, Rob. *London Calling: V. S. Naipaul: Postcolonial Mandarin* (Oxford: Oxford University Press, 1992).

Andrew Muldoon

NEUMANN, JOHN LOUIS VON (1903–1957)

Born in Budapest, Hungary, to Max Neumann, a wealthy Jewish banker who purchased the German honorific title "von" for his sons, János Neumann was called "Jancsi" as a boy, "Johann" early in his career, and "Johnny" after moving to

America in 1933. He was first educated at home by Max and tutors. Always a voracious reader, Max kept a huge personal library and partially succeeded in conveying this bibliophilia to Jancsi, who, after mathematics and science, loved history best. He read all 44 volumes of Wilhelm Oncken's *Allgemeine Geschichte* in Max's library as a boy, later enjoyed Edward Gibbon, and came to know ancient history and the American Civil War very well. But friends and family recalled his prodigious memory more than the breadth or regularity of his reading. He became proficient in the classics, learning Greek from Max and Latin in school. Except during a brief political exile in Austria in 1919, he attended the academically excellent Lutheran Gymnasium in Budapest from 1914 to 1921, where Laszlo Rácz was among his teachers and William Fellner, Leo Szilard, and Eugene Paul Wigner were among his schoolmates. Because of his obvious genius, he received special tutoring in mathematics from Lipót Fejér, Michael Fekete, Alfred Haar, Joseph Kürschak, Frigyes Riesz, and Gabriel Szego. Sandor Ferenczi, a relative, taught him some psychology. He pondered the philosophical implications of Luigi Pirandello's *Six Characters in Search of an Author*.

By the 1920s he was conversant with every strain of mathematics then under discussion, especially the work of Charles Babbage, René-Louis Baire, Émile Borel, Georg Cantor, Torsten Carleman, Arthur Cayley, David Hilbert, Henri Lebesgue, Jules Henri Poincaré, Heinz Prüfer, **Bertrand Russell**, Hermann Weyl, and Ernst Zermelo. From 1921 to 1923 he studied chemistry at the University of Berlin, where Erhard Schmidt taught mathematics; then from 1923 to 1926 chemical engineering at the Swiss Institute of Technology in Zürich, where he discussed mathematics with George Polya and Weyl. He met Edward Teller in 1925 when both studied under Fejér in Budapest. On the basis of exceptional examination scores and a dissertation about set theory, the University of Budapest awarded him a doctorate in mathematics in 1926, despite his never having taken courses there.

Already world-famous, he studied with Hilbert at the University of Göttingen from 1926 to 1927. Inspired by Borel, he developed minimax theory in the late 1920s. He taught mathematics from 1926 to 1929 at the University of Berlin, from 1929 to 1930 at the University of Hamburg, and in 1929 lectured on quantum physics at Princeton University, at that time probably the world's most fertile environment for mathematical and scientific research. From 1930 until his death, he taught mathematical physics at Princeton, where he was almost as famous for his parties as for his mathematics. Always a "party boy," he had frequented the notorious Berlin cabaret circuit throughout the 1920s. Rather than read, he preferred to acquire and test new ideas in conversation. His wild social life also fueled his intellectual achievements.

In 1933 he became one of the five original mathematics professors at the Princeton Institute for Advanced Study, along with James Waddell Alexander II, **Albert Einstein**, Oswald Veblen, and Weyl. Among his colleagues there were Alonzo Church, Leon Henkin, Solomon Lefschetz, Oskar Morgenstern, **Robert Oppenheimer**, Alan Turing, and Wigner. Early in his Princeton career, inspired by Haar, he solved the "compact group problem," the fifth of twenty-three challenges that Hilbert presented in 1900. In the 1930s and early 1940s he collaborated with Morgenstern and Francis J. Murray. Ulam (1958, 5) reported that von Neumann himself considered Schmidt and Weyl his two greatest influences.

Archives

Library of Congress. Correspondence, papers, memoranda, journals, speeches, rough drafts, notes, charts, graphs, patents, and family memorabilia, from 1912, but most from 1935 to 1957.

Printed Sources

Macrae, Norman. *John von Neumann* (New York: Pantheon, 1992).

Poundstone, William. *Prisoner's Dilemma* (New York: Doubleday, 1992).

Ulam, Stanislaw. "John von Neumann, 1903–1957," *Bulletin of the American Mathematical Society*, 64, 3 (May 1958), 1–49.

Vonneuman, Nicholas A. *John von Neumann as Seen by His Brother* (Meadowbrook, Pa.: N.A. Vonneuman, 1987).

Eric v.d. Luft

NIEBUHR, REINHOLD (1892–1971)

Reinhold Neibuhr was born in Wright City, Missouri. He attended Elmhurst College, Illinois (1910), Eden Theological Seminary, St. Louis (1910–13), and conducted his postgraduate study at the Yale Divinity School (1914–15). Ordained to the ministry in the Evangelical Synod of North America (later part of the United Church of Christ) in 1915, he accepted a pastorate at the Bethel Evangelical Church in Detroit, where he would grow his small congregation into a large, influential church (1915–28). In 1928 Niebuhr accepted a faculty position as chair of Christian ethics at Union Theological Seminary in New York and remained there until his retirement in 1960. A man of vigorous and keen intellect, his life's calling was the continuing attempt to apply a comprehensive and historical Christian ethic to practical sociopolitical concerns. His view of history emphasized the role of man as a physical and spiritual being. These themes dominated his famous Gifford Lectures in 1939 and constitute the framework of his later writings, namely his greatest works, *The Nature and Destiny of Man* (1941 and 1943) and *Faith and History* (1949).

Niebuhr credited his father with providing him his first formative religious influences, notably introducing him to the thought of the liberal theologian Adolf von Harnack. Seminary influenced his interest in—and understanding of—philosophy and theology, particularly the New Testament and what Niebuhr later in his life referred to as the "ethics of Jesus." It was, however, the social realities of industrial Detroit, especially his personal involvement with the worker's plight in the factories of **Henry Ford** and the outbreak and horror of World War I, that furthered his intellectual development "more than any books which I have read" (Niebuhr quoted in Kegley and Bretall 1956, 5) and undermined his youthful optimism and moralistic idealism. He organized and led the pacifist organization, the Fellowship of Reconciliation, and his advocacy of "pragmatic pacifism" reflected the influences of William James and the Social Gospel as propounded by Walter Rauschenbusch. These themes transcend his early writings, specifically *Moral Man and Immoral Society* (1932), which critique secular and Christian liberalism from a dominantly Marxist perspective, a view bolstered by Niebuhr's reflection that the Depression served as the conclusive refutation of liberal hopes. His tentative Marxist orientation led to his "Christian radicalism" and his involvement in organizing the Fellowship of Socialist Christians in the late 1920s and his unsuccessful congressional bid on the Socialist ticket in 1930 (resigning from the Socialist party in 1940). At Union, however, he began an earnest consideration of his theological heritage. In Søren Kierkegaard, Niebuhr discovered a kindred spirit who wrestled with the "paradox" of the Christian message and a form of Christian existentialism. Blaise Pascal's penetrating critique of the limits of human reason resound in Niebuhr's work as does Reformation theology as embodied foremost in Martin Luther and John Calvin. The thought of St. Augustine of Hippo, a theologian who Niebuhr credits for answering "so many of my unanswered questions" and finally freeing him from moral idealism (Niebuhr quoted in Kegley and Bretall 1956, 9), drove him on to further studies in the New Testament, Pauline theology and Greek antiquity. His theological pilgrimage produced an understanding of man as fallen and resulted in his philosophy of Christian realism, strongly influenced by the neo-orthodoxy of **Karl Barth.** Juxtaposed with the horror of now two world wars and the idolatries of Nazism and Communism, Niebuhr became increasingly critical of both liberal and Marxist utopianism, as evidenced in *The Irony of American History* (1952). His final years were marked by the great influence he exerted in the field of international relations and his unceasing polemic against the pragmatism of **John Dewey.**

Archives

Library of Congress, Manuscript Division, Washington D.C.: Niebuhr's private papers, correspondence, articles, sermons, reviews, lectures, typescripts of books, and biographical material.

Printed Sources

Brown, Charles C. *Niebuhr and His Age: Reinhold Niebuhr's Prophetic Role in the Twentieth Century* (Harrisburg, Penn.: Morehouse Publishing, 2002).
Kegley, Charles W., and Robert W. Bretall (eds.). *Reinhold Niebuhr: His Religious, Social, and Political Thought* (New York: Macmillan, 1956).

Rouven J. Steeves

NIEMÖLLER, MARTIN (1892–1984)

Martin Niemöller was born in Lippstadt, Germany. He attended the secondary school in Lippstadt and the gymnasium in Elberfeld, graduating Primus Omnium in 1910. Taught that a good German Protestant is also a citizen and soldier, he entered the German navy as an officer-candidate and served as a U-boat commander in World War I before attending the University of Münster as a theological student (1919–23). He was ordained in 1924 and served for seven years with the Westphalian Inner Mission. In 1931 he became a pastor in the suburb of Dahlem, Berlin, where his religious convictions brought him into ever greater conflict with the rising power of the National Socialists. In 1933 he founded the *Pfarrernotbund* (Pastors' Emergency League) and was integrally involved in creating the Confessing Church at the Synod of Barmen (1934) in opposition to the German Christians and their "positive Christianity"—a movement closely allied with the Nazis. In 1937 he was arrested by the Gestapo leading to his imprisonment as "Hitler's personal prisoner" in Sachsenhausen, Dachau, and Tirol until his liberation in 1945. Niemoller was instrumental in rebuilding the German Evangelical Church, serving as president of the Hesse-Nassau regional church (1947–64) and head of the foreign-relations council (1945–56). Convinced of the Germans' collective guilt, he played a crucial role in drafting the *Stuttgarter Schuldbekenntnis* (Stuttgart Confession of Guilt) in 1945 and became a controversial pacifist and internationalist. He served as a president of the World Council of Churches from 1961 to 1968.

Martin Niemöller's faith was Protestant, steeped in the Reformation, and highly conscious of his Reformed roots as embodied in the teachings and lives of Martin Luther, John Calvin, and Ulrich Zwingli. The teachings of his mother regarding the sufferings of their forefathers, especially the French Huguenots, and the reality of living in the dominantly Catholic areas of the Rhineland and Westphalia fermented in Niemöller an anti-Catholic bias. For the young Niemöller, piety implied Protestantism and German nationalism inextricably intertwined and shaped by an anti-intellectualism that stressed the spiritual life over theological studies. Following in his father's footsteps, he was deeply drawn to the "social question"—the plight of the working class. Influenced by Pastor Johann Hinrich Wichern's German "Inner Mission," formed in 1848, and the self-proclaimed Christian Socialist Adolf Stöcker, Niemöller was increasingly drawn to the Social Gospel. His experiences during World War I fortified his passionate nationalism, and his desire to see Germany return to greatness led to his initial support of the Nazis. However, Nazi infringement on the autonomy of the church and the ever-increasing virulence of the Nazi's anti-Semitism led Niemöller to assist in the formation of the Young Reformation Movement in 1933. It is through this forum that Niemöller influenced and was influenced by **Dietrich Bonhoeffer** and **Karl Barth,** the latter becoming a lifelong friend and theological mentor. After World War II, Niemöller became an outspoken internationalist and political pacifist strongly influenced by Frédéric Joliot-Curie's world peace movement and **Mohandas Gandhi**'s technique of nonviolent protest embodied in "provoking peacefully." Central to his postwar stance was a keen interest in the state of Russia, attacking racism and poverty internationally, and promoting nuclear disarmament.

Archives

Das Zentralarchiv und die Zentralbibliothek der Evangelischen Kirche in Hessen und Nassau, Darmstadt, Germany: Niemöller's personal papers, correspondence, works, and sermons as well as letters, documents, and publications relating to the church in general.

Printed Sources

Bentley, James. *Martin Niemöller: 1892–1984* (New York: The Free Press, 1984).

Davidson, Clarissa S. *God's Man: The Story of Pastor Niemoeller,* reprint ed. (Westport, Conn.: Greenwood Press, 1979).

Helmreich, Ernst Christian. *The German Churches Under Hitler: Background, Struggle, and Epilogue* (Detroit: Wayne State University Press, 1979).

Rouven J. Steeves

NIJINSKY, VASLAV (1889–1950)

Vaslav Nijinsky was born in Kiev to two Polish dancers, Thomas and Eleanora, who toured throughout Russia and were his first dance teachers. At age nine, Nijinsky was accepted as a student into the Imperial Theatrical School, where his phenomenal talent quickly became evident. Before Nijinsky was elevated to solo status at the Maryinsky Ballet in 1907, the St. Petersburg press had already proclaimed him a prodigy. In 1909, Serge Diaghilev, whose goal was to introduce Russian art and dance to the West, convinced Nijinsky to join his fledgling Ballets Russes in its first Paris season. Nijinsky's sensational dancing in *Le Spectre de la Rose* made him an overnight idol. His role as the Golden Slave in *Scheherazade* (1910) contributed to both his fame and that of the Ballets Russes, which for 20 years stood as the ultimate symbol of sophistication and artistic innovation in the West. Critics wrote that Nijinsky's technical virtuosity transcended the limits of what seemed physically possible; this extraordinary athleticism combined with his mimetic ability enabled Nijinsky to establish the centrality of the male classical dancer. Nijinsky choreographed three ballets, *L'Apres-midi d'une Faune* (1912), *Le Sacre du Printemps* (1913), and *Jeux* (1913), that radically broke with the tenets of classical ballet and ushered ballet into modernism. All provoked a scandalous, critical response. While the two-dimensional movements of the dancers in *Faune* reflected the geometric shapes of cubist art, it was the final masturbatory gesture of Nijinsky's faun that shocked the audience and added to the atmosphere of decadence and daring that surrounded the artist. The dissonance of **Igor Stravinsky**'s music, the violent stomping of the dancers, and the visual primitivism of the sets made the opening performance of *Le Sacre* a hallmark of modernism and created a riot in the audience. *Jeux*, too, with its modern dress and sexual theme, offended bourgeois sensibilities. A hasty marriage to Romola de Pulszky in 1913 led to his dismissal from the Ballets Russes. Nijinsky then formed his own dance troupe. In 1916–17, Nijinsky toured with Diaghilev's enterprise throughout the United States once more before succumbing to the schizophrenia that cut short his brilliant career. At the time of his tragic retirement at the end of 1917, Nijinsky was the most celebrated dancer in the world and is still considered the greatest male dancer of the twentieth century.

Off stage Nijinsky rarely talked, was socially incompetent, and even seemed simple-minded, fueling the legend of his being an idiot savant, a naive genius. His academic record at school was dismal, and his younger sister Bronislava Nijinsky, who turned into a noted ballerina, often tutored him in his general studies. Yet he had a perfect ear for music, memorizing entire scores of the operas that played at the Maryinsky. At the time of his graduation from the Imperial Theatrical School, he received the complete works of Lev Tolstoy. On his 1917 American tour, he fell under the spell of Dmitri Kostrovsky, another dancer, who espoused the religious philosophy of Tolstoy. Nijinsky embraced some of Tolstoy's teachings, including vegetarianism, pacifism, and anarchism. He began wearing peasant shirts and practicing sexual celibacy. Nijinsky's diary, written in six weeks in a secluded villa in Switzerland, revealed that he read not only Tolstoy, but also Nikolai Gogol and Fyodor Dostoyevsky, and was generally familiar with Russian literature. He began his descent into madness at this time, so it is difficult to separate Tolstoy's influence from his inner demons. Nijinsky imagined that he was God, expressed his desire to return to Russia, and echoed the nineteenth-century sentiment of the Slavophiles that Russia will be the world's spiritual center (the Third Rome). He also compared himself to Dostoyevsky's hero in the *The Idiot* and cited passages about salvation from Dostoevsky's *The Brothers Karamazov*. His references to Gogol, Guy de Maupassant, and Friedrich Nietzsche seemed self-prophetic, since they too suffered nervous breakdowns. The diary, heavily edited by his wife, was published in 1936. An unexpurgated version appeared in 1999.

Archives

Gabriel Astruc Papers, Dance Collection, Lincoln Center, New York Public Library, New York.

Serge Diaghilev Papers and Correspondence, Dance Collection, Lincoln Center, New York Public Library, New York.

Boris Kochno Papers, Bibliotheque de l'Opera, Paris.

Nijinsky Archives, Phoenix, Arizona.

Printed Sources

Benois, Alexandre. *Reminiscences of the Russian Ballet*, Mary Britnieva (trans.), (London: Chatto and Windus, 1941).

Buckle, Richard. *Nijinsky* (London: Weidenfeld & Nicolson, 1971).

Garafola, Lynn. *Diaghilev's Ballets Russes* (New York: Oxford University Press, 1989).

Nijinska, Bronislava. *Early Memoirs* (New York: Holt, Rinehart, and Winston, 1981).

Nijinsky, Vaslav. *The Diary of Vaslav Nijinsky*, Kyril FitzLyon (trans.), Joan Acocella (ed.), (New York: Farrar, Straus and Giroux, 1999).

Ostwald, Peter. *Nijinsky: A Leap into Madness* (New York: Carol Publishing, 1991).

Ulle V. Holt

NIXON, RICHARD MILHOUS (1913–1994)

Richard Nixon was born in Yorba Linda, California. He attended Whittier College and Duke University Law School. From 1946 to 1950 he served in the U.S. House of Representatives, where he was instrumental in exposing the communist traitor Alger Hiss. He went on to enter the U.S. Senate in 1950 and later served as vice president from 1952 to 1960. Nixon won the presidency in 1968. He engaged in a complex game of geopolitics to exploit cracks in the communist bloc, fashioning an arms control agreement with the Soviet Union, developing a diplomatic opening to China, and withdrawing troops from Vietnam. Reelected in 1972, he resigned two years later because of his involvement in a series of scandals collectively known as "Watergate."

He read diligently throughout his life. He developed a childhood fascination with *National Geographic*; though his family was too poor to afford it, he read a neighbor's copy. An interest in travel and a taste for reading periodical literature would serve him well: he would spend much of his adult life doing both. Of course during his political career, Nixon consumed a vast and constant diet of newspapers and news magazines. Nixon's own books also show a wide range of reading in political philosophy, referring to Thomas Hobbes, Niccolo Machiavelli, Friedrich Nietzsche, Immanuel Kant, and others.

Appropriately for a budding politician, he also read Dale Carnegie's *How to Win Friends and Influence People* while a youth. While in school he studied Latin literature and French literature. During his undergraduate studies at Whittier College, he read steadily and seriously and would continue to do so throughout his life. In addition, he developed a strong affection for the works of Lev Tolstoy; an interesting taste, since Tolstoy, particularly in the character of Marshal Kutuzov in *War and Peace*, presents a picture of the world in which human beings have a limited role in controlling the outcome of great events.

By contrast, Nixon also displayed a strong interest in the stories of great men performing great deeds. Throughout his career Nixon exhibited a fondness for the writings and speeches of Theodore Roosevelt. One quotation in particular recurs throughout Nixon's writings, in which Roosevelt praises the "man in the arena" and disparages critics. Nixon referred to the quotation in his memoirs and used part of it as the title of his book *In the Arena*. The quotation held obvious appeal for one who spent so much time in the arena and was hounded by such a vast army of critics. In addition, during his farewell speech to the White House staff in August 1974, Nixon paid tribute to his own deceased mother by quoting from a tribute that Roosevelt wrote upon the death of his first wife. He then contrasted the loss that Roosevelt expressed with his future political triumphs, attempting to sound a note of hope and renewal in one of his darkest hours.

British guerrilla warfare expert Sir Robert Thompson exercised a strong influence on Nixon. Thompson wrote about the successful counterinsurgency program conducted by the British during the 12-year (1948–60) struggle to root out communist guerrillas in Malaya. An example of a successful counterinsurgency campaign against communist guerrilla forces in Asia held obvious interest for Nixon during his first term, as Nixon struggled to end the Vietnam War on his own terms. Nixon showed a strong interest in Thompson and his work; in his memoirs, however, Nixon never states explicitly whether he read Thompson's books, but he mentions several meetings with Thompson in which the guerrilla warfare expert urged him to display the resolve to stay the course to final victory in Vietnam.

Nixon also drew inspiration from other periods of British history. One of Nixon's favorite books was Robert Blake's *Disraeli*. Nixon received the biography of the nineteenth-century statesman as a gift from Daniel Patrick Moynihan, and his copy of the book is displayed at the Richard Nixon Library and Birthplace in Yorba Linda, California. Nixon relished the story of the triumphant conservative prime minister of Great Britain scoring domestic and international triumphs. In particular, Nixon admired Disraeli's successful passage of the Reform Bill of 1867; by passing that bill, Disraeli, the conservative statesman, succeeded where his liberal opponents had failed. Nixon would describe his diplomatic opening to China in similar terms.

In his retirement Nixon continued a vigorous reading program. In particular he enjoyed Paul Johnson's *Modern Times*, a history of much of the twentieth century from a conservative perspective. And he continued to show a strong interest in British history, reading Martin Gilbert's mammoth biography of Sir **Winston S. Churchill,** another statesman who proved of profound and perpetual interest to Nixon.

Archives

Richard Nixon Library, Yorba Linda, California. Includes pre- and postpresidential papers, along with a collection of books and photographs.
National Archives, College Park, Maryland. Houses the Nixon presidential materials.

Printed Sources

Aitken, Jonathan. *Nixon, A Life* (Washington, D.C.: Regnery Publishing, 1993).
Ambrose, Stephen E. *Nixon*, 3 vols. (New York: Simon and Schuster, 1987–89).
Crowley, Monica. *Nixon in Winter* (New York: Random House, 1998).
———. *Nixon Off the Record* (New York: Random House, 1996).
Nixon, Richard. *In the Arena: A Memoir of Victory, Defeat, and Renewal* (New York: Simon and Schuster, 1990).

————. *RN: The Memoirs of Richard Nixon* (New York: Grosset and Dunlap, 1978).

Reeves, Richard. *President Nixon: Alone in the White House* (New York: Simon and Schuster, 2001).

Mitchell McNaylor

NUREYEV, RUDOLPH (1938–1993)

Nureyev was born into a Tatar, Muslim family from the Urals and raised in Ufa, the capital of the Bashkir Autonomous Republic, U.S.S.R. Educated in Russian and English at Ufa's School Number Two, where he was an indifferent student, Nureyev began his formal ballet instruction at the age of 10. At 17, he was accepted into the prestigious Vaganova Choreographic Institute in Leningrad, and at 21, he landed the starring role of the slave in the Kirov Ballet's "Le Corsaire," electrifying the Soviet dance world with his sexual magnetism and flamboyant technique. Nureyev quickly rose to the highest ranks of the Soviet ballet system. During the height of the cold war in 1961, he defected to the West for personal and artistic liberty while on a state-sponsored tour to promote Soviet cultural supremacy. His defection unleashed an international media furor, embarrassed the Soviet Union, made him a political symbol, and fueled his fame as an international celebrity. Dazzling audiences with his exotic looks and brilliant leaps, he reignited the career of Margot Fonteyn, elevated the prominence of the male dancer, and transformed ballet from an elite art form to a middle-class pastime. When the 20-year-old Nureyev partnered the 43-year-old Fonteyn, the Royal Ballet's prima ballerina, in *Giselle* in his Covent Garden debut (February 21, 1962), their performance sparked a boom in British ballet and launched a golden partnership that lasted for twelve years. The two were feted by diplomatic and social circles and were lionized by the press and the public. For 20 years he was a top box office draw in the major ballet companies in the West. Nureyev not only worked with classical choreographers such as Frederick Ashton and George Balanchine, but he also ventured into the field of modern dance by performing for **Martha Graham** and Paul Taylor. His appearance on the American *Ed Sullivan Show* attracted a record 52 million viewers. In 1983, he became artistic director of the Paris Opera Ballet.

While a student at the Vaganova, Nureyev was greatly influenced by two teachers, Nikolai Ivanovsky and Maria Marietta Frangopulo, who tutored him in the history of ballet. He became a voracious reader, devouring the works of Alexander Pushkin, William Shakespeare, and Fyodor Dostoyevsky. He also developed his lifelong passion for art and art history with frequent visits to the Hermitage Museum. Later when he started to choreograph, he visualized each dancer as a painting on the stage. It was during this time that he discovered J. D. Salinger's *The Catcher in the Rye*, a book censored by the Soviets; as an outsider due to his Tatar heritage and homosexual leanings, he identified with Holden Caulfield, whose rebellious stance mirrored his own dissatisfaction with a puritanical, repressive Soviet society.

In 1966, Nureyev embarked on his choreographic career, making dramatic innovations in Marius Petipa's *The Sleeping Beauty*, the embodiment of the classical repertoire of the Maryinsky and Kirov Ballets. He had the sets painted to reflect the splendor of Versailles, and he spent months researching the court of the Sun King by reading the memoirs of Count de Saint-Simon. He added several male solos to the revised production, as well as using subdued shades of browns, blacks, and golds on the staging to suggest a masculine elegance. In 1976, when he created his own version of *Romeo and Juliet*, he turned to Shakespeare's play for inspiration, studying not only Shakespeare's text, but also the stories on which the master built his play. The result was a ballet that highlighted the violence of medieval Verona and stressed the sexual lustiness between the two young lovers, a break from the original, chastely Victorian production. Nureyev fashioned Juliet as a willful tomboy, a reference to the custom of Shakespeare's times when boys played all the female parts. A year later he constructed a ballet, *Manfred*, loosely based on Lord Byron's poem with the same name. Like Byron, Nureyev was a genius with a turbulent sexual history. The ballet was set to Peter Tchaikovsky's *Manfred Symphony*. The central role, danced by Nureyev, was a romantic figure, tormented by the contradictions between sacred and profane love. Despite the technical virtuosity of the dancing, this ballet had disappointing reviews and revenues. In 1986, Nureyev created one final ballet around a literary work, *Washington Square*, titled after Henry James's novella. Charles Ives composed the musical score and Nureyev danced the part of the heiress's father.

Archives

Archive of the Central Committee of the CPSU, Moscow.
Russian State Military Archive, Moscow.

Printed Sources

Bland, Alexander. *Fonteyn and Nureyev: The Story of A Partnership* (New York: Times Books, 1979).
Houseal, Joseph. "Nureyev in the West," *Ballet Review* 22, 1 (Spring 1994), 32–40. Interview with Maude Gosling.
Nureyev, Rudolph. *Nureyev* (New York: E. P. Dutton, Inc., 1963).
Percival, John. *Nureyev: Aspects of the Dance* (New York: G. P. Putnam's Sons, 1975).
Solway, Diane. *Nureyev: His Life* (New York: William Morrow and Co., 1998).
Stuart, Otis. *Perpetual Motion: The Public and Private Lives of Rudolph Nureyev* (New York: Simon & Schuster, 1995).

Ulle V. Holt

O

O'CONNOR, FLANNERY (1925–1964)

Flannery O'Connnor was born in Savannah, Georgia, but lived much of her life in the small town of Milledgeville, Georgia, where she graduated from the Women's College of Georgia in 1945. She received an M.F.A. in 1947 from the renowned writers' program of the University of Iowa. During the late 1940s and throughout the 1950s she established a growing reputation as a writer of fiercely funny but deeply provocative short stories, and she also produced two novels. All of her writing—including her exceptionally interesting letters—show the influence of her abiding commitment to Christianity, particularly to Roman Catholicism. This commitment helped her deal with the growing ravages of lupus, which had already killed her father when O'Connor was a teenager and which kept O'Connor herself largely confined to her mother's farm in Milledgeville during the most productive years of her life. Along with writing, reading was one of O'Connor's great passions and consolations. Her work is haunted by intimations not only of fleshly mortality but also of spiritual transcendence.

The indispensable guide to O'Connor's reading is Arthur Kinney's *Flannery O'Connor's Library*, although much useful information can also be gleaned from other sources, including O'Connor's own correspondence in *The Habit of Being;* letters she exchanged with the Brainerd Chaineys; her interviews; her occasional prose; and her book reviews. O'Connor was a voracious, active, and often highly opinionated reader, as her reviews, letters, and marginalia show. Kinney indicates which pages of the books he lists contain markings, and often he gives brief representative quotations of the passages O'Connor marked. As might be expected, the Bible was a crucial text, and writings by Catholic authors were also especially prominent in O'Connor's library, particularly works by Thomas Aquinas, Saint Augustine, Dante, Martin C. D'Arcy, Dom Aelred Graham, Romano Guardini, Baron Friedrich von Hügel, Saint John of the Cross, Ronald Knox, William F. Lynch, François Mauriac, Gabriel Marcel, Jacques Maritain, John Henry Cardinal

Newman, Pierre Teilhard de Chardin, Edith Stein, and Claude Tresmontant. Guardini, Hügel, and Teilhard were unusually important.

Other authors in whom O'Connor took a particularly strong interest included Joseph Warren Beach, **Henri Bergson,** Louis Bouyer, **Martin Buber,** Joseph Conrad, **T. S. Eliot, William Faulkner,** Caroline Gordon, Nathaniel Hawthorne, Raymond Hostie, Henry James, Madison Jones, **Carl Jung,** Russell Kirk, Percy Lubbock, Emmanuel Mounier, Stephen C. Pepper, Katherine Anne Porter, Charles Raven, Alexis de Tocqueville, Eric Voegelin, and Victor White. Copies of their books were often extensively marked. Meanwhile, her letters reveal her intense interest in a number of other authors, especially Elizabeth Bishop, Cleanth Brooks, Truman Capote, Fyodor Dostoyevsky, Sigmund Freud, **André Gide,** Etienne Gilson, **Graham Greene,** John Hawkes, **Ernest Hemingway,** Gerard Manley Hopkins, Randall Jarrell, Samuel Johnson, **Franz Kafka,** Wyndham Lewis, Elizabeth and Robert Lowell, Andrew Lytle, Mary McCarthy, Carson McCullers, Bernard Malamud, Iris Murdoch, **Vladimir Nabokov, Frank O'Connor,** Walker Percy, J. F. Powers, **Marcel Proust,** Muriel Spark, Jean Stafford, Allen Tate, Peter Taylor, **Paul Tillich,** Robert Penn Warren, **Evelyn Waugh, Simone Weil,** Eudora Welty, **Tennessee Williams,** and even Dr. Frank Crane, an advice columnist whom O'Connor found endlessly amusing.

Archives

The Flannery O'Connor Collection, Ina Dillard Russell Library, Georgia College and State University, Milledgeville, Georgia. Contains copies of many (probably most) of the surviving books from O'Connor's personal library. Many of these are marked and/or annotated.

Printed Sources

DiRenzo, Anthony. *American Gargoyles: Flannery O'Connor and the Medieval Grotesque* (Carbondale: Southern Illinois University Press, 1993).

Flannery O'Connor Bulletin. Milledgeville, Georgia. Vols. 1–27, 1972–2000. Renamed *Flannery O'Connor Review,* effective Fall 2001.

Getz, Lorine M. *Flannery O'Connor: Her Life, Library, and Book Reviews* (New York: E. Mellen Press, 1980). Largely superseded by Kinney's volume and by the volume edited by Zuber and Martin.

Giannone, Richard. *Flannery O'Connor, Hermit Novelist* (Urbana: University of Illinois Press, 2000).

Kessler, Edward. *Flannery O'Connor and the Language of Apocalypse* (Princeton: Princeton University Press, 1986).

Kinney, Arthur F. *Flannery O'Connor's Library: Resources of Being* (Athens: University of Georgia Press, 1985).

Montgomery, Marion. *Why Flannery O'Connor Stayed Home* (LaSalle, Ill.: Sherwood Sugden, 1981).

O'Connor, Flannery. *Conversations with Flannery O'Connor,* Rosemary M. Magee (ed.), (Jackson: University of Mississippi Press, 1987).

———. *The Correspondence of Flannery O'Connor and the Brainard Cheneys,* C. Ralph Stevens (ed.), (Jackson: University of Mississippi Press, 1986).

———. *The Habit of Being: Letters,* Sally Fitzgerald (ed.), (New York: Farrar, Straus, and Giroux, 1979).

———. *Mystery and Manners: Occasional Prose,* Sally and Robert Fitzgerald (eds.), (New York: Farrar, Straus, and Giroux, 1969).

———. *The Presence of Grace, and Other Book Reviews,* Leo J. Zuber and Carter W. Martin (comp. and ed.), (Athens: University of Georgia Press, 1983).

Robert C. Evans

O'CONNOR, FRANK (1903–1966)

Born Michael Francis O'Donovan in Cork, Ireland, he adopted his pen name in the 1920s so that his sometimes-controversial writings would not threaten his means of earning a conventional livelihood (for a time as a librarian) in a country that was often both politically and religiously intolerant. Although a highly bookish and imaginative only child of poor parents (including a father he sometimes feared and a mother he always adored), O'Connor did not shrink from either literal or literary combat. He served the Republican cause during the Civil War but was often highly critical of the Republic it produced, and he later battled metaphorically on behalf of a variety of social and literary ideals. An avid reader and prolific writer (of novels, nonfiction, poetry, and especially short fiction), by the end of his life he was widely regarded as one of the best writers of short stories in Ireland and indeed the world. His writing was well-informed by his reading, although he sought to give his stories the sound of a true speaking voice and to avoid "literary" artifice and contrivance.

Many of O'Connor's opinions about writers are easily available in four of his own books: *Towards an Appreciation of Literature* (1945), *The Art of the Theatre* (1947), *The Mirror in the Roadway: A Study of the Modern Novel* (1956), and *The Lonely Voice: A Study of the Short Story* (1963). He also produced a highly idiosyncratic study of Shakespeare *(Shakespeare's Progress)* and a survey of Irish literature called *The Backward Look*. He wrote extensively on **James Joyce** (a contemporary whose importance he appreciated but whose writings he sometimes disliked) and on William Butler Yeats (who influenced him both as a writer and as a mentor). He offered opinions on such varied writers as AE (George Russell), Sherwood Anderson, Jane Austen, Honoré de Balzac, Robert Browning, **Willa Cather,** Anton Chekhov, A. E. Coppard, Charles Dickens, **William Faulkner,** Gustave Flaubert, **André Gide,** Nikolai Gogol, Lady Gregory, Thomas Hardy, **Ernest Hemingway,** Patrick Kavanagh, Rudyard Kipling, Mary Lavin, **D. H. Lawrence,** Nikolai Leskov, Katherine Mansfield, Guy de Maupassant, George Moore, Liam O'Flaherty, Edgar Allan Poe, Katherine Anne Porter, J. F. Powers, J. D. Salinger, William Saroyan, George Bernard Shaw, Stendhal, **Gertrude Stein,** James Stephens, Jonathan Swift, J. M. Synge, William Thackeray, Lev Tolstoy, Anthony Trollope, Ivan Turgenev, and **Virginia Woolf,** among many others. He personally knew and closely read many of the important writers of his day, particularly Irish authors or authors anywhere of short fiction, and he brought to all his reading a passionate conviction about the importance of literature to the wider community. This conviction is evident also in his various translations, particularly of ancient Irish poets.

Among novelists, O'Connor admired Austen for treating moral problems realistically; he deeply admired many nineteenth-century writers, especially from England and Russia; he found Thackeray full of intriguing contradictions; and he particularly esteemed Flaubert's *Madame Bovary*. At the same time, he was suspicious of the overemphasis on clever artistry sometimes exhibited by such novelists as Flaubert, Joyce, and Henry James, and he felt that modern novelists such as

399

Joyce, **Marcel Proust,** and Faulkner sometimes created characters who exhibited insufficient free will. He admired Faulkner's humor more than his technical innovations, and he valued detective fiction because he felt that it properly emphasized the importance of plot.

Commenting on short fiction, O'Connor mentioned that he had been significantly influenced by Isaac Babel early in his career; that much could be learned from Chekhov if Chekhov was studied correctly; that Coppard was a particularly worthy writer; that Turgenev's *A Sportman's Sketches* "may well be the greatest book of short stories ever written" and that the same author's "Old Portraits" may be the best story ever penned; that Kipling insufficiently emphasized the theme of human loneliness (which O'Connor regarded as crucial to short fiction); that Mansfield's stories are mostly forgettable; that Lawrence, along with Coppard, was one of England's best authors of short fiction; that Hemingway's stories sometimes fail to balance narrative and drama, and also that Hemingway's material is often either slight or overblown.

O'Connor's motives as a reader were clearly self-interested: he read other writers for what they could teach him about literature, whether through their virtues or their alleged errors. He seems to have been influenced, in one way or another, by nearly every text he encountered, and the impact of his reading can be seen not only in his published criticism but also in his own creative writing.

Archives

Important collections are held at Boston University, the British Broadcasting Corporation, the Cork Public Museum, Harvard University, the National Library of Ireland, Northwestern University, Stanford University, Trinity College (Dublin), the University of California at Berkeley, the University of Kansas, Manchester University, the University of Texas at Austin, the University of Toronto, the University of Tulsa, the University of Victoria, and especially the University of Florida.

Printed Sources

Evans, Robert C., and Richard Harp (eds.). *Frank O'Connor: New Perspectives* (West Cornwall, Conn.: Locust Hill, 1998).
Matthews, James. *Voices: A Life of Frank O'Connor* (New York: Atheneum, 1983).
O'Connor, Frank. *An Only Child* and *My Father's Son* (London: Pan Books, 1988).
Sheehy, Maurice (ed.). *Michael/Frank: Studies on Frank O'Connor* (New York: Knopf, 1969).
Tomory, William M. *Frank O'Connor* (Boston: Twayne, 1980).

Robert C. Evans

O'KEEFFE, GEORGIA (1887–1985)

Georgia O'Keeffe's career as an artist spanned over half a century. Yet she hardly personified the typical expectations of females; she flatly refused to be defined, and her artistic career, lasting until her death in 1985, spanned cityscapes, abstract art, and paintings reflecting her intimacy with nature. She claimed that her first memory was of the brightness of light, and many of her paintings represent her focus on the contrast between light and dark. She discovered at the age of eight that she wanted to be an artist, and her parents indulged her talent by sending her to art school. She enrolled at the Art Institute of

Chicago, studying under John Vanderpoel, who taught her that line and shading should be used with the awareness that both represented the external appearance of a complete living entity.

In an attempt to define more narrowly her artistic focus, O'Keeffe attended a summer course at the University of Virginia in 1912 taught by Alon Bement, who, using the theories of Arthur Dow, emphasized the careful arrangement of all elements in a composition and stressed the significance of the relationship between light and dark. O'Keeffe would later write in her autobiography, "It was in the fall of 1915 that I first had the idea that what I had been taught was of little value to me except for the use of my materials as a language. . . . I had become fluent with them when I was so young that they were simply another language that I handled easily. . . . I decided to start anew—to strip away what I had been taught—to accept as true my own thinking" (O'Keeffe 1976, 20). Her paintings began to evolve into an evident tension between light and dark; motion and stasis; and weight and levity, all of which led to a sense of vitality in her art. **Vassily Kandinsky's** *On the Spiritual in Art*, which Bement had recommended, became her justification for pursuing the intellectual in artistry and for completely breaking with traditional painting conventions.

While in New York in 1917, O'Keeffe met **Alfred Stieglitz,** whom she would marry in 1924. Coincidentally, since much of her artwork mirrored her life, her paintings in the 1920s featured flowers, perhaps to celebrate her happiness. O'Keeffe would often present a single, centrally-positioned object, many times a flower, enlarged to an unnatural size. Yet she still struggled to find her own way; she had to essentially free herself from Stieglitz's shadow. She knew that she was an enigma in the art world and that her male peers felt she could not compete with their work or that they did not take her work seriously. Often critics would degrade her work by misconstruing it as sexually based, comparing her flower artistry to human genitalia. She flatly denied any such accusations, despite the sort of sensuality and exotic flavor that her artwork exudes. She believed her art represented the whole psyche, not just one aspect.

O'Keeffe found inspiration in the Southwest, particularly in New Mexico, an enthusiasm not shared by Stieglitz, and their emotional separation is reflected in O'Keeffe's work during the 1930s. Her paintings throughout this period reveal a sense of yearning to reveal nature and often feature isolated animal skulls, painted with wave patterns and zigzag lines. The symbolic juxtaposition of life (flower imagery) and death (skulls) was a dramatic feature of many of her paintings. O'Keeffe rejected the critic's rather morbid metaphor of death in describing her paintings; to her, these were images of life and happiness.

While O'Keeffe's career was flourishing in New Mexico, Stieglitz suffered his third heart attack, and died on July 13, 1946, in O'Keeffe's arms. She spent two years settling their estate in New York and then moved permanently to Abiquiu, New Mexico. After her eyesight began to deteriorate, she enlisted the assistance of a sculptor, Juan Hamilton, as well as Sarah Greenough, a research curator at the National Gallery of Art in Washington, D.C., to help preserve elements of her life. After her death in 1985, her ashes were scattered on the grounds of her home by Hamilton, since a proper burial would have been incongruous for the woman who spent her life as an artist attempting to explain the unexplainable.

Archives

Georgia O'Keeffe Museum Research Center, Santa Fe, New Mexico.

Printed Sources

Benke, Britta. *Georgia O'Keeffe, 1887–1986: Flowers in the Desert* (Koln: Taschen, 2000).
Frazier, Nancy. *Georgia O'Keeffe* (North Dighton, Mass.: World Publications Group, Inc., 2001).
Mitchell, Brenda Maria. "Music That Makes Holes in the Sky: Georgia O'Keeffe's *Visionary Romanticism*" (Ph.D. diss., University of Illinois at Urbana-Champaign, 1996).
O'Keeffe, Georgia. *Georgia O'Keeffe* (New York: The Viking Press, 1976).
Richter, Peter-Cornell. *Georgia O'Keeffe and Alfred Stieglitz* (Munich: Prestel Verlag Press, 2001).

Jennifer Harrison

O'NEILL, EUGENE GLADSTONE (1888–1953)

Eugene O'Neill was born in a New York City hotel, the Barrett House. He attended Princeton University (1906–7) before being suspended for misbehavior and Harvard University (1914–15), where he took George Pierce Baker's famed English 47 workshop but did not matriculate. An intensely autobiographical playwright (his father was the stage actor James O'Neill), O'Neill won four Pulitzer Prizes (one posthumously) and the Nobel Prize for literature in 1936. Arguably America's greatest dramatist and certainly among its most important writers, O'Neill revolutionized American stagecraft in his early career by incorporating European expressionistic techniques into such plays as *The Emperor Jones* (1920) and *The Hairy Ape* (1921) and by using a mixture of Greek myth and Freudian psychoanalysis in *Desire Under the Elms* (1924) and the *Mourning Becomes Electra* (1931) trilogy. O'Neill's later, more classic works, such as *The Iceman Cometh* (1939) and *Long Day's Journey Into Night* (1941), both masterpieces of tragic psychological realism, solidified his lasting reputation and importance not only to American drama, but to the world.

While O'Neill was often loath to ascribe the influence of other writers on his work, his letters were often explicit on this matter where his plays were merely implicit. He noted early in his career (Bogard and Bryer 1988, 119) his dependence on the good opinion of his former professor, George Pierce Baker. Other early influences include his compatriots in the Experimental Theatre, Inc.: Robert Edmond Jones, whom O'Neill relied on for his expressionistic sets (Bogard and Bryer 1988, 161), and literary critic/producer Kenneth Macgowan, with whom O'Neill frequently and voluminously corresponded on business and artistic matters. In a 1927 letter, O'Neill made perhaps his most explicit declaration of influence, noting the profound impact of Friedrich Nietzsche's *Thus Spake Zarathustra* (1891) on O'Neill's play *Lazarus Laughed* (1926), among other works (Bogard and Bryer 1988, 245). Especially important for this play was Nietzsche's affirmation of man's supremacy over God as well as Nietzsche's theory of the opposition of the Dionysian and Apollonian aspects of human existence. This opposition was also rendered in the plays and short stories of Swedish writer Augustus Strindberg, whose collection *Married* was cited by O'Neill as an exploration of poverty's incompatibility with "the dictates of nature," a contrast often explored to tragic effect in O'Neill's own work (Bogard and Bryer 1988, 33). This tragic impulse was profoundly echoed in virtually all of O'Neill's plays, prompting him to defend his tendency of "always seeing things black" by citing several of whom he considered to be the best writers, including Henrik Ibsen, German writer **Gerhart Hauptmann,** and Russian Leonid Andreyev. Finally, one must include the influences of Aeschylus, from whose *The Oresteia* trilogy (458 B.C.E.) O'Neill borrowed the mythic structure and interest in the workings of destiny he incorporated in *Mourning Becomes Electra*, as well as Sigmund Freud, whose psychoanalytic theories O'Neill cited as an "unconscious influence" (Bogard and Bryer 1988, 192).

Archives

Eugene O'Neill Papers. Yale Collection of American Literature, Beinecke Rare Book and Manuscript Library, New Haven, Conn.: professional and family correspondence, manuscripts, photographs, legal and financial records, personal and professional memorabilia, primarily 1930s to 1950s.

Princeton University Library, Princeton, N.J.: 15 autographed manuscripts of O'Neill plays, most of which are first drafts and include preliminary notes (1913–24). Also includes photograph collection and correspondence from throughout O'Neill's life.

Eugene O'Neill Foundation, Tao House, Danville, Calif.: a large collection of manuscripts, first editions, inscribed books, photographs, correspondence, ephemera, and Carlotta Monterey O'Neill's diaries, including other materials.

Eugene O'Neill Papers. The Clifton Waller Barrett Library, Special Collections Department, University of Virginia Library, Charlottesville, Va.: correspondence and manuscripts.

Printed Works

Bogard, Travis, and Jackson R. Bryer (eds.). *Selected Letters of Eugene O'Neill* (New Haven: Yale University Press, 1988).

Ranald, Margaret Loftus. *The Eugene O'Neill Companion* (Westport, Conn.: Greenwood Press, 1984).

Shaeffer, Louis. *O'Neill: Son and Artist* (Boston: Little, Brown and Company, 1973).

Todd R. Robinson

OPPENHEIMER, ROBERT (1904–1967)

Robert Oppenheimer was the son of Julius Oppenheimer, a prosperous New York textile importer, and his wife, Ella Friedman, an artist. The cosmopolitan Oppenheimers were nonobservant Jews, and their sons attended the Ethical Culture School of New York. Oppenheimer, a precocious student, excelled in all subjects, mastering several languages, including Latin, Greek, French, and German, and showing particular ability in English and chemistry. After graduation he studied at Harvard University, obtaining a degree in chemistry summa cum laude in three years, carrying a maximum credit load, and auditing still more courses. Now enthralled by physics, Oppenheimer spent 1925–26 at the Cavendish Laboratory, Cambridge, England, proving inept at experimentation. Switching to the University of Göttingen, Germany, and the exciting new field of theoretical quantum physics, in March 1927 Oppenheimer received his doctorate. After two years' postdoctoral study in the United States, Holland, and Switzerland, Oppenheimer accepted a joint teaching appointment at the California Institute of Technology (Caltech) and the University of California, Berkeley. An inspiring teacher, Oppenheimer quickly attracted a generation of enthusiastic graduate students to Caltech and Berkeley, which became leading international centers of quantum physics. Although Oppenheimer published extensively on spectra, particles, neutron stars, and black holes, his personal scientific contribution was less outstanding, and he was never a serious contender for a Nobel Prize.

In October 1941 Oppenheimer began fast-neutron research for the United States government in connection with atomic bomb development and one year later became director of the central laboratory for bomb design and development at Los Alamos, New Mexico. In this enormously demanding position Oppenheimer revealed new self-discipline, and his skillful intellectual leadership, capacity to absorb and process information, concern for those working under him, and ability to negotiate the often difficult relationship between individualistic scientists and governmental demands for conformity, became legendary. After the 1945 atomic explosions over Hiroshima and Nagasaki, an exhausted Oppenheimer shared his Danish colleague **Niels Bohr**'s hope that the bomb's destructiveness might eventually force nations to abandon war. Leaving Los Alamos in late 1945, two years later Oppenheimer became director of the Institute of Advanced Study at Princeton, quickly transforming it into the world's top center for theoretical physics and simultaneously enhancing its existing reputation in humanistic studies. As the most prestigious American adviser to the United States Atomic Energy Commission, Oppenheimer advocated international control of atomic energy and lectured extensively, seeking to enhance popular scientific understanding. In 1953 growing domestic McCarthyist anti-Communist sentiment and some colleagues' resentment of Oppenheimer's reluctance to develop a thermonuclear bomb led the American government to withdraw his security clearance, on the grounds that his wartime evasiveness over potential security problems and prewar left-wing and Communist associates, including his brother, a former fiancée, and his wife, had permanently compromised his status. A full-scale inquiry held in 1954 on Oppenheimer's insistence confirmed this verdict. Although excluded from governmental counsels, Oppenheimer retained his academic position at Princeton until June 1966, dying of cancer in 1967.

From early childhood Oppenheimer read voraciously and omnivorously, a habit his father encouraged by buying him complete sets of any author whose books appealed to him. Although enormously well-read scientifically, Oppenheimer, a latter-day Renaissance man, was equally conversant with literature and poetry, an abiding passion, history of all periods and areas, architecture, and philosophy. The adult Oppenheimer acquired Dutch, Italian, and Sanskrit, the latter so that he could read the Hindu *Bhagavad-Gita* in the original; after the first successful atomic test took place, he recalled its words: "I am become death, the shatterer of worlds." Politics and contemporary affairs he initially ignored, but in the 1930s when Oppenheimer finally developed an interest in the Left, he read all the writings of Karl Marx, **Vladimir Ilyich Lenin,** and other communist theoreticians. Some even suggested that Oppenheimer's failure to produce any single outstanding personal intellectual contribution to theoretical physics resulted from his compulsion to acquire deep understanding of so many other fields.

Archives

J. Robert Oppenheimer Papers, Manuscripts Division, Library of Congress, Washington, D.C. Major collection of Oppenheimer's personal correspondence and manuscripts.

Printed Sources

Goodchild, Peter. *J. Robert Oppenheimer: Shatterer of Worlds* (Boston: Houghton Mifflin, 1981).

Kunetka, James W. *Oppenheimer: The Years of Risk* (Englewood Cliffs, N.J.: Prentice-Hall, 1982).

Schweber, S. S. *In the Shadow of the Bomb: Bethe, Oppenheimer, and the Moral Responsibility of a Scientist* (Princeton: Princeton University Press, 2000).

Smith, Alice Kimball, and Charles Weiner (eds.). *Robert Oppenheimer: Letters and Recollections* (Cambridge, Mass.: Harvard University Press, 1980). Gives much detailed insight into Oppenheimer's wide reading.

Priscilla Roberts

ORTEGA Y GASSET, JOSÉ (1883–1956)

One of the great thinkers of twentieth-century Spanish letters, José Ortega y Gasset was born in Madrid. His father was a fiction writer and director of an important literary journal, *Los Lunes del Imparcial*. His mother was from a family of politicians and journalists. It is not surprising that Ortega began reading at age four, 1897, and by 1890 his parents gave him a toy horse after his having memorized the first chapter of *Don Quixote*. He treasured Honoré de Balzac's *La comédie humaine* and works by Alexandre Dumas, Jules Verne, and Benito Pérez Galdós. Ortega studied at the Jesuit School in Málaga. At age 21, he became a doctor of philosophy at the University of Madrid and began to write for his father's journal. Inclined more to ideas and science than to writing, Ortega expressed admiration for French poet Ernest Renan's philosophy of the importance of reason and truth, elites in societies and democracy, and Saint-Simonian socialism. Ortega declared that Renan's "books have been with me ever since I was a child." He also became friends with **Miguel de Unamuno** at this time. His postdoctoral studies continued for two years at the German Universities of Leipzig, where he studied philology and came in contact with Neokantianism, Berlin, where Ortega studied the life philosophy of Georg Simmel, and Marburg, where he studied the work of Hermann Cohen. He also showed a predilection for Simmel regarding the relationship between man and culture, placing man at the center of philosophy. These were years he supported socialism as a "scientific conception" following Paul Natorp's concept that only the socialized individual is fully human, and he studied how to apply Kant's scientific methodologies to a philosophical system of grand synthesis of reason and empiricism. Ortega continued reading other German philosophers such as Oswald Spengler, the physicist Max Born, and the biologist Von Uexkull. In particular, from the works of phenomenologist Edmund Husserl's *Logical Investigations* (1900, 1901) and his "philosophy of rigorous science" (1910–11), Ortega extracted the concept of cognitive value of intuition and direct experience. Later in *Preface for Germans* (1958), Ortega declared that during these years he already felt somehow that the neo-Kantian thought was "contrived . . . profound, serious, acute, full of truth, and nevertheless, without veracity." He rejected Nietzsche's "live dangerously!" in favor of Ludovico Ariosto's more sober "vivere risolutamente!" (live resolutely). Upon his return to Spain in 1910, he taught Metaphysics at the University of Madrid and founded a short-lived party of intellectuals, the League of Political Education. He founded and published *Revista de Occidente* in 1923 and was a very prolific essayist.

In *El tema de nuestro tiempo* (1923), Ortega broke away from his neo-Kantian upbringing and began to propound the concept of *razón vital;* the vital reason that is more flexible and responds to the concrete lived experience of the individual. This tension between pure reason and vital reason (pure vitality) is the essence of the "theme of our time." From Husserl's 1927 *Yearbooks,* Ortega read **Martin Heidegger**'s ontology of existence theory in *Being and Time.* In his latest writings, Ortega also attested to an appreciation of Wilhem Dilthey's "historical reason." In *Historia como sistema* (1935), Ortega synthesized Husserl and Dilthey's ideas into a "vital and historical reason." A man is the sum of all human experiences as shown by history contrary to a scientifically measurable moment in time.

When the Spanish Civil War began, Ortega moved to France, Holland, Portugal, and later on to Buenos Aires where he occupied an important role in the intellectual circles of Latin America for several decades. He returned to Spain in 1945 to found the Institute de Humanities where he lectured along with his disciple Julián Marías in 1948. Between 1949 and 1951 he lectured also in the United States, Germany, and Switzerland. In his later works from 1933 to his death, Ortega studied the works of Ferdinand de Saussure and the Prague linguistic circle as well as German philosophy of language, and phenomenology, existentialism, structuralist linguistics.

Archives

Fundación Ortega y Gasset, Madrid.
Centro de Estudios Orteguianos, Universidad de la Coruña.
Archivo Histórico Nacional, Biblioteca Nacional, Madrid.

Printed Sources

Dobson, Andrew. *An Introduction to the Politics and Philosophy of José Ortega y Gasset* (Cambridge: Cambridge University Press, 1989).
Durán, Manuel (ed.). *Ortega hoy: Estudio, ensayos, y bibliografía sobre la vida y la obra de José Ortega y Gasset* (Xalapa, México: Universidad Veracruzana, 1985).
Ferrater Mora, José. *José Ortega y Gasset: An Outline of His Philosophy* (New Haven: Yale University Press, 1963).
Graham, John Thomas. *Theory of History in Ortega y Gasset: The Dawn of Historical Reason* (Columbia: University of Missouri Press, 1997).
Huéscar Rodríguez, A. *José Ortega y Gasset's Metaphysical Innovation: A Critique and Overcoming of Idealism* (Albany: University of New York Press, 1995).
Marías, Julián. *José Ortega y Gasset, Circumstance and Vocation,* Frances M. López-Morillas (trans.), (Norman: Unviersity of Oklahoma Press, 1970).
Orringer, Nelson R. *Nuevas fuentes germánicas de ¿Qué es filosofía? de Ortega* (Madrid: CSIC, 1979).
Ouimette, Victor. *José Ortega y Gasset* (Boston: Twayne, 1982).
Silver, Philip W. *Ortega as Phenomenologist: The Genesis of "Meditations on Quixote"* (New York: Columbia University Press, 1978).

Andrés Villagrá

ORWELL, GEORGE (1903–1950)

George Orwell, the pseudonym of Eric Arthur Blair, was born at Motihari in Bengal, India, where his father was a civil servant. In 1904 he moved to England with his mother and sister. In 1911 he entered St. Cyprian's preparatory school,

Eastbourne, winning a scholarship to Wellington College in 1917 and another to Eton later that year. He left Eton in 1921 but instead of going to Oxford or Cambridge like many of his contemporaries, he took the India Office civil service examination. He went to Burma in 1922, serving in the Indian Imperial Police until 1927. He returned to England on leave, decided to stay, and resigned his commission. He felt uncomfortable working in a position of what he saw as oppressive imperial authority.

He determined to turn himself into a writer to make his living. Already writing and politics were linked in his mind. Just for the experience, he lived rough in the East End of London, went on the road with tramps, and worked as a dishwasher in Paris, the sources of *Down and Out in Paris and London* (1933). In 1929 he began to write reviews and literary articles for *The Adelphi* and later for *The New English Weekly* and *The New Statesman and Nation*. His first novel, *Burmese Days*, was published in 1934, followed by *A Clergyman's Daughter* (1935), *Keep the Aspidistra Flying* (1936), and *Coming Up For Air* (1939). Financed by the Left Book Club, he traveled through coal-mining areas of northern England in 1936 and published *The Road to Wigan Pier* (1937), as critical of socialism as of the mine owners. Late in 1936 he went to Spain to join the socialist military party, POUM, fighting Franco's fascists in the Civil War. He was wounded and returned to England to write an account of his experiences and of socialism and equality in action in *Homage to Catalonia* (1938). From 1936 to 1941 he wrote reviews for *Time & Tide*, as many as three a week, and for *Horizon*. His health deteriorated and following a lung hemorrhage, he was forbidden to work. Coinciding with the outbreak of war in 1939, it contributed to his frustration and depression. From 1941 to 1943 he worked at the BBC Indian section as a radio talks producer, writer, and broadcaster. He left to be literary editor of *Tribune*. He began writing *Animal Farm* (1945), although progress was slow because of ill health, his wife's death, and commitments to the *Partisan Review*, *Manchester Evening News*, and *The Observer*. *Animal Farm* and later *Nineteen Eighty-Four* (1949) made him rich and famous, and alone would account for his reputation today, but he died too soon to enjoy the rewards.

At the age of eight he had read Jonathan Swift's *Gulliver's Travels*, a book he found inexhaustible and which he claimed to have reread every year of his life. At St. Cyprian's he and his friends read together Dickens, Carlyle, Shakespeare, and, inevitably, boys' weekly magazines filled with adventure stories. They particularly enjoyed H. G. Wells's *The Country of the Blind* and Compton Mackenzie's *Sinister Street*, not least because these were books to be read literally under cover, away from the eyes of authority. He was instructed in the merits of the Authorized Version of the Bible, and the values of its language were clearly still in his mind when he wrote his 1946 essay on style, "Politics and the English Language." At Wellington and Eton he studied Greek and Latin literature but his favorite authors were all modern—Jack London, George Bernard Shaw, and Wells. He enjoyed books that took him away from the world he knew—nature in London's *The Call of the Wild* and the descriptions of poverty in *People of the Abyss*. The more imaginative and fantastic the work, the more it appealed to him. Shaw's plays he liked for their anti-establishment ideas and skepticism. But Orwell's own growing skepticism eventually led to a certain disillusion with these early favorites, as illustrated by his 1941 essay, "Wells, Hitler and the World State." Meanwhile he was developing a taste for romantic poetry, especially Shelley, Ernest Dowson, and A. E. Housman.

He memorized *A Shropshire Lad*, wallowing in the language and the beauty and self-pity of its sentiments. Housman's defiant paganism and sexual pessimism appealed to him to the point that at the age of 15 he wrote a love poem entitled "The Pagan." In Burma in his early twenties there was plenty of time for reading. He later recalled the books that made the biggest impression on him at this stage: Lev Tolstoy's *War and Peace*, Samuel Butler's *Notebooks*, and **D. H. Lawrence**'s *Women in Love*. He read English newspapers and magazines when they eventually arrived by the long sea crossing, and he subscribed to John Middleton Murry's *Adelphi* monthly. Returning to England, he wrote reviews for a string of literary magazines, the work that made his living. While on the one hand it took time that he might have preferred to devote to writing his own books, on the other it might be seen as a source of literary inspiration. He was forced to read a lot. He learned the difference between good and bad writing. He developed a sense of literary style and refined the no-nonsense writing for which he is now famous.

In the mid-1930s he worked in a secondhand bookshop in Hampstead. Not only did this give him the opportunity to read extensively from the stock, but it also showed him how the book market worked and what readers wanted. Increasingly he was aware of books as a commodity and, disillusioned, he turned to old Victorian volumes of the *Gentleman's Magazine*, the *Cornhill Magazine*, *The Strand*, and, oddly, *The Girl's Own Paper*. In them he was intrigued by the way political and other ideas date, the mixture of sincerity and ignorance, and the way yesterday's burning issues are largely ignored by general history books.

Later in the 1930s in Spain, Orwell not only saw socialism in action, but also experienced the blurring of meaning that abuse of language and distortion of words can cause. He went as a socialist to fight against fascism but found communism fighting under the name of socialism and in reality fighting against socialist principles. Far from bringing about social revolution the communists were conservative, determined to grab and hold on to power. *Animal Farm* is about that abuse of power and the betrayal of good intentions, notably the principle of equality. Anxious to save socialism from communism and totalitarianism, he wrote *Nineteen Eighty-Four*, a warning about the suppression of individual freedom in the quest for power for its own sake. It is a book about contradictions, not least the distortion of language. The influences behind these two books go back to his youth. Even at Eton he was engaging in debate with Marxists, and throughout his reviewing career he was drawn to writings on power, power politics, and the abuse of power. He knew Jack London's *The Iron Heel* and **Aldous Huxley**'s *Brave New World*. In 1939 he reviewed **Bertrand Russell**'s *Power: A New Social Analysis*, and in a 1940 review of Jack Hilton's *English Ways* he wrote "If there is hope it lies in the proles," a sentiment repeated in *Nineteen Eighty-Four*. In the early 1940s he had read Yevgeny Ivanovich Zamyatin's 1923 futuristic fantasy novel, *We*, which inspired him to begin making notes for his own book. He read **Arthur Koestler**'s *Darkness at Noon* and in 1946 wrote at length on James Burnham's *The Managerial Revolution*. This was perhaps the strongest influence on *Nineteen Eighty-Four*, inspiring Orwell to one of his sharpest critical attacks on power. He argued that what seems powerful today is often, because of its ambition and apparent strength, overthrown tomorrow. His argument in the essay, as in his novel, is that the common man will prevail.

In the 1946 essay "Why I Write," Orwell describes his early determination to become a writer and his joy in words, sounds, and their associations. Writing became a way to take revenge on his other failures in life. Not to write was to out-rage his true nature. He identifies four driving forces in his writing: egoism, plea-sure in words, the historical impulse to record the truth, and the political impulse to push the world in a particular direction. His experiences in Spain had changed his outlook, and afterward his thinking and writing took a new and more seriously political turn. His hatred of authority was strengthened by those experiences, and thereafter he concentrated his writing attention against totalitarianism and toward democratic socialism. He was pessimistic because he recognized that there is some-thing in human nature that seeks violence, conflict, and power over others. He determined to make political writing into an art to expose deceit, while caring deeply about prose style and scraps of seemingly useless information. He loved the construction of language and the nature of truth in words. Both *Homage to Catalo-nia* and *Nineteen Eighty-Four* contain chapters about the distortion of truth through the manipulation of words. Orwell was committed to the exact use of words and increasingly in his later work he fused that artistic purpose with political purpose.

Archives

University College London, Department of Rare Books and Manuscripts, has the Orwell Archive containing manuscripts, typescripts, proofs, editions including translations, jour-nalism, books from his library, and secondary materials.

BBC Written Archive, Caversham Park, Reading, has correspondence, typescripts, radio scripts, and details of programs Orwell organized, arranged, and produced.

Printed Sources

Crick, Bernard. *George Orwell: A Life* (London: Secker & Warburg, 1980).

Fenwick, Gillian. *George Orwell: A Bibliography* (Winchester: St. Paul's Bibliographies, 1998).

Myers, Jeffrey. *George Orwell: The Critical Heritage* (London: Routledge & Kegan Paul, 1975).

Orwell, George. *Complete Works of George Orwell*, Peter Davison (ed.), 20 vols. (London: Secker & Warburg, 1986–98). Includes essays on each work.

Shelden, Michael. *Orwell: The Authorised Biography* (London: Heinemann, 1991).

Gillian Fenwick

OSBORNE, JOHN (1929–1994)

John Osborne was born in Fulham, London. The son of an advertising copy-writer, Osborne attended St. Michael's school and was expelled at age 16 for speak-ing derisively of the royal family and for an altercation with the headmaster. He arrived on the national scene in 1956 with the debut of his play *Look Back in Anger* about the frustrations and conflicts of a working-class man and his middle-class wife. In that work and in 1957's *The Entertainer*, Osborne launched a blistering attack on the class system, moral hypocrisy, and nostalgia for imperial glories. The plays made him the first of the "angry young men" of mid-twentieth-century English drama, and throughout his career, he was at his best depicting alienation, not only from society but also in intimate relationships.

Osborne recorded that while a teenager, he had been prompted to read Oscar Wilde's plays by his grandfather's "prurient obsession" with that author. The young Osborne soon moved on to Wilde's other works, such as *The Ballad of Reading Gaol* and *The Soul of Man under Socialism*. That last book led him to the writings of

George Orwell and other publications of Victor Gollancz's Left Book Club, which strongly influenced his later political allegiances (Osborne 1981, 83–4). In Osborne's early days working as an actor and fledgling playwright, his agent and his mentors in theater pressed him to study the plays of Arthur Pinero and Terence Rattigan. He did so, but remained skeptical as to whether those writers' craftsmanship was accompanied by meaningful content. Osborne compared Pinero's and Rattigan's plays to "the construction of an artefact like a carriage clock, which revealed its beautiful precision to all, particularly . . . those who were obliged to write and explain its workings to their readers" (Osborne 1981, 196).

Jean Anouilh, **Tennessee Williams,** and **D. H. Lawrence** were far more important figures in Osborne's development. Not only did those writers' frank—and often stark—studies of humanity influence Osborne's style, but he also credited the trio's controversial works with helping to prepare English audiences for his plays (Carter 1969, 15). Many critics have cited **Bertolt Brecht** as a seminal influence on Osborne but have often overstated the case. The two did share a realist approach and an interest in political topics, but Osborne's plays were driven by emotional intensity, while Brecht's goal was to achieve detachment from the emotions (Carter 1969, 177–79). The Brecht case is a salutary example of the limits to the search for antecedents, particularly in the case of such an original and pioneering playwright

Archives

The largest collection of Osborne material is found at the John Osborne Papers, Harry Ransom Humanities Research Center, University of Texas at Austin.
The British Library, St. Pancras, London, also holds a number of Osborne manuscripts.

Printed Sources

Carter, Alan. *John Osborne* (Edinburgh: Oliver and Boyd, 1969).
Hinchcliffe, Arnold P. *John Osborne* (Boston: Twayne, 1984; Copyright by G.K. Hall & Company).
Osborne, John. *Almost a Gentleman: An Autobiography, Volume II, 1955–1966* (London: Faber, 1991).
———. *A Better Class of Person: An Autobiography, 1929–1956* (London: Faber and Faber, 1981).
———. *Plays, Volumes I–III* (London: Faber, 1993–). This is the most complete collection of Osborne's dramatic works.

Christopher Pepus

OWENS, JAMES CLEVELAND (1913–1980)

James Cleveland Owens was born in Oakville, Alabama. The youngest child in the sharecropping family of Henry and Mary Emma Owens, Jesse Owens spent his youth and adolescence on the east side of Cleveland, Ohio, among enclaves of Polish and Italian immigrants and southern black migrant families. Owens's years of education were remarkable not so much for classroom performance, but for records broken in track and field events and for the people who would continue to influence and guide Owens throughout the rest of his life. Junior high track coach Charles Riley taught Owens focus and form. Minnie Ruth Solomon eventually became his wife, while fellow athlete David Albritton remained a lifelong friend. Running for Larry Snyder and Ohio State, Owens set world records in the 220-yard dash, long jump, and 220-yard low hurdles, propelling himself into a place on the track team representing the United States at the 1936 Olympiad XI in Berlin. Owens's four gold medals at the Berlin Games, against the backdrop of Hitler and Nazi Germany, gave Owens space on the public stage. In the years following the Olympics, Owens looked back on his early years in Alabama and the chance his family took in moving to Cleveland in search of a better life. Using his post-Olympic name recognition and profile, Owens engaged in multiple business ventures. At the core of his most meaningful work, however, was championing the cause of youth around the world and using sports as a means to give children focus and meaning. Running gave Owens a voice, and in his later years Owens spearheaded, along with the Atlantic Richfield Company (ARCO) of Los Angeles, the ARCO Jesse Owens Games for boys and girls between the ages of 10 and 15. Likewise, Owens continued to be an ambassador for the Olympic movement. Responding to the death of Owens in 1980, then-president **Jimmy Carter** declared the athlete a symbol of the human struggle against tyranny, poverty, and racial bigotry.

Inscribed on Owens's gravestone are the words athlete and humanitarian, the seeds of which are evident in Owens's own account of his childhood as told to friend and ghostwriter Paul Neimark and recorded in three autobiographical writings. Owens recalled being asked as a child who he wanted to be like when he got older, to which he replied, George Washington Carver. Owens also recalled wanting to be a runner. The oral tradition was strong in the Owens's Alabama home, with Sunday mornings given to Baptist services and dinners time for conversation. In *Blackthink*, Owens writes that his parents did not know how to read. There was no one in Oakville to teach them and no time to learn. Neither Owens's parents or grandparents had been allowed to own a book, but when the Owens family moved to Cleveland, Emma Cleveland saved to buy a Bible. The Bible was kept on a shelf above the fireplace and Owens remembers reading passages aloud. During the course of his grade school and high school education, Owens came across the principles of Booker T. Washington, adopting Washington's code of self-reliance rather than the militant confrontations promoted by **Marcus Moziah Garvey** and W.E.B. DuBois. Coming out of his own experience in Alabama, Owens advocated goals for breaking the cycle of poverty and enjoyed promoting his ideas through public speaking appearances and work with underprivileged inner-city children. Though Owens did not nurture an active reading life, he admired the noted orators of his time, including **Martin Luther King Jr.**, Adam Clayton Powell, and Roscoe Conkling Simmons.

Archives

Atlantic Richfield Company (ARCO), Los Angeles, California, typescript interviews for ARCO Jesse Owens Games.

Illinois State Historical Library, Springfield, Illinois, typescript interviews with Jesse Owens and Ruth Owens.

Jesse Owens Foundation, Chicago, Illinois.

Ohio State University Archives, miscellaneous letters and correspondence.

Printed Sources

Baker, William J. *Jesse Owens: An American Life* (New York: The Free Press, 1986).

Owens, Jesse, with Paul Neimark. *I Have Changed* (New York: William Morrow, 1972).

———. *The Jesse Owens Story* (New York: Putnam's, 1970).

———. *Jesse: The Man Who Outran Hitler* (Brooklyn, N.Y.: Fawcett Books Group, 1978).

Devon Niebling

P

PADEREWSKI, JAN IGNACY (1860–1941)

Jan Paderewski was a Polish pianist, composer, and statesman born in Podolia (part of Russian-occupied Poland) to an impoverished noble family. His education started at home with tutoring in music and Polish and French literature (his literary self-education continued throughout his lifetime). Paderewski studied piano and music theory at the Music Institute of Warsaw (1872–78), composition with Friedrich Kiel and Heinrich Urban in Berlin (1881–83), and piano with Theodore Leschetitzky in Vienna (1884-86). His international fame commenced with his Parisian debut in 1888; until his death, Paderewski gave thousands of concerts in all European countries, North and South America, Africa, Australia, and Asia. His activities prior to 1914 focused on performance and composition (opera *Manru*, 1901; Symphonia "Polonia," 1909; Piano Concerto in A, 1889; numerous pieces for solo piano, songs, etc.). During World War I, he campaigned for the independence of Poland, giving over 300 speeches and becoming a charismatic orator. In 1918–19 he served as the first prime minister of independent Poland, subsequently returning to his career as a piano virtuoso. Paderewski published numerous articles and speeches on musical and political subjects and was himself the topic of almost 20 poems. He was the most decorated pianist in history, knighted by George V, and recipient of honorary doctorates from such universities as Lwów (1912), Yale (1917), Cracow (1919), Oxford (1920), Columbia (1922), University of Southern California in Los Angeles (1923), Poznań (1924), Glasgow (1925), Cambridge (1926), and SUNY, New York (1933).

Fluent in Polish, Russian, German, English, and French, Paderewski was a voracious and discriminating reader. He preferred "classicizing" and "romantic" literature to either expressionist or modernist texts, even though he knew **Marcel Proust** and numerous members of the literary establishment. Dedicated to a lifetime of self-improvement, Paderewski amassed a huge library and continuously read novels, poetry, and drama. His favorite writers included Turgenev, Gogol, Molière, and

Shakespeare. He did not like either Dostoyevsky or Tolstoy, considering one too melancholy, the other a pretentious fake. In Polish literature, he was best acquainted with the nationalistic historical novels of Henryk Sienkiewicz (whose patriotic zeal he shared), realistic stories of Józef Ignacy Kraszewski (one was used as the basis for his opera *Manru*), romantic dramas of Adam Mickiewicz, and simple poems of Adam Asnyk. His poetic preferences may be seen in the choice of texts he set as songs: Asnyk and Mickiewicz are juxtaposed with a French proto-modernist, Catulle Mendès. Paderewski's speeches reveal his talent as an orator through the use of rhetorical figures and effective, though old-fashioned and lofty, language. The composer befriended a number of American and Polish poets who made him the subject of their work, including Richard Watson Gilder, Charles Phillips, Charles Underwood Johnson, John Huston Finley, and Maryla Wolska.

Archives

Paderewski Studies Center at the Jagiellonian University, Cracow, Poland: Paderewski's library and archives, including most personal letters.

Archivum Akt Nowych, Warsaw, Poland: Paderewski's political archives.

Library of the F. Chopin Academy of Music, Warsaw, Poland: Paderewski's manuscripts.

Polish Museum in Chicago, Illinois: Documents about his American years.

Société and Musée Paderewski in Morges, Switzerland: Swiss archives, memorabilia.

Other holdings at the Polish Institute of Arts and Sciences of America, Stanford University; Piłsudski Institute in New York; Polish Music Center at University of Southern California.

Printed Sources

Annales Paderewski. Periodical published since 1977 by Société and Musée Paderewski in Morges. With popular articles and historical source studies.

Opieński, Henryk. *Ignacy Jan Paderewski*, 2nd ed. (Kraków: PWM, 1960). With valuable musical insights by a musicologist and composer.

Orłowski, Józef, ed. *Ignacy Jan Paderewski i odbudowa Polski* (*Ignacy Jan Paderewski, the Reconstruction of Poland*), 2 vols. (Chicago: The Stanek Press, 1939–40). Comprehensive collection of political documents and photographs ca. 1910–20.

Paderewski, Ignancy Jan, and Mary Lawton. *The Paderewski Memoirs*, Stephen Citron (pref.), DeCapo Press [1930] (New York: Charles Scribner's Sons, 1938, 1939). Lawton's text based on interviews, covering the period to 1914.

———. *Pamiętniki 1912–1932*, Andrzej Piber (intro., trans., ed.), (Kraków: PWM, 1992). Second part of the memoirs, edited from notes.

Perkowska, Malgorzata. *Diariusz koncertowy Ignacego Jana Paderewskiego* (*Paderewski's Concert Diary*) (Kraków: PWM, 1990). Fundamental reference work cross-listing all of Paderewski's concerts and his whole repertoire; with a chronicle of life.

Piber, Andrzej. *Droga do sławy. Ignacy Paderewski w latach 1860–1902* (*The Road to Fame; Ignacy Paderewski in the Years 1860–1902*) (Warszawa: PIW, 1982). Source-based biography of Paderewski's early career, with numerous quotes and references to archival material.

Trochimczyk, Maja (ed.). "The Unknown Paderewski," special issue of the *Polish Music Journal* 4, 2 (Winter 2001). http://www.usc.edu/dept/polish_music/PMJ/index.html. Articles, libretto of *Manru*, reprints of numerous source readings, bibliography, list of works.

Zamoyski, Adam. *Paderewski* (New York: Atheneum, 1982). First critical biography, based on thorough archival research in numerous collections outside of Poland, with new information about the biography and personality of the composer.

Maja Trochimczyk

PAISLEY, IAN RICHARD KYLE (1926–)

Ian Paisley was born in Armagh, Northern Ireland, the son of a Baptist minister. Educated at the Barry School of Evangelism in South Wales (1942) and the Theological Hall of the Reformed Presbyterian Church of Ulster (1942–46), Paisley also received an honorary doctorate of divinity from Bob Jones University in South Carolina in 1966. The minister of the Ravenhill Mission Church in East Belfast (renamed Martyrs Memorial Church) since 1946, Paisley founded and served as moderator of the Free Presbyterian Church of Ulster since 1951, a church that espoused fundamentalism, anti-ecumenism, and militant anti-Catholicism. Paisley entered politics in the 1960s, leading a campaign against reforms seen as aiding Roman Catholics. A member of Parliament at Westminster for North Antrim since 1970, in 1971 Paisley founded the Democratic Unionist Party, which occupies the extreme Unionist position in Northern Ireland's political spectrum. Although he has expressed opposition to both bodies, Paisley has served as a member of the European Parliament since 1979 and as a representative to the Northern Irish Assembly since 1999. Paisley has built a formidable reputation as a charismatic preacher and orator and as an advocate for his constituents, both Protestant and Catholic. However, he is also the most visible spokesman for uncompromising, if nonviolent, Unionism, steadfastly opposing any solution for the Irish Troubles that involve cooperation or power-sharing with Irish Catholics or the Irish Republic. Paisley has also denounced British and Unionist politicians who advocate compromise, famously preaching for divine vengeance on Margaret Thatcher for her role in the Anglo-Irish Agreement of 1985 and claiming David Trimble had betrayed Unionists by signing the Good Friday Agreement in 1998.

Founder, editor, and frequent contributor to the Free Presbyterian Church journal *Revivalist* (1951–) and the newspaper *Protestant Telegraph* (1966–), Paisley has written numerous sermons and religious tracts as well as a number of political polemics and autobiographical sketches. Paisley claims as his literary influences Protestant Reformers such as Martin Luther and John Calvin as well as evangelical ministers such as George Whitefield and Presbyterian Divines such as Charles Hodge and Henry Cooke (Cooke 1996, 45–53).

Archives

Paisley's private papers are not available for research. Many public records may be found at the European Institute of Protestant Studies, Free Presbyterian Church, Belfast.

Printed Sources

Bruce, Steve. *God Save Ulster! The Religion and Politics of Paisleyism* (Oxford: Oxford University Press, 1986).
Cooke, Dennis. *Persecuting Zeal: A Portrait of Ian Paisley* (Dingle: Brandon Press, 1996).
Moloney, Ed, and Andy Pollak. *Paisley* (Dublin Swords: Poolbeg Press, 1986).
Paisley, Rhonda. *Ian Paisley, My Father* (Basingstoke: Marshall Pickering, 1988).
Smyth, Clifford. *Ian Paisley, the Voice of Ulster* (Edinburgh: Scottish Academic Press 1987).

Padraic Kennedy

PANKHURST, EMMELINE GOULDEN (1858–1928)

Emmeline Goulden Pankhurst was born in the industrial English city of Manchester into an affluent liberal manufacturing family. Her mother, a supporter of women's suffrage, took Emmeline from a young age to women's rights meetings, where she heard such prominent suffragists as the American Elizabeth Cady Stanton. Pankhurst attended a day school in Manchester, and at age 15 was sent to a boarding school in Paris that was based on the then-radical idea that girls' education should be as rigorous as that of boys. In 1879 she married the radical socialist and women's rights advocate Dr. Richard Pankhurst and they had five children. Living in London and later in Manchester, they mixed with the avant-garde late-Victorian society, including William Morris, Grant Allen, and Annie Besant. Emmeline participated with her husband in radical reform efforts, especially relating to women's rights. After the death of her husband in 1898, Pankhurst continued radical activism, serving as a Poor Law Guardian and as a member of the Manchester School Board. Prioritizing the cause of women's rights and rejecting the ineffective tactics of the moderate suffragists, in 1903 she and her two daughters, Christabel and Sylvia, founded the Women's Social and Political Union (WSPU). To bring attention to the cause of votes for women, they developed dramatic militant tactics of civil disobedience and violent action. Frequently arrested, the Pankhursts and their supporters went on much publicized hunger strikes while in prison. When Britain entered World War I, Emmeline Pankhurst, along with her daughter Christabel, suspended the actions of the WSPU and supported the government in its war effort. In contrast, Sylvia, an opponent of the war and a socialist who was concerned with the rights of working-class rather than elite women, broke with her mother and sister and was expelled from the WSPU. After the war, satisfied that women over 30 had gained the vote and no longer active in the campaign for equal political rights, Emmeline Pankhurst joined the Conservative Party. She died in the same month that British women finally achieved political rights equal to men's.

Pankhurst's childhood readings had decisive influence on the development of her later feminist activism. She was profoundly impacted by Harriet Beecher Stowe's *Uncle Tom's Cabin*, which awakened in her "that spirit of fighting and heroic sacrifice . . . and appreciation of the gentler spirit which is moved to mend and repair the ravages of war" (Pankhurst 1914, 3). She was also drawn to John Bunyan's *Pilgrim's Progress* and his lesser-known *Holy War*. Another favorite was Homer's *Odyssey*, with the same motif of heroic journey and struggle that could be seen as a metaphor for her activist career.

Thomas Carlyle's *French Revolution* probably had the greatest influence on her thought and career. Strongly identifying with the French throughout her youth, Pankhurst relished Carlyle's romantic glorification of rebellion and the emphasis he placed on the role of great people in shaping history.

In adulthood, Pankhurst read the radical visionary literature that was popular with the fin de siècle social and political rebels. Family reading in the Pankhurst household included the *Fabian Essays in Socialism*, Edward Bellamy's *Looking Backward*, Prince Kropotkin's *Fields, Factories, and Workshops*, and Robert Blatchford's *Merrie England*. These radical books also shaped the political ideas of her home-educated daughters, especially Sylvia. In addition to the political works, Sylvia was also drawn to the poetry of Percy Bysshe Shelley, Lord Byron, Walt Whitman, and especially Robert Burns. She also read the contemporary playwrights Henrik Ibsen and George Bernard Shaw and the novelists Anatole France and John Galsworthy. Neither Emmeline nor Christabel apparently read extensively after founding the

WSPU—the motto of the organization, "Deeds, not Words," probably also included written words.

Archives

Home Office Papers, Public Record Office, London.
Suffragette Fellowship Collection, Museum of London.
Fawcett Library, London. Includes letters by the Pankhursts and extensive collection of suffragette periodicals and other memorabilia of the WSPU.
Sylvia Pankhurst Papers, International Instituut voor Sociale Geschiedenis, Amsterdam.

Printed Sources

Holton, Sandra Stanley, "In Sorrowful Wrath: Suffrage Militancy and the Romantic Feminism of Emmeline Pankhurst." In *British Feminism in the Twentieth Century*, Harold Perkins (ed.), (Amherst: University of Massachusetts Press, 1990). Analysis of the cultural influences shaping Pankhurst's worldview.
Jorgensen-Earp, Cheryl R. *"The Transfiguring Sword": The Just War of the Women's Social and Political Union* (Tuscaloosa: The University of Alabama Press, 1997). Analysis of the philosophic traditions that shaped the Pankhursts' justification of violent militancy.
Pankhurst, Christabel. *Unshackled: The Story of How We Won the Vote* (London: Hutchinson, 1959). Discussion of early influences on her mother.
Pankhurst, Emmeline, *My Own Story* (New York: Hearst's International Library, 1914).
Pankhurst, Sylvia. *The Life of Emmeline Pankhurst* (London: T. Werner Laurie, 1935).
Winslow, Barbara. *Sylvia Pankhurst: Sexual Politics and Political Activism* (New York: St. Martin's Press, 1996). Discussion of the literary influences on Sylvia and Christabel Pankhurst and on the adult Emmeline Pankhurst.

Nancy Fix Anderson

PASOLINI, PIER PAOLO (1922–1975)

Pier Paolo Pasolini was born in Bologna on March 5, 1922. His father, Carlo Alberto Pasolini, was an officer in the fascist army; Suzanna Colussi, his mother, was a teacher. Raised in a family of only two sons, the young Pasolini attended a famous Bolognese high school, the Liceo Ginnasio Statale Luigi Galvani (1935–41). He studied art history and Italian literature at the University of Bologna from 1942 to 1944. From 1942, he wrote essays and book reviews about Italian poetry and published a first book of poems about the small town where he lived, *Poesie a Casarsa*. He also gave private lessons in Latin, Greek, and Italian literature. On November 26, 1945, Pasolini defended a master's degree thesis about Giovanni Pascoli. That same year, he began writing poems using Frioulan, his mother's Italian dialect. In 1947, he joined the Italian Communist Party but was expelled in 1949 for homosexuality. Between 1961 and 1975, Pasolini directed 24 movies (half of them were short films). He was the author of some fifty books, half of them published after his death. Very few of Pasolini's books were translated into English. Friend and novelist Alberto Moravia considered Pasolini "the major Italian poet" of the second half of the twentieth century; outside Italy, he was better known as a film director. Three days after the release of his controversial film *Salo: The 120 Days of Sodom* (1975), his body was discovered on waste ground near Ostia, not far from Roma. Pasolini was one of the most polyvalent authors of the twentieth century, writing poetry, novels, plays, essays, and film scripts; he also was a journalist and book critic, painter, actor, film director, and even cameraman for some of his short film essays. During the 1960s he wrote many articles about semiotics and film theory, speaking against prominent positions held by **Roland Barthes** and Christian Metz.

Pasolini was a book critic for newspapers and journals for most of his adult life. In high school, Pasolini read Ugo Foscolo, Giacomo Leopardi, Bartolommeo Carducci, Giovanni Pascoli, Gabriele D'Annunzio, and William Shakespeare. He admitted that his discovery of Arthur Rimbaud in 1938 changed his life. During World War II, Pasolini read **André Gide,** Jules Barbey d'Aurevilly, Arthur Schopenhauer, and many Italian poets including Giuseppe Ungaretti and Eugenio Montale. In 1966, while convalescent for a month, he rediscovered Plato and Mircea Eliade, then wrote his first plays in just a few weeks: six tragedies in an ancient Greek style. In October 1966, Pasolini went to New York City, where he discovered **Allen Ginsberg** and visited Harlem. In most of his films, Pasolini told stories as if they were myths; this is specially true with *Oedipus Rex* and *Medea*, but also in *Salo: The 120 Days of Sodom* (freely adapted from Sade) and *The Gospel According to St. Matthew*, his most beautiful and respectful movie. In his adaptations, Pasolini often transposed situations from other contexts into contemporary settings to make them clearer and stronger.

Archives

Associazione "Fondo Pier Paolo Pasolini," Rome. Personal archives, books, manuscripts, photos, drawings, correspondence, films.

Printed Sources

Bax, Dominique (ed.). *Pier Paolo Pasolini. Alberto Moravia* (Bobigny, France: Théâtres au cinéma, No. 11, 2000). Includes many good articles about Pasolini's books and films.

Boyer, Alain-Michel. *Pier-Paolo Pasolini. Qui êtes-vous?* (Lyon: La Manufacture, 1987). Excellent essay that deals precisely with his literary influences; includes a vital 30-page biography.

Pasolini, Pier Paolo. *Descrizioni di descrizioni* (Turin: Einaudi, 1979). Includes hundreds of book reviews written by Pasolini.

———. *The Letters of Pier Paolo Pasolini: 1940–54*, N. Naldini (ed.), Stuart Hood (trans.), (London: Quartet Books, 1992).

———. *Poesie a Casarsa* (Bologna: Libreria Aniquaria Landi, 1942).

Yves Laberge

PASTERNAK, BORIS LEONIDOVICH (1890–1960)

Boris Pasternak was born to a Jewish family in Moscow. His father was a famous impressionistic painter, his mother a pianist. In his youth he showed a dedication to music. Under the impact of Alexander Scriabin he wished to become a composer. In 1909 Pasternak began his studies of philosophy at the Moscow State University, then in 1912 at the University of Marburg, Germany. Back in Russia, he became in 1913 a member of the futurist literary circle "Tsentrifuga" (Centrifuge). In 1935 Pasternak traveled to Paris to the Congress of Defense of Culture against Fascism in Europe. In the following years he translated *Hamlet* by William Shakespeare and *Faust* by Johann Wolfgang von Goethe into Russian. In 1947 Pasternak began to write his famous opus, *Doctor Zhivago*, which was published in 1957 in Italy by Fel-

trinelli Press. On October 23, 1958, Pasternak received the Nobel Prize for literature. Just in the same month he had been excluded from the Soviet Writers' Union.
On May 31, 1960, Pasternak died of cancer in Moscow. In 1989 when **Mikhail
Gorbachev** was Soviet general secretary, Pasternak's *Doctor Zhivago* was published
in Russia for the first time.

There were various Western influences in Pasternak's creative life. In grammar
school he learned German with high proficiency and read the works of Goethe *(Die
Leiden des jungen Werthers, Dichtung und Wahrheit, Faust)*. Later, in 1912, Pasternak
studied at the University of Marburg in Germany under Professor Hermann
Cohen, a neo-Kantian philosopher of international repute. Cohen suggested that
Pasternak teach philosophy, but the young Russian rejected an academic career.
Nevertheless, metaphysics deeply influenced his later literary work as Pasternak
studied the works of Immanuel Kant *(Kritik der Reinen Vernunft)* and Edmund
Husserl *(Logische Untersuchungen)*, which provided a basis for the writer's symbolism. Under the influence of German philosophers Pasternak showed a special sen-
sitiveness to human existence. Influenced by Rainer Maria Rilke *(Das Stundenbuch)*,
the rhythm of lyrics symbolized for Pasternak the heartbeat of human life. During
the First World War, Pasternak became acquainted with Shakespeare *(Merry Wives
of Windsor)*, and he referred to his poem "Marburg," written in the Urals in May
1916, as a "Shakespearean drama." In his novel *Doctor Zhivago*, the writer is very
critical of the Russian revolution and Marxist ideology. The main figures in the
novel, Jurii Zhivago and Lara, are not socialist heroes but ordinary beings who are
caught by the cataclysms of Russian revolution and civil war, "the demonic forces."
Pasternak stood in the tradition of liberal and humanist Russian literature of the
nineteenth century; additionally his concept of good and evil shows a great affinity
to Goethe and Shakespeare: the protagonists Jurii Zhivago and Lara resemble
Goethe's Werther and Lotte. Jurii Zhivago has also some Shakespearean traits that
Pasternak called "a drama of duty and self-denial." In this context, Pasternak was
also influenced by Edward Young's *Night Thoughts on Life, Death, and Immortality*.
For his individualism Pasternak was frequently criticized by the Soviet press. The
main reproach was that he was too apolitical and too skeptical of the feats of socialism. Moreover, the Christian themes in the novel provoked harsh criticism in the
Soviet Union. Khrushchev wanted to deprive him of Soviet citizenship. The manuscript of *Doctor Zhivago* was smuggled out of the Soviet Union and became a bestseller in the West. But in contrast to his stigmatized novel *Doctor Zhivago*,
translations of *Hamlet* and *Romeo and Juliet* won Pasternak the highest Soviet literary prize.

Archives

Rossiiskii Gosudarstvennyi Arkhiv Literatury I Iskusstva (Russian State Archive of Literature and Arts), Moscow.

Printed Sources

Barnes, Christopher J. *Boris Pasternak: A Literary Biography* (Cambridge, N.Y.: Cambridge
University Press, 1998).
Conquest, Robert. *Courage of Genius. The Pasternak Affair. A Documentary Report on Its Liter-
ary and Political Significance* (London: Collins and Harvill Press, 1961).
Fleishman, Lazar. *Boris Pasternak. The Poet and His Politics* (Cambridge: Harvard University
Press, 1990).

Gladkov, Aleksandr K. *Meetings with Pasternak: A Memoir* (New York: Harcourt Brace Jovanovich, 1977).

Leonidze, Georgi. *Boris Pasternak: Materialy fonda gosudarstvennogo muzeia gruzinskoi literatury* (Tbilisi: Diogene, 1999).

Markov, Vladimir. "Notes on Pasternak's Doctor Zhivago, *Russian Review* 18 (1959), 14–22.

Moravia, Alberto. "Visite à Pasternak. Un adolescent aux cheveux gris," *Preuves* 8, 88 (1958), 3–7.

Eva-Maria Stolberg

PAUL VI (1897–1978)

Giovanni Battista Montini was born at Concesio, a village just north of Brescia. The scion of a prominent, patriotic Brescian family, he combined his father's sense of sociopolitical engagement with his mother's introspective spirituality. Exempted from military duty due to his frail constitution, Montini entered the priesthood in 1920. As ecclesiastical assistant to the Federation of Catholic University Students (FUCI) from 1925 to 1933, he mentored many future leaders of Italy's Christian Democratic Party. Astute, discrete, and diligent, Montini was well suited for the Vatican diplomatic service, which he entered in the early 1920s. In 1944 he and Monsignor Domenico Tardini jointly became Pope Pius XII's undersecretaries of state. Ten years later he was unexpectedly named Archbishop of Milan—a "promotion" which may in fact have reflected deepening differences between the "liberal" Montini and the "Roman Party" surrounding Pius XII. Thrust into the rough and tumble of Milanese life during Italy's "economic miracle," the bookish Montini gained invaluable pastoral experience. Montini supported John XXIII in calling the Vatican II Church Council in 1962. Elected John's successor the following year, he took the name of Paul VI. Vatican II's culminating proclamation, the Pastoral Constitution of the Church in the Modern World (*Gaudium et Spes*, 1965), clearly reflects Paul VI's values—both in its collegial mode of drafting and in its engaged, optimistic tone. The fruit of painful soul-searching, Paul VI's 1968 encyclical on birth control, *Humani generis*, heralded the more conflictual last decade of his pontificate.

Montini's worldview was shaped by a broad array of writers and thinkers. As a youth he was captivated by the lyrical piety of Alessandro Manzoni's (1785–1873) *The Betrothed* (1825–27) and Antonio Fogazzaro's (1842–1911) *The Saint* (1905). **Thomas Mann** (1875–1955), Georges Bernanos (1888–1948), and **Albert Camus** (1913–60) were among his favorite novelists later in his life. The son of a journalist, Montini was a voracious reader of newspapers; as pope, he urged reporters to exercise their influential vocation with moderation and charity. *The Intellectual Life* (translated into Italian in 1925) by Antonin Sertillanges, OP (1863–1948) convinced him of the inherent spirituality of both intellectual and artistic endeavor: in his view, learning could not remain merely an end in itself, but naturally led to the service of others. His ecclesiology was shaped by the German bishop and historian Karl Joseph Hefele's (1809–93) *History of the Councils* (1855–74) and the Jesuit liturgist Josef Jungmann's (1889–1975) concept of the church not as hierarchy but as community of the faithful.

Philosophically, Montini owed his greatest debts to the French. The prolific neo-Thomist writer Jacques Maritain (1882–1973) exercised a continuing influence on Montini's thinking from the 1920s onward. Particularly important for him during the interwar period was Maritain's conception of modern history, especially as demonstrated in his *Three Reformers: Luther, Descartes and Rousseau* (1925 in the French original, subsequently translated by Montini into Italian) and the French philosopher's aesthetics, set forth in his *Art and Scholasticism* (1920). Like so many Catholics of his generation, he was captivated by Maritain's evocation of a "new Christendom," particularly as set forth in his *Integral Humanism* (1936), as well as the opening to modern pluralism and parliamentarism offered in *Christianity and Democracy* (1943). Montini's ecumenism owed much to the writings of Dominican theologian Yves Congar (1904–95) and to the example of Louis Massignon's (1883–1962) "Badaliya" groups, dedicated to Catholic–Muslim dialogue. Also noteworthy is the unique friendship which Montini formed with Jean Guitton (1901–), a member of the Academie Francaise and a brilliant, if very conservative, philosopher, essayist, and painter. Beginning in 1950, the two men met annually for the remarkably candid, far-reaching intellectual colloquies which Guitton has documented in the works cited below in the bibliography.

Archives

Istituto Paulo VI, Brescia (contact e-mail: info@istitutopaulovi-bs.org). The institute's archives include edited and unedited manuscripts, correspondence, photographs, and documents pertaining to Paul VI's radio and television addresses. The institute's *Notiziario*, generally published twice a year, covers unpublished material from Paul VI, including news of work in progress, manuscripts discovered, and theses written. The *Quaderni*, published periodically, included the pope's writings and speeches. Of particular note are the *Discorsi e scritti sul Concilio, 1959–1963* and the *Discorsi e documenti sul Concilio, 1963–65*. See also the *Insegnamenti*, cited below.

Vatican guidelines bar access to archival holdings until 75 years have elapsed since the end of a pontificate.

Printed Sources

Clancy, John G. *Apostle for Our Time: Pope Paul* VI (New York: P. J. Kennedy, 1963). Particularly helpful with regard to Italian, French, and German literary influences on Montini (see especially pp. 35, 79–80).

Cremona, Carlo. *Paolo VI* (Milan: Rusconi, 1991).

Finotti, Fabio. *Critica stilistica e linguaggio religioso in Giovanni Battista Montini* (Rome: Edizioni Studium; Saggi I for the Istituto Paolo VI, 1989).

Guitton, Jean. *Dialogues avec Paul* VI (Paris: Fayard, 1967); translated by Anne and Christopher Freemantle as *The Pope Speaks* (London: Weidenfeld and Nicolson, 1968).

———. *Paul VI, secret* (Paris: Desclee de Brouwer, 1979).

Hebblethwaite, Peter. *Paul VI: The First Modern Pope* (New York: Paulist Press, 1993). Deals broadly with Montini's tastes and practices as a reader, writer, and correspondent.

Insegnamenti di Paolo VI, vols. I–XVI (Vatican City: Libreria editrice Vaticana, 1963–74).

Macchi, Pasquale. *Ricordo di Paolo VI* (Milan: Rusconi, 1979).

Paul VI et la Modernite dans l'Eglise. *Actes du colloque organise par l'Ecole francaise de Rome* (Rome: Ecole francaise de Rome and Istituto Paolo VI, 1984).

Steven F. White

PAZ, OCTAVIO (1914–1998)

Octavio Paz was born in Mexico City, Mexico, and educated in Roman Catholic elementary and secondary schools. He attended the University of Mexico and originally studied law and literature before shifting his focus to poetry. He published his first volume of poems, *Luna Silvestre*, in 1933, before traveling to Spain to support the loyalists during the Spanish Civil War as a member of the Republican brigade. From 1939 onward, Paz founded a number of literary reviews including *Workshop*, *Plural*, *The Prodigal Son*, and *Vuelta*. In 1943 he received a Guggenheim Fellowship to travel to the United States, then joined the diplomatic corps after World War II and traveled to Japan, Paris, and India as Mexico's representative to UNESCO. Throughout his career, Paz's work centered on the major theme of man's ability to overcome isolation through artistic creativity and erotic love. His masterpieces *The Labyrinth of Solitude* (1950) and *The Sun Stone* (1957) contain a more regional focus, however, as they analyze the history and culture of Paz's native Mexico. In 1962, Paz became Mexico's ambassador to India but resigned in 1968 when Mexican student protestors were shot at Tlatelolco. Paz was a visiting professor of Spanish American literature at the Universities of Texas and Pennsylvania (1968–70), Simón Bolívar Professor of Latin American Studies at Churchill College (1970–71) and Charles Eliot Norton Professor of Poetry at Harvard, Cambridge (1971–72). He was awarded an honorary doctorate at Harvard University in 1980 and a decade later became the first Mexican to be awarded the Nobel Prize for literature.

Paz was an avid reader of traditional and contemporary literature, and his grandfather had an extensive library of works that the poet read as a youth. These included *Sinbad*, *El Cid*, and Daniel Defoe's *Robinson Crusoe*, as well as the works of **Ezra Pound**, Walt Whitman, and **Thomas Stearns Eliot.** South American authors that Paz read included the Nobel Prize winner Pablo Neruda, who focused on the political struggles faced by the Chilean peasantry, and the seventeenth-century Jeronymite nun Sor Juana Ines de la Cruz, who dealt with existential concepts that Paz would emulate as the major themes of his poetry. Paz believed that poetry constituted a form of religion for the modern age and that through its reading, one could leave historical time to reenter other eras. This idea is closely linked to the concept of the timeless atman, or self, that Paz would have been familiar with from his frequent readings of Hindu texts such as the *Ramayana*, the *Upanishads*, and the *Bhagavad-Gita*. Paz was an admirer of both metaphysical writers, such as the poet Stephane Mallarmé, as well as Arthur Rimbaud and the French symbolists. He was also influenced by the manner in which surrealist writers, like his friend **André Breton,** creatively transformed experience in their works. Surrealist literature also often negated the contemporary world and the values of democratic, bourgeois society in favor of a more artistic and imaginative worldview. In much the same way, Paz shunned Mexico's plans for modernization and instead urged its citizenry to become independent of the influences of both communism and the United States.

Archives

Rare Book and Manuscript Library, University of Pennsylvania, Philadelphia, control no. PAUR01-A2540.
Berg Collection, The New York Public Library, control no. NYPW87-A420.
Houghten Library, Harvard University, Cambridge, control no. MAHV00-A18.

Printed Sources

Castanon, Adolfo, and Beatriz Zeller. *The Passing of Octavio Paz* (Mexico: Mosaic Press, 1999).

Grenier, Yvon. *From Art to Politics: The Romantic Liberalism of Octavio Paz* (New York: Rowman and Littlefield, 2001).

Quiroga, Jose, and James Hardin. *Understanding Octavio Paz* (Columbia: University of South Carolina Press, 1999).

Gregory L. Schnurr

PEI, IEOH MING (1917–)

I. M. Pei was born in Canton, China, in 1917 and emigrated to the United States to study architecture at the age of 17. He received a bachelor of architecture degree from the Massachusetts Institute of Technology in 1940 and upon graduation was awarded the Alpha Rho Chi Medal and the MIT Traveling Fellowship. World War II interrupted Pei's plans to return to China, and in 1942 he enrolled in the Harvard Graduate School of Design. Upon completion of his master's degree in 1946, Pei received the Wheelwright Traveling Fellowship, which allowed him to travel extensively throughout Europe. Pei returned to the United States and became a naturalized citizen, forming the partnership I. M. Pei and Associates. In 1978 Pei became the first architect to hold the position of chancellor of the American Academy, and in 1979 he received the gold medal of the American Institute of Architecture. This was followed by the Pritzker Architectural Prize in 1983, which honored Pei's outstanding work in designing over 50 major projects worldwide, more than half of which had received architectural awards. His choice of materials such as concrete, glass, and stone coupled with his use of uncomplicated geometric shapes allow Pei's designs to exude a cool clear rationalism while at the same time appearing refined and elegant. Notable projects Pei has completed include the controversial pyramidal addition to the Louvre in Paris, the East Building of the National Gallery of Art in Washington, D.C., and the Bank of China, which is currently Asia's tallest building. In late 1990, after more than four decades of practice, Pei retired from his firm in order to pursue smaller projects of personal interest.

Pei was first and foremost influenced by the theories of modernist architecture. The pioneers of this twentieth-century movement such as **Le Corbusier** (1887–1965) and **Ludwig Mies Van der Rohe** (1886–1969) believed in the prominence of functionalism and abstraction in their buildings and the need for the architect to experiment with both form and technique. While at MIT, Pei studied the treatises of these men and was also a student of **Walter Gropius** (1883–1969), who was the founder of the Bauhaus school in Berlin and Munich. Throughout his early career, Pei became familiar with the written work of both Louis Henri Sullivan and **Frank Lloyd Wright.** Wright believed that elementary geometric forms held a spiritual quality and that an architect should attempt to design his buildings in harmony with nature. Pei followed Wright's treatises and also Sullivan's basic precept that making architecture was an important social, symbolic, and intellectual endeavor. The principles of these men meshed nicely with Pei's early Eastern literary influences. As a youth, Pei was familiar with the precepts of Buddhism and would frequently accompany his mother on mountain retreats during which he would enjoy a sense of spiritual fulfillment through the appreciation of the beauty of nature. While in China, Pei also read many traditional fables, including Xiyouji's *The Journey to the West* and *The Golden Lotus.* In latter life, Pei would incorporate the settings associated with such tales directly into his architecture, as he did with the processional entrance to the Miho

Museum that reflects in a tangible form the lost paradise processional referenced in the ancient Chinese tale *Peach Blossom Spring*.

Archives

Archives of American Art and Design, Smithsonian Institution, Washington, D.C.

Printed Sources

Cannell, Michael T. *I. M. Pei: Mandarin of Modernism* (New York: Clarkson Potter, 1995).
Chester, Nagel. *The Indomitable Ieoh Ming Pei* (Denver: Aurora Library, 1985).
Wiseman, Carter. *I. M. Pei: A Profile in American Architecture* (New York: Harry N. Abrams, 2001).

Gregory L. Schnurr

PELÉ (1940–)

Edson Arantes do Nascimento, known as Pelé, was born in Três Corações, in the Brazilian state of Minas Gerais. His father, João Ramos do Nascimento, played professional soccer as Dondinho in the way Brazilian players are given single-word names. In 1944 the family moved to Baurú in São Paulo, where Dondinho was promised a playing contract and a state job. But he was thwarted by injuries and red tape and the family lived in poverty. Edson played street soccer with a stuffed sock for a ball. In school he resented the discipline, and by the age of seven he was working as a shoeshine boy and selling peanuts. By 10 he had become Pelé, a name he then detested, concocted by his friends from mispronunciations of the Portuguese for foot, the Turkish for stupid, and the name of a famous local player. He graduated to his own teams, September 7 and Ameriquinha, with whom he scored goals, won trophies, and gained a reputation as a budding phenomenon. At 14 he was working in a shoe factory and playing for the Baurú youth team and later for other local teams, Radium and Noroestinho, where, alongside professionals, he was soon leading scorer. At 15, small, skinny, and homesick, he went to play with the state champions, Santos, for $10 a month. Within a year he was the leading club and state goal-scorer. At 16 he was selected for the national team. In 1958 he made his first World Cup appearance in Sweden against the Soviet Union and scored his first World Cup goal against Wales. He scored three goals in the semifinal and two in the final as Brazil won the championship. Pelé was the center of media attention because he was so young and talented, full of speed, power, and creativity. He was a national hero and had already won his place in football history. He played in three more World Cups, in 1962 in Chile, 1966 in England, and 1970 in Mexico. Brazil won in 1962 and 1970. Meanwhile Santos became one of the best clubs in the world, exploiting the fact that they had Pelé. He scored his one-thousandth goal in 1969 and finished his professional career of 1,363 games with 1,281 goals, almost a goal a match. He retired in 1974 but came out of retirement because of financial problems and played for the New York Cosmos from 1975 to 1977.

Pelé played what he calls the Beautiful Game with obvious joy, inspiring his fellow team members and making his fans exuberant. He remains a legend not just because of his outstanding ability and performances but because no other player has done or possibly can ever again do what he did. He is famous for being famous, yet modest and accessible and deeply religious. He had little education and yet heads of state respect his views and take his advice. The myths say that war temporarily stopped in his name in Biafra in 1967. He has worked for UNESCO. From 1994 to 1997 he was Brazilian minister of sports, determined to stamp out football corruption and working to get poor youth off the streets in Brazil. He won the 1978 International Peace Award, and as the twentieth century closed he was Reuters Sportsman of the Century. He became a soccer ambassador, working to improve the game through youth. He is the greatest soccer player the world has known, ahead of his time as a media superstar, before the mammoth salaries and sponsorships today's players earn. His name is known far beyond soccer by people who know little about the game, as shown by his media success in the United States. Although his business affairs have not always run smoothly or profitably, Pelé has an astute eye for an opportunity whether in finance or the media. Recently he has made more from credit card and sports equipment endorsements than he ever did in soccer.

Archives

No significant archives. The small but developing Federation Internationale Football Association (FIFA) Archives is accessible on-line, www.fifa.com; and at Hitzigweg 11, P.O. Box 85, 8030 Zurich, Switzerland.

Printed Sources

Harris, Harry. *Pelé: His Life and Times* (London: Robson Books, 2000).
Kissinger, Henry. "The Phenomenon," *Time* (14 June 1999).
Morrison, Ian. *The World Cup: A Complete Record 1930-1990* (Derby: Breedon Books, 1990).
Pelé. *My Life and the Beautiful Game* (London: Horizon, 1977).

Gillian Fenwick

PERÓN, EVA (1919–1952)

Born Eva María Ibargueren in the small town of Los Todos, Perón was the illegitimate child of Juan Duarte, an *estanciero*, who took Eva's mother, Juana Ibarguren, as a mistress shortly after he arrived. Eva was always aware of her illegitimacy, and once she became Juan Perón's wife, she buried this part of her life forever. In 1935, Eva moved to Buenos Aires, where she intended to conquer the city and become a famous actress. For 10 years, she struggled to make a name for herself, and by 1943, she found success as one of the highest-paid radio stars in Argentina.

In 1944, Evita was introduced to Colonel Juan Domingo Perón. The experience was memorable for both. Eva recalled it as "marvelous," and to Perón, it was "destiny." From that moment on, she took on a new role. After her last film, *The Prodigal*, was completed, she ended her life as an actress and began her job as Perón's political activist, in which role she used the name "Evita." They were married on October 17, 1945, and on February 24, 1946, Perón was voted president of Argentina. As the president's wife, Evita familiarized herself with labor and union issues, and in 1947 she became the proprietor of *Democracia*, a newspaper designed as the propaganda tool for the Perón regime. She became the bridge between Perón and his constituents, whom she acknowledged as her "people." Outspoken, Evita drew criticism from the Parliamentary opposition, for her influence with Perón and her freedom to pursue political agendas, such the promotion of family members into government positions. She worked tirelessly for the poor, the sick, and the *descamisada*, with whom she felt she most identified. According to one biography, she created what would be the cabinet appointed in the middle of 1950 (Taylor 1979, 53). She was quoted as being "the woman behind the throne" (Fraser 1980, 82). However, her activism would be cut short when she was diagnosed with uterine cancer in 1950. Evita remained in the public eye until her illness rendered her incapacitated. Eva Perón passed away on July 26, 1952, at the age of 33.

It is hard to determine what Eva Perón's literary influences were, given that she buried much of her past and that she never went beyond an elementary school education. Most biographies point to her love of poetry, but never mention any titles. In her autobiography, *In My Own Words (Mi Mensaji)*, Evita mentioned that Perón became her mentor: "I remember asking him to be my teacher. In the respites of his fight, he would teach me a little of as much as I could learn. I like to read by his side. We started with Plutarch's *The Parallel Lives* and *The Complete Letters of Lord Chesterfield to His Son Stanhope*" (Perón 1996, 53).

Archives

Hoover Institution Library, Stanford University, California.
Stanford University Library, Stanford University, California.
Archivo General de la Nacion, Buenos Aires, Argentina.

Printed Sources

Alexander, Robert J. *The Perón Era* (New York: Columbia University Press, 1951).
Flores, María. *The Woman with the Whip: Eva Perón* (New York: Doubleday & Company, Inc., 1952).
Fraser, Nicholas, and Marysa Navarro. *Evita: The Real Life of Eva Perón* (New York: W. W. Norton & Company, 1980).
Ortiz, Alicia Dujovne. *Eva Perón: A Biography*, Shawn Fields (trans.), (New York: St. Martin's Press, 1996).
Perón, Eva. *In My Own Words*, Laura Dail (trans.), (New York: The New Press, 1996).
———. *My Mission in Life*, Ethel Cherry (trans.), (New York: Vantage Press, Inc. 1953).
Taylor, J. M. *Eva Perón: The Myths of a Woman* (Chicago: The University of Chicago Press, 1979).

Cheryl Lemus

PIAGET, JEAN (1896–1980)

The oldest child of Arthur Piaget, professor of medieval literature at the Académie de Neuchâtel, and of Rebecca Jackson, Jean Piaget was born in Neuchâtel, Switzerland, where he studied at the Latin College from 1907, at the gymnasium from 1912, and at the Université de Neuchâtel from 1915. At age 11, while he was a pupil at the Latin High School, he published a short notice in a local nature magazine *(Rameau de Sapin)* on an albino sparrow (1907). After high school graduation, he studied natural sciences at the University of Neuchâtel, where he obtained a Ph.D. in 1918. That year, Piaget wrote his second book, titled *Recherche (Research)*, in which he explained what questions still remained without answers for him. Piaget was professor of the history of scientific thought (1929–39), and later professor of sociology (1939–51) at the University of Geneva; he was also professor at the Université de Lausanne (Switzerland). In 1952, he was apointed professor of genetic psychology at he Université de Paris Sorbonne. Piaget published over 60 books and some seven hundred articles and was honored with the 1969 Distinguished Scientific Contribution Award by the American Psychological Association.

Piaget's religious, protestant education was in conflict with the Darwinian theories he was aware of between 1912 and 1915, leading to a religious crisis. At 16 he discovered a book in his father's library, written by a protestant theologian, Auguste Sabatier, titled *La philosophie de la religion fondée sur la psychologie et l'histoire*. Piaget later recalled that he "devoured that book with immense delight . . . a new passion took possession of me: philosophy" (quoted by Evans 1981, 110). Several months later, Piaget admitted that he was moved by French philosopher **Henri Bergson,** who wrote *L'Évolution créatrice*, although he later disagreed with him. In his *Autobiography*, Piaget remembered what he read around 1914: "everything which came to my hands after my unfortunate contact with the philosophy of Bergson: some Kant, Spencer, Auguste Comte, Fouillée and Guyau, Lachelier, Boutroux, Lalande, Durkheim, Tarde, Le Dantec; and, in psychology, W. James, Th. Ribot, and Janet" (quoted by Evans 1981, 112). Piaget also said: "If I had known at that time [1913–15] the work of Wertheimer and of Köhler, I would have become a Gestaltist" (quoted by Evans 1981, 115). After getting his Ph.D. in 1918, Piaget went to Zurich, where he attended lectures by Oskar Robert Pfister, Paul Eugen Bleuler, and **C. G. Jung**; he also discovered the work of Sigmund Freud. French philosopher Léon Brunschvicg also inspired Piaget, who often quoted two of his books: *Les étapes de la philosophie mathématique* (1912) and *L'expérience humaine et la causalité physique* (1922). Much later, Piaget was influenced by the numerous books in English given to him by a philosopher from the United States, Wolfe Mays, from 1953; they worked together on research on genetic epistemology, which became one of Piaget's most important contributions to scientific knowledge.

Archives

Archives Jean Piaget, Uni-Mail, 40 boulevard du Pont d'Arve, 1205 Genève, Switzerland (http://www.unige.ch/piaget/). Manuscripts, correspondence, diaries, notebooks.

Printed Sources

Bringuier, J. C. *Conversations with Jean Piaget* (Chicago: University of Chicago Press, 1980).
Ducret, Jean-Jacques. *Jean Piaget. Biographie et parcours intellectuel* (Neuchâtel: Delachaux et Niestlé, 1981).
Evans, Richard I. *Jean Piaget, the Man and His Ideas* (New York: Praeger, 1981).
Jean Piaget Archives Foundation. *The Jean Piaget Bibliography* (Geneva: Jean Piaget Archives Foundation, 1989).
Piaget, Jean. "Autobiography." In E. Boring (ed.), *History of Psychology in Autobiography*, Vol. 4. (Worcester, Mass.: Clark University Press, 1952).
Smith, L. *Necessary Knowledge* (Hove: Erlbaum Associates, 1993).

Yves Laberge

PICASSO, PABLO RUIZ Y (1881–1973)

Pablo Picasso was born in Malaga, Spain, and attended the School of Fine Arts in La Coruna (1892–95), the Barcelona Provisional School of Fine Arts (1895–96), and the Royal Academy of San Fernando (1897–98). In Barcelona, Picasso became a member of a group of intellectuals who would meet at El Quatre Gats café and exchange ideas on art, poetry, and literature. At the age of 19, Picasso moved to

Paris and painted through both his blue and rose periods before becoming interested in the simplified, iconic forms of African and Iberian art. By amalgamating these forms with Paul Cézanne's simplified geometric shapes, Picasso produced his early masterpiece *Les Demoiselles d'Avignon* (1907). Faceting the subject matter and exploring it from a variety of viewpoints, Picasso and his contemporary Georges Braque developed analytical cubism and later, through the inclusion of collage, its synthetic counterpart. Picasso became affiliated with the surrealist painters during the 1920s and in 1937 produced his monumental masterpiece *Guernica* in response to the bombing of a Basque town during the Spanish Civil War. Like the Andalusian society of his origin, Picasso's art was often misogynistic and phallocentric in nature, fusing the sacred and the profane in extremely personal, inventive, and abstract artistic expressions. Picasso continued his prolific production of paintings, sculpture, and ceramics well into his eighties, leaving behind more than 20,000 works at the time of his death.

From an early age, Picasso was exposed to classical and mythological tales, including Aristophanes's *Lysistrata*, Sophocles's *Oedipus Rex*, Ovid's *Metamorphoses*, and the stories of the fall of Icarus and Perseus and Medusa. Much of Picasso's work includes depictions of composite beasts such as the centaur and the minotaur that he first encountered in the traditional tales of the mithraic ritual of bull worship and which he would re-encounter in the books of Ramon Reventos, such as *El Centaure Picador*. Picasso would illustrate many of these tales in later life, as well as George Hugnet's *Le Chèvre-Feuille* and *Non Vouloir* and the Comte de Buffon's *Histoire Naturelle*. Living among the Paris intellectuals of the early twentieth century, Picasso read the works of those individuals with whom he was acquainted, including the philosopher and writer Eugenio d'Ors and the art historian Miguel Utrillo. While in Paris, Picasso also became familiar with the work of Paul Verlaine and Fernando de Roja, upon whose *La Tragicomedia de Calisto y Melibea* of 1499 Picasso based his painting *Celestina*. The subject matter of many of Picasso's blue and rose period paintings can be traced directly to his reading of Rudolph Lothar's *Harlequin King*, Maurice Maeterlinck's play *L'Intruse: La Vie*, and a familiarity with his acquaintance **Guillaume Apollinaire**'s poems dealing with magicians and circus performers. His love of poetry as a whole led Picasso to the work of Jean Cocteau, the French Dadaist writer Tristan Tzara, Andre Salmon, Max Jacob, and the surrealist poets **André Breton,** Paul Eluard, and Louis Aragon. The highly imaginative and bizarre writings of Alfred Jarry, such as *The Exploits and Opinions of Doctor Faustroll*, aided Picasso in understanding the contradictory use of symbols in art. Jarry's work frequently contained biomorphic and geometric descriptions of objects that may have provided Picasso with an impetus for the development of analytical cubism.

Archives

Getty Research Institute for the History of Art and Humanities, Special Collections, Los Angeles, California, control no. CJPA86-A917.

Printed Sources

Penrose, Roland. *Picasso: His Life and Work* (Los Angeles: USC Press, 1983).
Richardson, John. *A Life of Picasso 1881–1906* (New York: Random House, 1991).
Shapiro, Meyer. *The Unity of Picasso's Art* (New York: George Braziller, 2000).

Gregory L. Schnurr

PINTER, HAROLD (1930–)

Harold Pinter was born in Hackney, London, on October 10, 1930. He grew up in this predominantly working-class neighborhood, being evacuated to Cornwall for a part of the time London was bombed during World War II, but also spending a portion of the war years at home and at first hand witnessing flying bombs and widespread destruction. He studied on scholarship at Hackney Downs Grammar School, where he played football and cricket and ran track as well as acted the roles of Macbeth and Romeo. He won a grant to study at the Royal Academy of Dramatic Arts but left after a few months. Later he briefly attended the Central School of Dramatic Arts.

For roughly a decade starting in 1951, he acted under the stage name of David Baron, touring Ireland and England, appearing in over 90 plays including *Oedipus*, *King Lear*, *Othello*, *An Ideal Husband*, and *The Importance of Being Earnest*. While acting, he came under the influence of two theatrical figures, Anew McMaster and Donald Wolfit, both of whose views on plays and theater influenced Pinter greatly. During this time he began work on his only novel, *The Dwarfs* (written 1952–56, published 1990). Late in the 1950s Pinter began to write plays, having been exposed to the work of Samuel Beckett while touring with McMaster. Initially through correspondence, Pinter and Beckett became friends, with the older writer commenting on his work and offering advice on writing and literary subjects. Pinter was also influenced during this time by Hollywood gangster films, noir writing, and extensive reading in twentieth-century fiction, poetry, and drama.

Much of Pinter's work can be read from a political perspective. Certainly the experience of growing up Jewish in a time of anti-Semitism and widespread persecution of European Jews in part formed Pinter's political views. He has spoken of facing threats and violence from local bullies and thugs while growing up. He has been active in a number of left-wing causes, particularly marching for and writing on behalf of imprisoned or silenced or oppressed writers. His early plays—for instance, *The Room* (1957) and *The Birthday Party* (1958)—can be seen as political only figuratively, depicting metaphorically the forces of society as they act in concert to coerce conformity or obedience from individuals, to exert hegemony over members of the society. His one-act play *The Dumb Waiter* (1959)—in which two mysterious characters obey increasingly difficult orders from an unknown, off-stage figure until one is ordered to kill the other—is often read as a metaphor for service in the armed forces (Pinter himself declined national service as a conscientious objector, facing tribunals twice, but escaping both times without being sentenced to prison but having to pay fines).

Pinter's later plays—especially *One for the Road* (1984), *Mountain Language* (1988), *Party Time* (1991), *Ashes to Ashes* (1996), and *Celebration* (2000)—are more overtly political in their nature, and their social content can be read directly and not through the prism of metaphor. He also wrote the screenplay for the political dystopian film *The Handmaid's Tale* (1987), based on the Margaret Atwood novel.

Printed Sources

Billington, Michael. *The Life and Work of Harold Pinter* (London: Faber and Faber, 1996).

Bold, Alan (ed.). *Harold Pinter: You Never Heard Such Silence* (Totowa, N.J.: Barnes and Noble, 1984).

Esslin, Martin. *Pinter the Playwright* (New York and London: Methuen, 1984).

Gale, Steven H. *Butter's Going Up: A Critical Analysis of Harold Pinter's Work* (Durham: Duke University Press, 1977).

—— (ed.). *Harold Pinter: Critical Approaches* (Rutherford, N.J.: Fairleigh Dickinson University Press, 1986).

Merritt, Susan Hollis. *Pinter in Play: Critical Strategies and the Plays of Harold Pinter* (Durham: Duke University Press, 1990).

Peacock, D. Keith. *Harold Pinter and the New British Theatre* (Westport, Conn.: Greenwood Press, 1997).

Prentice, Penelope. *The Pinter Ethic: The Erotic Aesthetic* (New York: Garland, 2000).

Sakellaridou, Elizabeth. *Pinter's Female Portraits: A Study of Female Characters in the Plays of Harold Pinter* (Totowa, N.J.: Barnes and Noble, 1988).

Thompson, David T. *Pinter: The Player's Playwright* (New York: Schocken, 1985).

D. S. Lawson

PIRANDELLO, LUIGI (1867–1936)

Luigi Pirandello, Italian playwright, novelist, and literary essayist and winner of the Nobel Prize for literature in 1934, was born in the Sicilian town of Agrigento and educated in Palermo (1880–86); Rome (1887–89); and Bonn, Germany (1889–91), where he graduated with a degree in romance philology. The author of over 200 short stories, he gained wide acclaim for his anti-naturalistic novels *The Late Mattia Pascal* (1904), *The Old and the Young* (1913), *Shoot!* (1925), and *One, None, and a Hundred-Thousand* (1926), focusing on the turmoil of consciousness and on the predicament of civilization that emerged from other European modernist writers such as **Marcel Proust, James Joyce, Franz Kafka,** and Robert Musil. A subsequent interest in theater made Pirandello one of the most influential dramatists in twentieth-century Europe. From regional plays in Sicilian dialect such as *Better Think Twice About It* and *Liolà* (1916) to the drama of the human condition in *If You Think So* (1917), *The Pleasure of Honesty* (1917), *Six Characters in Search of an Author* (1921), and *Henry IV* (1922), Pirandello radically renovated the conception of the drama as a genre and of the stage as a space of representation.

Pirandello's early readings included the poetry of Giosué Carducci and Arturo Graf, combined with a fascination for tales of magic and local folklore that announce the regional rural setting of his first short story, "Capannetta" (1884), in which Pirandello's debt toward Giovanni Verga's novella *Jeli il pastore* was also evident. While an interest in poetry and in romanticism persisted during his studies in Germany, where he translated Goethe's *Roman Elegies* and read Tieck, Chamisso, and Heine, Pirandello also approached thirteenth-century Italian poet Cecco Angiolieri as the starting point for a meditation on the concept of humor, the topic of his eponymous 1908 essay in which Ariosto's *Orlando Furioso* and Cervantes's *Don Quixote* proved equally crucial.

Another 1908 essay, "Arte e scienza," provides insights into Pirandello's polemical reception of **Benedetto Croce**'s *Aesthetics,* separating intuitive from intellectual knowledge and also documenting the influence exerted on Pirandello by Alfred Binet's *Les altérations de la personnalité* (1892). Binet's analysis of the coexistence of different personalities in the same subject and of the action of involuntary memory contributes to a dynamic and complex vision of the individual that foreshadowed the disturbing plurality of Pirandello's major characters.

Although Pirandello's art soon transcended the naturalistic slant of Italian *verismo*, he owed a great deal not only to Verga for his idea of the character as a loser, but also to Luigi Capuana, who initiated him to fiction and then to theater and included him in his Roman intellectual circle (1892), where Pirandello developed solid ties with Ugo Ojetti (who later stirred in him the curiosity for films), and playwright Massimo Bontempelli, with whom he shared a brief experience of the permanent Teatro d'Arte (1924–25), becoming the director. A direct link with another representative of *verismo*, Grazia Deledda, emerged from Pirandello's novel *Her husband* (1912), which takes Deledda herself and her husband as models for the two protagonists.

In Pirandello's shift toward theater and in his development of the grotesque mode, intellectual exchanges with Sicilian playwright and impresario Nino Martoglio and with Pier Maria Rosso di San Secondo, author of *Marionette, che passione!*, were also pivotal. But the turning point in Pirandello's theater and life was certainly the encounter with actress Marta Abba (1926), who became not only the interpreter of his plays but also his muse, inspiring such new scripts as *As You Want Me*, *The Wives' Friend*, and *To Find Oneself*.

Archives

Biblioteca-Museo Luigi Pirandello, Agrigento, Italy. Photographs, first editions, manuscripts, and unpublished documents.

Printed Sources

Aguirre D'Amico, Maria Luisa (ed.). *Album Pirandello* (Milano: Mondadori, 1992).
Bassanese, Flora. *Understanding Luigi Pirandello* (Columbia: University of South Carolina Press, 1997).
Bini, Daniela. *Pirandello and His Muse: The Plays for Marta Abba* (Gainesville: University Press of Florida, 1998).
Giudice, Gaspare. *Pirandello: A Biography.* Alastair Hamilton (trans.), (London and New York: Oxford University Press, 1975).

Nicoletta Pireddu

PLANCK, KARL ERNST LUDWIG MAX (1858–1947)

Max Planck was born in Kiel, Germany, to Johann Julius Wilhelm von Planck, professor of jurisprudence, and his second wife, Emma (Patzig) Planck. At school, Planck was a gifted student, with a strong aptitude for music and philology, though not much for mathematics. He received the school prize in catechism almost every year. He began his studies at the University of Munich during the winter semester of 1874–75 majoring in mathematics and physics. In 1877 he transferred to the University of Berlin, where he met two professors whose teaching and philosophies would help to shape his own thinking: Hermann von Helmholtz and Gustav Kirchhoff, both of whom were leading physicists of the second half of the nineteenth century.

Though Planck enjoyed moments of music and frivolity at home with colleagues and friends, and long walks in the Alps, his activities seldom strayed far from the scientific world. His meticulous notes demonstrate his continual commitment to the latest research in physics. Articles by Rudolf Clausius on thermodynamics were especially influential on the young Planck and in part led him to write his dissertation "On the Second Law of the Mechanical Theory of Heat," which he defended successfully in 1879 in Munich.

In 1885, Planck gained a measure of financial security with his appointment at the University of Kiel as associate professor of theoretical physics. In 1887 after the death of Gustav Kirchhoff, Planck was appointed as his successor. While at the University of Berlin during the 1890s, Planck began to investigate radiative equilibria. Very little was known about the properties of thermal radiation. Planck had to construct a "black body" and attempt to find the universal function. With this new concept, Planck had to assume among other things that the energy e was not a continuous quantity but a discrete one, proportional to its frequency n $(e = hn)$. The introduction of a natural constant h, the Planck quantum of action, was a significant step, since it contradicted commonly held assumptions. For his work, Planck received the Nobel Prize in physics in 1918.

The last years of Max Planck's life were made difficult by wartime and its aftermath. In February 1944, his home in the Berlin suburb of Grunewald was totally destroyed by a fire after an air raid. He lost almost everything, including his scientific notebooks and diaries. In May 1945 some American colleagues found Planck and took him to Göttingen to live out his final years.

Archives

Max Planck Society (Max-Planck-Gesellschaft zur Förderung der Wissenschaften e.V.) Hofgartenstraße 8, 80539 Munich, Germany.

Printed Works

Greenberg, Valerie D. *Transgressive Readings: The Texts of Franz Kafka and Max Planck* (Ann Arbor: University of Michigan Press, 1990).

Heilbron, J. L. *The Dilemmas of an Upright Man: Max Planck as Spokesman for German Science* (Berkeley: University of California Press, 1986).

Planck, Max. *The New Science*. 3 complete works: *Where Is Science Going? The Universe in the Light of Modern Physics; The Philosophy of Physics*, James Murphy and W. H. Johnston (trans.), (New York: Meridian Books, 1959).

Peter E. Carr

POPPER, KARL RAIMUND (1902–1994)

Karl Popper was born in Vienna. The social and intellectual milieu of Popper's early years was largely progressive and socialist embodied in anticlerical secularism, political pacifism, and social reform. From 1908 to 1913, he attended the *Freie Schule*. His stints in three different Viennese gymnasiums (1913–18) ended with Popper leaving school without his *Matura* and attending the University of Vienna at first as a nonmatriculated student—though he eventually passed the *Matura* in 1921. Studying mathematics, physics, philosophy, and psychology, Popper earned his doctorate in 1928. He taught secondary school in Vienna (1930–36) until increasing apprehension of Nazism caused him to pursue a philosophy lectureship at Canterbury University College in Christchurch, New Zealand (1937–45). In 1945, with the assistance of Friedrich von Hayek, Popper was hired as a reader in logic and scientific method at the London School of Economics. Promoted to full professorship in 1949, he retired as professor emeritus in 1969.

Popper's earliest scientific and ethical considerations were spurred by the fantasies of Selma Lagerlöf and the real-life adventures of Norwegian explorer and humanitarian Fridtjof Nansen. Arthur Arndt, a family friend and mentor to the young Popper, explained Karl Marx and Charles Darwin to him, shaped Popper's lifelong engagement with socialism, and exposed Popper to the pacifism of Bertha von Suttner. Most influentially, Arndt introduced him to the Monists—an Ernst Mach–inspired association dedicated to the scientific reform of society. There he was introduced to the progressive monist Josef Popper Lynkeus with whom he shared a concern for social welfare and individualism. In the mid-1920s, Popper's involvement with the socialist Karl Frank's Youth Scout movement led to his conversion to communism, which quickly ended in disillusionment. Popper temporarily found relief in Søren Kierkegaard's theology but wrestled throughout his life with Kierkegaard's existential dilemmas. Interest in educational reform led to Popper's interaction with Karl Bühler and into confrontation with the psychoanalysis of Sigmund Freud and the individual psychology of Alfred Adler. He adopted Edgar Zilsel's critique of both. Popper's interest in the natural sciences led him to the theoretical physics of **Albert Einstein** and mathematics as propounded in the lectures of Hans Hahn. Also unmistakable are the influences of Karl Polanyi on Popper's social science methodology and the exposure to Heinrich Gomperz's work on logic and psychology. A friendship with Julius Kraft introduced Popper to the controversial Kantian philosophy of Jakob Fries and Leonard Nelson, especially the latter's epistemology. Nelson spurred Popper's critique of David Hume, neo-Kantianism, preeminently the form expounded by Georg Wilhelm Friedrich Hegel, and Marxism. Popper was greatly indebted to Immanuel Kant, specifically Kant's ethical individualism and cosmopolitanism. Popper's scientific paradigm and critical philosophy were a synthesis of Kant and Einstein embodying a hope of progress but remaining open to critique. His thoughts found parallel roots in Alfred Tarsk's theory of truth and the liberal Christian teachings of universal emancipation and individual responsibility. Popper's philosophical development was deeply rooted in his critical dialogue with the Vienna Circle. He read Ludwig Wittgenstein and critiqued the logical positivism of **Rudolf Carnap**, Moritz Schlick, and Otto Neurath as well as the Circle's synthesis of thought found in Herbert Feigl. Neurath's model of social planning along with Felix Kaufmann's *Methodenlehre der Sozialwissenschaften* (1936) and Hayek's *The Road to Serfdom* (1944) found voice and critique in Popper's *The Open Society and Its Enemies* (1945) and *The Poverty of Historicism* (1957). At the core of Popper's critique resided a deep concern for an ethical individualism and an open society opposed to any form of ethical collectivism and historicism. The latter themes Popper saw embodied in such diverse areas as the aesthetic modernism of Arnold Schönberg's music, the philosophies of Plato, Aristotle, Hegel, and Marx, and the sociology of **Max Weber**.

Archives

Karl Popper Collection, The Hoover Institute, Stanford University, Calif.: majority of Karl Popper's papers, including works, letters and correspondence, teaching materials, and photographs.

Karl-Popper-Sammlung, University of Klagenfurt, Austria: Karl Popper's library including annotated books.

433

Printed Sources

Hacohen, Malachi Haim. *Karl Popper, The Formative Years, 1902–1945: Politics and Philosophy in Interwar Vienna* (New York: Cambridge University Press, 2000).

Schilpp, Paul Arthur (ed.). *The Philosophy of Karl Popper* (La Salle, Ill: Open Court, 1974).

Rouven J. Steeves

POUND, EZRA LOOMIS (1885–1972)

Ezra Pound was born in Hailey, Idaho, and in childhood moved near Philadelphia, Pennsylvania. Raised a Presbyterian, the adult Pound rejected Christianity, embracing pagan mysticism. He attended the University of Pennsylvania (1901–3) and Hamilton College (1903–5), returning to Pennsylvania for a master's degree in romance languages (1905–6). Afterward, Pound received an appointment at Pennsylvania as Harrison Fellow in Romanics (1906–7). He taught briefly at Wabash College before leaving for England and Europe. Through his poetry, criticism, and personal association with W. B. Yeats, **James Joyce, T. S. Eliot,** and others, he helped pioneer the modernist movement in arts and letters. During World War II Pound ran afoul of the U.S. government for making profascist radio broadcasts in Italy. After being found incompetent to stand trial, he spent 12 years at St. Elizabeths Hospital in Washington, D.C. Upon release, he returned to Italy to live out his last years.

Pound's writing testifies to his voluminous reading. He knew the troubadors and read sources such as Justin H. Smith's *The Troubadors at Home* and Sâr Péladan's *Le Secret de Troubadors*. He researched Lope de Vega, basing a chapter in *The Spirit of Romance* (1910) on his unfinished dissertation on de Vega's plays. References to Guido Cavalcanti and Dante abound in his writing, and Pound based an opera on François Villon's verse. Pound knew Robert Browning's poetry, and both Sappho's and Catullus's influences mark his work (Laughlin 1987, 67, 86, 128–39). Pound's *Homage to Sextus Propertius* is an adaptation of that Latin author's poetry. As Orientalist Ernest Fenollosa's executor, Pound edited and published Fenollosa's papers on Japanese Noh drama and on Chinese poetry (Stock 1970, 148). Pound thereby became fascinated with Chinese authors, especially with Confucius and Mencius. Pound studied economics and politics, reading C. H. Douglas's *Economic Democracy* and *Credit Power and Democracy*, the Adams–Jefferson letters, John Quincy Adams's *Diary*, Allan Nevins's *American Political, Social and Intellectual Life*, and Martin Van Buren's autobiography (Tytell 1987, 226–27). Saint Ambrose influenced his thought on usury, and his reading included studies of monetary theory and economics by Alexander Del Mar and Silvio Gesell. Pound's knowledge of German anthropologist Leo Frobenius probably came via Douglas Fox's translation in *African Genesis* (Laughlin 1987, 38, 123–27, 193). Finally, French author Remy De Gourmont and British writer T. E. Hulme both influenced Pound's thought (Stock 1970, 241–42; Ackroyd 1980, 19).

Archives

Harry Ransom Humanities Research Center, University of Texas at Austin, Austin, Texas: Manuscripts and correspondence relating to Pound's art and politics ranging from 1905 to 1975.

Ezra Pound Archives, Brunnenberg Castle, Merano, Italy: Extensive holdings at the home of Pound's grandson, including much of his personal library.

Department of Special Collections and Archives, University of Idaho Library, University of Idaho, Moscow, Idaho: First editions of Pound's poetry, criticism, and translations; also works about him by supporters and detractors. The collection also contains facsimiles of over 2,000 articles, essays, poems, etc., from a wide range of rare or obscure publications.

Yale Collection of American Literature, Beinecke Rare Book and Manuscript Library, Yale University, New Haven, Conn.: General and family correspondence, Pound's manuscripts and those written by others; also financial and personal papers.

Printed Sources

Ackroyd, Peter. *Ezra Pound and His World* (New York: Charles Scribner's Sons, 1980).

Kenner, Hugh. *The Pound Era* (Berkeley and Los Angeles: University of California Press, 1971).

Laughlin, James. *Pound as Wuz: Essays and Lectures on Ezra Pound* (St. Paul: Graywolf Press, 1987).

Stock, Noel. *The Life of Ezra Pound* (New York: Pantheon Books, 1970).

Tytell, James. *Ezra Pound: The Solitary Volcano* (New York: Anchor Press, 1987).

Donald Carlson

PRESLEY, ELVIS AARON (1935–1977)

Elvis Presley was born in Tupelo, Mississippi. At 13 his family moved to Memphis, Tennessee, his hometown for the remainder of his life. In 1954, a year after graduating from Humes High School, Presley began recording with Sun Records, where he continued to record for over a year until he signed with RCA Victor in late 1955. Presley then became hugely popular due to songs such as "Heartbreak Hotel" and "Love Me Tender." Presley's career was temporarily halted in 1958 when he was drafted for a two-year tour of military service. Throughout the 1960s, he appeared in 33 films that coincided with a decline in his career; a decline eventually salvaged with his 1968 television special and a return to live performances. Presley devoted the 1970s to recording songs that were pseudobiographical in nature and to over 1,000 live performances. One concert performed in 1973 was broadcast via satellite and viewed by over one billion people. Though this was the peak of his superstardom, his life began to spin out of control. After a 1973 divorce from wife Priscilla Belleau, Presley became increasingly dependent on prescription medication, which led to a fatal heart attack on August 16, 1977.

During the mid 1960s, Presley, under the influence of hairdresser Larry Geller, began to read on a regular basis. Though Presley was deeply committed to Christianity and knowledgeable about the Bible, he nonetheless tried constantly to comprehend and explain the dramatic changes in his life. Presley's most frequently read books were those that offered religious and philosophical insight. The most influential were the Bible, Joseph Banner's *The Impersonal Life*, Paramahansa Yogananda's *Autobiography of a Yogi*, Larry Geller's *Beyond the Himalayas*, Jiddu Krishnamurti's *Last Freedom*, and the Madame Blavatsky's translations of *Voice of Silence* and *Leaves of Morya's Garden*. To help remember passages of importance or to cross-reference works or even to show approval or disapproval, Presley would underline, write, and/or fold the passages or pages. So strong was the influence of *The Impersonal Life* that Presley spent hours at a time discussing its meaning with personal friends and people he had just met, whether celebrities or excited fans. Presley would also give away copies of the book, often with his favorite passages underlined. The most frequently cited line was "Be still and know that you are

God." During the 1970s, Presley became increasingly interested in and highly influenced by numerology. He would often consult *Cheiro's Book of Numbers* before making serious decisions and he would discuss it with anyone who was willing to listen.

Archives

Elvis Presley Library Archive at Graceland. Contains Presley's large personal library.

Printed Sources

Esposito, Joe. *Elvis: A Legendary Performance* (Buena Park, Calif.: West Coast Publishing, 1990).

Guralnick, Peter. *Careless Love: The Unmaking of Elvis Presley* (New York: Little, Brown and Company, 1999).

———. *Last Train to Memphis: The Rise of Elvis Presley* (New York: Little, Brown and Company, 1997).

Hopkins, Jerry. *Elvis* (New York: Simon and Schuster, 1971).

Presley, Priscilla, with Sandra Harmon. *Elvis and Me* (New York: G.P. Putnum's Sons, 1985).

Aaron N. Coleman

PROKOFIEV, SERGEI SERGEEVICH (1891–1953)

Sergei Prokofiev, the son of a landowner, was born in Sonzovka, southern Russia. At the age of 10 he composed his first opera, "The Giant," and set the lyrics of the Russian poets Alexander Pushkin and Michail Lermontov to music. He studied at the St. Petersburg Conservatory (1904–9) and gave several concerts in France, England, Switzerland, and Italy before he left—after the October Revolution—Soviet Russia for the United States. Here he came into contact with the Christian Science movement of Mary Baker Eddy, and her seminal publication, *Science and Health with Key to the Scriptures* (1875). His tours through the United States in the 1920s and 1930s laid the foundation for his international fame. Prokofiev cooperated with the great orchestras in Chicago, Boston, and New York. *Time* and *Newsweek* praised him as Russia's greatest modern composer. In 1929 Prokofiev moved with his family to Paris and seven years later he returned permanently back to the Soviet Union. In 1939 he became vice chairman of the Soviet Composers' Union. During the war he had been evacuated like many other Soviet musicians to the Caucasus and Central Asia. In Alma-Aty (Kazakhstan) he worked together with film producer **Sergei Eisenstein.** In 1942 Prokofiev received the Stalin prize, in the next years the medal of the Red Workers' Movement and of the Red Army. In June 1945 the Royal Philharmonic Society in London awarded him the golden medal. Prokofiev died on March 5, 1953, the same day that his mentor Stalin died.

In his youth, Prokofiev became acquainted with Goethe's *Faust*, and he dreamt about setting it to music. As a youth, he appreciated Shakespeare's *Julius Caesar* and *Romeo and Juliet.* Due to his interest for Roman history, he also read Henryk Sienkiewicz's novel *Quo Vadis.* At the conservatory he had been attracted to the fantastic literature of Jules Verne *(Voyage to the Moon).* All these works Prokofiev read in the original languages. When Prokofiev later belonged to the Soviet music avant-garde, he was deeply influenced by Western symbolism, as he loved the poems of Charles Baudelaire *(Les Fleurs du Mal).* This explains why the composer was soon attracted by experimental music. Prokofiev's work reflects the popularity of West European modernism in Russia, but without neglecting Russia's own traditions. In his early period Prokofiev stood for a symbiosis between Western and Russian culture. Cultural policy under Lenin approved the Soviet artists' affinity to Western influences and propagated a cultural pluralism. At the same time, when Prokofiev introduced his work to a Western audience, Western composers like Arnold Schönberg, Paul Hindemith, and Alban Berg gave concerts in the Soviet Union. This free exchange of cultural influences ended abruptly under Stalin. In 1936, during the Great Purges, Prokofiev returned to the Soviet Union as a patriotic Russian, feeling that he could not get musical inspiration so far from his homeland. Under Stalin, Prokofiev enjoyed many privileges, and he was not sensitive to the deep changes in Soviet society when numerous artists vanished in the labor camps. Instead, Prokofiev cooperated with the regime. In contrast to his early experimental work in the 1920s influenced by Western modernism, in the following decades until his death in 1953 Prokofiev dedicated his music to the "socialist achievements" such as the October Revolution, industrialization, the Soviet constitution, and the victory in World War II and increasingly dissociated himself from Western influences.

Archives

Rossiiskii Gosudarstvennyi Arkhiv Literatury I Iskusstva (Russian State Archive of Literature and Arts), Moscow.

Printed Sources

Blok, Vladimir. *Sergei Prokofiev: Materials, Articles, Interviews* (Moscow: Progress Publishers, 1978).

Prokofiev, Oleg (ed.). *Sergey Prokofiev 1891–1953. Soviet Diary, 1927, and Other Writings* (Boston: Northeastern University Press, 1992).

Roberts, Peter Deane. *Modernism in Russian Piano Music. Scriabin, Prokofiev, and Their Russian Contemporaries*, 2 vols. (Bloomington/Indianapolis: Indiana University Press, 1993).

Robinson, Harlow. *The Operas of Sergei Prokofiev and Their Russian Literary Sources* (Berkeley: University of California Press, 1980).

Eva-Maria Stolberg

PROUST, MARCEL (1871–1922)

Marcel Proust's 16-volume novel *À la recherche du temps perdu* (1922–32) is regarded as one of the greatest achievements in world literature. Proust was born in Paris. He was raised as a Roman Catholic, the religion of his father, a professor of medicine. His mother kept the Jewish faith of her family. At her death, she advised Marcel, who as far as anyone could tell was not a believer, to remain a Catholic. During his final school year, Proust studied idealists such as Immanuel Kant. For Proust, his reading of Kant was inspirational, prompting speculations on metaphysics and human behavior.

Having completed his studies at the lycée Condorcet (1882–89) and after a year of military service, Proust continued his studies in law at the École des Sciences politiques and the Sorbonne. It was during this time that he began to develop his genius as a writer. He frequented Parisian literary salons where he met Anatole France, from whom he obtained a preface (1896) to his first novel, *Les Plaisirs et les jours.* He secluded himself in his apartment on the Boulevard Haussmann, going out only in the darkest of night. The Prix Goncourt that he won in 1919 brought him national renown by a public that until then had scarcely heard of him. From 1919 his reputation increased both at home and abroad. Sick with asthma since childhood, Proust knew that his life would be short, but before his death he wanted to finish the enormous work that he had undertaken. On November 18, 1922, he died as a result of his condition that was worsened by bronchitis.

Until age 35, Proust lived a carefree life in the salons, although he worked for a brief period as a lawyer and was active in the Dreyfus Affair, like Émile Zola and other artists and intellectuals. He was financially independent and had the freedom to begin his great novel, *Remembrance of Things Past*, which was influenced by the autobiographies of François Chateaubriand and Johann Wolfgang von Goethe. Proust admired the works of Vigny, Hugo, and Leconte de Lisle, but it was in Baudelaire's poetry that he found the greatest inspiration. Many of Proust's contemporaries cited **Henri Bergson**'s influence on Proust's work, which Proust denied, although they both were much occupied with time and memory.

Proust's entire work is written as an interior monologue and is semiautobiographical. His compact style has often put off readers who are unwilling to follow the labyrinths that he creates. To categorize his work as merely a memoir or a novel is to miss its central function. The importance of Proust's novel lies both in the psychological development of its characters and in his philosophical obsession with time. In addition, Proust wrote the annals of his society: the aristocracy of late nineteenth-century France. It is a psychological portrait of the people that made up this society, which was marked by such feelings as love, jealousy, and truth. Proust examined his society under a microscope, and he gave a poetic dimension to the characters that he painted. The most famous of Proust's essays is that on Flaubert's style, in which he compares Flaubert's grammatical use of tenses to Kant's revolution in philosophy.

Archives

Le Centre de Recherche Kolb-Proust, Correspondence of Marcel Proust, University of Illinois at Urbana-Champaign, Rare Book & Special Collections Library.
La Bibliothèque Nationale de France, Paris, France, Marcel Proust, Cabinet des Manuscrits.

Printed Sources

Carter, William C. *Marcel Proust: A Life* (New Haven: Yale University Press, 2000).
Duchêne, Roger. *L'Impossible Marcel Proust* (Paris: R. Laffont, 1994).

Richard J. Gray II

R

RAND, AYN (1905–1982)

Ayn Rand, born Alissa Rosenbaum in St. Petersburg, Russia, was an autodidact who taught herself to read at age six and began writing with professional aspirations by age nine. After graduating in 1924 from the University of Petrograd with majors in philosophy and history, Rand became disenchanted with the communist mindset taking over academia; she turned her attention toward Western films and plays and entered the State Institute for Cinema Arts, where she began to study screenwriting. By 1926, Rand departed from Russia and arrived in the United States, where she traveled from New York to Chicago and finally on to Hollywood where, after two days of standing in front of Cecil B. DeMille's studio, she was offered a job as an extra and script reader for his movie *The King of Kings*. Alissa Rosenbaum then changed her name to Ayn Rand and met actor Frank O'Connor, whom she would marry in 1929. Rand's first professional attempts at writing were failures—her first screenplay, *Red Pawn*, and stage play, *Night of January 16th*, as well as her first novel, *We the Living* (1933), were rejected most probably because Rand's approach clashed with pro-communist culture during the period often labeled "the Red Decade." Two years later Rand began writing *The Fountainhead*, a text that outlines her own spin on philosophy, known as objectivism, via Howard Roark, the ideal man and hero of the text. *The Fountainhead* appeared in 1943 after being rejected by 12 publishers and became a bestseller two years later just as Rand began working on a screenplay for the text. War delayed production of the film until 1948 and Rand shifted her focus back to novels, devoting most of her time to completing *Atlas Shrugged*.

Rand's main contribution is objectivism, a philosophy that was nascent in her mind as early as age eight when she encountered her first fictional hero in a French magazine for children. Objectivists hold that there is no greater moral goal than achieving happiness via objective principles, including moral integrity, capitalism, limited government, and individualism; hence, Rand was greatly influenced by writers who created nonmystic and noncollectivist works, such as the playwright Edmond Rostand, Walter Scott, and her lifetime favorite, Victor Hugo, as well as the general body of texts in Western political philosophy. Perhaps, as Michael Berliner suggests, an often overlooked but seminal influence in Rand's writings is the screenplays she read, edited, and enacted during her initial experiences in Hollywood.

Archives

The Ayn Rand Institute, Marina del Rey, California.

The Library of Congress—Manuscript Division. Donation from Leonard Peikoff, drafts, typescripts, and galley proofs of *We the Living, Anthem, The Fountainhead,* and *Atlas Shrugged,* plus some administrative material.

Margaret Herrick Library, Academy of Motion Picture Arts and Sciences Library, Beverly Hills, California.

Printed Sources

Binswanger, Harry (ed.). *The Ayn Rand Lexicon: Objectivism from A to Z* (New York: Meridian, 1988).

Branden, Barbara. *The Passion of Ayn Rand* (New York: Doubleday, 1986).

Gladstein, Mimi. *The Ayn Rand Companion* (Westport, Conn.: Greenwood Press, 1984).

Paxton, Michael. *Ayn Rand: A Sense of Life* (Layton, Utah: Gibbs-Smith, 1998).

Peikoff, Leonard. "My Thirty Years with Ayn Rand: An Intellectual Memoir." In *The Voice of Reason: Essays in Objectivist Thought* (New York: Meridian, 1990).

Rand, Ayn. *The Romantic Manifesto: A Philosophy of Literature* (New York: World, 1969); rev. [expanded] ed. (New York: Signet, 1975).

———. *Russian Writings on Hollywood,* Michael S. Berliner (ed.), Dina Garmong (trans.), (Los Angeles: Ayn Rand Institute Press, 1999). Essays by A. Rosenbaum (Ayn Rand).

Tucille, Jerome. *It Usually Begins with Ayn Rand: A Libertarian Odyssey* (New York: Stein and Day, 1971).

Dana Milstein

RATHENAU, WALTHER (1867–1922)

Walther Rathenau was born in Berlin and remained a Berlin resident for most of his life. He received his *Abitur* in 1885 from the Königlichen Wilhems Gymnasium and studied physics, chemistry, and philosophy at the Universities of Berlin and Strasbourg between 1886 and 1889. In 1890, Rathenau received additional training in chemistry at the Technischen Hochschüle in Munich. His most valued educational experience was as an officer candidate with a cavalry regiment in Berlin in 1890–91. Rathenau desired a career as an officer, but the German military excluded Jews from becoming officers. Instead, he studied industrial sciences anticipating controlling his father's business, Germany's first electrical company, but Rathenau's mother encouraged him to pursue literature, history, and philosophy. Rathenau developed into a true Renaissance man; he was an influential businessman, a prolific author, and a member of Berlin's cultural elite. Rathenau's greatest contribution was as an eloquent commentator on German–Jewish relations during a time when anti-Semitism grew into a permanent feature of German society. Rathenau passionately advocated Jewish assimilation into the German state. He revered his Prussian roots but quickly realized that even educated Jews like himself would never be accepted until Germany evolved into a meritocracy. The majority of

Rathenau's writings delineated an ideal society in which the personal and collective "soul" of German citizens could develop unencumbered by artificial boundaries like class. The key threat to the soul's development was "mechanization," the amalgamation of the world into a net of production and world trade.

The only author Rathenau quoted directly was St. Paul (Kessler 1969, 81), but Rathenau had a myriad of literary influences. Rathenau developed his vision in three books published between 1912 and 1918. His most important influence was Johann Gottlieb Fichte (1762–1814), whose articulation of a Spartan–Prussian spirit and description of a "perfect society" in *The Characteristics of the Present Age* (1806) and *Addresses to the German Nation* (1808) inspired Rathenau's vision of the "realm of the soul." Rathenau was also an avid reader of Friedrich Nietzsche (1844–1900). Nietzsche's *Beyond Good and Evil* (1886) helped Rathenau argue his point that humanity's potential mattered more than tradition and binding social standards. Rathenau was attracted to Benedict de Spinoza's (1632–77) *Ethics* (1678) because of its conception of God as an infinite substance and humans as transitory manifestations. An avid devotee to Prussian classicism and a frequent traveler to Greece, Rathenau admired Greek philosophy but was especially interested in Plato's (428–347 B.C.) *Republic* (360 B.C.). To complement the Prussian influences in his work, Rathenau also explored the Jewish side of his personality. Rathenau was influenced by Jewish mysticism, specifically Hassidism, because the movement advocated exploring the soul. Rathenau befriended Jewish mysticism's young historian, **Martin Buber** (1878–1965). Buber's seminal work, *I and Thou* (1923), remains the best interpretation of Hassidism. A victim of the anti-Semitism he fought to eradicate, Rathenau was assassinated in 1922 by right-wing extremists soon after accepting the post of foreign minister in the Weimar government.

Archives

Nachlass Walther Rathenau, N 1048, Bundesarchiv, Koblenz, Germany. Contains official and unofficial correspondence, including drafts of writings from different periods of his life.

Printed Sources

Berglar, Peter. *Walther Rathenau: Seine Zeit, sein Werk, sein Persönlichkeit* (Bremen: Schünemann, 1970).

Kessler, Harry Count. *Walther Rathenau: His Life and Work* (New York: Fertig, 1969).

Rathenau, Walther. *Walther Rathenau—Industrialist, Banker, Intellectual, and Politician: Notes and Diaries, 1907–1922*, Hartmut Pogge (ed.), (New York: Clarendon Press, 1985).

Brian Crim

REAGAN, RONALD (1911–)

Ronald Reagan was born in Tampico, Illinois. He was an active member of the Christian Church throughout his childhood and graduated from Eureka College, a liberal arts institution founded by the Disciples of Christ in Eureka, Illinois. He served two terms as governor of California before he was elected fortieth president of the United States. President Reagan's two terms in office have been dubbed "The Reagan Revolution" because of the many political and economic changes he initiated. He revived the Republican Party with his campaign promises to lower taxes, shrink government, and establish an aggressively anti-Communist foreign policy. He maintained his dedication to these core principles throughout his presidency, and though some critics have characterized his tactics as shortsighted, it is generally recognized that his Economic Recovery Act revived a depressed U.S. economy and his aggressive foreign policy contributed to the eventual collapse of the Soviet Union. His political rhetoric appealed to traditional middle-class conservative values of patriotism, religious piety, personal initiative, and economic progress.

Reagan in his second autobiography recalls that he learned to read at an early age and was "already a bookworm of sorts" by the time he entered the first grade. "I remember my father coming into the house one day before I'd entered school and finding me on the living room floor with the newspaper in front of me" (Reagan 1990, 25). He was an avid reader of news periodicals throughout his life and describes a morning routine in the White House that began with the *New York Times* and the *Washington Post* (Reagan 1990, 249). He often cited Mark Twain's *The Adventures of Tom Sawyer* in describing his youth in Dixon, Illinois. A "voracious reader," young Reagan consumed books on wildlife, such as *Northern Lights*, which he "read over and over, imagining myself with the wolves in the wild" (Reagan 1990, 31), and he especially enjoyed books with fictional heroes, particularly the *Rover Boys* books. He cites *Frank Merriwell at Yale* and *Brown of Harvard* as "books about college life, with exciting stories about Ivy League life and gridiron rivalries . . . my childhood dream was to become like those guys in the books" (Reagan 1990, 32). Reagan recalled that at age 12 his mother's copy of *That Printer of Udell's* by Harold Bell Wright inspired him to be baptized as a Disciple of Christ. He told his authorized biographer the book had a profound influence on him and "made him a practical Christian" (Morris 1999, 40). Subtitled *A Story of the Middle West*, the novel is a morality tale of a boy who overcomes poverty and an alcoholic father to revive his community and become its leading spokesman. The novel's last scene depicts the protagonist kneeling in prayer before pursuing his ambition in Washington, D.C. Morris conjectures, "The book's larger themes of self-indulgence versus practical Christianity, of institutional apathy yielding to passion, of oratory as a tool and private values as public policy, unmistakably nurtured the embryo president" (Morris 1999, 42). A long-time Democrat, Reagan registered with the Republican Party in 1962 when he felt "the liberal Democrats wanted to rein in the energy of free enterprise and capitalism, create a welfare state, and impose a subtle kind of socialism" (Reagan 1990, 134). He supported Barry Goldwater's 1964 presidential campaign and felt "his book, *Conscience of a Conservative*, contained a lot of the same points I'd been making in my speeches" (Reagan 1990, 138). Reagan became increasingly critical of what he felt was federal government's encroachment on state powers, often quoting Thomas Jefferson and James Madison in his attempts to return decision-making authority to what he termed "the grassroots level." Reagan's hand was on his mother's Bible when he took his first presidential oath of office, and in fact his childhood association with the Bible probably contributed to his effective rhetorical skills. Ritter and Henry identify Reagan's use of the "jeremiad" sermon structure and attribute the power of his political speeches to his "skill at adapting this old Puritan sermon form to contemporary campaigning" (Ritter and Henry 1992, 38). The jeremiad's three distinct parts are the promise, the declension, and the prophesy. Reagan's frequent use of apocalyptic imagery in later life is examined by Pierard and Linder (1988, 257–83).

Archives

Ronald Reagan Presidential Library, Simi Valley, California. Material from Reagan's presidential years.

Ronald Reagan Collection, Hoover Institution on War, Revolution and Peace, Stanford University. Papers and transcripts from eight years as governor of California.

Ronald Reagan Files, Dixon Public Library, Dixon, Illinois. News clippings, student yearbooks, material from his youth in and visits to Dixon.

Printed Sources

Bosch, Adriana. *Reagan: An American Story* (New York: TV Books, 1998). Extensive use of primary sources and fastidious citation.

Morris, Edmond. *Dutch* (New York: Random House, 1999). Detailed but impressionistic, authorized biography.

Pierard, Richard, and Robert Linder. *Civil Religion and the Presidency* (Grand Rapids, Mich: Zondervan, 1988). Introduction to Reagan's religious background, beliefs, and practices.

Reagan, Ronald. *An American Life* (New York: Simon and Schuster, 1990).

———. *I Love You, Ronnie: The Letters of Ronald Reagan to Nancy Reagan* (New York: Random House, 2000).

———. *Reagan, In His Own Hand,* Kiron Skinner, Annelise Anderson, and Martin Anderson (eds.), (New York: Simon and Schuster, 2001). Essays, short stories, notations, and speech transcripts from 1925 to 1994.

Reagan, Ronald, and Richard Hubler. *Where's the Rest of Me?* (New York: Duell, Sloan and Pearse, 1965).

Ritter, Kurt, and David Henry. *Ronald Reagan: The Great Communicator* (New York: Greenwood Press, 1992). Thoughtful analysis of Reagan's speech rhetoric that suggests biblical influences.

Richard N. Swanson

REMARQUE, ERICH MARIA (1898–1970)

Erich Maria Remarque, Erich Paul Remark by birth, was born in Osnabrück, Lower Saxony, one of four children, to Peter Franz Remark a bookbinder and former captain of the German Merchant Marine and his wife, Anna Maria, née Stallknecht. He grew up in a devoutly religious home, receiving a Catholic education at the Domschule (1904–8) and Johannisschule (1908–12), followed by a Catholic Preparatory School (1912–15) in Osnabrück, which prepared him for the career of an elementary school teacher. In November 1916 he was drafted into the German army, serving until being seriously wounded on the first day of the Battle of Flanders (July 31, 1917). Starting out as a teacher, salesman, and accountant after the war, he only began to get a hold on life when employed as a journalist and editor. In the early 1920s he changed "Paul" to "Maria," Rilke's—as well as his mother's—second Christian name, and adopted the original spelling of the family name. It was in Berlin, the seething metropolis he had moved to in 1925, that he put down his look back to the years of fighting in the form of a novel. *All Quiet on the Western Front*, published in 1929 by Ullstein, was an instant success in Germany and abroad. Although he wrote 13 novels, most of them bestsellers and many, like this first great success, popularized as a film version, it is for the scathing attack on the evils of war and, in the character Himmelstoss, of the evils of German militarism, that Remarque is most famous. Though he left Germany in 1931, in 1933 for good to live in Switzerland and, from 1939 to live mostly in the

United States until returning to Switzerland after 1945, many of his novels mirror life in decisive periods of twentieth-century German history: the experience of two wars, the Weimar years, flight from Nazism and exile, existence in a Nazi concentration camp.

Since Remarque was fascinated by a wide range of subjects, including music, literature, and the arts as well as by sports, fast cars, good food, and drink, he was a voracious reader throughout his life. Having already developed a love for literature in his youth, he was well versed in the works of Knut Hamsun, Jack London, Gottfried Keller, Honoré de Balzac, Stendhal, Gustave Flaubert, the poetry of Friedrich Hölderlin, Edgar Allan Poe, Rainer Maria Rilke, and Franz Werfel, the works of **Thomas** and **Heinrich Mann,** Hugo von Hofmannsthal, and **Hermann Hesse.** After the war experience he was even more strongly attracted to the ideas of Arthur Schopenhauer and Friedrich Nietzsche. Thomas Mann's *Der Zauberberg* and **Marcel Proust**'s *A la recherche du temps perdu* had a profound impact on him, as did **Franz Kafka**'s unveiling of the automatism of evil. With **Ernest Hemingway,** whom he admired, he shared the feeling of belonging to a lost generation. At the time of writing *All Quiet on the Western Front*, the Great War had become the subject of many fictional and nonfictional publications, some of which Remarque reviewed, Ernst Jünger's *In Stahlgewittern* and Franz Schauwecker's *Ringen an der Somme* among them.

A childhood spent in relative poverty and the war experience may account for the epicurean lifestyle he adopted sometime in the twenties, later to be explained by a parable by Friedrich Rückert, *Es ging ein Mann im Syrerland*, in an interview on his sixty-fifth birthday. It encapsulated his motto for life: to live every day as if it were the last (quoted in Habe 1963, 64). Erich Maria Remarque, whose German citizenship had been revoked by the National Socialists in 1938 and who had become an American citizen in 1947, was married three times, twice to Jutta Ilse Zambona and, in 1958, to Paulette Goddard. He died in 1970 of a heart attack.

Archives

Niedersächsisches Staatsarchiv Osnabrück.
Erich Maria Remarque-Archiv/Forschungsstelle Krieg und Literatur, Universität Osnabrück.
Remarque Collection, Fales Library, New York University, New York (holder of diaries).

Printed Sources

Habe, Hans. "Umstellt, umlagert, umdroht," *Epoca* (August 1963), 63–67.
Owen, Claude R. *Erich Maria Remarque: A critical bio-bibliography* (Amsterdam: Rodopi, 1984).
Remarque, Erich Maria. *Das unbekannte Werk. Frühe Prosa, Werke aus dem Nachlaß, Briefe und Tagebücher*, Thomas F. Schneider, Tilman Westphalen (eds.), vol. 5: *Briefe und Tagebücher* (Cologne: Kiepenheuer & Witsch, 1998).
Sternburg, Wilhelm von. *"Als wäre alles das letzte Mal": Erich Maria Remarque, eine Biographie* (Cologne: Kiepenheuer & Witsch, 1998).
Taylor, Harley U. Jr. *Erich Maria Remarque. A Literary and Film Biography* (New York, Bern, Frankfurt/Main, Paris: Peter Lang, 1988).

Angela Schwarz

RICHLER, MORDECAI (1931–2001)

Mordecai Richler was born in Montreal, Canada. He studied at Sir George Williams College (now Concordia University) in Montreal (1949–51). In 1951 Richler tired of college life and left Canada for Europe, spending almost two years in England, Spain, and France (in Paris he was part of an expatriate circle that included James Baldwin, Mavis Gallant, and **Allen Ginsberg**) before returning to Canada in 1952. In 1954, Richler again traveled to London, where he spent 18 years building an international literary reputation and establishing himself as one of Canada's most important contemporary novelists. Upon his return to Canada in 1972, Richler became a vocal opponent of Canadian cultural nationalism, criticizing both national institutions (such the Canadian Broadcasting Corporation where he worked in the 1950s) and a number of prominent Canadian writers. Although Richler produced fiction with less regularity in his later career, he continued to write for magazines and journals on both sides of the Atlantic, producing more than 300 articles on cultural and political topics by the end of his life. In the 1990s he generated considerable controversy with his loud criticism of Quebec nationalism. Richler's 10 novels are among the most acclaimed works of Canadian fiction, and he is among the most honored of Canadian writers, having won two Governor General's Awards, the Giller Prize, and the Commonwealth Writers Prize, and having been appointed to the Order of Canada.

All accounts of Richler's life note the formative influence of his early religious training: he grew up in an insular, predominantly Jewish part of Montreal and attended parochial school with the expectation of becoming a rabbi. Later, Richler's novels would critique and satirize Jewish Montreal, and a number of his novels—most notably *The Apprenticeship of Duddy Kravitz* (1959)—have been called anti-Semitic. Richler's early works are somewhat similar in style to those of some of his Paris acquaintances, notably Baldwin and Gallant, although Richler himself reveals that his most significant influences were the earlier generation of American modernists, including **Ernest Hemingway, F. Scott Fitzgerald, John Dos Passos,** and **William Faulkner** (Cohen 1957, 34). The "cynical world-weariness" that characterizes much of Richler's fiction can be traced back to his interest in existentialism and the works of French writers, including **Jean-Paul Sartre** and **André Malraux** (Brown 1983, 704). Within the Canadian tradition, Richler has compared himself to those writers whose works have a cosmopolitan inclination: Hugh MacLennan, Robertson Davies, Morley Callaghan, Malcolm Lowry, and Brian Moore (McSweeney 1985, 134–35). While Richler's brand of satire continues in the Canadian tradition established by Stephen Leacock, it is more Juvenalian, recalling both the work of two of his Paris friends from the 1950s, Terry Southern and Mason Hoffenberg, and works of black humor by Nathanael West, **Evelyn Waugh,** and Louis-Ferdinand Céline, all of whom Richler has acknowledged as influences (McSweeney 1985, 137).

Archives

University of Calgary Library, Special Collections, *Mordecai Richler Fonds:* correspondence, manuscripts of novels, short fiction, articles, screenplays, radio, television, and dramatic plays, interviews, other materials.

Printed Sources

Brown, Russell. "Mordecai Richler." In William Toye (ed.), *The Oxford Companion to Canadian Literature*. (Toronto: Oxford University Press, 1983).

Cohen, Nathan. "A Conversation with Mordecai Richler," *The Tamarack Review* 2 (Winter 1957), 6–23.

McSweeney, Kerry. "Mordecai Richler." In Robert Lecker, Jack David, and Ellen Quigley (eds.), *Canadian Writers and Their Works*. Fiction Series, vol. 6 (Toronto: ECW Press, 1985). Includes a detailed summary of influences on Richler's fiction.

Ramraj, Victor. "Biocritical Essay." In Apollonia Steele and Jean F. Tener (eds.), *The Mordecai Richler Papers: First Accession* (Calgary: University of Calgary Press, ca. 1987).

Shwartz, Ronald B. *For the Love of Books: 115 Celebrated Writers on the Books They Love Most* (New York: Grosset/Putnam, 1999).

Colin Hill

RIEFENSTAHL, HELENE (1902–2003)

Helene "Leni" Riefenstahl was born in Berlin, where she studied music and art history at the State School of Arts and Crafts. In 1919 she entered the Lohmann School in Thale, where she began acting in and directing stage plays. She was confirmed in the Kaiser Wilhelm Memorial Church in Berlin. Riefenstahl was a rising star as an actress in German cinema of the 1920s before becoming a film director of "bergfilms," a film genre with mountain settings. She so impressed **Adolf Hitler** that he put her in charge of filming the 1934 Nazi Party rally at Nuremberg and the 1936 Olympics in Berlin. The two films, *Triumph of the Will* and *Olympia*, are considered landmark documentaries because of Riefenstahl's innovative camera work, editing, and powerful combination of images and music. While she has always insisted that her art was entirely separate from politics, her critics accuse her of being a willing propagandist for the Nazis. But regardless of what Riefenstahl's personal motivations may have been in the 1930s, her *Triumph of the Will* glorified the Nazi Party and was a driving force in unifying Hitler's political power in Germany. Later in her career she continued to innovate with her work in underwater and anthropological still photography.

Riefenstahl maintained that she remained politically naive well into early adulthood. "My favorite pastime was reading fairy-tales and this taste lasted well beyond childhood," Riefenstahl wrote in her autobiography (Riefenstahl 1992, 4). At 15 she was still buying the weekly magazine *Fairy-Tale World*. She would lock herself in her room and "read and re-read, over and over again" stories such as "The Girl with the Three Walnuts," which she "has never forgotten" (Riefenstahl 1992, 4). Her other youthful passion was drama, and while in boarding school she was moved by such German classics as Friedrich von Schiller's *The Brigand*, Gotthold Lessing's *Minna Von Barnhelm*, and Johann Goethe's *Faust*. She received the works of Friedrich Holderlin and Friedrich Nietzsche from an admirer while in her early twenties (Riefenstahl 1992, 47) and indicates in her autobiography that she read *Thus Spake Zarathustra* and especially admired Nietzsche's poetry and use of language (Riefenstahl 1992, 130). She has stated that she first read *Mein Kampf* in 1932, shortly before her first meeting with Adolf Hitler. "I had jotted such comments in the margins as 'Untrue, Wrong, Mistaken,' though sometimes I put 'Good,'" she recalled in her autobiography (Riefenstahl 1992, 125). A different account describes a more enthusiastic response to *Mein Kampf*. "She came over to my apartment one day holding the book high above her head and said . . . 'you must sit down and read this man's book through. I must meet him!' Up until that day she was as much interested in and knew probably less about politics than my housemaid" (Sokal 1976, 14). While Riefenstahl defends *Triumph of the Will* as merely a documentary of an historical event, critics argue that it employs the subtle propaganda techniques outlined in *Mein Kampf*. Riefenstahl's loudest critics see fascist ideology at the root of her focus on physical perfection and natural beauty. But more cogent analyses of her work consider the literary and artistic tradition Riefenstahl was heir to. One must understand that the adoration of perfect bodies and beautiful nature was a romantic principle subjugated by Nazi ideology. As Von Dassanowski observes: "Essentially a Bergfilm maker and a nature-mystic, Riefenstahl gave Hitler's set pieces the needed emotional association with German tradition and culture. The concept of the nature-bound outsider as prophet, so prevalent in Riefenstahl's work, is also to be found throughout the German Romantic literary canon, in the works of Novalis [Friedrich von Hardenberg], [Ludwig] Tieck, Goethe, [Joseph] von Eichendorff, and Holderlin, where it is anything but reactionary or authoritarian" (Von Dassanowski 1995/96, 1). Riefenstahl's decision late in life to photograph in Africa was inspired by her reading of *The Green Hills of Africa*. "I read until dawn," she recalls, "by which time **Hemingway**'s lifelong fascination with Africa had taken hold of me" (Riefenstahl 1992, 407). Riefenstahl's unrealized project is a film production of Heinrich von Kleist's play about the queen of the Amazons, *Penthesilea*. She said reading it in 1926 was an unforgettable, intense experience. "I feel myself so akin to [Kleist] that . . . everything is spoken from the depths of my soul. In Penthesilia I found my own individuality as in no other character" (Riefenstahl 1973, 194).

Archives

Riefenstahl file, Berlin Document Center: Third Reich records including official documents and correspondence between Riefenstahl and party officials.

Archives of the Federal Republic of Germany, Koblenz: Third Reich records including official documents and correspondence between Riefenstahl and party officials.

Printed Sources

Berg-Pan, Renata. *Leni Riefenstahl* (Boston: Twayne Publishers, 1980).

Dassanowsky, Robert von. "Wherever You May Run, You Cannot Escape Him: Leni Riefenstahl's Self-Reflection and Romantic Transcendence of Nazism in Tiefland," *Camera Obscura* 35 (1996), 107–30.

Riefenstahl, Leni. *Leni Riefenstahl: A Memoir* (New York: St. Martin's Press, 1992).

———. "Why I Am Filming Penthesilea," *Film Culture* 56 (Spring 1973), 192–215.

Sokal, Harry R. "Uber Nacht antisemitin geworden?" *Der Spiegel* 30, 46 (1976), 14.

Richard N. Swanson

RIVERA, DIEGO (1886–1957)

José Diego Rivera Barrientos was born in Guanajuato, Mexico, and moved with his family to Mexico City at the age of six. He was enrolled in the San Carlos Academy (1896) and the National School of Fine Arts (1898), where he studied under noted engraver José Guadalupe Posada until the time of his expulsion in 1906. The following year, Rivera earned a four-year Veracruz scholarship for European study and traveled to Spain and Paris, where he became influenced by cubism, post-impressionism, and Renaissance painting, exhibiting at the 1911 Salon d'Automne as well as with **Pablo Picasso** at numerous cubist exhibitions. Upon returning to his homeland in 1921, Rivera was commissioned to decorate the convent of St. Peter and St. Paul in Mexico City with a mural program. The artist traveled to the ancient Mexican sites of Chichen Itza and Uxmal before embarking on the production of the first of literally hundreds of murals that would celebrate Mexican culture and heritage. In 1923 Rivera formed the Mexican Union of Technical Workers, Painters and Sculptors and the Escuela Mexicana de Pintura with fellow muralists David Alfaro Siqueiros and José Clemente Orozco. In 1929 he was appointed director of the Academy of San Carlos, and during the next two decades continued to accept numerous commissions, producing series of murals for the National Palace in Mexico City (1930–35), the Detroit Art Institute and Rockefeller Center (1932), and the Mexican Hotel del Prado (1948). Rivera died of heart failure in his San Angel Studio and is buried at the Rotonda de los Hombres Ilustres in Mexico City.

Rivera's artistic promotion of a traditional and independent Mexican culture was influenced by the wave of social realist writers who dominated Mexican literature during the early part of the twentieth century. South American authors such as Mariano Picon Salas, German Arciniegas, and Mexican Minister of Education José Vasconcelos detailed the injustices imposed upon the Mexican working classes in their novellas and essays. Novels such as *The Underdogs* by Mariano Azuela and Martin Luiz Guzman's *The Eagle and the Serpent* cast the Mexican indigenous population and the poor as the protagonists of their stories and dealt with contemporary social ills and issues of social reform as subject matter. As well, Mexican regionalism and history was popularized by such authors as Horatio Quiroga and Eduardo Acevedo Diaz, who wrote the gaucho novels that Rivera read as a youth. As a Marxist Leninist and a member of the Mexican Communist Party (1923–30 and again from 1954 until the time of his death), Rivera's style and subject matter were often influenced by his left-wing, anti-Stalinist views. Rivera analyzed the writings of **Vladimir Lenin** and exiled Russian Revolution leader **Leon Trotsky** and expressed his own ideology in various literary submissions to the New York magazine *The Partisan Review*. After his exposure to cubism and modern art during his European sojourn, Rivera studied the work of surrealist founder **André Breton,** and the two men collaborated in preparing a manifesto entitled *Towards a Free Revolutionary Art.* In this work Diego espoused his notion that the major function of modern art should be to aid in the revolution of the working class against oppression, in whatever form it may take.

Archives

Archives of American Art, Smithsonian Institution, Washington, D.C., control no. DCAW220208-A.

Printed Sources

Marnham, Patrick. *Dreaming With His Eyes Open: A Life of Diego Rivera* (New York: Knopf, 1998).

Rivera, Diego, and Gladys March. *My Art, My Life: An Autobiography* (New York: Dover Press, 1991).

Wolfe, Bertram D. *The Fabulous Life of Diego Rivera* (New York: Cooper Square Press, 2000).

Gregory L. Schnurr

ROBESON, PAUL LEROY BUSTILL (1898–1976)

Paul Robeson—actor, singer, orator, athlete, and civil rights activist—was born in Princeton, New Jersey, to clergyman William Drew Robeson, a former escaped slave of Nigerian Ibo origin, and Maria Louisa Bustill Robeson, a descendant of African Bantus, Delaware Indians, and American Quakers. Robeson challenged discrimination early in life. He was the third African American to officially attend Rutgers College and graduated as valedictorian with numerous honors in 1919. He was the first Rutgers player to earn a place on Walter Camp's All-American football team in 1917–18, and he began to play professional football in 1920. After earning a law degree from Columbia University in 1923, Robeson left the profession to pursue a theatrical career and gained early experience with the experimental Provincetown Players. Robeson is noted for his many performances of *The Emperor Jones* and *Show Boat*, from which came one of his most beloved songs, "Ol' Man River." He also distinguished himself in feature films. A popular concert singer, Robeson and collaborator Lawrence Brown (1893–1972) began to include African American spirituals in their concert program in 1925, stressing the history and culture of African Americans to diverse audiences.

Robeson's career became overtly political in the 1930s. He performed with the Unity Theater and helped found the Council on African Affairs in 1937 and the Negro Playwrights Company in 1940, the same year he released the patriotic *Ballad for Americans*. In 1942 he abandoned film-acting to protest stereotypical casting and in 1944 performed the title role in a Broadway production of Shakespeare's *Othello* that broke racial barriers in casting. He received numerous awards, including a citation from the Secretary of the Treasury for "patriotic service" (1942), the Abraham Lincoln Medal (1943), the American Academy of Arts and Letters medal (1944), and the NAACP's Spingarn Medal (1945). But Robeson's criticism of American racism and his support of Soviet Marxism drew the investigation of the U.S. House Un-American Activities Committee and in 1950 the State Department revoked his passport, the same year he shared the International Peace Prize with **Pablo Picasso** (1881–1973). In 1952 Robeson was awarded the International Stalin Peace Prize. His passport was reinstated following a 1958 Supreme Court decision, and he returned to the international stage and the recognition of a new generation of civil rights activists. He was inducted into the College Football Hall of Fame in 1995.

In 1944 Robeson said "I consider art a social weapon," and his literary influences reflect his desire to combine art and politics (Duberman 1989, 273). His traditional education included rigorous study of the Bible, Latin, Greek, and Shakespeare. His legal training influenced his position on civil rights, and he frequently cited the Declaration of Independence and the United States Constitution. Literature of the African American historical and cultural experience inspired Robeson throughout his life. In his autobiography in *Here I Stand* (1958), Robeson often referred to Black writers and activists **Marcus Garvey** (1887–1940), Frederick Douglass (ca. 1817–95) and W.E.B. DuBois (1868–1963). Robeson's experience collaborating with and reading the works of prominent African American writers such as **Richard Wright** (1908–60) and reading publications that focused on race relations, including the NAACP's *The Crisis* (1910–), further contributed to his emphasis on African American culture and racial equality.

In the 1930s Robeson's interest in Marxism drew him toward works such as *Soviet Communism: A New Civilization?* (1935) by Sidney (1858–1947) and **Beatrice**

(1858–1943) **Webb.** He frequently read and contributed to leftist journals such as *Freedom* (1950–55). Finally, Robeson's dedication to learning about his own heritage led him to study African and other languages as well as philology. He combined this with sustained examination of international folk songs and scholarly literature on the folk tradition in order to develop his thesis that such songs revealed the unified struggles of oppressed people everywhere. His concert repertoire of spirituals, international folk songs, and works like William Blake's *The Little Black Boy* reflect Robeson's wide-ranging literary background.

Archives

Robeson Family Archives, Moorland-Spingarn Research Center, Howard University, Washington, D.C.
The Paul Robeson Collection (microform). Bethesda, Md.: University Publications of America, 1991.

Printed Sources

Boyle, Sheila Tully, and Andrew Bunie. *Paul Robeson: The Years of Promise and Achievement* (Amherst: The University of Massachusetts Press, 2001).
Duberman, Martin Bauml. *Paul Robeson: A Biography* (New York: Ballantine Books, 1989).
Foner, Philip S. (ed.). *Paul Robeson Speaks: Writings, Speeches, Interviews, 1918–1974* (New York: Citadel Press, 1978).
Robeson, Eslanda Goode. *Paul Robeson, Negro* (London: Victor Gollancz, Ltd., 1930).
Robeson, Paul. *Here I Stand* (New York: Othello Associates, 1958).
Robeson, Paul Jr. *The Undiscovered Paul Robeson: An Artist's Journey, 1898–1939* (New York: John Wiley & Sons, Inc., 2001).
Seton, Marie. *Paul Robeson* (London: Dobson Books, Ltd., 1958).

Jill Silos

ROBINSON, JACK ROOSEVELT (1919–1972)

Jackie Robinson was born near Cairo, Georgia. Mallie Robinson named her youngest child for former president Theodore Roosevelt who spoke out against peonage, or new slavery, in the rural South. It was also Mallie who moved her family of five children to Pasadena, California, in 1920. Growing up on Pepper Street in Pasadena, Robinson watched his mother build a life for her family at a time when Jim Crow laws permeated all aspects of American life. From his mother, Robinson learned about faith and God, lessons and practice that would both challenge and sustain him throughout the rest of his life and in particular during the early years of his baseball career. The young Robinson distinguished himself immediately on the playing fields in Pasadena and at UCLA. An early influence included the Reverend Karl Everette Downs, pastor of Mallie's Scott United Methodist Church, who brought the teenaged Robinson back to Christ, encouraged him to teach Sunday school, and reminded him that he had a responsibility to help people that went beyond sports. Following time in the U.S. Army, Robinson began his professional baseball career with the Kansas City Monarchs of the Negro Leagues. In August 1945 he met with Branch Rickey, president of the Los Angeles Dodgers, agreeing to become the first African American player in the Major Leagues. At that meeting, Rickey handed Robinson a copy of Giovanni Papini's *Life of Christ*. Rickey opened the book to the passage concerning turning the other cheek, exactly what Robinson would be asked to do as the first Black ballplayer in the major leagues. Writer

Roger Kahn knew Robinson during his playing days with the Dodgers and notes that though Robinson was bright, he was not bookish, enjoying the racetrack and cards, reading newspapers and *Life* magazine. In his seasons with the Dodgers, Robinson was honored with Rookie of the Year and National League Most Valued Player honors while helping the Dodgers to six pennants. In those years he also nurtured friendships with Edward R. Murrow and Ed Sullivan, bridge master Charles Goren, and writers Roger Kahn and Milton Gross. Though he read few books, it appears Robinson's passion for words come through in the letters and essays he began to write about social justice and civil rights. Robinson contributed the essay "Free Minds and Hearts at Work" to Murrow's 1952 volume *This I Believe: The Living Philosophies of One Hundred Thoughtful Men and Women in All Walks of Life*. In the years following baseball, Robinson used the recognition from his playing days to bridge the civil rights movement and mainstream society. One of his primary causes included lobbying for Black managers in baseball.

After baseball, Robinson found ways to position himself to strike a balance between sports and civil rights. His years at UCLA had given him an intellectual framework, and after baseball, Robinson began having regular conversations with Columbia University professor Franklin Williams, who was also the secretary-counsel of the West Coast branch of the National Association for the Advancement of Colored People (NAACP). Through those conversations and his own experience growing up in Jim Crow Pasadena and breaking baseball's color barrier, Robinson expanded his role as a voice for civil rights. Visible as a businessman and through various chairmanships for the NAACP and the Student Nonviolent Coordinating Committee (SNCC), Robinson also put many of his thoughts on paper. Not necessarily an avid reader, Robinson was a prolific writer, starting a magazine directed primarily at Blacks called *Our Sports*. Writers for the magazine included Robinson himself, as well as Roger Kahn and Joe Louis. In his tri-weekly sports column for the *New York Post*, Robinson wrote about events on the international stage in Cuba, Africa, Tibet, and Israel, as well as local domestic issues such as housing discrimination in New York, juvenile delinquency, and migrant workers, and about personalities such as Harry Belafonte, Howard Cosell, and Sidney Poitier. The young playwright William Branch was his ghostwriter. In his column, titled at various times "Jackie Robinson Says" and "Home Plate," for the New York Black weekly, *Amsterdam News*, Robinson and ghostwriter Alfred Duckett addressed politics and civil rights. Robinson's columns were aggressive and controversial, usually bringing in loads of reader mail to both the *Post* and the *Amsterdam News*. In his youth, Robinson found his outlet in sports. As an adult, Robinson found in sports a bridge to other causes. Putting his own voice alongside the voices of **Martin Luther King Jr.** and **Malcolm X,** and having public arguments on the pages of the *Amsterdam News* with Malcolm X, Robinson continued to challenge barriers and bring issues to the forefront of American consciousness.

Archives

Arthur Mann Papers, Library of Congress, Washington D.C.; Branch Rickey Papers, Library of Congress, Washington D.C.; Jackie Robinson Papers, Jackie Robinson Foundation, New York; Major League Baseball archives, New York; National Archives and Records Administration, College Park, Maryland (civil rights advocacy letters); National Association for the Advancement of Colored People Records, Library of Congress, Washington D.C.; Negro League Collection, National Baseball Library, Cooperstown,

New York; Our Sports archives, Library of Congress, Washington D.C.; Player Clipping Files, National Baseball Library, Cooperstown, New York.

Printed Sources

Rampersad, Arnold. *Jackie Robinson: A Biography* (New York: Alfred A. Knopf, 1997).

Robinson, Jackie, and Alfred Duckett. *I Never Had It Made* (New York: Fawcett, Crest, 1974).

Tygiel, Jules. *Baseball's Great Experiment: Jackie Robinson and His Legacy*, expanded ed. (New York: Oxford University Press, 1997).

——— (ed.). *The Jackie Robinson Reader: Perspectives on an American Hero* (New York: Dutton, 1997).

Devon Niebling

ROCKEFELLER, JOHN DAVISON SR. (1839–1937)

John D. Rockefeller was born in Richford, New York. He quit high school two months before graduation in 1855 and completed a three-month business college course in Cleveland. In 1857 he entered his first business partnership and in 1863 invested in the burgeoning petroleum industry. He married Laura Celestia "Cettie" Spelman in 1864; they had four daughters and one son, John D. Rockefeller Jr., his father's successor at the Standard Oil Company and the primary heir to the Rockefeller fortune. By 1865 Rockefeller Sr. was a partner in two oil refineries, and in 1870 he organized Standard Oil, of which he remained president until 1896. Key to Standard Oil's early success was Rockefeller's discovery that collusion with railroads and pipeline companies enabled him to form an airtight trust that eliminated competition. One of the first major trusts in the United States, Standard Oil controlled 90 percent of U.S.-refined oil by 1877 and for years encountered opposition to its aggressive business practices before being dissolved by the Supreme Court in 1911. The enormous wealth that Rockefeller accumulated through business enabled his generous philanthropy; he donated millions of private dollars to charities and helped to found such enduring institutions as the University of Chicago, Spelman College, Rockefeller University, and the Rockefeller Foundation. In 1939 Rockefeller died at his country home in Ormond Beach, Florida, at the age of 97.

In boyhood and adolescence, Rockefeller was a serious student interested primarily in principles of mathematics and investment and in current events and social issues. He attended small schools and is known to have studied from a book of compositions entitled *Parker's Aids*; he is likely also to have read *Cobb's Spelling Book* or the *English Reader* and various history and travel books. A more specific record of his literary influences does not exist, for Rockefeller himself "could not recall" having "read widely" in his youth (Nevins 1940, 46) and throughout his lifetime was not interested in music, art, literature, or philosophy. Rockefeller did read the Bible, Baptist periodicals, and the newspaper, all of which had a more lasting influence on him than did most of his schoolbooks. At church he formed lifelong habits of altruism and temperance as well as the belief that his ability to make money was a gift from God. While literature did not directly influence him, Rockefeller certainly captured the late-nineteenth-century American literary imagination and embodied the expansionist spirit of an era that Mark Twain named "The Gilded Age." To some Rockefeller exemplified author Horatio Alger Jr.'s vision of the independent, brave, and ambitious American hero (Chernow 1998, 48), and to others, as represented by Henry Demarest Lloyd's *Wealth against Commonwealth* (1894) and Ida Tarbell's *The History of the Standard Oil Company* (1904), Rockefeller was the symbol of the corruption and ruthlessness of the American capitalistic enterprise. The figure of "the American millionaire," inspired by the likes of Rockefeller, Andrew Carnegie, Andrew Mellon, and J. Pierpont Morgan, and the unstoppable forces of capitalism and social Darwinism are also featured in such fiction as Henry James's *The American* (1877), William Dean Howells's *The Rise of Silas Lapham* (1885), and Frank Norris's *The Octopus* (1901).

Archives

The Rockefeller Archive Center, Pocantico Hills, Sleepy Hollow, N.Y.: exhaustive collection; 30,000 cubic feet of documents; records of family-founded philanthropic and educational institutions; 500,000 photographs; 2,000 films.

Printed Sources

Chernow, Ron. *Titan: The Life of John D. Rockefeller, Sr.* (New York: Random House, 1998).
Nevins, Allan. *John D. Rockefeller: The Heroic Age of American Enterprise*, 2 vols. (New York: Charles Scribner's Sons, 1940).
———. *Study in Power: John D. Rockefeller, Industrialist and Philanthropist*, 2 vols. (New York: Charles Scribner's Sons, 1953).

Tiffany Aldrich

ROCKWELL, NORMAN (1894–1978)

Norman Rockwell was born in New York City and began studies at the New York School of Art in 1908. He pursued further studies at the National Academy of Design in 1910, and later at the Art Students League founded by noted American illustrator Howard Pyle. Rockwell's gift for figurative painting and illustration was recognized and nurtured by the academic George Bridgeman, who encouraged the young artist to utilize a traditional rather than a modernist approach in his work. Upon graduation, Rockwell accepted a position as art director for *Boy's Life*, the official magazine of the Boy Scouts of America. In 1915 he moved to New Rochelle and began work as a freelance illustrator for such magazines as *Life, Ladies' Home Journal*, and *Country Gentleman*. The following year he produced the first of over 300 covers for the *Saturday Evening Post*, garnering the attention and admiration of the magazine's publisher, George Lorimer. During the First World War, Rockwell had a short career painting insignia on warplanes and producing officer portraits at Queenstown, Ireland, before receiving an inaptitude discharge. He returned home to continue work for the *Saturday Evening Post* and to produce various advertising campaigns for companies such as Jell-O and Orange Crush. During the Second World War, Rockwell painted *The Four Freedoms*, four large panels based on **Franklin Delano Roosevelt**'s 1941 State of the Union Address that were used to encourage war bond sales. In 1947 Rockwell helped found the Famous Artists School in Westport, Connecticut, and for the next several decades was commissioned to produce the official portraits of such presidents as **Dwight D. Eisenhower, John F. Kennedy,** and **Richard Nixon.** In 1977 he was awarded the Presidential Medal of Freedom by President Gerald Ford.

The anti-intellectual style of Rockwell's art and his choice of nostalgic subject matter reflect to a large extent the artist's rather conventional literary influences. As a child, Rockwell was read the stories of Charles Dickens by his father and learned caricature drawing by imaginatively sketching figures such as Mr. Micawber from that author's *David Copperfield*. The young artist also read Horatio Alger's *The River Boys, From Canal Boy to President*, and *Phil, the Fiddler*, and began to produce illustrations to accompany these works in a style that reflected the regional settings of the novels. Rockwell was also an avid reader of Thomas Hardy and Mark Twain and would professionally illustrate the latter's *Huckleberry Finn* and *Tom Sawyer* while at the pinnacle of his career. The Rockwells were socially acquainted with many writers of their era, including **F. Scott Fitzgerald** and Dorothy Canfield Fisher, an author and editor of the Book of the Month Club. Fisher lived next to the Rockwell residence in Vermont during the 1940s and regularly supplied the couple with new pieces of literature to peruse. Rockwell was known to have a penchant for the work of American authors, such as Anita Loos's *Gentlemen Prefer Blondes*, and that of American historians, such as **Woodrow Wilson**'s comprehensive *A History of the American People*. Despite his interest in home-grown literature, Rockwell also enjoyed the work of the author Edgar Allan Poe, especially his *Tales of Mystery and Imagination*.

Archives

Archives of American Art, Smithsonian Institution, Washington, D.C., control no. DCAW209851-A.

University of Iowa Libraries, Special Collections Department, Iowa City, control no. IAUG92-A1613.

George Arents Research Library for Special Collections at Syracuse University, Manuscript Collections, Syracuse, N.Y., NXSV653-A.

Printed Sources

Rockwell, Norman. *My Adventures as an Illustrator* (New York: Harry N. Abrams, 1988).

Watson, Donald. *A Rockwell Portrait: An Intimate Biography* (Kansas City: Sheed, Andrews and McMeel Inc., 1978).

Gregory L. Schnurr

ROGERS, WILLIAM PENN ADAIR (1879–1935)

Will Rogers was born on the 60,000-acre ranch of his father, Clem Vann Rogers, one-eighth Cherokee, and his wife, Mary America, one-quarter Cherokee, between the Verdigris and Caney Rivers in Indian Territory, later the state of Oklahoma. When he was six his father sent him to Drumgoole School, a one-room log cabin, but he hated to be indoors and soon proved to be a terrible student. Next his father briefly tried him at Harrell International Institute in Muskogee and at Tahlequah Male Seminary, but Will did not succeed at either. Seeking more discipline for his boy, Clem enrolled him at Willie Halsell College in Vinita, where Will lasted four years. He was happier there and won a medal for declamation, but he was still not a good student. He was expelled after one term at Scarritt Collegiate Institute in Neosho, Missouri, because he refused to study, still preferred the outdoors, and spent every possible minute practicing rope tricks. He later claimed that after spending three years with William Holmes McGuffey's *Fourth Reader* he knew it better than McGuffey did. Annoyed and desperate, Clem sent Will to Kemper Military School in Boonville, Missouri, in 1896. Will learned Azel Storrs Lyman's *Historical Chart* and consistently scored near 100 percent in American history but was mediocre in most other subjects. His verbal skills were considerable, his memory was powerful, but his mathematical and quantitative abilities were limited.

After two years at Kemper, which seemed to him like "one in the guardhouse and one in the fourth grade," he dropped out of school at 18 and worked on W. P. Ewing's ranch in Higgins, Texas. He toured the nation and the world with several Wild West shows, doing rope tricks, and by 1904 he was a headliner. Gradually he moved toward vaudeville and, between his tricks, began talking to his audience, mostly about current events, soon acquiring his reputation as a gentle but insightful critic of contemporary politics and culture, "The Cowboy Philosopher." He summed up his life's reading in 1931: "I am fifty-two years old, sound of body, but weak of mind, and I never did read hardly any books. . . . But I do a lot of newspaper reading. . . . If they would just quit printing newspapers for about a year, I could get some books read . . . All educated people started in reading good books. Well I didn't. I seem to have gone from Frank Merriwell and Nick Carter . . . right to the *Congressional Record*, just one set of low fiction to another" (Ketchum 1973, 312-13).

Archives

Will Rogers Memorial Commission, Museum and Library, Claremore, Oklahoma.

Printed Sources

Alworth, E. Paul. *Will Rogers* (New York: Twayne, 1974).
Carter, Joseph H. *Never Met a Man I Didn't Like: The Life and Writings of Will Rogers* (New York: Avon, 1991).
Day, Donald. *Will Rogers: A Biography* (New York: McKay, 1962).
Hitch, Arthur Martin. *Will Rogers, Cadet: A Record of His Two Years as a Cadet at the Kemper Military School, Boonville, Missouri, Compiled from Letters from His Fellow Cadets and Interviews with Them and from School Records* (Boonville, Mo.: Kemper Military School, 1935).
Ketchum, Richard M. *Will Rogers: His Life and Times* (New York: American Heritage, 1973).
Milsten, David Randolph. *Will Rogers: The Cherokee Kid* (Tulsa, Oklahoma: Coman, 1993).
Robinson, Ray. *American Original: A Life of Will Rogers* (New York: Oxford University Press, 1996).
Rogers, Betty Blake. *Will Rogers: The Story of His Life Told by His Wife* (Garden City, New York: Garden City Publishing, 1943).
Rogers, Will. *The Autobiography of Will Rogers* (New Brunswick, New Jersey: Transaction, 1998).
Yagoda, Ben. *Will Rogers: A Biography* (Norman: University of Oklahoma Press, 2000).

Eric v.d. Luft

ROOSEVELT, ANNA ELEANOR (1884–1962)

Eleanor Roosevelt was born in New York City to an affluent yet troubled family. When Eleanor was 15 her grandmother, who was raising her at the time, enrolled her in a private boarding school in England named Allenswood. In 1905, she married **Franklin Delano Roosevelt,** her cousin. A shy, diffident woman, Eleanor blossomed into one of the most influential women of the twentieth century, who championed minority causes, wrote the Universal Declaration of

Human Rights, promoted liberal social policies on behalf of the Democratic Party, worked to further women's rights, and served for 12 years as first lady to the thirty-second president.

It is difficult to pinpoint specific literary influences in Roosevelt's life; however, when she was a young girl, books quelled her feelings of loneliness and alienation in a troubled family. Her mother was distant and uncaring; she labeled her daughter "Granny" (an epithet that shamed Eleanor greatly) because she considered her homely. In contrast, Eleanor's father doted on her; however, as an alcoholic, he behaved unreliably and erratically. He often called her "Little Nell," alluding to Charles Dickens's character described in *The Old Curiosity Shop* as "a child of beautiful purity and character." Tragedy hit the family early; by her tenth birthday, both of her parents and one brother had died. Consequently, Eleanor's maternal grandmother raised her, though from a sense of duty to the family more than love for the little girl. In *The Autobiography of Eleanor Roosevelt*, Eleanor recalls finding solace in the library, among Dickens, Scott, and Thackeray because she was "much alone" (Roosevelt 1961, 15). She also remembers that her grandmother would restrict her reading on Sundays to religious verses and hymns because Eleanor was required to teach Sunday school to the servants' children. On weekdays, she was allowed to read liberally in the family library; however, when she "asked difficult questions" about certain books, they would somehow disappear. She adds, "I remember this happened to Dickens' *Bleak House*. I spent days hunting for it" (Roosevelt 1961, 16).

During her schooling at Allenswood, Roosevelt also notes a love of books. In her autobiography, she recalls enthusiastically reading Dante and Shakespeare in a rigorous curriculum that also included French, German, Latin, history, music, and gym. Roosevelt flourished at Allenswood because the school matron, Marie Souvestre, adopted Eleanor and provided the love and guidance she so desperately sought. Daughter of the radical French philosopher Emil Souvestre, the schoolmistress passionately embraced causes of the dispossessed, such as Dreyfus in France and the Boers in South Africa. She also traveled throughout Europe with Roosevelt, emphasizing the need to "acquire languages," as Roosevelt writes, "because of the enjoyment you missed in a country when you were deaf and dumb" (Roosevelt 1961, 31). In the first volume of her autobiography, Roosevelt called the years at Allenswood "the happiest" of her life adding, "Whatever I have become since had its seeds in those three years of contact with a liberal mind and a strong personality" (Roosevelt 1961).

Roosevelt's accomplishments are innumerable. She is probably most known for serving as her husband's "legs and ears" when he was stricken with polio in 1921. Roosevelt traveled extensively for her husband and then reported to him, thus becoming a savvy, seasoned politician in her own right. Among her many causes were poverty-stricken coal miners in West Virginia, unemployed Black and white youth, as well as disenfranchised artists, writers, and musicians. Always an advocate for women, she led four important organizations: the League of Women Voters, the Women's Trade Union League, the Women's City Club, and the Women's Division of the New York State Democratic Committee. By the late 1940s, she was popularly called "First Lady of the World" because of her appointment to the United Nations by President **Harry S. Truman**. Serving on the UN Human Rights Commission, she crafted the renowned Declaration of

Human Rights, which the General Assembly enacted in 1948. Throughout her life, she was prolific: between 1933 and 1945, for example, she dictated 2,500 syndicated newspaper columns, wrote 299 magazine articles, and delivered more than 70 speeches a year (Ward 1999, 814). She also wrote several memoirs: *This is My Story* (1937), *This I Remember* (1949), *On My Own* (1959), and *Autobiography* (1961).

Archives

Eleanor Roosevelt Papers, Franklin D. Roosevelt Library, Hyde Park, New York.

Printed Sources

"Anna Eleanor Roosevelt." In *Notable American Women of the Modern Period: A Biographical Dictionary*, Barbara Sicherman and Carol H. Green (eds.), (Cambridge: Belknap Press of Harvard University Press, 1980), 595–601. Concise overview of Roosevelt's life.

Black, Ruby. *Eleanor Roosevelt: A Biography* (New York: Duell, Sloan, and Pearce, 1940).

Hareven, Tamara. *Eleanor Roosevelt: An American Conscience* (Chicago: Quadrangle Books, 1968).

Lash, Joseph. *Eleanor and Franklin: The Story of Their Relationship Based on Eleanor Roosevelt's Private Papers* (New York: W.W. Norton, 1971).

———. *Eleanor: The Years Alone* (New York: W.W. Norton, 1972).

Roosevelt, Eleanor. *The Autobiography of Eleanor Roosevelt* (New York: Harper, 1961).

Ward, Geoffrey C. "Eleanor Roosevelt." In John Garraty and Mark Carnes (gen. eds.), *American National Biography*, vol. 18 (New York: Oxford University Press, 1999). Concise overview of Eleanor's life.

Rosemary King

ROOSEVELT, FRANKLIN DELANO (1882–1945)

Franklin Roosevelt was born at Hyde Park, New York, to James Roosevelt, a well-to-do country gentleman, and his second wife, Sara Delano. Both parents traced their American lineage back well before the Revolution, and Franklin accepted unquestioningly his father's Episcopalian religion and Democratic political loyalties. In childhood Roosevelt traveled extensively with his parents in Europe, spending the summer of 1891 at a German school, and quickly acquired both the French and German languages. Initially educated by private governesses and tutors, in 1896 he entered the elite Groton School, graduating in 1900. Roosevelt attended Harvard College for four years, in 1903 obtaining a "gentleman's C" in his bachelor's degree, and half-heartedly took master's courses for another year before spending three years at Columbia Law School. Eager to emulate the political success of President **Theodore Roosevelt,** his wife Eleanor's uncle, in 1910 Roosevelt ran for the New York Senate, serving two terms. In 1913 President Woodrow Wilson appointed him assistant secretary of the navy, where he strongly supported American intervention in World War I, and in 1920 Roosevelt campaigned unsuccessfully as the Democratic vice-presidential nominee. Shortly afterward poliomyelitis left him partially paralyzed. In 1928 Roosevelt became governor of New York State, serving two terms before winning an unprecedented four terms as president. Between 1933 and his death in April 1945, Roosevelt substantially reshaped the United States. His 1930s New Deal programs, intended to combat the Great Depression, established a broad array of national welfare and labor legislation and economic regulatory agencies. From 1940 on, Roosevelt transformed U.S. foreign policy, steering the country into World War II and facilitating postwar American participation in multilateral institutions designed to promote international peace and stability.

Roosevelt's associates agreed that for information he relied on people rather than books (Freidel 1952, 32; Daniels 1955, 104). Even so, his wife recalled that he "always read a great deal, chiefly biography and history, but occasionally a detective story," and "had an amazing ability to skim through any kind of book and get everything out of it" (Roosevelt 1949, 117). An often solitary childhood, and later the restrictions disability imposed, encouraged Roosevelt to resort to books and his impressive stamp collection. The cherished only child of his father's second marriage, he received numerous beautifully produced American and European children's books. At an early age his mother read him such classics as *Little Men*, *Robinson Crusoe*, and *The Swiss Family Robinson*. Roosevelt also ranged freely in his parents' extensive library, favoring American military and naval history, science, and natural history, while knowing most standard British and American literary classics (Freidel 1952, 31–32). A solid but unexceptional Groton student, Roosevelt won the Latin Prize, a 40-volume set of Shakespeare. Roosevelt later appropriated his Groton headmaster's annual Christmas practice of reading Charles Dickens's *A Christmas Carol* aloud to his assembled family.

Roosevelt's absorption in extracurricular activities, as librarian of the Fly Club his junior year and editor of the *Harvard Crimson* and librarian of the Hasty Pudding Club his senior year, contributed to his undistinguished academic college record. At Harvard he also began to amass a notable personal library of naval history, supplemented constantly throughout his lifetime, especially on trips abroad, together with smaller collections on his native Hudson Valley, children's books, and miniature books (Freidel 1952, 59–60; Ward 1985, 237). A maritime enthusiast who owned a small sailing boat, the teenaged Roosevelt received copies of Alfred Thayer Mahan's *The Influence of Sea Power on History, 1660–1773* and *The Interest of America in Sea Power, Present and Future* (Harper 1994, 23–24). The anti-German Mahan, with whom Roosevelt as assistant secretary of the navy corresponded, forcefully supported American naval expansion, arguing that past American security had rested upon the British fleet, but the United States should now assume independent great-power status and acquire naval bases and colonies, albeit in partnership with Britain. Roosevelt subsequently read admiringly Homer Lea's *Day of the Saxon* (1913), which predicted a forthcoming death struggle between the Anglo-American Saxon and German Teutonic races (Harper 1994, 33; Freidel 1952, 232). Though extensive, Roosevelt's reading was somewhat unadventurous, essentially representing the conventional mental furniture of the contemporary American upper-class gentleman and giving little indication of his subsequent atypical dedication to extensive social reform. His lifelong interest in naval history and strategic writings anticipated Roosevelt's eventual support for American intervention in both world wars and activist United States international policies.

Archives

Franklin D. Roosevelt Presidential Library, Hyde Park, New York: repository for the Personal and Political Papers of Franklin D. Roosevelt, together with those of many family members and political and personal associates.

Printed Sources

Daniels, Jonathan. "Franklin Roosevelt and Books." In Jonathan Daniels, Arthur Bestor, and David C. Mearns, *Three Presidents and Their Books* (Urbana: University of Illinois Press, 1955).

Freidel, Frank. *Franklin D. Roosevelt: The Apprenticeship* (Boston: Little, Brown, 1952).

Harper, John Lamberton. *American Visions of Europe: Franklin D. Roosevelt, George F. Kennan, and Dean G. Acheson* (Cambridge: Cambridge University Press, 1994).

Roosevelt, Eleanor. *This I Remember* (New York: Harper and Brothers, 1949).

Ward, Geoffrey. *Before the Trumpet: Young Franklin Roosevelt, 1882–1905* (New York: Harper & Row, 1985).

Priscilla Roberts

ROSSELLINI, ROBERTO (1906–1977)

Born in Rome, Italy, on May 8, 1906, film director Roberto Rossellini had a happy and uncommon childhood. Raised in a Catholic milieu but without faith, Rossellini was a bad student at the Collegio Nazareno in Rome. Rossellini shot some minor movies between 1936 and 1943, but did not adopt neo-realism until *Open City* (*Roma città aperta*, 1945), a feature film that was shot in the ruins of Rome before the end of World War II. *Open City* went unnoticed at the Cannes Film Festival in 1946, but was acclaimed by an influential Parisian critic a few weeks later, sparking worldwide acclaim for the film. His next films would follow the same aesthetic trend: *Paisan* (1946) and *Germania Anno Zero* (1947). Rossellini adapted many books for his films, including Jean Cocteau's *La Voix humaine* in Paris for *L'Amore* (1948), Stefan Zweig's novel for the film *Fear* (1954), and Paul Claudel's oratorio, *Jeanne au bûcher* (1955). From 1965, Rossellini chose humanity's greatest men as his film subjects, using television instead of cinema in order to reach the masses. This biographical cycle is the last of his career: *La Prise de Pouvoir par Louis XIV* (1966), *Socrates* (1970), *Blaise Pascal* (1972), *Cartesius* (on René Descartes, 1974), and *Il Messiah* (1975).

Roberto Rossellini's father owned a fabric business, but he was also an intellectual who wrote books that Roberto reread many times through his life. Italian author Raul Maria De Angelis wrote in *Cinema* that Rossellini asked him in 1943 to show him how to write novels, not in **James Joyce**'s style, but rather in a **Dos Passos** fashion (Maria De Angelis 1990). In the postscript of Rossellini's autobiography, Italian journalist Stefano Roncoroni mentions that the two main literary influences on Rossellini were probably *De vita propria* by Jérôme Cardan and Saint Augustine's *Confessions* (Bellour 1990). But Rossellini didn't talk much about what he read; he preferred to say that he only read biographies and books about science. In an essay about media and education published the year of his death, Rossellini repeatedly quoted Karl Marx and Alexis de Tocqueville. In 1962, Rossellini defined himself as an Aristotelian. He also was interested in history and psychology. Roberto Rossellini didn't like American movies, although he admired Orson Welles's *Citizen Kane* and, above all, films by **D. W. Griffith** and German director F. W. Murnau (1888–1931). He hated sports.

Archives

Cineteca Nazionale, Rome. Manuscripts, correspondence.
RAI, Rome. Films, correspondence.

459

Istituto Luce, Rome. http://www.luce.it/index.html.

Institut national d'audiovisuel (INA), Paris. Inathèque. Films, correspondence.

Cinémathèque française, Paris. Copies of some rare films, including *Vanina Vanini* (1961).

The Menil Collection, Media Center, Rice University, Houston, Texas. Rossellini was teaching there in 1972; he recorded many hours of video, mainly about scientific experiments.

Printed Sources

Bellour, Raymond. "Le cinéma, au-delà." In Alain Bergala et Jean Narboni (eds.), *Roberto Rossellini* (Paris: Éditions de l'Étoile/Cahiers du cinéma/Cinémathèque française, 1990), 17.

De Angelis, Raul Maria. "Rossellinin romancer." In Alain Bergala et Jean Narboni (eds.), *Roberto Rossellini* (Paris: Éditions de l'Étoile/Cahiers du cinéma/Cinémathèque française, 1990), 17.

Gallagher, Tag. *The Adventures of Roberto Rossellini* (New York: Da Capo Press, 1998).

Maria de Angelis, Raul. In *Cinema* 29 (December 30, 1949).

Rossellini, Roberto. *Fragments d'une autobiographie* (Paris: Ramsay, 1987). Written in French in 1977; postscript by Stefano Roncoroni.

———. *Un esprit libre ne doit rien apprendre en esclave*, Paul Alexandre (trans.), (Paris: Fayard, 1977).

———. *My Method: Writings and Interviews*, Annapaola Cancogni (trans.), (New York: Marsilio Publishers, 1993).

Rossi, Patrizio. *Roberto Rossellini: A Guide to References and Resources* (Boston: G.K. Hall, 1988).

Yves Laberge

RUSHDIE, SALMAN (1947–)

The literary world first took notice of author and critic Salman Rushdie in 1981 when his second novel, *Midnight's Children*, took the prestigious Booker Prize. The work, a mix of magic realism, deft wordplay, and history, recreated the first 30 years of India's independence through its narrator, Saleem Sinai, one of the "midnight's children" born in the hour when India gained its independence in August 1947. In 1993 the novel gained the "Booker of Bookers," as the best work in the prize's history. Rushdie's next novel, however, brought him global attention. *The Satanic Verses*, a tale of south Asian migration to Britain that made reference to Islamic and Koranic motifs and figures, drew heavy criticism from some Muslims upon its publication in 1988. In early 1989 the ruler of Iran, the ayatollah Khomeini, pronounced a fatwa, or death sentence, on Rushdie for blasphemy and exhorted Muslims to carry out the decree. The author, then living in London, was forced into hiding for nearly a decade, protected by British police, in a sort of internal exile. He continued to publish, though, including reviews, novels, and a children's book. In 1998 the Iranian government lifted the fatwa formally, and Rushdie began to move again in public circles, living first in London and then New York, from where he continues to write and work. Rushdie is credited with having created, alongside authors like Anita Desai, a surge of interest in Indian writing in English in the last 20 years.

Rushdie has given many interviews over the past 20 years, some from secret locations during the period of the fatwa, and the subject of his literary influences has figured prominently in these conversations. Critics have also tried to pin down some of these same influences in an effort to describe Rushdie's imaginative and intellectually agile work. Born in Mumbai (Bombay) and educated at Rugby and

Cambridge, the Muslim Rushdie has cited a wide array of influences from literature to comic books to the wild worlds created by the "Bollywood" film industry of his birthplace. A voracious reader from his youth, Rushdie once related that some Muslims kiss holy books, but that he grew up kissing every book, from "dictionaries and atlases" to "Enid Blyton novels and Superman comics" (Rushdie 1991, 415). He credits both Indian mythology and such books as *The Arabian Nights* for some of the fantastical elements in his writing, and his fantastical use of language draws in some part on **James Joyce.** Rushdie once noted that he always traveled with a copy of *Ulysses* at hand.

Rushdie has consistently noted his most important influences, those that have fostered his own embrace of sweeping narratives told from multiple perspectives and filled with digressions and asides. Among these were Gunter Grass and Italo Calvino, but especially Nikolai Gogol, the Russian satirist, and Charles Dickens, both of whom, in Rushdie's opinion, possessed "that ability to be on the edge between the surreal and the real" (Reder 2000, 111). Rushdie has also acknowledged a great debt to two earlier authors known both for their satiric work and their inventiveness: Jonathan Swift and, especially, Laurence Sterne, whose *Tristram Shandy* was a revelation to Rushdie when he discovered it as an undergraduate. *Tristram Shandy*, with its nonlinear narrative, eccentric characters, and asides to the reader, must have, Rushdie once admitted, been at least an unconscious influence on *Midnight's Children*.

Beyond these varied literary and cultural influences, though, there remains Rushdie's own life, which has had an equally profound impact on his work. He has tackled the histories of both India and Pakistan, often in thinly veiled yet devastating portraits of figures such as Indira Gandhi, Benazir Bhutto, and Bal Thackeray. The narrator of *The Moor's Last Sigh*, a novel written while Rushdie was in hiding, is a condemned man himself, locked away in isolation. With a keen eye for the surreal aspects of what is often a very harsh reality, Rushdie has asserted a place among English literature's premier exponents, and there is little doubt that future writers, not just from India but from around the world, will soon be uttering his name when interviewers ask them to describe their own influences.

Archives

There are no archival sources currently available.

Printed Sources

Cundy, Catherine. *Salman Rushdie* (Manchester: Manchester University Press, 1997).

Goonetilleke, D. C. R. A. *Salman Rushdie* (London: Macmillan, 1998).

Reder, Michael (ed.). *Conversations with Salman Rushdie* (Jackson, Mississippi: University Press of Mississippi, 2000).

Rushdie, Salman. *Imaginary Homelands: Essays and Criticism, 1981–1991* (London: Granta Books, 1991).

Andrew Muldoon

RUSSELL, BERTRAND (1872–1970)

Bertrand Russell was born at Ravenscroft in Monmouthshire in western England. Since Russell came from one of the great Whig families, he grew up with a point of view that was both aristocratic and progressive. He matriculated to

Trinity College, Cambridge, to study mathematics but would serve as a fellow (1895–1901) and eventually lecturer in philosophy. Over the course of his long life and career Russell would be prolific, publishing more than 3,000 works; in addition, more than 40,000 of his letters survive. Russell's contributions can be divided into two areas; first, he made a significant contribution as an academic philosopher, with much of his energy devoted to understanding the relationships between mathematics and logic; second, his commitment to political causes and social questions meant that his career could be seen as a textbook example of that of a public intellectual.

At the heart of Russell's philosophical work lay a commitment to empiricism, which would first find expression in his deep interest in the foundations of mathematics. These ideas (with the help of Alfred North Whitehead) culminated in the publication of *Principles of Mathematics* (1903) and *Principia Mathematica* (1910–13). Russell rejected the earlier idealist position that what is known is conditioned by the knower, holding instead that logic provided adequate foundations for mathematics. This included developing a definition of number which would be consistent with logical expression. At the same time, Russell also postulated a theory of types (to overcome the contradiction between classes and members) and put forward a theory of definite descriptions. This theory was an attempt to provide a secure means to refer to nonexistent objects without being committed to believing in the reality of their existence.

At the same time, Russell was also interested in broader philosophical issues. In *The Problems of Philosophy* (1913), he attempted to address a more general line of inquiry. His distinction between knowledge based upon acquaintance and knowledge derived from description would become paradigmatic for some areas of twentieth-century philosophy. Later, he would respond to **Ludwig Wittgenstein**'s criticism of his work by creating a theory of logical atomism. At the core of this theory was the premise that the world is made up of atomic facts which can be successfully represented by elementary propositions. Finally, in the effort to provide a foundational basis for sense-data, Russell also developed an idea of neutral monism.

These achievements ensured that Russell would be remembered as a significant philosopher; his extensive involvement with social and political causes meant that his career would be regarded as one of Britain's major public intellectuals. Most prominent, however, was the loss of Russell's position at Trinity and his later imprisonment for his objections to the First World War. He also articulated a strong secular point of view with *Why I Am Not a Christian* (1927). Ultimately Russell became a spokesman in the 1950s and early 1960s for the Campaign for Nuclear Disarmament.

Russell's development was shaped by his encounter with several key writers. Reading Shelly proved to be very important for his self-understanding; studying Spinoza—through Sir Frederick Pollock's *Spinoza: His Life and Philosophy* (1880)—helped him develop a pantheistic view of the universe that was not Christian. Russell came of age prior to the Edwardian period, but like so many other early twentieth-century figures, he was responsive to ideas that challenged conventional attitudes. His social vision was shaped, then, by reading Turgenev's novels (especially *Fathers and Sons*), Ibsen's plays, and Whitman's *Leaves of Grass.*

Russell's growth and maturation as a philosopher came through knowing and interacting with some of the twentieth century's major analytic philosophers. Although Russell would later reject idealism, John McTaggart Ellis McTaggart was an early philosophical influence. Alfred North Whitehead, a fellow at Trinity College, developed and later coauthored *Principia Mathematica* with him. G. E. Moore's impact upon Russell is not easy to measure, but it is clear that the latter's "The Nature of Judgement" (1899) was significant. Finally, Russell's close and tortured relationship with Ludwig Wittgenstein ensured that he would receive harsh criticism, which ultimately pushed him to develop a theory of atomic factuality.

Friendships also played a formative role in the development of Russell's social thought and criticism. Most important, Russell's connection to the world of Bloomsbury meant that he lived and thought among **D. H. Lawrence, Aldous Huxley,** Leonard and **Virginia Woolf, John Maynard Keynes,** Clive Bell, **Lytton Strachey** and other significant minds. While it is difficult to determine the extent of any one of these figures' impact upon Russell, it is clear that collectively they helped to further his rejection of conservatism and conventional social values.

Archives

Russell Archives, McMaster University, Hamilton, Ontario.
Humanities Research Center, University of Texas, Austin, Texas.

Printed Sources

Monk, Roy. *Bertrand Russell: The Ghost of Madness 1921–1970* (New York: Free Press, 2000).
———. *Bertrand Russell: The Spirit of Solitude* (New York: Free Press, 1996).
Moorehead, Caroline. *Bertrand Russell. A Life* (London: Sinclaire-Stevenson, 1992).
Russell, Bertrand. *The Autobiography of Bertrand Russell 1872–1967*, 3 vols. (Boston: Little, Brown, 1967–69).
———. *The Collected Papers of Bertrand Russell* Kenneth Blackwell (ed.), (London: G. Allen and Unwin, 1983–94).
———. *The Collected Stories of Bertrand Russell*, Barry Feinberg (ed.), (London: G. Allen and Unwin, 1972).
———. *The Selected Letters of Bertrand Russell. Volume 1: The Private Years, 1884–1914*, Nicholas Griffin (ed.), (London: Routledge, 1992).
Ryan, Alan. *Bertrand Russell: A Political Life* (London: Allen Lane, 1988).

Stephen L. Keck

RUTH, GEORGE HERMAN (BABE) JR. (1895–1948)

George Herman Ruth was born in Baltimore, Maryland. He began his baseball career as a left-handed catcher at St. Mary's Industrial School, where his parents placed him at age seven. Under the direction of the Xaverian Catholic Brothers, Ruth received religious, academic, and vocational training. He finished his formal academic curriculum at age 14 and continued to study the trade of shirt-making. In 1914, at age 19, Ruth left St. Mary's to join the Baltimore Orioles, a minor-league baseball team. He became the team's youngest member and was appropriately nicknamed "Babe." Within five months, Ruth moved up to the major leagues and on his way to greatness. At the time of his death, he held 54 major-league records. There is no doubt that St. Mary's greatly influenced the young boy and the hero he became. He referred to his time at St. Mary's as the most constructive period of his life and was "as proud of it as any Harvard man is proud of his school" (Ruth and Considine 1948, 13). It was at St. Mary's that Ruth met Brother Matthias, whom he believed was the greatest man he ever knew. Marshall Smelser summarized the importance of Babe Ruth in American life. "No other person outside of public life so stirred our imaginations or so captured our affections" (Smelser 1975, 560). He might well be considered the sport's greatest celebrity and most enduring legend.

There is little written evidence of Ruth's literary influences. During his education at St. Mary's, daily readings from the Bible were one of his earliest exposures to the written word. St. Mary's had two libraries, scaled to the ages of the boys, who were encouraged to read each night in bed. There are unconfirmed reports that Ruth knew the Nick Carter detective stories and the Frank Merriwell boy athlete stories (Smelser 1975, 146). According to his adopted daughter Julia, "Babe didn't read much because he was afraid it would damage his eyes. As a result, mother read books and magazines to him" (Beim 1998, 36). Referring to *The Babe Ruth Book of Baseball*, his ghostwritten autobiography full of baseball tips for kids, Ruth said that it was the only book he'd ever read cover to cover (Wagenheim 1974, 175). During a 1929 interview in Florida, Carl Sandburg is said to have asked him what books he would recommend to young boys if they asked. He simply said that they never ask him that question, only how to play ball. Ruth kept close company with many sportswriters through his relationship with Christy Walsh, a syndicated agent, who arranged payment to Ruth for baseball commentaries used in sports columns. Perhaps the literary works having the most influence on Ruth as an adult were simply the daily newspapers or the thousands of letters he received from fans young and old. "It was the letters of the kids that really touched me" (Ruth and Considine 1948, 232).

Archives

National Baseball Library, A. Bartlett Giamatti Research Center, Cooperstown, New York: scrapbooks and official player files, photo files, published works.
Enoch Pratt Free Library, Baltimore, Maryland: St. Mary's Industrial School Annual Reports and additional loose material.

Printed Sources

Beim, George, with Julia Ruth Stevens. *Babe Ruth: A Daughter's Portrait* (Dallas, Texas: Taylor Publishing Company, 1998).
Ruth, Babe, and Bob Considine. *The Babe Ruth Story* (New York: American Book-Stratford Press, Inc., 1948).
Ruth, Claire, with Bill Slocum. *The Babe and I* (New Jersey: Prentice-Hall, Inc., 1959).
Smelser, Marshall. *The Life that Ruth Built* (New York: Quadrangle/The New York Times Book Co., 1975).
Wagenheim, Kal. *Babe Ruth: His Life and Legend* (New York: Praeger Publishers, 1974).

Deborah K. O'Brien

S

SAID, EDWARD W. (1935–2003)

Born in Jerusalem, this Palestinian-American writer and professor of English and comparative literature at New York's Columbia University, where he taught from 1963, had a broad influence in European art, literature, cinema, music, and history through the wider "postcolonial" critique that he helped engender. He attended schools in both Jerusalem and the Victoria College in Cairo, receiving his B.A. from Princeton and his M.A. and Ph.D. from Harvard University. He held prestigious professional posts including president of the Modern Language Association (1999) and member of the governing council of the PLO, the Palestine National Council (1977–91). Said is widely regarded by students of literature and cultural studies as one of the founders of the postcolonial movement in criticism and of multiculturalism in politics. Professor Said's intellectual sophistication, candid political opinions, and articulate nature have made him an important voice in a whole genre of twentieth-century literature by and about exiles, symbolizing the age of the refugee. Edward Said's *Orientalism* (1978), the founding text of what eventually was to become "postcolonial theory," argues that British and French academic scholarship had constructed the "Orient" as "Other," or the cultural politics of difference, the "subaltern" consciousness. British cultural studies began to explore the multiculturalism of its own society through a similar critique of the ways in which white racism had come to constitute blackness as "Other." In the more recent *Culture and Imperialism* (1993), Said espouses a philosophy of making connections, complementarity, and interdependence rather than separation and distinctiveness. *The New Circle*, an Arab-American magazine, named Professor Said "Arab-American of the Year 2000" for his scholarly and political contributions to society.

The literary influences on Edward Said span a variety of disciplines and English, French, American, and Greek scholars and writers from a variety of countries. Following **Antonio Gramsci,** cofounder of the Italian Communist Party and author of the monumental *Prison Notebooks*, he treats culture as an instrument of political control in the recurring images of the Other in his works. Said found Gramsci's thinking about fascism, Marxism, and cultural revolution still relevant to contemporary struggles trying to defeat a resurgent fascistic culture and build a totally new socialist world culture. Said was also influenced by literature, journalism, travel books, and religious and philosophical studies in the production of his broadly historical and anthropological perspective, especially in his most famous work, *Orientalism*. He holds culpable such authors as Joseph Conrad, Rudyard Kipling, Jane Austen, and Charles Dickens for depicting native peoples as marginally visible, a people without history. He analyzes the impact of English literature from *Jane Eyre*, *Vanity Fair*, Daniel Defoe's *Robinson Crusoe* and *Great Expectations* to Raymond William's *Culture and Society* on the shaping of unconscious imperialist attitudes. Fielding, Richardson, Smollett, and Sterne, to a lesser extent, also helped to support a relationship of domination and authority in English cultural forms, according to Said. Even the literary traditions of Shakespeare, Chaucer, Dante, and the ancient Greeks, such as Homer and Aeschylus *(The Persians)* impacted this distribution of geopolitical awareness that developed into aesthetic, scholarly, economic, sociological, historical, and philological discourses of political, cultural, intellectual, and moral power. For Said, Oriental studies is a composite area of scholarship comprising philology, linguistics, ethnography, and the interpretation of culture through the discovery, recovery, compilation, and translation of Oriental texts. Said espoused Marxist readings of canonical texts, linking varied disciplines to the political arena of gender, race, and class, as well as nation.

Archives

The Edward Said Archive (TESA), New York: Columbia University Libraries Collection. Articles, editorials, interviews, bibliographies, biographies.

The Edward Said Archive, Rhode Island: Brown University Library Collection. Biographies, bibliographies, theoretical relations, historical contexts, political discourse.

Printed Sources

Ashcroft, Bill, and Pal Ahluwalia. *Edward Said: The Paradox of Identity* (London and New York: Routledge, 1999).

Bové, Pail A. (ed.). *Edward Said and the Work of the Critic: Speaking Truth to Power* (Durham and London: Duke University Press, 2000).

Hart, William D. *Edward Said and the Religious Effects of Culture* (Cambridge and New York: Cambridge University Press, 2000).

Said, Edward. *Beginnings: Intention and Method*, reprint ed. (Baltimore: Johns Hopkins University Press, 1978). Won the first annual Lionel Trilling Award given at Columbia University.

———. *Culture and Imperialism*. The T. S. Eliot Lectures at the University of Kent 1985 (New York: Knopf/Random House, 1993).

———. *Joseph Conrad and the Fiction of Autobiography* (Cambridge, Mass.: Harvard University Press; London: Oxford University Press, 1966).

———. *Orientalism* (New York: Pantheon Books; London: Routledge & Kegan Paul; Toronto: Random House, 1978). Runner-up in the criticism category of the National Book Critics Circle Award.

———. *Out of Place: A Memoir* (New York: Knopf, 1999).

———. *Reflections on Exile and Other Essays* (Cambridge, Mass.: Harvard University Press, 2000).

———. "Spurious Scholarship and the Palestinian Question," *Race & Class* 29, 3 (Winter 1988), 23–39.

Varadharajan, Asha. *Exotic Parodies: Subjectivity in Adorno, Said, and Spivak* (Minneapolis: University of Minnesota Press, 1995).

Elena M. De Costa

SANDBURG, CARL AUGUST (1878–1967)

Carl Sandburg was born in Galesburg, Illinois. He studied at Lombard College in Galesburg (1898–1902) but did not receive a degree. Sandburg was not only a nationally renowned poet, but a biographer, folk singer, and lecturer. Sandburg is chiefly remembered as a voice of the disenfranchised and overlooked, a radical populist, and a Democrat. In his first widely acclaimed collections, *Chicago Poems* (1916), *Cornhuskers* (1918), and *Smoke and Steel* (1920), he used the vernacular of the common man and woman and the free-verse style of Walt Whitman to ruminate on the plight of the poor, celebrate the spirit of the masses, and depict the landscapes of the Midwest, from urban streets to rural fields. Sandburg, who often peppered his poetry with folk songs and political commentary, shifted to biography in 1926 with the two-volume *Abraham Lincoln: The Prairie Years*. A four-volume sequel on Lincoln, *The War Years*, received the Pulitzer Prize in 1939 and continued to bring Sandburg a wide audience. By the time his *Complete Poems* received the Pulitzer in 1950, he was one of America's most widely known and beloved poets. Though his critical reputation suffered somewhat after his death, Sandburg remains one of the best-known American poets and the quintessential poetic chronicler of America's geographic and spiritual heartland.

An early and seminal influence on Sandburg and his work was his professor at Lombard, Philip Green Wright, who paid for the publication of Sandburg's first collection of poetry, *Reckless Ecstasy* (1904). After Wright, Harriet Monroe, editor of *Poetry: A Magazine of Verse*, began to publish Sandburg's poems and to encourage him to write free-verse poetry with homely speech and subject matter, much like Sandburg's literary forbear Walt Whitman, on whom Sandburg gave many public lectures. Whitman's subject matter and robust persona greatly influenced Sandburg, shaping both his work and his performance. Harriet Monroe's assistance helped to launch Sandburg's career and make him a leader in Chicago's literary renaissance along with Sherwood Anderson, whom Sandburg deeply admired (Sandburg 1968, 260), and Edgar Lee Masters, with whom Sandburg enjoyed a long literary friendship. Masters credited Sandburg with much of the inspiration for *Spoon River Anthology*. Another member of the Chicago Renaissance, Theodore Dreiser, shared Sandburg's interest in the urban poor, if not the poet's optimism. Sandburg was also influenced by the Illinois poet Archibald MacLeish, whom he called a "major poet." Another seminal influence on his work was George Bernard Shaw, whom Sandburg described as "for the ages" and whose radical politics inspired Sandburg's own populist poetry (Sandburg 1968, 66). Like Harriet Monroe, poet Amy Lowell was a close friend of Sandburg's and worked hard to advance his art and reputation. Perhaps the most important personal and literary influence on Sandburg was Abraham Lincoln, who served not only as one of the poet's chief intellectual and biographical influences throughout his life, but as a metaphor for both America's tragedies and triumphs (Sandburg 1968, 398). It is his spirit, even more than Whitman's, that infuses the poetry, prose, and song of Carl Sandburg.

Archives

Carl Sandburg Collection, University of Illinois Library. Champaign-Urbana, Illinois: The major repository of Sandburg's papers.

Conemara, Carl Sandburg National Historic Site. Flat Rock, North Carolina: personal effects, manuscripts, correspondence.

Carl Sandburg Collection, Clifton Walter Barrett Library of American Literature, University of Virginia. Charlottesville, Virginia: original manuscripts and correspondence.

Printed Sources

Niven, Penelope. *Carl Sandburg: A Biography* (New York: Charles Scribner's Sons, 1991).

Sandburg, Carl. *The Letters of Carl Sandburg,* Herbert Mitgang (ed.), (New York: Harcourt Brace Jovanovich, 1968).

Todd R. Robinson

SANGER, MARGARET LOUISA HIGGINS (1879–1966)

"Maggie" Higgins was born in Corning, New York, the sixth of eleven children of a freethinking Irish immigrant, Michael Hennessy Higgins, and his traditional, submissive wife, Anne Purcell. After he engaged socialist atheist Robert Ingersoll to speak at a public meeting in Corning in 1894, the locally predominant Roman Catholic community boycotted the Higgins stonecutting business and ostracized the family. She continued to attend the local parish school at St. Mary's Church, enduring the taunts of her teachers and classmates until 1896, when, with financial help from her older sisters, she was able transfer to Claverack College and Hudson River Institute, a Protestant boarding school far from her detested Corning. For the first time in her life she had regular access to secular books. Corning had no public library. After graduating in 1900, she enrolled in the nursing program at the White Plains, New York, hospital, because she could not afford to study medicine. In 1902 she married Jewish architect William Sanger and was credentialed as a nurse. From 1910 to 1912 she was a nurse midwife to impoverished women on Manhattan's Lower East Side and in 1916 opened America's first birth control clinic. In 1920 she divorced Sanger and in 1922 married millionaire J. Noah H. Slee. In 1922 she founded the American Birth Control League and in 1923 the Birth Control Clinical Research Bureau. In 1939 the two merged into the Birth Control Federation of America, which, in 1942, against her wishes, changed its name to the Planned Parenthood Federation of America.

Her father read to his children from *Gulliver's Travels* and taught them phrenology, history, and popular pseudoscience. She never forgave him for sexually tyrannizing her mother, but she admired his leftist radical iconoclasm and adopted as her political and ideological heroes many of his own, such as **Eugene Debs,** Henry George, and Ingersoll. The Sangers were already involved with both the Socialist Party and the International Workers of the World when they moved to Manhattan in 1910. There they frequented Mabel Dodge's Salon, patronized the Francisco Ferrer Center, known as the "Modern School," and associated with such socialists and anarchists as Alexander Berkman, Theodore Dreiser, Will Durant, Max Eastman, Elizabeth Gurley Flynn, Emma Goldman, Bill Haywood, **Walter Lipp-**

mann, Jack London, **Eugene O'Neill,** Man Ray, John Reed, **Upton Sinclair,** Rose Pastor Stokes, Frank Tannenbaum, and Carlo Tresca. Through Goldman, she learned of Thomas Malthus. During this time she also became familiar with the feminist theories of Susan B. Anthony, Carrie Chapman Catt, Matilda Joslyn Gage, Ellen Key, Elizabeth Cady Stanton, and especially Charlotte Perkins Gilman. In England, she met Havelock Ellis in 1914 and **Marie Stopes** in 1915. Ellis became her mentor and introduced her to the writings of Olive Schreiner and Alice Stockham. After 1920, the socialists Ellis and Sanger conspired against the patrician eugenicist Stopes. Sanger's entire circle considered the theories of Sigmund Freud a major topic throughout the 1910s and 1920s.

Archives

In 1985 the New York University Department of History began "The Margaret Sanger Papers Project" (http://www.nyu.edu/projects/sanger/) to locate, catalog, edit, microfilm, and publish all her papers and correspondence. Smith College and the Library of Congress own the only two large collections. The remainder is scattered among hundreds of repositories and private owners.

Printed Sources

Chesler, Ellen. *Woman of Valor: Margaret Sanger and the Birth Control Movement in America* (New York: Simon and Schuster, 1992).

Coigney, Virginia. *Margaret Sanger: Rebel with a Cause* (Garden City, N.Y.: Doubleday, 1969).

Douglas, Emily Taft. *Margaret Sanger: Pioneer of the Future* (Garrett Park, Md.: Garrett Park Press, 1975).

Grant, George. *Killer Angel: A Short Biography of Planned Parenthood's Founder, Margaret Sanger* (Nashville: Highland, 2001).

Gray, Madeline. *Margaret Sanger: A Biography of the Champion of Birth Control* (New York: Marek, 1979).

Kennedy, David M. *Birth Control in America: The Career of Margaret Sanger* (New Haven: Yale University Press, 1970).

Lader, Lawrence. *The Margaret Sanger Story and the Fight for Birth Control* (Westport, Conn.: Greenwood Press, 1975).

Sanger, Margaret, *The Margaret Sanger Papers: Collected Documents Series*, Esther Katz, Cathy Moran Hajo, and Peter C. Engelman (eds.), (Bethesda, Md.: University Publications of America, 1996). 18 microfilm reels plus printed guide.

———. *The Margaret Sanger Papers: Documents from the Sophia Smith Collection and College Archives, Smith College*, Esther Katz, Peter Engelman, Cathy Moran Hajo, and Anke Voss Hubbard (eds.), (Bethesda, Md.: University Publications of America, 1994). 83 microfilm reels plus 526-page guide.

———. *The Papers of Margaret Sanger.* (Washington, D.C.: Library of Congress, 1976). 145 microfilm reels.

Eric v.d. Luft

SANTAYANA, GEORGE (1863–1952)

Born in Madrid to Josefina Sturgis and Augustin Ruiz de Santayana, George remained a Spanish citizen with a global influence. Santayana lived with his American relatives after the physical separation (not a divorce) of his parents. Returning to Boston, Josefina raised the children of her first marriage. In 1872, Santayana joined her. His parents' permanent separation affected Santayana, a retiring artistic boy. His early childhood experience of desertion contributed to his mature thought. Years later, in the first volume of his autobiography, *Persons and Places, The Background of My Life* (1944), he candidly and ironically examined how the circumstance of his birth and early years shaped his philosophy. Although never physically abused, Santayana cast a cold eye upon the world, and by temperament, by experience, and by reading widely he was always the outsider. He wrote essays and poetry. He painted and drew. Poets such as Horace, Racine, and others were a part of his reading. Spinoza was a major influence.

Santayana graduated from Boston Latin School and went on to study philosophy at Harvard and in Germany. He received his Ph.D. and taught at Harvard, where he had a small student following, from 1889 to 1912. **Walter Lippmann** claimed Santayana was essential to a sound education. Santayana influenced **T. S. Eliot**'s development as a poet. Wallace Stevens, **Robert Frost,** Samuel Eliot Morison, and Felix Frankfurter, among others, felt Santayana's influence. By 1912 an inheritance and his own economies allowed him to leave America. He never returned.

His unpleasant childhood experiences, his alienation from America, and possibly his being a repressed homosexual meant a critical distance between himself and the world. Three events led to his metanoia: the death of a young student, witnessing his father's death in 1883, and the marriage of his half-sister Susanna. The personal became the philosophical. "To possess things and persons is the only pure good to be got out of them; to possess them physically or legally is a burden and a snare." It was a naturalism without the Darwinian desires of conflict and conquest, expressing his reading in classical materialism. In *Three Philosophical Poets* (1910)—Lucretius, Dante, and Goethe—Santayana examined such a creed. His "The Genteel Tradition in American Philosophy" caught the spirit of his age as an ascetic dedicated to work and sexual repression while believing itself to be an acme of moral material progress. *The Last Puritan* (1936), a novel, analyzed the Boston of his youth. It was one of three books selected by the Book-of-the-Month Club.

Santayana was conservative, believing the Enlightenment had limits. Politics provided limited goods and services. Freedom (that is, order) was problematic in this naturalistic world for the mind had the same essence (*Dominations and Powers*, 1951). Never religious, *Scepticism and Animal Faith* (1923) demonstrated that humans sought the eternal despite the evidence that no such condition existed.

In 1941 he took shelter in the Clinica delle Piccola Compagna di Maria, governed by Roman Catholic nuns. Santayana died in 1952 and is buried in the Panteon de la Pia española located in Rome's Campo Verano cemetery.

Archives

The University of Texas, Harvard University, Columbia University, and the University of Waterloo (Canada) have major holdings of Santayana's manuscripts. The MIT Press will publish 20 volumes of a critical edition of Santayana writings.

Printed Sources

Butler, Richard. "Catholic Atheist," *Spirituality Today*, 38 (Winter 1986).

Flower, Elizabeth, and Murray G. Murphey. *A History of Philosophy in America*, 2 vols. (New York: G.P. Putnam's Sons, 1977). A basic source.

Kuklick, Bruce. *The Rise of American Philosophy, Cambridge, Massachusetts, 1860–1930* (New Haven: Yale University Press, 1977). Essential for historical context.

Levinson, Henry. *Santayana, Pragmatism, and the Spiritual Life* (Chapel Hill: University of North Carolina Press, 1992). Demonstrates Santayana's far-ranging influence.

Lyons, Richard C. (ed.). *Santayana on America: Essays, Notes and Letters on American Life, Literature, and Philosophy* (New York: Harcourt Brace, 1968). Explores Santayana's complex attitude toward the United States.

McCormick, John. *George Santayana: A Biography* (New York: Knopf, 1986).

Michelson, John Magnus "The Place of Buddhism in Santayana's Moral Philosophy," *Asian Philosophy* 5 (March 1995).

Saatkamp, Herman J. Jr., and John Jones. *George Santayana: A Bibliographical Checklist, 1890–1980* (Baltimore: The Johns Hopkins University Press, 1982).

Donald K. Pickens

SARTRE, JEAN-PAUL (1905–1980)

Jean-Paul Sartre was born in Paris, France. His childhood and his early intellectual formation are described in the autobiographical novel *Les Mots* (1964)/*The Words* (tr. 1964). He studied at the École Normale Supérieure, where he became friends with Raymond Aron and Paul Nizan, taught for a short time at the lycée du Havre, and then continued his studies in philosophy at the Institut Français in Berlin. In 1929, he took first place at the *Agrégation de philosophie*, and met **Simone de Beauvoir** shortly after, who, in spite of his numerous affairs, remained his lifelong companion. Sartre was taken prisoner by the Nazis in 1940, managed to escape, and was later involved in the Resistance. He confessed that his imprisonment was a turning-point in his life: from an individualist he was transformed into a "socialist" deeply concerned with the values of the community. After the war (1945), he founded together with Maurice Merleau-Ponty the periodical *Les Temps Modernes*. Sartre's political sympathies have always been communist, and his refusal to criticize the Stalinist trials contributed to his estrangement from his friend **Albert Camus,** which culminated in 1951 after the publication of Camus's *L'Homme révolté*. In 1958, Sartre was among those who realized that **de Gaulle**'s personality was dangerous for a "republican state," and 10 years later, he participated at the students' movement in Paris. When he was offered the Nobel Prize in literature in 1964, he declined. In 1973, he founded another important periodical, *Libération*.

The philosophers that most influenced Sartre's thought and who are at the basis of his existentialist philosophy are Edmund Husserl and **Martin Heidegger** and, to a lesser degree, Sigmund Freud and Karl Marx. According to Simone de Beauvoir, Sartre had been reading Heidegger (both in the original and in translation) since the late thirties. The Heideggerian concept of *Dasein* (which literally means in German "being there," and which was transformed by Heidegger into a philosophy of the openness of Being) inspired Sartre's vision of man as a Being-in-the-World. This idea, as well as the critique of the Western subject-object relation (also taken from Heidegger) has permeated many of Sartre's works, from *Being and Nothingness* (tr. 1953)/*L'Être et le néant* (1943) to the novel *Nausea* (tr. 1949)/*La Nausée* (1938). The latter, catalogued by literary critics as belonging to the "literature of the absurd," was also influenced by two other important figures in Sartre's intellectual formation: Friedrich Nietzsche and **Andre Gide.** The novel is reminiscent of the Nietzschean definition of subjectivity as self-production and of Gide's continuous regeneration of the self. As a whole, Sartre's philosophy is known as "existentialist," that is, a coherent system of thought founded on several principles: existence precedes essence, individual freedom is the source of all human values, man can become free through his choices and actions. From the phenomenology of Husserl, Sartre developed the idea that all consciousness is consciousness *of* something; therefore what man is, is revealed in his acts. Echoes of this philosophy are present in many of Sartre's plays, which usually present a hero confronted with a *situation-limite*—an event which forces him to act in an *authentic* way. Some of Sartre's most famous plays are: *Les mouches* (1943), *Huis clos* (1945), *La putain respectueuse* (1946), *Les Mains sales* (1948), *Le diable et le bon dieu* (1951).

As a writer of fiction (novels, short-stories, plays), Sartre expressed his views on literature in his critical essays on Flaubert (*L'Idiot de la famille*, 1972), Baudelaire (*Baudelaire*, 1947, tr. 1950), Genet (*Saint Genet, Actor and Martyr*, tr. 1963/*Saint Genet, comédien et martyr*, 1952), and, more specifically in *What Is Literature?* (tr. 1966)/*Qu'est-ce que la littérature?* (1947). His view on literature is based on the premise that language in poetry and language in prose are essentially different. This distinction comes from Stephane Mallarmé and has informed an aesthetic ideal (which is also that of Heidegger) according to which all true literature is written in poetic language. Sartre, however, uses the distinction in order to prove that prose should be a vehicle for moral principles, or, in other words, it should be *engagé*. This view is complemented by an opposite idea, namely that art, "of its essence, is opposed to that which exists," and, as such, art has as its own and only goal freedom itself. These two views of art and literature are often confounded in Sartre.

Archives

Bibliothèque Nationale de France, Paris, France: Miscellaneous correspondence and draft manuscripts.

Printed Sources

Goldthorpe, Rhiannon. *Sartre: Literature and Theory* (Cambridge: Cambridge University Press, 1984).

Halpern, Joseph. *Critical Fictions. The Literary Criticism of Jean-Paul Sartre* (New Haven and London: Yale University Press, 1976).

Hollier, Denis. *The Politics of Prose* (Minneapolis: University of Minnesota Press, 1986).

———. *Politique de la prose* (Paris: Gallimard, 1982).

Jameson, Fredric. *Sartre: The Origins of a Style* (New Haven: Yale University Press, 1961).

Jeanson, Francis. *Sartre par lui-même* (Paris: Seuil, 1969).

Kern, Edith (ed.). *Sartre. A Collection of Critical Essays* (Englewood Cliffs, N.J.: Prentice Hall, 1962).

Lévy, Bernard-Henri. *Le siècle de Sartre* (Paris: Grasset, 2000).

Lilar, Suzanne. *À propos de Sartre et de l'amour* (Paris: Grasset, 1967).

Daniela Hurezanu

SCHÖNBERG, ARNOLD (1874–1951)

Arnold Schönberg was born in Vienna, the son of a Jewish salesman and of Pauline Nachod, who taught him his first musical notions. As a result of his father's death he was forced to leave school when he was 15, but he continued his musical study as an autodidact: he wrote to a friend that his teachers had been primarily Bach and Mozart and secondarily Beethoven, Brahms, and Wagner. The influence of Richard Wagner and of Gustav Mahler is evident in his first important compositions: *Transfigured Night* (1899) and the *Songs of Gurre* (1899–1901). In these works Schönberg clearly shows he has moved beyond the post-romantic harmonic tradition toward expressionist music, as in *Pelleas and Melisande* op. 5 (1902–3) and in the *Kammersymphonie* op. 9 (1906).

The first years of the century were particularly important for the development of his musical theory: his association with the artists of the *Blaue Reiter*, such as Franz Marc and **Vassily Kandinsky,** led to the publishing of a fundamental essay, "The relationship to the text" (1911–12). Schönberg developed in this article the aesthetic and ethical principles of expressionism. The theory found a practical application in the *Lieder op. 15* (1908), after some verses by Stefan George, and in the *Pierrot Lunaire op. 21* (1912), one of Schönberg's most famous compositions and the actual manifest of musical expressionism. Starting from 1904 the composer had gathered around him a group of disciples, among whom were Alban Berg and Anton Webern: the results of those years of theoretical meditations and teaching activity are contained in *The Manual of Harmony* (1911), a very strong criticism of the traditional teaching being done in music academies. In this work Schönberg explains the concepts of atonality and of *Klangfarbe Melodie*, looking to social commitment and religion for new themes allowing him to create a new poetic that was evident in *Die Jakobsleiter* (1912), inspired by Swedenborg, and *Die Satiren* op. 28 (1925).With the accession to power of **Adolf Hitler,** Schönberg fled to France and then took refuge in the United States, where he decided to abjure the Catholic faith and to convert to Judaism as a protest against Nazism. To this period belong the compositions *Moses and Aron* (1946) and *Survivor from Warsaw* op. 46 (1947), *Fantasy* op. 47 (1949), *De Profundis* op. 50 b (1950) and *Dreimal Tousend Jahre* op. 50 (1949). Arnold Schönberg died in Los Angeles in 1951.

From the point of view of the musical language, Schönberg has gone along the most radical and progressive path of postromanticism, from the negation of tonality to atonality and finally to the development of dodecaphony. This last puts all the twelve notes of the chromatic scale on the same level, all of them being fundamental for the composition and not in a hierarchical rank as in traditional harmony.

Both the musical and the theoretical heritages of Arnold Schönberg were gathered by his disciples Berg and Webern and, partially, by **Igor Stravinsky. Thomas Mann** was inspired by Schönberg's theories in his depiction of the composer Adrian Leverkuhn in *Doctor Faustus*. Relevant evidence of Schönberg influences can be seen in the musical aesthetics of Theodor Wiesengrund Adorno, and in the works of John Cage and of Karlheinz Stockhausen.

Archives

Arnold Schönberg Center, Vienna: Music manuscripts, text manuscripts, paintings and drawings, correspondence.
Library of Congress, Washington, D.C.: Correspondence to and from Arnold Schönberg.

Printed Sources

Milstein, Silvina. *Arnold Schönberg. Notes, Sets, Forms* (Cambridge: Cambridge University Press, 1992).

Rosen, Charles. *Arnold Schönberg* (Princeton, N.J.: Princeton University Press, 1981).

Schönberg, Arnold. *Coherence, Counterpoint, Instrumentation, Instruction in Form* (Lincoln and London: University of Nebraska Press, 1994).

———. *The Musical Idea and the Logic, Technique and Art of Its Presentation* (New York: Columbia University Press, 1993).

Maria Tabaglio

SCHUMAN, JEAN-BAPTIST NICOLAS ROBERT (1886–1963)

Robert Schuman was born in Luxembourg, the son of an originally French Lorrainer, Jean-Pierre Schuman, half-Luxembourgeois by birth, a prosperous *rentier* who chose to take German nationality in 1872 after France ceded Alsace-Lorraine to Germany, and his Luxembourgeoise wife, Eugénie Duren. Schuman grew up in Luxembourg, speaking Luxembourgeois, French, and German fluently, and attending the academically rigorous Atheneum of the Grand Duchy of Luxembourg, where he also learned Greek, Latin, and English and became known as a brilliant student. Schuman, then aged seventeen, chose to study law in German-speaking Lorraine at the Universities of Bonn, Berlin, and Munich, where he again excelled, and in 1910 he began to practice law in Metz. During the First World War he fought in the German army, and when Germany's defeat returned Alsace-Lorraine to France, Schuman remained in Metz, specializing in German legal problems, especially those arising from the region's repeated transfers. In 1919 Schuman, a devout Catholic and committed Democrat, joined the Catholic Popular Democratic Party and won election to the French chamber of deputies, remaining there for 40 years. When Germany invaded France in 1940, he refused to join Marshal Pétain's collaborationist Vichy government, but returned to Alsace-Lorraine, where his public condemnation of German expulsions of French residents soon caused his arrest. Escaping the Gestapo, Schuman participated in wartime resistance propaganda efforts, helping to found the Popular Republican Movement, France's Christian Democratic Party. As French governments rapidly succeeded each other after liberation in 1944, Schuman became France's finance minister (1945–47), premier for seven months (1947–48), foreign minister (1948–52), and justice minister (1955–58). Working closely with **Jean Monnet,** in 1950 Schuman was instrumental in creating the European Coal and Steel Community (ECSC), the foundation of the future European Union, which integrated key sectors of the French, German, Italian, and Benelux economies, thereby greatly reducing the possibility of future European hostilities. In 1958 he became the first ECSC and European Economic Community president.

Known for his intellectual brilliance, in high school Schuman excelled in Latin, history, and mathematics (Lejeune 2000, 31) and at university studied both philosophy and law, preferring the civil law's careful detail to broad legal theory (Pennera 1985, 29). A somewhat austere bachelor and, like his parents, a lifelong devout Roman Catholic, in 1904 Schuman joined the ultra-Catholic student organization "Unitas," and became a leading Catholic layman, deeply versed in religious literature, whose pronounced social conscience and commitment to democracy made him a prominent founder of France's Christian Democrat political movement. During his wartime refuge in assorted monasteries, orphanages, and churches, Schuman read extensively in theology, including the works of St.

John of the Cross and Thomas Aquinas, history from the Roman Empire onward, and current political affairs (Lejeune 2000, 118–19). Schuman's borderland heritage, liberal Catholicism, and democratic outlook all guided his dedicated efforts to accomplish West European reconciliation and prevent further devastating wars.

Archives

Papers of Robert Schuman. Archives of the French Foreign Ministry, Paris, France. Official correspondence and papers.

Papers of Robert Schuman. Series 34J, Departmental Archives of Metz, France. Official correspondence and papers as deputy for Metz.

For security reasons many of Schuman's pre-1940 personal and official papers were destroyed.

Printed Sources

Lejeune, René. *Robert Schuman: Pére de l'Europe 1886–1963: La politique, chemin de sainteté* (Paris: Fayard, 2000).

Pennera, Christian. *Robert Schuman: La jeunesse et les débuts politiques d'un grand européen, de 1886 à 1924* (Sarreguemines: Éditions Pierron, 1985).

Poidevin, Raymond. *Robert Schuman: Homme d'État, 1886–1963* (Paris: Imprimerie Nationale, 1986). Fullest biography.

Rochefort, Robert. *Robert Schuman* (Paris: Cerf, 1968).

Priscilla Roberts

SEUSS, DR. (1904–1991)

Born Theodore Seuss Geisel in Springfield, Massachusetts, he attended Dartmouth College, where he edited the school's humor magazine and graduated in 1925. He pursued a Ph.D. in English literature at Oxford University from 1925 to 1927, where he met and married Helen Palmer. He lost interest in his studies, dropped out of Oxford, and returned to America, where he began publishing cartoons and humorous articles for magazines such as *Judge, Life, Vanity Fair,* and *Liberty.* He first attained national exposure as the ad illustrator for the pesticide Flit. In 1937, he published *And to Think That I Saw It on Mulberry Street,* his first children's book, set in rhyme. During World War II, he served as a documentary writer for the U.S. Army and won an Academy Award for his short animated work, *Gerald McBoing-Boing.* In 1954, a critical story in *Life* magazine by American novelist John Hersey suggested illiteracy rates among children were caused by their boring textbooks. In response, Geisel and his Houghton Mifflin editor compiled and narrowed a list of important words children should know, and 225 of them formed the principle vocabulary of *The Cat in the Hat.* The tremendous success of the book led Geisel to write and illustrate over 44 children's books including *How the Grinch Stole Christmas* (1957), *Green Eggs and Ham* (1960), and *Horton Hatches an Egg* (1966). In 1984, he received the Pulitzer Prize, and he eventually accumulated a Peabody, two Emmy Awards, and three Academy Awards. He continued to write and illustrate children's books until his death in 1991.

In high school, Geisel came under the influence of Edwin A. "Red" Smith, an English teacher, who introduced him to the works of Hilaire Belloc, two of which in particular—*The Bad Child's Book of Beasts* and *Cautionary Tales*—stimulated Geisel's interest in rhyme, and he attributes the bulk of his artistic style to Belloc's influence.

Though he was exposed to the major British authors at Oxford (Geoffrey Chaucer, William Shakespeare, John Milton, William Wordsworth, and John Keats, among others), their influence is more ephemeral. His notebooks from the Oxford period (1925–27) do portray occasional scenes illustrating literary episodes in a whimsical proto-Seussian style. He did find Jonathan Swift's satire, *Gullivar's Travels*, particularly enjoyable, and Swiftian stylistic elements are evident in his later writing, such as *The Lorax* (1971). While traveling in Europe in mid-1926, he read **Lytton Strachey**'s biography, *Queen Victoria* (1921), and C. Grant Robertson's *Bismarck* (1918). He even thought of translating Emile Ludwig's *Napoleon* (1926), but he quickly abandoned the attempt. Indeed, in 1926 he lost interest in any systematic study of literature, which coincides with his departure from Oxford. The remainder of his life exhibits the topical reading he engaged in typically dealing with historical and cultural events of the moment, which eventually filtered into his work.

Archives

Mandeville Special Collections Library, University of California, San Diego, California. Principle repository: contains original drawings, sketches, proofs, notebooks, manuscript drafts, books, audio- and videotapes, photographs, and memorabilia spanning 1919–91.

Printed Sources

Morgan, Judith, and Neil. *Dr. Seuss and Mr. Geisel: A Biography* (New York: Da Capo Press, 1996).

Weidt, Maryann N. *Oh, the Places He Went: A Story about Dr. Seuss–Theodore Seuss Geisel* (New York: First Avenue Editions, 1995).

Joseph E. Becker

SHOLOKHOV, MIKHAIL ALEKSANDROVICH (1905–1984)

Mikhail Sholokhov, the only Soviet establishment writer to receive the Nobel Prize (1965), was born in Russia's Don Cossack Military Region to lower-class merchants with roots as gunners in service to Peter the Great (1715) and serfs in Ukraine's Chernihiv area. Sholokhov grew up amid widespread illiteracy and was heavily influenced by the oral culture and traditions of the Don Cossacks. His father collected a classical library and hired a teacher to teach him to read, later sending him to Moscow's Grigorii Shelaputin School and Boguchar Gymnasium (1914–18). Sholokhov's early readings included Nikolay Gogol's *Evenings on a Farm near Dikanka* and *Taras Bulba*, Aleksandr Pushkin's *Eugene Onegin*, and stories by Lev Tolstoy. In Boguchar, in the home of the teacher-priest Dmitri Tishansky, where he boarded, Sholokhov heard discussions about Maxim Gorky, Aleksandr Értle, Aleksandr Kuprin, Vladimir Korolenko, and Ivan Bunin. Additionally he read works by Mikhail Lermontov, Fyodor Tyuchev, and Nikolay Nekrasov, and he tried his hand at writing poetry, fiction, and comical plays based on Gogol. Later he also had access to the works of Immanuel Kant, Arthur Schopenhauer, Friedrich Nietzsche, Søren Kierkegaard, Baruch Spinoza, Friedrich Hegel, and Karl Marx.

Civil war (1918) ended Sholokhov's formal education and forced the 14-year-old to make life-defining decisions. During the War, Sholokhov joined the Bolsheviks, becoming a tax collector. At the same time he took part in a theatrical group that performed comedies by Denis Fonvizin, Gogol, Nikolay Ostrovsky, and Anton Chekhov, secretly composing farcical plays and recording his horrific, formative war experiences in autobiographical short stories.

In postwar Moscow (1923), Sholokhov joined the proletarian group "Young Guard" and briefly participated in seminars led by the Formalists Viktor Shklovskii and Osip Brik. He married at age 18 and had four children. In 1925, he met his mentor, the Cossack writer Alexander Serafimovich, who introduced his *Tales of the Don* (1926), critiqued his works, and recommended publication of his controversial epic, *And Quiet Flows the Don*. Later he was befriended by Gorky, whose intervention with **Josef Stalin** facilitated publication of book three of his epic.

Sholokhov always described himself first as a communist. He joined the Party in 1932 and took part in the formation of the Writers Union (1934), serving on its board from 1934 to 1984. He promoted socialist realism and spoke out against literary modernism and writers who resisted the Party line. Although his loyalty was questioned, he survived the purges and became a member of the Supreme Soviet (1936), a delegate to Party Congresses (1936–84), and a member of the Presidium (1966–81), the Soviet Academy of Sciences (1939), and the Central Committee (1961). His early autobiographical works were influenced by Gogol and Chekhov. His epic novel additionally shows traces of Tolstoy's novels *War and Peace* and *The Cossacks;* Slavic folklore, especially the medieval epics *Zadonshchina* and *The Song of Igor's Campaign;* and historical sources. Gorky and Socialist realism influenced Sholokhov's collectivization novel *Virgin Soil Upturned.*

Archives

Sholokhov's papers remain uncollected. Moscow's State Publishing House (GIXL), the Gorky Institute of World Literature (IMLI), the Russian State Archive of Literature and Art (RGALI), and the Russian Institute of Literature and Art (IRLI), St. Petersburg, hold some papers.

Printed Sources

Abramov, Fedor, and Viktor Gura. *M. A. Sholokhov: seminarii* (Leningrad: Gosudarstvennoe uchebno-pedagogicheskoe izdatel'stvo, 1962).

Ermolaev, Herman. *Mikhail Sholokhov and His Art* (Princeton: Princeton University Press, 1982).

Klimenko, Michael. *The World of Young Sholokhov* (North Quincy, Mass.: The Christopher Publishing House, 1972).

Medvedev, Roy A. *Problems in the Literary Biography of Mikhail Sholokhov* (New York: Cambridge University Press, 1977).

Petelin, Viktor, and Vladimir Vasil'ev (eds.). *Sholokhov na izlome vremeni* (Moscow: Nasledie, 1995).

Sholokhov, Mikhail Aleksandrovich. *Collected Works* (Moscow: Raduga Publishers, 1984).

———. *Sobranie sochinenii v vos'mi tomakh* (Moscow: Khudozhestvennaia literatura, 1985–86).

Shtavdaker, L. A. *Mikhail Aleksandrovich Sholokhov: Bibliograficheskii ukazatel'* (Rostov-na-Donu: Rostovskoe knizhnoe izdatel'stvo, 1980).

Stewart, David. *Mikhail Sholokhov: A Critical Introduction* (Ann Arbor: The University of Michigan Press, 1967).

Yakimenko, Lev. *Sholokhov: A Critical Appreciation* (Moscow: Progress Publishers, 1973).

Ludmilla L. Litus

SHOSTAKOVICH, DMITRI DIMITRIEVICH (1906–1975)

Dmitri Shostakovich was born in St. Petersburg. From 1919 to 1925 he studied at the Leningrad Conservatory. The Soviet government invested in this talented composer and sent him in 1927 on a trip to Berlin for the First Symphony's premiere under Bruno Walter. In 1928 Shostakovich worked as pianist and dramaturge at the Meyerhold Theater in Moscow. At this time he also composed music for some Soviet films. The most innovative of Shostakovich's early works was the opera *Lady MacBeth of Mtsensk* (1932) performed in the next years in New York, Cleveland, Philadelphia, Buenos Aires, and Prague. The newspaper *Pravda* defamed him as a lackey of capitalism and bourgeois society. In 1941 during the Nazi invasion of the Soviet Union, Shostakovich composed his monumental Seventh ("Leningrad") Symphony. After the war, Shostakovich had been elected chairman of the Leningrad Composer's Union and the Supreme Soviet of the Russian Republic before he fell into disgrace. A Central Committee Resolution condemned him for decadent Western tendencies in his music. Nevertheless, in 1949 **Josef Stalin** allowed him to visit the United States. However, in the cultural thaw after Stalin's death Shostakovich became the undisputed head of Soviet composers. In the 1960s Shostakovich's works that had been condemned in the 1930s and 1940s saw their revival. After Shostakovich had a severe heart attack, his late compositions such as the *Fifteenth Symphony* (1971) were more pessimistic and focused on the theme of death. On August 9, 1975, Shostakovich died of heart disease at the Kremlin hospital in Moscow.

Like his contemporary **Sergei Prokofiev**, Shostakovich was deeply influenced by Shakespeare's *Macbeth*, *Hamlet*, and *King Lear*, which he set to music in the 1930s and 1940s for the Soviet theater. Together with Prokofiev, Shostakovich stood for experimentalism in Soviet music and he found Shakespeare's masterpieces a breeding ground for his own creative work. In the U.S.S.R., Shostakovich set the formative tone of Soviet music and it stood for the East–West symbiosis. This, however, evoked sharp criticism by Soviet propaganda. Stalin found that Shostakovich's compositions smacked of Western vulgarism. In the 1960s Shostakovich composed the music for the film *Hamlet* after the translation by **Boris Pasternak.**

Archives

Rossiiskii Gosudarstvennyi Arkhiv Literatury I Iskusstva (Russian State Archive of Literature and Arts), Moscow.

Printed Sources

Norris, Christopher (ed.). *Shostakovich. The Man and His Music* (London: Lawrence and Wishart, 1982).

Roseberry, Eric. *Shostakovich. His Life and Times* (New York: Midas Hippocrene, 1982).

Shostakovich, Dmitrii D. *O vremeni I o sebe (About Himself and His Times)* (Moskva: Sovetskij Kompozitor, 1976).

Eva-Maria Stolberg

SILONE, IGNAZIO (1900–1978)

Ignazio Silone was the pseudonym of Secondo Tranquilli. He was marked as a social activist more by his early years in Pescina dei Marsi, Italy, than by his readings in world literature. His lifelong devotion to the cafoni (impoverished farmers) made him a rebel, first in politics and later in literature. After the premature deaths of five of six siblings and then his father in 1911, in January 1915 he witnessed the Marsica earthquake that killed his mother, followed by looting and murder among his extended family. His brother Romolo would be tortured to death by the Fascists. Silone's political activism dates from the earthquake at age 15. He became a Socialist and then a Communist in 1921 at the founding of the Italian party, remaining a member until his official expulsion in 1931. For his editorial and other political activities he fled Italy and Germany, then was expelled from Spain, France, and even Switzerland, though he finally settled in Davos. Disillusioned by "red Fascism," he launched his literary production with *Fontamara* (first in German translation in 1933, revised 1953), denouncing Fascist exploitation in his small Abruzzi village. In his subsequent fiction, drama, and essays he sought to reconcile Christianity and politics through social realism and ethical idealism around the abstract struggle for justice to the humble and oppressed. *Bread and Wine* (1937, in German), revised as *Wine and Bread* (1955), brings anti-Fascist Pietro Spina home, much as Silone returned at the end of the European war. While commanding respect in Italy for his quasi-Christian socialist politics, he was until recently more admired abroad for his writing. In 1944 he married Irish student Darina Elizabeth Laracy, who translated some of his works and edited the posthumous *Severina*.

With *Emergency Exit* Silone analyzes his experiences in essays that together constitute a spiritual autobiography incorporating his contribution to Crossman's collection of memoirs by lapsed Communists. After his primary and secondary schooling in private Catholic institutions, poor health and political activism had left him no time for university. A "silent and meditative" boy, Silone read Phaedrus's *Fables* at six. At 17 he read Lev Tolstoy and Maxim Gorky to Abruzzi peasants. Tolstoy's compassion and courage in stories like "Polikushka" attracted the future author's admiration. Fifty years later, in 1966, Silone again cited Tolstoy first among foreign writers to whom his generation turned for "an echo of their most personal sufferings." Tolstoy also figures alongside Cervantes and Giovanni Verga as Silone's favorite storytellers (Rawson 1981, 563). Cervantes's picaresque work had earlier reconciled Silone's rebellious activity and spiritual quest. But unlike Verga, Silone was no defeatist. His choice of pseudonym reflects the doubly positive thrust of his lifework. He called himself Ignazio following St. Ignatius of Loyola, but as a spiritual descendant of Q. Pompaedius Silo, he paid homage to the Abruzzese commander of the revolt against Rome in 90 B.C. All his life Silone wrote about local saints and proletarian heroes, of whom the final exemplar is Pietro da Morrone, better known as Pope Celestine V, who abdicated on finding religious faith incompatible with secular government. Morrone is the subject of Silone's play *The Story of a Humble Christian*. **Albert Camus,** too, furnished a compassionate model of escape from contemporary nihilism: their respect was mutual. In 1950 Silone's wife gave him **Simone Weil**'s *Attente de Dieu*. Read and reread with Weil's other works, his scored copy led to *Severina*. In his mature years he read more history and economics. The political writings were inspired by Gandhi and especially Giuseppe Mazzini, whose works were scorned in school but later introduced by Silone as "the sincerest prophet and most devoted apostle" of international solidarity and political reform leading to socialism. Finally, among literary figures he knew personally, he singled out Alois Musil for separate treatment. From their shared exile in Switzerland, Silone retained the isolation of "an artist who gave himself totally to his work."

Archives

Centro di Studi Siloniani, Pescina, preserves copies of his papers.
Fondazione Turati, Florence, holds under seal the papers donated to the Centro di Studi e Documentazione Socialista.
Zurich Central Library has Silone correspondence.

Printed Sources

Crossman, Richard (ed.). *The God That Failed* (New York: Harper, 1949).
Lewis, R. W. B. *The Picaresque Saint* (Philadelphia: Lippincott, 1959).
Paynter, Maria Nicolai. *Ignazio Silone* (Toronto: University of Toronto Press, 2000).
Rawson, Judy. " 'Che fare?': Silone and the Russian 'Chto Delat?' Tradition," *Modern Language Review* 76 (1981), 556–65.
Silone, Ignazio. *Emergency Exit* (New York: Harper, 1968).
———. "Encounters with Musil," *Salmagundi* 61 (1983), 90–98.
———. *Severina* (Milan: Mondadori, 1981).

Roy Rosenstein

SINCLAIR, UPTON BEALL JR. (1878–1968)

Upton Sinclair was born in Baltimore, Maryland, the son of an alcoholic salesman of Southern origin and Priscilla Augusta Harden, the daughter of a prosperous Maryland railroad executive. When Sinclair was 10 his family moved to New York City. He attended an East Side public school for three years before spending four years at the College of the City of New York, graduating with a B.A. in 1897. Sinclair originally intended to pursue graduate law studies at Columbia University, but a growing interest in politics and literature persuaded him to become a professional journalist and writer. Always fluent and prolific, in college Sinclair wrote pulp fiction to support himself and during his long life produced over 80 books, including novels, plays, and social and economic studies. Whether fiction or reportage, his books were invariably enormously well-researched repositories of factual information. Sinclair had early success with *The Journal of Arthur Stirling* (1903), purportedly written by an obscure, impoverished dead poet, and *Manassas* (1904), a Southern epic of a plantation heir's embrace of abolitionism. Sinclair's most famous novel was *The Jungle* (1905), written to expose appalling working conditions in the Chicago meatpacking industry. To Sinclair's annoyance, his graphic descriptions of unhygienic food preparation in the meat factories, not labor injustices, attracted public attention, providing final impetus for congressional passage of pure food and drugs legislation. Now among the foremost muckrakers, Sinclair published several further novels and nonfiction works on financial malpractices, the coal and oil industries, the 1920s Sacco and Vanzetti case, and the absence of integrity in journalism, religion, the arts, and education.

Sinclair joined the American Socialist Party in 1902 and throughout his life remained a committed non-Marxian socialist and crusader for social justice. In 1906 he ran unsuccessfully for Congress in New Jersey and, after moving to California in 1915, repeatedly sought to become that state's congressman (1920), senator (1922), and governor (1926 and 1930). From 1917 to 1919 he briefly left the Socialist Party in protest against its antiwar stance, and again in 1934, to run as the Democratic candidate for governor in California. This last campaign attracted national attention, as Sinclair advocated sweeping government agricultural and industrial subsidies to combat the Depression. Democratic Party leaders and Republicans alike considered him far too radical, and collaborated, assisted by President **Franklin D. Roosevelt,** to bring about his defeat by 1,138,000 votes to 879,000. Well into his eighties Sinclair still wrote prolifically, producing an 11-volume novel series covering early twentieth-century United States history. His autobiography gives a classic account of the Progressive era.

Sinclair took refuge in books from his sordid childhood surroundings. At age five he taught himself to read, requesting relatives send him only books as Christmas gifts. He devoured contemporary childhood classics, including Bible stories, the fairy tales of Hans Christian Andersen and the Brothers Grimm, the works of G. A. Henty, Captain Mayne Reid, and Horatio Alger. Sinclair quickly progressed to reading encyclopedias and William Shakespeare's plays at an uncle's house, together with most major American and British literature, poetry, and political philosophy. To encounter European countries' literature in the original, the teenaged Sinclair taught himself German, Italian, and French, finding Goethe especially inspiring, and in his early twenties Friedrich Nietzsche's *Also sprach Zarathustra* equally enthralled him. In his teens Sinclair briefly taught Sunday school but became increasingly agnostic, an outlook that religious works provided him by his mentor, the Episcopalian New York minister William Wilmerding Moir, paradoxically reinforced, since Sinclair found their arguments unconvincing. Jesus Christ, however, he always considered a great teacher and thinker, drawing political guidance from his communitarian social preachings, a perspective which effectively inoculated Sinclair against Marxism's emphasis on class conflict. Sinclair often stated that his three greatest heroes and models were Christ, the romantic revolutionary British poet Percy Bysshe Shelley, and Shakespeare's character Hamlet.

Archives

Upton Sinclair Papers. Lilly Library, University of Indiana, Bloomington, Indiana. Major collection of Sinclair's manuscripts, letters, and other papers.

Printed Sources

Bloodsworth, William A. *Upton Sinclair* (Boston: Twayne, 1977).

Harris, Leon. *Upton Sinclair: American Rebel* (New York: Thomas J. Crowell Company, 1975).

Mitchell, Greg. *The Campaign of the Century: Upton Sinclair's Race for Governor of California and the Birth of Media Politics* (New York: Random Books, 1992).

Sinclair, Upton. *The Autobiography of Upton Sinclair* (New York: Harcourt, Brace, 1962).

———. *My Lifetime in Letters* (Columbia: University of Missouri Press, 1960).

Yoder, Jon A. *Upton Sinclair* (New York: Ungar, 1975).

Priscilla Roberts

SINGER, ISAAC BASHEVIS (1904–1991)

Isaac Bashevis Singer was born on July 14 in Radzymin, Poland. His parents were Rabbi Pinchas Menachem Singer and Bathsheba Singer. Singer was fascinated by his father's offering of advice on religion and family matters, and how his father settled arguments in a judicious way among the people who visited his rabbinical court. His parents also influenced him with the telling of mythical folk tales to strengthen Singer's religious faith. He studied traditional Jewish literature, including the Torah, the Talmud, and the Kabala. He also studied at the Tackemoni Rabbinical Seminary in Warsaw. Singer first started writing in Hebrew, but decided to write in the language of his childhood—Yiddish. He migrated to the United States in 1935 and began working as a freelance writer for the Yiddish newspaper *Jewish Daily Forward*. Singer had immediate success with the publication of the English version of his novel *The Moskati*. His writing connects the mysticism of Jewish folklore and the realities of the life of Eastern European communities that no longer exist. Singer has been compared to Nathaniel Hawthorne, as both write moral fables. Singer had also been praised for his children's literature, including *Zlateh the Goat and Other Stories* (1966) and *Fearsome Inn* (1967). His writings have appeared in such publications as *Partisan Review*, *Commentary*, *New Yorker*, *Saturday Evening Post*, *Esquire*, and *Chicago Review*, and have been translated into many languages. He won the Nobel Prize for Literature in 1978.

Singer's greatest literary influence was his older brother, Israel Joshua Singer, who was himself a distinguished Yiddish writer. Israel Singer left the family's orthodoxy and became a secular writer and painter, writing stories that were philosophical in nature. Isaac Singer soon followed in his brother's footsteps and became a secular writer. In his memoir, *Love and Exile*, Singer wrote that one of his major literary influences was the rationalist philosopher Baruch Spinoza, who believed that the laws of nature were also the laws of God, and that there was no ultimate paradise of bliss to look forward to. Spinoza, especially in *Ethics*, made Singer question the place of Jews in the afterlife. Singer was also influenced by Nicolaus Copernicus and Sir Isaac Newton (in *Book of the Covenant*) and Moses Maimonides in *Guide for the Perplexed*. Judah Halevi's novel *Khuzari* greatly influenced Singer. He also read Arthur Schopenhauer's *The World as Will and Idea* and Friedrich Nietzsche's *Thus Spake Zarathustra*. Charles Bedouin's volumes on hypnotism and autosuggestion and Rob Moshe Haim Luzzato's novel *The Path of Righteousness* were important to Singer. In interviews with Richard Burgin, Singer mentioned other authors who impacted his life. He was moved by Lev Nikolavich Tolstoy's *Anna Karenina* and *War and Peace*, and Knut Hamsun's *Hunger* and *Pan*. Singer also claimed an intellectual debt to Fyodor Dostoyevsky, Nikolai Gogol, Charles Baudelaire, Paul Verlaine, August Strindberg, and Edgar Allan Poe.

Archives

Harry Ransom Humanities Research Center, University of Texas, Austin, Texas. Singer's Yiddish and English manuscripts, proofs, published texts, correspondence, photographs, and financial papers.

Columbia University, University Libraries, Butler Library, New York, N.Y., MS 70–140. Literary manuscripts, 1960–67.

Printed Sources

Ethridge, James M., and Barbara Kopala. "Isaac Bashevis Singer." In *Contemporary Authors*, Volumes 1–4, 1st ed. (Detroit: Gale: 1967), 872–73.

Goran, Lester. *The Bright Streets of Surfside: The Memoir of a Friendship* (Kent, Ohio: Kent State University Press, 1994).

"Isaac Bashevis Singer." *Current Biography*, Third Annual Cumulation (New York: H.W. Wilson, 1969).

Kresh, Paul. *Isaac Bashevis Singer: The Magician of 86th Street* (New York: Dial Press, 1979).

Miller, David Neal. *Bibliography of Isaac Bashevis Singer, 1924–1949* (New York: Peter Lang, 1983).

Singer, Isaac Bashevis. *Love and Exile: A Memoir* (Garden City, New York: Doubleday & Company, 1984).

———. "Nobel Lecture." *Nobel.e.Museum*, accessed Nov. 5 2001, http://www.nobel.se.

Singer, Isaac Bashevis, and Richard Burgin. *Conversations with Isaac Bashevis Singer* (Garden City, New York: Doubleday & Company, 1985).

Zamir, Israel. *Journey to My Father: Isaac Bashevis Singer* (New York: Arcade, 1996).

Cassandra Noel Kreischer

SKINNER, BURRHUS FREDERICK (1904–1990)

American psychologist and advocate of the school of behaviorist psychology, B. F. Skinner is considered one of the world's most influential modern psychologists and a founder of radical behaviorism. Skinner was born in Susquehanna, Pennsylvania, on March 20, 1904. His father, William, was a local attorney for the Erie Railroad; his mother, Grace, was a homemaker. After completing high school, Skinner attended Hamilton College in Clinton, New York, where he majored in English literature. Not satisfied with his progress as a writer after graduation, after a year he began graduate studies at Harvard University, receiving his masters in psychology in 1930 and his doctorate in psychology in 1931. He received a Junior Fellowship from Harvard and remained there over five years studying operant behavior. In 1936, he married Yvonne Blue with whom he later had two daughters, Julie and Deborah. He spent the remainder of his career on the faculty of the University of Minnesota (1936–45), Indiana University (1945–48), and Harvard University (1948–74). Skinner wrote over 20 books and more than 100 journal articles in his career. He continued his professional involvement until his death from leukemia on August 18, 1990.

Skinner said "we shouldn't teach great books, we should teach a love of reading." His recollection of the library at home included many sets of books purchased by his father, whom Skinner recalled as a "sucker for a book salesman." These included the *World's Greatest Literature* and *Masterpieces of World History*, among others. Skinner also read the articles by Reuben "Rube" Goldberg in the *Philadelphia Inquirer*, which featured inventions that would accomplish in a complex form something that could be done in a simple manner. Skinner's schoolteacher, Mary Graves, encouraged him to read and exposed him to all forms of material as well as teaching him the Old and New Testaments as literature and exciting his interest in Shakespeare and Francis Bacon, whose writings influenced his later research. Skinner dedicated his book *The Technology of Teaching* to Graves.

At Hamilton College, Skinner was introduced to Alexander Woollcott, **Carl Sandburg,** and **Robert Frost.** Skinner's goals at this time were more focused on professional writing than the behavioral science that later would make him famous. In 1926, he moved to Greenwich Village, where he reevaluated his career. He discovered behavioral science and began reading biology and psychology, including works by Jacques Loeb, James Watson, Ivan Pavlov, and Edward Thorndike. Thorndike and Skinner had a brief correspondence regarding Thorndike's *Studies in the Psychology of Language.* Also during this time, Skinner critiqued Louis Berman's *The Religion Called Behaviorism* and submitted it to the *Saturday Review of Literature*, though it was never published.

Skinner's literary influences at Harvard were broad. He was particularly enthused about reading Charles Scott Sherrington's *Integrative Action of the Nervous System.* At Harvard, Skinner expanded on Watson and Pavlov, integrating new ideas and methods into the already vast framework of behavioral science. *The Behavior of Organisms*, Skinner's first published work on behavioral psychology, was the beginning of many in his outstanding career that was marked by a dedication to the scientific method and superb research. In later life Skinner published several works on society. His most famous is *Walden Two*, inspired particularly by Francis Bacon's idea of the Royal Society in *New Atlantis* and by Diderot's *Encyclopedie.*

Archives

Harvard University Archives, Harvard University, Boston, Massachusetts. Includes biographical material, correspondence, reaction to Skinner's work, subject files, teaching machines, laboratory data, writings, *Walden Two* correspondence, newspaper clippings, and photographs.

Printed Works

Bjork, Daniel W. *B. F. Skinner: A Life* (New York: HarperCollins, 1993).

Nye, Robert D. *The Legacy of B. F. Skinner: Concepts and Perspectives, Controversies and Misunderstandings* (Belmont, California: Brooks/Cole, 1992).

Richelle, Marc N. *B. F. Skinner, A Reappraisal* (Mahwah, N. J.: Lawrence Erlbaum Associates, 1993).

Smith, L., and W. Woodward (eds.). *B. F. Skinner and Behaviorism in American Culture* (London: Lehigh University Press. 1996).

Arthur Holst

SOLZHENITSYN, ALEXANDR IVANOVICH (1918–)

Alexandr Solzhenitsyn was born in Kislovodsk, a town in the Russian Caucasus. In 1937, he entered the University of Rostov-on-Don, and while still a student married Natalia Reshetovskaia. He enrolled concurrently in correspondence studies at the Institute of History, Philosophy, and Literature in Moscow. Completing his degree in physics and mathematics in 1941, he was immediately taken into the Red Army and served for four years, rising to the rank of captain of artillery. In 1945 he was arrested and sent into exile for remarks critical of **Josef Stalin.** His experiences in labor camps and other correctional facilities, where he spent more than a decade, provided material for much of his fiction and nonfiction. In 1950, he and Natalia divorced, only to remarry in 1957 and divorce again in 1972. After being rehabilitated, he was sent to Central Asia, where he began writing. In 1962 his novel *One Day in the Life of Ivan Denisovich* was accepted for publication in *Novy Mir*. The vicissitudes of government policy toward writers caused him to fall out of favor quickly, however, and for 12 years he circulated work in *samizdat*, a form of underground publication. Some of his work reached the West and his reputation grew outside of the U.S.S.R.; nevertheless, when he was awarded the Nobel Prize in 1970, political tensions caused him to forego acceptance. In 1974, the Soviet government expelled him to West Germany. He took up residence briefly in Switzerland, then immigrated to the United States in 1976, remaining there until the post-Communist Russian government allowed him to return home in 1994. While in exile he prepared his major works for publication and established his reputation as the century's most important critic of communism.

In *Solzhenitsyn's Traditional Imagination* (1984), James Curtis identifies eight writers who influenced Solzhenitsyn's style and themes. Among the more important are Lev Tolstoy and Fyodor Dostoyevsky, while Nikolai Leskov, Anton Chekhov, Evgeny Zamyatin, **John Dos Passos,** and **Ernest Hemingway** are identified as lesser influences. From Dostoyevsky, critic Vladislav Krasnov asserts, Solzhenitsyn learned to write what the Russian critic **Mikhail Bakhtin** (1895–1975) has described as the polyphonic novel, a work with multiple themes and major characters that focuses principally on the exploration of important ideas and cultural phenomena.

While literary mentors are important, the more significant influences on Solzhenitsyn's writing are the works—and deeds—of figures whose development of communist ideology shaped the political system against which Solzhenitsyn rebelled. Primary among these are Karl Marx, **Vladimir Lenin,** and Stalin. By the time Solzhenitsyn entered the army, he had become imbued with communist doctrine and was a staunch supporter of the Soviet Union. His disillusionment with Stalinist policy led to his internment and internal exile. He spent more than a decade reflecting on the errors of communism as it was being practiced under totalitarian dictators. Hence, novels such as *Cancer Ward* (1969) and *The First Circle* (1968) highlight the weaknesses of the system and the dehumanization that results from the misapplication of Marxist ideology, while works such as *One Day in the Life of Ivan Denisovich* and the six volumes of *The Gulag Archipelago* (1973–75) illustrate the human cost of rebellion against the Soviet regime. By contrast, the influence of literary predecessors such as Tolstoy and Dostoyevsky can be seen more clearly in *August 1914* (1971) and the multivolume *The Red Wheel* (1983–91). Like Tolstoy's *War and Peace* (1865–69), these novels focus on the transformation of a nation during a period of crisis.

Archives

Amherst Center for Russian Culture, Amherst, Mass.: samizdat materials. (Much of Solzhenitsyn's work, including typescripts and correspondence, remains in private hands.)

Printed Sources

Curtis, James M. *Solzhenitsyn's Traditional Imagination* (Athens: University of Georgia Press, 1984).

Dunlop, John B., Richard S. Haugh, and Michael Nicholson (eds.). *Solzhenitsyn in Exile: Critical Essays and Documentary Materials* (Stanford, Calif.: Hoover Institute Press, 1985). Essays on the influence of political writers and novelists; contains two useful bibliographic chapters.

Kodjak, Andrej. *Alexander Solzhenitsyn* (Boston: Twayne Publishers, 1978).

Krasnov, Vladislav. *Solzhenitsyn and Dostoevsky: A Study in the Polyphonic Novel* (Athens: University of Georgia Press, 1980).

Pontuso, James F. *Solzhenitsyn's Political Thought* (Charlottesville: The University Press of Virginia, 1990). Focuses on the influence of political ideology, especially works by Marx, Lenin, and Stalin. Also notes the impact of the Western political tradition that gave rise to Communist ideology.

Scammell, Michael. *Solzhenitsyn: A Biography* (London and New York: W. W. Norton, 1984). Careful analysis of influences of friends, professional acquaintances, and the Soviet government on Solzhenitsyn's writings. Also discusses literary and cultural influences.

Siegel, Paul N. *The Great Reversal: Politics and Art in Solzhenitsyn* (San Francisco: Walnut Publishing, 1991). Discusses influence of Marx, Lenin, and Stalin.

Laurence W. Mazzeno

SOYINKA, WOLE (1934–)

Wole Soyinka, the Nigerian playwright, poet, and commentator, received the 1986 Nobel Prize in literature. A very public and at times controversial figure, Soyinka has made his name not only as an author, but also as an outspoken champion of political and social causes throughout Africa. Throughout his distinguished career, Soyinka has used his work to denounce apartheid in South Africa, European colonialism in the continent, and especially the corrupt and abusive regimes which have ruled Nigeria for much of the time since its independence. Despite imprisonment and exile, Soyinka has remained a thorn in the side of Nigeria's rulers, publishing in 1996, among other works, a scathing critique of the nation's military rulers: *The Open Sore of a Continent*. Soyinka was able to return to Nigeria in 1998, his having been an influential voice in gaining the return of civilian government there.

Educated in Nigeria and Britain, Soyinka has acknowledged that the works of many dramatists and writers have informed his own efforts, though he has staunchly resisted any attempt to categorize himself or his work as the successor to one tradition or another. Instead, Soyinka has maintained that a writer or artist must of necessity avail himself or herself of a wide range of influences, sources, and material. As he told an interviewer in 1985: "There's no way at all that I will ever preach the cutting off of any source of knowledge: Oriental, European, African, Polynesian or whatever" (Jeyifo 2001, 123). He has found fault mainly in those who refuse to encounter or explore literature or art outside their own experiences or narrow worldviews, saying, "The barrier is self-created. By now it has to be a two-way traffic" (Jeyifo 2001, 130). Among those he has cited as significant in his own development, Soyinka has included the following, reflecting his own universal approach to art and literature: John Donne, Derek Walcott, Sean O'Casey, and **Eugene O'Neill.**

Soyinka's plays have often centered on mythological subjects and religious rituals, especially those of the ancient Greeks and those of traditional Yoruban society in Nigeria. Elements of Greek drama have appeared throughout Soyinka's work. The most notable instance was his 1973 reinterpretation of Euripides's *The Bacchae*, but Soyinka has included devices such as the chorus or the individual set-piece in many of his works. Soyinka's reworking of *The Bacchae*, however, also included the insertion of new elements drawn from African myth and folklore, reflecting what seems to have been the greatest influence on his creations.

Though born to Christian parents, Soyinka was exposed from early in his life to the religious stories and rituals of the larger Yoruba community into which he was born. He was particularly taken by the god Ogun, a patron of hunters and a god who can be both just and destructive. Ogun appears in several of Soyinka's early plays, and several critics have argued that Soyinka reconstructed the character of Dionysus in *The Bacchae* in the image of Ogun. If Soyinka was taken by the figure of Ogun, though, he may have been even more influenced by the Yoruban festivals and ritual celebrations which center not only on this figure, but on other deities and often mark important moments in the various seasons. These celebrations included extensive dramatic performances, filled with elaborate costuming, broad physical comedy, and singing and dancing, all of which have found their way into Soyinka's plays, even those most overtly concerned with politics or social justice. These aspects of Yoruban drama are visible in an early play such as *The Lion and the Jewel*, which focused on the African encounter with Europeans, and in the later *Kongi's Harvest*, a work dealing with the rise of autocratic rule in Africa.

His most direct political play, *A Play of Giants*, published in 1984, eschewed many of these Yoruban devices, relying only on powerful and acerbic satire as Soyinka attacked the rise of dictatorship in Africa, specifically the horrific reign of Idi Amin in Uganda. The play's aggressive stance was a telling reminder of Soyinka's devotion both to justice and to his beloved Africa. Most of all, it was an affirmation of his own professed belief that "(t)he artist has always functioned in African society as the record of mores and experience of his society and as the voice of vision in his own time" (quoted in Gibbs 1986, 34–35).

Archives

None available.

Printed Sources

Gibbs, James. *Wole Soyinka* (London: Macmillan, 1986).

Jeyifo, Biodun. *Conversations with Wole Soyinka* (Jackson, Miss.: University Press of Mississippi, 2001).

Soyinka, Wole. *Ake: The Years of Childhood* (London: Rex Collings, 1981).

———. *Myth, Literature and the African World* (Cambridge: Cambridge University Press, 1976).

———. *The Open Sore of a Continent: A Personal Narrative of the Nigerian Crisis* (Oxford: Oxford University Press, 1996).

Andrew Muldoon

SPEER, ALBERT (1905–1981)

Albert Speer was born in Mannheim, Germany. He completed his studies in architecture at the Institute of Technology in Berlin-Charlottenburg. Speer hailed from a line of architects, as his father and his grandfather had also entered into this profession. After graduation, Speer became an assistant to Professor Heinrich Tessenow, who advocated simplicity in architecture. In 1931, Speer joined the NDSAP after hearing one of **Adolf Hitler**'s speeches. This speech became a determining factor in Speer's fate, for Germany was in a state of chaos; however, Speer had never given a serious thought to politics before. To Speer, Hitler's regime seemed at the time to be a good remedy against the threat of communism from the east. He saw this as an opportunity to help rebuild Germany, to design new buildings, and to keep Germany architecturally beautiful. He ignored the atrocities the Nazis committed around him, such as Kristallnacht, the transports of Jews to the east, and the hostile propaganda. This later disturbed him deeply at the end of the war. When he discovered that Hitler was planning to blow up everything as Germany was spiraling into defeat, Speer vowed to kill Hitler if he attempted to do so. Speer was tried at the Nuremberg Tribunal in 1946 and pleaded guilty to all charges, making him one of the few in the Nazi regime to readily admit his participation in Hitler's mad scheme. However, Speer was spared the death penalty, which the Russians had advocated, and instead received 20 years in Spandau Prison, a term that he served until the very last minute of his sentence in 1966.

Speer began to write about the Third Reich while imprisoned. He had intended for his children to read his work, but as he continued to analyze his past, he began to wonder why he had become such a willing participant in Hitler's plans. He saw the Third Reich for what it was and what it could not have possibly attained. In the afterword of his work *Inside the Third Reich: Memoirs* (1970), Speer writes, "In writing this book my intention has been not only to describe the past, but to issue warnings about the future. During the first months of my imprisonment, while I was still in Nuremberg, I wrote a great deal, out of the need to relieve some of the burden that pressed so heavily upon me" (Speer 1970, 525). As Speer began to publish, he felt motivated to further his study of the Third Reich and his part in the political machinery of the Nazi Party. His work *Spandau: The Secret Diaries* (1976), describes his prison experience and the deep struggle within himself. Thus, Speer's influence behind his writing was the desire to come to terms with his own conscience. He readily admitted that he was drawn into the vision that Hitler and Himmler had painted for Germany. He read over 5,000 works while imprisoned and was certainly influenced by Sigmund Freud's *Civilisation and Its Discontents* (1929) and *Interpretation of Dreams* (1900). Karl May's three-volume *Winnetou* series (1876–93) also played a role in Speer's writing, for May's works were favorites of Adolf Hitler. Speer's fascination with the outrageous behavior of these two men, the evil around him, and the atrocities committed in the name of Germany spurred him to write in an attempt to release himself from the burden of his Nazi past.

Archives

Yad Vashem, Jerusalem, Israel. Photos, manuscripts, correspondence, Nuremberg Tribunal records.

The Hoover Institution Archives, Stanford University, Stanford, California. European collection.

The Auschwitz-Birkenau State Museum, Auschwitz (Oswiecim), Poland. Correspondence, photos, documentation.

Bundesarchiv, Koblenz, Germany. Photos, correspondence, documentation.

Modern Military Branch, National Archives and Records Administration, College Park, Maryland. Nuremberg Tribunal records, investigatory records, audiovisual records.

Printed Sources

Boelke, Willi. *Deutschlands Rüstung im Zweiten Weltkrieg: Hitlers Konferenzen mit Albert Speer* (Frankfurt am Main: Akademische Verlagsgesellschaft Athenaion, 1969).

King, Henry T. Jr., and Bettina Ellis. *The Two Worlds of Albert Speer* (Lanham, Md.: University Press of America, 1997).

Schmidt, Mathias. *Albert Speer: The End of a Myth* (New York: St. Martin's Press, 1984).

Sereny, Gitta. *Albert Speer: His Battle with Truth* (New York: Alfred Knopf, 1995).

Speer, Albert. *Inside the Third Reich: Memoirs* (New York: Touchstone Books, 1997[1970]).

Van der Vat, Dan. *The Good Nazi: The Life and Lies of Albert Speer* (Boston: Houghton-Mifflin, 1997).

Cynthia A. Klima

SPIELBERG, STEVEN ALLAN (1946–)

Steven Spielberg was born in Cincinnati's Jewish Hospital, the first son of Arnold, a General Electric computer engineer, and Leah, a classically trained pianist and dancer. During his formative years, Spielberg's family moved frequently, first to New Jersey, then to Phoenix, Arizona, and finally to Saratoga, California, where the creative and inquisitive youngster attended high school. Spielberg's involvement with movie-making began with the use of his father's Kodak 8mm camera to document family camping trips. His early attempts at producing original short films, including *Fighter Squad, Escape to Nowhere,* and the sophomoric *Firelight* demonstrated Spielberg's developing talent for editing, creating originally framed compositions, and formulating on-screen special effects. Upon graduating from high school, Spielberg was accepted into California State's Department of Radio and Television at Long Beach, but he structured his classes to allow for three full days a week of unpaid work at Universal Studios. His independent short film *Amblin'* (1968) had precipitated a meeting with Universal Television's vice president of production, Sid Sheinberg, who arranged for Spielberg to informally train on the Universal lot and who eventually honored the young director with a seven-year contract. Spielberg's initial assignments for Universal included directing Joan Crawford in an episode of Rod Serling's *Night Gallery* and working on such popular television series as *Columbo* and *Marcus Welby M.D.* Spielberg's first foray into full-length feature films came with his movie adaptation of the made-for-TV adventure *Duel* (1971) which was followed by the slightly more successful *Sugarland Express* (1974). Large-scale commercial success evaded the young director until the release of *Jaws* (1975), which was followed by a string of box office hits including *Close Encounters of the Third Kind* (1977), *Raiders of the Lost Ark* (1981), *Poltergeist* (1982), *E.T.* (1982), *The Color Purple* (1985), and *Jurassic Park* (1993). Spielberg has twice won the Academy Award for Best Director, once in 1993 for *Schindler's List* and again in 1998 for *Saving Private Ryan.* In October 1994, Spielberg teamed with David Geffen and Jeffrey Katzenberg to form the highly successful Dreamworks SKG studios, which develops, produces, and distributes motion pictures, animated feature films, and a wealth of entertainment-related consumer products.

In his youth, Spielberg passionately avoided the classic literature of his era, refusing a friend's suggestion to read **James Joyce**'s *Ulysses* and publicly defacing a school copy of Nathaniel Hawthorne's *The Scarlet Letter* by turning it into an animated flip book. His literary interests lay in the realm of science fiction and fantasy, developed through his father's bedtime readings of serial adventure stories. Spielberg collected comic books from a young age and frequently read his father's collection of the John W. Campbell series *Analog Science Fiction/Science Fact,* which regularly featured such prominent science fiction authors as Ron L. Hubbard and

Frank Herbert. Other magazines that Spielberg perused on a regular basis included Forest J. Ackerman's *Famous Monsters of Filmland*, the content of which reflected the young director's early fascination with Hollywood movies. Spielberg avidly read the work of science fiction authors **Ray Bradbury**, Isaac Asimov, Jules Verne and H. G. Wells and has cited **J. R. R. Tolkien**'s *The Two Towers*, Arthur C. Clarke's *The City of the Stars*, and Ralph Ellison's *Invisible Man* as his favorite fantasy epics. His choice of light and fantastical literature was developmental to the formation of his powerful imagination and creativity, which would contribute directly to his later successes.

Archives

California State Archives, Sacramento.

Printed Sources

Baxter, John. *Steven Spielberg: The Unauthorized Biography* (London: HarperCollins Publishers, 1996).

McBride, Joseph. *Steven Spielberg: A Biography* (New York: Simon and Schuster, 1997).

Perry, George. *Steven Spielberg* (London: Orion Books, 1998).

Gregory L. Schnurr

SPOCK, BENJAMIN MCLANE (1903–1997)

Benjamin Spock was born in New Haven, Connecticut. When he was finally allowed to read (his mother didn't believe that children should learn to read until the age of seven), he began with Beatrix Potter's *Peter Rabbit* and, over his childhood years, moved on to Robert Louis Stevenson's *Treasure Island* and *The Book of Knowledge* encyclopedias before devouring the works of Charles Dickens and Mark Twain. He was educated at Hamden Hall preparatory school and Phillips Academy and earned a B.S. at Yale University (1925), where he read—in addition to the standard curriculum of Chaucer, Shakespeare (whose "seven ages of man" were later to influence the concepts underlying *Decent and Indecent: Our Personal and Political Behavior* [1969]), Pope, Samuel Johnson, Byron, and Shelley—*The Glories of Yale Athletics*, which reinforced his desire to go out for what became the gold-medal U.S. Olympic crew of 1924.

After medical training at Yale University School of Medicine (1925–27) and Columbia College of Physicians and Surgeons (earning his M.D. in 1929), and internships and residencies at New York's Presbyterian Hospital (1929–31), New York Nursery and Child's Hospital (1931–32), and Payne Whitney Clinic of New York Hospital (1932–33), Spock's training analysis was conducted in 1933–34 by Dr. Bertram Lewin, a disciple of Freud's. In 1933 Spock opened a private pediatric practice in New York, attracting an avant-garde clientele including anthropologist **Margaret Mead.** After serving as a psychiatrist in the U.S. Navy (1944–46), he joined the Mayo Clinic (1947–51), concurrently serving on the Mayo Graduate School of Medicine (part of the University of Minnesota) faculty. From 1951 to 1955 he was a teacher and administrator at the Western Psychiatric Institute. His final academic appointment was as a professor of child development and child psychiatry at the Western Reserve University Medical School in Cleveland, Ohio, 1955–67.

Publication of the immediately bestselling *Baby and Child Care* (first edition, 1946, initially published as *The Common Sense Book of Baby and Child Care;* sixth edition, coauthored with Dr. Michael Rothenberg, 1992) led to Spock's national prominence as a popular advisor to parents, not only in the successive editions of his book but in monthly (and later more intermittent) columns in *The Ladies Home Journal* (1954–62) and *Redbook* (1963–92). Impelled to oppose nuclear testing in the 1960s because of the threat to children's health from nuclear fallout in milk, Spock retired to devote full time to opposing the Vietnam War as cochair of SANE, the National Committee for a SANE Nuclear Policy, and a member of other opposition groups. As a member of the "Boston Five," Spock was tried and convicted for conspiracy to encourage draft resistance (1968) and acquitted on appeal (1969). He ran for president in 1972 as the People's Party candidate.

Although Spock's political activism continued throughout his life, he will remain best known for revolutionizing American child-rearing practices, primarily through *Baby and Child Care*, which considered the psychological as well as the physical aspects of child development. Although his medical training and inclinations were strongly Freudian, he was influenced as much by his experience as a training analysand as by his reading of such works as Freud's *Interpretation of Dreams* (1900), *Psychopathology of Everyday Life* (1904), and *Three Essays on the Theory of Sexuality* (1905). Spock's major works—all writings for parents—deliberately eschewed Freudian language, even when discussing toilet training and attachment to parents. Yet his implicit Freudianism was made manifest in *Decent and Indecent:* "The little girl's envy of the boy's penis and the boy's envy of the little girl's ability to grow babies create rivalries that persist into adulthood." His reading of earlier texts on child development, including Luther Emmett Holt's *The Care and Feeding of Children: A Catechism for the Use of Mothers and Children's Nurses* (1894) and behaviorist John B. Watson's *Psychological Care of Infant and Child* (1928), provided negative models against which to present his positive one, both in substance and in Spock's reader-friendly style. Spock was also influenced by **John Dewey**'s ideas on progressive education, such as those expressed in *Experience and Education* (1938), and he combined these with psychoanalytic educational theory by his mentor, Caroline Zachry, in seminars and in such works as *Emotion and Conduct in Adolescence* (1940).

Archives

Dr. Benjamin Spock Collection, George Arents Research Library, Syracuse University, Syracuse, New York.

Printed Works

Bloom, Lynn Z. *Doctor Spock: Biography of a Conservative Radical* (Indianapolis: Bobbs Merrill, 1972).

Hubbard, Mary Ellen. "Benjamin Spock, M.D.: The Man and His Work in Historical Perspective." Ph.D. diss., Claremont Graduate School, 1981.

Maier, Thomas. *Dr. Spock: An American Life* (New York: Harcourt Brace, 1998).

Sulman, A. Michael. "The Humanization of the American Child: Benjamin Spock as a Popularizer of Psychoanalytic Thought," *Journal of the History of the Behavioral Sciences* 9 (1973), 258–65.

Weiss, Nancy Pottishman. "Mother, the Invention of Necessity: Dr. Benjamin Spock's Baby and Child Care," *American Quarterly* 29 (Winter 1977), 519–46.

Lynn Z. Bloom

STALIN, JOSEF VISSARIONOVICH (1879–1953)

Josef Stalin was born to Vissarion and Ekaterina Djugashvili in Gori, Georgia. At the persistence of his mother, Josef, nicknamed Soso, was sent to the local church school in Gori. In 1894, he entered Tiflis Seminary. It was at seminary that Stalin became interested in revolutionary ideas and activities. He left seminary in 1898 without graduating to work full-time with the Social-Democratic Party. He experienced his first state arrest and exile in 1902. By 1907, Stalin was a committed revolutionary and even attended the Fifth Congress of the Russian Social-Democratic Party in London. His article, "Marxism and the National Question," written in 1913, brought him to the attention of **V. I. Lenin.** After the Revolution of 1917, he served on the Central Committee and then the Politburo of the Communist Party. In 1922, he was elected secretary-general of the Communist Party. He solidified his power as dictator by 1930. Stalin allied the U.S.S.R. with Great Britain and the United States during the Second World War. Then he led the U.S.S.R. against the West in the beginning of the ideological conflict of the cold war. In 1953, Stalin suffered a stroke and died.

Stalin was a practical revolutionary, not a philosophical intellectual. He was a Bolshevik Communist and dealt with ideology as it furthered the revolution and party interests. As a young boy, he devoured Georgian literature in rebellion against the Russification policies of the czarist government. Writers such as Ilie Chavchavadze and Daniel Chonkadze attracted his attention, but none captivated him so much as the author Alexander Kazbegi in *The Patricide.* So fascinated was Stalin with this heroic adventure that he nicknamed himself "Koba," the name of the main character and hero. Even at seminary, he supplemented his required readings of theology, Russian history and literature, Latin, and Greek with the illicit readings of "The Men in the Panther's Skin," an old, twelfth-century Georgian epic by Shota Rustaveli, as well as *Vanity Fair* by William Makepeace Thackeray and the works of Victor Hugo. Though not allowed by the seminary, Stalin also studied the works of Charles Darwin, Karl Marx, and Georgi Plekhanov.

Stalin's communist writings of 1906–7 reveal a studied knowledge of the works of Marx and Friedrich Engels, Paul Louis, and Peter Kropotkin. As leader of the Communist Party, he was attentive to the literature in the Soviet Union. His library consisted of works by Dmitrii Furmanov, Vsevolod Ivanov, Fedor Gladkov; the poetry of Alexander Bezymensky, Demian Bednyi, and Sergei Yesenin; and especially the works of Maxim Gorky, which he greatly admired. Special location and notes in the margins indicate that Stalin was deeply interested in the thoughts and ideas of Lenin, Karl Kautsky, **Leon Trotsky, Nikolai Bukharin,** Grigori Zinoviev, Lev Kamenev, and Paul Lafargue. Stalin readily admitted that he did not understand philosophy and did not grasp the role of the dialectic, a foundational Marxist principle. He employed a private teacher who tutored him with the readings of G.W.F. Hegel, Immanuel Kant, Ludwig Feuerbach, Johann Fichte, and Friedrich Schelling. Marginal annotations suggest that Stalin enjoyed the study of history over philosophy. He read I. Bellyarminov's *Course of Russian History* and R. Vipper's *History of the Roman Empire* and found especially fascinating Alexei Tolstoy's histories of Ivan the Terrible and the Romanovs. Showing limited interest in literature generally, Stalin was mainly concerned with works that practically affected revolution and the Communist Party.

Archives

Archive of the President of the Russian Federation, Moscow.

Stalin's personal archive, Moscow.

Russian Center for the Preservation and Study of Documents Relating to Modern History (formerly Central Party Archives), Moscow.

Annotated Books from Stalin's Private Library, Moscow.

Printed Works

Bullock, Alan. *Hitler and Stalin: Parallel Lives* (New York: Alfred A. Knopf, 1992).

Radzinsky, Edvard. *Stalin*, H. T. Willetts (trans.), (New York: Doubleday, 1996). Includes a substantial listing of available manuscript documents.

Tucker, Robert C. *Stalin as Revolutionary, 1879–1929* (New York: W.W. Norton, 1973).

Volkogonov, Dmitri. *Stalin: Triumph and Tragedy*, Harold Shukman (ed. and trans.), (London: Weidenfeld and Nicolson, 1991).

Katherine Matthews

STEICHEN, EDWARD (1879–1973)

Edward Steichen was born in Luxembourg but moved to Michigan with his family when he was two years old. An avid lover of nature, Steichen spent much of his childhood outdoors before going on to Pio Nono College in Milwaukee and entering an apprenticeship with the American Lithographing Company there. In 1899 Steichen displayed his first exhibition in the Second Philadelphia Salon; however, the failure to attract interest in his work led him to travel to France, where he encountered and became heavily influenced by the sculpture of Auguste Rodin. By 1904 Steichen was experimenting with multi-color separation and began to find success as a photographer. In 1947 he became the director of the Department of Photography at New York's Museum of Modern Art, where he remained until his death.

Steichen was repeatedly heard to comment that "all [his] work [wa]s commercial." From Rodin and as in the case of the poet Rainer Maria Rilke, Steichen adopted a strong work ethic that embodied hours of research and study to improve his own works. He was fascinated with Theodore Andrea Cook's text, *The Curves of Life* (1914), as well as the writings of Leonardo da Vinci. By 1920, Steichen developed an interest in conveying meaning through ordinary objects, and hence was influenced by French symbolist writers including Charles Baudelaire, Arthur Rimbaud, and Paul Verlaine, and also by the philosophy and writings of **Albert Einstein.** Nevertheless, nature remained the most important object of Steichen's attention, and he avidly read the American transcendentalist writers Henry David Thoreau and Ralph Waldo Emerson as well as Maeterlinck's *Intelligence of Flowers*, which encouraged him to discard artifice in artistic production. Steichen made repeated trips to Walden Pond to create a limited edition of Thoreau's *Walden* and produced photos and illustrations for a nature-based text written by his daughter entitled *First Picturebook: Everyday Things for Babies* (1930).

Archives

The Museum of Modern Art, New York, Audio-Visual Archives: complete works, the most extensive collection of papers, interviews, and works available.

Archives of American Art at the Smithsonian Institute, Washington, D.C.: Bowden Papers, Arthur Carles' Papers, Day Papers, Beaumont Newhall Interview, Peter Belz Papers.

Beinecke Rare Book and Manuscript Library at Yale University: 354 leaves of correspondence.

Center for Creative Photography, University of Arizona, Tucson.

International Museum of Photography, George Eastman Library, Rochester, New York.

Printed Sources

Gedrim, Ronald. *Edward Steichen: Selected Texts and Bibliography* (New York: G.K. Hall and Company, 1996).

Niven, Penelope. *Steichen: A Biography* (New York: Clarkson Potter, 1997).

Sandburg, Carl. *Steichen, the Photographer* (New York: Doubleday, 1961).

Smith, Joel. *Edward Steichen: The Early Years* (Princeton: Princeton University Press, 1999).

Dana Milstein

STEIN, GERTRUDE (1874–1946)

Gertrude Stein, modernist, avant-garde author and poet, was born in Allegheny, Pennsylvania, to Daniel and Amelia (Keyser) Stein. The Steins and their five children moved throughout Europe, subsequently settling in Oakland, California, in 1880. By the time Stein turned seventeen, she had lost both parents and moved to San Francisco to live with her brother Michael. In 1892, Stein and sister Bertha moved again to Baltimore to live with their maternal aunt. A year later following her brother Leo, she entered the Harvard Annex (Radcliffe College) and studied under Hugo Münsterberg, William Vaughn Moody, and William James, her mentor and greatest influence. In 1896 Stein and Leon Solomons published the "Normal Motor Automatism" in *Psychological Review*. While in Radcliffe she failed her Latin exam and was refused her degree, ultimately awarded to her in 1898. She entered Johns Hopkins Medical School in 1897, but failed four courses and did not receive a degree. In 1903 Gertrude joined Leo in Paris, at 27 rue de Fleurus, and started working on the early drafts of *The Making of Americans* and *Things as They Are*. Fascinated by Charles Loeser's collection of Cézannes in Florence, the Steins began collecting postimpressionist art works. In 1905 they purchased Henri Matisse's *La Femme au Chapeau* and met **Pablo Picasso**, Gertrude's most admired friend and artist, who painted her illustrious portrait. In 1909 Stein published her first book, *Three Lives*, and Alice B. Toklas, whom she met in 1907, moved in with her. Their lesbian relationship lasted for 39 years until Stein's death. The couple kept a hectic literary salon in their apartment, frequented by prominent figures such as Henri Mattisse, Picasso, **Guillaume Apollinaire,** Georges Braque, Sherwood Anderson, Carl van Vechten, and **Ernest Hemingway.** Remarkably, Stein and Toklas survived the two world wars, and the two decades between the wars were Stein's most productive and prolific years. In 1933 Stein attained celebrity status with the publication of *The Autobiography of Alice B. Toklas*, an instant bestseller. In the mid-1930s, Stein toured and lectured throughout England and the United States, promoting her writings and her modernist worldview.

The end of the nineteenth century was characterized by a belief in science and progress, termed "evolution" in Stein's *Wars I Have Seen*. In an era in which utopianism and optimism ended, Stein's interest and preoccupation with psychology and philosophy should not be underestimated as she explored the ideas of **Henri Berg-**

son, **Alfred North Whitehead,** I. A. Richards, and **Ludwig Wittgenstein.** In her *Autobiography of Alice B. Toklas,* the narrator claims that "the most important person in Gertrude Stein's Radcliffe life was William James." The sum of what she absorbed from him transpires in her lecture *The Gradual Making of The Making of Americans:* "When I was working with William James I completely learned one thing, that science is continuously busy with the complete description of something, with ultimately the complete description of anything with ultimately the complete description of everything." Still some critics argue that she had taken James's expression "keep your mind open" (and his pragmatism) too literally. In *Picasso* she admitted to using the "cubistic vision" in her writings, citing three reasons: "First. The composition, because the way of living had changed the composition of living had extended and each thing was as important as any other thing. Secondly . . . the faith in what the eyes were seeing . . . commenced to diminish . . . [and] Thirdly, the framing of life, the need that a picture exist in its frame, remain in its frame was over." Though an American expatriate all her life, Stein was close linguistically and conceptually to Shakespearian English in particular and to the Elizabethan writers in general. Her idea of the exemplary novel came from her fascination with Samuel Richardson's *Clarissa,* the first epistolary novel and one of the longest novels in the English literature, which she ritually reread every year. In 1946, the year she died of cancer, her first nonmusical play *Yes Is for a Very Young Man,* was performed in New York.

Archives

The main repository for Gertrude Stein's works is the Beinecke Library, Yale University, which carries most of her manuscripts, correspondence, and unpublished notebooks. Other extensive collections are housed at the Bancroft Library, University of California at Berkeley, and the University of Texas at Austin.

Printed Sources

Brinnin, John Malcolm. *The Third Rose: Gertrude Stein and Her World* (Boston: Little, Brown, 1959).

Hobhouse, Janet. *Everybody Who Was Anybody: A Biography of Gertrude Stein* (New York: Putman's, 1975).

Stein, Gertrude. *Everybody's Autobiography* (New York: Random House, 1937; London & Toronto: Heinemann, 1938).

———. *Last Operas and Plays,* Carl van Vechten (ed.), (New York & Toronto: Rinehart, 1949).

———. *The Making of Americans, Being a History of a Family's Progress* (Paris: Contact Editions, 1925; New York: A. & C. Boni, 1926; London: Owen, 1968); abridged as *The Making of Americans, The Hersland Family* (New York: Harcourt, Brace, 1934).

———. *Wars I Have Seen* (New York: Random House, 1945; enlarged edition, London: Batsford, 1945).

Toklas, Alice B. *What Is Remembered* (New York, Chicago & San Francisco: Holt, Rinehart & Winston, 1963).

Dina Ripsman Eylon

STEINBECK, JOHN (1902–1968)

John Steinbeck was born in Salinas, California, and grew up in the Salinas Valley, where he would eventually set a number of his works. He graduated from high school and entered Stanford University in 1919, attending sporadically until 1925 but never earning a degree. While working at various jobs to finance his education, Steinbeck learned firsthand of the labor struggles he would later write about in works such as *In Dubious Battle* (1936) and *The Grapes of Wrath* (1939). Although he did not want to be labeled a political writer, he is best remembered for his novels depicting the socioeconomic problems involving agricultural workers in 1930s California. Steinbeck won the Pulitzer Prize in 1940 for *The Grapes of Wrath* and the Nobel Prize for literature in 1962.

Steinbeck's childhood reading varied; along with the Bible and Greek myths, he specifically recalled reading *Crime and Punishment*, *Madame Bovary*, *Paradise Lost*, *The Return of the Native*, *Pilgrim's Progress*, *Morte d'Arthur*, and the works of George Eliot and William Shakespeare as well as various poets and writers of adventure. Sir Thomas Malory's *Morte d'Arthur* was clearly important to Steinbeck in later years, as its influence is evident in *Tortilla Flat* (1935), *Cannery Row* (1945), and implicitly in nearly all his published work. When Steinbeck graduated from high school, he had a solid background in world literature, and as he matured, his interests expanded into anthropology, biology, ecology, sociology, and philosophy. He was also widely read in psychology and profoundly affected by the works of **Carl Jung**.

As an adult, Steinbeck read voraciously and was especially fond of ancient classics and poetry, particularly that of Walt Whitman and Robinson Jeffers. While he read contemporary fiction, he was keenly aware of his susceptibility to influence, a tendency he attempted to restrain, although he was sometimes accused of being imitative. Steinbeck's fiction frequently refers or alludes to other works, demonstrating his vast range of knowledge in numerous areas. To his later embarrassment, *Cup of Gold* (1929) was obviously influenced by fantasy writers such as James Stephens, Donn Byrne, and James Branch Cabell. *To a God Unknown* (1933) shows the influence of Sir James Frazer's *The Golden Bough*, and we can see the influence of the Bible on *The Grapes of Wrath* and *East of Eden* (1952); *Paradise Lost* on *In Dubious Battle*; *Tao Te Ching* on *Cannery Row*; and the plays of William Shakespeare on *The Winter of Our Discontent* (1961). In the last decade of his life, Steinbeck worked to create a modern edition of *Morte d'Arthur*, translating a substantial portion, but never completing it. The work was published posthumously as *The Acts of King Arthur and His Noble Knights* (1976).

Perhaps the largest single influence on Steinbeck's work was Edward F. Ricketts, a marine biologist whom he befriended in 1930. Steinbeck's ongoing dialogue with Ricketts helped to shape Steinbeck's own worldview, and a number of his novels have a philosophical Ricketts-like character as a central figure. The two collaborated on *The Sea of Cortez* (1941).

Archives

Martha Heasley Cox Center for Steinbeck Studies, San Jose State University, San Jose, California. Manuscripts, letters, first editions, secondary works, photographs, films, cassettes, reviews.

The John Steinbeck Collection, Stanford University, Palo Alto, California. Joined by recently acquired Wells Fargo Steinbeck Collection. Manuscripts, letters, photographs, letters written by Steinbeck to his close relatives, unpublished poems and stories written during young adulthood.

Printed Sources

Benson, Jackson J. *The True Adventures of John Steinbeck, Writer* (New York: Viking, 1984).
DeMott, Robert. *Steinbeck's Reading: A Catalogue of Books Owned and Borrowed* (New York: Garland, 1984).

Wendy Pearce Miller

STEINEM, GLORIA (1934–)

Gloria Steinem was born in Toledo, Ohio. A granddaughter of Pauline Steinem, who was closely involved in the suffrage movement, Steinem lived in poverty after the divorce of her parents. She graduated from Smith College in 1956 with a B.A. and began graduate studies at the University of New Delhi and the University of Calcutta in 1957–58. Returning to New York, she had difficulty in finding her place in the publishing industry and worked freelance until becoming a contributing editor to *Glamour* from 1962 to 1969. She also contributed to *Cosmopolitan, Esquire, Family Circle, Life, Show,* and *Vogue.* Dubbed "The World's Most Beautiful Byline" by *Newsweek* staff writer Harvey Aronson, she is most known for her 1963 article "I Was a Playboy Bunny" in which she infiltrated the New York Playboy Club, investigated, and exposed the daily degradations women tolerated. In 1968 Steinem and Clay Felker founded *New York* magazine. Correct in her belief that stories featuring feminist issues were unacceptable to the male-controlled magazines, with Felker's backing she and her staff worked without pay to publish the first issue of *Ms.* in January 1972. That same year *McCall's* named her "Woman of the Year." Undoubtedly, she is the most recognized face of the women who organized the second wave of feminism. Steinem's first collection of essays, *Outrageous Acts and Everyday Rebellions* (1983) was soon followed by *Marilyn: Norma Jeane* (1986), which she wrote essentially to balance Norman Mailer's indifferent work *Marilyn, a Biography* (1973). Though her next book, *Revolution from Within: A Book of Self-Esteem* (1992), met with criticism for being too "New Age," her most recent book, *Moving Beyond Words* (1994), provided perspective on the women's movement.

Early on Steinem developed a keen interest in reading as a means to escape from her impoverished home and the demands of her mother's mental illness. Given a white leather Bible one Christmas, she tried religion as a means of escape as well. She described her childhood as "indiscriminately bookish, during which I did not go to school but worked my way through the entirety of *Nancy Drew, Godey's Lady's Book,* and the Theosophical Library" (Heilbrun 1995, 46). Additionally, she read "the *Hardy Boys;* a series by Mazo de la Roche called the *Whiteoaks of Jalna* (1927–1968); and isolated books of a series on the Civil War, and learned about sex from books her parents said she should not have read" (Stern 1997, 26). Like most girls at a certain age, she relished horse stories. From the age of six on, Steinem read *Little Women* annually. Identifying with Louisa May Alcott's strongest character, Jo March, she later read Alcott's adult novels and fancied her as an imaginary friend. She also enjoyed comic books, especially *Wonder Woman,* but also *Superman, Sheena of the Jungle,* and *Batman.* While it is uncertain that Sylvia Plath's poetry and, later, *The Bell Jar* influenced Steinem, they were contemporaries at Smith College, where Steinem "loved curling up in a big chair in the library. She loved the library's open stacks with 381,390 volumes" (Stern 1997, 66). *A Passage to India* was one of her favorite books, and **E. M. Forster** one of her favorite authors, as she found his gentle voice and strong female characters especially appealing (Heilbrun 1995, 51). At Smith she also read Plato, Aristotle, and Marx. Alice Walker's novels and nonfiction were particularly influential upon Steinem, as was their close friendship. Sven Lindqvist's *Exterminate All the Brutes* (1997) has also been mentioned as a recent influence.

Archives

Sophia Smith Collection, Smith College, Northampton, Massachusetts: 300 boxes and documents dating back to 1940. Materials in the collection include correspondence, speeches, court testimony, news articles, photographs, and other memorabilia once owned by Steinem.

Interview

Richards, Amy, personal assistant to Gloria Steinem. Interview by author, 20 February 2002, New York. By telephone.

Printed Sources

Heilbrun, Carolyn G. *The Education of a Woman: The Life of Gloria Steinem* (New York: Dial Press, 1995).

Stern, Sydney Ladensohn. *Gloria Steinem: Her Passions, Politics, and Mystique* (Secaucus, N.J.: Carol Pub. Group, 1997).

Rebecca Tolley-Stokes

STIEGLITZ, ALFRED (1864–1946)

Alfred Stieglitz, one of the most important photographers in the history of the medium, was also a tireless promoter of photography as a fine art and, more generally, a champion of modernism in America. He exerted considerable influence through his art magazine, *Camera Work* (1903–17) and through his New York gallery *291*, "The Little Galleries of the Photo-Secession." Born in Hoboken, New Jersey, and raised there and in Manhattan, Stieglitz read Horatio Alger stories, *Uncle Tom's Cabin*, and Charles Carleton Coffin's *The Boys of '76*. As a 20-year-old he listed William Shakespeare, Lord Byron, Edward Bulwer-Lytton, and Mark Twain as his favorite authors (Whelan 1995, 65). The hero of *David Copperfield* was his favorite in all literature, Johann Goethe's *Faust* his favorite childhood book altogether. After a private school education in New York, Stieglitz's parents sent him to Berlin to finish his education. Between 1882 and 1886 he was enrolled at the Technische Hochschule (the Polytechnic) to study mechanical engineering and then became committed to technical photography courses. He read much Russian literature, then in vogue, including works by Mikhail Lermontov, Nikolai Gogol, Aleksander Pushkin, Ivan Turgenev, and Lev Tolstoy. By the end of the 1880s, he revered the naturalism of Émile Zola. He was especially moved by *Madeleine Férat*—he once sat up all night reading it aloud to friends—and avidly read the entire Rougon-Macquart series. Stieglitz's photograph *Sun Rays—Paula* (1889), actually a picture of a prostitute, may be something of an homage to Zola. As a student he also assisted at innumerable operas and plays by William Shakespeare, Pedro Calderón, Goethe, Gotthold Lessing, Johann Schiller, Henrik Ibsen, and José Echegaray. Years later, Stieglitz was a regular attendee at the Greenwich Village productions of the Provincetown Players.

Literature was an important influence on early art photography. Pictorialism, the movement in photography with which Stieglitz is associated, had intense literary pretensions. Walt Whitman's *Leaves of Grass* was held in the highest regard by Stieglitz's circle for its espousal of Americanism and romantic individualism. Stieglitz's awareness of contemporary literature was acute since he promoted and/or was personally acquainted with many of the most famous literary figures of his day. Contributors to *Camera Work* included figures such as George Bernard Shaw, Maurice Maeterlinck, and **Gertrude Stein,** among others. He counted among his friends **Carl Sandburg,** Marianne Moore, Hart Crane, Sherwood Anderson, Van Wyck Brooks, Carl Van Vechten, Edmund Wilson, Frank Harris, and Theodore Dreiser. Stieglitz so admired Dreiser's *Sister Carrie* (1900) that he gave copies to many of his friends. A photograph of locomotives, *Hand of Man* (1902), may demonstrate Stieglitz's predilection for Dreiser's realism. In the summer of 1924, during a retreat to Lake George, New York, Stieglitz is known to have read **James Joyce**'s then-notorious *Ulysses*. When **D. H. Lawrence** sent Stieglitz a copy of *Lady Chatterly's Lover* in 1928, Stieglitz called the book "one of the grandest that had ever been written, a sort of Bible, on a par with Goethe and Shakespeare." His own earlier nude studies reveal a similarly frank eroticism.

Archives

The Metropolitan Museum of Art in New York houses the largest collection of Stieglitz's photographs. The National Gallery (Washington, D.C.), the Library of Congress, the Art Institute of Chicago, and the San Francisco Museum of Modern Art also have significant holdings. The Philadelphia Museum of Art hosts the Alfred Stieglitz Center.

Beinecke Rare Book and Manuscript Library, Yale University, New Haven, Conn. Correspondence.

Printed Sources

Green, Jonathan. *Camera Work: A Critical Anthology* (Millerton, N.Y.: Aperture, 1973).

Greenough, Sarah, and Juan Hamilton (eds.). *Alfred Stieglitz: Photographs and Writings.* 2nd ed. (Washington, D.C.: National Gallery of Art/Bulfinch Press/Little, Brown, 1999).

Whelan, Richard. *Alfred Stieglitz: A Biography* (Boston: Little, Brown and Co., 1995).

Mark B. Pohlad

STOPES, MARIE CHARLOTTE CARMICHAEL (1880–1958)

Marie Stopes was born in Edinburgh to the English architect, archeologist, and geologist Henry Stopes and his feminist wife, Charlotte Carmichael, one of the first women to attend a Scottish university. The family moved to London when Marie was six weeks old. She and her younger sister Winnie were raised in a curious mixture of socially progressive scientific thought and stern Scottish Protestantism. Her authoritarian mother trusted the Bible but still supported women's suffrage, clothing reform, and free thought. Her father was a gentle soul who cared mainly for science. Marie was educated at home until 1892, then attended St. George's High School for Girls in Edinburgh until 1894, when she transferred to North London Collegiate School for Girls. She enrolled at University College, London, in 1900 on a science scholarship, graduating with a B.Sc. in 1902 with honors in botany and geology. She did graduate work there until 1903 and then at the University of Munich, where she received her Ph.D. in paleobotany in June 1904. In October she became the first woman scientist on the faculty of the University of Manchester. In 1905 University College made her the youngest Briton of either gender to earn the D.Sc. She studied at the Imperial University of Tokyo from 1907 to 1908, then returned to Manchester in 1909. She married geneticist Reginald Ruggles Gates in 1911 but obtained an annulment in 1916. Inspired by meeting **Margaret Sanger** in 1915, she began crusading for sexual freedom and birth control. With her second husband, Humphrey Verdon Roe, she opened the first birth control clinic in Great Britain on March 17, 1921. By her own account she had three distinct careers: as a scientist until about 1914, as a social reformer until the late 1930s, and as a poet thereafter.

As a young girl she met many of her father's friends in the British Association for the Advancement of Science, including Francis Galton, Thomas Henry Huxley, Norman McColl, and Charles Sayle. Through them came her interest in Charles Darwin. Her mother was a published scholar of William Shakespeare and Francis Bacon, a friend of Constance and Oscar Wilde, and would read aloud to preteens Marie and Winnie from a great variety of serious history and literature, expecting the girls to correlate the events with locations in the atlas. Marie wrote later that she developed a lifelong antipathy toward Jane Austen from this experience. As a teenager, she immersed herself in philosophy and spirituality, reading Immanuel Kant, Emanuel Swedenborg, and Henry David Thoreau. Her mentors at North London were headmistress and chemist Sophie Bryant and teacher Clothilde von Wyss; at University College, botanist Francis Wall Oliver, who in many ways was a father figure after her own father died in 1903; in Munich, Karl Goebel; and in Tokyo, Kenjiro Fujii, who became her first lover and introduced her to Chinese and Japanese poetry.

Archives

The largest part of Stopes's vast estate of papers and correspondence is in the British Library Department of Manuscripts. Other significant collections are in the Wellcome Trust (London) Contemporary Medical Archives Centre and in the private holdings of her son, Harry Verdon Stopes-Roe.

Printed Sources

Begbie, Harold. *Marie Stopes: Her Mission and Her Personality* (London: G.P. Putnam's Sons, 1927).

Briant, Keith Rutherford. *Marie Stopes: A Biography* (London: Hogarth, 1962); American edition: *Passionate Paradox: The Life of Marie Stopes* (New York: Norton, 1962).

Coldrick, Jack. *Dr. Marie Stopes and Press Censorship of Birth-Control: The Story of the Catholic Campaign against Newspaper Advertising in Ireland and Britain* (Belfast: Athol, 1992).

Eaton, Peter, and Marilyn Warnick. *Marie Stopes: A Checklist of Her Writings* (London: Croom Helm, 1977).

Hall, Ruth. *Marie Stopes: A Biography* (London: Andre Deutsch, 1977); American ed.: *Passionate Crusader: The Life of Marie Stopes* (New York: Harcourt Brace Jovanovich, 1977).

Maude, Aylmer. *The Authorized Life of Marie C. Stopes* (London: Williams & Norgate, 1924).

———. *Marie Stopes: Her Work and Play* (New York: G.P. Putnam's Sons, 1933).

Reynolds, Moira Davison. *Women Advocates of Reproductive Rights: Eleven Who Led the Struggle in the United States and Great Britain* (Jefferson, N.C.: McFarland, 1994).

Rose, June. *Marie Stopes and the Sexual Revolution* (London: Faber and Faber, 1992).
Stopes-Roe, Harry Verdon. *Marie Stopes and Birth Control* (London: Priory, 1974).

Eric v.d. Luft

STOPPARD, TOM (1937–)

Born Thomas Straussler in Ziln, Czechoslovakia, Stoppard was five years old when his father died. His mother later married a British officer, from whom the boy received his surname. He was educated at various private schools in India and England and landed a job as a theater critic in 1954, working in that capacity until 1960. **John Osborne**'s plays and Kenneth Tynan's reviews championing them inspired Stoppard to try his hand as a playwright. He scored his first big success with *Rosencrantz and Guildenstern are Dead* (1966), a play about fate and free will involving two minor characters from *Hamlet*. *The Real Inspector Hound* (1968) solidified Stoppard's reputation for mixing philosophical speculation and sharp wit, and invited justifiable comparisons with the works of George Bernard Shaw. In his most recent efforts, such as *The Invention of Love* (1997), Stoppard brings a thorough knowledge of history to bear on the issues that puzzle him, revealing himself to be a historian's playwright as much as a philosopher's.

Stoppard's criticism exhibited an appreciation for the realist masters Henrik Ibsen and **Bertolt Brecht,** and in terms of technique, many authors have seen the traces of Robert Bolt's style of language in Stoppard's earliest stage works (Billington 1987, 17; Fleming 2001, 12). Even so, it is the absurdist influence that is most evident in Stoppard's early plays, particularly *Rosencrantz* and *Inspector Hound,* in which the characters are trapped by outside forces, and the logical distinctions between real and unreal, on-stage and off, prove unreliable. Stoppard has expressed admiration for the plays of **Samuel Beckett** and **Harold Pinter,** even hinting that those authors' works possess a more timeless quality than his own (Gussow 1995, 6). However, among absurdists, Stoppard is probably most similar to **Eugene Ionesco,** whose plays take a more explicitly humorous approach to existential dilemmas. In terms of his humor and his belief that the aesthetics of plays are more important than their political or social value, Stoppard follows Oscar Wilde, another author that he specifically mentions as an influence.

Archives

Archives have not been established.

Printed Sources

Billington, Michael. *Stoppard: The Playwright* (London: Methuen, 1987).
Fleming, John. *Stoppard's Theatre: Finding Order amid Chaos* (Austin, Texas: University of Texas Press, 2001).
Gussow, Mel. *Conversations with Tom Stoppard* (London: Nick Hern Books, 1995).
Stoppard, Tom. *Plays,* 5 vol. (London: Faber and Faber, 1996–99).

Christopher Pepus

STRACHEY, LYTTON (1880–1932)

Giles Lytton Strachey was born in London on March 1, 1880, to a family with strong connections to Indian administration. His father, Sir Richard Strachey, had an important career as an engineer, a scientist, and a man of letters in India. His mother Jane (née Grant) had, in fact, been born on a boat bound for India. Strachey's elder brothers also had prominent careers in Indian affairs. After school at Abbotsholme and Leamington, he went to what was then called Liverpool University College, where his kinsman Walter Raleigh was King Alfred Professor of English Literature. Then he went up to Trinity College, Cambridge, where he moved in that circle of intellectuals known as the Apostles (**John Maynard Keynes, E. M. Forster,** and Leonard Woolf) who would form the core of Bloomsbury. Strachey sat for both parts of the History Tripos but did not take a distinguished degree. He sought a Trinity fellowship with a dissertation on Warren Hastings, but was defeated in two tries. Thence he went down to London where he served as a critic for his cousin's (St. Loe Strachey) *Spectator.*

Strachey's first published works were collections of verse: *Prolusiones Academicae* (1902) and *Euphrosyne* (1905). His major works followed: *Landmarks in French Literature* (1912), *Eminent Victorians* (1918), *Queen Victoria* (1921), *Books and Characters, French and English* (1922), *The Son of Heaven, a Play* (1925), *Elizabeth and Essex, A Tragic History* (1928), *Portraits and Miniatures, Critical Essays* (1931). *Characters and Commentaries* came out the year after he died. Strachey is famous for the revolution he produced in the writing of biography. With his slashing style, Strachey, as he put it in the preface to *Eminent Victorians*, imposed nothing, proposed nothing, he only exposed. Rescuing biography from Victorian reticence, Strachey directed attention to questions of time, memory, and character, examining the dynamics of the inner lives of his subjects. He led the way for generations of experimenters to liberate biographical writing from sterile forms and illusions.

Strachey's intellectual and literary background included modest amounts of the usual classical and mathematical training. However, the force of his mental preparation was in modern English and French literature. His family was a literary hothouse. Some of this was the result of his family's experience in India with its exotic and sensually immediate impulses. From an early age, however, Strachey's mother exposed him to the ideas and forms of French letters. His influence in things French was further promoted by Marie Souvestre, who conducted a famous school for girls at Fontainebleau and who later taught his sisters at her school in Wimbledon, and by his own travels in France. Jane Strachey raised Lytton and his siblings on French songs and verses. She introduced them to the fables of La Fontaine and read to them from Racine every evening. Elinor, Lytton's eldest sister, recalled that once, when she and her mother arrived in Paris by rail, Jane Strachey rose to her full height in the carriage and saluted the city. When **André Gide** visited England, Jane Strachey tutored him. Lytton's sister, Dorothy, fell in love with Gide and translated his work into English. Dorothy married the French artist Simon Bussy and wrote on Eugene Delacroix and Charles Baudelaire. Pernel Strachey, another sister who became principal of Newnham College, Cambridge, wrote and taught the writings of Honoré de Balzac and **Marcel Proust.** At Cambridge, G. E. Moore's *Principia Ethica* (1903) was the most important literary and philosophical influence upon Strachey. Its pursuit of the true and the good followed Strachey all of his life. One cannot dismiss the importance of his family, the Apostles, and his friends in Bloomsbury, all of whom acted as kinds of knowledge communities and continued to stimulate Strachey's mental formation.

Archives

A large collection of Strachey papers, including the correspondence of his brother James, is found in the British Library (Add. Mss. 60706–60712), along with letters to and from his cousin Duncan Grant (Add. Mss. 57932–57933). An important collection of family letters and papers are in the India Office Library (Mss., Eur. F. 127). Strachey's correspondence with Maynard Keynes, letters essential to understanding both men's lives and careers, is located in King's College, Cambridge. Strachey's letters to G. E. Moore are located in the University of Cambridge Library and his letters to R. C. Trevelyan are in Trinity College, Cambridge. The Harry Ransom Humanities Research Center at the University of Texas holds an extensive collection of Strachey family correspondence as well as Strachey's letters to and from Lady Ottoline Morrell and Leonard Woolf. The Berg Collection in the New York Public Library holds a small but very interesting series of letters between Strachey and Keynes. The Taylor Collection at Princeton University contains the holographs of Strachey's dissertation on Warren Hastings and correspondence with his sister, Dorothy Bussy, and Vanessa Bell.

Printed Sources

Holroyd, Michael (ed.). *Lytton Strachey By Himself: A Self-Portrait* (London: Heinemann, 1971).

Strachey, James (ed.). *Spectatorial Essays* (New York: Harcourt Brace, 1964).

Strachey, Lytton. *The Shorter Strachey*, Michael Holroyd and Paul Levy (ed. and intro.), (Oxford: Oxford University Press, 1980).

Woolf, L., and J. Strachey (eds.). *Virginia Woolf and Lytton Strachey: Letters* (London: Hogarth Press, 1956).

W. C. Lubenow

STRAVINSKY, IGOR (1882–1971)

Igor Stravinsky was born at Oranienbaum, near St. Petersburg, into a family with pronounced intellectual and musical interests. His father, Fyodor Ignatievich, a prominent bass-baritone at the Maryinsky Imperial Theatre, provided the young Stravinsky with a strong musical education. Stravinsky found pleasure in reading opera scores from his father's library. While attaining his law degree from the University of St. Petersburg (1905), he studied composition with Nikolai Rimsky-Korsakov. Beginning with *L'Oiseau de Feu* in 1910 (Alexander Golovin, Michel Fokine), Stravinsky collaborated with Serge Diaghilev and his circle of avant-garde artists on numerous projects for the Ballets Russes, which won him international recognition: *Petrouchka* in 1911 (Alexandre Benois, **Vaslav Nijinsky**); *Le Sacre du Printemps* in 1913 (Nikolai Roerich, Nijinsky); *Pulcinella* in 1920 (**Pablo Picasso,** Tamara Karsavina, Leonide Massine); *Le Chant du Rossignal* in 1920 (Henri Matisse, Massine, Karsavina); *Le Renard* in 1922 (Michel Larionov, Bronislava Nijinska); *Les Noces* in 1923 (Natalia Gontcharova, Nijinska); *Apollon Musagete* in 1928 (George Balanchine, Coco Chanel). *Le Sacre*, Stravinsky's revolutionary masterpiece, changed the face of music with its block harmonies, primitive rhythms, and complex innovations. Its debut created both a riot in the audience and a myth of the birth of modern music. *Le Sacre* is regarded as a manifesto of modern music, the touchstone of modernity. Its impact and iconoclastic status remain unprecedented in the music world. Stravinsky turned from the Bacchanalianism of *Le Sacre* to neoclassical forms, then he continued experimenting with different styles, conventions, and aesthetics in opera, symphonies, sacral music, and serial works. After the Russian Revolution, he became a French citizen, but during World War II he immigrated to the United States, where he obtained American citizenship and composed his final block of work. In 1939–40, Stravinsky delivered the Charles Eliot Norton Lecture Series at Harvard University, in which he pointed out the key to his diverse creations: music is about music, and its essence is the expression of sound.

Trilingual (Russian, French, and English), Stravinsky wrote half a dozen books of memoirs and commentaries, displaying a prodigious mastery of world literature. As a young man, he was caught up in the intellectual ideas of Diaghilev's journal, *Mir iskusstva* (1898–1904). He admired Alexander Pushkin because he united the most characteristically Russian elements with Western style, and based *Mavra* (1922), on Pushkin's *The Little House of Kolomna*. Sharing the neonationalist fascination of Diaghilev's circle with Russia's mythic past and pre-Petrine culture, he studied Alexander Afanasyev's *Russian Folktales* and Peter Kireevsky's collection of folk songs. *Les Noces, Renard Suite, Pribaoutki* (1914), and numerous choral works had their origins in Russian folklore, as did *Le Sacre*, which was textured by Kireevsky's ethnographic research on ceremonial and ritual music and Lithuanian folk songs compiled by Anton Juszkiewicz. Stravinsky translated some of his favorite Russian fairy tales into French.

Stravinsky's *Three Japanese Lyrics* (1913) were inspired by his extensive reading of Japanese poetry; his *Scherzo fantastique* (1909) by Maurice Maeterlinck's *La Vie des abeilles*, which he read in 1907. In 1910, he created *Two Poems of Verlaine*, songs based on Paul Verlaine's poems, *La lune blanche* and *Un grand sommeil noir*. Versed in Western classics as well as in Russian literature (he preferred Fyodor Dostoyevsky to Pushkin), he was influenced by modern writers such as **Jean-Paul Sartre, T. S. Eliot, Wystan Auden, Vladimir Mayakovsky,** and **Dylan Thomas.** He revered Eliot, creating a requiem mass for him, *Introitus T. S. Eliot in Memoriam* (1966). Auden, a close friend, wrote the libretto for his opera, *The Rake's Progress* (1951), and Stravinsky constructed *Elegy for J. F. K.* (1964) around Auden's poem on that subject. In 1953, he was commissioned to write an opera with Thomas, but the project ended with the untimely death of the poet. Stravinsky wrote a dirge, *In memoriam Dylan Thomas* (1954), using Thomas's poetry for the song lyrics. Stravinsky was familiar with the writings of the Spanish philosopher **Ortega y Gasset** citing *Castles in Castile* as reading material in 1955. Stravinsky's dictum that form is everything in music correlates with Gasset's thinking on the structure of aesthetic principles. The literary collaboration between Robert Craft and Stravinsky, published in many volumes, provides the richest sources on the composer's thoughts on music and literature.

Archives

Central State Historical Archives, St. Petersburg.
Maryinsky Theatre Collection, State Museum of Theatre and Music, St. Petersburg.
Serge Diaghilev Correspondence, Dance Collection, Lincoln Center, New York Public Library, New York.

Printed Sources

Stravinsky, Igor. *Chronicle of My Life* (New York: Simon and Schuster, 1936).
———. *The Poetics of Music* (New York: Simon and Schuster, 1947).

———. *Selected Correspondence*, 3 vols., Robert Craft (ed.), (New York: Alfred A. Knopf, 1985).

———. *Themes and Conclusions* (Berkeley: University of California Press, 1982).

Stravinsky, Igor, and Robert Craft. *Conversations with Igor Stravinsky* (Garden City: Doubleday, 1959).

———. *Memories and Commentaries* (New York: Doubleday, 1960).

Taruskin, Richard. *Stravinsky and the Russian Traditions: A Biography of the Works Through Marva*, 2 vols. (Berkeley: University of California Press, 1996).

Van den Toorn, Peter C. *Stravinsky and the Rite of Spring: The Beginnings of a Musical Language* (Berkeley: University of California Press, 1987).

Ulle V. Holt

STRESEMANN, GUSTAV (1878–1929)

Gustav Stresemann was the youngest of eight children of the Berlin publican and beer wholesaler Ernst August Stresemann and his wife, Mathilde. The ideals and virtues of the Protestant Prussian middle classes, such as devotion to duty, hard work, patriotism, and loyalty toward state and monarch, were imprinted upon him even before he began to attend school. The lessons at the Andreas-Realgymnasium in Berlin, where Stresemann spent all of his twelve and a half years at school (1884–97), intensified those values. He studied literature, history, and national economy at the universities of Berlin and Leipzig, attending lectures on national economy held by Gustav Schmoller and Karl Theodor Reinhold, among others, and graduated in 1901 with a Ph.D. on the beer trade in Berlin. The Prussian ethos of work affected his later career as spokesman or, in modern terms, public relations manager of an association of industrialists and as politician and statesman most strongly, since he was to tax himself often beyond the limits of his physical strength. Though Stresemann started out on his political career as a member of the National Liberal Party in the German Reichstag in 1907, it was as chancellor for only 103 days in 1923 and foreign secretary of the Weimar Republic from 1923 to 1929 that he influenced the course of German politics most markedly. In the position of chancellor he took the then-unpopular decision to end passive resistance in the Ruhr area against French and Belgian occupation, thus paving the way to a political consolidation of the Weimar Republic. Even more momentous was his impact on German foreign policy and on international relations in the second half of the 1920s in general. Not aggression, but negotiations aiming at reconciliation were his instrument in the attempt to pave the way to peaceful relations and international exchange and to reestablish Germany as a great power. Together with his French counterpart, Aristide Briand, he successfully worked for a rapprochement between Germany and France, which ushered in a new phase of international stability after World War I. The consummation of this policy was reached with the Locarno Treaty of 1925. For this outstanding feat of diplomacy, Stresemann and Briand were awarded the Nobel Peace Prize in 1926.

With two parents working in the family business, Stresemann was left alone quite often as a child. He filled much of his time with reading, preferably with literary texts and books on history and geography. Early in his life, Adalbert vom Berge's *Napoleons Leben* instilled in him a lifelong interest in Napoleon and other great personalities in history, an interest which led him to read Johann Wolfgang von Goethe, whose ideas and writings accompanied him throughout his life. Publications of speeches held at the time of the revolution of 1848–49 attracted him in his youth. Being rhetorically talented himself, he upheld an appreciation of powerful rhetoric, such as the one found in Thomas Babington Macaulay's writings or in the parliamentary debates on the Education Bill in England in 1870. Quotations from Goethe and other high-ranking German poets had their place in his own speeches, as did ideas voiced by the people in the street. While at university, Stresemann kept a detailed record of his readings, among them Werner Sombart's *Sozialismus und soziale Bewegung;* Ernest Renan's *Leben Jesu,* which impressed Stresemann, a freemason from the mid-1890s to 1923, very much; Macaulay's *Machiavelli* as well as fictional writings from Henrik Ibsen's *Hedda Gabler;* Adalbert Stifter's *Studien;* Theodor Fontane's *Irrungen und Wirrungen;* and works popular at the time, such as Friedrich Spielhagen's novels, among them *Angela,* and Lewis Wallace's *Ben Hur.*

After a second stroke, Stresemann died in October 1929, at the time trying to rally his fellow party members to vote for a ratification of the Young Plan. He left a wife, Käte, née Kleefeld, and two sons.

Archives

Stresemann-Nachlaß, Politisches Archiv des Auswärtigen Amtes, Bonn (most of the documents are available on microfilm in the National Archives of the United States).

Printed Sources

Bernhard, Henry (ed.). *Gustav Stresemann. Vermächtnis. Der Nachlaß in drei Bänden* (Berlin: Ullstein, 1932–33).

Harttung, Arnold (ed.). *Gustav Stresemann. Schriften. Mit einem Vorwort von Willy Brandt* (Berlin: Berlin Verlag, 1976).

Koszyk, Kurt. *Gustav Stresemann. Der kaisertreue Demokrat. Eine Biographie* (Cologne: Kiepenheuer & Witsch, 1989).

Stresemann, Gustav. *Reden und Schriften. Politik—Geschichte—Literatur. 1897–1929,* 2 vols. (Dresden: Reissner, 1926).

Stresemann, Wolfgang. *Mein Vater Gustav Stresemann* (Munich: Herbig, 1979).

Turner, Henry Ashby Jr. *Stresemann and the Politics of the Weimar Republic* (Princeton, N.J.: Princeton University Press, 1963).

Angela Schwarz

SUNDAY, WILLIAM ASHLEY (1862–1935)

Billy Sunday was a Presbyterian minister, reformer, and athlete who helped establish the forms of modern fundamentalist evangelism. After a childhood characterized by a broken family and scattered education, Sunday was hired to play outfield for the Chicago White Stockings in 1883 but experienced a religious conversion in Chicago's Pacific Garden Mission in Chicago in 1886. He left his lucrative professional baseball career playing for teams in Pittsburgh and Philadelphia to pursue his religious calling in 1891. He first worked for the YMCA in Chicago and then for other evangelists but began his own revival campaigns in 1896 and was ordained as a Presbyterian minister in 1903.

Sunday's revivals were highly organized, publicized campaigns directed toward a mass audience. Stressing the importance of personal conversion, Sunday's sermons were characterized by a fiery rhetorical style characterized by colloquial language and rousing music. As a result, he was widely criticized by both liberal critics and members of the clergy but gained widespread popularity. A leading proponent of the Prohibition movement, his famed "Booze" sermon, entitled "Get on the Water Wagon," was a revival mainstay. Sunday also vigorously supported American involvement in World War I and spoke at the U.S. House of Representatives in 1918. His activity was not limited to public preaching; he published *Love Stories of the Bible* in 1917 and other articles and sermons throughout his life and was involved with the Winona Bible Conference in Indiana. In 1935 Sunday received an honorary Doctor of Divinity degree from Bob Jones College.

Sunday lacked a formal education and disdained the academic intellectualism practiced by many of his contemporaries. He rejected modern theological doctrines such as the Social Gospel and scientific theories such as evolution, declaring "I want to say that I believe the word of the Bible is the word of God from cover to cover" (Bruns 1992, 127). Sunday therefore was most influenced by the Bible, from which he drew both spiritual inspiration and possibly the practice of using parables and literary allusions in his sermons. However, he also drew literary inspiration from past revivalists and Christian workers, including Charles Grandison Finney, "Uncle" John Vassar, and Dwight L. Moody. *Receive Ye the Holy Ghost* (1894) by the evangelist John Wilbur Chapman, a disciple of Moody and Sunday's one-time employer, also strongly influenced Sunday's fundamentalism.

Archives

Papers of William Ashley "Billy" Sunday and Helen Amelia (Thompson) Sunday, Grace College and Theological Seminary, Winona Lake, Indiana.

Printed Sources

Bruns, Roger A. *Preacher: Billy Sunday and Big Time American Evangelism* (New York: W.W. Norton & Company, 1992).

Dorset, Lyle W. *Billy Sunday and the Redemption of Urban America* (Grand Rapids, Michigan: William B. Eerdmans, 1991).

Gullen, Karen. *Billy Sunday Speaks* (New York: Chelsea House Publishers, 1970).

Marsden, George. *Fundamentalism and American Culture: The Shaping of Twentieth Century Evangelicalism, 1870–1925* (New York: Oxford University Press, 1982).

Jill Silos

T

TARKOVSKY, ANDREI (1932–1986)

Soviet filmmaker Andrei Arsen'evic Tarkovsky was born in Zavroje, near the Volga River, not far from Ivanovo, Russia (U.S.S.R.), on April 4, 1932. His father, Arseny (or Arseniy, Arsenii) Aleksandrovich Tarkovsky was a poet of merit. Andrei Tarkovsky spent his childhood in Peredelkino (not far from Moscow), receiving a religious education from his mother. He went to art schools and studied music, fine arts, and sculpting. He found a job as a geologist and worked for a time in Siberia. From 1956 to 1961, Tarkovsky studied with Mikhail Romm at the official film school in Moscow, the V.G.I.K. His films feature long shots, minimal editing, slow movements, and no reaction shots. Most of Tarkovsky's feature films won important prizes in film festivals: in 1962 at the Venice Festival, with his first feature film titled *My Name is Ivan (Ivan's Childhood)*, and later at the Festival de Cannes, when *Solaris* (1972), *Nostalgia* (1983), and *The Sacrifice* (1986) got the highest awards. In 1984, Tarkovsky defected, emigrating to Italy, where he lived for two years. He died of cancer in Paris in 1986, the same year his masterpiece, *The Sacrifice* (*Offret*), was released in Sweden.

In a 1985 interview with Swedish journalist Boleslaw Edelhajt, Tarkovsky named his main literary influences, the Russian authors Alexandr Pushkin, Nikolai Gogol, Fyodor Dostoyevsky, and Lev Tolstoy. Curiously, Tarkovsky admitted he was more influenced by nineteenth-century Russian poets than by any filmmaker. His favorite directors were mainly European: **Ingmar Bergman,** Michelangelo Antonioni, Robert Bresson, **Federico Fellini, Akira Kurosawa,** and above all **Luis Bunuel.** He didn't like **Sergei Eisenstein**'s aesthetics, though he mentions his films and writings in his book, *Sculpting in Time* (1986). Elsewhere in *Sculpting in Time*, Tarkovsky mentions as his favorite directors **Charles Chaplin,** Alexander Dovjenko, and Kenji Mizoguchi. Tarkovsky considered American films "garbage" (Tarkovsky 1986, 83). While he was still at the V.G.I.K. film school, Andrei Tarkovsky adapted **Ernest Hemingway**'s novel *The Killers*. Although made in

1956, this early film was only released in the 1990s in a few countries, most prominently France. Tarkovsky became more widely known when his true story of a painter of icons, *Andrei Rouble*, was finally released in 1966 after many problems with Soviet authorities. Although similar to Stanley Kubrick's *2001: A Space Odyssey* (1968), Tarkovsky's *Solaris* (1972) was a more spiritual science fiction essay adapted from a novel by Stanislaw Lem. Poems by Andrei Tarkovsky's father are quoted in his *The Mirror* (1974) and *Stalker* (1979). He directed only two plays for the stage: *Hamlet* at the Moscow Theater in 1976 and *Boris Godounov* at Covent Garden in London (1983 and 1984). With only seven feature films, Andrei Tarkovsky is still considered the Soviet Union's most important filmmaker of the second half of the twentieth century.

Archives

Archives of Mosfilm Studios, Moscow. Manuscripts, correspondence.

Svenska Filminstitutet, Stockholm. Materials related to Tarkovsky's last film, *The Sacrifice* (*Offret*), shot in Sweden.

Tarkovsky Archives, Moscow. Still in preparation; includes diaries, correspondence.

Tarkovsky Museum Centre, Ulitsa, Sovetskaya, Russia. Souvenirs from childhood; the museum is built in the house where he lived during World War II.

Printed Sources

Edelhajt, Boleslaw. "Entretien avec Andreï Tarkovski," *Les Cahiers du cinéma*, 392, février 1987, 39–43. In this interview Tarkovsky talks about his main literary and cinematic influences.

Laberge, Yves. "Andreï Tarkovski. *Sculpting in Time*," *Études littéraires*, Ste-Foy (Canada), Université Laval 20, 3 (Hiver 1987–88), 151–53.

Tarkovsky, Andrei. *Collected Screenplays*, William Powell and Anastasia Synessiou (trans.), (London: Faber and Faber, 1999).

———. *Sculpting in Time: Reflections on the Cinema*, Kitty Hunter-Blair (trans.), (Austin: University of Texas Press, 1989). In his unique book, the director writes about his vision of life and about his conception of cinema.

———. *Time Within Time: The Diaries 1970–1986*, Kitty Hunter-Blair (trans.), (London: Verso Books, 1993). Tarkovsky's intimate, personal diary.

Tarkovsky, Arseny. *Life, Life*, Virginia Rounding (ed.), (Kent, U.K.: Crescent Moon Publishing, 2001). English translations of poems written by Andrei Tarkovsky's father.

Turovskaya, Maya. *Tarkovsky: Cinema as Poetry*, Natasha Ward (trans.), (London: Faber and Faber, 1990). The best analysis of the cultural, religious, and literary influences on Tarkovsky's movies.

Yves Laberge

THATCHER, MARGARET HILDA (1925–)

Margaret Thatcher, along with **Winston Churchill** and **Clement Attlee,** was one of the dominant political personalities in Britain (and the West) in the latter half of the twentieth century. In her 11 years as prime minister of Britain (1979–90), she fundamentally altered the direction of both the Conservative Party and British politics generally. Her influence, along with that of **Ronald Reagan** in the United States, in redirecting Western economies toward free markets and away from Keynesian planning, proved to have a lasting impact.

Thatcher has famously traced the roots of her economic policies to the practical lessons in economics and morality that she learned at the knee of her father, Alfred Roberts, and at the counter of the family grocery, above which the family lived, in the English market town of Grantham. Early on, her father instilled an ethic of reading. The first book she remembered receiving was an almanac of "homespun philosophy and religion," but under the influence of her father, a local councilor, she was primarily exposed to nonfiction works, sharing the books he borrowed from the public library and discussing them. She therefore was exposed to tracts in the contemporary debates on socialism and appeasement by the likes of John Strachey. She seems to have read less fiction, although in her memoirs she does mention being exposed to "the classics," such as Dickens, as well as the poetry of Milton and Kipling (Thatcher 1995, 7, 16, 28; Campbell 2000, 28). Her parents' Methodist faith instilled in her a strong sense of individualistic values, including charity, frugality, and work (Thatcher 1995, 11–12; Campbell 2000, 16). She remained an active Methodist until her marriage to Denis Thatcher, when she joined the Anglican Church.

Thatcher attended the local grammar school where she did well, eventually focusing upon chemistry. Although her headmaster discouraged her from seeking a place at Oxford and prevented her from taking Latin, she eventually won a place at Somerville College, Oxford, to study chemistry. She finished her degree with a second and was generally remembered as an able, if not gifted, chemist by her teachers, who included the Nobel-prize winning chemist Dorothy Hodgkin. She remains the only British prime minister whose education was directed to a physical science. On the other hand, she failed to get the broad, liberal education that her colleagues in the Oxford University Conservative Association were receiving by reading history or politics. In general, her reading does not seem to have expanded significantly during these years, though she read *The Times* and famously did purchase a copy of F. A. Hayek's *The Road to Serfdom*, a work that would have much more influence on her three decades later. Another work she later recalled was Karl Popper's *The Open Society and Its Enemies,* which debunked the Marxist claim of "scientific" socialism (Thatcher 1995, 38, 50). As one biographer has described her, "She arrived in Oxford with her political views already settled and spent four years diligently confirming them. . . . she read little or no history at university; and neither then nor later did she read much literature. . . . Her mind dealt in facts and moral certainties" (Campbell 2000, 64–5).

Thatcher was defeated in the 1951 and 1955 elections, but began to establish a name within the Conservative Party and was eventually elected to Parliament in 1959. At the same time, she began reading for the bar, which she had decided was a better basis than chemistry for a political career. Passing the bar and working as a tax lawyer contributed to the "elevated, almost mystical, reverence for the rule of law as the foundation of English liberty" already present in her mind from her childhood. Here, the works of A. V. Dicey, the late Victorian legal scholar, with his stress on the rule of law within a framework of classical liberalism, was particularly influential (Thatcher 1995, 84).

Although she held ministerial posts in the Tory governments of the 1960s and early 1970s, it was a surprise when she challenged and defeated Edward Heath for the leadership of the Conservative Party in 1975. Under the tutelage of Keith Joseph, she was given a rapid education in the new, monetarist economic thinking, reading the remainder of Hayek's works as well as those of **Milton Friedman,** Alan Waters, and others. She was a quick convert and integrated these ideas with the more homespun lessons in economics she had learned from her father. As she later wrote, "Before I ever read a page of Milton Friedman or Alan Walters, I just knew that these [collectivist] assertions could not be true. Thrift was a virtue and profligacy a vice" (Thatcher 1995, 567).

She seized upon the opportunity of the economic crises that Britain faced in the late 1970s to lead the Conservative Party to victory in the general election of 1979. Pursuing policies of monetarism, individualism, and reducing the obligations of government, she was reelected in 1983 and 1987 before being forced to resign from the leadership of the Conservative Party in 1990, primarily as a result of disagreements on European policy. The changes that her governments brought about with regard to public welfare, state ownership, and economic policies proved lasting and brought about a restriction of the welfare state and an end to the post–World War II "collectivist" consensus in Britain.

Mrs. Thatcher was created Baroness Thatcher of Kesteven, a life peerage, after her retirement from office.

Archives

Lady Thatcher's private papers have not yet been deposited in an archive.

Official papers will be available at the Public Record Office, subject to the Thirty Year Rule, and the Conservative Party Archive at the Bodleian Library, University of Oxford, holds the party's official records.

Printed Sources

Campbell, John. *Margaret Thatcher: Volume One, The Grocer's Daughter* (London: Jonathan Cape, 2000).

Thatcher, Margaret. *The Collected Speeches,* Robin Harris (ed.), (London: HarperCollins, 1997).

———. *Complete Public Statements, 1945–1990* on CD-ROM, Christopher Collins (ed.), (Oxford: Oxford University Press, 1999).

———. *The Downing Street Years* (London: HarperCollins, 1993).

———. *The Path to Power* (London: HarperCollins, 1995).

Young, Hugo. *One of Us: A Biography of Margaret Thatcher* (London: Macmillan, 1989; revised 1991).

Derek W. Blakeley

THOMAS, DYLAN MARLAIS (1914–1953)

Dylan Thomas was born in Swansea, Wales, where he studied at the grammar school under his father David John Thomas, the English master, and had several of his poems printed in the school magazine. Thomas began his writing career as a journalist for the *Herald of Wales* and *South Wales Evening Post.* When Thomas was 19, *New English Weekly* published his poem "And Death Shall Have No Dominion." After moving to London (although he would later return repeatedly to Wales), Thomas continued as a journalist for a time and went on to publish seven volumes of poetry, plays, film scripts, and short stories in his lifetime; a number more were published posthumously. He supplemented his income as a radio scriptwriter and reader for the British Broadcasting Corporation. He married Caitlin Macnamara in 1937; despite Thomas's womanizing, the couple stayed together until his death. They had a daughter, Aeronwy, and two sons, Llewelyn and Colm. An infamous pub-frequenter, Thomas died of alcohol poisoning at the age of 39 while in the United States on the last of four lecture tours there.

Determining Dylan Thomas's literary influences is challenging. On one hand, Thomas was quite well read, beginning with his father's extensive library. On the other hand, Thomas did not attend university, eschewed academia, and even chided those who would classify him by literary school or identify his writing with a particular poet, such as Gerard Manley Hopkins, to whom he was frequently compared. Although Thomas identified himself first as a Welshman, he could not read or speak Welsh. However, he heard Welsh poetry read and was said to be influenced by the rhythm and rhyme of its words in his poems as well as its subjects of death, nature, and spirituality. Many termed Thomas a "bardic poet," referring to the early Welsh poets.

Responding to a question on his early inspirations, Thomas remarked: "I wanted to write poetry in the beginning because I had fallen in love with words. The first poems I knew were nursery rhymes, and before I could read them for myself I had come to love just the words of them, the words alone." He proceeded to list the influences on his early poetry as "folk tales, the Scottish Ballads, a few lines of hymns, the most famous Bible stories and the rhythms of the Bible, Blake's *Songs of Innocence*, and the quite incomprehensible magical majesty and nonsense of Shakespeare heard, read, and near-murdered in the first forms of my school" (Maud 1992, 12). The use of biblical language and allusions is particularly noticeable in his poetry; despite his father's agnosticism, the elder Thomas still quoted from the Bible at home, and Thomas attended a Presbyterian church. Two of Dylan Thomas's uncles as well as his grandfather were also ministers.

As he records in his correspondence and radio programs, Thomas's subsequent reading ranged from ancient through medieval epics (in translation), including Dante's works, to seventeenth-century poets, particularly John Donne, George Herbert, whose shaped poem "Easter Wings" Thomas adapted to his own work "Vision and Prayer," John Milton, and Henry Vaughan, up to his contemporaries. His close friend was fellow Welsh poet Vernon Watkins, from whom he would sometimes solicit writing advice, as recorded in Thomas's letters. Often outspoken, Dylan Thomas was vocal in both his praise and castigation of other writers. William Wordsworth earned Thomas's scorn for his lack of true mystical insight and poetic language. Thomas criticized **W. H. Auden** for his obscurity and paucity of emotions, and derided **T. S. Eliot**'s influence. Thomas praised and was influenced by **William Butler Yeats,** his favorite to read aloud at lectures, Walter de la Mare, Thomas Hardy, and some of **D. H. Lawrence**'s works, and he imitated **James Joyce** in his own collection of autobiographical short stories, *Portrait of the Artist as a Young Dog.*

Archives

British Library, London: MS. 48,217, Thomas's early typewritten and corrected poems; MS 52,612, correspondence with Vernon Watkins.
Lockwood Memorial Library, State University of New York at Buffalo: Four notebooks, 1930–33; Pamela Hanson Johnson letters.
Harry Ransom Humanities Research Center, University of Texas at Austin: Thomas letters.

Printed Sources

Ackerman, John. *Dylan Thomas: His Life and Work* (New York: St. Martin's, 1996).

Ferris, Paul (ed.). *The Collected Letters: Dylan Thomas*, new ed. (London: J. M. Dent, 2000).

———. *Dylan Thomas: The Biography*, new ed. (Washington, D.C.: Counterpoint, 2000).

Maud, Ralph (ed.). *On the Air with Dylan Thomas: The Broadcasts* (New York: New Directions, 1992).

Moynihan, William T. *The Craft and Art of Dylan Thomas* (Ithaca, N.Y.: Cornell University Press, 1966).

Thomas, Dylan. *Poet in the Making: The Notebooks of Dylan Thomas*, Ralph Maud (ed.), (London: J. M. Dent, 1968).

Tindall, William York. *A Reader's Guide to Dylan Thomas* (New York: Octagon Books, 1973).

Carol Blessing

TILLICH, PAUL JOHANNES (1886–1965)

Paul Tillich was born in Starzeddel, Prussia, the son of Johannes Tillich, a conservative Lutheran minister, and Mathilde Dürselen, whose attitudes were more liberal. In the 1890s his father was superintendent of parishes in the Diocese of Schönfliess-Neumark. Tillich began school in the walled medieval town of Schönfliess, then from age 12 to 14 he attended the humanistic gymnasium as a boarding student in nearby Königsberg-Neumark, where he immersed himself in German romantic poetry, literature, and philosophy. During this period he read Joseph von Eichendorff, Stefan George, Johann Wolfgang von Goethe, Friedrich Hölderlin, Novalis, Friedrich Nietzsche, and especially Friedrich Wilhelm Joseph von Schelling, with whom he felt a lifelong affinity. Schelling's emphasis on nature, the aesthetic, and the dilemmas of life that can only be overcome by mysticism enthralled Tillich. Life in the Schönfliess parsonage between the Lutheran school and his father's church intensified Tillich's deep feeling of the close relationship, if not neo-Platonic identity, among nature, the beautiful, the spiritual, and the holy. In this conducive atmosphere he first encountered the works of Jakob Böhme, Rudolf Otto, and Friedrich Daniel Ernst Schleiermacher.

Tillich's father was transferred to Berlin in 1900. After graduating in 1904 from the humanistic gymnasium in Berlin, where he enjoyed ancient Greek language and literature and the poetry of Rainer Maria Rilke, Tillich studied theology at the universities of Berlin, Tübingen, Breslau, and Halle, receiving his Ph.D. at Breslau in 1911 with a dissertation on Schelling and his licentiate in theology at Halle in 1912. Besides Schelling, his reading at this time centered on Immanuel Kant, Johann Gottlieb Fichte, Georg Wilhelm Friedrich Hegel, and Søren Kierkegaard. He was ordained in 1912, served as a chaplain in the German army throughout World War I, and began teaching theology at the University of Berlin in 1919. Throughout the 1920s he wrestled with the ideas of Kierkegaard, Nietzsche, and Karl Marx. He allied himself with liberals such as **Rudolf Bultmann** against the neo-Orthodoxy of **Karl Barth.** From 1924 to 1925 he taught at the University of Marburg, where his colleague **Martin Heidegger** encouraged his interest in existentialism. From 1925 to 1929 he taught at the universities of Dresden and Leipzig, then became professor of philosophy at the University of Frankfurt. When **Adolf Hitler** fired Tillich and many other religious liberals from their teaching positions in 1933, **Reinhold Niebuhr** invited him to Union Theological Seminary in New York City.

Tillich wrote in *My Search for Absolutes*, his brief intellectual autobiography, that "the way of synthesis . . . my own way . . . follows the classical German philosophers from Kant to Hegel and has remained a driving force in all my theological work. It has found its final form in my *Systematic Theology*."

Archives

The largest collection of Tillich's papers is in the Manuscripts and Archives Department of the Andover–Harvard Theological Library, Cambridge, Massachusetts.

Printed Sources

Albrecht, Renate. *Paul Tillich: sein Leben* (Frankfurt am Main: Peter Lang, 1993).

Calí, Grace. *Paul Tillich, First-Hand: A Memoir of the Harvard Years* (Chicago: Exploration Press, 1996).

Carey, John Jesse. *Paulus, Then and Now: A Study of Paul Tillich's Theological World and the Continuing Relevance of His Work* (Macon, Ga.: Mercer University Press, 2002).

Dourley, John P. *Paul Tillich and Bonaventure: An Evaluation of Tillich's Claim to Stand in the Augustinian-Franciscan Tradition* (Leiden: Brill, 1975).

O'Meara, Thomas F., and Donald M. Weisser (eds.). *Paul Tillich in Catholic Thought* (New York: Image, 1969).

Pauck, Wilhelm. *Paul Tillich: His Life and Thought* (San Francisco: Harper & Row, 1989).

Stenger, Mary Ann, and Ronald H. Stone. *Dialogues of Paul Tillich* (Macon, Ga.: Mercer University Press, 2002).

Stumme, John R. *Socialism in Theological Perspective: A Study of Paul Tillich, 1918–1933* (Missoula, Mont.: Scholars Press, 1978).

Tillich, Paul. *My Search for Absolutes* (New York: Simon & Schuster, 1969).

———. *On the Boundary: An Autobiographical Sketch* (London: Collins, 1967).

Eric v.d. Luft

TITO, JOSIP BROZ (1892–1980)

Born Josip Broz, he became known to the world under the alias Tito, which he adopted in the 1930s. Tito was born in the village of Kumrovec in the Zagorje region of the Austro-Hungarian Empire (now in Croatia), into a Roman Catholic family as the seventh of 15 children. His father was a Croatian peasant while his mother was of a slightly more affluent Slovenian descent. He spent his early childhood in Slovenia with his grandparents, attended school in the native village from the age of 7 to 12, and was trained as a locksmith. He traveled throughout the empire and worked at different places, supposedly even as a test-driver at the Daimler-Benz factory near Vienna. As a young trade-union member he was exposed to labor issues and became a socialist sympathizer. Tito was drafted into the Austro-Hungarian army and during the First World War he fought on the eastern front until he was wounded and captured by the Russians in 1915. By the time he was released in 1917, he was a committed communist who supported the Bolsheviks and joined the Red Guard during the Russian Civil War. In 1920 Tito returned from the Soviet Union and became a prominent member of the outlawed Communist Party. Following a series of imprisonments for his underground communist activity, Tito was appointed secretary general of the Communist Party of Yugoslavia in 1937. During the Second World War the communists under Tito's leadership engaged in partisan warfare and successfully fought the Nazis as well as the domestic royalist, nationalist, and fascist factions. After winning the war and ruthlessly eliminating the opponents, in 1945 Tito reestablished Yugoslavia as a federal, centralized, communist state. Tito soon broke the ties with the Soviet Union and the Cominform (1948), subdued ethnic nationalisms, introduced a unique brand of market socialism and worker's self-management, and pursued a foreign policy of nonalignment. A skilled manipulator of power politics with aristocratic pretensions and an insatiable appetite for luxury, Tito served as secretary general of the Party, head of government, commander-in-chief, and president of Yugoslavia, which disintegrated in a bloody civil war only a decade after his death.

Although Tito's education was inadequate for him to be considered an intellectual, he bequeathed numerous speeches, interviews, articles, and books, many of which have been widely translated. Some of the most prominent compiled and edited works are of a political nature and deal with issues, such as neutrality, that defined Yugoslav foreign policy: *Non-Alignment, the Conscience and Future of Mankind* (1979); on nationalism, *The National Question* (1983); on the Second World War communist struggle for power, *Selected Works on the People's War of Liberation* (1969); and on domestic politics, *Self-Management* (1983). Vladimir Dedijer, **Milovan Djilas,** Richard West, and other Tito biographers suggest that Tito possessed a meager knowledge of socialist theory, economy, and history. During his prison sentences Tito read the *Communist Manifesto*, and he acquainted himself with the major works of Karl Marx, Friedrich Engels, and **Vladimir Ilich Lenin.** Tito possessed considerable mechanical skill, had a solid understanding of technical matters, and learned languages easily. In addition to knowing Slovenian, German, and French, Tito was so fluent in Russian that he confused Serbo-Croatian and Russian idioms. He was never an avid reader, though his closest associates, such as Edvard Kardelj and others, kept Tito abreast of current events. Tito was not an excellent military strategist but was considered to be an exemplary military commander and a brilliant and charismatic political leader who had an unquenchable drive for power.

Archives

Arhiv Jugoslavije, Beograd.
Hrvatski Državni Arhiv, Zagreb.
Arhiv Republike Slovenije, Ljubljana.
Public Record Office, Kew, U.K.
United States National Archives and Records Administration, Washington, D.C.

Printed Works

Beloff, Nora. *Tito's Flawed Legacy: Yugoslavia and the West since 1939* (Boulder: Westview Press, 1985).
Dedijer, Vladimir. *Novi Prilozi za Biografiju Josipa Broza Tito*, 3 vols. (Zagreb: Mladost, 1980).
———. *Tito Speaks: His Self Portrait and Struggle with Stalin* (London: Weidenfeld and Nicolson, 1953).
Djilas, Milovan. *Tito: The Story from Inside* (New York: Harcourt Brace Jovanovich, 1980).
Pavlowitch, Stevan K. *Tito: Yugoslavia's Great Dictator: A Reassessment* (Columbus: Ohio State University Press, 1992).
West, Richard. *Tito and the Rise and Fall of Yugoslavia* (New York: Carroll & Graf, 1996).

Josip Mocnik

TOLKIEN, JOHN RONALD REUEL (1892–1973)

Born on January 3, 1892, in Bloemfontein, in the Orange Free State, J.R.R. Tolkien was four and on holiday in England with his mother when his father died. Having limited resources, Mabel Tolkien settled south of her native Birmingham in the small village of Sarehole. In 1900 Ronald entered King Edward VI's School in Birmingham. He excelled especially at languages and was soon learning Anglo-Saxon and Chaucerian English. His mother died when he was 12, leaving her sons to the care of Father Francis Morgan of the Birmingham Oratory. Tolkien's deep Catholic faith formed one of the underlying foundations of all his "fairy stories" in later life. In 1911, he entered Exeter College, Oxford, receiving his B.A. in 1915 and an M.A. in 1919. Between degrees Tolkien got married but was also called to war. He survived the Battle of the Somme uninjured but fell ill with trench fever and was sent home to recover. After the Armistice, Tolkien became a philologist and spent several months working on what would become the *Oxford English Dictionary*. In 1920 he was appointed reader in English studies at the University of Leeds, where he produced an edition of the medieval poem *Sir Gawain and the Green Knight* (1925). Elected Rawlinson and Bosworth Professor of Anglo-Saxon at Oxford University in 1925, he immediately began working with other young scholars, among them **C. S. Lewis,** to improve the English syllabus. Though he published a few scholarly essays (including the acclaimed "Beowulf: the Monster and the Critics," 1936), his time was chiefly devoted to teaching, examinations, and the creation of the fantastic literary world of Middle Earth. This world was first revealed to a select group of friends and scholars, the Inklings, whose encouragement, particularly Lewis's, led Tolkien to publish *The Hobbit* in 1937. The book was an unexpected success, and the publisher asked for a sequel, which Tolkien agreed to do although he took 17 years to complete it. When the epic *Lord of the Rings* appeared in three volumes during 1954 and 1955, it received mixed reviews. Some complained about its escapism, but many others, including the poet **W. H. Auden,** declared it an achievement of lasting importance. Medieval historian Norman Cantor, normally unsympathetic to fantasy literature, has credited it with helping to bring modern readers into contact with a "realm of imagination that at the same time communicates how medieval people thought of themselves" (Cantor 1991, 232). More empathetic evaluators have sought to put Tolkien into the top echelon of twentieth-century writers, especially as *Lord of the Rings* remained among the most read and recommended of contemporary books.

Tolkien was certainly familiar with the revival of medieval romances and "fairy stories" in the late nineteenth century. But Middle Earth was not inspired by the works of such predecessors as William Morris or George MacDonald. Rather, Tolkien drew his creative breath directly from the classical epics, from the Norse and Icelandic Sagas, and from Anglo-Saxon poetry. Indeed, the very language of northern European mythology and poetry is echoed throughout Tolkien's stories, with many place and personal names coming directly from Norse, Anglo-Saxon, or even medieval Finnish (which served as the basic inspiration for the elvish languages Tolkien created). While some have decried Tolkien's apparent endorsement of medieval hierarchical society, others have noted that it is the small and ordinary folk, the Hobbits and their counterparts among elves, dwarves, and men, who are the real heroes of the stories, observing that the high and the mighty (which we always have with us) are nothing without the struggle for goodness and decency being won by the common members of society.

Archives

Manuscripts and notes, Marquette University Memorial Library, Milwaukee, Wisconsin. Manuscripts and proofs of *The Hobbit, Lord of the Rings*, and *Farmer Giles of Ham*.
Maps relating to the *Lord of the Rings*, Bodleian Library, Oxford, England.

Printed Sources

Cantor, Norman. *Inventing the Middle Ages: The Lives, Works, and Ideas of the Great Medievalists of the Twentieth Century* (New York: William Morrow, 1991).
Carpenter, Humphrey. *J. R. R. Tolkien: a Biography* (London: Allen & Unwin, 1977). The "official" biography.
——— (ed.). *The Letters of J. R. R. Tolkien* (New York: Houghton Mifflin, 2000). A useful biographical and literary resource.
Shippey, Tom. *J. R. R. Tolkien: Author of the Century* (New York: Houghton Mifflin, 2001). The latest attempt to raise Tolkien's literary status.
Stimpson, Catherine R. *J. R. R. Tolkien* (New York: Columbia University Press, 1969). An early and useful, if unsympathetic, literary evaluation.

Richard R. Follett

TOMASI, GIUSEPPE (1896–1957)

Giuseppe Tomasi, Duke of Palma and Prince of Lampedusa, was born in Palermo. He spent most of his life in Sicily but died in Rome. Reading was not just the most important thing in his life, it was the only thing he did. Inertia kept him from beginning his novel, *Il gattopardo (The Leopard)*, until 1954. It was rejected for publication in 1956 and 1957 but after his death it was published to wide acclaim, going through 52 editions in 17 months. He was agnostic. He was cosmopolitan, yet emotionally tied to Palermo and Sicily. He was proud, contemptuous, and reserved, taciturn in public, preferring solitude. Late in life he taught two students English and French literature. For his lectures he wrote notebooks of critical essays, some of which were published posthumously.

He was educated at home with access to the family library of Enlightenment classics, modern literature and histories, and later at schools in Rome and Palermo. In 1914 he studied law in Rome, then joined the artillery. He was taken prisoner by the Austrians at Asiago, eventually escaping to Trieste. After 1918 he suffered physical and nervous disorders and abandoned his law studies. Like many intellectual aristocrats, scornful of ineffectual liberalism and afraid of revolution, he was attracted to fascism in the 1920s. But later he was bored by it and by life in Sicily. He traveled in northern Italy, France, Germany, Austria, and England. He learned French, German, and later Spanish and Russian, and knew English well enough to read Shakespeare and **James Joyce.** In London he undertook private study of British essayists and poets. His favorite authors were John Keats, Homer, Cervantes, Jane Austen, Montaigne, Balzac, **André Gide,** Dickens, **Marcel Proust,** Tolstoy, Petrarch, D'Annunzio, and Leopardi. He published three articles on foreign literature in the 1920s. He was disdainful of Italy's part in World War II and after 1942 was exempt from active service because of ill health. He was depressed, especially after 1943 when the family palace in Palermo was bombed. From 1944 he was president of the Palermo and later Sicilian Red Cross, but was frustrated by shortages, rivalries, and internal disputes.

He met Montale, Bassani and other European and American writers. He was inspired by Stendhal's immediacy and sincerity. But more than formal education or people he met it was extensive reading that shaped his thinking. His book, *The Leopard*, is a historical novel set in 1860s Sicily at the time of Garibaldi's landing and Italian unification. The protagonist is Fabrizio Salina, a portrait of Tomasi's great-grandfather but to some extent also a self-portrait. It is a ruthlessly bitter picture of stagnant Sicilian society, tied to ancient values, prejudices, and indolence. Fabrizio's deep introspective personal analysis of the collapse of values is dominated by a dark suffocating funereal sense of decay, uselessness, and death. The style—historical, poetic, and elusive, and like Tomasi skeptical and pessimistic—has been compared to Tolstoy, Stendhal, Proust, Conrad, and **Thomas Mann.**

Tomasi's ancestors were ascetics, mystics, and fanatics who placed family survival in jeopardy by renouncing everything for the church, left their estates to distant branches of the family or, like his grandfather, failed to make a will, until there was little left to inherit. Tomasi was a literary dilettante who dedicated his life to reading to the detriment of his estates. Family decadence literally brought about the collapse of their properties, yet he did nothing to prevent it. The Lampedusas had never worked for a living and Giuseppe was no exception. His final burst of artistic creativity coincided with his rapid physical decline. After his death the remaining family properties fell into ruins. The only legacy of the Lampedusas was Giuseppe's memory and understanding of its traditions, which he transformed into literature.

Archives

Tomasi's papers, diaries, files, correspondence, unpublished works, and commonplace book are held by his adopted son, Gioacchino Lanza Tomasi, in Palermo.

Printed Sources

Cordona, Caterina. *Lettere a Licy* (Palermo: Sellerio, 1987).
Gilmour, David. *The Last Leopard* (London: Quartet, 1988). With bibliography.
Orlando, Francesco. *Ricordo di Lampedusa* (Milano: Vanni Scheiwiller, 1963).
Tomasi, Giuseppe. *The Leopard* (London: Collins, 1961).

Gillian Fenwick

TROTSKY, LEON (1879–1940)

Leon Trotsky was born Lyov Davidovich Bronstein in Yanovka, Ukraine, Russia, and died in Coyoacán, Mexico. Trotsky spent the first nine years of his life on his parents' farm, where all aspects of life were regulated by the toils of agrarian existence. He was, however, tutored in Russian, mathematics, and biblical Hebrew, and as a high school student, he attended the St. Paul Realschule in Odessa and the Nikolayev Realschule in Nikolayev. In Nikolayev, he came into contact with radical intelligentsia and became interested in revolutionary politics. His further schooling came in the form of incarcerations in czarist prisons, multiple banishments to Siberia, and foreign exile. When he heard that the March Revolution had installed a provisional government under Aleksandr Kerensky, Trotsky returned to Russia, arriving in Petrograd on May 4, 1917. He accepted **Vladimir Lenin**'s invitation to join the Bolshevik Party and played a leading role in preparations for the October uprising. This raised Trotsky to the pinnacle of his power, serving first as Bolshevik commissar for foreign relations and then as commissar for war.

As Bolshevik commissar of war, he galvanized the Russian peasantry and led them to several victories during the Russian Civil War. He accepted and collaborated with Lenin's style of leadership which involved ruthless centralism, iron discipline, and a cult of authority.

Trotsky's political fortunes drastically declined after Lenin's death in 1924. **Josef Stalin**'s politics of "Socialism in One Country" trumped Trotsky's theory of Permanent Revolution, which was seen as having the potential of involving Russia in international adventures of a dangerous nature. Trotsky's theory of Permanent Revolution maintained that revolution could not stop at the bourgeois/democratic stage but would have to follow up the liquidation of absolutism and feudalism with an immediate socialist transformation which would set the stage for socialist revolutions throughout the world.

In 1928, Trotsky was banished to Alma-Alta in Soviet Turkestan; in 1929 he was expelled from the Soviet Union and forced to take up residence on the Turkish island of Prinkipo. Efforts to reside in France and Norway were undermined by harassment by the respective governments of those countries, and in 1936, he moved to Mexico. In 1940, Ramon Mercador, believed to be a Stalinist agent, murdered Trotsky outside of Mexico City.

In *My Life: An Attempt at an Autobiography* (1931), Trotsky observes: "In my inner life, not only during my school years but throughout my youth, nature and individuals occupied a lesser place than books and ideas." He eagerly read such authors as Lev Tolstoy, Nikolay Nekrassov, Aleksandr Pushkin, and Charles Dickens. The social critical impulses in Dickens's *Oliver Twist* in terms of a sympathy for the impoverished made a strong impression on him.

As he developed toward becoming a revolutionary, Trotsky was strongly drawn toward such philosophers as John Stuart Mill and Jeremy Bentham and the nineteenth-century socialist Nikolay Chernyshevsky. He also mentions François Mignet's *History of the French Revolution* as having exerted a profound influence. Writing in 1824, Mignet expressed horror at the violence of the French Revolution but nonetheless maintained that it was a necessary outcome of social and economic conditions.

During his first imprisonment in Kherson and Odessa in 1898, Trotsky read the holdings of the prison libraries, which consisted of conservative historical and religious magazines covering many years. He immersed himself in a study of sects and heresies of ancient and modern times. He developed a special interest in the movement of freemasonry. In the eighteenth century, the freemasons existed as a secret society and enabled the progression of uncensored political and theological discussions that advanced the social agenda of the bourgeoisie in ways the absolutist state would not have allowed had these discussions taken place in a more public manner. Something in the conspiratorial nature of freemasonry appealed to Trotsky.

When his own books arrived at the prison, Trotsky read essays by the Italian Hegelian-Marxist Antonio Labriola, who brilliantly applied the concept of materialist dialectics to the philosophy of history. During his banishment to Ust-Kut, Siberia, in 1900, Trotsky began studying the works of Karl Marx and he also read Lenin's works, *What Is to Be Done?* and *The Development of Capitalism in Russia*. He also studied such Marxist philosophers as Eduard Bernstein, Karl Kautsky, and Geórgy Plekhanov.

Archives

Leon Trotsky Archives, Houghton Library, Harvard University.

Printed Sources

Smith, Irving H. (ed.). *Great Lives Observed: Trotsky* (Englewood Cliffs, N.J.: Prentice-Hall, 1973).
Trotsky, Leon. *My Life: An Attempt at an Autobiography* (New York: Scribner, 1931).
Wistrich, Robert S. *Trotsky: Fate of a Revolutionary* (London: Robson, 1979).

Peter R. Erspamer

TRUDEAU, PIERRE ELLIOTT (1919–2000)

Pierre Trudeau, Canada's most erudite prime minister (1968–79, 1980–84), was born in Montreal to a French-Canadian father and a mother, Grace Elliott, whose ancestry was partially Scottish-Canadian. Educated at the Jesuit-run Jean-de-Brébeuf College (B.A., 1940) and at the University of Montreal where he received a law degree in 1943, Trudeau obtained the A.M. in political economy at Harvard University in 1946 before pursuing graduate studies at the École libre des sciences politiques in Paris and the London School of Economics. Deeply Roman Catholic but iconoclastic, Pierre Trudeau experienced a personal epiphany around the age of 30 when he encountered the philosophy of personalism, whose foremost exponent in France was Emmanuel Mounier (Clarkson and McCall 1990/94, 1: 58). This left-wing Catholic approach allowed Trudeau to criticize the traditional outlook of Quebec's episcopate while still adhering to religious beliefs. He became a fierce critic of Quebec political and intellectual practices, but as prime minister he reformed the country's criminal code, legislated bilingualism for the federal government, instituted a policy of multiculturalism, and patriated the constitution from Britain in 1982 with a new Canadian Charter of Rights and Freedoms. On the international scene he attempted to promote detente and nuclear arms reduction during the later phases of the cold war.

At Jean-de-Brébeuf, a Montreal classical college combining high school and undergraduate instruction, Pierre Trudeau was introduced to French, Greek, and Latin literature as well as major thinkers such as John Locke, Alexis de Tocqueville, and Thomas Jefferson (Trudeau 1993, 22; Radwanski 1978, 57). He was deeply influenced by lines from Cyrano de Bergerac as presented in the sentimental 1897 drama by Edmond de Rostand: "To sing, to laugh, to dream, to walk in my own way. I'll climb, not high perhaps, but all alone" (Clarkson and McCall 1990/94, 1:43). Plato's and Aristotle's writings on politics and justice retained a lifelong interest, informing his view that a democracy needed to aim at being a "Just Society" (Trudeau 1970, throughout; Trudeau 1998, 15). He continued to quote Blaise Pascal's *Pensées* throughout his life and from Michel Montaigne's essays he adopted the need for tolerance. Montesquieu's *The Spirit of the Laws* (1748) confirmed Trudeau's belief in the value of parliamentary institutions in guaranteeing liberty and that reason should master emotion. At Harvard he deepened his interest in Western democratic thought, being particularly struck with British Victorian philosopher

Thomas Hill Green's liberal doctrine that liberty was impossible without an active state to provide security against abuses caused by industrialism. The argument made by his economics professor Joseph A. Schumpeter in *Capitalism, Socialism and Democracy* (1942) that capitalism was doomed to self-destruct left an impress that was deepened when studying with London's Harold Laski, who criticized liberalism's individualist failings.

Pierre Trudeau spent the post–Second World War period publishing essays about law, society, federalism, and Quebec that were later collected in *Approaches to Politics* (1970), *Federalism and the French Canadians* (1968), *Against the Current: Selected Writings, 1939–1996* (1996), and *The Essential Trudeau* (1998). Practicing law and appointed associate professor at the University of Montreal in 1961, he moved from a left-wing perspective to a left-of-center liberalism that extolled progressive ideas about democracy, human freedom, pluralism, and federalism, but he essentialized French-Canadian nationalism as intolerant, discriminatory, and totalitarian. The ideas of McGill University constitutional law professor and poet Frank Reginald Scott influenced his view of the creative possibilities for the law and the manner in which French Canadians had merely adhered to democracy rather than embracing it. He read British liberal historian and Catholic editor Lord John Dalberg Acton to bolster his argument that nationalism was retrograde and self-serving. Trudeau was also attracted to Catholic philosopher Jacques Maritain's critical realism and emphasis on human freedom, pluralism, and natural rights (Trudeau 1968, 105, 169, 181). Maritain reintroduced him to theologian Thomas Aquinas, but Trudeau also sometimes quoted the Bible (Trudeau 1998, 2; Trudeau 1996, 326).

With enduring literary interests, Pierre Trudeau spent much time discussing nineteenth-century poet Charles Baudelaire when he met French writer and politician **André Malraux** during the 1970s. In retirement he returned to literature, quoting the poetry of **T. S. Eliot** and **W. B. Yeats** extensively in accepting the J. H. Ralston prize from Stanford University in 1990 (Trudeau 1996, 325). Pierre Elliott Trudeau was a remarkable embodiment of Canada's linguistic and cultural dualism.

Archives

National Archives of Canada, Ottawa, Ontario.

Printed Sources

Clarkson, Stephen, and Christina McCall. *Trudeau and Our Times*, 2 vols. (Toronto: McClelland & Stewart, 1990, 1994).

Cook, Ramsay. *The Maple Leaf Forever: Essays on Nationalism and Politics in Canada* (Toronto: Macmillan, 1971).

Couture, Claude. *Paddling with the Current: Pierre Elliott Trudeau, Étienne Parent, Liberalism, and Nationalism in Canada* (Edmonton: University of Alberta Press, 1998).

Graham, Ron, and Lloyd Axworthy (eds.). *Towards the Just Society: The Trudeau Years* (Toronto: Viking, 1990).

Radwanski, George. *Trudeau* (Toronto: Macmillan, 1978).

Trudeau, Pierre Elliott. *Against the Current: Selected Writings, 1939–1996*, Gérard Pelletier (ed.), (Toronto: McClelland & Stewart, 1996)

———. *Approaches to Politics* (Toronto: Oxford University Press, 1970).

———. *The Essential Trudeau*, Ron Graham (ed.), (Toronto: McClelland & Stewart, 1998).

———. *Federalism and the French Canadians* (Toronto: Macmillan, 1968).

———. *Memoirs* (Toronto: McClelland & Stewart, 1993).

Terry Crowley

TRUFFAUT, FRANÇOIS (1932–1984)

Truffaut was born in Paris in 1932 and had a troubled childhood. The son of factory workers, he failed to complete his studies and was often imprisoned for theft and hooliganism. He also spent some time in a psychiatric hospital. But he was never without books in prison or without his journals and letter-writing. At the age of 13 he began to read the *Fayard* classics in alphabetical order, from Aristophanes to Voltaire: his favorite authors were **Marcel Proust,** Honoré de Balzac, Georges Bernanos, Gustave Flaubert, **André Gide, Graham Greene,** Guy de Maupassant, Georges Simenon, **Jean-Paul Sartre,** and Oscar Wilde. The turning point was his friendship with André Bazin, the film critic who directed the influential *Cahiers du Cinéma.* Bazin encouraged young Truffaut's interest in film, and the result was an article, "Une certaine Tendance du Cinéma Français" ("A Certain Tendency in French Cinema," 1954), which called for a more personal cinema. It became an informal manifesto for the nouvelle vague (new wave). Truffaut's first works as a film director were shorts, but already in 1959 he completed his first feature-length film, the semi-autobiographical *Les Quatrecents Coups* (*The Four Hundred Blows*), about a troubled adolescent, Antoine Doinel. The same character is the protagonist of an episode, *Antoine et Colette, in L'amour à Vingt* (*Love at Twenty*, 1962), of *Baisers Volés* (*Stolen Kisses*, 1968), of *Domicile Coniugal* (*Bed and Board*, 1970), and of *L'amour en fuite* (*Love on the Run*, 1979), all films featuring the actor Jean-Pierre Léaud as Antoine. The principal influence on Truffaut's cinematography came from the humanistic tradition of Jean Renoir, and through this perspective Truffaut gives expression to a vision of the life always continuing, always flourishing in spite of all difficulties and everyday dramas. The above-mentioned titles belong in this category, together with *Jules et Jim* (1961), *L'Enfant Sauvage* (*The Wild Child*, 1969), *La Nuit Americaine* (*Day for Night*, 1973), *Une Belle Fille Comme Moi* (*Such a Gorgeous Kid Like Me*, 1973), and *L'Homme Qui Aimait Les Femmes* (*The Man Who Loved Women*, 1977). Another somewhat contradictory tendency was deeply influenced by **Alfred Hitchcock**, representing the darker side of life in fatalistic, even cynical movies: *La Mariée Etait En Noir* (*The Bride Wore Black*, 1968), *Les Deux Anglaises* (*Two English Girls*, 1972), *Adèle H.* (*The Story of Adèle H.*, 1975), *La Chambre Verte* (*The Green Room*, 1978), *Le Dernier Metro* (*Last Metro*, 1980), *La Femme D'Acoté* (*The Woman Next Door*, 1981), and *Virement Dimanche* (1983). Truffaut won an Oscar for *La Nuit Américaine* (*Day for Night*, 1973).

The main themes around which the cinema of Truffaut develops are childhood, represented according to the patterns of Jean Vigo and of Charles Dickens, the violation of the cinematographic genre, the quest for absolute values, the quest for absolute and therefore impossible love, and the predominance of an anti-hero, who fights for freedom without weapons and loses, becoming part of a social order that strangles him. Truffaut's films and acute film criticism exercised a strong influence on many European film directors, especially on Eric Röhmer, Louis Malle, Bertrand Tavernier, Jacques Rivette, Alain Tanner, and Tony Richardson.

Archives

No archives available

Printed Sources

Crisp, C.G. *François Truffaut* (London: November Books, 1972).

Homes, Diana, and Robert Ingram. *François Truffaut* (Manchester: Manchester University Press, 1998).

Truffaut, François. *The Films in My Life* (New York: De Capo Press, 1995).

Maria Tabaglio

TRUMAN, HARRY S. (1884–1972)

Harry Truman was born in Lamar, Missouri. Around the age of six, his family moved to Independence, Missouri, where he met his wife, Elizabeth ("Bess") Wallace. He later attended Noland, Columbian, and Independence grade and high schools, and his favorite subject was history. Although he did not graduate from college, as Truman himself noted, books, especially historical biographies, definitively influenced his entire career. A book that was perhaps the most influential was Edward Creasy's *Fifteen Decisive Battles of the World.* In 1905, Truman joined the National Guard. When World War I erupted, he enlisted in the army. Truman was sent to France and was discharged on May 6, 1919. He married Bess on June 28, 1919, and they lived in Independence. Truman opened a store, but the business failed. In 1922, he was elected as a judge of the Missouri county courts. On February 17, 1924, his only child, Mary Margaret, was born. Truman ran for reelection that year, and was defeated. In 1926, he won the seat of presiding judge of Jackson County, Missouri, and was reelected in 1930. In 1934, he ran for the Senate, winning by a large majority. While preparing for his new position as senator, Truman read every book he could find on the Senate. In 1940, Truman ran for reelection and won. In response to manufacturing corruption during World War II, Truman organized the Special Committee Investigating the National Defense Program. In 1944, **Franklin D. Roosevelt** selected Truman for vice president. Roosevelt was reelected, and Truman became vice-president on January 20, 1945. Roosevelt died on April 12, 1945, and Truman became the thirty-third president of the United States. Truman ordered atomic bombs to be dropped on Japan in August of 1945 after Japan failed to agree to peace terms. Japan surrendered in September 1945. In 1947, Truman established the Truman Doctrine to help other countries fight against Communism, and in 1948, signed the Marshall Plan to assist European economic recovery. Truman ran for president in 1948 and won, but in 1952 refused to run again. Truman returned to Independence where he wrote *Memoirs: Years of Decision* (1955) and *Years of Trial and Hope* (1956). In 1956, he received an honorary degree from Oxford. In 1957, the Truman Library opened. In 1960, he published *Mr. Citizen*, about his post-presidential years. He died on December 26, 1972, and was interred in the courtyard of his library. His wife Bess died in 1982 and was buried alongside him.

Usually because of requests, Truman continually described his literary influences. In 1950, his press secretary listed some of his favorite books, including George Eliot's *Silas Marner.* She noted Truman enjoyed Dryden and Shakespeare (Truman Library, information sheet on literary influences, 1950). In a 1958 letter to the governor of Minnesota, Truman listed his greatest literary influences as anything by Mark Twain, **Carl Sandburg**'s *Abraham Lincoln*, Marquis James's books on Andrew Jackson, Claude Bowers's collection on Thomas Jefferson, and other various American memoirs. He made particular note that by 14, he had read all of the books in the Independence Public Library, including the Bible, which he read four times. Plutarch's *Lives*, Edward Gibbons's *Decline and Fall of the Roman Empire*, and the poetry of Tennyson also influenced him. Thucydides, the state papers of George Washington, and **Herbert Hoover**'s *The Ordeal of Woodrow Wilson* were also of particular personal importance. A favorite and influential work was Charles Horne's *Great Men and Famous Women*. Truman, when writing legislation or embarking on a new phase of his life, would always read any document he could find relating to his subject. Throughout his life, he always took great pride in his self-taught literary background.

Archives

Harry S. Truman Library and Museum. 500 W. U.S. Hwy. 24, Independence, Mo. 64050. Photographs, government documents, personal papers, manuscripts, personal memorabilia, correspondence.

National Archives and Records Service, *National Archives Microfilm Publications; Microcopy No. M835*, Washington, D.C. Over a thousand photographs of Harry S. Truman.

Printed Sources

Truman, Harry S. *Years of Decision: Memoirs by Harry S. Truman*, vol. 1 (New York: Doubleday & Co. Inc., 1955).

———. *1946–1952, Years of Trials and Hope: Memoirs by Harry S. Truman*, vol. 2 (New York: Doubleday & Co. Inc., 1956).

Truman, Margaret. *Harry S. Truman* (New York: Morrow, 1973).

———. *Letters from Father: The Truman Family's Personal Correspondence* (New York: Arbor House, 1981).

Wendy A. Maier

U

ULBRICHT, WALTER (1893–1973)

Walter Ulbricht was born in Leipzig to working class parents; his father was a tailor active in the tailors' union and the Social Democratic party (SPD). His parents were not religious, and Ulbricht was not confirmed; he remained hostile to religion his entire life. Ulbricht attended elementary school until 1907, and then completed a carpenter's apprenticeship. He worked as a carpenter in Leipzig from 1912, was a member of the carpenters' union, and also served as a functionary for the local SPD. In 1917 Ulbricht joined the fledgling USPD. During World War One he served in the army; he opposed the war and in 1918 was imprisoned for political agitation. After the war, Ulbricht wrote for several communist papers and in 1920 joined the new Communist Party (KPD). Thereafter he rose steadily in state and national party ranks. A year in Moscow, 1928–29, was especially influential: Ulbricht came into contact with important Soviet leaders and returned determined to work for a Soviet-style state on German soil. In 1933, Ulbricht fled the Nazis, first to Paris, then Prague; from 1933 to 1938 he performed underground work for the KPD and was steadfastly loyal to the Stalinist line. In 1938 he settled in the Soviet Union and remained until 1945. Desirous of power, Ulbricht positioned himself close to **Josef Stalin;** he also demonstrated a willingness to attack and destroy rivals. In early 1945 Ulbricht was Stalin's choice to head the KPD delegation established in defeated Germany. Ulbricht labored tirelessly to build KPD influence in the Soviet occupation zone. In 1946, he pushed a KPD–SPD merger, thus creating one working-class party under communist control, the Socialist Unity Party (SED). With the 1949 founding of the German Democratic Republic (GDR), Ulbricht became one of three deputy chairmen of the Council of Ministers. Thereafter he worked opportunistically to add new positions that permitted him to consolidate power and eliminate all rivals. Always keen to act in the interests of Moscow, in 1961 Ulbricht suggested the construction of the Berlin Wall, and in 1968 supported the suppression of the liberal "Prague Spring." By 1970, though, differences of opinion were evident between Ulbricht and the new generation of Soviet leaders, specifically in the areas of economic policy and relations with West Germany. In 1971 Ulbricht was removed from all major positions. He essentially disappeared from public life, and he died in 1973. Ulbricht is representative of the postwar generation of Stalinist political figures, individuals who worked to create Soviet-style states. As times changed and new leadership emerged in the Soviet Union, Ulbricht appeared increasingly inflexible and outdated; this ultimately led to his ouster.

As a young man, Ulbricht was politically engaged in different SPD cultural and political organizations; in both he encountered the works of Karl Marx, Friedrich Engels, and August Bebel, but also classics by Friedrich Schiller, Johann von Herder, Gotthold Lessing, and Johann Wolfgang von Goethe. He attended numerous lectures on different subjects and read widely. His future life was decisively influenced by these early, formative years; Marx and Engels especially provided a view of class conflict and revolution that appealed to him. For much of his life, but especially after the 1930s, Ulbricht lived a private existence and read little outside of party literature and political tracts. He had no close friends and seldom interacted with others outside the workplace; politics consumed his energies. Many publications appeared during the 1950s and 1960s under Ulbricht's name; these reveal a consistent vision of a planned economy and a centralized state under party control. After 1949, when time allowed, he read novels of Hans Fallada and the East German author Johannes Becher, because they portrayed politically acceptable views of working-class life.

Archives

Russian Center for the Storage and Investigation of Documents, Moscow. Records of Comintern; covers period to 1944.

Bundesarchiv Potsdam. Records of GDR Council of State.

Central Archive of the Former GDR Ministry of State Security, Berlin.

Records for GDR Council of Ministers, other state bodies, Berlin.

Printed Sources

Frank, M. *Walter Ulbricht. Eine deutsche Biografie* (Berlin: Siedler, 2001). The new standard biography.

Podewin, Norbert. *Walter Ulbricht. Eine neue Biografie* (Berlin: Dietz, 1995).

Stern, C. *Ulbricht: A Political Biography* (New York: Praeger, 1965). Good on early years.

Ulbricht, Walter. *On questions of socialist construction in the GDR.* (Dresden: Zeit im Bild, 1968).

———. *Whither Germany?* (Dresden: Zeit im Bild, 1966). Speeches and essays on the national question.

Thomas Saylor

UNAMUNO, MIGUEL DE (1864–1936)

Miguel de Unamuno cultivated almost every literary genre: the essay, the novel, the short story, poetry, and drama, and hundreds of articles published in Spain and Latin America. His work is engraved with human passion and the accent of his personality as if it were a spiritual and self-critical autobiography.

Unamuno was born to a fervent Catholic family from the Basque city of Bilbao. He studied philosophy at the University of Madrid. An avid reader, Unamuno declared in his posthumous *Diario Intimo* (published in 1970): "I can tell that French writers introduced me to European thought . . . but I have forgotten them long ago with the exception of the best." Between 1892 and 1897, Unamuno was influenced by Marxist socialism, which he rejected after his last religious and intellectual crisis. His fictional autobiography *Paz en la Guerra* (1897) explores a time of civil war in his native city from a metaphysical aspect of life.

After a few years back in Bilbao, Unamuno became professor of Greek at the University of Salamanca. He married his childhood sweetheart, Concepción Lizárraga, and had nine children. From 1901 to 1914, he acted as rector of the University of Salamanca until his strong anti-German sentiments provoked his dismissal.

Unamuno learned German and English so that he could read Immanuel Kant, G.W.F. Hegel, Herbert Spencer, and Thomas Carlyle. He was attracted to Hegelian dialectic and applied the concept of paradox in many of his works. Among his favorite writers were Blaise Pascal, Etienne Sénancour, Lev Tolstoy, and Henrik Ibsen. He also read the works of other controversial authors of the time, such as Ernest Renán and Georg Buchner, who were concerned with the conflict between science and religion. Unamuno also translated Giacomo Leopardi *La ginestra*, Samuel Taylor Coleridge from English and Joan Maragall from Catalan. His finest translation is considered Seneca's *Medea*.

Banished to the Canary Islands for his opposition to the Primo de Rivera dictatorship in 1924, he fled to France. He exultantly returned to Salamanca in 1930 when the dictatorship fell. Being critical of authoritarian Spanish regimes, he maintained an ongoing battle with the Spanish regimes of the early twentieth century: monarchy, dictatorship and republic. As such, he at first supported the uprising of General **Francisco Franco** in 1936 against the Second Republic, but soon after he recanted and denounced the military leaders of the rebellion and was then put under house arrest. A few months after the Spanish Civil War began, Unamuno died on December 31, 1936. Spain lost a great philosopher and the best in-depth interpreter of the times.

The period of "regenerationism" in the literary essay provided a forum for reformers. From Unamuno's time as a university professor, Castilian idiosyncrasy and landscape became a social concern as well as for other members of the generation of 1898, which included Angel Ganivet and Antonio Machado, among others. Unamuno's readings from George Bernard Shaw and Maurice Barrès led him to embark on a new attitude toward Spain as a cultural and spiritual entity and to discover the eternal and universal qualities of "Hispanidad" (Spanishness) after the national consternation over the loss of the last colonies in the Spanish-American war in 1898. In *En torno al casticismo* (1902), Unamuno perceives that excessive individualism produced decadence and isolation. Spain's need is to integrate itself in Europe. Two central and converging principles appear in his doctrine: "eternal tradition," alive and present, and the concept of "intrahistory" that searches for the essential and lasting in human life versus the purely chronological and accidental of history. In *La vida de don Quijote y Sancho* (1905), Unamuno returns to the idea of individualism, his personal vision, and his faith, due to his disillusion with reason. The "madman" Don Quixote symbolizes the virtues of disinterested heroism, optimism, and self-confidence, which should inspire the aim for spiritual rather than technological supremacy in Spanish people. With a similar approach, Unamuno visited Portugal between 1907 and 1914 and was interested in "*saudade*" (sadness) and Portugal's self-examination and religion through the poetry of Texeira de Pascoaes and Antero de Quental.

Unamuno's other basic preoccupation is that of the immortality of the soul and the finality of life. He trusts "el hombre de carne y hueso," the man of flesh and bone who struggles against death. After his religious crisis, Unamuno taught himself Danish in order to study Søren Kierkegaard in 1901. From William James and **Henri Bergson,** Unamuno expanded his doctrine on faith, reason, and intuition. *Del sentimiento trágico de la vida en los hombres y en los pueblos* (1913) shows an anguished quest for immortality. Man does not explain rationally the existence of God; man feels the need for God. He chose to make the "mortal leap" from denial to affirmation of God; he desires a God so he can extend his existence beyond death. Denying the validity of any inflexible philosophical system, he declares: "faith that does not doubt, is a dead faith." This agonizing struggle between reason and Christian faith forms the basis for *La agonía del Critianismo* (1925), also entitled "Pascalian Faith."

Unamuno mixes literature with ideas, as others mix philosophy with literature. Thus, he creates a very personal genre, "nivola," a type of fiction abstracted from time and space to show variants of the tragic feeling of life. The character Augusto Pérez in *Niebla* (1914) protests against Unamuno's intention to terminate his fictional life, on the grounds that he has an autonomous life, separate from Unamuno's pen. The autonomy of the literary character derives from *Don Quixote* as well as his being a precursor of **Luigi Pirandello**'s theater. Unamuno's work is a preexistential hagiography, the fictional balance to Saint Augustine's and Jean Jacques Rousseau's *Confessions*. Brotherly war and fraticide closely linked with the biblical story of Cain and Abel is the central theme of *Abel Sánchez* (1917).

Unamuno's voice speaks for the present in as unmistakable a style as that of Friedrich Nietzsche and Walt Whitman. He declares "My thought derives not from reason but (from) life, although I need to rationalize it to express it to you. Most of it cannot be reduced to a theory or logical system; but like Walt Whitman, the great yanqui poet, no theory or school should be created without me." As a national record, the novella reflects the political and ideological struggles of Spain that culminated in the Spanish Civil War. Unamuno's intellectual independence, originality, emotional intensity, and personal style make him a unique and unclassifiable artist.

Archives

Archivo de Don Miguel de Unamuno, Universidad de Salamanca.
Casa-Museo de Unamuno, Universidad de Salamanca.
Archivo Histórico Nacional, Biblioteca Nacional, Madrid.

Printed Sources

Ferrater Mora, José. *Unamuno, a Philosophy of Tragedy,* Phillip Silver (trans.), (Berkeley: University of California Press, 1962).

Ilie, Paul. *Unamuno. An Existential View of Self and Soul* (Madison: University of Wisconsin Press, 1967).

Marías, Julián. *Miguel de Unamuno,* Frances M. López-Morillas (trans.), (Cambridge, Mass.: Harvard University Press, 1966).

Nozick, Martín. *Miguel de Unamuno* (New York: Twayne Publishers, 1971).

Pérez-Lucas, M. D. *Unamuno en el recuerdo (retazos de su vida)* (Salamanca: Hespérides, 1998).

Sánchez, Barbudo A. *Miguel de Unamuno* (Madrid: Taurus, 1974).

Unamuno, Miguel de. *The Private World: Selections from the Diario Intimo and Selected Letters, 1890–1936*, Anthony Kerrigan, Allen Lacy, Martin Nozick (trans.), Martin Nozick and Allen Lacy (ed.), (Princeton: Princeton University Press, 1984).

Wyers, Frances. *Miguel de Unamuno: The Contrary Self* (London:Tamesis Books, 1976).

Andrés Villagrá

UNGARETTI, GIUSEPPE (1888–1970)

Giuseppe Ungaretti was born in Alexandria, Egypt. Having spent his childhood in North Africa, where he was greatly influenced by nomadic culture, he later completed his studies at the Sorbonne, where he focused on the writing and thought of Charles Baudelaire, Racine, and Nietzsche. During his stay in France, Ungaretti made strong ties to the literary and artistic avant-garde in Paris and continued his studies there until recalled back to Italy to serve in the war. After serving as an infantryman in Italy during World War I, Ungaretti taught at the University of São Paolo in Brazil until 1942, after which he accepted a chair at the University of Rome. An Italian poet, critic, and translator, Ungaretti is primarily known for having developed a "purist" style of poetic expression: intense and condensed, Ungaretti's writings display an unconventional syntax and elaborate rhetorical structure. His poem "Il porto sepolto" (1916; "The Buried Port") reoriented modern Italian poetry and permitted critics to dub him the founder of the Hermetic movement in literature.

In 1904 Ungaretti met and befriended the poet Mohammed Sceab at the meetings of the literary group L'Ecole Suisse Jacot, during which time he was introduced to European literature. Dabbling in the writings of subversive writers including William Blake, Charles Baudelaire, Jules Laforgue, Giacomo Leopardi, and Stéphane Mallarmé, Ungaretti was able to confer with some well-known avant-garde thinkers during meetings of the socialist-anarchist literary group "Baracca Rossa," which was established by the Tuscan writer Enrico Pea and Sceab in 1908. The Italian members of the circle proscribed a nostalgia for pre-Industrial Italy as well as a desire to adopt France as its new "motherland." It was primarily during his acquaintance (ca. 1913) with French symbolist poets and avant-garde artists including **Guillaume Apollinaire** and Giuseppe Prezzolini that Ungaretti's style reached maturation.

Archives

Wylie, Andrew, 1947– , collector. MC 217 (SUNY at Stony Brook) West Campus: Correspondence, drafts of poems and translations, newsletters, programs, photographs, clippings, telegrams, audiotapes, and phonograph records related to Ungaretti's reading tour of the United States in 1969.

Biblioteca Nazionale di Firenze: correspondence and rare manuscripts.

Printed Sources

Giachery, Emerico. *Vita d'un uomo: itinerario di Giuseppe Ungaretti* (Modena: Mucchi, 1990).

Piccioni, Leone. *Vita di Ungaretti* (Milan: Biblioteca universale Rizzoli, 1979).

Ungaretti, Giuseppe. *Ungaretti: la biblioteca di un nomade* (Rome: De Luca, 1997). Catalog of an exhibition of books most appreciated by Ungaretti, unedited manuscripts, and works by artists and writers with whom he was in touch.

Dana Milstein

UPDIKE, JOHN HOYER (1932–)

John Updike was born in West Reading, Pennsylvania—an only child—and raised in nearby Shillington and Plowville. Growing up, Updike enjoyed humorists who appeared in *New Yorker* magazine: Ogden Nash, James Thurber, and E. B. White, among others. Much of Updike's early fiction is set in Pennsylvania, including *Rabbit, Run* (1960), *Pigeon Feathers* (1962), and National Book Award–winning *The Centaur* (1963). Updike's Lutheran upbringing also informs his fiction; he undertook to "hymn" the "whole mass of middling, hidden, troubled America" (Updike 1989, 103), most famously through the Pulitzer Prize–winning *Rabbit* tetralogy.

Updike graduated from Shillington High School in 1950 as covaledictorian, earning a scholarship to Harvard, where he wrote and drew cartoons for the *Harvard Lampoon*. He studied English literature; his senior thesis concerned seventeenth-century poet Robert Herrick's debt to Horace. Updike also read William Shakespeare, with whom he engages in *Gertrude and Claudius* (2000), a prequel to *Hamlet*.

After graduating summa cum laude in 1954, Updike and his first wife spent a year in Oxford, England, where he studied at the Ruskin School of Fine Art and Drawing. As they started a family, Updike read **C. S. Lewis, T. S. Eliot,** G. K. Chesterton, **Miguel de Unamuno,** and Thomas Aquinas to soothe "existential terrors" and maintain his Christian faith (Updike 1989, 55, 230). Those struggles account for much of his fiction; *In the Beauty of the Lilies* (1996), for example, explores religious faith and doubt in America over the twentieth century.

Updike joined the *New Yorker* staff in 1955 and lived in New York City. Though he left for Ipswich, Massachusetts, in 1957, hundreds of Updike's poems, short stories, and reviews appeared in the *New Yorker* over the next several decades.

In the late 1950s and early 1960s, when Updike was in his late twenties, he read Swiss theologian **Karl Barth** and nineteenth-century Danish Lutheran Søren Kierkegaard; Barth's *The Word of God and the Word of Man* and Kierkegaard's *Fear and Trembling* gave Updike "a philosophy to live and labor by" (Updike 1999, *More Matter*, 843). Updike thought of his novels as illustrations from the texts of the two theologians: Kierkegaard's existentialist anxiety pervades Updike's character Rabbit Angstrom, while Barth's doctrine of God as "Wholly Other" encouraged Updike to hold a mirror to domestic life without moralizing (Updike 1999, "Remarks," 5).

Updike also acknowledges debts to French writer **Marcel Proust,** whom he read the summer after finishing college, and English novelist Henry Green for their "styles of tender exploration that tried to wrap themselves around the things, the tints and voices and perfumes, of the apprehended real" (Updike 1989, *Self-Consciousness* 103–4). Other notable influences are **James Joyce, Vladimir Nabokov, Jack Kerouac, Thomas Mann,** and J. D. Salinger (De Bellis 2000, 253–56).

Archives
Harvard University's Houghton Library, Cambridge, Mass.: Notes, manuscripts, drawings, proofs.

Printed Sources

De Bellis, Jack. *The John Updike Encyclopedia* (Westport, Conn.: Greenwood Press, 2000). A comprehensive secondary source which has entries devoted to Updike's influences and reading—and a helpful bibliography.

Plath, James (ed.). *Conversations with John Updike* (Jackson: University Press of Mississippi, 1994). Updike discusses his influences in many of these collected interviews.

Updike, John. *More Matter* (New York: Knopf, 1999). Updike's seventh collection of nonfiction, like those before it, contains reflections on a lifetime of wide reading.

———. "Remarks Upon Receiving the Campion Medal." In James Yerkes (ed.), *John Updike and Religion: The Sense of the Sacred and the Motions of Grace* (Grand Rapids: Eerdmans, 1999). Explores Updike's religious thought. The editor also maintains a comprehensive Updike Web site, "The Centaurian," at http://userpages.prexar.com/joyerkes/.

———. *Self-Consciousness: Memoirs* (New York: Knopf, 1989).

Stephen J. Rippon

VALÉRY, PAUL AMBROISE (1871–1945)

Paul Valéry, French poet and man of letters, is one of the greatest of modern philosophical writers in both verse and prose. Valéry was born in Sète to a bourgeois family of Italian and Corsican descent and was educated at the Université de Montpellier. After a year of voluntary military service, he enrolled in law school. It was there that he met **André Gide,** one of the most outstanding writers of the day. In 1892, he settled in Paris, where he entered the literary circle of symbolist poets and made friends with some very prominent writers including Henri de Régnier and Joris-Karl Huysmans. Valéry was the protégé of Stephane Mallarmé, who encouraged his early works, and whose other young disciples, such as Pierre Louis, had Valéry's work published. Valéry's reading of Mallarmé's works was the prime source from which his own poetic expression emerged. In the musicality of Valéry's verse, the influence of Mallarmé is clearly identifiable.

At the time of his acquaintance with Mallarmé, Valéry was also being greatly influenced by his reading of Edgar Allan Poe. He became interested in Poe's constructivist principle of poetry as he explained it in his 1846 essay *The Philosophy of Composition*, a description of the genesis of his work *The Raven*. He was further interested in the fame that Poe had gained in France through the translations of his work by Charles Baudelaire and Mallarmé. Valéry's reading of Baudelaire's description of Poe motivated him to attempt to perfect his own understanding of the mind. Valéry's early poems, which were written between 1889 and 1898, were influenced by the symbolists that he had met in Paris. In his poetry, Valéry attempted to make abstract ideas concrete through symbolic imagery.

Following these publications, Valéry began a long period of literary silence, opting instead to work at a publishing house in London and in a news agency (1900–1922). Valéry's *Introduction à la méthode de Léonard de Vinci* (1895) was an opportunity to test many of his arguments on the nature of thought. His constructivist version of Leonardo da Vinci owes much to his reading of René Descartes, who was the first to argue for the predominance of logical relationships in scientific inquiry. In Valéry's second published essay, *Une soirée avec Monsieur Teste* (1896), these Cartesian undercurrents surface. Indeed, through its depiction of the fictional Monsieur Tête, the essay traces the intellectual outline of the seventeenth-century philosopher.

His works from the World War I period include *La Jeune Parque* (1917). In 1920, he published *Cimetière marin*, one of his best-known poems. Other works include *Album des vers anciens* (1921), *Eupalinos* (1921), *Charmes* (1922), *L'Âme et la danse* (1925), and *Regards sur le monde actuel* (1931). Valéry's later prose works consist of philosophical studies and meditations. Valéry's poetry is best described as the painting of his thoughts. It is a philosophical poetry that centers on the problems of our existence and of our destiny. His prose follows a similar intellectual and philosophical angle. He was appointed a lecturer in politics at the Collège de France in 1937. Valéry was elected to the Académie française in 1925. Upon his death on July 20, 1945, he was given a national funeral.

Archives

Jacques Doucet Literary Library, Paris, France, Collection Valéry.
Bibliothèque St. Geneviève, Paris, France, Collection Doucet, Paul Valéry. Including manuscripts and original editions.

Printed Sources

Anderson, Kirsteen. *Paul Valéry and the Voice of Desire* (Oxford: European Humanities Research Centre, 2000).
Kluback, William. *Paul Valéry: A Philosopher for Philosophers, the Sage* (New York: Peter Lang, 1999).

Richard J. Gray II

VAUGHAN WILLIAMS, RALPH (1872–1958)

Ralph Vaughan Williams was born in Down Ampney, Gloucestershire, but lived most of his life in London and in the town of Dorking in Surrey. Considered one of the greatest English composers of the twentieth century or indeed of any era, he wrote in a wide variety of forms, and his music was often influenced by his broad range of reading. His first symphony, for instance, is a vast choral work that powerfully sets stirring music to the verse of Walt Whitman, one of Vaughan Williams's favorite poets. The ninth (and final) symphony, meanwhile, seems to have been largely inspired by the composer's reading of Thomas Hardy's *Tess of the D'Urbervilles*. First recorded on the very day the aged composer died, the final symphony exemplifies the strong links between literature and music that typify his whole career.

Many of Vaughan Williams's most significant works show the impact of his reading. His fifth symphony, for instance, draws (especially in its sublime third movement) on inspiration from John Bunyan's *Pilgrim's Progress*, and Vaughan Williams explained the eerily enigmatic final movement of his sixth symphony by alluding to a passage from Shakespeare's *The Tempest*. Meanwhile, each movement of the seventh symphony—*The Sinfonia Antarctica*—is headed by an epigraph from a separate literary source (Percy Shelley, Psalm 104, Samuel Coleridge, John Donne, and the journal of Captain R. F. Scott). Likewise, *Job, A Masque for Dancing*, was influenced not only by the Bible (a key source for many of the composer's works, even though Vaughan Williams himself was an agnostic) but also by the engravings and poems of William Blake. *Flos Campi*, a ravishing work for orchestra and solo viola, draws inspiration from the biblical Song of Songs, while the ever-popular work *The Lark Ascending*, for violin and orchestra, was inspired by a poem by George Meredith. *Riders to the Sea*, perhaps the composer's best opera, is a setting of the play by J. M. Synge, while another opera—*The Pilgrim's Progress*—exemplifies Vaughan Williams's enduring fascination with Bunyan. *The Poisoned Kiss*, yet another opera, was inspired by a short story by Richard Garnett, while the opera *Sir John in Love* is one of numerous works reflecting Vaughan Williams's lifelong love of Shakespeare.

It is obviously in his numerous songs and larger choral works that Vaughan Williams's literary interests are most apparent. Among the latter, *Dona Nobis Pacem* used words from Whitman, the Bible, and other texts to appeal for peace in prewar Europe; the oratorio *Sancta Civitas* draws on the Book of Revelation; while the exquisitely beautiful *Serenade to Music* takes its words from Shakespeare's *Merchant of Venice*. *Toward the Unknown Region* borrows again from Whitman, while *The Oxford Elegy* is a setting of Matthew Arnold's memorable poems "The Scholar Gypsy" and "Thyrsis." One of the most compelling of Vaughan Williams's large-scale choral works is *Hodie*, a Christmas cantata that sets texts from such varied sources as the Bible, Miles Coverdale, William Drummond, Thomas Hardy, George Herbert, John Milton, and even Ursula Vaughan Williams, the composer's second wife and herself a poet whose words he frequently used. His *Five Mystical Songs* do rich justice to the poems of George Herbert, while his *Five Tudor Portraits* set poems by John Skelton.

Vaughan Williams wrote music for numerous hymns and other liturgical works, and he was equally active as a composer of art songs and song-cycles, often drawing (as so often elsewhere) on the music and lyrics of the English folk song tradition, which he vigorously championed. Among the more obviously "literary" sources for his songs were poems by such notable writers as Blake, Robert Bridges, Robert Burns, Coleridge, Richard Crashaw, Hardy, Herbert, A. E. Housman, Christina Rossetti, Dante Gabriel Rossetti, Shelley, Fredegond Shove, Robert Louis Stevenson, Alfred Tennyson, and Paul Verlaine. Vaughan Williams drew on these and many other literary sources throughout his long career, but he seems to have been especially attracted to the words of Whitman, Shakespeare, anonymous "folk" poets, and (in his later years) his second wife. His musical legacy shows everywhere the deep, abiding impact of his reading.

Archives

Important sources include the Vaughan Williams Memorial Library, London; the Royal Academy of Music Library, London; the Cambridge University Library, Cambridge; the Bodleian Library at Oxford University; and especially The British Library, London.

Printed Sources

Day, James. *Vaughan Williams*, 3rd ed. (Oxford: Oxford University Press, 1998).
Dickinson, A. E. F. *Vaughan Williams* (London: Faber and Faber, 1963).
Foss, Hubert J. *Ralph Vaughan Williams: A Study* (London: Harrap, 1950).
Frogley, Alain (ed.). *Vaughan Williams Studies* (Cambridge: Cambridge University Press, 1996).

————. *Vaughan Williams's Ninth Symphony* (Oxford: Oxford University Press, 2001).

Howes, Frank. *The Music of Ralph Vaughan Williams* (London: Oxford University Press, 1954).

Kennedy, Michael. *The Works of Ralph Vaughan Williams* (London: Oxford University Press, 1971).

Mellers, Wilfrid. *Vaughan Williams and the Vision of Albion* (London: Barrie and Jenkins, 1989).

Vaughan Williams, Ursula. *R.V.W.: A Biography of Ralph Vaughan Williams* (Oxford: Oxford University Press, 1964).

Robert C. Evans

WALDHEIM, KURT (1918–)

Kurt Waldheim was born at St. Andrä-Wördern, Lower Austria. In 1936 when military service became compulsory in Austria, he joined the Austrian cavalry and was put on the reserve list. He began to study law at the University of Vienna and attended the Vienna Consular Academy in 1937 but his studies were interrupted when he was called up at the beginning of World War II. After the war, Waldheim worked as a diplomat until 1968 when he became foreign minister of Austria (1968–70). In 1971, he was nominated as the presidential candidate for the conservative People's Party (ÖVP) but he lost the election to the Social Democrat Franz Jonas (1899–1974). From 1971 to 1981, Waldheim served two terms as the United Nations secretary general. During this time he earned a reputation as a tough negotiator; critics, however, depicted him as an opportunist. As a visiting professor at Georgetown University, he taught international relations from 1981 to 1982. He became Austrian president in 1986. The scandal surrounding Waldheim's candidacy for Austrian president was triggered by his alleged involvement in war crimes. In his autobiography *The Challenge of Peace* (1980), he concealed his SA membership and his interest in becoming a member of the National Socialist Party, NSDAP. Furthermore, Waldheim was accused of having been involved in deportations of Jews from Greece. Although he insisted that he had no knowledge of the persecutions of Jews in Nazi Germany, he later contradicted himself. An international investigating commission of historians suggested that Waldheim covered up the truth about his actions during the war.

In 1944 Waldheim completed his dissertation on the federalist notions of Konstantin Frantz, a German diplomat who was known for his anti-Semitic attitude. Waldheim discussed Frantz's idea of a "Greater Germany Solution," and praised Frantz for predicting the emergence of a powerful "pan-Germany." In his autobiography, however, Waldheim depicted himself as a dissident and stated that, although a soldier of the *Wehrmacht*, he had read all of the anti-Nazi literature which had circulated during the war years. Waldheim claimed that the Catholic Church and the Bible had the most significant effect on him. Accordingly, in his political speeches, he quoted Austrian and European authors and scientists, whose sayings corresponded to his Catholic worldview. In addition, Antoine de Saint-Exupery's *Le Petit Prince* (1940) was a source of constant inspiration for Waldheim. In his speeches, he lauded the Austrian law professor and former president of the Austrian Constitutional Court, Walter Antoniolli, for his democratic notions, and the Swedish botanist and physician Carl von Linné for his euphoric attitude toward Europeans. At times, Waldheim referred to the German poet Johann Wolfgang von Goethe and to Austrian poets, such as Peter Rosegger, Josef Weinheber, and Karl-Heinrich Waggerl, who consistently praised their homeland. It should be noted that both Weinheber and Waggerl were committed National Socialists during the Third Reich. However, two of Waldheim's favorite Austrian writers, Stefan Zweig and Egon Fridell, were of Jewish descent. Waldheim admired Zweig's *Schachnovelle* (1942), *Die Welt von Gestern* (1942), and *Sternstunden der Menschheit* (1928) as well as Fridell's essayistic work *Kulturgeschichte der Neuzeit* (1927). Later in life, Waldheim was particularly influenced by Arnold Toynbee's *Mankind and Mother Earth: A Narrative History of the World* (1976), Alan Palmer's *The Chancelleries of Europe* (1983), and Frederic Morton's *Thunder at Twilight—Vienna 1913–1914* (1989). The renowned Jewish psychiatrist and founder of Logotherapy, Viktor Frankl, played an important role in the aftermath of Waldheim's presidential election. Frankl, a Holocaust survivor, publicly asked the victims of the Nazi regime to forgive and move on. Time and again, Waldheim referred to and extensively quoted Frankl's speech "Die Stimme der Vernunft" to defend himself against critics in Austria and abroad.

Archives

Dr. Kurt Waldheim-Archiv, Austrian National Library, Vienna, Austria. Includes United Nations documents, guest lectures at Georgetown University, book manuscripts, photos, correspondence, and a large collection of German and Austrian newspaper and magazine articles documenting Waldheim's role as UN General Secretary.
Personal Correspondence, Kurt Waldheim to Gregor Thuswaldner, 4 October 2002.

Printed Sources

Bom, Hanspeter. *Für die Richtigkeit: Kurt Waldheim* (Munich: Schneekluth, 1987).
Dickinger, Christian. *Österreichs Präsidenten: Von Karl Renner bis Thomas Klestil* (Vienna: Ueberreuter, 2000).
Finger, Seymour Maxwell, and Arnold A. Saltzman. *Bending with the Winds: Kurt Waldheim and the United Nations* (New York: Praeger, 1990).
Kurz, Hans Rudolf et al. *The Waldheim Report*, Williiam Templer (trans.), (Copenhagen: Museum Tusulanum, 1993).
Sassmann, Hanns (ed.). *Kurt Waldheim. Worauf es mir ankommt. Gedanken, Appelle, Stellungnahmen des Bundespräsidenten 1986–1992* (Graz: Styria, 1992).
Waldheim, Kurt. *The Challenge of Peace* (New York: Rawson, Wade, 1980).
———. *Die Antwort* (Vienna: Almathea, 1996).

Gregor Thuswaldner

WAŁESA, LECH (1943–)

Lech Wałesa, labor activist, political leader, and Nobel laureate, was born in Popowo in northern Poland into a moderately poor farm family during the Second

World War. His father was imprisoned as a slave laborer by the Nazis and died shortly after the war due to maltreatment. Wałesa attended local primary schools and high school and in 1961 graduated from the state-run technical school in Lipno. After a short stint in the army, he worked as an electrician in a state agricultural depot. In 1967, he went to work in the Lenin Shipyards in Gdańsk. Wałesa was a participant in the bloody 1970 strikes in the shipyards when the communist authorities massacred protesting workers. In about 1976, Wałesa became active in an illegal but open movement to defend the rights of workers and protest against increasingly bad economic conditions. In 1980, he rose to prominence when he was catapulted into the leadership of Solidarity, the first independent free trade union in the communist world. He became the movement's most recognized leader, facing the power of Poland's communist leaders with cool courage and sardonic humor. He was imprisoned during a period of martial law in 1981 but released a year later. In 1983, he was awarded the Nobel Peace Prize for his contribution to the cause of nonviolent change. The forces unleashed by Solidarity soon made themselves felt across the communist bloc, and in 1989 the Polish communist regime surrendered power. In 1990, Wałesa was elected the first independent leader of Poland since the 1930s, in which position he served until 1996.

Although few of Wałesa's immediate family were well educated, quite a few were self-educated. His maternal grandmother, for example, had worked in the United States prior to World War I and possessed a small library of the works of Ignacy Kraszewski and postivist writers Henryk Sienkiewicz and Bolesław Prus. These authors were apparently passed on to Wałesa's mother, who often read to her children. In his memoirs, Wałesa remembers her reading Sienkiewicz's historical novels *Teutonic Knights* and his trilogy (*With Fire and Sword, The Deluge*, and *Pan Wolodyjowski*), as well as Kraszewski's *Ancient Tale*.

At home and in church, Wałesa was also exposed to the rich liturgical tradition of Polish Catholicism and in particular to Marian devotions. Although Wałesa claims to have done poorly in history classes, this was probably due to the official communist historiography of the time. Historical stories and myths that ran counter to the official party propaganda were in wide circulation, passed by word of mouth and in underground publications. In school, Wałesa was required to study the work of communist leaders and ideologues such as Karl Marx and **V. I. Lenin** as well as of officially sanctioned writers and poets, many of whom were of dubious quality. Later, he was also exposed to a variety of underground workers' newspapers and to a lesser extent Radio Free Europe, which broadcast news and cultural programs in Polish. The influence of literature on Wałesa's life and career was indirect, mainly as part of a larger cultural milieu that kept alive a spirit of resistance against foreign-imposed rule.

Archives

National Archives, Warsaw. State and presidential papers.

Printed Sources

Brolewicz, Walter. *My Brother, Lech Wałesa* (New York: Tribeca Communications, 1983).
Wałesa, Lech. *A Way of Hope: An Autobiography* (New York: Henry Holt, 1987).
Wałesa, Lech, and Arkadiusz Rybicki. *The Struggle and the Triumph* (New York: Arcade, 1992).

John Radzilowski

WALLACE, GEORGE CORLEY (1919–1998)

George Wallace rose from humble roots in rural Alabama to become a state representative, judge, governor, four-time presidential candidate, and a key figure in the New Conservatism that slowly reshaped the American political landscape in the final four decades of the twentieth century. After losing an Alabama gubernatorial campaign in 1958, Wallace modified his message to include a harder edge on racial matters to go with a distinct class-based rhetoric honed by his life experiences and career in the legislature. He won the governorship easily in 1962. By appealing to a southern memory which indicted the federal government with a hundred years of extralegal intrusion into the South, Wallace became stunningly popular with whites in state and region. His use of racial politics and vigorous defense of segregation led to dramatic events including the Birmingham Civil Rights Campaign, the "Stand at the Schoolhouse Door," where he attempted to block the admission of Black students, and the Selma-to-Montgomery March. He entered Democratic presidential primaries in 1964, 1972 (where he was paralyzed by would-be assassin Arthur Bremer), and 1976, but he achieved his greatest national success by appearing on the ballot in all fifty states in 1968 as the standard-bearer of the American Independent Party. Though he lost to **Richard Nixon,** Wallace carried five southern states and 13.6 percent of the national vote. All told, Wallace was elected governor four times (1962, 1970, 1974, and 1982), not including the 1966 election of his first wife Lurleen as a stand-in. Emblematic of his political skills, Wallace reconciled with Black leaders before his last gubernatorial election and garnered a strong majority of Black votes in his last campaign.

Wallace was an avid reader of history and he was greatly influenced by the works he read in his formative years. According to interpretations made famous by William Dunning and his students, the South was ravaged during Reconstruction by scurrilous carpetbaggers, treasonous scalawags, the corrupt federal government, and incapable freed slaves. Among the best known of Dunning's students was Walter Fleming, whose works included *Civil War and Reconstruction in Alabama* and *Deportation and Colonization: An Attempted Solution of the Race Problem.* Wallace was a friend and regular correspondent with University of Alabama historian A. B. Moore, who led the Alabama Civil War Centennial Commission during Wallace's first term. Moore's most celebrated book, *History of Alabama,* was the authoritative text on state history for decades and characterized slaves as contented and carefree, masters as benevolent, and Reconstruction as a perversion of the natural order. This antigovernment philosophy with concomitant presuppositions of Black inferiority was reinforced in the Wallace home, at the University of Alabama where Wallace matriculated, and in nearly all political circles of the era. These influences are readily apparent in Wallace's brand of backlash conservatism that rebuked the federal government and Civil Rights protesters for meddling in the affairs of the states.

As governor, Wallace used his office to recommend books to his supporters that went beyond history and into pseudo-science. Carleton Putnam's *Race and Reason* and *Race and Reality,* W. C. George's *The Biology of the Race Problem,* and Carleton Stevens Coon's *The Origin of Races* were suggested to White Citizens Council members and others who wrote the governor to inquire about scientific explanations for maintaining segregation. These works argue for genetic differences which presage substandard intelligence for African Americans and make various other claims such as George's assertion that Blacks are prone to "indolence, imprudence, and consequent pauperism." Not coincidentally, when C. Vann Woodward and a host of southern historians and intellectuals challenged Old South interpretations of history, race, and sociology, Wallace sharpened his attacks on "pointy-headed" liberals and professors who "can't even park their bikes straight." Even so, during the bulk of his active years in politics, Wallace relied more on his own instincts and a stable of speechwriters to formulate rhetoric and policy than on his reading.

In his later years when numerous health problems stemming from the bullets in his spine led to constant pain, depression, and poor sight and hearing, Wallace, an indifferent Methodist for much of his life, turned to his Bible for comfort.

Archives

Administrative Files of Governor George C. Wallace, Alabama Department of Archives and History, Montgomery, Alabama.
Administrative Files of Governor Lurleen B. Wallace, Alabama Department of Archives and History, Montgomery, Alabama.

Printed Sources

Carter, Dan T. *The Politics of Rage: George Wallace, the Origins of the New Conservatism, and the Transformation of American Politics* (Baton Rouge: Louisiana State University Press, 1996).
Frady, Marshall. *Wallace* (New York: World Publishing Company, 1968).
Frederick, Jeff. "Stand by Your Man: Race, Alabama Women, and George Wallace in 1963," *Gulf South Historical Review* 18 (Fall, 2002), 47–75.
Lesher, Stephan. *George Wallace: American Populist* (Reading, Mass.: Addison-Wesley, 1994).

Jeff Frederick

WAUGH, EVELYN ARTHUR ST. JOHN (1903–1966)

Born in Hampstead, England, on October 28, 1903, Waugh was educated at Lancing and Hertford College, Oxford, 1922–24, and worked as a schoolmaster to 1927. An early book on the pre-Raphaelites appeared in 1926 and another on Rossetti in 1928, the year of his marriage to Evelyn Florence Margaret Winifred Gardner (whom he divorced in 1930; the marriage was annulled in 1936). In 1930 he was received into the Roman Catholic Church. In 1937, he married Laura Herbert.

Through the 1930s he published a series of works, beginning with a first and highly successful novel, *Decline and Fall, Vile Bodies* (1930), *Black Mischief* (1932), *A Handful of Dust* (1934), *Scoop* (1938), and travel books. His biography of the sixteenth-century English Jesuit martyr, Edmund Campion, appeared in 1935. Following his war service, during which he completed *Put Out More Flags* (1942) and his best-known novel, *Brideshead Revisited* (1945), he published *The Loved One* (1948), *Saint Helena* (1950), *The Ordeal of Gilbert Pinfold* (1957), a biography of his contemporary, the English convert priest, Ronald Knox (1957), and other travel and autobiographical works in addition to his *Sword of Honour* trilogy based on his war experiences: *Men at Arms* (1952), *Officers and Gentlemen* (1955), and *Unconditional Surrender* (1961).

Although Waugh's later autobiographical writing placed much emphasis on his ancestry both near and far, direct influences on his work were more immediate. Already as a youth at Lancing College he displayed a satiric tendency toward the world in which he found himself. At Oxford he was much attracted and influenced by the avant-garde literary and artistic tastes and the modernism of the group formed around Harold Acton, Bruce Howard, and others, including the novelists Anthony Powell and Henry Yorke ("Henry Green") and his later fellow-Catholic, Christopher Hollis (whose reception into the Church Waugh initially opposed). His early study of Rossetti reflects a general interest in the aesthetics, Gestalt psychology, and psychoanalytical theories of the day, as well as an anti-Victorianism somewhat similar to that of **Lytton Strachey.** In his first novel his reading of the German cultural theorist Oswald Spengler and, much more so, that of the French philosopher **Henri Bergson** is immediately evident, the dynamism of the life-force being depicted as merging the past in the present and overcoming the stasis in the human world. These influences were on the wane by the time of his second novel, however, in which the importance of the satiric work of Ronald Firbank and of Firbank's lesser-known literary disciple, William Gerhardi, remains evident.

In the late 1920s Waugh grew ever less enamored of modernist forms of art and on September 29, 1930, was received into the Roman Catholic Church by Father Martin D'Arcy at the Jesuit Church at Farm Street, London. Many of Waugh's friends at the time were Roman Catholics or High Church Anglicans, but none appears to have been directly influential in this regard. Even the philosopher and cultural theorist D'Arcy was introduced to Waugh after he had effectively made his decision to convert. By whatever the manner he came to the church, however, he wrote thereafter firmly as a Catholic, albeit avoiding propagandizing and for a time finding it necessary to defend his novels among some of his own co-believers who considered their content risqué.

Working primarily out of his own experience, the impact of his travels is regularly marked in his novels: for example, that of his trips to Abyssinia and British Guiana in *A Handful of Dust* and *Scoop* and to the United States in *The Loved One*. His initial enthusiasm with the British military at the beginning of World War II soon passed into disillusionment, and in the post-1945 period he grew increasingly anti-modern. The ongoing influence of significant friends before and after this period remains important but is difficult to specify. The novelist Nancy Mitford, a friend of his first wife, remained an important confidante throughout his life.

Archives

British Library, Manuscript Collections, 1921–66: correspondence; 1932–66: letters to Lady Diana Cooper (3 vols.); 1948: correspondence with Edward Sackville-West.

University of Texas at Austin: Harry Ransom Humanities Research Center Library: papers.

Columbia University Libraries, Rare Book and Manuscript Library, 1930–53: letters and literary manuscripts.

Georgetown University, Special Collections, Lauinger Library: letters to Handasyde Buchanan; letters to Graham Greene; correspondence with Bruce Marshall; letters to Leonard Russell; 1948–65: letters to Christopher Sykes, copies of letters to A. D. Peters 1930–45, copies of diaries 1916–63.

Cambridge University Library, Department of Manuscripts and University Archives, 1952–61: letters and postcards to F. J. Stopp.

Printed Sources

Hastings, Selina. *Evelyn Waugh: A Biography* (London: Sinclair-Stevenson, 1994).

Mosley, Charlotte (ed.). *The Letters of Nancy Mitford & Evelyn Waugh* (London: Hodder and Stoughton, 1996).

Stannard, Martin. *Evelyn Waugh: The Early Years 1903–1939* (London: J.M. Dent, 1986).

Waugh, Evelyn. *The Diaries of Evelyn Waugh*, Michael Davie (ed.), (London: Weidenfeld and Nicholson, 1976).

———. *Evelyn Waugh: The Later Years 1939–1966* (New York: W. W. Norton, 1992).

———. *The Letters of Evelyn Waugh*, Mark Amory (ed.), (London: Weidenfeld and Nicholson, 1980).

Peter C. Erb

WAYNE, JOHN (1907–1979)

John Wayne was born Marion Morrison in Winterset, Iowa. The family moved to Glendale, California, when Wayne was nine years old. He was nicknamed "Duke," after the family's dog. In 1925 he attended the University of Southern California on a football scholarship. The same year, he took a job at Fox Film Studio as a scenery mover, which led to work as an extra in westerns and movies about college athletes. During this time, he met John Ford, the movie director who was to have a decisive impact on his career. Ford gave Wayne his first starring role in 1930, but the film was a failure and it would be nine years and almost 70 B films later before Wayne achieved notable success as an actor. Wayne became politically active in 1944 as a founding member of the Motion Picture Alliance for the Preservation of American Ideals, an organization dedicated to expelling Communists from the film industry. As a vocal proponent of American involvement in the Vietnam War, Wayne again became as famous for his political opinions as his acting. With films that have grossed more than any other performer's, he is regarded as one of the great heroes of American cinema and a legend in American culture.

Wayne became a confirmed reader when growing up in Glendale, where he frequented the library. He told a reporter in 1972, "I've loved reading all my life" (Roberts 1995, 42). Adventure novels like Walter Scott's *Ivanhoe* and Daniel Defoe's *Robinson Crusoe* helped him escape the pressures of everyday life. He became an avid reader of Zane Grey's western novels. Biography, especially the stories of heroic men who triumphed over adversity and made a place for themselves in history, intrigued him. He read almost anything by or about **Winston Churchill,** the public figure he most revered. "After all," Wayne said, "he took a nearly beaten nation and kept their dignity for them" (Davis 1998, xii). Maintaining dignity became a guiding principle for Wayne. Aissa Wayne wrote that her father often read four newspapers a day when not doing a movie and likely read thousands of books in his lifetime (Wayne 1991, 38). Wayne loved the poetry of Walt Whitman and one of his favorite Whitman passages was "I contradict myself? Very well . . . I contradict myself. I am large; I contain multitudes" (Roberts 1995, 646). *The Shootist* is the story of J. B. Brooks, an aging gunfighter who has outlived the Old West. Wayne was so taken by the book that he tried to buy the movie rights. *The Shootist* became John Wayne's dialogue with death, spoken by J. B. Brooks (Roberts 1995, 614).

Archives

Mayer Library of the American Film Institute, Los Angeles: Charles K. Feldman Papers, including letters, telegrams, and memos.

Lilly Library, Indiana University, Bloomington, Indiana: John Ford Collection consisting of correspondence, scripts, production records, photographs, and interviews.

Madison County Historical Society, Madison County, Iowa, houses a scrapbook that details Wayne's years in Winterset and Earlham, Iowa, and various newspaper accounts have been preserved in the John Wayne birthplace in Winterset.

City of Lancaster Museum, Lancaster, California.

Wayne's private papers are still in the possession of the actor's family.

Printed Sources

Davis, Ronald L. *Duke: The Life and Image of John Wayne* (Norman, Okla.: University of Oklahoma Press, 1998).

Roberts, Randy, with James S. Olson. *John Wayne: America* (New York: The Free Press, 1995).

Wayne, Aissa, with Steve Delsohn. *John Wayne, My Father* (New York: Random House, 1991).

Wayne, Pilar, with Alex Thorleifson. *John Wayne: My Life with the Duke* (New York: McGraw-Hill Book Company, 1987).

Zolotow, Maurice. *Shooting Star: A Biography of John Wayne* (New York: Simon and Schuster, 1974).

Deborah K. O'Brien

WEBB, BEATRICE POTTER (1858–1943)

Beatrice Potter was born near Gloucester, in western England, into a wealthy liberal middle-class family. Without much formal education, she was largely self-educated through her unrestricted reading in the extensive parental library. By the age of 16, Webb lost her faith in orthodox Christianity and styled herself an agnostic. As a young woman she devoted herself to what became her lifelong work as a social investigator. Impacted by the social misery of late-nineteenth-century England, she embraced Fabian socialism in 1890 and in 1892 married Sydney Webb, a founder and leading member of the Fabian Society. In partnership with her husband, she wrote extensively on the conditions of the working classes and the poor in England and formulated policies of reform based on collectivism and state control of the economy, work that had a strong impact on the development of the Labour Party in the twentieth century and on the establishment of the welfare state after World War II.

Setting for herself even in her youth a rigorous reading program, a habit that continued throughout her life, Webb read in her childhood the major works of classical and modern philosophy and history. The classical writer who influenced her the most was Marcus Aurelius, whose stoicism appealed to and strengthened her own sense of duty and self-control. The modern author to whom she was most drawn was Johann Wolfgang von Goethe. She was also attracted to the social realism novels of Honoré de Balzac. Her favorite Victorian novelist was George Eliot, and especially her novel *Middlemarch*, in whose duty-ridden self-denying heroine Dorothea, Webb found strong identification. Webb was impressed by the novel *Jean Inglesant* by J. H. Shorthouse, an author who "had experienced that striving after inward purity of heart and mind" (Webb 1982/85, 1: 46). The modern historical works that had the greatest influence on her were Henry Buckle's *History of Civilisation in England* and W.E.H. Lecky's *History of European Morals*. Reading widely in liberal political economy, she was most impacted by the writings of her close family friend Herbert Spencer. Although she later rejected his anti-statism, she attributed to Spencer the lasting influence of his example of "amazing loyalty to a disinterested aim, the patience, endurance, the noble faith manifested in his daily life" (Webb 1982/85, 2: 308). Similarly, she was attracted to the writings of Thomas Carlyle, whose Gospel of Work found embodiment in her own life. Auguste Comte with his positivist union of science and social progress in a Religion of Humanity shaped her general intellectual framework. The positivist writings of Frederic Harrison influenced her decision to sign an anti-suffrage petition in 1889, an anti-feminist position that she later rejected. In young adulthood she read poetry and beautiful prose for the first time and found special delight in Ralph Waldo Emerson's essays. Clearly the strongest literary influence on her thinking was the 1889 *Fabian Essays in Socialism*, and particularly the essay by Sidney Webb, which literally changed her life. Fabianism gave her the theoretical framework of social democracy as a solution to poverty and economic inequality. Throughout the rest of her life, despite her tireless outpourings of tracts and reports, she continued to read contemporary literature and history. She was especially drawn to what she called the "literature of exposure" of **Upton Sinclair**'s *The Jungle* and T. W. Lawson's *Frenzied Finance*, which she thought would force greater change than all of her and her husband's labors. Her readings in adulthood also reflected her unsatisfied spiritual longings, and she was drawn to such works as Edward Carpenter's *The Art of Creation*, with its synthesis of the scientific and mystical spirit. When Annie Besant and other Fabians converted to the new occult religion of theosophy, Webb had no interest in following their path, but she was attracted to Besant's theosophical work *Thought Power* with its emphasis on the control of the will and the dominance of the mind over the body, which was a persistent goal in Webb's own life.

Archives

Passfield Papers, British Library of Political and Economic Science, London School of Economics, London. Manuscript diaries of B. Webb, other manuscripts, letters.
Fabian Society Papers, Nuffield College, Oxford.

Printed Sources

Harrison, Royden J. *The Life and Times of Sidney and Beatrice Webb, 1858–1905: The Formative Years* (New York: St. Martin's Press, 2000). Discusses the common intellectual inheritance of Sidney and Beatrice Webb.
Mackenzie, Norman (ed.). *Letters of Sidney and Beatrice Webb*, 3 vols. (London: Weidenfeld and Nicolson, 1978). Includes references to readings.
Seymour-Jones, Carole. *Beatrice Webb: A Life* (Chicago: Ivan R. Dee, 1992).
Webb, Beatrice. *The Diary of Beatrice Webb*, 4 vols., Norman and Jeanne MacKenzie (eds.), (Cambridge, Mass.: Harvard University Press, 1982–85).
———. *My Apprenticeship* (New York: Longmans, Green, 1926).
———. *Our Partnership* (New York: Longmans, Green, 1948). *My Apprenticeship* and *Our Partnership*, both autobiographies, include reflections on literary influences.

Nancy Fix Anderson

WEBER, MAX (1864–1920)

Max Weber was born in Erfurt, Prussia, the first child of Helene Fallenstein and Max Weber (Sr.), a professional politician and heir to the Bielefeld linen fortune of Weber, Laer, & Niemann. Weber's father was elected to the Prussian House of

Deputies in 1868 and the Reichstag in 1872. After the family relocated to Charlottenburg, a wealthy suburb of Berlin, in 1869, their home was frequented by important professors, writers, artists, and National Liberal Party members, including Ludwig Karl Aegidi, Rudolf von Bennigsen, Wilhelm Dilthey, Artur Hobrecht, James Friedrich Hobrecht, Levin Goldschmidt, Friedrich Kapp, Johannes von Miquel, Theodor Mommsen (whose son, physician Ernst Mommsen, Weber's younger sister Klara later married), Heinrich Rickert, Heinrich Julian Schmidt, Heinrich von Sybel, and Heinrich von Treitschke. At school in Charlottenburg, Weber preferred Latin and history. He became an enthusiastic reader. Besides history and classics, he read Immanuel Kant, Martin Luther, Niccolo Machiavelli, Arthur Schopenhauer, and Baruch Spinoza. Already steeped in influences as diverse as Frederick the Great, Homer, Ossian (James Macpherson), and Johann Wolfgang von Goethe, Weber began writing serious, adult-level historical essays at the age of 13.

Before he graduated from the Charlottenburg Gymnasium in 1882, Weber knew intimately the works of Cicero, Herodotus, Livy, Sallust, Virgil, Willibald Alexis, Ernst Curtius, Gustav Freytag, Victor Amadeus Hehn, Joseph Viktor von Scheffel, Sir Walter Scott, and Christoph Martin Wieland, as well as Mommsen and Treitschke. He also studied the history of religion on his own and taught himself Hebrew in order to read the original Old Testament.

Weber entered the University of Heidelberg as a law student in 1882. Among his professors were Ernst Immanuel Bekker, Bernhard Erdmannsdörfer, Kuno Fischer, and Karl Knies. He read Knies, Gustav Biedermann, G.W.F. Hegel, Friedrich Albert Lange, Rudolf Hermann Lotze, Otto Pfleiderer, Plato, Leopold von Ranke, Wilhelm Roscher, Friedrich Daniel Ernst Schleiermacher, and David Friedrich Strauss. A year spent in Strasbourg with his uncle Hermann Baumgarten and cousin Otto Baumgarten also stimulated his intellectual development, as they read many of the same books and frequently held family roundtable discussions about them. Surprisingly, for all his famous sociological work on the "Protestant ethic," he did not study John Calvin until much later.

In 1886 Weber continued his law studies at the University of Berlin and took his LL.D. there in 1889 with a dissertation on medieval commerce. After writing his habilitation thesis on Roman agriculture in 1891, he completed his military obligation, taught briefly at Berlin and the University Freiburg im Breisgau, then succeeded Knies at Heidelberg, where he remained until 1918. He taught at the University of Vienna in 1919, and was just beginning an appointment at the University of Munich when he died.

Archives

Most of Weber's papers are at either the University of Heidelberg or the University of Munich. His *Complete Works (Gesamtausgabe)*, sponsored by the Max Weber Institute of the University of Munich and the Commission for Social and Economic History of the Bavarian Academy of Sciences, edited by Horst Baier, M. Rainer Lepsius, Wolfgang J. Mommsen, Wolfgang Schluchter, and Johannes Winckelmann, is in preparation.

Printed Sources

Albrow, Martin. *Max Weber's Construction of Social Theory* (New York: St. Martin's Press, 1990).
Bendix, Reinhard. *Max Weber: An Intellectual Portrait* (London: Routledge, 1998).

Bologh, Roslyn Wallach. *Love or Greatness: Max Weber and Masculine Thinking: A Feminist Inquiry* (London; Boston: Unwin Hyman, 1990).

Lash, Scott, and Sam Whimster. *Max Weber: Rationality and Modernity* (London: Allen & Unwin, 1987).

Lehmann, Hartmut, and Guenther Roth (eds.). *Weber's Protestant Ethic: Origins, Evidence, Contexts* (New York: Cambridge University Press, 1993).

Mommsen, Wolfgang J., and Jürgen Osterhammel (eds.). *Max Weber and His Contemporaries* (London: Allen & Unwin, 1987).

Portis, Edward Bryan. *Max Weber and Political Commitment: Science, Politics, and Personality* (Philadelphia: Temple University Press, 1986).

Turner, Stephen (ed.). *The Cambridge Companion to Weber* (New York: Cambridge University Press, 2000).

Weber, Marianne. *Max Weber: A Biography*, Harry Zohn (trans.), (New Brunswick, N.J.: Transaction, 1988).

Weiss, Johannes. *Weber and the Marxist World* (London; New York: Routledge, 1998).

Eric v.d. Luft

WEIL, SIMONE ADOLPHINE (1909–1943)

Simone Weil was born in Paris to freethinking Jewish parents. Throughout her life she demonstrated a deep compassion for those less fortunate than herself. She completed her *baccalauréat* in philosophy at the Lycée Henri IV in Paris in 1925 under the tutelage of her lifelong friend and mentor, Alain (Emile Chartier). Weil continued her studies at the Sorbonne before winning a place at the École Normale Supérieure in 1928. In 1930, she began to suffer from debilitating migraines which were to affect her all her life. In 1931, she obtained her first teaching post in Le Puy. There, as in subsequent posts in Auxerre and Roanne, she shocked the educational establishment not only by her unconventional teaching, but by openly engaging in Trade Union activities and political demonstrations. In 1934, she requested unpaid leave to work in various factories in order to observe working conditions first-hand. She pursued this aim between December 1934 and August 1935, but was forced to abandon her positions due to ill health. While recuperating in Portugal, she had the first of three mystical experiences which were to turn her toward the Christian religion, although she never joined the Catholic church. Her correspondence with Father Perrin and the Catholic thinker Gustave Thibon details her spiritual struggles. During World War II, she traveled to England to join the Free French. She died in Ashford, Kent, in 1943 of tuberculosis exacerbated by a refusal to eat more than those suffering in France.

Weil's writings show that she revised certain of her ideas during her life while remaining faithful to particular writers that she encountered in her youth. In a letter to the minister of education in 1940 (Pétrement 1988, II, 291) she states that she learned to read through the French classics, notably Racine, Corneille, and Pascal. She admired Greek tragedy and classical French literature, while her *Lettre aux* Cahiers du sud *sur les responsabilités de la littérature* (1951) expresses a mistrust of twentieth-century literature. Alain's teaching instilled in her a passion for all aspects of the Hellenic tradition and formed the basis of her political and theological thought. She deeply respected Descartes, devoting her thesis to his ideas on science and perception. In her essay *Quelques réflexions autour de la notion de valeur* (1941) she lists those she deems true philosophers, including Plato, Descartes,

Kant, Jean Lagneau, and Edmund Husserl. Spinoza, too, had a profound effect on her (Pétrement 1988, I, 91). For Weil, science, work, and social organization were aspects of the same problem. She believed that oppression was linked to the layman's ignorance of higher mathematics and developed an educational program for the working class based on the Greek mathematical tradition (Pétrement 1988, II, 256–58). She admired the genius of Karl Marx, but her criticisms of aspects of his thought stem from reflections on both Homer and Plato. The *Iliad* and **T. E. Lawrence**'s *Seven Pillars of Wisdom* encouraged her to revise her pacifist ideals (Pétrement 1988, II, 190). Weil's religious thought was not informed by the Western tradition alone. She was greatly touched by *The Epic of Gilgamesh*, the *Bhagavad-Gita*, and the *Upanishads*, long passages of which are quoted in her numerous notebooks and referred to in her later writings.

Archives

Fonds Simone Weil, Bibliothèque Nationale de France, Paris.

Printed Sources

Cabaud, Jacques. *L'expérience vécue de Simone Weil* (Paris: Plon, 1957).

Perrin, J. M., and G. Thibon. *Simone Weil telle que nous l'avons connue* (Paris, La Colombe, 1952).

Pétrement, Simone. *La Vie de Simone Weil*, 2 vols. (Paris: Fayard, 1973). Translated as *Simone Weil: A Life*, Raymond Rosenthal (trans.), (New York: Random House, 1988).

Weil, Simone. *Œuvres complètes*, (Paris, Gallimard NRF, 1988–). Some volumes still to appear.

Linda Ness

WELLES, GEORGE ORSON (1915–1985)

Orson Welles was born in Kenosha, Wisconsin, and early in life showed signs of genius. As a youth, he loved optical illusions and vaudeville. These loves later became strong influences in his movie productions, keeping him from being a fan of the "realistic" school of movie-making because he always enjoyed the director's ability to craft a movie. On a trip to Ireland, Welles enjoyed his first professional stage work with the Gate Theatre of Dublin. Upon returning to America in the mid-1930s, he joined a road company and met John Houseman, which led to the subsequent creation of the New York Federal Theatre and the Mercury group, a socially conscious project to entertain and inform a mass public through revivals and adaptations of classics, reflecting the ideals of **Franklin Roosevelt**'s New Deal. Successful Mercury stage productions helped the group obtain a contract with CBS radio where Welles became famous as the voice of *The Shadow* and became even better known for his production of *War of the Worlds* in 1938, which guaranteed his going to Hollywood in a wave of publicity. Welles began work for RKO Studios and in 1941 he starred in, directed, produced, and cowrote his first movie, *Citizen Kane*. Innovative, original, and groundbreaking, *Citizen Kane* is generally considered the greatest movie ever made and garnered Welles his only Academy Award, which he shared for original screenplay. However, **William Randolph Hearst** tried to get the movie destroyed because it closely echoed his career and *Kane* was not a financial success. Coupled with the poor marketing of Welles's next movie, *The Magnificent Ambersons* (which he directed but did not star in), and RKO's loss of personnel who supported the Mercury group, Welles became branded as an outsider and individualist whose films were not commercial successes. All of Welles's later pictures were created under contractual constraints not imposed on *Citizen Kane*, and he could not recapture the greatness he had achieved by the age of 26. Nevertheless, his later career was wide-ranging. He starred in such movies as *The Third Man* (1949) and *A Man for All Seasons* (1966), directed movies from *Macbeth* (1948) to *The Trial* (1962), and starred in and directed *Touch of Evil* (1958). In a career spanning four decades and over 30 years in both Europe and America, Welles directed 13 films, narrated 15 others, and starred in at least 55 in all.

Literary classics heavily influenced Welles over the course of his career. One of the most successful of his radio broadcasts was H. G. Wells's *War of the Worlds*, after which Wells actually threatened to sue for the misuse of his novel. Welles also broadcast *Treasure Island, A Tale of Two Cities, Hamlet*, and other classics for CBS Radio with the Mercury Theatre, and one of their most acclaimed and popular productions was an expressionist play of Shakespeare's *Julius Caesar*. Critics often consider Welles's expressionistic *MacBeth* (1948) with Republic Pictures the most controversial Shakespeare production. As a transition figure between the medieval and modern worlds, Welles could associate with Shakespeare because of his boyhood years and the transition of the United States from an agricultural to an industrial society. A constant theme in his movies was a battle between the quest for power and a need for constraints in industrial society, nowhere better seen than in Welles's first two movies, *Kane* and *Ambersons*. *Ambersons* was the film version of Booth Tarkington's 1918 Pulitzer Prize–winning novel and depicted a midwestern town passing into the twentieth century while longing for the past. Welles's European movies were never as artful as his American efforts because they took him out of his social context and away from the easy association he had with his selected subject matter. His views of the individual's clash with the modern world are also seen in his admiration for **Franz Kafka**'s writings on modern sensibilities, present in his direction of Kafka's *The Trial*. Also interested in social consciousness, Welles wrote his own editorial column for the *New York Post* in 1945 in which he expressed his growing anger that America felt a complacent moral superiority, as shown in John Hershey's *A Bell for Adano*, and that more people needed to be aware of the Black race, as shown in **Richard Wright**'s *Black Boy*.

Archives

American Film Institute Archives: film and archival material.
Library of Congress, Film Archives, Washington, D.C.: film and archival material.
Museum of Modern Art's Film Study Center: stills, film, and archival material.
Weissberger Collection at the University of Wisconsin, Madison: personal correspondence and papers, archival material.

Printed Sources

Higham, Charles. *The Films of Orson Welles* (Berkeley: University of California Press, 1970).
McBride, Joseph. *Orson Welles* (New York: Viking Press, 1972).
Naremore, James. *The Magic World of Orson Welles* (Dallas: Southern Methodist University Press, 1989).
Noble, Peter. *The Fabulous Orson Welles* (London: Hutchinson, 1956).
Welles, Orson. *This Is Orson Welles: Orson Welles and Peter Bogdanovich* (New York: Harper Collins, 1992).

Christopher C. Strangeman

WHARTON, EDITH (1862–1937)

Edith Newbold Jones was born in Manhattan, New York. She was educated in her father's "gentleman's library" and by a governess. The first female writer to win the Pulitzer Prize (for *The Age of Innocence*, 1920), Wharton established her reputation as a premier novelist of manners with *The House of Mirth* (1905) and solidified it with a steady stream of critically and commercially successful novels and short stories, including *Ethan Frome* (1911), *The Custom of the Country* (1913), and *Summer* (1917). Wharton, the grand dame of American letters for the first two decades of the twentieth century, achieved popular success in spite of her generally tragic point of view, which often focused on the profound frustrations of men and women crushed beneath the stultifying conventions of genteel society, especially the conventions of marriage and divorce. Even as she skewered the corrupt social values of America's aristocracy, though, Wharton eulogized the passing age of gentility, chronicling the upper-class "Old New York" of the 1870s with both an artist's and an anthropologist's eye and, in so doing, making a convincing case for the preeminence of American literature in the new century.

Wharton's greatest influence was undeniably Henry James (1843–1916), who was both her close friend and literary model, especially for her early work as the progenitor of psychological realism. Wharton strongly disagreed with claims that she was derivative of James, but she did admit in her autobiography, *A Backward Glance* (1934), that she "cannot think of herself apart from the influence" of James (Wharton 1934, 169). James was also an influence as a writer obsessed with technique, as was her friend Paul Bourget, with whom Wharton shared "profitable" discussions about style (Wharton 1934, 199). *Backward Glance* elaborates on the exact impact of many of Wharton's influences, including Walter Berry, who is cited as a "guide" with great "influence" over each of Wharton's "literary steps" (Wharton 1934, 112–15). Here also she notes the good taste of her friend and "literary advisor" Edward Burlingame, her editor at Scribner's and thoughtful correspondent over Wharton's revision process (Wharton 1934, 145). In *The Writing of Fiction* (1925), Wharton's book on the craft of writing, the author places herself firmly within the tradition of literary realism and cites the influences of the great continental realists Honoré de Balzac and George Eliot, both of whom were technical virtuosos and profound psychological writers. Wharton's praise of Balzac's view of each character as "a product of particular material and social conditions" (Wharton 1925, 7) demonstrates the profundity of his and other realists' influence on Wharton, who explored the often tragic implications of this quasi-determinism in nearly everything she wrote. It is only for the great psychological novelist **Marcel Proust**, however, that Wharton devotes an entire section of *The Writing of Fiction*. Wharton returns to Proust in *A Backward Glance*, observing that Proust had "a new mastery, a new vision, and a structural design as yet unintelligible" (Wharton 1934, 324). The realists, then, not only shaped Wharton's appreciation of character, but of form.

Archives

Edith Wharton Collection. Yale Collection of American Literature. Beinecke Rare Book and Manuscript Library. New Haven, Conn.: approximately 50,000 items including manuscripts, letters, photographs, and miscellaneous personal papers.

Harry Ransom Humanities Research Center. University of Texas at Austin: correspondence, primarily between Wharton and Morton Fullerton, 1907–31.

William Royal Tyler Collection. Dumbarton Oaks, Washtingon, D.C.: correspondence, diaries, and manuscripts, 1900–37.

Printed Sources

Lewis, R. W. B. *Edith Wharton: A Biography* (New York: Fromm International Publishing Corporation, 1985).

Wharton, Edith. *A Backward Glance* (New York: Charles Scribner's Sons, 1934).

———. *The Writing of Fiction* (New York: Charles Scribner's Sons, 1925).

Todd R. Robinson

WHITEHEAD, ALFRED NORTH (1861–1947)

Alfred North Whitehead was born to Maria Sarah Buckmaster and Alfred Whitehead, a Church of England cleric of modest means. With a solidly Victorian upbringing, Alfred studied Latin and Greek with his father. As the last of four children, he was the "baby of the family." The works of Dickens, Wordsworth, and Shelley were read to him. He received a first-rate education at Sherborne School in Dorsetshire. He achieved both academic and athletic success. Later, personal tragedies stemming from the Great War led to his own development of philosophical theism. Meanwhile at Trinity College, Cambridge University, his major was mathematics; he read widely in the humanities and classics and discussed literature and Kantian philosophy with his classmates. He belonged to "The Apostles," an exclusive social and academic club. His undergraduate days were a success.

In 1890 he married Evelyn Willoughby Wade; they had three children, one of whom died in the Great War. Two major factors marked his career. First, he studied mathematics before turning to metaphysics, and second, he spent 25 years in the Department of Philosophy at Harvard.

For 30 years as student and tutor at Cambridge University, Whitehead investigated mathematics. With **Bertrand Russell** as coauthor, Whitehead published *Principia Mathematic* (1910–13). In 1910 he moved to London where, in time, he was at the Imperial College of Science and Technology. Indicative of his influence on British education was his *Introduction to Mathematics*, commissioned by the Home University Library of Modern Knowledge. From 1919 to 1924 he led Goldsmith's College, a teacher college. *The Organization of Thought* (1917) and *The Aims of Education* (1929) demonstrated his Victorian concern with the educational opportunities for the working class.

Whitehead was active in the Aristotelian Society from 1915 to 1924. Exchanging views with the leading philosophical minds in England prepared him for a wider American audience. *An Enquiry Concerning the Principles of Natural Knowledge* (1919), *The Concept of Nature* (1920), and *The Principles of Relativity* were the results of this education.

Harvard University offered him a five-year contract to teach in the Department of Philosophy. The relationship lasted until his retirement in 1937. For a time, Whitehead's influence extended in and outside the academy. In 1925, he published *Science and the Modern World*. His thesis was that the Copernican/Newtonian scientific revolution meant that many basic philosophical assumptions needed significant revision. Whitehead's revisions came four years later in *Process and Reality*. Unfortunately, Whitehead's text was filled with neologisms. He believed that a new philosophical language was necessary for a full understanding of his analysis. The result was interesting. Echoes of his interpretation can be found in the works of various thinkers. In a way, *Process and Reality* was for the philosophical profession while *Science and the Modern World* and *Adventures in Ideas* (1933) were more for the general reader.

Adventures in Ideas was multifaceted, like so much of Whitehead's work. As well as a philosophy of civilization, the book used his metaphysical system in explaining the cultural desires of the modern age. He related philosophical concepts with particular historical developments, combining thought with human action and institutions. In the nineteenth century, the industrial revolution and democracy were deeply related in the process of existence.

Whitehead's interest turned to philosophical theology in the late 1920s and 1930s. *Religion in the Making* (1926), *Symbolism: Its Meaning and Effect* (1927), *The Function of Reason* (1929), and *Modes of Thought* (1938) influenced a wide array of writers, both Christian theologians and secularists.

Always retiring and shy, Whitehead's thought did not spawn disciples or any organized school of thought. He believed that the development of an individual's creative articulation of his own ideas was the important educational objective—not a scholarly dispute over details. Undoubtedly this attitude contributed to the decline of his influence after his death in 1947.

Archives

In accordance with Whitehead's request, upon his death, the bulk of his papers were destroyed. The Center for Process Studies at the School of Theology in Claremont, California, maintains a research facility dealing with thought. The center also publishes the journal *Process Studies* and holds conferences dealing with various aspects of Whitehead's philosophy.

Printed Sources

Kuklick, Bruce. *The Rise of American Philosophy, Cambridge, Massachusetts, 1860–1930* (New Haven: Yale University Press, 1977). First-rate history of Harvard's Department of Philosophy, argues for a limited legacy from Whitehead.

Lowe, Victor. *Alfred North Whitehead: The Man and His Work*, 2 vols. (Baltimore: Johns Hopkins University Press, 1985, 1990). As *the* biography, it has details of the varied influences on Whitehead's life and thought.

———. *Understanding Whitehead* (Baltimore: Johns Hopkins University Press, 1962). Guides the interested reader through Whitehead's metaphysics.

Schilpp, Paul A. (ed.). *The Philosophy of Alfred North Whitehead*, 2nd reprint ed. (New York: Tudor Publishing Co., 1951; LaSalle, Ill.: Open Court, 1991). Includes a complete bibliography of his writings including an essay entitled "Autobiographical Note."

Donald K. Pickens

WIESEL, ELIEZER (1928–)

Elie Wiesel, Romanian Jewish journalist, essayist, and novelist, was born in Sighet, Transylvania, on September 30, 1928. Wiesel's early education, which focused upon his family's Jewish religion, was interrupted when in 1945 his family was rounded up with other Romanian Jews and shipped to Auschwitz where his father, mother, and younger sister died. Following the death of his family, Wiesel was sent to camps at Buna, Buchenwald, and Gleiwitz but was liberated in 1946. Following his release from the French orphanage which had been his home from the end of World War II until 1948, Wiesel resumed his education by studying philosophy, psychology, and literature at the Sorbonne in Paris. Wiesel's writing career began as a journalist covering the birth of the new nation of Israel; however, he would neither write nor speak about his experiences in the concentration camps until the publication of his autobiographical novel *Night* in 1958. From that point on, he spent much of his writing life commenting upon the Holocaust and the inhumanity which lay behind it in such works as *Dawn* (1960), *The Jews of Silence* (1966), and *One Generation After* (1970). Wiesel is currently Andrew Mellon Professor of Humanities at Boston University and was awarded the 1986 Nobel Peace Prize for his work as a writer and a human rights activist.

Wiesel discusses his love of reading in his autobiography *All Rivers Run to the Sea* (1995) and in a lengthy 1996 Academy of Achievement interview. Wiesel admits a lifelong propensity for reading and stories but contends that from his earliest memories, his most pronounced interest lay in the religious stories that arose in his Jewish family and in his early education. Most prominent of these early influences were the debates revolving around the Talmud and the Midrashic legends, which would become central in Wiesel's *Five Biblical Portraits* (1981), and the mysteries of the Kabbala. However, his favorite Jewish stories were the Hasidic stories which he would retell in *Souls of Fire* (1971), especially those recounted by Rabbi Nahman of Bratslav. Central to all of Wiesel's spiritual readings were the Old Testament stories of Isaac, Jacob, and Moses.

Following his release from the French orphanage in 1948 and during his matriculation at the Sorbonne (1948–51), Wiesel was introduced to French, American, and European literary classics by philosopher Gustave Wahl, even meeting **Martin Buber,** author of the influential *I and Thou* (1923) and voice of the Hassidic movement. While still a student, Wiesel began his venture in journalism. One of his early assignments was to interview French Catholic novelist and Nobel laureate François Mauriac, who would later write an introduction to Wiesel's *Night*. Wiesel developed an appreciation for such writers as **Albert Camus** and his "The Myth of Sisyphus" (1942), **André Malraux,** and the voice of French existentialism, **Jean-Paul Sartre,** creator of the existential portrait of Hell in *No Exit* (1944), all of whom are echoed in Wiesel's own writing.

It was Czechoslovakian novelist **Franz Kafka,** author of *The Metamorphosis* (1912), that Wiesel sees being most closely associated with his work. According to Wiesel, he felt most associated with Kafka because of the way Kafka could move his readers with words that came across almost like prayers.

Archives

Special Collections, Mugar Memorial Library, Boston University. Contains manuscripts, correspondence, and various versions of Weisel's work.

Printed Sources

Estess, Ted L. *Elie Wiesel* (New York: Frederick Ungar, 1980).
Wiesel, Elie. *All Rivers Run to the Sea: Memoirs* (New York: Alfred A. Knopf, 1995).

———. Interview. The Hall of Public Services, Academy of Achievement, June 29, 1996. http://www.achievement.org/autodoc/page/wie0int-1, accesed October 26, 2003. Necessary for understanding Wiesel's development through reading.

Tom Frazier

WILDER, THORNTON NIVEN (1897–1975)

Thornton Wilder was born in Madison, Wisconsin. He was raised in the New England Protestant tradition by his father, who was a devout Congregationalist, and his mother, the daughter of a Presbyterian minister. He studied at Oberlin College (1915–17) and Yale University (1917–20) and received an M.A. in French literature from Princeton University (1924–25). Wilder taught French at the Lawrenceville School in New Jersey (1921–28) but resigned following the success of his novel *The Bridge of San Luis Rey* (1927), which won the Pulitzer Prize. He lectured at the University of Chicago (1930–36) and continued writing novels, such as *Heaven's My Destination* (1935) and *The Ides of March* (1948). However, he achieved his greatest fame as a playwright, with his dramas *Our Town* (1938) and *The Skin of Our Teeth* (1942), both winning the Pulitzer Prize. During World War II he served in Africa and Europe as an officer with U.S. Air Corps Intelligence (1942–45) and afterward became the Charles Eliot Norton Professor of Poetry at Harvard University (1950–51). His later works included the play *The Matchmaker* (1954) and the novel *The Eighth Day* (1967), which won the National Book Award.

At the start of his career, Wilder wrote, "The training for literature must be acquired by the artist alone, through the passionate assimilation of a few masterpieces" (Wilder 1928, xiv), and throughout his life he was inspired by his shifting enthusiasms for various authors. For example, his first novel, *The Cabala* (1926), shows the influence of **Marcel Proust;** his second, *The Bridge of San Luis Rey*, reveals his interest in Madame Marie de Sevigne, while his third, *The Woman of Andros* (1930), is based on Terence's comedy *The Andria* (166 B.C.). Wilder was unapologetic about his indebtedness to earlier works, questioning "why this dependence on the art of the past . . . cannot be looked upon as a mode for the transmission of the real" (Harrison 1983, 303).

This pattern of changing literary influences is also apparent in his three most famous plays. He acknowledged that *The Skin of Our Teeth* was "deeply indebted to **James Joyce's** *Finnegans Wake*," his literary passion of the moment (Wilder 1957, xiv). He adapted *The Matchmaker* from Johann Nestroy's 1842 comedy *Einen Jux will er sich machen;* and in a letter to **Gertrude Stein,** he said of *Our Town*, "its third act is based on your ideas, as on great pillars" (Burns and Dydo 1996, 175). Indeed, Stein, with her belief in portraying eternal and universal human truths, had perhaps the most lasting influence on Wilder. The two were close friends for many years, and toward the end of his life he declared, "she took on the task of 'putting me right' as a writer. The works I wrote . . . may not reflect her influence on the surface; it is all the better for being internal" (Wilder 1965, 37).

Archives

Thornton Wilder Papers, Yale Collection of American Literature, Beinecke Rare Book and Manuscript Library, Yale University, New Haven, Conn.: correspondence, manuscripts, personal and business papers, printed materials, photographs, memorabilia, audio tapes.

Printed Sources

Burns, Edward, and Ulla E. Dydo (eds.). *The Letters of Gertrude Stein and Thornton Wilder* (New Haven: Yale University, 1996).

Harrison, Gilbert. *The Enthusiast: A Life of Thornton Wilder* (New Haven: Ticknor and Fields, 1983).

Wilder, Thornton. *The Angel That Troubled the Waters and Other Plays* (New York: Coward-McCann, 1928).

———. *Three Plays* (New York: Harper, 1957).

———. Untitled article, *Writer's Digest*, September 1965, 37.

Charles Trainor

WILHELM II (1859–1941)

Wilhelm II was German emperor and king of Prussia (1888–1918). Born in Berlin, he received his education through his rigid tutor Georg Ernst Hinzpeter at the gymnasium in Kassel (1873–77) and the University of Bonn (1877–79). The son of Crown Prince Friedrich (later Emperor Friedrich III) and the British princess Victoria, his acknowledged legacy is a vehement opposition to his parents' liberal attitude in his attempt to form a "personal reign." Soon after his accession to the throne in 1888 he fell foul of Bismarck. Wilhelm's sociopolitical ambitions drove the chancellor into resigning in 1890, but Wilhelm quickly dropped his plans to reconcile the working classes as soon as he ran into court opposition. Wilhelm's mostly constitutional conduct in political practice during an outwardly grand epoch in German history should not obscure the severe tensions within society marking his reign. The emperor's impulsive character and delight in the military culminated in inconsiderate speeches that gave the impression of a despotic and bellicose inclination. The *Daily Telegraph* crisis of 1908 led Wilhelm to play a less prominent role in public affairs. During World War I he receded into the background and allowed his generals to direct the war's conduct. After chancellor Prinz Max von Baden had announced the emperor's abdication on his own initiative on November 9, 1918, Wilhelm sought asylum in The Netherlands.

Most of the time Wilhelm II showed little inclination toward serious reading. Nevertheless, he was exposed to a considerable range of literary thought through education and social contacts. In his intellectual heritage he drew from Houston Stewart Chamberlain's *The Foundations of the Nineteenth Century*, which he called "the greatest and most meaningful work" (Cecil 1989/96, 2: 56), memorizing long passages and reading excerpts to his courtiers. He appreciated Chamberlain's pretension for the Germans to restore the Roman Empire and purge Christianity of the influence of the Jews. Chamberlain and Wilhelm engaged in frequent correspondence and shared a disdain for the alleged worship of mammon in Anglo-Saxon culture. Heinrich von Treitschke's admiration of Prussia had influenced Wilhelm in his youth, but later the fiery historian fell from grace because he failed to adopt a reverential tone toward the throne. Wilhelm's conviction that the navy was the decisive force in warfare can be traced back to his thorough reading and annotating of Alfred Thayer Mahan's *The Importance of Sea Power in History*.

In his historical and theological worldview, Wilhelm repeatedly spoke of two traditions of revelation: one stemming from biblical sources, the other from sages, priests, and kings. Among the latter he liked to name Homer and Goethe as well as his grandfather, Kaiser Wilhelm I. As his poet laureate Wilhelm II chose Ernst von Wildenbruch, whose patriotic poems and historical plays seldom rose above mediocrity. This was in accordance with the kaiser's general denouncement of everything that even remotely savored of modernism or socialism.

Works immediately connected with his rule were of especial interest to Wilhelm in his exile. When he read the third volume of Bismarck's reminiscences he took excited notes in the margins of every page. Taking criticism very hard, he occasionally burst into tears; among the most damaging were the memoirs of minister Zedlitz-Trützschler and of Wilhelm's former instructor Ludwig Raschdau. Wilhelm found Tirpitz's *Politische Dokumente* "perfectly outrageous" (Cecil 1989/96, 2: 309) and wrote an article attempting to correct the admiral's account.

Archives

Geheimes Staatsarchiv Preußischer Kulturbesitz, Berlin: among various pertinent collections the remnant of the Hohenzollern family archive.

Archiv des vormals regierenden preußischen Königshauses, Burg Hohenzollern: restricted access.

Rijksarchief, Utrecht: files from his exile.

Printed Sources

Cecil, Lamar. *Wilhelm II*, 2 vols. (Chapel Hill: University of North Carolina Press, 1989, 1996).

Röhl, John C. G. *Wilhelm II. Die Jugend des Kaisers 1859–1888* (München: C.H. Beck, 1993).

———. *Wilhelm II. Der Aufbau der Persönlichen Monarchie 1888–1900* (München: C.H. Beck, 2001).

Wilhelm II. *Aus meinem Leben, 1859–1888* (Berlin, and Leipzig: K.F. Koehler 1927).

———. *Ereignisse und Gestalten aus den Jahren 1878–1918* (Berlin and Leipzig: K.F. Koehler 1922).

Alexander Sedlmaier

WILLIAMS, THOMAS LANIER (1911–1983)

Tennessee Williams was born in Columbus, Mississippi, to Edwina Dakin and Cornelius Coffin Williams. He briefly attended both the University of Missouri at Columbia and Washington University, Saint Louis, before graduating with a degree in English at the University of Iowa in 1937, moving to Chicago and then to New Orleans. At the age of 24, Williams's first play, *Cairo, Shanghai, Bombay*, was produced in Memphis, an event that began his long and prolific artistic career. Compared to great writers of the romantic Southern Gothic tradition such as **William Faulkner,** Williams's writing often captured intimate details of family life in the South. Much of Williams's writing drew upon his family portrait for inspiration: a combination of revered grandparents, genteel mother, drunken father, favored younger brother Dakin, and mentally disturbed sister Rose highly influenced all of his writings.

Williams traveled extensively throughout his life writing fiction, plays, and poetry, living most of it in hotel rooms between publication paychecks, as noted in his letters to a friend, Donald Windham. Although much of his work obligated him to live in New York and his family obligated him to visit Saint Louis, Williams had a distaste for both cities and spent any free time he had in places such as Provincetown, Key West, New Orleans, and parts of Mexico. Williams remained most famous for his plays that painted violent and sexual, and oftentimes depressing and disturbing, portraits of society, such as the two Pulitzer Prize–winning plays, *A Streetcar Named Desire* (1947) and *Cat on a Hot Tin Roof* (1955), as well as *Sweet Bird of Youth* (1959), *Orpheus Descending* (1958), and *Suddenly Last Summer* (1958).

Besides modeling characters in his plays on autobiographical influences, Williams also notes his influences as English writer **D. H. Lawrence,** collaborating with Donald Windham on a one-act play about Lawrence's life entitled *I Rise in Flame, Cried the Phoenix* (1951), as well as writing the play *You Touched Me!* (1947), based on Lawrence's short story of the same name. Other influences include Russian physician and writer Anton Chekov, Swedish author August Strindberg, American playwright **Eugene O'Neill,** German poet and writer Rainer Maria Rilke, French poet Arthur Rimbaud, and American poet Hart Crane, whose work "The Broken Tower" appears as an epigraph to *A Streetcar Named Desire.* Another Crane epigraph appears in *Sweet Bird of Youth,* and Crane's name is mentioned in the character dialogue of *You Touched Me!* The title of Williams 1961 play, *Summer and Smoke,* was also influenced by Crane's poem, "Emblems of Conduct." Crane remains the author of the only published volume of poems that stayed with Williams throughout his travels, *The Collected Poems of Hart Crane* (1933).

Archives

Harry Ransom Humanities Research Center, University of Texas at Austin: primary manuscripts, letters, photos, miscellaneous papers.

Columbia University's Rare Books and Manuscript Library, New York, New York: contents of Key West house.

Miscellaneous materials can be found at Harvard University, Cambridge, Massachusetts; University of California, Los Angeles; University of Delaware, Newark; New York Public Library's Theater Collection, New York.

Printed Sources

Fritscher, John J. "Love and Death in Tennessee Williams" (Ph.D. diss., Loyola University Library, 1967).

Hayman, Ronald. *Tennessee Williams: Everyone Else Is an Audience* (New Haven: Yale University Press, 1993).

Williams, Dakin, and Shepherd Mead. *Tennessee Williams: An Intimate Biography* (New York: Arbor House, 1983).

Windham, Donald. *Tennessee Williams' Letters to Donald Windham 1940–1965* (New York: Holt, Rinehart and Winston, 1977).

Jennifer Clary-Lemon

WILLIAMS, WILLIAM CARLOS (1883–1963)

William Carlos Williams was born in Rutherford, New Jersey. His English father was transplanted first to Saint Thomas and Santo Domingo and later to New Jersey. His mother was of Puerto Rican and French descent. Williams's ethnic background was reflected in his education, which included the Château de Lancy school near Geneva and Horace Mann School in New York City. He received his degree from the Medical School of the University of Pennsylvania and interned at the French Hospital in New York. He also studied pediatrics for a year in Leipzig.

Williams decided at the University of Pennsylvania that he wanted to be a poet but that he would practice medicine to support himself. Returning to Rutherford in 1910, Williams began his career as a physician, largely in the poor immigrant neighborhoods in and around Paterson. In 1912 he married Florence Herman, with whom he had two sons, William Eric and Paul Herman Williams. Williams published his first important book, *Al Que Quiere!*, in 1917. This was followed in 1920 by *Kora in Hell: Improvisations* and in 1923 by *Spring and All*. As part of the New York avant-garde, Williams associated with writers and artists who were introducing modernism to art. By the end of his career, Williams had published 49 books and won the National Book Award (1950), the Bollingen Award (1953), and the Pulitzer Prize (1963). Early poems such as "The Red Wheelbarrow," "The Widow's Lament in Springtime," and "To Elsie" shaped much of American modernist poetry and influenced many poets of the 1950s and 1960s. In the final years of his career, Williams published *Paterson*, his book-length epic poem for a new urban America.

Williams grew up in a home where Spanish, French, and English were frequently heard, but one of his most vivid early memories was his father reading the Negro dialect poems of Paul Laurence Dunbar. His father also introduced him to Shakespeare. Another favorite was Francis Palgrave's *Golden Treasury of English Verse*. His father once promised Williams a dollar apiece to read Charles Darwin's *The Origin of the Species* and *The Descent of Man*. His father's encouragement to read difficult books prompted Williams to read Dante's *The Divine Comedy* and Herbert Spencer's *Principles of Philosophy*. His Sunday school teacher at the Unitarian Church read to him from Kant and the Dialogues of Plato. He was impressed with his reading of major British poets, especially Keats's *Endymion* and Milton's "Lycidas," "Comus," "L'Allegro," and "Il Penseroso." At Horace Mann School, a favorite teacher, "Uncle Billy Abbott," introduced him to a wider range of great books and poets. In medical school, Williams remembered reading Victor Hugo's *Les Miserables* when he should have been studying anatomy. His lifelong friendship with **Ezra Pound** began when both were students at the University of Pennsylvania. Williams read many books that Pound recommended, such as Longinus's *On the Sublime*, Dante's *Vita Nuova*, and John Newman's *Apologia pro Vita Sua*, but he ultimately rejected much of Pound's influence. Williams's early poetry written during medical school showed the influence of Keats, but his notebooks of the period were full of what Williams called in his *Autobiography* his "Whitmanesque" thoughts.

Although Williams's education introduced him to many of the traditional great books of British literature, the diverse influences through his family and his effort to combine medicine with art led him to read a much more diverse group of writers than Shakespeare, Keats, Dante, Milton, Wordsworth, and Whitman. Both his parents spoke Spanish, and before his father's death in 1918, they collaborated on the translation of works from several South American writers. At school in Geneva, Williams became fluent in French. In Leipzig he read the poetry of Heinrich Heine and took in the plays of Ibsen and the operas of Wagner. At home he had read Gilbert and Sullivan and performed in *The Mikado* and *H.M.S. Pinafore*. In Philadelphia and New York, Williams became close friends with painters such as Charles Sheeler and Charles Demuth. He read the early poetry of Marianne Moore, Wallace Stevens, Pound, and many others of less fame. This eclectic range of reading and exposure to literary work in four languages—English, French, Spanish, and German—produced a poet most noted for writing in the American vernacular and choosing for his subject the local scene around Paterson, New Jersey. When other writers of his generation sought the European artistic world, Williams stayed home. His poetry, informed by his reading of the literature of more than one culture and one language, sought in the particulars of one place and its language a transformation through art of the timeless human experience.

Archives

Lockwood Memorial Library, State University of New York; the American Collection, Yale University Library; Research Center, University of Texas at Austin.

Printed Sources

Mariani, Paul. *William Carlos Williams. A New World Naked* (New York: McGraw-Hill, 1981).

Whittemore, Reed. *William Carlos Williams. Poet from Jersey* (Boston: Houghton Mifflin, 1975).

Williams, William Carlos. *The Autobiography of William Carlos Williams* (New York: New Directions, 1951).

Linda Ray Pratt

WILSON, EDMUND (1895–1972)

Edmund Wilson was born in Red Bank, New Jersey. He attended the Hill School in Pottstown, Pennsylvania (1908–12), a preparatory school in the Calvinist tradition, although it did little to encourage him in the path of orthodox piety. Wilson became distrustful of organized religion, a stance he owed, at least in part, to an introductory sentence in George Bernard Shaw's *Major Barbara* (1905) in which Shaw discounted the credibility of the world's organized religions. Wilson then attended Princeton University (1912–16), where he gravitated toward the study of literature, graduating in 1916. He served in the U.S. Army in France during the First World War (1917–19), and the experience changed him: he became more socially conscious and suspicious of established authority. Attracted to a career in the literary world, Wilson became the managing editor of *Vanity Fair* in 1920. The following year, he became the drama critic for the *New Republic*, rising to associate editor in 1926. In 1931, his first major work of literary criticism, *Axel's Castle: A Study of the Imaginative Literature of 1870–1930*, was published. The book established Wilson's reputation as a literary critic and he quickly followed with other works, some of which evidenced his growing, yet essentially apolitical, fascination and eventual dissatisfaction with Marxism. Over the next four decades, Wilson maintained a prolific and eclectic publishing regimen that included such diverse subjects as *The Scrolls from the Dead Sea* (1955) and *The Cold War and the Income Tax: A Protest* (1963). In 1966, he was awarded the National Medal for Literature. During his lengthy career, Wilson distinguished himself as the leading literary critic in the United States.

Since Wilson was an avid reader and a professional critic, his literary influences are numerous and varied, although some authors are more significant than others. In "A Modest Self-Tribute" (1952), Wilson relates how Hippolyte-Adolphe Taine was one of his earliest literary influences. Taine's *History of English Literature* (written in 1864; translated 1871–72) introduced him to the skillful use of literary biography, or a novelistic approach to describing an author's background (Groth 1989, 8–9; Castronovo 1984, 24; Castronovo 1998, 31–32). Other early influences included, as mentioned above, Shaw, who Wilson acknowledged in his essays in the *New Yorker* entitled "A Prelude" (1967), and **H. L. Mencken,** both of whom Wilson saw as "prophets of new eras in their national cultures" (Kriegel 1971, 9). In fact, much of Wilson's early writing appears to be modeled after Mencken, although Leonard Kriegel suggests that the student outgrew the teacher (Kriegel 1971, 8). One teacher whose influence stayed with Wilson throughout his life was Christian Gauss, his professor of European literature at Princeton who Wilson later honored in "Christian Gauss as a Teacher of Literature" (Dabney 1983, 45–66). Other documented literary influences included James Huneker, Henry James, Voltaire, Jules Michelet, and Karl Marx (Dabney 1983, xvi-xvii).

Archives

Beinecke Rare Book and Manuscript Library, Yale University, New Haven, Conn.
Edmund Wilson Library, University of Tulsa, Tulsa, Oklahoma. Wilson's personal library. This is the best primary source for Wilson's literary influences.

Printed Sources

Castronovo, David. *Edmund Wilson* (Frederick Ungar Publishing, 1984).
———. *Edmund Wilson Revisited* (New York: Twayne Publishers, 1998).
Dabney, Lewis M. (ed.). *The Portable Edmund Wilson* (New York: Viking, 1983).
Frank, Charles P. *Edmund Wilson* (New York: Twayne, 1970).
Groth, Janet. *Edmund Wilson: A Critic For Our Time* (Athens, Ohio: Ohio University Press, 1989).
Kriegel, Leonard. *Edmund Wilson* (Carbondale, Ill.: Southern Illinois University Press, 1971).
Wain, John (ed.). *Edmund Wilson: The Man and His Work* (New York: New York University Press, 1978).

Scott Lupo

WILSON, THOMAS WOODROW (1856–1924)

Woodrow Wilson was born in Staunton, Virginia. Son of a Presbyterian minister, he studied at Princeton (1875–79) and Johns Hopkins (1883–85), gaining his Ph.D. Thereafter he taught at Bryn Mawr and Wesleyan and became a professor of jurisprudence and political economy at Princeton in 1890. He was chosen president of the university in 1902. In 1910, he began a political career and successfully ran for governor of New Jersey as a Democrat. An energetic reformer, he became the Progressive movement's hope and won the presidential election of 1912 owing to the split in the Republican Party. He continued a domestic reformist program called "New Freedom" and repeatedly intervened in Latin America. During the Great War and its diplomatic conflicts resulting from Great Britain's naval blockade and Germany's unlimited submarine campaign, Wilson strove for the role of mediator. But the Imperial German government's uncompromising position drew the United States in, and on April 6, 1917, war was declared. In January 1918 Wilson announced his war aims in the form of the "Fourteen Points" and quickly became the preeminent supporter of an international collective security system. In much of the world he was therefore hailed as a savior. In 1919 at the Paris Peace Conference, the compromises of *realpolitik* fell short of Wilson's idealist program, although he championed a League of Nations. But Wilson refused concessions to his domestic opponents, and the ratification of the Versailles Treaty failed in Congress (November 19, 1919, and March 19, 1920) after the president's health had collapsed.

Wilson's general reading was intensive rather than extensive. Toward the end of his professorship at Princeton he intended to read a play of Shakespeare's each night but probably never carried out this goal systematically; *Henry V* was one of his favorite plays. As a young student Wilson recorded his reading interests in an *Index Rerum* (*The Papers of Woodrow Wilson*, 1:83–127), a notebook revealing his affection for English life and letters, its quotations largely coming from historians and politicians, including Edmund Burke, Thomas Carlyle, and Thomas Babington Macaulay.

In a talk with his friend Edward M. House in 1914, Wilson mentioned the British writers Edmund Burke and Walter Bagehot as the major influences on his development (Link 1966–94, 31:279). In his essay *Edmund Burke: The Man and His Times* (1893) Wilson proclaimed the urgency of reform and insisted with Burke that "it is both better and easier to reform than to tear down and reconstruct" (Link 1966–94, 8:342–43). Earlier he had been inspired by Bagehot's *English Constitution*, after which he deliberately modeled his own *Congressional Government* (1885). Wilson also drew on Sir Henry Maine's writings in comparative law to shape the boundaries of his studies on democratic government. In 1898 he lectured on Burke, Bagehot, and Maine at Johns Hopkins (Link 1966–94, 10:408–61). Alexis Clérel de Tocqueville and Charles de Secondat, Baron de la Brède et de Montesquieu also figured prominently in Wilson's numerous lectures on great leaders of political thought. With Tocqueville Wilson shared the notion of political habit (Link 1966–94, 9:374–76). Francis Amasa Walker's ideas on the social preconditions of industrial progress were of great interest to Wilson in his unpublished *History of Political Economy in the United States* (Link 1966–94, 4:628–63), especially Walker's criticism of orthodox liberalism arguing that economic forces were not self-correcting. James Bryce in *The American Commonwealth* had high praise for Wilson's scholarly achievements; when in 1889 Wilson reviewed Bryce's book for the *Political Science Quarterly*, he found it admirable but also thought that it fell short of the highest excellence. Another contemporary theoretician of the American Constitution was Hermann Eduard von Holst, whose works Wilson knew well and reviewed favorably (Link 1966–94, 5:490–99). Wilson followed an early ambition to match John Richard Green's *History of the English People* when he wrote a popular history of the United States entitled *A History of the American People* (1902).

In his academic works of the 1880s Wilson drew extensively on German scholarship on law and administration. In particular he used Otto von Sarwey's *Allgemeines Verwaltungsrecht* and the writings of Adolf Merkel, part of which he carefully translated and digested (Link 1966–94, 7:249–69). Wilson based *The State* (1889), considered his most important scholarly work, on the series entitled *Handbuch des Oeffentlichen Rechts der Gegenwart* edited by Heinrich Marquardsen. John Mulder, author of a study of Wilson's scholarly career, even finds some "rather thinly veiled plagiarism" in Wilson's culling from German political and administrative historians (Mulder 1978, 103; cf. Link 1966–94, 6:244–52).

Archives

Library of Congress, Manuscript Division, Washington, D.C., *The Papers of Woodrow Wilson:* 278,700 items relating to Wilson's life.

Seeley G. Mudd Manuscript Library, Princeton University, Princeton, N.J., *Woodrow Wilson Papers:* mainly material relating to Wilson's years as university president.

Printed Sources

Ambrosius, Lloyd E. *Wilsonian Statecraft: Theory and Practice of Liberal Internationalism during World War I* (Wilmington: Scholarly Resources, 1991).

Axson, Stockton. *"Brother Woodrow": A Memoir of Woodrow Wilson*, Arthur S. Link (ed.), (Princeton: Princeton University Press, 1993). Contains reminiscences on Wilson's taste in literature by his brother-in-law, 107–11.

Bragdon, Henry W. *Woodrow Wilson: The Academic Years* (Cambridge: Harvard University Press, 1967).

Link, Arthur S. *Wilson*, 5 vols. (Princeton: Princeton University Press, 1947–65).

Link, Arthur S. et al. (eds.). *The Papers of Woodrow Wilson*, 69 vols. (Princeton: Princeton University Press, 1966–94).

Mulder, John M. *Woodrow Wilson: The Years of Preparation* (Princeton: Princeton University Press, 1978).

Schulte Nordholt, Jan W. *Woodrow Wilson: A Life for World Peace* (Berkeley: University of California Press, 1991).

Thorsen, Niels A. *The Political Thought of Woodrow Wilson, 1875–1910* (Princeton: Princeton University Press, 1988).

Alexander Sedlmaier

WITTGENSTEIN, LUDWIG JOSEF JOHANN (1889–1951)

Ludwig Wittgenstein was born in Vienna, Austria, the youngest of eight children of Karl Wittgenstein, a wealthy industrialist, and his wife, Leopoldine, née Kalmus. Both sides of his family were Jewish but led secular lives and had converted to Roman Catholicism in order to be accepted into the highest echelons of Viennese society. He was home-schooled until age 14. Two brothers and possibly a third were suicides. His parents frequently hosted Eduard Hanslick, Gustav Mahler, Bruno Walter, Johannes Brahms, and other prominent figures in the musical world. Wittgenstein early learned to love Johann Sebastian Bach, Ludwig van Beethoven, and Felix Mendelssohn, and lifelong he preferred talking about music to talking about philosophy.

Wittgenstein and **Adolf Hitler,** born six days apart, were schoolmates at the Realgymnasium (high school) in Linz, Austria, but only conflicting evidence exists of the extent and nature of their contact with each other. Wittgenstein's adolescence coincided with an extraordinary Viennese cult of enthusiasm for *Sex and Character*, whose bizarre 23-year-old author, Otto Weininger, committed suicide a few months after its publication in 1903. Wittgenstein never ceased to admire this book, even later recommending it to such steadfastly unreceptive colleagues as George Edward Moore.

Wittgenstein attended the Technische Hochschule in Berlin from 1906 to 1908 to study mechanical engineering, then pursued aeronautical engineering at the University of Manchester from 1908 to 1911. His visit to Gottlob Frege in 1911 persuaded him toward mathematical logic and philosophy. Frege urged him to study under **Bertrand Russell** at the University of Cambridge. From 1912 to 1913 he was supervised but not favorably influenced by William Ernest Johnson at Kings College, Cambridge. He abandoned Cambridge, spent much time from 1913 to 1950 in Norway, enlisted in the Austrian artillery in 1914, fought on several fronts, and spent the last 10 months of World War I as a prisoner of war in Italy.

After the war he finished the *Tractatus Logico-Philosophicus* that he had begun at Cambridge. He earned his living as a schoolteacher from 1920 to 1926, during which time he read Fyodor Dostoyevsky and Lev Tolstoy. He served in 1926 as gardener at a monastery, and from 1926 to 1928 as co-architect of his sister Gretl's mansion. He returned as a fellow to Trinity College, Cambridge, in 1929, and was professor there from 1939 to 1947 but worked as an orderly at Guy's Hospital, London, from 1941 to 1944. He was naturalized British in 1938. Among his Cambridge friends was the economist Piero Sraffa.

Wittgenstein never read Hume or several other key philosophers and never became well-read in philosophy. He did not understand G. W. F. Hegel and seemed to confuse Hegel's project with that of Friedrich Wilhelm Joseph von Schelling. He labeled some thinkers "deep," such as Immanuel Kant and George Berkeley, and others "shallow," such as Arthur Schopenhauer. He believed that he had finished philosophy with the *Tractatus*, but in the 1930s realized that philosophy remained unfinished, and returned to it. His subsequent philosophical work was almost entirely self-critical, directed toward repudiating the *Tractatus*.

Wittgenstein had many character flaws, yet, to his credit, he was explicitly aware and ashamed of most of them. He was a self-confessed coward and sneak, intolerant of intellects lesser than his, and quick-tempered. He was ascetic but cultured. His secretive, intensely private nature is attributable to paranoia about his homosexuality. In England, he had semi-secret homosexual relationships with Frank Plumpton Ramsey, Francis Skinner, and other intellectuals.

For Wittgenstein, the world's two most profound thinkers were St. Augustine and Søren Kierkegaard. He admired William James's *Varieties of Religious Experience*. Among the other writers he favored were Oswald Spengler, Franz Grillparzer, Charles Dickens, **John Maynard Keynes,** Max Kalbeck, Richard Wagner, Johann Georg Hamann, Karl Kraus, Rainer Maria Rilke, Georg Trakl, Samuel Johnson, physicists Ludwig Boltzmann and Heinrich Hertz, and architect Adolf Loos. Some interpreters have noted similarities between Wittgenstein's *Philosophical Investigations* and Blaise Pascal's *Pensées*, but there is no evidence that Pascal influenced Wittgenstein.

Archives

Wittgenstein's papers and especially his correspondence are in widely scattered repositories, the six most significant being Trinity College Library, Cambridge; the Austrian National Library, Vienna; Bodleian Library, Oxford; Bertrand Russell Archives, McMaster University, Hamilton, Ontario; Brenner-Archiv, University of Innsbruck, Austria; and the Wittgenstein Archives, University of Bergen, Norway, which, since its founding in 1990, has aimed to create a complete digital version of Wittgenstein's literary estate.

Printed Sources

Cornish, Kimberley. *The Jew of Linz: Wittgenstein, Hitler and Their Secret Battle for the Mind* (London: Century, 1998).

Flowers, F. A. (ed.). *Portraits of Wittgenstein* (Bristol, England: Thoemmes, 1999).

Janik, Allan. *Wittgenstein's Vienna Revisited* (New Brunswick, New Jersey: Transaction, 2001).

Janik, Allan, and Hans Veigl. *Wittgenstein in Vienna: A Biographical Excursion through the City and Its History* (New York: Springer, 1998).

Klagge, James C. (ed.). *Wittgenstein: Biography and Philosophy* (Cambridge: Cambridge University Press, 2001).

McGuinness, Brian. *Wittgenstein: A Life: Young Ludwig, 1889–1921* (Berkeley: University of California Press, 1988).

McGuinness, Brian, and Georg Henrik von Wright (eds.). *Ludwig Wittgenstein, Cambridge Letters: Correspondence with Russell, Keynes, Moore, Ramsey, and Sraffa* (Oxford: Blackwell, 1997).

Malcolm, Norman. *Ludwig Wittgenstein: A Memoir, with a Biographical Sketch by G. H. von Wright*, 2nd edition, with Wittgenstein's Letters to Malcolm (Oxford: Oxford University Press, 2001).

Rhees, Rush (ed.). *Recollections of Wittgenstein* (New York: Oxford University Press, 1984).

Sluga, Hans, and David G. Stern (eds.). *The Cambridge Companion to Wittgenstein* (Cambridge: Cambridge University Press, 1996).

The Wittgenstein Archives at the University of Bergen: Project Report 1990–1993 and Critical Evaluation (Bergen, Norway: Wittgensteinarkivet, 1995).

Eric v.d. Luft

WOJTYLA, KAROL

See John Paul II.

WOOLF, VIRGINIA (1882–1941)

Virginia Woolf was born in London, the daughter of Leslie Stephen, eminent Victorian agnostic, historian, and man of letters. She was educated informally at home; when she was 16, she took lessons in Latin and Greek. After her father's death, she joined her siblings in setting up house in the Bloomsbury district of London, which became the focus of the "Bloomsbury Group." She became an accomplished book reviewer, and in 1912 married Leonard Woolf (1880–1969). Two serious mental breakdowns in her youth were followed by a third after the completion of her first novel, *The Voyage Out* (1915). A printing press bought for occupational therapy was the origin of the Hogarth Press, a successful business through which the Woolfs published many notable books, including **T. S. Eliot**'s *The Waste Land* (1922) and the Standard [English] Edition of Sigmund Freud, as well as her own novels. *Jacob's Room, Mrs. Dalloway* (1925), *To the Lighthouse* (1927), *Orlando* (1928), and *The Waves* (1931) established her as a literary novelist of high distinction; *The Years* (1937), a family saga, brought commercial success. In *A Room of One's Own* (1929) she protested the economic and intellectual subjection of women. In 1941, distressed by the war and the threat of renewed mental illness, she committed suicide.

Conscious of her own intellectual powers and resentful of her exclusion, as a female, from formal education, Woolf was a passionate but conflicted reader. Her father had guided her early reading, first of T. B. Macaulay and other Victorian writers, then, starting with Richard Hakluyt's *Voyages*, in English literature of the Renaissance. Much of what she read and her reactions to it may be traced in her diaries, and in her published reviews and essays; the notes she made while reading have been calendared by Brenda Silver. Her series title for her two collections of literary essays, *The Common Reader* (1925, 1932), asserts amateur status, although she had become as professional and productive a writer as her father. At the time of her death she was planning a history of women's contributions as writers and readers to English literature. Allusions in her novels, which play a crucial role in the development of meaning, show that her creative imagination drew heavily on her reading of earlier literature, especially of the Renaissance. She was less engaged by contemporary writers. One exception is **James Joyce,** whose *Ulysses* (1922), a novel that she disliked yet uneasily respected, suggested the possibilities of a novel set in a single day and thus contributed a structural principle to *Mrs. Dalloway.*

Archives

Berg Collection, New York Public Library, New York, N.Y. Diaries, letters, literary manuscripts, reading notebooks.

Special Collections, Sussex University Library, Brighton, England. Letters, literary manuscripts, family papers, reading notebooks.

Library, Washington State University, Pullman, Wash. The Library of Leonard and Virginia Woolf. Short-title catalogue at: http://www.wsylibs.wsu.edu/holland/masc/woolflibrary.htm.

Printed Sources

Bell, Quentin. *Virginia Woolf: A Biography* [1972], rev. ed. (London: Pimlico, 1996).

Dusinberre, Juliet. *Virginia Woolf's Renaissance: Woman Reader or Common Reader?* (Iowa City, Iowa: University of Iowa Press, 1997).

Fox, Alice. *Virginia Woolf and the Literature of the English Renaissance* (Oxford: Clarendon Press, 1990).

Schlack, Beverly Ann. *Continuing Presences: Virginia Woolf's Use of Literary Allusion* (University Park, Pa.: Pennsylvania State University Press, 1979).

Silver, Brenda R. *Virginia Woolf's Reading Notebooks* (Princeton, N.J.: Princeton University Press, 1983).

Woolf, Virginia. *The Diary of Virginia Woolf* (1915–1941), 5 vols. Anne Olivier Bell (ed.), (New York: Harcourt Brace Jovanovich, 1977–84).

———. *The Essays of Virginia Woolf,* Andrew McNeillie (ed.), 6 vols. projected (London: Hogarth Press, 1986–).

———. *A Passionate Apprentice: The Early Journals 1897–1909,* Mitchell A. Leaska (ed.), (New York: Harcourt Brace Jovanovich, 1990).

John D. Baird

WRIGHT, FRANK LLOYD (1867–1959)

Frank Lloyd Wright was born at Richland Center, Wisconsin, into a conservative Unitarian family. At the age of 12, Wright moved to Madison, Wisconsin, where he attended high school and enjoyed a placid life amid the rural countryside. In 1885 he began studying under Allan Conover, the dean of the University of Wisconsin's Engineering Department. Two years later, he moved to Chicago to work under the architect Joseph Lyman Silsbee, with whom he produced his first building, the Wright family's Unity Chapel. Wright also worked for the team of engineer Dankmar Adler and renowned architect Louis Sullivan, producing residential designs from their Chicago firm. By 1893, Wright had established his own firm in Chicago, which he would later move (along with his place of residence) to Oak

Park, Illinois. The first decade of the twentieth century saw Wright formulate his highly influential prairie house style, typified in such buildings as the Robie House in Chicago and the Martin House in Buffalo, New York. In 1909, Wright moved to Germany but returned two years later to construct his Taliesin home at Spring Green, Wisconsin. Wright established a fellowship at Taliesin and lived there until fire claimed the dwelling in 1914. In the years to come, Wright would rebuild the structure as well as design and construct several of the most important buildings of the twentieth century. These include the Imperial Hotel in Tokyo, "Fallingwater" in Mill Run, Pennsylvania, and Taliesin West in Scottsdale, Arizona, where he spent the last 20 years of his life. By the time of his death Wright had published many influential and significant treatises on architecture. Over 400 of his uniquely designed structures remain standing at the time of this publication.

Influential to Wright's style of architecture were the copious writings of his mentor, Louis Sullivan, who espoused that form should always follow function in design. Sullivan was critical of architectural styles that had their basis in classicism and believed that architecture should always visually reflect the intent for which a building was to be used. This led Wright to develop a level of unprecedented geometric abstraction best typified by the designs for his prairie style dwellings. Abandoning traditional floor plans and contemporary ornamentation, Wright focused on the use of horizontal planes and low pitched rooflines with deep overhangs to give the interior space of his dwellings a sense of shelter without confinement. Following the notions of organic form found in John Ruskin's *The Seven Lamps of Architecture* and *The Stones of Venice*, Wright ensured that the design of his structures allowed for the connection of interior spaces with their natural surroundings. This notion of using natural forms and materials in architecture was paralleled by the arts and crafts movement in design during the early twentieth century, which Wright became acquainted with during his extensive European lecture circuits. The reverence of nature and the primacy of unity, truth, harmony, and simplicity in all manner of production were concepts that Wright first heard espoused in his childhood introductions to the works of Ralph Waldo Emerson, Henry David Thoreau, Walt Whitman, and William Blake.

Archives

The Frank Lloyd Wright Archives, Taliesin West, Scottsdale, Arizona. Drawings, manuscripts, books (including volumes from the libraries of Wright's father and paternal grandfather, some dating back to 1666), periodicals, correspondence.

The Getty Institute for the History of Art and the Humanities, Los Angeles, California.

State Historical Society of Wisconsin, Madison. Major collection of materials about Wright's life and times.

Printed Sources

Meehan, Patrick J. (ed.). *The Master Architect: Conversations with Frank Lloyd Wright* (New York: John Wiley and Sons, 1990).

Secrest, Meryle. *Frank Lloyd Wright* (New York: Alfred A. Knopf, 1992).

Twombly, Robert. *Frank Lloyd Wright: His Life and His Architecture* (New York: John Wiley and Sons, 1987).

Wright, Frank Lloyd. *Frank Lloyd Wright: Collected Writings*, Bruce Brooks Pfieffer (ed.), vols. 1–5 (New York: Rizzoli International Publications, 1992–95).

Gregory L. Schnurr

WRIGHT, RICHARD NATHANIEL (1908–60)

Richard Wright was born on a plantation near Natchez, Mississippi. When he was five years old, his father deserted the family to live with another woman, leaving his mother to raise him and his younger brother without his father's financial and emotional support. Two years later, Wright's mother was stricken with the first of many paralytic strokes; thus, Wright spent much of his childhood in the home of his maternal grandparents under the care of his grandmother. Wright's grandmother, Margaret Bolden, a devout Seventh-Day Adventist, insisted that her home's occupants follow her religious beliefs. Although Wright rejected religion, the fiery sermons and metaphorical biblical stories he heard as a child evoked his budding imagination and proved to have great impact on his work. In 1925, Wright left his mother in the care of his grandmother and moved to Memphis, Tennessee. A year later, he moved to Chicago where he joined the Communist Party. With only a high school education, he began his successful writing career. By the time he published *The Outsider* in 1953, Wright, his wife, and his two children had become residents of France, joining other American expatriates. He died from a heart attack while living in France.

In his autobiography, *Black Boy (American Hunger)*, Wright tells readers of his voracious reading habits. According to Wright, after reading *A Book of Prefaces* by **H. L. Mencken,** he learned that words could be used as weapons. Reading Mencken led him to discover other writers. Among those mentioned is Theodore Dreiser, author of *Jennie Gerhardt* and *Sister Carrie*. Dreiser's two novels informed Wright's sense of realism and naturalism, two elements characteristic of Wright's fiction. He also notes that **Sinclair Lewis's** *Main Street* helped him to realize the importance of point of view in narrative construction. Wright credits **Josef Stalin's** *The National and Colonial Question* with inspiring the idea that the unification of diverse minorities is possible. This idea is expressed in his first anthology of short stories, *Uncle Tom's Children* (1938), and in his most famous novel, *Native Son* (1940). The novel, which is set in Chicago, features a 20-year old Black male who accidentally murders his white employer's daughter and is subsequently represented by a Communist Jewish attorney. While living in France, Wright wrote *The Outsider* (1953), an existentialist novel that best expresses his disillusionment with communism and his rejection of religion. This novel shows the influences of existentialists **Simone de Beauvoir** and **Jean-Paul Sartre,** but **Albert Camus's** novel *The Stranger* seems to have been most influential. Readers may also note the influences of Friedrich Nietzsche and of Joseph Conrad's *Heart of Darkness*. Wright was also greatly interested in psychology. *Savage Holiday* (1954) reflects the influences of Frederic Wertham's *Dark Legend*, a book based on the case of Clinton Brewer, a teenager who murdered his mother in the 1930s. Further, Wright's novella, "The Man Who Lived Underground," was clearly inspired by his reading of Fyodor Dostoyesky's *Notes from the Underground*.

Wright's interests in religion and politics are present in his travel narratives. In *Black Power* (1954), which is about his trip to the reformed Gold Coast under the leadership of Kwame Nkrume and his observations of the country's traditional religious practices, Wright references a number of works. Among those named are Eric Williams's *Capitalism and Slavery* and W. Walton Claridge's *A History of the Gold Coast*, v. 1. Later in *Pagan Spain* (1957), Wright documents his trip to Spain and criticizes Catholicism and ruler **Francisco Franco.** In preparation for this trip and the impending book, Wright consulted nineteenth-century travelogues, including America Castro's *Structure of Spanish History* (Fabre 1973, 411).

Archives

Richard Wright Papers. Yale Collection of American Literature. Beinecke Rare Book and Manuscript Library, New Haven, Conn. This collection includes drafts of Wright's published works and unpublished works. It also includes letters written by Wright and to Wright.

Printed Sources

Gates, Henry Louis, and K. A. Appiah (eds.). *Richard Wright: Critical Perspectives Past and Present* (New York: Amistad, 1993).

Fabre, Michael. *Richard Wright: Books and Writers* (Jackson: University Press of Mississippi, 1990).

———. *The Unfinished Quest of Richard Wright*, Isabel Barzan (trans.), (New York: William Morrow, 1973).

Kinnamon, Keneth, and Michel Fabre, (eds.). *Conversations with Richard Wright* (Jackson: University Press of Mississippi, 1993).

Walker, Margaret. *Richard Wright Daemonic Genius: A Portrait of a Man* (New York: Warner Books, 1988).

Webb, Constance. *Richard Wright: A Biography* (New York: G.P. Putnam's Sons, 1968).

Wright, Ellen, and Michel Fabre (eds.). *Richard Wright Reader* (New York: Da Capo, 1997).

Tara D. Green

WRIGHT, WILBUR (1867–1912) AND ORVILLE (1871–1948)

Wilbur and Orville Wright were born to Bishop Milton Wright of the United Brethren in Christ Church and his wife, Susan, and grew up in Dayton, Ohio, together with their sister Katharine. Neither brother graduated from high school. They first operated a printing business (and invented a process for folding newspapers) and later, beginning in 1892, a bicycle shop. While recovering from a bout of typhoid fever in 1896, Wilbur Wright read of the death of German flight pioneer Otto Lilienthal in a gliding accident. He and his brother decided to learn about the work done to date on solving the problem of heavier-than-air flight. They then conducted their first glider experiments at Kitty Hawk, N.C., in 1900. By late 1902, they had assembled new information based on their own experiments, which included construction of a wind tunnel to understand why some theoretical calculations had not proven correct during glider trials. This experience laid the groundwork for the design of their first powered airplane, the Flyer I, which Orville successfully piloted on December 17, 1903. The following three years, they perfected their flying technique and, in 1906, received a patent for the plane. In 1908, they became the subject of public attention with demonstrations at Ft. Myers, Virginia, and in France, where they achieved several world records. Demonstrations continued in the following years, and the brothers spent much time selling their patent and taking to court other pioneers who had copied their wing-warping principle, which allowed controlled turns. Orville died unexpectedly of typhoid fever in 1912, and Wilbur retired from flying. In 1913, he won the Collier trophy for a device to automatically balance airplanes. Two years later, he sold his interest in the Wright Company. In 1929, he received the first Daniel Guggenheim Medal for his and Wilbur's contributions to the advancement of aeronautics. He died in 1947.

As youths, Orville and Wilbur read avidly from their father's book collection, housed in two libraries in their home (the theology library was upstairs in their father's study, the general library downstairs). The progressive attitude of their parents meant the boys had access to all readings, which included Darwin's *Origin of Species*, Plutarch's *Lives*, James Boswell's *Life of Samuel Johnson*, Edward Gibbon's *Decline and Fall of the Roman Empire*, and books by Sir Walter Scott and Nathaniel Hawthorne. The brothers also read anthologies, such as J. L. Cornstock's *An Introduction to the Study of Botany* (1857) and Sidney Norton's *The Elements of Natural Philosophy* (1870). The family also owned an *Encyclopedia Britannica* and the *Chamber's Encyclopedia*. This abundant exposure to reading influenced the brothers' capacity to assimilate large amounts of information and become self-taught in a number of trades.

In fact, many of the books the Wrights kept in their own library contain underlined passages and remarks in the margins, especially the aviation volumes that they acquired or received throughout their lives. When they first began researching flight, the brothers read classics of early aviation that had been recommended by the Smithsonian Institution, including English summaries of Lilienthal's *The Problem of Flying* and *Practical Experiments in Soaring* (1894), which the brothers acknowledged as their greatest inspiration, and of Jules Marey's *Animal Mechanism* (1874). They also read Samuel P. Langley's *Experiments in Aerodynamics* (1891); Louis Mouillard's *Empire of the Air* (1881), which they termed "one of the most remarkable pieces of aeronautical literature"; Octave Chanute's *Progress in Flying Machines* (1891); and the *Aëronautical Annual* volumes of 1895, 1896, and 1897. The writings of Chanute, Lilienthal, and Mouillard convinced them, as they later recalled in *The Century Magazine* (September 1908), of the advantage of experimenting first with gliders before switching to expensive powered airplanes.

Archives

Library of Congress Manuscripts Division, papers of the Wright brothers; papers of Octave Chanute.

Wright State University Libraries, papers of the Wright brothers, 1881–1948, including part of their personal library. (http://www.libraries.wright.edu/special/wright_brothers/ms1_scope.html)

Printed Sources

Combs, Harry B. *Kill Devil Hill: Discovering the Secret of the Wright Brothers* (Boston: Houghton Mifflin, 1979).

Crouch, Tom. *The Bishop's Boys: A Life of Wilbur and Orville Wright* (New York: W. W. Norton, 1989).

———. *A Dream of Wings: Americans and the Airplane 1875–1905* (Washington, D.C.: Smithsonian, 1989).

Howard, Fred. *Wilbur and Orville: A Biography of the Wright Brothers* (New York: Alfred A. Knopf, 1987).

Jakab, Peter L. *Visions of a Flying Machine* (Washington, D.C., Smithsonian, 1990).

Jakab, Peter L., and Rick Young (eds.). *The Published Writings of Wilbur and Orville Wright* (Washington, D.C.: Smithsonian, 2000).

Kelly, Fred C. *Miracle at Kitty Hawk: The Letters of Wilbur and Orville Wright* (New York: Da Capo Press, 1996).

———. *The Wright Brothers: A Biography* (New York: Dover, 1989).

Guillaume de Syon

INDEX

Page numbers in **bold** indicate the individual's own entry.

Abba, Marta, 431
Abbott, Billy, 560
ABC, 178
Abel, Theodora Mead, 357
Acevedo Diaz, Eduardo, 448
Achebe, Chinua, **1–2**, 209.
  Works: *Anthill of the Savan-
  nah*, 1; *Arrow of God*, 1; *A
  Man of the People*, 1; *No
  Longer at Ease*, 1; *Things Fall
  Apart*, 1
Ackerman, Forest J., *Famous
  Monsters of Filmland*, 490
Acton, Harold, 543
Acton, John Emerich Dalberg,
  Lord, 105, 522
Actualidad Económica, 275
Adam, Villiers de Lisle, 125
Adams, Henry, 68; *The Educa-
  tion of Henry Adams*, 64
Adams, John, 434
Adams, John Quincy, *Diary*,
  434
Adams, Samuel Hopkins,
  "Night Bus," 92
Addams, Jane, **3–4**. Works:
  Democracy and Social Ethics,
  81; *Hull House Maps and
  Papers*, 4; *A New Conscience
  and an Ancient Evil*, 64; *Peace
  and Bread in Time of War*, 4;
  Twenty Years at Hull-House, 4

Ade, George, 359
Adelphi, 407, 408
Adenauer, Konrad, **4–6**, 70,
  126, 302
Adler, Alfred, 40, 223, 350, 433.
  Works: *The Nervous Charac-
  ter*, 166; *Understanding
  Human Nature*, 166
Adler, Dankmar, 567
Adorno, Theodor, 345, 473
Advocate, 142
Ady, Endre, 301
AE (George Russell), 399
Aegidi, Ludwig Karl, 548
Aeronautical Annual, 571
Aeschylus, 119, 125, 262.
  Works: *Oedipus*, 429;
  Oresteia, 200, 291, 403; *The
  Persians*, 466; *Prometheus*, 291
Aesop, 67
Afanasyev, Alexander, *Russian
  Folktales*, 504
African Communities League,
  192
Aganbegyan, Abel, 208
Agee, James, 135; *Let us Now
  Praise Famous Men*, 96
Aitken, William Maxwell, Lord
  Beaverbrook, **6–8**. Works:
  *The Decline and Fall of Lloyd
  George*, 7; *Men and Power,
  1917–1918*, 7; *Politicians and*

the Press, 7; *Politicians and the
  War*, 7
Akhmatova, Anna, **8–9**, 79,
  183. Works: "Autobiographi-
  cal Prose;" 8, *Evening*, 8;
  Rosary, 8; *My Half Century*, 8
Alacro, Geraldo, 224
Alain. *See* Chartier, Emile
Alberti, Rafael, 178, 264, 265
Albritton, David, 410
Alcott, Louisa May: *Little Men*,
  458; *Little Women*, 40, 497
Aleichem, Sholem, 358
Alexander, James Waddell II,
  387
Alexander (the Great), xv
Alexander III, 314
Alexis, Willibald, 548
Alfonso XIII, 274
Alger, Horatio, 115, 139, 452,
  481, 498. Works: *From Canal
  Boy to President*, 454; *Phil, the
  Fiddler*, 454; *The River Boys*,
  454
Algonquin Round Table, 52
Algren, Nelson, 39
Ali, Duse Mohammed, *African
  Times and Orient Review*, 192
Ali, Muhammad, **9–10**, 338
Ali, Noble Drew, 376
Allen, Grant, 416
Allen, Paul, 194

Index

Allende, Isabel, **10–11**. Works: *Daughter of Fortune*, 10; *The House of Spirits*, 10; *Love and Shadows*, 10, *Portrait in Sepia*, 10; *The Stories of Eva Luna*, 10, 11

Allgemeine Zeitschrift fur Psychiatrie, 277

Almqvist, Jonas Love, 49

Alsopf, Kenneth, 37

Alterman, Nathan, 48

Althusser, Louis, 204

Althusser, Pierre, 130

Altmeier, Peter, 302

Amado, Jorge, **11–12**. Works: *Captains of the Sands*, 11; *Clove and Cinnamon*, 11; *Dona Flor and Her Two Husbands*, 11; *Gabriela*, 11; *The Two Deaths of Quincas Wateryell*, 11; *The Violent Land*, 11

Ambrose, 434

America, Mary, 454

American Civil Liberties Union, 3

American Heritage, 320

Amiel, Henri Frédéric, 371, *Amiel's Journal*, 200

Amin, Idi, 487

Amsterdam News, 451

Andersen, Hans Christian, 481

Andersen-Nexo, Martin, 69

Anderson, Lale, *Der Himmel hat viele Farben*, 167

Anderson, Maxwell, *Valley Forge*, 92

Anderson, Poul, *The Twilight World*, 88

Anderson, Sherwood, 65, 399, 467, 494, 499; *Winesburg, Ohio*, 169, 241

Andopov, Yuri, 207

Andreyev, Leonid, 403

Andrić, Ivo, **12–13**. Works: *Bosnian Chronicle*, 13; *The Bridge on the Drina*, 12; "The Development of Spiritual Life in Bosnia under the Influence of Turkish Rule," 12; *The Woman from Sarajevo*, 13

Angell, Norman, *The Fruits of Victory*, 4

Angelou, Maya, **13–15**. Works: *All God's Children Need Traveling Shoes*, 15; *The Heart of a Woman*, 14; *I Know Why the Caged Bird Sings*, 14; "On the Pulse of Morning," 14

Angioliere, Cecco, 430

Annalen der Physik, 158

Annales, 56, 71, 72

Annals of Xahil, 21

Annensky, Annokenty, 8

Anouilh, Jean, 49, 410

Anselm of Canterbury, 34

Ansen, Alan, 87

Anthony, Susan B., 123, 469

Antoniolli, Walter, 540

Antonioni, Michaelangelo, 509

Apollinaire, Guillaume, **15–16**, 67, 76, 103, 144, 340, 365, 428, 494, 531. Works: *The Cubist Painters—Aesthetic Meditations*, 103; *Le poete assassine*, 15; *Zone*, 144

Apostles, The (Cambridge), 294, 502, 553

Appleton's Cyclopedia, 124

Apuleius, 353

Aquinas, Thomas, 153, 269, 273, 276, 353, 361, 397, 475, 522, 532; *Summa Theologica*, 208, 328

Arabian Nights, 10, 103, 200, 249, 461; *Sinbad*, 422

Aragon, Louis, 20, 21, 75, 121, 365, 428; *Le creve-coeur*, 368

Arciniegas, German, 448

Ardigò, Roberto, 118; *Positivist Morality*, 378

Arendt, Hannah, **16–18**, 240; "The Concept of Love in St. Augustine," 17

Arevalo, Juan José, 21

Arguedas, José María, 224, 325. Works: *Todas Las Sangres*, 224; *El Zorro de ariba e el zorro de a baja*, 224

Ariosto, Ludovico, 405; *Orlando Furioso*, 430

Aristophanes, 147, 299, 523

Aristotle, 50, 147, 239, 273, 276, 284, 312, 332, 353, 433, 459, 498, 521

Armstrong, Louis, **18–20**

Arndt, Arthur, 433

Arndt, Ernest Moritz, 5

Arnold, Matthew, 68, 255. Works: "The Scholar Gypsy," 537; *Sohrab and Rustum*, 151; "Thyrsis," 537

Arnold, Thomas, 255

Aron, Raymond, 371, 471; *The Opium of the Intellectuals*, 43

Aronson, Harvey, 497

Arp, Jean, **20–21**

Arrospide, Cesar, 224

Artaud, Antonin, 76

Aschaffenburg, Gustav, 277

Ashton, Frederick, 394

Ashvaaghosa, *The Life of Buddha*, 292

Asimov, Isaac, 490

Asnyk, Adam, 414

Asquith, Raymond, 289

Asturias, Miguel Angel, **21–22**. Works: *Hombres de maiz*, 21; *El papa verde*, 21; *El Señor Presidente*, 21; *Weekend in Guatemala*, 21

Athanasius, 34

Atlantic Monthly, 94

Atlases, 461

Attlee, Clement, **22–24**, 111, 337, 510

Attridge, Derek, 131

Atwood, Margaret, **24–25**. Works: *The Handmaid's Tale*, 429; *Survival*, 24

Auden, Wystan Hugh, 24, **25–26**, 53, 77, 79, 229, 364, 504, 513, 517. Works: "The Age of Anxiety," 25; "For the Time Being," 25; "September 1, 1939," 25; "The Shield of Achilles," 25

Auerbach, Berhold, 332

Augustine, 34, 118, 125, 193, 239, 240, 267, 361, 389, 397, 530, 565; *Confessions*, 123, 200, 459

Austen, Jane, 24, 32, 109, 175, 327, 337, 373, 399, 466, 500, 518

Avanti!, 379

Avedon, Richard, 19

Avenarius, Richard, 93

Avison, Margaret, 24

Awoonor, Kofi, 209

Azuela, Mariano, *The Underdogs*, 448

Babbage, Charles, 387

Babel, Isaac, 316, 400; *Red Cavalry*, 11

Bach, Johann Sebastian, 196, 473, 564

Bachelard, Baston, *La philosophie du non*, 146

Bacon, Francis, 353, 483, 500; *New Atlantis*, 484

Baczko, Bronislaw, 263

Baden, Max von, 557

Baeck, Leo, **27–28**. Works: "Benedikt de Spinoza's First Influences on Germany," 27; *The Essence of Judaism*, 28

Baez, Joan, 148

Bagehot, Walter, *English Constitution*, 563

Bahr, Hermann, 248, 249, 342, 344

Bahro, Rudolf, 346

Baire, René-Louis, 387

Baker, George (Father Divine), 376

Baker, George, Pierce, 402

Baker, Josephine, **29–30**

Bakhtin, Mikhail, **30–31**, 485

Bakunin, Mikhail, 378

Balabanoff, Angelica, 378

Balanchine, George, 394, 503

Bălcescu, Nicolae, 100

Baldwin, James, 14, 339, 445

Baldwin, Stanley, **31–33**, 104, 112

Balfeuf, Marquise de, 113

Baliño, Carlos B., 98

Ball, Hugo, 20

Balmes, Jaime, 50

Balmont, Constantin, 352

Baltimore Morning Herald, 359

Baltimore Sun, 94, 359

Balzac, Honoré, 35, 61, 125, 157, 168, 309, 332, 399, 444, 502, 518, 523, 546, 552. *La Comédie humaine*, 113, 405; *Les Chouans*, 340; *Les Contes Drolatiques*, 299; *The Magic Skin*, 263

Bambara, Toni Cade, 373

Bandaranaike, Sirimavo, 357

Bang, Herman, 377

Banim, John, 114

Banner, Joseph, *The Impersonal Life*, 435–36

Baratynsky, Evgeny, 79

Barbey d'Aurevilly, Jules, 418

Barbour, John, 116

Barbusse, Henri, 215

Barker, George, 135

Barlâdeănu, Alexandru, 198

Barnefield, Richard, 116

Barney, Nathalie, 40

Baron, David (Harold Pinter), 429

Barrès, Maurice, 44, 125, 529

Barrie, James, 114

Barron, Frank, 312

Barth, Johann Friedrich, 33

Barth, Karl, **33–35**, 62, 85, 240, 389, 390, 514, 532. Works: *Barmen Declaration*, 34; *Church Dogmatics*, 34; *Epistle to the Romans*, 33–34, 147; *The Word of God and the Word of Man*, 532

Barthes, Roland, **35–36**, 418. Works: *Elements of Semiology*, 35; *Empire of Signs*, 35; *The Fashion System*, 35; *Mythologies*, 35; *The Pleasure of the Text*, 35; *Roland Barthes by Roland Barthes*, 35; *Sade, Fourier, Loyola*, 35; *S/Z*, 35; *Writing Degree Zero*, 35

Bartlett's Familiar Quotations, 320

Baruch, Bernard, **36–37**

Bashkirtsev, Marie, 39

Bassani, Giorgio, 519

Bataille, Georges, 176

Bateson, Gregory, 356

Bauch, Bruno, 93

Baudelaire, 8, 40, 76, 93, 125, 149, 163, 223, 248, 264, 280, 332, 340, 345, 372, 438, 472, 482, 493, 502, 522, 531, 535; *Les Fleurs du Mal*, 436

Bauer, Felice, 280

Bauer, Georg, *De Re Metallica*, 253

Bauer, Johannes, 85

Bauer, Otto, 84

Baum, Oskar, 280

Baumgarten, Alexander, 118

Baumgarten, Hermann, 548

Baumgartner, Walter, 85

Baykedagn, Gebre Heywet, 228

Bazin, André, 203, 523

Beach, Joseph, 398

Beatles, **37–39**

Beauvoir, Simone de, **39–40**, 179, 471, 569. Works: *Adieux: A Farewell to Sartre*, 39; *All Said and Done*, 39; *L'Amerique au jour le jour*, 40; *The Ethics of Ambiguity*, 39; *The Force of Circumstance*, 39; *Les Mandarins*, 39; *Memoirs of a Dutiful Daughter*, 39; *The Prime of Life*, 39; *Pyrrhus et Cenéas*, 39; *The Second Sex*, 39

Bebel, August, 69, 378, 528

Becher, Johannes, 528

Beckett, Samuel, **40–42**, 76, 170, 232, 258, 345, 429, 501. Works: "Dante . . . Bruno. Vico . . . Joyce," 41; *En attendant Godot*, 41; *Film*, 41; *Fin de partie*, 41; *Krapp's Last Tale*, 41; *Malone Dies*, 41; *Molloy*, 41; *More Kicks than Pricks*, 41; *Murphy*, 41; "Proust," 41; *The Unnamable*, 41; *Watt*, 41; *Whoroscope*, 41

Bécquer, Gustavo Adolfo, 264

Bednyi, Demian, 492

Bedouin, Charles, 482

Beebe, Ford, 307

Beethoven, Ludwig von, 473, 564

Begin, Menachem, 341

Behan, Brendan, 61

Behmann, Heinrich, 93

Behrens, Peter, 220, 313

Beissman, Adolf, 61

Bekker, Ernst, 548

Belafonte, Harry, 451

Belfrage, Leif, 229

Bell, Clive, 256, 463; *Vision and Design*, 372

Bell, Daniel, **42–44**; *The Cultural Contradictions of Capitalism*, 43

Bell, Myrta, 319

Bellah, James Warner, 174

Bellamy, Edward, 81. Works: *Looking Backward*, 81, 124, 416; *Equality*, 81

Belleau, Priscilla, 435

Belloc, Hilaire: *The Bad Child's Book of Beasts*, 475; *Cautionary Tales*, 475

Bellyarminov, I., *Course of Russian History*, 492

Bely, Andrey, 282. Works: *Gold on Azure*, 352; *Petersburg*, 382

Bement, Alon, 401

Benchley, Robert, 52

Benda, Julien, **44–45**. Works: *Le Bergsonisme*, 44–45; *Dialogues à Byzance*, 44; *The Treason of the Intellectuals*, 44

Benedek, Elek, 332

Benedek, Marcell, 332

Benedict, Ruth, 350, 356; *Patterns of Culture*, 356

Beneš, Edvard, **45–47**, 349

Beneš, Václav, 46

Ben-Gurion, David, **47–48**

Benjamin, Walter, 17

Bennett, Arnold, 114, 358

Bennett, Charles, 245

Bennigsen, Rudolf von, 548

Benois, Alexandre, 503

Ben Sira, 68
Bentham, Jeremy, 520
Beowulf, 236
Bérard, Victor, *Les Phoeniciens et
l'Odysee*, 273
Berdyaev, Nikolai, 79
Berg, Adalbert vom, *Napoleons
Leben*, 505
Berg, Alban, 437, 473
Berger, Victor L., 124
Bergman, Ingmar, **49–50**, 307,
509
Bergmann, Gustav, 93
Bergson, Henri, 44–45, 46,
50–51, 67, 89, 91, 125, 168,
240, 284, 285, 300, 382, 398,
438, 494–95, 530, 544.
Works: *Creative Evolution*,
71, 169, 182, 427
Berio, Luciano, 154
Berkeley, George, 118, 565
Berkman, Alexander, 468
Berlin, Irving, **51–53**
Berlin, Moses, 51
Berman, Louis, *The Religion
Called Behaviorism*, 484
Bernanos, Georges, 61, 62, 146,
420, 523; *Diary of a Country
Priest*, 123
Bernard, Claude, 51, 118
Bernstein, Aaron, *Popular Books
on Physical Science*, 157
Bernstein, Eduard, 17, 521
Bernstein, Leonard, **53–54**
Berr, Henri, 72
Berry, Walter, 552
Besant, Annie, 416; *Thought
Power*, 547
Bethmann Hollweg, Theobald
von, **54–55**
Beyle, Marie Henri (Stendhal),
125, 301, 332, 399, 444, 519.
Works: *The Charterhouse of
Parma*, 142, 200–201; *The
Red and the Black*, 375
Bezymensky, Alexander, 492
Bhagavad Gita, 38, 163, 187,
243, 404, 422, 550
Bhutto, Benazir, 461
Bible, xvii, 7, 8, 22, 25, 32, 47,
53, 62, 66, 79, 81, 85, 86, 96,
102, 123, 124, 128, 138, 149,
151, 159, 160, 169, 178, 187,
188, 200, 213, 214, 228, 238,
244, 252, 266, 273, 276, 280,
309, 310, 320, 351, 355, 371,
397, 411, 435, 442, 449, 452,
464, 481, 496, 497, 499, 507,

513, 522, 524, 540, 557, 569;
American Revised Standard,
329; Authorized Version
(1611), 169, 407; Cain and
Abel, 530; New Testament,
59, 85, 128, 230, 363, 388,
389, 483; Old Testament, 48,
54, 66, 106, 128, 169, 182,
193, 269, 363, 483, 555, 548;
Sermon on the Mount, 3, 81;
Ten Commandments, 28, 81.
Books of the *Bible*: Daniel,
66; Ezekial, 355; Isaiah, 3;
Job, 193, 316; Psalms, 123,
536; Matthew, 59, 418;
Romans, 193; Song of Songs,
537; Revelation, 537
Biedermann, Alois, 276
Biedermann, Gustav, 548
Bierce, Ambrose, 238, 359
Binet, Alfred, 277; *Les altéra-
tions de la personalité*, 430
Bion, Wilfred, 41
Biran, Maine de, 51
Bishop, Elizabeth, 398
Bismarck, Otto von, 70, 298,
557
Bissett, Bill (bissett, bill), 24
Blache, Paul Vidal de la, 56
Black, Jack, *You Can't Win*, 87
Blake, Robert, *Disraeli*, 393
Blake, William, 32, 199, 200,
201, 299, 309, 363, 531, 537,
568. Works: "Ah! Sun-
flower," 201; *The Little Black
Boy*, 450; "The Sick Rose,"
201; *Songs of Innocence and
Experience*, 201, 513
Blanchot, Maurice, 176
Blanqui, Louis, 368
Blast, 142
Blatchford, Robert, 124; *Merrie
England*, 416
Blavatsky, Elena (Helena)
Petrovna, 282, 369. Works:
Leaves of Morya's Garden, 435;
Voice of Silence, 435
Bleuler, Eugen, 276, 427
Blin, Roger, 41
Bliss, William D. P., 81
Bloch, Ernst, 332
Bloch, Joseph, 17
Bloch, Marc, **56–57**. Works:
French Rural History, 56, 72;
Feudal Society, 56; *The Histo-
rian's Craft*, 56; *Rois et serfs*,
56; *The Royal Touch*, 56, 72;
Strange Defeat, 56

Bloch, Robert, 65
Blok, Alexander, 282, 382
Blok, Alexander, 382
Blom, Frans, *Tribes and Temples*,
372
Blondel, Maurice, 146
Bloy, Léon, 61, 229; *The Blood
of the Poor*, 61
Blue, Yvonne, 483
Blum, Leon, 368
Blumenfeld, Kurt, 17
Blumhardt, Christoph, 34
Blumhardt, Johann Christian,
34
Bluwstein, Rachel, *Flowers of
Perhaps*, 358
Blyton, Enid, 461
Boas, Franz, 317, 356; *The
Mind of Primitive Man*, 356
Boccaccio, Giovanni, 243; *The
Decameron*, 230
Boccioni, Umberto, 103
Bodmer, Frederick, *The Loom of
Language*, 338
Bogdanov, Alexander, 84, 315
Böhm-Barwerk, Eugen von,
234, 366, 367
Bohme, Jakob, 82, 514
Bohr, Niels, **57–59**, 404
Boileau, Pierre, 245
Bojaxhiu, Agnes Gonxja
(Mother Teresa), **59–60**
Bolden, Margaret, 569
Bolintineanu, Dimitrie, 101
Böll, Annemarie, 61
Böll, Heinrich, 5, **60–61**.
Works: *The Silent Angel*, 61;
*Stranger, Bear Word to the
Spartans We . . .* , 61; *The
Train Was on Time*, 61
Boltzmann, Ludwig, 93, 565
Bolyai, Farkas, 50
Bonar Law, Andrew, 7, 31
Bonaventura, 239
Bonhoeffer, Dietrich, **61–63**,
390; *Letters and Papers from
Prison*, 62
Bontempelli, Massimo, 431
Booker Prize, 24, 208, 384, 460
Book of Kells, 273
Book of Knowledge, 213, 490
Book of the Dead, Tibetan, 38;
Egyptian, 273
Booth, Charles, 4
Borel, Émile, 387
Borges, Jorge Luis, **63–64**, 209,
279, 382. Works: *Aleph*, 63;
The Book of Imaginary Beings,

63; *The Book of Sand*, 63; *Dr. Brodie's Report*, 63; *Ficciones*, 63, 154; *A History of Eternity*, 63; *Nine Essays on Dante*, 63; *Other Inquisitions*, 63; *A Universal History of Infamy*, 63
Born, Max, 405
Bornkamm, Gunther, 85
Bosanquet, Bernard, 118
Bosch, Hieronymous, 147
Bossuet, Bishop Jacques, *De la connaissance de Dieu*, 200
Boswell, James, *Life of Samuel Johnson*, 571
Botticelli, Sandro, 67
Bougle, Celestin, 146
Bouillon, Jo, 29
Boulanger, Nadia, 115
Bourget, Paul, 125, 552
Bourke-White, Margaret, **64–65**. Works: *Eyes on Russia*, 64; *A Portrait of Myself*, 64
Boutroux, Émile, 427
Boutroux, Etienne, 125
Bouvier, Jacqueline, 289, 291
Bouyer, Louis, 398
Bowers, Claude, 524
Boxer Rebellion, 253
Boy's Life, 453
Brackett, Leigh, 65
Bradbury, Ray, **65–66**, 490. Works: *Dark Carnival*, 65; *Fahrenheit 451*, 65; *From the Dust Returned*, 65; *The Martian Chronicles*, 65; "The Veldt," 66
Brady, Matthew, 174
Brahms, Johannes, 473, 564
Braig, Carl, 239
Brancusi, Constantin, **66–67**, 102, 120, 369
Brandeis, Louis, **67–68**
Brandes, Georg, 342
Brandhuber, Camillo, 239
Brandt, Willy, **69–70**
Braque, Georges, **70–71**, 428, 494
Brathen, Oscar, *Decent People*, 49
Braudel, Fernand, **71–73**. Works: *The Mediterranean and the Mediterranean World in the Age of Philip II*, 72; *The Structure of Everyday Life*, 72
Braun, Wernher von, **73–74**
Brecht, Bertolt, 17, **74–75**, 79, 136, 147, 149, 203–4, 222, 258, 308, 332, 343, 410, 501.

Works: *Baal*, 74; *Er treibt den Teufel aus*, 74; *Der Jasager und der Neinsager*, 74; *Die höflichen Chinesen*, 75; *Die Kleinbürgerhochzeit*, 74; *Legende von der Enstehung des Buches Taoteking auf dem Weg des Latse in die Emigration*, 75; *Lux in Tenebris*, 74; *Die Maßnahme*, 75; *The Threepenny Opera*, 49, 75; *Trommeln in der Nacht*, 74
Bremer, Arthur, 542
Brentano, Clemens, 20
Brentano, Franz, *The Multivalent Meaning of Being in Aristotle*, 239
Bresciani, Antonio, 118
Bresson, Robert, 167, 509
Breton, André, **75–77**, 86, 121, 127, 144, 188, 281, 292, 345, 365, 422, 428. Works: *Anthologie de l'humour noir*, 76; *Les Champs magnétiques*, 76; *Manifeste du surréalisme*, 21, 75, 103; *Nadja*, 76; *Second Manifeste du surréalisme*, 75; *Towards a Free Revolutionary Art*, 448
Breuer, Josef, 277
Brew, 167
Brewer, Clinton, 569
Briand, Aristide, 505
Bridgeman, George, 453
Bridges, Robert, 537
Brightman, E. S., 297
Brik, Osip, 477
British poetry, 312
Britten, Benjamin, **77–78**, 176. Works: *Young Person's Guide to the Orchestra*, 77
Broch, Hermann, 303
Brod, Max, 230, 279
Brodsky, Joseph, **78–79**
Brody, Sandor, 332
Brontë, Charlotte, 214, 309; *Jane Eyre*, 309, 466
Brontë, Emily, 175, 214
Brooke, Rupert, **79–80**
Brooks, Cleanth, 398
Brooks, Van Wyck, 499
Brother Matthias, 463
Brothers, Thomas, 18
Broun, Heywood, 52
Brown, Katherine Tupper, 348
Brown, Lawrence, 449
Brown, Pat, 107
Browning, Robert, 149, 219, 363, 381, 399, 434. Works:

"That Toccato of Gallupis," 151
Brown of Harvard, 442
Bruno, Giordano, 41, 273, 312
Brunschvicg, Léon, *Les étapes de la philosophie mathématique*, 427; *L'expérience humaine et la causalité physique*, 427
Bruntière, Ferdinand, 44
Bruyere, Jean de La, 125
Bryan, William Jennings, **81–82**, 206
Bryant, Arthur, 22
Bryant, Clara Jane, 173
Bryant, Sophie, 500
Bryant, William Cullen, "To a Waterfowl," 81
Bryce, James, *American Commonwealth*, 329, 563
Brzozowski, Stanislaw, 364
Buber, Martin, **82–83**, 332, 398. Works: *Der Jude*, 82; *I and Thou*, 82, 229, 441, 555
Buchan, John, 22. Works: *Green Mantle*, 64; *Pilgrim's Way*, 289, 290; *Thirty-Nine Steps*, 64, 245, 290
Büchner, Georg, 74, 147, 529; *Lenz*, 231
Büchner, Ludwig, *Force and Matter*, 157
Buckle, Henry, 315; *History of Civilisation in England*, 546
Budde, Karl, 85
Buddha, 243
Buddhism, 202, 221, 273, 285, 292, 312; *The Buddhist Bible*, 292; Buddhist texts, 276; Zen Buddhism, 20
Buffon, Comte de, *Histoire Naturelle*, 428
Buhler, Karl, 433
Bukharin, Nikolai, **83–84**, 315, 492. Works: *ABC of Communism*, 252; *The Economic Theory of the Leisure Class*, 83; *Historical Materialism*, 83; *Imperialism and World Economy*, 83
Bulgakov, Sergei, 314
Bultmann, Rudolf, 17, 62, **84–86**, 240, 514
Bulwer-Lytton, Edward, 498
Bunin, Ivan, 381, 476
Bunuel, Luis, 75, 86–87, 106, 121, 167, 188, 189, 264, 307, 509

Bunyan, John, 326. Works:
Holy War, 416; *Pilgrim's Progress,* 32, 99, 151, 159, 416, 496, 536, 537
Burckhardt, Jacob, 243, 276, 332
Burdick, Eugene, *The Ugly American,* 289
Burke, Edmund, 132, 156, 293, 294, 563
Burke, Kenneth, 122
Burke, Thomas, *Limehouse Nights,* 219
Burlingame, Edward, 552
Burlyuk, David, 352
Burne-Jones, Edward, 32
Burnett, Frances Hodgson, *The Secret Garden,* 250
Burnham, James, *The Managerial Revolution,* 408
Burns, Arthur, *Production Trends in the United States,* 181
Burns, Robert, 327, 416, 537
Burroughs, Edgar Rice, 65, 241; *Tarzan* stories, 65, 213
Burroughs, John, 173
Burroughs, William S., 38, **87–88,** 201, 292, 312. Works: *Junky,* 87, 202; *Naked Lunch,* 87, 88; *Nova Express,* 87; *Queer,* 87; *The Soft Machine,* 87; *The Ticket That Exploded,* 87; *The Wild Boys,* 88
Burton, Richard, 311
Bussy, Simon, 502
Butler, Judith, 131
Butler, Samuel, *Erewhon,* 175; *Notebooks,* 408
Byrne, Donn, 496
Byron, George Gordon, Lord, 8, 149, 171, 231, 264, 265, 289, 301, 327, 352, 357, 395, 416, 490, 498

Cabell, James Branch, 496
Cabrera, Manuel Estrada, 21
Cadon, René Guy, 135
Caesar, Julius, 125
Cage, John, 473
Cahier d'un retour, 165
Cahiers du cinema, 203
Cajetan, Thommasio de Vio, 328
Calderón, Pedro, 189, 498
Caldwell, Erskine, 171, 191
Călinescu, George, 198. Works: *The Black Chest,* 198; *Poor Ioanide,* 198

Callaghan, Morley, 445
Calthrop, Gladys, 117
Calvin, John, 34, 240, 389, 415, 548
Cambio 16, 275
Camera Work, 498, 499
Cameron, A. C. 206
Camp, Walter, 449
Campbell, John W., *Analog Science Fiction/Science Fact,* 489
Campbell, Joseph, 214; *The Masks of God,* 214
Campion, Edmund, 169, 543
Camprubi, Zenobia, 264
Camus, Albert, 35, 43, **89–90,** 135, 147, 191, 223, 224, 291, 325, 340, 382, 420, 479. Works: *The Downfall,* 49; *The First Man,* 89; "The Myth of Sisyphus," 555; *Notebooks,* 291, *The Plague,* 368; *The Rebel,* 471; *Resistance, Rebellion, and Death,* 291; *The Stranger,* 89, 291, 569
Cannon, Jimmy, 137
Cantar del Mío Cid, El, 178
Cantor, Georg, 93, 387
Cantor, Norman, 517
Čapek, Josef, 90, 91
Čapek, Karel, **90–91,** 232, 349. Works: *From the Life of Insects,* 90; *Hordubal,* 90; *The Macropolous Case,* 90; *Meteor,* 90; *An Ordinary Life,* 90; *R.U.R.,* 90
Capote, Truman, 19, 398
Capra, Frank, **91–92,** 174
Capuana, Luigi, 431
Caragiale, Ion Luca, 257
Cardan, Jérôme, *De vita propria,* 459
Carducci, Bartolommeo, 418
Carducci, Giosuè, 118, 430
Carey, Harry, 174
Carleman, Torsten, 387
Carlyle, Thomas, 23, 99, 111, 309, 327, 407, 529, 547, 563. Works: *Cromwell,* 104; *The French Revolution,* 416; *On Heroes, Hero-Worship, and the Heroic in History,* 3
Carmichael, Charlotte, 500
Carnap, Rudolf, **92–94,** 109, 433; "Space," 93
Carnegie, Andrew, 453
Carnegie, Dale, *How to Win Friends and Influence People,* 392

Carpenter, Edward, 176, 199; *The Art of Creation,* 547
Carr, Lucien, 201
Carra, Carlo, 103
Carrel, Alexis, 323
Carrière, Jean-Claude, 86
Carroll, Lewis, 24, 38. Works: *Alice in Wonderland,* 38, 381
Carson, Rachel, **94–95.** Works: *The Edge of the Sea,* 94; *The Sea Around Us,* 94; *The Sense of Wonder,* 95; *Silent Spring,* 95; *Under the Sea-Wind,* 94
Carter, James Earl, Jr., **95–97,** 411
Carter, Nicholas, *Nick·Carter* stories, 455, 464
Carus, Carl Gustav, 276
Carver, George Washington, 411
Cary, Joyce, 1, 117
Cassady, Neal, 201, 312
Cassirer, Ernst, 31, 93, 240. Works: *The Philosophy of Symbolic Forms,* 30
Castaneda, Carlos, 170, 222, 312
Castro, America, *Structure of Spanish History,* 570
Castro, Fidel, **97–99,** 223
Castro, Raúl, 97
Castro, Rosalía de, 264
Cather, Willa, **99–100,** 399. Works: *Alexander's Bridge,* 99; *April Twilights,* 99; *My Antonia,* 99; *O Pioneers!,* 99; *One of Ours,* 99; *The Troll Garden,* 99
Catherine of Siena, 123
Catholic Missions, 59
Catt, Carrie Chapman, 469
Catton, Bruce, *Never Call Retreat,* 290
Catullus, 119, 182, 434
Cavalcanti, Guido, 434
Cayley, Arthur, 387
Ceauşescu, Nicolae, **100–101,** 198
Cecchi, Emilio, 215
Cecil, David, *Lord Melbourne,* 289
Celan, Paul, 316
Celestine V, 479
Céline, Louis-Ferdinand, 201, 445; *Journey to the End of the Night,* 292
Celtic poetry, 312
Century Magazine, 571

Cervantes Saavedra, Miguel de, 13, 169, 189, 230, 303, 381, 479, 518; *Don Quixote*, 48, 230, 299, 352, 405, 430, 529, 530

Césaire, Aimé, **101–2**, 165. Works: *Beheaded Sun*, 101; *L'Etudiant noir*, 101, *Miraculous Weapons*, 101; *Notebook of a Return to My Native Land*, 101

Céspedes, Carlos Manuel de, 98

Cézanne, Paul, 71, 120, 428, 494

Chabrol, Claude, 167, 203

Chagall, Marc, **102–3**

Chainey, Brainerd, 397

Chamberlain, Austen, 104

Chamberlain, Houston Stewart, *Foundations of the Twentieth Century*, 331, 557

Chamberlain, Joseph, 104

Chamberlain, Neville, **103–5**, 112, 155

Chamber's Encyclopedia, 571

Chamfort, Nicolas, 125

Chamisso, Adelbert von, 430

Champy, James, *Reenginering the Corporation*, 195

Chanel, Coco, 503

Chanute, Octave, *Progress in Flying Machines*, 571

Chaplin, Charles, 41, **105–6**, 161, 509

Chapman, Everett, 64

Chapman, John Wilbur, *Receive Ye the Holy Ghost*, 507

Charcot, Jean, 51

Chardin, Pierre Teilhard, 329, 398

Chartier, Emile, 549

Chateaubriand, François-René, Vicomte de, 40, 125, 382; *Autobiography*, 438

Chatwin, Bruce, 63

Chaucer, Geoffrey, 119, 466, 476, 490; "The Miller's Tale," 38

Chavchavadze, Ilie, 492

Chávez, Cèsar, **107–8**

Cheiro's Book of Numbers, 436

Chekhov, Anton, 208, 236, 344, 381, 399, 400, 477, 485, 559

Chénier, André, 125

Chernenko, Konstantin, 207

Chernyshevski, Nikolai, *What is to be Done?*, 315

Chernyshevsky, Nikolay, 381, 382, 520

Chesterfield, Philip Stanhope, Lord, *Letters to his Son*, 426

Chesterton, G. K., 63, 91, 532; *The Man Who Was Thursday*, 114

Chewelos, Nick, 312

Cheyney, Peter, 371

Chíbas, Eduardo, 97

Chicago Review, 482

Chinese literature, 13, 434

Chomsky, Noam, **108–10**. Works: *The Logical Structure of Linguistic Theory*, 109; *Syntactic Structures*, 109

Chomsky, William (Zev), 108

Chonkadze, Daniel, 492

Church, Alonzo, 387

Churchill, John, Duke of Marlborough, 110, 111

Churchill, Winston (U.S. novelist), *The Crisis*, 159

Churchill, Winston Leonard Spencer, 7, 23, 64, **110–12**, 155, 159, 178, 237, 289, 310, 348, 393, 510, 545. Works: *Lord Randolph Churchill*, 111; *Marlborough*, 111; *The Second World War*, 111, 342

Cicero, 159, 238, 267, 284, 353, 548

Cid, El, 178, 422

Cipriani, André, 261

Claridge, W. Walton, *A History of the Gold Coast*, 569

Clark, Colin, *Condition of Economic Progress*, 43

Clark, John Maurice, *Studies in the Economics of Overhead Costs*, 181

Clark, Walter H., 312

Clarke, Arthur C., 316; *The City of the Stars*, 490

Clarke, John Henrik, 14

Class, Heinrich, 55

Claudel, Paul, 146, 228, 258, 340. Works: *Jeanne au bucher*, 459; *Tête d'Or*, 102

Clausewitz, Karl von, *On War*, 160

Clausius, Rudolf, 431–32

Clemens, Samuel. *See* Twain, Mark

Cleveland, Grover, 81

Clinton, Bill, 14

Clouzot, Henri-Georges, 245

Clytemnestra, 214

Cobbett, William, 196, 385

Cobb's Spelling Book, 452

Cocteau, Jean, 136, 428; *La Voix humaine*, 459

Coffin, Charles, *The Boys of '76*, 498

Cohen, Hermann, 28, 30, 62, 85, 405, 419; *The Religion of Reason*, 28

Cohen, Sidney, 312

Coleridge, Samuel Taylor, 88, 529, 536, 537

Coles, Elizabeth, 347

Coles, Robert, 123

Colette, Sidonie-Gabrielle, 39, **112–13**. Works: Claudine novels, 113

Collier, John, 66

Collins, Michael, xvi, **114–15**

Colum, Padraig, 114

Comic books, 24, 137–38, 170, 461, 489; *Batman*, 497; *Sheena of the Jungle*, 497; *Superman*, 137, 461, 497; *Wonder Woman*, 497

Commentary, 482

Compton's Encyclopedia, 109

Comstock, Anna Botsford, 64

Comte, Auguste, 118, 146, 350, 427, 547

Conan Doyle, Arthur. *See* Doyle, Arthur Conan

Condorcet, Nicolas de Caritat, Marquis de, 437

Cone, James Hal, *A Black Theology of Liberation*, 224

Confucius, 243, 434

Congar, Yves, 421

Congressional Record, 271, 455

Conner, Fox, 159

Conrad, Joseph, 94, 114, 168, 217, 228, 316, 327, 386, 398, 466, 519. Works: *Heart of Darkness*, 569; *Lord Jim*, 171; *The Nigger of the "Narcissus,"* 171; "The Secret Sharer," 171; *Typhoon*, 200; *Under Western Eyes*, 88

Constant, Benjamin, 125

Cook, Theodore, *The Curves of Life*, 493

Cooke, Henry, 415

Coolidge, Calvin, 192, 253

Coon, Carleton Stevens, *The Origin of Races*, 542

Cooper, James Fenimore, 340; *The Last of the Mohicans*, 332

Cooper, Mrs. Astley, 116

Cooperative Commonwealth, 241
Copernicus, Nicolas, 482, 553
Copland, Aaron, **115–16**
Coppard, A. E., 399, 400
Corbiére, Tristan, 340
Cormack, Bartlett, 129
Corneille, Pierre, 146, 371, 549
Cornell, Drucilla, 131
Cornhill Magazine, 408
Cornstock, J. L., *An Introduction to the Study of Botany*, 571
Corso, Gregory, 201
Corum, Bill, 137
Cosbuc, George, 101
Cosell, Howard, 451
Cosmopolitan, 92, 497
Cottin, Sophie, 118
Coulanges, Numa-Denis Fustel de, 56; *The Ancient City*, 72
Country Gentleman, 453
Courier, Paul-Louis, 125
Cournot, Antoine, 50
Courtenay, Baudoin de, 30
Coverdale, Miles, 537
Coward, Noël, **116–18**, 136. Works: *Blythe Spirit*, 117; *I'll Leave it to You*, 117; *In Which We Serve*, 117; *The Vortex*, 117; *The Young Idea*, 117
Cowell, Henry, 196
Cowley, Malcolm, 122
Crabbe, George, The Borough, 77
Craft, Robert, 504
Crane, Frank, 398
Crane, Hart, 499. Works: "The Broken Tower," 559; *The Collected Poems of Hart Crane*, 559; *Emblems of Conduct*, 559
Crane, Stephen, 38, 99, 359
Crashaw, Richard, 537
Crawford, Joan, 489
Creasy, Edward S., *Fifteen Decisive Battles of the World*, 291, 524
Crisis, 449
Criterion, 162
Croce, Benedetto, 84, **118–19**, 156, 215. Works: *Aesthetics*, 430; *La Critica*, 118
Crockett, Davy, 139
Crookes, William, 276
Crowley, Aleister, 312
Cruz, Sor Juana Ines de la, 422
Cummings, E. E. (e. e. cummings), 116, **119–20**
Curzon, George Nathaniel, 31, 155

Cyclopaedic Survey of Chamber Music (Cobbett), 196
Cyprian of Carthage, 62

Dahl, Vladimir, *Dictionary of the Living Russian Language*, 381
Dahrendorf, Ralf, *Class and Class Conflict in an Industrial Society*, 43
Daily Express, 7
Daily Mail, 7
Daily Telegraph, 557
Daily Worker, 141
Daley, Arthur, 137
Dalí, Salvador, 75, 86, 103, **121–22**, 188, 189, 264
Dana, Mrs. William Star, *How to Know the Golden Flowers*, 182
Daniel, *Bible* story of, 66
Daniel, Jean, 368
Danish classics, 58
D'Annunzio, Gabriele, 118, 264, 343, 379, 418, 518
Dante, Alighieri, 3, 8, 41, 63, 236, 267, 273, 289, 312, 379, 397, 434, 456, 466, 470, 513, 560. Works: *Divine Comedy*, 163, 175, 231, 316, 560; *Inferno*, 236; *Purgatorio*, 236; *Vita Nuova*, 560
D'Arcy, Martin C., 397, 544
Darío, Rubén, 188, 264
Darrow, Clarence, 81
Darwin, Charles, 46, 50, 55, 104, 300, 315, 355, 360, 370, 381, 427, 433, 470, 492, 500. Works: *Descent of Man*, 378, 560; *Origin of Species*, 86, 188, 378, 560, 571; *Voyage of the Beagle*, 182
Daubler, Theodor, *Northern Lights*, 378
Daudet, Alphonse, *Sappho*, 115
D'Aurevilly, Barney, 125
David, King, 7
Davies, Lord, 158
Davies, Robertson, 24, 186, 445. Works: *Fifth Business*, 186; *The Manticore*, 186; *World of Wonders*, 186
Da Vinci, Leonardo, 67, 162, 195, 493; *Codex Leicester*, 195
Davis, Angela, 61, 373
Davis, John M. 206
Davis, Peter, 18
Davis, Thomas, 114, 132
Dawson, Christopher, 328

Day, Dorothy, **122–23**. Works: *Catholic Worker*, 122; *From Union Square to Rome*, 123; *The Long Loneliness*, 123
Dayrell-Browning, Vivien, 216, 217
Debs, Eugene V., **123–25**, 468. Works: *Fireman's Magazine*, 124; "How I Became a Socialist," 124
Debussy, Claude, 51
Dedijer, Vladimir, 516
Defoe, Daniel, 61, 142, 326. Works: *Robinson Crusoe*, 182–83, 422, 458, 466, 545; *Swiss Family Robinson*, 99, 458
Degas, Edgar, 305
De Gaulle, Charles, **125–27**, 159, 340, 367, 471. Works: *Memoires de guerre*, 368
Dekker, Thomas, "Golden Slumbers," 38
De Kooning, Willem, 127–28
Delacroix, Eugene, 174, 502
Delaunay, Robert, 103
Delaunay, Sonia, 102
Delboeuf, René, 51
Deledda, Grazia, 215, 431
Deleuze, Gilles, *Qu'est-ce que la philosophie*, 368
Delland, Clarence. Works: *Buddington*, 92; *Opera Hat*, 92
Del Mar, Alexander, 434
De Mille, Cecil B., **128–29**, 174, 439
De Mille, William C., 129
Democracia, 425
Demuth, Charles, 560
Derain, André, 15, 70
Der Blaue Reiter, 299
Derrida, Jacques, 35, **130–31**. Works: *The Margins of Philosophy*, 130; *Of Grammatology*, 130; *The Post-Card*, 131; "The Problem of Genesis in the Philosophy of Edmund Husserl," 130; *Speech and Phenomena*, 130; *Truth in Painting*, 131; "Two Words for Joyce," 130; "Ulysses Gramophone," 130
Derzhavin, Gavrila, 79, 352
Desai, Anita, 460
Descartes, René, 41, 46, 89, 118, 121, 125, 371, 421, 459, 535, 549
Des Knaben Wunderhorn, 20

Desnos, Robert, 76. Works: *Deuil pour deuil*, 21; *La liberté ou l'amour*, 21

Despedes, Carlos Manuel de, 98

Detective stories, 105, 371, 464

Deufrene, Maurice, 313

De Valera, Eamon, **131–33**

Dewey, John, 4, 91, **133–34,** 389, 491. Works: *Experience and Education*, 491; *Human Nature and Conduct*, 134; *The Public and Its Problems*, 134; *The Quest for Certainty*, 134; *Reconstruction in Philosophy*, 134; *The School and Society*, 134

Diaghilev, Serge, 391, 503; *Mir iskusstva*, 504

Diakonova, Helena, 121

Dicey, A. V., 511

Dickens, Charles, xvii, 24, 36, 61, 65, 99, 109, 123, 139, 157, 169, 219, 237–38, 267, 318, 321, 327, 337, 348, 356, 358, 381, 385, 399, 407, 461, 466, 490, 511, 518, 520, 523, 553, 565. Works: *Bleak House*, 456; *A Christmas Carol*, 458; *The Cricket on the Hearth*, 219; *David Copperfield*, 11, 77, 252, 280, 454, 498; *Dombey and Son*, 237–38; *Great Expectations*, 466; *The Old Curiosity Shop*, 106, 456; *Oliver Twist*, 106, 520; *Pickwick Papers*, 32, 151, 230; *A Tale of Two Cities*, 32, 551

Dickey, James, **134–35**. Works: *Alnilam*, 135; *Buckdancer's Choice*, 135; *Deliverance*, 135; *Into the Stone*, 134; *Self-Interviews*, 135; *To the White Sea*, 135

Dickinson, Emily, 116, 119, 214, 228, 265

Dictionaries, 461; *Dictionary of the Living Russian Language*, 381; *Dictionary of National Biography*, 22, 32; *Oxford English Dictionary*, 517; *Webster's English Dictionary*, 338

Diderot, Denis, *Encyclopedie*, 484

Die christliche Welt, 85

Die Sammlung, 343

Dietrich, Marlene, **136–37**

Die Zukrunft, 361

Dilthey, Wilhelm, 62, 118, 240, 332, 406, 548

DiMaggio, Joseph Paul, **137–38**

Dingler, Hugo, 93

Director, Rose, 180

Disney, Walt, **138–40**, 161

Ditman, Keith, 312

Ditmar, Raymond, 64

Dixon, Campbell, 245

Dixon, Franklin W., Hardy Boys books, 497

Djilas, Milovan, **140–41**, 516. Works: *Conversations with Stalin*, 140, *Fall of the New Class*, 140; *The New Class*, 140; *Njegoš: Poet, Prince, Bishop*, 140; *The Unperfect Society*, 140

Döblin, Alfred, 301, 343; *Berlin Alexanderplatz*, 167

Dobrogeanu-Gherea, Constantin, 100

Dobrovský, Josef, 351

Dodge, Mabel, 468

Dominik, Hans, 308

Donne, John, 66, 79, 149, 169, 486, 513, 536

Donovan, Frances, *The Woman Who Waits*, 64

Doppo, Kunikida, 305

D'Ors, Eugenio, 428

Dos Passos, John, 122, **141–43,** 171, 179, 191, 242, 445, 459, 485. Works: *Manhattan Transfer*, 142; *Three Soldiers*, 142; *U.S.A.*, 142

Dostoyevsky, Mikhail, 34, 40, 61, 79, 102, 109, 123, 127, 140, 169, 176, 200, 243, 258, 279, 298, 299, 315, 332, 340, 344, 358, 362, 373, 377, 381, 382, 391, 394, 398, 414, 482, 485, 504, 509, 565. Works: *The Brothers Karamazov*, 157, 305, 363, 391; *Crime and Punishment*, 92, 231, 280, 496; *The Idiot*, 231, 305, 391; *Notes from the Underground*, 569; *The Possessed*, 301

Doucet, Jacques, 75

Doughty, Charles, *Travels in Arabia Deserta*, 311

Douglas, C. H., *Credit Power and Democracy*, 434; *Economic Democracy*, 434

Douglass, Frederick, 14, 449

Dovjenko, Alexander, 509

Dow, Arthur, 401

Downs, Karl, 450

Dowson, Ernest, 407

Doyle, Arthur Conan, 24, 65, 381; *The Refugees*, 248; *Sir Nigel*, 348; *White Company*, 174

Dragoumis, Ion, 284

Dreiser, Theodore, 99, 142, 171, 179, 241, 359, 467, 468, 569. Works: *Jennie Gerhardt*, 569; *Sister Carrie*, 499, 569

Dreyfus, Alfred, 113, 456

Dreyfus Affair, 44, 438

Drummond, William, 537

Dryden, John, 524

Dubček, Alexander, **143–44**, 232, 303

Duble, Josie, 165

DuBois, W. E. B., 192, 262, 411, 449

Duchamp, Marcel, 41, 67, 120, **144–45**, 354

Duckett, Alfred, 451

Duffy, Charles Gavan, 132

Dujardin, Édouard, *Les lauriers sont coupées*, 273

Dumas, Alexandre (pere), 152, 325, 327, 340, 405

Du Maurier, Daphne, 245; *Rebecca*, 245

Dumont, Fernand, **145–47**. Works: *Le Lieu de l'homme*, 145; *Livre blanc*, 145

Dunbar, Paul Laurence, 297, 560; "Sympathy," 11

Duncan, Robert, 202

Dunning, William, 542

Duns Scotus, John, 239

Durant, Will, 312, 468

Duras, Marguerite, *L'amour*, 368

Dürkheim, Émile. 43, 46, 51, 57, 72, 84, 146, 258, 317, 427. Works: *The Division of Labor in Society*, 72; *Elementary Forms of the Religious Life*, 72; *Primitive Classification*, 317; *Rules of Sociological Method*, 72; *Suicide*, 72

Dürrenmatt, Friedrich, 147–48

Dylan, Bob, 37, **148–49**

Eakins, Thomas, 92

Earhart, Amelia, **151–53**

Eastman, Max, 468, *A Sense of Humour*, 106

Ebbinghaus, Julius, 85
Echegaray, José, 498
Eckhart, Meister, 82, 229, 240, 276
Eco, Umberto, 63, **153–54**. Works: *Baudolino*, 253; *Foucault's Pendulum*, 153; *The Island of the Day Before*, 143; *The Limits of Interpretation*, 153; *The Name of the Rose*, 153; *The Open Work*, 153; *The Role of the Reader*, 153; *A Theory of Semiotics*, 153
Economist, 156, 195
Eddington, Arthur, 361
Eddy, Mary Baker, *Science and Health*, 436
Eden, Anthony, 105, **155**
Edison, Thomas, 300
Ed Sullivan Show, 37, 394
Edwards, Jonathan, 214
Egoist, 162
Ehrenburg, Ilya, *The Extraordinary Adventures of Julio Jurenito and His Disciples*, 11
Eichendorff, Joseph von, 242, 447, 514
Einaudi, Luigi, **156–57**. Works: *Riforma sociale*, 156
Einstein, Albert, 93, **157–59**, 161, 264, 387, 433, 493
Eisenhower, Dwight D., **159–60**, 183, 253, 337, 453
Eisenstein, Sergei, **160–62**, 203, 305, 436, 509
Ekman, Bertin, 229
El Cid, 178, 422
El Espectador, 191
El Greco (Domenicos Theotocopoulous), 5
Eliade, Mircea, 418
Eliot, George, 109, 152, 309, 327, 552. Works: *Middlemarch*, 104, 546; *The Mill on the Floss*, 309; *Silas Marner*, 524
Eliot, T. S., 1, 24, 78, 80, 135, 142, 149, **162–64**, 171, 217, 236, 269, 316, 327, 354, 363, 370, 372, 398, 422, 434, 470, 504, 513, 522, 532. Works: *The Cocktail Party*, 163; *The Family Reunion*, 163; *The Four Quartets*, 163; "The Love Song of J. Alfred Prufrock," 163; *Murder in the Cathedral*, 163; *Notes Toward a Definition of Culture*, 163;

The Sacred Wood, 163; *Selected Essays, 1917–1932*, 163; *The Use of Poetry and the Use of Criticism*, 163; *The Waste Land*, 25, 162–63, 566
Elliot, William, 298
Ellis, Havelock, 115, 469
Ellison, Ralph, 261; *Invisible Man*, 490
El Moudjahid, 165
Éluard, Paul, 20, 75, 76, 86, 121, 428
Elvin, Kells, "Twilight's Last Gleaming," 87
Ely, Richard T., *Political Economy*, 81
Emerson, Ralph Waldo, 68, 92, 99, 119, 173, 187, 312, 326, 493, 547, 568. Works: *Essays*, 138, 199, 291; "Monadnoc," 182; "Self-Reliance," 106, 291
Eminescu, Mihai, 257
Encyclopedia Britannica, 571
Encyclopedias, 481; *Appleton's Cyclopedia*, 124; *Book of Knowledge*, 213, 490; *Compton's Encyclopedia*, 109; Diderot's *Encyclopedie*, 484; *Encyclopedia Britannica*, 571
Engels, Friedrich, 84, 98, 100, 118, 206, 223, 314, 315, 332, 378, 384, 492, 516, 528. Works: *Anti-Duhring*, 315; *The Communist Manifesto*, 70, 205, 206, 223, 254, 295, 384, 516; *The Condition of the Working Class in England*, 254, 315; "Preface to a Contribution to the Critique of Political Ideology," 166
English literature 10, 114, 276; British poetry, 312. *See also under names of specific authors*
English Reader, 452
Eötvös, József, 332
Epic of Gilgamesh, 550
Epstein, Brian, 37
Equiano, Olaudau, *The Interesting Narrative of the Life of Olaudau Equiano*, 14
Erasmus, Desiderius, 353
Erdmannsdorfer, Bernhard, 548
Erickson, Erik, 356
Ermatinger, Emil, 147
Ernst, Max, 75, 86
Ernst, Paul, 91, 332

Értle, Aleksandr, 476
Eschenmayer, Karl August von, 276
Eshkol, Levi, 357
Espronceda, José de, 264
Esquire, 482, 497
Euripides, 62, 147, 291; *The Bacchae*, 486, 487
Evening Standard, 7
Everyman, 249
Ewing, W. P., 455

Fabian Essays in Socialism, 416, 547
Fabre, Jean-Henri, 64; *Souvenirs Entomologiques*, 86
Fadeyev, Aleksandr, *The Rout*, 11
Fairy-Tale World, 446
Fallada, Hans, 528. Works: *Kleiner Mann was nun?*, 49; *A Wolf among Wolves*, 49
Fallersleben, Hoffmann von, *Lied der Deutschen*, 205
Family Circle, 497
Fanon, Frantz, **165–66**. Works: *L'An V de la révolution algerienne*, 166; *Les damnés de la terre*, 166; *Peau noire masques blancs*, 166
Faraday, Michael, 158
Fard, Wallace, 375, "The Supreme Lessons," 376
Farrere, Claude, 125
Fassbinder, Rainer, **166–68**: *The Bitter Tears of Petra von Kant*, 167; *Bremer Freiheit*, 167; *Only a Slice of Bread*, 166
Faulkner, William, **168–69**, 191, 340, 373, 382, 398, 399, 400, 445, 558. Works: *Absalom, Absalom!*, 168, 169; *As I Lay Dying*, 168, 169; *A Fable*, 168; *Father Abraham*, 169; *Go Down Moses*, 168; *The Hamlet*, 168; *Intruder in the Dust*, 168; *Light in August*, 168; *Mosquitoes*, 168; *Pylon*, 169; *Sanctuary*, 169; *Sartoris*, 168; *Soldiers' Pay*, 168; *The Sound and the Fury*, 168, 169; *The Reivers*, 168; *The Wild Palms*, 326; Yoknapatawpha saga, 326
Fayard classics, 523
Febvre, Lucien, 56, 72. Works: *The Coming of the Book*, 72; *A Geographical Introduction to History*, 72; *Martin Luther*, 72

Fechner, Gustav, 313
Federalist Papers, 159, 238, 330
Feigl, Herbert, 93
Feininger, Lyonel, 220
Fejér, Lipót, 387
Fekete, Michael, 387
Felker, Clay, 497
Fellini, Federico, **170**, 509; *The Funny Face Shop*, 170
Fellner, William, 387
Feminism, 11, 39, 358, 469
Fénélon, François, *Traité de l'existence de Dieu*, 200
Fenollosa, Ernest, 434
Ferenczi, Sandor, 277, 387
Ferlinghetti, Lawrence, 189, 202, 293
Fermi, Enrico, 58
Fernandéz, Macedonio, 63
Ferry, Jules, 368
Feudal Society, 72
Feuerbach, Ludwig, 492
Fichte, Johann Gottlieb, 50, 239, 332, 441, 492, 514. Works: *Addresses to the German Nation*, 441; *The Characteristics of the Present Age*, 441
Fielding, Henry, 142, 168
Fielding, Joseph, 466
Fillipiak, Izabella, 263
Finke, Heinrich, 239
Finley, John Huston, 414
Finney, Charles Grandison, 507
Fiorentino, Francesco, *History of Philosophy*, 378
Firbank, Ronald, 544
First, 341
Fischer, Kuno, 548
Fishcer, Bram, 341
Fisher, Dorothy Canfield, 454
Fisher, Irving, 367
Fisher, Leck, *Morderdyret*, 49
Fisher, Louis, *The Life of Gandhi*, 107
Fitzgerald, F. Scott, 141, **171–72**, 242, 288, 445, 454. Works: *The Beautiful and Damned*, 171; *The Crack-Up*, 171; *The Great Gatsby*, 171; *The Last Tycoon*, 171; *This Side of Paradise*, 171, 287; *Tales of the Jazz Age*, 171; *Tender is the Night*, 171
Flagg, Abbie, 123
Flake, Otto, 20
Flammarion, Camille, 73
Flaszen, Ludwig, 221

Flaubert, Gustave, 125, 142, 169, 170, 171, 258, 273, 279, 303, 332, 342, 373, 381, 438, 444, 472, 523. Works: *Bouvard et Pécuchet*, 340; *Madame Bovary*, 326, 399, 496; *Salammbô*, 340; *Sentimental Education*, 279–80
Fleming, Ian, 289; James Bond novels, 289, 290
Fleming, Wallace. Works: *Civil War and Reconstruction in Alabama*, 542; *Deportation and Colonization*, 542
Flournoy, Theodore, 277
Flynn, Elizabeth Gurley, 468
Foerster, Friedrich, 239
Fogazzaro, Antonio, 118; *The Saint*, 420
Fontane, Theodor, *Irrungen und Wirrungen*, 506
Fonteyn, Margot, 394
Fonvizin, Denis, 477
Forbes, 195
Ford, Ford Madox, 217, 242; *The Good Soldier*, 217
Ford, Francis, 174
Ford, Gerald, 453
Ford, Henry, **172–73**, 388; *The International Jew*, 172
Ford, John, **173–75**, 305, 545
Foreign Affairs, 287
Forman, Miloš, 303
Forster, E. M., 77, **175–76**, 208, 294, 502. Works: *Abinger Harvest*, 175; *Aspects of the Novel*, 175; *Howard's End*, 175; *Maurice*, 176; *A Passage to India*, 175, 497; *Two Cheers for Democracy*, 175
Fort, Paul, 76
Fortune, 42, 64, 185, 329
Foscolo, Ugo, 418
Foucault, Michel, 154, **176–77**. Works: *Discipline and Punish*, 177; *History of Sexuality*, 177; *Madness and Civilization*, 176; *The Order of Things*, 177, 368
Fouillée, Alfred, 50, 427
Fox, Douglas, 434
France, Anatole, 76, 125, 358, 416, 437
Francis of Assisi, 107, 123, 243; *Canticle of the Sun*, 366
Franco, Francisco, **177–78**, 274, 529, 569. Works: *Diario de una bandera*, 178; *Masoneria*, 178; *Raza*, 178

Frangopulo, Maria, 394
Frank, Erich, 85
Frank, Karl, 433
Frank, Philipp, 93
Frankenstein, Karl, 17
Frankfurter, Felix, 470
Frankl, Viktor, "Die Stimme der Vernunft," 540
Franklin, Benjamin: *Autobiography*, 329; *Poor Richard's Almanac*, 329
Frank Merriwell stories, 455, 464; *Frank Merriwell at Yale*, 442
Frantz, Konstantin, 539
Franz Ferdinand, 12
Frazer, James G., 168; *The Golden Bough*, 4, 169, 496
Frazier, Joe, 9
Frederick the Great, 3, 244, 548
Freedom, 450
Frege, Gottlob, 93, 109, 564–65
Frenaud, André, 135
French literature, 13, 99, 234
French troubadours, 119
Freud, Sigmund, 22, 25, 30, 93, 102, 109, 115, 128, 131, 162, 166, 168, 177, 179, 223, 224, 258, 273, 277, 317, 345, 346, 356, 361, 370, 382, 398, 403, 427, 433, 469, 471, 566. Works: *Civilisation and Its Discontents*, 488; *Interpretation of Dreams*, 122, 169, 279, 488, 491; *Moses and Monotheism*, 281; *Psychopathology of Everyday Life*, 138, 491; *Three Essays on the Theory of Sexuality*, 491
Fridell, Egon, 540, *Kulturgeschichte der Neuzeit*, 540
Friedan, Betty, **179–80**. Works: *Beyond Gender*, 179; *The Feminine Mystique*, 179; *The Fountain of Age*, 179; *It Changed My Life*, 179; *The Second State*, 179
Friedländer, Paul, 85
Friedman, Milton, **180–82**, 512. Works: *Incomes from Independent Professional Practice*, 181; *Theory of the Consumption Function*, 181
Friedrich III, 557
Fries, Jakob, 277, 433

Frisch, Max, 147
Frisch, Otto, 58
Frobenius, Leo, *African Genesis*, 434
Fromm, Erich, 345, 350
Frost, Robert, 65, 79, 160, **182–83**, 265, 470, 484; *A Boy's Will*, 182
Fry, Maxwell, 220
Fry, Roger, 256, 294; *Vision and Design*, 372
Frye, Northrop, 24
Fučík, Julius: *Božena Němcová is Fighting*, 254; *In the Country Where Tomorrow No Longer Means Yesterday*, 254
Fuentes, Carlos, 63
Fujii, Kenjiro, 500
Fuller, Margaret, 312
Fuller, Samuel, 174
Furmanov, Dmitrii, 492

Gadamer, Hans-Georg, 85
Gadea, Hilda, 223
Gadium et Spes, 224
Gage, Matilda Joslyn, 469
Gail, Willi, 308
Galbraith, John Kenneth, **185–86**. Works: *The Affluent Society*, 185; *Economics and the Public Purpose*, 185; *The New Industrial State*, 185
Galdós, Benito Pérez, 405
Galilei, Galileo, 379
Gallant, Mavis, 445
Galsworthy, 171, 416
Galton, Francis, 277, 500
Gance, Abel, 162
Gandhi, Indira, 461
Gandhi, Mohandas, 48, 64, 107, **186–88**, 297, 390, 480. Works: "My Experiments with Truth," 187; *Hind Swaraj*, 187
Ganivet, Angel, 529
Gans, Eduard, 28
García Lorca, Federico, 86, 165, **188–90**, 210, 264. Works: *Bernarda Alba*, 189; *Blood Wedding*, 189; *Gypsy Ballads*, 188; *Imprisiones y paisages*, 188; *Lament for Ignacio Sánchez Mejías*, 190; *My Village*, 188; *Poet in New York*, 189; *The Public*, 190; *Yerma*, 189; *La zapatera prodigiosa*, 189

García Márquez, Gabriel, 10, 63, **190–91**, 209. Works: *The Autumn of the Patriarch*, 191; *In Evil Hour*, 191; *The General in His Labyrinth*, 191; *Leaf Storm*, 191; *Love and Other Demons*, 191; *Love in the Time of Cholera*; *One Hundred Years of Solitude*, 191; *Strange Pilgrims*, 191
Garcilaso de la Vega, Sebastia, 264
Garibaldi, Giuseppe, 378, 379, 519
Garnett, Richard, 537
Garnett, Tay, 174
Garrigue, Charlotte, 349
Garvey, Marcus, **192–93**, 262, 347, 376, 411, 449; *The Philosophy and Opinions of Marcus Garvey*, 192
Gasperi, Alcide de, 156, **193–94**. Works: "The Moral Basis of Democracy," 194; *Reconstructive Ideas of Christian Democracy*, 193
Gates, Bill, **194–96**
Gates, Reginald, *Ruggles*, 500
Gaudier-Brzeska, Henri, 372
Gauguin, Paul, 92, 282
Gaulle, Charles de, **125–27**, 159, 340, 367, 471; *Mémoires de guerre*, 368
Gauss, Christian, 562
Gauthier-Villars, Henri, 112
Gay, John, *Beggar's Opera*, 75
Gebhard, Heinrich, 53
Geffen, David, 489
Geiger, Abraham, 28
Geijer, Erik Gustaf, 229
Geisel, Theodore Seuss. *See* Seuss, Dr.
Geissler, Lotti, 147
Gelek, Ngawang, 202
Geller, Larry, *Beyond the Himalayas*, 435
Genet, Jean, 131, 472; *Querelle de Brest*, 167
Gentile, Giovanni, 118
Gentleman's Magazine, 408
George, Henry, 81, 327, 468; *Progress and Poverty*, 206
George, Stefan, 204, 248, 249, 473; *Blätter für die Kunst*, 248
George, W. C. *The Biology of the Race Problem*, 542
George V, 413
Gerarchia, 379

Gerhardi, William, 544
Gerlash, Arthur, von, 308
German literature, 13, 104, 242; Germanic mythology, 276
Gershwin, George, **196–97**
Gershwin, Ira, 196–97
Gerstacker, Friedrich, 276
Gesell, Silvio, 434
Geulincx, Arnold, 41
Geyser, Josef, 239
Gheorghiu-Dej, Gheorghe, **197–98**; *A Romanian Politics*, 198
Gibbon, Edward, 22, 105, 110, 326, 374, 387; *Decline and Fall of the Roman Empire*, 175, 213, 287, 525, 571
Gibran, Kahlil, **198–99**. Works: *The Broken Wings*, 199; *The Garden of the Prophet*, 199; *Jesus, Son of Man*, 199; *The Madman*, 199; *The Prophet*, 198, 199; *Sand and Foam*, 199; *A Tear and a Smile*, 199
Gibson, Graeme, 24
Gide, Albert, 35
Gide, André, 89–90, 121, **200–201**, 340, 343, 398, 399, 418, 471, 502, 518, 523, 535. Works: "Concerning Influence in Literature," 200; *The Counterfeiters*, 200; *The Immoralist*, 113; *Journal*, 201; *La Nouvelle Revue Francaise*, 44
Giedion, Sigfreid, 354
Gilbert, Martin, *Churchill*, 393
Gilbert, William Schwenck, 560
Gilder, Richard Watson, 414
Gillespie, Dizzy, 293
Gilman, Charlotte Perkins, 469
Gilmore, Gary, 250–51
Gilson, Etienne, 398
Ginsberg, Allen, 87, 149, 189, **201–3**, 292, 312, 418, 445. Works: *Empty Mirror*, 202; *Howl*, 202; *Kaddish*, 201
Ginsburg, Asher, 109
Girl's Own Paper, 408
"The Girl with the Three Walnuts," 446
Gissinger, Theodor, 246
Gladen, Washington, 81
Gladkov, Fedor, 492
Gladstone, William, 22, 104

Glamour, 497
Glazer, Nathan, 43
Gleason, Jackie, 137
Glob, P. V. *The Bog People,* 236
Glories of Yale Athletics, 490
Gneist, Rudolf von, 55
Gobineau, Joseph Arthur, Comte de, 111
Godard, Jean-Luc, 167, **203–4,** 307. Works: *Défense et Illustration du découpage classique,* 203; *Mon Beau Souci,* 203; *Montage,* 203; *Pour un cinema politique,* 203
Goddard, Paulette, 444
Gödel, Kurt, 93
Godey's Lady's Book, 497
Goebbels, Joseph Paul, **204–5,** 361. Works: *Michael,* 204; *Wilhelm von Schaetz as Dramatist,* 204
Goebel, Karl, 500
Goethe, Johann Wolfgang von, 3, 5, 20, 30, 62, 93, 136, 147, 158, 204, 232, 234, 243, 264, 276, 279, 301, 308, 342, 344, 345, 447, 470, 481, 499, 505, 506, 514, 528, 540, 546, 548, 557. Works: *Autobiography,* 438; *Faust,* 200, 205, 276, 277, 287, 375, 418, 419, 436, 446, 498; *Kindred by Choice,* 375; *Poetry and Truth,* 419; *Unerhaltungen deutscher Ausgewanderter,* 249; *Roman Elegies,* 430; *The Sorrows of Young Werther,* 419; *Wilhelm Meister,* 55, 205
Goffin, Robert, *On the Frontiers of Jazz,* 19
Gogarten, Friedrich, 85
Gogol, Nikolai, 315, 358, 382, 391, 399, 413, 461, 477, 482, 498, 509. Works: *Dead Souls,* 103; *Evenings on a Farm,* 476; *Inspector General,* 279; *Spiritual Letters,* 267; *Taras Bulba,* 476
Gold, Michael, *Jews Without Money,* 11
Goldberg, Rube, 483
Golding, William, 24
Goldman, Emma, 358, 468
Goldmark, Rubin, 115
Goldschmidt, Levin, 548
Goldsmith, Oliver, 132
Goldwater, Barry, *Conscience of a Conservative,* 442

Gollancz, Victor, 410
Gombrowicz, Witold, 304
Gompers, Samuel, **206–7,** 320
Gomperz, Heinrich, 433
Góngora, Luis de, 189
Gontcharova, Natalia, 103, 503
Gorbachev, Mikhail, **207–8,** 419
Gordimer, Nadine, **208–9,** 341. Works: *Face to Face,* 208; *The Lying Days,* 208
Gordon, Aaron David, *Selected Essays,* 358
Gordon, Caroline, 398
Górecki, Henryk, **209–11**
Goren, Charles, 451
Gorgeous George, 9
Gorin, Jean-Pierre, 203
Göring, Hermann, **211–12**
Gorky, Arshile, 127
Gorky, Maxim, 69, 476, 479, 492
Gorres, Joseph von, 276
Goudeket, Maurice, 113
Gourmont, Remy de, 434
Goya, Francisco, 299
Graetz, Heinrich, 28
Graf, Arturo, 430
Graham, Billy, **212–13**
Graham, Dom Aelred, 397
Graham, John D., *System and Dialectics in Art,* 128
Graham, Martha, **214–15,** 394
Graham, W. S., 135
Gramsci, Antonio, 98, 215–16; *Prison Notebooks,* 215, 465–66
Grant, Ulysses S., 159, 252
Grass, Gunter, 61, 302, 461
Graves, Mary, 483
Graves, Robert, 26
Gray, Jennie, 252
Gray, Thomas, *Elegy,* 160
Greek literature, 79, 407, 521; classics, xv, xvii, 99, 266, 315, 336; drama, 3, 269, 549; mythology, 66, 71, 276, 318, 356, 496; philosophy, 371
Green, Henry, 532, 543
Green, John Richard, 111; *History of the English People,* 104, 563
Green, T. H., 521–22
Greene, Graham, 123, **216–18,** 398, 523. Works: *Brighton Rock,* 216; *A Burnt Out Case,* 216; *England Made Me,* 216; *The Fugitive,* 174; *A Gun for Sale,* 216; *The Heart of the*

Matter, 216; *It's a Battlefield,* 216; *Journey Without Maps,* 216; *The Man Within,* 216; *The Power and the Glory,* 174, 216, 217; *Stanboul Train,* 216
Greenough, Sarah, 401
Gregory, Horace, *Poems of Consolations,* 77; *The Triumph of Life,* 77
Gregory, Lady Augusta, 399
Gresham, Joy Davidman, 318
Greshoff, Jan, 370
Grey, Edward, *The Charm of Birds,* 104
Grey, Zane, 213, 327, 545
Griffith, Arthur, 114; *United Irishmen,* 114
Griffith, D. W., 129, 161, 174, 203, 218–19, 459
Grillparzer, Friedrich, 279, 565; *Das Kloster bei Sendomir,* 231
Grimm, Jakob and Wilhelm, 29, 481. Works: "Cinderella," 139; "Snow White," 139
Gröber, Conrad, 239
Gronlund, Lawrence, *The Cooperative Commonwealth,* 124
Gropius, Walter, **220–21,** 360, 423
Gross, Milton, 451
Gross, Otto, 277
Grosse, Ernst, 91
Grossi, Tommaso, 118
Grosz, George, 147
Grosz, Karl, 313
Grotowski, Jerzy, **221–22**
Groulx, Lionel, 146
Grove Dictionary of Music, 196
Grumach, Ernst, 17
Guardini, Romano, 17, 397
Guéranger, Dom, 267
Guevara, Ernesto "Che," 97, 98, **222–23;** *Guerrilla Warfare,* 223
Guillén, Jorge, 178, 264
Guiteras, Antonio, 98
Guitton, Jean, 421
Gumilyov, Nikolay, 8
Gunberg, Carl, 366
Gundolf, Friedrich, 17, 204
Gunkel, Hermann, 85
Gurdijieff, Georges, 222, 312
Gusman, Martin Luiz, *The Eagle and the Serpent,* 448
Guthrie, Woody, *Bound for Glory,* 148

Gutierrez Merino, Gustavo, **224–25**
Guyau, Jean-Marie, 50, 427
Gysin, Brion, 87

Haar, Alfred, 387
Haberler, Gottfried, 233
Hadden, Briton, 330
Haeckel, Ernst, 93, 377; *Mysteries of the Universe*, 300
Haeering, Theodor, 85
Hagen, Alice Caldwell, *Mrs. Wiggs of the Cabbage Patch*, 355
Haggard, H. Rider, 217
Hahn, Hans, 93
Haiku, 364
Haile Selassie, **227–28**, 347
Hakluyt, Richard, *Voyages*, 566
Halberstadt, Vitali, *Opposition et cases conjugees sont reconciles*, 41
Halbwachs, Maurice, 146
Halevi, Judah, *Khuzari*, 482
Haliburton, Thomas Chandler, 24
Hall, G. Stanley, 133, 277
Hallam, Henry, 110
Ham, Mordecai, 213
Hamann, Johann Georg, 565
Hambitzer, Charles, 196
Hamburger, Natalie, 27
Hamilton, Alexander, 238, 330
Hamilton, Edith, *The Greek Way*, 291
Hamilton, Juan, 401
Hammann, Otto, 55
Hammarskjöld, Dag, **228–29**
Hammer, Michael, *Reenginering the Corporation*, 195
Hammett, Dashell, 340
Hamon, Louis (Cheiro), *Cheiro's Book of Numbers*, 436
Hamsun, Knut, 300, 444. Works: *Hunger*, 482; *Pan*, 482; *Sult*, 377
Hanslick, Eduard, 564
Harbou, Thea von, 308
Hardenberg, Friedrich von. *See* Novalis
Harding, Warren G., 253
Hardy, Thomas, 22, 26, 38, 109, 114, 135, 219, 310, 399, 454, 513, 537. Works: *The Return of the Native*, 496; *Tess of the D'Urbervilles*, 536
Hardy Boys books, 497

Harland, Henry, *The Yellow Book*, 142
Harlem Renaissance, 14, 102, 376
Harmsworth, Alfred Charles William, Lord Northcliffe, 7
Harnack, Adolf von, 33, 61, 62, 85, 388; *The Essence of Christianity*, 28
Harper, Frances Ellen Watkins, 14
Harper's, 65
Harper's Weekly, 152
Harris, Ed, 250
Harris, Frank, 499
Harris, George Washington, 169
Harris, Joel Chandler, *Br'er Rabbit*, 36; Uncle Remus stories, 139
Harris, Zellig Sabbetai, 109
Harrison, Frederic, 327, 547
Harrison, George, 37–38
Hartmann, Eduard von, 51, 276
Hartmann, Nikolai, 62
Harvard Advocate, 53
Harvard Crimson, 458
Harvard Law Review, 383
Hašek, Jaroslav, **229–30**, 232; *The Fortunes of the Good Soldier Švejk*, 230
Hasse, Henry, 65
Hastings, Warren, 348
Hauptmann, Gerhart, 147, **231–32**, 332, 403. Works: *Der Apostel*, 231; *Bahnwärter Thiel*, 231; *Before Sunrise*, 231; *Elga*, 231; *Fasching*, 231; *Peace Celebrations*, 231; "Phantom," 231; *Promethidenlos*, 231; *The Weavers*, 231; *The Sunken Bell*, 231
Havel, Václav, 143, **232–33**, 254. Works: *The Garden Party*, 232; *The Increased Difficulty of Concentration*, 232; *Largo Desolato*, 232; *Letters to Olga*, 232; *The Memorandum*, 232; "Power of the Powerless," 232; *Temptation*, 232
Havlíček, Karel, 350
Hawkes, John, 398
Hawks, Howard, 203
Hawthorne, Nathaniel, 92, 99, 106, 398, 482, 571; *The Scarlet Letter*, 99, 489

Hawtrey, Charles, 116
Hawtrey, Ralph, 294
Hayek, F. A., **233–35**, 432, 512. Works: *The Constitution of Liberty*, 235; *The Fatal Conceit*, 235; *Law, Legislation and Liberty*, 235; *The Road to Serfdom*, 156, 235, 433, 511; *The Sensory Order*, 234
Hayes, Alfred, 116
Hayes, John Michael, 245
Hayford, J. E. Casely, 192
Haywood, Bill, 468
Hazlitt, William, 106, 385
Heaney, Seamus, **235–36**. Works: *Death of a Naturalist*, 235; *Door into the Dark*, 235; *Electric Light*, 236; *Field Work*, 235; *The Haw Lantern*, 235; *North*, 235; *Place and Displacement*, 236; *The Spirit Level*, 236; *Station Island*, 235; *Sweeney Astray*, 235; *Wintering Out*, 235
Heard, Gerald, 256, 312, 329
Hearst, William Randolph, 213, **237–39**, 550, 551; *In the News*, 238
Heath, Edward, 511
Hebbel, Friedrich, 299, 332
Hebel, Johann Peter, 61
Hébert, Anne, 24
Hefele, Karl Joseph, *History of the Councils*, 420
Hegel, 17, 30, 39, 50, 55, 118, 146, 147, 166, 176, 204, 215, 239, 240, 247, 262, 276, 297, 298, 332, 345, 352, 384, 433, 476, 492, 514, 529, 548, 565. Works: *Phenomenology of Spirit*, 146, 166
Heidegger, Martin, 17, 39, 62, 85, 127, 147, 166, 177, 232, **239–41**, 345, 471, 472, 514. Works: *Being and Time*, 130, 240, 406; "Release," 240
Heilbroner, Robert, 43
Heine, Heinrich, 5, 200, 230, 243, 264, 308, 344, 430, 560; *Book of Songs*, 200
Heinlein, Robert, 66
Heisenberg, Werner, 58, 361
Heisterbach, Casarius, 243
Heitmuller, Wilhelm, 84
Helfferich, Karl, 55
Hellman, Lillian, 54, 116

Helmholtz, Hermann von, 93, 431

Hemingway, Ernest, 92, 136, 141, 171, 191, **241–42**, 300, 301, 382, 398, 399, 400, 444, 445, 485, 494. Works: *A Farewell to Arms*, 241; *For Whom the Bell Tolls*, 241; *The Green Hills of Africa*, 447; *In Our Time*, 241; *The Killers*, 509; *A Moveable Feast*, 241; *The Old Man and the Sea*, 138; *The Sun Also Rises*, 241; *Three Stories and Ten Poems*, 241; *To Have and Have Not*, 241

Henkin, Leon, 387

Henley, W. T., 245

Henry, Charles, 377

Henry, Patrick, 192

Henty, G. A., 171, 348, 481

Heraclitus, 125, 135

Herald of Wales, 512

Herbart, Johann, 118

Herbert, Frank, 489

Herbert, George, 79, 537; "Easter Wings," 513

Herbert, Laura, 543

Herbert, Zbigniew, 236

Herbertz, Richard, 147

Herder, Johann Gottfried, 349, 528

Herman, Florence, 560

Herodotus, 548

Herrick, Robert, 169, 532

Herrmann, Wilhelm, 33, 85

Herron, George, 81

Hershey, John, *A Bell for Adano*, 551

Hertz, Heinrich, 300, 565

Hertz, Paul, 93

Hervé, Gustave, 378

Hesiod, *Theogony*, 71, 188

Hess, Rudolf, 247

Hesse, Hermann, 228, **242–43**, 312, 444; *Demian*, 243

Hewlett, Maurice, *Life and Death of Richard Yea-and-Nay*, 310

Heydrich, Reinhard, 211

Heym, Georg, 147

Heyward, DuBose, *Porgy*, 196

Higgs, Joe, 346

High School Physical Geography, 355

High-Wood, Vivien, 162

Hilbert, David, 93, 387

Hilferding, Rudolf, *Finance Capital*, 84

Hill, Robert, 307

Hillman, Carl, *Emancipation Hints*, 206

Hilton, Jack, *English Ways*, 408

Hindemith, Paul, 196, 437

Hindenburg, Paul von, 55, **243–44**, 247, 330

Hinduism, 221, 243, 276

Hinzpeter, Georg Ernst, 557

Hirsch, David, 206

Hita, Arcipreste de, 189

Hitchcock, Alfred, 203, **245–46**, 307, 523

Hitler, Adolf, 5, 6, 17, 25, 34, 105, 112, 172, 177, 204, 211, 237, **246–48**, 250, 288, 302, 330, 342, 344, 345, 366, 380, 389, 407, 473, 487, 514, 564. Works: *Mein Kampf*, 103, 205, 212, 223, 247, 446–47

Hobbes, Thomas, 392; *The Elements of Law*, 208

Hobrecht, Artur, 548

Hobrecht, James, 548

Hobson, J. A., 375

Hocking, William Ernest, 329

Hodge, Charles, 415

Hodgkin, Dorothy, 511

Hoennicke, Gustav, 85

Hofer, Abram, 312

Hoffenberg, Mason, 445

Hoffmann, August. See Fallersleben, Hoffmann von

Hoffmann, E. T. A., 242

Hofmann, Albert, 312

Hofmannsthal, Hugo von, 136, 228, **248–49**, 444. Works: *Die ägyptische Helena*, 249; *Andreas*, 248; *Ariadne auf Naxos*, 249; "Ein Brief," 249; *Das Erlebnis des Marschalls von Bassompierre*, 249; *Elektra*, 249; *Die Frau ohne Schatten*, 249; *Das gerettete Venedig*, 249; *Jedermann*, 248; "Märchen der 672. Nacht," 249

Hogarth, David, *A Wandering Scholar in the Levant*, 311

Hokusai Katsushika, 305

Hölderlin, Friedrich, 147, 239, 243, 301, 444, 446, 447, 514

Holl, Karl, 61

Holland, Agnieszka, **249–51**

Hollingshead, Michael, 312

Hollis, Christopher, 544

Holms, John Clellon, 201

Hölscher, Gustav, 85

Holst, Adrian, 370

Holst, Hermann Eduard von, 563

Holt, Luther, *The Care and Feeding of Children*, 491

Holy Koran of the Moorish Science Temple, 376

Holz, Arno, 231

Homer, xv, 92, 119, 142, 316, 466, 518, 548, 557. Works: *Iliad*, 30, 99, 200, 285, 332, 550; *Odyssey*, 30, 182, 273, 285, 416

Honecker, Erich, **251–52**

Hook, Sidney, 43

Hoover, Herbert, **252–54.** Works: *Addresses Upon the American Road*, 253; *An American Epic*, 253; *American Individualism*, 253; *The Challenge to Liberty*, 253; *The Ordeal of Woodrow Wilson*, 525

Hope, Laurence, 117

Hopkins, Gerard Manley, 135, 398, 513

Hopper, Edward, 92

Horace, 8, 125, 470, 532

Horizon, 407

Horkheimer, Max, 345

Horne, Charles, *Great Men and Famous Women*, 525

Horney, Karen, 350

Horst, Louis, 214

Hostie, Raymond, 398

Hotelling, Harold, 181

House, Edward M., 563

Houseman, John, 550

Housman, A. E., 99, 169, 382, 407, 537; *A Shropshire Lad*, 408

Howard, Bruce, 543

Howe, Irving, 43

Howells, 99; *The Rise of Silas Lapham*, 453

Hubbard, L. Ron, 489

Hugel, Friedrich von, 397

Hughes, Everett C., *French Canada in Transition*, 146

Hughes, Langston, 102, 297; *Famous American Negroes*, 19

Hughes, Richard, *A High Wind in Jamaica*, 363

Hughes, Ted, 236

Hugnet, George: *Le Chèvre-Feuille*, 428; *Non Vouloir*, 428
Hugo, Victor, 109, 125, 128, 152, 168, 200, 230, 258, 340, 358, 438, 440, 492. Works: *Les Misérables*, 124, 327, 368, 378, 560
Huizinga, Johan, 156
Hull House, 3, 4
Hulme, T. E., 434
Hume, David, 235, 350, 433, 565
Huneker, James, 359, 562
Hurston, Zora Neale, 14
Hus, Jan, 350
Husák, Gustáv, 232, **254–55**
Husserl, Edmund, 17, 39, 62, 130, 239, 240, 269, 345, 471, 472, 550. Works: *Logical Investigations*, 405, 419; *The Origin of Geometry*, 130; *Yearbooks*, 406
Huston, John, 65
Huxley, Aldous, 24, **255–56**, 312, 337, 343, 359, 463. Works: *Antic Hay*, 255; *Brave New World*, 255, 408; *Crome Yellow*, 255; *Mortal Coils*, 255; *Point Counter Point*, 255, 258
Huxley, Julian, 255, 361
Huxley, Thomas Henry, 255, 359, 360, 500; *Lessons in Elementary Physiology*, 133
Huysmans, Joris-Karl, 535; *Là-bas*, 86
Hyppolite, Jean, 176

Ibsen, Henrik, 80, 147, 273, 299, 309, 332, 403, 416, 498, 501, 529, 560. Works: *A Doll's House*, 152, 167; *Ghosts*, 152, 231; *Hedda Gabler*, 152, 506; *Rosmersholm*, 231; *The Wild Duck*, 231
Icelandic literature, *Eddas*, xvi, 58, 517. *See also* Norse literature
I Ching, 20, 38, 312
Idea, 284
Ignatius of Loyola, 479
Ilf, Ilya, *The Twelve Chairs*, 11
Illustrated London News, 129
Il Popolo d'Italia, 379
Index of Prohibited Books (Roman Catholic), 50, 200, 267
Ingarden, Roman, 269
Ingersoll, Robert, 124, 355, 468; *Essays and Lectures*, 106

International Migration Society, 376
Invernizio, Carolina, 215
Ionesco, Eugène, 76, 232, **257–59**, 501. Works: *The Bald Primadonna*, 257; *La leçon*, 257; *No*, 257; *Rhineocérous*, 257; *Le roi se meurt*, 257
Irish Poverty, 206
Irish Republican Army, 2
Irving, Washington, 106, 252
Isaac, 555
Iskra, 314
Itten, Johannes, 220
Ivan IV, 161
Ivanovsky, Nikolai, 394
Ivanov, Vsevolod, 492
Ivan the Terrible, 492
Ives, Charles, 395

Jabtinsky, Vladimir, 301
Jackson, Helen Hunt, *Ramona*, 219
Jacob, Old Testament story of, 555
Jacob, Max, 340, 428
Jacobsen, Jens Peter, 377
Jacoby, Georg, 136
Jacques, Norbert, 308
Jaeger, Hans, *Homo Sapiens*, 378
Jagow, Gottlieb von, 55
Jakobson, Roman, 318
James, C. L. R., **261–62**. Works: *Black Jacobins*, 262; *The Life of Captain Cipriani*, 261; *Mariners, Renegades and Castaways*, 262; *Minty Allen*, 262; *Toussaint L'Ouverture*, 261; "Triumph," 262
James, Henry, 64, 92, 99, 116, 398, 552, 562. Works: *The American*, 453; *The Turn of the Screw*, 77; *Washington Square*, 250, 395
James, Marquis, 524
James, William, 4, 51, 91, 92, 277, 309, 312, 324, 427, 495, 530 . Works: *Pragmatism*, 309; *Psychology: The Briefer Course*, 182; *Varieties of Religious Experience*, 123, 565
Janáček, Leoš, 90
Janet, Pierre, 39, 276, 277, 427
Janiger, Oscar, 312
Janion, Maria, **262–63**. Works: *Romanticism*, 163; *The Romantic Fever*, 263; *The Time*

of the Open Form, 263; "Transgressions," 262
Janouch, Gustav, 280
Japanese literature: drama, 434; haiku, 364; poetry, 504
Jarrell, Randall, 135, 398
Jarret, Bede, 217
Jarry, Alfred, 258; Works: *The Exploits and Opinions of Doctor Faustroll, Pataphysician*, 145, 428; "The Passion Considered as an Uphill Bicycle Race," 145; *The Supermale*, 145
Jaspers, Karl, 17, 85, 146, 166, 240
Jaurès, Jean, 50; *Historie socialiste*, 368; *L'Humanité*, 368
Jeanneret, Charles Edouard. *See* Le Corbusier
Jeffers, Robinson, 496
Jefferson, Thomas, 238, 434, 442, 521, 524
Jeremiah, 54
Jesse Brown, 129
Jessup, John, 329
Jesus, 7, 286, 297, 323, 351, 388, 450, 459, 481
Jewett, Sarah Orne, 99; *Country of the Pointed Firs*, 99
Jewish Daily Forward, 482
Jiménez, Juan Ramón, **264–66**. Works: *Almas de Violeta*, 264; *Animal de fondo*, 265; *Arias Tristes*, 265; *Estío*, 264; *Jardines Lejanos*, 264; *Ninfeas*, 264; *Platero y yo*, 264; *Romances de Coral Gables*, 265; *Sonetos espirituales*, 264; *Tiempo y muerta*, 265
John XXIII, **266–68**, 420; *Journal of a Soul*, 267
John of the Cross, 188, 229, 258, 264, 265, 269, 397, 475
John Paul II, **268–70**. Works: *David*, 269; *The Doctrine of Faith in St. John of the Cross*, 268; *Jeremiah*, 269; *Job*, 269; *Love and Responsibility*, 269; *Our God's Brother*, 269; *Person and Deed*, 269
John the Baptist, 266
Johnson, Charles Underwood, 414
Johnson, Georgia, 14
Johnson, James Weldon, "The Creation," 14

Johnson, Lyndon Baines, **270–72,** 290, 298

Johnson, Paul, *Modern Times,* 393

Johnson, Samuel, 398, 490, 565

Johnson, William Ernest, 565

Johst, Hanns, *Der Einsame,* 74

Joinville, Jean de, 125

Jolas, Eugene, 41

Joliot-Curie, Frédéric, 390

Jonas, Franz, 539

Jonas, Hans, 17

Jones, D. G., 24

Jones, Gayle, 373

Jones, Homer, 181

Jones, Madison, 398

Jones, Owen, *Grammar and Ornament,* 313

Jones, Robert Edmond, 402

Jones, Thomas, 32

Jonson, Ben, 169, 353

Jorgenson, Josef, 239

Joseph, Keith, 511

Joshua, 48

Jouvenael, Henry de, 113

Joyce, James, 8, 130, 153, 162, 168, 171, 191, 208, 236, 242, **272–74,** 303, 353, 354, 359, 382, 399, 400, 430, 434, 459, 513, 518, 532. Works: *Dubliners,* 272; *Exiles,* 273; *Finnegans Wake,* 38, 41, 273, 556; *Our Exgamination round his Factification for Incamination of Work in Progress,* 41; *A Portrait of the Artist as a Young Man,* 272; *Ulysses,* 130, 138, 142, 169, 217, 242, 272, 312, 382, 461, 489, 499, 567

Juan Carlos I De Bourbon, **274–76**

Judina, Maria Veniaminovna, 30

Juhos, Bela von, 93

Jülicher, Adolf, 84

Jung, Carl, 22, 41, 128, 214, 223, 243, 258, **276–77,** 300, 356, 375, 398, 427, 496; *On the Psychology of the Unconscious,* 309

Jünger, Ernst, 147; *In Stahlgewittern,* 444

Jungmann, Josef, 350, 420

Juszkiewicz, Anton, 504

Juvenal, 267

Kabbala, 482, 555

Kabir, 364

Kabuki theater, 162

Kadar, Janos, 384

Kafka, Franz, 63, 147, 149, 171, 201, 223, 233, **279–80,** 303, 382, 398, 430, 444. Works: *Amerika,* 280; *The Castle,* 363; "The Judgment," 279; *The Metamorphosis,* 382, 555; *The Trial,* 280, 551

Kaftan, Julius, 85

Kagan, Matvei Isaevich, 30

Kahlo, Frida, **281–82**

Kahn, Rober, 451

Kaiser, Georg: *Coral,* 308; *Gas I,* 91

Kalbeck, Max, 565

Kamenev, Lev, 492

Kandinsky, Vassily, 20, 220, **282–83,** 299, 473. Works: *The Blaue Reiter Almanac,* 282; *On the Spiritual in Art,* 282, 372, 401

Kanellopoulos, Anayiotis, 284

Kansas City Star, 241

Kant, Immanuel, 17, 39, 44, 45, 50, 62, 82, 118, 121, 141, 147, 177, 239, 276, 298, 312, 328, 332, 371, 392, 405, 427, 433, 438, 476, 492, 500, 514, 529, 548, 550, 560, 565; *Critique of Pure Reason,* 30, 93, 157, 419

Kantemir, Antioch, 79

Kantzow, Karin von, 211

Kapp, Friedrich, 548

Karadžić, Vuk, 13

Karamanlis, Konstantinos, **283–85**

Kardelj, Edvard, 516

Karmel, Alex, 116

Karno, Fred, 106

Karp, Frieda, 53

Karsavina, Tamara, 503

Kasprowicz, Jan: *The Book of the Poor,* 269; *Hymns,* 269

Katazenberg, Jeffrey, 489

Kathimerini, 284

Katz, Harold A., 383

Katzenelson, Berl, *What is Socialist Zionism?,* 358

Kaufman, George, 52

Kaufmann, Felix, 93; *Methodenlehre der Sozialwissenschaftern,* 433

Kautsky, Karl, 124, 315, 378, 492, 521

Kavanagh, Patrick, 236, 399

Kazan, Elia, 362

Kazantzakis, Nikos, **285–86.** Works: *Freedom or Death,* 285; *The Last Temptation of Christ,* 286; *The Odyssey: A Modern Sequel,* 285; *St. Francis,* 286; *Zorba the Greek,* 285

Kazbegi, Alexander, *The Patricide,* 492

Keaton, Buster, 41

Keats, John, 8, 120, 169, 318, 332, 357, 381, 476, 581; *Endymion,* 560

Kędzierski, Paweł, 250

Keelere, Leo W., 328

Keene, Carolyn, 497

Keller, Gottfried, 243, 249, 332, 444

Kelsey, George, 296

Kemnitz, Mathilde, 331

Kempis, Thomas à, 229; *Imitation of Christ,* 123

Kennan, George F., **286–88.** Works: "Long Telegram," 287; "The Sources of Soviet Conduct," 287

Kennedy, Jacqueline, 291

Kennedy, John F., 69, 98, 107, 182, 266, 270, **288–90,** 298, 342, 453, 504. Works: *Profiles in Courage,* 289; *Why England Slept,* 289

Kennedy, Joseph P., 288, 290

Kennedy, Robert F., **290–92**

Kepler, Johannes, 300

Kerensky, Aleksandr, 382, 519

Kern, Jerome, 52

Kerner, Justinus, 276

Kerouac, Jack, 87, 201, **292–93,** 312, 532. Works: "And the Hippos Were Boiled in Their Tanks," 87; *Big Sur,* 292; *The Dharma Bums,* 292; *Mexico City Blues,* 292; *On the Road,* 202, 292; *The Subterraneans,* 292; *The Town and the City,* 292

Kerr, Alfred, 136, 332

Kesey, Ken, 312

Key, Ellen, 469; *The Woman Movement,* 64

Keynes, John Maynard, 156, 223, 256, 264, **293–94,** 463, 502, 565. Works: *Economic Consequences of the Peace,* 293; *Essays in Biography,* 293; *Essays in Persuasion,* 293; *The General Theory of Employment, Interest and Money,* 293;

"The Political Doctrines of Edmund Burke," 294; *A Tract on Monetary Reform*, 293, 375; *A Treatise on Money*, 293

Khodasevich, Vladislav, 382

Khomeini, Ayatollah, 460

Khrushchev, Nikita, 98, 144, 183, 207, 266, **294–96**

Kickham, Charles, *Knocknagow, or the Homes of Tipperary*, 3, 114

Kidd, Benjamin, *Social Evolution*, 81

Kiel, Friedrich, 413

Kielland, Alexander, 344

Kierkegaard, Søren, 17, 25, 34, 40, 82, 85, 135, 147, 166, 239, 258, 279, 308, 332, 389, 398, 433, 476, 514, 530, 565. Works: *Concepts of Dread*, 378; *Either-Or*, 13; *Fear and Trembling*, 532

Kieślowski, Krzysztof, 250

Killens, John, 14

King, Henry, 174

King, Martin Luther, Jr., 14, 107, 108, 186, **296–97**, 411, 451. Works: "Letter from a Birmingham Jail," 296; *Strength to Love*, 297; *Stride Toward Freedom: The Montgomery Story*, 297; *Trumpet of Conscience*, 297; *Where Do We Go From Here: Chaos or Community*, 297; *Why We Can't Wait*, 297

King, Martin Luther, Sr., 296

Kingsley, Charles, 327; *Heroes*, 32

Kingston, Maxine Hong, 14

Kinsey, Alfred, *Sexual Behaviour in the Human Male*, 39

Kipling, Rudyard, 7, 22, 32, 152, 168, 288, 330, 359, 399, 400, 466, 511; *The Jungle Book*, 139

Kirchhoff, Gustav, 431, 432

Kirevsky, Peter, 504

Kirkpatrick, William Thompson, 318

Kissinger, Henry, **297–99**

Klee, Paul, 103, 220, 283, 299–300; *The Thinking Eye*, 299

Kleist, Heinrich von, 279; *Penthesilea*, 447

Klimke, Friedrich, 239

Klossowski, Pierre, 176

Kluge, Alexander, 167

Klyuchevsky, Vasili, *Peter the Great*, 337

Knapp, Georg, 366

Knies, Karl, 548

Knight, Frank, *Risk, Uncertainty and Profit*, 181

Knox, Ronald, 397, 543

Kochanowski, Jan, 269

Koestler, Arthur, **300–301**, 312. Works: *Darkness at Noon*, 408; "Freud or Marx?," 300; *The Gladiators*, 301; *Insight and Outlook*, 301

Koffka, Kurt, 350

Kohl, Helmut, **302–3**

Köhler, Wolfgang, 93, 427

Kojeve, Alexandre, 40

Kołaczkowski, Stefan, 269

Kolakowski, Leszek, 263

Kollár, Ján, 350

Kollwitz, Käthe, 17

Komenský, Jan Amos, 350

Konkret, 167

Konopnicka, Maria, 210

Koran, 9, 187, 338, 460

Korolenko, Vladimir, 476

Korzybski, Alfred, *Science and Sanity*, 88

Kosofsky-Sedgwick, Eve, 131

Kotlarczyk, Mieczysław, 268

Koussevitzky, Serge, 53, 115

Kraemer, Fritz, 298

Kraepelin, Emil, 277

Krafft-Ebing, Richard von, 276, 277

Kraft, Julius, 433

Kraft, Vicktor, 93

Krasiński, Zygmunt, *Un-divine Comedy*, 269

Kraszewski, Ignacy, 541; *Ancient Tale*, 541

Kraszewski, Józef, 414

Kraus, Karl, 565

Krishnamurti, Jiddu, 256; *Last Freedom*, 435

Kristeva, Julia, 35

Kristol, Irving, 43

Krohg, Christian, 377

Kropotkin, 123, 258, 378, 379, 492; *Fields, Factories, and Workshops*, 416

Krug, Wilhelm, 276

Kruger, Gerhard, 85

Krupskaya, Nadezhda, 314

Kubrick, Stanley, 510

Kuhn, Thomas S., *The Structure of Scientific Revolutions*, 179

Kukharchuk, Nina, 295

Kundera, Milan, 90, **303–4**. Works: *The Art of the Novel*, 303; *The Book of Laughter and Forgetting*, 303; *Farwell Party*, 303; *Immortality*, 303; *Identity*, 303; *Jacques and His Master*, 303; *The Joke*, 303; *Slowness*, 303; *Testaments Betrayed*, 303; *The Unbearable Lightness of Being*, 303, 304

Kuprin, Aleksandr, 476

Kurosawa, Akira, **304–5**, 509

Kürschak, Joseph, 387

Kuttner, Henry, 65

Kuznets, Simon, *Incomes from Independent Professional Practice*, 181

Labriola, Antonio, 118, 520; *The Materialist Conception of History*, 215

Lacan, Jacques, 35; *Of Paranoiac Psychosis in its Relationship to Personality*, 122

Lachelier, Jules, 50, 427

Laclos, Pierre Choderlos, *Dangerous Liaisons*, 200

L'Action francaise, 146

L'Action nationale, 146

Lada, Josef, 230

Ladies' Home Journal, 453, 491

LaFarge, Oliver, *Tribes and Temples*, 372

Lafargue, Paul, 492

La Fontaine, August, 67, 502; *Fables*, 103

Laforgue, Jules, 144, 163, 354, 531; *Moral Tales*, 144

Lagerlöf, Selma, 433; *Wonderful Adventures of Nils*, 364

Lagneau, Jean, 550

Lalande, André, 427

La Lotta di Classe, 379

Lamantia, Philip, 202

Lamartine, Alphonse, 264; *Histoire des Girondins*, 368

Lamb, Charles, *Tales from Shakespeare*, 32

Lampedusa, Duke of Palma and Prince. *See* Tomasi, Giuseppe

Lamprecht, Karl, 55

Landauer, Gustav, 82

Lang, Fritz, 86, 205, **307–8**

Lang, Matthäus, 239

Lange, Friedrich Albert, 548
Langer, Frantisek, 230
Langley, Samuel, P., *Experiments in Aerodynamics*, 571
L'Année Sociologique, 317
Lao Tzu, 67, 243, 323, 366
Laracy, Arina, 479
Lardner, Ring, 171, 241
La revolution surrealiste, 76
La revue Blanche, 103
Larionov, Mikhail, 102, 503
La Rochefoucauld, François de, 125
Lars, Krystyna, 263
Lask, Emil, 239, 332
Lassalle, Ferdinand, 69, 206
Lasswitz, Kurd, 308; *Auf zwei Planeten*, 73
Latin literature, 79, 407; 521; Latin (Roman) classics, xvii, 99, 266, 312, 315, 336; Roman mythology, 66, 318, 356
Lattuada, Alberto, 170
Laurencin, Marie, 15
Laurendeau, André, 146
Laurents, Arthur, 54
Laurrell, Karl, 206
Lautreamont, Comte de (Isidore Ducasse), *Les Chants de Maldoror*, 76
L'Avanti, 215
Lavelle, Louis, 102
L'Avenire del Lavoratore, 378
Lavin, Mary, 399
Lawrence, D. H., 80, 99, 149, 176, 208, 255, **308–10**, 340, 399, 400, 410, 463, 513. Works: *Lady Chatterley's Lover*, 499; "A Modern Lover," 309; *The Plumed Serpent*, 372; *Sons and Lovers*, 242; *Study of Thomas Hardy*, 309; *You Touched Me!*, 559; *Women in Love*, 408
Lawrence, T. E., **310–11**, 340; *Seven Pillars of Wisdom*, 176, 310, 550
Lawson, T. W., *Frenzied Finance*, 547
Layard, A. H., 310
Lea, Homer, *Day of the Saxon*, 458
Leacock, Stephen, 24, 445
Lear, Edward, 37
Leary, Timothy, **311–12**
Leaud, Jean-Pierre, 523
Lebesgue, Hermann, 387

Le Bon, Gustave, 379
Lecky, W. E. H., *History of European Morals*, 546
Leconte de Lisle, Charles, 200, 438
Le Corbusier, 162, **313–14**, 360, 423. Works: *The City of Tomorrow*, 313; *The Decorative Art of Today*, 313; *Towards a New Architecture*, 313
Le Dantec, 427
Lederer, Emil 332
Lederer, William, *The Ugly American*, 289
Le Devenir, 118
Leduc, Violette, 39
Lee, Dennis, 24
Lefschetz, Solomon, 387
Legends of the Rhine, 238
Leibniz, Gottfried, 39, 50
Leiris, Michel, 39
Lem, Stanislaw, 510
Lemaître, Jules, 44
Le Matin, 113
Lembede, Anton, 341
Le Monde, 284
Lenin, Alexander, 315
Lenin, V. I., 76, 84, 98, 109, 143, 166, 207, 215, 220, 223, 262, 330, 384, 404, 485, 492, 516, 519–20, 541. Works: "April Thesis," 314; *The Development of Capitalism in Russia*, 520; *Imperialism*, 208, 254; *Lessons of the Moscow Uprising*, 254; "New Economic Trends in Peasant Life," 314; *What is to be Done?*, 154, 314, 315, 520
Lennon, John, 37–38; *In His Own Write*, 37
Le Nouvel Observateur, 368
Lenz, Siegfried, 61
Leo XIII, *Rerum Novarum*, 193
Leopardi, Giacomo, 418, 518, 531; *La ginestra*, 529
LePan, Douglas, 24
L'Eplattenier, Charles, 313
Lermontov, Mikhail, 223, 436, 476, 498
Leschetitzky, Theodore, 413
Le Senne, Rene, 102
Leskov, Nikolai, 399, 485
Lesley, Cole, 117
Leslie's Weekly, 219
Lessing, Gotthold Ephraim, 147, 498, 528; *Minna Von*

Barnhelm, 446; *Nathan der Weise*, 205
Les Temps Modernes, 471
Lester, Julius, 14
Le Temps modernes, 39
Levi, Primo, **315–17**. Works: *The Periodic Table*, 316; *The Reawakening*, 316, *The Search for Roots*, 316; *Survival in Auschwitz*, 316
Levi-Città, Tullio, 158
Levinas, Emmanuel, 40, 146
Lévi-Strauss, Claude, 188, **317–18**; *Mythologiques*, 317
Lewin, Bertram, 490
Lewin, Kurt, 93
Lewis, C. S., **318–19**, 517, 532. Works: *The Allegory of Love*, 318; *The Great Divorce*, 319; *Narnia Chronicles*, 319; *Perelandra*, 319; *Preface to "Paradise Lost,"* 319; *Out of the Silent Planet*, 319; *That Hideous Strength*, 319; *Till We Have Faces*, 319
Lewis, John, **319–20;** *The Miners' Fight for American Standards*, 320
Lewis, Sinclair, 65, 179, **321–22**, 358. Works: *Arrowsmith*, 321; *Babbit*, 321; *Elmer Gantry*, 321; *Main Street*, 241, 321, 569
Lewis, Warren H., 319
Lewis, Wyndham, 354, 398
Ley, Willy, 73
Liberation, 471
Lidové noviny, 90
Lie, Jonas, 344
Liebig, Hans von, 55
Liebknecht, Karl, 17, 252
Life, 64, 329, 451, 453, 497
Lij Iyasu, 227
Lilienthal, Otto, 570; *The Problem of Flying*, 571; *Practical Experiments in Soaring*, 571
Lilly, John, 312
Lincoln, Abraham, 3, 252, 290–91, 326, 467; *Gettysburg Address*, 160
Lindbergh, Charles, **322–23**
Lindqvist, Sven, *Exterminate All the Brutes*, 498
Lindsay, David, *Voyage to Arcturus*, 319
Lindsay, Vachel, "The Broncho that Would Not Be Broken of Dancing," 151–52

Linne, Carl von, 540
Lippmann, Walter, **323–25,** 330, 468–69, 470. Works: *Essays in Public Philosophy,* 324; *The Stakes of Diplomacy,* 324; "Today and Tomorrow," 324
Lipset, Seymour Martin, 43
Lister, Joseph, 158
Liston, Sonny, 8
Litterature, 121
Little, Malcolm. *See* Malcolm X
Livy, 125, 548; "Horatius at the Bridge," 151
Lizárraga, Concepción, 529
Llosa, Mario Vargas, **325–26.** Works: *Aunt Julia and the Scriptwriter,* 325; *Captain Pantaja and the Special Service,* 325; *Conversation in the Cathedral,* 325; *A Fish in the Water,* 325; *The Green House,* 325; *Perpetual Orgy,* 326; *The Time of the Hero,* 325; *The War at the End of the World,* 325
Lloyd George, David, 7, 23, **326–27**
Lloyd, Henry Demarest, *Wealth Against Commonwealth,* 81, 453
Lloyd's Bulletin, 245
Lobachevski, Nikolai, 50
Locke, John, 118, 521; *Two Treatises of Civil Government,* 208
Loeb, Jacques, 484
Loeser, Charles, 494
Loewenson, Erwin, 17
Lombroso, Cesare, 118
London, Jack, 61, 69, 123, 223, 312, 241, 444, 469. Works: *The Call of the Wild,* 219, 407; *The Iron Heel,* 408; *People of the Abyss,* 407
Lonergan, Bernard, **327–28;** *Insight,* 327; *Method in Theology,* 327
Longfellow, Henry Wadsworth, 68, 99, 119
Longinus, *On the Sublime,* 560
Loos, Adolf, 565; *Ornament and Crime,* 313
Loos, Anita, *Gentlemen Prefer Blondes,* 454
Loraine, Lorn, 117
L'Ordine Nuovo, 215
Lorenz, Hendrik, 158

Lorimer, George, 453
Los Lunes del Imparcial, 405
Lothar, Rudolph, *Harlequin King,* 428
Loti, Pierre, 125
Lotze, Rudolf, 51, 548
Louis XIV, 394, 459
Louis, Joe, 451
Louis, Paul, 492
Louis, Pierre, 535
Louÿs, Pierre, 200; *La femme et le pantin,* 86
Lovecraft, H. P., 65
Lowell, Amy, 467
Lowell, Elizabeth, 398
Lowell, James Russell, 68, 99
Lowell, Robert, 398
Lowenthal, Leo, 345
Lowes, John Livingston, 88
Lowie, Robert Harry: *Primitive Society,* 317; *The History of Ethnological Thought,* 317
Löwith, Karl, 85, 240
Lowry, Malcolm, 445
Lubac, Henri de, *The Mystery of the Supernatural,* 224
Lubbock, Percy, 217, 398
Luce, Henry Robinson, 64, 185, **329–30**
Lucian, 353
Lucretius, 50, 470
Ludendorff, Erich, 55, 244, **330–31**
Ludlow, Fitz Hugh, 312
Ludwig, Emile, *Napoleon,* 476
Lueger, Karl, 247
Lukács, György, 209, **332–33;** *The Theory of the Novel,* 30
Lunacharsky, Anatoly, 315
L'Unione Sarda, 215
Luther, Martin, 34, 62, 85, 240, 389, 415, 421, 548
Lutosławski, Witold, 210
Luxemburg, Rosa, 17, 109, 332
Luzzato, Rob Moshe Haim, *The Path of Righteousness,* 482
Lyman, Azel Storrs, *Historical Chart,* 455
Lynch, William F., 397
Lynkeus, Josef, 433
Lytle, Andrew, 398

Mabovitch, Sheyna, 358
MacArthur, Douglas, 159, **335–36**
Macaulay, Thomas Babbington, 37, 105, 110, 163, 326, 348,

374, 506, 563, 566; *Machiavelli,* 506
Macdonald, Dwight, 109
MacDonald, George, xvi, 319, 517
Macdonald, Nancy, 109
MacDonald, Ramsay, 31
MacEwen, Gwendolyn, 24
Macgowan, Kenneth, 402
MacGreevy, Thomas, 41
Mach, Ernst, 93, 234, 249, 300, 433
Machado, Antonio, 529
Machen, Arthur, *The Hill of Dreams,* 142
Machiavelli, Niccolò, 392, 548; *The Prince,* 216, 379
Machlup, Fritz, 233
Mackenzie, Compton, 46; *Sinister Street,* 407
MacLeish, Archibald, 242, 467
MacLennan, Hugh, 445
Macmillan, Harold, **337–38;** *The Middle Way,* 337
Macnamara, Caitlin, 512
Macpherson, James. *See* Ossian
Macpherson, Jay, 24
MacPherson, Jeannie, 128
Madach, Imre, 332
Mademoiselle, 65
Madison, James, 442
Madonna, "Express Yourself," 307
Maeterlinck, Maurice, 243, 258, 365, 499. Works: *Blue Bird,* 49; *Intelligence of Flowers,* 493; *L'Intruse: la vie,* 428; *The Treasure of the Humble,* 199; *La Vie des abeilles,* 504
Mahabharata, 187
Mahan, Alfred Thayer: *The Influence of Sea Power on History,* 458, 557; *The Interest of America in Sea Power,* 458
Mahfouz, Naguib, 209
Mahler, Gustav, 136, 473, 564
Mahler-Gropius, Alma, 136
Maier, Heinrich, 85
Mailer, Norman, *Marilyn: A Biography,* 497; *The Naked and the Dead,* 137
Maimonides, Moses, *Guide for the Perplexed,* 482
Maine, Henry, 563
Maiorescu, Titu, 257
Makhinia, Pantelei, 295
Makonnen, Ras, 227
Malamud, Bernard, 398

Malcolm X, 15, 107, **338–39,** 376, 451; *The Autobiography of Malcolm X,* 338

Malebranche, Nicolas, 41

Malevich, Kazimir, 283

Malinowski, Bronislaw, *Argonauts of the Western Pacific,* 356

Mallarmé, Stéphane, 63, 76, 102, 130, 144, 153, 168, 188, 200, 248, 354, 422, 472, 531, 535

Malle, Louis, 523

Mallon, Paul, 237

Mallory, Thomas, 321; *La Morte D'Arthur,* 32, 311, 496

Malraux, André, 136, **339–40,** 445, 522, 555; *Lunes en papier,* 340

Malthus, Thomas, 469

Manchester Evening News, 407

Manchester Guardian, 261

Mandel, Eli, 24

Mandela, Nelson, **341–42**

Mandelstam, Osip, 79, 236

Mann, Heinrich, **342–43,** 344, 444. Works: *The Breath,* 343; *Eine Freundschaft,* 342; *Die Göttinnen,* 342; *Henry, King of France,* 343; *In the Land of Cockaigne,* 343; *Lidice,* 343; *Professor Unrat,* 342; *Voltaire—Goethe,* 342; *Young Henry of Navarre,* 343; *Zola,* 342

Mann, Thomas, 13, 69, 168, 200, 208, 228, 301, 316, 332, **343–45,** 382, 420, 519, 532. Works: *Die Buddenbrooks,* 69, 169, 343; *A Death in Venice,* 77; *Doctor Faustus,* 473; *Reflections of a Nonpolitical Man,* 344; *Der Zauberberg,* 444

Manning, Henry, 329

Mansfield, Katherine, 228, 399, 400

Mantegazza Paolo, 118, 312

Manzoni, Alessandro: *The Betrothed,* 193, 267, 420; *La Pentacoste,* 267

Mao Zedong, 204, 341; *On Guerrilla Warfare,* 223

Maragall, Joan, 529

Marc, Franz, 282, 473; *The Blaue Reiter Almanac,* 282

Marcel, Gabriel, 229, 397

Marconi, Guglielmo, 300

Marcus Aurelius, 13, 546

Marcuse, Herbert, **345–46.** Works: *Eros and Civilization,* 345; *One-Dimensional Man,* 345; *Reason and Revolution,* 345

Marcuse, Ludwig, 343

Mare, Walter de la, 513

Maréchal, Joseph, 328

Marey, Jules, *Animal Mechanism,* 571

Marías, Julián, 406

Mariátegui, José Carlos, 325; *Peranicemosal Peru,* 224

Marinetti, Filippo Tommaso, 103, 309

Maritain, Jacques, 123, 194, 397, 522. Works: *Art and Scholasticism,* 421; *Christianity and Democracy,* 194, 421; *Integral Humanism,* 421; *Three Reformers,* 420–21

Marley, Bob, **346–47**

Marlowe, Christopher, 79–80, 169; *The Troublesome Raigne and Lamentable Death of Edward II,* 75

Marquardsen, Heinrich, *Handbuch des Oeffentlichen Rechts der Gegenwart,* 563

Marsh, Edward, *Georgian Poetry,* 80

Marshall, Alfred, *Principles of Economics,* 181

Marshall, George C., 73, 159, **347–49**

Marshall, Paul, 14

Marson, John, 80

Martí, José, 97, 98

Martin, George, 37

Martini, Ferdinando, 118

Martoglio, Nino, 431

Martov, Yuli, 314

Marx, Karl, 17, 23, 30, 43, 45, 46, 70, 83, 98, 100, 102, 109, 118, 140, 141, 161, 162, 177, 179, 204, 215, 216, 220, 224, 252, 258, 262, 314, 327, 330, 332, 341, 345, 352, 367, 378, 379, 384, 404, 419, 433, 459, 466, 471, 476, 485, 492, 498, 514, 520, 528, 541, 550, 562. Works: *Capital,* 70, 124, 146, 208, 223, 254, 315, 342; *Communist Manifesto,* 70, 205, 206, 223, 254, 295, 384, 516; *Economic and Philosophical Manuscripts of 1844,*

345–46; *The 18th Brumaire of Louis Napoleon,* 143, 166; *The Poverty of Philosophy,* 315; "Preface to a Contribution to the Critique of Political Ideology," 166; *Wage-Labor and Capital,* 384

Masaryk, Tomáš, 46, 47, 90, 233, **349–50**

Masina, Giulietta, 170

Maslow, Abraham, **350–51;** *Motivation and Personality,* 351

Massignon, Louis, 421

Massine, Leonide, 503

Masterman, Charles, 327

Masterpieces of World History, 483

Masters, Edgar Lee, 142; *Spoon River Anthology,* 467

Mastroianni, Marcello, 170

Matisse, Henri, 20, 70, 282, 494, 503

Maugham, Somerset, 117, 245; *The Moon and Sixpence,* 241

Maupassant, Guy de, 208, 219, 309, 344, 358, 399, 523

Maurer, Ion Gheorge, 198

Mauriac, François, 76, 123, 397, 555

Maurin, Peter, 122, 123

Mauss, Marcel, 146, 317; *Primitive Classification,* 317

Mauthner, Fritz, 41

May, Karl, 61, 308; *Winnetou* series, 488

Mayakovsky, Vladimir, 78, **352–53,** 504

Mayfield, Julian, 15

Mays, Benjamin, 296

Mays, Wolfe, 427

Mazzini, Giuseppe, 379, 480

McCall's, 497

McCarey, Leo, 174

McCarthy, Joseph, 92, 363

McCarthy, Mary, 398

McCarthyism, 261, 344, 404

McCartney, Paul, 37–38

McClure, Michael, 202

McClure's Magazine, 99

McColl, Norman, 500

McCullers, Carson, 398

McDonnell, Donald, 107

McGuffey, William Holmes, *McGuffey's Eclectic Readers,* 172, 454

McLuhan, Marshall, 153–54, 312, **353–54.** Works: *From*

Cliché to Archetype, 354; *The Gutenberg Galaxy*, 353; *The Mechanical Bride*, 354; *Thomas Nashe and the Learning of His Time*, 353; *The Vanishing Point*, 354; *War and Peace in the Global Village*, 354
McPherson, Aimee Semple, **355–56**
McPherson, Harold, 355
McTaggart, John McTaggart, 462
Mead, Margaret, **356–57**, 490. Works: *Coming of Age in Samoa*, 356; *A History of Psychology in Autobiography*, 356
Medzini, Regina, 358
Meer, Ismail, 341
Meir, Golda, **357–58**
Meitner, Lise, 58
Melas, Spyros, 284
Mella, Juan Antonio, 98
Mellon, Andrew, 453
Melville, Herman, 66, 94. Works: *Billy Budd*, 77, 176; *Moby Dick*, 65, 262
Memoirs, 337
Mencius, 434
Mencken, H. L., 186, 321, **359–60**, 434, 562. Works: *The American Language*, 359; *A Book of Prefaces*, 569
Mendelssohn, Felix, 17, 265, 564
Mendelssohn, Moses, 17; *Jerusalem or On Religious Power and Judaism*, 28
Mendès, Catulle, 414
Mendes-France, Pierre, 368
Menger, Carl, 234. Works: *Investigations into the Method of the Social Sciences*, 234; *Principles of Economics*, 234, 367
Menger, Karl, 93
Menilek II, 227
Menzel, Jiří, 303
Mercador, Ramon, 520
Mercier, Honore, 146
Meredith, George, 114, 116, 537; *Modern Love*, 309
Meredith, H. O., 294
Merezhkovsky, Dmitri, 282
Merkel, Adolf, 563
Merleau-Ponty, Maurice, 166, 203, 471; *Phenomenologie de la perception*, 40
Mesmer, Franz, 51

Metchnikoff, Ilya, *La civilization et les grands fleuves historiques*, 273
Metternich, Klemens von, 298
Metz, Christian, 418
Meyerhold, Vsevelod, 221
Michelet, Jules, 562
Michels, Robert, 83
Mickiewicz, Adam, 210, 221, 263, 269, 364, 414; *Pan Tadeusz*, 269
Midrash, 555
Mies van der Rohe, Ludwig, 220, **360–62**, 423
Miéville, Ann-Marie, 203
Mignet, François, *History of the French Revolution*, 520
Milarepa, 67
Mill, John S., 50, 118, 235, 327, 350, 520; *On Liberty*, 156
Miller, Arthur, **362–63**. Works: *After the Fall*, 362; *All My Sons*, 362; *The American Clock*, 362; *Broken Glass*, 362; *The Creation of the World and Other Business*, 362; *The Crucible*, 362, 363; *Death of a Salesman*, 362; *Incident at Vichy*, 362; *The Man Who Had All the Luck*, 362; *The Price*, 362; *A View from the Bridge*, 362
Miller, Theodore A., 120
Milner, Alfred, 289
Milosevic, Slobodan, 140
Milosz, Czeslaw, 236, **363–65**. Works: *The Captive Mind*, 364; *Chronicles*, 364; *City Without a Name*, 364; *The Native Realm*, 364; *Three Winters*, 363; *Treatise on Morals*, 364; *Treatise on Poetry*, 364; *The Valley of the Issa*, 364
Milosz, Olcar, 363
Milton, 22, 64, 68, 327, 476, 511, 513, 537. Works: "L'Allegro," 560; "Comus," 560; "Lycidas," 560; *Paradise Lost*, 319, 323, 496; "Il Penseeroso," 560
Miner's Leaflet, 295
Miquel, Johannes von, 548
Mirbeau, Octave, *Diary of a Chambermaid*, 86
Mirbt, Carl, 85
Miro, Joan, 75, 86, **365–66**

Mises, Ludwig von, 233–34, **366–67**. Works: *Socialism*, 234, 367; *The Theory of Money and Credit*, 366, 367
Mitchel, John, 132
Mitchell, Wesley C., 181, 234
Mitford, Nancy, 544
Mitterand, François, **367–69**. Works: *L'abeille et l'architecte*, 368; *Le Grain et la paille*, 368
Mizoguchi, Kenji, 509
Modern Music, 53
Modigliani, Amedeo, 102
Modotti, Tina, 281
Moholoy-Nagy, Laszlo, 354
Moir, William Wilmerding, 481
Molière, 49, 66, 413
Molnar, Ference, *Liliom*, 308
Mommsen, Ernst, 548
Mommsen, Theodor, 548
Mondrian, Pieter, **369–70**
Monnet, Jean, 370–71, 474
Monroe, Harriet, 467
Monroe, Marilyn, 137–38, 362, 497
Montaigne, Michel de, 40, 125, 200, 353, 518, 521
Montalbán, Manuel Vázques, *Autobiografía del general Franco*, 178
Montale, Eugenio, 153, 418, 519
Montesquieu, Baron Charles de Secondat, 146, 563; *The Spirit of the Laws*, 521
Montherlant, Henri de, *Pitie pour les femmes*, 167
Montini, Giovanni. *See* Paul VI
Moody, Anne, 14
Moody, Dwight L, 355, 507
Moore, A. B., *History of Alabama*, 542
Moore, Brian, 445
Moore, George Edward, 293–94, 399, 564; "The Nature of Judgement," 463; *Principia Ethica*, 293, 502
Moore, Henry, **371–73**
Moore, Marianne, 499, 560
Moore, Thomas, 114
Moran, D. P., *The Leader*, 114
Moravia, Alberto, 417
More, Thomas, 353; *Utopia*, 81
Morgan, J. Pierpont, 453
Morgenstern, Oskar, 387
Mörike, Eduard, 243
Morison, Samuel Eliot, 470

Moro, César, 325
Morpurgo, Lucia, 316
Morrell, Ottoline, 217, 255
Morris, George Sylvester, 133
Morris, William, xvi, 4, 23, 220, 319, 416, 517. Works: *Hollow Land and other Tales*, 310–11; *Roots of the Mountains*, 311; *Sigurd the Volsung*, 311; *Well at the World's End*, 311; *Wood Beyond the World*, 311
Morrison, Harold, 373
Morrison, Marion. *See* Wayne, John
Morrison, Toni, **373–74**. Works: *Beloved*, 373; *The Black Book*, 374; *The Bluest Eyes*, 373; *Jazz*, 373; *Paradise*, 373; *Song of Solomon*, 373; *Sula*, 373
Morrone, Pietro da. *See* Celestine V
Morrow, Anne Spencer, 322
Morton, Frederic, *Thunder at Twilight*, 540
Moses, 48, 555
Mosley, Oswald, **374–75**
Mouillard, Louis, Empire of the Air, 571
Mounier, Emmanuel, 123, 146, 258, 398, 521
Moynihan, Daniel Patrick, 383, 393
Mozart, Wolfgang Amadeus, 473
Ms., 497
Muenzenberg, Willy, 301
Muhammad, Elijah, 9, 338, **375–77**
Müller, Admiral von, 55
Müller, Friedrich von, 276
Müller, Karl, 85
Mumford, Lewis, 354
Munch, Edvard, **377–78**
Munich Agreement, 46
Munro, Hector Hugh (Saki), 117
Munter, Gabriele, 282
Murdoch, Iris, 398
Muriedas, Luisa Grimm de, 265
Murnau, F. W., 174, 308, 459
Murray, Francis, J., 387
Murray, John Courtney, 329
Murray, John Middleton, 217
Murrow, Edward R., 451; *This I Believe*, 451

Murry, John Middleton, 408
Musil, Alois, 480
Musil, Robert, 147, 249, 303, 430
Musset, Alfred de, 125, 264
Mussolini, Benito, 177, 223, 237, **378–80**. Works: *Claudia Particella*, 379; *Il Trentino veduto da un socialista*, 379
Myerson, Morris, 357
Myrdal, Gunnar, 40
Mysteries, 320
Mystery novels, 327

NAACP (National Association for the Advancement of Colored People), 3, 29, 192, 296, 449, 451
Nabokov, Vladimir, **381–82**, 398, 532. Works: *Despair*, 167; *Lolita*, 381; *Mary*, 381; *The Real Life of Sebastian Knight*, 382
Nader, Ralph, **382–83**. Works: "The Safe Car You Can't Buy," 382; *Unsafe at Any Speed*, 382
Nagy, Imre, **384–85**. Works: *On Communism: In Defense of the New Course*, 384
Nahman, Rabbi, 555
Naipaul, V. S., **385–86**. Works: *Among the Believers*, 385; *An Area of Darkness*, 385; *A Bend in the River*, 385; *The Enigma of Arrival*, 386; *A House for Mr. Biswas*, 385; *In a Free State*, 385
Nancy Drew stories, 497
Nansen, Fridtjof, 433
Napoleon, 195, 212
Narcejac, Thomas, 245
Národní listy, 90
Nascimento, Edson Arantes do. *See* Pele
Nash, Ogden, 532
Nashe, Thomas, 353
Nasser, Gamal Abdel, 155
Nation, 382
National Association for the Advancement of Colored People (NAACP), 3, 29, 192, 296, 449, 451
National Book Award, 94, 373, 532, 556, 560
National Geographic, 392
National Labor Tribune, 206

National Organization for Women, 179
Nation of Islam, 8
Natorp, Paul, 62, 85, 93, 405
Nebraska State Journal, 99
Nechaev, Sergei, 315
Neimark, Paul, 411
Nekrasov, Nikolay, 352, 476, 520
Nelson, Leonard, 433
Neruda, Pablo, 10, 223, 422
Nerval, Gerard de, 8
Nestroy, Johann, 147; *Einen Jux will er sich machen*, 556
Neuberger, Louise, 51
Neumann, Erich, 17
Neumann, Franz, 346
Neumann, John Louis von, **386–88**
Neurath, Otto, 93, 433
Nevins, Allan, *American Political, Social and Intellectual Life*, 434
New English Weekly, 407, 512
New Leader, 42
New Left Review, 332
New Masses, 141
New Music, 196
New Republic, 216, 561
New Statesman and Nation, 407
New York, 497
New Yorker, 65, 482, 532
New York Herald-Tribune, 324
New York Post, 451, 551
New York Times, 137, 195, 271, 442
Newlove, John, 24
Newman, James R., *Tools of War*, 65
Newman, John Henry, 267, 398. Works: *Apologia pro Vita Sua*, 560; *Grammar of Assent*, 328
Newsweek, 180, 436, 497
Newton, Isaac, 158, 300, 482, 553
Nicholas of Cusa, 273
Nichols, Dudley, 174
Nicholson, Mike, 52
Nick Carter stories, 455, 464
Niebuhr, Reinhold, 96, **388–89**, 514. Works: *Faith and History*, 388; *The Irony of American History*, 389; *Moral Man and Immoral Society*, 388; *The Nature and Destiny of Man*, 388
Niemöller, Martin, **389–90**

Nietzsche, Friedrich, 17, 30, 35, 45, 51, 71, 82, 89, 111, 127, 135, 147, 159, 176, 200, 223, 240, 243, 247, 258, 264, 285, 286, 308, 309, 332, 340, 360, 370, 379, 380, 391, 392, 405, 444, 446, 471, 472, 476, 514, 530, 531, 569. Works: *Beyond Good and Evil*, 344, 441; *The Case of Wagner*, 344; *Gotzen-Dammerung*, 128; *Thus Spake Zarathustra*, 121, 166, 199, 276, 277, 375, 402, 446, 481, 482
Nijhoff, Martinus, 370
Nijinska, Bronislava, 391, 503
Nijinsky, Vaslav, **390–92,** 503
Nixon, Richard M., 290, 297, **392–94,** 453, 542; *In the Arena*, 393
Nizan, Paul, 471
Njegoš, Petar Petrović, 13, 140
Nkrume, Kwame, 569
Nobel prizes, 13, 21, 41, 58, 59, 60, 69, 78, 89, 110, 158, 163, 180, 191, 200, 207, 208, 228, 234, 236, 241, 242, 265, 297, 321, 323, 344, 348, 363, 373, 381, 402, 404, 419, 422, 471, 482, 486, 496, 511, 540–41, 55
Noerdlinger, Henry S., 129
Noguchi, Isamu, 214
Nohl, Hermann, 93
Nordau, Max, 332
Nordic mythology, 344
Norris, Frank, 142, 241, 359; *A Deal in Wheat*, 219; *The Octopus*, 453
Norris, Margot, 131
Norse literature: mythology, 318, 344; *Sagas*, xvi, 517. *See also* Icelandic literature
Northern Lights, 442
Norton, Sidney, *The Elements of Natural Philosophy*, 571
Norwid, Cyprian, 210, 269
Nottingham Journal, 216
Novalis, 50, 243, 249, 447, 514
Novotný, Antonín, 254
Novy Mir, 485
Nunez, Juan, 121
Nureyev, Rudolph, **394–95**

Oberth, Hermann, "The Rocket into Interplanetary Space," 73
O'Brien, Flann, 61

Observer, 407
O'Casey, Sean, 61, 486
O'Connor, Flannery, **397–99**
O'Connor, Frank (Irish author), 114, 398, **399–400.** Works: *The Art of the Theatre*, 399; *The Backward Look*, 399; *The Lonely Voice*, 399; *The Mirror in the Roadway*, 399; *Shakespeare's Progress*, 399; *Towards an Appreciation of Literature*, 399
O'Connor, Frank (U.S. actor), 439
Oettingen, Wolfang von, 55
Offroy de La Mettrrie, Julien, 312
O'Flaherty, Liam, 399
Ogai Mori, 305
O'Hara, John, 171
O. Henry, 241, 359
Ojetti, Ugo, 431
O'Keeffe, Georgia, **400–402**
Olcott, Henry, 369
Oliver, Francis Wall, 500
Oliver, Joe "King," 18
Ollé-Laprune, Léon, 50
Omar Khayyám, 117; *Rubáiyát*, 163, 188, 357
Oncken, Wilhelm, *Allgemeine Geschichte*, 387
O'Neill, Eugene, 122, **402–3,** 469, 486, 559. Works: *Desire Under the Elms*, 402; *The Emperor Jones*, 402; *The Iceman Cometh*, 402; *The Hairy Ape*, 402; *Lazarus Laughed*, 402; *Long Day's Journey Into Night*, 402; *Mourning Becomes Electra*, 402, 403
O'Neill, Gerard, 312
Opel, Fritz von, 73
Oppenheimer, Robert, 58, 387, **403–5**
Orlovsky, Peter, 87, 202
Orozco, José, 448
Ortega y Gasset, José, 62, 264, **405–6.** Works: *Castles in Castile*, 504; *Preface for Germans*, 405; *Revista de Occidente*, 405; *The Revolt of the Masses*, 330; *El tema de nuestro tiempo*, 406
Orwell, George, 123, 300, 301, **406–9,** 410. Works: *Animal Farm*, 407, 408; *Burmese Days*, 407; *A Clergyman's Daughter,*

407; *Coming Up for Air*, 407; *Down and Out in Paris and London*, 407; *Homage to Catalonia*, 109, 407, 409; *Keep the Aspidistra Flying*, 407; *Nineteen Eighty-Four*, 407, 408, 409; "The Pagan," 408; "Politics and the English Language," 407; "Wells, Hitler and the World State," 407; "Why I Write," 408
Ory, Kid, 18
Osborne, John, **409–10,** 501. Works: *The Entertainer*, 409; *Look Back in Anger*, 409
Osmond, Humphrey, 312
Ossian, 548
Osterwa, Juliusz, 222
Ostrovsky, Nikolay, 477
Ostwald, Wilhelm, 93
Otto, Rudolf, 85, 277, 514
Otway, Thomas, *Venice Preserv'd*, 249
Our Sports, 451
Overbeck, Franz, 34
Ovid, 67, 353; *Metamorphoses*, 188, 428
Owen, Wilfred, 77
Owens, Jesse, **410–11;** *Blackthink*, 411
Oxford English Dictionary, 517
Ozenfant, Amedee, *Apres Le Cubisme*, 313

Paderewski, Jan, **413–14**
Page, P. K., 24
Paine, Thomas, 355
Paisley, Ian, **415**
Palacký, František, 350
Palgrave, Francis, *Golden Treasury of English Verse*, 182, 560
Palmer, Alan, *The Chancelleries of Europe*, 540
Panassie, Hugues, *Le Jazz Hot*, 19
Pankhurst, Christabel, 416
Pankhurst, Emmeline, **415–17**
Pankhurst, Richard, 416
Pankhurst, Sylvia, 416
Papal *Index*, 50, 200, 267
Paparighopoulos, Konstantinow, 284
Papini, Giovanni, *Life of Christ*, 450
Paracelsus, 51, 277, 312
Parain, Brice, *Recherches sur la nature et les functions du langage*, 203

Pareto, Vilfredo, 83, 118, 379
Parker, Charlie, 293
Parker's Aids, 452
Parks, Gordon, 339
Parks, Rosa, 296
Parmenides, 125
Parsons, Wilfrid, *Mexican Martyrdom*, 217
Partisan Review, 407, 448, 482
Pascal, Blaise, 50, 125, 239, 279, 353, 389, 459, 529, 530, 549; *Pensées*, 228, 521, 565
Pascoaes, Texeira de, 530
Pascoli, Giovanni, 118, 418
Pasolini, Pier Paolo, **417–18;** *Poesie a Casarsa*, 417
Passavant, Johann Carl, 276
Pasternak, Boris, 78, **418–20,** 478. Works: *Dr. Zhivago*, 295, 382, 418, 419; "Marburg," 419
Pasteur, Louis, 146, 158
Patchen, Kenneth, 135, 149
Pater, Walter, 80
Patočka, Jan, 232
Patten, Gilbert: *Frank Merriwell* stories, 455, 464; *Frank Merriwell at Yale*, 442
Paul VI, 420–21; *Humani generic*, 420
Paul, 84, 193, 441
Pavlov, Ivan, 484
Payn, Graham, 117
Paz, Octavio, **421–23.** Works: *The Labyrinth of Solitude*, 422; *Luna Silvestre*, 422; *The Sun Stone*, 422
Pea, Enrico, 531
Peach Blossom Spring, 424
Pears, Peter, 77
Péguy, Charles, 125, 146, 228, 267; *Cahiers de la Quinzaine*, 44, 368
Pei, I. M., **423–24**
Pei, Louis, *Cour Napoléon*, 368
Peirce, Charles, 154
Péladan, Joseph "Sâr," *Le Secret de Troubadors*, 434
Pelé, **424–25**
Pellicer, Carlos, 22
Pellico, Silvio, 118
Penderecki, Krzysztof, 210
Penjon, Auguste, 51
Pepper, Stephen C., 398
Percy, Walker, 398
Peres, Shimon, 48
Péret, Benjamin, 75, 86
Peretz, Y. L. 358

Perkins, G. H., 133
Perkins, Maxwell, 171
Perlis, Vivian, 115
Perón, Eva, **425–26**
Perón, Juan, 63, 425, 426
Perrin, Father, 549
Pershing, John J., 347
Peter the Great, 476
Petrarch, 267, 518
Pfeiderer, Otto, 548
Pfister, Oskar, 427
Phaedra, 214
Phaedrus, *Fables*, 479
Philadelphia Inquirer, 483
Phillips, Charles, 414
Piaget, Jean, 4, 356, **426–27.** Works: *Autobiography*, 427; *Research*, 426
Picasso, Pablo, 15, 20, 70, 103, 120, 214, 340, **427–28,** 448, 449, 494, 503
Pick, Georg, 158
Pietrov, Yevgeny, *The Twelve Chairs*, 11
Pigoń, Stanisław, 269
Pinero, Arthur, 410
Pinter, Harold, **429–30,** 501. Works: *Ashes to Ashes*, 429; *The Birthday Party*, 429; *Celebration*, 429; *The Dumb Waiter*, 429; *The Dwarfs*, 429; *Mountain Language*, 429; *One for the Road*, 429; *Party Time*, 429; *The Room*, 429
Pirandello, Luigi, **430–31,** 530. Works: "Arte e scienza," 430; *As You Want Me*, 431; *Better Think Twice About It*, 430; "Capannetta," 430; *Henry IV*, 430; *Her Husband*, 431; *If You Think So*, 430; *The Late Mattia Pascal*, 430; *Liolà*, 430; *The Old and the Young*, 430; *One, None, and a Hundred-Thousand*, 430; *The Pleasure of Honesty*, 430; *Six Characters in Search of an Author*, 387, 430; *Shoot!*, 430; *To Find Oneself*, 431; *The Wives' Friend*, 431
Pisarev, Dmitri, 84
Piscator, Erwin, 343
Pittsburgh Leader, 99
Pius XII, 59, 194, 420
Planck, Max, 58, 93, 158, **431–32;** "On the Second Law of the Mechanical Theory of Heat," 432

Planno, Mortimo, 346
Platen, August, 228
Plath, Sylvia, 24, 497; *The Bell Jar*, 497
Plato, 48, 67, 125, 130, 146, 147, 159, 214, 240, 276, 284, 312, 328, 369, 418, 433, 498, 521, 548, 549, 550. Works: *Dialogues*, 188, 351, 560; *Republic*, 441
Plautus, 299
Plekahanov, Geórgi, 314, 492, 521; *Our Disagreements*, 315
Plunkett, Joseph, 114
Plural, 422
Plutarch, 62, 92, 284; *Parallel Lives*, 426, 525, 571
Poe, Edgar Allan, 21, 24, 38, 65, 92, 99, 106, 154, 168, 171, 219, 299, 312, 363, 381, 399, 444, 482. Works: *The Philosophy of Composition*, 535; "The Raven," 535; *Tales of Mystery and Imagination*, 454
Poetry: A Magazine of Verse, 467
Poetsch, Leopold, 246
Pohl, Admiral von, 55
Poincaré, Jules Henri, 67, 93, 158, 387
Poitier, Sidney, 451
Polanyi, Karl, 433
Polanyi, Michael, 43
Polish literature, 13
Political Science Quarterly, 563
Politics, 109
Pollard, Percival, 359
Pollock, Freidrich, 345; *Spinoza*, 462
Pollock, Jackson, 365
Polya, George, 387
Polybius, 125
Poole, Billie, 376
Poole, Elijah. *See* Elijah Muhammad
Popaedius Silo, 479
Pope, Alexander, 66, 353, 490; *The Dunciad*, 354
Popiełuszko, Jerzy, 250
Popper, Karl, 93, 234–35, **432–34.** Works: *Logic of Scientific Discovery*, 235; *The Open Society and Its Enemies*, 433, 511; *The Poverty of Historicism*, 433
Popular Electronics, 195
Popul Vuh, 21
Porten, Henny, 136
Porter, Gen Stratton, 94

Porter, Katherine Anne, 65, 398, 399
Porter, William Sydney (O. Henry), 241, 359
Posada, José, 447
Potinus, 50
Potter, Beatrix; *The Tale of Peter Rabbit*, 94, 490
Pound, Ezra, 24, 67, 116, 142, 163, 182, 242, 265, 272, 354, 422, **434–35**, 560. Works: *The Cantos*, 202; *Homage to Sextus Propertius*, 434; *The Spirit of Romance*, 434
Powell, Adam Clayton, 411
Powell, Anthony, 543
Powers, J. F., 398, 399
Prabhavananda, Swami, 256
Pravda, 83, 295, 478
Prel, Carl du, 276
Prem, Sri Krishna, 312
Présence africaine, 166
Presley, Elvis, **435–36**
Pre-Socratic philosophers, 240, 276, 309
Primo de Rivera, Miguel, 529
Pro, Miguel, 217
Proctor, Richard, *Our Place Among the Infinities*, 182
Prodigal Son, 422
Prokofiev, Sergei, **436–37**, 478
Protestant Telegraph, 415
Protocols of the Wise Men of Zion, 247
Proudhon, Jean-Joseph, 367–68; *La philosophie de la misère*, 368
Proust, Marcel, 41, 51, 75, 113, 117, 168–69, 208–9, 303, 398, 400, 413, 430, **437–38**, 502, 518, 519, 523, 532, 552, 556. Works: *A la recherché du temps perdu*, 169, 175, 368, 382, 437, 438, 444; *Les Plaisirs et les jours*, 437
Prüfer, Heinz, 387
Prus, Bolesław, 541
Pryzbyszewski, Stanislaw, 377–78
Przywara, Erich, 62
Psichari, Joan, 125
Psychological Review, 494
Puccini, Giacomo, 343
Puck, 152
Pulitzer, Joseph, 238
Pulitzer Prize, 241, 321, 362, 402, 467, 475, 496, 532, 551, 552, 556, 560

Pumpianskii, Lev Vasilievich, 30
Purdy, Al, 24
Pushkin, 8, 223, 230, 394, 436, 498, 504, 509, 520. Works: *Eugene Onegin*, 381, 476; *The Little House of Kolomna*, 504
Putnam, Carleton. Works: *Race and Reason*, 542; *Race and Reality*, 542
Putnam, George, Palmer, 151
Putnam, J. P., *The Kingdom of Heaven Is at Hand*, 81
Pynchon, Thomas, 312

Quasimodo, 153
Queen of Sheba, 227
Quental, Antero de, 530
Quevedo y Villegas, Francisco Gomez de, 189
Quincy, Thomas de, *Murder as One of the Fine Arts*, 245
Quinet, Edgar, 273
Quiroga, Horatio, 448

Rabaté, Jean-Michel, 131
Rabelais, François, 31, 125, 230, 316, 353; *Gargantua and Pantagruel*, 230
Rabotnitsa, 384
Racine, Jean, 41, 470, 502, 531, 549
Rácz, Laszlo, 387
Rade, Martin, 85
Rahner, Karl, *Theological Investigations*, 224
Raleigh, Walter, 502
Ramayana, 422
Rameau de Sapin, 426
Ramon Jimenez, Juan, 189
Ramsey, Frank Plumpton, 565
Rand, Ayn, **439–40**. Works: *Atlas Shrugged*, 439; *The Fountainhead*, 439; *We the Living*, 439
Ranke, Leopold von, 548
Raschdau, Ludwig, 558
Rathenau, Walter, 70, 234, **440–41**
Rattigan, Terence, 410
Rauschenbusch, Walter, 81
Ravaisson-Mollien, Jean Gaspard, 50
Raven, Charles, 398
Ray, Man, 75, 469
Raynaud, Georges, 21
Read, Herbert, 217
Reade, Charles, 327

Reagan, Ronald, **441–43**, 510
Realistic Manifesto, 103
Reaney, James, 24
Recherches sociographiques, 145
Redbook, 491
Reed, John, 469
Reglamento provisional para la instruction de las tropes de Infanteria, 178
Regnier, Henri de, 535
Reich, Wilhelm, 292, 312; *The Cancer Biopathy*, 88
Reichenbach, Hans, 93
Reid, Mayne, 381, 481
Rein, Yevgeny, 79
Reiner, Fritz, 53
Reinhardt, Max, 136, 248
Reinhold, Karl Theodor, 505
Remarque, Erich Maria, 69, 136, **443–44**; *All Quiet on the Western Front*, 443
Rembrandt, Harmensz van Rijn, 102; *Aristotle Contemplating the Bust of Homer*, 247
Remington, Frederic, 174
Renán, Ernest, 45, 50, 199, 327, 405, 529; *Leben Jesu*, 506
Renoir, Jean, 203, 308, 523
Renouvier, Charles, 44, 50
Reshetovskaia, Natalia, 484
Retz, Cardinal de, 125
Reventos, Ramon, *El Centaure Picador*, 428
Reverdy, Pierre, 135, 365
Reville, Brompton Alma, 245
Revivalist, 415
Revue historique, 57
Rexroth, Kenneth, 202, 293
Ribot, Théodule, 44, 51, 427
Ricardo, David, 315
Ricci, Gregorio, 158
Rice, Grantland, 137
Richards, I. A., 495
Richardson, Samuel, 466; *Clarissa*, 495
Richardson, Tony, 523
Richet, Charles, 51
Richler, Mordecai, **445–46**; *The Apprenticeship of Duddy Kravitz*, 445
Richmond, Kenneth, 217
Richmond, Zoe, 217
Richthofen, Baron Manfred von, 211
Rickert, Heinrich, 239, 332, 548
Ricketts, Edward F., 496; *The Sea of Cortez*, 496

Rickey, Branch, 450

Riefenstahl, Leni, 106, **446–47;** *Triumph of the Will,* 406

Riehl, Alois, 361

Riemann, Bernhard, 158

Riemann, George, 50

Riesman, David, "Leisure and Work in Post-Industrial Society," 43

Riesz, Frigyes, 387

Riis, Jacob. Works: *The Children of the Poor,* 81; *How the Other Half Lives,* 81

Riley, Charles, 410

Rilke, Rainer, 62, 135, 136, 301, 444, 493, 514, 559, 565; *Das Stundenbuch,* 419

Rimbaud, Arthur, 63, 74, 102, 142, 149, 153, 188, 201, 250, 292, 345, 354, 381, 418, 422, 493, 559; *Les Illuminations,* 77–78

Rimsky-Korsakov, Nikolai, 503

Riskin, Robert, 92

Ritschl, Albrecht, 276

Rivarol, Antoine, Comte de, 125

Rivas, Duge de, 189

Rivera, Diego, 281, **447–48;** *Towards a Free Revolutionary Art,* 448

Rivette, Jacques, 203, 523

Riviere, Jacques, 228

Robbe-Grillet, Alain, 76, 382

Robbins, Lionel, 234

Roberts, Charles G. D., 24

Robertson, C. Grant, *Bismarck,* 476

Robeson, Paul, 14, 261, **449–50;** *Here I Stand,* 449

Robin Hood, 213

Robinson, Edward Arlington, 116

Robinson, Jackie, **450–52.** Works: "Free Minds and Hearts at Work," 451; *Home Plate,* 451; *Jackie Robinson Says,* 451

Roche, Mazo de la, *Whiteoaks of Jalna,* 497

Rockefeller, John D., Jr., 452

Rockefeller, John Davison, **452–53**

Rocker, Rudolf, 109

Rockwell, Norman, **453–54**

Rodchenko, Alexander, 283

Rodin, Auguste, 199, 493

Rodo, José Enrique, 281

Roe, Humphrey, *Verdon,* 500

Roepke, Wilhelm, 156

Roerich, Nikolai, 503

Roethke, Theodore, 135

Rogers, Buck, 65

Rogers, Robert Athlyi, *Holy Piby,* 346, 347

Rogers, Will, **454–55**

Rohmer, Éric, 167, 203, 523

Roja, Fernando de, *La Tragicomedia de Calisto y Melibea,* 428

Rolfe, Frederick, 217

Rolland, Romain, 215; *Colas Breugnon,* 381; *Jean Christophe,* 115

Roman (Latin) classics, xvii, 99, 266, 312, 315, 336

Roman mythology, 66, 318, 356

Romero, Emilio, *Letters to a Prince,* 275

Romm, Mikhail, 509

Roncalli, Angelo Giuseppe. *See* John XXIII

Roncoroni, Sefano, 459

Roosevelt, *African Game Trails,* 241

Roosevelt, Eleanor, **455–57,** 458. Works: *Autobiography,* 455; *On My Own,* 457; *This I Remember,* 457; *This is My Story,* 457

Roosevelt, Franklin Delano, 64, 178, 182, 237, 25, 253, 320, 324, 453, 455, 456, **457–59,** 481, 524, 550

Roosevelt, Theodore, 3, 393, 450, 457

Roscher, Wilhelm, 548

Rosegger, Peter, 540

Rosenbaum, Alissa. *See* Rand, Ayn

Rosenzweig, Franz, 82

Rosmini, Antonio, 118

Ross, Bertram, 214

Ross, Harold, 52

Rossellini, Roberto, 170, 203, **459–60**

Rossetti, Christina, 537

Rossetti, Dante Gabriel, 119, 537, 544

Rostand, Edmond, 440

Rostow, W. W., *Stages of Economic Growth,* 43

Roth, Joseph, 343

Rothenberg, Michael, 491

Rotolo, Suze, 149

Rouble, Andrei, 510

Rouch, Jean, 203

Rousseau, Jean-Jacques, 40, 67, 141, 421. Works: *Confessions,* 530; *Discours sur l'origine et les fondements de l'inégalité parmi les homes,* 368

Roussel, Raymond, *Impressions d'Afrique,* 76, 145

Rouvroy, Henri de, 51

Roux, Saint-Pol, 76

Rover Boys books, 442

Rowntree, Seebowm, 327

Royce, Josiah, *The Spirit of Modern Philosophy,* 4

Royer-Collard, Pierre Pau, 51

Ruckert, Friedrich, *Es ging ein Mann im Syrerland,* 444

Rumilly, Robert, Mercier, 146

Rushdie, Salman, 63, **460–61.** Works: *Midnight's Children,* 460–61; *The Moor's Last Sigh,* 461; *The Satanic Verses,* 460

Ruskin, John, 23, 99, 309, 327. Works: *The Seven Lamps of Architecture,* 568; *Stones of Venice,* 310, 568; *Unto This Last,* 3, 187

Russell, Bertrand, 93, 109, 256, 387, **461–63,** 553, 565. Works: *Power: A New Social Analysis,* 408; *Principia Mathematica,* 462, 463; *Principles of Mathematics,* 462; *The Problems of Philosophy,* 462; *Why I am Not a Christian,* 462

Russell, George. *See* AE

Russian literature, 11, 13, 53, 287, 344; novels, 10; poetry, xvii. *See also* names of specific authors

Rustaveli, Shota, "The Men in the Panther's Skin," 492

Ruth, Babe, **463–64;** *The Babe Ruth Book of Baseball,* 464

Rutherford, Ernest, 58

Sabatier, Auguste, *La philosophie de la religion fondee sur la psychologie et l'historie,* 427

Sabato, Ernesto, 63

Sacco and Vanzetti case, 480

Sachs, Hans, 308

Sade, Marquis de, 76, 86, 418

Safarim, Mendele Mokher, 358

Said, Edward, 209, **465–67.** Works: *Culture and Imperialism,* 465; *Orientalism,* 465

Saint-Exupery, Antoine de, *The Little Prince*, 138, 540

Saint-Simon, Louis de Rouvroy, duc de, 51, 125, 394, 405; *Le catéchisme des industriels*, 367

Saki, 117

Salas, Mariano Picon, 448

Salazar Bondy, Sebastián, 325

Salinas, Pedro, 264

Salinger, J. D., 382, 399, 532; *The Catcher in the Rye*, 394

Sallust, 125, 548

Salmon, André, 428

Salvemini, Gaetano, 215

Samiou, Eleni, 285

Sanctis, Francesco De, 118, 215

Sand, George, 342

Sandburg, Carl, 64, 238, 242, 464, **467–68**, 483, 499. Works: *Abraham Lincoln*, 138, 524; *Chicago Poems*, 467; *Cornhuskers*, 467; *Reckless Ecstasy*, 467; *Smoke and Steel*, 467

Sanders, Betty, 338

San Francisco Examiner, 238

Sanger, Margaret, xvi, **468–69**, 500

Sanger, William, 468

Sanguineti, Edoardo, 154

San Secondo, Pier Rosso de, 431

Santayana, George, 324, **469–71**. Works: *Dominations and Powers*, 470; "The Genteel Tradition in American Philosophy," 470; *The Last Puritan*, 470; *Persons and Places*, 470; *Scepticism and Animal Faith*, 470; *Three Philosophical Poets*, 470

Sapir, Edward, *Language: An Introduction to the Study of Speech*, 356

Sappho, 119, 434

Saramago, José, 63

Sargent, John Singer, 92

Saroyan, William, 399

Sarrain, Albert, 125

Sartiliot, Claudette, 131

Sartre, Jean-Paul, 35, 39, 89, 90, 165–66, 170, 223, 258, 325, 445, **471–72**, 504, 523, 569. Works: *Anti-Semite and Jew*, 165; *Being and Nothingness*, 165, 471; *Le diable et le bon die*, 472; *Les Mains sales*,

472; *Le Mouches*, 472; *Nausea*, 471; *No Exit*, 472, 555; *Orphée noir*, 165; *La putain respectueuse*, 472; *What is Literature*, 472; *The Words*, 471

Sarwey, Otto von, *Allgemeines Verwaltungsrecht*, 563

Sassoon, Siegfried, 310

Satie, Eric, 67

Satta, Sebastiano, 215

Saturday Evening Post, 171, 453, 482

Saturday Review of Literature, 484

Saussure, Ferdinand de, 30, 35, 130, 154, 203, 318

Savonarola, 3

Sayle, Charles, 500

Scandinavian literature, 13. *See also names of specific authors*

Sceab, Mohammed, 531

Schaffer, Aaron, 115

Schauwecker, Franz, *Ringen an der Somme*, 444

Scheler, Max, 62, 240, 269

Schell, Hermann, 239

Schelling, Friedrich Wilhelm Joseph von, 17, 50, 118, 239, 492, 514, 565

Schickele, Rene, 20

Schiller, Friedrich, 5, 74, 99, 147, 308, 332, 344, 345, 498, 528. Works: *The Brigand*, 446; *Kabale und Liebe*, 205

Schlatter, Adolf, 33, 85

Schlegel, Friedrich von, 30

Schleiermacher, Friederich, 33, 514, 548

Schlick, Moritz, 93, 433

Schlieffen, Alfred von, 244

Schlier, Heinrich, 85

Schmarsow, August, 91

Schmid, Christoph von, 118

Schmidt, Erhard, 387

Schmidt, Heinrich, 548

Schmidt, Konrad, 17

Schmitz, Sybille, 167

Schmoller, Gustav, 505

Schneider, Arthur, 239

Schnitzler, Arthur, 248

Schoenerer, Georg Ritter von, 247

Schönberg, Arnold, 433, 437, **472–74;** *The Manual of Harmony*, 473

Schopenhauer, Arthur, 41, 51, 147, 243, 276, 308, 309, 312, 344, 379, 418, 444, 476, 548,

565. Works: *Philosophie der Kunst*, 378; *World as Will and Representation*, 106, 200, 243, 344, 482

Schreiner, Olive, 469

Schrodinger, Erwin, 361

Schubert, Franz, 196, 264

Schubert-Doldern, Richard von, 93

Schultz, Henry, *The Theory and Measurement of Demand*, 181

Schuman, Robert, **474–75**

Schumpeter, Joseph A., *Capitalism, Socialism and Democracy*, 43, 522

Schuppe, Wilhelm, 93

Schwartz, Stephen, 54

Schweitzer, Albert, 228

Scopes monkey trial, 81

Scott, Frank Reginald, 522

Scott, Ridley, 307

Scott, Robert F., 536–37

Scott, Walter, xvii, 7, 13, 24, 99, 118, 125, 139, 171, 237, 267, 288, 321, 326, 337, 340, 440, 456, 548, 571. Works: *Ivanhoe*, 1, 32, 171, 252, 545; *Guy Mannering*, 32; *Rob Roy*, 32

Scribner's Magazine, 171

Second Vatican Council, 224, 266, 267, 268, 420

Seeberg, Reinhold, 61

Seeger, Alan, "I Have a Rendezvous with Death," 289

Seerafimovich, Alexander, 477

Seghers, Anna, 332

Seldes, George, 383

Selznick, David O., 245

Semple, Robert, 355

Sénancour, Etienne, 529

Seneca, 353; *Medea*, 529

Senghor, Léopold, 101

Sennett, Mack, 92

Serafimovich, Aleksandr, *The Iron Flood*, 11

Serbian literature, 13

Serer, Calvo, *The New Democracies*, 275

Serling, Rod, 489

Sertillanges, Antonin, *The Intellectual Life*, 420

Service, Robert W., 323

Seton, Ernest Thompson, 24

Seuss, Dr., **475–76**. Works: *And to Think That I Saw It on Mulberry Street*, 475; *The Cat in the Hat*, 475; *Green Eggs* *and Ham*, 475; *Horton Hatches an Egg*, 475; *How the Grinch Stole Christmas*, 475; *The Lorax*, 476

Sevigne, Marie de, 556

Sewanee Review, 134

Sextus Empiricus, 239

Sextus Propertius, 434

Sfetcu, Paul, 198

Shakespeare, William, 8, 14, 32, 37, 49, 53, 65, 68, 80, 99, 105, 114, 132, 146, 147, 158, 160, 168, 175, 182, 219, 230, 238, 262, 264, 273, 289, 308, 326, 329, 332, 338, 342, 352, 353, 372, 381, 382, 394, 399, 407, 413, 418, 456, 458, 466, 476, 481, 483, 490, 495, 496, 498, 499, 500, 513, 518, 524, 560. Works: *Hamlet*, 38, 128, 144, 200, 231, 418, 419, 478, 481, 532, 551; *Henry V*, 563; *Julius Caesar*, 342, 436, 551; *King Lear*, 354, 429, 478; *Macbeth*, 478, 551; *Merchant of Venice*, 371, 537; *Merry Wives of Windsor*, 419; *A Midsummer Night's Dream*, 77; *Othello*, 429, 449; *Romeo and Juliet*, 54, 238, 395, 419, 436; *The Taming of the Shrew*, 136; *The Tempest*, 536; *Twelfth Night*, 152

Shaw, George Bernard, 38, 61, 65, 80, 91, 114, 275, 310, 359, 399, 407, 416, 467, 499, 501, 529, 562. Works: *Back to Methuselah*, 375; *Caesar and Cleopatra*, 375; *Major Barbara*, 561; *The Perfect Wagnerite*, 375; *You Never Can Tell*, 117

Sheeler, Charles, 560

Sheldon, Charles, *In His Steps*, 81

Shelley, Mary, *Frankenstein*, 91

Shelley, Percy Bysshe, 8, 169, 264, 332, 357, 407, 416, 481, 490, 536, 537, 553

Sheridan, Charles Brinsley, 38

Sherrington, Charles Scott, *Integrative Action of the Nervous System*, 484

Sherwood, Robert E., 52

Shestov, Lev, 79

Shils, Edward, 43

Shipiro, Karl, 364

Shklovskii, Viktor, 477

Sholokhov, Mikhail, **476–77.** Works: *And Quiet Flows the Don*, 477; *Tales of the Don*, 477; *Virgin Soil Upturned*, 477

Shonoagon, Sei, *Pillow Book*, 305

Shorthouse, J. H., *Jean Inglesant*, 546

Shostakovich, Dmitri, **478**

Show, 497

Showve, Fredegond, 537

Shure, Edward, *Les Grand Inites*, 313

Sibelius, Jan, 196

Sienkiewicz, Henryk, 414, 541. Works: *The Deluge*, 541; *Pan Wolodyjowski*, 541; *Quo Vadis*, 436; *Teutonic Knights*, 541; *With Fire and Sword*, 541

Silone, Ignazio, 301, **479–80.** Works: *Bread and Wine*, 123, 479; *Emergency Exit*, 479; *Fontamara*, 479; *Severina*, 479; *The Story of a Humble Christian*, 479

Silone, Romolo, 479

Silsbee, Joseph Lyman, 567

Simenon, Georges, 523

Simiand, François, 72, 146

Simmel, Georg, 82, 240, 332, 405

Simmons, Roscoe Conkling, 411

Simon (Paul) and Garfunkle (Art), "Mrs. Robinson," 138

Simonds, Frank, 238

Simonofsky, Elsie, 108

Simpson, Albert, 355

Sinbad, 422

Sinclair, Upton, 69, 161, 383, 469, **480–81.** Works: *The Journal of Arthur Stirling*, 480; *The Jungle*, 123, 480, 547; *Manassas*, 480

Sing, Jaydew, 341

Singer, Isaac Bashevis, **482–83.** Works: *Book of the Covenant*, 482; *Fearsome Inn*, 482; *Love and Exile*, 482; *The Moskati*, 482; *Zlateh the Goat*, 482

Singer, Israel Joshua, 482

Singh, Sundar, 228

Siqueiros, David, 448

Sir Gawain and the Green Knight, 517

Sirk, Douglas, 167

Sitwell, Edith, 327

Siwertz, Siegfried, 49

Sjöberg, Leif, 229

Sjostrom, Victor, 49

Skelton, John, 537

Skinner, B. F., **483–84.** Works: *The Behavior of Organisms*, 484; *The Technology of Teaching*, 483; *Walden Two*, 484

Skinner, Francis, 565

Slattery, Mary Grace, 362

Slee, J. Noah, 468

Sloane, Alfred P., *My Years with General Motors*, 195

Slonim, Véra, 381

Słowacki, Juliusz, 210, 221. Works: *Beniowski*, 269; *King-Spirit*, 269; *Samuel Zborowski*, 269

Slutsky, Boris, 79

Smart Set, 171

Smilansky, Yizhar, *The Days of Ziklag*, 48

Smith, Adam, 110, 156, 223, 235, 327

Smith, Clark Ashton, 65

Smith, Edwin A., 475

Smith, Justin, *The Troubadors at Home*, 434

Smith, Red, 137

Smith Academy Record, 163

Smollett, Tobias, 142, 466

Snow, Edgar, 341

Snyder, Gary, 202

Snyder, Larry, 410

Socrates, 3, 131, 284, 459

Soden, Hans von, 85

Söderblom, Nathan, 228

Söderblom, Yvonne, 228

Sollers, Philippe, 35

Sollertinskii, Ivan Ivanovich, 30

Solomon, 227

Solomon, Minnie Ruth, 410

Solomons, Leon, "Normal Motor Automatism," 494

Soloviev, Vladimir, 282, 363

Solzhenitsyn, Alexandr, 61, 382, **484–86.** Works: *August 1914*, 485; *Cancer Ward*, 485; *The First Circle*, 485; *Gulag Archipelago*, 485; *One Day in the Life of Ivan Denisovich*, 484; *The Red Wheel*, 485

Sombart, Werner, *Sozialismus und soziale Bewgung*, 506

Song of Igor's Campaign, 381, 477

Sonnemann, Emmy, 211

Sophocles. 125, 147, 236, 291, 299. Works: *Ajax*, 25; *Oedipus Rex*, 191, 428

Sorel, Georges, 44, 118, 332, 378, 379

Soseki, Natsume, 305

Soupault, Philippe, 75, 76, 121, 292, 365

Southern, Terry, 445. Works: *Candy*, 38; *The Magic Christian*, 38

Southern folktales, 36

South Wales Evening Post, 512

Soutine, Chaim, 102

Souvestre, Emil, 456

Souvestre, Marie, 502

Soyinka, Wole, 209, **486–87**. Works: *Kongi's Harvest*, 487; *The Lion and the Jewel*, 487; *The Open Sore of a Continent*, 486; *A Play of Giants*, 487

Spanish drama, 234

Spark (Romania), 98

Spark, Muriel, 398

Spaventa, Bertrando, 118

Spaventa, Silvio, 118

Spectator, 216, 502

Speer, Albert, **487–89**. Works: *Inside the Third Reich*, 488; *Spandau*, 488

Spelman, Cettie, 452

Spencer, Herbert, 50, 118, 300, 360, 427, 529, 546–47; *Principles of Philosophy*, 560

Spender, Stephen, 135, 301

Spengler, Oswald, 361, 405, 544, 565; *Decline of the West*, 220, 287, 292, 361, 375

Spenser, Edmund, *Faerie Queen*, 318

Spiegel, 167

Spielberg, Steven, **489–90**

Spielhagen, Friedrich, *Angela*, 506

Spillane, Mickey, 138

Spinks, Leon, 8

Spinoza, 45, 48, 50, 93, 121, 332, 470, 476, 482, 548, 550. Works: *Ethics*, 441, 482; *Tractatus Theologico-Politicus*, 28

Spock, Benjamin, **490–91**. Works: *Baby and Child Care*, 491; *Decent and Indecent*, 490, 491; *Emotion and Conduct in Adolescence*, 491

Sraffa, Piero, 216, 565

Stafford, Jean, 398

Staiger, Emil, 147

Stalin, Josef, xvii, 64, 75, 83, 144, 161, 207, 223, 252, 262, 295, 340, 383, 436, 437, 471, 477, 478, 484, 485, **492–93**, 520, 527. Works: *Foundations of Leninism*, 252; "Marxism and the National Question," 492; *The National and Colonial Question*, 569; "Workingwomen and Peasantwomen Remember and Carry Out Lenin's Behests," 384

Stanislavsky, Konstantin, 222

Stanley, Thomas J. and William Danko, *The Millionaire Next Door*, 138

Stanton, Elizabeth Cady, 416, 469

Starkey, Marion, *The Devil in Massachusetts*, 362

Starr, Ellen Gates, 3

Starr, Ringo, 37–38

Steffens, Lincoln, 383

Steichen, Edward, **493–94**

Stein, Edith, 398

Stein, Gertrude, 162, 169, 171, 242, 399, **494–95**, 499, 556. Works: *The Autobiography of Alice B. Toklas*, 494–95; *The Making of Americans*, 494; "Normal Motor Automatism," 494; *Picasso*, 495; *Things as They Are*, 494; *Three Lives*, 494; *Wars I Have Seen*, 494; *Yes is For a Very Young Man*, 495

Steinbeck, John, 65, 116, 148, 179, **495–97**. Works: *The Acts of King Arthur*, 496; *Cannery Row*, 496; *Cup of Gold*, 496; *East of Eden*, 496; *Grapes of Wrath*, 174, 341, 496; *In Dubious Battle*, 496; *Lifeboat*, 245; *The Sea of Cortez*, 496; *To a God Unknown*, 496; *Tortilla Flat*, 496; *The Winter of Our Discontent*, 496

Steinem, Gloria, **497–98**. Works: "I Was a Playboy Bunny," 497; *Marilyn: Norma Jeane*, 497; *Moving Beyond Words*, 497; *Outrageous Acts and Everyday Rebellions*, 497; *Revolution From Within*, 497

Steinem, Pauline, 497

Steiner, Rudolf, 280, 282

Stendhal, 125, 301, 332, 399, 444, 519. Works: *The Charterhouse of Parma*, 142, 200–201; *The Red and the Black*, 375

Stephen, Leslie, 566

Stephens, James, 114, 399, 496

Stern, Isaac, 53

Sternberg, Josef von, 136, 342

Sterne, Laurence, 353, 466; *Tristram Shandy*, 461

Stevens, Wallace, 24, 470, 560

Stevenson, Robert Louis, 7, 68, 94, 219, 327, 537; *Treasure Island*, 1, 139, 490, 551

Stewart, John Alexander, 328

Stieglitz, Alfred, 401, 498–99

Stifter, Adalbert, *Studien*, 506

Stirner, Max, 332, 379

St. Nicholas, 94, 171, 329

Stöcker, Adolf, 390

Stockham, Alice, 469

Stockhausen, Karlheinz, 473

Stoica, Gheorghe, 198

Stokes, Rose Pastor, 469

Stopes, Henry, 500

Stopes, Marie, 469, **499–501**

Stoppard, Tom, 79, 167, **501**. Works: *The Invention of Love*, 501; *The Real Inspector Hound*, 501; *Rosencrantz and Guildenstern are Dead*, 501

Storm, Theodor, 5, 344

Stowe, Harriet Beecher, *Uncle Tom's Cabin*, 315, 416, 498

Strachey, Dorothy, 502

Strachey, Jane, 502

Strachey, John, 511; *The Coming Struggle for Power*, 64

Strachey, Lytton, 294, 463, **501–3**, 544. Works: *Books and Characters*, 502; *Characters and Commentaries*, 502; *Elizabeth and Essex*, 502; *Eminent Victorians*, 502; *Landmarks in French Literature*, 502; *Portraits and Miniatures*, 502; *Queen Victoria*, 476, 502; *The Son of Heaven*, 502

Strachey, Pernel, 502

Strachey, Richard, 502

Strachey, St. Loe, 502

Strand, 408

Stratemeyer, Edward, *Tom Swift* series, 171

Strauss, David Friedrich, 55, 548

Strauss, Richard, 248

Stravinsky, Igor, 196, 391, 473, **503–5**
Stresemann, Gustav, 70, **505–6**
Strich, Fritz, 147
Strindberg, August, 17, 80, 147, 279, 280, 377, 482, 559. Works: *The Dream Play*, 49; *Lucky Per's Travels*, 49; *Married*, 402; *Master Olof*, 49; *Miss Julie*, 167; *The People of Hemsö*, 49; *Black Banners*, 49; *The Red Room*, 49; *To Damascus*, 49
Strong, Josiah. Works: *Our Country*, 81; *The Twentieth Century City*, 81
Struve, Petr, 314
Stur, L'udovit, 144
Suarez, Francisco, 239, 328
Sue, Eugene, *The Wandering Jew*, 348
Sufism, 222, 282
Sullivan, A. M., 114, 132
Sullivan, Arthur, 560
Sullivan, Ed, 394, 451
Sullivan, Louis Henri, 423
Sullivan, Louis, 567, 568
Sullivan, Mark, 238
Sullivan, T. D., 114
Sully, James, 50
Sumner, William Graham, 360
Sunday, Billy, **506–7**. Works: "Get on the Water Wagon," 507; *Love Stories of the Bible*, 507
Sunday Express, 7
Sun-tzu, 195
Superveille, Jules, 135
Suttner, Bertha von, 433
Suzuki, D. T., *Essais sur le Bouddhisme Zen*, 71
Swedenborg, Emanuel, 276, 363, 473, 500
Swift, Jonathan, 68, 132, 353, 399, 461; *Gulliver's Travels*, 407, 476
Swinburne, Algernon, 68, 80, 114, 199, 332
Sybel, Heinrich von, 548
Sydney-Turner, Saxon, 294
Synge, J. M. 399, 537
Szabelski, Boleslaw, 209
Szego, Gabriel, 387
Szilard, Leo, 387

Tacitus, 125, 159
Taggard, Genevieve, 116

Tagore, Rabindranath, 200, 228; *The Crescent Moon*, 265
Taine, Hippolyte, 50, 118; *History of English Literature*, 561
Talmud, 47, 53, 109, 280, 482, 555
Tanak (Old Testament), 48, 54, 66, 106, 128, 169, 182, 193, 269, 363, 483, 555, 548. Books and divisions of *Tanak*: Daniel, 66; Ezekial, 355; Isaiah, 3; Job, 193, 316; Psalms, 123, 536; Song of Songs, 537; Ten Words (Ten Commandments), 28, 81; *Torah*, 102, 297, 482
Tannenbaum, Frank, 469
Tanner, Alain, 523
Tannéry, Jules, 50
Taoism, 285
Tao Te Ching, 38, 496
Tarbell, Ida, 383; *The History of the Standard Oil Company*, 453
Tarde, Gabriel de, 427
Tardini, Domenico, 420
Tarkington, Booth, *The Magnificent Ambersons*, 551
Tarkovsky, Andrei, xvii, **509–10**; *Sculpting in Time*, 509
Tarsk, Alfred, 93, 433
Taruc, Louis, *Born of the People*, 341
Tasso, 267
Tate, Allen, 398
Tatlin, Vladimir, 283
Tavernier, Bertrand, 523
Taylor, Deems, 52
Taylor, Jeremy. Works: *Holy Dying*, 169; *Holy Living*, 169
Taylor, Paul, 394
Taylor, Peter, 398
Tchaikovsky, Peter, 395
Teller, Edward, 58, 387
Tennyson, Alfred, Lord, 68, 163, 537. Works: *Enoch Arden*, 219; *Idylls of the King*, 310
Terence, *The Andria*, 556
Teresa, Mother (Agnes Gonxja Bojaxhiu), **59–60**
Teresa of Avila, 123, 229
Tertullian, Quintus Septimius Florens, 62
Tessenow, Heinrich, 487
Tetmajer, Kazimierz, 210
Thackeray, Bal, 461

Thackeray, William Makepeace, 99, 128, 152, 237–38, 252, 267, 359, 399, 456. Works: *Vanity Fair*, 142, 466, 492
Thalberg, Irving, 171
Thatcher, Denis, 511
Thatcher, Margaret, 415, **510–12**
Theodore of Mopsuestia, 84
Theotocopoulous, Domenicos, (El Greco), 5
Thérèse of Lisieux, 59, 60, 123; *Story of a Soul*, 59
Thibon, Gustave, 549
Thienemann, Marie, 231
Thomas, David John, 512
Thomas, Dylan, 24, 96, 135, 504, **512–14**. Works: "And Death Shall Have No Dominion," 512; "Fern Hill," 38; *Portrait of the Artist as a Young Dog*, 513; *Vision and Prayer*, 513
Thompson, Francis, 265; *The Hound of Heaven*, 142
Thompson, J. J., 58
Thompson, Robert, 393
Thom's Dublin Directory, 273
Thoreau, Henry David, 119, 173, 292, 297, 323, 493, 500, 568. Works: *Walden*, 4, 182, 199, 493
Thorndike, Edward, *Studies in the Psychology of Language*, 484
Thousand and One Nights, 10, 103, 200, 249, 461; *Sinbad*, 422
Thucydides, 125, 284, 525
Thurber, James, 532
Tieck, Ludwig, 242, 430, 447
Tillich, Paul, 297, 329, 398, 514–15. Works: *My Search for Absolutes*, 515; *Systematic Theology*, 515
Time, 139, 297, 329, 436
Times (London), 216, 238, 511
Time & Tide, 407
Tirpitz, Admiral, 55
Tirpitz, Alfred von, *Politische Dokumente*, 558
Tishansky, Dmitri, 476
Tito, Josip Broz, 13, 140, **515–16**. Works: *National Question*, 516; *Non-Alignment*, 516; *Self-Management*, 516

Tkachëv, Pëtr, 315

Tocqueville, Alexis de, 146, 332, 398, 459, 521, 563; *Democracy in America*, 287

Todd, John, *Index Rerum*, 68

Toennies, Ferdinand, 82, 332

Togliatti, Palmiro, 194, 215; *Jalta memorandum*, 254

Toklas, Alice B., 494

Tolkein, J. R. R., xvi, **517–18.** Works: "Beowulf: The Monster and the Critics," 517; *The Hobbit*, 319, 517; *Lord of the Rings*, 38, 319, 517; *Sir Gawain and the Green Knight*, 517; *The Two Towers*, 490

Toller, Ernst, *Masse Mensch*, 69

Tolstoy, Alexei, 492

Tolstoy, Lev, 4, 81, 109, 123, 169, 219, 243, 299, 315, 332, 337, 358, 362, 363, 381, 391, 399, 414, 476, 479, 485, 498, 509, 518, 520, 529, 565. Works: *Anna Karenina*, 92, 309, 352, 482; *The Cossacks*, 477; *Grammar*, 8; *The Kingdom of God is Within You*, 187; *War and Peace*, 64, 96, 138, 341, 392, 408, 482, 485

Tolstoy, Sophie, 39

Tomasi, Giuseppe, **518–19;** *The Leopard*, 518

Tomson, Aleksandr Ivanovich, 30

Tom Swift stories (Stratemeyer), 171, 213

Toniolo, Giuseppe, 193

Torah, 102, 297, 482

Toronto Star, 241

Torres Bodet, Jaime, 22

Torry, H. A. P., 133

Tostand, Edmond de, 521

Toynbee, Arnold, 329; *Mankind and Mother Earth*, 540; *A Study of History*, 329

Toynbee Hall, 3, 23

Trakl, Georg, 147, 565

Traven, B., 69

Treitschke, Heinrich von, 548, 557

Tresca, Carlo, 469

Tresmontant, Claude, 398

Trevelyan, G. M., 105, 111, *Social History of England*, 22

Tribune, 407

Trilling, Lionel, 43, 201

Trimble, David, 415

Tristan, Flora, 368

Trollope, Anthony, 327, 337, 399. Works: *Barchester Towers*, 186; *The Last Chronicle of Barset*, 186; *The Warden*, 186

Tropiques, 101

Trotsky, Leon, 76, 101, 109, 166, 261, 281, 340, 448, 492, **519–21.** Works: *History of the Russian Revolution*, 262; *My Life*, 520

Trudeau, Pierre, **521–22.** Works: *Against the Current*, 522; *Approaches to Politics*, 522; *Federalism and the French Canadians*, 522

Truffaut, François, 203, 307, **523–24**

Truman, Harry S., 159, 213, 253, 336, 348, **524–25.** Works: *Memoirs*, 524; *Years of Trial and Hope*, 524

Trungpa, Chogyam, 202

Tsatsos, K., 284

Tsvetaeva, Marina, 78, 79

Tuchman, Barbara, *The Guns of August*, 291

Turgenev, Ivan, 109, 208, 243, 309, 315, 344, 399, 413, 498. Works: *Fathers and Sons*, 462; "Old Portraits," 400; *The Rendezvous*, 305; *Sportsman's Sketches*, 182, 242, 400

Turing, Alan, 387

Turner, Desmond, 294

Turner, Henry McNeal, 376

Tuwim, Julian, 210

Twain, Mark (Samuel Clemens), 11, 66, 105, 106, 109, 115, 139, 169, 219, 318, 358, 359, 452, 490, 498. Works: *A Connecticut Yankee in King Arthur's Court*, 160; *Huckleberry Finn*, 32, 99, 241, 332, 454; *Life on the Mississippi*, 312; *Tom Sawyer*, 32, 332, 442, 454

Tynan, Kenneth, 136, 501

Tyuchev, Fyodor, 476

Tzara, Tristan, 21, 67, 258, 365, 428

Uexkull, Von, 405

Ugarte, Augusto Pinochet, 10

Ulbricht, Walter, 251, **527–28**

Unamuno, Miguel de, 188, 264, 405, **528–31**, 532. Works: *Abel Sánchez*, 530; *La agonía del Critianismo*, 530; *Del sentimiento trágico de la vida en los hombres y en los publos*, 530; *Diario Intimo*, 529; *En torno al casticismo*, 529; *Niebla*, 530; *Paz en la Guerra*, 529; *La vida de don Quijote y Sancho*, 529

Ungaretti, Giuseppe, 153, 418, **531–32;** "The Buried Port," 531

United Nations, 10

Universal Declaration of Human Rights, 456

Universal Negro Improvement and Conservation Association, 192

Universal Negro Improvement Association, 262, 376

Upanishads, 243, 422, 550

Updike, John, 382, **532–33.** Works: *The Centaur*, 532; *Gertrude and Claudius*, 532; *In the Beauty of the Lillies*, 532; *Pigeon Feathers*, 532; *Rabbit, Run*, 532; Rabbit tetralogy, 532

Upham, Charles W., *Salem Witchcraft*, 362–63

Urban, Heinrich, 413

USA Today, 195

Uspensky, Gleb, 315

Utrillo, Miguel, 428

Valentin, Karl, 74

Valéry, Paul, 76, 113, 121, 264, 354, **535–36.** Works: *Album des vers anciens*, 536; *L'Âme et la danse*, 536; *Charmes*, 536; "Cimetière marin," 536; *The Esthetic Invention*, 128; *Eupalinos*, 536; *Introduction à la méthode de Léonard de Vinci*, 535; *La Jeune Parque*, 536; *Regards sur le monde actuel*, 371, 536; *Une soirée avec Monsieur Teste*, 536

Vallejo, Cesar, 224

Vallery-Radot, René, *La vie de Pasteur*, 146

Vallier, Max, 73

Van Buren, Martin, *Autobiography*, 434

Vanderpoel, John, 401

Van Doren, Mark, 201

Van Gogh, Vincent, 17, 305

Vanguardia, 275

Vanity Fair, 561

Van Vechten, Carl, 261, 494, 499
Varela y Morales, Félix, 98
Varharen, Emile, 142
Varnhagen, Rahel, 17
Varona, Enrique José, 98
Varro, 353
Vasconcelos, José, 281, 448; *Prometeo Vencendor,* 22
Vassar, John, 507
Vaughan, Henry, 513
Vauvenargues, Marquis de, 125
Veblen, Oswald, 387
Veblen, Thorstein, 43, 179, 186; *Theory of the Leisure Class,* 142
Vega, Lope Felix de, 189, 434
Verdi, Giuseppe, 379
Verga, Giovanni, 431, 479; *Jeli il pastore,* 430
Verlaine, Paul, 63, 125, 153, 188, 248, 250, 264, 332, 381, 428, 482, 493, 537. Works: *La lune blanche,* 504; *Un Grand sommeil,* 504
Verne, Jules, 13, 66, 125, 138, 308, 352, 381, 405, 490. Works: *From the Earth to the Moon,* 73, 436; *20,000 Leagues Under the Sea,* 139
Vico, Giambattista, 41; *The New Science,* 118, 273
Victorian novelists, 329
Vigny, Alfred, Comte de, 438
Vigo, Jean, 523
Villa, Pancho, 223
Villiers de L'Isle Adam, *L'Ève future,* 145, 308
Villon, François, 74, 434
Viner, Jacob, 181
Vipper, R., *History of the Roman Empire,* 492
Virgil, 8, 548; *Aeneid,* 99
Visconti, Luchino, *The Damned,* 167
Vivien, Renee, 39
Vögelin, Eric, 233, 398
Vogue, 497
Vollmer, Joan, 87
Voltaire, 168, 200, 219, 342, 355, 523, 562. Works: *Candide,* 54, 188, 299; *Lettres philosophiques,* 368; *Philosophical Dictionary,* 121, 124
Voronca, Ilarie, 67
Vorster, Balthazar, 342
Vuelta, 422

Wade, Evelyn Willoughby, 553
Waggerl, Karl-Heinrich, 540
Wagner, Richard, 86, 162, 246, 273, 344, 473, 560, 565
Wahl, Gustave, 555
Waismann, Friedrich, 93
Wajda, Andrzej, 250
Walcott, Derek, 486
Waldheim, Kurt, **539–40;** *The Challenge of Peace,* 539
Wałesa, Lech, **540–41**
Walker, Alice, 498
Walker, Francis Amasa, 563
Wallace, Elizabeth, 524
Wallace, George, **542–43**
Wallace, Lewis, *Ben Hur,* 506
Wallace, Lurleen, 542
Wall Street Journal, 195
Walpole, Horace, 68
Walsh, Christy, 464
Walsh, Raoul, 167, 174
Walter, Bruno, 53, 478, 564
Walters, Alan, 512
Ward, James, 51
Ward, Mrs. Humphry, 255
Warren, Robert Penn, 135, 398
Washington, Booker T., 411; *Up from Slavery,* 192
Washington, George, 252, 525
Washington Post, 271, 442
Wasson, Robert, 312
Watkins, Vernon, 513
Watson, James, 484
Watson, John B., *Psychological Care of Infant and Child,* 491
Watts, Alan, 312
Waugh, Evelyn, 24, 186, 217, 398, 445, **543–45.** Works: *Black Mischief,* 543; *Brideshead Revisited,* 543; *Decline and Fall,* 543; *A Handful of Dust,* 543, 544; *The Loved One,* 543, 544; *Men at Arms,* 543; *Officers and Gentlemen,* 543; *The Ordeal of Gilbert Pinfold,* 543; *Put Out More Flags,* 543; *Saint Helena,* 543; *Scoop,* 186, 543, 544; *Unconditional Surrender,* 543; *Vile Bodies,* 543
Wayne, John, **545–46**
Weaver, Harriet Shaw, 272
Webb, Beatrice, 4, 23, 80, **546–47;** *Soviet Communism,* 449
Webb, Constance, 261
Webb, Phyllis, 24

Webb, Sidney, 4, 23, 80, 546, 54; *Soviet Communism,* 449
Weber, Max, 17, 82, 84, 330, 332, 433, **547–49;** *The Protestant Ethic and the Spirit of Capitalism,* 43, 548
Webern, Anton, 473
Webster, John, 80
Webster's English Dictionary, 338
Wedekind, Frank, 74, 80
Weekley, Frieda, 309
Weil, Anne Mendelssohn, 17
Weil, Simone, 123, 364, 398, **549–50.** Works: *Attente de Dieu,* 479; *Lettre aux* Cahiers du sud *sur les responsabilités de la littérature,* 549; *Quelques réflexions autour de la notion de valeur,* 549
Weill, Kurt, *The Threepenny Opera,* 49, 75
Weinheber, Josef, 540
Weininger, Otto, *Sex and Character,* 564
Weir, Lorraine, 131
Weiss, Johannes, 84
Welch, Denton, 88
Welles, Orson, 307, **550–51;** *Citizen Kane,* 459, 550
Wells, H. G., 4, 38, 66, 80, 114, 310, 319, 321, 381, 385, 490. Works: *Brief History, of the World,* 223; *The Country of the Blind,* 407; *The History of Mr. Polly,* 321; *Island of Dr. Moreau,* 91; *The Outline of History,* 158; *Tono-Bungay,* 321; *War of the Worlds,* 73, 551
Welty, Eudora, 65, 398
Werfel, Franz, 343, 444
Wertham, Frederic, *Dark Legend,* 5l69
Wertheimer, Max, 93, 350, 427. Works: "Being and Doing," 350; "Some Problems in the Theory of Ethics," 351; "A Story of Three Days," 351
Wesley, John, 355
West, Jessamyn, 65
West, Mae, 217
West, Nathanael, 171, 445
West, Richard, 516
Western novels, 320, 327, 348, 545
Westminster Shorter Catechism, 213
Weyl, Hermann, 387

Whalen, Philip, 202, 293
Wharton, Edith, 66, 171, **552–53.** Works: *The Age of Innocence*, 552; *A Backward Glance*, 552; *The Custom of the Country*, 552; *Ethan Frome*, 552; *The House of Mirth*, 552; *Summer*, 552; *The Writing of Fiction*, 552
White, Andrew D., 253
White, E. B., 532
White, Victor, 398
Whitefield, George, 415
Whitehead, Alfred North, 330, 495, **553–54.** Works: *Adventures in Ideas*, 554; *The Aims of Education*, 553; *The Concept of Nature*, 553; *An Enquiry Concerning the Principles of Natural Knowledge*, 553; *The Function of Reason*, 554; *Introduction to Mathematics*, 553; *Modes of Thought*, 554; *The Organization of Thought*, 553; *Principia Mathematica*, 462, 463, 553; *The Principles of Relativity*, 553; *Process and Reality*, 554; *Religion in the Making*, 554; *Science and the Modern World*, 553; *Symbolism*, 554
Whiteman, Paul, 196
Whitman, Walt, 13, 21, 63, 176, 200, 219, 309, 330, 363, 416, 422, 467, 468, 496, 530, 536, 537, 545, 560, 568. Works: *I Hear America Singing*, 115; *Leaves of Grass*, 138, 199, 202, 462, 499
Wiazemsky, Anne, 203
Wichern, Johann, 390
Wieland, Christoph, 147, 548
Wien, Max, 93
Wiener, Charles, 99
Wiese, Benno Georg Leopold von, 17
Wiesel, Eli, **554–56.** Works: *All Rivers Run to the Sea*, 555; *Dawn*, 555; *Five Biblical Portraits*, 555; *The Jews of Silence*, 555; *Night*, 555; *One Generation After*, 555; *Souls of Fire*, 555
Wieser, Friedrich von, 234, 367
Wigner, Eugene Paul, 387
Wilbrandt, Adolf, von, 299
Wilde, Constance, 500

Wilde, Oscar, 38, 80, 117, 200, 301, 500, 501, 523. Works: *Aesthetic Manifesto*, 300; "Ballad of Reading Gaol," 114, 409; *De Profundis*, 188; *An Ideal Husband*, 429; *The Importance of Being Earnest*, 429; *The Picture of Dorian Gray*, 152, 300; *Salome*, 38; *The Soul of Man Under Socialism*, 300, 409–10
Wildenbruch, Ernst von, 558
Wilder, Billy, 129
Wilder, Thornton, 116, 147, 301, **556–57.** Works: *The Bridge of San Luis Rey*, 556; *The Cabala*, 556; *The Eighth Day*, 556; *Heaven's My Destination*, 556; *The Ides of March*, 556; *The Matchmaker*, 556; *Our Town*, 556; *The Skin of Our Teeth*, 556; *The Woman of Andros*, 556
Wilhelm I, 558
Wilhelm II (Germany), 55, **557–58**
Williams, Charles, 319
Williams, Eric, *Capitalism and Slavery*, 569
Williams, Franklin, 451
Williams, Ralph Vaughan, **536–38**
Williams, Raymond, *Culture and Society*, 466
Williams, Tennessee, 189, 398, 410, **558–59.** Works: *Cairo, Shanghai, Bombay*, 558; *Camino Real*, 38; *Cat on a Hot Tin Roof*, 559; *I Rise in Flame, Cried the Phoenix*, 559; *Orpheus Descending*, 559; *A Streetcar Named Desire*, 559; *Suddenly Last Summer*, 559; *Summer and Smoke*, 559; *Sweet Bird of Youth*, 559; *You Touched Me!*, 559
Williams, Ursula Vaughan, 537
Williams, William Carlos, 24, 202, **559–61.** Works: *Al Que Quiere!*, 560; *Kora in Hell*, 560; *Paterson*, 202; "The Red Wheelbarrow," 560; *Spring and All*, 560; "The Widow's Lament in Springtime," 560; "To Elsie," 560
Wilson, Edmund, 171, 499, **561–62.** Works: *Axel's Castle*, 561; *The Cold War and the*

Income Tax, 561; "A Modest Self-Tribute," 561; *The Scrolls from the Dead Sea*, 561
Wilson, Robert Anton, 312
Wilson, Thomas Woodrow, 3, 36, 37, 68, 81, 324, **562–64.** Works: *Congressional Government*, 563; *Edmund Burke*, 563; *A History of the American People*, 563; "History of Political Economy in the United States," 563; *Index Rerum*, 563; *The State*, 563
Winchell, Walter, 137
Windelband, Wilhelm, 239, 332
Windham, Donald, 558, 559
Winfield, Arthur M., *Rover Boys* books, 442
Wired, 353
Wisden, 22
Wister, Owen, *The Virginian*, 241
Witkiewicz, Stanislaw, 363
Wittgenstein, Ludwig, 93, 109, 433, 462, 495, **564–66.** Works: *Philosophical Investigations*, 565; *Tractatus Logico-Philosophicus*, 234, 565
Wojtyła, Karol. See John Paul II
Wolf, Immanuel, 28
Wolfe, Thomas, 65, 163, 171, 228, 292; *You Can't Go Home Again*, 171
Wolfsohn, Leopold, 115
Wolska, Maryla, 414
Woman's Home Companion, 95
Women's International League for Peace and Freedom, 3
Woodward, C. Vann, 543
Woolf, Leonard, 256, 294, 463, 502, 566
Woolf, Virginia, 63, 175, 191, 208, 256, 373, 399, 463, **566–67.** Works: *The Common Reader*, 567; *Jacob's Room*, 566; *Mrs. Dalloway*, 39–40, 179, 566; *Orlando*, 566; *A Room of One's Own*, 179, 566; *The Voyage Out*, 566; *To the Lighthouse*, 566; *The Waves*, 566; *The Years*, 566
Woollcott, Alexander, 52, 484
Wordsworth, William, 182, 236, 309, 476, 513, 553, 560. Works: *Prelude*, 235
Workingmen's Advocate, 206
Workshop, 422
World, 238

World's Greatest Literature, 483
Wright, Frank Lloyd, 360, 423, **567–68**
Wright, Harold Bell, *That Printer of Udell's*, 442
Wright, Philip Green, 467
Wright, Richard, xvii, 261, 449, **569–70**. Works: *Black Boy*, 39, 551; *Black Power*, 569; "The Man Who Lived Underground," 569; *Native Son*, 39, 569; *The Outsider*, 569; *Pagan Spain*, 569; *A Record of Childhood and Youth*, 39; *Savage Holiday*, 569; *Uncle Tom's Children*, 569
Wright, Wilbur and Orville, 195, **570–71**
Wright, Willard Huntington, *Modern Art*, 120
Wyatt, Thomas, 236
Wyspianski, Stanislaw, 210; *The Wedding*, 269
Wyss, Clothide Von, 500

Xenepol, A. D., 100
Xenophon, 125
Xiyouji: *The Journey to the West*, 423, *The Golden Lotus*, 423

Yamamoto, Kajiro, 304

Yavnieli, Samuel, *A Journey to Yemen and Its Jews*, 358
Yeats, Jack B., 41
Yeats, William Butler, 24, 114, 182, 199, 201, 236, 265, 370, 399, 434, 513, 522; *The Second Coming*, 1
Yesenin, Sergei, 492
Yogananda, Paramhansa, *Autobiography of a Yogi*, 435
Yorke, Henry. *See* Green, Henry
Young, Edward, *Night Thoughts*, 419
Young, Lester, 293
Yourcenar, Marguerite, *Memoires d'Hadrien*, 368
Youth's Companion, 152

Zachry, Caroline, 491
Zadonshchina, 477
Zambona, Jutta Ilse, 444
Zamyatin, Yevgeny, *We*, 408, 485
Zanussi, Krzysztof, 250
Zaslavskaya, Tatyana, 208
Zdziechowski, Marian, 363
Ze-ami, *Kadensho*, 305
Zedlitz-Trutzschler, Count R., 558
Zeising, Adolf, 313

Zelinskii, Fadei Frantsevich, 30
Zen Buddhism, 20
Zenchiku, *Taniko*, 75
Zeno, 50
Zermelo, Ernst, 387
Zilsel, Edgar, 93, 433
Zimmerman, Robert. *See* Dylan, Bob
Zimmermann, Otto, 239
Zinoviev, Grigori, 252, 492
Zinzendorf, Nikolaus von, 231
Zmigrodzka, Maria, 263
Zoellner, Karl, 276
Zola, Emile, 40, 46, 109, 113, 118, 332, 342, 438. Works: "J'accuse" letter, 113; *Germinal*, 295; *Madeleine Ferat*, 498; *L'Oeuvre*, 377; *Les Rougon-Macquart*, 368, 498
Zorilla, José, 189
Zschokke, Johann, 276
Zuckmayer, Carl, 136
Zunz, Leopold, 28
Zurn, Unica, *Man of Jasmine*, 167
Zweig, Stefan, 343; *Fear*, 459; *Schachnovelle*, 540; *Sternstunden der Menschheit*, 540; *Die Welt von Gestern*, 540
Zwingli, Huldreich, 240, 389

ABOUT THE
CONTRIBUTORS

Tiffany Aldrich is a Ph.D. candidate in the Department of English at the University of California, Davis. Her field of interest is nineteenth-century American literature, and she is writing a dissertation that interrogates tropes, symbols, and images of racial and cultural contact in that period.

Charles Allan is the Reference Librarian at the Charles C. Sherrod Library at East Tennessee State University in Johnson City, Tennessee. He has a masters degree in Latin American history from Tulane University.

Nancy Fix Anderson is a professor of history at Loyola University, New Orleans. She has published extensively on Victorian women and the family. Her most recent publication is "'Mother Besant' and Indian National Politics," *Journal of Imperial and Commonwealth History* (Fall 2002).

Eugene M. Avrutin is a doctoral candidate in history at the University of Michigan. He is currently completing a dissertation tentatively entitled "A Legible People: Population Politics and Jewish Accommodation in Tsarist Russia."

Philip Bader received his bachelor of arts degree in English from the University of Nebraska at Lincoln in 1996. He lives in Pasadena, California, where he works as a freelance writer and photo editor.

John D. Baird is professor of English at the University of Toronto. His interests lie in British literature of the eighteenth through the twentieth centuries, especially poetry and fiction. He is coeditor of *The Poems of William Cowper* (1980–95).

Linda A. Barnes received her Ph.D. in 1987 from Vanderbilt University with a dissertation on Flannery O'Connor. Since 1991 she has been at Austin Peay State

University in Clarksville, Tennessee, where she is now an associate professor. Most of her work has been in contemporary southern literature.

Harry McBrayer Bayne, associate professor of English at Brewton-Parker College in Mount Vernon, Georgia, teaches Southern, romantic, and Victorian literature. He is at work on a critical biography of musician and author Henry Bellamann.

Joseph E. Becker earned his Ph.D. in comparative literature at the University of Arkansas, where he specialized in European romanticism. He plans to expand his dissertation into a book and explore romantic myths and archetypes.

Bruce R. Berglund is assistant director of the Center for Russian and East European Studies at the University of Kansas, where he completed his Ph.D. in East European history. A former Fulbright Fellow in the Czech Republic, he has published articles on Czech history in the journals *Kosmas: Czechoslovak and Central European Journal, National Identities, Stredni Evropa, and Historie a vojenstvi.*

Derek W. Blakeley earned a Ph.D. at Washington University in St. Louis, examining the career of Lord Curzon and the development of the Conservative Party in the twentieth century. He currently teaches history in Virginia.

Carol Blessing, Ph.D., is an associate professor of literature and women's studies at Point Loma Nazarene University in San Diego, where she teaches British and world literature, literary theory and scholarship, and women writers. She has had eight essays published in *Reader's Guide to Women's Studies* (London: Fitzroy Dearborn, 1998), an article in *Asides Magazine* (The Shakespeare Theatre of Washington, D.C.) on the Duchess of Malfi, and works published on women in the church.

Lynn Z. Bloom is the Board of Trustees Distinguished Professor of English and Aetna Chair of Writing at the University of Connecticut. Among her publications are *Doctor Spock: Biography of a Conservative Radical* (Bobbs-Merrill, 1972); the NEH-funded *American Autobiography, 1945–1980: A Bibliography* (Wisconsin, 1982); and two diaries of American women civilian prisoners in the Philippines in World War II: Natalie Crouter's *Forbidden Diary* (Burt Franklin, 1980, 2001) and Margaret Sams's *Forbidden Family* (Wisconsin, 1989, 1996). Her *The Essay Canon* is forthcoming from Wisconsin in 2004.

Geoffrey S. Cahn is chair of the History Department, Yeshiva University High School for Boys, New York, New York. As a cultural historian, he has contributed several articles for publications in music history. He received his Ph.D. from St. John's University, New York. He lives with his wife and daughter in Riverdale, New York.

Donald Carlson holds a Ph.D. in literature from the University of Dallas. He lives in Fort Worth, Texas, and is a fellow at the College of Saint Thomas More. Dr. Carlson is also a principal and an English teacher at Trinity Valley School, a college preparatory school in Fort Worth.

Peter E. Carr is a professional archaeologist, historian, and author. He is publisher and editor of the *Caribbean Historical and Genealogical Journal.*

Peter P. Catterall lectures in history and politics at Queen Mary, University of London. As well as editing the journal *Contemporary British History*, he is currently preparing a two-volume edition of Harold Macmillan's diaries.

Kathleen M. Cioffi is a writer and editor at Associated University Presses. She has taught and directed in the United States and Poland and is the author of many articles and reviews about Polish theater as well as the award-winning book *Alternative Theatre in Poland 1954–1989.*

Jennifer Clary-Lemon is a teaching associate and doctoral candidate at Arizona State University. Her current research is in the area of critical multiculturalism, and has recently presented her findings at the Western States Composition Conference in Seattle and the Conference on College Composition and Communication in New York City.

Craig T. Cobane is an assistant professor of political science at Culver-Stockton College. His primary area of research is the tensions between civil liberties and national security policy. His numerous articles and essays have appeared in a variety of journals and encyclopedias. He is the recipient of several teaching awards.

Aaron N. Coleman, a graduate of Cumberland College, received his M.A. degree in History from the University of Louisville. He is currently a doctoral student at the University of Kentucky studying the American Revolution and the Early Republic. He lives in Lexington with his wife, Emily.

Arika L. Coleman holds bachelor of arts and master of arts degrees from Vermont College of Norwich University. She is currently an American studies Ph.D. candidate at the Union Institute and University. In addition, she is an adjunct professor of English at the University of Delaware as well as a lecturer and evaluator for the Delaware Humanities Speakers Bureau.

Philip M. Coupland earned his Ph.D. at the University of Warwick in 2000. He has published widely on British fascism, including articles in the *Journal of Contemporary History* and *Twentieth Century British History*. He served as a research assistant on the European Commission-funded project on "The Churches and European Integration."

Don M. Cregier, University of Prince Edward Island, Canada, is a specialist in twentieth-century British and Irish history. He has published several books on the Liberal Party and a biography of David Lloyd George.

Brian Crim graduated from Rutgers University in 2003 with a Ph.D. in modern European history. His research interests are twentieth-century Germany and the Holocaust. Crim is currently an intelligence analyst for the Joint Personnel Recovery Agency, a component of Joint Forces Command.

Terry Crowley of the University of Guelph in Canada has been teaching and writing Canadian history for more than 30 years. He is a graduate of Bishop's, Carleton (Ottawa), and Duke universities.

Elena M. De Costa holds a Ph.D. from the University of Wisconsin–Madison and is currently an associate professor of Spanish at Carroll College in Wisconsin. She is the author of *Collaborative Latin American Popular Theatre* and numerous articles and book chapters on Spanish and Latin American politics, literature, and culture. She is currently completing a manuscript on visual and sound constructs in contemporary Hispanic poetry. Her research interests also include oral testimony, syntactic theory, and the verbal art of storytelling.

Yücel Demirer holds M.A. degrees from Fisk University and Istanbul University and is a Ph.D. candidate in the Near Eastern Languages and Cultures department of Ohio State University. She has recently edited *The Second Palestinian Intifada: Before and After* (2002).

Eva Dobozy teaches in the School of Education at Murdoch University in Perth, Western Australia, and is in the finishing stages of her doctoral degree. The title of her Ph.D. thesis is *Democracy and Human Rights in Education: From Utopian Ideals to Grounded Practice*. She has a special interest in alternative educational practices and human rights education as a tool for human emancipation.

Todd Douglas Doyle is employed in the tax department of the law firm of Paul, Hastings, Janofsky and Walker in New York City. He holds a J.D. from Brooklyn Law School and a Ph.D. from the University of Toledo, where he completed a dissertation on Wall Street fiction.

Alexander Drace-Francis is a lecturer in Romanian studies at the School of Slavonic and East European Studies, University College, London. He is the author of numerous articles on Romanian cultural history and a Ph.D. thesis (London, 2001) on literature and national identity in nineteenth-century Romania.

Jill E. Eichhorn is Assistant Professor of English and Women's Studies at Austin Peay State University. As director of the Women's Studies Program, she coordinates the Clothesline Project and forums on violence and women. She is working on the significance of public testimony through writing and the Clothesline Project in the healing of sexual trauma.

Peter C. Erb is professor of religion and culture at Wilfrid Laurier University at Waterloo, Ontario. He has published on the Radical Reformation, German pietism, German Catholicism in the romantic era, and British Anglo-Catholics and Roman Catholics in the nineteenth century. He is currently editing the Gladstone–Manning correspondence for Oxford University Press.

Peter R. Erspamer is a freelance writer and the author of the book *The Elusiveness of Tolerance: The "Jewish Question" from Lessing to the Napoleonic Wars* (1997), which received the Choice Outstanding Academic Book Award. He is currently completing his second book, *The Holocaust and the Survival of Human Dignity.*

Robert C. Evans has been, successively, Alumni Professor, Distinguished Research Professor, and Distinguished Teaching Professor in the Department of English at Auburn University, Montgomery. Although most of his research focuses on Renaissance writers, he has a secondary interest in short fiction and has published several essays on Flannery O'Connor.

Dina Ripsman Eylon is a former instructor of Jewish studies at the University of Toronto. She received her B.A. from Haifa University, an M.A. from Carleton University, and a Ph.D. from the University of Toronto. She is the publisher and editor of *Women in Judaism: A Multidisciplinary Journal.*

Gentil de Faria, professor of comparative literature at Universidade Estadual Paulista–Unesp, Brazil, has written extensively on Anglo-American and Brazilian literature and culture, especially on influence issues. Currently he is working on the literary influences of Thomas Hardy and D. H. Lawrence upon Jose Lins do Rego, a major Brazilian novelist of the first half of the twentieth century. His doctoral dissertation was about the literary reception and influence of Oscar Wilde in Brazil.

Ricardo Faucci is professor of the history of economic thought at the University of Pisa, Italy. He was a founding member of the European Society for the History of Economic Thought in 1994, and served as president of the Italian Association for the History of Economic Thought, 1997–2001. His books include *Luigi Einaudi* (1986), *Breve storia dell'economia politica* (1988) and *L'economia politica in Italia dal Cinquecento ai nostri giorni* (2000). He has served as editor of the *History of Economic Ideas* since 1993.

Gillian Fenwick is associate professor of English at the University of Toronto. She is the author of *The Contributors' Index to the Dictionary of National Biography 1885–1901; Leslie Stephen's Life in Letters; Women and the Dictionary of National Biography; George Orwell: A Bibliography;* and *Understanding Tim Parks.* She is currently writing a history of the *Dictionary of National Biography* and a book on Jan Morris.

Richard R. Follett received his Ph.D. from Washington University in St. Louis in 1996. His publications include *Evangelicalism, Penal Theory and the Politics of Criminal Law Reform in England, 1808–1830* (2001). Dr. Follett currently teaches European history at Covenant College.

Tom Frazier is professor of English at Cumberland College, Williamsburg, Kentucky, and holds degrees in English from Cumberland College, Eastern Kentucky University, and Middle Tennessee State University. He continues his eclectic research interests by expanding an already completed manuscript on the Turner Thesis and examining literary presentations of Joan of Arc.

Jeff Frederick specializes in the twentieth-century history of the American South. He has written extensively on Southern politics and its relationship to society at large. His next major work will be a biography of George Wallace focusing broadly on policies, issues, and events within Alabama.

Robert Genter recently completed his Ph.D. in the department of history at Columbia University, where he studied American intellectual and cultural history. He has previously published in *History of Philosophy Quarterly* and *Twentieth-Century Literature*.

Indira Falk Gesink is the assistant professor for Middle Eastern and Asian history at Baldwin-Wallace College. She completed her Ph.D. examining the Azhar Reform Movement in Egypt during the late nineteenth and early twentieth centuries. She continues to research nationalism, religion, and educational reform in Egypt.

Rose Giltzow is a student at Roosevelt University, in Schaumburg, Illinois. She is an English major with a concentration in creative writing. Several of her poems and an interview article have been published in *The Delano*, a history journal published at Roosevelt and sponsored by the Kappa Upsilon Chapter.

E. Stanly Godbold Jr. is a professor of history at Mississippi State University. He has published several books, including *Christopher Gadsden and the American Revolution* (1981, with Robert H. Woody), and *Confederate Colonel and Cherokee Chief: The Life of William Holland Thomas* (1990, with Mattie U. Russell, Winner of the Thomas Wolfe Literary Prize, 1991). He is currently writing a biography of Jimmy Carter.

Ernst Grabovszki received his doctorate in comparative literature at the University of Vienna, where he is a lecturer in the Department of Comparative Literature and an assistant editor of the *Internationales Archiv für Sozialgeschichte der deutschen Literatur*. He is the author of *Methoden und Modelle der deutschent* (2002) and has coedited *Literature in Vienna at the Turn of the Centuries: Continuities and Discontinuities Around 1900 and 2000* (2002).

Richard J. Gray II is a Ph.D. candidate in French and francophone literature at the University of Texas at Austin. He is writing a dissertation on French radio drama from the interwar to post–World War II periods.

Tara D. Green, Ph.D., is an assistant professor of English at Southern University in Baton Rouge, Louisiana. She teaches African American literature and contemporary American literature. Her recent article, "Mother Dearest: The Motivations of Tina McElroy Ansa's Mudear" is published in *The Griot*, Spring 2002.

Erika Haber received her Ph.D. in Slavic languages and literatures from the University of Michigan in 1993. Currently an associate professor at Syracuse University, she has published *Myth of the Non-Russian: Iskander and Aitmatov's Magical Universe* (2003), *Russian-English/English-Russian Dictionary and Phrasebook* (2003), and *Mastering Russian* (1994).

Jennifer Harrison studied American social history at the University of Richmond, where she earned a master's degree. Her research focused on nineteenth-century secondary schooling for women in Virginia. She currently serves as a technology support specialist at the College of William and Mary.

Susan Hamburger (Ph.D., Florida State University, 1995), manuscripts cataloguing librarian at Penn State University, has published essays in *Biographical Dictionary of Literary Influences: The Nineteenth Century, 1800–1914* (2001), *American Book and Magazine Illustrators to 1920* (1998), *Encyclopedia of Rural America* (1997), and *American National Biography* (1999), and a chapter in *Before the New Deal: Southern Social Welfare History, 1830–1930* (1999).

Colin Hill is a Ph.D. candidate and sessional lecturer at McGill University in Montreal working on a dissertation entitled "Realizing Modernism: Prose Fiction in Canada, 1920–1950." He is coeditor of *English Canadian Literary Anthologies: An Enumerative Bibliography*, and has published on a variety of aspects of Canadian literature.

Paul Allan Hillmer is professor of history at Concordia University in St. Paul, Minnesota. A graduate of the University of Minnesota, he has also contributed to the *Encyclopedia of Cleveland History, Dictionary of Cleveland Biography*, and *Encyclopedia of the Home Front: WWI & WWII.*

J. Brandon Hinman holds a B.A. in philosophy from Furman University. He has lived and studied in Chile, Norway, and China. His interest in Che stems from a Lilly Endowment–funded trip to Cuba in 2001, where he worked on the photo documentary *40 Years, 40 Days.*

Arthur Holst earned his Ph.D. from Temple University in 1999 when he was serving as executive director of the Betsy Ross House in Philadelphia (1996–99). Since becoming government affairs manager for the Philadelphia Water Department, he has published widely on environmental topics in a variety of newspapers, journals, and magazines.

Richard P. F. Holt is associate professor of economics at Southern Oregon University. He has published in many scholarly journals such as the *Review of Political Economy*, the *Eastern Economic Journal*, and the *Journal of Economic History*. He is coeditor of *Economics and Discontents: Twentieth Century Dissenting Economist and the New Guide to Post Keynesian Economics*. He also serves as general editor and electronic manager of *Post Keynesian Thought.*

Ulle V. Holt was visiting assistant professor in history at Brown University in 2001–2. She is currently an adjunct lecturer at Brown in the International Relations Program while turning her dissertation, "Style, Fashion, Politics, and Identity: The Ballets Russes in Paris from 1909–14," into a book. She is also doing research on treatment of women political prisoners in the twentieth century.

Phil Huckelberry has a B.A. in history and political science from Illinois Wesleyan University (1998) and an M.A. in history from Ohio State University (2001) with an emphasis on twentieth-century American history. His M.A. thesis is entitled "In Proseperity's Wake: A Study of Community and Economic Stagnation in Centralia Illinois, 1938–1978."

Daniela Hurezanu received her Ph.D. in Romance languages and literatures from the University of Florida, and her DEA from the Universite de Stasbourg II. She currently serves as a lecturer in French at Arizona State University.

Millie Jackson is an associate librarian at Grand Valley State University in Allendale, Michigan, where she is the head of periodicals. She holds a Ph.D. in English from Michigan State University. Her research interests include nineteenth-century women's reading practice and popular culture.

Allan Johnston is a lecturer at DePaul University and at Columbia College, Chicago. He has written on William S. Burroughs for *Review of Contemporary Fiction* and for the *Dictionary of American Literary Characters*. Other studies of modern and contemporary literature have appeared in *Twentieth Century Literature*, *ISLE*, and *AUMLA*.

Guillemette Johnston is a professor of French at DePaul University. A specialist in Jean-Jacques Rousseau, she has also written on Frantz Fanon for the *Dictionary of Literary Biography* and regularly teaches courses on African and West Indian francophone literature.

Andrzej Karcz is an assistant professor in the Department of Slavic Languages and Literatures at the University of Kansas. He is a specialist in nineteenth- and twentieth-century Polish literature, formalism, literary theory, and Polish prose fiction. He has published articles on many Polish and Russian authors, as well as Polish autobiography and American literary criticism. He is author of the upcoming book, *The Polish Formalist School and Russian Formalism*.

Barry Keane has recently completed his doctorate at Trinity College Dublin on the Polish inter-war poetry group, Scamander. He is a renowned translator of and commentator on the Polish Renaissance poet Jan Kochanowski. Currently he is a senior lecturer at Warsaw University's English Department.

Anne Kelsch is an assistant professor in the Department of History at the University of North Dakota. She completed her Ph.D. in history at Texas A&M University in 1993, writing on Lord Beaverbrook's introduction into the British political world, 1910–18. More recently she has published articles on the Selkirk settlement in the Red River Valley of North Dakota and Manitoba.

Stephen L. Keck teaches historiography and modern European intellectual history at the National University of Singapore. His research is focused on John Ruskin, mid-Victorianism and British perceptions of Burma. He has also taught European history at the College of Charleston.

Padraic Kennedy is an assistant professor of history at McNeese State University in Louisiana. In 1996, he received his Ph.D. from Washington University in St. Louis, where he completed a dissertation entitled: "Political Policing in a Liberal Age: Britain's Responses to the Fenian Movement, 1858–1868."

Susan Eastbrook Kennedy, professor of history at Virginia Commonwealth University, earned her Ph.D. at Columbia University. She is the author of books on the banking crisis of 1933 and on working-class women in America. A former Guggenheim fellow, she is currently writing a book of essays about Herbert Hoover after the presidency.

Michael Keren, a native of Israel, is a professor and Canada Research Chair in Communication, Culture and Civil Society at the University of Calgary. He is the author of many books and articles on intellectuals and politics, political communication, and Israeli political culture.

Rosemary King is an assistant professor in the Department of English and Fine Arts at the U.S. Air Force Academy. Her area of specialty, literature of the U.S.–Mexico borderlands, is highlighted in her forthcoming book, *Border Confluences: Narratives from the Mexican War to the Present* (University of Arizona Press, 2004).

Cynthia A. Klima researched her Ph.D. in German from the University of Wisconsin–Madison. She is associate professor of German and Slavic languages at SUNY–Geneseo. Her major research includes Prague German-Jewish-Czech literature, the cultural history of the Czech lands, and Russian literature. She has contributed to the *Reader's Guide to Judaism, Guide to Holocaust Literature*, and *History in Dispute: The Holocaust.*

Cassandra Noel Kreischer grew up in the northwest suburbs of Chicago. She is a member of Phi Theta Kappa and was recognized in *Who's Who among College Students.* Currently, she is a student at Roosevelt University, majoring in English and minoring in journalism.

Yves Laberge is film historian and associate professor at the Department of Sociology at Université Laval in Québec City, Canada. His articles have appeared in *CinémAction, International Journal of Canadian Studies, Hermès,* and *Laval théologique et phiosophique.* He has served as guest editor for a number of refereed journals including *Cahiers de l'imaginaire, Cap-aux-Diamants, Revue d'histoire du Quebec,* and *Museum International.*

Theodoros Lagaris studied political science and sociology in Athens and Berlin. He received his doctorate at the Free University of Berlin for a study on the authoritarian state in Greece after the Second World War. He is currently a lecturer in political science and working on a project about democratization in southern Europe.

D. S. Lawson is associate professor of English at Lander University in Greenwood, South Carolina, where he also serves as director of Honors and International Programs. He has published widely in postwar British and American literature, including essays on Joe Orton, David Storey, James Merrill, Lanford Wilson, David Leavitt, and Craig Lucas, as well as on AIDS theater in New York.

Cyana Leahy is a bilingual writer and translator from Brazil. An associate professor at Rio's Federal University, she earned a Ph.D. in literature education from London University. She has published books of poetry, essays, and short stories. She is the 1993–94 recipient of the ORS Award in England.

Cheryl Lemus is a Ph.D. student at the University of California, Santa Cruz, and is expected to reach candidacy in 2003. Her interest is American history, with a focus on the Gilded Age and Progressive Era, gender, emotions, consumerism, and public history. Her dissertation will look at Valentine's Day and examine the commercialization of love and the shaming of the consumer.

Ludmilla L. Litus received her Ph.D. from the University of Michigan. She has taught Russian, Ukrainian, and German at the University of Michigan and Michigan State University. Her recent publications include "Intertextuality in *Shkola dlia durakov* Revisited: Sokolov, Gogol, and the *Others*"; "Two Paradigms for Teaching Russian Business Language"; and a biography, *Mikhail Aleksandrovich Sholokhov.*

E. D. Lloyd-Kimbrel is a freelance writer/editor and sometime poet. She also is the assistant to the vice president for enrollment at Mount Holyoke College. She holds undergraduate and graduate degrees in English with concentrations in biography and medieval studies. She has published in several scholarly journals and academic reference works, including OUP's *American National Biography* and Greenwood's *Biographical Dictionary of Literary Influences: The Nineteenth Century.*

Sheri Spaine Long (Ph.D., UCLA) is an associate professor at the University of Alabama in Birmingham, where she teaches Spanish language and literature in the Department of Foreign Languages and Literatures. She researches and publishes on Madrid studies and writes Spanish textbooks.

W. C. Lubenow, F.R.Hist.S., is professor of history at Stockton College of New Jersey. He is the author of *The Politics of Government Growth* (1971), *Parliamentary Politics and the Home Rule Crisis* (1988), and *The Cambridge Apostles, 1820–1914.* His current research includes a book on liberalism called *Making Words Flesh: Authority, Society, and Thought in Modern Britain, 1815–1914* and a book on the British Roman Catholic peerage, 1815–1914.

Eric v.d. Luft (Ph.D., M.L.S.) is curator of Historical Collections at the State University of New York (SUNY) Upstate Medical University and is included in the fifty-fourth edition of *Who's Who in America,* the twenty-seventh edition of *Who's Who in the East,* and the twenty-eighth edition of *Dictionary of International Biography.*

Scott Lupo is a lecturer in United States history at California State University, Sacramento, where he teaches introductory survey courses and an upper-division course in popular culture. His research focuses on apocalyptic thought in American popular culture. He holds a Ph.D. in history from the University of Nevada.

Mitchell McNaylor earned an M.A. degree in history from Ohio State University, and is now an adjunct instructor at Our Lady of the Lake College in Baton Rouge, Louisiana. His most recent article on "G. M. Trevelyan" was published in the *Madison Historical Review* (2003).

Linda Macrì received her Ph.D. in English from the University of Maryland in 2000. Her dissertation, currently being prepared for publication, was entitled "Revising the Story: A Rhetorical Perspective on Revisionary Fiction by Women Writers."

Peter Mahon received his doctorate from the University of British Columbia, Vancouver, Canada, where he is now a lecturer in the Department of English. His main research interests have to do with the texts of James Joyce and Jacques Derrida.

Wendy A. Maier is an adjunct professor of history, and is also an instructor for an adult general studies program. She has published several articles, book reviews, and essays. Research interests include the Holocaust, Nazi Germany, and early modern European women's history.

George Mariz earned his Ph.D. from the University of Missouri, Columbia. He is professor of history and honors director at Western Washington University and has published widely on intellectual and cultural history. He is currently at work on a study of Thomas Arnold.

Robert O. Marlin IV is a graduate student in history at the University of Houston–Clear Lake and the John W. Stormont Recipient for "The Death Penalty Case of a Mexican National and the Pardon and Parole Reforms It Helped to Spawn," *South Texas Studies Journal*, 2002.

Katherine Matthews recently earned a Bachelor of Arts degree in history from Cumberland College in Williamsburg, Kentucky. She is preparing for a career with the U.S. State Department.

Laurence W. Mazzeno is president of Alvernia College, Reading, Pennsylvania. He is the author of four books and dozens of articles on Victorian and modern literature. He is currently working on *Alfred Tennyson: The Critical Heritage* (Boydell & Brewer, forthcoming 2004).

David A. Meier, professor of history, Dickinson State University, received his Ph.D. from the University of Wisconsin–Madison in 1990. Currently chair of the Social Science Department, he is a regular contributor to the *German Studies Review* and has written numerous articles on postwar German politics.

James Mellis is currently completing his Ph.D. dissertation at Tulane University in New Orleans. His dissertation, "Writing Blackface: An Analysis of Jewish and

African American Stereotypes in Jazz Age Literature," examines racial stereotypes in the works of Langston Hughes, Zora Neal Hurston, Fanny Hurst, and Gertrude Stein. He holds a B.A. from Colgate University and an M. Phil from Trinity College Dublin.

Holly Messitt teaches composition and literature at Berkeley College in New York City. She is currently working on a study combining dance and literary theory.

Wendy Pearce Miller is a Ph.D. candidate and graduate instructor at the University of Mississippi. Her primary fields of interest are twentieth-century American literature and Southern literature. She is currently writing a dissertation focusing on the works of Mary Lee Settle.

Jim Millhorn is the History Librarian and Head of Acquisitions for the Northern Illinois University libraries. He is the author of the *Student's Companion to the World Wide Web* (Scarecrow, 2000).

Dana Milstein is a doctoral candidate in French at the Graduate Center in New York. Also a professor of literature at Baruch College, she has published and presented papers concerning nineteenth- and early twentieth-century art and literature as well as contemporary underground culture and media studies.

Carl Mirra teaches American studies and social studies at the State University of New York–Old Westbury. He is completing a dissertation titled "U.S. Foreign Policy and the Prospects for Peace Education" at Teachers College, Columbia University.

Josip Mocnik earned an M.A. degree from University College, London, and is now a Ph.D. candidate at Bowling Green State University. His dissertation is on United States–Yugoslav relations and the collapse of Yugoslavia.

Georg Modestin was born in 1969 in Berne, Switzerland, and graduated from Lausanne and Exeter. He specialized in medieval history and is particularly interested in the political symbolism of repression in the later Middle Ages. He has published a monograph and several articles and teaches general history courses in Biel, Switzerland.

Andrew Muldoon received his Ph.D. in 1999 from Washington University and works on British imperialism in India. He has taught at Tufts University and Saint Anselm College and is currently a lecturer in the Program in History and Literature at Harvard University.

Linda Ness is a graduate student in the Department of French at the University of Toronto. Her principal area of interest is the literature of early twentieth-century France. She is currently preparing a doctoral thesis on the *Journal* of André Gide.

Devon Niebling recently completed her Ph.D. in English from the University of Nebraska with a dissertation on baseball ecology. She currently teaches English as a second language at the University of Nebraska and is beginning work on her next baseball project.

Deborah K. O'Brien is an assistant professor, acquisitions librarian at East Tennessee State University, Sherrod Library, in Johnson City, Tennessee. She received a master of arts degree in 1994 from the University of South Florida.

Richard Penaskovic is a professor of religious studies at Auburn University in Alabama. He has written three books and 75 articles. His research interests include spirituality, Augustine and Newman Studies, and critical thinking and the academic study of religion.

Christopher Pepus is a teaching fellow and Ph.D. candidate in history at Washington University in St. Louis, Missouri.

Donald K. Pickens is semi-retired from the University of North Texas, where he has taught since 1965. He graduated from the University of Oklahoma (B.A., 1956; M.A., 1957) and received his Ph.D. in 1964 from the University of Texas. Widely published, he established the women in U.S. history course in addition to teaching social and intellectual history and a large number of special topic courses at UNT.

Nicoletta Pireddu is associate professor of Italian and comparative literature at Georgetown University. Her research and publications focus on European literary and cultural relations from the nineteenth century to the present. She is the author of the volume *Antropologi alla corte della bellezzal* (Fiorini, 2001) and of numerous articles on decadence, modernism, and postmodernism.

Mark B. Pohlad is an associate professor and teaches courses on modern art and photohistory at DePaul University in Chicago. A frequent contributor to the journal *History of Photography*, he writes on Marcel Duchamp's historicizing and self-canonizing behaviors, the subject of his dissertation (University of Delaware, 1994).

John Grady Powell is a graduate of Furman University with a bachelor of arts degree in economics. Recent publications include "The Immediate Returns to Career Mobility" with Todd Carroll (2002), and "The Value of Chinese Immigrants during the Building of the First American Transcontinental Railroad, 1852–1869" (2002).

Tessa Powell is majoring in English literature and political science at the University of Kentucky, where she is enrolled in the Honors Program. She has served as a page for the U.S. House of Representatives (1999–2000), an intern in the office of Senator Mitch McConnell (2000), and an intern at the Truman Presidential Library (2003).

Linda Ray Pratt is professor and chair of the Department of English at the University of Nebraska, Lincoln. Specializing in Victorian and modern poetry, her most recent book is *Matthew Arnold Revisited*. A former national president of the American Association of University Professors, Pratt also publishes widely on higher education.

John Radzilowski received his Ph.D. in history in 1999 from Arizona State University and is currently an associate at the Hubert H. Humphrey Institute at the University of Minnesota. He has written extensively on central and eastern Europe and on ethnic communities in the United States.

Todd W. Reeser is an assistant professor of French at the University of Utah in Salt Lake City. His research focuses on gender and sexuality in the Renaissance and on French cultural studies.

Stephen J. Rippon is assistant professor of English at the U.S. Air Force Academy and a captain in the U.S. Air Force. He is an assistant editor for *War, Literature, and the Arts: An International Journal of the Humanities*, for which he has written several pieces.

Priscilla Roberts received her undergraduate and doctoral degrees from King's College, Cambridge. She is a lecturer in history and director of the Centre of American Studies at the University of Hong Kong. She is the author of *The Cold War* (Sutton, 2000) and editor of *Sino-American Relations Since 1900* (1991) and *Window on the Forbidden City: The Beijing Diaries of David Bruce, 1973–1974* (2001).

Todd R. Robinson is in the Ph.D. program at the University of Nebraska–Lincoln, where he specializes in nineteenth-century American literature and American poetry and poetics. His essay on neurasthenia in Willa Cather's *The Professor's House* appeared in the June 2001 issue of *M/C: A Journal of Media and Culture*.

Roy Rosenstein is professor of comparative literature and English at the American University of Paris, where he has been teaching since 1977. He has also taught at the University of Rochester, the University of Oregon, the Sorbonne, elsewhere in Europe, and in South America.

Michael A. Rutz is an assistant professor of history at the University of Wisconsin, Oshkosh. He received his Ph.D. from Washington University in 2002, completing a dissertation on "The British Zion: Evangelization and the Politics of Dissent in Britain and the Empire." His research explores aspects of religion and politics, the history of Christian missions, and cross-cultural exchange in the British Empire.

Martine Sauret is associate professor of French at Western Michigan University on a professional leave of absence. He is currently finishing a book on early explorers and cartographers entitled *Voies Cartographiques*. He received his Ph.D. with honors at the University of Minnesota in 1991 under the direction of Professor Tom Conley, Harvard University. His most recent article, "Victor Hugo: Itinéraires" appears in *L'Etoile du Nord* in January 2003.

Thomas Saylor studied at the University of Akron, the Free University of Berlin, and the University of Rochester, where he received a Ph.D. in history in 1993. He is currently associate professor of history at Concordia University, St. Paul, and offers courses on modern Germany, the Holocaust, and the world wars.

Carl L. Schmider earned the Ph.D. in speech communication from the University of Denver with the dissertation, "The Precision Which Creates Movement: The Stylistics of E. E. Cummings" (copyright 1972, unpublished). Currently teaching for the University of Maryland University College–Maryland in Europe, he has performed Cummings's poetry as a reader in residence at several U.S. universities and in Iceland, Japan, and China.

Mary Ellen Heian Schmider earned a Ph.D. at the University of Minnesota, completing her dissertation on "Jane Addams Aesthetic of Social Reform" (copyright 1983, unpublished). She has lectured on Addams for the U.S. Information Service in Austria, Italy, Iceland, and Japan and as a U.S. Fulbright Lecturer at Lanzhou University, China, in 1997. After 18 years at Minnesota State University Moorhead, the last 10 as dean of graduate studies and research, she joined the University of Maryland University College–Maryland in Europe.

Gregory L. Schnurr (B.A., B. ED, H.B.A., M.A., Dip. Arts) was born in Chepstow, Ontario, Canada, and attended Sheridan College, the University of Toronto, Queen's University, and the Ontario Institute for Studies in Education. He is currently an artist and educator with the Bruce-Grey Catholic District School Board.

Angela Schwarz is assistant professor in modern history at the University of Duisburg, Germany. She has most recently published *Vom Industriebetrieb zum Landschaftspark* (Essen: Klartext, 2001). In 1991 she received the Fraenkel Prize in Contemporary History and in 1998 wrote a postdoctoral thesis on popular science in Britain and Germany, which was published in 1999 as *Der Schluessel zur modernen Welt, ca. 1870–1914.*

Alexander Sedlmaier is a postdoctoral research fellow at the history department of Technichal University, Berlin. He wrote a doctoral dissertation on *Images and Policy: The Wilson Administration and Germany (1931–1921).* He is currently at work on a comparative cultural history of department stores in divided Germany.

Keith D. Semmel is a professor of communication arts and chair of the Communication and Theatre Arts Department at Cumberland College. He teaches classes in mass media, film history, and popular culture studies, including a class on the Beatles. His master's thesis and doctoral dissertation also examined the Beatles.

Ann Shillinglaw is completing her doctoral dissertation in English at Loyola University in Chicago. She is Director of Development at the Stuart Graduate School of Business at the Illinois Institute of Technology. Her areas of interest include literature, folklore, and fairy tales.

Jerry Shuttle is reference/instruction librarian at East Tennessee State University. Before becoming a librarian he taught at Montana State University, Billings. His interests include environmentalism, Zen Buddhism, Chinese and Japanese poetry, Beat literature, and the works of California poet Gary Snyder. He lives north of the Middle Fork of the Holston River in East Tennessee.

Jill Silos is a doctoral candidate in history at the University of New Hampshire, where she has taught courses in United States history and American culture for several years. Her specialization is modern American cultural and intellectual history.

Phyllis Soybel is currently an associate professor of history at the College of Lake County in Illinois. Her teaching areas include World War II and Western civilization. She is currently finishing her book, *The Necessary Relationship: The Development of Anglo-American Co-operation in Naval Intelligence during the Second World War*, to be published by Praeger.

Melissa Stallings is publications coordinator for the California Veterinary Medical Association. She has worked as an editor and managing editor in the interactive media division of ABC-CLIO. She has a bachelor's degree in journalism from Abilene Christian University.

Rouven J. Steeves was educated at the United States Air Force Academy and the Naval Postgraduate School. He teaches in the departments of political science and foreign languages at the United State Air Force Academy in Colorado Springs, Colorado.

Eva-Maria Stolberg is a lecturer at the Institute of East European and Russian History, University of Bonn, and serves on the advisory board of the Eurasian Studies Society (Harvard University). She has recently published *Stalin and the Chinese Communists* (Stuttgart, 1997) and "Interracial Outposts in Siberia: Nerchinsk, Kiakhta, and the Russo-Chinese Trade in the Seventeenth/Eighteenth Centuries" in *Journal of Early Modern History* (2000).

Christopher C. Strangeman is currently working full-time on his Ph.D. at Southern Illinois University–Carbondale in historical studies. Recently, he served as a full-time social science instructor at a community college. His historical interests lie in modern Western intellectual thought.

Richard N. Swanson heads the journalism program at Lassen Community College in Susanville, California, where he also instructs film and English. He received master's degrees in journalism and English from Michigan State University. He has worked as a reporter and copyeditor for newspapers in Michigan, and in book publishing in New York City.

Guillaume de Syon teaches European history and the history of technology at Albright College in Reading, Pennsylvania. His research focuses on the impact of aviation on Western culture and society. He recently published *Zeppelin! Germany and the Airship, 1900–1939* (Johns Hopkins, 2002).

Maria Tabaglio received her M.A. in German philology from the University of Verona with a thesis on Hildegard of Bingen. She has published several articles on medieval Latin literature and is now translating works from Old French and Old German into Italian. She teaches German literature at a high school in Brescia.

Gregory F. Tague is an assistant professor of English at St. Francis College in Brooklyn Heights, New York. He is a speaker in the New York Council for the Humanities Program, and has published widely on the work of D. H. Lawrence.

Donald F. Theall, former president of Trent University and previously Molson Professor and Director of the Graduate Communications Program at McGill University, is author of *Beyond the Word*, *James Joyce's Techno-Poetics*, two books on McLuhan, and numerous articles in literature, aesthetic theory, communications, media, modernism, science fiction, and the prehistory of cyberspace.

Gregor Thuswaldner has studied German and English at the University of Salzburg, Bowling Green State University, and the University of Vienna and is currently completing his dissertation at the University of North Carolina at Chapel Hill. He has published numerous articles, reviews, and essays in scholarly journals and newspapers.

Rebecca Tolley-Stokes is a librarian and assistant professor at the University Libraries of East Tennessee State University. Her contributions to several reference works include the *Encyclopedia of Appalachia*, the *Dictionary of Literary Biography: American Radical and Reform Writers*, the *Encyclopedia of Labor History Worldwide*, and the *Dictionary of American History*.

Charles Trainor received his B.A. from Dartmouth, his M.A. from Cambridge, and his Ph.D. from Yale. He has taught at Yale and at Illinois College and is currently a professor of English at Siena College. His publications include *The Drama and Fielding's Novels* and articles on several playwrights and novelists.

Annette Trefzer is assistant professor of English at the University of Mississippi, where she teaches Southern literature and literary theory, and she is coeditor of *Journal X: A Journal in Culture and Criticism*.

Maja Trochimczyk is a native of Poland, a citizen of Poland and Canada, and a resident of California. She is the Stefan and Wanda Wilk Director of the Polish Music Center, Thornton School of Music at the University of Southern California. She holds a Ph.D. from McGill University, Montreal, and specializes in twentieth-century Polish music. She is the author of two books—*After Chopin: Essays in Polish Music* (USC, 2000) and *The Music of Louis Andriessen* (Routledge, 2002)—and over 40 articles and book chapters.

Wim van Mierlo is Administrator of the Records Management and Alumni Scheme and of the Bibliographical Society of the Institute for English Studies, School of Advanced Study at the University of London. He has a masters degree from the University of Antwerp and a doctorate from the University of Miami. In addition to publishing articles in *European Joyce Studies* and *Joyce Studies Annual*, he is co-editor of *The Reception of James Joyce in Europe* (Continuum, 2004).

Andrés Villagrá is associate professor of Spanish at Pace University, New York. He is the author of the upcoming book *Funciones y operaciones de la autobiografía hispánica moderna*. He is a contributor to *Romance Quarterly, Cuadernos de ALDEEU, Ojancano, Confluencia, Draco: Revista de Literatura*, and *Bulletin of Academy of Asturian Letters*.

Durthy A. Washington, M.A., M.S., has published more than 100 articles, essays, and book reviews as well as several literary study guides. A former technical writer, textbook editor, and manuscript consultant, she currently serves as Writing Center director at the U.S. Air Force Academy in Colorado Springs, Colorado, and teaches in the Department of English and Fine Arts.

Linda S. Watts received her Ph.D. in American Studies from Yale University in 1989. She authored *Rapture Untold: Gender, Mysticism*, and the "Moment of Recognition" in *Writings by Gertrude Stein* (1996) and *Gertrude Stein: A Study of the Short Fiction* (1999), and has published in a variety of scholarly journals. She is currently at work on an encyclopedia of American folklore. Watts is Professor of Interdisciplinary Arts and Sciences at the University of Washington, Bothell.

Steven F. White is associate professor of history at Mount Saint Mary's College. A two-time Fulbright Fellow, he now chairs the Italy/Spain/Portugal advanced area studies course at the Foreign Service Institute, U.S. State Department. He is the author of *Progressive Renaissance: America and the Reconstruction of Italian Education, 1943–1962* (New York, 1991).

Marianne Wilson has been teaching music in the Woodbridge Township School District for the past twenty years. She is a doctoral student at Drew University in Madison, New Jersey, preparing a dissertation on twentieth-century American music.

David E. Woodard received a Ph.D. in history from the University of Minnesota in 1996. He currently teaches history and American government at Concordia University in St. Paul, Minnesota. Professor Woodard's primary areas of study are diplomatic history and the U.S. Civil War.

Gelareh Yvard-Djahansouz is an associate professor (*maître de conférence*) in American studies at the University of Angers, France, and has been teaching courses on American history and political institutions. She obtained her Ph.D. in environmental policy and politics in the United States from the University of

Nantes in 1993 and has continued her research and published several articles in the field of environmental policy and ecology in the United States.

Katarzyna Zechenter teaches at University College London and has a Ph.D. from the University of Michigan. She has written a monograph on a contemporary Polish writer, Tadeusz Konwicki. She is currently working on a book on the representation of Krakow, the previous capital of Poland, in literature and in Polish national mythology.